The Irwin Business and Investment Almanac 1995

The IRWIN
Business and Investment Almanac 1995

Edited by

Sumner N. Levine
Professor Emeritus
State University of New York
at Stony Brook
and Editor
Financial Analyst's Handbook
and
The Investment Manager's Handbook

and

Caroline Levine

Professional Publishing
Chicago • Bogotá • Boston • Buenos Aires • Caracas
London • Madrid • Mexico City • Sydney • Toronto

Senior sponsoring editor: Amy Hollands Gaber
Project editor: Karen J. Nelson
Production supervisor: Ann Cassady
Compositor: Quebecor Printing/Kingsport
Typeface: 8/9 Caledonia
Printer: Quebecor Printing Book Press Inc.

ISSN 1072-6136
ISBN 0-7863-0240-2 ISBN 0-7863-0406-5 (Paperback edition)

Printed in the United States of America
1 2 3 4 5 6 7 8 9 0 BP 1 0 9 8 7 6 5 4

Preface

This 19th edition of the annual *Irwin Business and Investment Almanac* contains a number of new features in response to the rapidly changing business and investment scene as well as updates on our standard features.

The editors and publisher are, of course, pleased with the acceptance of the *Irwin Business and Investment Almanac* as a standard and unique reference for the business and investment community. As always, we continue to invite suggestions from our readers. All suggestions should be sent to: *Irwin Business and Investment Almanac,* P.O. Box 2118, Setauket, New York 11733.

TO ORDER COPIES

If copies are not available at your local bookstore call 1-800-634-3966 or write: Order Department, 1333 Burr Ridge Parkway, Burr Ridge, IL 60521.

We appreciate your suggestions.

The Editors

References to companies, securities, and other investment information do not constitute a recommendation or endorsement.

Foreword

The *Irwin Business and Investment Almanac* is one book I would take to a desert island if I had to start a new economy. Why? A virtual library in one book, this almanac is a very effective business tool kit, providing summaries, graphs, and statistics from a variety of respected business sources. You didn't save the Fortune 500? No problem. You don't know where to find the Lipper Gauge in Barron's? Don't worry. You don't know how to read a financial statement. No sweat. It's all here in this attractive, extensively indexed annual compendium.

The Editors, Sumner and Caroline Levine, have created a text that should delight the student, the investor, business people, and the information professional. The book is easy to use, with a detailed table of contents, bibliography, and index.

How does one use the *Irwin Business and Investment Almanac*? There are so many uses for the data that it really depends on you, your project, and where you've already looked. This book is a great place to start, and often you will find that it has sufficiently answered your question. If you need to go into more detail, the authors have clearly sourced and footnoted each chart and provided a bibliography for more searching.

Here are a few more examples and the chapters where you can find information.

Starting your own business?

- Small Business Investment Companies

Getting up to speed?

- How to Read Mutual Fund Quotations
- How to Understand Options and Futures

Investing in the stock market?

- Quarterly Dow Jones Averages
- Industry Surveys
- General Business & Economic Indicators

Doing business in another state?

- State Information Guide
- State Business Assistance Publications
- State Information Offices

Creating a new woman-owned business?

- Women in Business

Where else can I look?

- Business Information Directory
- General Reference Sources
- Selected Bibliography

Whether you are a professional researcher or a consumer, it's a value-added asset to have all the work done for you and to know that the Editors have used the most reliable publications found in business libraries.

Colin McQuillan, Manager
GE Investments Library

Contents

Business in Review

October 1993–September 1994

October 1993

4 The dollar surged against the mark in early Asia-Pacific trading Monday in the wake of an outbreak of chaos in Moscow. The events are expected to take only a limited toll on U.S. stock and bond prices today, with most of the damage felt in European markets, especially Germany's, analysts said.

5 Ford named Alexander Trotman to succeed Harold Poling as chairman. Trotman, head of Ford's world-wide auto operations, will take charge at a time of intense global competition.

Stock and bond prices ended mixed, as Russia's bloody clash sparked only a muted reaction in the financial markets. The dollar fell. Overseas, the stock markets' reaction was more subdued than expected. German and French stocks rose 0.6% and British shares climbed 0.9%.

U.S. stock mutual funds earned 5.3% in the third quarter. International stock funds earned 9.35%, though overseas economies continue to struggle. Technology shares made winners out of many growth stock funds and real-estate funds rallied sharply.

6 Metropolitan Life Insurance is being investigated in several states for questionable sales practices that affected thousands of life insurance policyholders across the country.

The Big Three car makers accounted for 73% of the new cars and light trucks sold in the U.S. in the 1993 model year, up from 72% in 1992. Japan's U.S. market share fell to 23%, the first drop in at least a decade.

7 South Africa offers enormous business promise, many U.S. firms say, but they are still somewhat wary about investing in a country where there are so many political uncertainties.

The International Energy Agency revised downward again its estimates of world oil demand. The lower figure would represent the first annual decline in global demand since 1983.

8 Retail sales rose 5.6% in September from the previous year, as cool weather spurred apparel purchases. Gap's sales increased 2%, Ann Taylor's sales rose 8.8% and Charming Shoppes' sales were up 6%.

Consumer credit rose at a 5.7% annual rate in August, suggesting that despite economic concerns, many are still willing buyers and borrowers.

Layoffs at big companies are being offset by a healthy pace of job growth in the service industries, resulting in an overall rise in employment. But some of the new jobs don't provide the level of economic confidence likely to spark a surge in consumer activity.

A widely followed survey of employers to calculate job growth may not be as accurate as a survey of households because of the peculiarity of the current economic recovery.

Six more underwriters that deal in municipal bonds announced they are halting political contributions in states and cities where they do business.

11 The economy continued its slow expansion in September. Employers added 156,000 jobs, although the jobless rate was unchanged at 6.7%.

12 Eli Lilly Chairman Tobias unveiled plans to cut 4,000 salaried and contract jobs through early retirements and reassignments. Tobias said the reduction in the work force is just the start of a shake-up at the drug maker.

13 BellSouth plans to acquire a 22.5% stake in Prime Management, giving the regional Bell company the entree it has been seeking into the cable television business. BellSouth would loan Prime as much as $250 million that would be used for a $450 million recapitalization of a cable operator partially owned by Prime. One individual familiar with the deal said BellSouth will pay less than $100 million for its initial stake in Prime.

Wal-Mart illegally engaged in predatory pricing by selling pharmacy products below cost, a state court in Arkansas ruled. Antitrust attorneys said the ruling, if it survives on appeal, could encourage more predatory-pricing suits in state courts against Wal-Mart and other big firms.

14 Bell Atlantic's bid to acquire cable giant Tele-Communications and its Liberty Media spinoff could vault the Baby Bell to the forefront of shaping an interactive video world for the 21st century. The deal, which could spur a flurry of other mergers and alliances, has a value of $11.8 billion, and could rise to over $20 billion. The role of TCI's John Malone in the Bell deal throws into uncertainty the cast of players in the battle for Paramount.

The Bell-TCI merger would be a major step toward creating the national information infrastructure the White House is pushing, but the administration has yet to spell out what its antitrust policy is in such a deal.

Merger activity this year is more than double the 1992 pace and is being spurred by high stock prices and rapid change in several industries. The latest deals are being funded largely by stocks, unlike the 1980s buyouts, which were financed by junk bonds.

Woolworth plans to close 970 of its stores in the U.S. and Canada, eliminate 13,000 jobs and take a $480 million charge in its third quarter. The cuts, which mark Woolworth's second major downsizing in two years, represent about 10% of the company's stores world-wide and 9% of its work force.

The selling pace of vehicles built in North America in early October rose to its highest level since the summer, signaling a brisk start for 1994 models.

15 Chrysler's profit more than doubled, surprising analysts and marking the car maker's best third quarter ever. Chrysler's stock rose $3.25, or 6.7%, to $51.75, a 52-week high. The results, which also lifted GM and Ford shares, could make a dividend increase likely before year end.

Producer prices edged up 0.2% last month, indicating that inflation remained low. Retail sales rose 0.1%. Sales at department, apparel and furniture stores were particularly strong. Separately, initial claims for state unemployment aid rose 8,000 last week.

Stock and bond prices rallied on the positive inflation news. The Dow Jones industrials climbed 18.44 points to 3621.63 in the second-heaviest trading on the Big Board this year. The Treasury's 30-year benchmark gained over ¾ point. Its yield fell to 5.85%.

18 Cox Enterprises and Advance Publications agreed to invest $500 million each in QVC Network, contingent on a successful QVC acquisition of Paramount. The stock investments appear to further strengthen QVC's hand in its bid for Paramount and to reduce the likelihood that QVC will seek further financial backing from Tele-Communications' John Malone.

A ruling allowing Bell Atlantic to sell its own cable service in areas where it provides phone service will be appealed by the Justice Department. Bell said the move has little bearing on its plans to buy cable giant TCI.

Medical-price inflation slowed to a moderate 4.2% annual rate in the third quarter from 7% in the second quarter, reflecting lower overall inflation and state cost-cutting efforts. Last month, overall consumer prices rose 0.1% while industrial output climbed 0.2%.

19 J. P. Morgan cut its prime lending rate, becoming the first big bank in over a year to do so, but it's unclear whether other banks will follow suit. Morgan lowered the rate to 5.5% from 6%, citing weak loan demand.

Chase, PNC Bank and First Interstate said third-quarter earnings jumped, while NationsBank's profit fell 2.6% because of one-time charges.

Major securities firms signed a pact to stop making political contributions that give the appearance they are buying bond-underwriting business from state and local officials.

20 Clinton decided on a cigarette tax increase of 75 cents a pack to help pay for his proposed health-care plan. The decision represents a retreat from the $1-a-pack increase the White House had once contemplated. The new figure is a bow to the strength of the lobbyists and lawmakers who represent tobacco-growing areas.

Philip Morris's profit fell 25% in the third quarter, reflecting the food and tobacco company's costly decision to cut prices of cigarettes in the U.S. The company also predicted earnings in the fourth quarter will be lower.

Pfizer, Upjohn and American Cyanamid said they plan to eliminate 7,000 jobs and take huge restructuring charges, in the latest round of pharmaceutical industry cutbacks. Pfizer took a $750 million charge, which led to a third-quarter loss, and plans to cut its work force by about 3,000.

Warner-Lambert reported a 5.2% drop in third-quarter earnings, while C. R. Bard posted a loss and Smith-

Kline Beecham's profit rose 13%. Eli Lilly reported a profit for the period, compared with a year-earlier loss.

Housing starts gained in September, increasing 2.8% to the highest level in more than three years.

21 London and Frankfurt stocks rose to records on encouraging British economic data and hopes that Germany will reduce interest rates.

22 Germany cut its two key lending rates, triggering rate cuts in other European nations. The Bundesbank cut its discount rate to 5.75% from 6.25% and its Lombard rate to 6.75% from 7.25%. Germany's move sent European equity markets up about 1%. The dollar rose 1.8% against the mark.

Big corporations are reining in their health-benefit costs even before a Clinton health-care system is installed, a survey indicates. Companies such as Mobil, Ford and Citicorp are holding down costs by making greater use of managed-care programs.

Clinton plans to set a ceiling on the total amount of subsidies available to low-income people and small businesses under his health-care plan.

Bond prices dropped after the Philadelphia Fed released an upbeat survey on the business outlook. The Treasury's 30-year benchmark lost over 1⅜ points. Its yield rose to 5.92%.

25 Viacom sweetened its bid for Paramount, countering rival QVC's $9.4 billion offer with its own two-step cash-and-stock offer that Viacom values at $10 billion. Viacom said its strategy gives Paramount holders the prospect of an immediate payoff because Viacom has already received most of the required regulatory approvals for acquiring Paramount.

26 General Motors' stock fell $1.25 to $44.75 in response to GM's tentative agreement with the UAW. After the market closed, GM announced it will take a third-quarter $950 million charge. S&P changed its outlook for GM to "negative" from "stable," citing the contract as well as GM's unfunded pension liability. GM said it was recalling 8,700 1994 Cadillacs to fix defects in the engines.

Sales of North American-built vehicles surged in mid-October, reaching the fastest pace in 18 months, as consumers headed to showrooms to take advantage of favorable interest rates and better inventory of 1994 models.

The Dow Jones industrials climbed 24.31 points to a record 3673.61 amid continued good earnings and further signs of an improving economy. Bond prices slumped, and the dollar rose.

Sales of existing homes grew a steady 2.6% in September from the previous month as pent-up demand and low interest rates continued to power a national housing recovery.

France undermined its commitment to restore the country's state-owned companies to financial health, agreeing to override Air France's plan to cut 4,000 jobs that led to a strike.

27 Consumer confidence fell this month, nearly wiping away September's gain, amid increasing pessimism about economic and employment prospects, a new survey shows. Separately, an employment cost index for the third quarter suggests that inflation is still well under control.

28 Durable-goods orders rose 0.7% in September, with gains posted across most major industries. The increase was the third in four months.

Japan's big banks are expected to make their largest-ever provisions against bad loans when they announce fiscal first-half results next month.

29 Gross domestic product grew at a 2.8% annual rate in the third quarter, apparently spurred by lower interest rates. But the growth is still quite moderate. Stronger economic data are leading many economists to increase their estimates for fourth-quarter growth, although they aren't yet as optimistic about next year.

The Dow Jones industrials hit a record, climbing 23.20 points to 3687.86, as stocks rallied on the government's figures on GDP.

The budget deficit at the end of the fiscal year was $254.95 billion, smaller than the White House and Congress anticipated a couple of months ago.

November 1993

1 Corporate profits surged in the third quarter, reflecting cost-cutting efforts. A *Wall Street Journal* survey shows that 597 major companies' earnings rose a cumulative 24% from the 1992 period, a sharp acceleration from the 11% gain in the second quarter. But even though some profits were stellar and most exceeded expectations, analysts now worry that companies may

have trouble sustaining the recent strong pace of growth.

Consumer spending rose 0.3% in September even though personal income gained only 0.1%. The trend is making many economists very upbeat about the recovery's strength.

The White House is urging U.S. companies to pledge not to move jobs to Mexico if the North American Free Trade Agreement passes, but corporations are balking at the request.

2 Manufacturing expanded in October for the first time in five months, a purchasing managers' poll shows. But growth still hasn't translated into job opportunities at U.S. factories. Separately, new construction spending rose 0.7% in September after a revised increase of 0.2% in August.

The Dow Jones industrials hit the third record in a week, climbing 12.02 points to 3692.61, on the October survey of purchasing managers. The Treasury's 30-year benchmark fell nearly 1 point. Its yield was 6.03%.

3 New home sales shot up in September to the highest level in seven years, another indication that low interest rates are stimulating the economy. Home sales surged 20.8% in September, following a 2.2% fall in August. Separately, the government's index of leading indicators rose 0.5% in September, suggesting continued moderate growth into 1994. The index rose a revised 0.9% in August.

Bond prices fell more than a point on the new-home sales data, but then rebounded somewhat. The Treasury 30-year benchmark ended down ⅜ point. Its yield climbed to 6.06%, as investors are acknowledging that the economy really is gaining strength. The Dow rose 5.03 to a record 3697.64.

Auto makers plan to increase fourth-quarter U.S. production 13% from year-ago levels, an indication that the industry is continuing to bet on the economy's moderate recovery.

Frankfurt stock prices soared 1.6% to a record, partly on hopes for further reductions in interest rates. Hong Kong shares rose to another record.

4 Stocks tumbled as skittish investors bailed out of utility and financial stocks amid fears that interest rates are headed higher. The Dow Jones Industrial Average sank 35.77 points to 3661.87. Long-term bond prices slumped for the fourth straight day. The yield on the Treasury's 30-year benchmark rose to 6.10%.

The pace of economic growth showed virtually no acceleration during the six weeks ended October 26, a new survey by the 12 Fed banks said.

Residential fixed-rate mortgages jumped to 7.16%, the first time since August they have been above 7%. Some analysts said that home-loan rates may finally have bottomed out.

5 Bond prices plunged as traders unloaded Treasurys before today's employment report. Rising long-term interest rates pulled down stocks. The Dow Jones Industrial Average sank 36.89 points to 3624.98. The Nasdaq Composite Index dropped 15.69, or 2%, to 757.26. The Treasury's benchmark 30-year issue lost almost one point. Its yield rose to 6.17%.

QVC is seeking to have Liberty Media sell its 22% stake in QVC to BellSouth. The move could defuse antitrust concerns in QVC's bid for Paramount, while giving QVC more cash to boost its $9.8 billion offer, according to people familiar with the talks.

Productivity rose at a 3.9% annual rate in the third quarter, reinforcing the notion that companies are on a long-term trend to raise efficiency.

Big U.S. retailers reported slightly disappointing October sales, as warm weather at the end of the month kept people from buying winter apparel.

8 Bond prices fell further, with the Treasury's 30-year bond losing about ½ point and its yield rising to 6.20%. Last week's sell-off was triggered by the economy's moderate show of strength, but worries of accelerating inflation are overblown, experts said.

U.S. stock market indexes rebounded after two days of sharp losses. European and Japanese stocks sank further. Most European indexes finished the week 2% to 3% lower.

The unemployment rate edged up to 6.8% in October, but factories added 12,000 employees to their payrolls, the first time since February that manufacturers haven't cut workers.

9 A Japanese advisory panel called for greater deregulation to benefit consumers and boost the economy, but it's unclear whether the government will follow its suggestions. Meanwhile, the relationship between Japan and the U.S. is improving, said Walter Mondale, the ambassador to Japan.

10 Mexico's currency sank 4% against the

dollar after Mexico's central bank, unwilling to defend the peso against speculators who are betting against Nafta, abandoned long-held currency stabilization levels. Investors have grown increasingly fearful that the U.S. Congress will defeat Nafta in a crucial vote next week.

The White House stepped up its assault on Ross Perot, with trade chief Mickey Kantor attacking the Texas billionaire before his televised debate last night with Gore. Meanwhile, the administration is negotiating possible changes in its plan to increase grazing fees in an effort to win Nafta votes.

The producer price index fell 0.2% in October, suggesting inflation is under control despite recent pickups in economic activity. Wholesale prices are up only 0.4% so far this year.

Bond prices rose on the producer prices report. The benchmark Treasury 30-year bond's price climbed 5/8 point. Its yield dropped to 6.14%.

Tokyo stocks sank 2.7% amid growing fears that the government will be unable to support share prices or revive the economy. The Nikkei Index dropped 499.45 points to 18125.71. The Nikkei has lost 2184 points, or 10.8%, over the past 10 trading sessions.

11 Consumer prices in October rose 0.4%, their biggest rise in six months, but analysts said the increase didn't signal a big new round of inflation. A good part of the October gain stemmed from the gasoline-tax increase.

Economists are raising their food inflation forecasts for 1994 in the wake of a report that the Midwest crop disaster is shrinking grain stockpiles.

12 BellSouth agreed to invest $1.5 billion in QVC, joining the battle against Viacom to acquire Paramount. The intricate pact rearranges QVC's ownership to remove antitrust obstacles to QVC's bid for Paramount. With BellSouth's new backing, QVC is widely expected to sweeten its $9.6 billion offer for Paramount before a crucial courtroom showdown Tuesday.

Tele-Communications is seeking to link up with another movie studio. The cable-TV giant has approached the parents of Universal Studios, 20th Century Fox and Columbia Pictures.

Mexican stocks climbed 1% to a second straight record, fueled by continuing optimism about prospects for the North American free trade pact.

15 The savings-and-loan cleanup agency is at a near standstill, plagued by unfilled positions, disputes over asset sales and a holdup in funds.

Retail sales jumped 1.5% in October, the largest increase since April and the seventh rise in a row.

16 General Motors said it may contribute $5.7 billion of its Class E stock to its pension fund for hourly workers, in a bid to rein in its $24 billion unfunded pension liability. The shares are linked to the earnings of its Electronic Data Systems unit. But the No. 1 auto maker cautioned that, in addition to board clearance, the plan is subject to a number of hurdles.

Chrysler contributed $2.6 billion to its pension fund in the first three quarters of 1993 as part of an effort to cut the car maker's unfunded liability. But Chrysler said its liability will rise by year end as a result of low interest rates and its new labor contract.

Bank regulators are preparing community-investment rules that would require banks to incorporate low- and moderate-income neighborhoods into their service areas.

Tokyo stocks tumbled 2.3%, with the Nikkei Index sinking 418.94 points to 18074.61. But Mexico City stocks hit another record, as investors seemed convinced the U.S. will pass Nafta.

Industrial production jumped 0.8% in October, another sign that the sector began perking up this fall after a dismal performance most of the year.

17 Stock prices rallied, with the Dow Jones Industrial Average jumping to a record as investors responded bullishly to signs that Nafta will pass Congress. The industrial average rose 33.25 points to 3710.77, closing above the 3700 mark for the first time. The dollar ended higher.

Stocks in Mexico City surged 1.7% to a fifth straight record on the Nafta optimism. Tokyo stocks posted strong gains, recovering some lost ground.

The unemployment rate could rise by half a percentage point because of changes taking effect in January in the government's tallying system.

18 Housing starts rose in October for the third month in a row, climbing 2.7% to the highest level since February 1990. The increase was driven largely by construction postponed by flooding in the Midwest region.

19 Businesses anticipate big benefits from the North American Free Trade Agree-

ment. Executives at large and small companies, in sectors ranging from agriculture to banking to transportation, are talking optimistically about expanded opportunities south of the border and increased jobs in the U.S. The successful fight for Nafta is the latest example of how the Clinton administration is aggressively wooing big business.

Clinton's Nafta victory raised hopes among world trade negotiators that they could meet the December 15 deadline for concluding talks on the General Agreement on Trade and Tariffs. But the optimism is tempered by a growing feeling that a GATT pact may not be as broad as once envisioned.

22 The U.S. plans to begin hard bargaining today on world trade talks now that Nafta cleared its final hurdle in Congress. But the EC said the U.S. isn't proposing adequate cuts in tariffs on textiles and apparel. Canada's prime minister said he wants further negotiations on Nafta side pacts.

The U.S. trade deficit widened to $10.9 billion in September from a revised $10.05 billion in August. But the gap looks better, and the country appears far more competitive, when trade in services is considered.

The price of the Treasury's 30-year bond plunged more than 1⅛ points, sending its yield up to 6.33%, the highest level in more than three months. Money managers predicted long-term yields will rise through the holidays but could drop in the first quarter.

23 Stock prices dropped on the conclusion that the bond market slump is worse than first thought. After diving more than 40 points, the Dow Jones industrials rebounded moderately to finish 23.76 points lower at 3670.25. The price of the 30-year Treasury bond fell ¾ point. Its yield rose to 6.38%.

Tokyo stock prices plunged 3.1% Monday, the largest percentage-point drop this year. The Nikkei Index closed at 17384.84, down 556.35 points.

24 Bond prices soared in a rebound from recent depressed levels, and stock prices rose. The Treasury's 30-year issue gained more than a point, while its yield fell to 6.31%. The Dow Jones Industrial Average edged up 3.92 points to end at 3674.17.

The Bank of England cut its base lending rate to 5.5% from 6% in a move to give consumer confidence a boost before the Treasury unveils a package of tax increases next week.

Oil prices plunged as OPEC's oil ministers deferred discussion of their oversupply problem until today. Even as formal OPEC talks began, skepticism mounted that the ministers will be able to end the oil glut. January crude fell 47 cents a barrel to $16.63.

26 OPEC members decided not to cut their oil production, a move that threatens to send prices tumbling. The shift in policy has wide-ranging implications for the world oil industry and for regions that produce petroleum.

Durable-goods orders rose 2% last month, the third consecutive monthly gain, pushing orders to a record level. The improvement reflects slow but steady growth in manufacturing.

Sales of North American-built cars and trucks in mid-November rose 20.5% as a recovery in the U.S. car industry remained robust amid low interest rates and a stronger economy.

29 Japan and the U.S. agreed on a plan to open Japan's markets to rice imports, giving an important boost to world trade talks in Geneva. Japan is expected to formally agree around December 10 to lift its longstanding ban on rice imports. U.S. officials said the agreement would add to pressure on the European Community to sweeten its offer on agricultural products in the trade negotiations.

Retailers rang up respectable gains during the weekend after Thanksgiving, although shoppers launched the holiday season with bargain hunting, a lot of window shopping and only cautious spending.

Employment in the first quarter is expected to continue to expand moderately, with significant improvement in durable-goods manufacturing and in the finance, insurance and real-estate sectors, Manpower said.

Machine-tool orders fell 8.5% in October from September but jumped 25% from the year-earlier month as manufacturers continued to seek equipment to cut costs and boost productivity.

Tokyo stocks dropped 2.9% Friday and analysts noted the potential for more selling pressure this week. The Nikkei Index closed at 16726.37, down 496.55 points, contributing to a loss of 22% over the past four weeks.

World oil prices fell further in the wake of OPEC's decision to leave its production ceiling untouched. Another test of the announcement comes today, when the New York Merc reopens following the Thanksgiving holiday. Prices declined $1 a barrel just since Wednesday, when OPEC members adjourned their winter meeting.

30 Oil prices fell further, with U.S. crude losing more than $1 a barrel in the wake of OPEC members' decision not to lower production. Some fuel prices were down even more steeply than crude, with January unleaded gasoline dropping nearly three cents a gallon on the New York Merc. Lower oil prices spurred a bond-market rally, but bond prices surrendered most of their gains. Stock prices also reversed course, ending lower.

Existing-home sales rose a robust 3.6% in October, with continued low interest rates fueling the highest monthly level of activity in 14 years.

Tokyo stocks plunged 3.9%, and the slide shows no signs of abating. The Nikkei Index dropped 647.66 to 16078.71 Monday, a new low for the year. Meanwhile, Japan's new reformist government isn't showing any signs it intends to try to stem the plunge.

December 1993

1 The Japanese government raised the prospect of emergency measures to combat an economic downturn, reversing slumping stock prices. The Nikkei rose 327.83 points to 16406.54.

AT&T is planning a major work-force cutback in its consumer long-distance unit as it struggles to fight stiff competition from MCI Communications. The reduction could run as high as 15%, or 4,500 jobs, in the 32,000-member unit, said individuals close to the telecommunications firm.

Boeing is expected to announce today more production cuts and further job losses, reflecting a continued dearth of major airplane orders. The production cuts will increase the number of jobs lost by as many as 3,000, or 3.5%, of Boeing's work force, adding to 27,000 cuts already under way.

The consumer confidence index jumped nearly 11 points in November to its highest reading since January. Bond prices dropped on signs of a strengthening economy. The Treasury's benchmark 30-year issue lost ⅞ point. Its yield rose to 6.30%. The Dow industrials rose 6.15 points to 3683.95.

The inflation rate is likely to fall further because of the slide in oil prices. The result could be an economy that gains momentum at the start of the year from consumer spending. Lower jet-fuel prices are producing a windfall for the airlines, but not enough to offset fourth-quarter losses. Oil prices rose slightly yesterday.

Russia is considering slashing crude-oil exports by up to 75% this month because frigid weather has increased demand within former Soviet republics. The cut, if instituted, could slow the price decline that followed OPEC's decision not to cut output.

2 Stock prices surged amid powerful rallies overseas and further evidence the economy is improving. Bond prices also rose. The Dow Jones industrials jumped 13.13 points to 3697.08. The Treasury's 30-year issue gained more than ½ point. Its yield fell to 6.25%.

Tokyo stocks rallied 4.4% after Japanese government officials promised to treat the ailing economy. The Nikkei climbed 718.77 points to 17125.31. But some stock traders predicted the recovery would be short-lived.

The manufacturing sector expanded in November for the second consecutive month, a survey of purchasing managers indicated. But the employment component of the index declined again last month. Separately, the economy grew at a 2.7% annual rate in the third quarter.

3 Big U.S. retailers posted slightly lower-than-expected sales in November, signaling a slow start to the crucial holiday shopping period. But analysts generally agreed that an improving economy, rising consumer confidence and low interest rates promise a good holiday shopping season.

Disposable personal income rose 0.2% in October, while spending increased 0.4% in the month, indicating that consumers are spending money faster than they're making it.

The U.S. and the European Community appear ready to strike a deal on world trade talks on Monday, despite some remaining differences. Comments by U.S. Trade Representative Kantor and EC Trade Minister Brittan indicate that both sides made substantive progress in their two days of talks this week and are looking for final approval to cut a deal.

6 The unemployment rate dropped to 6.4% in November from 6.8% the month before, as the lowest interest

rates in two decades began kicking in and stimulating the sectors of the economy that normally lead recoveries. Manufacturing jobs rose by 30,000, mostly in industries making durable goods, and construction jobs rose by 27,000.

Sales of North American-built cars and light trucks surged in the last 10 days of November as the Big Three continued to rack up market-share gains at the expense of the Japanese.

7 Mellon Bank agreed to acquire Dreyfus in a stock swap valued at $1.7 billion, in a bold move to grab a big chunk of the mutual-fund market. The acquisition, the biggest ever of a mutual-fund company, will give Mellon the largest mutual-fund business owned by any bank and mesh Dreyfus's lucrative portfolio of mutual funds with the bank's vast processing capabilities and customer base.

Securities brokerage firms are taking measures to clean up their images, amid lawsuits and unprecedented levels of consumer contempt.

Tokyo shares plunged 3.6% Monday, in the second-deepest point loss for the benchmark index this year, on disappointment about the Japanese government's faltering commitment to act quickly to battle the recession.

8 Investors are choking on the nearly $3 billion in new issues of real-estate investment trusts scheduled for early this month. Underwriters were forced to postpone offers from three developers because they couldn't get enough buyers at favorable prices.

Late mortgage payments plunged to the lowest level in 19 years, indicating homeowners continue to benefit from historically low interest rates.

9 Xerox plans to cut at least 10,000 jobs, or 10% of its work force, shutter some facilities and take $854 million in charges, probably producing a loss for the year as the company imposes its third restructuring in as many years. The news sent Xerox shares up $5.625, or 7%, to $86.375.

The Fed offered an upbeat survey of regional economic conditions, adding to mounting evidence that the U.S. economy is improving significantly nearly everywhere but California. Retailers said sales picked up after Thanksgiving, and they are optimistic about Christmas, the Fed found.

The Dow Jones industrials hit a record for a second day on a surge in economically sensitive stocks. Bond prices edged higher. The industrials climbed 15.65 to 3734.53. S&P's 500-stock index fell 0.47 to 466.29.

Tokyo stocks plummeted 2.3% on growing concern that Japan's governing coalition could collapse, jeopardizing efforts to rescue the economy.

Accounting rulemakers voted to consider forcing banks and others to disclose more information about risks in their derivatives investments.

10 Paramount was told by the Delaware Supreme Court to consider QVC's $10.1 billion offer on an equal basis with Viacom's friendly bid. Upholding a lower court ruling, the three-judge panel rebuked Paramount's directors for ignoring unwelcome suitor QVC in favor of a lower offer from Viacom, which is now expected to increase its bid. Traders watched the hearing live on TV.

Tokyo stock prices jumped 3.4%, helped by political jawboning and an important stock-futures expiration. The Nikkei 225-stock index closed at 17061.91, up 553.96 points.

Producer prices were unchanged in November, a sign that inflation still isn't a problem despite increased economic activity. Prices fell 0.2% in October and rose 0.2% in September.

Most midsize manufacturers increased sales in each of the past three months and a growing number expect a broad economic recovery in the second half of next year, a survey said.

13 Consumer prices inched up 0.2% in November, with the rise restrained by a 1.3% drop in energy prices. Inflation slowed to a 2.8% annual rate in the first 11 months, compared with a 2.9% rate in the year-earlier period.

Japan said its economy grew at a 2% annual rate in the latest quarter, a surprise to Japan's business world. But the rise didn't seem to change a generally pessimistic outlook.

15 Trade negotiators from the U.S. and Europe resolved remaining disputes, paving the way for approval of a GATT accord. Officials agreed to sharply reduce average tariffs world-wide, but they failed to achieve a broad opening of world markets to the service sector. The U.S. lost efforts to whittle down European aircraft subsidies or open markets for U.S. financial firms and Hollywood.

Retail sales rose 0.4% in November, the eighth consecutive monthly increase and another sign that consumers are back in a buying mood. Strong sales of furniture, apparel and building materials helped boost sales.

North American-built vehicle sales fell moderately in early December, but U.S. auto makers remain bullish and are planning sizable production increases for the first quarter of 1994.

16 Trade officials from 117 nations wrapped up a trade pact under GATT that slashes tariffs and cuts subsidies globally, after seven years of tortuous negotiations. But nations will still continue to try to wrangle better deals from their trading partners before the pact takes effect July 1, 1995.

The U.S. business community was relieved the trade pact was completed, but doesn't see it creating a flood of new economic activity. Executives in Europe, Asia and Latin America, on the other hand, were enthusiastic.

Industrial production shot up 0.9% last month, a sign the sector is gathering steam after a long spell of inertia. The rise was the largest in a year and the sixth consecutive monthly gain.

17 IBM is charting a big push into the consumer market, forming a new division and searching for an outside marketing executive to run it. The division will include IBM PC and the company's new PowerPC group, and marks a shift after years of focusing on big corporate customers. While IBM PC is considered one of the more successful units of IBM, it is in a fierce battle to retain market leadership over Apple and Compaq Computer.

U.S. imports and exports rose to records in October, and the merchandise-trade deficit shrank to $10.46 billion from $10.62 billion in September. Despite the slight improvement in October, the trade deficit has mostly deteriorated during the past 18 months.

British firms are on a buying spree of U.S. companies, re-establishing the U.K. as the largest direct foreign investor in American businesses.

20 Viacom and its rival bidder, QVC, are each expected to sweeten their cash-and-stock takeover offers for Paramount today. Observers believe Paramount ultimately will fetch more than $10 billion, with a considerably higher cash portion to the offer than in previous bids. Before the three-month-long takeover battle began, industry executives and analysts estimated that Paramount was valued at between $8 billion and $9 billion.

Paramount left open the possibility of successive rounds of bidding. The auction would end when one of the offers draws 51% of Paramount shares.

Retail stores revved up promotions to combat a lull before the sales surge they hope will materialize this final week of the Christmas retail season. Sales are ahead of last year but aren't as robust as some had hoped.

Housing starts climbed 3.9% in November. The rise marks the fourth consecutive monthly increase, suggesting a strengthening sector that will spur economic growth in this quarter and next, economists said.

21 Tokyo stocks fell 3.6%, as investors dumped shares on concerns that political turmoil will delay government measures to lift Japan's economy. The Nikkei lost 647.67 points, the largest point drop this year, to 17404.24. Meanwhile, London stock prices rose to the fourth consecutive record finish.

Many mortgage lenders are trying to do more business with minorities, but the gap between black and white loan-denial rates is hard to narrow, a *Wall Street Journal* study shows. The black-white rejection gap widened last year, rising to a 2.06 ratio from 1.91.

The Organization for Economic Cooperation and Development ratcheted downward its economic forecasts for most developed nations in 1994, with the exception of the U.S.

22 Domino's Pizza said it will no longer guarantee delivery of pizzas within 30 minutes, in the wake of its loss of a $78 million lawsuit last week to a St. Louis woman who was injured by a Domino's delivery driver.

23 UAL agreed to sell a majority stake in the airline to its two main unions in exchange for huge labor concessions, in what would become the nation's largest company majority-owned by employees. The $5 billion transaction puts pressure on major rivals to reduce costs in similar equity-for-concession plans, and it portends lower fares for consumers, fulfilling one of the main goals of deregulation, begun 15 years ago.

Paramount agreed to sign an acquisition agreement with QVC, until now a hostile bidder, and advise shareholders to embrace QVC's $10 billion bid over Viacom's $9.5 billion. But Viacom could still sweeten its offer and is reportedly in tense talks to line up a hefty cash infusion to do so.

The economy grew at an inflation-adjusted 2.9% annual rate in the third quarter, according to revised data, higher than the estimate of 2.7% that officials issued a month ago.

27 Retailers had an unremarkable holiday season that met expectations overall, but distributed its gifts to shop owners unevenly. Sales picked up last week after a post-Thanksgiving lull, but only with the help of heavier-than-usual discounting, which put pressure on profit margins. Merchants say a new type of shopper, unafraid of buying but insisting on value, is dominating spending.

Strength in the economy continues to build, a string of data shows. Topping the good news is a 2% increase in durable-goods orders in November. Also, personal income rose 0.5% while consumer spending fell 0.3%, suggesting that consumers are saving more.

Machine-tool orders fell 4% in November from October, a sign that the industry, though improving, still isn't receiving enough orders to sustain steady growth in backlog. Compared with November 1992, orders rose 50%.

Vehicle sales' steady recovery continued in mid-December, building hope that the rebound in the U.S. auto industry will be sustained and robust. Sales rose 27.3% from a year ago.

28 The White House called for emergency talks on semiconductor trade with Japan as new figures showed the foreign share of the Japanese semiconductor market fell to 18.1% in the third quarter, below the 20% goal set under a 1986 agreement. Although expressing disappointment, U.S. industry officials reined in their criticism, saying they will wait to see what the talks in January produce.

Ford will send three senior executives to Japan to help rescue Mazda, in which it owns a 25% stake. The move, which symbolizes the changing fortunes of U.S. and Japanese auto makers, points to a future in which Mazda will act more as Ford's Asian arm than as an independent entity.

29 Consumer confidence posted a healthy increase of more than eight points in December. At 80.2, the index is at its highest since September 1990. Consumers grew slightly more positive about the current state of the economy, and markedly more optimistic about the next six months.

U.S. manufacturing shipments will increase by the biggest amount since 1988, the Commerce Department's industrial outlook for 1994 predicts. The rise will be helped by increased investment in capital equipment and consumer purchases of durable goods.

New York Life and possibly Prudential Insurance are included in a broadened investigation of life-insurance sales tactics by Florida officials. The inquiry has centered on Met Life and involved claims that agents misled clients into buying life insurance.

30 Sales of previously owned homes grew 2.9% to a record in November, driven by low interest rates and rising consumer confidence. All regions in the U.S. posted strong gains.

Construction contracts fell 1% in value for November as gains in housing were offset by declines in construction other than homes and buildings.

The Dow Jones Industrial Average crept to a third-straight record, up 0.56, to 3794.33, on positive economic news. The dollar posted strong gains against the German, Swiss and British currencies and bond prices fell. The Treasury's 30-year issue lost more than 1/4 point. Its yield rose to 6.24%.

London stocks soared 1.5% to a record on rising economic optimism. The FT 100-stock index rose 49.7 to 3462.0.

31 Sales of new single-family homes rose 11.3% in November to their highest level since April 1986. The West led the surge with a 33.8% rise, the South and Midwest had moderate gains, and sales fell 10.2% in the Northeast.

Many small-business owners think the economy is finally picking up steam. Growing markedly more optimistic in the last few weeks, they are gearing up to boost hiring and investment. With many big firms still paring back, small businesses could play a vital role in economic growth next year.

January 1994

3 The U.S. economy's recent strength will continue in the first quarter, prompting the Federal Reserve Board to raise short-term interest rates as a pre-emptive strike against inflation, according to most of the 51 economists queried in *The Wall Street Journal*'s semiannual survey.

Economically sensitive stocks began a surge in the fourth quarter that analysts say will continue into 1994 as the economy improves, marking a new phase in the prolonged bull market.

America West's Michael Conway, the

carrier's president, CEO and one of its founders, was ousted, ending his nearly yearlong struggle for power with Chairman William Franke.

A record $1.5 trillion in new stocks and bonds were helped to market by securities firms in 1993, shattering 1992's record by 36%. The three-year underwriting spree is likely to keep going in 1994, generating fees in its path. In 1993, firms pocketed a record $9.13 billion in disclosed underwriting fees.

The junk-bond market had its best year in 1993, and shows little sign of slackening. The total issuance in the market of over $68 billion last year is nearly twice 1992's high and equal to the total raised from 1982 through 1986.

Japan and the U.S. are still "very far apart" in talks to set a framework for trade relations in areas such as motor vehicles and auto parts, a senior commerce department official said. Garten sought to dispel speculation that the Clinton administration might ease up on the Hosokawa government.

Japan's Hosokawa all but ignored the nation's economic downturn in a New Year's Day speech, a sign that leaders are still groping for ways to restart the stalled economy. Tokyo stocks rose Thursday partly on hopes that the prime minister would discuss a proposed income-tax cut.

4 Manufacturing activity shot up in December to its highest level in nearly a year, a survey of purchasing managers shows. Prices fell for the fourth consecutive month in December, suggesting that inflation is still under control. Separately, construction spending increased 1.2% in November.

Bond prices tumbled amid further signs of an improving economy. The Treasury's benchmark 30-year issue fell more than a point. Its yield rose to 6.42%. The Dow Jones Industrial Average increased 2.51 to 3756.60.

5 Sales of pickups, vans and sport utility vehicles surged in 1993, and early results show four of the top six vehicles sold in the U.S. were trucks. The trend reflects the natural strength of trucks in an economic recovery and a sea change in buying habits.

6 The mortgage-refinancing boom has slowed sharply, after soaring to record levels last year as interest rates plunged. A weekly index of refinancing activity last week stood 65% below its high recorded in September.

The Dow industrials broke through the 3800 level to reach their second consecutive record, up 5.06 to 3803.88.

7 U.S. mutual stock funds gained 12.54% in 1993, a year in which investors saw across-the-board strength. Foreign-stock funds soared 39.40% on average and a few reaped 80% to 90% gains or better in the "emerging markets" of developing countries.

Big U.S. retail chains reported moderate sales gains for the holiday period. But the results were achieved only after steep discounting.

Hong Kong stocks plunged 6.5% and left many investors wondering whether the decline signaled the end of a long bull. The Hang Seng index fell 793.43 points to 11374.50.

10 The unemployment rate fell to 6.4% of the work force in December from 6.5% in November and 7.3% a year ago. But the manufacturing and construction sectors, which had offered encouraging signs of job growth recently, added virtually no new workers.

Boeing and four European partners tentatively agreed to go on with the next phase in their proposed joint effort to build the world's largest jet, despite the realization that the project will likely cost at least 50% more than the $10 billion estimated a year ago, people familiar with the talks say.

11 Big Three auto stocks surged on expectations of strong fourth-quarter profits and an even better 1994. GM rose $1.375 to $59.25, Ford $2.625 to $67.25, and Chrysler $1.625 to $58.75, as many analysts raised their earnings forecasts upon returning from last week's upbeat Detroit auto show.

Viacom shares plunged 6.7% on news of its proposed takeover of Blockbuster, a move aimed at allowing Viacom to top rival QVC's $9.8 billion bid for Paramount. But the $2.75-a-share drop in Viacom nonvoting Class B shares reduced the value of Viacom's offer by $153 million, to $9.3 billion.

13 Producer prices fell 0.1% in December, driven down by a big drop in energy prices. Lower energy prices helped keep wholesale prices in check for the entire year, led by a 16.8% drop in gasoline prices. For 1993, the price of finished goods rose only 0.2%. The core rate of inflation, which excludes the food and energy sectors, rose 0.2% in December and 0.4% for the year, the best showing since the U.S. began tracking these prices in 1974.

New York Stock Exchange trading volume was the second highest in exchange history last week, second only to the week of the October 1987 crash. And this week, Big Board volume has topped 300 million shares every day.

Program trading accounted for a record 11.9% of overall New York Stock Exchange volume last year.

The White House plans to press Russia to limit its exports of aluminum as part of Clinton's Moscow summit with Yeltsin. Trade negotiators from the U.S., Russia and Europe have haggled for months over charges that Russian firms are dumping aluminum on the market at unfairly low prices.

14 Consumer prices rose 0.2% in December and gained 2.7% for 1993. The U.S. inflation outlook is as promising as it has been in decades, holding big implications for economic decision-making by individuals and corporate America that has in the past hinged on the belief that inflation is inevitable.

Retail sales rose 0.8% in December and 1993 sales jumped 6.2%, the strongest annual gain in four years. Sales of durable goods increased 1.7% last month as many consumers took advantage of low interest rates to improve or furnish their homes.

Bond prices fell on the stronger-than-expected retail sales report. The Treasury's 30-year issue fell almost one point. Its yield was 6.25%. The Dow industrials declined 6.20 to 3842.43.

17 Industrial production rose 0.7% in December, driven by high auto production. An index of consumer sentiment for early January also jumped.

18 A recovery in Europe appears to have begun, though it could be quite a while before business really picks up. A European Union panel predicts 1.3% growth among its member states this year after a 0.4% contraction in 1993.

China agreed to limit growth in its textile exports to the U.S. over three years. U.S. Trade Representative Kantor said there was "no linkage" between the pact and other benefits, such as an extension of favored trade status, but said that it marks the beginning of a "healthier" relationship.

The U.S. is pushing Japan to agree to increase its purchases of U.S.-made auto parts by about 20% a year as the White House broadens its pressure on Japan to move on stalled trade talks.

Eli Lilly plans to sell or spin off its entire medical-device business, according to people familiar with the decision. The plan to shed the nine companies with total annual sales of about $1.2 billion is the first indication of a changed course for Lilly under its new chairman, Randall Tobias. The landscape of various medical fields would be altered by the moves, since Lilly is the market-share leader or a strong No. 2 in several areas.

19 Viacom increased its bid for Paramount to about $9.7 billion. Although the current market value still falls short of the $10.1 billion bid by rival QVC Network, many traders said they prefer Viacom's bid because it contains a new provision to protect shareholders against a downturn in Viacom's stock price, a major component of its cash-and-stock offer.

20 Pfizer reported surprisingly weak earnings and sales growth for the fourth quarter, an indication that even the strongest of drug companies is being overpowered by upheaval in the health-care industry. The results sent Pfizer's shares down $5, or 7.4%, to $62.875, and shook the stock of the entire pharmaceutical sector.

The Federal Reserve's regional economic survey was mostly optimistic, citing stronger manufacturing, home construction and consumer spending on big-ticket purchases.

21 Housing starts grew 6.2% in December, pushing homebuilding for 1993 to its highest level in four years. Separately, initial jobless claims increased 23,000 last week to 380,000.

Japan's year-end trade statistics are expected to show that U.S. exports to Japan have picked up, but the bilateral trade imbalance hasn't budged, illustrating only limited success for President Clinton's strong-yen policy.

24 The Dow Jones Industrial Average surged 22.52, to 3914.48, closing above the 3900 level for the first time.

QVC network is under increased pressure to improve its bid for Paramount following the Paramount board's endorsement of the latest $9.8 billion takeover bid by Viacom. Lazard Freres advised the directors that the Viacom bid was "marginally superior," even though its market value is currently lower than the QVC offer, valued at about $10.2 billion.

25 The Nikkei Stock Average plummeted 954.19, or 4.9%, Monday to 18353.24, hurt by the defeat of a plan to reform Japan's political system.

26 IBM reported its first quarterly profit since the second quarter of 1992, signaling that two years of big charges and restructuring may finally be taking

hold. But the company still managed to disappoint Wall Street with lower-than-anticipated earnings and an unexpected decline in sales. Jerome York, chief financial officer, said he expects at least a break-even first quarter, and that profit margins and revenue will stay flat or rise slightly.

Kodak plans to offer its first economy-brand film to compete with low-priced rivals, which have eaten away at the company's market share. Kodak long resisted the idea, saying consumers were willing to pay extra for its respected technology and name.

Sales of previously owned homes grew 6.7% in December, continuing their record climb. Analysts attributed the gain to greater consumer optimism and fear that interest rates are moving up. The Conference Board's consumer confidence index rose to 83.2 in January from 79.8 in December.

Tokyo shares rose 1.6% Tuesday, boosted by arbitragers and foreign investors buying after Monday's slide.

27 Ford plans to unveil a used-vehicle leasing program. It could lead to a shift in car-buying patterns, analysts say, with some customers never buying another car or truck again. The plan could help Ford handle more than 250,000 leased vehicles scheduled to be returned this year.

The value of construction contracts fell 4% in December, for the second month in a row. Total construction in 1993 increased 5% to $264 billion.

28 Stock mutual funds pulled in a record $14.5 billion from investors in December and fund executives say January's inflows may soar even higher. The huge cash inflow last month capped the biggest year in history for mutual-fund sales, which hit $128 billion in 1993. Mutual funds now rank among the most dominant buyers and sellers in the stock market.

Orders for durable goods rose 8.6% in 1993, their strongest increase in five years. In December, durable-goods orders grew 2.2%. Economists were particularly encouraged that despite continual cutbacks in defense spending, overall orders were still strong.

31 Economic growth shot up at an annual rate of 5.9% in the fourth quarter of 1993 while inflation stayed well in check. The extremely strong performance has boosted analysts' expectations about the first half of this year.

The Dow Jones industrials rose 19.13 to 3945.43, its second high in a row, after the upbeat economic news.

An accord to cut aluminum output world-wide by up to two million metric tons was set by big aluminum producing nations, putting the beleaguered industry on track for recovery.

February 1994

2 Viacom and QVC each increased slightly their offers for Paramount, moments before the 5 P.M. deadline yesterday. QVC raised the cash portion of its offer to $104 a share from $92, but cut the amount of QVC stock in the bid. Viacom left the cash portion of its offer unchanged at $107 a share, but boosted the value of securities being offered. Because of the complex structure of the bids, traders couldn't yet say which would win.

A healthy rise in orders helped the manufacturing sector expand again in January, according to a survey of purchasing managers, but the growth brought along new hints of inflation.

Bond prices plunged on the strong manufacturing activity report. The Treasury's 30-year issue lost over 1 point and its yield was 6.31%. The Dow Jones industrials fell 14.35 to 3964.01.

3 Viacom has a clear but narrow edge over rival bidder QVC after Tuesday's final round of bidding for Paramount, takeover-stock traders said. QVC stock surged $2.25 to $47, and Viacom Class B shares sagged 62.5 cents to $33.50, reflecting the view that the eventual winner will issue millions of new shares and take on debt.

Tokyo unveiled a tax cut as the first part of its stimulus package, which is expected to total about $138 billion and may be released in full this week.

4 The Clinton health plan received another broadside from business as the U.S. Chamber of Commerce warned Congress against even using the bill as a "starting point" for future legislation. The statement came on the heels of a Business Roundtable vote also rebuffing the administration plan. A senior Chamber official described the twin actions as a "wake-up call" to the president of eroding business support for his plan.

U.S. vehicle sales rose 13.7% in January from a year ago. The increase in sales to 1,022,543 cars and trucks seemed to underscore the strength of the economic recovery, coming as it did in the face of higher prices and the disruptions of unusually cold weather and the California earthquake.

7 The Fed's decision to raise short-term interest rates for the first time in nearly five years won't have a significant impact on the economy, most economists say. They say the Fed, by nudging up the federal funds rate to 3.25% from 3% before inflation had begun to accelerate, is waging a psychological war. The move drew a mild response from the White House, demonstrating that a Greenspan-Clinton alliance continues.

Stocks fell sharply on the Fed action, but many analysts don't think the rate rise will derail the bull market. The Dow Jones industrials plunged 96.24 points, or 2.4%, to 3871.42.

The unemployment rate rose to 6.7% of the work force in January, interrupting a string of encouraging job gains. But a healthy rise in factory employment suggests that the labor market is still on solid footing.

Japanese trade negotiators say U.S. officials are pressing Japanese car makers in the U.S. to produce cars that have 90% of their parts made in North America, local-content rules far tougher than for other foreign firms. An impasse continues at the trade talks with a deadline looming Friday.

8 Clinton proposed a $1.5 trillion fiscal 1995 budget that reflects the administration's priorities while hewing to spending caps. The big winners are the departments of justice, commerce, education and transportation, which oversee many of the investment programs important to the president. Debate over the defense budget, meanwhile, is expected to focus less on its allotment than on a new vision of the military's role.

The proposed budget would raise about $1.5 billion in new user fees in fiscal 1995, yielding about $8.4 billion through 1999, with Wall Street and the pharmaceutical industry getting hit the hardest. The proposal would shrink the deficit for the third year in a row, to $165.1 billion this year.

The Dow Jones industrials surged 34.90 to 3906.32, roaring back from Friday's 96-point plunge after the Fed's decision to lift short-term interest rates. Analysts said investors realized the small rise won't hurt the economy and will help prolong the bull market.

Stock markets world-wide tumbled as much as 7% following Friday's 2.4% drop on Wall Street. Based on the Dow Jones World Stock Index, Hong Kong fell 5.8%, Thailand 6.6%, the U.K. market fell 1.3%, and Germany 2.4%.

9 Clinton's health plan would cost more than the White House projects, and would increase the deficit over the first 10 years of the plan, a Congressional Budget Office analysis concludes. In another blow to the president, the CBO listed as federal receipts the insurance premiums that businesses and individuals would be required to pay, a point likely to aid critics charging that the plan amounts to a huge new government program.

Health-care costs for manufacturers would be lower under the president's plan, but would increase for construction firms, retailers and other service-sector employers, two Brookings Institution economists report.

Japan's Hosokawa hammered out a $140 billion stimulus package that analysts say may add one to two percentage points to the nation's economic growth. But they warn the temporary nature of the proposal's tax cut might blunt its stimulative effect.

10 The U.S. trade talks with Japan broke down on the eve of a summit between Clinton and Hosokawa. Trade Representative Kantor's suspension of the negotiations was clearly meant to signal U.S. displeasure at the pace of the talks and to put maximum pressure on Tokyo to make concessions. The stalemate continues over U.S. insistence that Japan agree to numerical goals to lift its imports.

Ford rebounded strongly in the fourth quarter to a profit of $719 million from a year-ago loss, but its stock slid $1, to $68.50, because investors were looking for even better results.

GM's three nonautomotive units posted a combined 2.5% decline in fourth-quarter earnings, reflecting lower profit at the finance unit.

11 A U.S. surgeons' group stunned the medical and health-policy world by endorsing a national "single-payer" health system for the U.S., in which the government would control medical fees and pay medical bills with taxpayer funds. The White House doesn't support a single-payer system, but it reacted with encouragement to the American College of Surgeons' stance—partly because such a plan would guarantee universal coverage.

The SEC is asking 30 mutual-fund groups for detailed information about personal trading by their portfolio managers, spurred by growing concerns about possible self-dealing.

14 The U.S. is poised to launch proceedings to impose trade sanctions against Japan involving cellular telephones, following the collapse of a trade summit between Clinton and Hosokawa that sought to fundamentally redesign trade relations, but instead ended in stalemate and frustration. The sanctions are part of a broad effort to increase pressure on Tokyo to initiate new negotiations and agree to the U.S. demand to set import goals.

Nearly all silicone breast-implant companies in the U.S., including Dow Corning, Bristol-Myers and Baxter, agreed to fund a $4 billion liability settlement plan, virtually assuring the world's biggest product-liability pact will be offered for court approval.

QVC ruled out changing its $10 billion offer for Paramount, increasing the odds that Paramount shareholders will choose a rival offer from Viacom by the deadline of midnight tonight.

Consumer spending fell 0.5% in January, ending nine months of solid gains, and a consumer-sentiment index also slipped. Many analysts point to January's record cold weather as the main reason for the drop in spending. Separately, producer prices of finished goods climbed 0.2% last month.

Merck is shifting its strategy to emphasize market share, rather than profit margins, and the 1993 purchase of Medco will erode Merck's high 35% margin, a Merck executive said.

15 The dollar plunged nearly 4% against the yen, amid speculation that the Clinton administration will try using a stronger yen to prod a Japanese market opening. The White House didn't move to stop the yen's rise, nor did it show any unusual concern over the movement. Still, officials have ruled out efforts to boost the yen, as broader market forces will tend to push down the Japanese currency.

The White House is preparing a two-pronged trade attack, deciding to renew the tough Super 301 trade provision and planning trade-sanction proceedings over cellular telephones. Most of corporate America, however, doesn't want a trade war with Japan that threatens to flare out of control.

Many takeover-stock traders tendered their shares of Paramount to Viacom as the five-month takeover battle with QVC neared a conclusion. Among those tendering shares to Viacom was Mario Gabelli, one of Paramount's biggest shareholders.

Retailers are returning to downtown urban areas, reversing a 20-year shift to suburban malls. Kmart, Montgomery Ward and Toys 'R' Us are among the firms opening stores in cities, seeking reasonable real-estate rates and lots of potential customers.

16 Viacom won the Paramount battle, receiving nearly 75% of Paramount shares tendered as rival bidder QVC bowed out of the contest. But many traders and analysts believe Viacom is paying a high premium for Paramount, and that without a new depth of management, a strong stock market and some luck, the five-month struggle may prove an empty victory.

The U.S. opened its trade offensive against Japan, threatening to levy sanctions on several hundred millions of dollars of Japanese imports because of a dispute over cellular telephones.

Commerce Secretary Brown reiterated the Clinton administration's hands-off policy on the yen, but suggested that it isn't unhappy about the yen's rise. The dollar made a modest recovery against the yen yesterday.

Industrial output rose 0.5% in January, a much slower pace than at the end of 1993. The U.S. blamed wintry weather and the Los Angeles quake.

17 A Japanese trade negotiator accused the U.S. of bad faith and a "betrayal of trust" in GATT talks over tariffs in Geneva, sending U.S.-Japanese trade relations spiraling further downward. The accusations, which were accompanied by threats of retaliation, represent a significant escalation of the Japanese response to a U.S. move toward trade sanctions after bilateral talks failed last week.

Japan's trade surplus widened 17% in January from a year ago. The increase was the second in as many months and, coming after months of steady narrowing in the surplus, may heighten U.S. trade tensions.

The number of nonprofit hospitals defaulting on their obligations in the tax-exempt markets is growing. While the default rate is still slow, potential problems lurk. No one knows how many hospitals have used the markets, or how much they raise a year.

Housing starts plunged 17.6% in January, as the big freeze in much of the nation chilled home-building after a strong surge late last year.

18 Consumer prices didn't increase at all in January, something that hasn't happened in more than four years. Analysts said the figures show, yet again, that inflation is well under control despite a noticeably improving economy. The severely cold weather didn't damage crops enough to force up prices, as the cost of food fell last month. Clothing, transportation and energy prices also declined.

Bond prices plunged after a report from the Federal Reserve Bank of Philadelphia sparked inflation concerns, after initially rising on the consumer prices report. The Treasury's 30-year issue lost nearly 1⅛ points and its yield was 6.54%. The Dow Jones industrials fell 14.63 to 3922.64.

22 Corporate profits turned in another sharp rise in the fourth quarter, nourished by strong economic growth and continued cost-cutting. For the period, 674 major corporations reported net income surged a cumulative 61% from the 1992 quarter, according to a *Wall Street Journal* survey. The result compared with a 24% increase in the 1993 third quarter.

Bond investors' inflationary fears are growing and, rather than inspiring confidence, the Fed's recent rate boost has many wondering when the next rate increase will be. On Friday, the 30-year Treasury bond's price sank over a point. Its yield rose to 6.62%.

Some stock analysts proclaim a stock-market correction has begun, citing the recent rise in interest rates and fears that further increases are near. Still, others point to the health of the economy and say a correction is far off. The Dow Jones industrials tumbled 35.18 Friday, to 3887.46.

Vanguard Group is shuffling managers at some of its stock mutual funds to try to improve the funds' returns.

23 The Federal Reserve is likely to raise short-term interest rates again, Greenspan told Congress, but the amount and timing of such an increase hinge on expectations about inflation. The central bank, he vowed, won't wait until inflation actually shows itself before acting. Instead, it is watching reflections of market expectations for inflation—particularly the price of gold and exchange rates.

Stock and bond prices jumped amid relief that the Fed chairman didn't unveil any unpleasant surprises. The Dow Jones Industrial Average gained 24.20, to 3911.66. Gold futures prices fell after Greenspan pointed to gold as "a very good indicator" of inflation.

The FCC voted unanimously to require what amounts to a 7% reduction in cable-TV rates. A 10% cut that the agency ordered last year actually led to higher bills for some customers. The FCC estimates that this time about 90% of the 11,000 cable systems nationwide will be required to cut prices.

Some Japanese political and business leaders are calling for a compromise to avoid a trade war with the U.S., including setting nonbinding import goals to narrow Japan's surplus.

An index of consumer confidence slipped to 80.8 this month from a revised 82.6 in January in the face of bad weather and rising interest rates.

24 Bell Atlantic's planned acquisition of Tele-Communications collapsed. It wasn't clear whether there is any chance of resurrecting the $20 billion-plus pact announced only four months ago. TCI said the two are "discussing other ways of working together." In recent weeks, Bell and TCI had been quarreling over renegotiating the value and terms of their deal.

A Senate panel voted to let banks operate nationwide branch networks, adding steam to a bill that would accelerate the wave of bank acquisitions and allow banks to consolidate, saving the industry billions of dollars a year.

The huge oil surplus that rocked petroleum markets in recent months is decreasing, analysts say, pointing to the harsh U.S. winter and an economic recovery in oil-consuming nations.

Bond prices fell amid a weak government auction of two-year notes and stocks followed. The Treasury's 30-year issue lost ⅝ point. Its yield was 6.65%. The Dow Jones Industrial Average sank 19.98 points, to 3891.68.

Auto makers recalled 11 million vehicles in 1993, the most since 1977. Honda Motor led the list, based on a percentage of 1993 vehicle sales.

25 The breakdown of the Bell Atlantic-TCI pact won't mean the death of similar proposed alliances, but it will slow the pace of the frenzied alliance-making. Potential partners will take their time—not to second-guess strategy—but because the looming threat of a giant Bell-TCI combination is now out of the picture, changing the landscape.

Instead of large-scale mergers, rivals may seek partnerships and technology-sharing pacts.

The Bell Atlantic-TCI scenario shows the down side of using stock instead of cash in megadeals. Some 37% of U.S. deals announced last year were stock-for-stock mergers, compared with only 5% in 1988. And that means the acquirer's stock price is a critical element in getting deals done.

Plunging bond prices and the collapse of the Bell Atlantic-TCI deal knocked stock prices into a tailspin. The Dow Jones industrials tumbled 51.78, or 1.3%, to 3839.90. The Treasury's benchmark 30-year bond fell more than a point, with the yield soaring to 6.73%, its highest since June.

Orders for durable goods jumped 3.7% last month from December, when they rose 2.1%. Much of the gain came from a 13.9% rise in transportation orders, particularly for aircraft.

28 The Group of Seven attributed recent increases in long-term interest rates to spreading economic recovery rather than to signs of inflationary pressure. The members devoted most of their meeting Saturday to Russian economic reform, and reiterated support for the effort. The finance ministers took no action on exchange rates and representatives of the U.S. and Japan made no progress toward resolving their trade dispute.

March 1994

1 MCI agreed to pay $1.3 billion for a 17% stake in Nextel, challenging rival efforts by AT&T and the Baby Bells to create a national cellular telephone service. Ever since AT&T moved last year to buy McCaw, MCI has sought a cellular partner and it aims to help Nextel build a nationwide digital cellular network in two years. The MCI deal is forcing industry players to quickly align with one of three emerging wireless technologies.

McCaw is behind schedule on rolling out a wireless communications service, and expects to be six months late in offering the service in all of its cellular markets. The service is a contender in the race to offer wireless transmission to pocket computers.

Cigarette makers' stocks fell as investors reacted to the FDA's suggestion that a legal basis exists for the regulation of cigarettes as a drug. The stance rekindled concern about White House plans to lift tobacco taxes and some lawyers said it could spur a fresh round of suits against tobacco firms.

Japan suggested it would retaliate if the U.S. imposes sanctions that are found to violate international trade rules. Under GATT rules, a favorable ruling would allow Japan to slap tariffs of up to 100% on U.S. imports.

2 Economic growth rocketed at a 7.5% pace in the fourth quarter, faster than the 5.9% the government initially reported. Prospects for continued fast growth, coupled with a report showing price increases in February, spurred inflation fears. The Treasury's 30-year benchmark plunged 1½ points, driving the yield to 6.77%. The Dow fell 22.79 to 3809.23. But the inflation picture is far more ambiguous than the markets' sell-off suggests.

European stocks declined on interest-rate fears. London prices dived 1.7%, Frankfurt equities slumped 1.2% and Paris stocks tumbled 2.5%.

Stock mutual-fund sales hit a record in January but small investors now are turning cautious, retreating from some bond mutual funds and choosing the least-risky stock funds.

Existing-home sales rose 12.3% in January from a year earlier as buyers rushed to close deals before mortgage rates climbed. The pace was the second highest on record, following the surge in home resales last December.

Japanese businesses remained negative on the economy's outlook, but a nine-month deterioration in their sentiment was halted, a survey said.

3 New-home sales tumbled 20.1% in January, partly reflecting the effects of cold weather and marking the first decline in sales in seven months. Separately, disposable income fell 0.4% in January from December's 0.6% rise.

4 Clinton renewed a tough trade provision known as Super 301, a step that moves toward, though doesn't actually launch, a trade war with Japan. The White House is using Super 301 as part of a plan to signal its seriousness over shrinking the $59.3 billion U.S. trade deficit with Japan. But it could take nearly a year before any trade sanctions are levied.

Fears that a U.S.-Japanese trade war will stoke inflation sent bond prices lower, while speculation that tensions might disrupt purchases of U.S. crops pushed grain futures down. The Treasury's 30-year bond fell more than ¾ point. Its yield shot up to 6.83%. The dollar fell against the yen.

The U.S. auto industry is adding more than a million units of additional North American car and truck production capacity and about 9,500 new jobs. Chrysler announced plans to spend $1.8 billion on additional capacity, which would add 6,000 new jobs.

Sales of new cars and trucks in the U.S. surged 19.9% in February from a year earlier to the highest seasonally adjusted pace in over two years.

The nation's big retailers reported strong sales gains for February, despite the harsh winter weather. Sales jumped 6.4%, according to a survey.

Factory orders rose 2.1% in January, the sixth monthly rise in a row. Orders gained 1.4% in December.

7 The economy's momentum is slowing from last year's sizzling pace, February's employment report shows. The unemployment rate edged down to 6.5% from 6.7%, though the total number of hours worked last month fell 1.3%. However, economic forecasters said the economy still seems to be expanding at a healthy 3% annual rate or better in the first quarter.

Apple today will sketch out plans to make Macintosh software better able to do things automatically. As the race to define the look and feel of personal computers heats up, Apple is battling Microsoft, which has been giving glimpses of its still-unfinished "Chicago" operating-system software.

Several PC makers plan to announce models this week that use a robust version of Intel's Pentium chip. They hope to steal some fire from Apple, which soon will launch a Macintosh line using the PowerPC chip, designed by Apple, IBM and Motorola.

8 Martin Marietta agreed to buy Grumman for $1.9 billion, or $55 a share, capping a streak of major acquisitions and increasing pressure in the beleaguered defense industry for further consolidation. The purchase would make Martin the nation's largest aerospace-electronics concern. The move supports the notion that Chairman Norman Augustine has assumed the mantle of industry leader.

Grumman's stock climbed 8.5% Friday, suggesting that material inside information was used in trading before Martin Marietta's announcement. Other target firms in major deals in the past month have seen their stocks climb sharply before any merger announcements were made.

Gold is trading near a three-month low, partly reflecting selling by hard-pressed hedge funds hurt in international bond and currency markets. Some traders said that if gold, which closed yesterday at $376.90 an ounce, down $1.70, falls below the $374–$375 level, it could tumble to $365.

9 Japan is expected to clear the way for Chrysler to sharply boost exports of Jeep Cherokees to Japan, in an apparent effort by Japan to ease growing trade friction with the U.S. Chrysler plans to more than double exports to Japan of right-hand-drive Jeep Cherokee sport-utility vehicles this year.

10 The U.S. and Japan tentatively settled several important issues in their dispute over cellular phones, and the two sides appear headed toward a compromise that would avert U.S. sanctions against Japanese goods. Although differences remain, an accord would signal compromise at a critical time in relations between the U.S. and Japan, and would be a boost to Motorola's effort to expand in Japan. It could, however, hurt AT&T.

The economy expanded moderately in January and February despite the California earthquake and a bitter winter, the Fed said. Moreover, the Fed's regional report suggested that many merchants expect solid sales growth in the coming months.

11 Northrop launched a hostile $2.04 billion bid to acquire Grumman, which had agreed to be acquired by Martin Marietta for $1.93 billion. Northrop, which failed in three separate aerospace-acquisition attempts in the past year, seemed to face a stark choice in the rapidly consolidating defense industry: Buy or be bought. In after-hours trading Grumman stock surged more than $7, indicating that traders expect a bidding war.

14 Northrop's hostile $2.04 billion bid for Grumman could face an obstacle in a 33% equity stake in Grumman that employees hold. The stake is held by two savings and retirement plans and the plans' trustees, all of whom are Grumman executives, have the power to decide whether to accept the Northrop offer, a rival $1.87 billion bid by Martin Marietta, or to let employee shareholders decide.

U.S.-Japan trade relations appear to be heading for a momentary calm, after the resolution of a dispute over cellular phones and the expected easing of tensions over semiconductors.

Retail sales rose 1.5% in February, but sales dropped 1.9% in January rather than the 0.5% decline reported originally, indicating that, perhaps because of bad weather, consumers lost some enthusiasm for spending.

15 Breast-implant makers and plaintiffs reached an accord on all major remaining issues in the $4 billion silicone-implant settlement, the largest product-liability pact in U.S. courts.

Deloitte & Touche agreed to pay $312 million to settle government claims linking the accounting firm to a number of costly thrift failures.

17 Consumer prices rose 0.3% in February from January, signaling a relatively low rate of inflation. Prices had been unchanged in January. The core inflation rate was also up 0.3%. Separately, housing starts last month rose 4.1% after falling 22% in January.

Bond prices soared on evidence that inflation remains in check. The price of the Treasury's benchmark 30-year issue rose nearly a point, while its yield declined to 6.79%.

The assets in Fidelity Investments' mutual fund for developing-country debt have dropped more than 40% since the end of January.

18 Kemper directors unanimously rejected the $2.2 billion bid from GE Capital amid intensifying pressure from shareholders to sell the company. Kemper's chairman accused GE of "stealing Kemper with a 'low-ball' proposal" and suggested that GE is a corporate raider. But the harsh language could also be a tactical move to force GE to up the ante.

Six major airlines settled federal charges that they fixed prices in a scheme that may have cost consumers nearly $2 billion from 1988 to 1992.

21 A global satellite communications system is planned by William Gates and Craig McCaw, who will seek to raise capital and attract dozens of partners to build the $9 billion system. The system would involve hundreds of small satellites circling the Earth in a low orbit, offering a broad array of interactive voice, data and video services at prices similar to conventional wired services. The plan is expected to be disclosed today.

GE Capital asked Kemper for a list of its shareholders, setting the stage for what could be a lengthy battle for control of Kemper. The request came in response to Kemper's rejection of GE's $2.2 billion bid to buy the firm.

Clinton's welfare-reform working group plans to recommend a gambling tax as part of a proposal to the president at a cabinet meeting tomorrow. The 4% excise tax on net gambling revenues, except state lotteries, is expected to raise $4 billion in five years.

The bond market faces a major test this week as the Fed's policy-making arm meets. Many expect the Fed to tighten credit again. The benchmark 30-year bond fell nearly ⅞ point Friday. Its yield rose to 6.90%, mainly in reaction to news of a meeting between Fed Chairman Greenspan and Clinton. Aides called the meeting routine.

The Dow Jones industrials surged 30.51 to 3895.65 in late trading amid very heavy volume tied to quarterly expirations of futures and options.

Japanese computer-chip imports rose, easing the U.S. trade battle with Japan somewhat. But neither side is ready for a truce as the U.S. awaits Tokyo's market-opening initiatives.

23 The Fed's policy makers voted to push up short-term interest rates for the second time in as many months, the latest in what is expected to be a series of rate increases. Although the Fed wasn't explicit in its statement, it decided to increase the benchmark federal-funds interest rate by ¼ percentage point, to 3½%.

Bond prices soared after the Fed's announcement. The Treasury's benchmark 30-year bond jumped 1¼ points, with the yield falling to 6.85%. Stock prices were mixed, with the Dow Jones industrials slipping 2.30 points to 3862.55. The dollar was steady.

The U.S. trade deficit in goods and services widened in January to $6.3 billion from $4.14 billion in December, as U.S. exports were hurt by economic slumps in some overseas markets.

Japan's economy contracted at a 2.2% annual pace in the quarter ended December 31, better-than-expected results that may prompt economists to moderate bearish forecasts for this year.

Crude-oil output in the North Sea has jumped almost 25% from a year ago, an increase that is a major headache for OPEC, which meets Friday.

24 Durable-goods orders fell 2.5% in February from January, reflecting a drop

in aircraft demand. But the rest of the manufacturing sector was solid.

Surging vehicle sales this month have prompted two of the Big Three U.S. auto makers to raise their 1994 sales projections, and led Ford to give a mid-month sales report to the Fed before this week's meeting at which the Fed nudged up short-term rates.

25 Stocks and bonds were battered by domestic and international political worries. The Dow Jones industrials tumbled 48.37 to 3821.09 as investors awaited Clinton's news conference at which Whitewater was expected to take center stage. Markets shuddered in the wake of the assassination of Mexico's ruling party candidate for president and on growing tensions in Korea.

Mexico shut its banks and financial markets in the wake of the assassination, but Mexican stocks and bonds fell sharply in trading around the world.

28 OPEC ministers failed to agree to reduce crude-oil output, setting the stage for at least a small drop in already weak oil prices. A move by a majority of the oil ministers to cut production significantly to stop the fall in oil prices failed after two days of talks. Analysts and oil traders expect prices to fall as little as 50 cents a barrel.

Accounting rule makers will look at proposals that could lead to a compromise over the FASB's efforts to require companies to deduct the cost of employee stock options from earnings. A compromise plan would consider stock that is held and not sold quickly an equity stake and not deductible.

Banks and insurers are flooding the market with pools of soured real-estate loans and properties, after years of waiting for prices to rise. Many say it is now a seller's market.

Existing-home sales slowed in February from January's boom, partly as a result of bad weather, but the pace was still healthy, a survey showed.

Machine-tool orders fell 22% in February from January, but analysts said orders remained relatively high.

Nissan plans to increase purchases of U.S.-made auto parts 75% to $3.4 billion by the year ending March 1998.

29 Japan unveiled a package of market-opening initiatives intended to persuade the White House to call off its trade offensive, but the plan isn't likely to bring U.S. negotiators back to the table anytime soon. Tokyo's measures are largely a repackaging of proposals made in the framework talks that failed last month.

Insurance losses from winter storms, the Los Angeles earthquake and other catastrophes are expected to exceed $7 billion for the first quarter, one of the worst periods ever for U.S. property and casualty insurers.

World oil prices plunged as a result of OPEC's decision this weekend to leave production levels unchanged. A price drop was expected, although the fall of more than $1 a barrel for some crudes was sharper than anticipated.

Slumping oil stocks set the stage for what looked like yet another round of broad selling in the stock market. But the Dow Jones Industrial Average battled back from a 46-point deficit.

30 Stocks plunged, sparked by tumbling bond prices. The Dow Jones industrials lost 63.33 points, or 1.7%, to 3699.02. The drop in bond prices was spurred by a report that consumer confidence in the economy surged in March to the highest level in nearly four years. The benchmark 30-year Treasury bond tumbled more than a point. Its yield rose to 7.06%, its highest level since February 1993.

Consumers are borrowing heavily again, and economists said that signals optimism about the future and a willingness to take on debt. Although total consumer debt as a percentage of disposable income is back to late-1980s levels, low interest rates have made that debt much more affordable.

The U.S. Commerce Department is expected to issue a preliminary ruling today that will propose tariffs that could be significant against Fuji Photo Film for illegally dumping color photographic paper in the U.S. The ruling would be a victory for Kodak, though maybe a short-lived one, as Fuji said it would try to speed up plans to build a U.S. plant if such a ruling is issued.

The U.S. rejected Japan's latest package of market-opening measures as lacking in substance, and prepared to intensify its trade battle with Tokyo. Anticipating that reaction, Tokyo's Nikkei 225-stock index sank 1.2%.

31 Ford is preparing a reorganization that will put major functions, such as product development, sales and engine/transmissions, each under an executive with authority to act globally.

The job market has turned a corner in recent months and jobs are being created at a faster rate than many think, economists and companies said.

April 1994

1 The economy grew at a 7% annual rate in the fourth quarter, slower than the previously estimated 7.5%. The new GDP figure still marks the highest quarterly jump in 10 years.

The U.S. moved to tighten pressure on Japan by identifying Japanese trading barriers that Washington could target for retaliation.

Rates on 30-year conventional mortgages have surged above 8% for the first time in more than a year.

4 March's employment report showing 456,000 additional jobs convinced all but the most pessimistic observers that the U.S. economy grew at better than a 3% pace in the first quarter. Despite the effects of bad weather and the California earthquake, the economy is showing undeniable strength.

Bond prices plunged on the jobs data in holiday-shortened trading. The Treasury 30-year bond lost nearly two points, driving its yield to 7.26%. Over the weekend, banking, securities and futures regulators watched for clues about how stocks will react today.

5 Stock and bond prices fell again, though stocks didn't fall as much as some expected. The Dow Jones industrials lost 42.61 to 3593.35. Bonds continued their dive despite a purchasing managers' report showing price increases in March had slowed. The Treasury's benchmark 30-year issue plunged 1½ points, driving the yield to 7.40%. The market downturn is forcing thousands of unsophisticated investors to decide whether to stick with their mutual funds or bail out.

The rise in long-term rates has caught Washington policy makers by surprise, and they are trying to figure out what, if anything, to do about it. While financial markets fear strong jobs growth will lead to wage inflation, many economists aren't alarmed.

Major Japanese banks plan to write off a record $28 billion in bad debts for the year ended March 31.

7 Individual investors fleeing the turmoil in stocks and bonds poured more than $7.6 billion into money-market mutual funds in the latest week. The inflow is more than half the $12 billion that was added to money funds in the first quarter and the largest weekly inflow in many months.

Prices of 30-year U.S. Treasury bonds fell 14% from January 28 to April 4, the biggest downturn since 1987, handing stunning losses to an array of investors. The plunge also brought down prices of so-called Latin American Brady bonds. Brady bonds, many backed by Treasurys, have lost 30%.

Stock Mutual funds lost 3.33% in the first quarter, their worst period in 3½ years. But they held up better than the S&P 500-stock index, which fell 3.79%. Taxable-bond mutual funds ended the quarter with a 2.47% loss, according to a Lipper survey.

Sales of new cars and light trucks boomed in March, rising 20% from a year earlier. But sales were so hot that some analysts predicted a marginal dropoff this month and in May.

The Big Three auto makers are expected to report strong combined first-quarter earnings of as much as $3.4 billion, and analysts say second-quarter profits could be even stronger.

8 Big retailers reported surprisingly strong sales gains in March, as an early Easter and warmer weather inspired shoppers to load up on spring goods. Even after accounting for the holiday and the sunshine, analysts were startled at the hearty, across-the-board sales increases—especially for apparel, where sales had been chronically weak. March sales for stores opened at least a year soared 11% from a year earlier.

A shift in consumer spending this year is expected to put more bounce in the sales of apparel, name-brand foods and other nondurable products.

U.S. businesses plan to spend 8% more on new plants and equipment in 1994 than in 1993, a survey shows. The report, along with two others, suggest the economy is growing, though more moderately than in the fourth period.

Businesses are increasing their borrowings from banks to help finance expansion plans, adding fuel to the economy and some much-needed revenue to the banking industry.

11 The economy could soon get an extra boost from rising inventories, as economists say companies will have to replenish stockpiles to keep up with growing demand and to provide customers a wider product selection.

A pharmacy trade group formed a company, linking chain and independent drugstores, that will seek some of the rapidly growing business of managing prescription-drug programs for employers' health-care plans. The new company will compete against Merck's Medco operation and McKesson's PCS Health Systems, and will use seed money from some of the largest chain drugstores.

12 The Pentagon and antitrust regulators reached an informal understanding that could make it substantially easier for mergers to occur in the defense industry. Under the accord, which is described in a report expected to be released today, antitrust regulators will consider the Pentagon's views in evaluating defense-industry mergers and give more consideration to the peculiar circumstances of the U.S. defense market.

World energy use will grow at a strong annual rate of 2.1% through the year 2010, but oil consumption will rise more slowly, according to an International Energy Agency forecast.

Texaco and three other oil giants formed a company to explore and develop huge fields beneath the isolated tundra of Russia's Arctic Circle.

13 Producer prices rose a moderate 0.2% in March, as the specter of inflation that has spooked the bond market for weeks is looking a little less menacing. The core index of wholesale prices, which excludes food and energy prices, also rose 0.2%. The rate, in line with analysts' projections, muted fears that an overheated economy will spark price increases.

Stock prices slid as weakness in technology issues overshadowed the positive inflation report. The Dow Jones industrials fell 7.14 to 3681.69. Bond prices and the dollar rose.

Procter & Gamble said it will take a one-time after-tax charge of $102 million in its fiscal third quarter to close out two interest-rate swap contracts.

14 Companies are trying to determine their exposure to derivatives in the wake of P&G's decision to take a charge to close out two interest-rate swap contracts that went bad. About 20% of firms in a survey saw their treasurers' offices as profit centers rather than only as financiers of operations.

Hedge fund activities appear to have had little effect on the recent volatility in the stock and bond markets, according to the federal regulators who oversee securities and banking.

Investors around the world purchased a record $159.2 billion of stocks in other countries last year, triple 1992's cross-border equity investments and above 1991's record $100.6 billion. U.S. investors accounted for about 42% of such investing in world markets.

Stock prices tumbled amid slumping bond prices and fears of inadequate earnings. The Dow Jones Industrial Average sank 20.22 to 3661.47. The Treasury's 30-year bond lost more than ½ point. Its yield rose to 7.25%.

15 Ford raised its dividend 12.5% and declared a 2-for-1 stock split, signaling its optimism for a sustained recovery. The car maker plans to sell its unprofitable thrift unit to First Madison for $1.1 billion, and will take a first-quarter charge of $440 million in connection with the sale. But analysts expect the car maker to be profitable in the quarter nonetheless. Ford also bought the 46% stake in car renter Hertz that it didn't already own.

The winning bidder for Ford's thrift is a unit of Ronald Perelman's MacAndrews & Forbes, which will get a relatively clean bank after Ford agreed to keep $1.2 billion in bad loans and buy up to $500 million more.

Business inventories rose 0.5% in February, the biggest climb since November. The increase could provide a boost to first-quarter growth.

Germany's central bank cut its discount rate to 5% from 5.25%, triggering rate reductions elsewhere in Europe.

18 Treasury Secretary Bentsen said he is prepared for the Federal Reserve to raise short-term interest rates another half percentage point this year.

Rising short-term interest rates are likely to eat into corporate profits over the next year, reversing a trend that helped jump-start the economy.

A municipal-bond fund agreed to a settlement after allegedly failing to disclose the risks it took by investing 40% of its money in derivatives. Regulators are probing other funds' disclosure of risks from fixed-income derivatives, especially inverse floaters.

Brazil completed a deal to restructure $52 billion of its foreign loans, but the accord hasn't yet received backing from the IMF and the Dart family.

Industrial production rose 0.5% last month, following a revised increase of 0.6% in February.

Canada's inflation rate has dropped to its lowest level in over 30 years, but it has failed to boost Canadian bonds or the Canadian dollar.

19 The Fed raised short-term interest rates

another ¼ percentage point, and is likely to keep boosting rates if the economy continues to show exuberance. The Fed raised its target for the federal funds rate, at which banks lend to each other, by ¼ percentage point to 3¾%, the third such increase since February. Citibank boosted its prime interest rate to 6.75% and other big banks followed.

The Fed's move drove down stock and bond prices. The Dow Jones Industrial Average sank 41.05 points, or 1.1%, to 3620.42. The price of the 30-year Treasury bond fell more than 1⅜ points. Its yield jumped to 7.42%, the highest rate since January 1993.

20 Chrysler's earnings soared 77% to a quarterly record, but its failure to produce even higher results in the first quarter and fears that rising interest rates could choke off the economic recovery sent car makers' stocks down. Chrysler's revenue rose 21% to a record $13.2 billion.

Japanese car makers are beginning to gain market share in the U.S., after slipping from their 1991 peak.

Citicorp and Bankers Trust New York reported drastic drops in trading revenue for the first quarter, reflecting the toll rising interest rates took on bond and currency trading operations. But both posted respectable results.

The Supreme Court said investors can't file suits charging that someone "aided or abetted" deceptive acts involving stock or bond deals, taking away a legal weapon investors use to allege securities-fraud schemes.

The U.S. trade deficit widened sharply and unexpectedly in February, prompting analysts to lower estimates for first-quarter growth.

21 Bankers Trust New York disclosed that it got most of its first-quarter profit from the sale of derivative products to clients, as Mead became the third company in recent weeks to disclose losses as a result of derivatives purchased from the big bank.

A top bank regulator is moving toward tighter regulation of nationally chartered banks' derivatives trading.

Caterpillar reported its best first quarter ever, but Wall Street drove down the company's stock along with those of other cyclical companies.

Investors sold cyclical stocks because of fears about rising interest rates. The Dow Jones industrials tumbled 21.11 points to 3598.71. The Treasury's 30-year issue gained more than ½ point. Its yield was 7.31%.

Treasury chief Bentsen said that the Fed's recent interest-rate increases won't hinder the economic recovery and that he still expects the economy to grow about 3% this year, provided the bond market cooperates.

Housing starts surged 12.1% in March, as construction rebounded from severe cold weather and storms in the first two months of the year.

Mexico's short-term interest rates soared to the highest level in more than a year, sending stocks reeling for a sixth consecutive loss.

25 Clinton picked economists Alan Blinder and Janet Yellen for the Fed, hoping that they can persuade the Fed to increase its emphasis on growth. Neither is likely to side with those on the Fed whose top priority is reducing the inflation rate below today's level.

Kidder fired a trader for hiding up to $10 million in losses on a bond-derivatives deal, as the GE unit's bond-trading woes appear to be deepening.

The U.S. urged Germany and Japan to spur growth in their economies at a weekend meeting of officials from the G-7 nations. But Germany and Japan seemed to resist the message.

26 Stocks rocketed on robust earnings reports from DuPont and Boeing and a buoyant bond market. The Dow Jones Industrial Average shot up 57.10 points to 3705.78, surpassing the 3700 mark for the first time in nearly a month. It was the biggest one-day gain for the industrials since April 5. The Treasury's 30-year bond rose over ¾ point. Its yield was 7.15%.

Existing-home sales rebounded in March, surging 5.7% on improved weather and rising interest rates that economists said brought more buyers into an already strong market.

IBM's chairman said the computer maker expects to be profitable this year, which would mark its first full year in the black since 1990.

27 The rise in businesses' employment costs slowed during the first quarter from 1993's last quarter, suggesting renewed economic strength hasn't increased wage pressures.

The Supreme Court said a 1991 job-bias law shouldn't be applied retroactively to discrimination that allegedly took place before the law was enacted. The ruling is a victory for employers.

The Senate approved legislation that would let banks operate interstate branch networks, a move expected to spark additional bank mergers.

The U.S., Mexico and Canada created a facility to counter exchange-rate turbulence in their currencies. In Mexico, the countries' $8.8 billion foreign-exchange swap facility was seen as a way to support the peso.

The White House picked five technology areas for research-and-development dollars, including genetics and making cars weigh less.

28 IBM has yet to fire 28,000 people, or 80% of the goal it had set last July. Those numbers, industry executives say, indicate IBM's top personnel official, who abruptly resigned Tuesday, was under pressure because he wasn't making cuts fast enough.

The White House plans to spend up to $500 million over a decade to help the U.S. counter Japan's domination of the $5 billion flat-screen market.

29 The economy expanded at a surprisingly slow 2.6% annual rate in the first quarter, suggesting it is nowhere near overheating as some market participants have feared. The growth was much slower than the 7% fourth-quarter pace and was less than the 3.5% economists expected. But broad inflation measures showed accelerating increases over the quarter.

Stocks slid on the prospects of slow growth and renewed inflation, and the dollar fell sharply. The Dow Jones industrials tumbled 31.23 to 3668.31. The price of the 30-year Treasury bond fell 1¾ points. Its yield rose to 7.26%.

The White House decided against pursuing trade sanctions over Tokyo's government-procurement practices.

May 1994

2 Corporate profits continued to grow in the first quarter, thanks to wider profit margins and strong product demand, a *Wall Street Journal* survey found. Profit from continuing operations rose 11%. But the pace of profit and economic growth is expected to slow later this year.

The Fed's intervention in support of the dollar signals concerns about rising long-term interest rates and about the dollar falling further. On Friday, the Fed bought dollars against the mark and yen, intervening for the first time since August. The move was directed mostly against the mark.

Disposable personal income rose 0.3% in March, outpacing consumption, which rose 0.1%, marking the second month in a row in which income grew faster than spending. Separately, new-home sales climbed 11% from February's revised rate.

3 Kodak's stock jumped $3.25, or 7.8%, to $44.75, propelled by speculation that the company today will divulge details of a plan to turn itself around. Such a plan could include the sale or spinoff of Kodak's Sterling Winthrop over-the-counter drug unit.

IBM Personal Computer imposed a sweeping reorganization in the wake of the departure of its president and promised a "redo" to fix troublesome weaknesses in its product line. The new structure links the unit more closely with IBM's top management.

IBM expects to launch a new generation of its important midsize computers today, paving the way for an even more crucial upgrade of the machines next year to the PowerPC chip. The computers will use new software that can more easily work with other computer brands and types.

Tobacco companies are facing a fresh assault from Florida lawmakers who are seeking to hold the industry liable for the state's cost of treating smoking-related ailments. A bill making it easier for Florida to sue for the costs, estimated at over $1 billion a year, awaits Gov. Chiles's signature.

The American Stock Exchange will begin trading tomorrow the first options on the Hong Kong stock market to be listed on a U.S. stock exchange.

4 Smithkline Beecham agreed to acquire United HealthCare's pharmacy-benefit services unit for $2.3 billion, as the drug industry continues to transform itself in an era of cost containment. The deal is a direct response to last year's $6 billion purchase of Medco by Merck. On a smaller scale, Pfizer announced a strategic alliance with Value Health.

Drug stocks have risen sharply amid takeover euphoria in the past several days, but some analysts warned not to expect a parade of big deals. Still, some money managers are betting more deals are bound to follow and are scanning for likely targets.

Kodak announced plans to sell its Sterling Winthrop drug unit and two other businesses in a surprisingly sweeping reorganization. The sales, which could raise $6 billion, reverses nearly a decade of diversification and shows Kodak's determination to regain prominence in photography.

The index of leading indicators rose 0.7% in March, suggesting the economy is continuing on a moderate growth rate and not overheating.

6 Productivity edged up at a 0.5% annual rate in the first quarter after jumping at a 6.4% rate in the fourth quarter, but analysts said the figures are misleading because companies are still making big strides in efficiency.

The dollar extended its rally a day after massive intervention by the Fed and other central banks, helping to lift bond prices. But stock prices ended mixed after losing earlier gains. The Dow Jones Industrial Average inched down 1.78 points to 3695.97.

9 Chevron is curtailing investment at its Tengiz project in Kazakhstan, scaling back production plans and cutting workers, in a setback for oil development in the former Soviet Union.

The unemployment rate fell to 6.4% in April from 6.5%, as employers added 267,000 jobs, demonstrating the economy's momentum and exacerbating Wall Street fears that growth is so fast it will lead to higher inflation.

The strong jobs data caused bonds to tumble, and stocks followed. The Treasury's 30-year bond fell 2⅛ points, while its yield jumped to 7.54%, its highest level since December 1992.

IBM will sell its prestigious 590 Madison Ave. office tower in New York City for an estimated $200 million.

The mutual-fund industry today will propose a crackdown on personal trading by its own money managers.

10 Bond prices tumbled further on disappointment with the Fed's failure to boost interest rates, bringing stocks down also. The Dow Jones Industrial Average sank 40.46 points to 3629.04. The Treasury's 30-year bond fell more than a point. Its yield rose to 7.64%.

11 Lobbyists are no longer allowed to deduct their lobbying expenses, under specific new tax rules announced by the Treasury Department. The rules apply even to costs for preparation and support work. Many lobbyists say the new rules will mean dues increases for their trade-group members.

12 Germany's central bank cut official short-term interest rates by an unexpectedly deep one-half percentage point, contributing to global efforts to lift the dollar but failing to give it a lasting boost. The dollar jumped after the announcement, but later fell to 1.6695 marks, from 1.6735 marks Tuesday. The Bundesbank cut its discount rate to 4.5% from 5% and the Lombard rate to 6% from 6.5%.

Japan's opposition Socialists called for early elections as a way of stabilizing the shaky minority government, but Prime Minister Hata immediately rejected the idea. The Socialists, who bolted the ruling coalition last month, are widely expected to try to topple the government after a budget bill is passed.

13 Wholesale prices fell 0.1% in April and retail sales were much weaker than expected, falling 0.8%, suggesting the economy is losing some steam.

Bond prices rallied on the weaker-than-expected signs of inflation, but most of the gains later eroded. The Treasury's benchmark 30-year issue rose ½ point, to yield 7.56%. The Dow industrials climbed 23.80 to 3652.84.

16 NBC is forming a broad alliance with Mexico's TV Azteca, a broadcaster attempting to take on the country's long-dominant Grupo Televisa. As part of the alliance, which was finalized last week and will be announced today, the GE unit will buy a significant stake in the broadcaster.

NBC made major changes in its schedule for next season, replacing seven hours of its 22 hours of prime-time programming. The third-place network will have nine new shows.

Consumer prices edged up 0.1% in April after rising 0.3% in each of the previous two months. April's small rise may help calm fears that larger increases in February and March were the start of an inflationary trend. The core inflation rate, which excludes the volatile food and energy components, fell to 0.2% in April.

17 The Supreme Court decided that cities and counties can't ban haulers from shipping garbage to other states where dump space is cheaper, in a favorable ruling for garbage haulers.

The National Association of Home Builders trimmed its forecasts for housing construction this year and in 1995, citing rising mortgage rates. The changes reflect growing concerns that rising interest rates in recent months will hamper the economy's growth.

18 The Fed boosted short-term interest rates by another ½ percentage point and, attempting to reduce uncertainty about its intentions, signaled that it expects to hold rates steady for a while.

Although banks quickly raised their prime lending rates ½ percentage point, financial markets cheered the Fed's move and its untraditionally clear statement.

The Dow Jones Industrial Average shot up 49.11 points to close at 3720.61 after the Fed's move. The Treasury's benchmark 30-year bond rose almost two points. Its yield fell to 7.26%.

19 Fifty law firms have promised an initial investment of $100,000 each to finance a class-action lawsuit against the tobacco industry on behalf of people who are addicted to cigarettes.

Scrap prices declined 13% in recent weeks, which could undermine prospects for steel industry price relief. The drop is likely to create pressure in coming months to ease flat-rolled steel prices, even as analysts have been expecting another rise, citing strong industry demand and tight capacity.

20 The Treasury's benchmark 30-year issue gained ⅜ point to yield 7.23%. The Dow Jones Industrial Average jumped 26.09 points to 3758.98.

The U.S. trade deficit shrank in March as exports rebounded with the end of the harsh winter. The March deficit was $7.46 billion, compared with February's $9.15 billion deficit.

23 Trade negotiators for the U.S. and Japan are working on a new formula to measure trade liberalization in anticipation of reviving the stalled "framework" trade talks soon. Among the positions emerging in the current round of talks, the U.S. would vow not to seek specific numerical targets for foreign imports into Japan.

UAL reached an agreement with its unions on new terms for the employee buyout of the airline, addressing the pilots' concerns about the recent drop in UAL's stock price.

24 News Corp.'s Fox plans to invest $500 million in New World Communications, which in turn will switch the affiliation of most of its stations from ABC, CBS and NBC to Fox's network.

Bond and stock prices fell as the CRB Index, a key inflation indicator, rose to its highest level since October 1990. The benchmark 30-year bond fell 1⅜ point. Its yield was 7.43%. The Dow Jones industrials, which were down nearly 40 points in trading, ended with a loss of 23.94 at 3742.41.

World oil prices have surged over 20% since early April on signs that Iraq won't soon return to the oil market.

Columbia/HCA agreed to acquire Medical Care America for stock valued at about $858.4 million. The deal combines the largest U.S. for-profit hospital chain with the largest operator of outpatient surgery centers.

The SEC is asking dozens of public companies, as part of their SEC filings, to provide details on their exposure to risk in holding derivatives.

Some hedge-fund investors are withdrawing their funds in the wake of major losses at many of these leveraged private investment partnerships.

25 The U.S. and Japan agreed to revive the "framework" trade talks, reflecting Washington's decision to court Tokyo rather than confront it.

Publicly traded "country funds" have been hammered by world market turmoil, resulting in the best deals in over a year for the funds specializing in stocks of a single foreign market.

The number of new construction contracts took its biggest drop in more than a year, falling 7% in April, the Dodge construction index showed.

26 Durable-goods orders edged up 0.1% in April, a sign that the economy could be slowing down. Orders in March rose 0.7%. April growth was held back by a decline in orders for primary metals and a drop in orders for transportation equipment.

Sales of existing homes in April were 1.2% above the previous month's healthy level as recent boosts in interest rates have yet to appreciably damp the spring house-hunting season.

A small-business owner became the first person to be indicted over alleged fraud involving the Small Business Administration loan program. SBA officials also said the agency decided to significantly tighten oversight of the popular loan program.

27 Clinton renewed China's trading status while administering a slap on the wrist, even though he conceded that Beijing hadn't fully met the human-rights standards he set last year. While insisting human rights will remain a U.S. priority, Clinton said he would delink human rights from China's "most-favored-nation" status. But the U.S. will ban Chinese guns and ammunition imports and leave in place other sanctions. Other bilateral trade snags still loom.

The ban on guns and ammunition is a blow to two big Chinese firms that have plenty of political clout and close ties to China's military but that also have product lines and markets diverse enough to limit the injury.

Philip Morris tried to quell speculation that it will soon split its food and tobacco businesses by saying the issue isn't expected to come before its board again in the "foreseeable future."

Rep. Henry Waxman attacked the work of a tobacco-funded research body as "public relations masquerading as science," a charge staunchly denied by the organization's head.

Mutual-fund investors pulled $4.8 billion out of bond funds in April, substantially less than the $7.7 billion they withdrew in the month before. Stock funds drew in $11.3 billion in April, up from $6.6 billion the previous month.

31 The economy grew faster than originally thought in the first quarter, and Fed Chairman Alan Greenspan said it is "well-balanced" and "doing well." Gross domestic product grew at a 3.0% annual rate in the first quarter, compared with the 2.6% rate originally estimated. The rate suggests that the economy is expanding and adding new jobs but that inflation is under control.

Employers plan to continue hiring new employees in the third quarter, a survey of 15,000 companies showed.

Orders for machine tools climbed 11.7% in April from March, signaling widening demand from manufacturers outside of the auto industry. Orders rose 18.8% from April 1993.

June 1994

1 The economy is showing signs of cooling, with declines in consumer confidence and disposable personal income as well as a drop in sales of newly built houses. Disposable personal income fell 0.5% in April and consumer spending dropped 0.4%. Sales of new homes fell 6.8% in April, while consumer confidence fell in May.

2 Euro Disney received another lifeline when a member of the Saudi royal family agreed to invest up to $500 million for as much as 24% of the struggling theme park and resort. The Saudi investor, Prince Al-Waleed, has proven a canny bottom-fisher in the past, profiting handsomely on a $590 million investment he made in Citicorp in 1991.

The prince's investment also could reduce Disney's exposure in the rescue effort for Euro Disney.

Manufacturing kept up its steady growth in May, according to a purchasing managers' survey. Of the 20 industries surveyed, 18 reported improvements, the most in four years.

Stock prices swung sharply before ending with small gains as conflicting evidence of inflationary pressures whipped through the markets.

3 The index of leading indicators was unchanged in April, after rising 0.7% in March and holding steady in February, suggesting the economy is sticking to a moderate rate of growth.

Sales at the biggest U.S. retailers rose a disappointing 2.4% in May, a survey said, reflecting unseasonably cool weather and cautious consumers.

6 The unemployment rate fell to 6% in May, a drop that overstates the rate at which the job market is improving. A moderate increase in payrolls was seen as a more accurate indicator.

7 European bonds are being roiled by fears that the German central bank is bent on a policy shift that could drive European interest rates higher. The uncertainty could be a boon to U.S. bond markets, whose relative calm would make them attractive.

Bond prices surged as traders bet the Federal Reserve won't boost interest rates again any time soon. The Dow Jones Industrial Average slipped 3.70 points to 3768.52.

8 Oil exploration has slowed sharply in the North Sea, dimming the chances of further big increases in production after an expected peak in 1996. Oil companies cite low oil prices, relatively steep operating costs and dismal prospects for new giant oil finds.

9 Hewlett-Packard and Intel announced a broad partnership aimed at developing a single computer chip capable of running two major strains of software by the end of the decade. The surprising alliance shows how crushing technology development costs and shifting alliances are changing the industry's balance of power.

IBM lawyers seeking to eliminate a 1956 consent decree filed a motion urging the judge who has overseen the case to recuse himself, the fourth time IBM has taken aim at the jurist.

10 A Japanese bank is quietly marketing a $200 million portfolio of soured U.S. real estate, amid signs that Japanese

investors are stepping up their sales of troubled U.S. properties.

Money-market funds are experiencing a rash of bailouts from fund managers anxious to protect shareholders from losses, SEC aides said.

Businesses now plan to boost their capital spending 8.3% this year, compared with plans for an 8.0% rise when they were surveyed in April.

U.S. car makers plan an aggressive 18.9% boost in third-quarter production compared with a year ago, despite a slowdown in sales growth. The confidence extends across the board from Detroit's Big Three to Japanese auto makers, who plan a 24.6% rise in output from their U.S. factories.

U.S. Electricar is getting a $15 million investment from a Japanese company, in a deal that could raise competitive concerns for U.S. car firms.

Kidder Peabody's former government-bond chief and now its No. 3 bond-trading executive is coming under scrutiny in an internal investigation of alleged trading fraud at the firm, people close to the case said.

Dow Corning said it might consider filing for bankruptcy-law protection if too many women opt out of a settlement over implants and pursue suits. But its chairman stressed Dow Corning isn't considering that option now.

13 Inflation pressures remained minimal at the wholesale level in May, as the producer price index slipped 0.1%, after a similar drop of 0.1% in April.

Canada's gross domestic product grew at a 4.2% annual rate in the first quarter. Analysts predicted robust, inflation-free expansion will continue.

More Russian oil is flowing into world petroleum markets, possibly slowing the rise in oil prices. A Russian energy official said production probably will rise further.

14 Exxon's "recklessness" caused the 1989 Valdez oil-tanker spill, an Alaska jury found, clearing the way for the rest of the trial in which plaintiffs will seek damages totaling $16.5 billion. Exxon shares slumped $2.50 to $59.625 following news of the verdict. The jury will begin to hear testimony next week on damages inflicted on the roughly 14,000 plaintiffs in the suit.

The market for derivatives has slowed in the past few months, following highly publicized losses at corporations such as Procter & Gamble, Dell Computer, and Gibson Greetings.

A First Boston fund lost money in derivatives. The fund's manager was fired last month, but a spokesman said the dismissal was unrelated.

15 GE has injected hundreds of millions of dollars into its Kidder Peabody unit to prop up its financial foundation. The brokerage firm is bracing for its worst quarter in three years, expecting an operating loss of as much as $50 million, say Kidder executives. Kidder has been hurt by rising interest rates, a probe by the SEC and the New York Stock Exchange, and the departure of key traders.

Consumer prices rose a modest 0.2% in May, and economists were encouraged that price increases in the service sector seem to be slowing.

Stocks shot up and bond prices rallied on the upbeat inflation report. The Dow Jones Industrial Average jumped 31.71 to 3814.83, surpassing the 3800 level for the first time since March.

Sprint agreed to sell a 20% stake to the national phone companies of France and Germany for $4.2 billion, opening the way for a new global telecommunications service—and sparking the possibility of a trade fight.

16 Bond prices tumbled and stocks dropped as renewed inflation fears swept through financial markets. Surging commodities prices helped send the Treasury's 30-year issue down nearly a point to yield 7.39%. Crop prices jumped on signs of a moderate drought in part of the U.S., while oil prices rose as OPEC affirmed plans to hold production at current levels. The Dow Jones Industrial Average declined 24.42 points to 3790.41.

Industrial output rose 0.2% in May, the 12th monthly gain in a row, despite declining automobile production.

17 Japan's trade surplus fell nearly 16% in May in the most dramatic sign to date that the imbalance is starting to shrink. The decline was only the second monthly narrowing of the politically troublesome trade surplus since December 1990. The strong yen caused imports to swell 12%.

A Toyota official said the auto maker's purchases of U.S.-made parts will top out at $6.45 billion in 1996 despite U.S. pressure to buy more.

May housing starts rose 2.6%, rebounding from a 3.1% decline in April. Economists said home-building is holding at an improved level, with starts for the first five months of 1994 running 21.7% ahead of last year.

21 Stocks were driven lower by investors

worried that the sinking dollar will prompt another interest rate increase. Bond prices also fell. The Dow Jones Industrial Average tumbled 34.88 points to 3741.90. The Treasury's 30-year issue lost more than an eighth of a point to yield 7.46%. European stocks continued their recent slide, pushed down in part by fears about the slumping dollar.

Currency markets are testing the U.S.'s resolve to halt the dollar's fall, raising prospects that the Clinton administration will have to support the currency again. The dollar fell yesterday against the mark and yen.

California's tax on multinational companies was upheld by the Supreme Court. The decision spares California from having to make costly refunds, but probably won't have a big long-term effect because of state tax-law changes that took effect this year.

22 The dollar fell to a post-World War II low against the yen, hitting the "parity level" of 100 yen to the dollar. Economists and others predict the dollar will continue to fall unless U.S. interest rates rise. Federal Reserve officials think rates have risen enough to slow the U.S. economy, but face pressure to lift rates again to help the dollar, which hit an intraday low of 99.92 yen before ending New York trading at 100.43 yen.

The dollar's slide drove down stock and bond markets. The Dow Jones industrials slid 33.93 points to 3707.97. The Treasury's 30-year issue lost three-eighths of a point to yield 7.49%. Japanese stocks also were caught in the turmoil, with the Nikkei falling 338.87, or 1.6%, to 20813.16.

The U.S. trade deficit widened significantly in April. Economists said the trend is likely to continue because export growth remains crimped by slow economies overseas and Americans' appetite for foreign goods.

23 GE forced out Kidder Peabody's head, Michael Carpenter, replacing him with two of its top financial executives. Dennis Dammerman, GE's chief financial officer, becomes Kidder's chairman for a transition period that may see more high-level dismissals. Denis Nayden was named president and chief operating officer and will become chief executive officer when the "transition" is complete.

Greenspan said the economic outlook is bright, with "subdued" price trends. The Fed's regional economic report found growth easing in some areas, making another increase in short-term interest rates less likely.

The U.S. said it is ready to support the dollar, but didn't intervene to lift it after Tuesday's fall to a record low. The dollar rebounded yesterday to 101.55 yen in New York trading.

The dollar's recovery sparked an advance in bond prices. The Treasury's 30-year bond gained more than a point to yield 7.40%. The Dow Jones industrials rose 16.80 to 3724.77.

Mutual funds are having growing difficulties reporting accurate daily price data. Fund-research firm Lipper says as many as 40 funds each day give incorrect prices to the NASD, which supplies the data to newspapers. A mutual-fund group is discussing the problem with the NASD.

27 The dollar's fall despite concerted intervention by 17 countries heightened concern that the Federal Reserve will have to increase interest rates again to support the beleaguered currency. The Fed and 16 other central banks spent more than $3 billion to buy dollars on Friday but failed to lift the currency, quoted at 100.45 yen in New York trading.

Stocks plummeted after the failed intervention. The Dow Jones industrials dropped 62.15, or 1.7%, to 3636.94. Other markets saw prices plunge as well, with stocks in London off 2.2%. In Tokyo, the Nikkei fell 1.3%.

IBM is running months behind schedule for the launch of its new PowerPC computers and has all but given up plans to use the PowerPC chip to regain leadership in the personal-computer market this year.

IBM will unveil a new generation of computer-networking gear for phone companies and corporate customers, filling a hole in its product line.

Money center banks and Wall Street firms are showing renewed willingness to lend for corporate takeover deals, even for firms without top credit ratings. The financing of Conseco's bid for Kemper on Thursday includes a $1.22 billion loan from Citibank, the bank's largest since the 1980s.

28 Stock and bond prices shot higher as the dollar stabilized. The Dow Jones industrials soared 48.56 points to 3685.50, but analysts said the rebound was deceptive, citing thin trading volume and a large number of declining issues. The Treasury's 30-year bond gained nearly ¾ to yield 7.45%. The dollar rose against the yen but slipped against the mark.

29 Bentsen backed a stronger dollar, making the firmest statement yet by the Clinton administration that the U.S. doesn't want to let the dollar fall to help improve the American trade position. The Treasury secretary asserted that "a stronger dollar is better for our economy and better for the world's economy" in remarks prepared for an address in New York.

Many U.S. export-industry executives are ambivalent about the dollar's recent slide even though it can give them a competitive advantage in overseas markets. Import prices, meanwhile, have climbed less in the past year than overall consumer prices, despite the dollar's weakness.

Japan introduced a package of deregulatory measures to stimulate the economy and promote imports. But critics doubted the plan would do much to open the economy to imports or reduce Japan's big trade surplus.

Rising interest rates haven't sapped new-home sales or consumer confidence, which both showed greater-than-expected strength.

30 Bell Atlantic and Nynex are expected to merge their cellular phone businesses in a bid to create a nationwide cellular service. The combination would create one of the top three cellular companies with about 1.8 million subscribers and annual revenue of $1.2 billion. The two Bell companies also hope to combine resources to compete for licenses for new personal communications services.

Stock and bond prices withstood another tumble by the dollar against the yen. The Dow Jones Industrial Average fell 2.59 to 3667.05, and broader measures managed moderate gains. Despite falling to 98.75 yen, the dollar rose against the mark.

Investors are cutting back on the money they are putting into stock funds, and analysts expect further declines through the summer. Stock funds took in $11.8 billion in May, about 4% more than in April, but inflows have fallen this month.

The FCC adopted rules intended to give smaller companies, particularly ones controlled by women and minorities, a chance to compete in new wireless telecommunications services. The agency, auctioning airwave space for the new services, set aside space available only to smaller firms.

Gross domestic product rose at an annual rate of 3.4% in the first quarter, showing the economy had more momentum than previously thought. The Commerce Department's final GDP measure was well above its first two estimates of 2.6% and 3.0%.

Auto sales and production figures, reported in seasonally adjusted annual rates, inaccurately portray a slowdown in the industry, some economists say. That may be warping broader measures showing moderate, sustainable economic growth.

Coffee futures prices surged again. Prices have jumped 40% since the weekend freeze in Brazil.

July 1994

1 GM will lift prices on 1995 cars and trucks by an average of 2.5%, more than last year's increase but less than the 4% to 6% hikes expected from Japanese firms hurt by the strong yen.

Disposable personal income rose an inflation-adjusted 1% in May, while personal consumption was up 0.2%. New orders for manufactured goods advanced 0.6% in the month.

Bond prices tumbled on concerns about the dollar and renewed inflation fears. The Treasury's 30-year issue lost a point to yield 7.61%. The Dow Jones industrials sank 42.09 to 3624.96, but the Nasdaq index rose a bit.

5 Four baby Bells plan to launch a battle to end the consent decree that has controlled their business for the past decade. The companies—Bell Atlantic, BellSouth, Nynex and Southwestern Bell—plan to file as early as tomorrow a legal motion urging U.S. District Judge Harold Greene to give up oversight of the local phone monopolies, opening the way for Bell companies to enter the long-distance market and make phones and switches.

A gradual slowing in the growth of the U.S. economy, rising short-term interest rates and more inflation are likely over the next 12 months, according to the majority of economists surveyed by *The Wall Street Journal.*

The latest economic reports suggest the economy remains strong but growth will ease in the second half.

6 Texaco said it will cut its work force by

2,500, or 7.8%, and try to sell half of its 600 producing U.S. oil fields. The restructuring will result in a second-quarter charge of $165 million.

The Big Three auto makers are expected to post combined profit for the second quarter of up to $4.56 billion, nearly double the year-earlier total.

7 Federal reserve officials left short-term interest rates unchanged despite speculation that the weak dollar could force an increase. But the Fed's decision doesn't preclude an increase later this summer, and most economists are predicting rates will rise before year end.

Stocks and bonds were mixed in muted trading following the Fed's meeting. The dollar rose a bit against the yen but slipped against the mark.

U.S. stock funds fell 2.64% on average in the second quarter. Bond funds fared better: The average taxable bond fund slipped 1.34%. The S&P 500 index inched up 0.42%.

U.S. sales of cars and light trucks remained relatively slow in June, largely reflecting tight supplies.

Ford is raising prices on its 1995 cars an average of 2.2%, a bit less than GM's planned increase of 2.9%.

8 Big retailers reported modestly higher sales in June as hot weather sent shoppers hunting for summer apparel and outdoor goods, boosting business at department stores and big discounters in particular. But the month was a disappointment for some specialty retailers.

The U.S. will push a broad agenda of trade and investment liberalization at the G-7 economic summit that begins today. But attention could focus on the plunging dollar, and the U.S. and its trading partners haven't put forth a plan to lift the currency.

The International Trade Commission is expected to release a report today on Canadian grain exports to the U.S. that could touch off a trade battle between the two countries.

11 The leaders of the world's seven major economies made no move to stabilize the sinking dollar and shot down a trade-liberalization plan pushed by the U.S. The limited results of the G-7 summit show the loss of power of the big industrial nations, which find it increasingly difficult to steer the volatile currency market. Analysts expect the lack of action to send the dollar still lower against the yen.

Breast-implant litigation costs are likely to soar for Dow Corning and other implant makers as thousands of women have chosen to individually sue the firms rather than join a proposed global $4.2 billion settlement.

The latest U.S. jobs report shows the economy still growing strongly, raising the likelihood that the Fed will lift interest rates in coming months.

12 The dollar declined in the wake of a G-7 meeting that resulted in no moves to bolster the currency. But U.S. stock and bond prices fell only modestly. During the day the dollar tumbled more than four pfennigs, or 2.7%, to 1.52 marks, before recovering a bit.

13 Comcast plans a $2.1 billion offer for the 87% of QVC it doesn't already own in a bid that appears to be aimed at breaking up the merger of CBS and QVC. Comcast, which would offer $44 a share for QVC, opposed the CBS merger on the grounds that it didn't value QVC highly enough.

UAL shareholders approved a plan to sell a 55% stake to workers, clearing the way for the parent of United Air to become the nation's largest company majority-owned by employees.

June wholesale prices were unchanged from May, the Labor Department said. Excluding food and energy prices, the rate dropped 0.1%.

The Agriculture Department raised its harvest forecast for corn, prompting some economists to lower their food inflation predictions.

14 CBS said it would buy back 22.6% of its shares for $1.1 billion, or $325 a share, after its planned merger with QVC was scuttled. The offer would allow Laurence Tisch, CBS's chairman and largest shareholder, to realize an immediate cash payout of at least $220 million for his holdings. CBS shares rose $8, or 2.7%, to $308, after gyrating on rumors about takeover bids for the network.

QVC's directors authorized the company to begin talks with Comcast a day after its surprise $2.2 billion offer to acquire the 85% of QVC it doesn't own. QVC's shares surged $6, or 17%, to $42, as Wall Street bet that Comcast will have to increase its offer.

Medical costs in the U.S. are rising at the lowest rate in two decades, new reports indicate, another sign that the health-care industry is managing to bring expenses under control.

Consumer prices rose 0.3% in June, about in line with forecasts, the

Labor Department reported, adding to evidence that inflation remains at bay.

PepsiCo plans to eliminate between 10% and 20% of 6,000 administrative jobs in its domestic soft-drink division, company executives said.

15 The Clinton administration forecast an economic slowdown in the second half of the year and raised its prediction for long-term interest rates a full percentage point from its previous forecast in February. Meanwhile, the Commerce Department reported June retail sales rose a modest 0.6%.

Stock and bond prices rose on the retail report and an increase in jobless claims, as inflation fears calmed. Bond prices surged more than a point and the Dow Jones industrials jumped 34.97 to 3739.25 in heavy trading.

18 The economy showed further signs of cooling in the second quarter. Inventories rose 1.1% in May. Industrial production was up 0.5% in June.

Japan's merchandise trade surplus jumped 15% in June on surprisingly strong growth in exports. The trade gap with the U.S. soared 43%.

19 Conservative business interests are lobbying to expand health-care tax deductions beneficial to their members and upper-income individuals while working against President Clinton's proposed health-care reform.

20 The U.S. trade deficit widened in May, suggesting that second-quarter economic growth was weaker than many analysts have anticipated.

21 Fed Chairman Alan Greenspan laid the groundwork for further increases in interest rates, pointing to scattered signs in the economy that inflation may worsen and emphasizing the weakness of the dollar "is clearly signaling inflationary pressures." He said it wasn't clear that previous interest-rate rises had checked inflation.

Greenspan's remarks rattled stock and bond investors, sending prices lower. The Dow Jones Industrial Average fell 21.04 to 3727.27. The Treasury's 30-year bond dropped seven-eighths of a point to yield 7.54%.

22 IBM reported second-quarter profit far surpassing Wall Street's expectations, and its shares rose $4.375, or 7.8%, to $60.25. Revenue rose 2.7% in the quarter, held back by a large oversupply of personal computers and lagging sales of midrange models.

26 Sales of existing single-family homes fell 3.6% in June, another sign that rising interest rates are slowing growth in the housing market.

27 Wages and benefits inched up 0.9% in the second quarter, helping to keep inflation in check. Consumer confidence declined slightly in July.

Short interest on the Nasdaq Stock Market, where selling pressure has been heavy in recent weeks, continued to climb, rising 4.5% in July.

28 IBM plans the first layoffs ever at its personal-computer unit, with 2,000 jobs set to be cut, as it speeds up the reorganization of the troubled unit.

Ford reported second-quarter profit more than doubled. The results topped expectations, but Ford's stock slipped on fears that rising interest rates could hurt the auto industry.

Chrysler is raising prices on its 1995 minivans and other hot-selling vehicles by as much as 9% to capitalize on booming sales, dealers say.

29 GM's second-quarter profit more than doubled, as the auto maker joined Ford and Chrysler in reporting record earnings for the latest period. Strong vehicle demand in North America and cost-cutting spurred a comeback at GM's massive domestic operations.

The U.S. is poised to declare that Japanese government-purchasing practices harm U.S. companies, administration officials say. That could lead to trade sanctions next year.

The dollar rallied, topping the 100 yen level for the first time in a month, as currency traders took a more optimistic view of U.S.-Japan trade talks. The dollar lifted bonds and stocks.

August 1994

1 Corporate profits soared in the second quarter, as companies posted surprisingly large gains despite rising cost pressures, a *Wall Street Journal* survey found. Profit from continuing operations rose 39%. In large part, the credit goes to continued strong domestic economic activity and a pickup in economies abroad.

The economy's 3.7% pace of growth in the second quarter confirmed the strength of the current expansion, while details of the report, especially a huge rise in inventories, eased fears that the economy is overheating.

Bond prices surged on the inventory growth, with the Treasury's 30-year issue rising more than 1¾ points.

Stocks also rallied, with the Dow Jones industrials climbing 33.67 to 3764.50, their highest level since June 17.

The U.S. declared that Japanese government-purchasing practices unfairly harm U.S. companies, a hard-line position that could lead to trade sanctions. Meanwhile, the U.S. and Canada continue to try to settle a dispute over Canadian wheat imports.

2 Crude oil prices surged as widening political chaos in Nigeria threatened to halt its oil production.

The U.S. and Canada averted a trade war after Canada agreed to cut the wheat it exports to the U.S.

3 American Home Products made a hostile $8.5 billion offer for American Cyanamid, seeking to scuttle a multibillion-dollar asset swap discussed by Cyanamid and SmithKline Beecham. The surprise proposal to pay $95 a share for Cyanamid represents a 50% premium over its stock price and is the latest in a wave of mergers in the health-care industry.

A Senate committee stripped the "fast-track" request from a ratification plan for the world-trade pact. The move is a big setback for the White House, and although the administration will seek to revive the request, its chances are considered to be slim.

Wheat prices jumped in the wake of Canada's agreement to limit U.S. shipments. The pact averted a trade war but could raise some food prices.

4 The economy is "continuing to expand at a solid pace," although there are signs of weakness in the South and Midwest, the Federal Reserve said in its periodic regional economic report.

U.S. sales of cars and light trucks slid in July, but auto makers and dealers faulted supply shortages, not a slowing economy, for the drop.

8 The economy continued to show strength, increasing the likelihood the Federal Reserve will push up interest rates next week. New job growth in July was slightly better than expected, and came on top of an upward revision of June's job-growth figure. If the Fed does raise rates, most economists are expecting a quarter-point boost, although some see an increase of as much as a half-point.

The jobs report sent stock and bond prices tumbling Friday. The 30-year Treasury bond plunged more than 1⅜ to yield 7.54%. The Dow Jones Industrial Average fell 18.77 to 3,747.02.

9 Wall Street is being hurt by the weak bond market. Merrill Lynch has laid off 4% of its employees in its fixed-income unit. PaineWebber and Prudential also have made trims.

10 American Home Products began its hostile $8.5 billion tender offer for American Cyanamid, putting pressure on Cyanamid to either accept the $95-a-share bid or find an alternative.

The SEC has launched an insider-trading investigation of stock-options trading ahead of American Home's proposed takeover of Cyanamid. The agency is studying options trading preceding other recent takeovers.

U.S. productivity fell at a 1.2% annual rate in the second quarter, the Labor Department reported, but wage pressures remained under control. The decline in productivity was the first since the first quarter of 1993.

12 Exxon was ordered to pay commercial fishermen $286.8 million for damages caused by the 1989 Exxon Valdez oil spill, less than one-third of what the fishermen were seeking. The decision was seen by some as a good sign for Exxon, which now enters the punitive-damages portion of the trial, where the same federal jury will consider damages of $15 billion.

Producer prices rose 0.5% in July, the largest increase in 18 months, leading many analysts to believe the Federal Reserve will increase interest rates when it meets next week.

Bond prices tumbled on the economic report and a weak Treasury auction. The Treasury's 30-year issue sank more than three-quarters of a point to yield 7.64%. Stock prices were mostly lower, with the Dow Jones Industrial Average off 15.86 to 3750.90.

16 Business groups are increasing pressure on an accounting-standards committee to modify or drop a proposal that would demand greater disclosure in corporate annual reports.

Industrial production rose 0.2% in July, led by business equipment and consumer goods, the Federal Reserve said. The report, slightly stronger than expected, isn't expected to have much impact on the Fed's Open Market Committee when it meets today to consider interest-rate rises.

17 The Federal Reserve pushed up short-term interest rates by one-half percentage point, sending a clear inflation-fighting message. The increase is likely to raise borrowing costs for consumers and businesses: Many big banks raised their prime lending rates

after the Fed announcement. The rise also is likely to bolster the dollar against foreign currencies.

The credit tightening sparked a rally in bond prices, pulling stocks higher. The benchmark 30-year Treasury bond soared nearly 1¾ points as its yield fell to 7.36%. The Dow Jones industrials rose 24.28 to 3784.57.

The U.S. and Japan resolved a longstanding dispute over intellectual property, signaling an improvement for the broader "framework" trade talks between the two countries.

United Airlines, which last year was laying off workers, said it will hire more than 1,700 employees by the end of the year to ease worker shortages.

Housing starts rebounded in July, rising 4.7%, the Commerce Department reported. Many analysts believe the increase shows the market is stabilizing after a sharp decline in June.

18 American Cyanamid agreed to be acquired by American Home Products for $9.7 billion, or $101 a share, in a deal to create the nation's fourth-largest prescription-drug company. The purchase would boost American Home's sales to about $12.6 billion. Cyanamid shares climbed $2.125 to $96.125 while American Home shares rose 37.5 cents to $59.25.

19 Insurers were dealt a blow as California's Supreme Court swept aside constitutional objections to a referendum designed to roll back insurance rates for consumers. The court ruled that imposing a 10% operating profit margin on insurers is neither unfair nor unconstitutional. Consumer advocates and others said the decision could embolden other states to push ahead with tough rules on insurers.

The U.S. trade deficit narrowed slightly in June as the strength of the economy made for strong imports and exports. Analysts predict the deficit will remain large, narrowing slightly at the end of 1994 or early 1995. Meanwhile, the trade deficit between the U.S. and Japan continued to widen.

The trade report and remarks by officials in the U.S. and Japan pushed the dollar lower against the yen.

22 Clinton suggested that recent interest-rate rises were necessary to fight inflation, saying the economy is growing faster than the Federal Reserve or the administration expected.

Wal-Mart Stores formed a joint venture to open three to four stores in Hong Kong this fall and eventually to operate discount stores in China.

25 Derivative investments made by a single portfolio manager at Piper Jaffray could result in more than $700 million in losses to investors. The losses include those already disclosed in the company's $800 million Institutional Government Income Portfolio short-term bond fund and additional losses from other investment funds and privately managed accounts.

The SEC is considering an accounting-rule change for a complex but popular derivative that could result in write-downs at many companies. The change would have broad implications for bank companies in particular.

Orders for durable goods fell 4.2% in July, pointing to an economy that is downshifting in the third quarter.

26 Toyota will raise prices substantially in the coming weeks on vehicles sold in North America, to reflect the yen's sharp rise against the dollar. Japan's largest auto maker said the move is necessary for it to avoid criticism for dumping cars in the U.S. market. Rival Honda has also said it will likely raise U.S. prices.

General Motors reached a tentative agreement with the UAW that would end a three-day strike at a tail-light plant and enable it to resume production at 13 idled assembly plants.

Existing-home sales held firm in July from June, despite fears that rising interest rates might curb buying. Analysts cited strong job growth and competition in mortgage lending as factors supporting the market.

29 The Commerce Department revised its second-quarter growth estimate to 3.8%, less than many analysts had expected. Many economists now expect slower third-quarter growth than they had first anticipated.

Stock prices jumped on optimism about inflation and interest rates as the Dow Jones Industrial Average soared 51.16, or 1.34%, to 3881.05.

30 Investors added $9.2 billion to stock funds in July, and have accelerated their purchases this month. But their retreat from bond funds continues.

Disposable personal income rose 0.2% in July on the strength of increased employment. The increase followed a 0.1% decline in June.

The Federal Reserve Board has lost some control of monetary policy because of the growing importance of the market for mortgage-backed securities, a study by the Federal Reserve Bank of New York suggests.

31 Defense industry stock prices jumped on the news of Lockheed's merger with Martin Marietta. The stock swap, valued at more than $10 billion, accelerates the consolidation of the defense industry as competitors look ahead to the broad influence that the new Lockheed Martin will have. Lockheed shares surged $10.75, or 16%, to $76.75, while Marietta shares rose 50 cents to $48.75.

The economy saw more signs of slower growth. August consumer confidence dipped, the Conference Board reported. July new-home sales rose 8.3% after June's 11.4% decline, but analysts saw a downward trend.

Japan's unemployment rate hit a seven-year high of 3% in July, a sign the job market is drooping although the economy is beginning to revive.

September 1994

1 Canada's economy, fueled by exports and business outlays for plant and equipment, recorded its strongest growth in seven years in the second quarter, as gross domestic product rose at an annual rate of 6.4%.

Philip Morris announced a $6 billion stock-buyback plan and raised its quarterly dividend nearly 20%, an aggressive move to boost its stock price that shows the confidence Philip Morris's new management has in the company's domestic tobacco operations. Philip Morris shares rose $2.50, or 4.3%, to $61, a 52-week high. The shares of tobacco rival RJR Nabisco also gained, rising 37.5 cents, or 5.7%, to $7 a share in heavy trading.

The U.S. and Canada signed a pact yesterday to make sharp cuts in tax rates on cross-border payments of dividends, interest and royalties.

The index of leading indicators was unchanged in July and factory orders tumbled 2.3% in the month, the biggest drop in nearly three years, further evidence that the economy is cooling off.

2 Sales at big U.S. retailers grew modestly in August, raising hopes for a strong Christmas season. Sales at stores open at least a year climbed 4.9% in August from a year earlier, according to an index of leading retailers compiled by Salomon Brothers.

The manufacturing sector lost some momentum in August, as the National Association of Purchasing Management index declined to 56.2% from 57.8%, further proof that the slowdown hitting other sectors of the economy is affecting the nation's factories.

A Japanese ministry responsible for nearly $200 billion in public pension funds sought permission to hire investment advisers, including foreign fund managers. U.S. fund managers have been barred by law from managing Japanese public pension funds.

6 Wage pressures remain virtually absent from the U.S. economy even though unemployment is staying at about 6%. In August, the jobless rate was unchanged at 6.1%, although hourly earnings in the nonfarm sector increased just 0.2% last month.

Some natural-gas producers have chosen to cut output, as price declines have convinced them that their reserves are more valuable in the ground than in the marketplace.

Toyota and Nissan raised prices on more of the cars they import to the U.S., reflecting the pressure Japanese auto makers are under because of the strong yen.

7 Johnson & Johnson agreed to buy Kodak's clinical diagnostics unit for $1.01 billion, a purchase that would transform J&J into the No. 3 firm in the industry. Like its offer last month for beauty-products concern Neutrogena, J&J's foray into clinical diagnostics is seen as an attempt to diversify beyond pharmaceuticals, where managed-care institutions are exerting pressure on drug prices.

The U.S. has replaced Japan as the world's most competitive economy for the first time since 1985, but middle-income Americans have paid a stiff price in the process, according to an annual global study.

Japanese business sentiment at major manufacturers has improved sharply, a survey showed. The results are the clearest sign yet that the nation's economy is recovering.

U.S. car and light-truck sales in August rose 10.1% from a year earlier and rebounded substantially from July's relatively weak level. The gain underscores that the economic expansion continues at a moderate pace.

8 U.S. productivity fell at a revised 2.5% annual rate in the nonfarm business sector in the second quarter. Despite the overall decline, productivity continued to rise in manufacturing.

China's inflation rate in August remained above an annual pace of 20%. The continued high level is keeping pressure on the nation's leaders.

9 Capital outlays by U.S. businesses are expected to rise 9.4% this year after inflation, a new survey shows.

12 Wholesale prices surged 0.6% in August, the largest rise in nearly four years, but several economists said the picture wasn't as bleak as it appeared. Many expect tomorrow's consumer price report to be less alarming.

Stocks and bonds tumbled. The Dow Jones industrials fell 33.65 to 3874.81. Treasury bonds skidded as much as 1⅝ points, with the yield on the 30-year issue jumping to 7.70%.

Antitrust arguments are being prepared against parts of the Lockheed-Martin Marietta merger plan. The opposition by competitors could force divestitures and slow approvals.

California's aerospace industry faces an estimated 23,000 added job cuts by the end of 1995, including 4,000 that are expected to be announced today by GM's Hughes Aircraft unit.

13 Britain raised its base lending rates 0.50 percentage point to 5.75%, the first major increase in five years.

14 Consumer prices rose 0.3% in August, for an increase of 2.9% over the past year. Stock and bond prices rose on the inflation report, with the Dow Jones industrials climbing 19.52 to 3879.86. Despite worries on Wall Street, inflation is likely to pick up only slightly from current levels.

Some investment experts say portfolios should be adjusted now for inflation, but not all the traditional inflation hedges have paid off recently.

The U.S. current account deficit widened to $36.97 billion in the second quarter, the biggest shortfall since 1987. However, in the short term, the gap may be a sign of economic vigor.

U.S. auto makers plan a 5.5% increase in fourth-period output. The move will put the quarter's production at a robust 3,028,168 units, reflecting industry expectations of continued strong sales.

Toyota plans to boost North American production nearly 50% by 1996 compared with last year, as the Japanese auto maker seeks refuge from the effects of the strong yen.

15 Big long-distance companies are talking to cable-TV firms about entering local-telephone markets. AT&T has discussed alliances that would turn cable systems into two-way interactive phone, video and data highways. Sprint is trying to entice cable players to join it in bidding for federal licenses to build networks for wireless services. And MCI is talking with cable firms about its plan to build networks in 20 major markets, bypassing local phone companies.

The Federal Reserve found more signs of labor shortages as the economy continues to expand. But the survey of the Fed's 12 district banks said that wage pressures are still modest despite increased worker shortages.

Japan's trade surplus fell sharply in August as imports surged, but its trade gap with the U.S. widened. The overall surplus dropped 19% to $6.08 billion. The surplus with the U.S. edged up 2% to $3.49 billion.

16 McCaw Cellular Communications will spend more than $1 billion to expand its national network and market cellular service in the next 18 months as it becomes the wireless subsidiary of AT&T. AT&T could win FCC approval of the $12.6 billion purchase as early as today, its final hurdle before closing the acquisition.

Investment bankers are busier with mergers and acquisitions than at any time since 1988, but their fees are about half what they were in the 1980s because of increasing competition.

Business inventories rose modestly in July, the fourth straight month they have increased. The 0.3% rise suggests that while the economy is expanding, the pace of growth appears to be slowing, economists said. Meanwhile, business sales fell 0.8%.

Ford said it is raising prices on some of its 1995 models for the second time. Its hot-selling new Windstar minivan will rise by $350 to $760 a vehicle, or 1.3% to 3.3%, although on average prices will go up 0.1%.

19 Industrial production rose 0.7% in August and the economy was operating closer to full capacity, the Federal Reserve reported. Economists said the reports suggest inflationary pressure may be stronger than anticipated.

Inflation fears sparked a bond-market rout, pushing stocks modestly lower. The Treasury's 30-year bond dropped more than 1½ points to yield 7.77%. The Dow Jones Industrial Average slipped 20.53 to 3933.35.

21 Federal investigators are probing several Wall Street firms on suspicion that some brokers are laundering illegal drug profits. Customer accounts totaling more than $10 million have been seized at Merrill Lynch, Dean Witter, Prudential Securities and PaineWebber, according to court records and people close to the investigation. Transactions at Bear Stearns are also being examined.

The U.S. trade deficit ballooned to $10.99 billion in July, and although many analysts considered the increase a fluke, the widened gap shook financial markets. A big drop in exports of civilian aircraft was the major reason for the deficit's increase.

Stocks tumbled on the trade report, with the Dow Jones Industrial Average showing its worst drop in six months, declining 67.63 to 3869.09. Bond prices also fell, as the Treasury's 30-year issue slipped one-quarter of a point to yield 7.77%. The dollar was mixed.

Clinton plans to adjust the 1990 census to add undercounted minorities.

The administration's expected move would reverse a Bush administration policy and alter the distribution of $34 billion of federal funds to states and municipalities. Big cities like New York and Los Angeles would receive millions more in outlays to account for the millions of minorities undercounted in the survey. The readjustment would increase the total population count for the nation by five million to 255 million.

The action is expected to help Democratic politicians, since two of their major constituencies, big city mayors and inner city residents, would benefit.

22 Housing starts grew modestly in August, rising 2.1% to an annual rate of 1,442,000 units. But single-family starts, which are the largest portion of new-home construction, fell 2.7%.

Japan's economy contracted unexpectedly in the quarter ended June 30, as GDP declined at a 1.6% annual rate.

Money-market mutual fund yields are close to the 5% level, which they haven't hit since February 1992. One fund cracked 5% in the latest week.

23 Japanese negotiators proposed a new way to measure Japan's progress in opening its markets, which U.S. officials took as a hopeful sign that stalled trade talks can be revived.

Four Chinese auto makers, including three funded by European interests, will receive special government support in order to increase production and squeeze out smaller rivals.

26 An effort to overhaul telecommunications regulation fell apart in the Senate. The regional Bells now are expected to step up their efforts with state regulators and in the courts to win permission to enter three areas: cable television, long-distance service, and equipment manufacturing.

Southwestern Bell is trying to sell cable-television systems it purchased less than a year ago. The regional Bell has approached Jones Intercable, Comcast and others about a possible sale. Separately, Microsoft agreed to provide software for Southwestern Bell's interactive video trial.

27 Health-care reform was abandoned for this year, as Senator Mitchell said he won't attempt to bring legislation to the Senate floor for the remainder of this session of Congress. Lawmakers vowed to return to the issue next year, but much depends on the outcome of the November elections. Support remains for modest reforms to make it easier for the sick to keep insurance or for workers to maintain coverage from job to job.

28 The Federal Reserve decided to hold short-term interest rates steady, but analysts say it is still likely to raise them before year end unless the economy shows signs of slowing substantially. Financial markets took the expected Fed decision calmly. Stocks were mixed, bond prices fell and the dollar weakened. The Dow Jones industrials gained 13.80 to 3863.04 while the Treasury's 30-year bond fell more than half a point.

A money-market fund is shutting down after its net asset value fell below $1 a share. Community Bankers U.S. Government Money-Market Fund was hurt by derivatives investments.

An SEC survey of mutual funds showed trading abuses by fund managers aren't a widespread problem.

29 Investors slowed their buying of stock mutual funds in September, after making big purchases in August. Stock-fund inflows jumped 53% to $14.1 billion in August. But investors, worried

about inflation and interest rates, pulled back this month, industry executives said. Meanwhile, the withdrawal from bond funds continues.

Durable-goods orders rose 6% in August, another sign that the economy is still expanding briskly. The rise was the largest since December 1992 and the 11th in the past 13 months.

World economic output will expand 3.1% this year and 3.6% next, twice the growth rate of the first three years of the decade, the IMF predicted.

Central banks from 12 countries are calling for more complete and regular disclosure of risky investments such as derivatives held by mutual funds, corporations, insurance companies, securities firms and others.

30 Gross domestic product was up 4.1% in the second quarter, a slight increase from the previous estimate of 3.8%, the Commerce Department said. Separately, the department said sales of new single-family homes rose 9.7% in August, but economists expect that figure to be revised downward.

Mergers and acquisitions in the third quarter totaled a record $110.4 billion. There were 1,841 combinations announced in the quarter, helping securities firms partly recoup trading losses from earlier in the year.

Highlights of the 1994 U.S. Industrial Outlook

*by Jonathan C. Menes**

Business investment in new capital equipment and growth in demand for consumer durables are the major forces that will drive manufacturers' real shipments in 1994 to the fastest rate of growth in 6 years (Table 1). These trends are reflected in the manufacturing industries analyzed in the 1994 edition of the *Industrial Outlook*. In addition, shipments of instruments and medical equipment will contribute to an escalation of manufacturing growth from 1993 to 1994.

Table 1: Growth Rates of Manufacturers' Shipments

(percent change in 1987 dollars)

Item	87-88	88-89	89-90	90-91	91-92[1]	92-93[1]	93-94[2]
Median . . .	3.4	-0.1	0.4	-3.7	1.7	2.0	2.8
Mean	5.2	0.4	0.7	-2.7	1.6	2.2	2.2

[1]Estimate.
[2]Forecast.
SOURCE: U.S. Department of Commerce, International Trade Administration.

Although data for service industries are less precise than for manufacturers, Department of Commerce analysts project that most of the service industries covered in *Outlook '94* will expand at a slightly faster rate than in 1993.

Outlook '94 demonstrates that industries contributing most to economic growth will be dependent on capital investment in business equipment and increased consumer spending for durable goods (Table 2). The two fastest-growing industries in 1994—metal cutting machine tools and electronic components—are benefiting from sharper demand for autos, computer equipment and telecommunications. Most of the weakest-performing

Table 2: Growth Rates for Selected Industry Groups

(in billions of 1987 dollars except as noted)

Item	Chapter	Value of Industry Shipments 1994	Percent Change (1987-94)						
			87-88	88-89	89-90	90-91	91-92	92-93	93-94
Electronic components	15	93.8	11.6	4.3	3.4	8.8	13.4	13.1	11.1
Motor vehicles and parts	35	256.5	6.4	-0.8	-7.2	-6.6	4.9	9.6	6.4
Computers	26	66.2[1]	12.4	-4.8	-1.3	-7.3	6.1	7.8	5.9
Metal working equipment	16	18.8	6.4	6.0	-1.2	-9.7	0.1	7.4	5.7
Instruments, controls, and medical equipment	22,44	70.9	9.0	2.1	6.2	3.0	4.1	5.0	5.2
Plastics and rubber	12	120.2	2.8	2.5	2.0	-1.5	1.2	3.6	4.7
Production machinery	17	37.1	10.1	6.6	-2.5	-8.1	-2.8	2.8	3.9
Electrical equipment	18	21.8	8.1	-0.2	-2.2	-6.3	-1.2	2.0	3.8
Durable consumer goods	36,37	74.3	3.9	1.5	-1.9	-3.3	4.6	4.0	3.3
Paper and allied products	10	118.6	2.9	1.0	0.0	0.0	1.0	0.5	3.0
Steel mill products	13	59.8	13.8	-2.6	-1.5	-7.8	8.4	5.0	2.5
Wood products	6	45.3	-1.2	-1.4	-3.2	-5.9	4.9	0.2	2.3
Construction	5	405.9[2]	1.2	-1.3	-2.9	-9.2	7.3	3.0	1.9
Printing and publishing	24	133.4	0.5	-1.2	0.6	-4.0	-0.8	1.1	1.9
Chemicals	11	50.7	3.0	0.9	5.1	-2.6	-0.6	-0.1	1.4
Food and beverages	34	355.5	2.8	-1.3	2.0	1.4	1.0	1.3	1.0
Petroleum refining	4	127.6	5.1	-1.6	-0.6	1.5	1.6	1.0	1.0
Construction materials	7	23.0	-0.2	0.6	0.9	-8.0	3.3	0.4	0.8
Telecommunications and navigation equipment	30	63.4	3.0	-4.7	5.6	-2.9	-2.9	-2.2	-2.6
Aerospace	20	92.3	3.0	2.9	6.5	0.1	-0.5	-11.0	-11.0

[1]In current dollars.
[2]Value of new construction put in place.
SOURCE: U.S. Department of Commerce, International Trade Administration.

* Director, Office of Trade and Economic Analysis.

Source: *U.S. Industrial Outlook 1994*, U.S. Department of Commerce, International Trade Administration.

industries in 1994 are expected to be aerospace and defense-related electronics.

Manufacturing Industries

The median growth rate for inflation-adjusted shipments of manufacturers is projected to increase 2.8 percent in 1994, up from 2 percent in 1993 and the fastest since the 3.4 percent rise in 1988.

Durables, driven by a 14-percent surge in shipments of pickup trucks, vans, and other light motor vehicles, will lead the way with anticipated growth of 2.8 percent, the highest since the 5.9 percent gain of 1988. Shipments of nondurables, led by leather goods for the auto industry, are projected to rise 1.9 percent, also the sharpest gain since 1988 when nondurables rose 2.7 percent.

Despite the prospect for higher shipments, 60 of the manufacturing sectors with growth forecasts (Table 8) are expected to cut employment in 1994. Electronic components, the second-fastest growing industry, for example, is expected to trim its work force by nearly 2 percent in 1994. Only two fast-growing sectors—analytical instruments and optical instruments and lenses—expect to have a record-high number of employees in 1994. The industries expanding shipments most rapidly are increasingly technology-driven.

For example, shipments of leather shoes, slippers, and other nonrubber footwear have rebounded from an 11 percent decline in 1991 to a projected 5.5 percent increase in 1994. Despite the closing of nearly 100 plants and the loss of nearly one-third of the industry's jobs over the past 7 years, shipments in 1994 are expected to be nearly as high as the record peak in 1989.

The nonrubber footwear industry has increased its use of computers for design, management, manufacturing, and marketing functions, and for improved quality and quicker delivery. As a result, tooling can be produced from computer-assisted-design data and linked to automatic stitching, milling, and turning machines. Computers also enable the industry to combine several operations or machines under fewer operators, reducing handling time and improving quality. The net effect has been to reduce production costs, which allows U.S. shoe manufacturers to compete more favorably with cheap labor producers in the Far East, but decreases employment in the United States.

All 10 of the fastest-growing manufacturing industries in 1994 are being propelled by domestic demand for automobiles, housing, computerization, health care and environmental equipment (Table 3). Machine tools, electronic components, automotive parts and accessories, and tanned leather goods are rising with the auto industry. Surgical appliances, surgical and medical instruments, and analytical instruments reflect the growing domestic and international demand for leading-edge health care and environmental equipment. Mobile home shipments will be strong, largely due to shipments to replace housing lost in the 1992 hurricanes in the Southeast and Hawaii. The recovering homebuilding and home improvement industries and mobile home industry are spurring demand for lighting fixtures and mattresses.

Table 3: Ten Fastest-Growing Manufacturing Industries in 1994
(percent change based on 1987 dollar shipments)

SIC	Industry	Percent Change 1993–94
3541	Machine tools, metal cutting types	12.8
367	Electronic components and accessories	11.1
3842	Surgical appliances	10.0
2451	Mobile homes	9.4
371A	Automotive parts and accessories	7.7
3841	Surgical and medical instruments	7.0
364A	Lighting fixtures	6.6
2515	Mattresses and bedsprings	6.4
3111	Leather tanning and finishing	6.0
3826	Analytical instruments	6.0

SOURCE: U.S. Department of Commerce, International Trade Administration.

The fast-growing sectors are also introducing new technologies and quality control into their production schedules. Exports of metal working equipment were up 12 percent in 1993 and are expected to gain an additional 8 percent in 1994 to $4.5 billion, largely due to the manufacture of cleaner and more precise cutting tools and the introduction of lasers.

There is strong evidence of a pickup in shipments of capital goods, with computers continuing to show significant gains in the business equipment sectors despite some uncertainty about the strength of the economy in early 1993. New orders climbed at the fastest annual rate in 9 years. U.S. business purchases of computer systems and peripherals reflected the efforts of many corporations to reduce costs and boost productivity through the use of this equipment. Private sector purchases offset a decline in Federal spending for computer hardware and slower growth in exports.

The construction industry is also showing signs of growth despite the overhang of excessive commercial construction in prior years. Residential housing starts are estimated to increase 4 percent to 1.3 million units, which

Table 4: Ten Slowest-Growing Manufacturing Industries in 1994
(percent change based on 1987 dollar shipments)

SIC	Industry	Percent Change 1993–94
3728	Aircraft parts and engines, nec	-24.3
3724	Aircraft engines and engine parts	-20.0
3721	Aircraft	-11.3
3812	Search and navigation equipment	-6.6
3731	Ship building and repairing	-6.6
3764	Space propulsion units and parts	-5.3
3172	Personal leather goods, nec	-5.2
2761	Manifold business forms	-5.0
2874	Phosphatic fertilizers	-4.8
3769	Space vehicle equipment, nec	-3.9

SOURCE: U.S. Department of Commerce, International Trade Administration.

will also stimulate household durables. The value of new residential housing put in place in 1993 increased 8 percent in current dollars from 1992.

Chemicals, which are important feedstocks in many manufacturing operations, are expected to increase 1 to 2 percent in real terms in 1994 and maintain their position as the top exporting industry. After posting, in 1993, the third highest balance of trade surplus in its history, uncertainty in many foreign economies and the impact on exports holds down growth estimates for chemical producers in 1994.

By contrast, 7 of the 10 most sluggish industries are defense-related (Table 4). Federal military expenditure restraint, relative in part to the dissolution of the Soviet Union, has trimmed demand for weapons systems. In the other three industries, changing business practices and foreign competition have eroded markets. Computerization has sharply reduced the need for manifold business forms. Manufacturers of phosphate-based fertilizers are losing important export markets in India and China to lower-cost producers in Morocco. China, South Korea, and India, which have low labor costs, have undercut U.S. production of handbags, luggage, gloves, and other leather goods for personal use.

For the first time in the 1990's, import growth of manufactured goods is expected to exceed export growth in 1994. Of 68 exporting industries with forecasts, exports are projected to increase 5.4 percent in 1994 while imports from competing foreign manufacturers are expected to rise 6.7 percent. By contrast, U.S. exports increased 7.5 percent and imports increased 6.5 percent in 1992 and both exports and imports increased by 5 percent in 1993.

Service Industries

Industries that are undergoing the most growth in services are also linked to the rise in spending for business equipment with computer-related and telecommunications services leading the way (Table 5). Space commerce, a communications services industry which emerged in the late 1980's, will follow 9 percent growth in 1993 with 23 percent growth in 1994.

After declining in 1991 and 1992, banks increased their lending in 1993 by an estimated 2 percent and are projected to increase lending by 4 percent in 1994. But loan demand will continue to be relatively modest compared with the unsustainable rates of the late 1980's, so banks will be increasing their investment portfolios at double-digit rates for the fifth consecutive year to absorb excess deposits.

Information services, including data processing and network services, are projected to grow more than 12 percent to $136 billion in 1994. A major factor in this expansion involves an industry marketing strategy that links computer skills with gains in worker productivity. The computer services industry, including custom programming, has also emerged as an important export industry for the United States, and expects to generate more than 10 percent of its estimated revenues in 1994 from providing computer education and consulting services in foreign markets.

Revenues of the commercial space service industries are expected to increase 23 percent to $6.5 billion, with satellite manufacturing dramatically reversing its 1993 decline with record-high deliveries in 1994. Surging demand for cable television and mobile communications is driving commercial space services.

The related telecommunications services industry is becoming increasingly international. Its total revenues are expected to rise 7.7 percent in 1994, but revenues generated by international services are projected to jump 20 percent.

In retail trade, sales at general merchandise stores are expected to swell by 14 percent in 1994. Discount retailers are taking a large segment of business from traditional department stores. But the discounting is apparently stimulating sales for both bargain outlets and traditional retailers, which are cutting prices to meet the competition. Projected increases for retail sales reflect the general view of business forecasters that consumer spending in 1994 will constitute the core of an ex-

Table 5: Trends in Selected Service Industries
(in billions of current dollars)

Item	Chapter	Unit of Measure	1994 Value	Percent Change (1990-94) 90-91	91-92	92-93	93-94
Accounting	51	Receipts	38.8	3.4	4.1	5.0	5.6
Advertising	51	Receipts	21.9	-3.8	0.5	1.0	3.8
Banks	45	Loans	2,420.0	-0.9	-0.3	2.0	4.0
Cable television	31	Revenues	28.8	11.1	9.1	9.6	9.5
Computer professional services	25	Revenues	66.7	12.2	12.1	9.7	9.6
Credit unions	45	Loans	157.9	5.9	5.1	4.4	7.0
Data processing	25	Revenues	53.6	14.1	14.3	14.0	15.5
Education and training	50	Expenditures	529.3	8.2	6.3	5.6	5.8
Electronic information services	25	Revenues	15.6	13.2	14.7	16.0	14.7
Equipment leasing	49	Original equipment cost	128.7	-3.3	1.2	2.8	3.0
Health services	42	Revenues	1,060.5	11.4	11.6	12.1	12.5
Legal services	51	Receipts	97.0	1.3	1.5	3.3	4.3
Life and health insurance	48	Premium receipts	316.8	-0.1	6.9	6.0	6.0
Management consulting	51	Receipts	77.0	4.7	5.0	5.9	6.9
Motion picture theaters	31	Receipts	5.3	-4.4	1.5	4.5	3.1
Prerecorded music	31	Manufacturers' value	11.8	3.9	15.2	15.0	13.5
Property and casualty insurance	48	Net premiums written	245.0	2.4	2.0	3.5	4.0
Railroads (class 1)	40	Revenue	29.4	-2.5	2.2	1.4	2.4
Retail sales, total	39	Sales	2,232.0	2.2	5.1	6.3	7.0
Apparel and accessories stores	39	Sales	112.0	3.2	8.2	2.9	3.7
General merchandise stores	39	Sales	320.0	7.5	8.3	13.4	14.3
Eating and drinking places	39	Sales	216.0	5.9	2.5	2.5	4.4
Food retailing	39	Sales	399.0	1.3	1.9	0.8	3.1
Savings institutions	45	Mortgage-related loans	710.0	-9.5	-6.8	-6.8	-5.1
Space commerce	28	Revenues	6.5	29.1	11.2	9.0	22.6
Telecommunications services	29	Revenues	193.1	6.1	5.0	6.0	7.7
Travel services	41	Expenditures	420.4	3.4	5.2	4.8	5.8
Trucking and courier services	40	Revenues	331.0	2.6	6.5	5.7	5.8
Venture capital	46	Capital commitments	2.7	-31.2	100.5	11.6	-6.8
Wholesale sales, total	38	Sales	1,973.0	-1.2	3.2	3.8	4.0

SOURCE: U.S. Department of Commerce, International Trade Administration.

pected 3 percent growth in real gross domestic product.

Health Care

The health care industry is expected again to be among the fastest-growing in 1994, with expenditures rising by more than 12 percent to exceed $1 trillion for the first time. Since Federally sponsored health care began in 1965, the nation's health care expenditures have increased from 6 percent of gross domestic product to an estimated 14 percent in 1993. But the health care industry has also contributed significantly to the development of new technologies and industries through the development of diagnostic tools and treatments.

Surgical appliances—such as wheel chairs, prosthetics, and implantable devices—and surgical instruments are expected to be among the 10 fastest-growing industry sectors in 1994. In addition to serving the domestic market, producers of surgical instruments and appliances are important exporters, posting a trade surplus of more than $2.4 billion in 1993.

Pharmaceutical manufacturing, which is another important component of the health care industry, is expected to sustain real growth of about 2 percent in 1994. Pharmaceutical firms exported more than $7.2 billion in products in 1993 and recorded a trade surplus of $500 million. Pharmaceutical manufacturers are also contributing to the rapid growth of an important support sector, producers of analytical instruments.

The health care industry has other secondary effects that influence production, particularly in the construction industry. Hospital construction is expected to rise 5 percent in 1994, about the same as in 1993. Over the next 5 years, however, construction of health care facilities is expected to be among the nation's fastest-growing industry sectors due to the rapid expansion of the aging population.

Environment

The enactment and implementation of comprehensive anti-pollution legislation in the United States, coupled with growing concerns about the risks and costs of pollution all over the world, has added new costs and challenges to a wide array of U.S. manufacturers. But increasingly, many industries have discovered that cleaner manufacturing processes not only mitigate waste, but ultimately produce cost savings and heightened competitiveness at home and abroad.

Industrial and analytical instruments, which will be one of the fastest-growing manufacturing sectors, is benefitting from both domestic and international demand for new technologies. Demand for valves and pipe fittings for use in environmental cleanup is more than offsetting a decline in defense-related orders for general components. The growth rate of exports of general components now exceeds the growth of domestic shipments.

The focus on cleaning the environment and preventing pollution has created new business opportunities with a huge export potential. The United States is the world's largest producer and consumer of environmental goods and services, accounting for about 40 percent—or $80 billion—of the world market, primarily in controlling and preventing water and air pollution. U.S. exports of environmental technologies and services are growing rapidly, particularly to the Far East, Eastern Europe and Latin America, and have the potential to grow faster because of the U.S. technological advantage over foreign competitors.

The Clean Air Act amendments of 1990 will continue to play a key role in near-term business opportunities as major U.S. industries invest in air-pollution reduction and monitoring equipment between 1995 and 1997, as required by the law. Utilities are expected to be the largest purchasers of pollution abatement equipment, followed by the chemical industry, the pulp and paper industry, and petroleum refining. Other industries that will be required to make substantial investments include primary metals, iron and steel mills, cement manufacturers, and mining.

Clean water regulations also have changed the way many U.S. manufacturers do business, such as the trend in carpet and textile mills to use new types of dyes that reduce water usage and chemical discharges.

The capacity problems of municipal landfills will spur new technologies in waste treatment, recycling, and disposal. From beverage cans and paper to computer components and car batteries, the emphasis is on recycling and reducing the amounts of waste that enter landfills each year. Carnegie Mellon University has estimated that about 15 million used computers could end up in U.S. landfills by the year 2005 at a cost to taxpayers of about $1 billion. Several U.S. computer firms have started recycling processor boards and power supplies, along with other reusable components such as batteries and printer toner cartridges.

Wastepaper recovery reached 42 percent in 1993, surpassing the 1995 goal of 40 percent. Recycled paper constituted nearly one-third of the fiber used at domestic paper and paperboard mills in 1993, and accounted for $560 million of the paper industry's exports in 1993. The recycling rate of aluminum beverage containers reached a record 68 percent in 1992, keeping more than 2 billion pounds of material out of landfills. Recycling aluminum saves 95 percent of the energy required to make primary aluminum, and electricity is the single most costly component in the production of this metal.

The automotive industry is investigating ways to produce environmentally friendly vehicles with improved fuel efficiency and lower pollutants. In 1993, the Big Three automakers formed a joint research group to develop new materials for use in lighter, cleaner, and safer vehicles. The automakers are now working with the Federal Government to develop an electric car. Another Big Three consortium that focuses on environmental issues is the Vehicle Recycling Partnership. Plastic products also represent a growing challenge for the auto industry. A recent study estimated that as much as 1 billion pounds of automotive plastic now end up in landfills. At the current rate, this figure could reach 2.5 billion pounds by the end of the decade. In a pilot program with GE plastics, Ford is making new materials from salvaged plastic bumpers to mold new tail light housings.

Industry Trends

Industry trends point to a swing from computers and semiconductors as the fastest-growing manufacturing sectors between 1973 and 1988 to health care equipment industries in the 1987 to 1994 cycle.

Of the 20 manufacturing industry sectors with the highest compound annual rates of increase between 1987 and 1994, 9 are manufacturers of health care products (Table 6). Electronic components, used in capital equipment, computerization and medical equipment, was among the leading growth industries in the 1973–88 cycle and continued to show strength in the 1987–94 cycle.

Further rapid growth for fluid meters and counting devices, which recorded the highest expansion rate between 1987 and 1994, is expected to slow in the late 1990's because of increased foreign competition. The auto in-

Table 6: Twenty Fastest-Growing Manufacturing Industries, 1987–94

(percent change based on 1987 dollar shipments)

Rank	SIC	Industry	Compound Annual Percent Change 1987–94
1	3824	Fluid meters and counting devices	11.4
2	3844	X-ray apparatus and tubes	11.3
3	2835	Diagnostic substances	10.9
4	367	Electronic components and accessories	9.3
5	3751	Motorcycles, bicycles, and parts	8.7
6	3842	Surgical appliances and supplies	7.9
7	3769	Space vehicle equipment, nec	7.6
8	3088	Plastic plumbing fixtures	7.3
9	3845	Electromedical equipment	7.1
10	2833	Medicinals and botanicals	7.1
11	3841	Surgical and medical instruments	6.1
12	3826	Analytical instruments	6.0
13	2836	Biological products, except diagnostic	5.9
14	3651	Household audio and video equipment	5.6
15	3635	Household vacuum cleaners	5.1
16	2451	Mobile homes	5.0
17	3949	Sporting and athletic goods, nec	4.9
18	3851	Ophthalmic goods	4.5
19	2822	Synthetic rubber	4.1
20	2841	Soap and other detergents	4.0

SOURCE: U.S. Department of Commerce, International Trade Administration.

Table 7: Compound Annual Growth Rates of Selected Services, 1987–94

(percent change based on current dollars)

Rank	Industry	Compound Annual Percent Change 1987–94
1	Space commerce	44.3
2	Electronic information services	36.1
3	Data processing	19.6
4	Health services	11.5
5	Prerecorded music	11.2
6	Management consulting	8.2
7	Travel services	6.9
8	Credit Unions	6.8
9	Life and health insurance	5.8
	U.S. gross domestic product	**5.8**
10	Trucking and courier services	5.7
11	Accounting	5.5
12	Retail sales, total	5.4
13	Legal services	5.4
14	Wholesale sales, total	4.1
15	Equipment leasing	4.0
16	Telecommunications services	4.0
17	Advertising	3.8
18	Property and casualty insurance	3.5
19	Banks	3.5
20	Motion picture theaters	3.0
21	Railroads (class 1)	1.4
22	Savings institutions	-5.9
23	Venture capital	-6.3

SOURCE: U.S. Department of Commerce, International Trade Administration.

dustry is the primary consumer of this equipment.

The manufacturing industries with annual compound real growth of 4 percent or more per annum between 1987 and 1994 are secular rather than cyclical.

High-tech services have dominated growth in the services area since 1987 (Table 7). Space commerce, which emerged as a new commercial industry in the late 1980's, grew at a compound annual rate of 44 percent and should fulfill the early projections that it would be a $10 billion industry by the end of the 20th century. Computer-related services have also grown at compound annual rates of 20 percent or more.

There are also fewer fast-growing sectors in the service industries in *Outlook '94* than in manufacturing. While 20 major manufacturing industries are showing compound annual growth rate that exceeds GDP, only 9 services are rising faster than GDP, and 2 of those are health-related. The largest and most important services industries, such as banking, retailing, wholesaling, telecommunications and mortgage lending have all lagged behind the growth in current-dollar GDP in which they are measured.

Table 8: Forecast Growth Rates for 136 Manufacturing Industries and Groups

(in billions of 1987 dollars except as noted)

SIC	Industry	Chapter	Value of Industry Shipments 1994	Growth Rate 1993–94 Percent	Growth Rate 1993–94 Rank	Compound Annual Growth 1987–94 Percent	Compound Annual Growth 1987–94 Rank
20	Food and kindred products	34	355.533	1.0	113	1.1	69
2386	Leather and sheep-lined clothing	34	0.157	5.4	16	-3.5	127
2411	Logging	6	9.627	2.0	85	-1.8	120
2421	Sawmills and planing mills, general	6	17.066	2.0	86	-0.2	94
2431	Millwork	6	8.473	3.0	60	-1.4	112
2435	Hardwood veneer and plywood	6	2.048	2.5	73	-0.1	90
2436	Softwood veneer and plywood	6	4.524	1.5	105	-1.2	107
2451	Mobile homes	5	5.765	9.4	4	5.0	16
2493	Reconstituted wood products	6	3.588	4.0	39	3.3	26

SIC	Industry	Chapter	Value of Industry Shipments 1994	Growth Rate 1993-94		Compound Annual Growth 1987-94	
				Percent	Rank	Percent	Rank
2511	Wood household furniture	36	7.977	3.7	45	0.0	85
2512	Upholstered household furniture	36	6.140	4.3	27	2.2	42
2514	Metal household furniture	36	2.000	2.8	68	-1.0	101
2515	Mattresses and bedsprings	36	3.030	6.4	8	3.3	25
26	Paper and allied products	10	118.600	3.0	61	1.2	67
2711	Newspapers	24	25.221	0.1	119	-3.3	126
2721	Periodicals	24	16.517	2.0	93	-0.7	97
2731	Book publishing	24	14.610	3.7	44	2.1	48
2732	Book printing	24	3.720	3.0	55	1.9	51
2741	Miscellaneous publishing	24	8.840	4.0	40	1.8	54
275	Commercial Printing	24	47.651	2.7	69	0.9	73
2761	Manifold business forms	24	5.486	-5.0	129	-4.2	129
2771	Greeting cards	24	3.278	2.0	95	1.7	57
2782	Blankbooks and looseleaf binders	24	2.645	1.9	100	-1.3	110
2789	Bookbinding and related work	24	1.140	0.4	116	-0.4	95
2791	Typesetting	24	1.470	-1.7	123	-2.7	123
2796	Platemaking services	24	2.800	3.5	47	2.4	37
281A	Industrial Inorganic chemicals, except pigments	11	20.437	1.2	108	2.3	38
2821	Plastics materials and resins	12	30.473	6.0	11	2.2	45
2822	Synthetic rubber	12	4.363	3.0	62	4.1	19
2833	Medicinals and botanicals	43	5.429	1.9	101	7.1	10
2834	Pharmaceutical preparations	43	35.710	2.0	89	1.5	60
2835	Diagnostic substances	43	4.542	2.0	90	10.9	3
2836	Biological products, except diagnostic	43	2.408	1.9	99	5.9	13
2841	Soap and other detergents	33	15.216	2.0	92	4.0	20
2842	Polishes and sanitation goods	33	5.575	1.4	107	0.0	85
2843	Surface active agents	33	2.722	2.0	98	-1.4	113
2844	Toilet preparations	33	16.438	2.0	91	1.7	56
2851	Paints and allied products	11	11.677	2.5	76	-1.2	108
2873	Nitrogenous fertilizers	11	2.549	2.0	88	0.6	80
2874	Phosphatic fertilizers	11	4.203	-4.8	128	1.4	63
2879	Agricultural chemicals, nec	11	7.249	2.5	77	2.0	50
2891	Adhesives and sealants	11	4.604	3.5	49	-0.2	93
2911	Petroleum refining	4	127.601	1.0	114	1.1	68
3011	Tires and inner tubes	12	11.153	1.0	112	1.0	72
3069	Fabricated rubber products, nec	12	6.170	3.0	64	2.3	40
308A	Miscellaneous plastic products, except bottles and plumbing	12	68.040	5.0	19	2.2	41
3088	Plastics plumbing fixtures	7	1.161	4.0	31	7.3	8
3111	Leather tanning and finishing	34	2.202	6.0	9	-0.1	91
3142	House slippers	34	0.256	-1.9	124	1.4	62
3143	Men's footwear, except athletic	34	1.719	2.0	82	-2.9	124
3144	Women's footwear, except athletic	34	1.063	3.0	59	-3.0	125
3149	Footwear, except rubber, nec	34	0.198	1.0	110	-10.2	136
3151	Leather gloves and mittens	34	0.132	0.8	115	-4.7	130
3161	Luggage	34	1.018	0.1	120	1.3	64
3171	Women's handbags and purses	34	0.384	3.5	48	-5.0	131
3172	Personal leather goods, nec	34	0.239	-5.2	130	-6.9	135
3211	Flat glass	7	2.386	2.0	84	-0.9	100
3241	Cement, hydraulic	7	3.944	2.0	96	-1.3	111
3253	Ceramic wall and floor tile	7	0.835	3.0	66	2.2	43
3261	Vitreous plumbing fixtures	7	0.693	2.5	72	-1.9	121
3275	Gypsum products	7	3.267	1.6	104	2.9	30
331A	Steel mill products (SIC 3312, 3315, 3316, 3317)	13	59.780	2.5	71	2.3	39
3431	Metal sanitary ware	7	0.754	1.9	102	-0.9	98
3432	Plumbing fixture fittings and trim	7	2.100	2.9	67	-1.6	117
3441	Fabricated structural metal	7	7.847	-2.0	125	-1.4	114
3451	Screw machine products	14	3.322	6.0	12	2.4	36
3452	Bolts, nuts, rivets, and washers	14	5.329	4.0	38	0.7	77
349A	Valves and pipe fittings (SIC 3491, 3494)	14	7.210	2.5	74	0.5	82
3523	Farm machinery and equipment	17	8.333	2.5	75	2.8	32
3524	Lawn and garden equipment	36	4.921	2.0	97	1.0	71
3531	Construction machinery	17	11.305	4.0	37	-1.7	119
3532	Mining machinery	17	1.360	3.0	58	-1.6	116
3533	Oil and gas field machinery	17	3.355	3.1	54	3.0	27
3541	Machine tools, metal cutting types	16	3.636	12.8	1	1.9	52
3542	Machine tools, metal forming types	16	1.542	3.6	46	1.4	61

(continued)

Table 8: Forecast Growth Rates for 136 Manufacturing Industries and Groups *(concluded)*

(in billions of 1987 dollars except as noted)

SIC	Industry	Chapter	Value of Industry Shipments 1994	Growth Rate 1993–94 Percent	Growth Rate 1993–94 Rank	Compound Annual Growth 1987–94 Percent	Compound Annual Growth 1987–94 Rank
3544	Special dies, tools, jigs and fixtures	16	8.986	4.0	35	2.5	33
3546	Power-driven handtools	16	2.459	5.1	17	1.9	53
3548	Welding apparatus	16	2.140	3.9	42	0.2	84
3552	Textile machinery	17	1.150	3.0	56	-1.1	104
3554	Paper industries machinery	17	1.715	3.9	43	-1.2	109
3555	Printing trades machinery	17	3.130	1.8	103	1.3	65
3556	Food products machinery	17	2.025	4.1	30	0.4	83
3562	Ball and roller bearings	14	3.706	4.5	23	-0.1	89
3565	Packaging machinery	17	2.753	3.9	41	3.3	24
357A	Computers and peripherals (SIC 3571, 3572, 3575, 3577)	26	66.200*	5.9*	14	2.5*	35
3585	Refrigeration and heating equipment	17	18.029	5.0	18	0.8	74
3612	Transformers, except electronic	18	3.301	3.3	52	0.0	85
3613	Switchgear and switchboard apparatus	18	4.577	3.0	63	-1.0	102
3621	Motors and generators	18	7.040	4.5	24	0.6	79
3625	Relays and industrial controls	18	6.882	4.0	34	1.7	55
3631	Household cooking equipment	36	3.270	3.1	53	-0.5	96
3632	Household refrigerators and freezers	36	4.060	4.4	26	2.1	49
3633	Household laundry equipment	36	3.530	4.0	33	2.2	44
3634	Electric housewares and fans	36	3.460	2.4	78	2.9	28
3635	Household vacuum cleaners	36	1.870	3.0	58	5.1	15
3639	Household appliances, nec	36	3.020	4.1	29	3.3	23
364A	Lighting Fixtures (SIC 3645, 3646, 3648)	8	6.425	6.6	7	0.5	81
3643	Current-carrying wiring devices	8	4.297	4.2	28	1.6	58
3644	Noncurrent-carrying wiring devices	8	2.471	0.3	117	-2.3	122
3651	Household audio and video equipment	36	8.656	2.0	83	5.6	14
3661	Telephone and telegraph apparatus	30	17.400	-.6	122	-0.1	92
3663	Radio and TV communications equipment	30	18.400	2.2	79	3.7	22
367	Electronic components and accessories	15	93.767	11.1	2	9.3	4
3711	Motor vehicles and car bodies	35	145.800	5.7	15	1.3	66
3715	Truck trailers	35	3.587	-3.8	126	0.6	78
371A	Automotive parts and accessories	35	107.158	7.7	5	2.1	46
3721	Aircraft	20	36.630	-11.3	134	-0.9	99
3724	Aircraft engines and engine parts	20	13.350	-20.0	135	-5.8	133
3728	Aircraft parts and equipment, nec	20	12.555	-24.3	136	-5.0	132
3731	Ship building and repairing	21	7.831	-6.6	132	-1.2	106
3732	Boat building and repairing	37	3.300	5.9	13	-6.7	134
3751	Motorcycles, bicycles, and parts	37	1.906	2.6	70	8.7	5
3761	Guided missiles and space vehicles	20	24.081	4.9	22	1.6	59
3764	Space propulsion units and parts	20	3.717	-5.3	131	0.7	75
3769	Space vehicle equipment, nec	20	1.980	-3.9	127	7.6	7
3812	Search and navigation equipment	30	27.570	-6.6	133	-3.8	128
3821	Laboratory apparatus and furniture	22	1.650	4.5	25	-1.0	103
3822	Environmental controls	22	2.072	1.0	109	0.0	85
3823	Process control instruments	22	5.679	5.0	21	2.5	34
3824	Fluid meters and counting devices	22	1.996	1.0	111	11.4	1
3825	Instruments to measure electricity	22	8.285	4.0	36	1.0	70
3826	Analytical instruments	22	5.210	6.0	10	6.0	12
3827	Optical instruments and lenses	22	2.280	4.0	32	2.9	29
3829	Measuring and controlling devices, nec	22	4.198	2.0	94	2.9	31
3841	Surgical and medical instruments	44	11.769	7.0	6	6.1	11
3842	Surgical appliances and supplies	44	14.488	10.0	3	7.9	6
3843	Dental equipment and supplies	44	1.847	3.5	50	3.8	21
3844	X-ray apparatus and tubes	44	3.279	5.0	20	11.3	2
3845	Electromedical equipment	44	5.799	0.2	118	7.1	9
3851	Ophthalmic goods	44	2.294	2.0	87	4.5	18
3861	Photographic equipment and supplies	23	20.200	2.0	81	0.7	76
3911	Jewelry, precious metal	37	3.775	3.0	65	-1.1	105
3931	Musical instruments	37	0.730	0.0	121	-1.5	115
394A	Dolls, toys, and games (SIC 3942, 3944)	37	4.262	2.0	80	2.1	47
3949	Sporting and athletic goods, nec	37	7.178	3.4	51	4.9	17
3961	Costume jewelry	37	1.233	1.5	106	-1.7	118

*In billions of current dollars.
SOURCE: U.S. Department of Commerce, International Trade Administration.

Industry Surveys[1]

Aerospace

This section covers the following Standard Industrial Classification (SIC) categories: Aircraft (3721), Aircraft Engines and Engine Parts (3724), Aircraft Equipment, NEC (3728), Guided Missiles and Space Vehicles (3761), Guided Missiles and Space Vehicle Propulsion and Parts (3764), and Guided Missiles and Space Vehicle Equipment NEC (3769).

The U.S. aerospace industry, one of America's most successful industries, is facing some difficult challenges. The three key issues confronting the aerospace sector are: continuing defense cuts, increasing international competition, and a weak global economy.

Still a global leader, the U.S. aerospace industry is a critical part of the country's domestic and export economies. The aerospace industry is the nation's leading net exporter of manufactured goods, selling products worth $40 billion in 1993. The aerospace industry produces the largest trade surplus of any U.S. manufacturing industry (approximately $28 billion in 1993). Aerospace is also a leading technology driver, utilizing a number of the technologies identified as critical by the White House Office of Science and Technology Policy, the Department of Defense (DOD), and the Department of Commerce. The industry accounts for more than 25 percent of all the nation's research and development (R&D) expenditures, making it the country's leader in R&D spending on new technologies.

Industry Sales Continue Down

The aerospace industry is facing serious challenges. Due to continued defense cuts, a weak global economy, and increased international competition, industry shipments (in constant dollars) will decline in 1994 for the third year in a row. The value of aerospace industry shipments, unadjusted for inflation, peaked in 1992 at $134 billion. Shipments in 1993 fell 11 percent, in real terms, and shipments in 1994 are expected to be 11 percent lower than 1993. Historically, at least half of the industry's revenues were derived from the military sector. Cuts in the defense budgets for aerospace products, both in the United States and in other developed countries, have reduced requirements for military aircraft, missiles, and related equipment from U.S. suppliers. Total U.S. defense spending peaked in 1985, and current budget requests indicate an annual average decline of overall spending of more than 5 percent per year through 1997. The major impact will be from procurement cuts, estimated to be down 47 percent from the peak years of the 1980's build-up. Increased emphasis on dual-use technology combined with funding for defense conversion should focus future attention on research and development. Rather than canceling ongoing projects, the 1994 defense budget recommends continuing development. By contrast, the defense industry's production will continue to fall.

In the past, significant growth in the civil sector sustained the aerospace industry during periodic downturns in defense spending. Between 1985 and 1991, when defense aerospace shipments were declining at a rate of approximately 2 percent per year, commercial aerospace shipments increased more than 11 percent per year. This counter-cyclical characteristic of the industry has disappeared. In 1992, civil orders represented 62 percent of the industry's total order backlog—down from 65 percent in 1991. The civil sector is facing the cumulative effect of the worldwide economic downturn and a decline in global airline passenger traffic. Airline traffic reached its peak of 466 million passengers in 1990. Thereafter, a series of events began which severely damaged the economic underpinning of the industry. The Persian Gulf crisis and the worldwide recession caused airlines' loss of $13 billion between 1990 and 1993. This weak financial performance of the airline industry has, in turn, affected aerospace equipment orders and shipments during 1992 and into 1993.

The downturn in the industry is reflected in a severe decline in employment. Between 1989 and 1993, total aerospace industry employment fell from 912,000 to 615,000, according to Bureau of Labor statistics. Total aerospace employment declined between

[1] Relevant tables are at the end of each industry section. See page 128 for the glossary.

Source: *U.S. Industrial Outlook 1994*, U.S. Department of Commerce.

The U.S. Industrial Outlook contains more complete discussions of the industries excerpted for the *Almanac* as well as discussions of many more. The *Outlook* is available for purchase from the Superintendent of Documents (202) 783-3238.

December 1989 and June 1993 at an average rate of almost 6,000 jobs per month. Layoffs have occurred in both the commercial and military sectors. Capacity utilization for the industry, as calculated by the Federal Reserve, fell from 85 percent in mid-1990 to only 69 percent by May 1993. As long as capacity utilization remains low, prospects for reversing or stabilizing employment trends remain poor.

INTERNATIONAL COMPETITIVENESS

The U.S. aerospace industry faces increasing international challenges as well. While the United States retains both market and technology leadership within the global aerospace industry, its position has eroded. In 1970, the United States led the global aerospace market with a share of almost 80 percent (excluding the former members of the Council for Mutual Economic Assistance, or COMECON, a group of nations led by the former Soviet Union). In 1993, U.S. aerospace shipments still led the world, but had shrunk to less than 60 percent of the worldwide market. This decline reflects the success of other countries in their efforts to foster the development and growth of their national aerospace industries, particularly Europe. Many foreign governments have ambitious plans for developing competitive aerospace industries and support the growth of these industries with subsidies for product development and production. Foreign governments have required U.S. aerospace companies to provide offsets and technology transfers and made sales contingent upon their own firms supplying some of the components. In addition, some governments have encouraged consolidation and cooperation among domestic companies to reduce competition within their borders, enabling their firms to compete more effectively with established U.S. companies.

Europe provides the most formidable competition to the U.S. aerospace industry. According to European Community (EC) statistics, the EC aerospace industry grew almost twice as fast as the U.S. industry during the period 1978–1989. In 1990, the EC industry was nearly half the size of the U.S. industry. The emergence of the Airbus Industrie consortium, composed of the member governments of France, the United Kingdom, Germany, and Spain, is primarily responsible for the erosion of global U.S. market share. Since its inception, Airbus has received an estimated $26 billion, including interest, in direct government supports to assist in the development of its fleet of aircraft. Historically, U.S. companies have not received government assistance. European governments also support their commercial space, smaller aircraft, rotorcraft, engine, and parts industries.

Most individual EC governments have encouraged concentration in their aerospace industries, leading to diversified, national monoliths such as Deutsche Aerospace (Germany), Aerospatiale (France), Alenia (Italy), Fokker (Netherlands), and British Aerospace (U.K.). Even though Deutsche Aerospace privatized their operations in 1992 and Aerospatiale has been offered by the French government as a candidate for future privatization, the trend toward intra-EC ventures will continue to lead to even larger industry consortiums as the EC governments work to integrate their economies. An example is the recent takeover of Fokker by Deutsche Aerospace, with a possible further consolidation with Aerospatiale and Alenia's regional jet programs, the ATR-42 and the ATR-72.

In the future, Japan will become a more significant competitor in several segments of the industry. Small by global standards, the Japanese aerospace industry production totaled only $8.5 billion in 1991, but the industry has grown at a rate of 9 percent a year since 1984. Targeted by the Japanese government, aerospace research and development efforts have focused on aircraft fuselage and systems components, electronics, high-speed propulsion systems, and space launch vehicles. Japan's growth in the aerospace industry stems from its partnerships and cooperative ventures with Western aerospace companies, most notably Boeing. These partnerships enabled Japanese aerospace output to grow from less than $1 billion in 1970 to more than $8.5 billion by 1991. Japan, a "program partner" in the new Boeing 777 aircraft, already possesses much of the expertise needed to produce a world-class aircraft of its own design in the future. In fact, discussions are underway for Boeing to assist its Japanese suppliers in building an 80-seat jetliner, the YSX.

China also has become a major market for U.S. aerospace products. In 1992, U.S. aerospace exports to China totalled over $2 billion. More than 40,000 U.S. aerospace jobs are estimated to have been created as a result of trade with China. It is estimated that China will need more than $40 billion in new aircraft over the next 20 years, making China one of the brighter spots in today's aerospace market. China's market remains fragile, as does its foreign relations with the United States, but the market potential is promising. China also plans to build an indigenous aerospace industry and will become both a growing subcontractor and competitor in segments of the aerospace industry, especially in lower-cost military and commuter aircraft.

The new spirit of international cooperation

prevalent in the Russian aerospace industry presents both opportunities and challenges for the U.S. industry. A market that contains the world's largest airline, largest space industry, and greatest pent-up consumer demand certainly provides new long-term opportunities for U.S. aerospace companies. It is estimated that the former Soviet market will require 2,000 new aircraft for domestic service and 250 aircraft for international routes during the next 18 years. Yet it also presents the challenge of new competition. An example is the 1993 roll-out and first flight of the IL-96M, a four-engine, long-range aircraft. While the IL-96M will be powered by U.S.-built Pratt & Whitney engines and fitted with U.S. advanced avionics, it will compete with the McDonnell Douglas' MD-11 and Boeing's future 777 twin-engine aircraft. Another recent product of Russian aerospace collaboration with the West is Tupolev's TU-204, a mid-range, 200-seater twin jet airliner with Rolls-Royce engines designed to compete against the Boeing 757. Prior to the dissolution of the former Soviet Union, Soviet aerospace factories produced at least as many aircraft, missiles, and spacecraft as the United States. Today, most of these facilities are operating at less than 30 percent capacity. Desire for new orders for those factories, for technology, and for hard currency will force the industries of the former Soviet republics to both collaborate and compete in the international market. These factors play a key role in Russia's future participation in the Space Station. In September 1993, Vice President Gore and Russian Prime Minister Chernomyrdin agreed to the construction of a space station blending elements from the U.S. Freedom and Russian Mir projects.

Other countries also seek larger shares of the global aerospace industry, including: Canada, Brazil, Indonesia, Sweden, South Korea, Israel, and Australia.

LONG-TERM PROSPECTS

The trend toward continued reductions in defense spending is forcing the industry into a major restructuring. The preliminary DOD budget projects a 7 percent decline in military spending in 1994. The Pentagon's bottom-up review process has focused on additional reordering of priorities. The industry will continue to consolidate operations and reduce R&D and capital investment. Layoffs are expected to continue at approximately the same rate as defense procurement reductions—about 7 percent in 1994—but the rate will slow as the major effects of reform are concluded by the mid-1990's. As this restructuring represents a fundamental change in the way the industry operates, only minor cyclical employment increases are anticipated in the future.

Commercial aircraft long-term prospects are more positive, but still uncertain. A strong world economy and recovery from the 1990–1993 global recession would ensure continued steady demand for airline, corporate, and general aviation aircraft and equipment. The introduction of a high-speed civil transport (HSCT)—an aircraft that can fly at speeds two to three times the speed of sound and have a range of 5,000–6,000 nautical miles—could have a major impact on the aircraft industry in the early 21st century. The expanding economies of Asia and the Pacific Rim also will significantly influence industry sales. Space exploration and commercialization face unreliable government funding and uncertain commercial demand. A successful conclusion of multilateral negotiations to reduce government supports to international aerospace industries would help level the playing field for U.S. manufacturers.—*Aircraft and Equipment: Ronald Green; Missiles and Space: Clayton Mowry; Office of Aerospace Policy and Analysis (202) 482-4222.*

U.S. Total Exports of Aerospace Vehicles and Equipment, 1990–94

(values in millions of dollars)

Items	1990		1991		1992[1]		1993[2]		1994[3]	
	Units	Value	Units	Value	Units	Value	Units	Value	Units	Value
Aerospace vehicles and equipment, total	—	39,081	—	43,794	—	45,030	—	40,118	—	34,777
Civilian Aircraft	3,779	18,148	3,329	22,388	2,086	24,337	1,808	21,077	1,735	15,489
Under 4,536 kg. unladen weight, new	1,134	324	911	311	586	297	500	187	510	191
4,536–15,000 kg. unladen weight, new	79	245	69	279	60	295	48	254	50	260
Over 15,000 kg. unladen weight, new	306	16,691	385	20,881	387	22,379	275	19,500	195	13,900
Rotocraft, new	349	161	318	168	212	118	190	106	180	100
Nonpowered aircraft, new	—	15	—	15	—	7	—	12	—	13
Used or rebuilt	1,911	712	1,646	734	841	1,241	795	1,018	800	1,025
Military aircraft	445	1,481	490	1,784	428	2,083	500	1,311	500	1,384
New	387	1,406	355	1,640	331	1,909	370	1,250	380	1,284
Used	58	75	135	144	97	174	130	61	120	100
Aircraft engines and parts	—	6,883	—	7,049	—	6,699	—	6,361	—	6,394
Piston engines and parts	—	421	—	417	—	315	—	291	—	294
Complete engines, new and used	6,411	110	7,812	111	7,278	104	7,170	108	7,200	109
Engine parts	—	311	—	306	—	211	—	183	—	185
Turbine engines and parts[4]	—	6,462	—	6,632	—	6,384	—	6,070	—	6,100
Complete engines, new and used	24,687	1,856	17,565	2,229	18,540	2,484	27,150	2,580	26,000	2,600
Engine parts	—	4,606	—	4,403	—	3,900	—	3,490	—	3,500
Propellers, rotors, and parts	—	343	—	317	—	289	—	296	—	300
Landing gear and parts	—	276	—	333	—	362	—	310	—	320
Aircraft parts and accessories, n.e.c.	—	8,982	—	9,386	—	8,496	—	8,321	—	8,400
Avionics	—	747	—	780	—	795	—	663	—	700
Flight simulators	—	255	—	245	—	205	—	200	—	210
Guided missiles and parts	—	1,306	—	1,204	—	1,428	—	1,200	—	1,210
Space vehicles and parts	—	660	—	308	—	336	—	379	—	370

[1]Revised.
[2]Estimate.
[3]Forecast.
[4]Category changed to include reaction engines, other than turbojets—except missile and rocket—and their parts.

NOTE: Totals do not correspond to SIC-based trade statistics because of slightly broader coverage. Data shown for certain products for 1990–1994 are not comparable to previous year because of category changes made under the Harmonized System.

SOURCE: U.S. Department of Commerce: International Trade Administration (ITA), Bureau of the Census. Estimates and forecasts by ITA.

U.S. Total Imports of Aerospace Vehicles and Equipment, 1990–94

(values in millions of dollars)

Items	1990		1991		1992[1]		1993[2]		1994[3]	
	Units	Value	Units	Value	Units	Value	Units	Value	Units	Value
Aerospace vehicles and equipment, total	—	12,235	—	13,391	—	14,473	—	13,154	—	11,463
Civilian Aircraft	640	2,775	749	3,305	620	3,866	664	3,442	649	3,474
Under 4,536 kg. unladen weight, new	150	228	142	200	118	104	122	60	125	62
4,536–15,000 kg. unladen weight, new	163	1,354	143	1,368	126	1,272	130	1,154	132	1,170
Over 15,000 kg. unladen weight, new	30	737	44	1,285	64	2,007	52	1,775	50	1,800
Rotocraft, new	167	162	244	289	148	179	140	192	142	195
Nonpowered aircraft, new	—	2	—	2	—	3	—	1	—	2
Used or rebuilt	130	292	176	161	164	301	220	260	200	245
Military aircraft	466	63	142	28	77	55	70	16	65	16
New (quantity of powered aircraft only)	460	55	129	20	26	50	32	14	30	13
Used	6	8	13	8	51	5	38	2	35	3
Aircraft engines and parts	—	4,750	—	4,999	—	6,124	—	5,344	—	4,116
Piston engines and parts	—	101	—	101	—	100	—	94	—	96
Complete engines, new and used	3,152	36	9,379	53	2,987	43	2,400	41	2,500	42
Engine parts	—	65	—	48	—	57	—	53	—	54
Turbine engines and parts[4]	—	4,649	—	4,898	—	6,024	—	5,250	—	4,020
Complete engines, new and used	5,891	2,409	2,941	2,371	2,849	3,017	2,480	2,630	2,158	2,020
Engine parts	—	2,240	—	2,527	—	3,007	—	2,620	—	2,000
Propellers, rotors, and parts	—	26	—	37	—	26	—	22	—	23
Landing gear and parts	—	47	—	86	—	78	—	61	—	53
Aircraft parts and accessories, n.e.c	—	3,526	—	4,094	—	3,284	—	3,347	—	2,920
Avionics	—	452	—	477	—	511	—	478	—	435
Flight simulators	—	200		173	—	205	—	75	—	80
Guided missiles and parts	—	83	—	106	—	108	—	103	—	96
Space vehicles and parts	—	313	—	86	—	216	—	266	—	250

[1]Revised.
[2]Estimate.
[3]Forecast.
[4]Category changed to include reaction engines, other than turbojets—except missile and rocket—and their parts.

NOTE: Totals do not correspond to SIC-based trade statistics because of slightly broader coverage. Data shown for certain products for 1990-1994 are not comparable to previous year because of category changes made under the Harmonized System.
SOURCE: U.S. Department of Commerce: International Trade Administration (ITA), Bureau of the Census. Estimates and forecasts by ITA.

Trends and Forecasts: Aerospace (SIC 372, 376)

(in millions of dollars except as noted)

Item	1987	1988	1989	1990	1991	1992[1]	1993[2]	1994[3]	Percent Change (1989–1994) 88–89	89–90	90–91	91–92	92–93	93–94
Industry Data														
Value of shipments[4]	103,589	107,746	113,477	125,194	131,345	133,613	120,742	101,962	5.3	10.3	4.9	1.7	-9.6	-15.6
Value of shipments (1987$)	103,589	106,681	109,736	116,815	116,911	116,287	103,510	92,313	2.9	6.5	0.1	-0.5	-11.0	-10.8
Total employment (000)	810	820	823	816	746	674	587	542	0.4	-0.9	-8.6	-9.7	-12.9	-7.7
Production workers (000)	407	399	400	396	362	323	279	267	0.3	-1.0	-8.6	-10.8	-13.6	-4.3
Average hourly earnings ($)	14.92	15.35	15.84	16.36	16.73	17.56	18.37	—	3.2	3.3	2.3	5.0	4.6	—
Capital expenditures	3,612	3,388	3,921	3,490	3,407	—	—	—	15.7	-11.0	-2.4	—	—	—
Product Data														
Value of shipments[5]	97,185	102,242	106,320	118,141	124,109	126,800	112,244	93,921	4.0	11.1	5.1	2.2	-11.5	-16.3
Value of shipments (1987$)	97,185	100,875	102,103	109,258	109,742	110,349	96,230	80,760	1.2	7.0	0.4	0.6	-12.8	-16.1
Trade Data														
Value of imports	—	—	9,672	10,985	12,422	12,914	11,277	10,973	—	13.6	13.1	4.0	-12.7	-2.7
Value of exports	—	—	30,688	37,304	42,343	43,562	39,560	33,745	—	21.6	13.5	2.9	-9.2	-14.7

[1] Estimate, except exports and imports.
[2] Estimate.
[3] Forecast.
[4] Value of all products and services sold by establishments in the aerospace industry.
[5] Value of products classified in the aerospace industry produced by all industries.

SOURCE: U.S. Department of Commerce: Bureau of the Census; International Trade Administration (ITA). Estimates and forecasts by ITA.

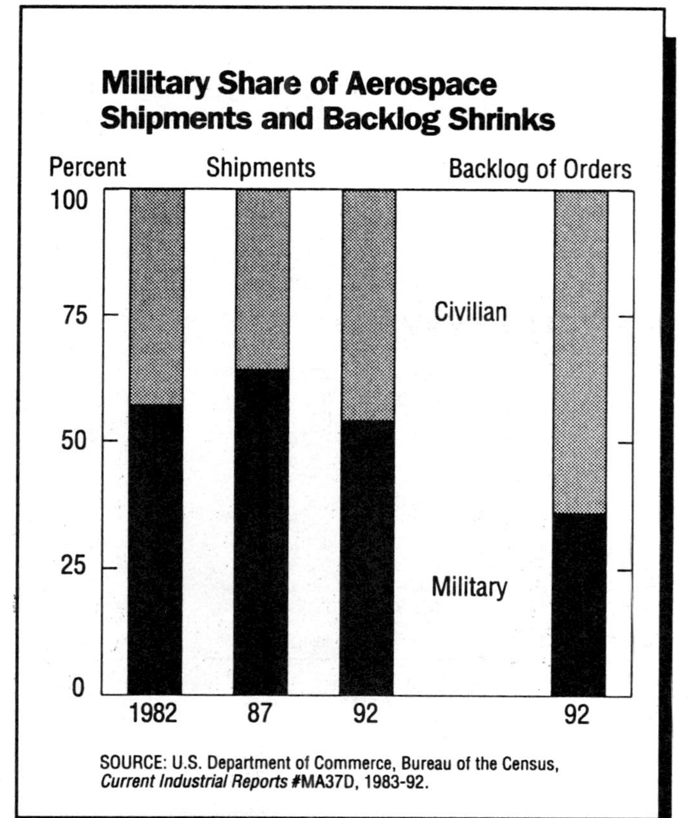
Military Share of Aerospace Shipments and Backlog Shrinks
Percent
Shipments
Backlog of Orders
100
75
50
25
0
Civilian
Military
1982
87
92
92
SOURCE: U.S. Department of Commerce, Bureau of the Census, *Current Industrial Reports* #MA37D, 1983-92.

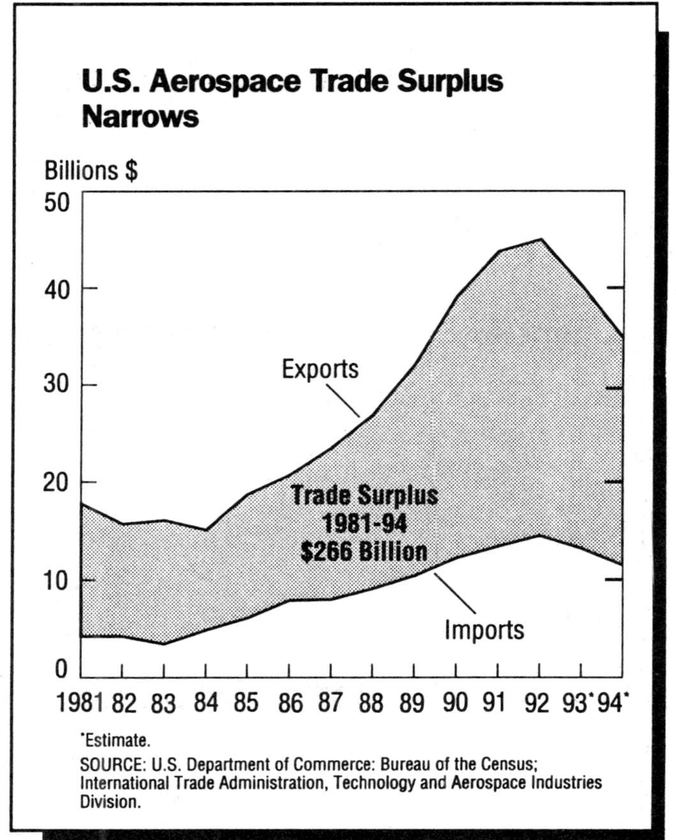
U.S. Aerospace Trade Surplus Narrows
Billions $
50
40
30
20
10
0
Exports
Trade Surplus
1981-94
$266 Billion
Imports
1981 82 83 84 85 86 87 88 89 90 91 92 93* 94*
*Estimate.
SOURCE: U.S. Department of Commerce: Bureau of the Census; International Trade Administration, Technology and Aerospace Industries Division.

Shipments of Complete U.S. Aircraft, 1971–94

(values in millions of dollars)

	Aircraft Total		Civil								Military Total	
			Total		Large Transports		General Aviation[1]		Rotocraft			
Year	Units	Value	Units	Value	Units	Value	Units	Value	Units	Value	Units	Value
1971	11,056	6,593	8,142	2,971	223	2,580	7,466	322	453	69	2,914	3,622
1972	13,072	6,220	10,542	3,417	199	2,787	9,774	558	569	72	2,530	2,803
1973	16,509	8,176	14,688	4,814	274	3,873	13,646	828	768	113	1,821	3,362
1974	16,805	8,595	15,292	5,270	317	4,207	14,166	909	809	154	1,513	3,325
1975	16,958	9,355	15,179	5,305	285	4,006	14,056	1,033	838	266	1,779	4,050
1976	17,807	9,001	16,489	4,705	217	3,155	15,451	1,226	821	324	1,318	4,296
1977	19,381	9,092	18,047	4,512	159	2,672	16,904	1,488	984	352	1,334	4,580
1978	19,881	10,179	18,885	6,460	241	4,308	17,811	1,781	833	371	996	3,719
1979	19,302	15,028	18,465	10,598	376	8,030	17,048	2,165	1,041	403	837	4,430
1980	14,660	18,845	13,613	12,953	383	9,793	11,877	2,486	1,353	674	1,047	5,892
1981	11,860	20,157	10,798	13,287	388	9,731	9,457	2,920	953	636	1,062	6,870
1982	6,248	19,266	5,089	8,619	236	6,254	4,266	2,000	587	365	1,159	10,647
1983	4,409	23,012	3,356	10,266	262	8,493	2,691	1,470	403	303	1,053	12,746
1984	3,931	22,570	2,995	8,354	188	6,343	2,431	1,681	376	330	936	14,216
1985	3,597	29,312	2,678	11,311	273	9,375	2,029	1,431	376	505	919	18,001
1986	3,261	35,622	2,154	12,670	329	11,120	1,495	1,262	330	288	1,107	22,952
1987	2,995	37,317	1,785	13,540	355	11,900	1,160	1,320	270	320	1,210	23,777
1988	3,285	33,840	1,980	14,820	380	13,000	1,270	1,420	330	400	1,305	19,020
1989	3,675	34,228	2,448	17,128	398	15,074	1,535	1,803	515	251	1,227	17,100
1990	3,486	39,206	2,268	24,476	521	22,215	1,144	2,007	603	254	1,218	14,730
1991	2,934	40,776	2,181	29,035	589	26,856	1,021	1,968	571	211	753	11,741
1992[1]	2,465	41,828	1,833	32,246	610	30,268	899	1,836	324	142	632	9,582
1993[2]	2,079	36,483	1,429	28,097	429	26,310	710	1,660	290	127	650	8,386
1994[3]	1,851	28,475	1,311	20,555	306	18,715	730	1,720	275	120	540	7,920

*Excludes off-the-shelf military aircraft
[1]Revised.
[1]Estimate.
[3]Forecast.

SOURCE: U.S. Department of Commerce; International Trade Administration (ITA); general aviation (through first half 1993), General Aviation Manufacturers Association; rotorcraft (through first half 1993); Aerospace Industries Association. Estimates and forecasts by ITA.

Apparel and Fabricated Textile Products

The apparel and fabricated textile products industry (SIC 23), also known as the sewn products industry, consists primarily of firms that produce wearing apparel, both cut and sewn and knit to shape, for all population groups. Apparel accounted for 74 percent of total SIC 23 shipments in 1992. However, fabricated textile products, which include home furnishings, canvas products, and automotive trimmings, are a growing segment of the industry.

Many of the data in this chapter have been revised. In particular, the foreign trade concordance between the SIC and the tariff schedules was revised. This caused the trade series presented in this chapter to be significantly different from that presented last year. For example, knit wearing apparel was moved from SIC 22 (Textile Products) to SIC 23 (Apparel and Fabricated Textile Products). These concordance changes are part of ongoing efforts to more accurately reflect the relationship of export and import data to domestic output. All of the revised time series shown in the tables are continuous.

The apparel and fabricated textile products industry increased its shipments by 2 percent in current-dollar value in 1993, about the same growth as in the previous year. In constant dollars, shipments were nearly 1 percent higher, following a small decline in 1992, because price increases for apparel products decelerated. The shipment gains have occurred in response to sharp increases in consumer spending for clothing, although imports also have benefited from higher spending. Some of the increased production, however, reflected inventory buildup in late 1992 and early 1993, similar to what occurred in the overall economy. This inventory rise probably will hold down production to some extent until stocks are worked down.

Total employment in the apparel and fabricated textile products industry was about 939,000 workers in 1993. Employment has been declining since 1977, and this is reflected in all product lines, particularly outerwear. In 1992, the number of production workers increased slightly, although total employment registered a small decline, reflecting cost-saving cuts in management positions. Production workers constituted 84 percent of the work force in 1993, compared with 68 percent for all U.S. manufacturing. The average number of hours worked weekly by production workers grew to 37.2 in 1992, the highest level in at least 20 years. This growth indicates not only the industry's increased activity, but also its hesitancy in hiring permanent workers until the economy is in a solid recovery. Average hours may increase marginally in 1993.

Despite improvements in technology, manufacturing processes in this industry are still quite labor-intensive. Wages and profit margins are low relative to other manufacturing industries. In 1993, the hourly earnings of production workers averaged $7.10, 2 percent above 1992. Employees making men's coats and suits averaged the highest hourly wages, while children's wear workers earned the least. Earnings of apparel and fabricated textile product workers were about 40 percent below the average for all U.S. manufacturing employees and about 35 percent below workers in nondurable goods industries in 1993.

Apparel

Inflationary pressures in the apparel industry continued to ease in 1993, with the rate of price increases slowing for the third year in a row. A slowdown in inflation in the overall economy, little pressure from raw materials costs, and continuing declines in employment due to productivity gains all contributed to keep inflation in check.

Personal consumption expenditures on clothing expanded sharply at the end of 1992 and the beginning of 1993, following declines the two prior years, but then tapered off somewhat around mid-year. Despite the second-half slowdown, constant-dollar personal consumption expenditures for clothing expanded at a faster rate than total consumption expenditures and at a much faster pace than other nondurable spending. (Usually, toward the beginning of an economic recovery, nondurable spending lags purchases of durable goods, such as autos and appliances, that had been postponed during the recession.)

Retail sales of apparel and accessory stores in mid-1993 were running about 5 percent higher than in 1992. This was slightly less than the previous year's increase but well ahead of the 1991 pace. Retail inventories increased in 1992 and, at mid-year 1993, were about 9 percent above mid-year 1992. Weather disasters may have contributed to the inventory buildup in 1993. The ratio of inventories to sales in 1993 rose for the first time in 6 years.

Because labor is such a significant cost component in apparel manufacturing, producers in low-wage developing countries enjoy a significant cost advantage over U.S. producers, creating intense competition and downward pressure on profits. In addition, consumers persisted in searching for value, buying more sale merchandise in department stores and shifting some purchasing to discount and factory outlet stores. Apparel manufacturers continued to shift sourcing out of the country, most recently to the Caribbean, Central America, or South America. Major companies produced an estimated 70 percent of their sales in U.S. plants in 1993.

Structurally, the domestic industry is made up of a few large companies and many small and medium-size firms. According to one study, in 1993, the larger apparel firms appear to have become more diversified, accounting for 75 percent of apparel sales and all of the growth in volume. The divergence between the performance of the larger firms and many of the smaller companies widened, as profits of the latter group declined in 1992. As a result, the larger companies had most of the funds needed for reinvestment in the industry.

Men's and Boys' Apparel

Shipments of men's and boys' clothing, which outperformed the apparel industry in 1992, slowed somewhat in 1993, although boys' wear was still strong. Production of suits and coats continued the uptrend begun in 1992, following years of decline, helped by a move toward European styling, industry consolidation, and the general absence of inflation in this sector. Production of men's and boys' shorts, sweatshirts, knit sport shirts, and jeans also showed significant increases. Dress shirts, ties, and slacks recorded only slight gains. Dress shirt purchases were mainly for replenishment. Underwear shipments grew only slightly in value as a result of overproduction and price competition. Shipments of both men's and boys' sweaters continued to decline. In terms of sales, brand-name apparel recorded an above-average performance, but consumers generally looked for value.

Women's, Girls', and Children's Apparel

Women's outerwear shipments outperformed the industry average in 1992 and 1993, partially because of a strong showing in exports. European women recently began buying more U.S. clothing, and now markets are opening up for high-status designer apparel in the Far East, including China. Employment in the women's outerwear sector continued to decline sharply, and earnings increases were below average, largely because of the heavy impact of imports on the women's apparel industry. Women's and children's underwear showed little change in shipments between 1992 and 1993.

Retail sales of women's apparel slowed somewhat in 1993, following a reasonable performance in 1992. The lackluster economic picture, coupled with a lack of significant fashion change, had a negative impact on sales. Designer apparel has been particularly hard hit as consumers turned more toward value in apparel purchases and discount pricing. Women's activewear, jeans, and skirts are the brightest spots in this segment of the apparel industry. Sweaters sales have been slow.

Girls' wear sales showed considerable strength in the beginning of 1993, following a good year in 1992. As with boys' wear, demographic trends have had a major impact on this segment of the market. More children have been born in recent years to older, better educated, and more affluent parents who tend to spend more money on them. Imports of girls' wear had little growth in 1993, but exports continued to make gains. Employment in girls' and children's wear manufacturers continued to decline steeply, while average hourly earnings increased modestly.

Fabricated Textile Products

The fabricated textile products industry (SIC 239) is made up of eight industry groups: curtains and draperies (SIC 2391), house furnishings (SIC 2392), textile bags (SIC 2393), canvas and related products (SIC 2394), pleating and stitching (SIC 2395), automotive and apparel trimmings (SIC 2396), schiffli machine embroideries (SIC 2397), and fabricated textile products, NEC (SIC 2399). Products in the latter group include such miscellaneous products as banners and flags, sleeping bags, nondisposable diapers, fishing nets, parachutes, and seat belts. Fabricated textile products accounted for a significant share (26 percent) of total SIC 23 industry shipments in 1993. Textile house furnishings and automotive and apparel trimmings constituted 65 percent ($11.5 million) of total SIC 239 industry shipments.

In 1993, industry shipments of fabricated textile products increased by 2 percent in current dollars and by 1 percent in constant dollars, to $17.5 million and $15.8 million, respectively. Growth was led by higher output of textile house furnishings, textile bags, pleating and stitching, and miscellaneous fabricated textile products. Shipments of textile house furnishings were buoyed by an upturn in housing sales in 1993, and steady growth in spending on home textile products as consumers responded to gradually improving economic conditions. Bed-in-a-bag packaging (sets that include a comforter, sheets, pillowcases, ruffles and shams) remains the most successful line of home linen products. As a result, companies have become more interested in marketing towel sets. In the home textiles market, the consolidation that took place in the 1980's, when most of the top companies changed ownership, has resulted in larger and more responsive home textile mills. Some manufacturers are making significant capital investments to streamline their operations and improve and speed up service to their customers.

Employment in the fabricated textile industry increased in 1993, following almost continuous declines since 1988. Most of the manufacturing processes in the industry are labor-intensive, with production workers accounting for more than 80 percent of total SIC 239 employment between 1988 and 1993. However, some manufacturers, particularly in textile house furnishings, are investing in high-technology machinery, such as computerized quilting and embroidery machines. Some manufacturers also are coordinating deliveries through their own electronic data interchange/quick response-equipped facilities, to improve the distribution of their goods.

Technological Advances

Research and development in apparel and fabricated textiles manufacturing continue to progress, with an increasing concentration on improving quality. However, only about 60 percent of the industry uses new technology. Large, specialized companies tend to make the greatest use of technological advances. Smaller firms tend to be the least efficient. Recent technological advances in this industry occurred in three main areas: computer-aided design (CAD), production, and communications; new modular manufacturing systems; and ergonomics (work place instruments designed to improve the safety, health, and efficiency of workers). Commitments in 1993 by the National Aeronautics and Space Administration (NASA) and the Department of Energy (DOE) to technology transfer and research in this industry could lead to further technological advances and a revitalization of the sewn products industry. NASA has begun several technology transfer projects with the apparel industry in an effort to adapt technology developed for the space program to commercial applications. Some of the ideas under consideration for industry use are planning operations, robotics, vision systems and sensor technology, and a device that reduces an electric motor's power consumption in sewing applications. The DOE research project links eight of its national labs with the American Textile Partnership (AMTEX) and has a projected cost of up to $200 million over the next few years. This project, which brings together for the first time a number of research interests in the industry, is an indication that the sewn products industry must improve productivity to remain internationally competitive. The five research areas now being targeted are analysis/simulation/integration, automation, improved materials and processes, environmental quality and waste minimization, and energy efficiency.

Apparel manufacturing has become more computer-based. New CAD applications greatly streamline front-end product development by allowing quick exchanges of ideas and design specifications with retailers. Using CAD systems for pattern design, marking, grading, and cutting reduces waste and speeds up the production process. Communications technology has been essential in the sewn products industry's ongoing effort to provide "quick response" to retail needs. Quick response now has evolved at the most advanced companies into "responsive manufacturing," whereby consumer demand at retail is quickly translated into production at the manufacturing facility. With responsive manufacturing, companies are able to offer a wider choice of styles, replenish retail stocks frequently at moderate cost, pare inventory levels, and forecast demand more accurately. Initially seen as a tool for manufacturers of standardized products such as underwear, quick response now is being used more frequently by "fashion" apparel companies.

The number of retailer-manufacturer quick response relationships has grown sharply in the past few years. Retailers use point-of-sale systems, bar coding, automated inventory management systems, and electronic data interchange for accepting and confirming purchase orders. These partnerships call for a high degree of cooperation. Information is shared on production schedules and forecasting. One study shows that, among large companies, order cycle time—the time to process an order—was cut from 17.6 days in 1985 to 12.5 days in 1990; there are plans to reduce this to 9 days by 1995.

INTERNATIONAL COMPETITIVENESS

The trade deficit in apparel and fabricated textile products has been growing in recent years. It increased from $28 billion in 1992 to an estimated $30 billion in 1993, despite a 20 percent gain in exports and import growth of 9 percent, half the rate in 1992. The increase in the value of imports overwhelmed the export advance because imports continue to be substantially larger than exports in value terms.

Although the sewn products industry (SIC

23) is historically not export-oriented, manufacturers have increasingly turned their attention to overseas markets in recent years, rather than depend solely on the slow-growing U.S. market. Exports accounted for about 9 percent of product shipments in 1993, up from 4 percent in 1989. The depreciation in the exchange rate value of the dollar and the growing demand abroad for quality apparel and fabricated textile products contributed to the surge in exports the past several years. In 1993, exports, which were affected by depressed economic conditions in all the major apparel markets abroad, grew at the slowest rate in more than 4 years, but still managed a 20 percent gain. Some of the export growth consisted of shipments of garment parts for assembly abroad and subsequent reimport, but exports of finished apparel for sale in foreign markets increased sharply as well. Apparel components that are shipped to other countries for assembly and eventual return to the U.S. market under the HTSUS 9802 (previously 807) program receive preferential duty treatment. (The importer pays duty only on the value added abroad under this program.)

U.S. manufacturers have taken advantage of their reputation for high quality, U.S. Government-sponsored foreign trade fairs and export seminars, and long-term export strategies to expand their shipments abroad. Occasionally, modifications in design and fit are necessary to sell in foreign markets, but many customers are looking for the American look and ease of care and wearing. In addition to direct exports, greater numbers of U.S. retailers and catalog houses have established sales outlets in other countries to sell U.S. apparel products. Men's outerwear and home furnishings remain the largest export categories. Men's and boys' trousers are the most important products exported to Japan, Canada, and the European Community (EC), followed by men's and boys' knit shirts. Menswear and women's outerwear exports recorded particularly steep increases in 1993. Children's wear and women's and children's underwear continue to make strong export gains.

Japan, the EC countries, and Canada are the largest customers for U.S. apparel, with steep gains in shipments the past few years. Sales of completed garments to Mexico also grew sharply. After the United States and Canada implemented a free trade agreement in 1989, the U.S. share of the Canadian apparel market grew sharply. During the same time period, however, the U.S. share of the Mexican market dropped following liberalization of Mexican import barriers. If the recently negotiated North American Free Trade Agreement (NAFTA) is implemented, U.S. exports are expected to regain some of their lost share in the Mexican market. Under the agreement, virtually all trade restrictions would be eliminated within 10 years, some much sooner. The expected benefit to the Mexican economy resulting from implementation of the agreement should boost demand for U.S. exports there.

Although small in value, exports of U.S. clothing have been growing rapidly to Eastern Europe and China, where demand is increasing for upscale goods, status symbols, and Western looks. U.S. manufacturers that are able to take advantage of opportunities in these countries should experience a surge in their exports. Exports of cut apparel parts to the Caribbean Basin countries have advanced sharply in recent years, particularly to the Dominican Republic and Costa Rica, which are the leading participants in HTSUS 9802 garment assembly operations.

Exports of fabricated textile products continued to expand in 1993. The largest export markets are Canada and Mexico, buying more than 50 percent of total SIC 239 exports since 1989. Exports of miscellaneous fabricated textile products (SIC 2399) have grown substantially since 1989, at an average annual rate of more than 25 percent, and now account for more than 50 percent of total SIC 239 exports.

Imports of most apparel and fabricated textile products are covered under the framework of the Multifiber Arrangement (MFA), an international agreement that sets out procedures whereby signatory countries can regulate textile and apparel trade through quantitative import restrictions to prevent disruption to domestic markets and ensure the orderly development of trade. In 1992, the MFA was extended for the sixth time, through December 1993. Potential future changes in the international trade of apparel and fabricated textile products are dependent on the successful completion of the current General Agreement on Tariffs and Trade (GATT) negotiations—the Uruguay Round, which encompasses a gradual phaseout of the MFA and the return of textile and apparel trade to regular GATT rules.

The largest suppliers of imports of apparel and fabricated textile products to the U.S. market in 1993 were China, Hong Kong, South Korea, and Taiwan, but only China increased its shipments of sewn products to the United States. These four countries accounted for nearly half of U.S. imports of all apparel and fabricated textile products. In 1993, the largest import increases, in addition to those from China, were from countries with large HTSUS 9802 operations, namely Mexico, the Dominican Republic, and the Philippines. Arrivals of HTSUS 9802 goods now account for 15 percent of all apparel imports, up from 9 percent as recently as 1990. Apparel imports in 1993 grew at less than half the 19 percent rate in 1992.

In 1993, imports of fabricated textile products, which accounted for only about 9 percent of total SIC 23 imports, rose 15 percent. The major supplying countries of SIC 239 imports expanded shipments to the U.S. market in 1993, with significant increases coming from Canada, China, India, and Mexico. Between 1992 and 1993, the U.S. trade deficit in fabricated textile products widened by 13 percent, to $2.1 billion.

LONG-TERM PROSPECTS

Factors contributing to a favorable long-term outlook for the industry include the growing recovery in economic activity and consumer spending, and continuing growth in exports and investment. Environmental and health issues and the need for further technological advancement and quality improvement are among the challenges facing the industry.

The continuing recovery of the economy should lead to a pickup in consumer confidence. The decline in consumer debt is expected to level off, while new housing starts should gain momentum. These factors should lead to increases in consumer spending on apparel and fabricated textile products. Favorable demographic and technological trends also should help boost shipments.

During the next several years, the U.S. apparel marketplace will become even more competitive, with more overseas producers vying with U.S. manufacturers for shares of the market. More U.S. companies also are shifting assembly operations to other countries to lower their production costs. U.S. producers can use new technology to strengthen the industry's productivity, quality, flexibility, and response time, thereby becoming stronger competitors in the international area.

Exports will continue to provide a significant share of the growth in shipments of apparel and fabricated textile products, even though U.S. firms will still encounter stiff challenges from foreign competitors. When major industrialized economies expand more rapidly, the favorably valued U.S. dollar should help companies increase sales abroad of quality U.S. goods. U.S. manufacturers should continue to take advantage of export opportunities in countries such as Japan, Canada, and Mexico, where trade barriers have been reduced. A successful conclusion to the NAFTA agreement should lead to increased opportunities south of the border, and may serve as a model for similar agreements with other Latin American countries. The increased economic integration of the European market is expected to benefit U.S. exporters by eliminating national barriers to trade. In addition, the economic and political reforms in Eastern Europe and the newly independent states of the former Soviet Union may create additional opportunities for U.S. exports and investment in the apparel sector.—*Joanne Tucker (Apparel) and Maria Corey (Fabricated Textile Products), Office of Textiles and Apparel (202) 482-4058.*

Trends and Forecasts: Apparel and Other Textile Products (SIC 23)

(in millions of dollars except as noted)

Item	1987	1988	1989	1990	1991	1992[1]	1993[2]	Percent Change (1989-93) 88-89	89-90	90-91	91-92	92-93
Industry Data												
Value of shipments[3]	64,243	65,032	63,398	64,414	65,345	66,652	68,052	-2.5	1.6	1.4	2.0	2.1
Value of shipments (1987$)	64,243	63,129	60,185	59,483	59,021	58,790	59,391	-4.7	-1.2	-0.8	-0.4	1.0
Total employment (000)	1,081	1,066	1,018	993	960	959	939	-4.5	-2.5	-3.3	-0.1	-2.1
Production workers (000)	912	895	865	845	815	816	799	-3.4	-2.3	-3.6	0.1	-2.1
Average hourly earnings ($)	6.11	6.34	6.46	6.54	6.73	6.91	7.06	1.9	1.2	2.9	2.7	2.2
Product Data												
Value of shipments[4]	62,119	62,750	61,447	61,962	62,649	64,115	65,461	-2.1	0.8	1.1	2.3	2.1
Value of shipments (1987$)	62,119	60,940	58,349	57,236	56,634	56,552	57,130	-4.3	-1.9	-1.1	-0.1	1.0
Trade Data												
Value of imports	—	—	25,372	26,602	27,230	32,462	35,449	—	4.8	2.4	19.2	9.2
Value of exports	—	—	2,362	2,864	3,708	4,625	5,556	—	21.3	29.5	24.7	20.1

[1]Estimate, except exports and imports.
[2]Estimate.
[3]Value of all products and services sold by establishments in the apparel and other textile products industry.
[4]Value of products classified in the apparel and other textile products industry produced by all industries.
SOURCE: U.S. Department of Commerce: Bureau of the Census; International Trade Administration (ITA). Estimates and forecasts by ITA.

Trends and Forecasts: Selected Womens' Outerwear (SIC 2331, 2335, 2337)

(in millions of dollars except as noted)

Item	1987	1988	1989	1990	1991	1992[1]	1993[2]	Percent Change (1989-93) 88-89	89-90	90-91	91-92	92-93
Industry Data												
Value of shipments[3]	13,726	14,316	13,009	13,810	13,790	14,329	14,767	-9.1	6.2	-0.1	3.9	3.1
2331 Women's/misses' blouses	3,831	3,574	3,402	3,733	3,801	3,797	3,884	-4.8	9.7	1.8	-0.1	2.3
2335 Women's/misses' dresses	5,448	6,037	5,366	5,915	5,665	6,176	6,379	-11.1	10.2	-4.2	9.0	3.3
2337 Women's suits and coats	4,447	4,705	4,241	4,163	4,324	4,356	4,504	-9.9	-1.8	3.9	0.7	3.4
Value of shipments (1987$)	13,726	13,818	12,277	12,688	12,351	12,705	13,020	-11.2	3.3	-2.7	2.9	2.5
2331 Women's/misses' blouses	3,831	3,473	3,219	3,375	3,322	3,274	3,344	-7.3	4.8	-1.6	-1.4	2.1
2335 Women's/misses' dresses	5,448	5,856	4,968	5,314	4,960	5,375	5,551	-15.2	7.0	-6.7	8.4	3.3
2337 Women's suits and coats	4,447	4,489	4,089	3,999	4,068	4,056	4,125	-8.9	-2.2	1.7	-0.3	1.7

Total employment (000)	241	235	215	217	210	195	176	-8.5	0.9	-3.2	-7.1	-9.7
2331 Women's/misses' blouses	73.4	67.0	64.6	64.4	59.5	58.5	55.0	-3.6	-0.3	-7.6	-1.7	-6.0
2335 Women's/misses' dresses	113	115	105	106	102	90.5	78.7	-8.7	1.0	-3.8	-11.3	-13.0
2337 Women's suits and coats	55.2	53.3	46.1	45.9	47.9	45.9	41.9	-13.5	-0.4	4.4	-4.2	-8.7
Production workers (000)	199	191	180	184	178	165	146	-5.8	2.2	-3.3	-7.3	-11.5
2331 Women's/misses' blouses	63.2	56.7	55.2	54.3	49.4	48.6	45.1	-2.6	-1.6	-9.0	-1.6	-7.2
2335 Women's/misses' dresses	91.5	91.8	89.2	93.3	89.6	78.6	67.3	-2.8	4.6	-4.0	-12.3	-14.4
2337 Women's suits and coats	44.6	42.2	36.0	36.6	39.3	37.8	34.1	-14.7	1.7	7.4	-3.8	-9.8
Average hourly earnings ($)	5.95	6.20	6.16	6.13	6.38	6.54	6.62	-0.6	-0.5	4.1	2.5	1.2
2331 Women's/misses' blouses	5.38	5.65	5.70	5.85	5.93	6.06	6.29	0.9	2.6	1.4	2.2	3.8
2335 Women's/misses' dresses	6.08	6.40	6.10	5.93	6.30	6.44	6.55	-4.7	-2.8	6.2	2.2	1.7
2337 Women's suits and coats	6.53	6.57	7.02	7.00	7.09	7.09	6.99	6.8	-0.3	1.3	0.0	-1.4
Product Data												
Value of shipments[4]	13,410	13,927	12,500	12,817	12,805	13,291	13,694	-10.2	2.5	-0.1	3.8	3.0
2331 Women's/misses' blouses	4,178	3,983	3,635	3,660	3,618	3,723	3,808	-8.7	0.7	-1.1	2.9	2.3
2335 Women's/misses' dresses	5,347	5,810	5,245	5,746	5,443	6,000	6,197	-9.7	9.6	-5.3	10.2	3.3
2337 Women's suits and coats	3,885	4,134	3,620	3,410	3,745	3,568	3,689	-12.4	-5.8	9.8	-4.7	3.4
Value of shipments (1987$)	13,410	13,450	11,786	11,748	11,451	11,755	12,049	-12.4	-0.3	-2.5	2.7	2.5
2331 Women's/misses' blouses	4,178	3,871	3,439	3,309	3,162	3,210	3,278	-11.2	-3.8	-4.4	1.5	2.1
2335 Women's/misses' dresses	5,347	5,636	4,856	5,163	4,766	5,222	5,392	-13.8	6.3	-7.7	9.6	3.3
2337 Women's suits and coats	3,885	3,944	3,491	3,276	3,523	3,323	3,379	-11.5	-6.2	7.5	-5.7	1.7
Trade Data												
Value of imports	—	—	5,881	6,190	6,119	7,073	8,098	—	5.3	-1.1	15.6	14.5
2331 Women's/misses' blouses	—	—	2,983	3,005	2,923	3,501	4,032	—	0.7	-2.7	19.8	15.2
2335 Women's/misses' dresses	—	—	937	1,028	981	1,054	1,150	—	9.7	-4.6	7.4	9.1
2337 Women's suits and coats	—	—	1,962	2,157	2,215	2,518	2,916	—	9.9	2.7	13.7	15.8
Value of exports	—	—	235	291	362	519	647	—	23.8	24.4	43.4	24.7
2331 Women's/misses' blouses	—	—	77.2	80.6	100	171	233	—	4.4	24.1	71.0	36.3
2335 Women's/misses' dresses	—	—	42.3	50.9	65.0	98.3	108	—	20.3	27.7	51.2	9.9
2337 Women's suits and coats	—	—	116	159	197	250	306	—	37.1	23.9	26.9	22.4

[1]Estimate, except exports and imports.
[2]Estimate.
[3]Value of all products and services sold by establishments in the selected women's outerwear industry.
[4]Value of products classified in the selected women's outerwear industry produced by all industries.
SOURCE: U.S. Department of Commerce: Bureau of the Census; International Trade Administration (ITA). Estimates and forecasts by ITA.

Trends and Forecasts: Selected Mens' and Boys' Apparel (SIC 231, 2321, 2323, 2325, 2326)

(in millions of dollars except as noted)

Item	1987	1988	1989	1990	1991	1992[1]	1993[2]	Percent Change (1989–93)				
								88–89	89–90	90–91	91–92	92–93
Industry Data												
Value of shipments[3]	14,969	15,101	14,772	14,484	15,386	15,197	15,654	-2.2	-1.9	6.2	-1.2	3.0
2311 Men/boys' suits/coats	2,863	3,169	2,918	2,622	2,467	2,766	2,880	-7.9	-10.1	-5.9	12.1	4.1
2321 Men's and boys' shirts	4,075	4,031	3,873	4,243	4,494	4,331	4,476	-3.9	9.6	5.9	-3.6	3.3
2323 Men's and boys' neckwear	476	500	534	500	532	486	493	6.8	-6.4	6.4	-8.6	1.4
2325 Men/boys' trousers	6,014	5,767	5,983	5,657	6,467	6,079	6,193	3.7	-5.4	14.3	-6.0	1.9
2326 Men/boys' work clothing	1,542	1,633	1,464	1,462	1,426	1,535	1,612	-10.3	-0.1	-2.5	7.6	5.0
Value of shipments (1987$)	14,969	14,508	13,719	13,070	13,561	12,941	13,082	-5.4	-4.7	3.8	-4.6	1.1
2311 Men/boys' suits/coats	2,863	3,010	2,596	2,239	2,057	2,269	2,400	-13.8	-13.8	-8.1	10.3	5.8
2321 Men's and boys' shirts	4,075	3,876	3,613	3,836	3,939	3,646	3,528	-6.8	6.2	2.7	-7.4	-3.2
2323 Men's and boys' neckwear	476	490	496	447	465	418	418	1.2	-9.9	4.0	-10.1	0.0
2325 Men/boys' trousers	6,014	5,562	5,655	5,224	5,847	5,272	5,370	1.7	-7.6	11.9	-9.8	1.9
2326 Men/boys' work clothing	1,542	1,570	1,360	1,324	1,253	1,336	1,366	-13.4	-2.6	-5.4	6.6	2.2
Total employment (000)	266	270	258	239	230	234	230	-4.4	-7.4	-3.8	1.7	-1.7
2311 Men/boys' suits/coats	55.2	60.0	54.5	48.4	43.6	41.0	39.0	-9.2	-11.2	-9.9	-6.0	-4.9
2321 Men's and boys' shirts	76.7	77.4	73.7	69.7	68.8	74.1	72.5	-4.8	-5.4	-1.3	7.7	-2.2
2323 Men's and boys' neckwear	7.4	7.5	8.0	7.4	6.4	7.0	7.0	6.7	-7.5	-13.5	9.4	0.0
2325 Men/boys' trousers	93.3	91.9	88.0	81.7	80.5	81.4	80.9	-4.2	-7.2	-1.5	1.1	-0.6
2326 Men/boys' work clothing	33.1	33.3	34.0	31.5	30.8	30.4	30.4	2.1	-7.4	-2.2	-1.3	0.0
Production workers (000)	232	236	225	208	201	206	203	-4.7	-7.6	-3.4	2.5	-1.5
2311 Men/boys' suits/coats	43.1	51.7	47.0	41.3	36.5	35.0	34.0	-9.1	-12.1	-11.6	-4.1	-2.9
2321 Men's and boys' shirts	66.6	68.0	65.1	61.7	60.9	65.7	64.7	-4.3	-5.2	-1.3	7.9	-1.5
2323 Men's and boys' neckwear	6.2	6.2	6.6	6.0	5.1	6.0	5.0	6.5	-9.1	-15.0	17.6	-16.7
2325 Men/boys' trousers	82.3	80.8	76.7	71.6	70.8	72.1	71.8	-5.1	-6.6	-1.1	1.8	-0.4
2326 Men/boys' work clothing	29.0	29.5	30.0	27.8	27.2	27.0	27.3	1.7	-7.3	-2.2	-0.7	1.1
Average hourly earnings ($)	5.92	6.18	6.42	6.61	6.79	7.03	7.20	3.9	3.0	2.7	3.5	2.4
2311 Men/boys' suits/coats	6.95	7.09	7.58	7.84	8.14	8.28	8.46	6.9	3.4	3.8	1.7	2.2
2321 Men's and boys' shirts	5.45	5.77	6.29	6.46	6.87	7.17	7.35	9.0	2.7	6.3	4.4	2.5
2323 Men's and boys' neckwear	6.98	7.15	7.04	7.28	8.02	8.15	8.40	-1.5	3.4	10.2	1.6	3.1
2325 Men/boys' trousers	5.88	6.26	6.17	6.43	6.36	6.57	6.70	-1.4	4.2	-1.1	3.3	2.0
2326 Men/boys' work clothing	5.17	5.17	5.41	5.46	5.68	5.88	6.08	4.6	0.9	4.0	3.5	3.4

Product Data												
Value of shipments[4]	14,035	14,174	14,383	13,771	14,143	14,459	14,893	1.5	-4.3	2.7	2.2	3.0
2311 Men/boys' suits/coats	2,877	2,977	2,915	2,633	2,450	2,777	2,892	-2.1	-9.7	-7.0	13.3	4.1
2321 Men's and boys' shirts	3,842	3,728	3,681	3,740	3,915	3,818	3,946	-1.3	1.6	4.7	-2.5	3.4
2323 Men's and boys' neckwear	422	457	526	498	525	484	491	15.1	-5.3	5.4	-7.8	1.4
2325 Men/boys' trousers	5,474	5,475	5,889	5,544	5,911	5,957	6,070	7.6	-5.9	6.6	0.8	1.9
2326 Men/boys' work clothing	1,420	1,537	1,372	1,355	1,341	1,423	1,494	-10.7	-1.2	-1.0	6.1	5.0
Value of shipments (1987$)	14,035	13,617	13,355	12,422	12,457	12,312	12,466	-1.9	-7.0	0.3	-1.2	1.3
2311 Men/boys' suits/coats	2,877	2,827	2,593	2,248	2,043	2,278	2,410	-8.3	-13.3	-9.1	11.5	5.8
2321 Men's and boys' shirts	3,842	3,584	3,433	3,382	3,431	3,213	3,110	-4.2	-1.5	1.4	-6.4	-3.2
2323 Men's and boys' neckwear	422	448	489	445	459	416	417	9.2	-9.0	3.1	-9.4	0.2
2325 Men/boys' trousers	5,474	5,279	5,566	5,119	5,345	5,167	5,263	5.4	-8.0	4.4	-3.3	1.9
2326 Men/boys' work clothing	1,420	1,478	1,274	1,228	1,179	1,238	1,266	-13.8	-3.6	-4.0	5.0	2.3
Trade Data												
Value of imports	—	—	5,566	5,716	6,167	7,624	8,232	—	2.7	7.9	23.6	8.0
2311 Men/boys' suits/coats	—	—	745	650	678	789	842	—	-12.8	4.3	16.4	6.7
2321 Men's and boys' shirts	—	—	2,749	2,792	3,039	4,028	4,577	—	1.6	8.8	32.5	13.6
2323 Men's and boys' neckwear	—	—	100	110	140	151	159	—	10.0	27.3	7.9	5.3
2325 Men/boys' trousers	—	—	1,971	2,164	2,310	2,657	2,654	—	9.8	6.7	15.0	-0.1
2326 Men/boys' work clothing	—	—	0.0	0.0	0.0	0.0	0.0	—	—	—	—	—
Value of exports	—	—	713	906	1,140	1,478	1,794	—	27.1	25.8	29.6	21.4
2311 Men/boys' suits/coats	—	—	84.0	129	161	197	239	—	53.6	24.8	22.4	21.3
2321 Men's and boys' shirts	—	—	217	268	333	457	572	—	23.5	24.3	37.2	25.2
2323 Men's and boys' neckwear	—	—	10.1	9.8	14.5	15.5	20.3	—	-3.0	48.0	6.9	31.0
2325 Men/boys' trousers	—	—	402	500	631	809	963	—	24.4	26.2	28.2	19.0
2326 Men/boys' work clothing	—	—	0.0	0.0	0.0	0.0	0.0	—	—	—	—	—

[1]Estimate, except exports and imports.
[2]Estimate.
[3]Value of all products and services sold by establishments in the selected men's and boys' apparel industry.
[4]Value of products classified in the selected men's and boys' apparel industry produced by all industries.
SOURCE: U.S. Department of Commerce: Bureau of the Census; International Trade Administration (ITA). Estimates and forecasts by ITA.

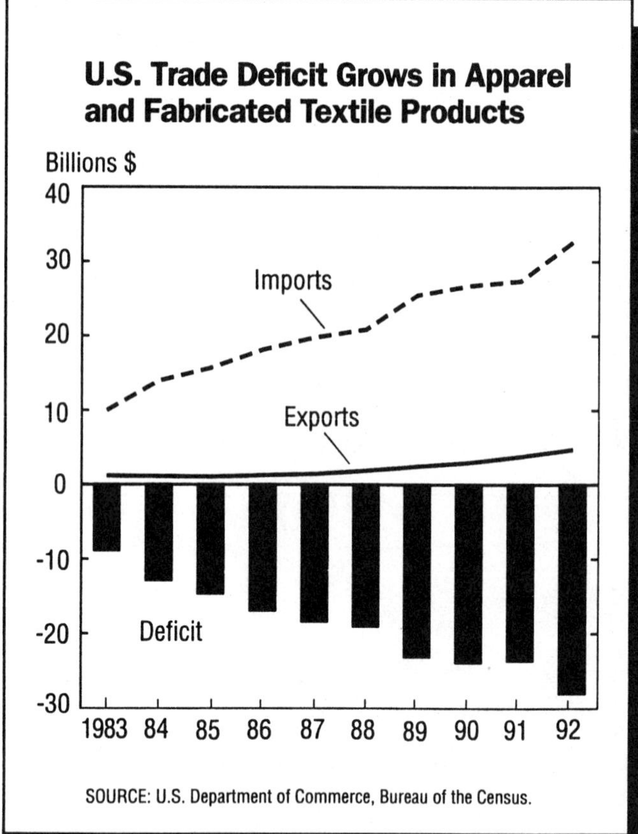
U.S. Trade Deficit Grows in Apparel and Fabricated Textile Products
Billions $
40
30
20
10
0
-10
-20
-30
Imports
Exports
Deficit
1983 84 85 86 87 88 89 90 91 92
SOURCE: U.S. Department of Commerce, Bureau of the Census.

Banking

Federally insured depository institutions held slightly more than $4.9 trillion in assets in 1993, down slightly from 1992. If the interest rates remain low and prices remain steady, however, assets in 1994 are expected to increase 1 percent to approximately $5 trillion.

Commercial banks, savings institutions, and credit unions in 1993 benefited from a widening of spreads between interest rates charged for loans and paid for deposits. Savings institutions reported a record high spread of 4.25 percent between interest earned from mortgage loans and interest paid on deposits.

Depositors in 1993 diverted funds in record volume from banks, thrifts, and credit unions to alternative investments, especially mutual funds and common stock. Commercial banks faced with higher deposit insurance and the need to improve loan quality slowed the growth of deposits and their lending activity.

Despite the slowdown in lending and runoff in deposits, commercial banks and savings institutions continued to increase profits in 1993. Banks in 1994 are expected to report profits for the third consecutive year. Savings institutions are expected to continue to decline in terms of numbers and assets, but should extend a streak of profitable quarters that dates from 1991.

Banks and savings institutions are also expected to continue their evolution into a structure featuring a regional bank holding company that operates independent depository, commercial and consumer lending, mortgage lending and mortgage servicing, insurance, and securities units. Banks expect securities activities to become a significant growth area.

In 1987 the Federal Reserve Board allowed certain subsidiaries of banks to underwrite and deal in asset-backed securities and municipal revenue bonds. The Fed in 1989 expanded the eligible securities to corporate debt and stock. Revenues from underwriting and dealing in these securities are limited to 10 percent of the subsidiary's total revenues, yet by early 1993 bank subsidiaries accounted for 6.2 percent of the capital of all securities firms. During the 12 months ending June 30, 1993, these subsidiaries underwrote 5.5 percent of all investment-grade corporate debt. Money center and large regional banks in 1993 also competed aggressively with traditional mutual fund sponsors by retailing mutual funds to their customers, in part as an effort to recapture some of the funds flowing from certificates of deposit to other investment vehicles. Some of these banks have limited their activity to retailing funds sponsored by traditional fund management companies. But more than 110 banks or bank-holding companies offered proprietary mutual funds, primarily to their existing client base. Bank-sponsored mutual funds in 1993 were the fastest growing segment of the mutual-fund industry, accounting for 10.6 percent of total assets, and 30 percent of new sales.

Community development banking also increased in prominence in 1993. Federal banking and savings institution regulators intensified their audits of lending to lower income communities, and gathered public information on means to increase lending in these neighborhoods. Credit union regulators chartered four new credit unions exclusively to provide services for lower income members, while another 140 credit unions focused services on lower income members.

Commercial Banking

As economic activity maintained its steady, but modest, upward trend, businesses began once again to turn to banks for their short-term capital needs. With low interest rates and steady price levels as a backdrop, bank lending was expected to fare a little better than in the most recent past, rising 2 percent to $2,327 billion in 1993, and 4 percent to $2,420 billion in 1994. Bank lending dropped slightly both in 1991 and 1992. The growth of bank investments, on the other hand, is expected to continue to decelerate from its recent peak increase of 16.5 percent in 1991 to about 10 percent in both 1993 and 1994.

The broad variety of savings and investments instruments marketed by competing depository and non-depository financial institutions is expected to result in a relatively small 3 percent increase in commercial bank deposits in 1993 and 1994. Over the past few years, consumer bank deposits have been especially hit due to the runoff of certificates of deposit, only partly offset by the growth of passbook and money market accounts. Most of the runoff has flowed into mutual funds providing the strength being experienced in the stock and bond markets. This continuous rivalry from competitors has compelled commercial banks to enter the mutual fund business and to keep up the pressure on legislators and regulators in an effort to open up areas, such as the securities market, that previously were off limits.

Specifically, the Federal Reserve Board has in recent years given approval to a number of banks for broader securities underwriting powers, under "Section 20" of the Glass-Steagall Act, which permits banks, through separately capitalized units, to underwrite and deal in corporate debt and equity. These activities, however, can contribute no more than 10 percent of the unit's revenues. Banks have long been able to deal in government securities.

Of the more than 30 banks that have received approval by the Board for securities underwriting privileges under Section 20, about one third are foreign banks while the rest are domestic money-center banks and big regional bank companies. It should be noted that 17 additional foreign banks have used "grandfathered" status under the International Banking Act of 1978 to deal in both commercial banking and securities underwriting activities in the United States.

Profitability of Banks

High net interest-rate margins—the spread between interest income and interest expense—and improved quality of commercial bank assets in 1992, set in a framework of a general economic upturn, resulted in lifting banks out of their 1989–1991 depressed profit picture. These trends continued in the first half of 1993.

The average return on assets, measured by income as a percentage of average fully consolidated assets for all size categories of banks went from 0.53 percent in 1991 to 0.92 in 1992. The most progress was experienced by large banks—those with more than $5 billion in assets—and the 10 largest banks, the return on assets of the former going from 0.50 to 1.01 percent, and the latter from 0.21 to 0.65 percent.

The average return on equity, measured by net income as a percentage of average equity capital, also grew substantially for the industry as a whole, going from 7.86 percent in 1991 to 12.80 in 1992. As with the return on assets, the greatest gains were shown by large banks and the 10 largest banks, the return on equity of the former increasing from 8.10 to 14.66 percent and the latter from 4.25 to 11.87 percent.

Failures and Problem Banks

The financial health of the commercial banking industry is also evident in the number of failures, which dropped from a peak of 206 in 1989 to 120 in 1992. Unofficial predictions for 1993 put the number of failures at 50 to 60. The number of banks on the problem list of the Federal Deposit Insurance Corporation (FDIC) also dropped considerably, falling by nearly half from the 1987 peak.

As a consequence of bank failures and the depletion of the Bank Insurance Fund, premium rates have been steadily increasing since 1989 when banks were paying 8.3 cents for every $100 of insured deposits. Beginning in January 1993, the FDIC instituted a risk-based system with premiums ranging from 23 cents for the best-performing banks to 31 cents for the weaker ones. It was at first predicted that by the year 2002 the bank fund would reach the required level of $1.25 for every $100 of insured deposits, at which time premiums would drop to 13.5 cents per $100 of deposits and to 10 cents a year later. More recent predictions, however, based on lower bank failure projections for the years ahead and a slowing in the growth rate of deposits, estimated that the $1.25 level for every $100 of insured deposits, might be reached much earlier than 2002, perhaps as early as 1996. Consequently, premiums are now expected to be reduced quicker than previously predicted.

INTERNATIONAL ACTIVITIES

The number of foreign bank offices in the United States rose steadily throughout the past two decades, reaching 747 by the end of 1992 and fell slightly to 720 a year later.

These offices include 8 branches, 224 agencies, 90 subsidiaries more than 25 percent owned by foreign banks, 17 Edge Act and Agreement Corporations, and 11 New York State Investment Companies. Nearly one-half of the offices are in New York, with most of the rest in California, Illinois, and Florida. Japan, Canada, France, and the United Kingdom have the largest number of bank offices in the United States. Assets of foreign bank offices in the United States have increased significantly in recent years, rising from $198 billion in 1980 to $865 billion in 1992 or approximately one-fourth of U.S. total banking assets.

In contrast to foreign banks in the United States, U.S. banks abroad have been restructuring and consolidating their activities during the past several years. By the end of 1992, 120 Federal Reserve member banks were operating 774 branches in foreign countries and overseas areas of the United States, a decline from 916 branches at the end of 1985. Of the 120 banks, 88 were national banks operating 660 branches, and 32 were state banks operating the remaining 114 branches.

Technological Developments

Customer use of automated teller machines (ATMs) has been rising significantly over the past few years with the result that branch operating costs have been falling, according to an ATM survey conducted in 1992 by the *American Banker*. Specifically, the annual growth rate for ATMs between 1989 and 1992 has ranged between 17 and 19 percent, with the top 5 users of teller machines being Bank of America with 4,500; Citibank 1,900; Wells Fargo 1,687; NationsBank 1,678; and First Interstate 1,332.

Increased ATM usage and the consequent decrease in teller transactions does not necessarily mean the demise of branches. There will always be customers who will prefer a live teller to a machine, but it will be bank officers with their sophisticated personal computers and software that will, with increased efficiency, meet new customers, handle their questions, and sell them new products.

Slower progress than the ATM growth is being shown by the debit card which can be used not only in conjunction with an ATM for the withdrawal of funds, but also in conjunction with a point-of-sale terminal for the transfer of funds from a buyer's account to a seller's account. The development of the debit card also remains quite modest in the United States, although it has had enormous success in other countries.

In the home banking field, it seems that the problems that existed in the 1980's still prevail in the 1990's. It is a relatively expensive service that requires a personal computer, a modem, and the necessary software. However, for the sophisticated customer, it offers the facility of paying bills, transferring funds, and opening new accounts. As the equipment becomes less expensive, however, and as banks offer a broader array of services, home banking could develop into a comprehensive information package that would include such non-bank activities as insurance, entertainment, travel, as well as business and sports news.

Legislative and Regulatory Issues

As a result of the passage of the Federal Deposit Insurance Corporation Improvement Act of 1991 (see *1993 U.S. Industrial Outlook*), with its mandated new disclosure rules and tougher auditing and underwriting standards, commercial bankers have been pressuring legislators and regulators to ease the regulatory burden that might have resulted from the implementation of the act. Consequently, regulators decided to rely on examiners to assure that banks are operating safely rather than to set specific managerial standards. Other examples of regulatory sensitivity to bankers' complaints include a proposal to exempt about 7,500 smaller banks from the act's proposed capital standards for banks facing unusual risk from interest rate swings, loan concentration and other nontraditional activities; and a proposal to let large banks use their own internal systems, with examiner approval, for measuring interest-rate risk.

The principal banking bills in Congress in 1993 concerned the issues of interstate banking (to authorize nationwide branching subject to restrictions on market share of deposits), community development lending (to establish a fund to support community development by financial institutions), overhauling the Federal Reserve System (to increase accountability of the central bank), Fair Credit Reporting Act Amendments (to make it easier for consumers to obtain copies of their credit reports and correct errors), a secondary market for small business loans (to create such a market by either establishing a federal agency or reducing regulatory impediments to securitization), regulatory relief (to give well-capitalized institutions more favorable treatment, or repeal or modify some of the congressionally mandated regulations), and agency consolidation (to create a single banking oversight agency).

At the state level, legislators aimed at using state law to break down interstate banking barriers. Among the latest states to favorably consider interstate banking reform legislation are North Carolina, Alaska, and Oregon. Several Southeastern states are expected to take up similar legislation in the near future, a move that is necessary to modify the regional banking pact system these states adopted in the mid-1980's. Twenty-two states, including California and New York, require reciprocity as a condition to interstate banking, meaning they will let an out-of-state bank into their state if that bank's home state will let their banks in.

Despite strong banking industry opposition, the Financial Accounting Standards Board (FASB) adopted rules which require banks to assign market value to a broader classification of securities holdings; and to value impaired or troubled loans at their current value, and to thereafter reserve against expected loss of interest on such loans. However, in a concession to the industry, FASB gave banks the option of adopting its market-value standard in the fourth quarter of 1993 instead of the first quarter of 1994, as requested by some large banks, and delaying the starting date for a new standard on valuing non-performing loans and setting loan-loss reserves to the first quarter of 1995.

Judicial Issues

Following many years of debate over the advantages and disadvantages of the separation of commercial banking and insurance, and with billions of dollars at stake, the U.S. Supreme Court in mid-1993 ruled that a 1916 law, which authorized national banks with branches in towns of less than 5,000 to sell insurance, remains in force. On remand, the U.S. Circuit Court of Appeals for the District of Columbia also decided that there is no geographic limit on where national banks affected by the Supreme Court ruling may sell insurance. In a related case, the U.S. Supreme Court declined to resolve the issue as to whether the Office of the Comptroller of the Currency may permit national banks to sell title insurance under authority of a federal law that permits national banks to exercise "all such incidental powers as shall be necessary to carry on the business of banking." In refusing to hear this appeal, the Court let stand a decision of the U.S. Court of Appeals for the Second Circuit which barred the sale of such insurance in New York, Vermont and Connecticut. In yet another insurance case, the U.S. Circuit Court of Appeals for the Fifth Circuit ruled that annuities are insurance products, and thus subject to the so-called town of 5,000 rule. Under the ruling, a national bank could sell annuities by mail in small towns, but it would not be able to offer them from branches in larger cities.

LONG-TERM PROSPECTS

During the late 1990's, legislators and regulators alike will feel increasing pressure to address many of the problems affecting the commercial banking industry. Most important among these issues is the need to expand the opportunities for risk diversification for banks by removing the boundaries separating the banking, securities and insurance businesses. With a combination of banks' application of its proven technological prowess and increasing sophistication of banking regulators' tools, consumers should benefit without compromising bank safety and soundness.

Another problem relates to the need to impose, on non-banking financial services companies, rules relating to community development, equal lending and other social requirements currently applied only to banks. This will level the playing field while providing improved access to capital for America's low-income individuals and neighborhoods.—*Wray O. Candilis, Office of Service Industries, (202) 482-0339; and John R. Shuman, Office of Finance, (202) 482-3050.*

Glossary

Types of Foreign Banks in U.S.

Branches of foreign banks—Full-service banking offices that compete directly with local banks and are subject to all local banking laws and regulations.

Agencies—Agencies make commercial and industrial loans, and finance international transactions, but cannot accept deposits or perform trust functions; not subject to reserve requirements or loan limits.

Commercial bank subsidiary—Any bank that is majority-owned or effectively controlled by a foreign bank. Unlike branches, which are administratively and legally integral parts of a foreign bank, subsidiaries are separate entities.

Edge Act corporations—Banks chartered by the Federal Reserve to engage only in international banking and financing. They are allowed to have offices in more than one state.

Agreement corporations—State-chartered Edge Act corporations.

New York State Investment Companies—New York State charters only for wholesale international commercial banking activities. Like agencies, the companies cannot accept deposits and they are limited to short- and medium-term lending.

Representative offices—These maintain contact with correspondent banks, monitor local business conditions, and serve as a contact point for clients, but handle no banking business.

Principal U.S. Banking Laws

McFadden Act of 1927—Prevents interstate deployment of bank branches and gives states authority to set branching standards for banks within their jurisdictions.

Bank Holding Company Act of 1956—Known as the Douglas Amendment, this prohibits multibank holding companies and one-bank holding companies from acquiring a bank in another state, unless the law of the state in which the bank to be acquired is domiciled affirmatively provides for such entry.

National Banking Act of 1933—Known as the Glass-Steagall Act, this bans affiliations between banks and securities firms, and generally prevents banks from engaging in the issue, flotation, underwriting, public sale, or distribution of stocks, bonds, debentures, notes, or other securities.

Trends and Forecasts: Commercial Banking (SIC 602)

(in billions of dollars except as noted)

Item	1987	1988	1989	1990	1991	1992	1993[1]	1994[2]	Percent Change (1987–1994)						
									87–88	88–89	89–90	90–91	91–92	92–93	93–94
Assets	2,847	3,036	3,246	3,400	3,545	3,653	3,689	3,763	6.6	6.9	4.7	4.3	3.1	1.0	2.0
Loans	1,899	2,040	2,207	2,309	2,288	2,281	2,327	2,420	7.4	8.2	4.6	-0.9	-0.3	2.0	4.0
Investments	514	533	551	606	706	799	878	966	3.7	3.4	10.0	16.5	13.2	10.0	10.0
Deposits	2,009	2,143	2,270	2,363	2,452	2,542	2,593	2,648	6.7	5.9	4.1	3.8	3.7	2.0	2.0
Employment (000)	1,540	1,535	1,556	1,565	1,529	1,488	1,473	1,458	-0.3	1.4	0.6	-2.3	-2.7	-1.0	-1.0

[1]Estimate.
[2]Forecast.

SOURCE: Board of Governors of the Federal Reserve System; U.S. Department of Labor, Bureau of Labor Statistics. Estimates and forecasts by U.S. Department of Commerce, International Trade Administration.

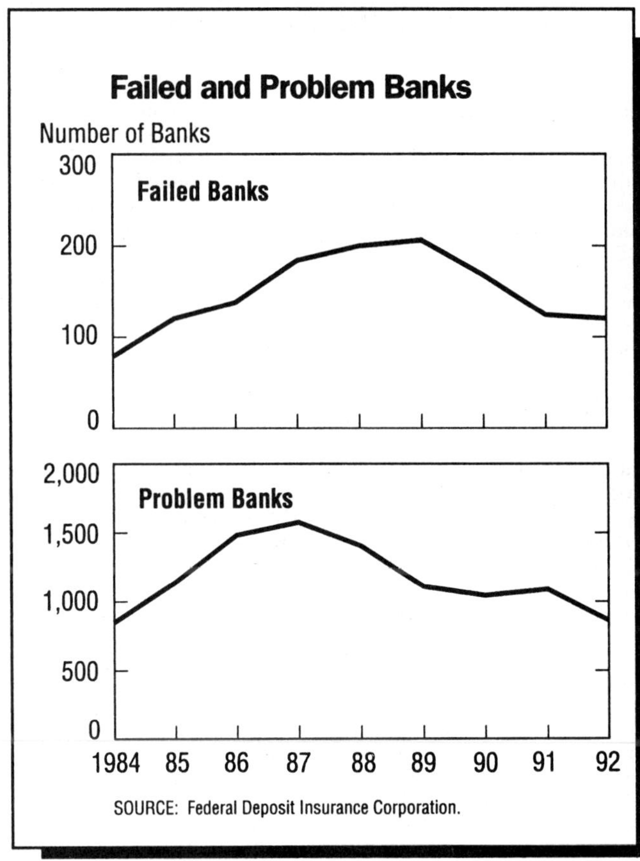
Failed and Problem Banks
Number of Banks
300
Failed Banks
200
100
0
2,000
Problem Banks
1,500
1,000
500
0
1984 85 86 87 88 89 90 91 92
SOURCE: Federal Deposit Insurance Corporation.

Chemicals and Allied Products

Chemicals and allied products industries (SIC 28) manufacture more than 50,000 different chemical substances. Most are used as basic materials in other industries, but some are used directly by consumers. These include such diverse products as organic chemicals (including petrochemicals) and inorganic chemicals (including industrial gases and alkalies and chlorine), plastic resins and synthetic rubber, drugs and pharmaceuticals, soaps and detergents, cosmetics, paints and coatings, agricultural chemicals (including fertilizers and pesticides), adhesives and sealants, and a variety of miscellaneous chemicals (including essential oils, salts, and distilled water).

The chemical and allied products industry is one of the largest U.S. industries. The industry employs about 850,000 persons, and manufacturing facilities are located in every state.

The industry is also the largest U.S. exporting sector and has maintained a positive trade balance for the last decade. This is in part due to its extensive globalization. Twenty-nine percent of the $71 billion in total U.S. chemical trade (exports plus imports) is estimated to be intra-company transfers.

Although 1993 was a difficult year for the chemical industry, it is positioned for slow sustained growth in 1994. Constant-dollar value of shipments grew less than 1 percent in 1993, to $249 billion, as a result of a sputtering domestic economy, turbulence in Japanese and EC currency markets, and a recessionary climate in Europe. The health of the industry is closely tied to the U.S. and global economy, as reflected in the movements of the GNP, personnel consumption expenditures, retail sales, and exchange rates. Resurgence in key industries such as automobiles, housing, and electronics are needed to lead to increased chemical industry shipments in 1994. Capacity utilization for the industry was sustained at slightly more than 81 percent, about the same as the previous year's operating rate. Apparent domestic consumption (product shipments plus imports minus exports) rose 1.4 percent, reflecting a slowdown in domestic economic activity.

INTERNATIONAL COMPETITIVENESS

The chemical industry is the United States' largest exporter, with a 1993 positive trade balance of $15.1 billion, the third largest in the industry's history. One hundred and seventy U.S. chemical companies have more than 2,800 affiliates abroad, and there are about 1,700 foreign subsidiaries or affiliates operating in the United States. U.S. chemical companies' direct investment abroad amounts to $43.8 billion, while foreign direct investment in the U.S. equals $50.3 billion. Although the book value of foreign investment in the U.S. is greater than U.S. investment abroad, U.S. investments have generally been established longer and possess greater earning power. Earnings from U.S. chemical investments abroad in 1992 (operating profits, licenses and royalties, and service charges) exceeded earnings of foreign chemical companies in the U.S. by about $4.1 billion.

In 1993, exports of $43.3 billion exceeded imports of $28.2 billion, producing a trade surplus of about $15.1 billion. This positive trade balance continued a decade-long trend. Due to the restructuring of the industry since the mid-1980's, U.S. chemical producers are well positioned, relative to the world's other major chemical production centers in Europe and Japan, to take advantage of a rebounding global economy. In addition, the industry's primary energy sources—natural gas, natural gas liquids, and crude petroleum—are abundant and inexpensive. The United States and Canada are the world's second- and third-largest producers of natural gas. In Europe and the Far East, naphtha is the primary feedstock. Currently the world enjoys cheap and plentiful supplies of naphtha. However, Saudi Arabia, the world's largest naphtha supplier, plans to build reformers to turn naphtha into gasoline, and this could cause a tight naphtha market in Europe and the Far East.

Marketing opportunities for U.S. producers are likely to open in Europe for select basic chemicals over the next few years, but on a very competitive basis. The European Commission proposal to speed up the process of giving East European countries open access to the EC market only compounds U.S. selling problems. The major chemicals growth market is Asia and the Pacific Rim, in spite of looming regional overcapacity in Taiwan and Korea for basic chemicals and the recessionary conditions in Japan. Indeed, the global economic slowdown has delayed planned construction of chemical facilities in Pacific Rim countries, which means that existing U.S. export markets remain for the short term. Markets in Latin America show no uniform trend for the coming year. Political instability and restraints in industrial development in countries such as Brazil, Venezuela, and Argentina will likely result in slower growth. Plans to privatize the chemical industry in Brazil and Mexico add to the uncertainty about chemical markets.

LONG-TERM PROSPECTS

Over the next five years, the U.S. chemical industry is expected to grow about 1.5 greater than GNP. Prescription pharmaceuticals will be the leading sector, with 5 percent growth expected each year. There is a promising outlook for commodity plastics, as the market is growing in North America, but depressed in Europe and Japan. In Europe, plastic producers are seeking strategic alliances to cut back capacity. By 1998 the European plastic industry is likely to have fewer players and a better balance between demand and supply. With an improved global economy, U.S. adhesive and sealant producers will be presented with export opportunities, especially in Far Eastern markets, where these products will further enhance already efficient manufacturing and assembly industries. The petrochemical industry in Europe is another sector where massive restructuring is overdue. When it occurs, U.S. petrochemical manufacturers will face fewer European competitors but more Middle Eastern suppliers of basic feedstocks.

Organic Chemicals

Organic chemicals are defined as chemicals that are compounds of carbon. They are derived primarily from petroleum and natural gas, and to a much lesser degree from agricultural products and coal. Primary organic chemicals are frequently components of fuels and can be obtained by separation and purification of petroleum refinery products or natural gas constituents. Many of the primary products can be used either as fuels or as basic materials from which other chemicals are made. Organic chemicals are the single largest segment of chemical exports, accounting for nearly one-half of total chemical shipments to foreign markets.

On a volume basis, 75 to 80 percent of organic chemicals are petrochemicals (SIC 2821, 2822, 2824, 2843, 2865, 2869, 2873, 2895). The remaining 20 to 25 percent are pharmaceutical or drug products, which on a value basis comprise 50 percent of organic chemicals.

Historically the United States, Western Europe, and Japan have dominated production of the primary petrochemicals—ethylene, methanol, propylene, butadiene, benzene, toluene, and xylene—serving approximately 70 percent of the world market. In the 1980's energy-rich countries in the Middle East—Saudi Arabia, United Arab Emirates, Kuwait, and Qatar—and the Pacific Rim countries—Japan, Korea, Singapore, Thailand, Indonesia, Malaysia, the Philippines, and Brunei—began development of world-scale petrochemical facilities. While some of these facilities will not come on line as early as planned because of the slowed global economy, they will decrease the three traditional production centers' global market share by about 10 percent.

The primary petrochemicals are precursors of plastics, fibers, elastomers, fertilizers, and chemical intermediates that are the raw material for numerous consumer and industrial products. This relationship with consumer and industrial products and the agricultural sector makes the petrochemical industry highly sensitive to domestic and global economic conditions. The industry is also sensitive to currency fluctuations, as small price differentials in its commodity products reverberate globally and can determine whether it is better to produce or import primary petrochemicals.

The value of petrochemical industry shipments increased in 1993 by about 1 percent in constant dollars, to $101 billion. Employment in the petrochemical industry declined between 1 and 2 percent, to 254,000, reflecting restructuring and initial personnel cutbacks. Despite this reduction, employees in petrochemicals still represent 30 percent of the chemical industry workforce. Exports declined almost 2 percent, to $21.8 billion, while imports increased 11 percent, to 12.3 billion, resulting in a positive trade balance of $9.5 billion in 1993.

INTERNATIONAL COMPETITIVENESS

The U.S. petrochemical industry faces growing competition in its export market despite rising world demand. World petrochemical demand is projected to grow from 320 million metric tons in 1992 to 575 million metric tons in 2010. The share of consumption accounted for by the United States, Western Europe, and Japan will drop from 71 to 63 percent at the same time, as the rest of the world experiences a sharp rise in per capita consumption. Simultaneously, product from Gulf Cooperation Council and Pacific Rim countries will begin to compete head-on with U.S. products in current export markets. European markets will also be adversely affected by the over-capacity problems facing European petrochemical firms. This problem is compounded because many of Europe's most inefficient plants are state owned and political pressure may prevent their closing. Still another problem confronting European producers is the European Community effort to help struggling Eastern

European economies by lifting its own custom duties on products, including chemicals, by the end of 1994.

The European and Japanese petrochemical industries are more dependent on naphtha as a feedstock than the U.S. petrochemical industry. This can have major consequences. For example, Japan, which lacks natural gas, became dependent on imported methanol in 1990 when importing became a more economical method of meeting its methanol requirements.

Naphtha is currently cheaply priced and in plentiful global supply. However, a number of Middle East refiners that are now major naphtha suppliers are planning to build reformers to turn naphtha into gasoline. This will drastically reduce the amount of naphtha available for export. Naphtha is the primary feedstock used to make ethylene in the Far East and Europe. Ethylene is the most important organic chemical in terms of volume, number of derivatives, and sales. It seems that the U.S. petrochemical advantage of lower prices for its natural gas and liquid feedstocks, lower utility costs, and lower fixed costs will serve to keep the U.S. industry a contender in an increasingly competitive market.

LONG-TERM PROSPECTS

With its supply of natural gas, an extensive pipeline system both to receive raw material and deliver product, and an economy expected to revive sooner than those of competing nations, the U.S. chemical industry should experience growth of 1 to 2 percent during the next five years. Given the importance of international trade to the industry, successful conclusions of the Uruguay Round and NAFTA will increase this growth rate. Average ethylene growth rates for 1991 to 1997 are projected at about 5 percent annually. For this major petrochemical product U.S. producers have sufficient flexibility to adjust to changing market conditions in either natural gas liquids or crude oil-derived feed. European producers are suffering from overcapacity and high production costs. As these producers attempt to push prices higher to cover costs, they lure more imports. However, not all of these imports are of U.S. origin. As East European petrochemical plants begin to reenter the market in force, they will bring fierce competition to the EC market. The other historical and much-expanded petrochemical producing center, Japan and the Pacific Rim countries, faces a supply imbalance that will take two years to resolve. Even then the supply/demand situation in that area is highly dependent upon a rapidly expanding Chinese market. During the next 10 years, more growth in production and consumption of petrochemicals is projected for Asia than for the rest of the world combined. Excluding Japan, ethylene demand in the seven other East Asian nations (South Korea, Taiwan, China, Thailand, Singapore, Malaysia, and Indonesia) is expected to reach 13 million metric tons by 1996, compared with 7.5 million metric tons in 1991. Joint ventures with these emerging petrochemical producing nations will sustain the U.S. industry, and increasing world supply of basic petrochemicals will enhance export opportunity for higher refined products.—*Michael Kelly, Chemicals and Allied Products Division (202) 482-0128.*

Trends and Forecasts: Chemicals and Allied Products (SIC 28)

(in millions of dollars except as noted)

Item	1987	1988	1989	1990	1991	1992[1]	1993[2]	1994[3]	Percent Change (1989–1994) 88–89	89–90	90–91	91–92	92–93	93–94
Industry Data														
Value of shipments[4]	229,546	259,699	278,085	288,184	292,326	304,604	310,696	320,016	7.1	3.6	1.4	4.2	2.0	3.0
Value of shipments (1987$)	229,546	239,529	242,930	248,952	245,187	248,374	249,616	253,360	1.4	2.5	-1.5	1.3	0.5	1.5
Total employment (000)	814	830	848	853	846	846	841	834	2.2	0.6	-0.8	0.0	-0.6	-0.8
Production workers (000)	463	475	484	484	477	476	474	470	1.9	0.0	-1.4	-0.2	-0.4	-0.8
Average hourly earnings ($)	3.04	13.21	13.82	14.40	14.98	15.13	15.28	15.43	4.6	4.2	4.0	1.0	1.0	1.0
Capital expenditures	8,711	10,858	13,480	15,202	16,009	—	—	—	24.1	12.8	5.3	—	—	—
Product Data														
Value of shipments[5]	214,618	244,515	260,649	268,505	268,934	—	—	—	6.6	3.0	0.2	—	—	—
Value of shipments (1987$)	214,618	225,097	227,632	232,379	226,554	—	—	—	1.1	2.1	-2.5	—	—	—
Trade Data														
Value of imports	—	—	20,351	21,919	23,329	26,221	28,232	29,982	—	7.7	6.4	12.4	7.7	6.2
Value of exports	—	—	36,170	38,286	41,892	42,366	43,376	43,940	—	5.9	9.4	1.1	2.4	1.3

[1]Estimate, except exports and imports.
[2]Estimate.
[3]Forecast.
[4]Value of all products and services sold by establishments in the chemicals and allied products industry.
[5]Value of products classified in the chemicals and allied products industry produced by all industries.

SOURCE: U.S. Department of Commerce: Bureau of the Census; International Trade Administration (ITA). Estimates and forecasts by ITA.

U.S. Trade Patterns in 1992
Chemicals and Allied Products
SIC 28

(in millions of dollars, percent)

Exports	Value	Share	Imports	Value	Share
Canada and Mexico	9,555	22.6	Canada and Mexico	5,469	20.9
European Community	11,733	27.7	European Community	10,910	41.6
Japan	4,502	10.6	Japan	2,935	11.2
East Asia NICs	7,242	17.1	East Asia NICs	1,677	6.4
South America	3,424	8.1	South America	750	2.9
Other	5,909	13.9	Other	4,479	17.1
World Total	42,366	100.0	World Total	26,221	100.0

Top Five Countries

Exports	Value	Share	Imports	Value	Share
Canada	6,810	16.1	Canada	4,663	17.8
Japan	4,502	10.6	Germany	3,319	12.7
Mexico	2,746	6.5	Japan	2,935	11.2
Belgium	2,472	5.8	United Kingdom	2,538	9.7
Netherlands	2,315	5.5	France	1,723	6.6

See "Getting the Most Out of *Outlook '94*" for definitions of the country groupings.

SOURCE: U.S. Department of Commerce: Bureau of the Census; International Trade Administration.

Computer Equipment

The computer-equipment sector encompasses electronic computers (SIC 3571), storage devices (SIC 3572), computer terminals (SIC 3575), and computer peripheral equipment, NEC (SIC 3577). Electronic computers include digital computers of all sizes, as well as computer kits assembled by the purchaser. Computer storage devices are such equipment as magnetic and optical disk drives and tape storage units. The category of computer terminals covers teleprinters. Computer peripherals are printers, plotters, graphics displays, and other input/output equipment. Parts and components for computers and peripherals are included, as appropriate, in each of these industries. However, since 1988, the U.S. Bureau of the Census has reclassified some parts, such as printed circuit boards and integrated microcircuits, originally reported in electronic computers, in their respective component industries.

In 1993, the U.S. computer industry experienced its second straight year of recovery from the 1990–91 recession, led by an increase in domestic computer demand of 20 percent to an estimated $69.4 billion. During the first half of 1993, shipments rose at a much higher rate than they did in the same period in 1992; new orders showed their strongest annual growth in 9 years; and inventories were at a relatively low level. Despite some uncertainty about the economy, U.S. business purchases of computer systems and peripherals increased substantially, reflecting the efforts of many corporations to reduce costs and boost productivity through the use of this equipment. These purchases helped the industry offset a decline in Federal computer hardware spending and slower growth in exports.

Product shipments of U.S.-based manufacturers were up an estimated 8 percent (in current dollars) in 1993, to $56.3 billion. Computer systems grew faster than peripheral equipment deliveries and represented more than 50 percent of total shipments. The mix of systems shipments was toward cheaper and increasingly more powerful workstations and personal computers, as users continued to shift many of their applications from mainframes and minicomputers to these smaller platforms. Peripheral shipments were largely storage devices and input/output equipment such as printers.

Computer manufacturers were concerned about the effect that mid-1993 shortages of dynamic random access memory (DRAM) chips, flash memory devices, and flat panel display screens would have on the production and pricing of their systems. Regarding DRAM supply, companies reported lead times for 1- and 4-megabit chip deliveries of up to 14 weeks and significant price increases for these devices. Many of the smaller U.S. computer systems firms were in a vulnerable position compared with the larger vendors, which were insulated to some extent by long-term contracts with DRAM suppliers. Debate arose within the industry over whether the explosion of a Japanese epoxy resin plant in July 1993 would further exacerbate the imbalance between DRAM supply and demand by late 1993. Some industry observers speculated in August that personal computer prices might rise as much as $150 per system by year end.

Faced with financial losses stemming from declining demand for some products and fierce price competition across a broad spectrum of computer equipment, several U.S. computer manufacturers continued to restructure their domestic and foreign operations and reduce the number of positions during 1993. Total industry employment in the United States fell 7 percent to 200,000 workers. The bulk of the 15,000 jobs lost came from administrative, technical, sales, and support personnel. Layoffs were greater among systems firms than peripheral equipment suppliers. IBM and Digital Equipment Corporation (DEC) announced cutbacks totaling about 70,000 employees worldwide. Many smaller U.S. firms and some subsidiaries of foreign companies in the United States also trimmed their work forces. U.S. production worker employment was once again adversely affected by plant closings. The number of factory workers declined nearly 5 percent to 69,100, but remained a little more than one-third of the industry's labor force.

The U.S. computer equipment industry has used automation as a competitive tool to raise productivity, lower costs, and bring products to market quickly. A 1992 survey by the Automation Forum showed that the industry's investment in automation reached $2.1 billion in 1991, a 23 percent increase over the 1989 level. Most of this investment was in production automation software (28 percent of the total) and computer-aided product design and engineering hardware and software (25 percent). The industry was the fifth-largest spender on automation in the United States, but actually led all other U.S. industries in investment per production worker at $20,220. In terms of the demand for computers to automate design, engineering, and manufacturing, U.S. industries spent $11.6 billion on computer equipment during 1991. Among the major users were the automotive, aircraft and aerospace, and electronics industries.

Research and development (R&D) has always been critical to this industry's ability to maintain its technological leadership. Data compiled by *Business Week* in its annual R&D Scoreboard survey shows that a combined sample of 87 U.S. computer firms raised their R&D spending by 4 percent, to $14.2 billion, in 1992. This growth was low relative to the 7 percent average increase for all U.S. industries. However, the computer equipment industry surpassed all other U.S. electronics industries and industrial sectors in absolute spending and only lagged behind health care in the percentage of sales devoted to R&D. Three U.S. computer firms—IBM, DEC, and Hewlett-Packard—ranked among the top 10 R&D spenders in the United States.

Legislation was introduced in Congress in mid-1993 to upgrade the 3-year old High Performance Computing and Communications Initiative (HPCCI), which focuses on developing a national high-speed communications network, primarily for the use of scientists and academic researchers. The High Performance Computing and High Speed Networking Applications Act of 1993 (H.R. 1757), if passed, will allocate $1 billion over 5 years to develop applications that allow broader use of this network in health care, public education, and manufacturing. It also will boost Federal funding of research on supercomputers, advanced networking technologies, and software. The European Commission is considering a proposal for a similar 5-year, large-scale, $4.5 billion project on high-performance computing and networking research.

INTERNATIONAL COMPETITIVENESS

The top 100 computer companies worldwide account for a majority share of the international market for information equipment and services. Their sales expanded at a healthy rate of almost 10 percent, to $318 billion, in 1992, according to *Datamation* magazine's annual survey of these companies. The U.S. suppliers' share of this group's total remained steady at 61 percent, while the Japanese share fell two percentage points to 25 percent. Major factors behind this share loss may have been the downturn in Japanese computer demand during 1992 and increased competition from U.S. firms in Japan, particularly in the personal computer segment of that market.

Many of the leading U.S. computer equipment suppliers have continued to move aggressively into software and computer services as price competition in hardware has intensified and their profits have dwindled. In 1991 (the latest year available for purposes of comparison), U.S. computer systems and peripheral sales were only slightly more than half of their total revenues. European companies were even more involved in computer software and services. In contrast, their competitors in Japan and other Asian nations still derived most of their revenues from computer equipment.

The U.S. computer industry appeared to have ceded its position as the world's leading computer-equipment producer to European Community (EC) manufacturers by 1992. However, because EC statistics include business machines, such as typewriters and electronic cash registers, the EC industry's computer production is overstated somewhat. Digital Equipment, Hewlett-Packard, IBM, and other U.S. firms also contribute substantially to this industry's output through their European subsidiaries. The production of the Japanese computer industry has risen at a rapid pace, 13 percent annually since 1982, and may surpass that of U.S.-based suppliers by the middle of this decade. Like their U.S. counterparts, both EC and Japanese computer-equipment manufacturers have suffered from recession in their domestic and key overseas markets during the early 1990's. They have reacted in much the same way to losses by restructuring their operations and by instituting hiring freezes or significantly cutting back their work forces. The European computer industry reduced employment, for example, by nearly 21,000 workers during 1992–93.

Although it has remained the top exporter of computers, the U.S. industry has lost considerable ground to the Japanese since 1982. Japanese computer exports have risen 21 percent annually over the past 10 years, nearly twice the rate of the United States and the EC. Peripherals have accounted for almost half of the value of these exports, followed by parts (more than a 30 percent share). Computer systems have played only a minimal role. The Japanese also have increased the amount of computer production that is exported from 28 percent to more than 50 percent during this period and have a computer trade surplus that currently exceeds $15 billion. In contrast, the EC industry has traditionally exported no more than 20 percent of its production outside the region, concentrating its efforts within the 12 EC member countries. The EC's trade deficit has more than quadrupled in 10 years to more than $20 billion. Imports from non-EC countries have accounted for one-third of European computer consumption, with the United States and Japan as the leading suppliers.

LONG-TERM PROSPECTS

While the 1980's brought the age of personal computing—mainframe computing power on the desk in businesses, schools, and the home—the decade of the 1990's should usher in an era of personal access to a vast array of interactive information and entertainment services, known as "infotainment." This new development is being shaped by the convergence of computer, communications, and consumer electronics technologies. The technological focus of personal computing on microprocessors and operating systems will shift in this new age to communications, particularly the development of the National Information Infrastructure. Phone and cable television suppliers have formed alliances with each other and with computer, consumer electronics, entertainment, and publishing companies to work on the best way to cheaply deliver large amounts of video, sound, graphics, and text in digital form to the public and to provide interactive services within an electronic network connecting every home, school, library, and hospital. U.S. computer firms have concentrated on creating the products for this nascent, but potentially lucrative, world infotainment market. Products will include set-top personal computers, back-end network servers, personal digital assistants, asynchronous transfer mode equipment, network protocols, and communications and systems software.

The U.S. computer industry will have enormous opportunities for growth, but will face significant challenges in the more complex infotainment market over the next 5 years. U.S. companies should play a critical role as suppliers of information systems, networking equipment, interactive services, and entertainment and educational software packages. They should likewise benefit from their strength in systems integration, which is based on providing users with cost-effective solutions to their business problems. However, they will have to compete against a broader range of both domestic and foreign firms, some of which have greater experience in consumer electronics and communications technologies.

The future survival of U.S. computer firms will depend on several factors. They must continue to innovate and to commercialize their technological advances quickly into marketable products. Their technological leadership, in turn, will rest on their ability to sustain a fairly high level of spending on R&D, to draw on a highly educated and skilled U.S. labor force, and to perform research efficiently, either on their own or in consortia. They must then aggressively protect their intellectual property rights around the world so that competitors and high-technology pirates do not reap undeserved rewards from their substantial investments of time and money in research. Strategy will be another crucial factor. Computer suppliers will have to weigh carefully the advantages and long-term costs of alliances involving significant technology transfer with partners in other industries and foreign firms that may emerge as their potential rivals. Before U.S. companies develop and market new infotainment products and services, they also must have a good understanding of their customers' needs and willingness to pay.

Asia, the countries of the former Soviet Union, and Latin America, especially Mexico, may become more important to the industry in the future. U.S. computer companies probably will increase their manufacturing of price-sensitive products and components in the lower labor rate areas of East Asia such as Malaysia, the Philippines, China, and Thailand, to remain competitive with Japanese and other Asian hardware suppliers. U.S. firms will continue to sell aggressively in Japan, the second-largest country market in the world, but may find themselves lured to rapidly growing markets in China, Russia, and many Latin American nations. Growth in U.S. computer exports to these areas will occur if U.S. suppliers are not constrained by trade barriers and if they are not concerned about political instability and the lack of adequate protection of intellectual property rights.—*Tim Miles, Office of Computers and Business Equipment (202) 482-2990.*

Revenues of Information Equipment and Services Firms, 1991

Item	Percent Hardware	Percent Software	Total Revenues (in billion dollars)
United States	54	46	174
Europe	42	58	29
Japan	69	31	78
Other Asia	93	7	3

SOURCE: *Datamation.*

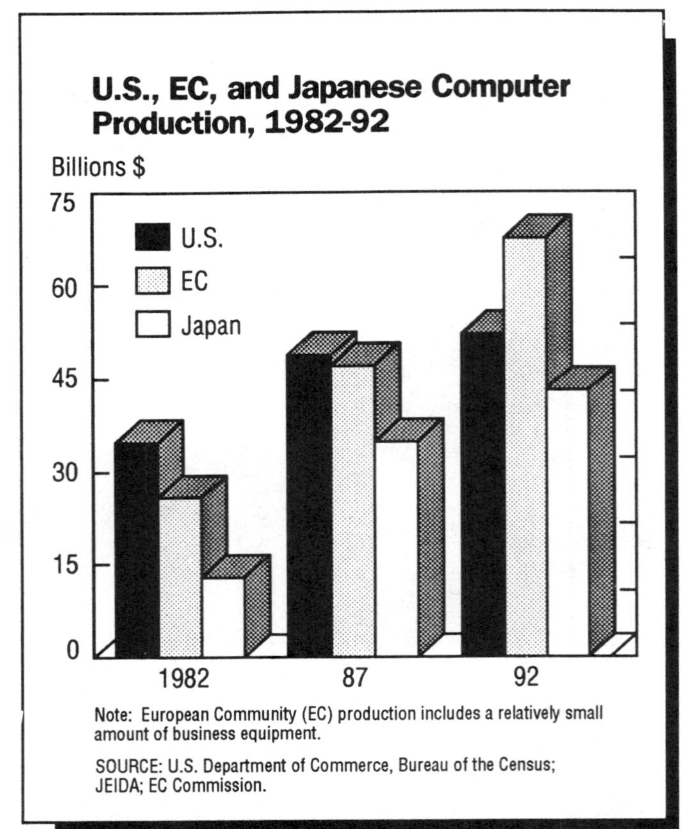

U.S., EC, and Japanese Computer Production, 1982-92

Note: European Community (EC) production includes a relatively small amount of business equipment.

SOURCE: U.S. Department of Commerce, Bureau of the Census; JEIDA; EC Commission.

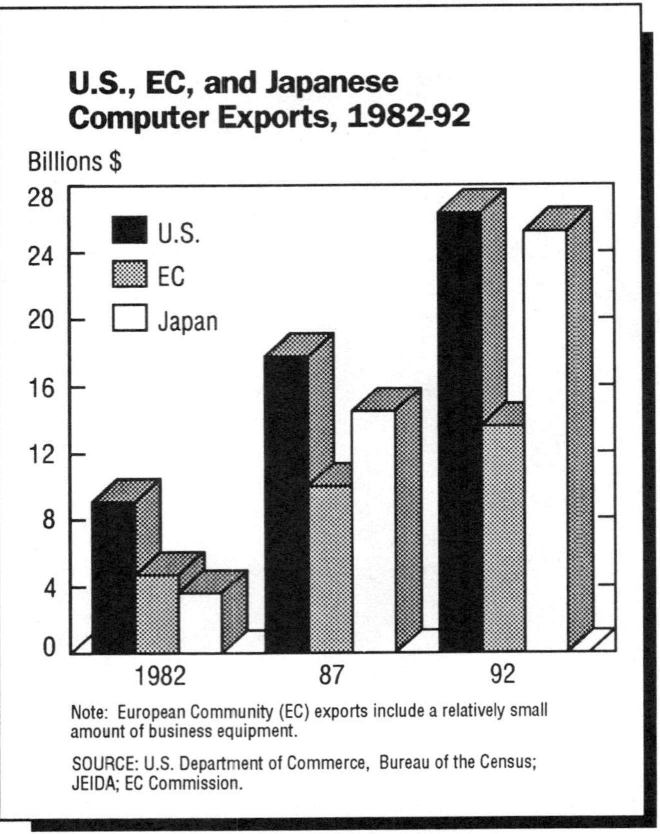

U.S., EC, and Japanese Computer Exports, 1982-92

Note: European Community (EC) exports include a relatively small amount of business equipment.

SOURCE: U.S. Department of Commerce, Bureau of the Census; JEIDA; EC Commission.

Trends and Forecasts: Computers and Peripherals (SIC 3571, 3572, 3575, 3577)

(in millions of dollars except as noted)

Item	1987	1988	1989	1990	1991	1992[1]	1993[2]	1994[3]	Percent Change (1989–1994) 88–89	89–90	90–91	91–92	92–93	93–94
Industry Data														
Value of shipments[4]	55,843	62,773	59,758	58,981	54,703	58,000	62,500	66,200	-4.8	-1.3	-7.3	6.0	7.8	5.9
Total employment (000)	286	290	263	248	227	215	200	190	-9.3	-5.7	-8.5	-5.3	-7.0	-5.0
Production workers (000)	101	105	96.8	89.6	76.2	72.5	69.1	66.4	-7.8	-7.4	-15.0	-4.9	-4.7	-3.9
Average hourly earnings ($)	10.47	10.93	11.68	11.72	12.52	12.72	12.81	—	6.9	0.3	6.8	1.6	0.7	—
Capital expenditures	2,020	2,213	2,148	1,993	1,813	—	—	—	-2.9	-7.2	-9.0	—	—	—
Product Data														
Value of shipments[5]	48,801	53,230	54,891	52,628	49,144	52,100	56,300	59,700	3.1	-4.1	-6.6	6.0	8.1	6.0
Trade Data														
Value of imports	—	—	21,714	23,323	26,424	32,137	40,170	46,196	—	7.4	13.3	21.6	25.5	14.5
Value of exports	—	—	22,360	24,138	25,182	26,304	27,066	29,231	—	8.0	4.3	4.5	3.1	7.8

[1]Estimate, except exports and imports.
[2]Estimate.
[3]Forecast.
[4]Value of all products and services sold by establishments in the computers and peripherals industry.
[5]Value of products classified in the computers and peripherals industry produced by all industries.

NOTE: Census reclassified some parts for electronic computers (3571) to component industries (367) for 1988–1990.

SOURCE: U.S. Department of Commerce: Bureau of the Census, International Trade Administration (ITA). Estimates and forecasts by ITA.

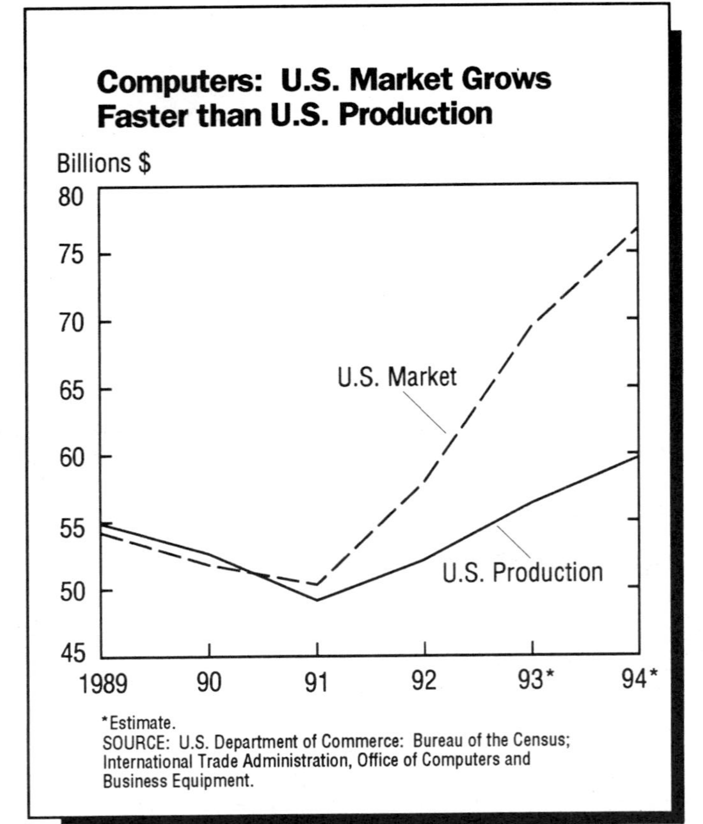

*Estimate.
SOURCE: U.S. Department of Commerce: Bureau of the Census; International Trade Administration, Office of Computers and Business Equipment.

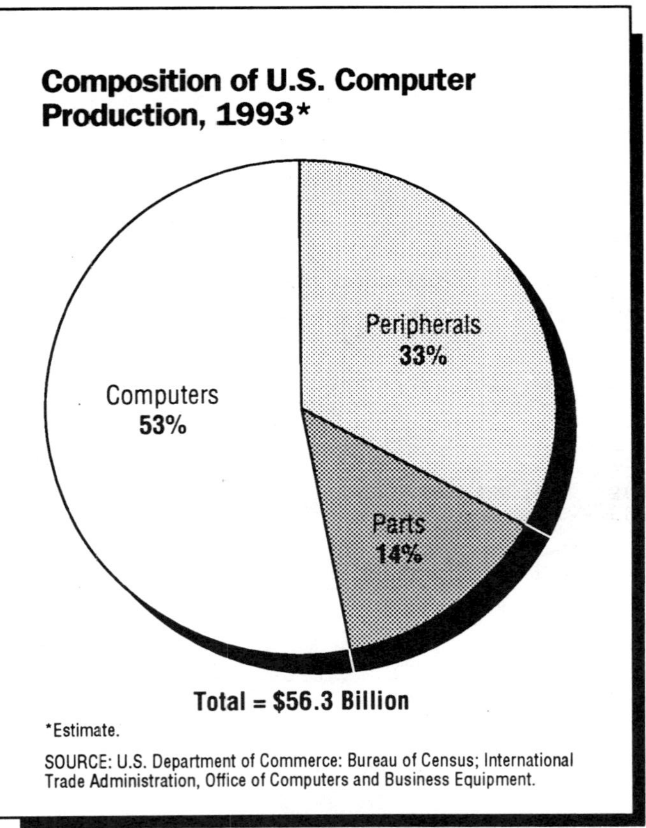

*Estimate.

SOURCE: U.S. Department of Commerce: Bureau of Census; International Trade Administration, Office of Computers and Business Equipment.

Computer Software

The computer software and networking sectors include three industries: computer programming services (SIC 7371), prepackaged software (SIC 7372), and computer-integrated-systems design (SIC 7373).

Employment in the U.S. software industry rose in 1993, as it has in each year since 1988, the first year employment data were available. The Bureau of Labor Statistics reported that the software industry employed nearly 435,000 people in June 1993, up 9 percent from June 1992. While each of the three major segments of the industry posted gains, growth varied among them during this period. Employment in the computer programming services industry (SIC 7371) increased the most—10 percent. Employment in both the prepackaged software (SIC 7372) and computer integrated systems design industries (SIC 7373) increased 8 percent. In June 1993, there were more than 182,000 employees in computer programming services; 142,500 in prepackaged software; and 110,000 in computer integrated systems design.

In spite of the weak worldwide economy, U.S. computer-software and networking industries fared relatively well in 1993, and are expected to continue to do so in 1994 and the next several years. In general, these industries are young, competitive, innovative, and entrepreneurial, and face good opportunities for increased sales worldwide. The United States is extremely competitive in computer software and networking, although Japanese and European suppliers are making advances in some areas.

Packaged Software

The U.S. packaged software industry remained one of the fastest-growing sectors of the U.S. economy in 1993. According to International Data Corp. (IDC), the U.S. packaged software market—comprised of application tools, application solutions, and systems software—increased 12.6 percent to $32 billion in 1993. Application tools, which include data access and retrieval, data management, data manipulation, and program design and development software, was the fastest-growing category, increasing 15.4 percent to $8.5 billion in 1993. Application solutions, defined as programs that perform specific industry or business functions, is the largest segment of the U.S. market and grew 11.8 percent to $12.4 billion. Systems software, which includes operating systems, operating system enhancements, and data center management software, increased 11.4 percent to $11.2 billion.

The U.S. software industry posted strong financial results in 1993. According to *Business Week*, sales of 19 major software and services firms (ASK Group, Cabletron Systems, Ceridian, Cisco Systems, Comdisco, Computer Associates, Computer Sciences, Electronic Data Systems (EDS), EMC, First Data, Gtech Holdings, Lotus, Microsoft, Novell, Oracle, Safeguard Scientifics, Shared Medical Systems, SynOptics Communications, and Western Digital) increased 15 percent between the second quarter of 1992 and the second quarter of 1993, reaching $8 billion. Profits also were up, rising 44 percent to $827 million during this 12-month period. Collectively, two firms, EDS and Microsoft, accounted for 40 percent of total sales and 54 percent of total profits.

PC Software

According to the Software Publishers Association (SPA), sales of PC applications software in the United States and Canada totaled more than $3 billion in the first half of 1993, up approximately 19 percent from the same period a year earlier. These figures are based on a survey of SPA members and exclude sales of operating systems (for PCs and networks) and video-game cartridges; they are not comparable to IDC data cited earlier.

Other productivity software, which includes communications, personal and business productivity, and project management software, was the largest of 14 categories, accounting for 27 percent of total PC application sales in the first half of 1993. Word processors were next, with a 15 percent share, followed by spreadsheets, databases, and finance programs. Each of the remaining categories accounted for less than 6 percent of the market.

Growth varied considerably among the different types of applications. Home education software increased the most, rising approximately 75 percent between the first half of 1992 and the first half of 1993. Databases and other productivity software also posted strong gains, rising more than 65 percent and 45 percent, respectively. Sales declined in desktop publishing, spreadsheets, utilities, and other graphics software.

In the first quarter of 1993, for the first time in Canada and the United States, Windows-based applications outsold DOS-based applications. Sales of Windows applications increased 75 percent in the first half of 1993, to approximately $1.4 billion, while sales of DOS applications decreased 13 percent, to approximately $1.1 billion. In all, Windows applications outsold DOS applications in 10 of the 14 categories, including the top 4 (other productivity, word processors, spreadsheets, and databases). DOS maintained the lead in finance programs, entertainment software, utilities, and home education software. Macintosh applications accounted for 16 percent of the PC market while applications for other platforms, including the UNIX and OS/1 operating systems and the Apple II, Commodore 64, Atari, and Amiga systems, accounted for 4 percent.

Price wars continued in the PC software market over the last 12 months. Price competition was particularly fierce in the Windows-based applications market, where vendors, including Microsoft, Lotus, and Borland, are fighting to increase market share. Vendors are using a variety of pricing strategies to woo new customers: low introductory prices, special upgrade deals, and suite pricing, in which several packages are sold together for a fraction of their individual cost. Industry analysts expect PC software prices to continue to fall over the next few years. The lower margins that result may cause the market to consolidate and encourage software vendors to reevaluate their business strategies.

INTERNATIONAL COMPETITIVENESS

The United States remained by far the largest single-country market for packaged software in 1993, and its share of the world market increased slightly, from 44.3 percent to 44.7 percent. Japan, with a nearly $7 billion market was second, followed by Germany, United Kingdom, and France. The market in 13 Western European countries was worth $25.7 billion, or 36 percent of the world market, in 1993.

U.S. packaged software suppliers also continued to be world leaders. According to IDC, the worldwide revenues of U.S. vendors increased 11 percent to $47.6 billion in 1992. As a result, U.S. vendors supplied 74 percent of the world packaged software market. Application solutions accounted for more than 31 percent of these revenues, systems software 38 percent, and application tools 30 percent.

While U.S. vendors supplied more than 50 percent of four regional packaged software markets in 1992, U.S. vendors' strength varied among regions. Internationally, U.S. packaged software vendors held the largest market share in countries outside Western Europe and Japan, supplying more than 73 percent of these markets. The strong U.S. position in these countries (generally in Asia and Latin America) reflects both the high quality of and receptivity to U.S. software as well as the relatively small international presence of European and Japanese software vendors. U.S. vendors supplied 60 percent of the packaged software markets in Western Europe and Japan, regions where domestic vendors hold stronger positions.

LONG-TERM PROSPECTS

Fueled by stronger economic growth, new product introductions, and ongoing price wars, the U.S. packaged software market should continue to post double-digit gains in the next few years. Many current trends should continue, including downsizing, the movement toward increased interoperability, and the growing importance of international markets. Over the next decade, several emerging technologies, including pen computers, multimedia and virtual products, and object-oriented software should develop into sizable markets.

IDC estimates that the U.S. packaged software market will increase almost 13 percent annually between 1994 and 1997, reaching nearly $52 billion or almost 45 percent of the world market. Application tools and solutions will remain the fastest-growing categories. Application solutions, the largest segment, is expected to increase more than 12 percent annually between 1994 and 1997 to almost $20 billion. Application tools and systems software are expected to post annual increases of more than 15 and 11 percent, respectively, during this period.—*Mary Smolenski, Office of Computers and Business Equipment (202) 482-0551.*

PC Software Sales in the United States and Canada, 1993[1]

(in millions of dollars)

Item	DOS	Windows	Macintosh	Other	Total
Total	**1,052.5**	**1,437.0**	**513.0**	**108.9**	**3,111.4**
Other productivity[2]	309.9	339.9	136.7	41.3	827.8
Word processors	134.9	267.3	47.9	10.6	460.7
Spreadsheets	82.8	253.8	34.4	10.7	381.7
Databases	96.8	131.5	34.0	—[3]	262.3
Finance	104.6	39.8	22.2	—[3]	166.6
Utilities	71.9	54.8	27.8	—[3]	154.5
Presentation graphics	25.4	94.2	26.1	2.7	148.4
Entertainment	116.7	6.7	12.9	2.6	138.9
Languages and tools	19.4	67.3	12.6	34.4	133.7
Drawing and painting	—[3]	56.4	64.8	1.7	122.9
Other graphics	27.4	37.6	39.7	1.2	105.9
Home education	43.1	16.4	13.1	2.2	74.8
Desktop publishing	1.2	47.9	19.8	—[3]	68.9
Integrated	18.4	23.4	21.0	1.5	64.3

[1]First half.
[2]Includes communications, personal and business productivity, and project management software.
[3]Sales of less than $1 million or inadequate reporting.
NOTE: Detail may not sum to total due to rounding.
SOURCE: Software Publishers Association.

Packaged Software Markets, 1991–97

(in millions of dollars except as noted)

	1991	1992	1993[1]	Percent Change (1991-1997) 91-92	92-93[2]	93-97[2]
World	57,022	64,313	71,864	12.8	11.5	12.8
United States	25,330	28,460	32,040	12.4	12.6	12.7
Western Europe[3]	21,091	23,850	25,699	13.1	7.8	10.3
Japan	5,270	5,967	6,938	13.2	16.3	18.7
Canada	1,078	1,188	1,374	10.2	15.7	10.4
Australia	941	980	1,094	4.1	11.6	13.3
Latin America[4]	1,054	1,242	1,471	17.8	18.4	18.0
Asia[5]	584	780	974	33.6	24.9	21.4
Other	1,674	1,846	2,094	10.3	13.4	14.9

[1]Estimate.
[2]Forecast of annual compound rate of change.
[3]Austria, Belgium, Denmark, Finland, France, Germany, Italy, Netherlands, Norway, Spain, Sweden, Switzerland, and United Kingdom.
[4]Argentina, Brazil, Chile, Mexico, and Venezuela.
[5]China, Hong Kong, India, Malaysia, Singapore, South Korea, Taiwan, and Thailand.
SOURCE: International Data Corp.

Construction

This section covers private residential construction (including single-unit, multiunit, and manufactured housing); prefabricated buildings; private nonresidential construction; publicly owned construction; and international construction and engineering.

The inflation-adjusted value of new construction put in place increased about 3 percent in 1993, but was about 8 percent lower than the record level of 1986. The 1993 value of about $460 billion was an all-time high in current dollars. The number of housing starts increased by about 4 percent to 1.25 million units in 1993. An additional 265,000 manufactured (mobile) homes were shipped, a 26 percent increase. Public works construction increased slightly, led by strong spending for highways. The decline in private nonresidential construction was largely attributable to high vacancy rates in commercial buildings. Some categories of private nonresidential construction, such as hospitals and electric utilities, were growing markets in 1993.

Remodeling and repair work increased faster than new construction in 1993. Although the data for maintenance and repair construction are not as complete as those for new construction, 1993 probably was a record year for maintenance and repair work. Nonresidential building improvements (commercial remodeling and renovation) declined slightly from the record levels set in 1992.

According to the 1987 Census of Construction, about 66 percent of the construction industry's work was for new construction; 19 percent was for additions, alterations, and reconstruction; 10 percent was for maintenance and repair; and 5 percent was unspecified. In 1993, new construction probably accounted for about 60 percent of the industry's business.

In 1993, the value of new construction put in place was equal to about 7.9 percent of gross domestic product (GDP). This is well below the post-World War II peak of 11.9 percent of GDP attained in 1966, and very close to the cyclical low of 7.7 percent in 1982. Construction's share of GDP is expected to remain constant in 1994. However, this measure tends to understate the importance of construction in the economy because several types of construction activity that are not included in new construction data have grown rapidly during the past decade. These include maintenance and repair, commercial/industrial renovation, and environmental restoration.

In 1993, construction costs increased by about 4 percent, as measured by the Census Bureau's fixed-weight construction cost deflator. This was about double the average annual rate of increase during the previous 5 years, and was slightly faster than the rate of increase of the Consumer Price Index. Building materials prices also rose an average of about 4 percent in 1993; lumber prices were especially volatile. (See section on construction materials for further information.) Land prices have been fairly stable, on average, and have even declined in many areas. (Land prices are not included in the construction cost index.) Insurance and bonding costs have continued to increase, although the availability of insurance appears to be better. Labor costs have been relatively steady, with average hourly earnings of construction workers increasing by about 1 percent in 1993. Interest rates declined to 15-year lows, but credit standards were tighter than they had been, especially for real estate and construction loans.

There were about 4.6 million employees in the construction industry in 1993. This is about 10 percent below the 1990 level, which was a near record. In addition, about 1.4 million people were self-employed as proprietors and working partners. Despite the recent moderation in construction wage increases, construction remained one of the highest-paying industries, as measured by average hourly and weekly earnings.

INTERNATIONAL COMPETITIVENESS

The construction business has become increasingly international during the past 20 years. Although only a small number of U.S. construction contractors are active internationally, they are among the most successful in the world. In 1992, U.S. contractors won about 49 percent of all international construction contracts, according to the *Engineering News-Record.* (This includes construction contracts won by foreign subsidiaries of U.S. firms.) U.S. international contractors face stiff competition, chiefly from European and Pacific Rim firms, which often have more government financial support at their disposal than U.S. companies. Economic problems in Europe and several countries in the Middle East will make it difficult for U.S. contractors to repeat the remarkable successes of 1991 and 1992.

Many of the world's largest foreign construction contractors have entered the U.S. construction market, but they have not made significant inroads here, except in a few specialized sub-markets. Most of these foreign contractors have bought U.S. construction companies, while some of the largest foreign contractors have established their own operations in the United States. Foreign-owned construction firms won about $8.9 billion in U.S. construction contracts in 1992, which was down 28 percent from 1991 and 43 percent lower than the record $15.5 billion in 1990. Foreign-owned companies accounted for only about 4 percent of all construction contracts awarded in the United States during 1992. Most of these foreign entrants are based in the United Kingdom, Germany, and Japan, although nearly a dozen additional nations are represented.

Exports of prefabricated buildings have increased impressively over the past 5 years, with 1993 exports of $285 million. This success is partly due to the cheaper dollar and more commercially oriented foreign aid programs. In addition, U.S. industry has become aware that there are viable but specialized foreign markets for prefabricated buildings, and firms are stepping up their foreign marketing efforts.

LONG-TERM PROSPECTS

During the 1994–98 period, new construction is expected to increase modestly from current levels, but with a slower growth rate than GDP. Remodeling and repair construction will increase substantially if interest rates remain moderate, with about the same growth rate as the overall economy.

The modest increase in new construction activities is partly due to the oversupply of commercial buildings, which will be gradually absorbed by attrition and a growing economy. The demand for new housing construction will be limited by demographic factors and by a slower buildup in homeowner equity. The Federal budget deficit will limit spending for public works, despite the well-publicized need for additional infrastructure investment.

The recovery of the U.S. manufacturing sector is expected to result in strong demand for industrial construction during the rest of this decade. Electric utility construction also will be a large and growing market. Hospital construction will continue to gain but will be influenced by the Federal health care initiative. Remodeling and repair work, both residential and nonresidential, is expected to remain a growth area, as the U.S. stock of structures becomes older and more extensive.

The commercial real estate slump is likely to persist through the middle of the decade. As measured by the value of new construction put in place, the sector will decline in 1994, but the bottom may be reached by 1995. Even so, the recovery is likely to be slow, and commercial construction will not even reach current levels by 1998. The downturn is exacerbated by the failure of record numbers of financial institutions. High vacancy rates and weak building prices have made new construction unprofitable in most cases, and reluctance to make real estate loans has further limited opportunities.

In addition to market factors, the U.S. construction industry will face a number of supply-side challenges during the next 5 years, including foreign competition, the availability of workers, and the cost of insurance. Most of the foreign construction contractors competing in the U.S. market are extremely well-financed and often possess construction expertise equal or superior to that of most U.S. builders. The number of young workers, who make up most of the construction labor force, is dwindling because of demographic trends. On the other hand, there is currently no construction labor shortage because of low economic growth and high levels of immigration. However, as the economic recovery continues, shortages of labor skills could become a major problem. The cost of liability insurance has stabilized temporarily, but the cost of health insurance and worker's compensation insurance has continued to increase at rapid rates.—*Patrick H. MacAuley, Office of Materials, Machinery, and Chemicals (202) 482-0132.*

Private Residential Construction

Housing recorded the strongest growth among the construction sectors in 1993. The current-dollar value of new residential construction amounted to $205 billion. After adjusting for inflation, this was a 6.5 percent rise over 1992, and the second year of recovery from the 1991 recession. The improvement in housing construction in 1993 was centered in single-unit homes, rising 8 percent over 1992. The market for homes in structures with two or more units remained at about the 1992 level after experiencing 3 years of declining activity. Total housing starts reached 1.25 million units in 1993, a 4 percent improvement over 1992, and the highest level since 1989. Home improvement expenditures rose in 1992 and 1993, when expenditures were about $64 billion.

Mortgage interest rates declined further in 1993. Thirty-year, conventional fixed-rate mortgages dropped to less than 7 percent in late summer. Interest rates were the major factor boosting new and existing home sales in a period of sluggish economic growth and vacillating consumer confidence.

LONG-TERM PROSPECTS

Although home maintenance and improvements spending is expected to continue to rise substantially over the next 5 years, new residential construction will grow slowly, probably less than the overall economy. Affordability and demographic factors will tend to dilute the demand for new housing, while the need to maintain and the desire to improve the growing stock of existing houses will tend to increase those expenditures. Over the 1994–98 period, annual housing starts probably will average about 1.3 million. Later in the decade, greater construction of multifamily owner and rental units could occur because more people are expected to find it difficult to afford a single family home.

Single-Unit Housing

Starts of new private single family housing units were an estimated 1.08 million in 1993, up from 1.03 million in 1992 and 840,000 in 1991. Detached homes account for about 90 percent of these units. In 1992, the median sales price for a new single family house was $121,500, up from $120,000 in 1991, when the price declined for the first time in many years. The median price in 1993 is estimated to be about $126,500, a 4 percent increase over 1992.

The size of and amenities for new housing units have grown over the years. (In 1991, the average size of new homes declined slightly from 1,905 square feet in 1990 to 1,890 square feet, however.) In 1992, the average unit reached 1,920 square feet. The growth in housing amenities, including more bedrooms and bathrooms, central air conditioning, two-car garages, full basements, and fireplaces, occurred again in 1992. The trend is expected to continue through 1998 at its historical average growth rate of 2 percent annually.

New housing reflects two major market segments: first-time buyers and buyers who are moving up. Lower mortgage rates in 1993 have assisted both these groups. There are, of course, other segments, including the growing number of persons who have raised their families, are close to retirement or retired, and who want to find smaller units.

Multiunit Housing

Multiunit housing consists of two or more dwelling units in a single structure. Some townhouses and most apartments are included in this category. About 80 percent of these units are rental apartments.

Multifamily housing starts were about 170,000 units in 1993, about the same level as in 1992, but the long-term trend has been down. In 1985, the recent peak year, 670,000 multifamily units were started and accounted for 38 percent of all housing starts, but by 1992 they were only 14 percent of the total.

Some of the factors that have affected the level of multifamily housing construction are changes in tax laws, diminished demand, the financial problems of the real estate industry and lending institutions, and regulatory requirements such as handicapped accessibility. Some factors may be favorable for renting, rather than buying, in the coming years, including the aging of the U.S. population, lower property appreciation values, affordability problems for many prospective home purchasers, and the expected improvement in the financing environment for apartment owners.

Manufactured Housing

The manufactured housing (mobile homes) industry is different from prefabricated housing, especially modular prefabs. "Manufactured" units are built to the U.S. Department of Housing and Urban Development national manufactured housing standard, while "prefabricated" (modular) units are built to either statewide factory-built housing codes or local building codes. Manufactured housing units are shipped from plants, either single wide or as single sections of multiwide housing units. Some manufactured housing is not used for dwellings, but for light commercial use, classrooms, or clinics.

Single-wide units now account for slightly more than half of total shipments, as the popularity of the larger multiwide units has grown. Many single-wide units are placed in manufactured home communities and on rural lots. A smaller number of the multiwide units end up in manufactured home communities; more are being placed on individual plots where allowed by zoning.

Prior to 1992, shipments of manufactured homes had declined each year since 1983. Shipments were down to about 171,000 units in 1991, but rose thereafter to 210,800 in 1992 and to about 265,000 in 1993, increases of 23 and 26 percent, respectively. Growth of about 9 percent, to 290,000 units, is expected in 1994.

Manufactured home markets are usually in exurban, small town, and rural areas. In 1992, about 7 percent of total shipments went to the Northeast, 19 percent to the Midwest, 58 percent to the South, and 14 percent to the West. The remainder involved government purchases and exported units.

Customers for the industry are primarily

first-time buyers, rural inhabitants, retired people, and various nontraditional households. Although most units are sold by retailers (mobile home dealers), developers have become the intermediate buyers for a growing number of mostly multiwide units.—*C. B. Pitcher, Office of Materials, Machinery, and Chemicals (202) 482-0132.*

Private Nonresidential Construction

In 1993, the value of new private nonresidential construction was $117 billion, about 1 percent less in constant dollars than in 1992, and about 20 percent below the record set in 1985. Of the 1993 total, $85 billion was for buildings, and $32 billion went for other structures. The declines were most severe for office buildings and hotels, while the construction of hospitals and electric utility plants registered solid increases. The South and West accounted for about 60 percent of total nonresidential construction.

The weakness in nonresidential construction reflects the aftermath of the phenomenal commercial building boom of the 1980's. The record amounts of new building space, combined with the slowdown in economic growth, have resulted in record vacancy rates for office buildings, stores, hotels, and warehouses. These high rates will depress the demand for new construction through the mid-1990's, until supply and demand for commercial space are brought into balance.

Although lower interest rates have tempered the decline in commercial construction, availability of credit for commercial construction has been tight. For the past several years, lenders have been reluctant to provide credit for real estate development because of poor loan experiences and government regulations.

LONG-TERM PROSPECTS

Growth in total private nonresidential construction is likely to lag increases in the overall economy over the next 5 years, given high vacancy rates for commercial buildings, continued liquidation of failing thrift institutions, and relatively modest growth in GDP. However, the decline will be entirely in commercial construction. Industrial, utility, and hospital construction probably will increase from 1993 to 1998.

By 1998, private nonresidential construction will have recovered to about current levels, but spending on factories, utilities, and hospitals will account for a much larger share of the total, and commercial construction will have a substantially lower proportion. The decline in commercial construction is likely to end before 1998, but a sustained recovery is unlikely until building prices increase enough to make new construction profitable.

The need to modernize the existing U.S. capital stock will provide strong underlying demand for new construction as well as for repair and renovations. The amount invested in structures will be large. The repair and renovation market will be stronger than the new construction market during the next 2 years, and spending for nonresidential building improvements may exceed that for new building construction by the end of the decade.—*Patrick H. MacAuley, Office of Materials, Machinery, and Chemicals (202) 482-0132.*

Value of New Construction Put in Place, 1990–98

(in billions of 1987 dollars except as noted)

Type of Construction	1990	1991	1992	1993[1]	1994[2]	1998[2]	Percent Change (1993–98) 92–93	93–94	93–98[3]
Total New Construction	**397.5**	**360.7**	**386.9**	**398.4**	**405.9**	**435.6**	**3**	**2**	**2**
Residential	164.0	141.3	165.4	176.2	183.9	198.7	7	4	2
Single family	97.5	85.4	102.6	110.8	115.2	122.3	8	4	2
Multifamily	17.3	13.6	11.5	11.5	12.1	14.0	0	5	4
Home improvement	49.2	42.3	51.3	53.9	56.6	62.4	5	5	3
Private Nonresidential	135.6	120.7	113.9	112.6	112.0	122.0	-1	-1	2
Manufacturing facilities	21.4	20.0	18.3	17.8	18.1	21.6	-3	2	4
Office	25.8	20.6	15.3	13.0	11.7	11.2	-15	-10	-3
Hotels and motels	8.7	5.6	3.1	2.6	2.2	2.0	-17	-15	-5
Other commercial	30.7	22.8	21.5	21.5	20.4	22.6	0	-5	1
Religious	3.0	3.0	3.0	3.2	3.3	*	6	3	*
Educational	3.8	3.5	3.8	3.9	4.0	4.5	3	2	3
Hospital and institutional	8.5	8.2	8.9	9.3	9.8	11.4	5	5	4
Miscellaneous buildings	4.1	3.8	3.3	3.4	3.4	*	3	0	*
Telecommunications	8.5	8.1	8.2	8.6	9.0	9.5	5	5	2
Railroads	2.2	2.1	2.9	2.9	3.0	*	0	2	*
Electric utilities	9.2	12.5	14.2	15.1	15.5	18.3	6	3	4
Gas utilities	4.2	4.8	5.5	5.3	5.4	*	-4	2	*
Petroleum pipelines	0.4	0.6	0.7	0.7	0.7	*	0	0	*
Farm structures	2.3	2.3	2.0	2.1	2.1	*	3	2	*
Miscellaneous structures	2.7	2.6	3.2	3.4	3.4	*	5	0	*
Public Works	97.5	98.7	107.6	109.6	110.0	114.9	2	0	1
Housing and redevelopment	3.4	3.4	3.7	3.8	3.8	*	2	2	*
Federal industrial	1.3	1.6	1.6	1.7	1.5	*	7	-10	*
Educational	18.4	20.5	20.7	20.3	20.3	21.3	-2	0	1
Hospital	2.3	2.3	2.7	2.7	2.6	2.7	0	-3	0
Other public buildings	15.6	16.2	17.1	16.2	14.8	14.7	-5	-9	-2
Highways	29.6	29.1	33.4	35.1	36.5	38.7	5	4	2
Military facilities	2.4	1.7	2.3	2.3	2.1	1.7	0	-10	-6
Conservation and development	4.1	4.3	5.1	5.5	5.7	5.8	8	4	1
Sewer systems	8.5	8.2	8.2	8.4	8.7	9.3	3	3	2
Water supplies	4.2	4.3	4.4	4.7	4.9	5.5	7	5	3
Miscellaneous public structures	7.7	7.1	8.4	8.8	9.0	9.7	5	2	2

[1]Estimate.
[2]Forecast.
[3]Average annual rate.
*Long–term forecast not made separately for this category.

NOTE: Totals may not add due to rounding. Percent changes are calculated on more detailed data.

SOURCE: U.S. Department of Commerce: Bureau of the Census; International Trade Administration (ITA). Estimates and forecasts by ITA.

Construction Expenditures by Type of Structure, 1990–98

(in billions of 1987 dollars except as noted)

Item	1990	1991	1992	1993[1]	1994[2]	1998[2]	Percent Change (1993-98) 92-93	93-94	93-98[3]
Total New Construction	**397.5**	**360.7**	**386.9**	**398.4**	**405.9**	**435.6**	**3**	**2**	**2**
New Building Construction	262.4	230.7	237.1	241.7	243.4	260.4	2	1	1
New housing units	114.8	99.0	114.1	122.3	127.3	136.3	7	4	2
Private nonresidential	106.1	87.6	77.2	74.7	72.9	79.8	-3	-2	1
Publicly owned	41.5	44.1	45.8	44.7	43.1	44.2	-2	-4	0
Other New Structures	85.9	87.7	98.5	102.8	106.0	112.8	4	3	2
Private nonresidential	29.5	33.1	36.7	38.0	39.0	42.1	3	3	2
Publicly owned	56.4	54.6	61.8	64.9	66.9	70.7	5	3	2
Home Improvements[4]	49.2	42.3	51.3	53.9	56.6	62.4	5	5	3
Selected Maintenance and Repair[5,8]									
Residential[5]	39.8	41.0	41.0	41.6	42.3	45.3	2	3	2
Nonresidential buildings[5,6]	32.9	34.5	35.5	36.6	37.7	40.4	3	3	2
Highway[5]	20.1	20.7	22.9	22.9	23.6	26.5	4	3	3
Utility[5]	23.1	25.2	27.3	28.7	29.8	34.9	5	4	4
Nonresidential Building Improvements[4,5,6,7,8]	53.8	54.5	61.1	59.9	59.9	62.9	-2	0	1

[1]Estimate.
[2]Forecast.
[3]Average annual rate of growth.
[4]Home Improvements are included in Total New Construction, but Nonresidential Building Improvements are not included.
[5]Estimates in constant 1987 dollars were derived by ITA, using current-dollar data developed by the Bureau of the Census, and the Census Fixed-Weight Composite Construction Cost Index as the deflator.
[6]Excludes industrial and agricultural buildings, as well as buildings owned by the Federal Government or private utilities. Also excludes buildings of 1,000 square feet or less.
[7]About half of all nonresidential building improvements are included in the value of new construction.
[8]Not included separately in Total New Construction.

NOTE: Totals may not add due to rounding. Percent changes are calculated on more detailed data.

SOURCE: U.S. Department of Commerce: Bureau of the Census, International Trade Administration (ITA). Estimates and forecasts by ITA.

Construction Materials

Demand for construction materials rose modestly in 1993, reflecting the 3 percent rise in constant-dollar construction put-in-place. This was the second consecutive small increase in construction work since the 1990–91 recession. New housing in 1993 was mixed, with single-family construction up slightly and multifamily construction flat. In 1991, total housing starts were slightly above 1 million units, the lowest annual volume since 1946. In 1992, housing starts were up 18 percent, to about 1.2 million units, and in 1993 they reached almost 1.3 million, an increase of about 4 percent. Multifamily housing starts were at about 170,000 in both 1992 and 1993. Shipments of the other new housing sector, manufactured (mobile) homes, had been in a long-term slide, with only 171,000 units shipped in 1991. The situation improved in 1992, with shipments up 23 percent. The 1993 total should reach 250,000 units, a 20 percent rise.

The long-term increase in the size and features of new single-family houses have tended to increase demand for construction materials. For the first time in many years, the average size of new houses declined to 2,075 square feet in 1991 (from 2,080 square feet in 1990). This compares with 2,035 square feet in 1989 and 1,780 square feet in 1984. With the improvement in new housing starts and sales in 1992, the trend to larger homes was evident again, with the average up to 2,095 square feet. As new houses have grown larger, the number of amenities has grown as well. These include two-car garages, central air conditioning, additional bedrooms and bathrooms, fireplaces, and full basements.

The demand for materials for use in the private nonresidential construction sector continued to decline in 1993. This sector experienced a 1 percent drop in activity on an inflation-adjusted basis. The important office building segment declined about 15 percent, hotels and motels were off 17 percent, and manufacturing facilities dropped 3 percent. Sectors experiencing some growth in 1993 were religious, educational, and institutional buildings and hospitals. Telecommunications and most utility construction were also up.

After rising about 9 percent in 1992, public construction increased about 2 percent in real terms in 1993. The important highway sector was up about 5 percent. Activity in most public categories rose in 1993, with the exception of educational buildings and other public buildings.

Construction work on existing structures continues to be an excellent market for construction materials. Manufacturers have developed product lines specifically designed for ease of installation by do-it-yourselfers and small contractors. Residential alterations, additions, and repair expenditures in current dollars rose to about $107 billion in 1990 and they declined sharply to about $97 billion in 1991, reflecting the recession. In 1992, these expenditures rose to more than $103 billion and in 1993 they are expected to increase to about $108 billion, or 5 percent over 1992. Nonresidential renovation and repair work increased in both 1992 and 1993.

Recent natural disasters have no doubt contributed to the demand for construction materials, and it will escalate toward the end of 1993, primarily in southern Florida and along the Midwest river basins. Much of the actual rebuilding, however, will take place in 1994 and beyond.

With demand improving, prices of construction materials rose between 4 and 5 percent in 1993, the largest increase since 1988. Large increases in lumber and wood building materials were major contributors to the rise in the Bureau of Labor Statistics Producer Price Index for all construction materials. All of the material indexes covered in the table "Construction Materials Price Trends, 1988–93" recorded price increases in 1993. The indexes for gypsum products, insulation, Portland cement, and sheet, plate and float glass increased 4 percent or more. Price indexes for ceramic tile and metal doors, sash and trim recorded the smallest increases.

INTERNATIONAL COMPETITIVENESS

U.S. exports of nonlumber construction materials increased in 1993 for the seventh consecutive year. Imports, after rising dramatically for many years, declined during the recession of 1990 and 1991, but rose again in 1992 and 1993. Both U.S. exports and imports rose about 8 percent in 1993. With exports and imports totalling about $4 billion, there was little or no surplus. Similar small trade surpluses of about $40 million were experienced in both 1991 and 1992. This compares with the peak U.S. trade surplus of about $700 million in 1981, and the deficits of more than $2 billion in 1986, 1987, and 1988.

The improving U.S. trade balance for these products in recent years primarily reflects the relative weakness in the U.S. construction market, a more competitive exchange rate, and the growing market for such products worldwide. Strong construction activity in most Asian countries, Mexico, the Middle East, Spain, and Portugal have helped increase demand for many U.S. construction materials. These factors have also affected U.S. imports, as foreign producers concentrate more on their own growing domestic markets and third-country markets than on exporting to the United States. Also bolstering U.S. exports are greater efforts by U.S. companies to market their products abroad.

U.S. construction materials enjoy a reputation for quality, innovation, and superior service. The U.S.-Canada Free Trade Agreement resulted in improved market access for both countries. Similar results could come from implementation of the North American Free Trade Agreement (NAFTA), although some building materials firms are concerned about the agreement's potential impact on their industries.

U.S. exports are significant in the flat glass, mineral wool, builders' hardware, fabricated structural metals, hard-surfaced floor coverings, prefabricated wood and metal buildings, plastics building materials, and cast iron pipe and fittings industries. Industries experiencing large import volumes include flat glass, cement, ceramic wall and floor tile, dimension stone, builders' hardware, some plumbing equipment, fabricated structural metals, and miscellaneous metal work products.

Canada is the largest customer of U.S. nonlumber building products. Other major customers include Mexico, Japan, the United Kingdom, Taiwan, Hong Kong, Saudi Arabia, and South Korea.

Major suppliers of these products to the United States are Canada, Mexico, Italy, Taiwan, Japan, Spain, and Germany.

LONG-TERM PROSPECTS

Longer-term demand for construction materials will continue to reflect the pace of the economic recovery. New residential construction should be the strongest sector, at least through 1994, with the recovery in the private nonresidential sector beginning in 1995 at the earliest. The projected number of new home buyers will limit the peak level of residential recovery cycle to not more than about 1.4 million housing units in the peak years. This is much below the previous cyclical housing peaks of the 1970's and 1980's. Over-building and weakness in commercial real estate and financial institutions will probably result in further declines in some types of private nonresidential building categories until at least 1995. Public construction, despite infrastructure needs, will grow only moderately because of tight Federal, state, and local budgets. As the recovery strengthens, higher tax revenues should support more public infrastructure renewal and improvement work, although there will be continuing pressure to decrease the Federal budget deficit. If implemented, a proposed infrastructure program to provide jobs and improve U.S. competitiveness would stimulate greater construction activity and improve materials demand. Total demand for construction materials should rise an average of 3 to 4 percent through 1999, although the usual cyclical downturn is likely before that time.

Long-term prospects for U.S. construction materials in the world market will depend on product and price competitiveness, the relative strength of the U.S. and other markets, and currency exchange rates. Bilateral and multilateral trade negotiations, such as NAFTA and the Uruguay Round of GATT negotiations, will play an important role. Most areas of the world have major housing and infrastructure needs. Canada, Asia, and Europe have been the U.S.'s major customers of construction materials. In the future, Mexico, other Latin American countries, African nations, China, Russia, and the other newly independent states in the former Soviet Union also should offer good growth prospects. Approval of NAFTA would offer easier access the Mexican, Canadian, and U.S. markets. Some U.S. building material industries are concerned about the prospects for increased U.S. imports of these products from Mexico and Latin American countries. Additional initiatives for free trade agreements with Central and South American countries would further enhance trade opportunities.

The fast pace of foreign investment in U.S. construction materials industries that marked the 1980's should slow in the 1990's. The level of overseas joint ventures between U.S. and foreign firms and increased exporting by U.S. firms show the growing awareness of the benefits of selling in foreign markets. These activities offer opportunities for higher sales and serve as a hedge against the cyclical fluctuations of the U.S. market. U.S. sales in foreign markets also helped provide some protection for U.S. markets by not allowing foreign firms to concentrate their efforts on the U.S. market.—*C. B. Pitcher, Office of Materials, Machinery and Chemicals (202) 482-0132.*

Trends and Forecasts: Construction Materials

(in millions of 1987 dollars except as noted)

Item	1991	1992[1]	1993[1]	1994[2]	Annual Growth Rate 91-94	Percent Change 91-92	92-93	93-94
Total	21,985	22,719	22,812	22,987	1.5	3.3	0.4	0.8
3088 Plastic plumbing fixtures	972	1,094	1,116	1,161	6.1	12.6	2.0	4.0
3211 Flat glass	2,248	2,293	2,339	2,386	2.0	2.0	2.0	2.0
3241 Hydraulic cement	3,605	3,825	3,867	3,944	3.0	6.1	1.1	2.0
3253 Ceramic wall/floor tile	705	773	811	835	5.8	9.6	4.9	3.0
3261 Vitreous plumbing fixtures	685	669	676	693	0.4	-2.3	1.0	2.5
3275 Gypsum products	2,744	3,153	3,216	3,267	6.0	14.9	2.0	1.6
3431 Metal sanitary ware	766	732	740	754	-0.5	-4.4	1.1	1.9
3432 Plumbing fixture fittings	2,007	2,010	2,040	2,100	1.5	0.1	1.5	2.9
3441 Fabricated structural metals	8,253	8,170	8,007	7,847	-1.7	-1.0	-2.0	-2.0

[1]Estimate.
[2]Forecast.

SOURCE: U.S. Department of Commerce: Bureau of the Census; International Trade Administration (ITA). Estimates and forecasts by ITA.

Construction Materials Price Trends, 1988–93

(annual percent change)

Industry	1987-88	1988-89	1989-90	1990-91	1991-92	1992-93[1]
Builders hardware	4.7	4.3	4.1	3.8	2.4	2.5
Ceramic tile	3.3	2.3	1.8	-1.1	1.1	0.4
Clay brick	2.5	1.2	2.6	1.0	1.5	3.4
Concrete products	0.5	1.1	2.1	2.7	0.5	2.1
Fabricated structural steel for buildings	6.4	3.6	-0.1	-1.3	-1.6	3.0
Gypsum products	-9.8	-2.6	-4.4	5.6	0.6	6.3
Hard surface floor coverings	5.5	6.0	2.4	4.7	2.0	2.4
Insulation materials	-0.8	-0.9	1.6	2.2	-7.7	-5.6
Metal doors sash and trim	9.3	6.2	1.1	2.4	0.3	0.9
Plumbing fixtures and fittings	7.3	7.0	4.8	3.7	2.3	2.1
Portland cement	0.1	-0.7	1.6	3.0	-0.5	4.7
Prefab metal buildings	5.6	4.5	1.2	0.6	0	3.9
Prepared asphalt roofing	2.6	1.3	0.1	0.5	-2.0	1.5
Sand, gravel, crushed stone	2.1	1.8	2.1	2.6	1.6	1.8
Sheet, plate, and float glass	4.2	-2.2	-6.5	-4.3	-0.2	4.9
All construction materials[2]	5.7	3.3	0.1	0.7	1.7	4.3

[1]Estimate.
[2]Includes lumber, wood products, and other construction products not covered in this chapter.

SOURCE: U.S. Department of Labor, Bureau of Labor Statistics; U.S. Department of Commerce, International Trade Administration (ITA). Estimates by ITA.

Drugs

In 1993, the value of shipments of the pharmaceutical industry (SIC 283) reached $69 billion, of which pharmaceutical preparations (SIC 2834) accounted for 78.4 percent, medicinals and botanicals (SIC 2833) 10.2 percent, diagnostics (SIC 2835) 7.6 percent and biologicals (SIC 2836) 3.8 percent. Industry shipments increased by 1.9 percent in constant dollars to $48.2 billion. Exports amounted to more than $7.2 billion in 1993, and imports increased to $6.7 billion.

The U.S. pharmaceutical industry is facing considerable change as a result of price discounting, weak foreign economies, increased use of generic and over-the-counter (OTC) drugs, and the prospect of increased governmental controls under health care reform. As a result, many firms are restructuring. This restructuring ranges from recent mergers of biotech and research and development (R&D) companies to the consolidation and reorganization of some of the industry's largest companies. Brand prescription manufacturing firms are increasingly entering the generic and OTC markets to boost sales and to help pay for increased R&D costs.

The U.S. pharmaceutical industry is adjusting to changing market conditions and remains the leader in world industry sector competitiveness and innovation. R&D investment has doubled every 5 years since 1970. In 1993 the industry invested more than $12.6 billion in R&D, a 14.5 percent increase over 1992. R&D expenditures now represent 16.7 percent of total sales. This is more than double the amount of R&D investment in any other high-technology industry. Recent discoveries, such as a drug that eases the acute pain of migraine headaches and products used to treat Alzheimer's disease, reinforce the industry's belief that R&D investment assures continued growth and success.

The FDA drug approval system and drug prices continued to be key issues affecting the industry in 1993. For the first time, in an effort to get new drugs to the market faster, drug companies will be paying the FDA to review their products. The Prescription Drug User Fee Act of 1992 is expected to bring in about $300 million over the next 5 years to help cover reviewing expenses. The user fee act expires after 5 years when the law will be reviewed to determine whether it was helpful in speeding up drug reviews.

Throughout 1993, a major topic of health care reform discussion was pharmaceutical prices. Primarily as a result of public opinion and domestic and foreign government pressure over prescription drug prices, 10 of the leading pharmaceutical firms have promised to increase their average prices at a rate no greater than the general inflation rate. Recent reports of economic research firms also suggest drug prices are being moderated by the formation of large buying groups under managed care programs. Other reports show that while the percentage of GDP devoted to health care has increased steadily, the percentage spent on prescription drugs has remained constant.

Those who favor Federal regulation of prescription drug prices contend that price increases severely strain the budgets of the biggest users of prescription drugs—the elderly and the chronically ill. They also argue that the pharmaceutical industry has used most of the higher profits generated by the price increases to develop duplicative—or "me-too"—medications and to undertake costly marketing campaigns. Conversely, there are those that believe price regulations would undercut the most potent incentive for investment in new drug development—the prospect of earning a return on a costly and risky investment. The opponents of government regulation also point out that, even with the increases in drug prices, many drug therapies are still much cheaper than alternative treatments, such as surgery and psychotherapy. While the argument over prices remains unresolved, drug prices are moderating.

INTERNATIONAL COMPETITIVENESS

U.S. manufacturers account for nearly half of the major pharmaceuticals marketed worldwide. While consistently maintaining a positive trade balance, the industry faces increasing international competition. To maintain competitiveness, the industry must overcome international obstacles such as price controls, illegal use of patents and copyrights, and foreign regulations on marketing and R&D.

Markets in Eastern Europe, China, Japan, Mexico, Canada, and the European Community (EC) offer mixed prospects for expanded pharmaceutical trade and investment. The new markets opened up in Russia and other countries in the Commonwealth of Independent States provide particularly strong potential, but at the same time present formidable challenges as a result of registration, testing, and license regulations. China is also a large potential pharmaceutical market, but is increasing pharmaceutical production. The Japanese market remains one of the best customers of the United States, but as a reaction to slumping domestic pharmaceutical prices, the Japanese industry is developing new markets in the United States and Europe, and acquiring foreign firms. Japanese companies are heavily investing in R&D in a bid to catch up with their foreign competitors.

The North America Free Trade Agreement (NAFTA) is expected to increase U.S. exports of pharmaceuticals, particularly, through the reduction of tariffs, the improvement of intellectual property rights protection, and the opening of the government procurement market in Mexico and Canada. These countries represent approximately 15 percent of total U.S. exports of pharmaceuticals goods.

The EC remains the largest importer of U.S. pharmaceuticals, purchasing nearly 50 percent of all U.S. exports. The European Community's single market emerged in 1993, but the U.S. pharmaceutical industry has yet to receive many benefits. Individual European governments still maintain control of pharmaceutical registration and pricing.

LONG-TERM PROSPECTS

The drug market is expected to continue to expand over the next 5 years, but industry will face increasing pressure to control prices. In addition to the uncertain impact of health care policy reform, the nature of the U.S. health care delivery system is changing. There is a shift away from the fee-for-service doctor/patient relationship and a corresponding increase in service by large, managed health care providers. Growth in the number of older people will boost demand for quality, low-cost health care services and products. Since R&D costs are expected to continue to rise, the ability to develop new drugs and new global markets is expected to play an even greater role in determining long-term prospects.

Pharmaceutical Preparations

Shipments of pharmaceutical preparations during 1993 increased by 5.5 percent to $54.1 billion, or by 2 percent in constant dollars. Both exports and imports increased by 13 percent with exports reaching $2.1 billion.

The establishments in this industry are primarily engaged in manufacturing, fabricating, and processing drugs into pharmaceutical preparations for human or veterinary use. The products of pharmaceutical preparations are usually finished in the form intended for consumption.

Pharmaceutical preparations are made by ethical brand drug manufacturers, generic drug manufacturers, and OTC pharmaceutical companies. Brand prescription drug manufacturers invent the prescription drugs which can be sold only with a doctor's prescription. OTC pharmaceuticals are those drug products that consumers can obtain and use on their own initiative. Generic forms of prescription drugs are made available once the innovator's patent expires. Generic drugs, like prescription drugs, can be obtained only through a doctor's prescription. The foundation for the success of the generic and OTC industries rests largely on the inventiveness of the brand prescription drug companies.

LONG-TERM PROSPECTS

The three major sectors of the pharmaceutical preparation industry are forecast to grow at a rate of 2.5 percent over the next 5 years. Brand name pharmaceuticals will continue to provide medical breakthroughs in the treatment of such complex diseases as cancer, AIDS, and heart disease. These innovations will require continued R&D investments. An important market trend is the increasing switch from prescription drug status to OTC drug status. The FDA is expected to receive more than 70 switch applications during the next 4 to 5 years. Generic substitutions will increase in popularity as the consumer becomes even more cost conscious. The generic market is expected to increase to more than $21 billion by 1995, as 51 of today's prescription drugs' patents expire. By the year 2000, due to patent expiration, more than one third of the industry's 300 best selling brand-name drugs may be available in generic form.—*William Hurt, Chemicals and Allied Products Division (202) 482-0128.*

Biological Products

Companies in the biological products industry are primarily engaged in producing bacterial and virus vaccines, toxoids, and analogous products, serums, plasmas, and other blood derivatives for human or veterinary use. Industry shipments of biological products increased by 4 percent to $2.6 billion in 1993, or by 1.8 percent in constant dollars. The industry had a positive trade balance of $554 million, with exports reaching $1.2 billion.

Although generally recognized as a small segment of the pharmaceutical industry, the vaccine market is growing with the emergence of innovative technology. Vaccine companies are striving to develop new vaccines, particularly for AIDS and malaria, while at the same time improving current vaccines. Worldwide growth for childhood disease vaccines continues with the support of organizations such as WHO and UNICEF.

Current market trends include the development of vaccines based on multiple antigens and microencapsulation, and a move toward genetically engineered bacterial or viral vectors for pathogenic antigens. Genetically engineered viral vectors will provide a safer and more efficient delivery system while simultaneously vaccinating against several diseases. However, these vaccines will have to meet the stringent guidelines set forth by the Center for Biologics Evaluation and Research, which require new vaccines to be at least as safe and efficient as traditional vaccines. Microencapsulation, which may be more cost effective and efficient, involves the use of biodegradable capsules for the administration of the vaccines, instead of the traditional use of injections.

LONG-TERM PROSPECTS

The industry will continue to face stringent regulations with a 1.5–2 percent growth rate in constant dollars over the next 5 years. Vaccines based on genetically engineered vectors will continue to grow as biotechnology-based products gain acceptance. The most important factor affecting future industry growth will be health care reforms.—*Melissa Harrington, Chemicals and Allied Products Division (202) 482-0128.*

U.S. Trade Patterns in 1992
Drugs
SIC 283

(in millions of dollars, percent)

Exports			Imports		
	Value	Share		Value	Share
Canada and Mexico	986	14.6	Canada and Mexico	325	5.5
European Community	3,260	48.1	European Community	3,245	54.5
Japan	963	14.2	Japan	685	11.5
East Asia NICs	329	4.9	East Asia NICs	150	2.5
South America	291	4.3	South America	27	0.5
Other	944	13.9	Other	1,526	25.6
World Total	6,774	100.0	World Total	5,958	100.0
Top Five Countries					
	Value	Share		Value	Share
Japan	963	14.2	United Kingdom	932	15.6
Canada	844	12.5	Germany	871	14.6
Germany	768	11.3	Switzerland	764	12.8
Italy	561	8.3	Japan	685	11.5
France	499	7.4	Ireland	410	6.9

See "Getting the Most Out of *Outlook '94*" for definitions of the country groupings.
SOURCE: U.S. Department of Commerce: Bureau of the Census; International Trade Administration.

Trends and Forecasts: Drugs (SIC 283)

(in millions of dollars except as noted)

Item	1987	1988	1989	1990	1991	1992[1]	1993[2]	1994[3]	Percent Change (1989–1994) 88–89	89–90	90–91	91–92	92–93	93–94
Industry Data														
Value of shipments[4]	39,263	43,987	49,114	53,720	60,835	65,317	68,973	70,452	11.7	9.4	13.2	7.4	5.6	2.1
2833 Medicinals & botanicals	3,350	4,150	4,753	4,919	6,308	6,548	7,044	7,178	14.5	3.5	28.2	3.8	7.6	1.9
2834 Pharmaceutical preps	32,094	35,825	40,028	44,182	47,376	51,295	54,101	55,183	11.7	10.4	7.2	8.3	5.5	2.0
2835 Diagnostic substances	2,20	2,261	2,325	2,462	4,746	4,940	5,188	5,340	2.8	5.9	92.8	4.1	5.0	2.9
2836 Bio prod ex diagnostic	1,614	1,750	2,008	2,156	2,406	2,534	2,640	2,751	14.7	7.4	11.6	5.3	4.2	4.2
Value of shipments (1987$)	39,263	40,942	41,998	42,773	45,470	46,277	47,153	48,089	2.6	1.8	6.3	1.8	1.9	2.0
2833 Medicinals & botanicals	3,350	3,960	4,213	4,274	5,141	5,234	5,328	5,429	6.4	1.4	20.3	1.8	1.8	1.9
2834 Pharmaceutical preps	32,094	32,988	33,581	34,144	33,767	34,357	35,010	35,710	1.8	1.7	-1.1	1.7	1.9	2.0
2835 Diagnostic substances	2,205	2,237	2,275	2,282	4,280	4,366	4,453	4,542	1.7	0.3	87.6	2.0	2.0	2.0
2836 Bio prod ex diagnostic	1,614	1,757	1,929	2,073	2,282	2,320	2,362	2,408	9.8	7.5	10.1	1.7	1.8	1.9
Total employment (000)	172	175	184	183	184	—	—	—	5.1	-0.5	0.5	—	—	—
2833 Medicinals & botanicals	1.6	11.3	11.4	10.9	12.5	—	—	—	0.9	-4.4	14.7	—	—	—
2834 Pharmaceutical preps	132	133	142	144	129	133	136	—	6.8	1.4	-10.4	3.1	2.3	—
2835 Diagnostic substances	15.4	16.2	16.1	14.9	30.5	—	—	—	-0.6	-7.5	104.7	—	—	—
2836 Bio prod ex diagnostic	13.3	13.7	14.5	13.3	12.1	—	—	—	5.8	-8.3	-9.0	—	—	—
Production workers (000)	79.6	81.0	82.8	81.4	82.7	—	—	—	2.2	-1.7	1.6	—	—	—
2833 Medicinals & botanicals	6.1	6.2	6.6	6.5	7.2	—	—	—	6.5	-1.5	10.8	—	—	—
2834 Pharmaceutical preps	59.9	60.8	62.4	61.5	59.2	60.4	61.6	—	2.6	-1.4	-3.7	2.0	2.0	—
2835 Diagnostic substances	6.8	7.5	6.8	6.6	9.9	—	—	—	-9.3	-2.9	50.0	—	—	—
2836 Bio prod ex diagnostic	6.8	6.5	7.0	6.8	6.4	—	—	—	7.7	-2.9	-5.9	—	—	—
Average hourly earnings ($)	12.22	12.67	13.48	14.22	15.36	—	—	—	6.4	5.5	8.0	—	—	—
2833 Medicinals & botanicals	15.32	16.09	16.29	17.35	20.06	—	—	—	1.2	6.5	15.6	—	—	—
2834 Pharmaceutical preps	12.42	12.93	13.83	14.71	14.77	—	—	—	7.0	6.4	0.4	—	—	—
2835 Diagnostic substances	10.74	10.93	11.54	11.80	18.17	—	—	—	5.6	2.3	54.0	—	—	—
2836 Bio prod ex diagnostic	8.87	9.13	9.30	9.15	11.00	—	—	—	1.9	-1.6	20.2	—	—	—
Capital expenditures	1,749	2,058	2,392	2,280	2,669	—	—	—	16.2	-4.7	17.1	—	—	—
2833 Medicinals & botanicals	115	151	219	195	487	—	—	—	45.0	-11.0	149.7	—	—	—
2834 Pharmaceutical preps	1,471	1,725	1,933	1,809	1,772	—	—	—	12.1	-6.4	-2.0	—	—	—
2835 Diagnostic substances	93.5	93.3	117	147	302	—	—	—	25.4	25.6	105.4	—	—	—
2836 Bio prod ex diagnostic	69.9	89.1	124	130	108	—	—	—	39.2	4.8	-16.9	—	—	—

(continued)

Trends and Forecasts: Drugs (SIC 283) *(concluded)*

(in millions of dollars except as noted)

Item	1987	1988	1989	1990	1991	1992[1]	1993[2]	1994[3]	Percent Change (1989–1994) 88–89	89–90	90–91	91–92	92–93	93–94
Product Data														
Value of shipments[5]	35,283	39,532	43,796	47,832	51,880	55,607	58,428	—	10.8	9.2	8.5	7.2	5.1	—
2833 Medicinals & botanicals	4,224	4,948	5,393	5,789	6,647	6,898	7,116	—	9.0	7.3	14.8	3.8	3.2	—
2834 Pharmaceutical preps	26,610	29,555	32,713	35,280	37,416	40,532	42,750	—	10.7	7.8	6.1	8.3	5.5	—
2835 Diagnostic substances	2,683	3,063	3,471	4,234	4,973	5,176	5,435	—	13.3	22.0	17.5	4.1	5.0	—
2836 Bio prod ex diagnostic	1,765	1,966	2,220	2,529	2,844	3,001	3,127	—	12.9	13.9	12.5	5.5	4.2	—
Value of shipments (1987$)	35,283	36,939	37,753	38,649	39,269	39,984	40,737	—	2.2	2.4	1.6	1.8	1.9	—
2833 Medicinals & botanicals	4,224	4,721	4,781	5,030	5,417	5,514	5,611	—	1.3	5.2	7.7	1.8	1.8	—
2834 Pharmaceutical preps	26,610	27,214	27,443	27,264	26,668	27,148	27,664	—	0.8	-0.7	-2.2	1.8	1.9	—
2835 Diagnostic substances	2,683	3,030	3,396	3,924	4,484	4,574	4,665	—	12.1	15.5	14.3	2.0	2.0	—
2836 Bio prod ex diagnostic	1,765	1,974	2,132	2,431	2,699	2,748	2,797	—	8.0	14.0	11.0	1.8	1.8	—
Trade Data														
Value of imports	—	—	3,531	3,884	4,812	5,958	6,743	—	—	10.0	23.9	23.8	13.2	—
2833 Medicinals & botanicals	—	—	2,354	2,303	2,854	3,277	3,604	—	—	-2.2	23.9	14.8	10.0	—
2834 Pharmaceutical preps	—	—	868	1,103	1,442	1,859	2,105	—	—	27.1	30.7	28.9	13.2	—
2835 Diagnostic substances	—	—	118	207	191	336	371	—	—	75.4	-7.7	75.9	10.4	—
2836 Bio prod ex diagnostic	—	—	191	271	325	486	662	—	—	41.9	19.9	49.5	36.2	—
Value of exports	—	—	4,345	5,050	5,731	6,774	7,207	—	—	16.2	13.5	18.2	6.4	—
2833 Medicinals & botanicals	—	—	1,794	1,908	2,064	2,444	2,442	—	—	6.4	8.2	18.4	-0.1	—
2834 Pharmaceutical preps	—	—	974	1,258	1,478	1,818	2,055	—	—	29.2	17.5	23.0	13.0	—
2835 Diagnostic substances	—	—	739	909	1,160	1,370	1,494	—	—	23.0	27.6	18.1	9.1	—
2836 Bio prod ex diagnostic	—	—	839	974	1,028	1,142	1,216	—	—	16.1	5.5	11.1	6.5	—

[1]Estimate, except exports and imports.
[2]Estimate.
[3]Forecast.
[4]Value of all products and services sold by establishments in the drugs industry.
[5]Value of products classified in the drugs industry produced by all industries.

NOTE: Changes in the mix of products produced by drug making establishments caused them to be reclassified among the SICs shown between 1990 and 1991 distorting the magnitude of the changes for the four-digit SICs.

SOURCE: U.S. Department of Commerce: Bureau of the Census; International Trade Administration (ITA). Estimates and forecasts by ITA.

Electronic Components and Equipment

This section covers electronic components, semiconductor manufacturing equipment (SME), and superconductivity, although Census data are not available on SME and superconductivity. Electronic components are the fundamental building blocks for the electronics industry. These components account for about 2 million jobs and production of almost $300 billion annually.

A wide variety of products comprises the electronics components category, including electron tubes (SIC 3671), printed circuit boards (SIC 3672), semiconductors and diodes (SIC 3674), capacitors (SIC 3675), resistors (SIC 3676), coils and transformers (SIC 3677), connectors (SIC 3678), and electronic components, NEC (SIC 3679). Many industries use these products. Demand for electronic components comes primarily from the computer, telecommunications, instrumentation, medical equipment, and transportation industries.

Market conditions in the United States improved in 1993, with the expansion in the overall economy. Supported by strong demand for computers and telecommunications equipment, industry sales of electronic components grew to almost $81 billion in current dollars, a significant improvement over the 1992 level of $73 billion.

Employment losses in the electronic component sectors continued in 1993. Jobs in semiconductor companies were down 3 percent, while the remaining electronic component firms had 3.2 percent fewer workers. Reflecting increasing efficiencies in production methods, total employment fell from 496,000 in 1992 to 479,000 in 1993, despite the increase in industry shipments.

The trade deficit in electronic components increased in 1993 to an estimated $6.8 billion, from $6.6 billion in 1993. Stagnant economies in many foreign countries, particularly Japan and the European Community (EC), dampened sales of U.S. exports. Demand for imports expanded, reflecting the recovery in the U.S. market. Although exports reached $19.1 billion in 1993, up about 18 percent, imports still outpaced them, rising to $25.9 billion from $22.8 billion in 1992.

Worldwide competition in the electronics components industry is fierce. The United States faces continued strong competition from Japan and other countries in technologically sophisticated products. Although U.S. firms frequently will be the first to introduce new products, the Japanese often have been able to refine the manufacturing process and produce large quantities at relatively low prices. In less sophisticated products, U.S. suppliers have difficulty competing with such countries as South Korea, Malaysia, and Taiwan, where production costs are low.

The other North American countries, Canada and Mexico, remained the largest trading market for U.S. suppliers. Many U.S. electronics companies have set up production and assembly facilities in Mexico to take advantage of low wage rates there. These companies import electronic components from the United States and export finished products back across the border. The proposed elimination of tariffs between the United States and Mexico, combined with simplified regulations affecting trade among Canada, Mexico, and the United States as envisioned under the North American Free Trade Agreement (NAFTA), should stimulate further growth of two-way trade in the region.

Today's customers demand higher performance, more functionality, and continued miniaturization of physical characteristics at ultra-competitive prices. International buying patterns for components are based on manufacturing costs and technological sophistication. A range of variables exists in global production costs, including labor and capital inputs, and regulatory enforcement costs for environmental and worker safety standards. Product sophistication depends on the development of technology and the commercialization of research.

The competitiveness of world producers of electronic components demands commitments by producers to meet increasingly costly production and product planning expenses. Because of intense international competition, the U.S. industry must:

- Maintain its domestic manufacturing base;
- Be first to market commercial applications of high-quality product innovations;
- Accommodate quick turnaround requests from customers;
- Maintain a leadership role in setting standards; and
- Further penetrate world markets.

Unlike their overseas competitors, U.S. component suppliers do not have the advantage of long-term supplier relationships with original equipment manufacturers (OEMs) that purchase components and integrate them into electronic systems. OEMs in the United States tend to emphasize supplier flexibility, rather than lasting alliances. If the U.S. component industry is to prosper in the face of global competition, better long-term supplier/customer relations are needed.

LONG-TERM PROSPECTS

Shipments of electronic components are forecast to grow at an annual rate of 6 to 8 percent through the late 1990's. Component suppliers will face continuing demand for higher performance products. The increased complexity of the packaging and the interconnection of high-performance systems place a premium on compatibility among components. Systems designers will select components that offer the best engineering solutions. Component suppliers will have to carefully track technology and product developments in their customer markets and anticipate needed changes in their own product development to ensure compatibility. The establishment of close working relationships between component suppliers and users will be critical if U.S. companies want to maintain their competitive position.

Within the next few years, new consumer products, such as HDTV, interactive multimedia, and handheld computers, will enter the U.S. market. These products will be based on developing technologies, including multichip modules, voice recognition synthesis, image processing, character recognition, and artificial intelligence. All of these products will require increasing quantities of electronic components, both sophisticated semiconductors and advanced components. Many will use digital technologies, where U.S. suppliers hold the lead. If U.S. suppliers focus on new developments in consumer electronics products, they have the opportunity to regain part of the consumer segment of the U.S. electronics market.—*Margaret T. Donnelly, Office of Microelectronics, Medical Equipment, and Instrumentation (202) 482-5466.*

Semiconductors and Related Devices

The U.S. semiconductor industry continued its recovery in 1993 because of renewed growth in major markets worldwide. Shipments by U.S. semiconductor firms rose an estimated 16 percent (in current dollars). U.S. companies experienced increased sales in every regional market, with the strongest growth occurring in North America and Asia/Pacific.

The domestic semiconductor book-to-bill ratio remained above 1.1 from October 1992 through July 1993. The ratio is a closely monitored indicator comparing the registration of new orders with the billing of customers for actual shipments. The ratio normally peaks in January and bottoms out in the summer. However, it rose in July 1993 for the second time in 10 years, reflecting continued strong demand as well as some panic buying inspired by fears of a possible shortage of certain chips.

The partial destruction on July 4, 1993 of a Sumitomo Chemical plant, which supplied 60 percent of the high-grade plastic resin for integrated circuit (IC) packaging, touched off a wave of speculative buying that temporarily drove up the price of ICs packaged in plastic. However, shortage fears dissipated as semiconductor manufacturers got a clearer picture of the size of the resin shortfall and formulated plans to deal with it.

The Sumitomo event diverted attention from the real price increases that occurred during 1993 because strong growth in semiconductor demand outpaced the growth of production capacity worldwide. The capacity utilization rate of U.S. electronics production facilities (including semiconductor plants) remained above 80 percent in 1993, indicating strong demand for electronic products as well as limited reserve production capacity.

Capital and R&D Spending

The U.S. semiconductor industry invests heavily in new capital equipment, facilities, and R&D for future growth. According to the Semiconductor Industry Association, from 1980 to 1992, U.S. companies spent an average 12 percent of annual revenue on R&D and 14 percent of annual revenue on capital equipment and facilities, well above the average of all U.S. industry.

Capital spending underwent a major adjustment from 1990 to 1992, to bring worldwide semiconductor production capacity into line with demand. Semiconductor manufacturers delayed or canceled new plants and closed older ones, contributing to the capacity crunch that began to be felt in 1993. According to the market research firm, Dataquest, worldwide capital spending decreased in 1992 in all areas except Asia/Pacific. The greatest retrenchment occurred in Japan, where capital spending plunged by almost 29 percent in 1992. For 1993, Dataquest estimates that capital spending continued to drop in Japan and Europe, though at a slower pace. Capital spending in North America and Asia/Pacific was estimated to have grown moderately in 1993, spurred by the continued growth of semiconductor consumption there.

The cost of a new semiconductor fabrication plant (fab) for high-volume production of dynamic random access memories (DRAMs) has risen from about $400 million in 1990 to a range of $600 million to $1 billion in 1993. These costs are driven by the need for constant product innovation and leading-edge manufacturing technology. DRAM prices have remained relatively low, however, resulting in insufficient profits to recoup the massive R&D and capital expenditures required.

High capital costs have led semiconductor companies to adopt various capital-saving strategies. Some firms have resorted to smaller, specialized "mini-fabs." Many companies no longer can pursue technology-driven growth strategies; instead, they seek to spread their costs by sharing manufacturing processes and equipment across their product mixes, and by partnering with other firms.

INTERNATIONAL COMPETITIVENESS

The U.S. trade deficit in semiconductors was $3.8 billion in 1992. Worldwide semiconductor sales in North America grew by 18.6 percent in 1993, and the region surpassed Japan in total sales for the first time in several years. The strong U.S. market was a magnet for semiconductor imports, which were up nearly 20 percent from 1992. Dataquest forecasts the North American semiconductor market to experience a compound annual growth rate of about 11 percent through 1997.

The dominant regional trading partner of the United States continues to be East Asia, which accounted for roughly half of U.S. semiconductor imports and exports in 1992. The strongest regional market growth in 1993 occurred in the Asia/Pacific region, which was up about 23 percent. The Japanese semiconductor market recovered somewhat in 1993 from the sharp decline in 1992.

LONG-TERM PROSPECTS

Product innovation in the design and fabrication of ICs has focused on the reduction of minimum feature size and the efficiency with which greater numbers of circuits can be packed onto a chip. Progress on these parameters will continue to be made with new generations of ICs. However, some observers feel that the semiconductor industry is maturing and that rapidly escalating costs for design, engineering, and production facilities threaten profit levels and growth rates. These increasing costs lengthen the return on investment while product life cycles remain relatively constant.

Semiconductor makers will strive to maintain profits by cutting costs and improving the productivity of new design, engineering, and fabrication tools. They also will seek to share costs, through horizontal partnering with other semiconductor firms and vertical partnering with semiconductor end users.

DRAMs will be a primary technology driver and a barometer of semiconductor costs and prices for several years to come. New DRAM makers in Singapore, Taiwan, and perhaps China and Malaysia will sharpen competition and hold down prices of memory products. Established DRAM manufacturers will continue to differentiate their products, expand to new product lines, develop more efficient manufacturing and engineering methods, and enter into strategic alliances.

Growing end-use markets for semiconductors include pen-based computers, HDTV, PCs, multimedia integrated services digital networks (ISDNs), portable cellular phones, and other communications products. Although the automotive market is not expected to grow dramatically, the value of automobile electronic devices will continue to expand. Semiconductor sales to auto parts companies are expected to grow, especially those used in safety features such as airbags, collision detection, and anti-lock brakes. Sales of specialized semiconductors for the government-military sector are not expected to be higher, but the military will use increasing numbers of commercial-grade semiconductor products.

Continuing technological development of integrated circuits will encourage further substitution of advanced ICs for discrete semiconductors in many applications. However, with increased power-carrying capability, discrete diodes and transistors will retain a significant share of the market for power control circuitry, despite growing competition from power ICs. Because of increasing demand from television set manufacturers, the cathode ray tube market will continue to expand during the next 5 years. The long-term outlook for the tube industry will continue to parallel the dynamic growth of end-product development in various consumer electronics markets, including HDTV, computer monitors, and multimedia applications.—*Robin Roark and Robert Scott, Office of Microelectronics, Medical Equipment, and Instrumentation (202) 482-2470.*

Trends and Forecasts: Electronic Components and Accessories (SIC 367)

(in millions of dollars except as noted)

Item	1987	1988	1989	1990	1991	1992[1]	1993[2]	1994[3]	Percent Change (1989–1994) 88–89	89–90	90–91	91–92	92–93	93–94
Industry Data														
Value of shipments[4]	50,258	56,999	59,913	60,844	65,233	72,767	80,863	88,337	5.1	1.6	7.2	11.5	11.1	9.2
Value of shipments (1987$)	50,258	56,075	58,502	60,514	65,849	74,650	84,410	93,767	4.3	3.4	8.8	13.4	13.1	11.1
Total employment (000)	546	552	551	536	519	496	479	471	-0.2	-2.7	-3.2	-4.4	-3.2	-1.9
Production workers (000)	329	337	339	325	314	310	305	—	0.6	-4.1	-3.4	-1.3	-1.6	—
Average hourly earnings ($)	9.32	9.78	9.96	10.22	10.34	10.48	10.60	—	1.8	2.6	1.2	1.4	1.1	—
Product Data														
Value of shipments[5]	46,719	52,688	57,009	59,307	62,766	69,881	77,499	84,506	8.2	4.0	5.8	11.3	10.9	9.0
Value of shipments (1987$)	46,719	51,853	55,666	58,843	63,174	71,453	80,597	89,346	7.4	5.7	7.4	13.1	12.8	10.9
Trade Data														
Value of imports	—	—	18,342	19,111	20,409	22,842	25,936	29,201	—	4.2	6.8	11.9	13.6	12.6
Value of exports	—	—	12,630	15,581	15,498	16,192	19,092	21,174	—	23.4	-0.5	4.5	17.9	10.9

[1]Estimate, except exports and imports.
[2]Estimate.
[3]Forecast.
[4]Value of all products and services sold by establishments in the electronic components and accessories industry.
[5]Value of products classified in the electronic components and accessories industry produced by all industries.
SOURCE: U.S. Department of Commerce: Bureau of the Census; International Trade Administration (ITA).

Food and Beverages

The processed food and beverage industry sector (SIC 20) is the nation's largest manufacturing sector. In 1993, the value of food and beverage industry shipments reached an estimated $404 billion, up more than 2 percent over 1992. Exports rose almost 3 percent, while exports of higher value-added processed foods and beverages rose almost 12 percent, a turbulent international economy notwithstanding. Adjusted for inflation, processed food and beverage sector industry shipments rose slightly more than 1 percent in 1993; between 1988 and 1992, real sectoral shipment value rose about 1 percent annually.

Industry expectations for 1994 are clouded by concerns about the pace of domestic and international economic recovery, a possible softening in export demand, and increasingly acrimonious food processor-food retailer relationships. Adjusted for inflation, total food and beverage industry shipments are likely to rise about 1 percent in 1994. A rebounding U.S. economy and a pickup in export demand would contribute to accelerated industry growth.

In 1993, aggregate food and beverage industry shipments value increased between 2 and 3 percent (nominal), or slightly more than 1 percent in real terms, as a number of factors dampened growth. Consumers continued to express concern about the overall economy by reducing their spending and, in some cases, by changing buying habits and purchase preferences.

For the first half of 1993, personal consumption expenditures (PCE) for food and beverages consumed at home and away from home rose at an annual rate of more than 2 percent over 1992. Interestingly, expenditures outside the home increased more than in-home food purchases. Many consumers, however, responded to unsettled economic times not only by spending less overall, but also by increasing their purchases of less costly, private-label foods and beverages. In addition, increasing numbers of shoppers have begun trading at "warehouse club" outlets, which stock extra large items at attractive prices.

Most industry analysts consider the U.S. food and beverage processing sector mature and developed. Population growth, economic conditions, and foreign trade patterns affect growth. In 1993, the U.S. population grew by less than 1 percent, consumers were concerned about their economic well-being, and foreign customers struggled with recession.

In addition, an increasing number of food and beverage processors adopted a wholesale pricing strategy centered around lower prices without discounts, merchandise deals, or other purchase incentives. This pricing approach results in smaller gross sales but does not necessarily affect net sales and may even increase them because it reduces promotional costs.

The economic troubles affecting most of the world in 1993 had a dampening effect on U.S. processed food and beverage exports. Total processed food and beverage export value rose only modestly, while exports of lower value-added products, such as meat, poultry, seafood, most dairy products, and grain-based intermediate products declined moderately. Foreign demand for U.S.-produced higher value-added products, such as processed fruits and vegetables, alcoholic beverages, ready-to-eat meals, bakery items, and candy products increased significantly in 1993.

Value-Added

The industry sector is divided here into two groups—higher value-added industries and lower value-added industries—for further analysis. (The Census Bureau derives value added by subtracting the cost of materials, supplies, containers, fuel, electricity, and contract work from the value of industry shipments.) The higher value-added industries manufacture retail-ready, packaged, consumer brand-name products of which at least 40 percent of the industry shipment value is added through sophisticated manufacturing.

Industry analysts attribute the increased foreign demand for higher value-added U.S. products, such as roasted nuts, frozen fruit and vegetables, ice cream, jellies, and canned fruits and vegetables to several factors. A rapidly growing middle class in developing and emerging countries accounted for some of the increased demand. Also, Russia, Ukraine, and other countries of the former Soviet Union had a great appetite for higher value-added foods and beverages, especially alcoholic beverages. Observers believe that some of these shipments moved through brokers and traders in several member states of the European Community.

Mirroring the strength of higher value-added food and beverages abroad, the value of industry shipments of the higher value-added group substantially out-performed lower value-added industries in 1993. The value of industry shipments of the higher value-added group increased an estimated 3 percent and accounted for 50 percent of total value; in contrast, the value of the lower value-added group's industry shipments rose about 2 percent.

Adjusted for inflation, the value of shipments of the higher value-added industry group rose more than 2 percent in 1993. The relatively large increase in real shipments value compared with nominal value change (3 percent) reflects processors' price restraints, new efficiencies, and a changing product mix. The lower value-added industry group did not fare as well; adjusted for inflation, group value of shipments contracted fractionally due to declines in the meat and poultry and the fats and oils industries of 1 percent and 3 percent, respectively.

INTERNATIONAL COMPETITIVENESS

Recognizing that domestic markets are expanding slowly, many U.S. food and beverage processors emphasized export sales in 1993. A weaker U.S. dollar and economic concerns abroad have contributed to record export sales in 1993. As U.S. firms become more skillful in cultivating overseas customers and the international economy improves, exports are likely to increase substantially.

U.S. exports of processed foods and beverages reached an estimated $22.5 billion in 1993, an increase of about 3 percent over 1992. Despite this marginal gain, U.S. processed food and beverage exports continued to out-pace imports, a pattern first established in 1991. U.S. imports of processed foods and beverages edged down an estimated 1 percent in 1993 to $20.8 billion, reversing an increase of more than 5 percent in 1992.

Foreign demand for lower value-added intermediate processed foods and beverages declined slightly in 1993. However, exports of higher value-added products were expected to rise a substantial 12 percent. Because of weakening foreign demand for lower value-added products, which represent the majority of U.S. food and beverage exports, total export value rose almost 3 percent.

Exports of higher value-added processed foods and beverages, including bakery products, breakfast cereal, and chewing gum reached about $7.5 billion in 1993, up nearly 12 percent from 1992. Between 1989 and 1993, exports of these products expanded more than 16 percent annually. Increases in foreign demand boosted the share of higher value-added food and beverage exports relative to total exports from more than 23 percent in 1989 to more than 32 percent in 1993.

In 1993, exports from five industries among the higher value-added group of industries accounted for 47 percent of the total. Processed nuts led the list with a share of more than 10 percent with exports of $776 million, unchanged from 1992. U.S. manufacturers of processed nuts have strong technical and marketing expertise.

LONG-TERM PROSPECTS

Over the next five years the processed food and beverage industries are likely to grow slowly; adjusted for inflation, the value of aggregate industry shipments is forecast to rise about 1 percent a year. Industry growth is likely to be less robust during the early years and rise to higher levels as the U.S. and international economies improve and the expected benefits of the pending NAFTA and Uruguay Round trade agreements begin to materialize.

U.S. alcoholic beverage processors must contend with the sales-dampening effects of prospective Federal excise tax increases. Some of the costs of the new national health-care system may be financed by excise tax increases on distilled spirits. Brewers and winemakers also are concerned that escalating health-care costs will bring about excise tax hikes for beer and wine.—*William Janis (202) 482-2250, Cornelius Kenney (202) 482-2428, and Elena Vasquez (202) 482-2624, Office of Consumer Goods.*

Trends and Forecasts: Food and Kindred Products (SIC 20)

(in millions of dollars except as noted)

Item	1987	1988	1989	1990	1991	1992[1]	1993[2]	1994[3]	Percent Change (1989–1994) 88–89	89–90	90–91	91–92	92–93	93–94
Industry Data														
Value of shipments[4]	329,725	351,515	364,403	384,009	387,601	394,039	404,342	415,406	3.7	5.4	0.9	1.7	2.6	2.7
Value of shipments (1987$)	329,725	337,265	333,011	339,697	344,351	347,649	352,013	355,533	-1.3	2.0	1.4	1.0	1.3	1.0
Total employment (000)	1,449	1,465	1,459	1,470	1,475	1,475	1,461	1,458	-0.4	0.8	0.3	0.0	-0.9	-0.2
Production workers (000)	1,029	1,046	1,049	1,061	1,070	1,068	1,068	1,066	0.3	1.1	0.8	-0.2	0.0	-0.2
Average hourly earnings ($)	9.36	9.52	9.68	9.82	10.10	10.36	10.58	—	1.7	1.4	2.9	2.6	2.1	—
Capital expenditures	7,197	7,493	8,330	8,858	9,362	—	—	—	11.2	6.3	5.7	—	—	—
Product Data														
Value of shipments[5]	305,753	326,728	340,733	359,713	363,943	369,988	379,661	390,051	4.3	5.6	1.2	1.7	2.6	2.7
Value of shipments (1987$)	305,753	313,412	311,497	318,608	323,763	326,835	330,977	334,341	-0.6	2.3	1.6	0.9	1.3	1.0
Trade Data														
Value of imports	—	—	18,744	19,834	19,779	20,869	20,785	21,087	—	5.8	-0.3	5.5	-0.4	1.5
Value of exports	—	—	17,070	18,473	19,918	22,504	23,101	24,307	—	8.2	7.8	13.0	2.7	5.2

[1]Estimate, except exports and imports.
[2]Estimate.
[3]Forecast.
[4]Value of all products and services sold by establishments in the food and kindred products industry.
[5]Value of products classified in the food and kindred products industry produced by all industries.

SOURCE: U.S. Department of Commerce: Bureau of the Census; International Trade Administration (ITA). Estimates and forecasts by ITA.

Health and Medical Services

The health care industry consists of public, private, and non-profit institutions. These institutions are hospitals; offices and clinics of medical doctors; nursing homes; other specialized health care facilities; managed care consisting of pre-paid plans such as health maintenance organizations (HMOs), preferred provider organizations (PPOs), and independent practice associations (IPAs).

The health care industry generated more than $942.5 billion in expenditures in 1993, and employed more than 10 million people including 2 million nurses, more than 650,000 doctors, and 150,000 dentists. The industry supports 126 medical schools and approximately 6,600 hospitals; 1,100 health insurance companies; and 25,600 nursing care facilities.

The nation's health care services industry includes thousands of independent medical practices and partnerships, as well as public and non-profit institutions, and major private corporations. America's complex health care system is a leader in the use of sophisticated and expensive technology.

Dynamics of the Health Care Industry

The dynamism of this industry is reflected in part by its contribution to the national output as well as the social well being of the population. Since Federally sponsored health care began in 1965, the nation's health care expenditures have risen from $41.6 billion, or about 6 percent of the gross domestic product (GDP), to an estimated $942.5 billion in 1993, representing more than 14 percent of GDP.

Modern technologies have contributed significantly to the worldwide delivery of high-quality health care. Besides developing new medical technologies, the United States probes the mysteries of disease through basic and clinical research. Through the development of new diagnostic tools and treatments, the United States increases the effectiveness of medical care worldwide. In 1991, total health research and development spending amounted to an estimated $25.6 billion with the Federal Government contributing more than half.

Many foreign students come to the United States to pursue their medical education. Upon completion, they return home to apply their knowledge and skills. In addition, many affluent foreign patients come to the United States for health care treatment. Education of foreign students and treatment of foreign patients contributes to a services surplus in the U.S. balance of payments.

Some aspects of the health care industry contribute to rising costs for consumers, businesses, states, and the Federal Government. There are also areas that most observers agree receive too few resources, such as immunizations against disease and other preventive procedures.

In regard to costs, the health care market is unique among industries. For most products and services, the purchaser knows the price, quantity, and quality of the goods before consumption. However, in the health care market price information is not generally available. To further complicate the cost issue, the health care industry is dominated by third-party providers in the form of private insurers and publicly funded Medicare and Medicaid that insulate patients from assessing price. The persistent rise in health care costs has absorbed much of the growth of employees' real compensation in the past two decades. Increasing health care costs discourage worker mobility, particularly among older workers who are concerned about losing insurance coverage. Approximately half the estimated 37 million uninsured Americans are in the 16-to-34 age group that is entering the workforce or generally undergoing the most frequent job changing. In the 1980's and 1990's, increasing health care costs have put pressures on budgets of Federal, state, and local governments. Both workers and governments have less to spend on other priorities.

Health Care Expenditures

The cost of the nation's health care (SIC 80) rose about 12 percent in 1993 to reach an estimated $942.5 billion, or about $3,900 per capita. By 1993, the U.S. health and medical care sector outlays amounted to 14 percent of the nation's economy. As health care expenditures have risen, there has been an accompanying shift from the private to the public sector. Private sector health care expenditures represented about 54 percent of total health care spending in 1992, down from 58 percent in 1980. Medicaid programs accounted for most of the 4 percent increase from 1980 to 1992.

International Comparisons

In 1990, on a per capita basis, health care expenditures among nations ranged from a low of $2 to more than $2,700. Low-income countries, such as Bangladesh, India, Pakistan, Egypt, and most sub-Saharan African countries with per capita income of $100 to $600 spend between $2 to $40 per individual on health care. Another set of countries called middle-income, whose per capita income ranges between $600 and $7,900, spend about $20 to $400 per capita on health care services. Among them are South Africa, Zimbabwe, Costa Rica, South Korea, Turkey, Poland, and the republics of the former Soviet Union. Established-market economies whose per capita income ranges between $5,000 and $34,000 consume per capita health care expenditures of $400 to $2,500. However, the United States, with a per capita income of $22,000, spent more than $2,700 on health care services in 1990.

With the exceptions of the United States and Egypt at the high and low extremes, per-capita expenditures fall in a general range for most countries, which suggests there are potential growth markets for health care in many countries. As countries become more developed, they spend a greater share of their income on health care services.

Health Care Services Revenue

Despite the 1.2 percent decline in the U.S. economy from 1990 to 1991, the Census Bureau estimated health care services revenue rose 9.5 percent from an estimated $521.7 billion to $571.3 billion. The highest revenue growth areas occurred in home health care services (19.2 percent), kidney dialysis centers (18 percent), specialty outpatient facilities (17.4 percent), and nursing and personal care facilities (15.7 percent). Hospitals realized a 10.8 percent increase, while offices and clinics of doctors of medicine grew 7.2 percent during that period. Hospitals accounted for 53 percent of all revenues for the health services industries in 1991. Hospital revenues rose by $29.7 billion to reach an estimated $305.9 billion in 1991, the Census Bureau reported.

According to the Census Bureau, these estimates are obtained from a sample of health care businesses and do not include income that self-employed individuals received for delivering health care services. From the estimated $521.7 billion in revenues, annual receipts for taxable firms in health services amounted to $245.7 billion. In 1990, hospital taxable receipts were estimated at $25.2 billion out of their $276.2 billion in revenue representing about 9.1 percent of total revenue.

Health Care Industry Employment

Health care is a leading employment sector in the economy. Employment rose steadily from 9.1 million in June 1990 to 10.2 million in June 1993, an average annual increase of 3.8 percent despite the 1990–91 recession and the weak economic recovery. Health care employment surpasses that of transportation and public utilities (5.7 million); wholesale trade (6.1 million); and finance, insurance, and real estate (6.6 million).

Employment has grown in all health care sectors, especially in home care, nursing, and personal care facilities, offices and clinics of medical doctors and dentists, and hospitals. The highest growth rate occurred in home health care services where employment rose an average annual pace of 17.6 percent from 290,900 in June 1990 to 473,100 in June 1993. Hospitals have the lowest rate of growth, but accounted for more than half of the total employment in the industry.

Medicare and Medicaid

Medicare and Medicaid programs are subject to statutory and regulatory charges; administrative rulings, interpretations, and determinations; and governmental restrictions. All such charges may materially increase or decrease payments to hospitals, physicians, and other medical providers. During the 1980's, as Medicare and Medicaid programs became costlier, their financing was reduced. Consequently, Federal and state governments tightened regulations on publicly financed medical programs.

Medicare and Medicaid pay hospitals, physicians, and other medical providers for services to qualified patients. In 1992, Medicare payments under its Hospital Insurance provision increased an estimated 8.5 percent to approximately $84 billion. Of the payouts, nearly $82 million was collected in the form of payroll taxes on employers and their workers. Medicare payments under the Supplementary Medicare Insurance program for physicians, outpatient hospital care, and other health services totaled nearly $51 billion in 1992. SMI enrollees paid premiums that covered less than 30 percent of the outlays. Government subsidies made up the difference.

Medicaid program expenditures grew by 33.2 percent to $100 billion in 1991, surpassing its 21.3 percent increase in 1990. This growth in expenditures was the result of 3 million additional people who qualified under the program due to the recession, Federal mandates to expand the program, and an increase in Federal payments to hospitals and nursing homes. In addition to the growth in the number of recipients, the growth in payment per recipient accelerated from $2,516 in 1989 to $3,412 in 1991.

Many states that administer the Medicaid program opted for donated funds and imposed provider-specific taxes to finance it. As states received more taxes and donations (T&D), the Federal matching fund share for

T&D automatically increased. These T&D programs increased both the Federal share to be paid for Medicaid and the Federal matching rate.

Home Health Care

Home-delivered health and medical services are being increasingly recognized as vital components of comprehensive health care and local health-planning activities. High hospital and nursing home care costs have underlined the need for alternative, less expensive ways to deliver care to the elderly sick who do not require continuous institutional care.

Many people with chronic illnesses can be adequately cared for in a home setting if some type of nursing care and supportive services are available. Home care agencies are filling this void. There were an estimated 12,500 home care agencies in the United States in 1992, including 6,129 Medicare certificate home health agencies, and 1,100 certified hospices. The remaining 5,258 were home health agencies, home care aid organizations, and hospices that do not participate in the Medicare program.

The number of Medicare-certified home health agencies increased nearly 6 percent from 5,785 in 1987 to 6,129 in 1992. During the same period, the number of proprietary home health agencies also increased nearly 6 percent from 1,846 to 1,953.

The latest National Medical Expenditure Survey indicates that a variety of health care providers administered home care services to 5.9 million Americans in 1987.

Demographics, technology, cost-effectiveness, and consumer choice should provide added momentum for the expansion of the home care sector. President Clinton's proposal for health care reform includes a significant initiative to expand home and community care for elderly and disabled Americans. Under health care reform, the nationally guaranteed benefit package also covers home-based care following an acute illness.

Continuing Care Retirement Communities

An estimated 900 continuing care retirement communities (CCRCs) in the United States provide continuing care for more than 270,000 residents who are still ambulatory. CCRCs provide coordinated housing and health-related services to older individuals under an agreement which may last as little as 1 year or as long as the life of the individual. CCRCs provide campus-style living with convenient services such as housekeeping, meals, and health care. The most significant of these is long-term nursing, which is often very expensive and usually not covered by Medicare.

Typically, a healthy, active elderly person moves into residential accommodations (apartment, townhouse, single-family home). Many activities and levels of care are available, such as assisted living and skilled nursing care. There is usually a resident health clinic that coordinates preventive health care and medical services.

Health care services are at the heart of the continuing care concept. These services include emergency response system, resident health clinic, wellness programs, health education, hospice services, nursing advice, physician services (primary and specialty), podiatry services, dental services, pharmacy services, therapies, assisted living, and nursing care.

Managed Health Care

Managed health care, a system of prepaid plans providing comprehensive coverage to voluntarily enrolled members, continues as the growth leader in the health care industry. Providers of managed care include health maintenance organizations (HMOs) and preferred provider organizations (PPOs), as well as traditional indemnity insurance companies.

Prepaid managed care is designed to control the use of health care services so that these services are provided cost effectively. Because traditional indemnity plans or programs do not control health care costs effectively, employers, including the U.S. Government, are offering their employees the opportunity to join HMOs and PPOs. Currently, HMOs and PPOs service more than 25 percent of the U.S. population, up from 3 percent in the 1970's.

The number of HMO plans decreased from 662 in 1987 to 544 in 1992, but the number of enrollees increased from 29.3 million to 41.4 million due to greater efforts by employers who prefer these plans. In 1993, HMO enrollment reached an estimated 45 million. The decline in the number of HMO plans is due to mergers and acquisitions and consolidations and terminations.

Every measure of HMO median rates of return was positive for 1990. Rates of return are measures of the ability of an HMO to generate funds. HMOs reported a median net rate of return on assets of 8.8 percent, a median net rate return on revenues of 2.5 percent, and a median net return on equity of 33 percent. Industry earnings in 1990 were $1.39 billion before taxes on revenue of

$45.61 billion. Eighty percent of HMOs reported positive gross income in 1990.

For the first quarter of 1993, industry data indicated HMOs had the highest overall profit gains for the 50 largest publicly traded U.S. health care companies. According to the *Jenks Health Care Business Report*, first-quarter earnings showed that seven HMOs listed among the Jenks Top 50 posted higher profits in the first quarter of 1993 than in the first quarter of 1992. The average gain was more than 40 percent.

PPOs, a modified version of HMOs, increased from 692 in 1987 to 978 in 1991. The number of eligible family members of those employees has increased from 28.0 million in 1987 to 85.0 million in 1991, a threefold increase.

PPOs have a weaker incentive to control utilization than do HMOs. PPOs permit enrollees to use non-plan providers (hospital and physicians), but cover less of non-plan provider costs. PPOs use various management programs such as recertification, concurrent review, and discharge planning to reduce patient use of unnecessary services.

The rapid growth of HMOs and other managed care organizations has somewhat restrained the expansion in hospital services, including the number of inpatient admissions. Some health care critics have expressed concern about the quality of care provided by managed health care organizations, although there is no real evidence that the trend toward managed care has had a negative effect on quality. Others maintain that managed care may have more of a positive effect on quality care than the traditional fee-for-service indemnity insurance system. Moreover, managed care plans offer more coverage than indemnity plans, especially in the area of preventive medical expenses where HMOs have ongoing wellness programs including programs for smoking cessation, prenatal care, and, diet and nutrition counseling.

Industry experts, health care administrators, legislators and various health care interest groups, realizing that managed care is rapidly expanding, are beginning to ask whether managed care companies can assure patients that the quality of care they receive will be protected. As a result, Congress has mandated peer review of HMOs and other competitive medical plans by professional review organizations. The indications are that with a few adjustments these managed care organizations will continue to play a leading role in providing health care to the nation.

Managed competition lies at the heart of the President's proposal to reduce health care costs, and to provide care for the uninsured. Reform or not, managed care through HMOs and PPOs is already dominating the market.

INTERNATIONAL COMPETITIVENESS

Without reform, the annual cost of health care for a family in the United States may reach $14,000 by the end of the decade. In 1992, average per capita spending for health care in the United States totaled $3,160 a year, up from $1,000 in 1980. The United States spends twice as much on health care as the average for the 24 industrialized countries in Europe and North America. The economic drain on U.S. society represented by higher and rising health care costs threatens to jeopardize the United States' competitive position in international trade.

Although the United States spends more on health care than any other industrialized nation, a lower proportion of U.S. citizens have health insurance coverage and a typical insurance policy provides less coverage than in any other industrialized nation.

According to industry studies, the greater amount of spending for health care in the United States goes to support:

- Inappropriate care and inefficient systems—some estimates put the level of unnecessary tests and procedures at $130 billion per year.
- Regulation and administration—estimates of insurance overhead account for nearly 25 percent of total spending. By contrast, administrative costs in other industrialized countries total 11 percent or less.

Over the past 20 years, the wages of U.S. workers have fallen in real terms while health care costs have climbed 10 to 15 percent each year. For small businesses, premiums have risen by as much as 50 percent annually. Skyrocketing health care costs make it harder for U.S. companies to compete in the global marketplace. Health care costs add more than $1,100 dollars to the price of every car manufactured in the United States—Japan spends half of this amount. In 1990, General Motors spent $3.2 billion in medical coverage for its 1.9 million employees and retirees. That is more than the company spent on steel.

Without health care reform, it is projected that the cost of health care will rise from 14 percent of GDP today to 18 percent in the year 2000. In other words, without reform, in less than 10 years, almost one dollar out of every five dollars earned by people living in the United States will go to cover the cost of health care.

If the United States were able through health reform to achieve a level of spending comparable to other countries, the United States could save about 4 percent of GDP. Those savings could be reallocated to investments in other areas such as training and production, thus enhancing the U.S. competitive position.

LONG-TERM PROSPECTS

The health care system will likely be reformed based on managed competition to provide health care access to the uninsured and accomplish cost efficiency. Comprehensive health care reform will take many years and its success will depend on controlling costs and maintaining quality. Increases in funding will most likely be directed at home nursing to accommodate long-term care needs. Consequently, home care will continue to gain market share. More medical technology will be developed to be used in the home care sector.

The implementation and success of health care reform will require the cooperation of providers, investors, and consumers. Strong measures will have to be introduced so as to eliminate billions of dollars of wasted resources in providing health care to the nation. The nation's schools and colleges may introduce health care consciousness into the curriculum as a way to help reduce costs.

It is difficult to accurately project health care costs for the next 5 years without knowing the outcome of health care reform. However, without reform, health care expenditures are projected to rise by an average annual rate of growth of 13.5 percent during the next 5 years.—*Simon Francis, Office of Service Industries (202) 482-2697.*

Reasons for Rising Health Care Expenditures

Factors contributing to the rising costs of health care are numerous and well-known. They include the following:

- Use of sophisticated, expensive technologies.
- Duplication of tests and sometimes duplication of technologies which yield similar results.
- Increases in variety and frequency of treatments including arguably unnecessary tests.
- Increasing number and longevity of the elderly.
- Regulations that result in cost shifting rather than cost reduction.
- Increasing number of accidents and crimes that require emergency medical services.
- Limited competition and restrictive work rules in the health care delivery system.
- Labor intensiveness and rapid average earnings growth for health care professionals and executives.
- Built-in inflation in the health care delivery system.
- Other major factors, which cost billions of dollars each year, are fraud, administrative waste, malpractice insurance, excessive surgical procedures, a wide range of prices for similar services, and double health coverage including medigap.

Glossary

Medicaid—Medicaid is a federally supported and state-administered assistance program providing medical care for certain low-income individuals and families. Medicaid covered more than 31.2 million people at a cost of $91.5 billion in 1992.

Medicare—A U.S. government program that pays hospitals, physicians, and other medical providers for serving patients aged 65 years and older, certain disabled people, and most persons with end-stage renal disease (ESRD).

Medicare enrolls approximately 34 million people, including 3.5 million disabled. An estimated 97 percent of Medicare enrollees are elderly. Medicare consists of two basic programs: Part A, or Hospital Insurance (HI) and Part B, or Supplementary Medical Insurance (SMI).

Hospital Insurance (HI)—HI is the Medicare program that pays for inpatient hospital care, skilled nursing facility care, home healthcare, and hospice care. Payments under the HI Program are made from a trust fund which is financed primarily from payroll taxes. In 1993, employees and employers each paid a payroll tax of 1.45 percent on income up to $135,000. Self-employed persons paid 2.9 percent in 1992 and 1993.

Supplementary Medicare Insurance (SMI)—The SMI program pays for services from physicians, outpatient hospital services, home health agencies, independent laboratories, and group practice prepayments. SMI funding comes primarily from government contributions, plus premiums paid by eligible people, those over 65 years old and disabled people under 65.

Continuing Care Retirement Communities (CCRCs)— CCRCs in the United States provide continuing care for more than 270,000 Americans aged 75 to 78. CCRCs provide coordinated housing and health-related services to older individuals under an agreement which may last as little as one year or as long as the life of the individual.

CCRCs services include emergency response system, resident health clinic, wellness programs, health education, hospice services, nursing advice, physician services (primary and specialty), podiatry services, dental services, pharmacy services, therapies, assisted living, and nursing care.

Continuing care has three different healthcare coverages based upon the agreement one has with the CCRC: extensive, fee-for-service, and modified.

Extensive Agreement—The extensive agreement covers most health-related services including long-term care. The services are provided without additional costs.

Fee-for-Service Agreement—The fee-for-service agreement requires payment for health-related services, including long-term care, as they are delivered.

Modified Agreement—The modified agreement covers some health-related services, including some long-term care. The agreement is expressed as a number of days per year or as a lifetime of long-term care.

Health Maintenance Organization (HMO)—HMOs provide "managed healthcare" services, usually in their own facilities.

Preferred Provider Organizations (PPO)—PPOs provide "managed healthcare" services. PPOs are a modified version of HMOs. PPO enrollees are offered incentives to limit their provider selection to preferred providers.

Home Health Care—Home healthcare is a method of providing services to disabled people in their homes rather than in medical facilities.

During 1992, general government contributions amounted to $38.7 billion or 72.7 percent of all SMI income. The remaining $14.5 billion or 27.3 percent came from premiums paid by SMI enrollees, interest, and other income. About 33.8 million persons were enrolled under SMI in 1992.

Home Care Agencies—Home health agencies, home care aid organizations, and hospices are known as home care agencies.

Managed Health Care—Managed healthcare is a system of prepaid plans providing comprehensive coverage to voluntarily enrolled members. Managed healthcare typically covers professional fees, hospital services, diagnostic services, emergency healthcare services, limited mental services, medical treatment for drug or alcohol abuse, home health services, and preventive healthcare.

Trends and Forecasts: Health and Medical Services

(in billions of dollars except as noted)

Item	1987	1988	1989	1990	1991[1]	1992[2]	1993[2]	1994[3]	Percent Change (1987-1994) 87-88	88-89	89-90	90-91	91-92	92-93	93-94
National health expenditures	495.2	547.2	605.4	676.3	753.1	840.4	942.5	1,060.5	10.5	10.6	11.7	11.4	11.6	12.1	12.5
Health services and supplies	476.9	526.2	583.6	652.4	728.6	813.9	914.0	1,029.6	10.3	10.9	11.8	11.7	11.7	12.3	12.6
Personal healthcare	439.3	482.8	530.9	591.5	660.2	739.0	830.2	934.8	9.9	10.0	11.4	11.6	11.9	12.3	12.6
Hospital	194.2	212.0	232.4	258.1	288.6	323.2	363.4	408.8	9.2	9.6	11.1	11.8	12.0	12.4	12.5
Physicians' services	93.0	105.1	116.1	128.8	142.0	157.1	175.2	194.9	13.0	10.5	10.9	10.2	10.6	11.5	11.2
Dentists services	27.1	29.4	31.6	34.1	37.1	40.4	44.2	47.5	8.5	7.5	7.9	8.8	8.9	9.4	7.5
Other professional services	21.1	23.8	27.1	30.7	35.8	41.7	47.4	54.0	12.8	13.9	13.3	16.6	16.5	13.7	13.9
Home health	4.1	4.5	5.6	7.6	9.8	12.7	16.5	22.2	9.8	24.4	35.7	28.9	29.6	29.9	34.5
Nondurable medical products	43.2	46.3	50.5	55.6	60.7	66.4	72.6	80.2	7.2	9.1	10.1	9.2	9.4	9.3	10.5
Durable medical equipment	9.1	10.1	10.4	11.7	12.4	13.2	14.2	15.5	11.0	3.0	12.5	6.0	6.5	7.6	9.2
Nursing home care	39.7	42.8	47.7	53.3	59.8	67.3	76.0	85.5	7.8	11.4	11.7	12.2	12.5	12.9	12.5
Other personal health care	7.8	8.7	9.8	11.5	14.0	17.0	20.7	25.2	11.5	12.6	17.3	21.7	21.4	21.8	21.7
Administration	23.0	26.9	33.8	38.9	43.9	48.6	54.3	61.9	17.0	25.7	15.1	12.9	10.7	11.7	14.0
Government public health activity	14.6	16.6	18.9	22.0	24.5	26.3	29.4	32.9	13.7	13.9	16.4	11.4	7.3	11.8	11.9
Research and construction	18.2	21.0	21.8	23.9	24.5	26.5	28.5	30.8	15.4	3.8	9.6	2.5	8.2	7.5	8.1
Research[4]	9.0	10.3	11.0	11.9	12.6	13.3	14.1	15.0	14.4	6.8	8.2	5.9	5.6	6.0	6.4
Construction[5]	9.2	10.7	10.8	12.0	11.9	13.2	14.4	15.8	16.3	0.9	11.1	-0.8	10.9	9.1	9.7

[1] Preliminary.
[2] Estimate.
[3] Forecast.
[4] Research and development expenditures of drug companies and other manufacturers and providers of medical equipment and supplies are excluded from "research expenditures," but they are included in the expenditure class in which the product falls.
[5] Benchmark data by HCFA.

NOTE: Numbers may not add to totals because of rounding.

SOURCE: U.S. Department of Health and Human Services: Health Care Financing Administration (HCFA), Office of the Actuary; U.S. Department of Commerce: International Trade Administration (ITA). Estimates and forecasts by ITA.

International Health Care Spending

(in dollars except as noted)

Country	Income per capita[1]	Spending per capita[2]	Health care expenditures as a percent of 1990 GDP		
			Public	Private	Total
Mozambique	80	5	4.4	1.5	5.9
Bangladesh	220	7	1.8	1.9	3.7
Egypt	610	18	1.0	1.6	2.6
India	330	21	1.3	4.7	6.0
Bolivia	650	25	2.4	1.6	4.0
Poland	1,790	83	4.1	1.0	5.1
Mexico	3,030	89	1.6	1.6	3.2
Brazil	2,940	132	2.8	1.4	4.2
South Africa	2,560	158	3.2	2.4	5.6
South Korea	6,340	377	2.7	3.9	6.6
United Kingdom	16,550	1,039	5.2	0.9	6.1
France	20,380	1,869	6.6	2.3	8.9
Canada	20,440	1,945	6.8	2.4	9.2
Sweden	25,110	2,343	7.9	0.9	8.8
United States	22,240	2,763	5.6	7.0	12.6

[1]Gross domestic product per capita in 1991.
[2]Health care expenditures per capita in 1990.

SOURCE: World Bank, *World Development Report 1993*.

Insurance

Life Insurance

Premium receipts of life insurance companies grew nearly 6 percent in 1993 to $298.9 billion. Strong annuity sales and modest growth in health premiums led this growth. Life insurance sales were flat. Life insurance in force—the total face value of all policies—grew very little in 1993.

The life insurance industry consists of more than 1,700 companies that engage in underwriting life insurance and annuities. Life insurance companies also engage significantly in underwriting accident and health insurance, and in managing pension and trust funds. These companies are classified mostly in SIC 631 "Life Insurance" and SIC 6321 "Accident and Health Insurance." Stock companies, owned by shareholders, and mutual companies, owned by policyholders, are the two main types of insurance providers.

Life insurance companies get their premium income from three major product areas: life insurance, annuities, and health insurance. There was little growth in premium receipts for life insurance products in 1993. Sales of traditional whole life and term insurance for individuals fell considerably. This was offset by growth in investment-type products—variable and universal and their hybrids—in which policyholders assume much or most of the financial risk of the underlying assets. Many consumers who bought investment-type life insurance were looking for long-term yields higher than banks and money market funds offered. Sales of group life insurance fell in 1993.

Income from individual and group annuities rose strongly to $132.6 billion in 1992 and this growth continued into 1993. Despite some consumer confidence problems, individual annuities sold extremely well in 1993 as people with maturing bank certificates of deposit or qualified retirement plans often rolled over the funds into higher-yielding annuities, especially variable products. Insurers with strong balance sheets did well with group annuities. In particular, guaranteed investment contracts (GICs) offered by insurers remained popular with 401(k) plans—the fastest growing part of the retirement investment market.

Premium growth from health insurance increased again in 1992 and 1993. Cost pressures were the chief reason for this growth. The trend toward managed health care, however, has tempered the increase of health premiums for life insurers. Life insurance companies are major providers of health insurance. Other providers of health insurance include Blue Cross/Blue Shield plans, property/casualty insurers, self-funded employer plans, and government programs.

Growth in investment income for insurers in 1992 and 1993 fell off as interest rates dropped. Other income fell in 1992 because insurers were taking capital losses on mortgages and other troubled assets.

The assets of life insurers increased an estimated 7.5 percent in 1993 to $1.79 trillion. The proportion of corporate bonds remained level from 1991 to 1992 because of the improvements in the bond market, while equities increased their proportion of life insurers assets. The commercial mortgage portfolio of insurers declined both absolutely and as a proportion of assets from 1991 to 1992. Assets consist mainly of financial instruments such as stocks and bonds. These assets back insurance and annuity reserves required to pay expected claims and provide the necessary surplus and capital to meet solvency standards.

The life insurance industry remained financially sound in 1993. Balance sheets improved in 1992 and 1993 for most companies as they adjusted to the new risk-based capital standards (see Key Developments section). In 1991, a stagnant economy, a depressed real estate market, excessive investments in low-grade corporate bonds, and a sharp drop in consumer confidence were the immediate causes of several large, well-publicized failures. Since then, the bond market has improved, the stock market has grown strongly, and the decline in real estate has leveled off in many regions, although real estate holdings remain the problem for many companies. The overall quality of assets in the portfolios of life insurance companies has improved, demonstrated by a shift from commercial mortgages to more conservative assets such as higher-grade bonds.

Life insurance companies cut operating costs by reducing staff and home office expenses and by focusing on reform of their agency and product distribution systems. As a result, employment in the industry fell again in 1993 to 520,800, down from 537,400. Merger and acquisition activity was strong. Many insurers acquired pieces of troubled companies, while some divested unprofitable product lines and operations. Foreign insurers have been active in acquisitions and investments in the United States, although there was a decrease in this activity in 1992.

Key Developments

Although the financial situation of the industry has improved, the solvency of the insurance industry was still the main issue of 1993, as it has been since 1991 when several large life insurers failed. Congressional inquiries on solvency have focused on the ability of the current state regulatory system to protect the public against insurance company failures. Critics of state regulation contend that the industry is too big, too diverse, and too international for 50 different state regulators to supervise the market and to protect consumers effectively.

Several pieces of legislation were introduced in Congress in 1993 calling for a direct federal role in insurance regulation. Some legislative proposals more narrowly address various aspects of insurance solvency regulation, such as setting federal requirements for foreign insurers and strengthening federal laws for insurance fraud and abuse.

Proponents of state regulation, led by the state regulators, claim the current system has done a good job of protecting policyholders and providing an efficient market, especially compared to what they label as "federal mismanagement" of the banking and savings and loan industries. The states, propelled by the solvency policing program of the National Association of Insurance Commissioners (NAIC), are moving to change licensing and financial standards, screening and surveillance procedures of insurers, and guaranty fund programs and insolvency procedures. New financial standards include risk-based capital requirements based on the amount of assets, underwriting, and other risks an insurer faces, in addition to the current minimum capital and surplus requirements. Under the program, the NAIC will certify any state meeting these standards. Thus, insurers from certified states are more easily received and recognized in other states. The NAIC has certified 22 states so far and more are expected by 1994.

The integration of financial services industries remains a key issue affecting competition in insurance. For years, the banking industry and others have argued that allowing banks to operate more fully in the insurance and securities industries would increase competition in financial services, provide stability to the financial marketplace, improve economic and capital market efficiencies, and provide greater convenience for consumers. In addition, regulatory and market developments in Europe and elsewhere point to a competitive need to integrate U.S. financial services markets. Opponents argue that current restrictions are necessary to protect consumers from unfair practices and to assure the soundness of financial institutions. They say, for example, that banks are in a strong position to unduly tie insurance sales to loans. Many also fear integrating the sectors will only compound current solvency problems in each.

Health care reform is a key U.S. public policy issue. It is widely recognized that health care costs are out of control and that many people have no health insurance or inadequate coverage. In September 1993, the Clinton Administration unveiled its health care plan focusing on universal coverage for all Americans and mandatory employer contributions to pay for health insurance premiums. The proposal is expected to be the subject of protracted congressional debate and intense lobbying from the health care industry and consumers.

LONG-TERM PROSPECTS

The long-term prospects for life insurance and annuity products of life insurance companies are fairly good. Demographic variables, such as income growth, wealth accumulation, population and workforce changes, and home ownership will determine the demand for insurance products over the long term. The rate of personal savings in the United States will rise with the movement of the baby-boom population into middle age. The aging of the baby-boom population will raise the demand of individuals for products that provide for retirement income and for health care financing. Health care reform, however, will likely diminish the growth of private health insurance, especially indemnity insurance. New health products and markets, such as long-term health insurance, probably will not replace business lost elsewhere.

Competition in insurance markets will increase. Banks may be authorized to sell and underwrite insurance. Banks, mutual funds and other financial institutions will be offering investment and savings products that directly compete with insurance and annuity products. Foreign insurers will continue to expand into the largely unrestricted U.S. market.

Increased competition, changes in health care financing, and lingering problems in real estate will keep the number of insolvencies up over the next few years. These real estate problems will persist for a couple of years as commercial mortgages mature, but then diminish as insurers restructure their portfolios or real estate markets turn around. The problem of insolvencies has already prompted state level action to strengthen financial standards and tighten the regulation of insurance companies. If the states fail to address the problems adequately, a larger Federal role in insurance regulation may follow.

These conflicting forces and issues will change the nature of industry. Profits margins will likely remain thin and returns on equity will remain below historical levels over the next few years. To compete, life insurance companies will have to specialize in certain market segments, reduce operating costs, increase efficiency and service quality, and improve management of their assets and liabilities. Larger, better capitalized companies will get a bigger share of the market, but smaller niche players will be strong competitors in selected markets.

There also will be pressure on the distribution system to reduce costs. Agents will have to accept less compensation or increase production. Insurers will be forced to look for more cost-efficient alternatives such as direct mail, other financial institutions, or financial advisors and consultants. Insurers will be seeking new information and communications technology to increase efficiency in underwriting, distributing, investment, claims, and administrative activities.

Diminished returns on life insurance in the United States also will prompt the stronger insurance companies to look for other investment opportunities. Many life insurance companies, mainly through holding companies, have moved or will move into related financial services including securities, banking activities, and real estate. More U.S. life insurance companies will take advantage of expanding foreign markets, especially in Europe, Asia, and Mexico with or without the North American Free Trade Agreement.

Property/Casualty Insurance

Net written premiums for property/casualty insurance increased 3.5 percent to an estimated $235.5 billion for 1993. Increasing rates in personal lines, such as automobile and homeowners' insurance, and selected commercial lines were the main reason for this growth. Rates in most commercial lines, however, remained flat in 1993 because of ample capital in the industry and competition from alternative risk-financing methods. In addition, a slow growing, low-inflation economy helped to minimize insured losses, which aided operating earnings. A decline in operating expenses, evidenced by sharp drops in industry employment, also benefitted earnings. Despite reduced investment income, realized capital gains added to overall earnings in 1993.

Although damage from the Midwestern floods in the summer of 1993 totaled an estimated $10 billion, less than $1 billion was privately insured and should not have a major impact on the insurance industry. Barring any other major disasters for the remainder of 1993, the industry's overall earnings and surplus increases should be positive.

The property/casualty insurance industry provides financial protection for individuals, commercial businesses, and others against losses of property or losses by third parties for which the insured is liable. P/C insurance companies are classified in SIC 633 "Fire, Marine and Casualty Insurance." There are an estimated 3,800 P/C companies. Most are organized as stock companies, some as mutual companies.

The biggest increase in premiums for property/casualty insurers in 1992 was private automobile insurance that grew $5.6 billion to $88.4 billion. Much of this growth is attributed to rate increases in many states because of prior underwriting losses.

In commercial lines, premiums for workers' compensation dropped 5 percent in 1992 to $29.7 billion following a decade of strong growth. The slow-growth economy and smaller rate increases helped spur the decline of premiums for workers' compensation. Premiums in other commercial lines either fell or were flat in 1992, continuing the trend begun in 1991. Most notably, liability other than automobile fell again for the fifth year in a row. The use of other risk financing alternatives has especially hit premium growth in liability lines. The decline in liability lines will likely continue in 1993 due to overcapacity, the slow-growth economy, and reduced inflation. A slow economy reduces the number of claims (excluding catastrophe losses) and a reduction in inflation reduces the increase in costs of those claims—thus premium increases can be reduced.

In addition, the abundance of capital kept commercial rates low. The amount of capital available to underwrite risks determines the supply of insurance protection. With an adequate supply of capital, rates (prices) will stay low. A relative decrease in capital—as often happens after major catastrophes—suggests rates in the industry will move upward.

The overall financial situation of P/C insurers diminished in 1992 due to the worst year ever for catastrophe losses. Operating losses were $3.3 billion, reflecting the impact of about $23 billion in catastrophe losses. Despite the operating losses, policyholders' surplus grew in 1992 due to earnings from investments. The rate of insolvencies remained at approximately the same levels of recent years. Hurricane Andrew and other catastrophes pushed many smaller insurers who were overexposed in the disaster areas into insolvency, and stressed the balance sheet of many larger insurers.

Reinsurance premiums to U.S. professional reinsurance companies—those companies that sell insurance that primary insurance companies buy to reduce and spread their risks—increased to nearly $14 billion in 1992, up from $12.7 billion. Reinsurance premiums to non-U.S. reinsurers increased to $10.5 billion in 1992, up from $10 billion. These premium increases were due mainly to rate increases for catastrophe risks and liability lines and reflect even stronger rate increases and tighter markets in Europe and elsewhere. The same trend continued through 1993. The upturn in reinsurance rates suggests that rates in the U.S. primary market may increase soon. However, increased reinsurance rates have not affected the primary market much yet because primary insurers retain most of their risks anyway and have adequate capital.

Asset quality is not a problem for P/C insurers as investments are relatively liquid and secure. There is a concern, however, that insurers have not increased reserves for losses sufficiently. This could affect future performance. Insurers cashed out many of their investments to pay for record losses. But the slow economy and continued low inflation allowed many insurers to reduce their reserves. In addition, some analysts question the reliability of collecting from reinsurance companies.

Insurers moved to streamline operations and reduce expenses in 1992 and 1993. Employment fell 1.6 percent in 1992 and another 1.4 percent in 1993 to stand at 545,400. Many insurers are restructuring and refocusing on core business. Merger and acquisition activity was strong in 1991 and 1992, highlighted by several large acquisitions by foreign firms in 1991. In addition, agents and brokers reported falling income because of reduced commissions and slower business. Many insurers are leaving personal lines to insurers that write the business through their own employees rather than through agents.

LONG-TERM PROSPECTS

The long-term prospects of the industry will depend mostly on how much and how fast rates increase over the next several years. Commercial rates will head upward, but will be sporadic and limited. A number of factors suggest rates are heading upward. Reinsurance rates for catastrophe risks are high and increasing. In addition, there is a general fear that many companies have inadequate loss reserves. Thus, insurers may need to start rate increases to bring reserves to adequate levels or face pressure from regulators, rating agencies, and stockholders.

Rate increases will be limited by line of business and concern about market share. Capital in the industry is relatively strong, and new capital keeps coming into the industry. Alternative risk-financing markets are strong and business would flee from commercial insurers to these markets if rates jumped. Rates will stay down if low inflation and slow economic growth keep losses in check. Also, pressure from consumer groups will hold rates in personal lines in check.

In this environment, stronger or more efficient companies with a better capital position will get larger market shares. This will be particularly true as the industry adjusts and restructures for risk-based capital standards. Weaker companies will need to streamline or consolidate. They may have to join with stronger companies or find other capital sources. Foreign investment may provide some of this capital. Thus, merger and acquisition activity will likely remain high for the next few years.

Some companies will not survive. Insolvencies could increase if the economy falls or catastrophe losses jump suddenly. The failure of a large P/C company, although not foreseen, could strain the capacity of state guaranty funds. This could lead to other failures as the effects of the failure move through the industry.—*M. Bruce McAdam, Office of Service Industries (202) 482-0346.*

Trends and Forecasts: Life/Health Insurance

(in billions of dollars except as noted)

Item	1987	1988	1989	1990	1991	1992	1993[1]	1994[2]	Percent Change (1989–1994) 88–89	89–90	90–91	91–92	92–93	93–94
Premium receipts	213.0	229.1	244.4	264.0	263.8	282.1	298.9	316.8	6.7	8.0	-0.1	6.9	6.0	6.0
Life insurance in force[3]	7,452.5	8,020.2	8,694.0	9,392.6	9,986.3	10,405.8	10,822.0	11,254.9	8.4	8.0	6.3	4.2	4.0	4.0
Life insurance assets	1,044.5	1,166.9	1,299.8	1,408.2	1,551.2	1,664.5	1,789.3	1,914.6	11.4	8.3	10.2	7.3	7.5	7.0
Employment: (000)[4]														
Life insurance (SIC 6311)	578.0	570.4	550.2	547.5	560.0	537.4	520.8	510.4	-3.5	-0.5	2.3	-4.0	-3.1	-2.0
Health insurance (SIC 6301)	202.1	216.5	228.1	241.6	258.7	268.3	270.3	273.0	5.4	5.9	7.1	3.7	0.7	1.0

[1]Estimate.
[2]Forecast.
[3]Excludes foreign business.
[4]Employees on payroll only. Does not include agents not directly employed by insurers.

SOURCE: American Council of Life Insurance; U.S. Department of Labor; Bureau of Labor Statistics. Estimates and forecasts by the U.S. Department of Commerce, International Trade Administration.

World Insurance Markets 1991 Premiums

(billions of dollars)

Countries	Total[1]	Life	Nonlife[2]
Total, all countries	1,414.4	743.6	670.7
United States	486.8	202.9	283.9
Canada	33.9	17.1	16.7
Europe	468.6	231.7	236.9
United Kingdom	114.7	75.6	39.1
Germany	104.3	40.6	63.8
France	80.6	44.1	36.5
Italy	34.5	9.2	25.3
Netherlands	25.9	14.1	11.8
Spain	20.5	6.2	14.3
Asia	371.6	266.7	104.9
Japan	307.8	225.6	82.2
South Korea	31.7	25.5	6.2
Taiwan	8.3	5.8	2.5
Latin America	14.9	3.2	11.6
Mexico	3.5	1.3	2.3
Africa	15.7	10.3	5.4
Oceania[3]	22.9	11.7	11.2

[1]Numbers may not add due to rounding.
[2]Nonlife business includes accident and health insurance as well as property/casualty insurance.
[3]Includes Australia, New Zealand, and South Pacific Islands.
SOURCE: *Sigma*, 1993, Swiss Reinsurance Company.

Trends and Forecasts: Property/Casualty Insurance

(in billions of dollars except as noted)

Item	1987	1988	1989	1990	1991	1992	1993[1]	1994[2]	Percent Change (1989–1994) 88–89	89–90	90–91	91–92	92–93	93–94
Net written premiums	193.2	202.0	208.4	217.8	223.0	227.5	235.5	244.9	3.2	4.5	2.4	2.0	3.5	4.0
Assets	426.7	476.9	527.0	556.3	601.4	637.3	661.5	689.3	10.5	5.6	8.1	6.0	3.8	4.2
Employment (000) (SIC 633)	526.1	540.7	547.8	557.3	561.9	552.9	545.4	539.5	1.3	1.7	0.8	-1.6	-1.4	-1.1

[1]Estimate.
[2]Forecast.

SOURCE: A.M. Best Co., *Best Aggregates and Averages;* U.S. Department of Labor, Bureau of Labor Statistics. Estimates and forecasts by U.S. Department of Commerce, International Trade Administration.

Net Written Premiums by Line of Business, 1987–92

(in billions of dollars)

Item	1987	1988	1989	1990	1991	1992
Total, all lines	193.2	202.0	208.4	217.8	223.0	227.5
Personal lines	80.9	86.6	91.2	97.0	102.1	108.9
Private automobile[1]	64.3	69.5	73.6	78.4	82.8	88.4
Homeowners' multiple peril	16.7	17.1	17.7	18.6	19.3	20.5
Commercial lines[2]	112.3	115.4	117.2	120.8	120.9	118.6
Commercial automobile[1]	16.9	16.9	17.3	17.0	16.6	16.1
Liability other than auto	24.9	23.1	22.7	22.1	20.9	21.1
Fire and allied lines	7.7	6.9	7.0	7.1	7.2	7.1
Commercial multiple peril	17.2	17.7	17.5	17.7	17.0	16.4
Workers' compensation	23.4	26.1	28.5	31.0	31.3	29.7
Marine, inland and ocean	5.5	5.5	5.6	5.7	5.5	5.5
Accident and health	3.8	4.7	4.6	5.0	5.1	5.4
Other lines	12.8	14.5	14.2	15.2	17.4	17.3

[1]Includes premiums for automobile liability and physical damage.
[2]May include some personal insurance, such as accident or health, but data cannot be broken out readily.

NOTE: Detail may not add to total due to rounding.
SOURCE: A.M. Best Co., *Best's Aggregates and Averages,* Property-Casualty Editions.

Medical and Dental Instruments and Supplies

The U.S. medical and dental instruments and supplies industry is a diverse and technologically dynamic field, consisting of five specific industry sectors. These five sectors are surgical and medical instruments (SIC 3841), surgical appliances and supplies (SIC 3842), dental equipment and supplies (SIC 3843), X-ray apparatus and tubes (SIC 3844), and electromedical equipment (SIC 3845). For the first time, this chapter also includes sections covering ophthalmic goods (SIC 3851), and used and refurbished medical equipment.

The five medical industries manufacture a wide range of health care products used to diagnose and treat patients, ranging from tongue depressors to highly sophisticated, diagnostic devices that can provide clear images of internal organs. Medical items not covered in this chapter include *in vitro* and *in vivo* diagnostics, classified under SIC 2835, and surgical gloves, condoms, and similar latex-based products that fall under fabricated rubber products, not elsewhere classified (SIC 3069).

Despite the slow growth in the domestic economy and buyers' resistance in a cost-conscious, health-care environment, the value of shipments by the U.S. medical equipment and supplies industry rose more than 8 percent in 1993. This increase was partly due to the strong overseas demand for U.S. medical equipment. Industry employment increased to an estimated 287,000. Among the major medical product groupings, the surgical appliances and supplies segment, which accounted for 38 percent of the total medical equipment shipments, experienced another year of strong growth, at a rate of nearly 10 percent in constant dollars, reaching $13.2 billion in 1993. Manufacturers of surgical and medical instruments also experienced solid growth, as shipments increased nearly 7 percent to $11 billion. However, the demand for capital-intensive electromedical equipment was adversely affected by cost-containment pressures and concerns over potential changes in reimbursement policy and health care reform. Constant-dollar shipments of electromedical equipment grew at less than 1 percent to $5.8 billion in 1993, compared to nearly 3 percent during 1992. Affected by similar factors, industry shipments of the dental equipment and supplies industry grew at a rate of only 2 percent in constant dollars to $1.8 billion in 1993, compared to the average growth rate of 5 percent from 1989 to 1991.

In the global market, exports continued to be the strength of the U.S. medical and dental equipment and supplies industry, accounting for 23 percent of 1993 industry shipments. Experiencing strong growth in many overseas medical equipment markets, U.S. vendors generated a record trade surplus of $3.5 billion in 1993. Of the total $8.1 billion in exports, 39 percent were shipped to the European Community (EC), 14 percent to Japan, and 18 percent to Canada and Mexico. Together, these markets represented 71 percent of the total U.S. medical equipment and supplies exports. In addition, several Asian markets provided significant growth for U.S. exports in 1993. For example U.S. exports of medical equipment to South Korea increased 25 percent from 1992; Singapore, 23 percent; Hong Kong, 20 percent; and China 13 percent.

Medical Device Regulations

After a series of congressional hearings on the U.S. Food and Drug Administration's medical device approval process, the Subcommittee on Oversight and Investigations of the House Committee on Energy and Commerce issued its findings. In a report entitled, "Reforms Needed in the Organization, Management, and Resources of the Food and Drug Administration's Center for Devices and Radiological Health," the subcommittee concluded that there had been a growing adversarial relationship between the FDA and the medical device industry because of increasing application processing time. The subcommittee recommended that FDA immediately undertake substantial reforms to speed the device review process so that the industry could maintain its global competitiveness.

Despite the fact that FDA has the most stringent and lengthy review and approval process in the world, the U.S. medical device industry, in some respects, may have benefited from its regulations. For example, U.S. exporters gain a competitive advantage from FDA-approved products because some international markets more readily accept them as being of high quality and safe. However, given the strong demand for U.S. exports, recent delays in the FDA's product-approval process have not only hindered the ability of U.S. firms to market leading-edge products domestically, but also adversely affected their competitiveness overseas.

In June 1993, in response to the industry's concerns over FDA's delays, FDA began to streamline its product-approval process so that safe and effective medical devices can reach markets in a more timely and competitive manner.

Global Harmonization

The FDA is participating in the Global Harmonization Task Force, which includes government and medical device industry representatives from the European Community, the United States, Japan, and Canada. The purpose of the task force is to develop an internationally accepted, quality standard for medical devices. Specifically, the task force is involved in developing common guidance documents, programs for joint inspections, and exchange of information. The objective is to set up a single quality inspection that might be accepted by regulators in any of the major world markets. This system would give companies in member countries better access to each other's markets.

INTERNATIONAL COMPETITIVENESS

U.S. medical and dental equipment manufacturers continued to be very active in the $81 billion global market, supplying 52 percent of the world output. U.S. exports of medical equipment and supplies generated a $3.5 billion trade surplus in 1993, the largest to date. Despite the international economic slowdown affecting several developed countries that are major buyers of U.S. medical equipment and supplies, the demand for U.S. medical products in developed countries continued to expand. For example, the EC economy, which grew at less than 1 percent in 1993, purchased $3.2 billion of U.S. medical equipment to contribute to a $1.2 billion overall U.S. trade surplus with the EC. Canada, recovering moderately from a recession, increased purchases from the United States by 8 percent to $988 million in 1993. Although Japan's economic growth was weak in 1993, Japan increased its purchases of U.S. medical and dental products by 18 percent. However, in Japan, the market share for U.S. medical equipment manufacturers, including U.S. subsidiaries in Japan, remained at 20 percent. The aging population, upgrading of health care systems, and the creation of a single market in Europe are some factors contributing to the increase in demand for medical equipment abroad.

LONG-TERM PROSPECTS

Progress in areas such as optical tomography, imaging, and laser technology is likely to further improve U.S. competitiveness in advanced medical equipment. Optical tomography is one example of an emerging U.S. technology with the potential to save lives and cut costs. This type of photonic technology is now being used for the early detection of breast cancer. Continuing progress on high-definition digital imaging transfer is expected to result in a significant increase in physicians' ability to exchange information and share knowledge, make diagnoses more rapidly, and perform surgery which might otherwise be impossible. The use of lasers in dentistry for periodontal surgery is another emerging technology. Introductions of such new technologies in medical applications will continue to help the U.S. industry maintain its competitive lead in advanced medical and dental devices into the 21st century.—*Victoria Kader and Matthew Q. Edwards, Office of Microelectronics, Medical Equipment, and Instrumentation (202) 482-2796 and (202) 482-0550.*

Surgical and Medical Instruments

The surgical and medical instruments industry (SIC 3841) includes such products as syringes, clamps, hypodermic and suture needles, stethoscopes, laparascopic devices, catheters and drains, and blood pressure measuring devices. Constant-dollar shipments by this industry segment rose by nearly 7 percent in 1993, to $11 billion. Shipments of these primarily non-electric diagnostic and therapeutic devices have shown steady growth at an average annual rate of 6 percent over the past five years.

Total employment in the United States in the surgical and medical instruments industry rose by more than 2 percent to more than 89,000 in 1993. The proportion of production workers among this total held steady at 61 percent.

INTERNATIONAL COMPETITIVENESS

U.S. medical and surgical instrument manufacturers demonstrated their international competitiveness with a record-high export total of $2.6 billion in 1993, leading to a second consecutive $1.4 billion trade surplus for this industry segment. Continued strong growth in exports helped to offset some sluggishness in the domestic market. In 1993, the primary competition for U.S. medical and surgical instruments came from Germany and Singapore, which, alone among major trading partners, ran surpluses with the United States in this product area during 1993.

LONG-TERM PROSPECTS

Average annual real growth for U.S. surgical and medical instruments shipments should range between 6 and 7 percent through 1998. As cost-containment pressures dictate reliance on less-invasive surgical procedures that reduce risk of complications, hospital stays, and labor costs, demand should rise most rapidly for devices used in minimally invasive surgery, such as internal stapling devices and laparascopic and endoscopic instruments. Also faring well will be products used in treatment of cardiovascular disorders, including instruments used in angiography and angioplasty procedures and other cardiovascular therapeutic devices.

Surgical Appliances and Supplies

In 1993, U.S. manufacturers of surgical appliances and supplies (SIC 3842) increased shipments nearly 10 percent to an estimated $13.2 billion in constant dollars. This industry segment encompasses a broad array of products, ranging from sutures and bandages to wheelchairs, prosthetics, and implantable devices.

Total employment expanded by slightly less than 1 percent in 1993, to more than 96,000, of whom 65 percent were production workers.

INTERNATIONAL COMPETITIVENESS

U.S. exports of surgical appliances and supplies rose by almost 11 percent in 1993 to an estimated $1.9 billion, the strongest increase within the overall medical instruments and supplies industry. This performance, combined with a drop in U.S. imports in 1993, contributed to more than a $1 billion trade surplus in this industry segment, a 37 percent improvement over 1992's $800 million surplus. Among major trading partners in 1993, the United States widened its trade surpluses with the EC and Japan in SIC 3842 by more than one-third (despite recessions in these markets), and cut its deficit with Mexico by 7 percent. China's market stood out as one which U.S. manufacturers of surgical appliances and supplies had difficulty penetrating in 1993.

LONG-TERM PROSPECTS

Industry shipments are expected to grow steadily at an average annual rate of between 8 and 9 percent through 1998. Demographic trends (predominantly the aging of populations) in the large Japanese and Western European export markets, as well as in the United States, will continue to be the primary influence upon demand for surgical appliances and supplies. Markets for wheelchairs and ambulatory aids, prosthetics, and other orthopedic devices and supplies should be robust, as cost-cutting pressures faced by hospitals and nursing homes will favor products which afford long-term care patients the opportunity for greater mobility and capacity for self-care. Examples of high-potential technologies include continuous ambulatory peritoneal dialysis, which affords mobility to patients with chronic renal disorders, and enteral nutrition therapy, which assists persons with digestive disorders. Manufacturers of wearable infusion devices also stand to benefit from new research indicating that more frequent daily insulin doses can forestall more expensive-to-treat complications of diabetes.—*Matthew Q. Edwards, Office of Microelectronics, Medical Equipment, and Instrumentation (202) 482-0550.*

Dental Equipment and Supplies Industry

The U.S. dental equipment and supplies industry (SIC 3843) covers U.S. manufacturers of equipment, instruments, and supplies used by dentists, dental laboratories, and dental colleges. Specific products include dental hand instruments, plaster, drills, amalgams, cements, sterilizers, and dental chairs.

In 1993, the worldwide market for dental equipment and supplies was estimated at $5.5 billion. The global market for consumer dental products, including toothbrushes and mouthwashes, was estimated at $4.3 billion. The U.S. share of the international market for both dental equipment and supplies and consumer dental products remained steady at 50 to 55 percent. The major players in this industry include Block Drug, Dentsply International, Unitek, 3M, and Kerr Manufacturing. However, the U.S. dental equipment and supplies industry is largely composed of small and medium-size firms.

Uncertainty about reforms in health care policy, coupled with the economic slowdown in domestic and international economies, hurt U.S. dental equipment and supply manufacturers. Consequently, U.S. dental industry shipments increased at a constant-dollar rate of only 2 percent to $1.8 billion in 1993, compared to an average annual growth rate of 5 percent between 1989 and 1991.

INTERNATIONAL COMPETITIVENESS

The U.S. dental equipment and supplies industry enjoyed a healthy $258 million trade surplus in 1993. Exports are the strength of this industry, and accounted for 35 percent of 1993 product shipments, a higher rate than the overall medical equipment industry. U.S. dental products, which employ the latest technology, are in demand worldwide. Canada, Germany, Japan, Italy, and France have offered excellent export opportunities for U.S. dental equipment and supply manufacturers in the past, and will continue to be strong future purchasers. U.S. manufacturers continue to face competition from Germany, Japan, Switzerland, Italy, and France.

LONG-TERM PROSPECTS

ISO 9000 certification will be the "passport" for doing business in the EC beginning in 1995. However, the initial capital outlay to comply with these standards may be burdensome for small and medium-size dental companies. In the United States, industry shipments are forecast to increase at an average annual rate of 3 percent in constant dollars between 1995 and 1998. Although employment of dentists is expected to increase no more than 1 percent between 1995 and 1998, growth of "private practitioners" will exceed that of active dentists. In 1998, there are expected to be 142,000 self-employed dentists in the United States and 130,000 "private practitioners"—dentists employed by clinics and government entities. Emerging areas of dentistry expected to spur growth in the manufacture of dental equipment include periodontal diagnosis and treatment with lasers. Laser surgery on the gums, for example, is an emerging technology that offers surgery with less pain than treatment with a scalpel, little-to-no bleeding, and shorter healing time. In addition to periodontics, cosmetic dentistry, such as bonding and bleaching, is also on the rise.

In addition to emerging technologies, Oral Health 2000, an initiative that unites government, consumer groups, industry, and health professionals to improve the oral health of both adults and children by the year 2000, will make dental health a national issue. Oral Health 2000 will strive to prevent oral diseases, eliminate unnecessary tooth loss, and alleviate barriers to dental care. This initiative will strive to increase the public's awareness of oral health, which, in turn, will spur demand for dental services into the next century.—*Patricia Anne Eyring, Office of Microelectronics, Medical Equipment, and Instrumentation (202) 482-2846.*

Trends and Forecasts: Surgical Appliances and Supplies (SIC 3842)

(in millions of dollars except as noted)

Item	1987	1988	1989	1990	1991	1992[1]	1993[2]	1994[3]	Percent Change (1989–1994) 88–89	89–90	90–91	91–92	92–93	93–94
Industry Data														
Value of shipments[4]	8,534	9,828	10,187	11,128	12,555	14,140	15,992	18,119	3.7	9.2	12.8	12.6	13.1	13.3
Value of shipments (1987$)	8,534	9,654	9,656	10,088	10,984	11,995	13,171	14,488	0.0	4.5	8.9	9.2	9.8	10.0
Total employment (000)	78.5	82.1	84.4	86.6	93.3	95.9	96.4	—	2.8	2.6	7.7	2.8	0.5	—
Production workers (000)	51.1	52.8	54.3	55.8	60.6	63.0	62.4	—	2.8	2.8	8.6	4.0	-1.0	—
Average hourly earnings ($)	8.79	8.98	9.35	9.60	10.12	—	—	—	4.1	2.7	5.4	—	—	—
Capital expenditures	215	220	240	266	425	—	—	—	9.1	10.8	59.8	—	—	—
Product Data														
Value of shipments[5]	7,981	8,895	9,474	10,355	11,514	12,945	14,573	16,466	6.5	9.3	11.2	12.4	12.6	13.0
Value of shipments (1987$)	7,981	8,738	8,980	9,388	10,074	10,981	12,002	13,166	2.8	4.5	7.3	9.0	9.3	9.7
Trade Data														
Value of imports	—	—	394	554	645	892	770	802	—	40.6	16.4	38.3	-13.7	4.2
Value of exports	—	—	965	1,226	1,450	1,693	1,870	2,096	—	27.0	18.3	16.8	10.5	12.1

[1]Estimate, except exports and imports.
[2]Estimate.
[3]Forecast.
[4]Value of all products and services sold by establishments in the surgical appliances and supplies industry.
[5]Value of products classified in the surgical appliances and supplies industry produced by all industries.

SOURCE: U.S. Department of Commerce: Bureau of the Census; International Trade Administration (ITA). Estimates and forecasts by ITA.

Trends and Forecasts: Dental Equipment and Supplies (SIC 3843)

(in millions of dollars except as noted)

Item	1987	1988	1989	1990	1991	1992[1]	1993[2]	1994[3]	Percent Change (1989–1994) 88–89	89–90	90–91	91–92	92–93	93–94
Industry Data														
Value of shipments[4]	1,421	1,473	1,277	1,365	1,576	1,601	1,595	1,685	-13.3	6.9	15.5	1.6	1.2	3.8
Value of shipments (1987$)	1,421	1,503	1,334	1,410	1,723	1,750	1,785	1,847	-11.2	5.7	22.2	1.6	2.0	3.5
Total employment (000)	14.6	14.9	12.9	12.9	13.8	13.8	13.8	13.9	-13.4	0.0	7.0	0.0	0.0	0.7
Production workers (000)	8.7	8.9	8.4	8.4	8.6	8.6	8.7	8.7	-5.6	0.0	2.4	0.0	1.2	0.0
Average hourly earnings ($)	9.35	9.45	10.31	11.34	11.23	11.33	11.43	11.53	9.1	10.0	-1.0	0.9	0.9	0.9
Capital expenditures	31.5	30.0	27.3	24.4	32.2	—	—	—	-9.0	-10.6	32.0	—	—	—
Product Data														
Value of shipments[5]	1,241	1,227	1,177	1,265	1,397	1,415	1,439	1,652	-4.1	7.5	10.4	1.3	1.7	14.8
Value of shipments (1987$)	1,241	1,252	1,230	1,307	1,527	1,551	1,582	1,637	-1.8	6.3	16.8	1.6	2.0	3.5
Trade Data														
Value of imports	—	—	138	168	183	230	244	268	—	21.7	8.9	25.7	6.1	9.8
Value of exports	—	—	265	312	376	448	502	512	—	17.7	20.5	19.1	12.1	2.0

[1]Estimate, except exports and imports.
[2]Estimate.
[3]Forecast.
[4]Value of all products and services sold by establishments in the dental equipment and supplies industry.
[5]Value of products classified in the dental equipment and supplies industry produced by all industries.

SOURCE: U.S. Department of Commerce: Bureau of the Census; International Trade Administration (ITA). Estimates and forecasts by ITA.

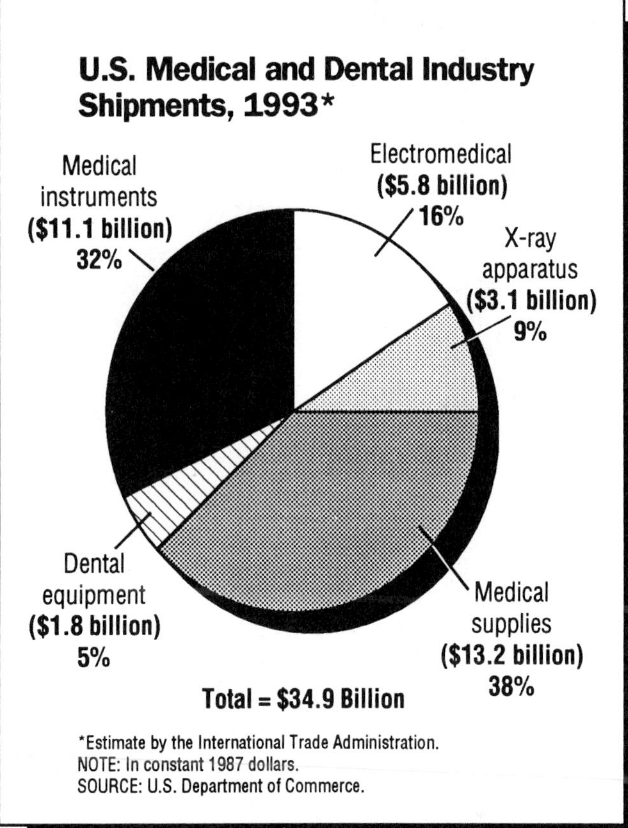

U.S. Trade Patterns in 1992
Medical Instruments and Supplies
SIC 384

(in millions of dollars, percent)

Exports	Value	Share	Imports	Value	Share
Canada and Mexico	1,335	17.5	Canada and Mexico	660	14.2
European Community	3,110	40.7	European Community	2,083	44.7
Japan	988	12.9	Japan	1,023	21.9
East Asia NICs	599	7.9	East Asia NICs	386	8.3
South America	337	4.4	South America	12	0.3
Other	1,263	16.6	Other	501	10.7
World Total	7,632	100.0	World Total	4,665	100.0

Top Five Countries

	Value	Share		Value	Share
Japan	988	12.9	Germany	1,152	24.7
Canada	911	11.9	Japan	1,023	21.9
Germany	822	10.8	Mexico	504	10.8
France	465	6.1	United Kingdom	239	5.1
United Kingdom	453	5.9	France	232	5.0

See "Getting the Most Out of *Outlook '94*" for definitions of the country groupings.
SOURCE: U.S. Department of Commerce: Bureau of the Census; International Trade Administration.

Trends and Forecasts: Surgical and Medical Instruments (SIC 3841)

(in millions of dollars except as noted)

Item	1987	1988	1989	1990	1991	1992[1]	1993[2]	1994[3]	Percent Change (1989–1994) 88–89	89–90	90–91	91–92	92–93	93–94
Industry Data														
Value of shipments[4]	7,780	8,259	8,972	10,262	10,710	11,519	12,524	13,803	8.6	14.4	4.4	7.6	8.7	10.2
Value of shipments (1987$)	7,780	8,161	8,553	9,546	9,817	10,318	10,999	11,769	4.8	11.6	2.8	5.1	6.6	7.0
Total employment (000)	73.1	75.7	83.9	88.9	87.7	87.4	89.4	—	10.8	6.0	-1.3	-0.3	2.3	—
Production workers (000)	45.4	46.7	50.7	53.8	53.1	53.0	54.6	—	8.6	6.1	-1.3	-0.2	3.0	—
Average hourly earnings ($)	8.91	9.57	9.58	9.81	10.59	—	—	—	0.1	2.4	8.0	—	—	—
Capital expenditures	355	385	403	469	536	—	—	—	4.7	16.4	14.3	—	—	—
Product Data														
Value of shipments[5]	7,232	7,959	8,655	9,857	10,474	11,276	12,283	13,550	8.7	13.9	6.3	7.7	8.9	10.3
Value of shipments (1987$)	7,232	7,865	8,251	9,169	9,600	10,100	10,787	11,553	4.9	11.1	4.7	5.2	6.8	7.1
Trade Data														
Value of imports	—	—	654	800	996	1,111	1,242	1,370	—	22.3	24.5	11.5	11.8	10.3
Value of exports	—	—	1,497	1,854	2,173	2,445	2,602	2,836	—	23.8	17.2	12.5	6.4	9.0

[1]Estimate, except exports and imports.
[2]Estimate.
[3]Forecast.
[4]Value of all products and services sold by establishments in the surgical and medical instruments industry.
[5]Value of products classified in the surgical and medical instruments industry produced by all industries.

SOURCE: U.S. Department of Commerce: Bureau of the Census; International Trade Administration (ITA). Estimates and forecasts by ITA.

Metals

Shipments by the major metals industries increased moderately in 1993. The principal factor influencing the boost in shipments was the increase in automotive vehicle production. This was a boon to all the industries, except titanium which is heavily dependent upon the flagging aerospace industry. Prices for steel mill products increased while prices for all nonferrous metals declined as a result of weak demand and mounting inventories worldwide. The large inventories are principally a result of export surges by the countries of the former Soviet Union.

Steel Mill Products

After experiencing a decline in the value of shipments in 3 of the last 4 years (measured in constant dollars), the U.S. steel industry (SIC 3312, 3315, 3316, and 3317) experienced a turnaround in 1993. Shipments through June increased 7.2 percent (on a tonnage basis) from year-earlier levels and were expected to exceed 78 million (metric) tons for the year, up about 5 percent from 1992 and the highest level since 1981. Imports dropped 3.7 percent for the first 6 months of 1993 and import penetration fell to its lowest level since 1980. Most importantly, steelmakers were able to boost prices, which had fallen every year since 1989. After registering a 7.1 percent decline between 1989 and 1992, the Bureau of Labor Statistics (BLS) price index for all steel mill products rose 2 percent during the first half of the year. Spot price increases were substantially greater. The aggregate index is less likely to demonstrate big shifts in price because more than half of all steel is sold on a long-term contract basis.

The relatively high level of shipments was attributable in large measure to strong demand from the automotive and construction sectors—historically steel's two largest consuming industries. With light vehicle production in the United States up 14 percent through June, steelmakers were able to increase shipments to this sector by nearly 13 percent. Shipments to the construction market rose 11 percent, a surprisingly large rise considering the persistent sluggishness of that sector. The oil and gas sector also experienced a significant upturn, as did steel service centers, which purchase steel from mills and distribute it to end users.

With the improvement in both prices and volume, and with the aid of continuous cost-cutting, a number of deficit-ridden steelmakers anticipated a return to profitability later in 1993. During the first 6 months of the year, the industry narrowed its operating loss to only $6 million, down from $220 million a year earlier. In addition to improved prices, major steelmakers credited higher volume, lower production costs, and a more favorable product mix for the improved earnings. The industry had sustained a cumulative operating deficit of $3.5 billion between 1989 and 1992, largely because of the losses of the major integrated producers. The specialty sectors and the smaller minimills, which melt steel from scrap, were generally profitable during this period. Even so, the minimills had difficulties of their own in the first half of 1993. Despite rising shipments, minimill profits were squeezed by higher raw material—especially ferrous scrap—and labor costs.

Due to the increased demand and a small reduction in capacity, the industry was able to boost its capacity utilization rate through June to 87.4 percent, up from 82.9 percent a year earlier and the highest level since 1989. Capacity utilization measures how much raw steel a mill could produce if it was running at its maximum capability. By maintaining high operating rates, steelmakers were able to make steel more efficiently and at lower costs. High operating rates allow the industry to spread high fixed costs over more units of production, reducing average total production costs.

Some experts were surprised that the industry was not operating at even higher levels—raw steel production was up only 2.5 percent through June—considering the strength of orders during the first half of the year. Apparently there was not sufficient incentive for companies to hire additional workers and restart higher-cost plants. To some extent, steelmakers improvised by substantially increasing imports of semifinished steel for further rolling.

The ongoing technological revolution in steelmaking had an important impact on industry restructuring in 1993. Nucor Corp., the nation's largest minimill, joined forces with a Canadian minimill and a joint venture between a Canadian integrated producer and Canadian minimill, to build a plant using the thin slab caster, a less capital-intensive and lower-operating cost alternative to traditional sheet manufacture. Some estimates put operating costs at about $80 per ton less. Nucor plans to expand capacity at its two current mills. The additional capacity, which is expected to exceed 6 million tons later in this decade, will clearly intensify competition in the flat-rolled market and threaten some integrated mill capacity. This market, which totalled 40 million tons in 1992, is expected to grow over the next decade.

The flat-rolled market had been the exclusive domain of integrated producers until Nucor began operating its first mill in 1988. Initially, the steels produced by this new process were used for low-end applications such as decking, but the quality of the steel products has since improved. Nevertheless, more than half of this market currently remains beyond minimill capability.

In recognition that costs would have to be reduced to improve competitiveness, a number of major steelmakers reached long-term contract agreements with the United Steelworkers of America (USW) in mid-summer that traded representation on the board and job security for improvements on productivity. Other provisions of the 6-year contract included two wage increases, bonuses, and improved pension benefits.

Huge pension and insurance costs potentially endanger the competitiveness of some integrated producers. Inadequate contributions by companies, deep cuts in the size of the work force, and improved benefits (including those in 1993) have left companies with enormous pension liabilities which must be covered by elusive profits. Also, retiree group health care costs are rising as the ratio of retired-to-active workers increases. (LTV, which went into bankruptcy in 1986 in part due to pension liabilities, has three retirees for every active worker.) Minimills, by contrast, are generally free of these costs because they have a relatively young work force, few retirees, and fewer benefits for retired workers.

INTERNATIONAL COMPETITIVENESS

Severe competitive pressures both in the United States and abroad forced the U.S. steel industry to reduce costs. Through investment of capital in new technologies, new management styles, and closing of inefficient plants, the U.S. industry has become one of the lowest-cost producers in the developed world. Productivity at U.S. mills grew rapidly in the last decade (6.7 percent annually, according to BLS) and is currently estimated to be equal to that of Japan and higher than in any other major steel-producing country.

A worldwide recession has intensified steel trade problems. Beginning in mid-1989, export prices for steel mill products began to fall, as weakening domestic demand in a number of countries encouraged producers to boost overseas sales. In the European Community, which has delayed the wrenching restructuring that the U.S. steel industry undertook over the last decade, domestic demand fell for a second straight year and the operating rate sank to only 66 percent. In Japan, a significant drop in domestic consumption led to a sharp decline in capacity utilization.

China is one exception to the weak demand overseas. That country's rapid economic growth has propelled demand for steel. Steel demand rose by 20 million tons between 1990 and 1992 and was expected to reach 100 million tons by 2000. The growth of Chinese demand is expected to be a stabilizing factor for the global market in the 1990's.

The recession affecting the steel industry in most countries prompted a series of bilateral disputes that disrupted world trade. In 1992, U.S. steelmakers filed more than 100 unfair (antidumping and countervailing duty) trade cases involving a wide range of products and a large number of countries. The largest number of cases involved flat-rolled carbon steel products. In 1992, imports of the four flat-rolled categories involved totalled $3.4 billion or 40 percent of all imports. In mid-1993, the U.S. Department of Commerce announced that flat-rolled imports from 19 countries were being dumped and that the same products from 12 countries were being subsidized. The U.S. International Trade Commission (ITC) commissioners voted in 32 of the 72 cases—principally plate and corrosion-resistant steel—that imports had caused material injury to domestic steel producers. The affirmative determinations affected half of the dollar value of subject imports. For the remainder of products—hot-and-cold rolled sheet—supplemental tariffs were effectively removed, creating the possibility that imports would rise and the recent price increases by U.S. producers would not stick. However, because of the strength of the market, the prices were still holding firm in late summer.

During the first half of the year, uncertainties generated by the trade cases discouraged imports. Until the ITC vote, importers were required to post a cash deposit in the amount of the estimated subsidies or dumping margin on all the products covered. Following the vote, the Commerce Department ordered the U.S. Customs Service to impose duties on those products where the ITC found injury.

Total imports fell by 3.7 percent through June. Among the four major product categories affected by the trade cases, the decline was 19 percent. However, integrated mills' need for semi-finished steel boosted imports of these products by more than 27 percent to 1.5 million tons, or to 20 percent of total imports.

U.S. exports were also affected by trade disputes. In apparent retaliation for the U.S. actions, steel producers in Canada and Mexico initiated antidumping cases on a variety of flat-rolled products from the United States and other sources in 1992. The Canadian government found in 1993 that U.S. products were being dumped, but in most cases they were not a cause of material injury, and the cases were terminated. However, Canada did find injury on imports of cold-rolled coil.

Mexican producers filed their cases in mid-1992. In April 1993, the Mexican government determined that steel from the United States was being dumped and supplemental duties of 3 percent to 81 percent were to be placed on imports. The Mexican government also initiated a countervailing duty investigation of coded steel flat-rolled products. Mexico and Canada accounted for about two-thirds of total exports in 1992.

To address the longstanding problem of unfairly traded steel, the United States has sought a multilateral steel agreement (MSA) since 1989. Most major steel-producing countries are participating in MSA negotiations that are taking place in Geneva under the auspices of the General Agreement on Tariffs and Trade. The U.S. objective in these talks is to address the underlying causes of trade distortions that have had such a debilitating effect on steel trade for two decades. The agreement would place strict disciplines over subsidies and eliminate tariffs and other trade-distorting practices in the steel sector. Dumping would be addressed indirectly; with the removal of trade barriers, companies would be less able to protect their domestic market and to engage in the sort of price discriminations that lead to dumping cases.

Concluding an MSA has been difficult because of disagreement over fundamental issues such as treatment of past subsidies, establishment of a permissible category of subsidies, and how to address dumping directly, if at all. The negotiations, which broke down in March 1992 over these issues, were restarted in the fall.

After little progress initially, the negotiations picked up new momentum at the July 1993 meeting of the Group of Seven in Tokyo when agreement was reached on a market access package linking the elimination of tariffs on steel mill products to a multilateral steel agreement. The outcome of the trade cases mitigated one stumbling block to concluding the agreement—the insistence by the European Community that there be a political settlement to the trade cases.

Soaring health care costs are also affecting steel industry competitiveness internationally. Major U.S. steel producers are now paying out an average of $5.30 per hour worked, 17 percent of total hourly employment costs, for health care. The steel industry argues that these high costs place it at a disadvantage with its major foreign competitors, some of whom pay no direct health care expenses.

LONG-TERM PROSPECTS

After years of losing market share to other materials, steel appears to be maintaining its competitive position against other materials. To some extent, this is the result of the development of new, lighter-weight products, bake hardenable grades, and high-strength steels. In the automotive market, for example, steel appears to be holding its own as some parts, recently made of plastic, are being returned to steel. These involve parts such as fuel tanks, fenders, pickup truck cargo boxes, roofs, and hoods. Moreover, the decades-long downtrend in steel content in automobiles appears to have slowed or at least temporarily reversed. According to the Ford Motor Company, the average vehicle built in 1993 contained 1,726 pounds of steel, up from 1,710 pounds in 1992, marking the second consecutive yearly increase. Total average vehicle weight increased from 3,059 pounds to 3,150 pounds. A further increase was anticipated in 1994 due to new and expanding applications of steel.

The residential construction sector is potentially a rich market for steel producers. Steel framing for houses is being promoted as a light-weight alternative to wood framing. A galvanized steel frame for a 2,000 square foot house would weigh approximately one-fourth the weight of a lumber structure. New interest in steel has also been sparked by the damage to wood-framed structures caused by recent natural disasters and the spurt in wood prices in late 1992 and early 1993.—*Charles L. Bell, Office of Metals, Machinery and Chemicals (202) 482-0608.*

Aluminum

In spite of sluggish domestic and global economies in 1993, shipments of ingot and semifabricated products by the U.S. aluminum industry increased an estimated 2.8 percent over 1992 to a record 8.2 million metric tons. Among the major aluminum consuming markets—the United States, Europe and Japan—the United States demonstrated the most strength. Therefore, although overall U.S. shipments increased, domestic shipments increased at a faster rate than total shipments, resulting in a trade deficit in aluminum. However, the United States did maintain a positive trade balance for aluminum semifabricated products in 1993. Shipments by aluminum distributors also increased at a greater rate than overall shipments.

Domestically, shipments to the three major end-use sectors—containers and packaging, transportation, and building and construction—accounted for approximately 60 percent of shipments. The dominant end use is the containers and packaging sector, principally beverage containers, which accounts for more than one-quarter of total shipments. A decrease in beer consumption was offset by an increase in soft-drink consumption which resulted in flat shipments to this sector. Shipments to the transportation sector increased more than any other aluminum-consuming sector, benefiting not only from an increase in motor vehicle production, but also a slight increase in the amount of aluminum used per vehicle. Residential and commercial building remained sluggish and shipments to this sector increased on par with overall shipments.

The primary aluminum capacity utilization rate in the United States—the amount of aluminum a plant could produce if working at full capacity—decreased considerably in 1993 from the previous year. This may be attributed to two factors. First, production curtailments occurred early in the year in response to the continued power cutbacks by the Bonneville Power Authority (BPA). The BPA found it necessary to reduce power service to the aluminum smelters in the Pacific Northwest, site of approximately 40 percent of U.S. capacity, because of a water shortage which hampered its hydro system. Second, some U.S. producers curtailed capacity considerably in mid-year, citing the impact of the continued high levels of exports by the countries of the former Soviet Union. Thus U.S. production was only 3.7 million metric tons, down 8.5 percent from 1992.

The price for primary aluminum fell to record-low levels (in constant dollars) during 1993 (54.5 cents per pound in July). Despite a moderate increase in global demand, a continued flood of exports from the former Soviet republics, estimated at more than 1 million metric tons annually for the period 1991–1993, depressed prices. As a result, there is a large accumulation of inventories of primary aluminum, especially of Russian metal, in London Metal Exchange warehouses. These historically high inventory levels are likely to continue to have a dampening effect on prices.

The rapid increase in exports of large quantities of aluminum from the countries of the former Soviet Union has hurt the U.S. industry. U.S. imports of Russian aluminum, which were only 16,000 metric tons in 1992 and represented slightly more than 1 percent of imports, increased dramatically in 1993 to several hundred thousand metric tons, accounting for nearly one-quarter of U.S. aluminum imports. As a result of these imports, and their overall affect on the global price of aluminum, several U.S. producers were forced to curtail production and lay off workers. The European Community responded to the situation by imposing a restriction on imports of aluminum from the former Soviet republics for the last third of the year.

INTERNATIONAL COMPETITIVENESS

The combined import volume of ingot and semifabricated aluminum products increased about 37 percent in 1993 from year-earlier levels. The rate of increase in ingot imports, a result of the surge in ingot imports from Russia, significantly exceeded that of semifabricated products. Exports of ingot declined due to a decrease in U.S. primary production and relatively strong domestic demand. Meanwhile, exports of semifabricated products were relatively flat, impeded by recessionary economic conditions in Europe and Japan, the major overseas markets for these products.

The aluminum industry is a modern and efficient producer of high-quality products with an international competitive advantage. From 1982 to 1992, semifabricated exports by the U.S. aluminum industry achieved an annual growth rate of over 10 percent. The international competitiveness of the industry would be further improved by reducing the barriers to foreign market access.

LONG-TERM PROSPECTS

U.S. aluminum shipments are expected to increase at a compound annual rate of approximately 3 percent through 1998. Beverage cans will remain the largest end use for aluminum. Can stock should also spur exports as aluminum cans become more prevalent in other markets. Exports of semifabricated products will provide the growth in the export market as exports of ingot decline. Imports will continue to increase, especially of ingot.

The automotive sector could be the next large volume, end-use for aluminum, perhaps exceeding the phenomenal growth resulting from the introduction of the aluminum beverage can. In the future, fuel economy standards could hasten the increased use of aluminum. Although a considerable part of the increase in aluminum consumption by the automotive sector will be based on current applications, such as aluminum wheels and engines, most aluminum companies remain sanguine regarding the use of aluminum in high-volume applications, such as in structural applications and body panels. However, through 1998, castings will likely retain their two-thirds share of the aluminum auto market.

In order to facilitate the introduction of aluminum into new automotive applications, aluminum companies have invested heavily in research and development and new facilities, and have formed partnerships with auto and metals companies worldwide.

Several plans are under consideration for the introduction of aluminum-intensive cars. Chrysler Corp. may begin building an aluminum-intensive car in 1996, employing 600 to 700 pounds of aluminum per vehicle. Currently, the U.S. average is about 195 pounds per vehicle.

Plans to mass produce electric vehicles by the late 1990's could create another opportunity for increased aluminum consumption. A General Motors version would probably utilize aluminum frame components. Meanwhile, incremental gains in aluminum consumption are being made by substituting aluminum for existing materials, such as in making hoods for Ford F-Series pickup trucks beginning in 1996.

The aluminum industry has been developing new materials employing aluminum as a means of ensuring its future. Although the early bright prospects for aluminum-lithium alloys have not been realized, there does seem to be considerable market potential for metal matrix composites (MMC)—which combine metals with a fiber to form a strengthened alloy—utilizing aluminum as a matrix material and typically reinforced with silicon carbide or alumina. The reinforcing materials impart their beneficial characteristics, such as lightweight and high strength, to the overall composite while simultaneously retaining aluminum's ease of fabrication.

Although autos are currently the most significant application for MMC, there are a variety of future applications for these materials, ranging from sports equipment to high-speed commercial aircraft and engines. As an example, Pratt and Whitney Aircraft is developing a fan blade for jet engines utilizing an aluminum matrix composite employing continuous boron fibers as the reinforcing material. In addition to MMC, laminated metal composites incorporating alternating layers of aluminum and aluminum MMC may open potential new, low-cost, high-performance uses for aluminum.—*David Cammarota, Metals Branch, Office of Materials, Machinery, and Chemicals (202) 482-5157.*

Copper

Conditions in the U.S. copper industry (SIC 1021, 3331, 3341, 3351, and 3357) continued to improve during 1993, despite uncertainty over new administration policies, questions over future demand, fluctuating prices, and uncooperative weather conditions. U.S. mine production for the first half of 1993 was approximately 3.4 percent higher than for the same period of 1992, even though production was disrupted by heavy rains early in the year. Refined copper production increased about 7 percent by mid-year compared to the first half of 1992. Annual copper consumption remained strong at slightly more than 3 million metric tons (mt), an increase of about 4 percent over 1992 levels. Copper consumption by wire rod mills increased about 2.5 percent; copper consumption by brass mills increased about 11 percent. The end-use markets for copper remained about the same in 1992, led by building construction materials.

Domestic stock levels remained stable at the higher levels established at the end of 1992. However, stock levels in the rest of the world rose significantly, mirroring market weakness in Europe and Asia. As of mid-September, about 7,800 mt of refined copper had been sold from the National Defense Stockpile.

Copper prices declined during the first 6 months of 1993, trading on the New York Commodity Exchange between 78 cents and $1.01 per pound compared with a price range of between 96 cents and $1.07 per pound over the same period in 1992. While financial performance of the major domestic copper mining companies was mixed at mid-year, largely due to lower metal prices, most U.S. copper companies were profitable. Production losses due to heavy rains in late 1992 and early 1993 contributed to slightly higher operating costs for some producers.

The domestic mining industry continued with major renovations and expansions intended to increase the productivity and efficiency of their domestic operations. Kennecott Corp. received approval for its copper smelter facility modernization. The $880 million project will increase the company's refined capacity from 215,000 tons to 282,000 tons per year and will eliminate the need to sell its excess concentrates. AMAX Inc. and Cyprus Minerals Co. announced a merger, creating one of the world's largest natural resources companies, and the second largest copper producer in the United States. Cyprus currently has a $200 million capital expenditure program underway to reduce copper production costs. Several labor contracts expired during the year; all contracts were renegotiated without disruption of production.

Meanwhile, plans for Magma Copper's proposed redevelopment of the Robinson Mining District in Nevada were put on hold, pending the resolution of an appeal by environmental groups filed with the Bureau of Land Management. Magma originally planned for the 55,000 ton-per-year mine to become operational by late 1994.

INTERNATIONAL COMPETITIVENESS

The trade picture for the U.S. copper industry has changed dramatically in the past several years. From 1986 through 1991, net imports of refined copper declined from approximately 489,000 mt to about 17,000 mt, primarily due to increasing levels of U.S. exports. This trend halted in 1992, however, as exports of refined copper decreased 33 percent and imports rose slightly higher than 1991 levels. Consequently, net imports increased during 1992 to about 112,000 mt, largely due to weaker demand from Europe and Asia.

During the first half of 1993, imports of all copper and copper alloy products increased by 11 percent, while exports remained near mid-year 1992 levels. During that same period, imports of refined copper increased about 7 percent compared to 1992 and exports increased by about 20 percent. At mid-year, the brass mill industry appeared to be on its way to reversing a 6-year trend of increased exports and declining imports. Exports decreased slightly while imports rose 11 percent in 1993. Canada, Mexico, and Japan are the primary export markets for U.S. brass mills, but these mills have recently made export gains in some European Community-member countries.

By mid-year, exports of wire mill products, traditionally a strong export sector, were approximately 25 percent above levels of the prior year. Mexico, Canada, Saudi Arabia, the United Kingdom, and the Philippines are the main export markets for these products. A relatively stronger economic recovery in the United States compared to several other countries was expected to drive imports of wire mill products in 1993, but the United States was expected to remain a net exporter in this sector. Export growth has spread across several product lines, including copper and copper alloy bars, rod, wire, pipe, tube, sheet, strip, plate, and foil. Antidumping and countervailing duty orders remained in place on brass sheet and strip during 1993.

Historically, the domestic copper mining industry has paid close attention to events in the developing world. Economic and legislative reforms in some developing countries, especially Chile and Peru, are a positive sign for U.S. investment in overseas mining. The countries of the former Soviet Union, in particular Russia and Kazakhstan, became an increasingly important factor in the world copper market during 1993 and are expected to become a much larger force among world copper producers in the future. For example, copper shipments from the former Soviet republics to recession-plagued European nations contributed to international stock buildups during late 1992 and early 1993.

Copper is generally mined in the developing countries of the southern hemisphere, but is consumed and processed into intermediate and final products in the developed northern hemisphere countries. The United States is the exception to this rule because it is both a major producer and consumer of copper. Consequently, the economic interests of domestic producers, the mining companies, and the consumers (the brass mills and wire mills) tend to diverge regarding the economic development of Eastern Europe, China, and the former Soviet republics.

Growth and reconstruction of these economies create demand for raw materials, thereby benefiting producers. But as the new economies develop, they also compete in the domestic and foreign markets with existing producers of mill products and for their customers, the domestic producers of finished products containing copper. The ability of the new domestic mills to compete on the basis of quality will be a major factor in their success in the international markets. So will continued efforts to eliminate trade barriers around the world.

During 1993, Phelps Dodge Corp., the largest U.S. copper company, continued with plans to develop the La Candelaria mine in northern Chile. The newly formed International Copper Study Group, headquartered in Lisbon, began its work at the First General Session in June, with the United States and 17 other countries participating. The group's mission is to improve world statistics on copper production and consumption and to provide a forum for the exchange of views between producing and consuming countries.

LONG-TERM PROSPECTS

Total world copper consumption is estimated to increase at a compound annual rate of approximately 2 percent through 2000. The largest increases are expected in China, provided progress continues on economic reforms. U.S. copper consumption is estimated to grow at a compound annual rate of approximately 1.5 to 1.7 percent through 2000.

U.S. productivity and market development are improving. The domestic copper mining companies, brass mills, and wire mills have increased productivity and efficiency and have controlled costs. These efforts will be important in meeting competition from foreign copper producers and manufacturers of copper substitutes. Market development efforts will be aimed at increasing copper use in existing markets and finding new applications in construction, telecommunications, and automotive electronics.—*Barbara Malès, Office of Materials, Machinery, and Chemicals (202) 482-0606.*

Trends and Forecasts: Steel Mill Products (SIC 3312, 3315, 3316, 3317)

(in millions of dollars except as noted)

Item	1987	1988	1989	1990	1991	1992[1]	1993[2]	1994[3]	Percent Change (1989–1994) 88–89	89–90	90–91	91–92	92–93	93–94
Industry Data														
Value of shipments[4]	50,971	62,783	63,054	60,941	55,182	—	—	—	0.4	-3.4	-9.5	—	—	—
Value of shipments (1987$)	50,971	57,998	56,464	55,595	51,234	55,525	58,300	59,780	-2.6	-1.5	-7.8	8.4	5.0	2.5
Total employment (000)	249	261	256	254	241	234	—	—	-1.9	-0.8	-5.1	-2.9	—	—
Production workers (000)	193	201	199	196	184	179	—	—	-1.0	-1.5	-6.1	-2.7	—	—
Capital expenditures	1,643	2,222	2,961	3,011	3,337	—	—	—	33.3	1.7	10.8	—	—	—
Product Data														
Value of shipments[5]	50,058	61,715	62,105	60,065	53,968	—	—	—	0.6	-3.3	-10.2	—	—	—
Value of shipments (1987$)	50,058	57,056	55,631	54,791	50,133	53,291	56,100	57,525	-2.5	-1.5	-8.5	6.3	5.3	2.5
Trade Data														
Value of imports	—	—	9,599	8,911	8,339	8,499	7,843	8,184	—	-7.2	-6.4	1.9	-7.7	4.3
Value of exports	—	—	2,953	2,921	3,819	3,167	2,954	3,024	—	-1.1	30.7	-17.1	-6.7	2.4

[1]Estimate, except exports and imports.
[2]Estimate.
[3]Forecast.
[4]Value of all products and services sold by establishments in the steel mill products industry.
[5]Value of products classified in the steel mill products industry produced by all industries.
SOURCE: U.S. Department of Commerce: Bureau of the Census; International Trade Administration (ITA). Estimates and forecasts by ITA.

Aluminum Ingot and Semifabricated Products, 1990–94

(in thousands of metric tons)

Item	1990	1991	1992	1993[1]	1994[2]	Percent Change (1990–1994) 90–91	91–92	92–93	93–94
Total shipments[3]	7,718[4]	7,722[4]	8,011	8,235	8,581	0.1	3.7	2.8	4.2
Primary ingot production	4,048	4,121	4,042	3,700	3,750	1.8	-1.9	-8.5	1.4
Exports	1,164	1,374	1,233	1,065	1,100	18.0	-10.5	-13.6	3.3
Ingot	686	746	606	450	450	8.8	-18.8	-25.7	0.0
Semifabricated products	478	578	627	615	650	20.9	8.5	-1.9	5.7
Imports	1,421	1,398	1,572	2,150	2,260	-1.6	12.4	36.8	5.1
Ingot	962	1,029	1,163	1,700	1,800	7.0	13.0	46.2	5.9
Semifabricated products	459	369	409	450	460	-19.6	10.8	10.0	2.2

[1]Estimate.
[2]Forecast.
[3]Aluminum ingot and semifabricated products.
[4]Revised.
SOURCE: U.S. Department of Commerce, International Trade Administration (ITA); The Aluminum Association. Estimates and forecasts by ITA.

Copper, 1990–94

(in thousands of metric tons except as noted)

Item	1990	1991	1992	1993[1]	1994[2]	Percent Change (1990–1994) 90–91	91–92	92–93	93–94
Copper production	2,017.4	2,000.6	2,020.6	2,121.2	2,206.1	-0.8	1.0	5.0	4.0
Copper consumption, total	3,090.5	2,888.5	2,980.9	3,100.0	3,149.6	-6.5	3.2	4.0	1.6
By wire rod mills	1,678.0	1,609.7	1,645.0	1,686.7	1,720.4	-4.1	2.2	2.5	2.0
By brass mills	1,023.4	956.7	1,008.0	1,118.9	1,141.3	-6.5	5.4	11.0	2.0
Exports									
Refined	212.7	271.2	181.7	205.0	215.3	27.5	-33.0	12.8	5.0
Wire mills	161.8	191.7	235.9	294.9	309.6	18.5	23.1	25.0	5.0
Brass mills	157.0	162.0	192.8	207.3	217.3	3.2	19.0	-1.5	3.8
Imports									
Refined	261.6	288.6	299.1	320.0	316.8	10.3	3.6	7.0	1.0
Wire mills	134.3	104.1	135.5	136.4	132.3	-22.5	30.2	0.7	-3.0
Brass mills	347.6	288.1	276.6	307.0	302.7	-17.1	-4.0	11.0	-1.4

[1]Estimate.
[2]Forecast.
NOTE: Production and consumption data include the use of scrap. Trade data on wire mills include insulated wire and cable. Other industries that consume copper include the foundry, powder metallurgy, and chemicals industries.

SOURCE: U.S. Department of the Interior, Bureau of Mines; American Bureau of Metal Statistics; U.S. Department of Commerce: Bureau of the Census, International Trade Administration (ITA); Copper Development Association, Inc. Estimates and forecasts by ITA.

Motor Vehicles and Parts

The motor vehicle and parts industry is a key component of the U.S. economy, accounting for a substantial percentage of direct and indirect employment and industrial output. An estimated 6.7 million persons were employed directly and in allied automotive industries in 1991, accounting for 6.2 percent of all U.S. nonfarm employment. Manufacturing employment in the industry was an estimated 1.2 million persons, 6.5 percent of all such jobs in the United States. Manufacturers of motor vehicles and equipment (SIC 371) generated annual shipments totaling $236 billion in 1992, nearly 16 percent of all shipments in the durable goods industries, and 8 percent of all product shipments in the manufacturing sector. During the first half of 1993, shipments of SIC 371 products were $146 billion, 18 percent of all durable goods output.

In 1992, product shipments by all producers of motor vehicles and car bodies (SIC 3711) totaled $138.8 billion, an increase of almost 8 percent. Sales of new light vehicles in the United States increased slightly after 3 consecutive years of decline, reaching a total of 12.9 million units.

Purchases by individuals, businesses, and government agencies for locally made and imported cars and new trucks totaled $216 billion in 1992, the equivalent of 3.6 percent of U.S. gross domestic product (GDP). Expenditures by individuals for cars and trucks reached $180.6 billion. Consumer purchases of tires, tubes, accessories, and parts were an additional $23.7 billion. Combined, these expenditures accounted for 41 percent of total outlays by consumers for durable goods. Excluding related services and nondurables (such as the $103 billion spent for gasoline and oil), these purchases represented 5 percent of the public's total consumption expenditures, and 4.5 percent of its total disposable income, in 1992.

Challenges of Competition

The U.S. market for new passenger cars and light trucks is essentially saturated. There is little prospect that annual growth on a long-term basis will be more than 1 or 2 percent. Despite, or perhaps because of this situation, competition in the United States among foreign and U.S. manufacturers is growing even more intense. In 1993, U.S. purchasers could choose from among 31 major domestic and foreign manufacturers offering 337 separate car and 143 separate light truck models, almost all of them superior in most respects to previous models. Moreover, virtually all of today's new vehicles were developed and brought to market more quickly than in the 1980's, and were manufactured more efficiently and with less negative impact on the environment.

Virtually all competitive, high-volume vehicle and parts manufacturers worldwide have become significant players in the U.S. market, and more are coming. BMW and Mercedes-Benz announced in 1993 that they will operate vehicle assembly plants in the United States in 1995 and 1997, respectively. Kia Motors, a South Korean automaker, began establishing a West Coast sales network in 1993. It has targeted an early 1994 introduction date for its compact sedan, to be followed by a sport utility at mid-year.

The genuine openness of the U.S. market has profoundly affected the operations of U.S.-owned producers, from the smallest parts supplier to the largest vehicle manufacturer. Many companies have declined or disappeared in the face of stiff competition, but others have funnelled substantial resources into new or renovated facilities. The latter have become more competitive and have increased their share, not only of the U.S. market, but worldwide as well. Motor vehicle and equipment manufacturers invested $8.7 billion in the United States in 1992 for new and refurbished manufacturing plant facilities and equipment, a decline from $10.3 billion in 1991. In the first quarter of 1993, investments were running at an annual rate of $10.4 billion, up from an annual rate of $9.4 billion in the same quarter of 1992. Based on realized and known third-quarter capital spending plans, total investments were an estimated $9.8 billion in 1993.

U.S.-owned firms have not been the only casualties of the U.S. market wars. Faced with fierce competition from Japanese vehicle producers, Sterling, a unit of the British Rover Group, and the French firm, Peugeot, withdrew completely from the United States in 1991. Yugo, which supplied the "entry level" small car market, ceased operations in 1992. Daihatsu, a small Japanese producer of entry-level cars and sport-utility vehicles, also left. Other withdrawals could occur in the near term.

The severity of the competition has taken its toll on domestic profits. It also has propelled the industry on a painful, but beneficial, journey to reduce operating expenditures through improvements in manufacturing technology and productivity and reductions in overhead expenses. In 1982, at the bottom of the last slump in domestic production, local manufacturers assembled 7 million cars and all types of trucks. The Department of Labor's Bureau of Labor Statistics

(BLS) reported average annual employment in the industry was 318,000 manufacturing employees, the equivalent of 22 vehicles per worker. In 1992, output totaled 9.7 million units, while BLS-reported employment averaged 323,000, or 30 vehicles per worker.

GM, Ford, Chrysler, and many U.S.-owned parts manufacturers obtain many products for the U.S. market from their foreign subsidiaries and from their competitors. Competitive pressures also have generated a bewildering array of cooperative manufacturing and marketing ventures. GM's "Geo" car brand is marketed as a single product line in the United States. The brand consists of compact sedans made in California in a 50-50 joint venture between GM and Toyota; subcompact and sport-utility vehicles made in Canada in a 50-50 joint venture between GM and Suzuki; and a compact made in Japan by Isuzu, of which GM owns 38 percent. Ford owns 50 percent of Mazda's Michigan plant, which builds the Mazda MX-6 and the Ford Probe on the same basic platform. Chrysler provides engines to Mitsubishi's Illinois plant that are used in vehicles that each firm sells under separate nameplates. In 1993, GM and Toyota petitioned the Federal Trade Commission (FTC) and won the right to continue to operate a $1.5 billion joint venture in California—New United Motor Manufacturing, Inc. The original 1984 FTC consent order required that they terminate operations at the end of 1996. In 1992, the two firms merged their separate manufacturing operations in Australia, where they now produce individual models on a common platform in a shared facility. In 1996, Toyota will begin marketing a GM U.S.-built car in Japan with a Toyota nameplate.

The entwining of the passenger car producers is duplicated by the light and heavy truck manufacturers, many of which are the same players. Chrysler initiated joint-venture production in 1992 with the Austrian firm, Steyer-Daimler-Puch, of a slightly modified version of Chrysler's U.S. market-leading minivan for the European markets. Since 1991, Ford has produced in the United States a "badge-engineered" sport-utility truck for Mazda. In 1994, it will supply all of Mazda's light pickup trucks. Mazda previously had imported all of its light trucks from its factories in Japan. Ford also assembles in Ohio a small passenger van that was designed principally by Nissan, using sheet metal panels and engines supplied by the latter from its Tennessee plant. Both firms market the minivan, but with different trim options and nameplates. In late 1993, General Motors and Isuzu announced that they are working out details for the U.S. production of an Isuzu-designed commercial truck. Mitsubishi is reported to be searching for a U.S. source for a light truck. Honda has contracted Isuzu to supply it with a sport utility made in Isuzu's Indiana plant.

Recognizing the high level of competition that exists in the United States, and the need to match or exceed it, General Motors, Ford, and Chrysler—the Big Three—have initiated several jointly funded "pre-competitive" product and manufacturing technology research projects under the umbrella of the United States Council for Automotive Research. USCAR was formed in June 1992 to coordinate more effectively existing and future jointly funded R&D programs. The directorship of the council rotates every 2 years among the three companies. USCAR, in compliance with the National Cooperative Research Act of 1984, cannot focus on the design or production of specific vehicles. It may, however, pursue the development of generic, fundamental technologies to bring vehicles to the market sooner and at less cost to customers and the environment. USCAR will generate new techniques to reduce vehicle emissions and to improve fuel economy, as well as to create more environmentally friendly manufacturing and recycling procedures (discussed later).

The Automotive Composites Consortium, which is under USCAR's purview, seeks to develop new materials for stronger, lighter, and more durable body panels. This consortium already has generated patents for new methods of fabricating polymer-based components. Other USCAR consortia include the Auto Oil/Air Quality Improvement feasibility research program, the CAD/CAM Partnership, the Environmental Science Research Consortium that seeks to improve understanding of the environmental impact of vehicle and manufacturing plant emissions, the High Speed Serial Data Communications Research and Development Partnership, the Low Emissions Technologies Research and Development Partnership, the Low Emission Paint Consortium, the Occupant Safety Research Partnership, the U.S. Advanced Battery Consortium, the U.S. Automotive Materials Partnership, and the Vehicle Recycling Partnership. Industrial research laboratories are participating in several of the consortia.

In September 1993, President Clinton proclaimed a major new undertaking involving the U.S. government and industry. USCAR will join with several agencies of the Federal Government, under the leadership of the Commerce Department's Technology Administration, to inaugurate the New Technology Initiative, a special partnership aimed at strengthening U.S. competitiveness. The initiative will enlist government and industry resources to develop within 10 years a new generation of vehicles having up to three times greater fuel efficiency than now exists. Cooperative research projects, involving private research facilities and the Federal Government's national defense research laboratories, will be launched to develop advanced manufacturing techniques for bringing new product ideas to the market quicker; implement near-term productivity improvements in manufacturing techniques that also will reduce the impact of auto production on the environment; and generate near-term improvements in vehicle fuel consumption, safety, and emissions.

Financial Performance

Domestic corporate earnings of motor vehicle and equipment companies (before taxes, inclusive of inventory adjustments) reached $3.1 billion in 1992, reversing losses of $6.9 billion in 1991. In the first half of 1993, vehicle sales were almost 7 million units, nearly 8 percent higher than the same period of 1992. According to the Commerce Department's Bureau of Economic Analysis, in the first quarter of 1993, total domestic corporate earnings jumped to $4.7 billion, compared with $1.8 billion in the first quarter of 1992.

The Big Three suffered global net income losses in 1992 of $30 billion on worldwide automotive sales and revenues of $236 billion. While Chrysler posted its first net income gain since 1988, Ford reported a loss of $7.4 billion. General Motors' net loss of $23.5 billion was the largest in U.S. corporate history. However, the net income figures of GM and Ford included one-time charges to net income of $20.8 billion and $7.5 billion, respectively, due to Federally required changes in the accounting methodology for post-retirement benefits. Essentially, these are paper losses. Without these charges, the Big Three loss in 1992 was "only" $2.4 billion (compared with a $7.6 billion loss in 1991 on worldwide operations totaling $208 billion).

The Big Three recovered somewhat in 1992. Total net sales and revenues rose for the first time since 1989; gross profits showed their first increase since 1988; and net losses before the nonrecurring accounting charges were less than those of 1991. Profit margins improved over 1991, but returns on sales and equity declined sharply due to one-time accounting charges. Liquidity indicators also improved, with cash and marketable securities continuing to grow and working capital accounts finally increasing. The total debt-to-equity ratio continued upward, however, while the quick and current ratios remained relatively unchanged.

Discounting Chrysler's first-quarter 1993 charge of $4.7 billion for its post-retirement benefits obligation, the three firms generated first-half 1993 gains of $4 billion on worldwide sales of $144 billion, compared with earnings of $245 million on sales of $140 billion during the same period of 1992. Their improved earnings are primarily the result of reduced manufacturing costs, but other factors include expanding market share, enhanced product offerings, less sales incentives, increasing domestic demand partly due to aging of the vehicle fleet, and a strong Japanese yen that reduces the competitiveness of Detroit's primary challengers.

U.S. automotive parts suppliers had increased revenues in 1992 and expected higher sales in 1993. In 1992, the top 50 U.S. original equipment (OE) suppliers had North American sales of $73 billion, an increase of 11 percent. This follows a period of increased losses since 1989, when major U.S. OE suppliers saw a sharp drop in profits due to lack of demand, pricing pressures from Detroit, and foreign competition. Financial pressures on the supplier sector have greatly increased as their customers often ask them to finance R&D, inventory, tooling, and logistics.

In 1992, the parts-producing affiliates of the Big Three—GM's Automotive Components Group (GMACG), Ford's Automotive Components Group (ACG), Chrysler's Acustar, and Chrysler/GM joint venture New Venture Gear—accounted for about 40 percent of North American sales by U.S. OE suppliers. The three companies had sales of $28.6 billion in North America. GMACG was number one in sales, both globally and in North America, with revenues of $23.6 billion and $19.5 billion, respectively. Ford ACG was the number two North American supplier with sales of $7.2 billion and fourth-largest supplier worldwide. Acustar was number 17 in North American sales, and New Venture Gear was 25th. Independent OE suppliers comprise the remaining top 50 OE vendors.

U.S. automotive parts manufacturers that produce replacement parts also posted sales increases in 1992. According to the Motor & Equipment Manufacturers Association (MEMA), U.S. retail sales of aftermarket parts totaled $76.4 billion in 1992, and were expected to rise about 4 percent to $80 billion in 1993.

INTERNATIONAL COMPETITIVENESS

Until recently, exports have played only a minor role in the profit-generating efforts of U.S. firms in this industry. However, recent actions to improve their product offerings, productivity, and prices for the domestic market also have resulted in increased international competitiveness. Automotive exports totaled $47.3 billion in 1992, up from $40.7

billion in 1991, even though total sales in most major foreign markets were flat or negative. The United States exported more automotive parts than motor vehicles ($28.5 billion vs. $18.8 billion) in 1992, while importing more vehicles than parts ($57.1 billion vs. $33.5 billion).

As has been the case for many years, most of the auto deficit is the result of trade with Canada and Mexico, where GM, Ford, and Chrysler operate plants producing vehicles for the U.S. market, and with Japan. The United States had an estimated trade deficit in motor vehicles of $43 billion in 1993, 12 percent higher than in 1992. The estimated 1993 trade deficit in automotive parts was $3.7 billion, compared with a deficit of $5.1 billion in 1992.

Total U.S. direct investment (the market value at the time the investment was made) in place in foreign motor vehicle and equipment manufacturing organizations was $24.5 billion in 1992, compared with $22.8 billion the year before. The foreign subsidiaries created by these investments generated income of $2.9 billion in 1992, up slightly from $2.8 billion in 1991, but far behind $5.1 billion earned in 1989. This trend reflects the intensifying strength of competition abroad and the weakness in demand in most foreign markets. In 1992, capital outflows by U.S. firms were $3.6 billion, mostly to establish operations in newly emerging markets, or to create facilities to supply their U.S. requirements.

The value of direct investment placed in the United States by automotive sector foreign-owned entities totaled $2.7 billion in 1992. However, there was an outflow of $11 million, primarily because of sales, income, and market share losses by U.S. subsidiaries of European and Japanese vehicle and equipment producers. Foreign investors reported losses of $284 million in 1992 on their U.S. motor vehicle and parts operations, following losses of $372 million in 1991. This pattern continued in 1993.

Passenger Cars and Light Trucks

Three American and eight Japanese-owned manufacturers with U.S. plants were active in the United States in 1993. They shared the market with an additional 20 foreign firms that maintain major marketing operations around the country. While the overall economic recovery was modest in 1993, total sales of light vehicles (passenger cars and light trucks, including vans, pickups, sport utilities, and other multipurpose vehicles) gained an estimated 9 percent to reach 14 million units. The portion of the market supplied by locally assembled vehicles did even better, advancing almost 14 percent to 12 million units. Sales of vehicles assembled in U.S. plants affiliated with Japanese firms reached 1.8 million units, an increase of 9 percent over 1992. Sales of traditional imports declined for the eighth consecutive year, falling 13 percent to an estimated 2.1 million units, equal to a 14.6 percent market share. The volume of Japanese-made imports sold in the United States by U.S. and Japanese automakers dropped 11 percent to 1.6 million units, their lowest level in more than 12 years. This volume represents an 11.7 percent share of the total market.

Although some analysts believe that it may be just a cyclical change in purchasing patterns—and one that is near its peak, the domestic market in 1993 continued to exhibit what well may be a fundamental shift toward light trucks (sport utilities, minivans, pickups) and away from station wagons and sedans. Light trucks supplied just 29 percent of the domestic light vehicle market in 1986, but by 1992 accounted for 36 percent of all sales. Light trucks supplied more than 38 percent of the U.S. market during the first 7 months of 1993, compared with 35 percent in the same 1992 period. The strength of the light truck segment, in fact, was responsible for most of the growth in the motor vehicle market. Light trucks increased an estimated 14 percent to 5.3 million units, while sales of passenger cars advanced just 6 percent.

Detroit is particularly competitive in the light truck sector, selling 4 million units—86 percent of that market—in 1992. Japanese firms supplied virtually the rest. Germany and Great Britain are the only other suppliers, selling a few thousand units each year, but they have major marketing efforts under way to increase their sales, if not their market shares.

The eight leading suppliers of light vehicles increased their share of the market from 90 percent in 1986 to 95 percent in 1992, leaving only a few customers for the 20 other companies. The top four firms (GM, Ford, Chrysler, and Toyota) supplied 80 percent of the 1992 market. GM's share has declined by four percentage points since 1986, but it remained by far the predominant individual supplier with 34 percent. Toyota had the largest foreign-owned share—8 percent.

INTERNATIONAL COMPETITIVENESS

In 1992, the United States ranked second to Japan as the leading country producing passenger cars, light trucks, and commercial motor vehicles. U.S. production was 9.7 million units, 20.7 percent of the world's total output. Japan's share was 26.7 percent (12.5

million units). Motor vehicle production in South Korea and Mexico has grown strongly, each having nearly tripled its share of the world market since 1986, and reaching 1.7 million units and 1.1 million units, respectively, in 1992.

On a corporate worldwide basis, GM, Ford, and Chrysler continued to rank first, second, and seventh, with 1992 production estimated by *Automotive News* magazine to have totaled 15.1 million units. The Big Three have major factories in Argentina, Australia, Austria, Belgium, Brazil, Canada, Germany, Great Britain, Mexico, and Spain, plus several smaller facilities in developing countries. According to corporate annual reports, the Big Three spent $11.3 billion worldwide on automotive R&D projects in 1992, an increase of 7 percent over the previous year. From 1986 to 1992, the Big Three invested $95.4 billion worldwide in plant and equipment, even though in the same period they suffered net income losses totaling $2.1 billion. New capital investment by Detroit was $13.5 billion in 1992, when they recorded a net income loss on their automotive operations of $30.1 billion.

General Motors produced 7.1 million vehicles worldwide in 1992, 15 percent of the world's total. Ford manufactured 5.8 million units worldwide (12 percent share). Chrysler's total production of 2.2 million units accounted for 5 percent.

Toyota, with worldwide output of 4.7 million units, was the third-largest producer in 1992. Nissan ranked fifth at 3 million units; Mitsubishi, 10th largest, produced 1.8 million units, as did Honda, in 11th place. *Automotive Industries* magazine estimates that worldwide expenditures by Honda, Nissan, and Toyota on automotive R&D projects totaled $6.7 billion in 1991, a 17 percent increase in dollar terms over 1990.

The Big Three have notable investment positions in several large and small foreign vehicle manufacturers, although there is no direct investment in the Big Three by any foreign vehicle maker. Among its several holdings, GM owns 37.5 percent of the shares of Isuzu, 5.3 percent of Suzuki, and 50 percent of Saab Automobile (Sweden). GM decided in mid-1993 to sell one of its English holdings, Lotus, to Bugatti of Italy. Ford owns 25 percent of Mazda, 10 percent of Kia Motors (South Korea), 100 percent of Jaguar, and 75 percent of Aston Martin (both United Kingdom). Chrysler owns 15.6 percent of Maserati (Italy). Chrysler sold Lamborghini (Italy) and its remaining holdings in Mitsubishi in 1993, and may sell its Maserati share in 1994.

In 1992, the Big Three supplied 24 percent of the 13.8 million unit West European markets, primarily from the several local manufacturing facilities that GM and Ford established or acquired in the 1920's and 1930's. GM's European automotive operations generated an estimated $1.2 billion profit in 1992, and continued to have substantial profits in 1993. During 1992–93, GM reduced its employment 14 percent to 78,000 persons, and increased its productivity 8 to 10 percent each year. Ford Europe lost $1.3 billion in 1992, and was forced subsequently to cut its 1993 work force by 17,000, or 17 percent of its staff. Further losses were expected in 1993. In 1991, Chrysler opened a joint-venture plant in Austria to produce minivans for the European markets. Production reached 15,300 units in 1992 and an estimated 33,000 units in 1993. Chrysler's partner, Steyer-Daimler-Puch, also will build annually up to 47,000 units of Chrysler's Grand Cherokee sport-utility vehicle, beginning in late 1994.

The Big Three have substantial manufacturing operations in Canada (11 plants) and in Mexico (6 plants). In 1992, they assembled 1.6 million vehicles in the former and 600,000 in the latter. In late 1993, GM announced that it will return to Argentina, after terminating operations there in 1978, investing $80 million in a $100 million joint venture with Cidea, the local assembler of Renault cars. Production will begin in 1994, with annual volume of 25,000 vehicles scheduled by 1996. GM's plant in Brazil was expected to assemble 250,000 vehicles in 1993, up from 198,000 units in 1992. GM is reportedly prepared to open a second plant in 1995, if the market continues to expand at its current pace. Ford holds 49 percent of a joint venture in Brazil and Argentina with Volkswagen. Ford produced a total of 177,000 units in the two plants in 1991.

LONG-TERM PROSPECTS

Since the early 1970's, the long-term trend for new car sales in the U.S. market has been flat. However, sales of light trucks have been growing so rapidly that the overall light vehicle market has increased, but only about 1 percent annually since 1981. This situation is expected to persist during the next 5 years, although sales in any given year will continue to oscillate on either side of the trend line.

Fewer residents will reach driving age in the next several years than in the past decade. The negative implication of this development could be offset somewhat, however, by the baby boom's entry into what has typically been their peak earning years, permitting them to own more expensive cars and more of them. Another factor affecting the industry's long-term growth is the response of Federal and local governments to increasingly congested urban streets and overburdened, deteriorating interstate highways. If the response is inadequate, or if a preference evolves for giving greater support to mass transit, future vehicle sales could be adversely affected. As part of its initial effort to address the deteriorating road infrastructure, Congress appropriated $660 million for R&D of "intelligent vehicle highway systems" during FY 1992–97. These funds could greatly reduce traffic congestion and accidents in several critical regional transportation corridors. The appropriation is part of a larger funding to revive and improve the surface transportation network under the Intermodal Surface Transportation Efficiency Act of 1991.

The U.S. light vehicle market will continue to become more competitive, with more producers offering new and revised models on ever-shortening time cycles. Market demand will splinter into smaller segments, aided by the success of the major manufacturers in adopting and refining the high degree of flexibility inherent in the lean manufacturing techniques that were pioneered by Japanese firms. Manufacturers will aggressively exploit their new capabilities by cultivating and filling new market niches with models constructed specifically for them. This strategy will place a heavier burden on product planners, market researchers, design and production engineers, and styling studios to generate new concepts, and to compress their development cycles. Manufacturers also must continue to improve their cost-control procedures so that they can extract profits from relatively small production runs of individual models.

The battle for U.S. market share will exert some downward pressure on prices. However, more stringent safety, environmental, and fuel economy regulations may be introduced; if so, they are likely to increase manufacturer costs and raise prices more rapidly than the average rate of inflation. Producers will thus have additional impetus to maximize manufacturing productivity and to keep costs under control. Consequently, labor relations will become increasingly important to the industry. This is especially true since vehicle assembly operations are becoming more vulnerable to total disruption by local strikes. The low parts inventory procedures being implemented as part of lean manufacturing allow no cushion, even for the temporary disruption of supplies. The new labor contracts signed by the Big Three with the United Auto Workers in late 1993 provides for base-pay increases of 3 percent in 1994, 2 percent bonus payments in the following 2 years, a continuation of existing health-care benefits, and up to $200 per month extra in pension benefits. The contract also renews the existing income-protection program for laid-off workers, providing up to 95 percent of salaries for 3 years.

International

The next several years should witness more cross-border mergers (like the proposed 1994 amalgamation of Volvo and Renault), takeovers, terminations, and the development of even more extensive cooperative production and marketing arrangements between or among firms in the United States, Europe, and Asia. The result will be fewer (perhaps no more than 10), but more equally matched, global contestants. If there are no new barriers, Japanese investment probably will continue to expand in the United States, Europe, and in Asia, as will investment by the Big Three.

European firms will remain focused in their own region, except for the three major German producers, which are all expanding or establishing production facilities in North America. Some analysts expect a turnaround in the European vehicle market to begin in late 1994. The Big Three remain confident that certain of their North American models will thrive in upscale niche markets throughout Europe. They will continue to pursue export sales there.

Detroit also will continue efforts to increase sales in Japan. Good opportunities exist in certain niche segments, although building a viable sales network will be a major challenge. Moreover, the Industrial Bank of Japan predicts that the local market will remain depressed until Japanese FY 1995, when registrations could grow to 7.2 million units. The bank predicts a peak of 7.9 million vehicles in FY 1997, with sales falling to 7 million in 2000.

Significant prospects are emerging quickly in the less-developed Asian markets, which some analysts believe will account for two-thirds of all growth in the world auto market over the next 7 years. The Big Three are moving to augment their local sales offices, as well as to establish and expand existing manufacturing operations in the region. GM is investing nearly $70 million in a $110 million joint venture in Indonesia for the production of right-hand drive light trucks and passenger cars, beginning in 1995. Chrysler is gearing up in Malaysia, with a joint venture assembly operation capable of producing 2,000 Jeep Cherokees per year. Ford already owns 70 percent of a joint venture in Taiwan, and has acknowledged that it is evaluating other sites in Asia for a new assembly plant. General Motors also assembles vehicles in Taiwan. All three companies are thought to be evaluating production sites in Thailand.

The Chinese government expects that auto sales in China, which were 180,000 units in 1992, could reach 1.5 million cars annually by 2003. GM and Chrysler already have joint-production facilities with separate Chinese partners to produce light trucks. Ford began to open a China sales network in 1993 to take part in this expanding market.

South Korea may represent the best near-term export prospect among the developing countries of Asia, with an estimated annual growth rate of 15 percent expected for several years. Sales reached an estimated 1.5 million units in 1993. Although foreign vehicle producers have been denied full market access, liberalizing changes are expected soon.

When the North American Free Trade Agreement (NAFTA) among the United States, Mexico, and Canada is implemented, U.S. producers will benefit from greatly improved access to one of the fastest-growing markets in the Western Hemisphere. Several forecasters expect that, if Mexico experiences the expected economic stimulus from NAFTA, the consumer vehicle market could grow 4 to 7 percent annually in the near term and at higher rates thereafter. The Big Three have a 51 percent share of Mexico's light vehicle market. Because of current import restrictions, however, they must supply the market primarily with local production. Under NAFTA, the elimination of investment and import requirements will allow imports to increase.

The Big Three can maximize their international opportunities if favorable dollar exchange rates continue and there is a sustained commitment to their export strategies. Detroit also must continue to reduce its U.S. operating costs and improve productivity and product quality, perhaps by adopting new "agile manufacturing" techniques that take lean manufacturing to the next plateau. Critical to Detroit's effort will be the availability of low-cost capital for the acquisition of even more flexible plant, tooling, and assembly machinery than now exist. Operating costs must be reduced by improving productivity through more intense employee training. The containment of health-care expenditures for current and retired employees also will be critical.—*Randall Miller and Mark Brectl (Financial Performance section), Office of Automotive Affairs (202) 482-0669.*

Trends and Forecasts: Motor Vehicles and Car Bodies (SIC 3711)

(in millions of dollars except as noted)

Item	1987	1988	1989	1990	1991	1992[1]	1993[2]	1994[3]	Percent Change (1989–1994) 88–89	89–90	90–91	91–92	92–93	93–94
Industry Data														
Value of shipments[4]	133,346	142,060	149,315	140,417	133,861	144,200	161,500	175,800	5.1	-6.0	-4.7	7.7	12.0	8.9
Value of shipments (1987$)	133,346	140,237	143,572	132,594	120,922	126,500	137,900	145,800	2.4	-7.6	-8.8	4.6	9.0	5.7
Total employment (000)	281	250	250	240	218	219	210	205	0.0	-4.0	-9.2	0.5	-4.1	-2.4
Production workers (000)	236	214	213	200	179	178	170	165	-0.5	-6.1	-10.5	-0.6	-4.5	-2.9
Average hourly earnings ($)	17.33	18.68	19.40	20.31	21.32	21.96	22.40	22.85	3.9	4.7	5.0	3.0	2.0	2.0
Capital expenditures	4,121	1,137	2,374	3,004	3,262	—	—	—	108.8	26.5	8.6	—	—	—
Product Data														
Value of shipments[5]	130,857	139,864	144,448	135,741	128,754	138,800	155,800	169,600	3.3	-6.0	-5.1	7.8	12.2	8.9
Value of shipments (1987$)	130,857	138,069	138,892	128,178	116,309	121,900	132,900	140,500	0.6	-7.7	-9.3	4.8	9.0	5.7
Trade Data														
Value of imports	—	—	58,729	60,568	59,131	60,398	62,100	65,200	—	3.1	-2.4	2.1	2.8	5.0
Value of exports	—	—	12,479	12,838	15,180	17,628	18,900	20,300	—	2.9	18.2	16.1	7.2	7.4

[1]Estimate, except exports and imports.
[2]Estimate.
[3]Forecast.
[4]Value of all products and services sold by establishments in the motor vehicles and car bodies industry.
[5]Value of products classified in the motor vehicles and car bodies industry produced by all industries.

SOURCE: U.S. Department of Commerce: Bureau of the Census; International Trade Administration (ITA). Estimates and forecasts by ITA.

U.S. New Light Vehicle Sales by Country of Manufacture, 1992–98

(in thousands of units)

Item	1992[1]	1993[2]	1994[3]	1995[3]	1996[3]	1997[3]	1998[3]
Automobiles							
Total	**8,214**	**8,700**	**9,000**	**9,200**	**9,300**	**8,800**	**8,500**
All local	6,260	7,000	7,400	7,650	7,850	7,400	7,200
Imports	1,954	1,700	1,600	1,550	1,450	1,400	1,300
Japan	1,453	1,300	1,200	1,100	1,000	950	900
Germany	221	200	200	225	225	225	200
Other	280	200	200	225	225	225	200
Light Trucks							
Total	**4,647**	**5,300**	**5,800**	**6,100**	**6,400**	**6,100**	**6,000**
All local	4,248	4,955	5,455	5,760	6,100	5,850	5,765
Imports	399	345	345	340	300	250	235
Japan	392	335	330	315	275	225	215
Other	7	10	15	25	25	25	20
Light Vehicles[4]							
Total	**12,861**	**14,000**	**14,800**	**15,300**	**15,700**	**14,900**	**14,500**
All local	10,508	11,955	12,855	13,410	13,950	13,250	12,965
Imports	2,353	2,045	1,945	1,890	1,750	1,650	1,535
Japan	1,845	1,635	1,530	1,750	1,275	1,175	1,115
Germany (cars)	221	200	200	225	225	225	200
Other	287	210	215	250	250	250	220

[1]Actual.
[2]Estimate.
[3]Forecast.
[4]Automobiles plus light trucks.

NOTE: "Local" includes sales of all vehicles made in the United States and Canada for the U.S. market, plus sales of Big Three units produced in Mexico.

SOURCE: U.S. Department of Commerce, International Trade Administration (ITA); 1992 data from *Ward's Automotive Reports*. Estimates and forecasts by ITA.

Plastics and Rubber

Plastic Materials

This category (SIC 2821) groups together various petroleum-derived monomeric and polymeric materials, whether used singly or in combination, to make a wide variety of molded plastic shapes. Production of plastics follows a well-defined sequence: three primary materials (petroleum, natural gas, and coal) are broken down by refining and fractionation processes into various light-to-heavy petrochemical feedstocks. These materials, also known as light, middle, and heavy oils, are then reacted with others to make more complex intermediates. These can be further reacted with accelerating agents to yield low molecular weight monomers and the heavier, more complex polymers.

General purpose, or commodity thermoplastics are usually manufactured in large quantities using well established technology. The bulk of total general purpose plastic goes to a relatively small number of large volume users. Among the general purpose materials are the simpler monomers, such as the polyethylenes, polystyrenes, and polyvinyls.

In contrast, specialty plastics are specifically developed to meet extreme environmental conditions and involve significant upfront research and development costs. These highly resistant materials are often produced on a customized basis to address the needs of individualized end uses. Typical specialty resins are the cellulosics, the polycarbonates, and the polyetheretherketones.

The final end use often determines how a given material may be classified. Thermoplastics differ from thermosets in that the former can be reheated and remolded repeatedly, while thermosets can be heated and molded to a final shape only one time. About three-quarters of total U.S. production of plastic materials covered by SIC 2821 is thermoplastics.

Total output of U.S. plastic materials producers in 1992 reached an estimated 66.6 billion pounds. Profit margins that had eroded in 1990 and 1991 were partially offset in 1992 as prices stabilized. In volume terms, demand in 1992 was highest for the low- and high-density polyethylenes, polypropylene, polyvinyl chloride, polystyrene, and acrylonitrile butadiene styrene. The fastest growing market segments in 1992, however, were the engineering resins, high-density polyethylene, polyvinyl chloride, and the polyolefins.

INTERNATIONAL COMPETITIVENESS

The United States remains a major net exporter of plastics to the world. Trade with Canada and Mexico accounted for about one-third of total U.S. exports in 1992, followed by the Netherlands, Belgium, Japan, Hong Kong, and Taiwan.

Chronic worldwide overcapacity, particularly in Europe and Japan, however, continues to depress long-term prospects across most product areas. Plant closures and capacity cutbacks have been partially successful in preventing further price declines. Joint ventures between high volume firms have become more frequent as producers see the advantages of pooling resources to prosper in a sagging market.

LONG-TERM PROSPECTS

Material substitution (e.g., plastic for metal, wood, or glass) as a major growth factor is expected to slow down considerably, reflecting the already high level of substitution of plastic now evident in areas once reserved for more traditional materials. However, new applications are emerging. These will place greater demand on convenience and safety features and are likely to generate interest in newer general purpose materials. The cost, low weight, and versatility advantages of newer plastic materials will also make them more attractive in the auto assembly industries. The demand for recycled and biodegradable materials is expected to continue, as well as drive development of more economical recycling technologies.

Plastic Products

The production process for most plastic shapes is well defined. Once a final use is established, the primary inputs (monomers and polymers) are reacted with a variety of chemical reagents (reaction accelerators, antioxidants, and emulsifiers) to impart desired characteristics, and then processed using one or more methods such as coating, extrusion, molding, laminating, and others. Consumption of plastic products is highest in the electronics, health care, construction, transportation, automotive, and food packaging industries.

INTERNATIONAL COMPETITIVENESS

In 1992, exports of about $4.5 billion only slightly exceeded imports of about $4.3 billion. The value of the total trade turnover (sum of imports plus exports) amounted to about 13.5 percent of total industry shipments, domestic and foreign, in 1993. U.S. exports compete favorably against lower cost producers in many third-country markets.

Canada, Taiwan, China, and Japan accounted for the bulk of imports in 1993.

LONG-TERM PROSPECTS

Greater reliance on computer-aided design and manufacturing is expected in the last half of the 1990's as the industry streamlines its production. These measures will be aimed at strengthening the industry's competitiveness in the areas of quality control and improved client relations.

Synthetic Rubber

Synthetic petroleum-based rubber materials in this sector (SIC 2822) are also known as elastomers.

The development of synthetic rubber parallels that of other materials: general purpose commodity materials used in bulk in the tire industry and elsewhere give rise to new applications that, in turn, become more refined over time and stimulate needs for more complex specialty materials. Synthetic rubber (SR) materials therefore fall into two broad categories: general purpose or commodity materials, and the specialty elastomers.

Among the most common general purpose elastomers are styrene-butadiene latex, polychloropropylene, nitrile, ethylenepropylene diene monomer, carboxylated styrene, polybutadiene, and solid elastomers. These are widely used in the production of tires and industrial rubber products. In contrast, specialty elastomers are used in applications where resistance to extreme environmental conditions or considerations of weight and volume are important. While relatively minor as a percentage of total SR volume, specialty elastomers continue to show growth rates far higher than the industry as a whole.

INTERNATIONAL COMPETITIVENESS

The United States now ranks first in production of synthetic rubber with about 26 percent of total world output in 1992. Other major world-class producers in 1992 include the former republics of the Soviet Union (18 percent), Japan (15 percent), Germany (5 percent), and China (4 percent).

Foreign trade is significant in the SR industry: total trade turnover (exports plus imports) accounted for more than one-third of industry shipments in 1993. The favorable U.S. trade balance in synthetic rubber grew steadily during four consecutive years starting in 1989. Recession in major world markets, however, tended to depress export levels during most of 1992. Canada remains both the largest supplier and export market. Other major suppliers in 1992 were Belgium and Mexico.

LONG-TERM PROSPECTS

Growth prospects for the domestic synthetic rubber industry remain mixed, reflecting the industry's dependence on tire manufacturing. Demand for tire-related uses is expected to remain uncertain. Declines, however, will be partially offset by increased use of synthetic rubber as a plastic additive, as well as higher rates of material substitution (rubber compounds for plastic) in the auto industry. Exceptionally high growth rates for high value elastomers are expected through the end of the decade.

Rubber Products

Tires

The tire industry includes companies whose main line of business consists of the production of pneumatic casings, inner tubes, and solid and cushion tires for a variety of vehicles (passenger cars, buses, trucks, bicycles, farm equipment, and airplanes). Also included are tiring, camelback, tire repair, and retreading materials. The primary production elements are natural and synthetic rubber materials, and carbon black.

The industry shows signs of stabilizing after undergoing a period characterized by massive restructuring, the effects of recession in the domestic market, and consistently high levels of imports. With tire durability virtually pushed to what many consider the practical limit, industry strategy has shifted to servicing the fast-growing emerging markets for high-performance, light truck, and recreational vehicle (RV) tires.

INTERNATIONAL COMPETITIVENESS

International restructuring of the industry in recent years has brought about the formation of multinational companies, particularly in Europe and Japan. Among the advantages to be realized by the surviving companies are the reallocation of global resources to spread out R&D costs, and economies of scale across procurement, manufacturing, distribution and service.

Imports continued to outpace exports at a nearly 2:1 ratio in 1993. But a steady growth of exports, starting in 1989, has slowly cut into this negative net trade position since then.

The foreign trade sector of the industry is stable, as evidenced by several consecutive years when the ratio of combined exports and imports to overall industry shipments remained relatively constant. Trade turnover remains at about 30 percent of total industry shipments. Canada is now the United States' largest trading partner, absorbing 40 percent of total U.S. exports, while supplying about 30 percent of imports in 1992.—*Raimundo M. Prat, Office of Metals, Machinery and Chemicals (202) 482-0128.*

Trends and Forecasts: Plastics Materials and Resins (SIC 2821)

(in millions of dollars except as noted)

Item	1987	1988	1989	1990	1991	1992[1]	1993[2]	1994[3]	Percent Change (1989–1994) 88–89	89–90	90–91	91–92	92–93	93–94
Industry Data														
Value of shipments[4]	26,246	32,110	33,257	31,326	29,566	30,406	31,623	—	3.6	-5.8	-5.6	2.8	4.0	—
Value of shipments (1987$)	26,246	26,893	27,622	27,870	27,100	27,642	28,748	30,473	2.7	0.9	-2.8	2.0	4.0	6.0
Total employment (000)	56.3	58.3	62.0	62.4	60.5	59.7	58.8	—	6.3	0.6	-3.0	-1.3	-1.5	—
Production workers (000)	34.9	36.0	37.8	37.9	36.7	36.9	37.4	—	5.0	0.3	-3.2	0.5	1.4	—
Average hourly earnings ($)	15.24	15.37	15.92	16.88	17.25	17.38	17.45	—	3.6	6.0	2.2	0.8	0.4	—
Capital expenditures	1,247	1,606	1,966	2,437	2,252	—	—	—	22.4	24.0	-7.6	—	—	—
Product Data														
Value of shipments[5]	27,812	34,235	34,692	33,038	31,723	32,659	33,930	—	1.3	-4.8	-4.0	3.0	3.9	—
Value of shipments (1987$)	27,812	28,673	28,814	29,393	29,077	29,659	30,845	32,696	0.5	2.0	-1.1	2.0	4.0	6.0
Trade Data														
Value of imports	—	—	1,554	1,811	1,776	2,063	2,570	—	—	16.5	-1.9	16.2	24.6	—
Value of exports	—	—	5,590	6,316	7,447	7,052	7,122	—	—	13.0	17.9	-5.3	1.0	—

[1]Estimate, except exports and imports.
[2]Estimate.
[3]Forecast.
[4]Value of all products and services sold by establishments in the plastics materials and resins industry.
[5]Value of products classified in the plastics materials and resins industry produced by all industries.
SOURCE: U.S. Department of Commerce: Bureau of the Census; International Trade Administration (ITA). Estimates and forecasts by ITA.

Trends and Forecasts: Synthetic Rubber (SIC 2822)

(in millions of dollars except as noted)

Item	1987	1988	1989	1990	1991	1992[1]	1993[2]	1994[3]	Percent Change (1989–1994) 88–89	89–90	90–91	91–92	92–93	93–94
Industry Data														
Value of shipments[4]	3,283	3,996	4,008	4,210	4,088	4,439	4,618	—	0.3	5.0	-2.9	8.6	4.0	—
Value of shipments (1987$)	3,283	3,609	3,630	3,696	3,771	4,073	4,236	4,363	0.6	1.8	2.0	8.0	4.0	3.0
Total employment (000)	10.4	11.3	11.2	11.4	11.5	11.6	11.6	—	-0.9	1.8	0.9	0.9	0.0	—
Production workers (000)	6.7	7.1	7.1	7.2	7.4	7.5	7.5	—	0.0	1.4	2.8	1.4	0.0	—
Average hourly earnings ($)	15.88	16.36	16.78	17.91	17.79	17.80	—	—	2.6	6.7	-0.7	0.1	—	—
Capital expenditures	171	216	266	379	360	—	—	—	23.1	42.5	-5.0	—	—	—
Product Data														
Value of shipments[5]	3,467	3,916	4,070	4,219	3,939	4,169	4,456	—	3.9	3.7	-6.6	5.8	6.9	—
Value of shipments (1987$)	3,467	3,537	3,686	3,704	3,634	3,925	4,088	4,204	4.2	0.5	-1.9	8.0	4.2	2.8
Trade Data														
Value of imports	—	—	514	514	466	530	605	—	—	0.0	-9.3	13.7	14.2	—
Value of exports	—	—	869	885	900	1,010	991	—	—	1.8	1.7	12.2	-1.9	—

[1]Estimate except exports and imports.
[2]Estimate.
[3]Forecast.
[4]Value of all products and services sold by establishments in the synthetic rubber industry.
[5]Value of products classified in the synthetic rubber industry produced by all industries.

SOURCE: U.S. Department of Commerce: Bureau of the Census; International Trade Administration (ITA). Estimates and forecasts by ITA.

Retailing

The retail trade sector (SIC 52–59) is one of the major sources of jobs in the U.S. economy, consistently accounting for about 21 percent of all non-farm jobs in the private sector. Retail establishments are primarily engaged in selling merchandise for personal or household consumption.

Retailers sell an ever-changing combination of durable and nondurable merchandise. The Census Bureau designates the several different types of retail stores according to their principal merchandise lines, such as food stores, or usual trade designations, such as department store or discount store.

A principal merchandise line is one that accounts for at least 50 percent of total sales. Thus, the Census Bureau would classify a retail establishment that derives at least half of its revenue from food as a food retail store, despite the fact that the store also receives part of its revenue from the sale of paper products, soaps, housewares, and services, such as renting rug cleaners or arranging flowers. The store's entire revenue would be recorded as food sales by the Census Bureau.

The Census Bureau's practice of reporting the total sales revenue of a retailer by the principal merchandise line makes it difficult to accurately interpret trends in retail sales of individual merchandise lines as retailers constantly alter their products to adjust to changing consumer demands.

Retail merchandise lines are divided into the following categories: building materials, hardware, garden supplies, and mobile home dealers (SIC 52); general merchandise stores (SIC 53); food stores (SIC 54); automobile dealers and gasoline service stations (SIC 55); apparel and accessory stores (SIC 56); home furniture, furnishings, and equipment stores (SIC 57); eating and drinking places (SIC 58); and miscellaneous retail stores (SIC 59).

In general, sales of retail establishments in SIC groups 52, 55, 57 and 59 are mostly from durable goods and sales of retail establishments in SIC groups 53, 54, 56, and 58 are mostly from nondurable goods.

Year-to-year changes in sales of retail stores concentrating on nondurable merchandise lines, such as food and clothing, tend to mirror changes in general business conditions as indicated by the gross domestic product (GDP), which is forecast to grow about 3 percent in 1994. In contrast, year-to-year changes in sales of retail stores concentrating in durable goods, such as furniture and major household appliances, tend to exaggerate changes in business conditions by increasing more than the GDP during good years and declining more than the GDP during slowdowns. In addition to overall business conditions, retail sales reflect changes in prices, merchandise mix, and shifts to alternative channels of distribution.

Industry Sales

In 1993, total retail sales reached nearly \$2.1 trillion, a gain of more than 6 percent in current dollars. A major portion of the increase was due to price hikes. It is difficult to measure the precise increase in "real dollars" because of the incompatibility of retail sales data and the Consumer Price Index which measures inflation.

Stores selling mostly nondurables accounted for nearly 64 percent of total retail sales, with 1993 revenues topping \$1.3 trillion, up 5.7 percent over 1992. Sales of durable goods totaled \$757 billion in current dollars, up more than 7 percent from 1992, and accounted for 36 percent of the total.

However, these year-to-year gains should be taken as only a rough approximation of the direction of change for the sales value of all consumer durables or nondurables because of the way Census Bureau data is reported. For example, K-Mart reported furniture sales totaling \$364 million in 1991. The Census Bureau reported all of these sales as retail sales of nondurables because K-Mart's principal merchandise lines are nondurable.

Retail stores selling primarily nondurable goods, for which Census Bureau data are available, include general merchandise stores, department stores, food stores, variety stores, apparel stores, restaurants, and drug stores. Other retailers for which Census data are not available include discount stores, warehouse clubs, convenience stores, and catalog and video sales firms.

A list of the top 100 retailing firms compiled by *Chain Store Age Executive* magazine combined the sales data for the top 100 retailing firms in 1992, including data for types of retailers not collected by Census. The results indicated that discount stores accounted for 21 percent of all sales by the top retail stores selling nondurable goods, second only to supermarkets, which represented 35 percent of total sales. Warehouse clubs, a relatively recent entrant into the retail market, accounted for 6 percent of nondurable sales in 1992.

According to the *Chain Store Age Executive*, discount stores and warehouse clubs achieved their current market position mainly by underpricing department stores, variety stores, and drug stores. Supermarkets also increased their market share at the expense of drug stores, and specialty apparel stores captured markets formerly claimed by department stores. A new category of retailer—"G" stores, operated by the major gasoline companies—encroached on the market share of traditional convenience stores.

Competitive Measures

Shifts in market position during the last 5 years prompted retailers to adopt competitive countermeasures, including downsizing and consolidation, merchandise mix changes, more consumer services, and greater use of advanced technologies, such as a quick response system, to control inventory costs and increase productivity.

A quick response system usually involves a strategic alliance between a retailer and manufacturer, coupled with an Electronic Data Interchange (EDI) system, which includes sharing sales, marketing, and inventory data with vendors; bar coding on packaging to track sales and inventory; and point-of-sale scanners to track sales and implement an automated stock replenishment system. It is also essential than an EDI system be able to issue invoices and payments electronically and track consumer buyer patterns.

The most frequently cited benefits of a quick response system include increased inventory turnover and reduced inventory levels, operating costs, and frequency of out-of-stock items. A recent Garr Consulting Group survey of a cross section of retailers conducted for *Chain Store Age Executive* magazine found that 61 percent of those surveyed had entered into strategic alliances with vendors to take advantage of the benefits of a quick response system.

The various competitive strategies undertaken by major types of retailers during the last few years are reviewed in the next section.

Department Stores

Department store sales increased from nearly $153 billion in 1988 to $183 billion in 1993, a 5-year increase of nearly 20 percent, according to Census Bureau data. Despite the growth in sales volume, department stores lost market share to discount stores, warehouse clubs, and specialty apparel shops, dropping from nearly 15 percent of the market for nondurable retailers in 1988 to slightly less than 14 percent in 1993.

To adjust to the competitive pressures from other types of retailers, several department stores, including R. H. Macy and Federated Stores, filed chapter 11 bankruptcy actions while they downsized and restructured their operations. Other department stores have changed their merchandise mix to de-emphasize their durable lines, and highlight their fashion apparel, gifts, and designer household items.

The Garr Consulting Group survey showed 78 percent of the department store managers interviewed reported they had entered into strategic alliances with their vendors to implement the quick response system. In terms of sales, the top five department stores are Mays, J. C. Penney, Federated, R. H. Macy, and Dillard.

Supermarkets

Food retailers increased their sales but accounted for a smaller share of nondurable goods purchased during the 1988–93 period. Sales rose from $326 billion in 1988 to $387 billion in 1992, a gain of nearly 19 percent, according to the Census Bureau. In terms of market share, food stores claimed more than 29 percent of the total market for nondurable retailers in 1993, down from the nearly 32 percent claimed in 1988. Supermarkets have consistently accounted for about 80 percent of all food store sales.

During the last several years, supermarkets lost sales to drugstores, discount stores, and warehouse clubs. To meet these competitive challenges, supermarkets changed their merchandise mix by dropping duplicated product lines and allocating more shelf space to fast-moving, non-food items and promotional items. Some supermarkets also have revised their marketing strategy, shifting some of their advertising dollars from weekly newspaper inserts to direct mail circulars.

According to the Garr Consulting Group survey, 46 percent of the supermarket managers surveyed said that they have entered into strategic alliances with their vendors to implement the quick response system. In addition, a few supermarkets have expanded their consumer services, such as accepting telephone orders of groceries for home delivery.

The top five supermarkets are Kroger, American Stores, Safeway, A&P, and Winn-Dixie.

Warehouse Clubs

The number of warehouse clubs increased from 15 in 1983 to 577 in 1992, experiencing double digit growth in sales and earnings until the early 1990's. Since then, warehouse club sales and earnings have declined.

Part of this deterioration in sales and earnings is due to competitive challenges from other types of retailers such as supermarkets. In response, warehouse clubs are downsizing and restructuring, changing their mix of merchandise, adding more services, and opening new markets. K-Mart's recent sale of Pace

Club to Sam's Club, and Costco's merger with Price Club, are examples of the new competitive strategies. Price Club and Sam's Club also entered new markets by forming joint ventures with retailers in Mexico.

The top warehouse clubs include Price Club, Sam's Club, and Waban.

Discount Stores

Sales of the big 10 discount stores grew at a robust average annual rate of 11.5 percent from 1987–1991, according to *Chain Store Age Executive* magazine. But discount stores' sales have begun to slow, increasing only 10.3 percent from 1990 to 1991—the latest period for which revenue figures are available. A closer look at the individual sales changes from 1990 to 1991, compared to the full 1987–1991 period, reveals a significant slowdown in the revenue of several discounters, including Hills, Ames, and Rose's. As a result, discount stores have implemented strategies to maintain their market standing, including downsizing and restructuring, changing their merchandise mix, adding services, and intensifying the use of their quick response systems.

The Garr Consulting Group report revealed that 50 percent of the discount store managers responding to the survey said they have entered into strategic alliances with their vendors to implement their quick response systems.

Discount stores also are changing their merchandise mix by adding groceries to their product lines. Others are adding more services, such as beauty shops and in-store opticians. A few discount stores also are expanding into new markets by forming joint ventures with retailers in Mexico.

The major discount stores include Walmart, K-Mart, Stop N Shop, Pacific Enterprises, and Ames.

Apparel Stores

Apparel and accessory stores posted sales of $108 billion in 1993, up 27 percent from the $85 billion recorded for 1988. In terms of market position, apparel and accessory stores have maintained a fairly stable 8 percent of total sales of all retailers of nondurable merchandise. Apparel and accessory stores have been effective in maintaining their market position by emphasizing fashion and value, thereby capturing consumer clothing sales previously claimed by department stores.

According to the Garr Consulting Group survey, 59 percent of the apparel store managers surveyed reported that they have entered into strategic alliances with their vendors to implement quick response systems.

The top retail firms selling mostly apparel and accessories are: Melville, The Limited, TJX Co., U.S. Shoe, and Gap.

Drug Stores

Drugstore sales increased nearly 37 percent from $57 billion in 1988 to $78 billion in 1993 while their market share remained relatively steady at about 6 percent, despite strong competition from supermarkets and discount stores. Part of this stability may be attributed to the strong sales position of two of the major discount drug stores, Phar-Mor and Drug Emporium. Traditional and chain drug stores, in contrast, have lost market position to supermarkets and discount stores.

In response to that competition, traditional and chain drug stores have changed their merchandise mix to include many food and convenience items and downsized their hardware and related departments. Some have expanded their services to include free delivery of medicines and drugs, a valuable service to the elderly and mothers of young children. Others have made shopping easier by relocating in strip malls and other easy in-and-out locations, rather than in large shopping malls.

The top drug stores are Walgreen, Eckerd, Rite Aid, Phar-Mor, and Drug Emporium.

Restaurants

Restaurant sales increased at an average annual rate of 4.5 percent from 1988 to 1993. During this same period, the number of restaurants also increased. However, as *Nation's Restaurant News* points out, the number of restaurants is constantly changing, as new entrants come and go and chains expand into new areas. In addition to the many single proprietorships, there are at least 100 chains that service one or more of the twelve niche markets. They include: dinner houses (e.g., Red Lobster), sandwich shops (e.g., McDonalds), family restaurants (e.g., Denny's), chicken shops (e.g., KFC), pizza shops (e.g., Pizza Hut), steak houses (e.g., Bonanza), seafood houses (e.g., Captain D's), snack restaurants (e.g., Dunkin' Donuts), cafeterias (e.g., Morrison's), contract food service (e.g., Marriott), hotel restaurants (e.g., Hilton Hotels), theme park food services (e.g., Disneyland), and in-store restaurants (e.g., K-Mart).

Each of these individual markets showed a different growth pattern between 1988 and 1993. *Nation's Restaurant News* reports that dinner houses posted the fastest growth rates, both in terms of sales and the number of outlets opened. Family restaurants were a close second. Sandwich shops lost sales to dinner houses and family restaurants during that period. Growth in hotel and theme park restaurants was less than 2 percent.

To meet the competitive challenge of dinner houses and family restaurants, sandwich shops are expanding into greater levels of service and providing more value for the customer's dollar. In addition, the sandwich shops are using computers to integrate order taking, food preparation and service, inventory control, and managerial and accounting functions.

According to *Restaurant News*, the top restaurant chains in terms of sales are McDonalds, Burger King, Pizza Hut, Hardee's and KFC.

INTERNATIONAL COMPETITIVENESS

Until recently, few retailers attempted to expand into foreign markets. But the easing of investment restrictions in some foreign countries, and the emerging trend of establishing affiliated firms abroad, has launched a new era in retailing.

The precise volume of exports and imports attributable to retailers is not known because merchandise trade flows are identified by type of product (e.g., manufactured, agricultural, metals, and minerals, etc.) rather than type of organization. The only export data identified by type of organization are listed in the *U.S. Direct Investment Abroad* (DIA) reports published every 5 years. The latest, the 1989 benchmark survey, shows the 50 U.S. retailers, with 211 foreign affiliates, exported merchandise valued at $200 million to affiliated firms in foreign markets. They included retailers of general merchandise, food, clothing, autos, garden supplies, hardware, as well as discount stores and catalog retailers. In addition, U.S. retailers reported $500 million in direct sales to foreign customers.

In 1989, major stores with at least one affiliated firm in a foreign market included Sears, J. C. Penney, Woolworth, and Carter-Hawley. The foreign affiliates of these retail parent firms were either wholly owned or majority owned by the U.S. firm. Since then, several other major U.S. retailers have established affiliated firms in foreign countries, including Toys-R-Us, Sam's Club, K-Mart, Price Club, Blockbuster, and Dillard.

Most recent investments in foreign affiliates have been in Mexico due to easing of government restrictions on joint ventures and other business activities that had previously been imposed on foreign investors. Further expansions are expected pending congressional approval of the North American Free Trade Agreement.

Foreign governments often impose restrictions on how or where foreign firms may operate or limit foreign investment to certain sectors or organizational arrangements. These constraints discourage U.S. retailers from expanding into new markets through affiliated firms in foreign countries. A major objective of the Uruguay Round of multilateral trade negotiations, as well as separate bilateral consultations, is to reduce or eliminate restrictions on investment. If the negotiations are successful, more U.S. retailers will be encouraged to expand to new foreign markets. For example, bilateral consultations with Japan have resulted in an easing of restrictions on the size of foreign retail stores, prompting Toys-R-Us and Blockbuster Video to establish affiliated firms there.

Additional U.S. investment in retail affiliates abroad may increase the demand for American exports from U.S. parent retail firms to their foreign affiliates.

LONG-TERM PROSPECTS

Retailers of nondurable merchandise face a dual challenge of a slow-growing market and changes in demographics and consumer buying habits that have spawned structural changes within the industry. The retailers that adjust their competitive strategies to these new realities, and take advantage of the new marketing techniques such as electronic retailing, catalog marketing, smaller stores, and improved customer service, should succeed in improving their market position in the changing retailing era of the 1990's.—*James Walsh, Office of Service Industries (202) 482-5131.*

Trends and Forecasts: Retail Sales (SIC 52–59)

(in billions of dollars except as noted)

Item	1988	1989	1990	1991	1992	1993[1]	1994[2]	Percent Change (1988–94) 88–89	89–90	90–91	91–92	92–93	93–94
All stores	1,650	1,734	1,826	1,866	1,962	2,086	2,232	5.1	5.3	2.2	5.1	6.3	7.0
Total nondurables	1,022	1,088	1,165	1,212	1,257	1,329	1,411	6.5	7.1	4.0	3.7	5.7	6.2
General merchandise	192	203	212	228	247	280	320	5.7	4.4	7.5	8.3	13.4	14.3
Apparel	85	91	94	97	105	108	112	7.0	3.3	3.2	8.2	2.9	3.7
Restaurants	166	174	186	197	202	207	216	4.8	6.9	5.9	2.5	2.5	4.4
Drugs	57	61	69	76	77	78	80	7.0	13.1	10.1	1.3	1.3	2.6
Food	326	349	372	377	384	387	399	7.1	6.6	1.3	1.9	0.8	3.1
Other	196	210	232	237	242	269	284	7.1	10.5	2.2	2.1	11.2	5.6
Total durables	628	646	661	654	705	757	821	2.9	2.3	-1.1	7.8	7.4	8.5
Employment (millions)	19.1	19.6	19.7	19.3	19.1	19.3	NA	2.6	.5	-2.0	-1.0	1.1	NA
Average hourly earnings ($)	6.31	6.53	6.76	6.95	7.14	7.26	NA	3.5	3.5	2.8	2.7	1.7	NA

[1]Estimate.
[2]Forecast.

SOURCE: U.S. Department of Commerce: Bureau of the Census, International Trade Administration (ITA); U.S. Department of Labor, Bureau of Labor Statistics. Estimates and forecasts by ITA.

1992 Retail Sales of Nondurable Products

(by type of store, ranked by total sales*)

Item	Market Share (in percent)
Super markets	35.0
Discount stores	21.0
Department stores	13.0
General merchandise	8.0
Specialty apparel	7.0
Warehouse clubs	6.0
Drug stores	5.0
Convenience stores	3.0
Variety stores	2.0
Total	100.0

*Based on total sales of the top 100 retailers of nondurable merchandise in 1992. Excludes revenues of catalogs and video sales channels, estimated at $2 billion.

SOURCE: *Chain Store Age Executive*, April 1993.

Telecommunications

The telecommunications equipment industry is composed of telephone and telegraph apparatus (SIC 3661) and radio and television broadcasting and communications equipment (SIC 3663). Telephone and telegraph apparatus includes both network equipment such as switching and transmission equipment, as well as customer premises equipment such as telephones and facsimile machines. Radio and television broadcasting and communications equipment encompasses fixed and mobile radio systems; cellular radio telephones; radio transmitters, transceivers and receivers (except household and automotive receivers); fiber optics equipment; satellite communications systems (space and ground segments); closed-circuit and cable television equipment; and studio (audio and video) equipment.

Navigation equipment refers to SIC 3812, search, detection, navigation, guidance, aeronautical, and nautical systems, instruments and equipment. It includes radar and sonar systems, light reconnaissance and surveillance equipment, and electronic warfare equipment.

The sluggish performance of the U.S. telecommunications equipment industry in 1993 reflected excess capacity in the wired network coupled with static demand pending commercial development of new services. Shipments were essentially unchanged, at slightly more than $35.5 billion in constant dollars, from 1992 to 1993. Shipments of telephone and telegraph apparatus (SIC 3661) remained steady at about $17.5 billion, while shipments of radio and television broadcasting and communications equipment (SIC 3663) edged up slightly to $18 billion from $17.8 billion in 1992.

Employment in the telecommunications equipment industry remained steady at about 230,000 in 1993, reflecting continuing efforts by manufacturers to control costs. New technology and improved productivity may contribute to employment declines in 1994, as will mergers and consolidations among manufacturers.

INTERNATIONAL COMPETITIVENESS

After stabilizing at about $500 million in 1991 and 1992, the U.S. telecommunications trade deficit was expected to narrow to about $200 million in 1993. U.S. telecommunications imports increased about 6 percent to an estimated $8.8 billion, up from $8.3 billion in 1992. Telecommunications exports increased about 10 percent to an estimated $8.6 billion, up from $7.8 billion in 1992. Although the industry registered a $100 million trade surplus in the first half of 1993, there is historically a deficit in the second half of the year. Figures for telecommunications trade in the first half of 1993 demonstrated a steady rise in import growth and a resurgence in export growth compared with the last several years.

Canada and Mexico continued to rank closely as the largest export markets for U.S. telecommunications products in 1993, accounting for 16 and 11 percent of the total, respectively. After declining sharply in 1992, telecommunications exports to Japan, the third largest U.S. export market, rose 70 percent in the first half of 1993. About 20 percent of U.S. telecommunications exports are shipped to the European Community.

Telecommunications imports from East Asia comprised 65 percent of the total in 1993. Japan alone accounts for about one-third of total U.S. telecommunications imports. Imports from new suppliers, particularly China, Malaysia, Thailand, and the Philippines, are experiencing high rates of growth and are supplementing those from traditional suppliers such as Hong Kong, South Korea, Singapore, and Taiwan. In fact, China and Malaysia now rank as the third and fourth largest suppliers of U.S. telecommunications imports, respectively. The European Community accounts for about 7 percent of total imports.

The U.S. continues to have a sizeable trade deficit in customer premises equipment (CPE), about $1.6 billion in the first half of 1993. This was offset to a large extent by trade surpluses in the areas of network/transmission equipment amounting to $800 million, and "other" telecommunications equipment (primarily radio communications, broadcasting, and categories that cannot be distinguished), also $800 million.

In addition, parts represent a significant amount of U.S. telecommunications trade. Parts exports of $1.6 billion accounted for almost 36 percent of the total in the first 6 months of 1993. By comparison, parts imports of $1 billion represented about 24 percent of total imports during the same period.

The leading telecommunications import categories are facsimile machines, line telephones and cordless telephones, accounting for more than $1.4 billion in the first half of 1993. These are followed by radio transceivers, parts for radio equipment, television transmission equipment, and cellular telephones.

On the export side, radio transceivers continued to be the leading product category, accounting for $900 million in January–June 1993. The next largest categories are parts for radio equipment, parts for switching equipment, parts for telephonic apparatus and switching equipment.

LONG-TERM PROSPECTS

The outlook for telecommunications equipment through 1998 is increasingly positive, with shipments forecast to grow an average of 2–4 percent per year. New service offerings and foreign procurements will drive demand for new equipment.

Once these services are authorized, new technologies will generate growth in many sectors of the telecommunications equipment industry. The trend towards deployment of fiber optic cable in the local loop will spark growth in both fiber optic equipment and new network equipment. The development of wireless personal communications services will fuel demand for radio base station equipment and antennas, low earth orbit satellite systems and new wireless customer premises equipment.

In the longer term, future telecommunications networks will be substantially transformed by the demand for customized, interconnected and wireless services. Networks will gradually evolve to new hybrids characterized by transparent interoperability and connectivity between technologies. The massive capital requirements of building unique telecommunications systems will drive service providers to use existing facilities, such as wired, cable, cellular and satellite systems to control costs and create mass markets. New services will demand enhanced intelligence capabilities in switching and transmission facilities. The thrust of the remaining 1990's decade will be to add more intelligence to switching and transmission facilities, enabling full interconnectivity between differing technologies.—*Linda L. Gossack and John R. Henry, Office of Telecommunications (202) 482-4466.*

Cellular Radiotelephone Systems

As the U.S. cellular industry marked its tenth anniversary in October 1993, its impressive growth trend continued unabated, despite highly publicized, unsubstantiated allegations of harmful radiation from handheld cellular telephones. The commercial availability of digital cellular equipment in 1993 spurred the transition from analog to digital technology, although continued industry divisiveness over digital standards has dampened momentum. Numerous technological advances enhancing the features and capacity of analog systems may further delay more aggressive digital deployment.

The Cellular Telecommunications Industry Association (CTIA) reported more than 13 million U.S. cellular subscribers by mid-1993. With a growth rate amounting to more than 300,000 new subscribers per month, the number of cellular users in the United States was expected to be nearly 15 million by the end of 1993, up 36 percent over 1992. Cumulative capital investment grew by $3.5 billion from mid-92 to mid-93, or 38 percent, to $12.8 billion. This increase stems from the network investment required to enhance analog systems as well as add digital channels.

Beginning with their 1992 survey, the Bureau of the Census collected data on cellular equipment shipments. Shipments of cellular radio equipment (base stations as well as subscriber units) were $3.2 billion in 1992, up from $2.9 billion in 1991. Shipments of cellular switching equipment were not reported. The total size of the cellular equipment market for 1993 is extrapolated from the expected increase in the number of subscribers during the year. Using this base, the market reached an estimated $3.7 billion in 1993, up about 23 percent from $3 billion in 1992.

As of June 1993, there were 1,523 cellular systems in operation, up from 1,506 at the end of 1992. The number of cell sites reached 11,551, up from 10,307 at the end of 1992. Statistics collected by the FCC indicate more than 17,000 cells installed. The discrepancy is due to a high degree of sectorization of cell sites into three cells to improve call quality.

Annual service revenues in 1993 approached $10 billion, up more than 30 percent over 1992. Roaming (using cellular outside of one's home service area) accounted for about 12 percent of total revenue. The average cost of local cellular service declined 2 percent in 1993 to about $67.30 per month, and the average cellular call lasted nearly 2.4 minutes.

U.S. Market Trends

The U.S. cellular market moved further toward its goal of a seamless national network with the selection of Independent Telecommunications Network, Inc. (ITN) to establish a Signalling System 7 backbone network to transport cellular calls between system operators. This development positively affects the entire cellular industry by facilitating nationwide automatic call delivery, thereby broadening user appeal.

Commercial deployment of digital cellular technology in the U.S. market began in 1993. As of September 1993, at least two carriers were providing digital service to an estimated

20,000 subscribers: McCaw and Southwestern Bell. Both companies planned to further expand digital coverage in their markets by the end of 1993.

These first digital systems use time division multiple access (TDMA), one of two competing U.S. digital cellular standards. Many carriers have also been testing the rival standard, code division multiple access (CDMA), and several plan deployment of the latter in late 1994, including US West New Vector Group, Bell Atlantic, and Pacific Telesis. BellSouth's test of extended-TDMA (E-TDMA), a technology developed and produced by Hughes Network Systems, achieved an elevenfold capacity increase.

In contrast, Ameritech has decided to delay its digital deployment indefinitely. Their decision was based on field tests of TDMA in which customers felt that the digital service could not meet the quality standards of the analog system. Many other carriers remain undecided as to which standard to use. As a result, the transition to digital cellular in the United States is proceeding more slowly than expected.

The major U.S. handset and infrastructure equipment manufacturers will sell products based on both standards. Many dual-mode (analog/digital) TDMA phones are already on the market, produced by Motorola, Ericsson-GE Mobile Communications and others. The first dual-mode phone for CDMA was introduced by Qualcomm in early 1993. The company has received FCC type-acceptance for the phone and at least one large order from US West New Vector Group. Motorola introduced a prototype dual-mode CDMA base station in early 1993. Although TDMA is the first digital system to be commercially available, deployment has been slower than initially forecast. CDMA will not be ready for commercial deployment until mid-1994 or later. Meanwhile, a number of carriers, especially those in smaller markets, seem willing to take advantage of sectorized antennas, cell enhancers, microcells and narrowband-AMPS (N-AMPS) and to wait and make their digital technology choice based on merit rather than speed. Dataquest Inc. predicts that in 1997, dual-mode TDMA will be in use in 24 percent of U.S. markets, dual-mode CDMA in 19 percent, while AMPS or N-AMPS analog systems will continue in 57 percent. The Department of Commerce estimates only 300,000 TDMA subscribers by the end of 1994.

The uncertainty over digital standards has created an unanticipated market for products to support multiple interfaces. For example, Motorola unveiled its next generation base station system that supports analog and TDMA or CDMA digital interfaces, giving operators flexibility in their technology choices and customers a smooth transition to digital. Steinbrecher Corp.'s MiniCell generic base station transceiver handles multiple calls using all modulation standards, including U.S. and foreign analog and digital standards, and data, transmission, simultaneously. Several versions are available for use with a variety of wireless networks, including paging and PCS.

About 5 million cellular telephones were sold in the United States in 1993, up 13 percent over 1992, according to Herschel Shosteck Associates. Phone sales tend to exceed the number of new subscribers by about 20 percent due to purchases of replacement and multiple phones by subscribers. The average wholesale price of cellular phones decreased to about $280 in 1993, although the decline was at a slower pace than in previous years. The continuing downward trend in wholesale phone prices, combined with deep carrier discounts on handsets, has helped spur the entrance of consumer users into a market traditionally dominated by business users. The entrance of dual-mode phones into the market during the longer term may push up average phone prices, though this will depend on the growth of digital subscribership.

Another important trend in the cellular telephone market is the availability of new features made possible by advances in electronic circuitry and the increasing intelligence built into the cellular network. These features include voice dialing and alphanumeric display for short messaging, among others.

In many cases cellular phones are crossing the lines that formerly defined distinct communications areas. For example, Telular introduced two products that allow consumers to switch between landline and cellular service: PCS One transforms a portable cellular phone into a landline telephone, and PhoneCell allows landline phones, faxes or modems to operate on a cellular system. NovAtel also developed a cellular phone that converts to a landline phone while retaining its cellular calling features.

Another growing area is the transmission of data over the cellular network. It is estimated that portable faxes and modems are being used by about 500,000 U.S. cellular subscribers. Several new products were introduced in 1993: Technophone launched a portable cellular phone with an optional cellular datafax interface; Motorola, ZyXel and others have cellular modems on the market; ORA Electronics developed a data link to allow portable computers to communicate through cellular phones.

Cellular data got a boost in 1993 with the publication of the cellular digital packet data

(CDPD) protocol, a technology originally developed by IBM for the transmission of data over analog cellular systems. The CDPD consortium's long-term goal is a nationwide overlay network for data transmission. Products meeting the CDPD specification started coming to market in mid-1993. AT&T announced a mobile data base station and mobile data intermediary system to work with AMPS equipment. Steinbrecher Inc., Pacific Communication Sciences, Inc., and Cellular Data, Inc. are supplying mobile data base stations for McCaw's new Wireless Data Division.

Another wireless data innovation is the personal computer memory card international association (PCMCIA), a format to ensure interoperability of data transmission hardware and software products for both cellular and noncellular data networks. Nokia (Finland) and AT&T developed the first PCMCIA cellular modem in early 1993, and Motorola introduced its line of four credit-card sized modems to plug into PCMCIA standard ports.

In another development, firms sought to tap the emerging rental market with the introduction of new products such as cellular vending machines and sophisticated interactive software. These products enable consumers to rent cellular phones at locations without technical representatives. Greater availability of rental units should stimulate sales to the rental companies and also expose prospective subscribers to the technology.

INTERNATIONAL COMPETITIVENESS

Due to the lack of official trade data for cellular infrastructure equipment, the U.S. trade balance on these products cannot be quantified. To date, available information suggests that the United States enjoys a considerable market presence in this area.

There are no official export statistics for cellular telephones, although a number of U.S. manufacturers sell abroad. Statistics indicate that about 40 percent of phones purchased in the United States are imported. Imports topped 2 million units, valued at more than $400 million in 1993. While the number of units imported was up 41 percent over 1992, the value of those units increased only 19 percent, indicating a decrease in the average price of imported phones. Japan, Hong Kong, and China had the highest shares of the import market, at 40, 21 and 17 percent of total volume, and 45, 16 and 16 percent of total value, respectively. Imports from China were up 75 percent over 1992. Imports from Finland jumped nearly 600 percent to more than 25,000 phones, while imports from the United Kingdom in 1993 fell by 87 percent from the 1992 figure.

Although portables are an estimated 50 percent of U.S. cellular phone sales, they accounted for only 21 percent of imports (26 percent of total value) in 1993. Vehicular units accounted for 57 percent (53 percent of value) and transportables 22 percent (21 percent of value).

The number of cellular subscribers worldwide neared 27 million in mid-1993, an increase of about 18 percent over 1992 figures. Nearly 110 countries now offer cellular service; an estimated 30 new systems started operation in 1993 (in some cases these are competing with existing systems). The United States continues to have almost half of all worldwide subscribers. Japan is the second largest market, with more than 2 million subscribers by mid-1993. Other leading markets include the United Kingdom, Germany, Canada, Italy, Sweden, and Australia. One notable trend: subscriber numbers in Mexico and several Southeast Asian countries have equalled or surpassed those of Norway and Finland, although the Scandinavian countries still have among the highest penetration rates in the world.

As of September 1993, there were 17 global system for mobile communications (GSM) digital cellular systems in operation in 10 European countries, with 13 more planned for the near future. Dataquest Inc. forecast 1 million GSM subscribers in western Europe by the end of 1993, about half of those in Germany. In addition to being the only digital standard in Europe, GSM has also been chosen by many countries outside of Europe, partly as a result of aggressive campaigns by European equipment manufacturers and governments, and partly because it was the first digital standard on the market. Many countries in the Asia-Pacific region (except Japan), Eastern Europe, Africa and the Middle East have committed to building GSM systems. In 1993, GSM licenses were awarded or pending in Hungary, India, Russia, Turkey, and South Africa.

By 1994 U.S. manufacturers will supply GSM equipment to carriers in at least nine countries, among them Pakistan, Spain, Sweden, and the U.K. AT&T won three GSM contracts, including one in the United Arab Emirates. Compatibility has been established between Motorola's GSM base station and switches produced by Ericsson, Alcatel, and Siemens. Motorola has cross-licensed patents with Ericsson and Nokia, and the company recently completed an expansion of a plant in the U.K. to produce GSM products. Motorola has had considerable success with its lightweight, inexpensive GSM handset.

GSM has experienced some deployment problems. In addition to extended delays in its introduction because of the complexity of the technology and lack of test equipment, its operation in Australia and Europe has caused interference at certain frequencies with analog cellular phones, hearing aids, car alarms and other radio spectrum users.

In Japan, new digital licensees awarded major contracts to Ericsson and Motorola for infrastructure equipment. Handset manufacturers are readying for the planned deregulation of cellular phone sales from the current lease-only market structure. Japan has authorized customer ownership of phones, effective in April 1994. Networks of retail outlets are forming to prepare for the nticipated exponential increase in demand.

Major equipment contracts for U.S. cellular firms in 1993 included Motorola's contract to expand the cellular network in the Shanghai region of China; Hughes Network Systems' selection to provide a fixed and mobile digital cellular system in Chengdu, China; and AT&T's sale of network equipment to Poland, Ghana, and South Korea. Qualcomm signed two agreements: with South Korean companies for the manufacture of CDMA equipment for South Korea's proposed digital system, and with the Russian Telecommunications Ministry for allocation of spectrum and implementation of a CDMA network. Qualcomm will also supply CDMA equipment to the Australian telephone company for technical trials.

In the international cellular infrastructure market, Ericsson of Sweden is the dominant supplier, with 33 percent of the market in 1990. Future sales opportunities will be affected by producers' willingness to make equipment for multiple standards. Ericsson, Motorola, and Northern Telecom are committed to produce equipment for all major digital standards, although Ericsson is the only one with proficiency in both cell sites and switches. As open system architecture becomes more prevalent, the specializations of Motorola in cell sites and Northern Telecom in switches may be a long-term advantage.

According to the U.S. International Trade Commission (ITC), Motorola has the largest segment of the global cellular telephone market, and likely will remain dominant because of its experience in radio electronics and its broad product line encompassing most standards.

In June 1993 the ITC concluded in a study that U.S. cellular companies are among the most competitive in the world. It also suggested that U.S. industry's inability to adopt a common digital standard has adversely affected U.S. foreign sales of cellular network equipment.

LONG-TERM PROSPECTS

By the late 1990's, the U.S. market is expected to grow to 30–35 million cellular subscribers. The size of the equipment market should slowly level out as digital technology lowers the incremental cost of adding new subscribers to the network. However, the market schism over digital technology is unlikely to be resolved for the next several years, until after CDMA is commercially deployed. In the meantime, domestic sales of analog equipment are expected to remain healthy as many carriers continue to expand their AMPS and N-AMPS networks.

Foreign equipment sales are likely to suffer as additional countries choose the more universally accepted GSM digital standard, a market that European vendors currently dominate. Average phone prices will be pushed up by the increasing penetration of more expensive dual-mode systems.

Advances in digital and microcellular technologies, as well as competition from personal communications services (PCS), will stimulate new equipment purchases by cellular carriers and customers over the five-year forecast period. Despite earlier concerns that PCS would capture some of cellular's future market, U.S. experience suggests that new communications technologies often enhance rather than supplant their predecessors. Competition from PCS is therefore likely to spark continued innovation and growth in the cellular industry.—*Linda L. Gossack and Stephanie W. McCullough, Office of Telecommunications (202) 482-4466.*

Trends and Forecasts: Telecommunications Equipment (SIC 3661, 3663)

(in millions of dollars except as noted)

Item	1987	1988	1989	1990	1991	1992[1]	1993[2]	1994[3]	Percent Change (1989–1994) 88–89	89–90	90–91	91–92	92–93	93–94
Industry Data														
Value of shipments[4]	31,811	33,594	32,754	36,057	35,590	—	—	—	-2.5	10.1	-1.3	—	—	—
Value of shipments (1987$)	31,811	33,898	32,843	36,408	35,528	35,350	35,500	35,800	-3.1	10.9	-2.4	-0.5	0.4	0.8
Total employment (000)	238	241	232	228	218	—	—	—	-3.7	-1.7	-4.4	—	—	—
Production workers (000)	117	116	111	109	101	—	—	—	-4.3	-1.8	-7.3	—	—	—
Average hourly earnings ($)	11.97	12.43	13.13	12.99	13.39	—	—	—	5.6	-1.1	3.1	—	—	—
Capital expenditures	1,175	1,330	1,271	1,345	1,051	—	—	—	-4.4	5.8	-21.9	—	—	—
Product Data														
Value of shipments[5]	29,784	32,130	31,014	33,772	32,531	—	—	—	-3.5	8.9	-3.7	—	—	—
Value of shipments (1987$)	29,784	32,404	31,101	34,092	32,436	—	—	—	-4.0	9.6	-4.9	—	—	—
Trade Data														
Value of imports	—	—	7,012	7,156	7,246	8,278	9,183	10,050	—	2.1	1.3	14.2	10.9	9.4
Value of exports	—	—	4,979	6,159	6,464	7,522	9,136	10,250	—	23.7	5.0	16.4	21.5	12.2

[1]Estimate, except exports and imports.
[2]Estimate.
[3]Forecast.
[4]Value of all products and services sold by establishments in the telecommunications equipment industry.
[5]Value of products classified in the telecommunications equipment industry produced by all industries.

SOURCE: U.S. Department of Commerce: Bureau of the Census; International Trade Administration (ITA). Estimates and forecasts by ITA.

Trends and Forecasts: Radio and TV Communications Equipment (SIC 3663)

(in millions of dollars except as noted)

Item	1987	1988	1989	1990	1991	1992[1]	1993[2]	1994[3]	Percent Change (1989–1994) 88–89	89–90	90–91	91–92	92–93	93–94
Industry Data														
Value of shipments[4]	14,229	15,693	17,287	18,759	18,165	—	—	—	10.2	8.5	-3.2	—	—	—
Value of shipments (1987$)	14,229	15,538	16,848	18,428	17,602	17,800	18,000	18,400	8.4	9.4	-4.5	1.1	1.1	2.2
Total employment (000)	126	129	135	135	123	—	—	—	4.7	0.0	-8.9	—	—	—
Production workers (000)	58.5	58.5	62.1	62.4	53.7	—	—	—	6.2	0.5	-13.9	—	—	—
Average hourly earnings ($)	11.17	11.55	12.10	11.90	12.51	—	—	—	4.8	-1.7	5.1	—	—	—
Capital expenditures	623	705	698	752	592	—	—	—	-1.0	7.7	-21.3	—	—	—
Product Data														
Value of shipments[5]	13,256	15,462	16,335	17,735	17,247	17,420	17,800	18,150	5.6	8.6	-2.8	1.0	2.2	2.0
Value of shipments (1987$)	13,256	15,309	15,921	17,422	16,712	—	—	—	4.0	9.4	-4.1	—	—	—
Trade Data														
Value of imports	—	—	2,723	3,049	2,696	3,107	3,486	3,850	—	12.0	-11.6	15.2	12.2	10.4
Value of exports	—	—	2,907	3,797	3,930	4,252	4,818	5,550	—	30.6	3.5	8.2	13.3	15.2

[1]Estimate, except exports and imports.
[2]Estimate.
[3]Forecast.
[4]Value of all products and services sold by establishments in the radio and TV communications equipment industry.
[5]Value of products classified in the radio and TV communications equipment industry produced by all industries.

SOURCE: U.S. Department of Commerce: Bureau of the Census; International Trade Administration (ITA). Estimates and forecasts by ITA.

Glossary

Advanced Research Projects Agency (ARPA) An organization in the Department of Defense responsible for sponsoring advanced research.

Antidumping duty A duty imposed by the United States to offset any profits that a foreign firm attempts to make by dumping merchandise on the U.S. market. (See dumping.)

Apparent consumption Product shipments plus imports minus exports.

CAD/CAM/CAE Computer-aided design, computer-aided manufacturing, and computer-aided engineering.

Caribbean Basin Initiative (CBI) An inter-American program, led by the United States, of increased economic assistance and trade preferences to Caribbean and Central American countries. CBI provides duty-free access to the U.S. market for most products from the region, and promotes private sector development in the region.

c.i.f. Cost, insurance, and freight.

Compact disc read-only memory (CD-ROM) High-density data storage media for computer databases and other applications, including entertainment.

Conference Board A nonprofit, nonpolitical group in New York City that specializes in short-term forecasts of GDP and its components, and the collection, analysis, and reporting of worldwide management practices and policies.

Constant dollars (or "real" dollars) Output values converted to a base price level, calculated by dividing current dollars by a deflator. Use of constant dollars eliminates the price changes between the year of measurement and the base year and allows calculation of real changes in output.

Consumer Price Index (CPI) Measures the price levels of various goods and services purchased by consumers.

Countervailing duty A retaliatory charge that a country places on imported goods to counter the subsidies or bounties granted to the exporters of the goods by their home governments.

Current dollars The actual amount paid in sales transactions.

Dumping A term used in international trade that refers to the sale of a product in export markets below the selling price for the same product in domestic markets.

Durable goods (durables) Items with a normal life expectancy of 3 years or more, such as automobiles, furniture, and major household appliances. Sales of durable goods are generally postponable and therefore are the most volatile component of consumer expenditures.

Eurodollars Deposits held in denominations of U.S. dollars in commercial banks outside the United States.

European Community (EC) A regional economic/political organization with a population of about 345 million forming the largest trading bloc in the world. Its 12 members are Belgium, Denmark, France, Germany, Greece, Ireland, Italy, Luxembourg, the Netherlands, Portugal, Spain, and the United Kingdom. Also called the European Union (EU) since November 1, 1993.

European Currency Unit (ECU) An international unit of account created for the European Monetary System (EMS), to be used as the denominator of EMS debts and credits and as a reserve credit in the European Monetary Cooperation Fund (EMCF). The ECU is composed of a weighted basket of currencies of EC members.

Exchange Rate Mechanism (ERM) Fixed exchange rate system created by the EC in March 1979 as part of the EMS. Participant countries (not all EC members joined the ERM at its inception) were expected to intervene in currency markets to keep the value of their respective currencies within plus or minus 2.5 percent of central parity to the ECU. The currency fluctuation bands were extended to plus-or-minus 15 percent on August 1, 1993.

Export-Import Bank (Eximbank) An autonomous agency of the U.S. Government created in 1934 to facilitate the export trade of the United States.

Fiscal Year (FY) Designation of a year for budget and accounting purposes. The U.S. Government's fiscal year runs from October 1 to September 30.

Foreign trade zones (FTZs) Designated areas in the United States, usually near ports of entry, considered to be outside the customs territory of the United States. Also known as free trade zones.

Free alongside ship (f.a.s.) The transaction price of an export product, including freight, insurance, and other charges incurred in placing the merchandise alongside the carrier in the U.S. port.

Free on board (f.o.b.) Without charge for delivery of export merchandise to and placing on board a carrier at a specified point.

Source: *U.S. Industrial Outlook 1994*, U.S. Department of Commerce, International Trade Administration.

G-7 (Group of Seven) Seven industrial countries: the United States, Japan, Germany, France, the United Kingdom, Italy, and Canada. G-7 leaders have met at annual economic summits since 1975 to coordinate their economic policies.

General Agreement on Tariffs and Trade (GATT) An international organization and code of tariffs and trade rules that has evolved out of the multilateral trade treaty signed in 1947. GATT is dedicated to equal treatment for all member trading nations, reduction of tariffs and nontariff barriers by negotiation, and elimination of import quotas. (See Uruguay Round.)

Generalized System of Preferences (GSP) A system approved by GATT in 1971 that authorizes developed countries to give preferential tariff treatment to developing countries.

Gross domestic product (GDP) The value of all goods and services produced in a country.

Gross national product (GNP) The value of all goods and services produced in a country plus income earned in foreign countries less income payable to foreign sources.

Harmonized System An international convention, implemented by the United States in 1989, for classifying imports and exports so that data from different countries are comparable.

High-definition television (HDTV) Standards and technology being developed by the United States, Europe, and Japan for commercial television broadcasting with at least twice the reception quality of current equipment.

Industry shipments The total value of products shipped by establishments classified as being in the industry, plus miscellaneous receipts.

Intellectual property Includes trademarks, copyrights, patents, and trade secrets.

International Monetary Fund (IMF) Established in 1945, the IMF is a permanent forum for its member countries to coordinate economic and financial policies. It monitors compliance with agreements to maintain orderly exchange rates, provides resources to members facing balance-of-payments difficulties, and offers technical and policy assistance.

ISO 9000 A series of five standards (9000–9004) of the International Standards Organization (ISO), an international agency that promotes quality standards in products and systems.

Joint venture An international business undertaking, usually between foreign interests and private parties from the host country, or between foreign interests and the host government.

Just-in-time (JIT) delivery A management technique in which a manufacturer works closely with its suppliers to assure that critical components are delivered as needed to avoid disruptions of the production process and the costs of maintaining excessive inventories.

Maquila (maquiladora) Mexican assembly plant generally near the U.S.-Mexican border; most of its production is exported to the United States.

Ministry of International Trade and Industry (MITI) Japanese government agency with broad powers over the country's trade policies.

Most-favored-nation (MFN) trade status An arrangement in which GATT countries must extend to all other members the most favorable treatment granted to any trading partner, thus assuring that any tariff reductions or other trade concession are automatically extended to all GATT parties.

Multifiber Arrangement (MFA) Trade agreements, under GATT auspices, between major textile importing and exporting countries covering most of the world trade in textiles and apparel. The MFA was in effect through December 1993, pending completion of the Uruguay Round.

National Defense Stockpile Materials deemed critical for national defense, and the amounts of each required to meet national security requirements, administered by the Department of Defense.

NEC Not elsewhere classified.

NIC Newly industrialized (or industrializing) country. Developing countries that have experienced rapid growth in GDP, industrial production, and exports in recent years. The economies listed in the *Outlook*'s Trade Patterns tables are China, Hong Kong, Indonesia, South Korea, Malaysia, Singapore, Taiwan, and Thailand.

Nondurable goods (nondurables) Items which last for less than 3 years, such as food, beverages, and clothing. Nondurables are generally purchased when needed.

North American Free Trade Agreement (NAFTA) Agreement to create a free trade area among the United States, Canada, and Mexico. Implementation began on January 1, 1994.

Organization for Economic Cooperation and Development (OECD) Group of 24 industrialized, market economy countries of North

America, Europe, the Far East, and the South Pacific. The OECD, which has headquarters in Paris, was established in 1961 to promote economic development and international trade.

Organization of Petroleum Exporting Countries (OPEC) An association of important oil-exporting countries that are highly dependent on oil revenues. Formed in 1960, its major purpose is to coordinate the petroleum production and pricing policies of its 12 members.

Pacific Rim A term that technically means all countries adjoining the Pacific Ocean, although it often refers only to East Asian countries.

Producers Price Index (PPI) Measures price levels of commodities produced or imported for sale in commercial transactions in the United States.

Product shipments The total value of specific products shipped by all establishments, irrespective of the industry classification of these establishments.

Real dollars See constant dollars.

Standard Industrial Classification (SIC) system The standard established by the Federal Government for defining industries and classifying individual establishments by industry.

Total quality management (TQM) A management technique to improve the quality of goods and services, reduce operating costs, and increase customer satisfaction.

Uruguay Round Eighth round of multilateral trade negotiations held under GATT auspices. Named for the country where initial discussions began in September 1986; most of the negotiations have taken place in Geneva, Switzerland.

U.S.-Canada Free Trade Agreement (FTA) Implemented in January 1989 to eliminate all tariffs on U.S. and Canadian goods by January 1998 and to reduce or eliminate many nontariff barriers.

Value added The difference between the value of goods produced and the cost of materials and services purchased to produce them. It includes wages, interest, rent, and profits. The sum of value added of all sectors of the economy equals GDP.

Voluntary restraint agreement (VRA) An import relief device to limit foreign trade in a particular commodity and protect domestic industry from injury by foreign competition. Sometimes referred to as a "voluntary export restraint" or an "orderly marketing agreement."

World Bank The International Bank for Reconstruction and Development (IBRD), the most important member of the World Bank Group, was created in 1945 as a companion organization to the IMF. The main purposes of the IBRD are to lend funds and provide technical and policy assistance to foster the economic development of its poorer member countries.

METRIC CONVERSION TABLE

(approximate conversions to metric measurements)

This table is included here to help readers who follow U.S. industry and business competition in world markets. The United States remains one of the few countries in the world still using inch-pound measurement. Beginning in January 1994, all bids and specifications for Federal construction projects are to be submitted in metric terms. For more information, contact the Metric Program, National Institute of Standards and Technology (NIST), at (301) 975-3690.

Symbol	When You Know	Multiply by	To Find	Symbol
		LENGTH		
in	inches	2.5	centimeters	cm
ft	feet	30	centimeters	cm
yd	yards	0.9	meters	m
mi	miles	1.6	kilometers	km
		AREA		
in^2	square inches	6.5	square centimeters	cm^2
ft^2	square feet	0.09	square meters	m^2
yd^2	square yards	0.8	square meters	m^2
mi^2	square miles	2.6	square kilometers	km^2
	acres	0.4	hectares	ha
		MASS (weight)		
oz	ounces	28	grams	g
lb	pounds	0.45	kilograms	kg
	short tons (2,000 lb)	0.9	metric tons	t
		VOLUME		
tsp	teaspoon	5	milliliter	mL
Tbsp	tablespoons	15	milliliter	mL
in^3	cubic inches	16	milliliter	mL
fl oz	fluid ounces	30	milliliter	mL
c	cups	0.24	liters	l
pt	pints	0.47	liters	l
qt	quarts	0.95	liters	l
gal	gallons	3.8	liters	l
ft^3	cubic feet	0.03	cubic meters	m^3
yd^3	cubic yards	0.76	cubic meters	m^3
		TEMPERATURE (exact)		
°F	degrees Fahrenheit	5/9 (after subtracting 32)	degrees Celsius	°C

SOURCE: U.S. Department of Commerce, NIST Metric Program.

Net Domestic Product and Domestic Income by Sector

[Billions of dollars]

	Line	1990	1991	1992	1993
Net domestic product	1	**4,943.5**	**5,098.3**	**5,361.7**	**5,674.2**
Business	2	**4,123.2**	**4,221.1**	**4,431.9**	**4,702.3**
Nonfarm	3	4,052.0	4,162.5	4,359.4	4,646.2
Nonfarm less housing	4	3,730.4	3,821.9	4,006.6	4,269.6
Housing	5	321.6	340.6	352.9	376.6
Farm	6	63.5	57.1	63.7	53.8
Statistical discrepancy	7	7.8	1.5	8.8	2.3
Households and institutions	8	**227.5**	**246.7**	**268.6**	**285.3**
General government	9	**592.8**	**630.5**	**661.2**	**686.6**
Domestic income	10	**4,469.3**	**4,592.2**	**4,824.0**	**5,126.9**
Business	11	**3,649.1**	**3,715.0**	**3,894.1**	**4,155.0**
Nonfarm	12	3,581.7	3,654.7	3,826.7	4,093.8
Nonfarm less housing	13	3,337.1	3,397.0	3,561.1	3,807.5
Housing	14	244.6	257.7	265.5	286.3
Farm	15	67.4	60.3	67.5	61.2
Households and institutions	16	**227.5**	**246.7**	**268.6**	**285.3**
General government	17	**592.8**	**630.5**	**661.2**	**686.6**

Net Domestic Product and Domestic Income by Sector in Constant Dollars

[Billions of 1987 dollars]

	Line	1990	1991	1992	1993
Net domestic product	1	4,342.5	4,297.6	4,383.5	4,535.1
Business	2	**3,636.1**	**3,580.8**	**3,662.9**	**3,809.9**
Nonfarm	3	3,577.1	3,527.7	3,593.5	3,754.9
Nonfarm less housing	4	**3,302.3**	**3,251.3**	**3,325.0**	**3,468.2**
Housing	5	**274.8**	**276.4**	**268.5**	**286.7**
Farm	6	52.1	51.8	62.0	53.1
Statistical discrepancy	7	6.9	1.3	7.3	1.9
Households and institutions	8	**196.9**	**202.4**	**208.5**	**215.6**
General government	9	**509.5**	**514.4**	**512.0**	**509.6**
Domestic income	10	**3,938.2**	**3,902.3**	**3,970.2**	**4,112.0**
Business	11	**3,231.8**	**3,185.5**	**3,249.6**	**3,386.8**
Nonfarm	12	3,170.2	3,123.9	3,177.3	3,322.8
Nonfarm less housing	13	2,959.2	2,912.1	2,974.1	3,103.2
Housing	14	211.0	211.8	203.2	219.6
Farm	15	61.6	61.6	72.3	64.0
Households and institutions	16	**196.9**	**202.4**	**208.5**	**215.6**
General government	17	**509.5**	**514.4**	**512.0**	**509.6**

Source: *Survey of Current Business,* U.S. Department of Commerce, Bureau of Economic Analysis.

MEDIA GENERAL P/E DISTRIBUTIONS BY MARKET
(for week ended 07/01/94)

P/E Ratios Now

Rankings as of July 1, 1994

Stocks by P/E Ranking*	Composite Now	Composite 52 Weeks Ago	NYSE Now	NYSE 52 Weeks Ago	ASE Now	ASE 52 Weeks Ago	OTC Now	OTC 52 Weeks Ago
Top 5%	50.0	56.3	47.5	47.5	50.0	63.8	51.6	59.4
10%	37.0	40.8	33.7	36.2	39.6	44.2	38.3	44.0
15%	30.7	33.1	28.3	29.0	30.7	34.8	31.8	35.1
20%	26.2	28.1	25.0	25.0	27.2	28.9	26.8	29.7
25%	23.5	24.6	22.2	23.2	24.1	25.6	23.9	26.3
30%	21.2	22.0	20.4	21.3	22.2	21.9	21.7	22.7
35%	19.2	20.1	18.6	20.0	19.0	19.4	19.6	20.4
40%	17.8	18.6	17.6	18.8	17.6	17.8	18.1	18.5
45%	16.7	17.4	16.6	17.9	15.8	16.7	16.8	17.1
50%	15.6	16.3	15.7	17.0	14.8	15.4	15.7	15.9
55%	14.6	15.3	14.8	16.1	14.0	14.6	14.6	14.7
60%	13.8	14.4	14.0	15.4	13.1	13.7	13.6	13.8
65%	13.0	13.6	13.4	14.7	12.6	12.9	12.9	12.9
70%	12.1	12.7	12.5	14.0	11.8	11.9	12.1	11.8
75%	11.4	11.7	11.7	13.2	10.8	11.1	11.2	11.0
80%	10.4	10.8	10.8	12.4	9.8	9.9	10.3	10.2
85%	9.5	9.8	10.0	11.3	8.9	9.1	9.3	9.3
90%	8.4	8.5	9.0	10.0	7.9	7.9	8.2	8.1
95%	6.9	7.1	7.5	8.2	6.0	6.6	6.9	6.8
No. of Companies	4,507	4,072	1,431	1,354	451	411	2,625	2,307

P/E Ratio Ranges	Composite Now	Composite 52 Weeks Ago	NYSE Now	NYSE 52 Weeks Ago	ASE Now	ASE 52 Weeks Ago	OTC Now	OTC 52 Weeks Ago
0.1 to 1.9	.1%	.1%	.0%	.0%	.5%	.2%	.1%	.1%
2.0 to 2.9	.2	.1	.1	.1	.1	.0	.2	.1
3.0 to 3.9	.3	.1	.1	.0	.6	.1	.3	.2
4.0 to 4.9	.5	.3	.4	.1	.5	.6	.5	.3
5.0 to 5.9	.8	.6	.7	.4	1.0	.6	.8	.8
6.0 to 6.9	1.0	1.1	.9	.9	.7	1.2	1.0	1.2
7.0 to 7.9	1.9	1.6	1.5	.9	1.9	2.3	2.1	1.8
8.0 to 8.9	2.2	1.8	2.0	1.4	2.6	1.9	2.3	2.0
9.0 to 9.9	2.7	2.2	3.0	1.7	3.0	2.6	2.4	2.4
10.0 to 11.9	6.4	5.4	7.4	4.7	4.9	4.5	6.2	5.9
12.0 to 13.9	6.8	5.3	7.1	6.4	6.8	5.2	6.7	4.8
14.0 to 15.9	5.9	5.7	7.3	8.1	5.6	5.1	5.2	4.6
16.0 to 17.9	4.9	4.4	6.2	6.2	3.5	3.8	4.4	3.6
18.0 to 19.9	3.7	3.6	3.7	5.5	2.8	3.0	3.8	2.7
20.0 to 24.9	6.0	5.5	6.7	8.3	4.0	3.2	6.0	4.6
25.0 to 29.9	3.6	3.5	4.1	3.4	4.0	3.4	3.2	3.5
30.0 to 39.9	4.0	3.7	3.6	3.8	3.7	3.4	4.3	3.7
40.0 to 49.9	1.8	1.9	1.6	1.7	2.3	1.4	1.9	2.0
50.0 And Over	3.0	3.3	2.6	2.4	2.6	4.0	3.2	3.7
Cannot Calculate	44.4	49.7	40.9	44.1	49.1	53.6	45.2	51.8
No. of Companies	8,099		2,422		886		4,791	

*Excludes negative and zero earnings companies.

Source: Media General Financial Services, Inc., Richmond, VA.

MEDIA GENERAL INDUSTRY INDEXES
(for week ended 07/01/94)

Jan. 2, 1970 = 100

M/G Composite Index 200 days Ago: 493.92

Industry	Index					Percent Change				Fundamental						
	Week's Close	Previous Week's Close	30 Days Ago	90 Days Ago	52-Wk Moving Average	For Week	30 Days	90 Days	Year To Date	P/E Ratio Now	5-Year Average P/E	12 Mos. Earnings Change - (%)	5-Year Earnings Growth - (%)	Dividend Yield - (%)	Return On Equity - (%)	Profit Margin - (%)
Composite	488.98	484.94	500.32	517.26	499.61	.8	-2.2	-5.4	-4.4	23.9	21.0	8	-8	2.4	10.0	4.0
01. Aerospace	834.03	832.55	826.27	861.49	805.34	.1	.9	-3.1	.3	14.5	12.6	-8	3	2.3	15.0	4.0
02. Airlines	294.49	287.72	287.20	295.72	300.13	2.3	2.5	-.4	2.3	NC	NC	NE	NC	.4	NE	-.8
03. Automotive	310.44	311.81	307.52	314.71	292.45	-.4	.9	-1.3	5.7	20.2	NC	783	NC	2.6	10.3	2.0
04. Banking	414.59	409.78	425.14	416.58	414.99	1.1	-2.4	-.4	1.2	13.3	17.6	27	7	2.8	13.0	9.5
05. Building	359.69	359.53	377.90	433.05	382.13	.0	-4.8	-16.9	-12.6	24.6	NM	0	-21	2.5	9.0	3.2
06. Building-Heavy	769.34	766.46	779.50	868.58	780.24	.3	-1.3	-11.4	-7.9	NM	NM	-78	NC	1.5	1.5	.4
07. Business Data Proc	217.50	213.60	227.90	236.04	219.79	1.8	-4.5	-7.8	-2.0	NC	NC	NE	NC	.7	NE	-1.6
08. Business Equipment	237.53	237.11	244.35	255.91	232.75	.1	-2.7	-7.1	-.9	54.5	68.6	20	-22	2.5	6.5	1.8
09. Business Services	315.93	313.72	318.98	334.43	324.45	.7	-.9	-5.5	-4.7	48.0	21.7	-60	-17	2.1	5.6	2.0
10. Chemicals	739.79	735.14	759.46	759.89	710.91	.6	-2.5	-2.6	5.5	39.6	17.8	-36	-24	2.8	6.5	2.3
11. Communications	646.62	641.67	671.06	738.88	701.35	.7	-3.6	-12.4	-10.3	28.7	20.1	-24	2	2.2	11.4	6.7
12. Cosmetic-Personal	436.71	431.45	442.64	420.97	408.54	1.2	-1.3	3.7	10.1	26.4	NC	-9	13	1.8	28.4	5.8
13. Credit	401.02	394.87	415.17	421.50	430.11	1.5	-3.4	-4.8	-6.2	10.7	16.2	25	9	1.8	13.8	11.4
14. Distillers-Brewers	635.07	620.83	646.79	607.86	621.97	2.2	-1.8	4.4	11.9	75.2	22.9	-22	-14	1.3	10.4	4.6
15. Drug Manufacturers	767.21	764.25	780.41	809.46	803.65	.3	-1.6	-5.2	-10.2	20.5	22.5	-1	5	3.3	19.5	11.6
16. Electrical Equip	691.90	684.24	697.44	722.02	679.34	1.1	-.7	-4.1	1.5	22.5	27.8	-6	-6	2.3	10.2	3.8
17. Electronics	659.43	649.50	647.32	675.31	625.13	1.5	1.8	-2.3	8.0	29.4	29.3	36	5	.6	7.6	3.4
18. Food Production	799.06	805.48	811.62	842.33	843.10	-.8	-1.5	-5.1	-8.6	17.8	20.5	31	6	2.2	16.5	4.1
19. Food-Packed Goods	1189.16	1186.88	1201.16	1289.09	1215.06	.1	-1.0	-7.7	-6.9	18.5	17.5	-9	5	2.5	23.4	4.4
20. Food-Meats-Dairy	926.55	912.99	901.95	952.93	924.16	1.4	2.7	-2.7	-4.1	NM	31.2	-97	NC	1.4	NE	-.4
21. Food-Confections	1325.47	1301.86	1407.49	1508.33	1432.94	1.8	-5.8	-12.1	-12.7	22.6	22.8	-2	9	1.8	19.0	6.4
22. Freight-Shipping	466.26	465.40	478.92	519.21	476.88	.1	-2.6	-10.2	-4.6	25.1	25.1	-1	-10	1.4	8.4	2.6
23. Health	526.98	526.91	548.49	570.70	523.43	.0	-3.9	-7.6	-2.7	34.1	30.0	-21	6	1.0	12.5	4.9
24. Hotels-Motels-Res	755.53	731.55	808.39	890.42	819.86	3.2	-6.5	-15.1	-11.7	97.3	23.6	-72	-15	1.0	4.0	1.6
25. Housewares-Furn.	544.77	539.25	559.16	588.73	557.94	1.0	-2.5	-7.4	-7.2	23.5	19.7	3	-4	1.4	9.6	2.9

26. Insurance	493.52	494.79	505.35	516.29	525.57	-.2	-2.3	-4.4	-5.2	14.5	13.8	29	-1	2.0	10.2	6.6
27. Investments	152.09	152.28	158.15	169.56	169.11	-.1	-3.8	-10.3	-11.7	7.7	11.9	62	16	6.0	21.3	10.3
28. Machinery-Heavy	534.98	529.39	546.60	566.60	534.87	1.0	-2.1	-5.5	-.4	25.8	NM	185	NC	1.5	9.9	2.9
29. Machine-Lt-Equip	439.30	452.92	461.29	494.95	468.97	-3.0	-4.7	-11.2	-7.9	32.0	56.4	205	-32	1.9	5.5	2.0
30. Metals Fabrication	602.70	598.34	589.62	652.99	597.73	.7	2.2	-7.7	-5.8	25.0	NM	9	-6	1.5	9.5	2.8
31. Metals-Iron-Steel	223.08	220.93	216.93	232.09	211.03	.9	2.8	-3.8	-1.2	NC	NC	NE	NC	.9	NE	-1.1
32. Metals-Nonf-Coal	218.95	217.01	224.25	226.34	204.28	.8	-2.3	-3.2	3.3	NC	NM	-100	NC	2.3	.1	.0
33. Metals, Rare	465.04	477.42	458.56	462.73	454.59	-2.5	1.4	.5	-8.6	61.5	83.8	19	NC	1.6	5.5	6.8
34. Multi-Industry	271.62	273.29	279.91	307.13	286.89	-.6	-2.9	-11.5	-8.3	18.0	26.5	88	-20	2.8	13.3	3.9
35. Oil, Nat Gas Svcs	470.30	472.08	471.64	467.32	475.20	-.3	-.2	.6	1.7	33.0	25.1	NE	NC	1.7	4.9	2.8
36. Oil, Nat Gas Prod	259.94	262.77	260.84	264.81	255.21	-1.0	-.3	-1.8	4.3	35.6	NM	79	NC	3.0	7.7	4.4
37. Oil Refin, Mkting	644.60	647.88	674.24	667.46	655.44	-.5	-4.4	-3.4	-1.1	19.6	18.0	3	-10	3.9	9.9	3.4
38. Paper, Packaging	640.75	639.56	643.78	685.08	626.74	.1	-.4	-6.4	-1.6	65.0	27.2	6	-38	2.2	3.5	1.3
39. Personal Services	321.33	316.88	329.11	360.99	340.01	1.4	-2.3	-10.9	-7.3	27.4	28.1	-22	-3	1.8	9.8	4.8
40. Precision Instruments	219.08	217.63	213.17	210.48	203.31	.6	2.7	4.0	-1.5	42.3	25.3	-29	-13	1.4	4.7	2.0
41. Publishing	800.06	798.97	837.46	865.31	835.96	.1	-4.4	-7.5	-8.4	26.2	35.3	28	-4	1.6	10.0	6.9
42. Railroads	753.58	751.26	774.01	852.28	797.34	.3	-2.6	-11.5	-9.7	19.3	63.3	42	NC	2.2	10.6	6.6
43. Real Estate Inves	178.97	176.66	178.86	180.08	176.86	1.3	.0	-.6	5.0	14.8	44.4	14	8	4.0	12.4	13.6
44. Real Estate	80.08	79.93	82.99	86.38	83.42	.1	-3.5	-7.2	-7.5	NC	NC	NE	NC	2.6	NE	-.8
45. Recreation-Luxury	294.32	288.12	315.46	322.08	310.60	2.1	-6.7	-8.6	-5.8	39.4	32.7	-29	-20	1.1	8.6	2.4
46. Recreation-Bdcstg	2859.20	2766.87	2839.28	3207.55	3097.30	3.3	.7	-10.8	-18.3	86.0	NM	NE	NC	.3	8.2	4.2
47. Recreation-Mov-Sp	1786.07	1795.23	1856.22	2071.42	1928.73	-.5	-3.7	-13.7	-14.0	34.8	65.0	-16	-19	1.4	6.6	4.4
48. Retail-Apparel	1547.20	1519.43	1645.41	1702.23	1701.42	1.8	-5.9	-9.1	-8.2	23.4	24.6	27	5	1.5	10.4	2.7
49. Retail-Dept Strs	384.79	367.15	383.57	382.04	378.19	4.8	.3	.7	1.1	17.4	46.9	361	-10	1.9	16.3	4.0
50. Retail-Disc, Drug	1134.32	1103.98	1131.77	1283.76	1220.65	2.7	.2	-11.6	-8.2	32.4	24.5	-33	1	1.2	10.1	1.6
51. Retail-Food Strs	867.16	863.59	870.96	882.27	856.40	.4	-.4	-1.7	3.5	19.4	39.7	23	NC	1.6	16.2	1.2
52. Retail-Misc	1007.02	989.19	1053.34	1081.29	1027.02	1.8	-4.4	-6.8	-3.8	27.7	22.9	21	-1	1.0	10.2	1.7
53. Rubber-Plastic	527.67	528.63	540.02	602.84	563.91	-.1	-2.2	-12.4	-10.7	16.1	18.3	10	-7	2.7	15.4	5.3
54. Savings and Loan	453.12	444.09	430.47	416.91	424.66	2.0	5.2	8.6	5.3	29.8	NC	-46	NC	2.0	7.3	7.0
55. Shoes-Leather	865.37	841.05	872.51	853.35	853.74	2.8	-.8	1.4	4.8	17.6	16.3	9	9	1.2	17.5	5.7
56. Textile Mfg	495.94	489.59	521.22	521.22	525.34	1.3	-4.8	-4.8	-2.0	34.4	19.8	-56	-4	1.3	7.7	2.7
57. Textiles-Apparel	532.41	530.60	563.89	551.96	538.75	.3	-5.5	-3.5	-3.9	17.1	NM	6	-4	1.3	12.0	3.8
58. Tobacco	1420.72	1377.04	1437.49	1599.07	1492.66	3.1	-1.1	-11.1	-11.5	12.3	12.5	-23	9	5.3	26.7	5.6
59. Utilities-Electric	157.09	154.16	162.90	180.48	187.89	1.9	-3.5	-12.9	-19.6	13.1	14.0	-6	0	6.7	10.5	8.8
60. Utilities-Gas-Oth	303.97	301.06	310.68	334.19	331.17	.9	-2.1	-9.0	-8.3	19.3	24.9	-6	-7	4.3	5.2	3.6

Source: Media General Financial Services, Inc., Richmond, VA.

General Business and Economic Indicators

SELECTED BUSINESS STATISTICS

SEASONALLY ADJUSTED WHERE APPLICABLE EXPANSION PEAKS (P), RECESSION TROUGHS (T)

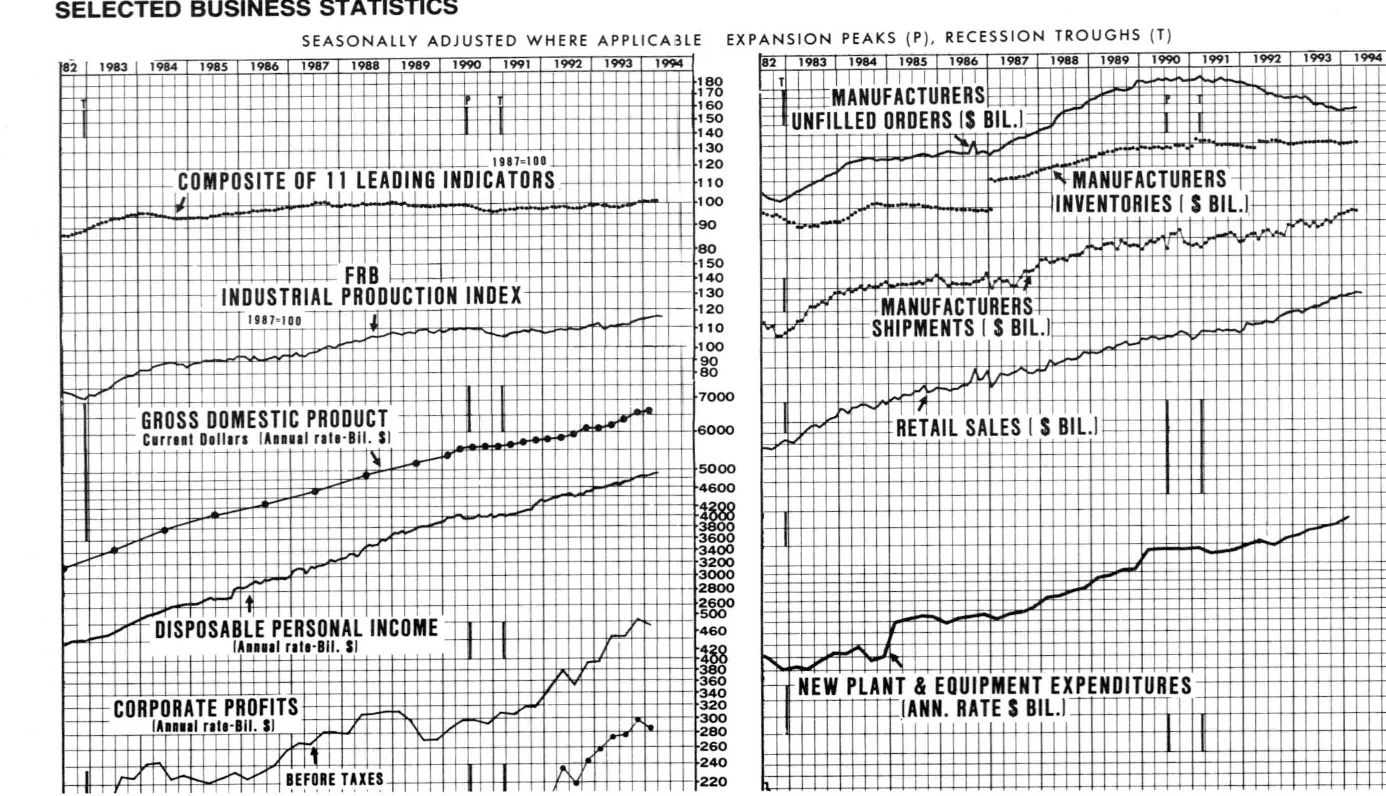

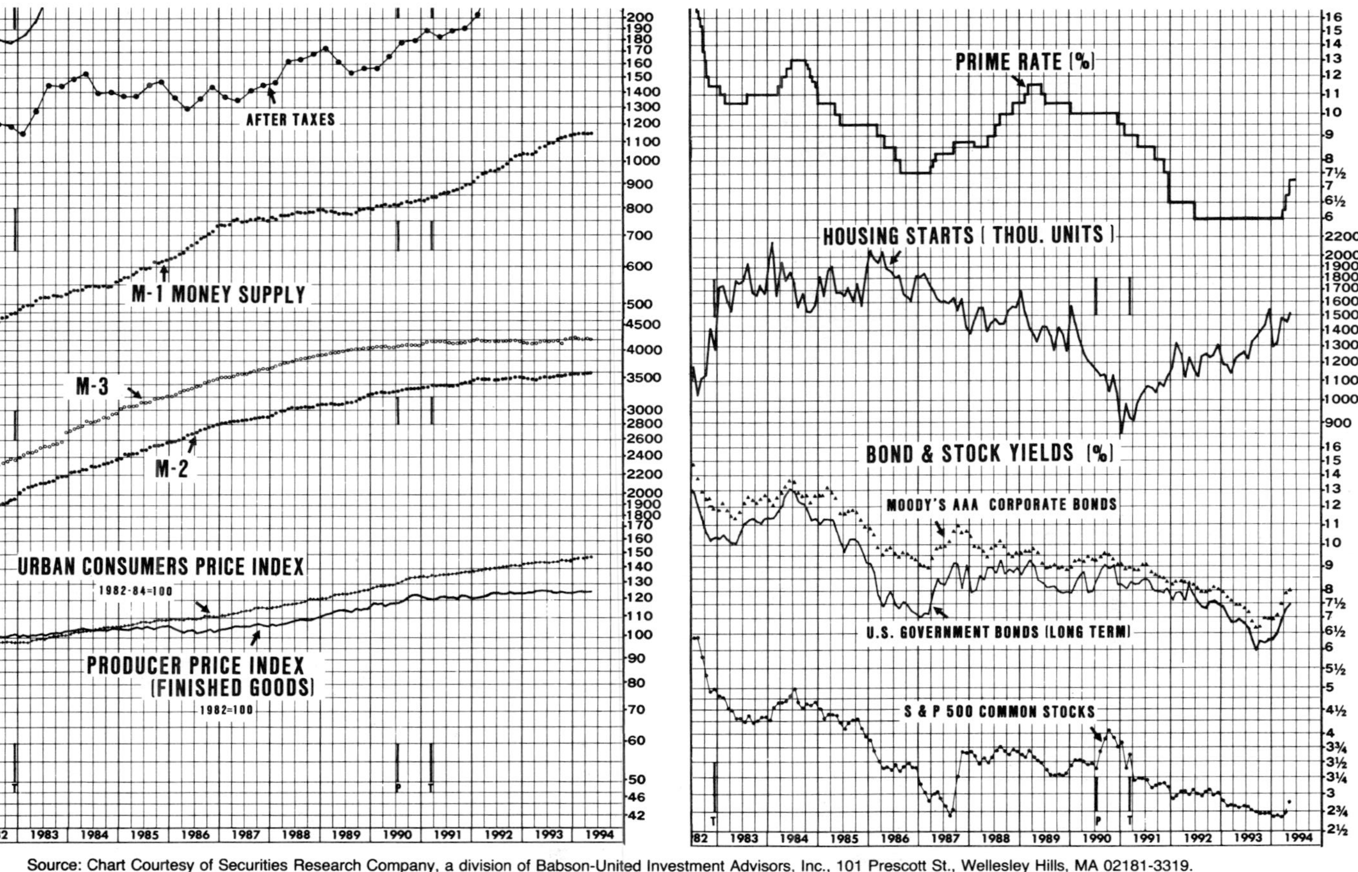

Source: Chart Courtesy of Securities Research Company, a division of Babson-United Investment Advisors, Inc., 101 Prescott St., Wellesley Hills, MA 02181-3319.

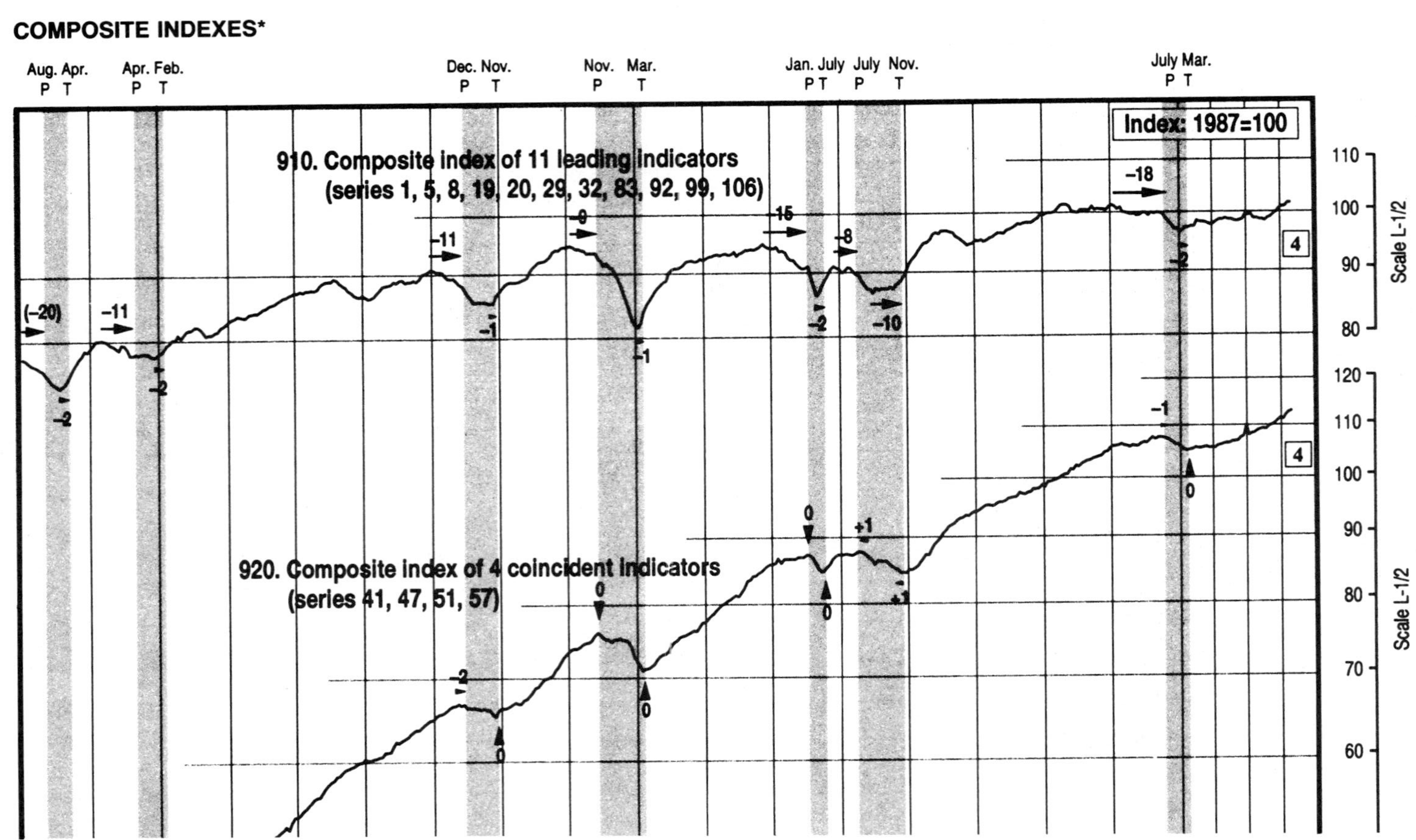
COMPOSITE INDEXES*
Aug. Apr. P T
Apr. Feb. P T
Dec. Nov. P T
Nov. Mar. P T
Jan. July P T
July Nov. P T
July Mar. P T
Index: 1987=100
910. Composite index of 11 leading indicators
(series 1, 5, 8, 19, 20, 29, 32, 83, 92, 99, 106)
920. Composite index of 4 coincident indicators
(series 41, 47, 51, 57)
Scale L-1/2
Scale L-1/2

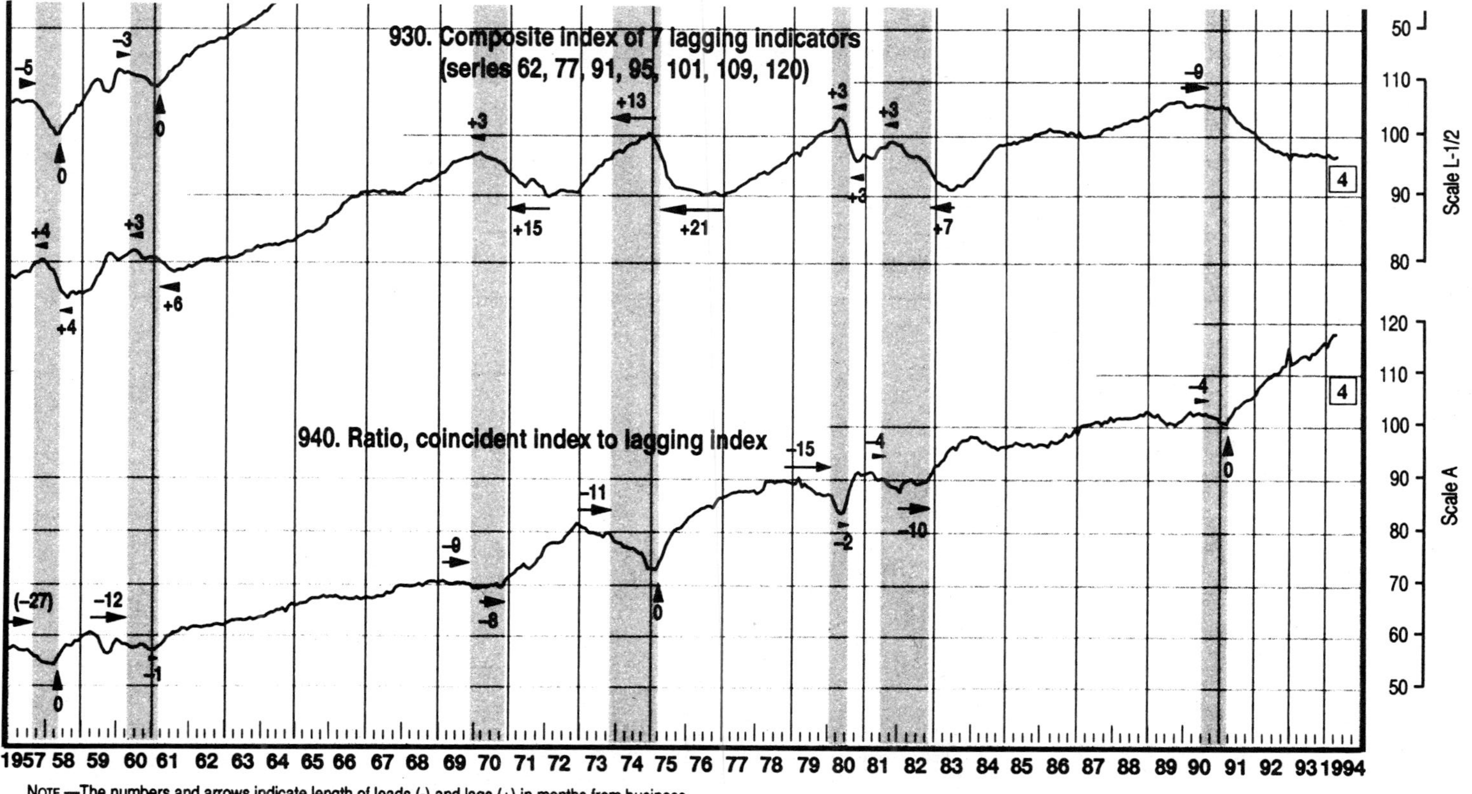

NOTE.—The numbers and arrows indicate length of leads (-) and lags (+) in months from business cycle turning dates.

* For definitions see page 140.

Source: *Survey of Current Business,* U.S. Department of Commerce, Bureau of Economic Analysis.

Composition of Leading, Coincident, and Lagging Indicators

I. THE ELEVEN LEADING INDICATORS

1. Average weekly hours of production or non-supervisory workers, manufacturing.
5. Average weekly claims for unemployment insurance, State programs.
8. Manufacturers' new orders in 1987 dollars, consumer goods and materials industries.
19. Index of stock prices, 500 common stock prices.
20. Contracts and orders for plant and equipment in 1987 dollars.
29. Index of new private housing units authorized by local building permits.
32. Vendor performance, slower deliveries diffusion Index.
83. Index of consumer expectations.
92. Change in manufacturer's unfilled orders for the durable goods industry.
99. Change in sensitive materials prices, smoothed.
106. Money supply (M2 in 1987 dollars).

II. THE FOUR COINCIDENT INDICATORS

41. Employees on non-agricultural payrolls.
47. Index of industrial production.
51. Personal income less transfer payments in 1987 dollars.
57. Manufacturing and trade sales in 1987 dollars.

III. THE SEVEN LAGGING INDICATORS

62. Change in index of labor costs per unit of output, manufacturing, smoothed.
77. Ratio, manufacturing, and trade inventories to sales in 1987 dollars.
91. Average duration of unemployment in weeks.
95. Ratio, consumer installment credit outstanding to personal income.
101. Commercial and industrial loans outstanding in 1987 dollars.
109. Average prime rate charged by banks.
120. Change in Consumer Price Index for services, smoothed.

Source: *Survey of Current Business.*

NATIONAL INCOME (Billions of dollars; quarterly data at seasonally adjusted annual rates)

Period	National income	Compensation of employees[1]	Proprietors' income with inventory valuation and capital consumption adjustments		Rental income of persons with capital consumption adjustment	Corporate profits with inventory valuation and capital consumption adjustments					Net interest
						Total	Profits with inventory valuation adjustment and without capital consumption adjustment			Capital consumption adjustment	
			Farm	Nonfarm			Total	Profits before tax	Inventory valuation adjustment		
1988	4,002.6	2,921.3	30.9	293.4	4.3	365.0	320.3	347.5	−27.3	44.7	387.7
1989	4,249.5	3,100.2	40.2	307.0	−13.5	362.8	325.4	342.9	−17.5	37.4	452.7
1990	4,491.0	3,297.6	41.9	321.4	−14.2	380.6	354.7	365.7	−11.0	25.9	463.7
1991 r	4,608.2	3,404.8	36.7	339.5	−10.5	390.3	370.9	365.2	5.8	19.4	447.4
1992 r	4,829.5	3,591.2	44.4	374.4	−5.5	405.1	389.4	395.9	−6.4	15.7	420.0
1993 r	5,131.4	3,780.4	37.3	404.3	24.1	485.8	456.2	462.4	−6.2	29.5	399.5
1982: IV	2,551.5	1,940.4	10.2	169.6	24.1	150.3	160.0	168.6	−8.6	−9.6	256.8
1983: IV	2,834.3	2,101.2	6.3	193.8	22.2	229.1	216.2	223.8	−7.6	12.9	281.8
1984: IV	3,134.4	2,288.1	21.9	217.7	24.3	261.3	223.6	220.1	3.5	37.7	321.1
1985: IV	3,341.9	2,442.5	17.8	250.9	14.0	284.9	228.0	231.8	−3.8	56.9	331.9
1986: IV	3,486.0	2,582.5	23.6	260.9	4.7	264.6	225.0	235.7	−10.7	39.6	349.7
1987: IV	3,828.8	2,785.1	42.4	282.6	6.8	343.3	293.4	311.2	−17.8	49.9	368.6
1988: IV	4,127.6	3,004.9	30.9	302.5	2.8	378.3	340.5	372.2	−31.7	37.9	408.1
1989: IV	4,305.2	3,162.8	38.4	311.4	−21.6	354.5	320.6	334.1	−13.5	33.9	459.8
1990: IV	4,539.2	3,344.2	43.8	325.1	−11.1	362.8	349.3	368.9	−19.5	13.5	474.4
1991: IV r	4,663.9	3,459.1	36.6	349.8	−8.1	394.7	372.3	373.1	−.8	22.4	431.8
1992: I r	4,752.4	3,514.2	49.0	361.9	−6.4	412.1	393.0	397.0	−4.0	19.0	421.6
II r	4,806.8	3,564.9	43.7	369.1	−5.4	412.6	396.9	413.5	−16.6	15.8	421.9
III r	4,793.9	3,614.7	38.8	374.0	−15.5	363.2	352.3	359.5	−7.3	10.9	418.7
IV r	4,964.9	3,671.0	46.0	392.4	5.1	432.5	415.6	413.5	2.1	16.9	418.0
1993: I r	5,031.1	3,713.1	49.6	394.8	16.5	442.5	421.5	432.7	−11.2	21.0	414.6
II r	5,094.0	3,761.1	39.4	399.4	23.4	473.1	446.6	456.6	−10.0	26.5	397.6
III r	5,138.5	3,801.7	15.8	404.5	26.3	493.5	461.7	458.7	3.0	31.7	396.7
IV r	5,262.0	3,845.8	44.4	418.5	30.3	533.9	495.1	501.7	−6.5	38.8	389.1
1994: I r	5,308.7	3,920.0	47.2	423.8	15.3	508.2	471.2	483.5	−12.3	37.0	394.2
II p	....	3,979.3	37.6	431.8	33.1	....	....	....	−10.3	37.3	....

[1] Includes employer contributions for social insurance.

Source: Department of Commerce, Bureau of Economic Analysis.

Source: *Economic Indicators,* Council of Economic Advisers.

Gross Domestic Product as a Measure of U.S. Production

As of late 1991, the Bureau of Economic Analysis (BEA) features gross domestic product (GDP), rather than gross national product (GNP), as the primary measure of U.S. production. This change in emphasis recognizes that GDP is more appropriate for many purposes for which an aggregate measure of the Nation's production is used. GNP will remain a key aggregate in the national income and product accounts (NIPA's) and will continue to be published regularly.

How Do the GDP and GNP Concepts Differ?

Both GDP and GNP are defined in terms of goods and services produced, but they use different criteria for coverage. GDP covers the goods and services *produced by labor and property located in the United States.* As long as the labor and property are located in the United States, the suppliers (that is, the workers and, for property, the owners) may be either U.S. residents or residents of the rest of the world. GNP covers the goods and services *produced by labor and property supplied by U.S. residents.* As long as the labor and property are supplied by U.S. residents, they may be located either in the United States or abroad.

As shown in table 1, to move from GNP to GDP one must subtract factor income receipts from foreigners, which represent the goods and services produced abroad using the labor and property supplied by U.S. residents, and add factor income payments to foreigners, which represent the goods and services produced in the United States using the labor and property supplied by foreigners. Factor incomes are measured as compensation of employees, corporate profits (dividends, earnings of unincorporated affiliates, and reinvested earnings of incorporated affiliates), and net interest.

Why Feature GDP?

GDP refers to production taking place in the United States. It is, therefore, the appropriate measure for much of the short-term monitoring and analysis of the U.S. economy. In particular, GDP is consistent in coverage with indicators such as employment, productivity, industry output, and investment in equipment and structures.

In addition, the use of GDP facilitates comparisons of economic activity in the United States with that in other countries. GDP is the primary measure of production in the System of National Accounts, the set of international guidelines for economic accounting that the U.S. economic accounts will be moving toward in the mid-1990's, and virtually all other countries have already adopted GDP as their primary measure of production. Canada, for example, began featuring GDP in 1986.

The emphasis on GDP is consistent with measurement considerations. Data from BEA's direct investment survey, which is one of the primary sources for estimating factor income payments and receipts, are not available for the first two of the three quarterly estimates of GNP. For these two estimates, factor income payments and receipts are based on judgments about trends in the pace of economic activity in the United States and abroad and about the value of the dollar in foreign countries, on announced profits of individual companies, and on other information. Even when all of the source data become available, BEA does not have the information needed to make a full set of adjustments to reflect the concepts underlying the NIPA's. For example, the profits of foreign affiliates do not include inventory valuation and capital consumption adjustments, and they are affected by intracompany transfer prices and exchange rates. In addition, the deflation of current-dollar factor incomes is problematic because incomes such as interest and dividends cannot be separated into price and quantity components. Lacking a component-specific deflator, BEA uses the implicit price deflator for net domestic product to derive constant-dollar estimates.

GNP, however, continues to be a useful concept. Because it refers to the income available to U.S. residents as the result of their contribution to production, it is appropriate for analyses related to sources and uses of income. For example, saving rates are normally expressed as a percentage of income, and GNP is the more appropriate measure for this purpose. In addition, GNP is better than GDP for analyses that focus on the availability of resources, such as the Nation's ability to finance expenditures on education.

How Much Do the Estimates of GDP and GNP Differ?

For the United States, the dollar levels of GDP and GNP differ little—that is, the net receipts (receipts from foreigners less payments to foreigners) of factor income have been small (tables 1 and 2). The main reason is that the value of the property owned abroad by U.S. residents (U.S. investment abroad) less the value of the property owned by foreigners in the United States (foreign invest-

Source: *Survey of Current Business,* Bureau of Economic Analysis, U.S. Department of Commerce.

Table 1.—Relation of GNP and GDP

	1990	
	Billion of dollars	Billions of 1982 dollars
GNP	5,465.1	4,157.3
Less: Factor income receipts from foreigners	137.4	102.2
Plus: Factor income payments to foreigners	95.7	70.3
GDP[2]	5,423.4	4,125.4

Table 2.—Differences Between GNP and GDP

Year or quarter	GNP less GDP (Billions of dollars)	GNP less GDP, as a percent of GDP	Growth rate of GNP less growth rate of GDP, based on 1982 dollars (Percentage points)
1980	47.6	1.8	0
1981	52.1	1.7	–.1
1982	51.2	1.6	0
1983	49.9	1.5	–.1
1984	47.4	1.3	–.2
1985	40.7	1.0	–.2
1986	34.4	.8	–.2
1987	29.0	.6	–.2
1988	33.5	.7	.1
1989	37.6	.7	0
1990	41.7	.8	.1
1990: I	41.6	.8	–.1
II	31.6	.6	–.8
III	42.9	.8	.7
IV	50.8	.9	.5
1991: I	54.8	1.0	.2
II	42.4	.8	–.9

NOTE.—The quarterly estimates are based on seasonally adjusted annual rates.

ment in the United States) has been small relative to the size of the U.S. economy. (The value of labor supplied to, and by, foreigners is even smaller.) Since 1929, the receipts by U.S. residents from their investments abroad have exceeded payments to foreigners for their investments here, so GNP has been larger than GDP. The largest percentage difference, 1.8 percent, was in 1980. In 1990, GNP was 0.8 percent larger than GDP.

In some countries, the difference between GDP and GNP is much larger. For example, there is much more foreign investment in Canada than Canadian investment abroad; consequently, its GNP was 3.6 percent smaller than its GDP in 1990. However, the difference in France, Japan, the United Kingdom, and several other industrialized countries is now similar, at 1 percent or less, to that in the United States.

Although the differences between the dollar levels of U.S. GNP and GDP are small, their growth rates sometimes differ. Table 2 shows that the annual growth rate of real GNP was slightly less than that of real GDP in most years of the 1980's. Differences between growth rates tend to be larger and to fluctuate more.

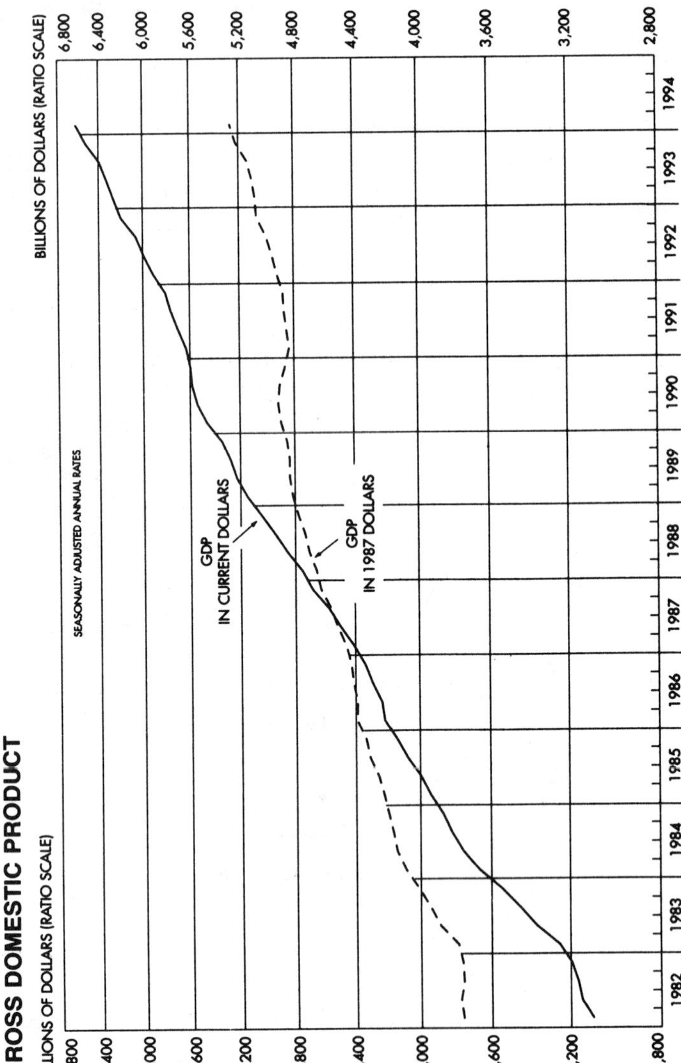
GROSS DOMESTIC PRODUCT
BILLIONS OF DOLLARS (RATIO SCALE)
BILLIONS OF DOLLARS (RATIO SCALE)
SEASONALLY ADJUSTED ANNUAL RATES
GDP
IN CURRENT DOLLARS
GDP
IN 1987 DOLLARS
6,800
6,400
6,000
5,600
5,200
4,800
4,400
4,000
3,600
3,200
2,800
1982
1983
1984
1985
1986
1987
1988
1989
1990
1991
1992
1993
1994
SOURCE: DEPARTMENT OF COMMERCE
COUNCIL OF ECONOMIC ADVISERS

[Billions of current dollars; quarterly data at seasonally adjusted annual rates]

Period	Gross domestic product	Personal consumption expenditures	Gross private domestic investment	Exports and imports of goods and services			Government purchases					Final sales of domestic product	Gross domestic purchases [1]	Addendum: Gross national product
				Net exports	Exports	Imports	Total	Federal			State and local			
								Total	National defense	Nondefense				
1986	4,268.6	2,850.6	717.6	−132.5	319.2	451.7	833.0	367.8	276.7	91.1	465.3	4,260.0	4,401.2	4,277.7
1987	4,539.9	3,052.2	749.3	−143.1	364.0	507.1	881.5	384.9	292.1	92.9	496.6	4,513.7	4,683.0	4,544.5
1988	4,900.4	3,296.1	793.6	−108.0	444.2	552.2	918.7	387.0	295.6	91.4	531.7	4,884.2	5,008.4	4,908.2
1989	5,250.8	3,523.1	832.3	−79.7	508.0	587.7	975.2	401.6	299.9	101.7	573.6	5,217.5	5,330.5	5,266.8
1990	5,546.1	3,761.2	808.9	−71.4	557.1	628.5	1,047.4	426.5	314.0	112.5	620.9	5,539.3	5,617.5	5,567.8
1991	5,722.9	3,906.4	736.9	−19.6	601.5	621.1	1,099.3	445.9	322.5	123.4	653.4	5,731.6	5,742.5	5,737.1
1992	6,038.5	4,139.9	796.5	−29.6	640.5	670.1	1,131.8	448.8	313.8	135.0	683.0	6,031.2	6,068.2	6,045.8
1993	6,377.9	4,391.8	891.7	−63.6	661.7	725.3	1,158.1	443.4	303.4	140.1	714.6	6,362.3	6,441.5	6,378.1
1982: IV	3,195.1	2,128.7	464.2	−29.5	265.6	295.1	631.6	281.4	205.5	75.9	350.3	3,241.4	3,224.6	3,222.6
1983: IV	3,547.3	2,346.8	614.8	−71.8	286.2	358.0	657.6	289.7	222.8	66.9	367.9	3,527.1	3,619.1	3,578.4
1984: IV	3,869.1	2,526.4	722.8	−107.1	308.7	415.7	727.0	324.7	242.9	81.9	402.2	3,818.1	3,976.2	3,890.2
1985: IV	4,140.5	2,739.8	737.0	−135.5	304.7	440.2	799.2	356.9	268.6	88.3	442.4	4,107.9	4,276.0	4,156.2
1986: IV	4,336.6	2,923.1	697.1	−133.2	333.9	467.1	849.7	373.1	278.6	94.5	476.6	4,355.4	4,469.8	4,340.5
1987: IV	4,683.0	3,124.6	800.2	−143.2	392.4	535.6	901.4	392.5	295.8	96.7	509.0	4,623.7	4,826.2	4,690.5
1988: IV	5,044.6	3,398.2	814.8	−106.0	467.0	573.1	937.6	392.0	296.8	95.2	545.7	5,027.3	5,150.7	5,054.3
1989: IV	5,344.8	3,599.1	825.2	−73.9	523.8	597.7	994.5	405.1	302.5	102.6	589.3	5,314.6	5,418.7	5,365.0
1990: IV	5,597.9	3,836.6	756.4	−71.6	577.6	649.2	1,076.5	436.5	322.5	114.0	640.0	5,621.8	5,669.5	5,630.0
1991: III	5,758.6	3,929.8	744.5	−19.8	603.0	622.8	1,104.0	446.8	321.2	125.6	657.3	5,759.1	5,778.4	5,766.2
IV	5,803.7	3,964.1	752.4	−13.0	625.7	638.8	1,100.2	437.4	311.2	126.2	662.8	5,794.8	5,816.7	5,815.5
1992: I	5,908.7	4,046.5	750.8	−7.0	633.7	640.7	1,118.5	445.5	312.3	133.1	673.0	5,913.9	5,915.8	5,927.6
II	5,991.4	4,099.9	799.7	−33.9	632.4	666.3	1,125.8	444.6	310.4	134.2	681.2	5,978.6	6,025.3	5,996.3
III	6,059.5	4,157.1	802.2	−38.8	641.1	679.9	1,139.1	452.8	316.7	136.1	686.2	6,049.9	6,098.3	6,067.3
IV	6,194.4	4,256.2	833.3	−38.8	654.7	693.5	1,143.8	452.4	315.7	136.7	691.4	6,182.5	6,233.2	6,191.9
1993: I	6,261.6	4,296.2	874.1	−48.3	651.3	699.6	1,139.7	442.7	304.8	137.9	697.0	6,227.1	6,309.9	6,262.1
II	6,327.6	4,359.9	874.1	−65.1	660.0	725.0	1,158.6	447.5	307.6	140.0	711.1	6,314.5	6,392.7	6,327.1
III	6,395.9	4,419.1	884.0	−71.9	653.2	725.1	1,164.8	443.6	301.9	141.7	721.2	6,388.2	6,467.8	6,402.3
IV	6,526.5	4,492.0	934.5	−69.1	682.4	751.5	1,169.1	440.0	299.2	140.7	729.2	6,519.6	6,595.6	6,520.9
1994: I r	6,623.1	4,563.7	970.0	−83.5	678.2	761.7	1,172.9	440.9	291.7	149.3	732.0	6,602.2	6,706.6	6,618.6

[1] GDP less exports of goods and services plus imports of goods and services.

Source: Department of Commerce, Bureau of Economic Analysis.

Source: *Economic Indicators*, Council of Economic Advisers.

GROSS DOMESTIC PRODUCT IN 1987 DOLLARS (Billions of 1987 dollars; quarterly data at seasonally adjusted annual rates)

Period	Gross domestic product	Personal consumption expenditures	Gross private domestic investment			Exports and imports of goods and services			Government purchases					Final sales of domestic product	Gross domestic purchases [1]	Addendum: Gross national product
			Nonresidential fixed investment	Residential fixed investment	Change in business inventories	Net exports	Exports	Imports	Total	Federal			State and local			
										Total	National defense	Nondefense				
1986	4,404.5	2,969.1	500.3	226.2	8.5	−155.1	329.6	484.7	855.4	373.0	280.6	92.4	482.4	4,395.9	4,559.6	4,413.5
1987	4,539.9	3,052.2	497.8	225.2	26.3	−143.1	364.0	507.1	881.5	384.9	292.1	92.9	496.6	4,513.7	4,683.0	4,544.5
1988	4,718.6	3,162.4	530.8	222.7	19.9	−104.0	421.6	525.7	886.8	377.3	287.0	90.2	509.6	4,698.6	4,822.6	4,726.3
1989	4,838.0	3,223.3	540.0	214.2	29.8	−73.7	471.8	545.4	904.4	376.1	281.4	94.8	528.3	4,808.3	4,911.7	4,852.7
1990	4,897.3	3,272.6	546.5	194.5	5.7	−54.7	510.5	565.1	932.6	384.1	283.6	100.4	548.5	4,891.6	4,951.9	4,916.5
1991	4,861.4	3,258.6	514.5	169.5	−8.4	−19.1	543.4	562.5	946.3	386.5	281.3	105.3	559.7	4,869.8	4,880.5	4,874.5
1992	4,986.3	3,341.8	529.2	197.1	6.5	−33.6	578.0	611.6	945.2	373.0	261.2	111.8	572.2	4,979.8	5,019.9	4,994.0
1993	5,136.0	3,453.2	591.8	214.2	14.3	−76.5	598.3	674.8	938.9	354.9	242.4	112.5	584.0	5,121.7	5,212.5	5,138.6
1982: IV	3,759.6	2,539.3	417.2	131.2	−44.9	−19.0	280.4	299.4	735.9	316.0	229.4	86.6	419.9	3,804.5	3,778.6	3,791.7
1983: IV	4,012.1	2,678.2	449.6	190.6	29.3	−83.7	291.5	375.1	748.1	322.2	242.9	79.3	425.9	3,982.8	4,095.8	4,046.6
1984: IV	4,194.2	2,784.8	509.6	198.8	47.9	−131.4	312.8	444.2	784.3	341.7	254.3	87.4	442.6	4,146.2	4,325.5	4,216.4
1985: IV	4,333.5	2,895.3	525.5	207.4	30.2	−155.4	312.0	467.4	830.5	363.7	272.1	91.6	466.7	4,303.3	4,488.9	4,349.5
1986: IV	4,427.1	3,012.5	495.5	230.5	−20.1	−156.0	342.9	498.9	864.8	377.5	282.2	95.3	487.3	4,447.2	4,583.1	4,430.8
1987: IV	4,625.5	3,074.7	510.6	223.3	59.9	−136.0	386.1	522.1	893.0	391.6	295.0	96.6	501.4	4,565.6	4,761.5	4,633.0
1988: IV	4,779.7	3,202.9	538.8	225.3	20.9	−102.7	438.2	540.9	894.5	378.4	285.7	92.7	516.1	4,758.7	4,882.4	4,789.0
1989: IV	4,856.7	3,242.0	536.7	208.0	24.9	−67.4	487.7	555.0	912.6	376.1	281.5	94.7	536.5	4,831.8	4,924.1	4,875.1
1990: IV	4,867.2	3,265.9	540.2	176.3	−20.9	−36.8	520.4	557.2	942.4	386.5	285.7	100.8	555.8	4,888.0	4,904.0	4,895.4
1991: III	4,872.6	3,267.1	512.8	171.0	−.9	−25.0	546.9	571.9	947.6	386.6	279.4	107.2	561.0	4,873.5	4,897.6	4,880.3
IV	4,879.6	3,267.5	506.1	179.1	7.1	−16.4	564.2	580.7	936.2	372.1	264.9	107.2	564.1	4,872.5	4,896.0	4,890.9
1992: I	4,922.0	3,302.3	510.5	186.2	−5.0	−15.2	571.0	586.2	943.1	372.1	261.2	110.9	571.0	4,926.9	4,937.1	4,939.0
II	4,956.5	3,316.8	528.8	195.6	12.6	−38.0	570.2	608.2	940.7	369.2	257.9	111.3	571.5	4,943.8	4,994.5	4,962.2
III	4,998.2	3,350.9	533.8	196.2	9.6	−42.5	579.3	621.8	950.2	377.0	264.4	112.5	573.2	4,988.6	5,040.7	5,006.4
IV	5,068.3	3,397.2	543.7	210.6	8.7	−38.8	591.6	630.3	946.9	373.7	261.3	112.4	573.2	5,059.6	5,107.1	5,068.4
1993: I	5,078.2	3,403.8	562.3	211.4	29.3	−59.9	588.0	647.9	931.3	357.6	246.0	111.5	573.7	5,048.9	5,138.1	5,080.7
II	5,102.1	3,432.7	584.3	206.2	13.0	−75.2	593.2	668.4	941.1	359.4	246.4	113.0	581.6	5,089.1	5,177.4	5,104.1
III	5,138.3	3,469.6	594.8	212.1	6.5	−86.3	591.9	678.2	941.7	353.7	240.1	113.7	588.0	5,131.8	5,224.6	5,145.8
IV	5,225.6	3,506.9	625.7	227.2	8.5	−84.5	620.0	704.5	941.7	349.0	237.1	111.8	592.8	5,217.1	5,310.0	5,223.7
1994: I r	5,269.5	3,551.9	636.8	231.9	20.6	−105.0	615.6	720.6	933.3	344.3	227.5	116.7	589.0	5,248.9	5,374.5	5,268.5

[1] GDP less exports of goods and services plus imports of goods and services.

Source: Department of Commerce, Bureau of Economic Analysis.

Source: *Economic Indicators*, Council of Economic Advisers.

PERSONAL CONSUMPTION EXPENDITURES IN 1987 DOLLARS (Billions of 1987 dollars, except as noted; quarterly data at seasonally adjusted annual rates)

Period	Total personal consumption expenditures	Durable goods				Nondurable goods						Services			Retail sales of new passenger cars (millions of units)	
		Total durable goods	Motor vehicles and parts	Furniture and household equipment	Other	Total nondurable goods	Food	Clothing and shoes	Gasoline and oil	Fuel oil and coal	Other	Total services [1]	Housing	Medical care	Domestics	Imports
1987	3,052.2	403.7	183.5	144.0	76.2	1,011.1	500.7	174.5	84.7	12.0	239.1	1,637.4	452.5	384.7	7.1	3.2
1988	3,162.4	428.7	194.8	155.4	78.5	1,035.1	513.4	178.9	86.1	12.0	244.7	1,698.5	461.8	399.4	7.5	3.1
1989	3,223.3	440.7	196.4	165.8	78.5	1,051.6	515.0	187.8	87.3	11.4	250.2	1,731.0	469.2	408.6	7.1	2.8
1990	3,272.6	443.1	192.7	171.6	78.7	1,060.7	523.9	186.2	86.4	10.5	253.8	1,768.8	474.6	424.6	6.9	2.6
1991	3,258.6	426.6	170.5	180.0	76.1	1,048.2	518.7	184.7	83.1	10.7	250.9	1,783.8	478.6	437.6	6.1	2.3
1992	3,341.8	456.6	182.3	194.8	79.5	1,062.9	520.5	193.7	83.9	11.9	252.9	1,822.3	484.2	449.2	6.3	2.1
1993	3,453.2	490.0	191.7	216.3	82.0	1,088.1	531.0	199.5	84.9	13.0	259.8	1,875.2	492.0	463.4	6.7	2.0
1982: IV	2,539.3	272.3	123.7	96.4	52.3	880.7	458.3	135.7	73.4	10.5	202.8	1,386.2	411.0	327.8	6.0	2.5
1983: IV	2,678.2	319.1	151.6	109.3	58.1	915.2	467.1	147.7	76.9	11.4	212.2	1,443.9	419.7	334.8	7.4	2.6
1984: IV	2,784.8	347.7	164.3	118.7	64.8	942.9	475.1	154.7	79.0	11.1	222.9	1,494.2	431.3	344.9	7.7	2.6
1985: IV	2,895.3	369.6	173.9	128.6	67.1	968.7	488.2	161.7	79.5	11.4	228.0	1,557.1	438.1	359.1	7.0	3.1
1986: IV	3,012.5	415.7	193.6	141.4	80.7	1,000.9	496.9	171.9	84.6	12.4	235.2	1,595.8	444.8	372.0	7.7	3.4
1987: IV	3,074.7	404.7	183.6	145.9	75.2	1,014.6	502.4	174.5	85.4	11.9	240.4	1,655.5	457.0	390.7	6.6	3.3
1988: IV	3,202.9	439.2	197.7	160.3	81.2	1,046.8	518.0	182.8	87.5	12.0	246.4	1,716.9	465.6	403.0	7.5	3.0
1989: IV	3,242.0	436.8	188.3	167.9	80.5	1,058.9	515.6	190.9	88.6	12.0	251.8	1,746.3	471.3	411.8	6.2	2.6
1990: IV	3,265.9	433.2	182.1	172.3	78.8	1,057.5	525.8	184.5	84.6	9.5	253.1	1,775.2	475.9	429.4	6.6	2.4
1991: III	3,267.1	432.6	173.7	182.7	76.2	1,049.3	518.8	185.9	83.4	11.4	249.8	1,785.2	479.4	438.8	6.2	2.3
IV	3,267.5	431.5	173.0	182.9	75.6	1,044.0	518.2	183.1	82.5	10.6	249.6	1,792.0	480.6	443.6	6.1	2.2
1992: I	3,302.3	446.6	180.6	188.2	77.8	1,052.0	518.8	188.3	82.7	11.1	251.1	1,803.7	481.7	445.3	6.1	2.3
II	3,316.8	447.5	179.5	189.8	78.2	1,055.0	515.7	191.1	83.7	12.8	251.7	1,814.3	483.2	447.9	6.3	2.2
III	3,350.9	459.0	180.6	197.1	81.3	1,062.9	518.2	195.4	84.7	11.7	252.7	1,829.0	485.1	450.4	6.2	2.0
IV	3,397.2	473.4	188.6	204.2	80.6	1,081.8	529.3	200.0	84.4	11.9	256.2	1,842.0	486.7	453.2	6.4	2.0
1993: I	3,403.8	471.9	185.7	206.5	79.7	1,076.0	526.7	194.8	83.9	12.9	257.7	1,855.9	488.8	458.0	6.4	2.0
II	3,432.7	484.2	191.3	212.4	80.6	1,083.1	528.6	197.8	84.1	12.6	259.9	1,865.4	490.7	461.1	6.9	2.1
III	3,469.6	493.1	189.9	219.4	83.7	1,093.0	532.6	200.6	86.2	13.2	260.4	1,883.5	493.3	465.1	6.6	2.0
IV	3,506.9	510.9	199.7	227.1	84.1	1,100.2	536.0	204.6	85.4	13.1	261.1	1,895.8	495.3	469.3	7.1	1.9
1994: I [r]	3,551.9	523.4	210.7	228.2	84.6	1,111.8	540.9	205.9	84.7	14.5	265.8	1,916.6	497.5	472.6	7.5	2.0

[1] Includes other items, not shown separately.

Source: Department of Commerce, Bureau of Economic Analysis.

Source: *Economic Indicators*, Council of Economic Advisers.

CORPORATE PROFITS

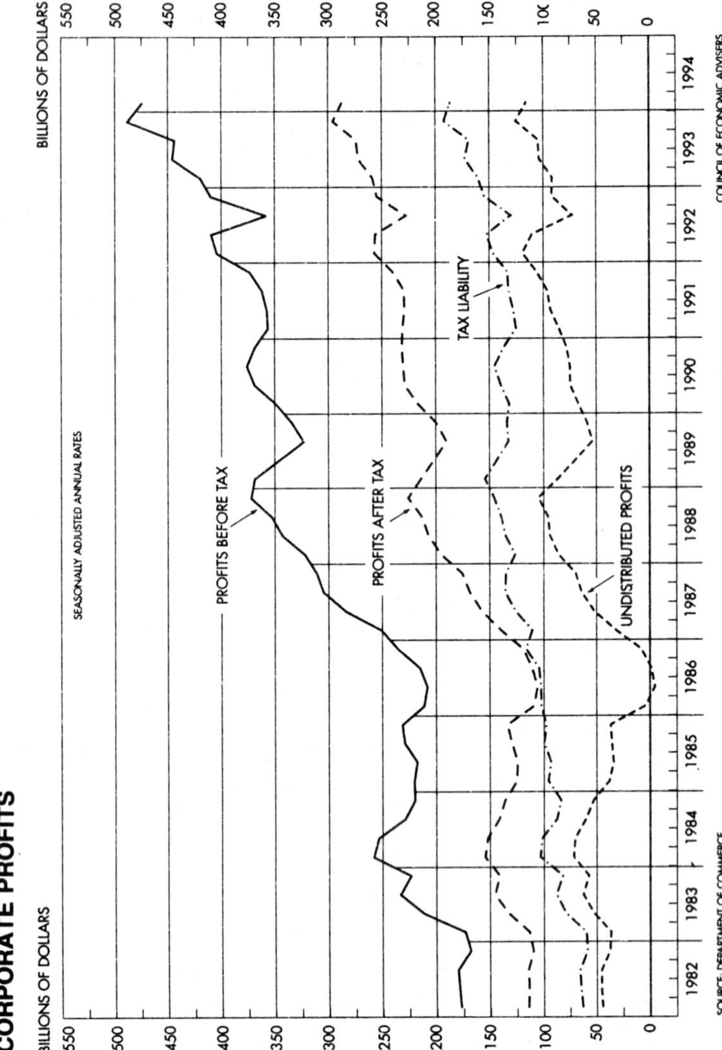
BILLIONS OF DOLLARS
SEASONALLY ADJUSTED ANNUAL RATES
PROFITS BEFORE TAX
PROFITS AFTER TAX
TAX LIABILITY
UNDISTRIBUTED PROFITS
550
500
450
400
350
300
250
200
150
100
50
0
1982
1983
1984
1985
1986
1987
1988
1989
1990
1991
1992
1993
1994
SOURCE: DEPARTMENT OF COMMERCE
COUNCIL OF ECONOMIC ADVISERS

[Billions of dollars; quarterly data at seasonally adjusted annual rates]

Period	Profits (before tax) with inventory valuation adjustment [1]						Profits before tax	Tax liability	Profits after tax			Inventory valuation adjustment
	Total [2]	Domestic industries							Total	Dividends	Undistributed profits	
		Total	Financial	Nonfinancial								
				Total [3]	Manufacturing	Wholesale and retail trade						
1986	227.6	194.6	35.8	158.9	59.0	46.3	217.8	106.5	111.3	109.8	1.6	9.7
1987	273.4	233.9	36.4	197.5	87.0	39.9	287.9	127.1	160.8	106.2	54.6	−14.5
1988	320.3	271.2	41.8	229.4	117.5	37.1	347.5	137.0	210.5	115.3	95.2	−27.3
1989	325.4	266.0	50.6	215.3	108.0	39.7	342.9	141.3	201.6	134.6	67.1	−17.5
1990	354.7	286.7	65.7	221.1	109.1	37.2	365.7	138.7	227.1	153.5	73.6	−11.0
1991	367.3	300.4	80.7	219.7	89.8	47.4	362.3	129.8	232.5	137.4	95.2	4.9
1992	390.1	327.8	78.1	249.8	115.5	46.3	395.4	146.3	249.1	150.5	98.6	−5.3
1993	442.3	383.6	99.0	284.6	131.7	54.4	449.4	174.0	275.4	169.0	106.4	−7.1
1982: IV	160.0	130.8	23.0	107.8	50.1	33.8	168.6	58.7	109.9	72.5	37.5	−8.6
1983: IV	216.2	182.6	22.1	160.5	90.5	40.7	223.8	82.2	141.6	84.2	57.4	−7.6
1984: IV	223.6	192.9	20.3	172.6	79.2	50.8	220.1	83.8	136.3	83.4	52.9	3.5
1985: IV	228.0	193.5	29.0	164.5	83.3	39.0	231.8	97.6	134.2	97.4	36.9	−3.8
1986: IV	225.0	192.5	34.7	157.8	63.9	43.1	235.7	116.6	119.2	111.0	8.2	−10.7
1987: IV	293.4	246.3	39.4	207.0	98.7	39.3	311.2	135.2	176.0	106.3	69.7	−17.8
1988: IV	340.5	285.9	46.1	239.7	129.3	39.3	372.2	146.2	226.0	121.0	105.0	−31.7
1989: IV	320.6	254.8	52.5	202.3	94.5	39.2	334.1	134.2	200.0	141.3	58.7	−13.5
1990: IV	349.3	273.8	66.6	207.2	98.5	36.2	368.9	137.0	231.8	153.7	78.1	−19.5
1991: III	359.0	299.3	84.2	215.1	89.3	45.6	362.0	132.5	229.5	133.4	96.1	−3.0
IV	375.4	306.8	81.6	225.2	88.9	47.8	373.5	133.4	240.1	133.9	106.1	1.9
1992: I	399.7	328.5	97.9	230.5	98.9	40.0	404.3	147.0	257.3	138.0	119.3	−4.6
II	395.7	334.2	87.7	246.5	115.7	46.0	409.5	153.0	256.5	146.1	110.4	−13.7
III	350.1	288.6	44.6	244.0	119.3	41.3	357.9	130.1	227.8	155.2	72.7	−7.8
IV	414.8	360.1	82.0	278.1	128.0	57.7	409.9	155.0	254.9	162.9	92.0	4.9
1993: I	407.0	348.0	92.3	255.7	118.9	46.0	419.8	160.9	258.9	167.5	91.4	−12.7
II	433.4	375.3	96.4	278.9	132.5	55.4	445.6	173.3	272.3	168.5	103.9	−12.2
III	444.8	382.1	99.3	282.8	126.7	55.1	443.8	169.5	274.3	169.7	104.6	1.0
IV	484.0	428.9	108.1	320.8	148.9	61.4	488.4	192.5	295.9	170.3	125.6	−4.3
1994: I [r]	458.0	403.6	82.9	320.7	154.1	57.0	474.2	186.7	287.5	171.8	115.7	−16.2

[1] See p. 141 for profits with inventory valuation and capital consumption adjustments.
[2] Includes rest of the world, not shown separately.
[3] Includes industries not shown separately.
Source: Department of Commerce, Bureau of Economic Analysis.

Source: *Economic Indicators*, Council of Economic Advisers.

Price Data

Definitions are applicable to the exhibit on pages 151–152.

Price data are gathered by the Bureau of Labor Statistics from retail and primary markets in the United States. Price indexes are given in relation to a base period (1982 = 100 for many Producer Price Indexes or 1982–84 = 100 for many Consumer Price Indexes, unless otherwise noted).

DEFINITIONS

The **Consumer Price Index** (CPI) is a measure of the average change in the prices paid by urban consumers for a fixed market basket of goods and services. The CPI is calculated monthly for two population groups, one consisting only of urban households whose primary source of income is derived from the employment of wage earners and clerical workers, and the other consisting of all urban households. The wage earner index (CPI–W) is a continuation of the historic index that was introduced well over a half-century ago for use in wage negotiations. As new uses were developed for the CPI in recent years, the need for a broader and more representative index became apparent. The all urban consumer index (CPI–U) introduced in 1978 is representative of the 1982–84 buying habits of about 80 percent of the noninstitutional population of the United States at that time, compared with 32 percent represented in the CPI–W. In addition to wage earners and clerical workers, the CPI–U covers professional, managerial, and technical workers, the self-employed, short-term workers, the unemployed, retirees, and others not in the labor force.

The CPI is based on prices of food, clothing, shelter, fuel, drugs, transportation fares, doctor's and dentist's fees, and other goods and services that people buy for day-to-day living. The quantity and quality of these items are kept essentially unchanged between major revisions so that only price changes will be measured. All taxes directly associated with the purchase and use of items are included in the index.

Data collected from more than 19,000 retail establishments and 57,000 tenants in 85 urban areas across the country are used to develop the "U.S. city average." Separate estimates for 15 major urban centers are presented in the table on page 152. The areas listed are as indicated in footnote 1 to the table. The area indexes measure only the average change in prices for each area since the base period, and do not indicate differences in the level of prices among cities.

NOTES ON THE DATA

In January 1983, the Bureau changed the way in which homeownership costs are measured for the CPI–U. A rental equivalence method replaced the asset-price approach to homeownership costs for that series. In January 1985, the same change was made in the CPI–W. The central purpose of the change was to separate shelter costs from the investment component of homeownership so that the index would reflect only the cost of shelter services provided by owner-occupied homes. An updated CPI-U and CPI-W were introduced with release of the January 1987 data.

For additional information on consumer prices, contact the Division of Consumer Prices and Price Indexes: 202-606-7000.

Source: *Monthly Labor Review*, U.S. Department of Labor Statistics, Bureau of Labor Statistics.

CONSUMER PRICE INDEX—U.S. CITY AVERAGE AND AVAILABLE LOCAL AREA DATA: ALL ITEMS

(1982-84=100, unless otherwise indicated)

Area[1]	Pricing schedule[2]	All Urban Consumers							Urban Wage Earners						
		1993			1994				1993			1994			
		Mar.	Apr.	Dec.	Jan.	Feb.	Mar.	Apr.	Mar.	Apr.	Dec.	Jan.	Feb.	Mar.	Apr.
U.S. city average	M	143.6	144.0	145.8	146.2	146.7	147.2	147.4	141.1	141.6	143.3	143.6	144.0	144.4	144.7
Region and area size[3]															
Northeast urban	M	150.9	151.1	152.7	153.2	154.0	154.3	154.4	148.7	148.9	150.4	150.8	151.4	151.7	151.8
Size A - More than 1,200,000	M	151.6	151.7	153.2	153.7	154.6	155.1	155.0	148.4	148.5	149.9	150.2	150.9	151.4	151.4
Size B - 500,000 to 1,200,000	M	149.3	150.1	151.7	152.5	153.0	152.7	153.3	147.3	148.0	149.4	150.3	150.7	150.6	151.1
Size C - 50,000 to 500,000	M	149.1	149.2	151.1	151.3	151.9	152.2	152.6	150.7	150.9	152.6	152.7	153.2	153.4	153.9
North Central urban	M	139.0	139.4	141.2	141.5	142.1	142.6	142.9	136.2	136.6	138.2	138.5	139.0	139.4	139.8
Size A - More than 1,200,000	M	140.1	140.5	142.2	142.5	143.2	143.9	144.1	136.5	136.9	138.5	138.8	139.4	140.0	140.3
Size B - 360,000 to 1,200,000	M	137.3	137.7	140.1	141.1	141.3	141.8	142.2	134.1	134.6	136.5	137.4	137.6	137.9	138.5
Size C - 50,000 to 360,000	M	140.4	140.7	142.4	142.4	143.0	143.1	143.7	138.2	138.6	140.0	140.0	140.6	140.6	141.2
Size D - Nonmetropolitan (less than 50,0000	M	134.7	134.8	136.8	136.7	137.2	137.8	137.9	133.8	133.9	135.6	135.3	135.8	136.3	136.4
South urban	M	139.7	140.2	142.2	142.5	142.9	143.6	143.8	138.3	138.8	140.8	141.0	141.2	141.9	142.2
Size A - More than 1,200,000	M	140.4	140.8	142.7	142.9	143.4	144.4	144.4	138.5	138.8	141.0	141.0	141.3	142.3	142.4
Size B - 450,000 to 1,200,000	M	141.6	141.9	143.8	144.4	144.6	145.4	145.5	138.2	138.6	140.7	141.1	141.2	141.8	141.8
Size C - 50,000 to 450,000	M	138.6	139.3	140.9	141.0	141.6	142.0	142.9	138.5	139.3	140.8	140.8	141.3	141.6	142.6
Size D - Nonmetropolitan (less than 50,000)	M	137.0	137.7	140.7	140.8	140.7	141.3	141.3	137.0	137.8	140.9	141.1	141.0	141.4	141.4
West urban	M	145.2	145.7	147.8	148.1	148.3	149.0	148.9	142.7	143.2	145.0	145.3	145.4	145.9	145.9
Size A - More than 1,250,000	M	147.2	147.7	149.5	149.7	149.9	150.5	150.4	143.0	143.5	145.2	145.3	145.4	145.9	145.8
Size C - 50,000 to 330,000	M	143.8	144.2	146.7	147.8	148.3	148.7	148.6	141.8	142.4	144.5	145.4	146.0	146.3	146.3
Size classes:															
A (12/86=100)	M	130.6	130.9	132.5	132.7	133.3	133.9	133.9	129.7	130.0	131.5	131.7	132.1	132.7	132.7
B	M	142.5	143.0	145.0	145.8	146.1	146.5	146.8	140.1	140.6	142.6	143.2	143.4	143.8	144.1
C	M	141.8	142.3	144.1	144.3	144.9	145.2	145.8	141.3	141.8	143.4	143.6	144.1	144.3	144.9
D	M	138.3	138.7	141.3	141.2	141.5	142.0	142.1	137.8	138.3	140.7	140.6	140.8	141.2	141.4

(continued)

CONSUMER PRICE INDEX—U.S. CITY AVERAGE AND AVAILABLE LOCAL AREA DATA: ALL ITEMS *(concluded)*

(1982-84=100, unless otherwise indicated)

Area[1]	Pricing schedule[2]	All Urban Consumers							Urban Wage Earners						
		1993			1994				1993			1994			
		Mar.	Apr.	Dec.	Jan.	Feb.	Mar.	Apr.	Mar.	Apr.	Dec.	Jan.	Feb.	Mar.	Apr.
Selected local areas															
Chicago, IL-Northwestern IN	M	144.1	144.7	146.1	146.5	146.8	147.6	147.9	139.5	140.3	141.7	142.0	142.3	143.0	143.3
Los Angeles-Long Beach, Anaheim, CA	M	149.8	149.9	151.9	152.2	152.2	152.5	152.0	144.8	144.9	146.7	146.8	146.9	147.0	146.6
New York, NY-Northeastern NJ	M	154.1	154.0	155.6	156.0	157.4	157.9	157.7	150.7	150.7	152.1	152.4	153.5	154.0	153.9
Philadelphia, PA-NJ	M	149.3	149.6	151.3	152.5	152.9	153.5	153.1	149.0	149.4	151.2	152.1	152.2	152.8	152.6
San Francisco-Oakland, CA	M	145.7	146.8	147.0	147.5	147.4	148.2	148.0	143.8	144.8	144.7	145.3	145.0	145.6	145.6
Baltimore, MD	1	142.6	–	–	143.8	–	145.0	–	141.8	–	–	142.7	–	144.2	–
Boston, MA	1	154.1	–	–	153.6	–	155.0	–	154.0	–	–	152.5	–	153.5	–
Cleveland, OH	1	138.8	–	–	142.4	–	143.3	–	131.8	–	–	135.1	–	135.7	–
Miami, FL	1	139.2	–	–	141.0	–	143.5	–	137.1	–	–	138.7	–	141.1	–
St. Louis, MO-IL	1	136.1	–	–	138.6	–	139.7	–	135.5	–	–	137.7	–	138.7	–
Washington, DC-MD-VA	1	148.5	–	–	150.9	–	151.5	–	146.2	–	–	148.3	–	148.9	–
Dallas-Ft. Worth, TX	2	–	137.0	138.8	–	139.2	–	140.3	–	136.3	138.6	–	138.1	–	139.3
Detroit, MI	2	–	138.7	140.2	–	141.7	–	142.6	–	134.6	135.7	–	137.0	–	137.9
Houston, TX	2	–	131.8	136.5	–	137.0	–	136.8	–	131.3	136.0	–	136.3	–	136.2
Pittsburgh, PA	2	–	139.6	141.1	–	142.6	–	143.9	–	133.6	135.1	–	136.3	–	137.4

[1] Area definitions are those established by the Office of Management and Budget in 1983, except for Boston-Lawrence-Salem, MA-NH, Area (excludes Monroe County); and Milwaukee, WI, Area (includes only the Milwaukee MSA). Definitions do not include revisions made since 1983. Excludes farms and the military.

[2] Foods, fuels, and several other items priced every month in all areas; most other goods and services priced as indicated:.

M - Every month.

1 - January, March, May, July, September, and November.

2 - February, April, June, August, October, and December.

[3] Regions are defined as the four Census regions.

– Data not available.

NOTE: Local area CPI indexes are byproducts of the national CPI program. Because each local index is a small subset of the national index, it has a smaller sample size and is, therefore, subject to substantially more sampling and other measurement error than the national index. As a result, local area indexes show greater volatility than the national index, although their long-term trends are quite similar. Therefore, the Bureau of Labor Statistics strongly urges users to consider adopting the national average CPI for use in escalator clauses.

Source: *Monthly Labor Review*, U.S. Department of Labor, Bureau of Labor Statistics.

Purchasing Power of the Dollar: 1950–1993

1950 to 1992

[Indexes: PPI, 1982=$1.00; CPI, 1982–84=$1.00. Producer prices prior to 1961, and consumer prices prior to 1964, exclude Alaska and Hawaii. Producer prices based on finished goods index. Obtained by dividing the average price index for the 1982=100, PPI; 1982–84=100, CPI base periods (100.0) by the price index for a given period and expressing the result in dollars and cents. Annual figures are based on average of monthly data]

YEAR	ANNUAL AVERAGE AS MEASURED BY—		YEAR	ANNUAL AVERAGE AS MEASURED BY—		YEAR	ANNUAL AVERAGE AS MEASURED BY—	
	Producer prices	Consumer prices		Producer prices	Consumer prices		Producer prices	Consumer prices
1950	$3.546	$4.151	1965	2.933	3.166	1979	1.289	1.380
1951	3.247	3.846	1966	2.841	3.080	1980	1.136	1.215
1952	3.268	3.765	1967	2.809	2.993	1981	1.041	1.098
1953	3.300	3.735	1968	2.732	2.873	1982	1.000	1.035
1954	3.289	3.717	1969	2.632	2.726	1983	0.984	1.003
1955	3.279	3.732	1970	2.545	2.574	1984	0.964	0.961
1956	3.195	3.678	1971	2.469	2.466	1985	0.955	0.928
1957	3.077	3.549	1972	2.392	2.391	1986	0.969	0.913
1958	3.012	3.457	1973	2.193	2.251	1987	0.949	0.880
1959	3.021	3.427	1974	1.901	2.029	1988	0.926	0.846
1960	2.994	3.373	1975	1.718	1.859	1989	0.880	0.807
1961	2.994	3.340	1976	1.645	1.757	1990	0.839	0.766
1962	2.985	3.304	1977	1.546	1.649	1991	0.822	0.734
1963	2.994	3.265	1978	1.433	1.532	1992	0.812	0.713
1964	2.985	3.220						

Source: U.S. Bureau of Labor Statistics. Monthly data in U.S. Bureau of Economic Analysis, Survey of Current Business.

Source: *Statistical Abstract of the United States,* U.S. Department of Commerce.

1993

YEAR	ANNUAL AVERAGE AS MEASURED BY—	
	Producer prices	Consumer prices
1993.........	.802	.692

Source: U.S. Department of Commerce, U.S. Bureau of Economic Analysis.

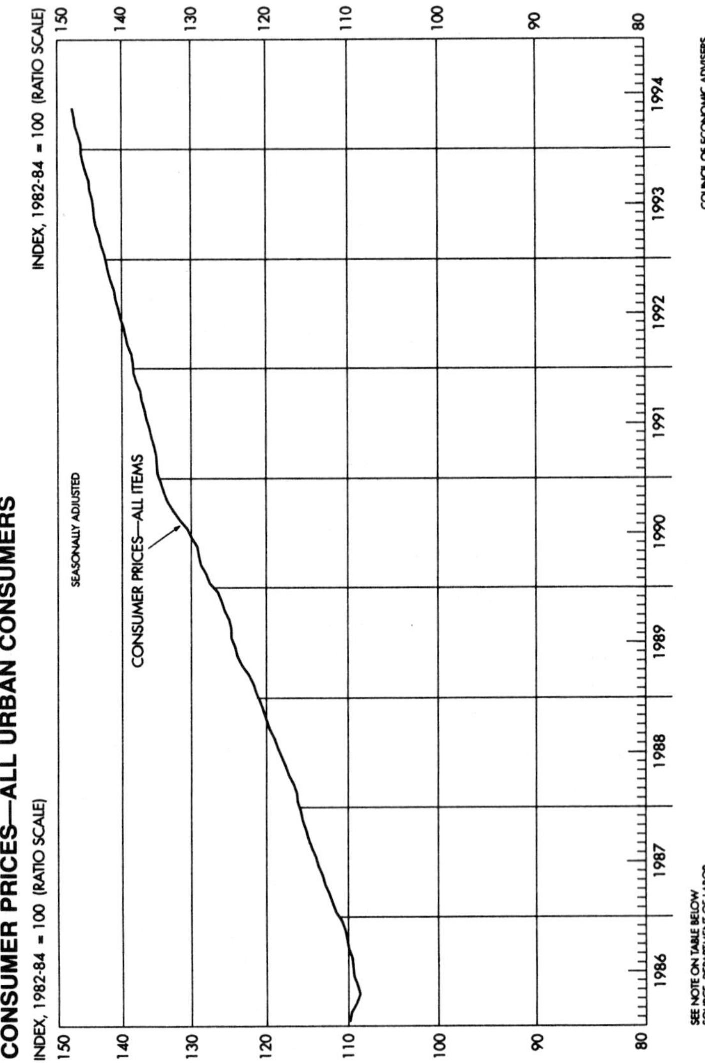
CONSUMER PRICES—ALL URBAN CONSUMERS
INDEX, 1982-84 = 100 (RATIO SCALE)
INDEX, 1982-84 = 100 (RATIO SCALE)
150
140
130
120
110
100
90
80
SEASONALLY ADJUSTED
CONSUMER PRICES—ALL ITEMS
1986
1987
1988
1989
1990
1991
1992
1993
1994
SEE NOTE ON TABLE BELOW
SOURCE: DEPARTMENT OF LABOR
COUNCIL OF ECONOMIC ADVISERS

[1982–84=100, except as noted; monthly data seasonally adjusted, except as noted]

Period	All items [1]		Food	Housing						Apparel and upkeep	Transportation			Medical care	Energy [2]	All items less food and energy
					Shelter											
	Not seasonally adjusted (NSA)	Seasonally adjusted		Total [1]	Total	Renters' costs (Dec. 1982=100)	Homeowners' costs (Dec. 1982=100)	Maintenance and repairs (NSA)	Fuel and other utilities		Total [1]	New cars	Motor fuel			
Rel. imp. [3]	*100.0*	....	*15.8*	*41.4*	*27.9*	*8.0*	*19.8*	*0.2*	*7.3*	*5.9*	*17.0*	*4.0*	*3.0*	*7.1*	*7.0*	*77.2*
1984	103.9	....	103.2	103.6	104.0	108.6	107.3	103.7	104.8	102.1	103.7	102.8	97.9	106.8	100.9	104.6
1985	107.6	....	105.6	107.7	109.8	115.4	113.1	106.5	106.5	105.0	106.4	106.1	98.7	113.5	101.6	109.1
1986	109.6	....	109.0	110.9	115.8	121.9	119.4	107.9	104.1	105.9	102.3	110.6	77.1	122.0	88.2	113.5
1987	113.6	....	113.5	114.2	121.3	128.1	124.8	111.8	103.0	110.6	105.4	114.6	80.2	130.1	88.6	118.2
1988	118.3	....	118.2	118.5	127.1	133.6	131.1	114.7	104.4	115.4	108.7	116.9	80.9	138.6	89.3	123.4
1989	124.0	....	125.1	123.0	132.8	138.9	137.3	118.0	107.8	118.6	114.1	119.2	88.5	149.3	94.3	129.0
1990	130.7	....	132.4	128.5	140.0	146.7	144.6	122.2	111.6	124.1	120.5	121.0	101.2	162.8	102.1	135.5
1991	136.2	....	136.3	133.6	146.3	155.6	150.2	126.3	115.3	128.7	123.8	125.3	99.4	177.0	102.5	142.1
1992	140.3	....	137.9	137.5	151.2	160.9	155.3	128.6	117.8	131.9	126.5	128.4	99.0	190.1	103.0	147.3
1993	144.5	....	140.9	141.2	155.7	165.0	160.2	130.6	121.3	133.7	130.4	131.5	98.0	201.4	104.2	152.2
1993:																
May	144.2	144.3	141.1	140.8	155.1	164.0	159.7	131.6	121.0	133.6	130.1	131.0	98.9	200.7	104.2	152.0
June	144.4	144.4	140.7	141.1	155.4	164.2	160.1	131.2	121.4	133.1	130.0	131.2	97.2	201.5	103.7	152.3
July	144.4	144.6	140.7	141.2	155.6	164.3	160.4	131.3	121.8	133.0	130.5	131.6	96.9	202.4	103.7	152.6
Aug	144.8	145.0	141.2	141.6	156.0	164.5	160.8	131.6	122.2	133.9	130.6	132.2	95.3	203.0	103.0	153.0
Sept	145.1	145.1	141.6	141.9	156.3	164.8	161.1	131.3	122.4	133.4	130.6	132.5	94.1	203.8	102.6	153.1
Oct	145.7	145.6	142.3	142.2	156.6	165.6	161.3	130.8	122.5	133.2	131.9	132.9	98.3	204.8	104.5	153.5
Nov	145.8	146.0	142.6	142.5	157.1	165.8	161.9	127.9	122.4	134.1	131.9	133.1	96.6	205.4	103.6	154.1
Dec	145.8	146.3	143.3	142.8	157.5	166.3	162.4	127.6	122.3	133.9	131.7	133.2	95.3	206.1	102.9	154.4
1994:																
Jan	146.2	146.3	143.1	142.9	157.8	166.3	162.8	128.9	121.8	133.8	131.4	133.3	94.8	206.7	102.1	154.6
Feb	146.7	146.7	142.7	143.5	158.6	167.0	163.6	129.4	122.9	133.4	132.0	133.9	96.8	207.3	103.7	155.0
Mar	147.2	147.2	142.9	144.0	159.2	167.7	164.3	129.3	123.3	134.0	132.8	134.5	97.0	207.8	104.1	155.5
Apr	147.4	147.4	143.0	144.0	159.3	167.7	164.4	130.2	122.9	133.6	133.2	135.0	96.8	209.1	103.7	155.8
May	147.5	147.7	143.5	144.3	159.7	168.4	164.8	131.0	122.8	134.2	132.7	135.4	95.3	209.9	102.7	156.3

[1] Includes items not shown separately.
[2] Household fuels—gas (piped), electricity, fuel oil, etc.—and motor fuel. Motor oil, coolant, etc. excluded beginning 1983.
[3] Relative importance, December 1993.

NOTE.—Data beginning 1983 incorporate a rental equivalence measure for homeownership costs and therefore are not strictly comparable with figures for earlier periods.
Data beginning 1987 and 1988 calculated on a revised basis.
Source: Department of Labor, Bureau of Labor Statistics.

Source: *Economic Indicators*, Council of Economic Advisers.

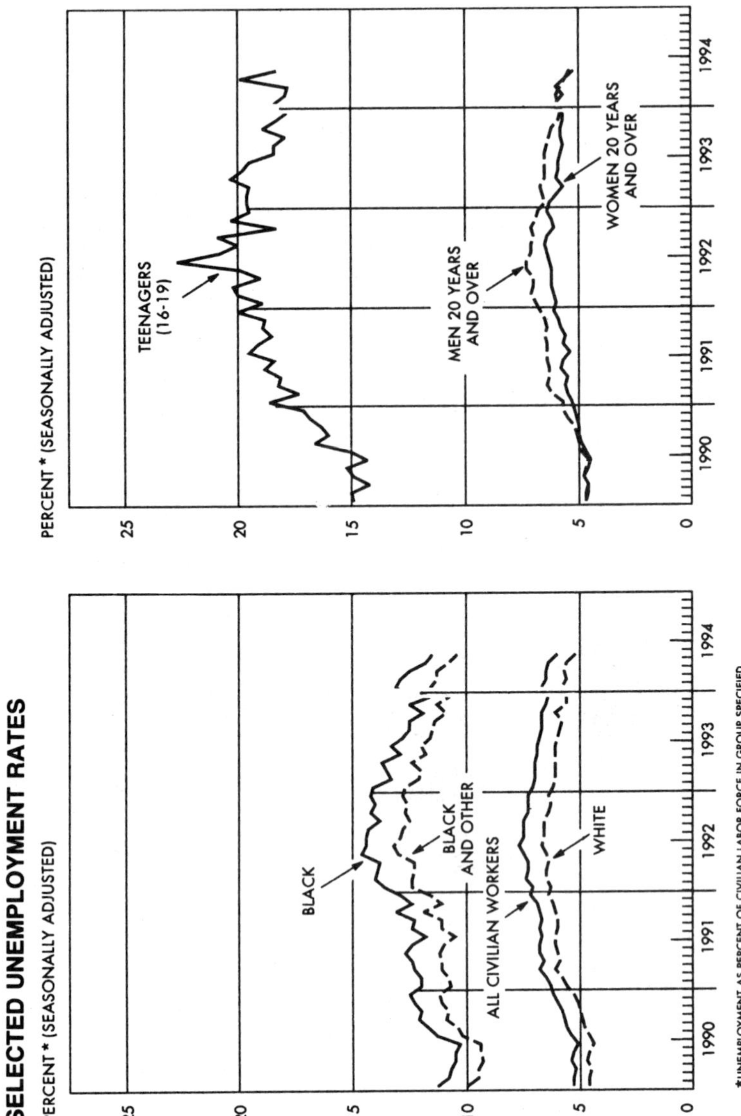
SELECTED UNEMPLOYMENT RATES
PERCENT * (SEASONALLY ADJUSTED)
25
20
15
10
5
0
BLACK
BLACK AND OTHER
ALL CIVILIAN WORKERS
WHITE
1990
1991
1992
1993
1994
*UNEMPLOYMENT AS PERCENT OF CIVILIAN LABOR FORCE IN GROUP SPECIFIED
SOURCE: DEPARTMENT OF LABOR
PERCENT * (SEASONALLY ADJUSTED)
TEENAGERS (16-19)
MEN 20 YEARS AND OVER
WOMEN 20 YEARS AND OVER
COUNCIL OF ECONOMIC ADVISERS

[Monthly data seasonally adjusted]

Period	Unemployment rate, all workers [1]	Unemployment rate (percent of civilian labor force in group)												Labor force time lost (percent) [3]
		All civilian workers	By sex and age			By race			By selected groups					
			Men 20 years and over	Women 20 years and over	Both sexes 16–19 years	White	Black and other	Black	Experienced wage and salary workers	Married men, spouse present	Women who maintain families	Full-time workers [2]	Part-time workers [2]	
1984	7.4	7.5	6.6	6.8	18.9	6.5	14.4	15.9	7.1	4.6	10.3	7.5	7.4	8.6
1985	7.1	7.2	6.2	6.6	18.6	6.2	13.7	15.1	6.8	4.3	10.4	7.1	7.5	8.1
1986	6.9	7.0	6.1	6.2	18.3	6.0	13.1	14.5	6.6	4.4	9.8	6.9	7.4	7.9
1987	6.1	6.2	5.4	5.4	16.9	5.3	11.6	13.0	5.8	3.9	9.2	6.0	6.9	7.1
1988	5.4	5.5	4.8	4.9	15.3	4.7	10.4	11.7	5.2	3.3	8.1	5.3	6.4	6.3
1989	5.2	5.3	4.5	4.7	15.0	4.5	10.0	11.4	5.0	3.0	8.1	5.1	6.2	5.9
1990	5.4	5.5	4.9	4.8	15.5	4.7	10.1	11.3	5.3	3.4	8.2	5.4	6.3	6.2
1991	6.6	6.7	6.3	5.7	18.6	6.0	11.1	12.4	6.5	4.4	9.1	6.7	6.9	7.6
1992	7.3	7.4	7.0	6.3	20.0	6.5	12.7	14.1	7.1	5.0	9.9	7.4	7.4	8.3
1993	6.7	6.8	6.4	5.9	19.0	6.0	11.7	12.9	6.5	4.4	9.5	6.8	7.1	7.7
1993: May	6.9	6.9	6.5	5.9	19.8	6.1	11.8	12.9	6.6	4.5	9.8	6.9	6.9	7.9
June	6.8	6.9	6.5	5.9	19.5	6.1	12.0	13.3	6.6	4.4	9.7	6.9	7.1	7.8
July	6.7	6.8	6.5	5.8	18.4	6.0	11.6	12.8	6.5	4.5	9.6	6.8	6.7	7.8
Aug	6.7	6.7	6.4	5.7	18.4	5.9	11.5	12.5	6.4	4.4	9.0	6.7	6.8	7.7
Sept	6.6	6.7	6.3	5.8	17.9	5.8	11.4	12.5	6.3	4.2	9.0	6.6	6.9	7.5
Oct	6.6	6.7	6.2	5.8	18.9	6.1	10.9	11.9	6.4	4.4	9.3	6.6	7.2	7.6
Nov	6.4	6.5	5.9	5.7	18.3	5.6	11.3	12.5	6.2	4.0	9.0	6.3	6.9	7.2
Dec	6.3	6.4	5.8	5.7	17.8	5.6	10.7	11.5	6.2	3.9	10.2	6.4	6.6	7.2
1994: Jan [4]	....	6.7	5.9	6.0	18.4	5.8	11.6	13.1	6.6	4.1	9.4	6.8	6.2	....
Feb	....	6.5	6.0	5.7	17.9	5.6	11.3	12.9	6.4	4.3	9.7	6.6	5.9	....
Mar	....	6.5	5.8	6.0	17.8	5.7	11.3	12.5	6.4	4.1	9.6	6.6	6.3	....
Apr	....	6.4	5.6	5.6	19.9	5.6	10.8	11.8	6.2	3.9	9.1	6.4	6.5	....
May	....	6.0	5.2	5.4	18.3	5.2	10.4	11.5	5.8	3.7	8.9	6.0	6.2	....

[1] Unemployed as percent of total labor force including resident Armed Forces.
[2] Revised definition; for details, see *Employment and Earnings*, February 1994.
[3] Aggregate hours lost by the unemployed and persons on part time for economic reasons as percent of potentially available labor force hours.
[4] Data beginning January 1994 are based on the revised Current Population Survey and are not directly comparable with data for earlier periods. For details, see *Employment and Earnings*, February 1994.

Source: Department of Labor, Bureau of Labor Statistics.

Source: *Economic Indicators*, Council of Economic Advisers.

MONEY STOCK, LIQUID ASSETS, AND DEBT MEASURES

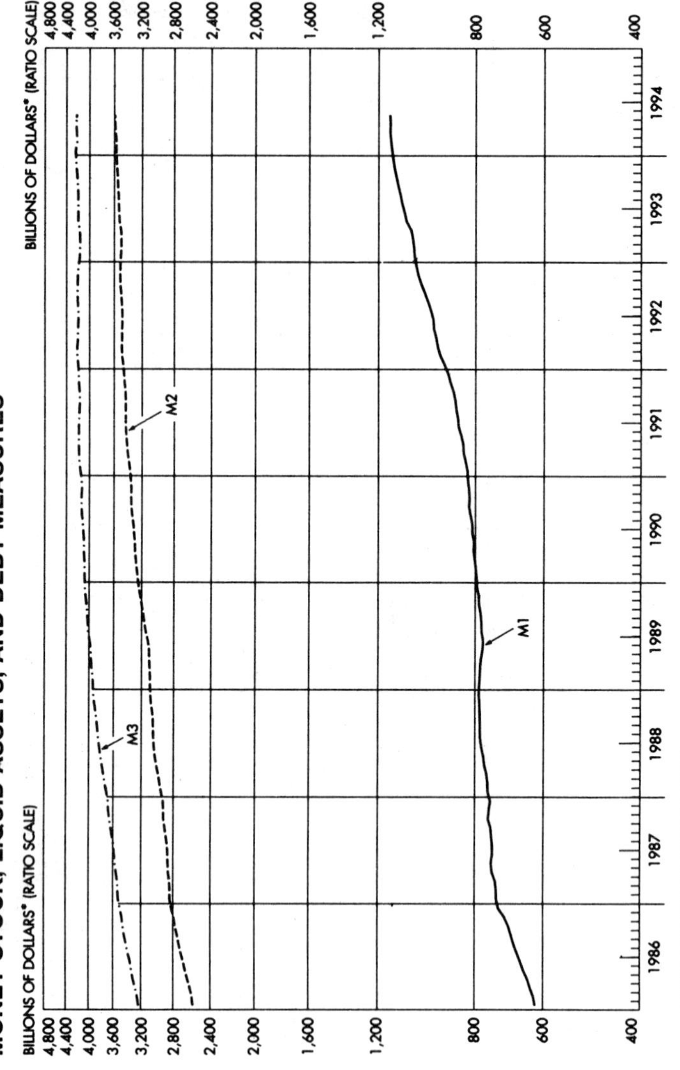

[Averages of daily figures, except as noted; billions of dollars, seasonally adjusted]

Period	M1	M2	M3	L	Debt	Percent change from year or 6 months earlier [2]			
	Sum of currency, demand deposits, travelers' checks, and other checkable deposits (OCDs)	M1 plus overnight RPs and Eurodollars, MMMF balances (general purpose and broker/dealer), MMDAs, and savings and small time deposits	M2 plus large time deposits, term RPs, term Eurodollars, and institution-only MMMF balances	M3 plus other liquid assets	Debt of domestic nonfinancial sectors (monthly average) [1]	M1	M2	M3	Debt
1984: Dec	552.1	2,377.8	2,994.6	3,536.0	6,006.1	6.0	8.7	11.1	14.2
1985: Dec	619.9	2,575.0	3,211.6	3,838.9	6,901.1	12.3	8.3	7.2	14.9
1986: Dec	724.5	2,818.2	3,497.3	4,137.5	7,778.6	16.9	9.4	8.9	12.7
1987: Dec	750.1	2,920.1	3,681.3	4,340.2	8,543.3	3.5	3.6	5.3	9.8
1988: Dec	787.4	3,081.4	3,920.4	4,674.6	9,306.1	5.0	5.5	6.5	8.9
1989: Dec	794.7	3,239.8	4,067.3	4,897.3	10,030.7	.9	5.1	3.7	7.8
1990: Dec	826.4	3,353.0	4,125.7	4,974.8	10,670.1	4.0	3.5	1.4	6.4
1991: Dec	897.7	3,455.3	4,180.4	4,992.9	11,147.3	8.6	3.1	1.3	4.5
1992: Dec	1,024.8	3,509.0	4,183.0	5,057.1	r 11,727.7	14.2	1.6	.1	5.2
1993: Dec r	1,128.4	3,567.4	4,229.4	5,131.8	12,309.8	10.1	1.7	1.1	5.0
1993: Apr	1,047.1	3,498.0	4,162.0	r 5,054.4	r 11,870.6	8.5	−.5	−1.7	r 4.1
May	1,067.7	3,521.9	4,187.6	r 5,088.2	r 11,918.1	10.1	.6	−.3	r 4.2
June	1,076.6	3,528.7	4,187.8	r 5,089.5	r 11,987.6	10.1	1.1	.2	4.4
July r	1,086.8	3,533.7	4,186.9	5,086.2	12,044.9	10.4	1.8	1.2	4.8
Aug r	1,095.3	3,536.0	4,186.8	5,094.8	12,097.1	11.6	2.4	1.5	5.4
Sept r	1,105.1	3,544.2	4,195.8	5,087.8	12,155.3	12.5	2.8	2.0	5.6
Oct r	1,113.4	3,547.8	4,203.4	5,098.3	12,190.5	12.7	2.8	2.0	5.4
Nov r	1,122.4	3,560.1	4,216.8	5,111.6	12,238.7	10.2	2.2	1.4	5.4
Dec r	1,128.4	3,567.4	4,229.4	5,131.8	12,309.8	9.6	2.2	2.0	5.4
1994: Jan r	1,133.5	3,572.6	4,233.5	5,151.9	12,370.9	8.6	2.2	2.2	5.4
Feb r	1,138.6	3,568.7	4,207.0	5,140.5	12,419.8	7.9	1.8	1.0	5.3
Mar r	1,142.4	3,582.7	4,215.3	5,141.0	12,473.3	6.8	2.2	.9	5.2
Apr r	1,141.3	3,590.0	4,224.0	p 5,159.5	p 12,520.2	5.0	2.4	1.0	5.4
May	1,143.2	3,591.3	4,215.4	....	....	3.7	1.8	−.1	....

[1] Consists of outstanding credit market debt of the U.S. Government, State and local governments, and private nonfinancial sectors; data from flow of funds accounts.

[2] Annual changes are from December to December and monthly changes are from 6 months earlier at a simple annual rate.

NOTE.—See p. 27 for components.

Source: Board of Governors of the Federal Reserve System.

Source: *Economic Indicators*, Council of Economic Advisers.

OUTPUT, CAPACITY, AND CAPACITY UTILIZATION[1] (Seasonally adjusted)

Series	1993			1994	1993			1994	1993			1994
	Q2	Q3	Q4[r]	Q1	Q2	Q3	Q4	Q1	Q2	Q3	Q4[r]	Q1
	Output (1987=100)				Capacity (percent of 1987 output)				Capacity utilization rate (percent)[2]			
1 **Total industry**	**110.3**	**111.1**	**112.9**	**115.0**	**135.9**	**136.5**	**137.2**	**138.0**	**81.2**	**81.4**	**82.3**	**83.3**
2 Manufacturing	111.2	111.8	114.1	116.3	138.4	139.2	140.0	140.9	80.3	80.3	81.5	82.5
3 Primary processing[3]	107.0	107.7	109.9	111.0	127.9	128.3	128.6	129.0	83.6	83.9	85.5	86.0
4 Advanced processing[4]	113.2	113.8	116.1	118.8	143.4	144.4	145.4	146.6	78.9	78.8	79.9	81.1
5 Durable goods	113.2	114.2	118.1	121.2	144.5	145.4	146.3	147.6	78.4	78.5	80.7	82.1
6 Lumber and products	98.0	100.8	104.9	104.5	114.8	115.0	115.2	115.4	85.4	87.6	91.1	90.5
7 Primary metals	105.2	106.7	109.6	110.6	123.3	123.0	122.6	122.4	85.3	86.8	89.4	90.3
8 Iron and steel	109.7	112.3	115.6	116.1	127.4	126.9	126.3	126.0	86.1	88.6	91.5	92.1
9 Nonferrous	99.0	98.9	101.4	103.1	117.6	117.6	117.6	117.5	84.1	84.1	86.2	87.7
10 Nonelectrical machinery	141.7	147.2	152.7	158.8	173.1	175.7	178.2	181.7	81.8	83.8	85.7	87.4
11 Electrical machinery	125.9	129.7	132.6	136.2	153.8	155.7	157.7	160.3	81.9	83.2	84.1	85.0
12 Motor vehicles and parts	118.1	112.0	131.7	144.7	153.4	154.8	156.1	157.8	76.9	72.3	84.4	91.7
13 Aerospace and miscellaneous transportation equipment	90.3	87.4	85.2	82.8	133.7	133.2	132.8	132.2	67.6	65.6	64.2	62.6
14 Nondurable goods	108.7	108.9	109.2	110.2	131.0	131.6	132.1	132.7	83.0	82.8	82.6	83.0
15 Textile mill products	108.4	108.0	107.7	108.4	118.8	119.4	119.9	120.5	91.3	90.5	89.8	90.0
16 Paper and products	113.2	111.7	114.2	115.7	124.3	124.8	125.3	125.8	91.1	89.6	91.2	92.0
17 Chemicals and products	117.7	118.6	118.6	120.5	145.1	145.9	146.8	147.7	81.2	81.2	80.8	81.6
18 Plastics materials	112.8	111.5	114.4	...	130.1	131.1	132.0	...	86.7	85.1	86.6	...
19 Petroleum products	104.0	104.0	107.7	105.4	115.8	115.7	115.6	115.4	89.8	89.9	93.2	91.3
20 Mining	97.5	96.8	97.3	98.4	111.4	111.1	110.8	110.6	87.5	87.1	87.8	88.9
21 Utilities	114.1	117.5	115.6	118.2	133.6	134.0	134.3	134.7	85.4	87.8	86.1	87.8
22 Electric	114.8	118.0	114.8	117.4	130.8	131.2	131.7	132.2	87.7	89.9	87.2	88.8

Series	1973	1975	Previous cycle[2]		Latest cycle[3]		1993	1993			1994		
	High	Low	High	Low	High	Low	Mar.	Oct.	Nov.	Dec.[r]	Jan.[r]	Feb.[r]	Mar.[p]
	Capacity utilization rate (percent)[2]												
1 **Total industry**	**99.0**	**82.7**	**87.3**	**71.8**	**84.8**	**78.3**	**81.2**	**81.7**	**82.2**	**82.9**	**83.1**	**83.4**	**83.6**
2 Manufacturing	99.0	82.7	87.3	70.0	85.1	76.6	80.1	80.8	81.5	82.3	82.2	82.5	82.8
3 Primary processing[3]	99.0	82.7	89.7	66.8	89.1	77.9	83.2	84.4	85.5	86.4	85.8	85.8	86.4
4 Advanced processing[4]	99.0	82.7	86.3	71.4	83.3	76.1	78.9	79.3	79.8	80.6	80.7	81.2	81.3
5 Durable goods	99.0	82.7	86.9	65.0	83.9	73.8	78.2	79.6	80.6	81.9	81.9	82.2	82.3
6 Lumber and products	99.0	82.7	87.6	60.9	93.3	76.8	85.9	90.9	91.0	91.3	90.9	90.1	90.4
7 Primary metals	99.0	82.7	102.4	46.8	92.9	74.3	84.4	86.5	89.5	92.2	90.2	90.2	90.7
8 Iron and steel	99.0	82.7	110.4	38.3	95.7	72.3	84.7	89.6	90.6	94.5	91.7	92.2	92.5
9 Nonferrous	99.0	82.7	90.5	62.2	88.9	75.9	84.1	81.8	88.0	88.9	87.9	87.2	87.9
10 Nonelectrical machinery	99.0	82.7	92.1	64.9	83.7	73.0	79.9	84.7	85.3	87.0	87.1	87.0	88.0
11 Electrical machinery	99.0	82.7	89.4	71.1	84.9	76.8	81.5	83.6	83.7	84.8	84.6	84.9	85.5
12 Motor vehicles and parts	99.0	82.7	93.0	44.5	84.5	57.9	79.1	79.7	84.8	88.5	90.2	94.7	90.4
13 Aerospace and miscellaneous transportation equipment	99.0	82.7	81.1	66.9	88.3	78.1	68.6	64.3	64.5	63.7	63.3	62.4	62.2
14 Nondurable goods	99.0	82.7	87.0	76.9	86.8	80.4	82.8	82.5	82.6	82.9	82.7	83.0	83.5
15 Textile mill products	99.0	82.7	91.7	73.8	92.1	78.7	90.5	90.0	90.0	89.4	89.8	89.7	90.4
16 Paper and products	99.0	82.7	94.2	82.0	94.9	86.0	89.8	90.1	91.4	92.1	90.9	92.0	93.2
17 Chemicals and products	99.0	82.7	85.1	70.1	85.9	78.5	81.0	80.4	81.0	81.2	81.4	81.6	81.8
18 Plastics materials	99.0	82.7	90.9	63.4	97.0	75.5	87.1	84.4	85.2	90.3	87.3	...	...
19 Petroleum products	99.0	82.7	89.5	68.2	88.5	84.2	89.8	93.6	93.3	92.7	90.5	91.4	92.0
20 Mining	99.0	82.7	96.6	80.6	87.0	86.8	86.8	88.4	87.5	87.5	87.5	89.2	90.1
21 Utilities	99.0	82.7	88.3	76.2	92.6	83.4	87.9	85.6	86.4	86.2	89.1	87.9	86.2
22 Electric	99.0	82.7	88.3	78.7	94.8	87.4	88.8	86.5	87.5	87.6	90.2	89.0	87.2

1. Data in this table also appear in the Board's G.17 (419) monthly statistical release. For ordering address, see inside front cover. For a detailed description of the series, see "Recent Developments in Industrial Capacity and Utilization," *Federal Reserve Bulletin*, vol. 76 (June 1990), pp. 411–35. See also "Industrial Production Capacity and Capacity Utilization Since 1987," *Federal Reserve Bulletin*, vol. 79, (June 1993), pp. 590–605.

2. Capacity utilization is calculated as the ratio of the Federal Reserve's seasonally adjusted index of industrial production to the corresponding index of capacity.

3. Primary processing includes textiles; lumber; paper; industrial chemicals; petroleum refining; rubber and plastics; stone, clay, and glass; and primary and fabricated metals.

4. Advanced processing includes food, tobacco, apparel, furniture, printing, chemical products such as drugs and toiletries, leather and products, machinery, transportation equipment, instruments, miscellaneous manufacturing, and ordnance.

5. Monthly highs, 1978 through 1980; monthly lows, 1982.

6. Monthly highs, 1988–89; monthly lows, 1990–91.

Source: *Federal Reserve Bulletin,* Board of Governors of the Federal Reserve System.

INDUSTRIAL PRODUCTION Indexes and Gross Value[1]

Monthly data seasonally adjusted

Group	1987 proportion	1993 avg.	1993r Mar.	Apr.	May	June	July	Aug.	Sept.	Oct.	Nov.	Dec.	1994 Jan.r	Feb.r	Mar.p
			Index (1987 = 100)												
MAJOR MARKETS															
1 **Total index**	**100.0**	**111.0**	**108.9**	**109.3**	**109.9**	**110.1**	**110.4**	**110.2**	**110.5**	**110.8**	**111.0**	**111.4**	**112.1**	**113.2**	**114.0**
2 Products	60.8	110.2	108.2	108.5	109.2	109.5	109.6	109.3	109.4	110.0	110.3	110.5	111.4	112.4	113.0
3 Final products	46.0	113.5	111.5	111.9	112.4	112.7	112.8	112.5	112.7	113.2	113.5	113.8	114.8	115.9	116.6
4 Consumer goods, total	26.0	108.1	107.5	107.6	108.5	108.6	108.1	107.3	107.3	107.7	107.8	107.4	108.6	109.6	109.8
5 Durable consumer goods	5.6	111.3	107.9	110.9	111.3	111.5	112.2	110.8	107.9	108.6	107.9	109.3	113.4	117.0	118.6
6 Automotive products	2.5	110.6	108.7	112.7	111.9	111.2	112.1	109.7	105.3	103.3	103.0	105.6	112.9	119.5	123.4
7 Autos and trucks	1.5	112.2	111.7	116.8	114.6	113.4	114.3	110.1	105.0	100.3	99.2	104.1	114.9	124.9	131.5
8 Autos, consumer	.9	86.1	86.9	86.6	90.2	90.5	90.2	86.5	83.5	78.2	71.8	75.4	85.2	95.4	98.8
9 Trucks, consumer	.6	157.3	154.6	169.1	156.9	153.1	155.9	150.9	142.3	138.6	146.7	153.9	166.4	176.0	188.0
10 Auto parts and allied goods	1.0	108.0	103.8	105.8	107.4	107.5	108.5	109.1	105.8	108.4	109.3	108.1	109.5	110.4	109.9
11 Other	3.1	111.9	107.2	109.3	110.7	111.7	112.3	111.8	110.2	113.2	112.2	112.5	113.8	114.9	114.4
12 Appliances, A/C, and TV	.8	122.9	110.5	116.0	117.6	125.0	124.3	121.1	116.1	127.3	123.8	125.9	129.6	131.9	128.5
13 Carpeting and furniture	.9	107.8	105.4	105.5	106.7	104.5	106.2	108.9	109.1	109.9	108.3	107.3	109.0	108.6	109.4
14 Miscellaneous home goods	1.4	108.3	106.6	108.0	109.5	108.9	109.6	108.4	107.6	107.4	108.1	108.2	108.0	109.3	109.6
15 Nondurable consumer goods	20.4	107.2	107.4	106.7	107.7	107.7	106.9	106.3	107.2	107.4	107.8	106.9	107.3	107.4	107.2
16 Foods and tobacco	9.1	104.5	104.8	104.6	105.5	104.3	103.9	104.3	104.7	104.9	105.5	104.2	104.8	104.5	104.4
17 Clothing	2.6	93.7	96.0	95.7	95.0	94.6	94.9	94.2	94.6	93.6	93.3	92.6	92.6	92.9	92.5
18 Chemical products	3.5	123.3	121.7	122.4	121.1	123.7	123.1	122.6	123.0	124.0	123.8	124.0	123.0	124.2	124.3
19 Paper products	2.5	100.9	100.9	100.2	101.8	102.1	101.7	101.8	102.6	101.3	100.8	100.8	101.3	100.6	99.4
20 Energy	2.7	114.0	114.4	109.5	115.5	116.0	111.5	107.4	110.4	112.9	114.7	112.9	114.6	115.4	115.7
21 Fuels	.7	108.3	106.1	106.5	108.9	107.1	106.6	106.5	105.8	105.0	104.0	108.2	113.1	114.6	112.0
22 Residential utilities	2.0	116.2	117.5	110.7	118.0	119.5	113.4	107.7	112.2	116.0	118.9	114.7	115.1	115.7	117.1
23 Equipment	20.0	121.2	117.2	118.1	118.0	118.7	119.7	119.9	120.4	121.2	121.6	122.9	123.8	125.2	126.6
24 Business equipment	13.9	137.0	129.6	131.2	131.7	133.4	134.8	135.4	136.1	137.1	137.6	139.4	140.8	142.9	144.9
25 Information processing and related	5.6	156.2	143.2	144.4	146.1	149.1	150.6	153.5	155.7	158.2	158.8	161.5	162.3	164.9	168.2
26 Office and computing	1.9	223.6	186.4	192.0	198.0	203.3	209.5	216.5	221.0	226.5	232.0	237.1	241.8	247.9	255.0
27 Industrial	4.0	115.8	112.3	113.1	112.2	113.7	115.0	115.0	115.6	117.2	117.3	117.8	117.6	118.5	119.5
28 Transit	2.5	141.2	144.1	146.7	146.5	145.0	145.0	142.5	138.0	133.2	132.5	135.3	141.3	145.7	147.7
29 Autos and trucks	1.2	134.5	131.4	136.7	136.8	135.8	136.2	133.1	127.2	118.9	119.6	126.5	139.6	150.5	154.9
30 Other	1.9	119.1	109.2	112.6	113.4	114.9	117.5	116.2	117.6	119.6	121.9	123.1	124.5	125.0	125.5
31 Defense and space equipment	5.4	78.7	82.5	82.0	81.5	80.7	80.5	79.5	78.6	78.6	78.0	77.5	76.9	76.6	76.1
32 Oil and gas well drilling	.6	82.5	91.2	89.0	77.9	71.1	72.4	75.1	82.4	81.0	87.8	90.5	88.9	85.7	85.0
33 Manufactured homes	.2	...	128.6	129.4	127.1	116.2	114.9	112.1	113.6	118.5	116.2	120.6	127.7	138.4	...
34 Intermediate products, total	14.7	100.1	98.3	98.2	99.3	99.6	100.0	99.7	99.4	100.4	100.6	100.4	101.0	101.8	101.9
35 Construction supplies	6.0	98.1	94.5	94.8	97.5	96.4	96.4	97.7	96.8	98.4	98.7	99.3	99.9	100.7	101.3
36 Business supplies	8.7	101.5	100.8	100.5	100.5	101.8	102.5	101.0	101.1	101.7	101.8	101.2	101.6	102.5	102.2
37 Materials	39.2	112.2	110.0	110.4	110.9	110.9	111.5	111.6	112.1	112.0	112.2	112.7	113.2	114.3	115.5
38 Durable goods materials	19.4	116.0	111.9	113.3	114.2	114.1	114.9	114.8	114.9	115.4	115.8	117.2	118.2	119.7	121.7
39 Durable consumer parts	4.2	112.7	107.5	110.8	111.8	112.2	112.6	111.6	110.2	109.8	110.3	112.0	114.2	118.6	123.6
40 Equipment parts	7.3	125.1	119.7	120.4	121.0	121.3	122.7	123.5	124.1	124.9	126.2	128.0	129.2	129.6	131.5
41 Other	7.9	109.9	107.5	108.6	109.7	108.9	109.5	109.2	109.4	110.2	109.7	110.6	110.8	111.9	112.8
42 Basic metal materials	2.8	111.4	108.8	110.4	113.2	109.9	110.3	111.1	111.3	111.3	109.7	110.8	112.2	112.8	114.3
43 Nondurable goods materials	9.0	114.0	111.5	112.4	112.1	112.8	113.8	114.1	114.8	114.2	115.2	113.8	114.4	115.5	115.3
44 Textile materials	1.2	104.0	102.9	104.2	103.2	104.2	102.7	104.3	104.9	105.9	105.6	102.9	103.9	104.1	104.2
45 Pulp and paper materials	1.9	113.3	110.7	110.7	111.9	112.8	115.3	114.1	115.9	113.4	113.5	112.6	112.1	114.2	113.1
46 Chemical materials	3.8	117.5	114.6	114.9	114.6	115.6	116.1	117.2	118.6	117.3	119.5	117.9	118.0	119.1	119.8
47 Other	2.1	113.8	111.3	114.1	112.5	112.6	114.2	113.6	112.3	114.0	114.2	113.3	115.8	116.7	115.6
48 Energy materials	10.9	103.5	105.1	103.4	103.8	103.5	103.4	103.4	104.6	103.7	102.8	103.3	102.9	103.0	103.9
49 Primary energy	7.2	98.8	101.3	100.4	98.3	97.4	99.9	101.6	100.9	98.2	96.7	98.7	97.9	97.6	98.5
50 Converted fuel materials	3.7	112.6	112.4	109.1	114.6	115.4	110.3	106.8	111.7	114.5	114.9	112.4	112.7	113.8	114.4
SPECIAL AGGREGATES															
51 Total excluding autos and trucks	97.3	110.7	108.6	108.9	109.5	109.7	110.1	110.0	110.4	110.9	111.1	111.3	111.8	112.6	113.2
52 Total excluding motor vehicles and parts	95.3	110.5	108.6	108.7	109.3	109.6	109.9	109.8	110.3	110.9	111.1	111.2	111.5	112.2	112.7
53 Total excluding office and computing machines	97.5	108.3	107.1	107.3	107.8	107.8	108.0	107.7	107.8	108.1	108.1	108.4	109.0	110.0	110.6
54 Consumer goods excluding autos and trucks	24.5	107.8	107.3	107.0	108.1	108.2	107.6	107.1	107.5	108.2	108.4	107.7	108.2	108.5	108.2
55 Consumer goods excluding energy	23.3	107.5	106.8	107.4	107.7	107.7	107.6	107.3	107.0	107.1	107.0	106.8	108.0	108.9	109.1
56 Business equipment excluding autos and trucks	12.7	137.2	129.5	130.7	131.3	133.2	134.6	135.6	136.8	138.7	139.1	140.6	140.9	142.2	144.1
57 Business equipment excluding office and computing equipment	12.0	122.4	120.1	121.0	120.6	121.6	122.2	121.8	121.8	122.1	121.7	123.0	123.8	125.2	126.4
58 Materials excluding energy	28.4	115.4	111.8	113.0	113.6	113.7	114.6	114.6	114.9	115.1	115.6	116.1	117.0	118.4	119.8

(continued)

INDUSTRIAL PRODUCTION Indexes and Gross Value *(concluded)*

	Group	SIC code[2]	1987 pro-portion	1993 avg.	1993[r] Mar.	Apr.	May	June	July	Aug.	Sept.	Oct.	Nov.	Dec.	1994 Jan.[r]	Feb.	Mar.[p]
					Index (1987 = 100)												
	MAJOR INDUSTRIES																
59	**Total index**	...	**100.0**	**111.0**	**108.9**	**109.3**	**109.9**	**110.1**	**110.4**	**110.2**	**110.5**	**110.8**	**111.0**	**111.4**	**112.1**	**113.2**	**114.0**
60	Manufacturing	...	84.3	111.9	109.2	109.9	110.5	110.8	111.4	111.3	111.3	111.6	111.9	112.3	113.2	114.5	115.3
61	Primary processing	...	27.1	107.5	105.0	105.8	106.9	106.4	107.1	107.1	107.5	107.6	108.0	107.6	108.2	109.5	109.9
62	Advanced processing	...	57.1	113.9	111.3	111.9	112.2	112.9	113.4	113.3	113.0	113.5	113.7	114.5	115.6	116.8	117.8
63	Durable goods	...	46.5	115.9	111.8	112.9	113.8	114.1	115.0	114.9	114.6	115.4	115.7	117.0	118.3	120.1	121.7
64	Lumber and products	24	2.1	100.0	98.0	99.3	101.8	98.0	98.1	97.4	96.5	99.1	99.9	100.7	104.0	104.2	104.6
65	Furniture and fixtures	25	1.5	109.4	103.9	105.2	106.0	107.3	108.8	108.4	109.5	111.1	111.1	111.3	111.4	111.5	110.9
66	Clay, glass, and stone products	32	2.4	100.5	98.0	97.0	98.9	98.6	99.8	99.6	100.5	100.8	100.9	102.4	101.4	102.9	103.0
67	Primary metals	33	3.3	105.5	102.4	102.8	108.0	104.2	104.4	104.2	105.7	105.3	106.2	106.0	105.0	107.1	109.1
68	Iron and steel	331,2	1.9	110.5	107.4	107.0	112.9	107.6	108.4	108.1	110.9	111.9	112.1	111.1	112.4	111.1	114.6
69	Raw steel	...	.1	...	104.6	103.4	105.9	102.0	102.6	105.1	106.8	108.2	106.2	105.3	106.7	106.8	...
70	Nonferrous	333–6,9	1.4	98.6	95.7	97.1	101.4	99.4	98.9	98.9	98.5	96.3	98.0	98.9	94.9	101.6	101.6
71	Fabricated metal products	34	5.4	100.9	97.8	99.8	99.7	100.3	101.4	100.6	100.1	101.2	101.0	100.9	101.6	102.7	103.3
72	Industrial and commercial machinery and computer equipment	35	8.5	146.8	133.8	135.0	136.7	139.6	142.8	144.2	145.4	148.5	149.9	152.1	153.7	156.2	158.8
73	Office and computing machines	357	2.3	223.6	186.4	192.0	198.0	203.3	209.5	216.5	221.0	226.5	232.0	237.1	241.8	247.9	255.0
74	Electrical machinery	36	6.9	131.7	124.8	125.8	127.1	128.5	129.0	129.7	130.1	132.3	133.5	135.2	136.0	137.2	138.
75	Transportation equipment	37	9.9	105.6	106.3	108.4	107.8	106.9	106.9	105.5	102.6	100.8	100.4	102.4	106.3	110.0	112.
76	Motor vehicles and parts	371	4.8	120.1	116.2	120.9	120.7	120.1	120.4	118.1	114.3	110.1	110.0	115.0	124.1	132.3	138.8
77	Autos and light trucks	...	2.2	114.9	114.4	118.2	117.8	116.9	117.5	113.1	108.2	102.8	104.0	104.8	116.3	127.3	133.
78	Aerospace and miscellaneous transportation equipment	372–6,9	5.1	92.0	97.1	96.7	95.8	94.6	94.2	93.7	91.8	92.0	91.3	90.5	89.5	89.0	88.
79	Instruments	38	5.1	102.2	103.3	103.0	102.2	103.3	102.6	102.5	102.5	102.8	101.3	102.0	101.7	101.5	102.
80	Miscellaneous	39	1.3	113.1	111.8	110.9	111.9	112.6	114.3	113.1	112.1	112.3	112.5	114.3	113.7	114.3	115.
81	Nondurable goods	...	37.8	106.8	106.0	106.4	106.4	106.6	106.9	106.9	107.2	107.0	107.3	106.5	107.0	107.6	107.
82	Foods	20	8.8	106.9	106.2	105.9	106.9	106.7	106.7	106.7	107.1	107.2	107.8	107.3	107.8	107.2	107.
83	Tobacco products	21	1.0	91.1	96.1	100.5	99.3	92.4	90.2	92.1	89.1	91.5	92.7	85.8	88.2	89.1	88.
84	Textile mill products	22	1.8	106.3	106.0	106.9	106.2	105.4	104.2	106.9	107.1	107.7	107.4	105.4	106.6	106.3	106.
85	Apparel products	23	2.3	90.8	92.7	93.1	92.5	92.1	92.0	91.2	91.1	90.7	90.6	89.6	89.4	90.0	89.
86	Paper and products	26	3.6	112.0	108.3	108.6	110.4	111.1	113.1	112.1	114.2	112.0	113.1	111.2	111.8	113.8	112.
87	Printing and publishing	27	6.5	94.1	94.7	94.7	94.0	94.7	95.6	94.7	94.5	93.8	93.4	93.8	94.3	94.4	93.
88	Chemicals and products	28	8.8	118.3	116.7	116.8	116.2	117.6	117.8	118.1	119.1	118.7	119.1	118.5	118.1	119.6	120.
89	Petroleum products	29	1.3	104.8	103.4	103.2	104.7	104.7	104.3	103.6	103.9	102.5	102.4	104.3	107.9	108.2	107.
90	Rubber and plastic products	30	3.2	113.7	111.3	113.6	112.7	112.9	113.6	113.8	112.8	114.7	114.8	113.9	113.9	115.4	116.
91	Leather and products	31	.3	98.1	96.7	97.1	99.0	99.1	100.1	98.2	97.0	96.8	97.0	98.2	99.1	99.3	99.
92	Mining	...	8.0	97.0	98.2	98.3	95.9	95.3	96.4	97.3	98.0	96.4	95.5	97.7	98.2	97.4	97.
93	Metal	10	.3	165.5	158.1	167.7	163.0	158.2	162.5	169.3	164.4	167.7	148.2	161.5	178.5	172.0	172.
94	Coal	11,12	1.2	103.6	107.9	108.2	101.7	102.3	108.2	106.4	106.7	101.0	95.9	103.9	104.7	100.7	104.
95	Oil and gas extraction	13	5.8	92.0	93.4	92.7	90.9	90.4	90.5	91.6	93.1	91.6	92.4	93.0	92.7	92.6	92.
96	Stone and earth minerals	14	.7	93.9	92.6	93.8	95.2	93.4	92.3	94.0	91.7	93.2	94.7	95.0	94.3	95.9	94.
97	Utilities	...	7.7	116.0	116.8	112.8	117.5	117.8	114.4	112.1	114.9	116.9	117.7	115.3	114.6	115.4	116.
98	Electric	491,3PT	6.1	115.7	116.4	112.9	116.5	116.3	114.5	114.0	115.6	118.1	118.9	115.1	113.6	114.8	116.
99	Gas	492,3PT	1.6	116.9	118.2	112.4	121.4	123.3	113.9	104.9	112.2	112.4	113.3	116.0	118.2	117.8	118
	SPECIAL AGGREGATES																
100	Manufacturing excluding motor vehicles and parts	...	79.5	111.4	108.8	109.3	109.8	110.2	110.8	110.9	111.1	111.7	112.0	112.1	112.6	113.4	113
101	Manufacturing excluding office and computing machines	...	81.9	108.7	107.0	107.6	108.0	108.1	108.6	108.3	108.1	108.3	108.5	108.7	109.5	110.7	111
					Gross value (billions of 1987 dollars, annual rates)												
	MAJOR MARKETS																
102	**Products, total**	...	**1,707.0**	**1,890.0**	**1,857.5**	**1,864.9**	**1,880.2**	**1,880.3**	**1,882.8**	**1,872.6**	**1,873.2**	**1,877.4**	**1,879.3**	**1,887.2**	**1,914.3**	**1,938.2**	**1,947**
103	Final	...	1,314.6	1,492.5	1,466.8	1,476.4	1,485.7	1,484.3	1,485.6	1,477.9	1,477.5	1,479.0	1,480.5	1,489.1	1,513.4	1,534.3	1,54
104	Consumer goods	...	866.6	944.8	936.3	940.0	949.4	946.1	943.6	936.1	935.5	935.5	935.6	936.7	953.8	965.7	96
105	Equipment	...	448.0	547.6	530.5	536.5	536.3	538.2	541.9	541.8	541.9	543.4	544.9	552.4	559.6	568.7	57
106	Intermediate	...	392.5	397.6	390.7	388.4	394.5	396.0	397.3	394.7	395.7	398.4	398.8	398.1	401.0	403.9	40

1. Data in this table also appear in the Board's G.17 (419) monthly statistical release. For ordering address, see inside front cover.

A revision of the industrial production index and the capacity utilization rates was released in May 1993. See "Industrial Production, Capacity, and Capac Utilization since 1987," *Federal Reserve Bulletin*, vol. 79 (June 1993), pp. 590–6

2. Standard industrial classification.

Source: *Federal Reserve Bulletin,* Board of Governors of the Federal Reserve System.

PERSONAL INCOME AND SAVING

Billions of current dollars except as noted; quarterly data at seasonally adjusted annual rates

Account	1991	1992	1993	1993				1994
				Q1	Q2	Q3	Q4	Q1
PERSONAL INCOME AND SAVING								
1 **Total personal income**	**4,850.9**	**5,144.9**	**5,388.3**	**5,254.7**	**5,373.2**	**5,412.7**	**5,512.7**	**5,576.8**
2 Wage and salary disbursements	2,815.0	2,973.1	3,080.5	2,974.3	3,082.7	3,115.4	3,149.6	3,201.9
3 Commodity-producing industries	738.1	756.5	763.6	740.7	765.1	769.4	779.3	789.6
4 Manufacturing	557.2	577.6	577.3	559.7	580.3	581.5	587.8	595.6
5 Distributive industries	648.0	682.0	706.6	682.9	709.1	714.4	720.1	733.4
6 Service industries	883.5	967.0	1,020.6	966.6	1,022.2	1,038.8	1,054.7	1,075.9
7 Government and government enterprises	545.4	567.5	589.7	584.1	586.3	592.8	595.4	603.0
8 Other labor income	296.9	322.7	350.7	338.5	346.6	354.7	362.9	371.9
9 Proprietors' income[1]	376.4	414.3	443.2	444.1	439.4	422.5	467.0	474.6
10 Business and professional[1]	339.5	370.6	397.3	388.4	392.4	397.6	410.6	416.6
11 Farm[1]	36.8	43.7	46.0	55.7	47.0	24.8	56.4	57.9
12 Rental income of persons[2]	−12.8	−8.9	12.6	7.5	12.7	13.7	16.4	2.5
13 Dividends	127.9	140.4	158.3	157.0	157.8	159.0	159.4	160.7
14 Personal interest income	715.6	694.3	695.2	695.4	693.1	695.7	696.7	700.2
15 Transfer payments	769.9	858.4	912.1	894.4	905.5	918.5	929.8	944.3
16 Old-age survivors, disability, and health insurance benefits	382.3	413.9	438.4	433.1	435.0	439.4	446.1	457.8
17 LESS: Personal contributions for social insurance	237.8	249.3	264.3	256.6	264.5	266.8	269.2	279.3
18 EQUALS: Personal income	4,850.9	5,144.9	5,388.3	5,254.7	5,373.2	5,412.7	5,512.7	5,576.8
19 LESS: Personal tax and nontax payments	620.4	644.8	681.6	657.1	681.0	689.0	699.2	715.8
20 EQUALS: Disposable personal income	4,230.5	4,500.2	4,706.7	4,597.5	4,692.2	4,723.7	4,813.5	4,860.9
21 LESS: Personal outlays	4,029.0	4,261.5	4,516.8	4,419.7	4,483.6	4,544.0	4,620.1	4,689.2
22 EQUALS: Personal saving	201.5	238.7	189.9	177.9	208.7	179.7	193.4	171.8
MEMO								
Per capita (1987 dollars)								
23 Gross domestic product	19,237.9	19,518.0	19,887.4	19,744.4	19,785.4	19,868.8	20,150.1	20,250.4
24 Personal consumption expenditures	12,895.2	13,080.9	13,371.3	13,234.2	13,311.6	13,416.2	13,522.7	13,642.2
25 Disposable personal income	13,965.0	14,219.0	14,330.0	14,163.0	14,326.0	14,341.0	14,491.0	14,549.0
26 Saving rate (percent)	4.8	5.3	4.0	3.9	4.4	3.8	4.0	3.5
GROSS SAVING								
27 **Gross saving**	**733.7**	**717.8**	**780.2**[r]	**762.0**	**766.7**	**774.3**	**817.8**[r]	**858.4**
28 Gross private saving	929.9	986.9	1,004.8[r]	1,024.8	988.3	988.7	1,017.5[r]	1,024.9
29 Personal saving	201.5	238.7	189.9	177.9	208.7	179.7	193.4	171.8
30 Undistributed corporate profits[1]	102.3	110.4	123.6[r]	103.7	116.3	129.3	145.1[r]	117.3
31 Corporate inventory valuation adjustment	4.9	−5.3	−7.1	−12.7	−12.2	1.0	−4.3	−16.0
Capital consumption allowances								
32 Corporate	383.2	396.6	408.8	402.2	405.2	414.0	413.9	433.3
33 Noncorporate	242.8	261.3	262.5	261.0	258.1	265.7	265.1	302.5
34 Government surplus, or deficit (−), national income and product accounts	−196.2	−269.1	−224.6[r]	−262.8	−221.5	−214.4	−199.7[r]	−166.5
35 Federal	−203.4	−276.3	−226.4[r]	−263.5	−222.6	−212.7	−207.0[r]	−164.7
36 State and local	7.3	7.2	1.8[r]	.8	1.1	−1.7	7.2[r]	−1.8
37 **Gross investment**	**743.3**	**741.4**	**795.4**	**796.5**	**778.7**	**787.6**	**819.0**	**853.7**
38 Gross private domestic	736.9	796.5	891.7	874.1	874.1	884.0	934.5	966.7
39 Net foreign	6.4	−55.1	−96.2	−77.6	−95.4	−96.4	−115.5	−113.0
40 **Statistical discrepancy**	**9.6**	**23.6**	**15.2**[r]	**34.4**	**12.0**	**13.3**	**1.2**[r]	**−4.7**

1. With inventory valuation and capital consumption adjustments.
2. With capital consumption adjustment.

SOURCE. U.S. Department of Commerce, *Survey of Current Business*.

Source: *Federal Reserve Bulletin*, Board of Governors of the Federal Reserve System.

EXPENDITURES FOR NEW PLANT AND EQUIPMENT

According to the Commerce Department April-May 1994 survey, business spending for new plant and equipment is expected to rise 8.3 percent in 1994, following a rise of 7.1 percent in 1993.

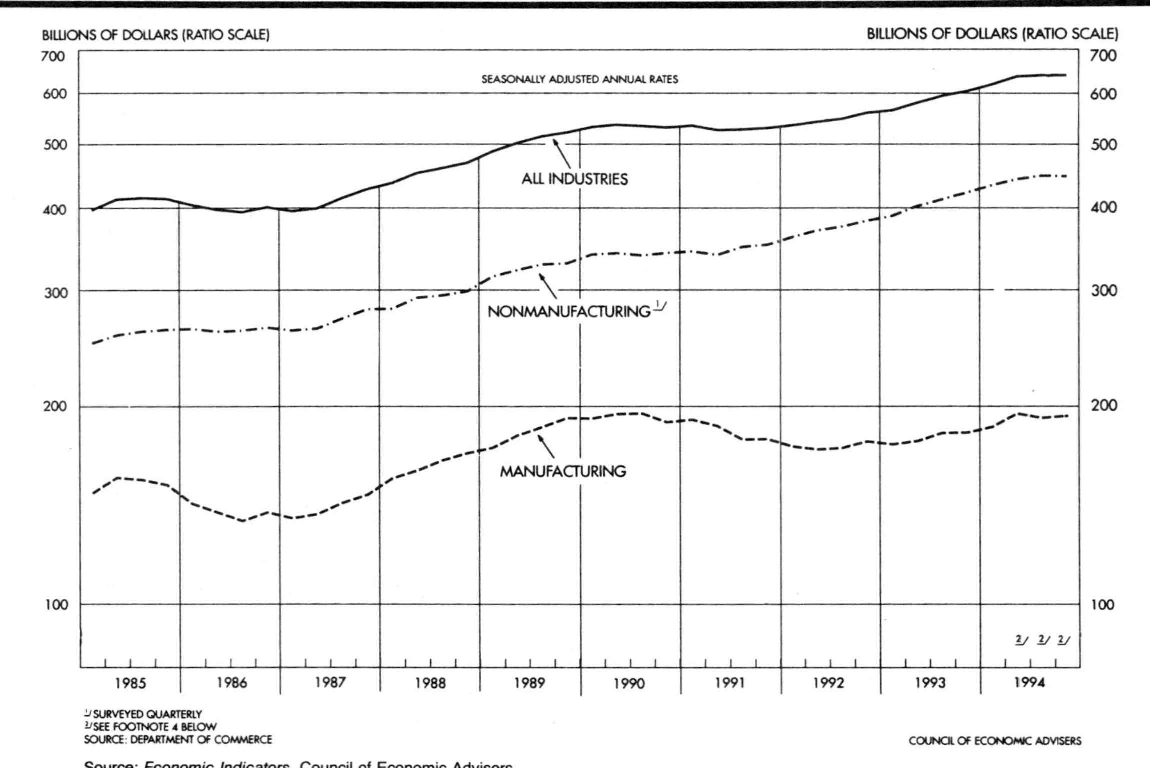

Source: *Economic Indicators*, Council of Economic Advisers.

Government Budget, Receipts, and Deficits: Historical Data[1]

Overview of the Budget Process

Executive Budget Formulation Process

During budget formulation, the President establishes general budget and fiscal policy guidelines. Under a multi-year planning system, policy guidance and planning ceilings are given to agencies for both the upcoming budget year and for the four following years and provide the initial guidelines for preparation of agency budget requests.

The budget formulation process begins not later than the spring of each year, at least nine months before the budget is transmitted. Executive branch agencies prepare their budget requests based on the guidelines provided by the President through the Office of Management and Budget (OMB) and the detailed instructions on preparation of budget estimates provided in this Circular. Executive branch departments and agencies are required to submit initial budget materials to OMB beginning in September, in accordance with the schedule in section 10.3. Other materials are submitted throughout the fall and winter on a schedule supplied by OMB. Budget data are required for the past, current, and upcoming budget year, as well as for the four years following the budget year.

Following submission of initial materials, hearings or less formal discussions with agencies are scheduled by OMB representatives. These hearings and discussions provide OMB an opportunity to obtain a better understanding of agency policies and programs, efforts to improve agency management (including highrisk areas) and program delivery, and to discuss specific problems. They also enable agencies to justify budget requests orally and provide additional information in response to specific questions.

After review of budget submissions, OMB staff prepare issue papers and recommendations on major issues for discussion with the Director.

After the review process is completed, decisions on budget requests are passed back to the agencies. If an agency disagrees with some aspect of the passback and considers it sufficiently important to pursue, it may submit an appeal to OMB. If OMB and the agency cannot reach agreement, appeals may be made to the President. Upon receipt of final decisions for the current and budget year, agencies revise their budget requests promptly to bring them into accord with these decisions. These final estimates are transmitted to Congress in the President's budget. In accordance with current law, the budget must be transmitted to Congress not later than the first Monday in February.

During the budget formulation process, management issues are reviewed, and proposals for improvements in agency management and program delivery are reflected in final budget decisions.

After transmittal of the budget, allowance letters are sent to agency heads formally advising them of decisions on budget and multi-year planning estimates; employment ceilings; goals for management improvements; and significant policy, program, and administrative matters. The multi-year planning estimates then become the starting point in planning for the budget to be transmitted to Congress the following year.

Executive and Congressional Budget Processes

The executive budget formulation process described above is prescribed by OMB, in accordance with the Budget and Accounting Act of 1921, as amended. The following timetable highlights significant dates culminating in transmittal of the President's budget and subsequent updates of the budget. It also reflects the congressional budget procedures established by the Congressional Budget Act of 1974 (2 U.S.C. 621), as amended, and by the Budget Enforcement Act of 1990 (BEA), Public Law 101–508, which amended the Gramm-Rudman-Hollings (G-R-H) law (Public Law 99–177, as amended by Public Law 100–119).

Source: Office of Management and Budget, Circular No. A-11.

[1] See page 192 for notes to Exhibits on pages 172–191.

THE BUDGET PROCESS

ACTION TO BE COMPLETED

The Executive Budget Process	Timing	The Congressional Budget Process
Agencies subject to executive branch review submit initial budget request materials.	September 1	
Fiscal year begins.	October 1	Fiscal year begins.
Agencies not subject to executive branch review submit budget request materials.	October 15	
	10 days after end of session	CBO issues its final sequester report.
OMB issues its final sequestration report;[1] President issues sequestration order, if necessary.	15 days after end of session	
	30 days later	Comptroller General issues compliance report.
Legislative branch and the judiciary submit budget request materials.	November–December	
	5 days before President's budget transmittal	CBO issues its sequestration preview report
President transmits the budget to Congress, including OMB sequestration preview report.	Not later than the first Monday in February	
OMB sends allowance letters to agencies.	February–March	
	February 15	Congressional Budget Office reports to the Budget Committees on the President's budget.
	Within 6 weeks of President's budget transmittal	Committees submit views and estimates to Budget Committees.

	April 1	Senate Budget Committee reports concurrent resolution on the budget.
	April 15	Congress completes action on concurrent resolution.
	May 15	House may consider appropriations bills in the absence of a concurrent resolution on the budget.
	June 10	House Appropriations Committee reports last appropriations bill.
	June 15	Congress completes action on reconciliation legislation.
	June 30	House completes action on annual appropriations bills.
	After completion of action on discretionary, direct spending, or receipts legislation.	CBO provides estimate of the impact of legislation as soon as practicable.
President transmits the Mid-Session Review, updating the budget estimates.	July 15	
OMB provides agencies with policy guidance for the upcoming budget.	July–August	
	August 15	CBO issues its sequestration update report.
OMB issues its sequestration update report	August 20	

[1] A "within session" sequestration is triggered within 15 days after enactment of appropriations that are enacted after the end of a session for the budget year and before July 1, if they breach the category spending limit for that fiscal year. A "lookback" reduction to a category limit is applied for appropriations enacted after June 30th for the fiscal year in progress that breach a category limit for that fiscal year and is applied to the next fiscal year.

Note.—OMB also reports to Congress on the impact of enacted legislation and provides an explanation of any differences between OMB and CBO estimates, within 5 calendar days of enactment of legislation.

Glossary of Budget Terms[1]

BALANCES OF BUDGET AUTHORITY—These are amounts of budget authority provided in previous years that have not been outlayed. Obligated balances are amounts that have been obligated but not yet outlayed. Unobligated balances are amounts that have not been obligated and that remain available for obligation under law.

BREACH—A breach is the amount by which new budget authority or outlays within a category of discretionary appropriations for a fiscal year is above the cap on new budget authority or outlays for that category for that year.

BUDGET—The *Budget of the United States Government* (this document) sets forth the President's comprehensive financial plan and indicates the President's priorities for the Federal Government.

BUDGET AUTHORITY (BA)—Budget authority is the authority provided by Federal law to incur financial obligations that will result in outlays. Specific forms of budget authority include:

- provisions of law that make funds available for obligation and expenditure (other than borrowing authority), including the authority to obligate and expend offsetting receipts and collections;
- borrowing authority, which is authority granted to a Federal entity to borrow (e.g., through the issuance of promissory notes or monetary credits) and to obligate and expend the borrowed funds;
- contract authority, which is the making of funds available for obligation but not for expenditure; and
- offsetting receipts and collections as negative budget authority.

BUDGETARY RESOURCES—Budgetary resources comprise new budget authority, unobligated balances of budget authority, direct spending authority, and obligation limitations.

BUDGET TOTALS—The budget includes totals for budget authority, outlays, and receipts. Some presentations in the budget distinguish on-budget totals from off-budget totals. On-budget totals reflect the transactions of all Federal Government entities except those excluded from the budget totals by law. Off-budget totals reflect the transactions of Government entities that are excluded from the on-budget totals by law. Currently excluded are the social security trust funds (Federal Old-Age and Survivors Insurance and Federal Disability Insurance Trust Funds) and the Postal Service. The on- and off-budget totals are combined to derive a total for Federal activity.

CAP—This is the term commonly used to refer to legal limits on the budget authority and outlays for each fiscal year for each of the discretionary appropriations categories. A sequester is required if an appropriation for a category causes a breach in the cap.

CATEGORIES OF DISCRETIONARY APPROPRIATIONS—Through 1993, discretionary appropriations are categorized as defense, international, or domestic. Separate spending limits (caps) are applied to each category. The appropriations in each of the categories are determined by lists of existing appropriations in a 1990 congressional report[2] or, in the case of new appropriations, in consultation among the Office of Management and Budget and the congressional Committees on Appropriations and the Budget. For 1994 and 1995, all discretionary appropriations constitute a single category.

COST—The term cost, when used in connection with Federal credit programs, means the estimated long-term cost to the Government of a direct loan or loan guarantee, calculated on a net present value basis. The term excludes administrative costs and any incidental effects on governmental receipts or outlays. Present value is a standard financial concept that allows for the time value of money, that is, for the fact that a given sum of money is worth more at present than in the future because interest can be earned on it. The cost of direct loans and loan guarantees is a net present value because collections are offset against disbursements.

CREDIT PROGRAM ACCOUNT—A credit program account receives an appropriation for the cost of a direct loan or loan guarantee program, from which such cost is disbursed to a financing account for the program.

DEFICIT—A deficit is the amount by which outlays exceed Governmental receipts.

DIRECT LOAN—A direct loan is a disbursement of funds by the Government to a non-Federal borrower under a contract that requires the repayment of such funds with or without interest. The term includes the purchase of, or participation in, a loan made by another lender. The term does not include the acquisition

[1] These basic terms and other budget terms, concepts, and procedures are described more fully in *The Budget System and Concepts of the United States Government,* a pamphlet available from the Government Printing Office. References to requirements in law generally refer to the Balanced Budget and Emergency Deficit Control Act of 1985 (also known as the Gramm-Rudman-Hollings Act), as amended. The Act was most recently amended by the Budget Enforcement Act of 1990 (Title XIII of Public Law 101–508). These requirements are discussed in various parts of the *Budget.*

[2] The joint statement of the managers accompanying the conference report on the Omnibus Budget Reconciliation Act of 1990 (Public Law 101–508).

of a federally guaranteed loan in satisfaction of default claims or the price support loans of the Commodity Credit Corporation. (*Cf.* LOAN GUARANTEE.)

DIRECT SPENDING—Direct spending, which sometimes is called mandatory spending, is a category of outlays from budget authority provided in law other than appropriations acts, entitlement authority, and the budget authority for the food stamp program. (*Cf.* DISCRETIONARY APPROPRIATIONS.)

DISCRETIONARY APPROPRIATIONS—Discretionary appropriations is a category of budget authority that comprises budgetary resources (except those provided to fund direct-spending programs) provided in appropriations acts. (*Cf.* DIRECT SPENDING.)

EMERGENCY APPROPRIATION—An emergency appropriation is an appropriation in a discretionary category that the President and the Congress have designated as an emergency requirement. Such appropriations result in an adjustment to the cap for the category.

FEDERAL FUNDS—Federal funds are the moneys collected and spent by the Government other than those designated as trust funds. Federal funds include general, special, public enterprise, and intragovernmental funds. (*Cf.* TRUST FUNDS.)

FINANCING ACCOUNT—A financing account receives the cost payments from a credit program account and includes other cash flows to and from the Government resulting from direct loan obligations or loan guarantee commitments made on or after October 1, 1991. At least one financing account is associated with each credit program account. For programs with direct and guaranteed loans, there are separate financing accounts for direct loans and guaranteed loans. The transactions of the financing accounts are not included in the budget totals. (*Cf.* LIQUIDATING ACCOUNT)

FISCAL YEAR—The fiscal year is the Government's accounting period. It begins on October 1st and ends on September 30th, and is designated by the calendar year in which it ends.

GENERAL FUND—The general fund consists of accounts for receipts not earmarked by law for a specific purpose, the proceeds of general borrowing, and the expenditure of these moneys.

LIQUIDATING ACCOUNT—A liquidating account includes all cash flows to and from the Government resulting from direct loan obligations and loan guarantee commitments prior to October 1, 1991. (*Cf.* FINANCING ACCOUNT.)

LOAN GUARANTEE—A loan guarantee is any guarantee, insurance, or other pledge with respect to the payment of all or a part of the principal or interest on any debt obligation of a non-Federal borrower to a non-Federal lender. The term does not include the insurance of deposits, shares, or other withdrawable accounts in financial institutions. (*Cf.* DIRECT LOAN.)

MANDATORY SPENDING—See DIRECT SPENDING.

MAXIMUM DEFICIT AMOUNTS—These are amounts specified in and subject to certain adjustments under law. If the deficit for the year in question is estimated to exceed the adjusted maximum deficit amount for that year by more than a specified margin, a sequester of the excess deficit is required.

INTRAGOVERNMENTAL FUNDS—Intragovernmental funds are accounts for business-type or market-oriented activities conducted primarily within and between Government agencies and financed by offsetting collections that are credited directly to the fund.

OBLIGATIONS—Obligations are binding agreements that will result in outlays, immediately or in the future. Budgetary resources must be available before obligations can be incurred legally.

OFF-BUDGET—See BUDGET TOTALS.

OFFSETTING COLLECTIONS—Offsetting collections are collections from the public that result from business-type or market-oriented activities and collections from other Government accounts. These collections are deducted from gross disbursements in calculating outlays, rather than counted in Governmental receipt totals. Some are credited directly to appropriation or fund accounts; others, called offsetting receipts, are credited to receipt accounts. The authority to spend offsetting collections is a form of budget authority. (*Cf.* RECEIPTS, GOVERNMENTAL.)

ON-BUDGET—See BUDGET TOTALS.

OUTLAYS—Outlays are the measure of Government spending. They are payments to liquidate obligations (other than the repayment of debt), net of refunds and offsetting collections. Outlays generally are recorded on a cash basis, but also include many cash-equivalent transactions, the subsidy cost of direct loans and loan guarantees, and interest accrued on public issues of the public debt.

PAY-AS-YOU-GO—This term refers to requirements in law that result in a sequester if the estimated combined result of legislation affecting direct spending or receipts is an increase in the deficit for a fiscal year.

PUBLIC ENTERPRISE FUNDS—Public enterprise funds are accounts for business or market-oriented activities conducted primarily with the public and financed by offsetting collections that are credited directly to the fund.

RECEIPTS, GOVERNMENTAL—Governmental receipts are collections that result primarily from the Government's exercise of its sovereign power to tax or otherwise compel payment. They are compared to outlays in calculating a surplus or deficit. (*Cf.* OFFSETTING COLLECTIONS.)

SEQUESTER—A sequester is the cancellation of budgetary resources provided by discretionary appropriations or direct spending legislation, following various procedures prescribed in law. A sequester may occur in response to a discretionary appropriation that causes a breach, in response to increases in the deficit resulting from the combined result of legislation affecting direct spending or receipts (referred to as a "pay-as-you-go" sequester), or in response to a deficit estimated to be in excess of the maximum deficit amounts.

SPECIAL FUNDS—Special funds are Federal fund accounts for receipts earmarked for specific purposes and the associated expenditure of those receipts. (*Cf.* TRUST FUNDS.)

SUBSIDY—This term means the same as cost when it is used in connection with Federal credit programs.

SURPLUS—A surplus is the amount by which receipts exceed outlays.

SUPPLEMENTAL APPROPRIATION—A supplemental appropriation is one enacted subsequent to a regular annual appropriations act when the need for funds is too urgent to be postponed until the next regular annual appropriations act.

TRUST FUNDS—Trust funds are accounts, designated by law as trust funds, for receipts earmarked for specific purposes and the associated expenditure of those receipts. (*Cf.* SPECIAL FUNDS.)

Source: *Budget of the United States Government, Fiscal 1994,* Executive Office of the President, Office of Management and Budget.

THE FEDERAL GOVERNMENT DOLLAR
FISCAL YEAR 1995 ESTIMATES

WHERE IT COMES FROM...

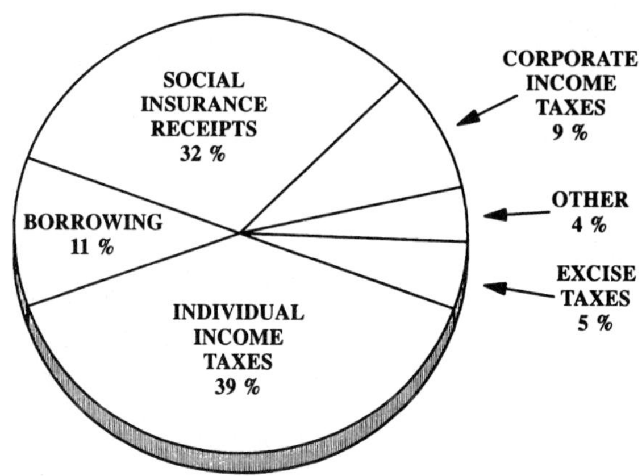

WHERE IT GOES...

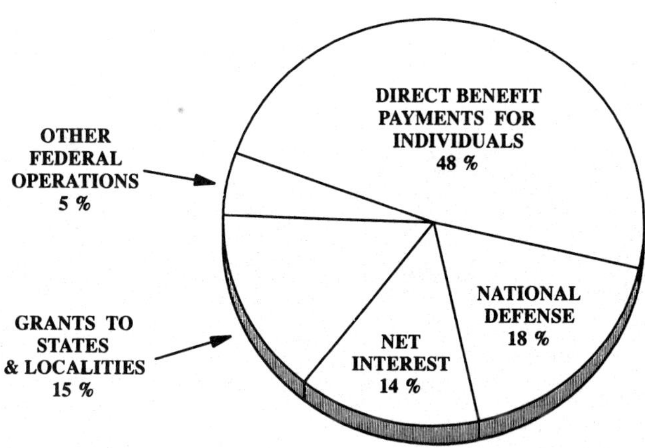

Source: *Budget of the United States Government,* Fiscal year 1995. Executive Office of the President, Office of Management and Budget.

RECEIPTS BY SOURCE AS PERCENTAGES OF GDP: 1934–1999

Fiscal Year	Individual Income Taxes	Corporation Income Taxes	Social Insurance Taxes and Contributions			Excise Taxes	Other	Total Receipts		
			Total	(On-Budget)	(Off-Budget)			Total	(On-Budget)	(Off-Budget)
1934	0.7	0.6	*	(*)	......	2.2	1.3	4.9	(4.9)	......
1935	0.8	0.8	*	(*)	......	2.1	1.6	5.3	(5.3)	......
1936	0.9	0.9	0.1	(0.1)	......	2.1	1.1	5.1	(5.1)	......
1937	1.3	1.2	0.7	(0.4)	(0.3)	2.2	0.9	6.2	(5.9)	(0.3)
1938	1.5	1.5	1.8	(1.3)	(0.4)	2.1	0.9	7.7	(7.2)	(0.4)
1939	1.2	1.3	1.8	(1.2)	(0.6)	2.1	0.8	7.2	(6.6)	(0.6)
1940	0.9	1.3	1.9	(1.3)	(0.6)	2.1	0.7	6.9	(6.3)	(0.6)
1941	1.2	1.9	1.7	(1.1)	(0.6)	2.3	0.7	7.7	(7.1)	(0.6)
1942	2.3	3.3	1.7	(1.1)	(0.6)	2.4	0.6	10.3	(9.7)	(0.6)
1943	3.7	5.4	1.7	(1.1)	(0.6)	2.3	0.5	13.7	(13.0)	(0.6)
1944	9.8	7.4	1.7	(1.1)	(0.6)	2.4	0.5	21.7	(21.0)	(0.6)
1945	8.7	7.5	1.6	(1.0)	(0.6)	3.0	0.5	21.3	(20.7)	(0.6)
1946	7.6	5.6	1.5	(0.9)	(0.6)	3.3	0.6	18.5	(17.9)	(0.6)
1947	8.0	3.9	1.5	(0.9)	(0.7)	3.2	0.6	17.3	(16.6)	(0.7)
1948	7.8	3.9	1.5	(0.9)	(0.7)	3.0	0.6	16.8	(16.2)	(0.7)
1949	5.9	4.3	1.4	(0.8)	(0.6)	2.9	0.5	15.0	(14.4)	(0.6)
1950	5.9	3.9	1.6	(0.8)	(0.8)	2.8	0.5	14.8	(14.0)	(0.8)
1951	6.9	4.5	1.8	(0.8)	(1.0)	2.8	0.5	16.5	(15.5)	(1.0)
1952	8.2	6.2	1.9	(0.8)	(1.1)	2.6	0.5	19.4	(18.4)	(1.1)
1953	8.2	5.8	1.9	(0.7)	(1.1)	2.7	0.5	19.1	(18.0)	(1.1)
1954	8.0	5.7	2.0	(0.7)	(1.2)	2.7	0.5	18.9	(17.7)	(1.2)
1955	7.5	4.6	2.0	(0.7)	(1.3)	2.4	0.5	17.0	(15.7)	(1.3)
1956	7.7	5.0	2.2	(0.7)	(1.5)	2.4	0.5	17.9	(16.4)	(1.5)
1957	8.1	4.8	2.3	(0.7)	(1.5)	2.4	0.6	18.3	(16.7)	(1.5)
1958	7.7	4.5	2.5	(0.7)	(1.8)	2.4	0.7	17.8	(16.0)	(1.8)
1959	7.6	3.6	2.4	(0.7)	(1.7)	2.2	0.6	16.5	(14.8)	(1.7)
1960	8.1	4.3	2.9	(0.8)	(2.1)	2.3	0.8	18.3	(16.2)	(2.1)
1961	8.0	4.1	3.2	(0.8)	(2.3)	2.3	0.7	18.3	(15.9)	(2.3)
1962	8.2	3.7	3.1	(0.9)	(2.2)	2.3	0.7	18.0	(15.7)	(2.2)
1963	8.1	3.7	3.4	(1.0)	(2.4)	2.3	0.8	18.2	(15.8)	(2.4)
1964	7.8	3.8	3.5	(0.9)	(2.6)	2.2	0.8	18.0	(15.4)	(2.6)

1965	7.3	3.8	3.3	(0.8)	(2.5)	2.2	0.9	17.4	(14.9)	(2.5)
1966	7.5	4.1	3.5	(0.9)	(2.6)	1.8	0.9	17.8	(15.2)	(2.6)
1967	7.8	4.3	4.1	(1.0)	(3.1)	1.7	0.9	18.8	(15.7)	(3.1)
1968	8.1	3.4	4.0	(1.1)	(2.9)	1.7	0.9	18.1	(15.1)	(2.9)
1969	9.4	4.0	4.2	(1.1)	(3.1)	1.6	0.9	20.2	(17.1)	(3.1)
1970	9.2	3.3	4.5	(1.1)	(3.4)	1.6	1.0	19.6	(16.2)	(3.4)
1971	8.2	2.5	4.5	(1.1)	(3.4)	1.6	1.0	17.8	(14.4)	(3.4)
1972	8.3	2.8	4.6	(1.1)	(3.5)	1.3	1.1	18.1	(14.6)	(3.5)
1973	8.1	2.8	5.0	(1.3)	(3.6)	1.3	0.9	18.1	(14.5)	(3.6)
1974	8.5	2.8	5.3	(1.5)	(3.8)	1.2	1.0	18.8	(14.9)	(3.8)
1975	8.1	2.7	5.6	(1.5)	(4.1)	1.1	1.0	18.5	(14.3)	(4.1)
1976	7.8	2.5	5.4	(1.4)	(3.9)	1.0	1.0	17.7	(13.8)	(3.9)
TQ	8.7	1.9	5.7	(1.6)	(4.0)	1.0	1.0	18.3	(14.2)	(4.0)
1977	8.2	2.9	5.6	(1.5)	(4.0)	0.9	1.0	18.5	(14.5)	(4.0)
1978	8.4	2.8	5.6	(1.7)	(4.0)	0.9	0.9	18.5	(14.6)	(4.0)
1979	9.0	2.7	5.7	(1.7)	(4.0)	0.8	0.9	19.1	(15.0)	(4.0)
1980	9.2	2.4	6.0	(1.7)	(4.3)	0.9	1.0	19.6	(15.3)	(4.3)
1981	9.6	2.1	6.2	(1.8)	(4.4)	1.4	1.0	20.2	(15.8)	(4.4)
1982	9.5	1.6	6.5	(1.9)	(4.6)	1.2	1.1	19.8	(15.2)	(4.6)
1983	8.7	1.1	6.3	(1.9)	(4.4)	1.1	0.9	18.1	(13.7)	(4.4)
1984	8.1	1.5	6.5	(2.0)	(4.5)	1.0	0.9	18.0	(13.5)	(4.5)
1985	8.4	1.5	6.7	(2.0)	(4.7)	0.9	0.9	18.5	(13.8)	(4.7)
1986	8.3	1.5	6.7	(2.0)	(4.7)	0.8	1.0	18.2	(13.5)	(4.7)
1987	8.8	1.9	6.8	(2.0)	(4.8)	0.7	0.9	19.2	(14.4)	(4.8)
1988	8.3	2.0	7.0	(1.9)	(5.0)	0.7	0.9	18.9	(13.9)	(5.0)
1989	8.6	2.0	6.9	(1.9)	(5.1)	0.7	0.9	19.2	(14.1)	(5.1)
1990	8.5	1.7	6.9	(1.8)	(5.1)	0.6	1.0	18.8	(13.7)	(5.1)
1991	8.2	1.7	7.0	(1.8)	(5.2)	0.7	0.9	18.6	(13.4)	(5.2)
1992	8.0	1.7	7.0	(1.9)	(5.1)	0.8	0.9	18.4	(13.3)	(5.1)
1993	8.1	1.9	6.8	(1.8)	(5.0)	0.8	0.8	18.3	(13.4)	(5.0)
1994 estimate	8.3	2.0	7.0	(1.9)	(5.1)	0.8	0.8	18.8	(13.7)	(5.1)
1995 estimate	8.5	2.0	7.0	(1.9)	(5.1)	1.0	0.8	19.3	(14.2)	(5.1)
1996 estimate	8.5	2.0	7.0	(1.9)	(5.1)	1.0	0.9	19.2	(14.2)	(5.1)
1997 estimate	8.5	1.9	7.0	(1.9)	(5.1)	0.9	0.9	19.2	(14.1)	(5.1)
1998 estimate	8.5	1.8	7.0	(1.9)	(5.1)	0.9	1.0	19.2	(14.1)	(5.1)
1999 estimate	8.5	1.8	7.0	(1.9)	(5.1)	0.9	1.0	19.1	(14.0)	(5.1)

* 0.05 percent or less.

Source: *Budget of the United States Government, Historical Tables, Fiscal Year 1995,* Executive Office of the President, Office of Management and Budget.

PERCENTAGE COMPOSITION OF RECEIPTS BY SOURCE: 1934–1999

Fiscal Year	Individual Income Taxes	Corporation Income Taxes	Social Insurance Taxes and Contributions			Excise Taxes	Other	Total Receipts		
			Total	(On-Budget)	(Off-Budget)			Total	(On-Budget)	(Off-Budget)
1934	14.2	12.3	1.0	(1.0)	......	45.8	26.7	100.0	(100.0)	......
1935	14.6	14.7	0.9	(0.9)	......	39.9	30.0	100.0	(100.0)	......
1936	17.2	18.3	1.3	(1.3)	......	41.6	21.6	100.0	(100.0)	......
1937	20.3	19.3	10.8	(5.9)	(4.9)	34.8	14.9	100.0	(95.1)	(4.9)
1938	19.1	19.1	22.8	(17.1)	(5.7)	27.6	11.5	100.0	(94.3)	(5.7)
1939	16.3	17.9	25.3	(17.3)	(8.0)	29.7	10.7	100.0	(92.0)	(8.0)
1940	13.6	18.3	27.3	(18.9)	(8.4)	30.2	10.7	100.0	(91.6)	(8.4)
1941	15.1	24.4	22.3	(14.4)	(7.9)	29.3	9.0	100.0	(92.1)	(7.9)
1942	22.3	32.2	16.8	(10.6)	(6.1)	23.2	5.5	100.0	(93.9)	(6.1)
1943	27.1	39.8	12.7	(8.0)	(4.7)	17.1	3.3	100.0	(95.3)	(4.7)
1944	45.0	33.9	7.9	(5.0)	(3.0)	10.9	2.2	100.0	(97.0)	(3.0)
1945	40.7	35.4	7.6	(4.7)	(2.9)	13.9	2.4	100.0	(97.1)	(2.9)
1946	41.0	30.2	7.9	(4.8)	(3.2)	17.8	3.1	100.0	(96.8)	(3.2)
1947	46.6	22.4	8.9	(5.1)	(3.8)	18.7	3.5	100.0	(96.2)	(3.8)
1948	46.5	23.3	9.0	(5.1)	(3.9)	17.7	3.5	100.0	(96.1)	(3.9)
1949	39.5	28.4	9.6	(5.3)	(4.3)	19.0	3.5	100.0	(95.7)	(4.3)
1950	39.9	26.5	11.0	(5.7)	(5.3)	19.1	3.4	100.0	(94.7)	(5.3)
1951	41.9	27.3	11.0	(4.9)	(6.0)	16.8	3.1	100.0	(94.0)	(6.0)
1952	42.2	32.1	9.7	(4.3)	(5.4)	13.4	2.6	100.0	(94.6)	(5.4)
1953	42.8	30.5	9.8	(3.9)	(5.9)	14.2	2.7	100.0	(94.1)	(5.9)
1954	42.4	30.3	10.3	(3.8)	(6.6)	14.3	2.7	100.0	(93.4)	(6.6)
1955	43.9	27.3	12.0	(4.2)	(7.8)	14.0	2.8	100.0	(92.2)	(7.8)
1956	43.2	28.0	12.5	(3.9)	(8.6)	13.3	3.0	100.0	(91.4)	(8.6)
1957	44.5	26.5	12.5	(4.0)	(8.5)	13.2	3.3	100.0	(91.5)	(8.5)
1958	43.6	25.2	14.1	(4.0)	(10.1)	13.4	3.7	100.0	(89.9)	(10.1)
1959	46.3	21.8	14.8	(4.3)	(10.5)	13.3	3.7	100.0	(89.5)	(10.5)
1960	44.0	23.2	15.9	(4.4)	(11.5)	12.6	4.2	100.0	(88.5)	(11.5)
1961	43.8	22.2	17.4	(4.6)	(12.8)	12.6	4.0	100.0	(87.2)	(12.8)
1962	45.7	20.6	17.1	(4.8)	(12.3)	12.6	4.0	100.0	(87.7)	(12.3)
1963	44.7	20.3	18.6	(5.3)	(13.3)	12.4	4.1	100.0	(86.7)	(13.3)
1964	43.2	20.9	19.5	(5.0)	(14.5)	12.2	4.2	100.0	(85.5)	(14.5)

1965	41.8	21.8	19.0	(4.7)	(14.3)	12.5	4.9	100.0	(85.7)	(14.3)
1966	42.4	23.0	19.5	(4.9)	(14.6)	10.0	5.1	100.0	(85.4)	(14.6)
1967	41.3	22.8	21.9	(5.5)	(16.4)	9.2	4.7	100.0	(83.6)	(16.4)
1968	44.9	18.7	22.2	(5.9)	(16.3)	9.2	5.0	100.0	(83.7)	(16.3)
1969	46.7	19.6	20.9	(5.4)	(15.5)	8.1	4.7	100.0	(84.5)	(15.5)
1970	46.9	17.0	23.0	(5.7)	(17.4)	8.1	4.9	100.0	(82.6)	(17.4)
1971	46.1	14.3	25.3	(6.1)	(19.2)	8.9	5.4	100.0	(80.8)	(19.2)
1972	45.7	15.5	25.4	(6.1)	(19.2)	7.5	6.0	100.0	(80.7)	(19.2)
1973	44.7	15.7	27.3	(7.4)	(20.0)	7.0	5.2	100.0	(80.0)	(20.0)
1974	45.2	14.7	28.5	(8.0)	(20.5)	6.4	5.2	100.0	(79.5)	(20.5)
1975	43.9	14.6	30.3	(7.9)	(22.4)	5.9	5.4	100.0	(77.6)	(22.4)
1976	44.2	13.9	30.5	(8.2)	(22.3)	5.7	5.8	100.0	(77.7)	(22.3)
TQ	47.8	10.4	31.0	(8.9)	(22.2)	5.5	5.3	100.0	(77.8)	(22.2)
1977	44.3	15.4	29.9	(8.3)	(21.6)	4.9	5.3	100.0	(78.4)	(21.6)
1978	45.3	15.0	30.3	(8.9)	(21.4)	4.6	4.8	100.0	(78.6)	(21.4)
1979	47.0	14.2	30.0	(8.8)	(21.2)	4.0	4.8	100.0	(78.8)	(21.2)
1980	47.2	12.5	30.5	(8.6)	(21.9)	4.7	5.1	100.0	(78.1)	(21.9)
1981	47.7	10.2	30.5	(8.8)	(21.7)	6.8	4.8	100.0	(78.3)	(21.7)
1982	48.2	8.0	32.6	(9.4)	(23.2)	5.9	5.3	100.0	(76.8)	(23.2)
1983	48.1	6.2	34.8	(10.3)	(24.5)	5.9	5.0	100.0	(75.5)	(24.5)
1984	44.8	8.5	35.9	(11.0)	(24.9)	5.6	5.2	100.0	(75.1)	(24.9)
1985	45.6	8.4	36.1	(10.8)	(25.4)	4.9	5.0	100.0	(74.6)	(25.4)
1986	45.4	8.2	36.9	(10.9)	(26.0)	4.3	5.2	100.0	(74.0)	(26.0)
1987	46.0	9.8	35.5	(10.5)	(25.0)	3.8	4.9	100.0	(75.0)	(25.0)
1988	44.1	10.4	36.8	(10.2)	(26.6)	3.9	4.8	100.0	(73.4)	(26.6)
1989	45.0	10.4	36.3	(9.7)	(26.6)	3.5	4.8	100.0	(73.4)	(26.6)
1990	45.3	9.1	36.9	(9.5)	(27.3)	3.4	5.4	100.0	(72.7)	(27.3)
1991	44.4	9.3	37.6	(9.7)	(27.9)	4.0	4.7	100.0	(72.1)	(27.9)
1992	43.6	9.2	37.9	(10.2)	(27.7)	4.2	5.0	100.0	(72.3)	(27.7)
1993	44.2	10.2	37.1	(10.1)	(27.0)	4.2	4.3	100.0	(73.0)	(27.0)
1994 estimate	44.0	10.5	37.0	(10.1)	(26.9)	4.4	4.2	100.0	(73.1)	(26.9)
1995 estimate	44.0	10.4	36.2	(10.0)	(26.2)	5.3	4.1	100.0	(73.8)	(26.2)
1996 estimate	44.0	10.2	36.3	(10.1)	(26.3)	5.0	4.5	100.0	(73.7)	(26.3)
1997 estimate	44.1	10.0	36.4	(10.0)	(26.4)	4.8	4.6	100.0	(73.6)	(26.4)
1998 estimate	44.2	9.6	36.5	(10.0)	(26.6)	4.6	5.0	100.0	(73.4)	(26.6)
1999 estimate	44.5	9.4	36.5	(9.9)	(26.6)	4.5	5.1	100.0	(73.4)	(26.6)

Source: *Budget of the United States Government, Historical Tables, Fiscal Year 1995,* Executive Office of the President, Office of Management and Budget.

COMPOSITION OF OUTLAYS IN CURRENT AND IN CONSTANT (FY 1987) DOLLARS: 1984–1999

Category	1984	1985	1986	1987	1988	1989	1990	1991
In millions of current dollars								
Total outlays	851,846	946,391	990,336	1,003,911	1,064,140	1,143,172	1,252,705	1,323,793
National defense [1]	227,413	252,748	273,375	281,999	290,361	303,559	299,331	273,292
Nondefense:								
Payments for individuals	401,209	427,302	451,261	471,277	500,656	536,030	584,090	650,263
Direct payments [2]	(355,856)	(377,950)	(397,036)	(413,522)	(438,222)	(468,677)	(506,958)	(557,766)
Grants to State and local governments	(45,353)	(49,352)	(54,225)	(57,755)	(62,434)	(67,353)	(77,132)	(92,497)
All other grants	52,129	56,388	57,978	50,498	52,760	54,370	58,004	61,889
Net Interest [2]	111,123	129,504	136,047	138,652	151,838	169,266	184,221	194,541
All other [2]	91,929	113,147	104,682	97,941	105,492	117,158	163,675	183,165
Undistributed offsetting receipts [2]	−31,957	−32,698	−33,007	−36,455	−36,967	−37,212	−36,615	−39,356
Total nondefense	624,433	693,643	716,961	721,912	773,780	839,613	953,374	1,050,501
In billions of constant (FY 1987) dollars								
Total outlays	933.5	1,001.3	1,017.3	1,003.9	1,027.1	1,057.2	1,110.2	1,122.8
National defense [1]	241.7	261.2	276.4	282.0	283.3	285.9	272.5	240.4
Nondefense:								
Payments for individuals	446.5	458.6	467.5	471.3	480.0	490.4	509.6	540.8
Direct payments [2]	(396.0)	(405.6)	(411.4)	(413.5)	(420.2)	(428.8)	(442.3)	(463.8)
Grants to State and local governments	(50.5)	(53.0)	(56.2)	(57.8)	(59.9)	(61.6)	(67.3)	(77.0)
All other grants	57.8	59.8	59.6	50.5	50.8	50.3	51.9	53.6
Net Interest [2]	122.3	137.3	140.1	138.7	146.5	156.3	163.1	165.3
All other [2]	100.0	118.7	107.6	97.9	102.4	108.6	145.5	155.8
Undistributed offsetting receipts [2]	−34.8	−34.3	−34.0	−36.5	−35.8	−34.4	−32.4	−33.2
Total nondefense	691.7	740.1	740.8	721.9	743.8	771.3	837.7	882.3

As percentages of GDP

Total outlays	23.1	23.9	23.5	22.5	22.1	22.1	22.9	23.3
National defense [1]	6.2	6.4	6.5	6.3	6.0	5.9	5.5	4.8
Nondefense:								
Payments for individuals	10.9	10.8	10.7	10.6	10.4	10.4	10.7	11.5
Direct payments [2]	(9.6)	(9.5)	(9.4)	(9.3)	(9.1)	(9.1)	(9.2)	(9.8)
Grants to State and local governments	(1.2)	(1.2)	(1.3)	(1.3)	(1.3)	(1.3)	(1.4)	(1.6)
All other grants	1.4	1.4	1.4	1.1	1.1	1.1	1.1	1.1
Net Interest [2]	3.0	3.3	3.2	3.1	3.2	3.3	3.4	3.4
All other [2]	2.5	2.9	2.5	2.2	2.2	2.3	3.0	3.2
Undistributed offsetting receipts [2]	−0.9	−0.8	−0.8	−0.8	−0.8	−0.7	−0.7	−0.7
Total nondefense	16.9	17.5	17.0	16.2	16.1	16.2	17.4	18.5
Addendum: GDP ($ billions)	3,695.0	3,967.7	4,219.0	4,452.4	4,808.4	5,173.3	5,481.5	5,673.3

As percentages of outlays

Total outlays	100.0	100.0	100.0	100.0	100.0	100.0	100.0	100.0
National defense [1]	26.7	26.7	27.6	28.1	27.3	26.6	23.9	20.6
Nondefense:								
Payments for individuals	47.1	45.2	45.6	46.9	47.0	46.9	46.6	49.1
Direct payments [2]	(41.8)	(39.9)	(40.1)	(41.2)	(41.2)	(41.0)	(40.5)	(42.1)
Grants to State and local governments	(5.3)	(5.2)	(5.5)	(5.8)	(5.9)	(5.9)	(6.2)	(7.0)
All other grants	6.1	6.0	5.9	5.0	5.0	4.8	4.6	4.7
Net Interest [2]	13.0	13.7	13.7	13.8	14.3	14.8	14.7	14.7
All other [2]	10.8	12.0	10.6	9.8	9.9	10.2	13.1	13.8
Undistributed offsetting receipts [2]	−3.8	−3.5	−3.3	−3.6	−3.5	−3.3	−2.9	−3.0
Total nondefense	73.3	73.3	72.4	71.9	72.7	73.4	76.1	79.4

See footnotes at end of table.

(continued)

COMPOSITION OF OUTLAYS IN CURRENT AND IN CONSTANT (FY 1987) DOLLARS: 1984–1999—*(concluded)*

Category	1992	1993	1994 estimate	1995 estimate	1996 estimate	1997 estimate	1998 estimate	1999 estimate
In millions of current dollars								
Total outlays	1,380,856	1,408,205	1,483,829	1,518,945	1,596,877	1,691,443	1,777,416	1,854,023
National defense [1]	298,350	291,086	279,824	270,725	261,015	256,429	256,594	257,534
Nondefense:								
Payments for individuals	727,646	782,214	830,030	878,967	934,601	994,271	1,030,581	1,076,630
Direct payments [2]	(615,461)	(657,926)	(689,235)	(727,898)	(773,074)	(826,220)	(864,784)	(913,479)
Grants to State and local governments	(112,185)	(124,289)	(140,795)	(151,069)	(161,527)	(168,051)	(165,797)	(163,150)
All other grants	65,613	69,223	76,295	79,462	87,238	94,170	98,052	102,338
Net Interest [2]	199,421	198,811	203,448	212,835	224,199	234,004	244,648	254,402
All other [2]	129,105	104,256	132,120	119,554	131,504	152,011	188,961	203,632
Undistributed offsetting receipts [2]	−39,280	−37,386	−37,887	−42,597	−41,679	−39,442	−41,420	−40,513
Total nondefense	1,082,506	1,117,119	1,204,005	1,248,220	1,335,862	1,435,014	1,520,822	1,596,489
In billions of constant (FY 1987) dollars								
Total outlays	1,132.1	1,120.6	1,149.0	1,141.7	1,164.0	1,195.2	1,217.5	1,230.4
National defense [1]	250.2	235.7	220.1	206.6	193.6	184.7	179.4	174.8
Nondefense:								
Payments for individuals	585.7	611.9	631.8	648.9	668.0	688.0	689.7	696.8
Direct payments [2]	(495.3)	(514.5)	(524.4)	(537.2)	(552.3)	(571.5)	(578.5)	(590.9)
Grants to State and local governments	(90.5)	(97.4)	(107.4)	(111.8)	(115.7)	(116.5)	(111.2)	(105.9)
All other grants	56.0	57.5	61.9	62.9	67.2	70.6	71.5	72.6
Net Interest [2]	164.4	159.6	159.4	162.2	166.0	168.2	170.8	172.4
All other [2]	107.5	85.2	104.8	92.7	99.2	111.3	134.3	140.5
Undistributed offsetting receipts [2]	−31.8	−29.3	−28.9	−31.6	−30.1	−27.6	−28.2	−26.8
Total nondefense	881.9	885.0	928.9	935.1	970.3	1,010.5	1,038.1	1,055.5

As percentages of GDP

Total outlays	23.3	22.4	22.3	21.6	21.5	21.6	21.5	21.2
National defense[1]	5.0	4.6	4.2	3.9	3.5	3.3	3.1	2.9
Nondefense:								
Payments for individuals	12.3	12.4	12.5	12.5	12.6	12.7	12.4	12.3
Direct payments[2]	(10.4)	(10.5)	(10.4)	(10.4)	(10.4)	(10.5)	(10.4)	(10.4)
Grants to State and local governments	(1.9)	(2.0)	(2.1)	(2.2)	(2.2)	(2.1)	(2.0)	(1.9)
All other grants	1.1	1.1	1.1	1.1	1.2	1.2	1.2	1.2
Net Interest[2]	3.4	3.2	3.1	3.0	3.0	3.0	3.0	2.9
All other[2]	2.2	1.7	2.0	1.7	1.8	1.9	2.3	2.3
Undistributed offsetting receipts[2]	−0.7	−0.6	−0.6	−0.6	−0.6	−0.5	−0.5	−0.5
Total nondefense	18.2	17.7	18.1	17.8	18.0	18.3	18.4	18.2
Addendum: GDP ($ billions)	5,937.2	6,294.8	6,641.2	7,022.0	7,418.9	7,841.5	8,284.9	8,750.3

As percentages of outlays

Total outlays	100.0	100.0	100.0	100.0	100.0	100.0	100.0	100.0
National defense[1]	21.6	20.7	18.9	17.8	16.3	15.2	14.4	13.9
Nondefense:								
Payments for individuals	52.7	55.5	55.9	57.9	58.5	58.8	58.0	58.1
Direct payments[2]	(44.6)	(46.7)	(46.4)	(47.9)	(48.4)	(48.8)	(48.7)	(49.3)
Grants to State and local governments	(8.1)	(8.8)	(9.5)	(9.9)	(10.1)	(9.9)	(9.3)	(8.8)
All other grants	4.8	4.9	5.1	5.2	5.5	5.6	5.5	5.5
Net Interest[2]	14.4	14.1	13.7	14.0	14.0	13.8	13.8	13.7
All other[2]	9.3	7.4	8.9	7.9	8.2	9.0	10.6	11.0
Undistributed offsetting receipts[2]	−2.8	−2.7	−2.6	−2.8	−2.6	−2.3	−2.3	−2.2
Total nondefense	78.4	79.3	81.1	82.2	83.7	84.8	85.6	86.1

[1] Includes a small amount of grants to State and local governments and direct payments for individuals.
[2] Includes some off-budget amounts; most of the off-budget amounts are direct payments for individuals (social security benefits).

Source: *Budget of the United States Government, Historical Tables, Fiscal Year 1995,* Executive Office of the President, Office of Management and Budget.

TOTAL GOVERNMENT EXPENDITURES AS PERCENTAGES OF GDP: 1947–1993

Fiscal Year	Total Government Expenditures	Federal Government Outlays			Addendum: Federal Grants	State and Local Government Expenditures From Own Sources (NIPA Basis)
		Total	On-Budget	Off-Budget		
1947	20.4	15.5	15.3	0.1	(0.7)	4.9
1948	17.7	12.1	11.9	0.1	(0.7)	5.6
1949	21.0	14.8	14.6	0.2	(0.8)	6.2
1950	23.1	16.0	15.8	0.2	(0.9)	7.1
1951	21.0	14.5	14.1	0.4	(0.8)	6.4
1952	26.3	19.9	19.4	0.5	(0.7)	6.4
1953	27.2	20.9	20.3	0.6	(0.8)	6.3
1954	26.0	19.3	18.5	0.8	(0.8)	6.8
1955	25.1	17.8	16.8	1.0	(0.8)	7.3
1956	24.2	17.0	15.8	1.2	(0.8)	7.2
1957	25.0	17.5	16.1	1.4	(0.8)	7.5
1958	26.4	18.4	16.7	1.7	(1.0)	8.0
1959	27.2	19.2	17.3	1.9	(1.3)	8.0
1960	26.1	18.3	16.1	2.2	(1.4)	7.8
1961	27.3	18.9	16.6	2.3	(1.3)	8.4
1962	27.7	19.2	16.8	2.4	(1.4)	8.4
1963	27.6	19.0	16.5	2.6	(1.4)	8.5
1964	27.5	19.0	16.4	2.5	(1.6)	8.6
1965	26.2	17.6	15.2	2.5	(1.6)	8.6
1966	27.0	18.3	15.6	2.7	(1.7)	8.7

1967	28.8	19.8	17.3	2.6	(1.9)	9.0
1968	30.3	21.0	18.4	2.6	(2.1)	9.3
1969	29.5	19.8	17.1	2.7	(2.1)	9.6
1970	29.7	19.9	17.1	2.8	(2.3)	9.8
1971	30.4	20.0	16.9	3.1	(2.5)	10.4
1972	30.3	20.1	16.9	3.2	(2.8)	10.2
1973	29.0	19.3	15.7	3.6	(3.2)	9.7
1974	29.1	19.2	15.5	3.7	(3.0)	10.0
1975	32.4	22.0	18.0	4.0	(3.2)	10.4
1976	32.4	22.1	17.9	4.1	(3.4)	10.4
TQ	32.1	21.6	17.2	4.4	(3.5)	10.5
1977	31.0	21.3	17.1	4.2	(3.5)	9.7
1978	30.4	21.3	17.1	4.2	(3.5)	9.1
1979	29.7	20.7	16.6	4.1	(3.3)	9.0
1980	31.5	22.3	18.0	4.3	(3.3)	9.2
1981	31.9	22.9	18.3	4.6	(3.0)	9.0
1982	33.3	23.9	19.0	4.8	(2.7)	9.4
1983	33.8	24.4	19.9	4.4	(2.6)	9.4
1984	32.1	23.1	18.6	4.5	(2.5)	9.0
1985	33.0	23.9	19.4	4.5	(2.5)	9.2
1986	32.9	23.5	19.1	4.3	(2.6)	9.4
1987	32.5	22.5	18.2	4.4	(2.3)	9.9
1988	32.0	22.1	17.9	4.2	(2.3)	9.9
1989	31.9	22.1	18.0	4.1	(2.2)	9.8
1990	33.0	22.9	18.7	4.1	(2.3)	10.2
1991	34.1	23.3	19.1	4.3	(2.6)	10.7
1992	34.2	23.3	19.0	4.3	(2.8)	11.0
1993	33.3	22.4	18.1	4.2	(2.9)	11.0

Source: *Budget of the United States Government, Historical Tables, Fiscal Year 1995,* Executive Office of the President, Office of Management and Budget.

TOTAL GOVERNMENT EXPENDITURES BY MAJOR CATEGORY OF EXPENDITURE AS PERCENTAGES OF GDP: 1947–1993

Fiscal Year	Total Government	Defense and International	Net Interest	Federal Payments For Individuals		Other Federal	State and Local From Own Sources (Except Net Interest)
				Social Security and Medicare	Other		
1947	20.4	8.3	1.9	0.2	3.9	1.2	4.8
1948	17.7	5.5	1.8	0.2	3.5	1.1	5.6
1949	21.0	7.3	1.8	0.2	3.6	1.9	6.1
1950	23.1	6.9	1.8	0.3	4.9	2.1	7.0
1951	21.0	8.7	1.5	0.5	2.8	1.1	6.4
1952	26.3	14.3	1.4	0.6	2.6	1.0	6.4
1953	27.2	15.1	1.4	0.7	2.3	1.4	6.3
1954	26.0	13.8	1.3	0.9	2.5	0.7	6.8
1955	25.1	11.7	1.3	1.1	2.6	1.1	7.3
1956	24.2	10.8	1.2	1.3	2.4	1.3	7.2
1957	25.0	11.1	1.2	1.5	2.4	1.3	7.5
1958	26.4	11.2	1.3	1.8	2.9	1.3	8.0
1959	27.2	10.9	1.2	2.0	2.8	2.4	8.0
1960	26.1	10.1	1.4	2.3	2.5	2.0	7.8
1961	27.3	10.2	1.3	2.4	3.0	2.1	8.4
1962	27.7	10.4	1.3	2.5	2.7	2.3	8.4
1963	27.6	10.0	1.3	2.6	2.7	2.4	8.5
1964	27.5	9.5	1.3	2.6	2.6	2.9	8.6
1965	26.2	8.3	1.2	2.5	2.4	3.1	8.6
1966	27.0	8.7	1.2	2.8	2.3	3.3	8.7
1967	28.8	9.7	1.2	3.1	2.4	3.4	9.1

1968	30.3	10.3	1.2	3.4	2.5	3.5	9.4
1969	29.5	9.4	1.3	3.6	2.6	2.9	9.7
1970	29.7	8.7	1.3	3.7	2.9	3.1	10.0
1971	30.4	7.9	1.3	4.1	3.6	3.0	10.5
1972	30.3	7.3	1.2	4.2	3.9	3.3	10.3
1973	29.0	6.3	1.2	4.5	3.7	3.4	9.9
1974	29.1	6.1	1.3	4.7	3.9	3.0	10.2
1975	32.4	6.2	1.2	5.1	5.0	4.1	10.7
1976	32.4	5.7	1.3	5.3	5.4	4.1	10.6
TQ	32.1	5.6	1.3	5.4	4.8	4.2	10.7
1977	31.0	5.4	1.3	5.4	4.8	4.1	9.9
1978	30.4	5.2	1.3	5.4	4.4	4.6	9.5
1979	29.7	5.1	1.3	5.4	4.2	4.2	9.5
1980	31.5	5.5	1.3	5.7	4.8	4.3	9.9
1981	31.9	5.8	1.6	6.0	4.9	3.9	9.8
1982	33.3	6.3	1.8	6.5	5.0	3.4	10.3
1983	33.8	6.7	1.8	6.8	5.2	3.0	10.3
1984	32.1	6.6	2.1	6.4	4.4	2.6	9.9
1985	33.0	6.8	2.3	6.5	4.3	3.0	10.1
1986	32.9	6.8	2.3	6.4	4.3	2.7	10.4
1987	32.5	6.6	2.2	6.4	4.2	2.3	10.8
1988	32.0	6.3	2.3	6.3	4.1	2.3	10.8
1989	31.9	6.1	2.3	6.3	4.1	2.4	10.8
1990	33.0	5.7	2.4	6.5	4.2	3.1	11.1
1991	34.1	5.1	2.6	6.7	4.8	3.3	11.6
1992	34.2	5.3	2.6	7.0	5.3	2.3	11.8
1993	33.3	4.9	2.4	7.1	5.4	1.9	11.7

Source: *Budget of the United States Government, Historical Tables, Fiscal Year 1995*, Executive Office of the President, Office of Management and Budget.

TOTAL GOVERNMENT EXPENDITURES BY MAJOR CATEGORY OF EXPENDITURE: 1947–1993

(in billions of dollars)

Fiscal Year	Total Government	Defense and International	Net Interest	Federal Payments For Individuals		Other Federal	State and Local From Own Sources (Except Net Interest)
				Social Security and Medicare	Other		
1947	45.4	18.6	4.3	0.4	8.6	2.6	10.8
1948	43.6	13.7	4.4	0.5	8.5	2.7	13.8
1949	55.0	19.2	4.6	0.6	9.5	5.0	16.1
1950	61.3	18.4	4.9	0.7	12.9	5.7	18.7
1951	65.7	27.2	4.7	1.5	8.8	3.4	20.1
1952	89.4	48.8	4.7	2.0	8.9	3.4	21.7
1953	98.9	54.9	5.2	2.6	8.3	5.1	22.8
1954	95.9	50.9	4.8	3.3	9.3	2.6	25.0
1955	96.5	45.0	4.9	4.3	10.0	4.3	27.9
1956	100.8	44.9	5.2	5.4	9.8	5.4	30.0
1957	109.6	48.6	5.4	6.5	10.5	5.6	32.9
1958	118.4	50.2	5.7	8.0	12.9	5.7	35.9
1959	130.6	52.2	5.9	9.5	13.2	11.4	38.4
1960	131.8	51.1	7.1	11.4	12.8	10.0	39.5
1961	141.3	52.8	6.8	12.2	15.3	10.7	43.5
1962	153.7	58.0	7.0	14.0	14.9	13.0	46.7
1963	161.1	58.7	7.9	15.5	15.5	13.9	49.6
1964	172.2	59.7	8.2	16.2	16.0	18.4	53.7
1965	176.0	55.9	8.4	17.1	16.0	20.6	58.0
1966	198.4	63.7	9.0	20.3	16.8	24.4	64.3
1967	228.7	77.0	9.5	24.5	18.7	27.0	72.0

1968	256.9	87.2	10.1	28.4	21.4	30.0	79.7
1969	272.7	87.1	11.7	33.0	24.2	26.6	90.1
1970	292.2	86.0	12.8	36.4	28.4	30.4	98.1
1971	319.2	83.0	13.2	42.6	38.0	31.7	110.6
1972	347.4	84.0	14.2	47.7	45.3	38.2	118.1
1973	369.1	80.8	15.3	57.2	47.5	42.8	125.5
1974	409.1	85.1	17.8	65.7	54.7	42.4	143.5
1975	489.6	93.6	18.7	77.7	76.2	61.6	161.9
1976	546.4	96.1	22.5	89.6	91.0	68.4	178.9
TQ	142.7	24.7	6.0	24.0	21.5	18.8	47.7
1977	594.7	103.6	25.6	104.5	92.5	78.7	189.8
1978	655.6	112.0	28.4	116.7	95.0	99.5	203.9
1979	721.8	123.8	30.8	130.8	103.1	103.2	230.1
1980	834.2	146.7	34.6	151.0	127.5	113.2	261.1
1981	945.1	170.6	46.3	179.1	145.5	114.2	289.4
1982	1,038.9	197.6	57.3	203.1	154.8	105.2	320.9
1983	1,120.2	221.8	59.3	224.0	172.5	100.3	342.4
1984	1,185.6	243.3	78.1	237.0	164.2	96.2	366.8
1985	1,311.0	268.9	91.9	256.1	171.2	120.7	402.2
1986	1,387.3	287.5	95.7	270.7	180.5	115.5	437.2
1987	1,445.6	293.6	97.8	285.0	186.3	100.3	482.6
1988	1,538.5	300.8	108.7	302.5	198.1	110.8	517.5
1989	1,651.5	313.1	118.9	324.4	211.6	124.7	558.7
1990	1,809.8	313.1	131.7	353.8	230.3	171.3	609.6
1991	1,932.9	289.1	146.8	380.7	269.6	189.8	656.9
1992	2,032.9	314.5	153.3	414.3	313.4	139.3	698.2
1993	2,098.0	307.9	153.4	444.7	337.6	119.2	735.2

Source: *Budget of the United States Government, Historical Tables, Fiscal Year 1995,* Executive Office of the President, Office of Management and Budget.

TOTAL GOVERNMENT SURPLUSES OR DEFICITS (–) IN ABSOLUTE AMOUNTS AND AS PERCENTAGES OF GDP: 1947–1993

Fiscal Year	In Billions of Current Dollars					As Percentages of GDP		
	Total Government	Federal Government			State and Local (NIPA Basis)	Total Government	Total Federal	State and Local
		Total	On-Budget	Off-Budget				
1947	5.6	4.0	2.9	1.2	1.6	2.5	1.8	0.7
1948	12.4	11.8	10.5	1.2	0.6	5.0	4.8	0.2
1949	0.4	0.6	–0.7	1.3	–0.2	0.2	0.2	–0.1
1950	–4.4	–3.1	–4.7	1.6	–1.3	–1.7	–1.2	–0.5
1951	5.6	6.1	4.3	1.8	–0.6	1.8	1.9	–0.2
1952	–2.0	–1.5	–3.4	1.9	–0.4	–0.6	–0.4	–0.1
1953	–6.2	–6.5	–8.3	1.8	0.3	–1.7	–1.8	0.1
1954	–1.4	–1.2	–2.8	1.7	–0.3	–0.4	–0.3	–0.1
1955	–4.6	–3.0	–4.1	1.1	–1.6	–1.2	–0.8	–0.4
1956	3.2	3.9	2.5	1.5	–0.8	0.8	0.9	–0.2
1957	2.5	3.4	2.6	0.8	–0.9	0.6	0.8	–0.2
1958	–4.8	–2.8	–3.3	0.5	–2.0	–1.1	–0.6	–0.5
1959	–14.6	–12.8	–12.1	–0.7	–1.8	–3.0	–2.7	–0.4
1960	0.7	0.3	0.5	–0.2	0.4	0.1	0.1	0.1
1961	–3.6	–3.3	–3.8	0.4	–0.2	–0.7	–0.6	–*
1962	–7.1	–7.1	–5.9	–1.3	*	–1.3	–1.3	*
1963	–4.5	–4.8	–4.0	–0.8	0.3	–0.8	–0.8	*
1964	–5.3	–5.9	–6.5	0.6	0.6	–0.8	–0.9	0.1
1965	–0.7	–1.4	–1.6	0.2	0.7	–0.1	–0.2	0.1
1966	–3.1	–3.7	–3.1	–0.6	0.6	–0.4	–0.5	0.1
1967	–10.2	–8.6	–12.6	4.0	–1.6	–1.3	–1.1	–0.2

1968	−24.7	−25.2	−27.7	2.6	0.5	−2.9	−3.0	0.1
1969	2.8	3.2	−0.5	3.7	−0.4	0.3	0.4	−*
1970	0.8	−2.8	−8.7	5.9	3.7	0.1	−0.3	0.4
1971	−23.6	−23.0	−26.1	3.0	−0.5	−2.2	−2.2	−0.1
1972	−15.2	−23.4	−26.4	3.1	8.2	−1.3	−2.0	0.7
1973	−0.1	−14.9	−15.4	0.5	14.8	−*	−1.2	1.2
1974	4.4	−6.1	−8.0	1.8	10.5	0.3	−0.4	0.8
1975	−47.4	−53.2	−55.3	2.0	5.9	−3.1	−3.5	0.4
1976	−66.7	−73.7	−70.5	−3.2	7.0	−4.0	−4.4	0.4
TQ	−16.5	−14.7	−13.3	−1.4	−1.8	−3.7	−3.3	−0.4
1977	−30.8	−53.7	−49.8	−3.9	22.9	−1.6	−2.8	1.2
1978	−26.3	−59.2	−54.9	−4.3	32.9	−1.2	−2.7	1.5
1979	−14.8	−40.2	−38.2	−2.0	25.3	−0.6	−1.7	1.0
1980	−50.5	−73.8	−72.7	−1.1	23.3	−1.9	−2.8	0.9
1981	−51.1	−79.0	−74.0	−5.0	27.9	−1.7	−2.7	0.9
1982	−101.0	−128.0	−120.1	−7.9	27.0	−3.2	−4.1	0.9
1983	−172.7	−207.8	−208.0	0.2	35.1	−5.2	−6.3	1.1
1984	−130.0	−185.4	−185.7	0.3	55.4	−3.5	−5.0	1.5
1985	−157.9	−212.3	−221.7	9.4	54.4	−4.0	−5.4	1.4
1986	−165.5	−221.2	−238.0	16.7	55.8	−3.9	−5.2	1.3
1987	−106.0	−149.8	−169.3	19.6	43.8	−2.4	−3.4	1.0
1988	−115.6	−155.2	−194.0	38.8	39.6	−2.4	−3.2	0.8
1989	−106.7	−152.5	−205.2	52.8	45.8	−2.1	−2.9	0.9
1990	−192.2	−221.4	−278.0	56.6	29.2	−3.5	−4.0	0.5
1991	−261.5	−269.5	−321.7	52.2	8.0	−4.6	−4.8	0.1
1992	−286.3	−290.4	−340.5	50.1	4.1	−4.8	−4.9	0.1
1993	−251.3	−254.7	−300.0	45.3	3.4	−4.0	−4.0	0.1

*If dollars, $50 million or less. If percent, 0.05 percent or less.

Source: *Budget of the United States Government, Historical Tables, Fiscal Year 1995,* Executive Office of the President, Office of Management and Budget.

SUMMARY OF RECEIPTS, OUTLAYS, AND SURPLUSES OR DEFICITS(−) IN CURRENT DOLLARS, CONSTANT (FY 1987) DOLLARS, AND AS PERCENTAGES OF GDP: 1940–1999

(dollar amounts in billions)

Fiscal Year	In Current Dollars			In Constant (FY 1987 Dollars)			Addendum: Composite Deflator	As Percentages of GDP		
	Receipts	Outlays	Surplus or Deficit (−)	Receipts	Outlays	Surplus or Deficit (−)		Receipts	Outlays	Surplus or Deficit (−)
1940	6.5	9.5	−2.9	67.0	96.8	−29.9	0.0978	6.9	9.9	−3.1
1941	8.7	13.7	−4.9	86.3	135.3	−49.0	0.1009	7.7	12.1	−4.4
1942	14.6	35.1	−20.5	131.2	315.1	−183.9	0.1115	10.3	24.8	−14.5
1943	24.0	78.6	−54.6	200.2	655.2	−455.0	0.1199	13.7	44.8	−31.1
1944	43.7	91.3	−47.6	377.1	787.1	−410.0	0.1160	21.7	45.3	−23.6
1945	45.2	92.7	−47.6	395.8	812.6	−416.8	0.1141	21.3	43.7	−22.4
1946	39.3	55.2	−15.9	329.4	463.0	−133.6	0.1193	18.5	26.0	−7.5
1947	38.5	34.5	4.0	257.4	230.6	26.9	0.1496	17.3	15.5	1.8
1948	41.6	29.8	11.8	269.3	192.9	76.4	0.1543	16.8	12.1	4.8
1949	39.4	38.8	0.6	249.1	245.5	3.7	0.1582	15.0	14.8	0.2
1950	39.4	42.6	−3.1	241.4	260.5	−19.1	0.1634	14.8	16.0	−1.2
1951	51.6	45.5	6.1	324.2	285.9	38.3	0.1592	16.5	14.5	1.9
1952	66.2	67.7	−1.5	406.7	416.0	−9.3	0.1627	19.4	19.9	−0.4
1953	69.6	76.1	−6.5	406.6	444.5	−37.9	0.1712	19.1	20.9	−1.8
1954	69.7	70.9	−1.2	394.9	401.4	−6.5	0.1765	18.9	19.3	−0.3
1955	65.5	68.4	−3.0	363.4	380.0	−16.6	0.1801	17.0	17.8	−0.8
1956	74.6	70.6	3.9	391.1	370.4	20.7	0.1907	17.9	17.0	0.9
1957	80.0	76.6	3.4	396.6	379.7	16.9	0.2017	18.3	17.5	0.8
1958	79.6	82.4	−2.8	374.9	388.0	−13.0	0.2124	17.8	18.4	−0.6
1959	79.2	92.1	−12.8	352.4	409.5	−57.1	0.2249	16.5	19.2	−2.7
1960	92.5	92.2	0.3	393.4	392.1	1.3	0.2351	18.3	18.3	0.1
1961	94.4	97.7	−3.3	392.1	406.0	−13.9	0.2407	18.3	18.9	−0.6
1962	99.7	106.8	−7.1	406.8	436.0	−29.2	0.2450	18.0	19.2	−1.3
1963	106.6	111.3	−4.8	418.9	437.6	−18.7	0.2544	18.2	19.0	−0.8
1964	112.6	118.5	−5.9	433.8	456.6	−22.8	0.2596	18.0	19.0	−0.9
1965	116.8	118.2	−1.4	440.8	446.1	−5.3	0.2650	17.4	17.6	−0.2
1966	130.8	134.5	−3.7	478.9	492.4	−13.5	0.2732	17.8	18.3	−0.5

1967	148.8	157.5	−8.6	529.2	560.0	−30.7	0.2812	18.8	19.8	−1.1
1968	153.0	178.1	−25.2	522.6	608.6	−86.0	0.2927	18.1	21.0	−3.0
1969	186.9	183.6	3.2	604.4	593.9	10.5	0.3092	20.2	19.8	0.4
1970	192.8	195.6	−2.8	587.5	596.1	−8.7	0.3282	19.6	19.9	−0.3
1971	187.1	210.2	−23.0	533.5	599.1	−65.7	0.3508	17.8	20.0	−2.2
1972	207.3	230.7	−23.4	554.9	617.5	−62.6	0.3736	18.1	20.1	−2.0
1973	230.8	245.7	−14.9	582.7	620.3	−37.6	0.3961	18.1	19.3	−1.2
1974	263.2	269.4	−6.1	611.2	625.4	−14.2	0.4307	18.8	19.2	−0.4
1975	279.1	332.3	−53.2	586.6	698.5	−111.9	0.4758	18.5	22.0	−3.5
1976	298.1	371.8	−73.7	584.7	729.3	−144.6	0.5098	17.7	22.1	−4.4
TQ	81.2	96.0	−14.7	153.6	181.5	−27.9	0.5287	18.3	21.6	−3.3
1977	355.6	409.2	−53.7	643.8	740.9	−97.2	0.5523	18.5	21.3	−2.8
1978	399.6	458.7	−59.2	674.0	773.9	−99.8	0.5928	18.5	21.3	−2.7
1979	463.3	503.5	−40.2	719.3	781.7	−62.4	0.6441	19.1	20.7	−1.7
1980	517.1	590.9	−73.8	728.1	832.1	−104.0	0.7102	19.6	22.3	−2.8
1981	599.3	678.2	−79.0	766.6	867.7	−101.0	0.7817	20.2	22.9	−2.7
1982	617.8	745.8	−128.0	738.2	891.1	−152.9	0.8369	19.8	23.9	−4.1
1983	600.6	808.4	−207.8	684.3	921.1	−236.8	0.8776	18.1	24.4	−6.3
1984	666.5	851.8	−185.4	730.4	933.5	−203.2	0.9125	18.0	23.1	−5.0
1985	734.1	946.4	−212.3	776.6	1,001.3	−224.6	0.9452	18.5	23.9	−5.4
1986	769.1	990.3	−221.2	790.0	1,017.3	−227.3	0.9735	18.2	23.5	−5.2
1987	854.1	1,003.9	−149.8	854.1	1,003.9	−149.8	1.0000	19.2	22.5	−3.4
1988	909.0	1,064.1	−155.2	877.3	1,027.1	−149.8	1.0361	18.9	22.1	−3.2
1989	990.7	1,143.2	−152.5	916.2	1,057.2	−141.0	1.0813	19.2	22.1	−2.9
1990	1,031.3	1,252.7	−221.4	914.0	1,110.2	−196.2	1.1284	18.8	22.9	−4.0
1991	1,054.3	1,323.8	−269.5	894.2	1,122.8	−228.6	1.1790	18.6	23.3	−4.8
1992	1,090.5	1,380.9	−290.4	894.0	1,132.1	−238.1	1.2197	18.4	23.3	−4.9
1993	1,153.5	1,408.2	−254.7	918.0	1,120.6	−202.7	1.2566	18.3	22.4	−4.0
1994 estimate	1,249.1	1,483.8	−234.8	967.2	1,149.0	−181.8	1.2914	18.8	22.3	−3.5
1995 estimate	1,353.8	1,518.9	−165.1	1,017.6	1,141.7	−124.1	1.3304	19.3	21.6	−2.4
1996 estimate	1,427.3	1,596.9	−169.6	1,040.4	1,164.0	−123.6	1.3719	19.2	21.5	−2.3
1997 estimate	1,505.1	1,691.4	−186.4	1,063.5	1,195.2	−131.7	1.4152	19.2	21.6	−2.4
1998 estimate	1,586.9	1,777.4	−190.5	1,087.0	1,217.5	−130.5	1.4599	19.2	21.5	−2.3
1999 estimate	1,672.9	1,854.0	−181.1	1,110.2	1,230.4	−120.2	1.5069	19.1	21.2	−2.1

Source: *Budget of the United States Government, Historical Tables, Fiscal Year 1995,* Executive Office of the President, Office of management and Budget.

SUMMARY OF RECEIPTS, OUTLAYS, AND SURPLUSES OR DEFICITS(−) AS PERCENTAGES OF GDP: 1934–1999

Year	GDP (in billions of dollars)	Total			On-Budget			Off-Budget		
		Receipts	Outlays	Surplus or Deficit (−)	Receipts	Outlays	Surplus or Deficit (−)	Receipts	Outlays	Surplus or Deficit (−)
1934	60.4	4.9	10.8	−5.9	4.9	10.8	−5.9	....	....	....
1935	68.7	5.3	9.3	−4.1	5.3	9.3	−4.1	....	....	....
1936	77.5	5.1	10.6	−5.6	5.1	10.6	−5.6	....	....	....
1937	86.8	6.2	8.7	−2.5	5.9	8.7	−2.8	0.3	−*	0.3
1938	87.8	7.7	7.8	−0.1	7.2	7.8	−0.6	0.4	−*	0.5
1939	87.8	7.2	10.4	−3.2	6.6	10.4	−3.8	0.6	−*	0.6
1940	95.4	6.9	9.9	−3.1	6.3	9.9	−3.7	0.6	−*	0.6
1941	112.5	7.7	12.1	−4.4	7.1	12.1	−5.0	0.6	*	0.6
1942	141.8	10.3	24.8	−14.5	9.7	24.7	−15.0	0.6	*	0.6
1943	175.4	13.7	44.8	−31.1	13.0	44.7	−31.7	0.6	0.1	0.6
1944	201.7	21.7	45.3	−23.6	21.0	45.2	−24.2	0.6	0.1	0.6
1945	212.0	21.3	43.7	−22.4	20.7	43.7	−23.0	0.6	0.1	0.6
1946	212.5	18.5	26.0	−7.5	17.9	25.9	−8.0	0.6	0.1	0.5
1947	222.9	17.3	15.5	1.8	16.6	15.3	1.3	0.7	0.1	0.5
1948	246.7	16.8	12.1	4.8	16.2	11.9	4.3	0.7	0.1	0.5
1949	262.7	15.0	14.8	0.2	14.4	14.6	−0.3	0.6	0.2	0.5
1950	265.8	14.8	16.0	−1.2	14.0	15.8	−1.8	0.8	0.2	0.6
1951	313.5	16.5	14.5	1.9	15.5	14.1	1.4	1.0	0.4	0.6
1952	340.5	19.4	19.9	−0.4	18.4	19.4	−1.0	1.1	0.5	0.5
1953	363.8	19.1	20.9	−1.8	18.0	20.3	−2.3	1.1	0.6	0.5
1954	368.0	18.9	19.3	−0.3	17.7	18.5	−0.8	1.2	0.8	0.5
1955	384.7	17.0	17.8	−0.8	15.7	16.8	−1.1	1.3	1.0	0.3
1956	416.3	17.9	17.0	0.9	16.4	15.8	0.6	1.5	1.2	0.3
1957	438.3	18.3	17.5	0.8	16.7	16.1	0.6	1.5	1.4	0.2
1958	448.1	17.8	18.4	−0.6	16.0	16.7	−0.7	1.8	1.7	0.1
1959	480.2	16.5	19.2	−2.7	14.8	17.3	−2.5	1.7	1.9	−0.1
1960	504.6	18.3	18.3	0.1	16.2	16.1	0.1	2.1	2.2	−*
1961	517.0	18.3	18.9	−0.6	15.9	16.6	−0.7	2.3	2.3	0.1
1962	555.2	18.0	19.2	−1.3	15.7	16.8	−1.1	2.2	2.4	−0.2
1963	584.5	18.2	19.0	−0.8	15.8	16.5	−0.7	2.4	2.6	−0.1
1964	625.3	18.0	19.0	−0.9	15.4	16.4	−1.0	2.6	2.5	0.1

1965	671.0	17.4	17.6	−0.2	14.9	15.2	−0.2	2.5	2.5	*
1966	735.4	17.8	18.3	−0.5	15.2	15.6	−0.4	2.6	2.7	−0.1
1967	793.3	18.8	19.8	−1.1	15.7	17.3	−1.6	3.1	2.6	0.5
1968	847.2	18.1	21.0	−3.0	15.1	18.4	−3.3	2.9	2.6	0.3
1969	925.7	20.2	19.8	0.4	17.1	17.1	−0.1	3.1	2.7	0.4
1970	985.4	19.6	19.9	−0.3	16.2	17.1	−0.9	3.4	2.8	0.6
1971	1,050.9	17.8	20.0	−2.2	14.4	16.9	−2.5	3.4	3.1	0.3
1972	1,147.8	18.1	20.1	−2.0	14.6	16.9	−2.3	3.5	3.2	0.3
1973	1,274.0	18.1	19.3	−1.2	14.5	15.7	−1.2	3.6	3.6	*
1974	1,403.6	18.8	19.2	−0.4	14.9	15.5	−0.6	3.8	3.7	0.1
1975	1,509.8	18.5	22.0	−3.5	14.3	18.0	−3.7	4.1	4.0	0.1
1976	1,684.2	17.7	22.1	−4.4	13.8	17.9	−4.2	3.9	4.1	−0.2
TQ	445.0	18.3	21.6	−3.3	14.2	17.2	−3.0	4.0	4.4	−0.3
1977	1,917.2	18.5	21.3	−2.8	14.5	17.1	−2.6	4.0	4.2	−0.2
1978	2,155.0	18.5	21.3	−2.7	14.6	17.1	−2.5	4.0	4.2	−0.2
1979	2,429.5	19.1	20.7	−1.7	15.0	16.6	−1.6	4.0	4.1	−0.1
1980	2,644.1	19.6	22.3	−2.8	15.3	18.0	−2.8	4.3	4.3	−*
1981	2,964.4	20.2	22.9	−2.7	15.8	18.3	−2.5	4.4	4.6	−0.2
1982	3,122.2	19.8	23.9	−4.1	15.2	19.0	−3.8	4.6	4.8	−0.3
1983	3,316.5	18.1	24.4	−6.3	13.7	19.9	−6.3	4.4	4.4	*
1984	3,695.0	18.0	23.1	−5.0	13.5	18.6	−5.0	4.5	4.5	*
1985	3,967.7	18.5	23.9	−5.4	13.8	19.4	−5.6	4.7	4.5	0.2
1986	4,219.0	18.2	23.5	−5.2	13.5	19.1	−5.6	4.7	4.3	0.4
1987	4,452.4	19.2	22.5	−3.4	14.4	18.2	−3.8	4.8	4.4	0.4
1988	4,808.4	18.9	22.1	−3.2	13.9	17.9	−4.0	5.0	4.2	0.8
1989	5,173.3	19.2	22.1	−2.9	14.1	18.0	−4.0	5.1	4.1	1.0
1990	5,481.5	18.8	22.9	−4.0	13.7	18.7	−5.1	5.1	4.1	1.0
1991	5,673.3	18.6	23.3	−4.8	13.4	19.1	−5.7	5.2	4.3	0.9
1992	5,937.2	18.4	23.3	−4.9	13.3	19.0	−5.7	5.1	4.3	0.8
1993	6,294.8	18.3	22.4	−4.0	13.4	18.1	−4.8	5.0	4.2	0.7
1994 estimate	6,641.2	18.8	22.3	−3.5	13.7	18.1	−4.4	5.1	4.2	0.8
1995 estimate	7,022.0	19.3	21.6	−2.4	14.2	17.4	−3.2	5.1	4.2	0.9
1996 estimate	7,418.9	19.2	21.5	−2.3	14.2	17.4	−3.2	5.1	4.2	0.9
1997 estimate	7,841.5	19.2	21.6	−2.4	14.1	17.5	−3.4	5.1	4.1	1.0
1998 estimate	8,284.9	19.2	21.5	−2.3	14.1	17.4	−3.4	5.1	4.0	1.1
1999 estimate	8,750.3	19.1	21.2	−2.1	14.0	17.2	−3.2	5.1	4.0	1.1

* 0.05 percent or less.

Source: *Budget of the United States Government, Historical Tables, Fiscal Year 1995*, Executive Office of the President, Office of Management and Budget.

NOTES TO HISTORICAL TABLES

Because of the numerous changes in the way budget data have been presented over time, there are inevitable difficulties in trying to produce comparable data to cover so many years. The general rule underlying all of these tables is to provide data in as meaningful and comparable a fashion as possible. To the extent feasible, the data are presented on a basis consistent with current budget concepts. When a structural change is made, insofar as possible the data are adjusted for all years.

In November 1990, the Omnibus Budget Reconciliation Act of 1990 was enacted. Part of this legislation was the Budget Enforcement Act, which not only provided new enforcement mechanisms, but also included significant changes in budget concepts. The major conceptual change concerns the measurement of Federal credit activity in the budget. Under current law, only the subsidy cost (the cost to the Government, including the cost associated with loan defaults) of direct loans or loan guarantees be recorded as budget authority and outlays. The remaining financial transactions are recorded as means of financing the deficit. This concept applies only to direct loan obligations and loan guarantee commitments made in 1992 and later years. Unfortunately, the historical data prior to 1992 could not be converted to this new measurement basis. Thus, data prior to 1992 are on a cash flow or pre-credit reform basis. Data for 1992 and beyond are on a cash flow basis for direct loans and loan guarantees obligated or committed in earlier years, but the budget program accounts providing direct loans or loan guarantees reflect the subsidy cost for subsequent obligations and commitments.

Coverage

The Federal Government has used the unified or consolidated budget concept as the foundation for its budgetary analysis and presentation since the 1969 budget. The basic guidelines for the unified budget were presented in the *Report of the President's Commission on Budget Concepts* (October 1967). The Commission recommended the budget include all Federal fiscal activities unless there were exceptionally persuasive reasons for exclusion. Nevertheless, from the very beginning some programs were perceived as warranting special treatment. Indeed, the Commission itself recommended a bifurcated presentation: a "unified budget" composed of an "expenditure account" and a "loan account." The distinction between the expenditure account and the loan account proved to be confusing and caused considerable complication in the budget for little benefit. As a result, this distinction was eliminated starting with the 1974 budget. However, even prior to the 1974 budget, the Export-Import Bank had been excluded by law from the budget totals, and other exclusions followed. The structure of the budget was gradually revised to show the off-budget transactions in many locations along with the on-budget transactions, and the off-budget amounts were added to the on-budget amounts in order to show total Federal spending.

The Balanced Budget and Emergency Deficit Control Act of 1985 (Public Law 99–177) repealed the off-budget status of all then existing off-budget entities, but it included a provision immediately moving the Federal old-age, survivors, and disability insurance funds (collectively known as social security) off-budget. To provide a consistent time series, the budget historical data show social security off-budget for all years since its inception, and show all formerly off-budget entities on-budget for all years. Subsequent law (OBRA 1989) moved the Postal Service fund off-budget, starting in fiscal year 1989. Prior to that year, the Postal Service fund is shown on-budget.

Though social security and the Postal Service are now off-budget, they continue to be Federal programs. Indeed, social security currently accounts for around one-third of all Federal receipts and one-quarter of all Federal spending. Hence, the budget documents include these funds and focus on the Federal totals that combine the on-budget and off-budget amounts. Various budget tables and charts show total Federal receipts, outlays, and surpluses and deficits, and divide these totals between the portions that are off-budget and the remainder of Federal transactions, all of which are on-budget.

Changes in Historical Outlays and Deficit

The outlay, receipt and deficit totals for 1992 have changed from those published in the Mid-Session Review of the 1994 budget. Receipts are lower by $9 million, outlays are lower by $48 million, and the deficit is lower by $39 million. These changes correct errors of various agencies in reporting actual spending to the Treasury Department.

NOTE ON THE FISCAL YEAR

The Federal fiscal year begins on October 1 and ends on the subsequent September 30. It is designated by the year in which it ends; for example, fiscal year 1993 began October 1, 1992 and ended on September 30, 1993. Prior to fiscal year 1977 the Federal fiscal years began on July 1 and ended on June 30. In calendar year 1976 the July–September period was a separate accounting period (known as the transition quarter or TQ) to bridge the period required to shift to the new fiscal years.

Concepts Relevant to the Historical Tables

Budget (or "on-budget") receipts constitute the income side of the budget; they are composed almost entirely of taxes or other compulsory payments to the Government. Any income from business-type activities (e.g., interest income or sale of electric power), and any income by Government accounts arising from payments by other Government accounts is offset in computing *budget outlays* (spending). This method of accounting permits users to easily identify the size and trends in Federal taxes and other compulsory income, and in Federal spending financed from taxes, other compulsory income, or borrowing. *Budget surplus* refers to any excess of budget receipts over budget outlays, while *budget deficit* refers to any excess of budget outlays over budget receipts.

The terms *off-budget receipts, off-budget outlays, off-budget surpluses*, and *off-budget deficits* refer to similar categories for off-budget activities. The sum of the on-budget and off-budget transactions constitute the consolidated or total Federal Government transactions.

The budget is divided between two fund groups, federal funds and trust funds. The Federal funds grouping includes all receipts and outlays not specified by law as being trust funds. All Federal funds are on-budget except for the Postal Service fund starting with fiscal year 1989. All trust funds are on-budget, except that, as explained in the general notes above, the two social security retirement trust funds are shown off-budget for all years.

The term *trust fund* as used in Federal budget accounting is frequently misunderstood. In the private sector, "trust" refers to funds of one party held by a second party (the trustee) in a fiduciary capacity. In the Federal budget, the term "trust fund" means only the law requires that the funds must be accounted for separately and used only for specified purposes and that the account in which the funds are deposited is designated as being a "trust fund." A change in law may change the future receipts and the terms under which the fund's resources are spent. The determining factor as to whether a particular fund is designated as a "Federal" fund or "trust" fund is the law governing the fund.

The largest trust funds are for retirement and social insurance (e.g., civil service and military retirement, social security, medicare, and unemployment benefits). They are financed largely by social insurance taxes and contributions and payments from the general fund (the main component of Federal funds). However, there are also major trust funds for transportation (highway and airport and airways) and for other programs that are financed in whole or in part by *user charges*.

The budget documents do not separately show user charges. Frequently there is confusion between the concept of user charges and the concept of offsetting collections. User charges are charges for services rendered. Such charges may take the form of taxes (budget receipts), such as highway excise taxes used to finance the highway trust fund. They may also take the form of business-type charges, in which case they are off-setting collections—offset against budget outlays rather than being recorded as budget receipts. Examples of such charges are the proceeds from the sale of electric power by the Tennessee Valley Authority and medical insurance premiums paid to the supplementary medical insurance trust fund. User charges may go to the general fund of the Treasury or they may be "earmarked." If the funds are earmarked, it means the collections are separately identified and used for a specified purpose—they are not commingled (in an accounting sense) with any other money. This does not mean the money is actually kept in a separate bank account. All money in the Treasury is merged for efficient cash management. However, any earmarked funds are accounted for in such a way that the balances are always identifiable and available for the stipulated purposes.

U.S. BUDGET RECEIPTS AND OUTLAYS (millions of dollars)[1]

Source or type	Fiscal year		Calendar year						
			1992		1993		1994		
	1992	1993	H1	H2	H1	H2	Jan.	Feb.	Mar.
RECEIPTS									
1 **All sources**	**1,090,453**	**1,153,209**	**560,318**	**540,484**	**593,212**	**582,054[r]**	**122,966[r]**	**72,874[r]**	**93,108**
2 Individual income taxes, net	475,964	509,680	236,576	246,938	255,556	262,073	74,167	28,107	29,917
3 Withheld	408,352	430,427	198,868	215,584	209,745[r]	228,429	36,838	37,335	42,805
4 Presidential Election Campaign Fund	30	28	20	10	25	2	1	10	14
5 Nonwithheld	149,342	154,772	110,995	39,288	113,495[r]	41,765	37,798	1,151	4,434
6 Refunds	81,760	75,546	73,308	7,942	67,468	8,114	470	10,388	17,336
Corporation income taxes									
7 Gross receipts	117,951	131,548	61,682	58,022	69,044	68,266	4,761	2,888	17,234
8 Refunds	17,680	14,027	9,403	7,219	7,198	6,514	844	1,294	1,660
9 Social insurance taxes and contributions, net	413,689	428,300	224,569	192,599	227,177	206,174	36,983	35,989	36,957
10 Employment taxes and contributions[2]	385,491	396,939	208,110	180,758	208,776	192,749	35,831	32,957	35,976
11 Self-employment taxes and contributions[3]	24,421	20,604	20,434	3,988	16,270	4,335	−1,589	1,577	1,630
12 Unemployment insurance	23,410	26,556	14,070	9,397	16,074	11,010	794	2,664	522
13 Other net receipts[4]	4,788	4,805	2,389	2,445	2,326	2,417	358	367	459
14 Excise taxes	45,569	48,057	22,389	23,456	23,398	25,994	4,011	3,249	5,285
15 Customs deposits	17,359	18,802	8,146	9,497	8,860	10,215	1,526	1,419	1,745
16 Estate and gift taxes	11,143	12,577	5,701	5,733	6,494	6,617	1,105	1,093	1,211
17 Miscellaneous receipts[5]	26,459	18,273	10,658	11,458	9,879	9,227[r]	1,258[r]	1,424[r]	2,418
OUTLAYS									
18 **All types**	**1,380,794[r]**	**1,407,892**	**704,266**	**723,527**	**673,340**	**728,207[r]**	**107,718[r]**	**114,440[r]**	**125,423**
19 National defense	298,350	290,590	147,065	155,231	140,535	146,177	18,861	21,996	24,476
20 International affairs	16,107	17,175	8,540	9,916	6,565	10,534	1,103	948	696
21 General science, space, and technology	16,409	17,055	7,951	8,521	7,996	8,904	1,299	1,269	1,685
22 Energy	4,499	4,445	1,442	3,109	2,462	1,641	465	159	510
23 Natural resources and environment	20,025	20,088	8,594	11,467	8,592[r]	11,077	1,447	1,449	1,631
24 Agriculture	15,205	20,257	7,526	8,852	11,872[r]	7,335	1,122	1,817	1,439
25 Commerce and housing credit	10,118	−23,532	15,615	−7,697	−15,112	−1,724	−1,124	−4,608	−1,260
26 Transportation	33,333	35,238	15,651	18,425	16,077	20,375	2,503	2,784	2,845
27 Community and regional development	6,838	10,395	3,903	4,464	4,929[r]	5,606	906	445	1,276
28 Education, training, employment, and social services	45,250	48,857	23,767	21,241	24,088[r]	25,515	2,693	2,666	2,285
29 Health	89,497	99,249	44,164	47,232	49,882	52,631	7,665	8,229	10,014
30 Social security and Medicare	406,569	435,137	205,500	232,109	195,933	223,735	36,009	37,224	40,350
31 Income security	196,891	207,788	104,537	98,382	108,090[r]	103,163	16,196	22,466	20,549
32 Veterans benefits and services	34,133	35,715	15,597	18,561	16,385	19,848	2,151	3,135	2,793
33 Administration of justice	14,426	15,001	7,435	7,238	7,486[r]	7,448	1,210	1,105	1,760
34 General government	12,945	13,039	5,050	8,223	5,205	6,565	669	782	779
35 Net interest[6]	199,439	198,870	100,161	98,692	99,635	99,963	17,095	15,524	16,594
36 Undistributed offsetting receipts[7]	−39,280	−37,386	−18,229	−20,628	−17,035	−20,407	−2,914	−2,815	−2,999

1. Functional details do not sum to total outlays for calendar year data because revisions to monthly totals have not been distributed among functions. Fiscal year total for outlays does not correspond to calendar year data because revisions from the *Budget* have not been fully distributed across months.
2. Old-age, disability, and hospital insurance, and railroad retirement accounts.
3. Old-age, disability, and hospital insurance.
4. Federal employee retirement contributions and civil service retirement and disability fund.
5. Deposits of earnings by Federal Reserve Banks and other miscellaneous receipts.
6. Includes interest received by trust funds.
7. Consists of rents and royalties for the outer continental shelf and U.S. government contributions for employee retirement.

SOURCES. U.S. Department of the Treasury, *Monthly Treasury Statement of Receipts and Outlays of the U.S. Government*, and the U.S. Office of Management and Budget, *Budget of the U.S. Government, Fiscal Year 1994*.

Source: *Federal Reserve Bulletin*, Board of Governors of the Federal Reserve System.

FEDERAL DEBT SUBJECT TO STATUTORY LIMITATION

Billions of dollars, end of month

Item	1992				1993				1994
	Mar. 31	June 30	Sept. 30	Dec. 31	Mar. 31	June 30	Sept. 30	Dec. 31	Mar. 31
1 **Federal debt outstanding**	**3,897**	**4,001**	**4,083**	**4,196**	**4,250**	**4,373**	**4,436**	n.a.	**4,576**
2 Public debt securities	3,881	3,985	4,065	4,177	4,231	4,352	4,412	4,536	↑
3 Held by public	2,918	2,977	3,048	3,129	3,188	3,252	3,295	↑	↑
4 Held by agencies	964	1,008	1,016	1,048	1,043	1,100	1,117	↑	↑
5 Agency securities	16	16	18	19	20	21	25	n.a.	n.a.
6 Held by public	16	16	18	19	20	21	25	↓	↓
7 Held by agencies	0	0	0	0	0	0	0	↓	↓
8 **Debt subject to statutory limit**	**3,784**	**3,891**	**3,973**	**4,086**	**4,140**	**4,256**	**4,316**	**4,446**	**4,491**
9 Public debt securities	3,783	3,890	3,972	4,085	4,139	4,256	4,315	4,445	4,491
10 Other debt[1]	0	0	0	0	0	0	0	0	0
MEMO									
11 Statutory debt limit	4,145	4,145	4,145	4,145	4,145	4,370	4,900	4,900	4,900

1. Consists of guaranteed debt of U.S. Treasury and other federal agencies, specified participation certificates, notes to international lending organizations, and District of Columbia stadium bonds.

SOURCES. U.S. Department of the Treasury, *Monthly Statement of the Public Debt of the United States* and *Treasury Bulletin*.

Source: *Federal Reserve Bulletin,* Board of Governors of the Federal Reserve System.

Largest Companies

The 100 Largest U.S. Industrial Corporations (ranked by sales)

RANK 1993	1992	Company	SALES $millions	SALES % change from 1992	PROFITS $millions	PROFITS Rank	PROFITS % change from 1992	ASSETS $millions	ASSETS Rank	STOCKHOLDERS' EQUITY $millions	STOCKHOLDERS' EQUITY Rank
1	1	**GENERAL MOTORS** Detroit	133,621.9	4.0	2,465.8	6	—	188,200.9	3	5,597.5	28
2	3	**FORD MOTOR** Dearborn, Mich.	108,521.0	8.4	2,529.0	5	—	198,938.0	2	15,574.0	5
3	2	**EXXON** Irving, Texas	97,825.0[E]	(5.2)	5,280.0	1	10.7	84,145.0	4	34,792.0	1
4	4	**INTL. BUSINESS MACHINES** Armonk, N.Y.	62,716.0	(2.8)	(8,101.0)	485	—	81,113.0	5	19,738.0	3
5	5	**GENERAL ELECTRIC** Fairfield, Conn.	60,823.0	(0.9)	4,315.0[†]	2	(8.7)	251,506.0	1	25,824.0	2
6	6	**MOBIL** Fairfax, Va.	56,576.0[E]	(0.5)	2,084.0	10	141.8	40,585.0	8	16,474.0	4
7	7	**PHILIP MORRIS** New York	50,621.0[E]	1.1	3,091.0[†]	4	(37.4)	51,205.0	6	11,627.0	9
8	11	**CHRYSLER** Highland Park, Mich.	43,600.0	18.2	(2,551.0)[†]	484	(452.8)	43,830.0	7	6,836.0	20
9	10	**TEXACO** White Plains, N.Y.	34,359.0[E]	(6.7)	1,068.0	22	50.0	26,626.0	15	10,279.0	12
10	9	**E.I. DU PONT DE NEMOURS** Wilmington, Del.	32,621.0[E]	(2.0)	555.0	41	—	37,053.0	10	11,230.0	10
11	8	**CHEVRON** San Francisco	32,123.0[E]	(3.6)	1,265.0	18	(19.4)	34,736.0	11	13,997.0	7
12	13	**PROCTER & GAMBLE** Cincinnati[1]	30,433.0	1.8	(656.0)[†]	477	(135.0)	24,935.0	17	7,441.0	19
13	14	**AMOCO** Chicago	25,336.0[E]	0.2	1,820.0	12	—	28,486.0	13	13,665.0	8
14	12	**BOEING** Seattle	25,285.0	(16.1)	1,244.0	20	125.4	20,450.0	21	8,983.0	15
15	15	**PEPSICO** Purchase, N.Y.	25,020.7	13.9	1,587.9	14	324.2	23,705.8	20	6,338.7	23
16	17	**CONAGRA** Omaha[2]	21,519.1	1.4	270.3[†]	77	(27.4)	9,988.7	53	2,054.5	82
17	18	**SHELL OIL** Houston[3]	20,853.0	(1.5)	781.0	25	—	26,851.0	14	14,624.0	6
18	16	**UNITED TECHNOLOGIES** Hartford	20,736.0	(5.9)	487.0	46	—	15,618.0	31	3,598.0	46
19	24	**HEWLETT-PACKARD** Palo Alto[4]	20,317.0	23.8	1,177.0	21	114.4	16,736.0	28	8,511.0	16
20	19	**EASTMAN KODAK** Rochester, N.Y.	20,059.0[1]	(0.6)	(1,515.0)[†]	482	(232.2)	20,325.0	22	3,356.0	51
21	20	**DOW CHEMICAL** Midland, Mich.	18,060.0	(4.8)	644.0	35	—	25,505.0	16	8,034.0	17
22	22	**ATLANTIC RICHFIELD** Los Angeles	17,189.0[E]	(1.8)	269.0	78	(66.4)	23,894.0	18	6,127.0	26
23	32	**MOTOROLA** Schaumburg, Ill.	16,963.0	27.5	1,022.0	23	125.6	13,498.0	34	6,409.0	22
24	25	**USX** Pittsburgh	16,844.0[E]	4.1	(259.0)	456	—	17,320.0	26	3,864.0	44
25	26	**RJR NABISCO HOLDINGS** New York	15,104.0[E]	(4.0)	(145.0)[*]	441	(148.5)	31,295.0	12	9,621.0	14
26	21	**XEROX** Stamford, Conn.	14,981.0	(17.2)	(126.0)	437	—	38,750.0	9	5,241.0	30
27	33	**SARA LEE** Chicago[1]	14,580.0	10.1	704.0	29	(7.5)	10,862.0	47	3,551.0	48
28	23	**MCDONNELL DOUGLAS** St. Louis	14,487.0	(17.3)	396.0	60	—	12,026.0	39	3,413.0	50
29	27	**DIGITAL EQUIPMENT** Maynard, Mass.[1]	14,371.4	3.2	(251.3)	453	—	10,950.3	44	4,885.4	31
30	29	**JOHNSON & JOHNSON** New Brunswick, N.J.	14,138.0	2.8	1,787.0	13	73.5	12,242.0	36	5,568.0	29
31	28	**MINNESOTA MINING & MFG.** St. Paul	14,020.0	1.0	1,263.0	19	2.4	12,197.0	37	6,512.0	21
32	34	**COCA-COLA** Atlanta	13,957.0	6.8	2,176.0	8	30.8	12,021.0	40	4,584.0	33
33	31	**INTERNATIONAL PAPER** Purchase, N.Y.	13,685.0	0.6	289.0	72	236.0	16,631.0	29	6,225.0	25
34	30	**TENNECO** Houston	13,255.0	0.1	426.0	52	—	15,373.0	32	2,601.0	65
35	45	**LOCKHEED** Calabasas, Calif.	13,071.0	29.4	422.0	53	—	8,961.0	59	2,443.0	68
36	39	**GEORGIA-PACIFIC** Atlanta	12,330.0	4.1	(34.0)[*]	396	—	10,545.0	50	2,402.0	69
37	37	**PHILLIPS PETROLEUM** Bartlesville, Okla.	12,309.0	3.2	243.0	82	35.0	10,868.0	46	3,033.0	54
38	36	**ALLIEDSIGNAL** Morris Township, N.J.	11,827.0	(1.8)	411.0[†]	54	—	10,829.0	48	2,390.0	70
39	42	**IBP** Dakota City, Neb.	11,671.4	4.9	90.1[‡]	169	41.6	1,538.9	247	612.8	232
40	38	**GOODYEAR TIRE** Akron	11,643.4	(1.2)	387.8[†]	62	—	8,436.1	63	2,300.8	73
41	44	**CATERPILLAR** Peoria, Ill.	11,615.0	13.9	652.0	34	—	14,807.0	33	2,199.0	77
42	35	**WESTINGHOUSE ELECTRIC** Pittsburgh	11,564.0[1]	(4.2)	(326.0)[†]	467	—	10,553.0	49	1,045.0	161
43	41	**ANHEUSER-BUSCH** St. Louis	11,505.3[E]	1.0	594.5	36	(35.2)	10,880.3	45	4,255.5	38
44	40	**BRISTOL-MYERS SQUIBB** New York	11,413.0	(2.7)	1,959.0	11	(0.2)	12,101.0	38	5,940.0	27
45	43	**ROCKWELL INTERNATIONAL** Seal Beach, Calif.[5]	10,840.0	(1.4)	561.9	40	—	9,885.1	54	2,956.0	57
46	47	**MERCK** Whitehouse Station, N.J.	10,498.2	8.6	2,166.2	9	9.2	19,927.5	23	10,021.7	13
47	46	**COASTAL** Houston	10,136.1	0.7	115.1	147	—	10,227.0	52	2,278.1	74
48	50	**ARCHER DANIELS MIDLAND** Decatur, Ill.[1]	9,811.4	6.3	567.5	38	12.7	8,404.1	64	4,883.3	32
49	48	**ASHLAND OIL** Russell, Ky.[5]	9,553.9[E]	—	142.2	121	—	5,551.8	91	1,454.8	122
50	51	**WEYERHAEUSER** Federal Way, Wash.	9,544.8	3.5	579.3	37	55.7	12,638.5	35	3,966.1	39

The definitions, explanations, and footnotes underlying the figures in this directory are on pages 198–200.

MARKET VALUE 3/4/94 $ millions	Rank	PROFITS AS % OF ... SALES %	Rank	ASSETS %	Rank	STOCKHOLDERS' EQUITY %	Rank	EARNINGS PER SHARE 1993 $	% change from 1992	1983–93 annual growth rate %	Rank	TOTAL RETURN TO INVESTORS 1993 %	Rank	1983–93 annual rate %	Rank	Industry table number	RANK 1993
44,556.5	5	1.8	296	1.3	326	44.1	9	2.13	—	(9.7)	238	73.2	27	10.4	224	17	1
32,543.8	9	2.3	272	1.3	330	16.2	114	4.55	—	2.9	179	55.0	48	22.3	46	17	2
81,040.5	2	5.4	152	6.3	145	15.0	140	4.21	11.1	3.8	173	7.9	239	19.2	77	18	3
30,595.4	11	(12.9)	461	(10.0)	451	(41.0)	434	(14.22)	—	—		15.6	183	(3.7)	340	6	4
89,526.6	1	7.1	87	1.7	314	16.7	107	5.05	(8.3)	8.5	107	26.0	131	17.2	105	7	5
31,554.8	10	3.7	204	5.1	187	12.7	181	5.07	152.2	3.2	177	31.0	118	16.9	107	18	6
48,130.4	4	6.1	114	6.0	152	26.6	30	3.52	(35.4)	14.7	57	(24.2)	400	24.6	33	8	7
21,046.8	22	(5.9)	431	(5.8)	427	(37.3)	429	(7.62)	(444.8)	—		68.7	35	20.2	64	17	8
17,095.3	27	3.1	233	4.0	226	10.4	224	3.74	57.8	(2.5)	211	13.8	194	14.3	155	18	9
35,657.5	8	1.7	303	1.5	322	4.9	307	0.81	—	(6.4)	226	6.1	256	15.5	129	5	10
28,746.5	15	3.9	193	3.6	239	9.0	254	3.89	(16.0)	(1.8)	207	30.6	120	15.5	130	18	11
38,845.5	7	(2.2)	398	(2.6)	404	(8.8)	392	(1.11)	(142.4)	—		8.8	229	18.6	86	23	12
26,123.1	17	7.2	85	6.4	142	13.3	168	3.66	—	1.4	186	12.8	200	12.9	180	18	13
16,029.0	28	4.9	166	6.1	150	13.8	157	3.66	125.9	12.9	72	10.7	219	15.6	126	1	14
30,353.7	12	6.3	103	6.7	135	25.1	35	1.96	326.1	19.3	23	(0.1)	299	28.0	16	3	15
6,696.0	67	1.3	324	2.7	277	12.0	192	1.06	(29.3)	10.7	91	(18.4)	386	20.6	59	8	16
N.A.		3.7	198	2.9	269	5.3	305	N.A.	—	—		—		—		18	17
8,523.9	52	2.3	270	3.1	259	13.5	164	3.53	—	(1.2)	199	33.1	105	9.2	241	1	18
22,525.2	19	5.8	128	7.0	119	13.8	158	4.65	113.3	10.7	92	14.5	187	7.3	268	6	19
14,751.5	31	(7.6)	442	(7.5)	437	(45.1)	439	(4.62)	(230.9)	—		44.5	68	10.0	229	22	20
17,704.3	25	3.6	211	2.5	284	7.9	267	2.33	—	7.4	124	3.8	273	14.6	149	5	21
15,915.4	29	1.6	308	1.1	337	4.4	316	1.66	(66.5)	(12.1)	243	(3.7)	320	15.3	132	18	22
29,183.4	13	6.0	121	7.6	107	15.9	119	3.56	318.8	13.1	71	77.5	24	16.6	109	7	23
N.A.		(1.5)	393	(1.5)	386	(6.7)	387	N.A.	—	—		—		—		18	24
7,823.8	59	(1.0)	383	(0.5)	378	(2.2)	369	(0.15)	(175.0)	—		(26.1)	402	—		25	25
10,151.9	40	(0.8)	381	(0.3)	376	(2.4)	370	(1.84)	—	—		17.2	173	11.9	199	22	26
10,348.8	39	4.8	168	6.5	140	19.8	68	1.40	(9.1)	14.6	59	(14.8)	373	26.3	23	8	27
4,655.4	97	2.7	250	3.3	252	11.6	207	10.10	—	3.9	171	126.7	8	9.6	235	1	28
4,257.3	108	(1.7)	394	(2.3)	398	(5.1)	380	(1.93)	—	—		1.5	281	(0.5)	333	6	29
25,558.5	18	12.6	26	14.6	23	32.1	20	2.74	75.6	15.6	47	(9.0)	347	18.6	85	19	30
22,171.8	20	9.0	56	10.4	51	19.4	71	5.82	3.4	7.5	123	11.4	213	14.1	157	22	31
54,006.5	3	15.6	20	18.1	13	47.5	7	1.67	32.5	17.2	36	8.3	233	29.4	12	3	32
8,905.3	47	2.1	282	1.7	312	4.6	314	2.34	229.6	0.2	192	4.4	270	12.2	190	9	33
9,572.7	45	3.2	230	2.8	276	15.8	123	2.44	—	(6.4)	227	33.8	99	8.9	247	11	34
4,153.9	111	3.2	229	4.7	204	17.3	93	6.70	—	4.8	161	24.9	136	9.0	245	1	35
6,420.4	71	(0.3)	374	(0.3)	375	(1.4)	365	(0.39)	—	—		13.0	196	14.1	156	9	36
7,060.0	63	2.0	290	2.2	294	8.0	266	0.93	34.8	(5.1)	223	19.8	159	16.2	119	18	37
10,962.3	38	3.5	218	3.8	233	17.2	95	1.45	—	42.1	4	32.7	107	13.5	170	1	38
1,157.6	271	0.8	341	5.9	158	14.7	144	1.88	40.3	—		29.8	121	—		8	39
6,622.7	69	3.3	225	4.6	210	16.9	102	2.64	—	5.6	153	35.7	94	15.7	125	21	40
11,421.3	35	5.6	139	4.4	216	29.6	26	6.43	—	—		67.4	36	8.3	253	11	41
5,106.5	84	(2.8)	407	(3.1)	408	(31.2)	424	(1.07)	—	—		8.6	231	4.2	293	7	42
13,116.4	34	5.2	161	5.5	173	14.0	156	2.17	(32.6)	7.2	132	(13.7)	370	19.4	75	3	43
27,706.9	16	17.2	15	16.2	16	33.0	18	3.80	0.3	9.7	99	(9.4)	350	14.7	146	19	44
9,179.8	46	5.2	159	5.7	163	19.0	75	2.55	—	15.0	54	31.9	113	12.0	198	7	45
38,870.9	6	20.6	10	10.9	46	21.6	53	1.87	8.7	18.6	29	(18.4)	387	24.2	35	19	46
3,363.5	130	1.1	330	1.1	338	4.9	312	1.00	—	(1.7)	205	20.2	156	12.6	183	18	47
8,333.4	55	5.8	130	6.8	131	11.6	206	1.66	13.0	16.9	37	(9.5)	351	15.9	123	8	48
2,540.2	170	1.5	312	2.6	283	9.6	243	2.26	—	6.3	147	33.8	100	13.1	176	18	49
9,767.4	43	6.1	117	4.6	211	14.6	146	2.83	54.6	12.1	79	24.5	140	11.5	205	9	50

(continued)

The 100 Largest U.S. Industrial Corporations (ranked by sales) *(concluded)*

RANK 1993	1992	Company	SALES $ millions	SALES % change from 1992	PROFITS $ millions	PROFITS Rank	PROFITS % change from 1992	ASSETS $ millions	ASSETS Rank	STOCKHOLDERS' EQUITY $ millions	STOCKHOLDERS' EQUITY Rank
51	93	**MARTIN MARIETTA** Bethesda, Md.	9,435.7	58.5	20.9	311	(94.0)	7,744.9	68	2,876.4	59
52	54	**RAYTHEON** Lexington, Mass.	9,201.2	1.6	693.0	30	9.1	7,257.7	72	4,297.9	36
53	53	**CITGO PETROLEUM** Tulsa[6]	9,107.4 E	(0.6)	162.1	112	388.7	3,866.3	124	1,349.6	132
54	49	**ALCOA** Pittsburgh	9,055.9	(4.6)	4.8	361	—	11,596.9	41	3,583.8	47
55	61	**BAXTER INTERNATIONAL** Deerfield, Ill.	8,879.0	4.8	(198.0)‡	447	(144.9)	10,545.0	50	3,185.0	52
56	91	**INTEL** Santa Clara, Calif.	8,782.0	50.3	2,295.0	7	115.2	11,344.0	43	7,500.0	18
57	63	**TEXTRON** Providence	8,668.5	8.6	379.1	64	—	19,658.4	24	2,780.2	61
58	71	**TEXAS INSTRUMENTS** Dallas	8,523.0	14.6	472.0	48	91.1	5,993.0	83	2,315.0	72
59	66	**ABBOTT LABORATORIES** Abbott Park, Ill.	8,407.8	7.1	1,399.1	16	12.9	7,688.6	69	3,674.9	45
60	67	**AMERICAN HOME PRODUCTS** Madison, N.J.	8,304.9	5.5	1,469.3	15	0.6	7,687.4	70	3,876.5	42
61	57	**AMERICAN BRANDS** Old Greenwich, Conn.	8,287.5 E	(6.3)	469.8†	49	(46.8)	16,339.0	30	4,271.4	37
62	70	**EMERSON ELECTRIC** St. Louis[5]	8,173.8	6.1	708.1	28	6.8	7,814.5	67	3,915.1	41
63	68	**GENERAL MILLS** Minneapolis[2]	8,134.6	4.6	506.1	43	2.1	4,650.8	109	1,218.5	144
64	56	**OCCIDENTAL PETROLEUM** Los Angeles	8,116.0	(4.5)	283.0	75	—	17,123.0	27	3,958.0	40
65	65	**HANSON INDUSTRIES NA** New York[3,7]	8,111.5	(1.0)	758.6	26	37.7	23,713.7	19	6,251.6	24
66	55	**UNOCAL** Los Angeles	8,077.0	(9.7)	213.0†	85	(3.2)	9,254.0	57	3,129.0	53
67	76	**APPLE COMPUTER** Cupertino, Calif.[5]	7,977.0	12.6	86.6	173	(83.7)	5,171.4	96	2,026.4	83
68	64	**TRW** Cleveland	7,947.9	(4.4)	195.4	95	—	5,336.0	92	1,534.0	113
69	69	**RALSTON PURINA** St. Louis[5]	7,902.2	1.9	122.6†	141	(60.9)	5,071.9	98	469.8	282
70	60	**MONSANTO** St. Louis	7,902.0	(6.4)	494.0	44	—	8,640.0	62	2,855.0	60
71	62	**UNISYS** Blue Bell, Pa.	7,742.5	(8.1)	565.4‡	39	56.5	7,519.2	71	2,695.5	62
72	79	**DEERE** Moline, Ill.[4]	7,693.8	11.0	(920.9)†	478	(2,560.5)	11,351.9	42	2,085.4	80
73	73	**WHIRLPOOL** Benton Harbor, Mich.	7,533.0	3.2	51.0*†	227	(75.1)	6,047.0	82	1,648.0	103
74	72	**PFIZER** New York	7,477.7	3.4	657.5	33	(18.9)	9,330.9	56	3,865.5	43
75	59	**SUN** Philadelphia	7,297.0 E	(15.4)	288.0	74	—	5,900.0	84	1,984.0	86
76	119	**COMPAQ COMPUTER** Houston	7,191.0	75.4	462.0	50	116.7	4,084.0	120	2,654.0	63
77	78	**COLGATE-PALMOLIVE** New York	7,141.3	1.9	189.9†	97	(60.2)	5,761.2	88	1,875.0	90
78	80	**H.J. HEINZ** Pittsburgh[8]	7,103.4	7.9	396.3†	59	(37.9)	6,821.3	75	2,321.0	71
79	75	**KIMBERLY-CLARK** Irving, Texas	6,972.9	(1.7)	510.9	42	278.4	6,380.7	79	2,457.2	67
80	77	**HOECHST CELANESE** North Somerville, N.J.[9]	6,899.0	(2.1)	101.0†	158	—	7,917.0	66	3,482.0	49
81	81	**CPC INTERNATIONAL** Englewood Cliffs, N.J.	6,738.0	2.1	454.5	51	103.1	5,060.8	99	1,769.1	97
82	74	**BORDEN** Columbus, Ohio	6,700.0	(6.2)	(630.7)	475	—	N.A.	498	N.A.	471
83	85	**CAMPBELL SOUP** Camden, N.J.[10]	6,586.2	5.2	8.2†	352	(98.3)	4,897.5	102	1,704.0	99
84	82	**MILES** Pittsburgh[11]	6,586.0	1.3	131.7†	129	88.7	5,242.3	94	2,268.8	75
85	84	**ELI LILLY** Indianapolis	6,452.4	4.6	480.2	47	(32.2)	9,623.6	55	4,568.8	34
86	87	**KELLOGG** Battle Creek, Mich.	6,295.4	1.7	680.7	32	57.9	4,237.1	117	1,713.4	98
87	89	**COOPER INDUSTRIES** Houston	6,273.8	2.3	367.1	65	—	7,147.8	73	2,984.6	56
88	105	**JOHNSON CONTROLS** Milwaukee[5]	6,181.7	19.9	15.9†	327	(87.1)	3,230.8	144	1,079.0	157
89	86	**HONEYWELL** Minneapolis	5,963.0	(4.2)	322.2	69	30.6	4,598.1	112	1,773.0	96
90	99	**LEVI STRAUSS ASSOCIATES** San Francisco[12]	5,892.5	5.8	492.4	45	36.5	3,108.7	152	1,251.0	141
91	92	**AMERADA HESS** New York	5,851.6 E	(0.4)	(268.2)‡	458	(3,654.7)	8,641.5	61	3,028.9	55
92	97	**WARNER-LAMBERT** Morris Plains, N.J.	5,793.7	3.5	331.0‡	68	(48.6)	4,828.0	104	1,389.6	126
93	94	**PPG INDUSTRIES** Pittsburgh	5,753.9	(1.0)	22.2†	303	(93.0)	5,651.5	89	2,473.1	66
94	83	**W.R. GRACE** Boca Raton, Fla.	5,736.6¶	(9.4)	26.0	295	—	6,108.6	80	1,517.6	114
95	98	**QUAKER OATS** Chicago[1]	5,730.6	2.8	167.1†	107	(32.5)	2,815.9	161	551.1	250
96	95	**LITTON INDUSTRIES** Beverly Hills[10]	5,480.2¶	(3.7)	65.2†	208	(62.6)	3,834.4	125	1,663.7	102
97	106	**COCA-COLA ENTERPRISES** Atlanta	5,465.0	6.6	(15.0)	382	—	8,682.0	60	1,260.0	136
98	108	**DANA** Toledo	5,460.1	12.1	79.6†	187	—	4,631.9	110	801.4	194
99	104	**GILLETTE** Boston	5,410.8	4.8	288.3†	73	(43.8)	5,102.3	97	1,479.0	119
100	103	**AMERICAN CYANAMID** Wayne, N.J.	5,305.6	0.7	(1,118.5)†	480	(383.1)	6,057.4	81	1,367.0	128

E Excise taxes equal to 5% or more of total sales have been deducted.
F FORTUNE estimate.
* Reflects an extraordinary charge of at least 10%.
** Reflects an extraordinary credit of at least 10%.
† Reflects a net SFAS 106, 109, and/or 112 charge of at least 10%.
‡ Reflects a net SFAS 106, 109, and/or 112 credit of at least 10%.
¶ Includes sales of discontinued operations of at least 10%.
1 Figures are for fiscal year ended June 30, 1993.
2 Figures are for fiscal year ended May 31, 1993.
3 Owned by Royal Dutch/Shell Group (1992 Global 500 rank: 4).
4 Figures are for fiscal year ended October 31, 1993.

MARKET VALUE 3/4/94 $millions	Rank	PROFITS AS % OF ... SALES %	Rank	ASSETS %	Rank	STOCKHOLDERS' EQUITY %	Rank	EARNINGS PER SHARE 1993 $	% change from 1992	1983–93 annual growth rate %	Rank	TOTAL RETURN TO INVESTORS 1993 %	Rank	1983–93 annual rate %	Rank	Industry table number	RANK 1993
4,282.4	105	0.2	362	0.3	361	0.7	352	(0.26)	(107.2)	—		30.8	119	17.2	104	1	51
8,586.1	51	7.5	74	9.5	62	16.1	115	5.11	8.3	11.2	85	31.9	112	15.2	135	7	52
N.A.		1.8	299	4.2	224	12.0	191	N.A.	—	—		—		—		18	53
6,671.4	68	0.1	368	—	370	0.1	360	0.03	—	(34.8)	262	(1.0)	306	7.8	263	15	54
6,221.6	72	(2.2)	399	(1.9)	391	(6.2)	382	(0.72)	(146.2)	—		(23.2)	396	3.9	299	22	55
29,103.3	14	26.1	7	20.2	10	30.6	22	5.20	109.3	31.0	12	43.0	71	16.1	120	7	56
5,083.7	85	4.4	177	1.9	306	13.6	163	4.21	—	13.4	68	33.3	104	17.9	94	1	57
7,693.2	60	5.5	145	7.9	96	20.4	65	5.03	101.2	—		37.8	87	5.1	290	7	58
21,862.6	21	16.6	18	18.2	12	38.1	15	1.69	15.0	16.8	39	(0.0)	298	20.6	58	19	59
18,425.6	23	17.7	14	19.1	11	37.9	16	4.73	1.7	9.0	104	0.3	292	14.8	142	19	60
6,430.6	70	5.7	136	2.9	272	11.0	215	2.32	(45.9)	3.2	176	(13.0)	365	13.7	168	25	61
14,337.0	32	8.7	60	9.1	69	18.1	87	3.15	6.4	8.4	111	12.3	204	14.1	158	7	62
8,764.9	49	6.2	108	10.9	45	41.5	11	3.10	3.7	9.8	98	(8.8)	346	21.8	48	8	63
5,348.1	80	3.5	217	1.7	317	7.2	277	0.80	—	(8.9)	236	5.2	264	4.2	294	5	64
N.A.		9.4	53	3.2	256	12.1	190	N.A.	—	—		—		—		16	65
6,696.7	66	2.6	256	2.3	290	6.8	284	0.73	(14.1)	(8.6)	234	12.2	206	9.1	243	18	66
4,281.2	106	1.1	331	1.7	316	4.3	318	0.73	(83.1)	1.3	187	(50.4)	422	9.9	231	6	67
4,663.3	96	2.5	264	3.7	238	12.7	178	3.01	—	0.9	189	24.0	142	9.6	236	17	68
N.A.		1.6	310	2.4	287	21.6	52	N.A.	—	—		—		—		8	69
8,669.2	50	6.3	105	5.7	161	17.3	92	4.10	—	5.3	157	32.2	111	15.2	137	5	70
2,343.0	178	7.3	81	7.5	108	21.0	59	2.69	84.2	5.8	152	24.7	139	0.0	327	6	71
7,447.6	61	(12.0)	457	(8.1)	439	(44.2)	437	(11.91)	(2,530.6)	—		74.9	26	9.9	230	11	72
4,986.8	87	0.7	345	0.8	343	3.1	329	0.67	(76.9)	(11.6)	242	52.1	53	14.6	150	7	73
17,411.7	26	8.8	58	7.0	117	17.0	98	2.05	(14.9)	4.2	168	(2.3)	313	17.9	93	19	74
3,703.0	122	3.9	192	4.9	197	14.5	147	2.70	—	(3.5)	215	11.9	209	7.9	261	18	75
8,339.9	54	6.4	100	11.3	41	17.4	91	5.45	111.2	46.5	2	51.5	56	28.0	15	6	76
9,589.7	44	2.7	255	3.3	251	10.1	233	1.08	(63.0)	(1.1)	198	14.7	186	23.3	39	23	77
8,171.2	56	5.6	142	5.8	159	17.1	97	1.53	(36.3)	7.4	127	(16.0)	378	17.6	99	8	78
8,812.0	48	7.3	80	8.0	92	20.8	61	3.18	278.6	11.7	82	(9.2)	348	20.3	62	9	79
N.A.		1.5	314	1.3	329	2.9	331	N.A.	—	—		—		—		5	80
7,228.7	62	6.7	91	9.0	71	25.1	34	2.95	109.2	15.4	49	(3.2)	316	21.4	51	8	81
2,098.1	190	(9.4)	446	—		—		(4.47)	—	—		(38.0)	417	9.7	234	8	82
10,044.0	42	0.1	367	0.2	365	0.5	356	0.03	(98.5)	(26.4)	260	(0.2)	303	21.3	52	8	83
N.A.		2.0	289	2.5	285	5.8	299	N.A.	—	—		—		--		5	84
15,808.4	30	7.4	77	5.0	194	10.5	222	1.63	(32.4)	0.6	190	2.4	279	18.8	82	19	85
11,343.5	37	10.8	39	16.1	17	39.7	13	2.94	62.4	14.0	62	(13.3)	367	24.8	32	8	86
4,353.1	103	5.9	124	5.1	186	12.3	188	2.75	—	15.6	48	6.7	250	14.7	145	7	87
2,391.2	176	0.3	360	0.5	353	0.6	354	0.17	(94.1)	(22.2)	256	21.7	147	12.1	195	22	88
4,440.1	100	5.4	151	7.0	121	18.2	86	2.40	34.8	14.3	60	5.7	260	11.3	209	22	89
N.A.		8.4	65	15.8	18	39.4	14	N.A.	—	—		—		—		2	90
4,363.2	102	(4.6)	420	(3.1)	409	(8.9)	393	(2.90)	(3,322.2)	—		(1.0)	307	6.6	279	18	91
8,467.6	53	5.7	133	6.9	126	23.8	38	2.45	(48.7)	6.9	139	1.0	286	20.0	68	19	92
8,066.5	57	0.4	356	0.4	356	0.9	350	0.21	(93.0)	(18.7)	251	18.7	166	19.8	71	5	93
4,035.3	116	0.5	354	0.4	354	1.7	342	0.28	—	(16.2)	250	4.6	269	11.4	208	5	94
4,273.6	107	2.9	242	5.9	154	30.3	25	2.34	(28.0)	13.5	67	12.5	201	21.0	53	8	95
3,085.9	141	1.2	326	1.7	315	3.9	322	1.56	(63.0)	(5.4)	224	43.7	70	6.7	277	7	96
2,244.5	183	(0.3)	373	(0.2)	373	(1.2)	364	(0.11)	—	—		24.9	135	—		3	97
2,755.2	159	1.5	315	1.7	313	9.9	239	1.72	—	(1.7)	204	31.4	115	12.6	184	17	98
13,778.0	33	5.3	153	5.7	165	19.2	73	1.29	(44.4)	8.0	117	6.4	255	29.4	10	14	99
4,031.3	117	(21.1)	471	(18.5)	467	(81.8)	448	(12.44)	(386.0)	—		(9.9)	355	10.3	226	19	100

[5] Figures are for fiscal year ended September 30, 1993.
[6] Owned by PDVSA (1992 Global 500 rank: 56).
[7] Owned by Hanson (1992 Global 500 rank: 105).
[8] Figures are for fiscal year ended April 30, 1993.
[9] Owned by Hoechst (1992 Global 500 rank: 37).
[10] Figures are for fiscal year ended July 31, 1993.
[11] Owned by Bayer AG (1992 Global 500 rank: 43).
[12] Figures are for fiscal year ended November 30, 1993.

DEFINITIONS AND EXPLANATIONS

Sales All companies on the list must derive more than 50% of their sales from manufacturing and/or mining and must publish financial data. Sales include operating revenues but in most cases do not include income from dividends, interest, royalties, etc. Sales of consolidated subsidiaries are included. So are sales from discontinued operations if these figures are published. If the sales are at least 10% higher for this reason, there is a symbol (¶) next to the sales figure. All figures are for the year ending December 31, 1993, unless otherwise noted. Sales figures do not include excise taxes collected by the manufacturer, so the numbers for some corporations—most of which sell gasoline, liquor, or tobacco—may be lower than those published by the corporations themselves. If they are at least 5% lower for this reason, there is a letter E next to the sales figures.

Profits are shown after taxes and after extraordinary credits or charges if any appear on the income statement, and after cumulative effects of accounting charges. An asterisk (*) signifies an extraordinary charge amounting to at least 10% of the profits shown; a double asterisk (**), an extraordinary credit of at least 10%. A single dagger (†) signifies a net SFAS 106, 109, and/or 112 charge amounting to at least 10% of the profits shown; a double dagger (‡) a net SFAS 106, 109, and/or 112 credit amounting to at least 10%. Figures in parentheses indicate a loss. Profit declines over 100% reflect swings from 1992 profits to 1993 losses. Cooperatives provide only 'net margin' figures, which are not comparable with the profits figures in these listings, and therefore N.A. is shown in that column.

Assets are those shown at the company's year-end total.

Stockholders' Equity is the sum of all capital stock, paid in capital, and retained earnings at the company's, year-end. Preferred stock capital that is technically construed to be debt has been excluded. Redeemable preferred stock whose redemption is either mandatory or outside the control of the company is therefore excluded. For purposes of calculating profits as percent of common stockholders' equity, all preferred stock is excluded. The dividends paid on such stock have been subtracted from the profit figures.

Market Value The figure shown was arrived at by multiplying the number of common shares outstanding by the price per common share as of March 4, 1994. Shares traded on a when-issued basis are excluded.

Earnings per Share The figures shown for each company are the primary earnings per share that appear on the income statement. Per share earnings for 1992 and 1983 are adjusted for stock splits and stock dividends. They are not restated for mergers, acquisitions, or accounting changes. Nor are the earnings per share numbers marked by any footnotes to indicate extraordinary charges or credits. However, if a company's profits are footnoted to indicate an extraordinary charge or credit, it can be assumed that earnings per share are affected as well. Results are listed as not available (N.A.) if the companies are cooperatives, joint ventures, or wholly owned subsidiaries of other companies; if the figures were not published; or if the stock traded on a limited basis and was not widely held. The 1983–93 growth rate is the average annual growth, compounded.

Total Return to Investors includes both price appreciation and dividend yield to an investor in the company's stock. The figures shown assume sales at the end of 1983 and 1992. It has been assumed that any proceeds from cash dividends, the sale of rights and warrant offerings, and stock received in spinoffs were reinvested when they were paid. Returns are adjusted for stock splits, stock dividends, recapitalizations, and corporate reorganizations as they occur; however, no effort has been made to reflect the cost of brokerage commissions or of taxes. Results are listed as not available (N.A.) if shares are not publicly traded or are traded on only a limited basis. If companies have more than one class of shares outstanding, only the more widely held and actively traded has been considered. Total return percentages shown are the returns received by the hypothetical investor described above. The 1983–93 return is the annual rate, compounded.

The World's 100 Largest Industrial Corporations (ranked by sales)

RANK 1993	1992			SALES $millions	SALES % change from 1992	PROFITS $millions	PROFITS Rank	PROFITS % change from 1992	ASSETS $millions	ASSETS Rank	STOCKHOLDERS' EQUITY $millions	STOCKHOLDERS' EQUITY Rank	EMPLOYEES Number	EMPLOYEES Rank	Industry table number
1	1	GENERAL MOTORS	U.S.	133,621.9	4.0	2,465.8	7	—	188,200.9	3	5,597.5	85	710,800	1	17
2	3	FORD MOTOR	U.S.	108,521.0	8.4	2,529.0	6	—	198,938.0	2	15,574.0	11	322,200	7	17
3	2	EXXON	U.S.	97,825.0[E]	(5.2)	5,280.0	1	10.7	84,145.0	7	34,792.0	3	91,000	66	18
4	4	ROYAL DUTCH/SHELL GROUP	BRIT./NETH.	95,134.4[E]	(2.0)	4,505.2	2	(16.7)	99,664.6	4	51,505.6	1	117,000	43	18
5	5	TOYOTA MOTOR[1]	JAPAN	85,283.2	10.1	1,473.9	21	(18.7)	88,150.0	5	44,593.1	2	109,279	51	17
6	10	HITACHI[2]	JAPAN	68,581.8	13.6	605.0	69	(2.3)	87,217.7	6	28,898.1	6	330,637	6	7
7	7	INTL. BUSINESS MACHINES	U.S.	62,716.0	(2.8)	(8,101.0)	494	—	81,113.0	8	19,738.0	9	267,196	9	6
8	12	MATSUSHITA ELECTRIC INDUSTRIAL[2]	JAPAN	61,384.5	8.6	227.0	164	(26.2)	80,006.2	9	32,118.6	5	254,059	11	7
9	9	GENERAL ELECTRIC	U.S.	60,823.0	(0.9)	4,315.0†	3	(8.7)	251,506.0	1	25,824.0	7	222,000	14	7
10	8	DAIMLER-BENZ	GERMANY	59,102.0	(6.3)	364.0	119	(59.9)	52,271.3	11	10,108.7	35	366,736	4	17
11	13	MOBIL	U.S.	56,576.0[E]	(0.5)	2,084.0	11	141.8	40,585.0	27	16,474.0	10	61,900	102	18
12	16	NISSAN MOTOR[2]	JAPAN	53,759.8	8.3	(805.5)	481	—	71,564.0	10	15,427.7	12	143,310	30	17
13	11	BRITISH PETROLEUM	BRITAIN	52,485.4	(10.5)	923.6	41	—	45,828.9	19	14,403.1	13	72,600	86	18
14	18	SAMSUNG	SOUTH KOREA	51,345.2	3.6	519.7	82	38.9	50,492.4	15	7,273.2	55	191,303	18	7
15	17	PHILIP MORRIS	U.S.	50,621.0[E]	1.1	3,091.0†	5	(37.4)	51,205.0	14	11,627.0	22	173,000	21	8
16	6	IRI[G]	ITALY	50,488.1	(25.3)	N.A.		—	N.A.		N.A.		366,471	5	15
17	15	SIEMENS[3]	GERMANY	50,381.3	1.4	1,112.6	35	(2.0)	46,194.6	18	11,700.7	21	391,000	3	7
18	14	VOLKSWAGEN	GERMANY	46,311.9	(15.3)	(1,232.4)	489	(2,568.6)	45,586.7	20	6,474.8	66	251,643	12	17
19	28	CHRYSLER	U.S.	43,600.0	18.2	(2,551.0)†	493	(452.8)	43,830.0	24	6,836.0	60	128,000	38	17
20	25	TOSHIBA[2]	JAPAN	42,917.2	15.8	112.5	255	(31.7)	52,252.8	12	10,915.3	26	175,000	20	6
21	20	UNILEVER	BRITAIN/NETHERLANDS	41,842.6	(4.0)	1,946.2	15	(14.6)	24,735.5	49	6,948.9	58	302,000	8	8
22	23	NESTLÉ[4]	SWITZERLAND	38,894.5	0.4	1,953.3	14	1.9	30,233.9	40	10,524.2	28	209,755	15	8
23	22	ELF AQUITAINE	FRANCE	37,016.3	(2.3)	188.9	195	(83.8)	45,455.5	21	14,206.5	14	94,000	60	18
24	30	HONDA MOTOR[2]	JAPAN	35,797.9	8.1	219.6	171	(28.4)	28,526.2	41	9,446.7	40	91,300	65	17
25	21	ENI[G]	ITALY	34,791.3[E]	(13.8)	266.6	153	—	51,912.7	13	9,453.3	39	106,391	53	18
26	19	FIAT	ITALY	34,706.7	(27.6)	1,134.3	33	153.9	48,898.4	17	10,660.8	27	260,351	10	17
27	32	SONY[2]	JAPAN	34,602.5	8.2	141.8	224	(51.2)	41,698.1	26	12,984.0	17	130,000	35	7
28	27	TEXACO	U.S.	34,359.0[E]	(6.7)	1,068.0	37	50.0	26,626.0	44	10,279.0	31	32,514	215	18
29	40	NEC[2]	JAPAN	33,175.9	17.8	61.2	311	—	39,451.3	28	7,637.3	51	147,910	27	7
30	26	E.I. DU PONT DE NEMOURS	U.S.	32,621.0[E]	(2.0)	555.0	77	—	37,053.0	31	11,230.0	24	114,000	44	5
31	24	CHEVRON	U.S.	32,123.0[E]	(3.6)	1,265.0	24	(19.4)	34,736.0	35	13,997.0	15	47,576	139	18
32	31	PHILIPS ELECTRONICS	NETHERLANDS	31,665.5	(4.8)	1,057.8	38	—	23,769.5	52	5,879.7	80	238,500	13	7
33	41	DAEWOO	SOUTH KOREA	30,893.4	9.0	482.6	91	25.7	44,352.1	22	7,367.6	54	76,986	81	7
34	36	PROCTER & GAMBLE[1]	U.S.	30,433.0	1.8	(656.0)†	479	(135.0)	24,935.0	47	7,441.0	53	103,500	54	23
35	29	RENAULT[G,4]	FRANCE	29,974.8	(11.5)	189.1	194	(82.4)	35,920.1	33	5,723.4	83	139,733	31	17
36	42	FUJITSU[2]	JAPAN	29,093.9	4.9	(349.1)	469	—	35,104.9	34	10,331.1	30	163,990	24	6
37	44	MITSUBISHI ELECTRIC[2]	JAPAN	28,779.8	10.2	191.8	190	(16.0)	32,764.5	38	7,909.1	50	111,053	47	7
38	33	ABB ASEA BROWN BOVERI	SWITZERLAND	28,315.0	(7.3)	68.0	304	(86.5)	24,904.0	48	3,528.0	139	206,490	16	7
39	37	HOECHST	GERMANY	27,844.8	(5.2)	281.8	144	(52.4)	22,484.6	61	6,418.5	68	170,161	22	5
40	34	ALCATEL ALSTHOM	FRANCE	27,599.4	(9.6)	1,246.7	27	(6.4)	43,938.3	23	10,142.9	34	196,500	17	7
41	47	MITSUBISHI MOTORS[2]	JAPAN	27,310.9	7.2	51.8	323	(75.0)	23,582.3	54	3,989.1	118	46,000	148	17
42	57	PEMEX (PETRÓLEOS MEXICANOS)[G]	MEXICO	26,572.9	24.8	970.8	40	(9.3)	49,294.0	16	34,710.9	4	106,951	52	18
43	49	MITSUBISHI HEAVY INDUSTRIES[2]	JAPAN	25,804.0	14.0	740.1	48	13.9	39,229.4	29	10,929.1	25	68,057	94	11
44	38	PEUGEOT	FRANCE	25,669.1	(12.7)	(249.5)	458	(139.2)	21,393.8	62	8,537.3	42	143,700	29	17
45	48	NIPPON STEEL[2]	JAPAN	25,480.5	7.8	(501.3)	476	(3,534.1)	42,444.2	25	9,491.0	38	50,458[5]	128	15
46	46	AMOCO	U.S.	25,336.0[E]	0.2	1,820.0	16	—	28,486.0	42	13,665.0	16	46,317	147	18
47	35	BOEING	U.S.	25,285.0	(16.1)	1,244.0	28	125.4	20,450.0	67	8,983.0	41	134,400	34	1
48	51	PEPSICO	U.S.	25,020.7	13.9	1,587.9	19	324.2	23,705.8	53	6,338.7	70	423,000	2	3
49	43	BAYER	GERMANY	24,797.1	(6.0)	802.4	46	(17.3)	23,093.4	59	10,164.4	33	151,900	26	5
50	39	BASF	GERMANY	24,531.9[E]	(8.6)	518.7	83	31.8	23,200.9	58	8,499.2	44	112,020	45	5

The definitions and explanations underlying the figures in this directory are on page 203.

[E] Excise taxes have been deducted.
[G] Government owned.
* Reflects an extraordinary charge of at least 10%.
** Reflects an extraordinary credit of at least 10%.
† Reflects an SFAS 106, 109, and/or 112 charge of at least 10%.
‡ Reflects an SFAS 106, 109, and/or 112 credit of at least 10%.
¶ Includes sales of discontinued operations of at least 10%.
[1] Figures are for fiscal year ended June 30, 1993.
[2] Figures are for fiscal year ended March 31, 1994.
[3] Figures are for fiscal year ended September 30, 1993.

(continued)

The World's 100 Largest Industrial Corporations (ranked by sales) *(concluded)*

RANK 1993	1992	Company	Country	SALES $ millions	SALES % change from 1992	PROFITS $ millions	PROFITS Rank	PROFITS % change from 1992	ASSETS $ millions	ASSETS Rank	STOCKHOLDERS' EQUITY $ millions	STOCKHOLDERS' EQUITY Rank	EMPLOYEES Number	EMPLOYEES Rank	Industry table number
51	45	TOTAL[4]	FRANCE	23,917.4	(7.3)	523.4	81	(2.6)	22,592.3	60	8,352.6	45	49,772	134	18
52	58	CONAGRA[6]	U.S.	21,519.1	1.4	270.3†	151	(27.4)	9,988.7	171	2,054.5	236	83,975	74	8
53	56	PDVSA[G]	VENEZUELA	21,275.0	(0.5)	1,089.0	36	222.2	34,120.0	36	23,066.0	8	55,218	119	18
54	53	UNITED TECHNOLOGIES	U.S.	20,736.0	(5.9)	487.0	90	—	15,618.0	92	3,598.0	134	168,600	23	1
55	50	THYSSEN[3]	GERMANY	20,672.8	(8.6)	(585.1)	477	(381.5)	14,554.1	103	2,168.9	224	136,975	33	15
56	71	HEWLETT-PACKARD[7]	U.S.	20,317.0	23.8	1,177.0	31	114.4	16,736.0	82	8,511.0	43	96,200	58	6
57	59	MAZDA MOTOR[2]	JAPAN	20,279.3	(2.4)	(454.0)	474	(4,527.3)	14,841.8	98	3,526.4	140	33,000	210	17
58	61	EASTMAN KODAK	U.S.	20,059.0¶	(0.6)	(1,515.0)†	491	(232.2)	20,325.0	68	3,356.0	149	110,400	48	22
59	52	ROBERT BOSCH	GERMANY	19,634.2	(10.9)	257.6	154	(21.4)	14,628.9	101	4,773.8	103	156,615	25	17
60	62	NIPPON OIL[2]	JAPAN	19,585.0[E]	2.6	215.1	173	(13.5)	26,062.8	45	6,042.1	75	12,247	416	18
61	54	INI[G]	SPAIN	18,639.3	(13.9)	(1,052.5)	487	—	33,230.9	37	5,420.9	90	129,435	37	11
62	63	DOW CHEMICAL	U.S.	18,060.0	(4.8)	644.0	64	—	25,505.0	46	8,034.0	48	55,400	118	5
63	66	XEROX	U.S.	17,790.0	(1.7)	(126.0)	438	—	38,750.0	30	5,241.0	94	97,000	57	22
64	60	BMW (BAYERISCHE MOTOREN WERKE)	GER.	17,546.1	(12.2)	316.9	132	(31.8)	17,415.9	79	3,975.3	119	71,034	90	17
65	64	REPSOL	SPAIN	17,411.1	(6.5)	629.3	66	(10.3)	10,632.5	159	3,688.6	129	18,797	352	18
66	67	ATLANTIC RICHFIELD	U.S.	17,189.0[E]	(1.8)	269.0	152	(66.4)	23,894.0	51	6,127.0	73	25,100	285	18
67	103	MOTOROLA	U.S.	16,963.0	27.5	1,022.0	39	125.6	13,498.0	112	6,409.0	69	120,000	42	7
68	65	MANNESMANN	GERMANY	16,909.1	(5.7)	(207.8)	453	(258.9)	12,192.1	128	3,569.1	136	127,695	39	11
69	84	CANON	JAPAN	16,507.4	9.3	189.7	193	(33.0)	19,385.6	74	6,458.5	67	64,535	98	6
70	68	BRITISH AEROSPACE	BRITAIN	16,158.6	(8.2)	(321.4)	466	—	15,134.5	97	2,231.1	218	87,400	69	1
71	74	USX	U.S.	16,137.0[E]	(0.3)	(259.0)	461	—	17,374.0	80	3,864.0	126	44,605	154	18
72	73	METALLGESELLSCHAFT[3]	GERMANY	16,101.5	(0.4)	(1,249.7)	490	(4,929.1)	10,200.0	168	(224.9)	490	43,292	161	15
73	55	IMPERIAL CHEMICAL INDUSTRIES	BRITAIN	15,966.4	(25.0)	207.2	177	—	13,636.2	110	5,885.0	79	67,000	96	5
74	90	SUNKYONG	SOUTH KOREA	15,912.4	12.8	56.6	318	(3.6)	13,851.8	106	3,460.9	145	21,229	324	18
75	76	CIBA-GEIGY[4]	SWITZERLAND	15,322.7	(5.0)	1,203.7	30	11.4	21,347.4	63	11,478.5	23	87,480	68	5
76	79	RJR NABISCO HOLDINGS	U.S.	15,104.0[E]	(4.0)	(145.0)*	442	(148.5)	31,295.0	39	9,621.0	37	66,500	97	25
77	89	PETROBRÁS[G]	BRAZIL	15,029.0	1.8	687.0	56	20.5	20,818.5	65	12,574.2	18	56,852	113	18
78	88	NKK[8]	JAPAN	14,891.4	2.7	(35.7)	408	—	28,453.6	43	4,076.1	117	22,942[5]	310	15
79	80	BTR	BRITAIN	14,674.9¶	(5.9)	1,211.9	29	1.5	13,299.3	115	3,105.8	161	129,814	36	11
80	104	SARA LEE[1]	U.S.	14,580.0	10.1	704.0	53	(7.5)	10,862.0	153	3,551.0	138	138,000	32	8
81	75	FERRUZZI FINANZIARIA	ITALY	14,507.1	(10.1)	(1,538.9)	492	—	23,235.5	57	(984.0)	493	41,392	173	8
82	87	SSANGYONG	SOUTH KOREA	14,479.6	1.8	86.3	282	(45.0)	13,022.0	118	3,730.0	128	25,470	283	18
83	69	MCDONNELL DOUGLAS	U.S.	14,474.0	(17.4)	396.0	108	—	12,026.0	134	3,413.0	148	70,016	92	1
84	123	KOÇ HOLDING	TURKEY	14,409.0	25.7	707.4	51	77.3	3,723.4	381	757.6	427	41,397	171	17
85	96	BRIDGESTONE	JAPAN	14,377.0	4.4	255.2	155	13.9	15,768.7	91	4,380.2	109	87,332	70	21
86	93	DIGITAL EQUIPMENT[1]	U.S.	14,371.4	3.2	(251.3)	460	—	10,950.3	150	4,885.4	101	94,200	59	6
87	82	PREUSSAG[3]	GERMANY	14,371.0	(7.2)	145.6	220	(51.0)	8,673.0	192	1,946.1	246	73,319	85	15
88	78	VIAG	GERMANY	14,351.8	(7.8)	179.2	201	(2.7)	12,849.7	119	2,545.2	200	80,683	78	15
89	85	VOLVO	SWEDEN	14,272.4	0.2	(445.0)	473	—	16,129.0	89	3,248.0	153	73,641	84	17
90	77	RHÔNE-POULENC	FRANCE	14,222.9	(7.8)	325.5	128	(21.1)	19,341.3	75	5,866.4	81	81,678	76	5
91	81	RUHRKOHLE	GERMANY	14,154.8	(9.9)	6.8	376	(79.1)	16,514.8	85	995.1	397	111,150	46	16
92	97	JOHNSON & JOHNSON	U.S.	14,138.0	2.8	1,787.0	17	73.5	12,242.0	126	5,568.0	86	81,600	77	19
93	95	MINNESOTA MINING & MFG.	U.S.	14,020.0	1.0	1,263.0	25	2.4	12,197.0	127	6,512.0	65	86,168	73	22
94	106	COCA-COLA	U.S.	13,957.0	6.8	2,176.0	9	30.8	12,021.0	135	4,584.0	106	34,000	204	3
95	108	SANYO ELECTRIC[9]	JAPAN	13,849.9	12.4	(13.9)	395	—	19,418.4	73	6,538.4	64	59,624	109	7
96	116	SHARP[2]	JAPAN	13,809.7	16.6	294.6	138	24.2	19,845.9	70	7,992.4	49	42,883	165	7
97	152	JAPAN ENERGY[2,10]	JAPAN	13,736.3[E]	48.5	63.5	310	—	15,357.6	94	1,507.1	310	14,232	395	18
98	110	ISUZU MOTORS[7]	JAPAN	13,730.8	10.8	(37.8)	413	—	12,770.3	121	586.1	451	13,084[5]	407	17
99	100	INTERNATIONAL PAPER	U.S.	13,685.0	0.6	289.0	140	236.0	16,631.0	84	6,225.0	72	72,500	87	9
100	98	SUMITOMO METAL INDUSTRIES[8]	JAPAN	13,521.0	(0.9)	5.4	378	—	23,484.7	55	5,008.3	96	30,926	229	15

[4] Figures prepared in accordance with International Accounting Standards.
[5] Parent company figure only.
[6] Figures are for fiscal year ended May 31, 1993.
[7] Figures are for fiscal year ended October 31, 1993.
[8] Figures are for fiscal year ended March 31, 1993.
[9] Figures are for fiscal year ended November 30, 1993.
[10] Name changed from Nikko Kyodo, December 1, 1993.

Source: Reprinted by permission from FORTUNE GLOBAL 500;

DEFINITIONS AND EXPLANATIONS

Sales All companies on the list must have derived more than 50% of their sales from manufacturing and/or mining. Sales include operating revenues but in most cases do not include other income from dividends, interest, royalties, etc. Sales of consolidated subsidiaries are included as well as sales from discontinued operations when these figures are published. Sales figures do not include excise taxes collected by manufacturers, and so the figures for some corporations—most of which sell gasoline, liquor, or tobacco—may be lower than those published by the corporations themselves. Figures have been converted to dollars using an exchange rate that consists of the official average rate during each company's fiscal year (ended December 31, 1993, unless otherwise noted).

Profits Profits are shown after taxes, after extraordinary credits or charges if any appear on the income statement, and after cumulative effects of accounting changes. An asterisk (*) signifies an extraordinary charge amounting to at least 10% of the profits shown; a double asterisk (**) an extraordinary credit of at least 10%. A single dagger (†) signifies a net SFAS 106, 109, and/or 112 charge amounting to at least 10% of the profits shown; a double dagger (‡) an SFAS 106, 109, and/or 112 credit amounting to at least 10%. Figures in parentheses indicate a loss. Profit declines over 100% reflect swings from 1992 profits to 1993 losses. Cooperatives provide only net margin figures, which are not comparable with the profit figures in these listings, and therefore N.A. is shown in that column. Figures have been converted to dollars using the average official exchange rate during each company's fiscal year (ended December 31, 1993, unless otherwise noted).

Assets Assets shown are those at the company's fiscal year-end. Figures have been converted to dollars at the official exchange rate at each company's fiscal year-end.

Employees The figure shown is either a fiscal year-end or yearly average number, as published by the corporation.

Stockholders' Equity Stockholders' equity is the sum of capital stock, paid-in capital, and retained earnings at the company's fiscal year-end. Minority interest is not included. Figures have been converted to dollars at the official exchange rate at each company's year-end.

Industry Tables Companies are included in the industry that represents the greatest volume of their industrial sales. Industry groups are based on categories established by the U.S. Office of Management and Budget.

The 25 Largest Diversified Service Companies (ranked by sales)

RANK BY SALES 1993	1992	(Major industry)	SALES $millions	SALES % change from 1992	PROFITS $millions	PROFITS Rank	PROFITS % change from 1992	ASSETS $millions	ASSETS Rank	STOCKHOLDERS' EQUITY $millions	STOCKHOLDERS' EQUITY Rank
1	1	**AMERICAN TELEPHONE & TELEGRAPH** New York (telecomm.)	67,156.0	3.5	(3,794.0)†	94	(199.7)	60,766.0	1	13,850.0	1
2	4	**FLEMING** Oklahoma City (wholesale)	13,092.1	1.5	35.2	67	(68.9)	3,102.6	38	1,060.4	29
3	5	**SUPERVALU** Eden Prairie, Minn. (wholesale)[2]	12,568.0	18.2	164.5	25	(15.4)	4,064.2	28	1,134.8	27
4	6	**MCI COMMUNICATIONS** Washington, D.C. (telecommunications)	11,921.0	12.9	582.0	3	(4.4)	11,276.0	8	4,713.0	3
5	7	**MCKESSON** San Francisco (wholesale)[3]	11,672.2	12.8	114.7	38	—	2,800.1	42	619.4	53
6	8	**SPRINT** Westwood, Kans. (telecommunications)	11,367.8	23.2	54.9*†	58	(88.0)	14,148.9	5	3,918.3	6
7	9	**SYSCO** Houston (wholesale)[4]	10,021.5	12.7	201.8	18	17.2	2,530.0	46	1,137.2	26
8	11	**WMX TECHNOLOGIES** Oak Brook, Ill. (waste)[5]	9,135.6	5.5	452.8	5	(46.7)	16,264.5	4	4,159.5	4
9	13	**WALT DISNEY** Burbank, Calif. (theme parks)[6]	8,529.2	13.7	299.8†	10	(63.3)	11,751.1	6	5,030.5	2
10	12	**ELECTRONIC DATA SYSTEMS** Plano, Texas (computing)[7]	8,507.3	4.3	724.0	2	13.9	6,942.1	10	3,617.4	7
11	2	**ENRON** Houston (natural gas)	7,972.5	(43.4)	332.5	8	8.6	11,504.3	7	2,623.4	11
12	15	**FLUOR** Irvine, Calif. (construction, engineering)[8]	7,971.2	18.2	166.8	24	2,767.0	2,588.9	44	1,044.1	33
13	●	**MARRIOTT INTERNATIONAL** Washington, D.C. (hotels)[9]	7,430.0	6.6	126.0†	34	(6.0)	3,092.0	39	696.0	48
14	17	**BERGEN BRUNSWIG** Orange, Calif. (wholesale)[10]	6,823.6	24.4	26.0	70	(57.2)	1,772.3	58	417.8	64
15	21	**ALCO STANDARD** Wayne, Pa. (wholesale)[6]	6,591.3	27.7	0.1	80	(99.9)	3,348.9	34	1,020.6	34
16	3	**TIME WARNER** New York (entertainment)	6,581.0	(49.6)	(221.0)*	90	(357.0)	16,892.0	2	1,370.0	23
17	16	**HALLIBURTON** Dallas (construction, engineering)	6,350.8	(3.3)	(161.0)	89	—	5,403.1	16	1,887.7	13
18	18	**CAPITAL CITIES/ABC** New York (broadcasting)	5,673.7	6.2	455.3	4	85.0	5,792.6	14	3,572.1	8
19	●	**COLUMBIA HEALTHCARE** Louisville (hospitals)[11]	5,653.0	590.0	139.0*	30	446.6	4,619.0	21	1,656.0	17
20	22	**HOSPITAL CORP. OF AMER.** Nashville (hospitals)[12]	5,122.0	(0.1)	368.0*	6	1,205.7	5,597.0	15	1,815.0	14
21	23	**ARA GROUP** Philadelphia (food service)[6]	4,890.7	0.5	77.1	48	14.5	2,005.4	53	124.1	91
22	34	**NATIONAL INTERGROUP** Carrollton, Texas (wholesale)[3]	4,851.6	42.2	0.6	79	(98.0)	1,562.1	62	360.1	72
23	24	**DUN & BRADSTREET** Westport, Conn. (information services)	4,710.4	(0.8)	38.1†	65	(93.1)	5,170.4	17	1,111.3	28
24	30	**GENUINE PARTS** Atlanta (wholesale)	4,384.3	19.5	257.8	14	17.3	1,870.8	55	1,445.3	22
25	25	**PARAMOUNT COMMUNICATIONS** New York (entertainment)[14]	4,164.5	0.9	137.9†	31	(40.4)	6,874.0	11	3,982.1	5

● Not on last year's list.
* Reflects an extraordinary charge of at least 10%.
† Reflects a net SFAS 106, 109, and/or 112 charge of at least 10%.
‡ Reflects a net SFAS 106, 109, and/or 112 credit of at least 10%.
[1] Sales include all operating revenues and revenues from discontinued operations when they are published. Sales also include consolidated subsidiaries, but they do not include excise taxes. All figures are for the fiscal year ended December 31, 1993, unless otherwise noted. All companies on the list must have derived more than 50% of their revenues from nonmanufacturing and nonmining businesses. Excluded from this list, bu[t] eligible for those that follow, are companies deriving more than 50% of their revenues solely from banking, life insurance, finance, savings, retailing, transportation, or utilities.
[2] Figures are for fiscal year ended February 28, 1993.
[3] Figures are for fiscal year ended March 31, 1993.
[4] Figures are for fiscal year ended June 30, 1993.

DEFINITIONS AND EXPLANATIONS TO FORTUNE'S SERVICE 500

Assets are those shown at the company's fiscal year-end.

Profits are shown after taxes, after extraordinary credits or charges if any appear on the income statement, and after cumulative effects of accounting charges. An asterisk (*) signifies an extraordinary charge amounting to at least 10% of the profits shown; a double asterisk (**) an extraordinary credit of at least 10%. A single dagger (†) signifies a net SFAS 106, 109, and/or 112 charge amounting to at least 10% of the profits shown; a double dagger (‡) a net SFAS 106, 109, and/or 112 credit amounting to at least 10%. Figures in parentheses indicate a loss. Profit declines over 100% reflect swings from 1992 profits to 1993 losses. Cooperatives provide only net margin figures, which are not comparable with the profit figures in these listings, and therefore N.A. is shown in that column.

Stockholders' equity is the sum of capital stock, paid-in capital, and retained earnings at the company's year-end. Preferred stock that is technically construed to be debt has been excluded. Redeemable preferred stock whose redemption is either mandatory or outside the control of the company is therefore excluded. For purposes of calculating profits as a percent of stockholders' equity, dividends paid on such stock have been subtracted from the profit figures.

Market Value The figure shown was arrived at by multiplying the number of common shares outstanding by the price per common share as of April 15, 1994. Shares traded on a when-issued basis are excluded.

Earnings per Share The figures shown for each company are the primary earnings per share that appear on the income state-

MARKET VALUE 4/15/94 $ millions	Rank	PROFITS AS % OF . . . SALES %	Rank	ASSETS %	Rank	STOCK-HOLDERS' EQUITY %	Rank	EARNINGS PER SHARE 1993 $	% change from 1992	1983–93 annual growth rate %	Rank	TOTAL RETURN TO INVESTORS 1993 %	Rank	1983–93 annual rate %	Rank	EMPLOYEES Number	Rank	RANK 1993
67,619.9	1	(5.6)	91	(6.2)	92	(27.4)	89	(2.80)	(197.9)	—		5.3	56	13.6	32	308,700	1	1
900.4	66	0.3	78	1.1	73	3.3	76	0.96	(69.6)	(8.6)	47	(18.5)	78	1.6	56	23,300	30	2
2,495.5	41	1.3	65	4.0	41	14.5	33	2.31	(11.2)	9.6	21	19.3	41	11.9	33	42,000	15	3
11,834.4	8	4.9	28	5.2	32	12.3	43	1.04	(52.9)	(4.7)	41	42.9	19	14.8	28	36,235	18	4
2,556.3	39	1.0	67	4.1	39	18.5	22	2.69	—	4.4	30	31.6	29	15.6	24	14,000	44	5
11,976.1	7	0.5	74	0.4	78	1.3	78	0.15	(92.8)	(19.5)	51	40.3	21	18.8	16	50,500	12	6
4,523.5	22	2.0	54	8.0	20	17.7	27	1.08	16.1	16.1	8	12.0	50	21.5	11	24,200	28	7
12,146.8	6	5.0	27	2.8	57	10.9	50	0.93	(45.9)	11.5	17	(32.9)	83	17.9	18	72,600	5	8
21,930.8	3	3.5	37	2.6	61	6.0	70	0.55	(63.8)	12.5	12	(0.3)	66	30.3	3	62,000	10	9
N.A.		8.5	11	10.4	11	20.0	15	N.A.	—	—		—		—		70,000	6	10
7,448.0	15	4.2	32	2.9	55	12.7	42	1.32	2.3	1.0	38	28.0	32	17.0	21	7,100	62	11
4,340.7	25	2.1	53	6.4	26	16.0	30	2.03	2,800.0	19.2	5	(2.2)	69	10.3	42	38,532	17	12
3,449.1	30	1.7	60	4.1	40	18.1	24	N.A.	—	—		—		—		166,000	2	13
536.6	77	0.4	75	1.5	68	6.2	69	0.72	(55.6)	3.0	32	(17.5)	77	6.9	45	4,395	78	14
2,744.1	36	—	80	—	80	(0.2)	79	(0.20)	(109.8)	—		53.6	12	15.4	25	28,500	23	15
14,044.4	4	(3.4)	90	(1.3)	85	(16.1)	88	(0.90)	—	—		52.4	13	14.8	27	27,000	25	16
3,451.5	29	(2.5)	89	(3.0)	88	(8.5)	85	(1.43)	—	—		14.1	48	1.4	57	64,700	9	17
10,645.0	9	8.0	12	7.9	21	12.7	41	27.79	87.5	12.5	13	22.0	37	15.8	23	19,250	37	18
13,467.1	5	2.5	47	3.0	52	8.4	62	0.92	(2.1)	—		56.0	9	—		65,500 F	7	19
N.A.		7.2	16	6.6	25	20.3	14	N.A.	—	—		—		—		65,500 F	7	20
N.A.		1.6	62	3.8	43	62.2	1	1.49	(72.0)	(10.5)	48	—		—		131,000	3	21
210.7	82	—	79	—	79	(1.3)	82	(0.24)	(121.2)	—		3.9	60	(8.7)	63	3,300	86	22
9,706.1	11	0.8	69	0.7	77	3.4	75	0.23	(92.6)	(17.0)	50	11.0	52	10.9	39	50,400	13	23
4,241.1	26	5.9	19	13.8	5	17.8	26	2.08	8.3	9.4	23	13.9	49	14.5	30	20,500	35	24
4,462.0	23	3.3	38	2.0	65	3.5	74	N.A.	—	—		75.3	7	20.0	14	12,833	45	25

[5] Name changed from Waste Management, May 14, 1993.
[6] Figures are for fiscal year ended September 30, 1993.
[7] Wholly owned by General Motors (1993 Industrial 500 rank: 1).
[8] Figures are for fiscal year ended October 31, 1993.
[9] Company spun off to shareholders of Marriott (1992 rank: S-10), October 8, 1993. Marriott renamed Host Marriott (1993 rank: S-86).
[10] Figures are for fiscal year ended August 31, 1993.
[11] Figures (except market value) do not reflect merger with Hospital Corp. of America (1993 rank: S-20), February 10, 1994.
[12] Figures do not reflect merger with Columbia Healthcare (1993 rank: S-19), February 10, 1994.
[13] Figures are for fiscal year ended April 30, 1993.
[14] Figures are for four quarters ended April 30, 1993.

Source: FORTUNE SERVICE 500;

ment. Per share earnings for 1983 and 1992 are adjusted for stock splits and stock dividends. They are not restated for mergers, acquisitions, or accounting changes. Nor are the earnings per share numbers marked by any footnotes to indicate extraordinary charges or credits. However, if a company's profits are footnoted to indicate an extraordinary charge or credit, it can be assumed that earnings per share is affected as well. Results are listed as not available (N.A.) if the companies are cooperatives, joint ventures, or wholly owned subsidiaries of other companies; if the figures were not published; or if the stock traded on a limited basis and was not widely held. The 1983–93 growth rate is the annual rate, compounded.

Total Return to Investors Total return to investors includes both price appreciation and dividend yield to an investor in the company's stock. The figures shown assume sales at the end of 1993 of stock owned at the end of 1983 and 1992. It has been assumed that any proceeds from cash dividends, the sale of rights and warrant offerings, and stock received in spinoffs were reinvested when they were paid. Returns are adjusted for stock splits, stock dividends, recapitalizations, and corporate reorganizations as they occur; however, no effort has been made to reflect the cost of brokerage commissions or of taxes. Results are listed as not available (N.A.) if shares are not publicly traded or are traded on a limited basis. If companies have more than one class of shares outstanding, only the more widely held and actively traded has been considered. Total return percentages shown are the returns received by the hypothetical investor described above. The 1983–93 return is the annual rate, compounded.

The 25 Largest Life Insurance Companies (ranked by assets)

RANK BY ASSETS 1993	1992		ASSETS[1] $ millions	% change from 1992	PREMIUM AND ANNUITY INCOME $ millions	Rank	NET INVESTMENT INCOME $ millions	Rank	NET GAIN FROM OPERATIONS[3] $ millions	Mutual rank	Stock rank
1	1	**PRUDENTIAL OF AMERICA*** Newark, N.J.	165,741.9	7.1	23,897.7	1	8,632.0	1	849.1	1	
2	2	**METROPOLITAN LIFE** * New York	128,225.2	8.5	19,441.5	2	7,298.9	2	265.1	5	
3	3	**TEACHERS INS. & ANNUITY** New York	67,483.2	9.2	3,198.1	20	5,150.4	3	511.6		1
4	5	**NEW YORK LIFE*** New York	53,570.9	14.2	8,874.5	4	3,598.0	4	313.4	4	
5	4	**AETNA LIFE** Hartford[8]	51,535.4	1.3	6,508.2	7	2,704.5	6	275.3		3
6	7	**CONNECTICUT GENERAL LIFE** Bloomfield, Conn.[9]	48,371.7	9.7	5,304.7	11	2,609.3	7	501.3		2
7	6	**EQUITABLE LIFE ASSURANCE*** New York	47,308.6	1.5	3,742.6	17	2,267.7	10	216.6	7	
8	8	**NORTHWESTERN MUTUAL LIFE** * Milwaukee	44,058.0	11.1	5,314.1	10	2,888.0	5	330.1	2	
9	9	**JOHN HANCOCK MUTUAL LIFE*** Boston	43,693.5	11.6	8,415.0	5	2,520.0	8	328.4	3	
10	10	**PRINCIPAL MUTUAL LIFE*** Des Moines	40,072.4	14.1	9,868.5	3	2,368.5	9	263.9	6	
11	12	**MASSACHUSETTS MUTUAL LIFE*** Springfield, Mass.	34,314.3	10.1	4,784.3	13	2,078.7	11	210.2	8	
12	13	**LINCOLN NATIONAL LIFE** Fort Wayne	34,040.3	18.2	5,569.6	9	1,590.3	14	220.8		5
13	11	**TRAVELERS** Hartford[10]	32,671.6	(4.5)	5,152.5	12	1,799.8	12	(88.8)		31
14	15	**HARTFORD LIFE** Simsbury, Conn.[11]	28,970.5	39.6	7,187.9	6	1,039.4	20	48.2		24
15	14	**IDS LIFE** Minneapolis[12]	28,040.9	20.5	3,925.3	16	1,542.5	15	259.1		4
16	17	**NATIONWIDE LIFE** Columbus, Ohio	23,050.2	19.7	4,322.9	14	1,110.6	19	83.2		17
17	16	**ALLSTATE LIFE** Northbrook, Ill.[13]	21,233.8	4.5	3,670.5	18	1,683.5	13	123.6		14
18	18	**VARIABLE ANNUITY LIFE** Houston[14]	19,943.8	15.5	2,131.8	25	1,436.0	16	162.3		8
19	22	**AETNA LIFE & ANNUITY** Hartford[8]	17,639.9	16.2	2,547.7	22	873.7	25	77.5		18
20	21	**STATE FARM LIFE** Bloomington, Ill.	17,090.3	11.2	2,234.1	23	1,253.7	18	204.6		6
21	23	**JACKSON NATIONAL LIFE** Lansing, Mich.[15]	16,953.9	14.7	2,063.6	27	1,363.1	17	156.3		9
22	20	**NEW ENGLAND MUTUAL LIFE*** Boston	16,240.6	(0.7)	1,881.1	30	792.4	29	57.2	17	
23	19	**MUTUAL OF NEW YORK*** New York	14,678.0	(13.1)	1,705.4	33	873.2	26	102.3	14	
24	24	**NEW YORK LIFE & ANNUITY** New York	13,679.7	8.6	1,321.2	39	1,021.9	21	165.5		7
25	25	**PACIFIC MUTUAL LIFE*** Newport Beach, Calif.	13,346.1	15.6	2,085.7	26	875.1	24	107.3	12	

The definitions and explanations underlying the figures in this directory are on page 204.

* Reflects an extraordinary charge of at least 10%.

[1] As of December 31, 1993.

[2] Includes premium income from life, accident, and health policies, annuities, and contributions to deposit administration funds.

[3] After dividends to policyholders and federal income taxes; excluding realized capital gains and losses. Figures in parentheses indicate a loss.

[4] After dividends to policyholders and federal income taxes; including realized capital gains and losses. Figures in parentheses indicate a loss.

[5] Face value of all life policies, including variable life insurance, as of December 31, 1993.

[6] Changes between December 31, 1992, and December 31, 1993.

NET INCOME[4]				NET INCOME AS % OF ASSETS		LIFE INSURANCE IN FORCE[5]		INCREASE IN LIFE INSURANCE IN FORCE[6]				EMPLOYEES[7]		
$ millions	Mutual rank	Stock rank	% change from 1992	%	Rank	$ millions	Rank	$ millions	Rank	%	Rank	Number	Rank	RANK 1993
644.5	1		18.8	0.4	36	913,825.2	2	89,813.0	2	10.9	14	66,100	1	1
133.1	10		(40.9)	0.1	44	1,156,579.9	1	94,516.1	1	8.9	19	47,300	2	2
293.5		2	(24.1)	0.4	35	39,371.4	35	5,988.1	21	17.9	6	4,008	30	3
335.7	4		90.2	0.6	25	367,985.9	4	34,170.3	5	10.2	16	17,169	8	4
13.7		26	(73.9)	—	45	310,457.4	6	(1,368.6)	47	(0.4)	31	24,232	5	5
396.7		1	(0.6)	0.8	16	544,770.6	3	62,303.1	3	12.9	10	—	49	6
408.5	3		—	0.9	14	216,075.1	10	(69,264.3)	50	—		12,358	13	7
510.3	2		46.2	1.2	8	313,241.6	5	35,906.7	4	12.9	9	9,305	16	8
200.2	7		60.6	0.5	33	253,378.5	8	8,564.8	16	—		10,190	15	9
212.2	6		(10.3)	0.5	31	151,830.3	12	19,439.7	11	14.7	8	13,444	12	10
133.4	9		21.5	0.4	36	139,373.2	15	6,915.2	18	5.2	27	8,777	17	11
195.7		4	19.4	0.6	26	136,210.1	16	2,245.1	31	—		4,459	28	12
(625.7)		31	—	(1.9)	50	181,797.4	11	(10,946.7)	48	—		28,000	4	13
74.2		17	8.6	0.3	41	103,540.0	25	9,970.3	15	10.7	15	2,967	33	14
235.7		3	47.3	0.8	15	43,191.7	34	5,072.6	24	22.1	4	8,371	18	15
185.9		7	449.9	0.8	17	32,663.3	39	3,367.2	28	11.5	12	8,247	19	16
55.4		20	(66.7)	0.3	40	121,440.2	19	13,077.2	13	12.1	11	16,673	11	17
154.2		9	125.7	0.8	18	1.6	50	(0.1)	39	—		1,976	37	18
77.6		16	24.1	0.4	34	33,701.3	37	(127.3)	43	—		2,144	36	19
190.2		6	66.1	1.1	11	244,874.4	9	24,327.7	8	11.0	13	19,619	6	20
149.2		11	1.1	0.9	13	132,833.6	17	5,685.2	22	—		1,050	42	21
89.4	14		15.0	0.6	27	84,513.9	27	217.5	38	0.3	30	6,159	21	22
104.2	13		(12.3)	0.7	21	74,775.4	30	1,843.1	33	2.5	28	5,658	23	23
104.5		14	(20.8)	0.8	19	47,561.2	32	2,770.4	30	6.2	23	17,169	8	24
118.5	11		49.1	0.9	12	37,783.0	36	3,482.5	27	10.2	17	4,145	29	25

[7] Includes home office, field force, and full-time agents.
[8] Wholly owned by Aetna Life & Casualty (1993 rank: F-6).
[9] Wholly owned by Cigna (1993 rank: F-9).
[10] Wholly owned by Travelers Inc. (1993 rank: F-4).
[11] Wholly owned by ITT (1993 rank: F-11).
[12] Wholly owned by American Express (1993 rank: F-8).
[13] 80.1% owned by Sears Roebuck (1993 rank: R-2).
[14] Wholly owned by American General (1993 rank: F-15).
[15] Wholly owned by Prudential Corp. PLC (1992 Global Service 500 rank: L-9).

Source: FORTUNE SERVICE 500

Companies That Rate Insurance Companies

Company	Telephone	Address
A.M. Best & Co.	908-439-2200	A.M. Best Road Oldwich, NJ 08858-9999
Duff & Phelps/ Credit Rating Co.	312-368-3157	55 East Monroe Street Chicago, IL 60603
Moody's Investor's Service, Inc.	212-553-0377	99 Church Street New York, NY 10007
Standard & Poor's Corp.	212-208-1527	25 Broadway New York, NY 10004
Weiss Research, Inc.	800-289-9222	P.O. 2923 West Palm Beach, FL 33402

The 25 Largest Commercial Banking Companies (ranked by assets)

RANK BY ASSETS 1993	1992	Company	ASSETS $millions	ASSETS % change from 1992	DEPOSITS $millions	DEPOSITS Rank	LOANS $millions	LOANS Rank	PROFITS $millions	PROFITS Rank	PROFITS % change from 1992
[illegible]	1	**CITICORP** New York	216,574.0	1.3	145,089.0	1	134,588.0	1	2,219.0	1	207.3
2	2	**BANKAMERICA CORP.** San Francisco	186,933.0	3.5	141,618.0	2	122,871.0	2	1,954.0	2	31.0
3	4	**NATIONSBANK CORP.** Charlotte, N.C.[3]	157,686.0	33.6	91,113.0	4	89,838.0	3	1,501.0‡	5	31.1
4	3	**CHEMICAL BANKING CORP.** New York	149,888.0	7.3	98,277.0	3	72,361.0	4	1,604.0	3	47.7
5	5	**J.P. MORGAN & CO.** New York	133,888.0	30.1	40,402.0	10	23,223.0	19	1,586.0	4	14.8
6	6	**CHASE MANHATTAN CORP.** New York	102,103.0	6.5	71,509.0	5	59,068.0	5	966.0‡	8	51.2
7	7	**BANKERS TRUST N.Y. CORP.** New York	92,082.0	27.1	22,776.0	26	13,876.0	33	995.0	7	30.7
8	8	**BANC ONE CORP.** Columbus, Ohio	79,918.6	30.1	60,943.2	6	52,927.5	6	1,140.0	6	45.9
9	11	**FIRST UNION CORP.** Charlotte, N.C.[4]	70,787.0	37.9	53,742.4	7	45,856.0	7	817.5	9	58.7
10	10	**PNC BANK CORP.** Pittsburgh	62,080.0	20.8	33,115.0	11	32,336.0	8	725.9	12	70.0
11	13	**FIRST CHICAGO CORP.** Chicago	52,560.0	6.7	28,186.0	19	22,420.0	21	804.5	10	760.4
12	9	**WELLS FARGO & CO.** San Francisco	52,513.0	—	41,644.0	9	30,977.0	9	612.0	14	116.3
13	12	**FIRST INTERSTATE BANCORP** Los Angeles	51,461.3	1.2	44,701.2	8	24,986.6	16	736.7‡	11	161.0
14	15	**NORWEST CORP.** Minneapolis	50,782.3	14.0	32,573.2	13	26,200.1	12	653.6	13	46.3
15	14	**FLEET FINANCIAL GROUP** Providence	47,922.5	2.1	31,084.8	15	25,310.3	14	488.0	17	74.4
16	17	**BANK OF NEW YORK CO.** New York	45,546.0	11.3	32,153.0	14	29,600.0	10	559.0	15	51.5
17	16	**NBD BANCORP** Detroit	40,775.9	(0.4)	29,821.1	17	25,127.8	15	485.8	18	61.9
18	20	**SUNTRUST BANKS** Atlanta	40,728.4	11.1	30,485.8	16	24,730.9	17	473.7	19	14.6
19	22	**BANK OF BOSTON CORP.** Boston[5]	40,587.9	25.5	29,614.1	18	28,011.7	11	299.0*‡	31	13.7
20	19	**REPUBLIC NEW YORK CORP.** New York	39,493.5	6.3	22,801.3	25	9,196.7	40	301.2	30	16.3
21	18	**BARNETT BANKS** Jacksonville	38,331.1	(2.9)	32,633.8	12	25,408.0	13	421.0	20	102.7
22	21	**WACHOVIA CORP.** Winston-Salem, N.C.	36,525.8	9.5	23,352.4	23	22,572.7	20	492.1	16	13.6
23	23	**MELLON BANK CORP.** Pittsburgh	36,139.0	14.5	27,538.0	21	23,873.0	18	361.0	24	(17.4)
24	24	**FIRST FIDELITY BANCORP.** Newark, N.J.	33,762.6	7.2	28,143.0	20	20,784.7	24	398.8	22	27.1
25	25	**KEYCORP** Albany, N.Y.[6]	32,648.0	8.4	26,618.0	22	21,876.0	22	362.8	23	24.7

The definitions and explanations underlying the figures in this directory are on page 204.
** Reflects an extraordinary credit of at least 10%.
‡ Reflects an SFAS 109 credit of at least 10%.
[1] As of December 31, 1993. All companies on the list must have more than 80% of their assets in chartered commercial banking institutions.
[2] Net of unearned discount and loan loss reserves. Figures include lease financing.
[3] Acquired MNC Financial (1992 rank: B-38), October 1, 1993.

STOCKHOLDERS' EQUITY		MARKET VALUE 4/15/94		PROFITS AS % OF . . .				EARNINGS PER SHARE				TOTAL RETURN TO INVESTORS				EMPLOYEES		
				ASSETS		STOCKHOLDERS' EQUITY		1993	% change from 1992	1983-93 annual growth rate		1993		1983-93 annual rate				
$ millions	Rank	$ millions	Rank	%	Rank	%	Rank	$		%	Rank	%	Rank	%	Rank	Number	Rank	RANK 1993
13,953.0	2	15,169.7	1	1.0	68	15.9	30	4.50	233.3	3.3	65	65.7	2	12.2	67	81,500	1	1
17,144.0	1	15,166.5	2	1.0	66	11.4	81	4.79	13.0	8.2	47	2.7	52	11.6	68	79,225	2	2
9,979.0	4	14,120.9	3	1.0	78	15.0	36	5.78	25.7	12.1	15	(1.5)	63	17.8	36	57,463	3	3
11,164.0	3	9,641.8	6	1.1	58	14.4	46	5.77	47.9	(0.9)	73	7.3	37	10.6	73	41,567	5	4
9,859.0	5	12,285.2	5	1.2	38	16.1	28	7.80	12.7	11.5	22	9.2	32	20.0	22	15,193	23	5
8,122.0	6	6,219.8	12	0.9	81	11.9	78	4.79	38.4	(1.3)	74	23.5	13	11.4	70	34,000	7	6
4,534.0	9	5,622.0	15	1.1	56	21.9	3	11.51	30.5	10.4	30	20.5	17	18.8	31	13,571	25	7
7,033.6	7	13,371.6	4	1.4	13	16.2	26	2.98	24.9	13.4	11	(5.6)	76	19.3	26	45,300	4	8
5,207.6	8	7,771.7	10	1.2	45	15.7	32	4.73	27.2	10.2	32	(2.3)	65	15.7	48	32,861	8	9
4,325.0	10	7,041.2	11	1.2	40	16.8	18	3.06	61.1	8.0	49	5.8	43	15.7	47	21,060	11	10
4,264.0	12	4,616.1	20	1.5	6	18.9	6	8.78	1,271.9	8.4	46	21.1	16	11.5	69	17,355	20	11
4,315.0	11	8,302.1	7	1.2	40	14.2	51	10.10	127.5	12.9	12	73.0	1	25.7	3	19,700	14	12
3,548.3	17	5,925.1	13	1.4	12	20.8	4	8.96	177.4	4.5	62	41.0	5	10.3	74	26,589	9	13
3,568.4	16	7,779.2	9	1.3	24	18.3	8	2.13	22.4	12.2	14	16.0	24	21.0	16	35,000	6	14
3,638.7	14	5,272.0	17	1.0	70	13.4	62	3.01	69.1	5.7	58	4.8	47	15.5	50	26,000	10	15
4,072.0	13	5,218.5	18	1.2	31	13.7	57	5.74	29.0	4.2	63	9.1	33	15.9	46	15,579	21	16
3,248.6	19	4,640.7	19	1.2	35	15.0	37	3.01	61.0	11.6	19	(6.1)	78	20.6	18	18,715	16	17
3,609.6	15	5,618.2	16	1.2	40	13.1	70	3.77	14.9	—		5.5	46	—		19,532	15	18
2,911.7	21	2,750.8	31	0.7	88	10.3	87	2.51	(15.2)	0.2	71	(8.3)	82	10.1	75	18,644	18	19
2,747.2	24	2,595.6	33	0.8	87	11.0	83	5.20	17.6	7.9	50	1.5	55	14.3	54	5,300	55	20
2,874.1	22	4,602.4	21	1.1	55	14.6	42	4.10	108.1	7.2	54	3.7	49	12.9	63	18,647	17	21
3,017.9	20	5,634.0	14	1.3	18	16.3	23	2.83	12.7	10.0	35	1.4	56	17.7	38	15,531	22	22
3,313.0	18	3,729.3	24	1.0	71	10.9	84	4.63	(33.5)	(4.6)	77	2.8	51	5.6	78	20,200	12	23
2,738.4	25	3,715.4	25	1.2	38	14.6	45	4.66	19.8	—		6.7	39	14.0	58	12,043	29	24
2,371.0	26	N.A.		1.1	51	15.3	34	3.43	8.2	10.6	28	(5.6)	77	20.5	19	17,500	19	25

[4] Acquired First American Bankshares (1992 rank: B-81), June 23, 1993.
[5] Acquired Society for Savings (1992 rank: I-38), July 9, 1993.
[6] Figures do not reflect merger with Society Corp. (1993 rank: B-29), March 1, 1994.

Source: FORTUNE SERVICE 500

America's Biggest Brokers

Rank 1992	Rank 1993	Firm	Total consolidated capital ($ millions)	Equity capital ($ millions)	Long-term debt ($ millions)	"Excess" net capital ($ millions)	Total assets ($ millions)
1	1	Merrill Lynch	$18,954.8	$5,485.9	$13,468.9	$1,653.7	$152,910.4
2	2	Salomon Inc.	17,023.0	5,331.0	11,692.0	883.4	184,835.0
4	3	Goldman, Sachs & Co.[1]	15,249.0	5,008.0	10,241.0	960.0	115,900.0
3	4	Lehman Brothers	11,951.0	2,052.0	9,899.0	1,293.0	80,474.0
5	5	Morgan Stanley[2]	8,208.8	3,906.2	4,302.6	463.6	98,248.6
7	6	Bear, Stearns & Co.	4,665.3	2,040.4	2,624.9	865.5	67,384.1
6	7	CS First Boston	4,649.0	1,324.0	3,325.0	572.0	67,925.0
8	8	PaineWebber	3,131.0	1,195.0	1,936.0	475.0	37,027.0
11	9	Smith Barney Shearson	2,742.0	2,055.0	687.0	785.0	30,549.0
9	10	Prudential Securities	1,842.0	1,379.0	463.0	554.0	28,207.0
12	11	Donaldson, Lufkin & Jenrette	1,709.0	975.0	734.0	374.0	37,406.0
10	12	Dean Witter Reynolds	1,615.0	1,286.0	329.0	495.0	13,499.0
15	13	Kidder, Peabody & Co.	1,385.0	773.0	612.0	583.0	72,887.0
14	14	J.P. Morgan Securities	1,106.0	556.0	550.0	350.0	34,667.0
16	15	Nomura Securities International	954.0	304.0	650.0	332.6	32,633.9
13	16	Shelby Cullom Davis & Co.	848.8	848.8	0.0	549.7	4,837.4
17	17	BT Securities Corp.	814.0	453.0	361.0	353.0	26,154.0
19	18	UBS Securities	811.5	436.5	375.0	210.4	29,065.2
18	19	A.G. Edwards, Inc.	752.0	752.0	0.0	471.0	2,213.0
20	20	Charles Schwab & Co.	459.0	326.0	133.0	207.0	6,795.0
21	21	Citicorp Securities	453.0	308.0	145.0	228.0	7,804.0
22	22	Greenwich Capital Markets	424.9	214.9	210.0	215.1	21,408.8
—	23	D.E. Shaw & Co.	372.0	372.0	0.0	40.2	750.0
23	24	Chemical Securities	363.0	363.0	0.0	210.0	10,988.0
24	25	Daiwa Securities America	343.5	193.5	150.0	104.1	26,943.4
30	26	Alex. Brown & Sons	334.0	314.0	20.0	211.0	1,158.0
25	27	Deutsche Bank Securities Corp.	331.6	135.8	195.8	182.7	10,610.8
29	28	Oppenheimer & Co.	321.0	241.0	80.0	112.0	4,815.0
35	29	Fidelity Brokerage Services	311.6	311.6	0.0	189.0	3,910.1
37	30	Legg Mason	308.0	205.5	102.5	91.3	910.6
32	31	Spear, Leeds & Kellogg	300.0	215.0	85.0	86.0	6,667.0
31	32	Yamaichi International (America)	295.2	145.2	150.0	161.7	17,062.5
27	33	Kemper Securities	294.4	250.1	44.3	76.4	1,452.9
28	34	Aubrey G. Lanston & Co.	282.0	272.0	10.0	125.0	3,367.0
32	35	Chase Securities	278.0	278.0	0.0	190.0	6,421.0
34	36	John Nuveen & Co.	275.0	275.0	0.0	211.0	411.0
40	37	Nikko Securities Co. International	260.8	160.8	100.0	196.1	12,611.5
36	38	Dillon, Read & Co.	248.0	183.0	65.0	105.0	3,173.0
39	39	Edward D. Jones & Co.	237.0	164.0	73.0	77.0	742.0
38	40	Allen & Co.	231.3	231.3	0.0	90.3	340.3
44	41	Raymond James Financial	218.0	218.0	0.0	163.0	1,772.0
41	42	Gruntal Financial Corp.	210.5	179.3	31.2	65.5	2,315.8
49	43	Quick & Reilly Group[1]	198.0	197.6	0.4	121.2	2,357.0
—	44	Instinet Corp.	186.0	186.0	0.0	53.0	228.0
52	45	S.G. Warburg & Co.	182.1	153.4	28.7	13.0	183.4
42	46	Sanwa Securities (USA) Co.	177.5	127.5	50.0	93.3	15,294.0
47	47	Wertheim Schroder & Co.	175.7	160.6	15.1	45.6	5,641.5
43	48	Barclays de Zoete Wedd Securities	175.0	125.0	50.0	117.0	11,573.0
45	49	D.H. Blair & Co.	173.0	173.0	0.0	26.6	279.0
48	50	M.A. Schapiro & Co.	166.2	166.2	0.0	112.7	958.2

Rank 1992	Rank 1993	Firm	Total consolidated capital ($ millions)	Equity capital ($ millions)	Long-term debt ($ millions)	"Excess" net capital ($ millions)	Total assets ($ millions)
56	**51**	**Piper, Jaffray Cos.**	$165.1	$165.1	$0.0	$65.7	$575.1
46	**52**	**Fuji Securities**	164.2	114.2	50.0	120.9	10,946.5
50	**53**	**Jefferies & Co.**	154.6	144.6	10.0	66.8	1,388.7
53	**54**	**Neuberger & Berman**	152.0	57.0	95.0	90.0	1,937.0
51	**55**	**Brown Brothers Harriman & Co.**	144.0	144.0	0.0	—	1,566.2
57	**56**	**First Chicago Capital Markets**	137.0	77.0	60.0	91.7	5,062.0
55	**57**	**Arnhold & S. Bleichroeder**	128.0	128.0	0.0	62.0	7,691.0
63	**58**	**Cowen & Co.**	126.0	103.5	22.5	41.6	1,670.9
58	**59**	**Glickenhaus & Co.**	125.0	125.0	0.0	44.0	1,445.0
61		**Lazard Frères & Co.**	125.0	125.0	0.0	34.0	1,172.0
72	**61**	**McDonald & Co. Securities**	124.5	99.5	25.0	50.8	639.6
69	**62**	**Morgan Keegan & Co.**	124.0	124.0	0.0	73.0	698.0
25	**63**	**Van Kampen Merritt**	122.0	122.0	0.0	38.0	191.0
53	**64**	**Stephens, Inc.**	119.0	119.0	0.0	55.0	437.0
59	**65**	**NYLife Securities**	112.0	112.0	0.0	16.0	176.0
67	**66**	**J.C. Bradford & Co.**	110.6	95.6	15.0	53.0	701.7
73	**67**	**Herzog Heine Geduld**	110.5	81.2	29.3	73.9	692.0
64	**68**	**Dain Bosworth**	107.7	102.2	5.5	18.4	354.0
62	**69**	**Janney Montgomery Scott**	105.5	81.5	24.0	66.0	421.4
60	**70**	**Toronto Dominion Securities (USA)**	103.5	18.5	85.0	62.0	782.5
70	**71**	**Bernard L. Madoff Investment Securities**	102.5	102.5	0.0	56.7	382.3
—	**72**	**Paribas Corp.**	102.0	80.0	22.0	64.0	1,701.5
74	**73**	**Wheat, First Securities**	98.1	98.1	0.0	41.1	632.2
76	**74**	**Interstate/Johnson Lane Corp.**	97.1	75.1	22.0	32.2	648.9
66	**75**	**SBCI Swiss Bank Corp. Investment Banking**	95.0	40.0	55.0	47.0	873.0
—	**76**	**Republic NY Securities Corp.**	92.8	92.8	0.0	73.9	1,902.0
77	**77**	**Mabon Securities Corp.**	91.0	44.0	47.0	16.0	3,340.0
68	**78**	**S.D. Securities**	89.8	89.8	0.0	70.0	475.1
78	**79**	**Robert W. Baird & Co.**	83.2	79.8	3.4	26.1	452.9
75	**80**	**Montgomery Securities**	80.1	50.1	30.0	37.3	323.2
65	**81**	**Tucker Anthony**	79.0	79.0	0.0	33.0	466.0
81	**82**	**Fahnestock & Co.**	76.5	63.9	12.6	56.2	425.3
80	**83**	**Chicago Corp.**	73.0	56.9	16.1	24.1	559.8
95	**84**	**Smith New Court**	70.0	52.0	18.0	10.0	480.0
86	**85**	**Rauscher Pierce Refsnes**	69.0	66.0	3.0	20.0	166.0
—	**86**	**Kleinwort Benson Holdings**	67.2	51.2	16.0	8.6	959.2
—	**87**	**Harris Nesbitt Thomson Securities**	66.0	21.0	45.0	52.0	4,314.0
85	**88**	**J.J.B. Hilliard, W.L. Lyons**	64.6	60.2	4.4	31.7	164.8
93	**89**	**BHC Securities**	64.1	2.1	62.0	45.4	483.2
79	**90**	**Weiss, Peck & Greer**	64.0	51.0	13.0	12.0	561.0
82	**91**	**Advest**	62.0	62.0	0.0	26.0	534.0
86	**92**	**William Blair & Co.**	60.0	60.0	0.0	33.9	210.7
83	**93**	**Miller Tabak Hirsch & Co.**	58.4	58.4	0.0	4.4	62.6
94	**94**	**Hambrecht & Quist**	57.3	57.3	0.0	16.6	157.3
90	**95**	**ScotiaMcLeod (USA)**	51.0	51.0	0.0	22.0	3,008.0
89	**96**	**Sanford C. Bernstein & Co.**	50.3	50.3	0.0	25.1	826.8
88	**97**	**The Principal/Eppler, Guerin & Turner**	49.0	49.0	0.0	17.0	135.0
91	**98**	**Crowell, Weedon & Co.**	46.4	40.2	6.2	19.6	109.9
99	**99**	**Wedbush Morgan Securities**	43.2	42.9	0.3	34.0	481.3
92	**100**	**ABD Securities Corp.**	43.0	43.0	0.0	17.0	93.0

[1] *As of 11/26/93.* [2] *As of 10/31/93.*

Source: © *Institutional Investor.* Reprinted with permission.

50 Leading Retained Executive Search Firms in North America*

Allerton Heneghan & O'Neill
70 W. Madison St., Ste. 2015
Three First National Plz.
Chicago, IL 60602
(312) 263-1075
Donald Allerton

Martin H. Bauman Assoc., Inc.
410 Park Ave., Ste. 1600
New York, NY 10022
(212) 752-6580
Martin H. Bauman

Bishop Partners, Ltd.
708 Third Ave., Ste. 2200
New York, NY 10017
(212) 986-3419
Susan K. Bishop

Boyden
375 Park Avenue, Ste. 1008
New York, NY 10152
(212) 685-3400
William E. Goodman, IV

The Caldwell Partners Amrop Int'l.
64 Prince Arthur Ave.
Toronto, ON M5R 1B4 Canada
(416) 920-7702
Steve Ashley

Callan Assoc., Ltd.
1550 Spring Rd.
Oak Brook, IL 60521
(708) 832-7080
Robert M. Callan

Cejka & Co.
222 S. Central, Ste. 400
St. Louis, MO 63105
(314) 726-1603
Susan Cejka

Clarey & Andrews, Inc.
1200 Shermer Rd., Ste. 108
Northbrook, IL 60062
(708) 498-2870
J. Douglas Andrews

Coleman Lew & Assoc., Inc.
326 W. Tenth St.
Charlotte, NC 28202
(704) 377-0362
Charles E. Lew

Conrey Paul Ray International
Palo Santo #6
Col. Lomas Altas
Mexico City, MX CP 11950 Mexico
52 5 5 70 74 62
Craig J. Dudley

Thorndike Deland Assoc.
275 Madison Ave., 13th Floor
New York, NY 10016
(212) 661-6200
Howard Bratches

Dieckmann & Assoc., Ltd.
180 N. Stetson Ave., Ste. 5555
Two Prudential Plaza
Chicago, IL 60601
(312) 819-5900
Ralph E. Dieckmann

Robert W. Dingman Co., Inc.
32129 W. Lindero Canyon Rd., Ste. 206
Westlake Village, CA 91361
(818) 991-5950
Robert W. Dingman

Diversified Search, Inc.
One Commerce Sq.
2005 Market St., Ste. 3300
Philadelphia, PA 19103
(215) 732-6666
Judith M. von Seldeneck

Bert H. Early Assoc., Inc.
55 E. Monroe St., Ste. 4530
Chicago, IL 60603-5805
(312) 236-6868
Bert H. Early

---

* Retained executive search firms primarily require an advance fee and progress payments versus payments contingent on hiring.

Source: Reprinted with permission of *Executive Recruiter News®*, published monthly by Kennedy Publications, Templeton Rd., Fitzwilliam, NH 03447, 603-585-6544, also publishers of *The Directory of Executive Recruiters*.

Fenwick Partners
57 Bedford St., Ste. 101
Lexington, MA 02173
(617) 862-3370
David F. Kehoe

Francis & Assoc.
6923 Vista Drive
West Des Moines, IA 50266
(515) 221-9800
Dwaine Francis

Jay Gaines & Company, Inc.
598 Madison Ave.
New York, NY 10022
(212) 308-9222
Jay Gaines

Gould & McCoy, Inc.
300 Park Ave.
New York, NY 10022
(212) 688-8671
William E. Gould

Hayden Group, Inc.
10 High St.
Boston, MA 02110
(617) 482-2445
James A. Hayden

Heidrick & Struggles, Inc.
125 S. Wacker Drive, Ste. 2800
Chicago, IL 60606-4590
(312) 372-8811
Robert E. Hallagan

The Heidrick Partners, Inc.
20 N. Wacker Drive, Ste. 2850
Chicago, IL 60606
(312) 845-9700
Robert L. Heidrick

The Hetzel Group
Williamsburg Village
1601 Colonial Pkwy.
Inverness, IL 60067
(708) 776-7000
William G. Hetzel

Hockett Assoc., Inc.
350 Second St., Ste. 7
P.O. Box 1765
Los Altos, CA 94023
(415) 941-8815
Bill Hockett

William C. Houze & Co.
48249 Vista De Nopal
La Quinta, CA 92253
(619) 564-6400
William C. Houze

Houze, Shourds & Montgomery, Inc.
Greater LA World Trade Ctr.
One World Trade
Long Beach, CA 90831-1840
(310) 495-6495
James Montgomery

Isaacson, Miller, Inc.
334 Boylston St., Ste. 500
Boston, MA 02116-3805
(617) 262-6500
John Isaacson

Pendleton James & Assoc., Inc.
200 Park Ave., Ste. 3706
New York, NY 10166
(212) 557-1599
E. Pendleton James

A. T. Kearney Executive Search
222 W. Adams St.
Chicago, IL 60606
(312) 648-0111
Charles W. Sweet

Kenny, Kindler, Hunt & Howe
1 Dag Hammarskjold Plaza, 34th Floor
New York, NY 10017
(212) 355-5560
James E. Hunt

Korn/Ferry Int'l.
237 Park Ave.
New York, NY 10017
(212) 687-1834
Richard Ferry

Lamalie Amrop Int'l.
489 Fifth Ave.
New York, NY 10017-6105
(212) 953-7900
John F. Johnson

Herbert Mines Assoc., Inc.
399 Park Ave., 27th Floor
New York, NY 10022
(212) 355-0909
Herbert Mines

Mirtz Morice, Inc.
One Dock St., 3rd Floor
Stamford, CT 06902
(203) 964-9266
P. John Mirtz

Nadzam, Lusk & Assoc., Inc.
3211 Scott Blvd., Ste. 205
Santa Clara, CA 95054
(408) 727-6601
Theodore E. Lusk

Norman Broadbent Int'l., Inc.
200 Park Ave.
New York, NY 10166
(212) 953-6990
William B. Clemens, Jr.

Preng & Assoc., Inc.
2925 Briarpark, Ste. 1111
Houston, TX 77042
(713) 266-2600
David E. Preng

Paul Ray Berndtson
301 Commerce St., Ste. 2300
Ft. Worth, TX 76102
(817) 334-0500
Paul R. Ray, Jr.

Russell Reynolds Assoc., Inc.
200 Park Ave.
New York, NY 10166
(212) 351-2000
Hobson Brown, Jr.

Norman Roberts & Assoc., Inc.
1800 Century Park E., Ste. 430
Los Angeles, CA 90067-1507
(310) 552-1112
Norman C. Roberts

Seitchik, Corwin & Seitchik, Inc.
1830 Jackson St., Ste. C
San Francisco, CA 94109
(415) 928-5717
Blade Corwin

Smith, Goerss & Ferneborg, Inc.
388 Market St., Ste. 860
San Francisco, CA 94111
(415) 543-4181
John R. Ferneborg

SpencerStuart
55 E. 52nd St.
New York, NY 10055-1021
(212) 407-0200
Robert A. Damon

Tanton/Mitchell Paul Ray Berndtson
710-1050 W. Pender St.
Vancouver, BC V6E 3S7 Canada
(604) 685-0261
Kyle Mitchell

Travis & Co., Inc.
325 Boston Post Rd.
Sudbury, MA 01776
(508) 443-4000
John A. Travis

Ward Howell International, Inc.
99 Park Ave., Ste. 2000
New York, NY 10016-1699
(212) 697-3730
John F. Raynolds, III

Daniel Wier & Assoc.
333 S. Grand Ave., Ste. 2980
Los Angeles, CA 90071
(213) 628-2580
Daniel C. Wier

Wilkinson & Ives
One Bust St., Ste. 550
San Francisco, CA 94104
(415) 433-2155
William R. Wilkinson

Witt/Kieffer, Ford, Hadelman & Lloyd
2015 Spring Rd., Ste. 510
Oak Brook, IL 60521
(708) 990-1370
Michael C. Kieffer

Egon Zehnder Int'l., Inc.
55 E. 59th St., 14th Floor
New York, NY 10022
(212) 838-9199
A. Daniel Meiland

America's Most Admired Corporations*

THE MOST ADMIRED

A new No. 1, Rubbermaid, replaces Merck, now No. 11. Home Depot, Microsoft, and Disney are new to the expanded survey. Note the three ties—for Nos. 3, 6, and 8.

RANK	LAST YEAR	COMPANY	SCORE
1	2	**Rubbermaid** Rubber & plastic products	8.68
2	*	**Home Depot** Specialist retailers	8.36
3	5	**Coca-Cola** Beverages	8.30
3	*	**Microsoft** Computer & data services	8.30
5	4	**3M** Sci., photo & control equip.	8.19
6	*	**Walt Disney** Entertainment	8.16
6	18	**Motorola** Electronics, electrical equip.	8.16
8	9	**J.P. Morgan** Commercial banking	8.14
8	6	**Procter & Gamble** Soaps, cosmetics	8.14
10	17	**United Parcel Service** Trucking	8.13

* Not ranked last year.

* HOW IT WAS DONE. The 12th annual Corporate Reputations Survey includes 404 companies in 42 industry groups that appeared in the 1993 FORTUNE 500 and FORTUNE Service 500 directories. More than 10,000 senior executives, outside directors, and financial analysts were asked to rate the ten largest companies (or sometimes fewer) in their own industry on eight attributes of reputation, using a scale of zero (poor) to ten (excellent). The attributes were quality of management; quality of products or services; innovativeness; long-term investment value; financial soundness; ability to attract, develop, and keep talented people; responsibility to the community and the environment; and wise use of corporate assets.

FORTUNE 500 companies are assigned to a group based on the activity that contributed most to their 1992 industrial sales; Service 500 companies to a group based on the activity contributing most to their service sales.

Source: FORTUNE,

America's Best 100 Growth Companies[1]

RANK THIS YEAR	RANK LAST YEAR	COMPANY / *BUSINESS*	FIVE-YEAR AVERAGE EPS GROWTH	FIVE-YEAR AVERAGE RETURN ON EQUITY	ESTIMATED EPS GROWTH '94 VS. '93	EARNINGS PER SHARE LATEST 12-MONTH	EARNINGS PER SHARE 1994 EST.	LATEST 12-MONTH SALES (MIL.)	LATEST 12-MONTH PROFITS (MIL.)	DEBT AS % OF EQUITY	STOCK PRICE	P/E 1994 EST.
1	NR	**Zoom Telephonics** *markets products that link personal computers to telephone networks*	62%	45%	54%	$0.63	$0.97	$55	$4	0%	$9.50	10
2	NR	**American Power Conversion** *manufactures uninterruptible power supply products for computer workstations*	64	36	40	0.53	0.74	250	49	0	22.00	30
3	NR	**Transmedia Network** *restaurant charge cards that provide customers with discounts*	88	23	49	0.45	0.64	40	3	0	20.75	32
4	NR	**Mid Atlantic Medical Svc** *owns three health maintenance organizations*	60	49	29	1.13	1.46	647	26	8	48.38	33
5	NR	**Speizman Inds** *distributes machinery used to make textiles*	56	35	31	1.26	1.35	53	3	2	10.50	8
6	NR	**Spartan Motors** *makes heavy-duty chassis for fire trucks, recreational vehicles and buses*	57	26	40	0.80	1.12	167	11	5	18.25	16
7	NR	**BMC Software** *makes software for large-scale data management systems*	50	31	30	3.10	3.25	274	81	0	61.00	19
8	NR	**International Game Tech** *world's largest manufacturer of gaming machines*	65	26	28	0.91	1.09	504	115	11	24.38	22
9	12	**Jean Philippe Fragrances** *makes fragrances and cosmetics*	47	21	62	0.61	0.81	57	6	2	10.50	13
10	NR	**SynOptics Communications** *manufactures local area network systems*	45	21	37	1.09	1.49	705	76	34	20.00	13
11	NR	**Mercury Finance** *finances the sale of used autos for new and used car dealers*	35	32	29	0.56	0.72	179	65	0	16.25	23
12	NR	**Jack Henry & Associates** *develops in-house data processing systems for financial institutions*	57	24	24	0.50	0.57	36	6	0	7.38	13
13	22	**Linear Technology** *produces integrated circuits*	40	20	42	1.22	1.41	175	45	0	47.75	34
14	NR	**KCS Energy** *engaged in oil and gas exploration mainly in Gulf coast*	94	15	133	1.61	2.77	304	19	61	24.75	9
15	NR	**Vicor** *manufactures power conversion devices for electronic data processing*	51	20	30	0.70	0.91	84	15	0	25.63	28
16	NR	**Chipcom** *makes computer networking products*	99	16	37	1.45	1.98	150	14	1	44.88	23
17	10	**Fastenal** *specialty retailing of industrial and construction supplies*	28	24	35	0.63	0.85	110	12	0	31.00	36
18	11	**US Healthcare** *operates health maintenance organizations in northeast*	109	34	18	1.84	2.17	2,645	300	0	43.25	20
19	NR	**ABS Inds** *makes transmission components and hitchballs for autos*	22	27	49	0.72	1.00	75	4	29	13.75	14

*NR: not rated. Est.: Consensus estimate. * Merger with Viacom pending.*
Sources: William O'Neil & Co.; Market Guide via OneSource; I/B/E/S, Inc.

[1] TO LOCATE AMERICA'S 200 BEST GROWTH COMPANIES FOR 1994, we used a mainframe and two Dell 486 PCs to sort through more than 9,000 publicly traded companies, applying rather strict screens.

Just to be eligible for our ranking required some pretty good numbers: a five-year annual earnings per share growth rate greater than 12%; a five-year average return on shareholders' equity of at least 10%; long-term debt not more than 150% of shareholder's equity; a positive book value; both higher EPS and sales during the most recent four quarters than one year earlier; and projected earnings growth this year versus 1993 better than 11%.

Individually, these criteria are not that difficult to meet. But in the aggregate they're so tough that only 300 companies could meet the challenge. After all, not that many companies can grow rapidly over a long period while remaining rock-solid financially.

Next, each company was ranked based on the three yardsticks that Wall Street deems the most important measures of corporate performance: historical earnings growth; historical return on equity; and forecasted earnings growth. Each of these counts equally in our rankings. If two or more firms tied on any of these yardsticks, the company with the greater earnings growth during the past 12 months was awarded the higher score.

A couple of observations about the tables: Most of the data comes from Los Angeles-based William O'Neil & Co. Earnings estimates were provided courtesy of New York City-based I/B/E/S Inc., and represent the average, or "consensus," of all analysts' opinions collected in the data base for each company. Most reported earnings data are as of Dec. 31, 1993. Balance sheet information is as of Sept. 30, 1993. Stock prices are as of April 22, 1994.

—*Michael Ozanian*

Source: Reprinted from *FINANCIAL WORLD*, 1328 Broadway, New York, N.Y. 10001

RANK THIS YEAR	RANK LAST YEAR	COMPANY *BUSINESS*	FIVE-YEAR AVERAGE EPS GROWTH	FIVE-YEAR AVERAGE RETURN ON EQUITY	ESTIMATED EPS GROWTH '94 VS. '93	EARNINGS PER SHARE LATEST 12-MONTH	EARNINGS PER SHARE 1994 EST.	LATEST 12-MONTH SALES (MIL.)	LATEST 12-MONTH PROFITS (MIL.)	DEBT AS % OF EQUITY	STOCK PRICE	P/E 1994 EST.
20	**16**	**Buffets** *owns and franchises family-style restaurants*	**35**	**21**	**33**	**0.66**	**0.88**	**335**	**20**	**0**	**23.13**	**26**
21	**NR**	**Concord EFS** *builds electronic payment networks for retailers*	**29**	**28**	**30**	**0.90**	**1.17**	**75**	**10**	**0**	**21.00**	**18**
22	**NR**	**Micros Systems** *produces point-of-sale computer systems*	**47**	**17**	**46**	**0.91**	**1.08**	**67**	**7**	**6**	**24.50**	**23**
23	**14**	**Blockbuster Entertainment*** *owns and franchises video rental and music stores*	**48**	**20**	**25**	**1.11**	**1.39**	**2,227**	**244**	**33**	**24.63**	**18**
24	**6**	**Surgical Care Affiliates** *operates freestanding surgical centers*	**52**	**20**	**24**	**0.85**	**1.05**	**197**	**32**	**35**	**12.50**	**12**
25	**NR**	**CML Group** *specialty retailer of excercise equipment and men's apparel*	**48**	**33**	**20**	**1.25**	**1.33**	**731**	**65**	**27**	**14.75**	**11**
26	**NR**	**Mattel** *designs and makes toys*	**24**	**31**	**28**	**1.30**	**1.66**	**2,704**	**226**	**57**	**24.50**	**15**
27	**NR**	**Seattle FilmWorks** *mail-order film and photofinishing services*	**31%**	**35%**	**22%**	**$1.34**	**$0.79**	**$44**	**$4**	**0%**	**$13.75**	**17**
28	**NR**	**Nature's Bounty** *makes multi-branded vitamins and nutritional supplements*	**99**	**13**	**45**	**0.56**	**0.77**	**146**	**11**	**11**	**19.00**	**25**
29	**45**	**Meridian Diagnostics** *makes immunodiagnostic test kits*	**66**	**14**	**41**	**0.28**	**0.38**	**17**	**2**	**106**	**9.00**	**24**
30	**66**	**Green Tree Financial** *originates and services sales contracts for manufactured homes*	**45**	**22**	**21**	**3.62**	**4.39**	**316**	**116**	**59**	**49.25**	**11**
31	**104**	**Cerner** *provides information systems run on digital vax computers*	**41**	**18**	**30**	**1.00**	**1.30**	**121**	**15**	**11**	**27.50**	**21**
32	**NR**	**Franklin Resources** *provides investment management services*	**19**	**27**	**33**	**2.39**	**2.81**	**712**	**200**	**57**	**36.13**	**13**
33	**20**	**Home Depot** *specialty retailer of building and home improvement supplies*	**36**	**18**	**32**	**1.01**	**1.33**	**9,239**	**457**	**31**	**41.38**	**31**
34	**NR**	**PacifiCare Health Systems** *operates health maintenance organizations*	**52**	**22**	**20**	**2.39**	**2.69**	**2,382**	**67**	**6**	**48.50**	**18**
35	**1**	**Microsoft** *develops microcomputer software*	**46**	**31**	**18**	**3.41**	**3.73**	**4,109**	**1,036**	**0**	**91.75**	**25**
36	**19**	**Atlantic Southeast Air** *largest regional airline in southeast*	**23**	**21**	**32**	**1.35**	**1.78**	**289**	**46**	**67**	**28.75**	**16**
37	**88**	**Heartland Express** *a medium-haul, irregular route trucker*	**24**	**23**	**26**	**1.12**	**1.41**	**116**	**14**	**0**	**33.50**	**24**
38	**NR**	**Countrywide Credit Inds** *originates, sells and purchases mortgage loans*	**60**	**14**	**36**	**2.88**	**3.37**	**694**	**171**	**0**	**20.50**	**6**
39	**NR**	**Maxim Integrated Products** *produces mixed signal analog circuits*	**28**	**19**	**29**	**1.30**	**1.48**	**128**	**20**	**0**	**46.13**	**31**
40	**5**	**Novell** *manufactures local area network software*	**53**	**26**	**17**	**0.90**	**1.05**	**1,174**	**284**	**0**	**16.44**	**16**
41	**NR**	**Wausau Paper Mills** *makes specialty papers*	**24**	**22**	**25**	**1.58**	**1.79**	**406**	**42**	**16**	**26.60**	**15**
42	**NR**	**Cordis** *makes medical instruments*	**44**	**20**	**21**	**2.24**	**2.41**	**276**	**33**	**1**	**46.88**	**19**
43	**58**	**System Software Assoc** *markets and supports business application software*	**22**	**28**	**23**	**0.87**	**1.06**	**281**	**24**	**30**	**15.50**	**15**
44	**121**	**Collective Bancorp** *largest thrift in New Jersey*	**42**	**15**	**31**	**2.78**	**3.01**	**250**	**57**	**0**	**20.63**	**7**
45	**13**	**Healthcare Compare** *provides cost management services to hospitals*	**71**	**17**	**20**	**1.08**	**1.30**	**158**	**38**	**0**	**16.88**	**13**
46	**NR**	**Respironics** *makes respiratory medical products*	**39**	**18**	**24**	**0.81**	**1.05**	**74**	**7**	**10**	**19.50**	**19**
47	**NR**	**Lund Intl Holdings** *produces sun visors and spoilers for autos, trucks and vans*	**17**	**23**	**30**	**1.03**	**1.17**	**31**	**4**	**0**	**19.00**	**16**
48	**63**	**Gainsco** *provides property and casualty insurance*	**33**	**21**	**20**	**0.74**	**0.89**	**84**	**13**	**0**	**8.50**	**10**
49	**89**	**Paychex** *provides computerized payroll accounting services*	**24**	**21**	**22**	**0.86**	**1.12**	**216**	**26**	**1**	**33.75**	**30**
50	**122**	**Briggs & Stratton** *world's largest producer of air cooled gasoline engines*	**59**	**15**	**22**	**5.80**	**5.93**	**1,190**	**84**	**21**	**80.25**	**14**

NR: not rated. Est.: Consensus estimate.

Sources: William O'Neil & Co.; Market Guide via OneSource; I/B/E/S, Inc.

(continued)

America's Best 100 Growth Companies *(concluded)*

RANK THIS YEAR	RANK LAST YEAR	COMPANY / *BUSINESS*	FIVE-YEAR AVERAGE EPS GROWTH	FIVE-YEAR AVERAGE RETURN ON EQUITY	ESTIMATED EPS GROWTH '94 VS. '93	EARNINGS PER SHARE LATEST 12-MONTH	EARNINGS PER SHARE 1994 EST.	LATEST 12-MONTH SALES (MIL.)	LATEST 12-MONTH PROFITS (MIL.)	DEBT AS % OF EQUITY	STOCK PRICE	P/E 1994 EST.
51	NR	**Rainbow Technologies** *develops software and information protection products*	32	18	25	1.06	1.32	35	6	6	15.50	12
52	87	**X-Rite** *produces quality control instruments for the photographic and medical industries*	23	18	36	0.72	0.98	39	8	0	22.00	22
53	119	**Fair, Isaac** *develops analytical scorecards used to evaluate consumer credit risk*	27	14	46	1.04	1.27	74	6	8	24.75	19
54	NR	**Nature's Sunshine Prods** *produces herbs, vitamins and food supplements*	17	24	26	0.66	0.83	127	7	0	15.00	18
55	60	**Amgen** *advanced cellular and molecular biology*	133	24	13	2.55	2.88	1,374	366	17	42.00	15
56	NR	**DiMark** *data base marketing and graphics services*	48%	12%	36%	$0.44	$0.64	$58	$3	14%	$16.63	26
57	NR	**Horizon Healthcare** *provides long-term nursing care*	88	10	31	0.86	1.17	287	11	59	22.50	19
58	NR	**Bombay** *markets traditionally styled furniture and accessories*	33	13	38	0.61	0.65	286	23	0	19.63	30
59	35	**Wal-Mart Stores** *discount department stores*	22	24	21	1.02	1.23	67,986	2,333	78	25.38	21
60	NR	**GAP** *specialty retailing of casual apparel*	27	29	16	1.78	2.07	3,296	258	7	46.00	22
61	71	**Coca-Cola** *world's largest producer of soft drink concentrates*	19	40	18	1.68	1.99	13,957	2,188	31	40.00	20
62	102	**Superior Inds Intl** *manufactures cast aluminum wheels for autos*	24	19	20	1.47	1.77	393	45	19	30.88	17
63	NR	**Consolidated Stores** *largest U.S. retailer of close-out merchandise*	101	10	28	0.90	1.15	1,055	43	43	17.50	15
64	NR	**Caremark Intl** *provides health care products and services outside the hospital*	24	23	19	1.06	1.26	1,783	78	29	17.25	14
65	NR	**Michaels Stores** *specialty retailing of home decorative items*	100	10	25	1.53	1.92	620	26	57	41.00	21
66	NR	**Lancaster Colony** *manufactures auto accessories, specialty foods and glassware*	24	19	20	2.28	2.43	673	52	16	40.25	17
67	42	**Stryker** *manufactures powered surgical instruments*	32	18	20	1.25	1.50	557	60	11	26.00	17
68	NR	**Keane** *designs software for the insurance and financial industries*	15	18	48	1.14	1.69	176	9	18	36.75	22
69	27	**Empi** *makes biomedical devices for electro-therapeutic applications*	91	13	19	1.08	1.29	66	9	4	10.13	8
70	52	**Brinker Intl** *owns and franchises family-style restaurants*	28	14	27	1.18	1.31	740	57	1	28.50	22
71	78	**Adaptec** *produces components that control data flow between microcomputers and peripherals*	62	16	17	1.04	1.12	355	55	4	16.50	15
72	97	**Merrill** *involved in commercial typesetting, printing and graphics*	54	17	16	1.47	1.92	166	12	4	23.13	12
73	180	**Paxar** *makes electronic bar code and labeling systems*	48	13	24	0.67	0.83	139	9	1	13.25	16
74	NR	**Designs** *retails Levi Strauss apparel exclusively*	188	10	24	0.92	1.14	241	15	7	15.50	14
75	40	**Cracker Brl Old Ctry Str** *family-style restaurants and gift shops*	34	14	24	0.85	0.97	578	51	6	25.38	26
76	159	**Tech Data** *distributes microcomputers and related hardware and software*	31	14	24	1.54	2.05	1,372	27	4	18.25	9
77	NR	**Thor Inds** *manufactures recreational vehicles and buses*	33	10	42	1.57	1.80	447	14	0	26.13	15
78	99	**Dollar General** *owns and franchises discount stores mainly in small towns*	36	14	21	1.13	1.37	1,133	49	3	24.63	18
79	18	**Utah Medical Products** *produces disposable medical products used in gynecology and critical care*	37	31	12	0.60	0.67	37	7	0	7.75	12
80	NR	**American Med Electronics** *makes medical devices for spinal fusions and recalcitrant bone fractures*	47	17	16	0.69	0.80	39	5	0	9.50	12

NR: not rated. Est.: Consensus estimate.
Sources: William O'Neil & Co.; Market Guide via OneSource; I/B/E/S, Inc.

RANK THIS YEAR	RANK LAST YEAR	COMPANY / *BUSINESS*	FIVE-YEAR AVERAGE EPS GROWTH	FIVE-YEAR AVERAGE RETURN ON EQUITY	ESTIMATED EPS GROWTH '94 VS. '93	EARNINGS PER SHARE LATEST 12-MONTH	EARNINGS PER SHARE 1994 EST.	LATEST 12-MONTH SALES (MIL.)	LATEST 12-MONTH PROFITS (MIL.)	DEBT AS % OF EQUITY	STOCK PRICE	P/E 1994 EST.
81	65	**UST Inc** *makes smokeless tobacco and wine*	19	52	16	1.61	1.86	1,110	347	30	26.00	14
82	24	**Medstat Group** *supplies specialized data bases to insurance companies*	29	17	19	0.66	0.75	53	7	1	15.25	20
83	NR	**Richfood Holdings** *largest wholesale food distributor in mid-Atlantic*	44	17	17	0.89	1.16	1,243	19	50	16.50	14
84	NR	**Gillette** *makes toiletries and cosmetics*	18	38	16	2.66	3.09	5,411	591	57	66.63	22
85	NR	**Hillenbrand Inds** *makes hospital beds and home infusion products*	17%	19%	23%	$1.86	$2.29	$1,448	$132	17%	$38.75	17
86	117	**American Management Sys** *provides computer services*	27	15	23	1.04	1.28	364	18	12	20.50	16
87	NR	**Kirby** *provides marine transportation and diesel repair services*	20	12	50	0.86	1.29	379	23	52	20.50	16
88	NR	**Quixote** *manufactures highway safety devices, stenographic machines and compact disks*	35	19	15	1.29	1.38	156	10	102	17.25	13
89	NR	**Clayton Homes** *builds prefabricated homes*	23	15	23	1.09	1.17	542	62	32	20.38	17
90	100	**Instrument Systems** *makes building products and specialty plastic films*	73	16	14	0.73	0.80	450	28	10	8.63	11
91	NR	**Jones Medical Inds** *manufactures drugs and vitamins*	26	14	22	0.65	0.79	43	8	18	10.50	13
92	62	**Invacare** *makes wheelchairs, beds and respiratory equipment*	42	15	18	1.50	1.77	366	22	67	25.75	15
93	124	**Phillips-Van Heusen** *makes apparel under the Van Heusen, Geoffrey Beene and Winsor brand names*	18	19	21	1.47	1.94	1,116	40	65	33.25	17
94	NR	**Falcon Products** *manufactures furniture for food service industry*	18	17	25	0.59	0.70	65	5	1	10.00	14
95	85	**TriMas** *manufactures specialty containers and precision tools for industrial use*	16	17	26	1.05	1.32	443	38	98	25.25	19
96	NR	**Communications Systems** *makes connecting devices for telephone systems*	31	13	23	0.75	0.92	61	7	1	11.25	12
97	79	**Great Lakes Chemical** *world's leading producer of bromine*	21	20	17	3.82	4.48	1,828	273	5	64.88	14
98	47	**Crompton & Knowles** *produces specialty chemicals and processing equipment*	22	23	15	1.00	1.15	558	52	6	20.00	17
99	34	**Intel** *manufactures microprocessors*	34	18	14	5.20	5.93	8,782	2,295	6	60.38	10
100	NR	**Shaw Inds** *produces tufted carpeting and rugs*	13	17	39	0.82	1.00	2,476	118	44	22.00	22

NR: not rated. Est.: Consensus estimate.
Sources: William O'Neil & Co.; Market Guide via OneSource; I/B/E/S, Inc.

Source: Reprinted from *FINANCIAL WORLD*, 1328 Broadway, New York, N.Y. 10001

Biggest Acquisition Deals

BIGGEST U.S. DEALS

	Target (Advisers)	Acquirer (Advisers)	Type of deal	Price ($ millions)	Effective date
1	**Medco Containment Services** (Kidder Peabody)	**Merck & Co.** (Morgan Stanley)	acquisition	$6,225.7	11/18/93
2	**Galen Health Care** (Goldman Sachs)	**Columbia Hospital Corp.** (Stephens, Inc.)	acquisition	4,187.7	9/1/93
3	**Centel Corp.** (Goldman Sachs, Morgan Stanley)	**Sprint Corp.** (Dillon Read)	merger via stock swap	3,967.0	3/9/93
4	**Travelers Corp.** (Wasserstein Perella, Merrill Lynch)	**Primerica Corp.** (Smith Barney Shearson, J.P. Morgan Securities, Salomon Brothers)	acquisition of remaining 73.4 percent interest	3,955.9	12/31/93
5	**Quantum Chemical Corp.** (Dillon Read)	**Hanson**	acquisition	3,219.7	10/1/93
6	**General Electric Co.'s GE Aerospace division** (Kidder Peabody)	**Martin Marietta Corp.** (Goldman Sachs, Lehman Brothers)	acquisition	3,050.0	4/2/93
7	**AMAX** (James D. Wolfensohn)	**Cyprus Minerals Co.** (Kidder Peabody, Dillon Read)	acquisition	2,657.0	11/15/93
8	**Gulf States Utilities Co.** (Goldman Sachs)	**Entergy Corp.** (Salomon Brothers)	acquisition	2,281.0	12/31/93
9	**Chrysler Corp.'s Chrysler Financial Corp.'s Chrysler First** (Salomon Brothers)	**NationsBank Corp.** (Bear Stearns)	acquisition	2,200.0	2/1/93
10	**Consumer loan portfolio of ITT Corp.'s ITT Financial Corp.** (Lazard Frères)	**Investor group of Goldman Sachs, Household International and ITT** (Goldman Sachs)	acquisition	2,100.0	6/4/93
11	**LDDS Communications** (Breckenridge)	**Resurgens Communications Group** (Donaldson, Lufkin & Jenrette)	acquisition	1,961.3	9/15/93
12	**IMC Fertilizer Group's phosphate fertilizer business** (Lehman Brothers)	**Freeport-McMoRan's phosphate fertilizer business** (Goldman Sachs)	merger	1,866.0	7/1/93
13	**Price Co.** (Lehman Brothers)	**Costco Wholesale Corp.** (Donaldson, Lufkin & Jenrette)	merger	1,666.2	10/22/93
14	**General Dynamics Corp.'s Fort Worth, Texas, Division** (Goldman Sachs)	**Lockheed Corp.** (Morgan Stanley)	acquisition	1,525.0	3/1/93
15	**American Express Co.'s Shearson Lehman Holdings' Boston Co.** (James D. Wolfensohn, Lehman Brothers, Lazard Frères)	**Mellon Bank Corp.** (Goldman Sachs)	acquisition	1,453.0	5/21/93

Source: Securities Data Co.

HOW THEY'RE CALCULATED

The table above shows the 15 largest deals involving a U.S.-target company that were completed between January 1 and December 31,1993.

In this table advisers received credit only for those deals on which they served as financial advisers; firms that acted only as providers of fairness opinions were not credited.

These deals do not include buybacks or repurchases, spin-offs, split-offs, self-tenders or minority stake purchases, unless the stake purchase was for the remaining interest of a company that the acquirer already partially owned.

Source: *Institutional Investor.*

BIGGEST CANADIAN AND LATIN AMERICAN DEALS

	Target (Advisers)	Acquirer (Advisers)	Type of deal	Price ($ millions)	Effective date
1	**Gentra's Canadian and international assets** (Canada) (S.G. Warburg, Burns Fry)	**Royal Bank of Canada** (N.M. Rothschild)	acquisition	$1,327.9	9/1/93
2	**El Chocón and Arroyito hydroelectric plants** (Argentina) (Banco General de Negocios, Kleinwort Benson, CS First Boston)	**Hidroinvest,** an investor group (Chile)	acquisition of 59 percent stake in state-owned plants	833.9	7/9/93
3	**Crown Forest Industries' forest product assets** (Canada)	**Fletcher Challenge's Fletcher Challenge Canada** (Canada) (Wood Gundy)	acquisition	704.1	2/18/93
4	**Media assets** (Mexico) (Donaldson, Lufkin & Jenrette)	**Investor group of Bancomer, Elektra and Organización Radio Centro** (Mexico)	acquisition of state-owned media firms	639.3	7/18/93
5	**Aseguradora Mexicana** (Mexico)	**Grupo Financiero Mexival-Banpais** (Mexico) (Bear Stearns)	acquisition of 51 percent stake in state-owned insurance company	583.0	9/20/93
6	**Minero Perú's Cerro Verde Copper** (Peru) (Morgan Grenfell)	**Amoco's Cyprus Minerals Co.** (United States)	acquisition from state-owned mining company	522.0	11/19/93
7	**Suramericana** (Colombia)	**Nacional** (Colombia) (J.P. Morgan Securities)	acquisition	449.9	9/30/93
8	**Encor** (Canada) (Wood Gundy)	**Talisman Energy** (Canada)	acquisition	376.1	5/21/93
9	**Hidroeléctrica Alicura** (Argentina) (Banco General de Negocios, CS First Boston, Kleinwort Benson)	**Southern Co.'s SEI Holdings' SEI y Asociados de Argentina** (United States) (Lehman Brothers)	acquisition of 59 percent stake	352.9	7/6/93
10	**Real Turismo** (Mexico) (Morgan Stanley)	**Investor group led by Alvaro Lopez Castro** (Mexico)	acquisition	315.0	7/16/93

Source: Securities Data Co.

HOW THEY'RE CALCULATED

The table above shows the ten largest deals involving a Canada- or Latin America–target company that were completed between January 1 and December 31, 1993.

In this table advisers received credit only for those deals on which they served as financial advisers; firms that acted only as providers of fairness opinions were not credited.

These deals do not include buybacks or repurchases, spin-offs, split-offs, self-tenders or minority stake purchases, unless the stake purchase was for the remaining interest of a company that the acquirer already partially owned.

Source: *Institutional Investor.*

Capital Sources for Startup Companies and Small Businesses

Sources of Venture Capital

Small Business Investment Companies (SBICs)

Small Business Administration (SBA)
409 Third Street, S.W.—6th Floor
Washington, D.C. 20416
Telephone: 202-205-7586

The Small Business Investment Companies (SBIC) are licensed by the SBA. They are privately organized and privately managed investment firms, yet they are participants in a vital partnership between government and the private sector economy. With their own capital and with funds borrowed at favorable rates from the Federal government, SBICs provide venture capital to small independent businesses, both new and already established. Today there are two types of SBICs—the original, or regular SBICs and SSBICs (Specialized Small Business Investment Companies). SSBICs are specifically targeted toward the needs of entrepreneurs who have been denied the opportunity to own and operate a business because of social or economic disadvantage.

For further information call your regional SBA office listed below or the Answer Desk at 800-827-5722. See also page 236.

Small Business Administration Regional Structure

Region I 617-451-2023

Connecticut
Maine
Massachusetts
New Hampshire
Rhode Island
Vermont

Region II 212-264-1450

New Jersey
New York
Puerto Rico

Region III 215-962-3700

Delaware
Dist. of Columbia
Maryland
Pennsylvania
Virginia
West Virginia

Region IV 404-347-2797

Alabama
Florida
Georgia
Kentucky
Mississippi
North Carolina
South Carolina
Tennessee

Region V 312-353-5000

Illinois
Indiana
Michigan
Minnesota
Ohio
Wisconsin

Region VI 214-767-7633

Arkansas
Louisiana
New Mexico
Oklahoma
Texas

Region VII 816-426-3208

Iowa
Kansas
Missouri
Nebraska

Region VIII 303-294-7186

Colorado
Montana
North Dakota
South Dakota
Utah
Wyoming

Region IX 415-744-6402

Arizona
California
Hawaii
Nevada

Region X 206-553-5676

Alaska
Idaho
Oregon
Washington

Source: *Directory of Operating Small Business Investment Companies*, U.S. Small Business Administration, Investment Division.

Note: In addition to the companies listed in this section of the *Almanac*, the *Directory of Small Business Investment Companies* includes SBICs designed to assist small businesses owned by socially or economically disadvantaged persons.

Region I

Connecticut

AB SBIC, Inc.
Adam J. Bozzuto, President
275 School House Road
Cheshire, CT 06410
PH: (203) 272-0203

All State Venture
Capital Corporation
Ceasar N. Anquillare, President
The Bishop House
32 Elm Street, P.O. Box 1629
New Haven, CT 06506
PH: (203) 787-5029

Capital Resource Co.
of Connecticut
Morris Morgenstein, General Partner
2558 Albany Avenue
West Hartford, CT 06117
PH: (203) 236-4336

Financial
Opportunities, Inc.
Ms. Robin Munson, Manager
One Vision Drive
Enfield, CT 06082
PH: (203) 741-4444

First New England
Capital, LP
Richard C. Klaffky, President
100 Pearl Street
Hartford, CT 06103
PH: (203) 293-3333

Marcon Capital Corp.
Martin A. Cohen, President
49 Riverside Avenue
Westport, CT 06880
PH: (203) 226-6893

RFE Capital
Partners, L.P.
Robert M. Williams, Managing Partner
36 Grove Street
New Canaan, CT 06840
PH: (203) 966-2800

SBIC of Connecticut
Inc. (The)
Kenneth F. Zarrilli, President
965 White Plains Road
Trumbull, CT 06611
PH: (203) 261-0011

Maine

Maine Capital Corp.
David M. Coit, President
Seventy Center Street
Portland, ME 04101
PH: (207) 772-1001

Massachusetts

Advent Atlantic
Capital Company, LP
David D. Croll, Managing Partner
75 State Street, Suite 2500
Boston, MA 02109
PH: (617) 345-7200

Advent Industrial
Capital Company, LP
David D. Croll, Managing Partner
75 State Street, Suite 2500
Boston, MA 02109
PH: (617) 345-7200

Advent V Capital
Company LP
David D. Croll, Managing Partner
75 State Street, Suite 2500
Boston, MA 02109
PH: (617) 345-7200

BancBoston Ventures,
Incorporated
Frederick M. Fritz, President
100 Federal Street
Mail: P.O. Box 2016 Stop 01-31-08
Boston, MA 02110
PH: (617) 434-2442

Business Achievement
Corporation
Michael L. Katzeff, President
1172 Beacon Street, Suite 202
Newton, MA 02161
PH: (617) 965-0550

Chestnut Capital
International II LP
David D. Croll, Managing Partner
75 State Street, Suite 2500
Boston, MA 02109
PH: (617) 345-7200

Chestnut Street
Partners, Inc.
David D. Croll, President
75 State Street, Suite 2500
Boston, MA 02109
PH: (617) 345-7220

First Capital Corp.
of Chicago
(Main Office: Chicago, IL)
One Financial Center
27th Floor
Boston, MA 02111
PH: (617) 457-2500

LRF Capital,
Limited Partnership
Joseph J. Freeman, Manager
189 Wells Avenue, Suite 4
Newton, MA 02159
PH: (617) 964-0049

Mezzanine Capital
Corporation
David D. Croll, President
75 State Street, Suite 2500
Boston, MA 02109
PH: (617) 345-7200

Northeast SBI Corp.
Joseph Mindick, Treasurer
16 Cumberland Street
Boston, MA 02115
PH: (617) 267-3983

Pioneer Ventures
Limited Partnership
Frank M. Polestra, Managing Partner
60 State Street
Boston, MA 02109
PH: (617) 742-7825

UST Capital Corp.
Arthur F.F. Snyder, President
40 Court Street
Boston, MA 02108
PH: (617) 726-7000

Rhode Island

Domestic Capital Corp.
Nathaniel B. Baker, President
815 Reservoir Avenue
Cranston, RI 02910
PH: (401) 946-3310

Fairway Capital Corp.
Paul V. Anjoorian, President
99 Wayland Avenue
Mail: 285 Governor Street
Providence, RI 02906
PH: (401) 454-7500

Fleet Venture
Resources, Inc.
Robert M. Van Degna, President
111 Westminster Street
4th Floor
Providence, RI 02903
PH: (401) 278-6770

Moneta Capital Corp.
Arnold Kilberg, President
99 Wayland Avenue
Mail: 285 Governor Street
Providence, RI 02906
PH: (401) 454-7500

NYSTRS/NV Capital,
Limited Partnership
Robert M. Van Degna, Managing Partner
111 Westminster Street
Providence, RI 02903
PH: (401) 276-5597

Richmond Square
Capital Corporation
Harold I. Schein, President
1 Richmond Square
Providence, RI 02906
PH: (401) 521-3000

Wallace Capital
Corporation
Lloyd W. Granoff, President
170 Westminister Street
Suite 300
Providence, RI 02903
PH: (401) 273-9191

Vermont

Green Mountain
Capital, L.P.
Michael Sweatman, General Manager
P.O. Box 659
Stowe, VT 05672
PH: (802) 253-8142

Queneska Capital
Corporation
Albert W. Coffrin, III, President
123 Church Street
Burlington, VT 05401
PH: (802) 865-1806

Region II

New Jersey

Bishop Capital, L.P.
Charles J. Irish, General Partner
500 Morris Avenue
Springfield, NJ 07081
PH: (201) 376-0495

CIT Group/Venture
Capital, Inc.
Colby W. Collier, Manager
650 CIT Drive
Livingston, NJ 07932
PH: (201) 740-5429

ESLO Capital Corp.
Leo Katz, President
212 Wright Street
Newark, NJ 07114
PH: (201) 242-4488

First Princeton
Capital Corporation
Michael Lytell, President
One Garret Mountain Plaza
9th Floor
West Paterson, NJ 07424
PH: (201) 278-8111

Fortis Capital
Corporation
Martin Orland, President
333 Thornall Street, 2nd Floor
Edison, NJ 08837
PH: (908) 603-8500

Tappan Zee Capital
Corporation
Jack Birnberg, President
201 Lower Notch Road
Little Falls, NJ 07424
PH: (201) 256-8280

New York

399 Venture Partners
Barbara Wolfson, Unit Leader
399 Park Avenue, 14th Floor/Zone 4
New York, NY 10043
PH: (212) 736-8170

767 Limited
Partnership
H. Wertheim and H. Mallement, G.P.
767 Third Avenue
c/o Harvey Wertheim
New York, NY 10017
PH: (212) 838-7776

ASEA-Harvest
Partners II
Harvey Wertheim, General Partner
767 Third Avenue
New York, NY 10017
PH: (212) 838-7776

Argentum Capital
Partners, LP
Daniel Raynor, Chairman
405 Lexington Avenue, 54th Floor
New York, NY 10174
PH: (212) 949-8272

Atalanta Investment
Company, Inc.
L. Mark Newman, Chairman of the Board
650 5th Avenue, 15th Floor
New York, NY 10019
PH: (212) 956-9100

BT Capital Corp.
Noel E. Urben, President
280 Park Avenue--32 West
New York, NY 10017
PH: (212) 454-1903

Barclays Capital
Investors Corp.
Graham McGahen, President
222 Broadway, 7th Floor
New York, NY 10038
PH: (212) 412-3937

CB Investors, Inc.
Edward L. Kock III, President
270 Park Avenue
New York, NY 10017
PH: (212) 286-3222

CIBC Wood Gundy
Ventures, Inc.
Gordon Muessel, Vice President
425 Lexington Avenue, 9th Floor
New York, NY 10017
PH: (212) 856-3713

CMNY Capital II, L.P.
Robert G. Davidoff, General Partner
135 East 57th Street
26th Floor
New York, NY 10022
PH: (212) 909-8432

CMNY Capital L.P.
Robert Davidoff, General Partner
135 East 57th Street
26th Floor
New York, NY 10022
PH: (212) 909-8432

Chase Manhattan
Capital Corporation
Gustav H. Koven, President
1 Chase Plaza--7th Floor
New York, NY 10081
PH: (212) 552-6275

Chemical Venture
Capital Associates
Jeffrey C. Walker, Managing Gen. Partner
275 Park Avenue, 5th Floor
New York, NY 10017
PH: (212) 270-3220

Citicorp Venture
Capital, Ltd.
William Comfort, Chairman of the Board
399 Park Avenue, 14th Floor/Zone 4
New York, NY 10043
PH: (212) 559-1127

Edwards Capital Company
Edward H. Teitlebaum, President
Two Park Avenue, 20th Floor
New York, NY 10016
PH: (212) 686-5449

Fifty-Third Street
Ventures, L.P.
Patricia Cloherty & Dan Tessler, G.P.
155 Main Street
Cold Spring, NY 10516
PH: (914) 265-4244

First Wall Street SBIC, LP
Alan Farkas, G.P.
26 Broadway, Suite 1320
New York, NY 10004
PH: (212) 742-3770

Fundex Capital Corp.
Howard Sommer, President
525 Northern Blvd.
Great Neck, NY 11021
PH: (516) 466-8551

Genesee Funding, Inc.
Stuart Marsh, President & CEO
100 Corporate Woods
Rochester, NY 14623
PH: (716) 272-2332

IBJS Capital Corp.
Peter D. Matthy, President
One State Street, 8th Floor
New York, NY 10004
PH: (212) 858-2000

InterEquity Capital
Corporation
Irwin Schlass, President
220 Fifth Avenue, 10th Floor
New York, NY 10001
PH: (212) 779-2022

J.P. Morgan Investment
Corporation
David M. Cromwell, Managing Director
60 Wall Street
New York, NY 10260
PH: (212) 483-2323

Kwiat Capital Corp.
Sheldon F. Kwiat, President
579 Fifth Avenue
New York, NY 10017
PH: (212) 223-1111

M & T Capital Corp.
Phillip A. McNeill, Vice President
One M & T Plaza
Buffalo, NY 14240
PH: (716) 842-5881

NYBDC Capital Corp.
Robert W. Lazar, President
41 State Street
P.O. Box 738
Albany, NY 12201
PH: (518) 463-2268

NatWest USA Capital
Corporation
Phillip Krall, General Manager
175 Water Street, 27th Floor
New York, NY 10038
PH: (212) 602-1200

Norwood Venture
Corp.
Mark R. Littell, President
1430 Broadway, Suite 1607
New York, NY 10018
PH: (212) 869-5075

Paribas Principal
Incorporated
Steven Alexander, President
787 Seventh Avenue
New York, NY 10019
PH: (212) 841-2000

Pyramid Ventures, Inc.
Annmarie O'Shea, Asst. Vice President
280 Park Avenue--29 West
New York, NY 10017
PH: (212) 454-1702

R & R Financial Corp.
Imre Rosenthal, President
1370 Broadway
New York, NY 10036
PH: (212) 356-1400

Rand SBIC, Inc.
Donald Ross, President
1300 Rand Building
Buffalo, NY 14203
PH: (716) 853-0802

Sterling Commercial
Capital, Inc.
Harvey L. Granat, President
175 Great Neck Road--Suite 408
Great Neck, NY 11021
PH: (516) 482-7374

TLC Funding Corp.
Phillip G. Kass, President
660 White Plains Road
Tarrytown, NY 10591
PH: (914) 332-5200

Tappan Zee Capital
Corporation
(Main Office: Little Falls, NJ)
120 North Main Street
New City, NY 10956
PH: (914) 634-8890

Vega Capital Corp.
Victor Harz, President
720 White Plains Road
Scarsdale, NY 10583
PH: (914) 472-8550

Winfield Capital Corp.
Stanley M. Pechman, President
237 Mamaroneck Avenue
White Plains, NY 10605
PH: (914) 949-2600

Region III

District of Columbia

Allied Investment Corp.
Cable Williams, President
1666 K Street, N.W., Suite 901
Washington, DC 20006
PH: (202) 331-1112

Allied Investment
Corporation II
William F. Dunbar, President
1666 K Street, N.W., Suite 901
Washington, DC 20006
PH: (202) 331-1112

Legacy Fund Limited
Partnership
John Ledecky, Manager & General Partner
1225 19th Street, N.W., 5th Floor
Washington, DC 20036
PH: (202) 659-1100

Maryland

American Security
Capital Corp., Inc.
Jim Henry, Investment Officer
100 S. Charles Street, 5th Floor
Baltimore, MD 21203
PH: (410) 547-4205

Greater Washington
Investments, Inc.
Haywood Miller, Manager
5454 Wisconsin Avenue
Chevy Chase, MD 20815
PH: (301) 656-0626

Pennsylvania

CIP Capital, L.P.
Winston Churchill, Jr., Manager
20 Valley Stream Parkway
Malvern, PA 19355
PH: (215) 695-8380

Enterprise Venture Cap
Corp of Pennsylvania
Don Cowie, CEO
111 Market Street
Johnstown, PA 15901
PH: (814) 535-7597

Erie SBIC
George R. Heaton, President
32 West 8th Street, Suite 615
Erie, PA 16501
PH: (814) 453-7964

Fidelcor Capital
Corporation
Elizabeth T. Crawford, President
Fidelity Building, 11th Floor
123 South Broad Street
Philadelphia, PA 19109
PH: (215) 985-3722

First SBIC of
California
(Main Office: Costa Mesa, CA)
Daniel A. Dye, Contact
P.O. Box 512
Washington, PA 15301
PH: (412) 223-0707

Meridian Capital Corp.
Pamela E. Davis, President
601 Penn Street
Reading, PA 19603
PH: (215) 655-2924

Meridian Venture
Partners
Raymond R. Rafferty, General Partner
The Fidelity Court Building
259 Radnor-Chester Road
Radnor, PA 19087
PH: (215) 254-2999

PNC Capital Corp.
Gary J. Zentner, President
Pittsburgh National Building
Fifth Avenue and Wood Street
Pittsburgh, PA 15265
PH: (412) 762-2248

Virginia

Rural America
Fund, Inc.
Fred Russell, Chief Executive Officer
2201 Cooperative Way
Herndon, VA 22071
PH: (703) 709-6750

Walnut Capital Corp.
(Main Office: Chicago, IL)
8000 Tower Crescent Drive, Suite 1070
Vienna, VA 22182
PH: (703) 448-3771

Region IV

Alabama

First SBIC of
Alabama
David C. DeLaney, President
16 Midtown Park East
Mobile, AL 36606
PH: (205) 476-0700

Hickory Venture
Capital Corporation
J. Thomas Noojin, President
200 W. Court Square, Suite 100
Huntsville, AL 35801
PH: (205) 539-5130

Florida

Allied Investment
Corporation
(Main Office: Washington, DC)
Executive Office Center, Suite 305
2770 N. Indian River Blvd.
Vero Beach, FL 32960
PH: (407) 778-5556

Florida Capital
Ventures, Ltd.
Warren E. Miller, President
880 Riverside Plaza
100 W. Kennedy Blvd.
Tampa, FL 33602
PH: (813) 229-2294

J & D Capital Corp.
Jack Carmel, President
12747 Biscayne Blvd.
North Miami, FL 33181
PH: (305) 893-0303

Market Capital Corp.
Donald Kolvenbach, President
1102 North 28th Street
Mail: P.O. Box 31667
Tampa, FL 33631
PH: (813) 247-1357

Quantum Capital
Partners, Ltd.
Michael E. Chaney, President
4400 NE 25th Avenue
Fort Lauderdale, FL 33308
PH: (305) 776-1133

Western Financial
Capital Corporation
(Main Office: Dallas, TX)
AmeriFirst Bank Building, 2nd Floor S
18301 Biscayne Boulevard
N. Miami Beach, FL 33160
PH: (305) 933-5858

Georgia

Investor's Equity,
Inc.
I. Walter Fisher, President
945 E. Paces Ferry Road, Suite 1735
Atlanta, GA 30326
PH: (404) 266-8300

North Riverside
Capital Corporation
Tom Barry, President
50 Technology Park/Atlanta
Norcross, GA 30092
PH: (404) 446-5556

Kentucky

Mountain Ventures,
Inc.
L. Ray Moncrief, President
P.O. Box 1738, 362 Old Whitley Road
London, KY 40743
PH: (606) 864-5175

North Carolina

First Union Capital
Partners, Inc.
Kevin J. Roche, Senior Vice President
One First Union Center, 18th Floor
301 South College Street
Charlotte, NC 28288
PH: (703) 374-6487

Heritage Capital Corp.
Richard N. Brigden, Vice President
2000 Two First Union Center
Charlotte, NC 28282
PH: (704) 372-5404

NationsBanc SBIC
Corporation
George W. Campbell, Jr., President
901 West Trade Street, Suite 1020
Charlotte, NC 28202
PH: (704) 386-7720

Springdale Venture
Partners, LP
S. Epes Robinson, General Partner
2039 Queens Road, East
Charlotte, NC 28207
PH: (704) 344-8290

South Carolina

Charleston Capital
Corporation
Henry Yaschik, President
111 Church Street
P.O. Box 328
Charleston, SC 29402
PH: (803) 723-6464

Floco Investment
Company, Inc. (The)
William H. Johnson, Sr., President
Highway 52 North
Mail: P.O. Box 919; Lake City, SC 29560
Scranton, SC 29561
PH: (803) 389-2731

Lowcountry Investment
Corporation
Joseph T. Newton, Jr., President
4444 Daley Street
P.O. Box 10447
Charleston, SC 29411
PH: (803) 554-9880

Tennessee

Sirrom Capital, LP
George M. Miller, II, Manager
511 Union Street, Suite 2310
Nashville, TN 37219
PH: (615) 256-0701

Region V

Illinois

Business Ventures,
Incorporated
Milton Lefton, President
20 North Wacker Drive, Suite 1741
Chicago, IL 60606
PH: (312) 346-1580

Continental Illinois
Venture Corp.
John Willis, President
209 South LaSalle Street
Mail: 231 South LaSalle Street
Chicago, IL 60693
PH: (312) 828-8023

First Capital Corp.
of Chicago
J. Mikesell Thomas, President
Three First National Plaza
Suite 1330
Chicago, IL 60670
PH: (312) 732-5400

Heller Equity
Capital Corporation
John M. Goense, President
500 West Monroe Street
Chicago, IL 60661
PH: (312) 441-7200

Walnut Capital Corp.
Burton W. Kanter, Chairman of the Board
Two North LaSalle Street, Suite 2410
Chicago, IL 60602
PH: (312) 346-2033

Indiana

1st Source Capital Corp.
Eugene L. Cavanaugh, Jr., Vice President
100 North Michgan Street
Mail: P.O. Box 1602; South Bend 46634
South Bend, IN 46601
PH: (219) 235-2180

Cambridge Ventures, LP
Ms. Jean Wojtowicz, President
8440 Woodfield Crossing, #315
Indianapolis, IN 46240
PH: (317) 469-9704

Circle Ventures, Inc.
Carrie Walkup, Manager
26 N. Arsenal Avenue
Indianapolis, IN 46201
PH: (317) 636-7242

Michigan

Capital Fund, The
Barry Wilson, President
6412 Centurion Drive Suite 150
Lansing, MI 48917
PH: (517) 323-7772

White Pines Capital Corporation
Mr. Ian Bund, President & Manager
2929 Plymouth Road, Suite 210
Ann Arbor, MI 48105
PH: (313) 747-9401

Minnesota

FBS SBIC, Limited Partnership
John M. Murphy, Jr., Managing Agent
601 Second Avenue South
Minneapolis, MN 55402
PH: (612) 973-0988

Northland Capital Venture Partnership
George G. Barnum, Jr., President
613 Missabe Building
Duluth, MN 55802
PH: (218) 722-0545

Northwest Venture Partners
Robert F. Zicarelli, Managing G.P.
2800 Piper Jaffray Tower
222 South Ninth Street
Minneapolis, MN 55402
PH: (612) 667-1650

Norwest Equity Partners IV
Robert F. Zicarelli, General Partner
2800 Piper Jaffray Tower
222 South Ninth Street
Minneapolis, MN 55402
PH: (612) 667-1650

Norwest Growth Fund, Inc.
Daniel J. Haggerty, President
2800 Piper Jaffray Tower
222 South Ninth Street
Minneapolis, MN 55402
PH: (612) 667-1650

Ohio

Banc One Capital Partners Corporation
(Main Office: Dallas, TX)
10 West Broad Street, Suite 200
Columbus, OH 43215

Clarion Capital Corporation
Morton A. Cohen, President
Ohio Savings Plaza, Suite 1520
1801 E. 9th Street
Cleveland, OH 44114
PH: (216) 687-1096

National City Capital Corporation
William H. Schecter, President & G.M.
1965 East Sixth Street, Suite 400
Cleveland, OH 44114
PH: (216) 575-2491

Society Venture Capital Corporation
Raymond Lancaster, President
127 Public Square, 4th Floor
Cleveland, OH 44114
PH: (216) 689-5776

Wisconsin

Banc One Venture Corp.
H. Wayne Foreman, President
111 East Wisconsin Avenue
Milwaukee, WI 53202
PH: (414) 765-2274

Bando-McGlocklin SBIC
George Schonath, Chief Executive Officer
13555 Bishops Court, Suite 205
Brookfield, WI 53005
PH: (414) 784-9010

Capital Investments, Inc.
James R. Sanger, President
Commerce Building, Suite 540
744 North Fourth Street
Milwaukee, WI 53203
PH: (414) 273-6560

M & I Ventures Corp.
John T. Byrnes, President
770 North Water Street
Milwaukee, WI 53202
PH: (414) 765-7910

MorAmerica Capital Corporation
(Main Office: Cedar Rapids, IA)
600 East Mason Street
Milwaukee, WI 53202
PH: (414) 276-3839

Polaris Capital Corp.
Richard Laabs, President
One Park Plaza
11270 W. Park Place, Suite 320
Milwaukee, WI 53224
PH: (414) 359-3040

Region VI

Arkansas

Small Business
Inv. Capital, Inc.
Charles E. Toland, President
10003 New Benton Hwy.
Mail: P.O. Box 3627
Little Rock, AR 72203
PH: (501) 455-6599

Southern Ventures, Inc
George Surgeon, CEO
605 Main Street, Suite 202
Arkadelphia, AR 71923
PH: (501) 246-9627

Louisiana

Premier Venture
Capital Corporation
G. Lee Griffin, President
451 Florida Street
Baton Rouge, LA 70821
PH: (504) 389-4421

Oklahoma

Alliance Business
Investment Company
Barry Davis, President
17 East Second Street
One Williams Center, Suite 2000
Tulsa, OK 74172
PH: (918) 584-3581

Texas

AMT Capital, Ltd.
Tom H. Delimitros, CGP
8204 Elmbrook Drive, Suite 101
Dallas, TX 75247
PH: (214) 905-9760

Alliance Business
Investment Company
(Main Office: Tulsa, OK)
911 Louisiana
One Shell Plaza, Suite 3990
Houston, TX 77002
PH: (713) 224-8224

Banc One Capital
Partners Corporation
Michael J. Endres, President
300 Crescent Court, Suite 1600
Dallas, TX 75201
PH: (214) 979-4360

Capital Southwest
Venture Corp.
William R. Thomas, President
12900 Preston Road, Suite 700
Dallas, TX 75230
PH: (214) 233-8242

Catalyst Fund,
Ltd. (The)
Richard L. Herrman, Manager
Three Riverway, Suite 770
Houston, TX 77056
PH: (713) 623-8133

Central Texas SBI
Corporation
Robert H. Korman II, Director
1401 Elm Street, Suite 4764
Dallas, TX 75202
PH: (214) 508-0900

Charter Venture Group,
Incorporated
Winston C. Davis, President
2600 Citadel Plaza Drive, Suite 600
P.O. Box 4525
Houston, TX 77008
PH: (713) 622-7500

Citicorp Venture Capital, Ltd.
(Main Office: New York, NY)
717 North Harwood
Suite 2920-LB87
Dallas, TX 75201
PH: (214) 880-9670

First City, Texas
Ventures, Inc.
Mr. J.R. Brlansky, Manager
1001 Main Street, 15th Floor
P.O. Box 4517
Houston, TX 77002
PH: (713) 658-5421

Ford Capital, Ltd.
C. Jeff Pan, President
200 Crescent Court, Suite 1350
Mail: P.O. Box 2140; Dallas, TX 75221
Dallas, TX 75201
PH: (214) 871-5177

HCT Capital Corp.
Vichy Woodward Young, Jr., President
4916 Camp Bowie Boulevard, Suite 200
Fort Worth, TX 76107
PH: (817) 763-8706

Houston Partners, SBIP
Harvard Hill, President, CGP
Capital Center Penthouse, 8th Floor
401 Louisiana
Houston, TX 77002
PH: (713) 222-8600

Jiffy Lube Capital
Corporation
Mark Youngs, Manager
700 Milam Street
Mail: P.O. Box 2967
Houston, TX 77252
PH: (713) 546-8910

Mapleleaf Capital Ltd.
Patrick A. Rivelli, Manager
Three Forest Plaza, Suite 1300
12221 Merit Drive
Dallas, TX 75251
PH: (214) 239-5650

NationsBanc Capital
Corporation
David Franklin, President
901 Main Street, 66th Floor
Dallas, TX 75202
PH: (214) 508-0900

SBI Capital Corp.
William E. Wright, President
6305 Beverly Hill Lane
Mail: P.O. Box 570368; Houston, TX 77257
Houston, TX 77057
PH: (713) 975-1188

UNCO Ventures, Inc.
John Gatti, President
520 Post Oak Blvd., Suite 130
Houston, TX 77027
PH: (713) 622-9595

Ventex Partners, Ltd.
Richard S. Smith, President
1000 Louisiana, Suite 1110
Houston, TX 77002
PH: (713) 659-7860

Victoria Capital Corp.
Kenneth L. Vickers, President
One O'Connor Plaza
Victoria, TX 77902
PH: (512) 573-5151

Victoria Capital Corp.
(Main Office: Victoria, TX)
750 E. Mulberry, Suite 305
Mail: P.O. Box 15616
San Antonio, TX 78212
PH: (512) 736-4233

Western Financial
Capital Corporation
Andrew S. Rosemore, President
17290 Preston Road, Suite 300
Dallas, TX 75252
PH: (214) 380-0044

Region VII

Iowa

MorAmerica Capital
Corporation
David R. Schroder, Vice President
101 2nd Street, SE
Suite 800
Cedar Rapids, IA 52401
PH: (319) 363-8249

Kansas

Kansas Venture
Capital, Inc.
Rex E. Wiggins, President
6700 Antioch Plaza, Suite 460
Overland Park, KS 66204
PH: (913) 262-7117

Kansas Venture Capital, Inc.
(Main Office: Overland Park, KS)
Thomas C. Blackburn, Vice President
One Main Place, Suite 806
Wichita, KS 67202
PH: (316) 262-1221

Missouri

Bankers Capital Corp.
Raymond E. Glasnapp, President
3100 Gillham Road
Kansas City, MO 64109
PH: (816) 531-1600

CFB Venture Fund I, Inc.
James F. O'Donnell, Chairman
11 South Meramec, Suite 800
St. Louis, MO 63105
PH: (314) 854-7427

CFB Venture Fund II,
Inc.
Bart S. Bergman, President
1000 Walnut Street, 18th Floor
Kansas City, MO 64106
PH: (816) 234-2357

Midland Capital Corp.
Neil E. Sprague, Manager
1010 Walnut Street
Kansas City, MO 64106
PH: (816) 471-8000

MorAmerica Capital
Corporation
(Main Office: Cedar Rapids, IA)
911 Main Street, Suite 2724A
Commerce Tower Building
Kansas City, MO 64105
PH: (816) 842-0114

United Missouri
Capital Corporation
Noel Shull, Manager
1010 Grand Avenue
Mail: P.O. Box 419226; K.C., MO 64141
Kansas City, MO 64106
PH: (816) 556-7333

Nebraska

United Financial
Resources Corp.
Joan Boulay, Manager
7401 "F" Street
Mail: P.O. Box 1131; Ohama, NE 68101
Omaha, NE 68127
PH: (402) 339-7300

Region VIII

Colorado

UBD Capital, Inc.
Dennis D. Erickson, President
1700 Broadway
Denver, CO 80274
PH: (303) 861-8811

Region IX

Arizona

First Commerce
& Loan LP
Ross M. Horowitz, GP & Manager
5620 N. Kolb, #260
Tucson, AZ 85715
PH: (602) 298-2500

First Interstate
Equity Corp.
Edmund G. Zito, President
100 West Washington Street
Phoenix, AZ 85003
PH: (602) 528-6647

Sundance Venture
Partners, L.P.
(Main Office: Cupertino, CA)
Gregory S. Anderson, Vice-President
2828 N. Central Avenue, Suite 1275
Phoenix, AZ 85004
PH: (602) 279-1101

California

AMF Financial, Inc.
Ron Arehart, President
4330 La Jolla Village Drive
Suite 110
San Diego, CA 92122
PH: (619) 546-0167

BNP Venture Capital
Corporation
Edgerton Scott II, President
3000 Sand Hill Road
Building 1, Suite 125
Menlo Park, CA 94025
PH: (415) 854-1084

BT Capital Corp.
(Main Office: New York, NY)
300 South Grand Avenue
Los Angeles, CA 90071
PH: NONE

Citicorp Venture
Capital, Ltd.
(Main Office: New York, NY)
2 Embarcadero Place
2200 Geny Road, Suite 203
Palo Alto, CA 94303
PH: (415) 424-8000

DSC Ventures II, LP
Daniel D. Tompkins, Jr., Managing G.P.
20111 Stevens Creek Boulevard
Suite 130
Cupertino, CA 95014
PH: (408) 252-3800

Developers Equity
Capital Corporation
Larry Sade, Chairman of the Board
1880 Century Park East
Suite 211
Los Angeles, CA 90067
PH: (310) 277-0330

Draper Associates,
a California LP
Timothy C. Draper, President
400 Seaport Court, Suite 250
Redwood City, CA 94063
PH: (415) 599-9000

First SBIC of
California
Robert L. Boswell, Senior Vice President
650 Town Center Drive
Seventeenth Floor
Costa Mesa, CA 92626
PH: (714) 556-1964

First SBIC of California
(Main Office: Costa Mesa, CA)
5 Palo Alto Square, Suite 938
Palo Alto, CA 94306
PH: (415) 424-8011

First SBIC of
California
(Main Office: Costa Mesa, CA)
155 North Lake Avenue, Suite 1010
Pasadena, CA 91109
PH: (818) 304-3451

G C & H Partners
James C. Gaither, General Partner
One Maritime Plaza, 20th Floor
San Francisco, CA 94110
PH: (415) 981-5252

Hall, Morris
& Drufva II, L.P.
Ronald J. Hall, Managing Director
25401 Cabbot Road, Suite 116
Laguna Hills, CA 92653
PH: (714) 707-5096

Imperial Ventures,
Inc.
Ray Vadalma, Manager
9920 South La Cienega Blvd.
Mail: P.O. Box 92991; L.A. 90009
Inglewood, CA 90301
PH: (310) 417-5710

Jupiter Partners
John M. Bryan, President
600 Montgomery Street
35th Floor
San Francisco, CA 94111
PH: (415) 421-9990

Marwit Capital Corp.
Martin W. Witte, President
180 Newport Center Drive
Suite 200
Newport Beach, CA 92660
PH: (714) 640-6234

Merrill Pickard
Anderson & Eyre I
Steven L. Merrill, President
2480 Sand Hill Road, Suite 200
Menlo Park, CA 94025
PH: (415) 854-8600

New West Partners II
Timothy P. Haidinger, Manager
4350 Executive Drive, Suite 206
San Diego, CA 92121
PH: (619) 457-0723

Northwest Venture
Partners
(Main Office: Minneapolis, MN)
3000 Sand Hill Road
Building 3, Suite 245
Menlo Park, CA 94025

Norwest Equity
Partners IV
(Main Office: Minneapolis, MN)
3000 Sand Hill Road
Building 3, Suite 245
Menlo Park, CA 94025
PH: (503) 223-6622

Norwest Growth Fund,
Inc.
(Main Office: Minneapolis, MN)
3000 Sand Hill Road
Building 3, Suite 245
Menlo Park, CA 94025

Ritter Partners
William C. Edwards, President
150 Isabella Avenue
Atherton, CA 94025
PH: (415) 854-1555

Sundance Venture
Partners, L.P.
Larry J. Wells, General Manager
10600 N. DeAnza Blvd., Suite 215
Cupertino, CA 95014
PH: (408) 257-8100

Union Venture Corp.
Kathleen Burns, Vice President
445 South Figueroa Street
Los Angeles, CA 90071
PH: (213) 236-5658

VK Capital Company
Franklin Van Kasper, General Partner
50 California Street, Suite 2350
San Francisco, CA 94111
PH: (415) 391-5600

Hawaii

Bancorp Hawaii SBIC
Robert Paris, President
111 South King Street
Suite 1060
Honolulu, HI 96813
PH: (808) 521-6411

Region X

Oregon

Northern Pacific
Capital Corporation
Joseph P. Tennant, President
937 S.W. 14th Street, Suite 200
Mail: P.O. Box 1658
Portland, OR 97207
PH: (503) 241-1255

U.S. Bancorp Capital
Corporation
Gary Patterson, President
111 S.W. Fifth Avenue
Suite 1090
Portland, OR 97204
PH: (503) 275-5860

Directories

Directory of Small Business Investment Companies. Contains a listing of SBICs by state including branch offices, contact persons, and types of businesses funded. Free of charge, the *Directory* is available by calling the Small Business Administration at 202-205-7586.

Pratt's Guide to Venture Capital Sources. Provides extensive information on all leading venture capital firms in the U.S.A. and around the world. Available from:

Venture Economics
40 West 57th Street
New York, NY 10102-0968

Corporate Finance Source Book. This volume provides a listing of thousands of US and world financial sources. Published by:

National Register Publishing Co.
3004 Glenview Road
Wolmette, IL 60091

National Venture Capital Association (NVCA) *Membership Directory* lists members of the association and information about it.

National Venture Capital Association
1655 North Fort Meyer Drive
Arlington, VA 22209
Telephone: 703-528-4370

Small Business Administration (SBA) Field Offices

REGIONAL OFFICES

REGION I
155 Federal St.
Ninth Floor
Boston, MA 02110
Tel: (617) 451-2023
TDD: (617) 451-0491

REGION II
26 Federal Plaza
Room 31-08
New York, NY 10278
Tel: (212) 264-1450
TDD: (212) 264-5669

REGION III
475 Allendale Road
Suite 201
King Of Prussia, PA 19406
Tel: (215) 962-3700
TDD: (215) 962-3739

REGION IV
1375 Peachtree St. N.E.
Fifth Floor
Atlanta, GA 30367-8102
Tel: (404) 347-2797
TDD: (404) 347-5051

REGION V
300 S. Riverside Plaza
Suite 1975 S
Chicago, IL 60606-6617
Tel: (312) 353-5000
TDD: (312) 353-8060

REGION VI
8625 King George Drive
Building C
Dallas, TX 75235-3391
Tel: (214) 767-7633
TDD: (214) 767-1339

REGION VII
911 Walnut St.
13th Floor
Kansas City, MO 64106
Tel: (816) 426-3608
TDD: (816) 426-2990

REGION VIII
999 18th St.
Suite 701
Denver, CO 80202
Tel: (303) 294-7186
TDD: (303) 294-7096

REGION IX
71 Stevenson St.
20th Floor
San Francisco, CA 94105-2939
Tel: (415) 744-6402
TDD: (415) 744-6401

REGION X
2615 Fourth Ave.
Room 440
Seattle, WA 98121
Tel: (206) 553-5676
TDD: (206) 553-2872

DISTRICT, BRANCH AND POST-OF-DUTY OFFICES

ALABAMA
2121 8th Ave., N.
Suite 200
Birmingham, AL 35203-2398
Tel: (205) 731-1344
TDD: (205) 731-2265

ALASKA
222 W. 8th Ave.
Room 67
Anchorage, AK 99513-7559
Tel: (907) 271-4022
TDD: (907) 271-4005

ARIZONA
2828 N. Central Ave.
Suite 800
Phoenix, AZ 85004-1025
Tel: (602) 640-2316
TDD: (602) 640-2357

300 W. Congress St.
Room 7-H
Tucson, AZ 85701-1319
Tel: (602) 670-4759
TDD: None Listed

ARKANSAS
2120 Riverfront Drive
Suite 100
Little Rock, AR 72202
Tel: (501) 324-5278
TDD: (501) 324-7849

CALIFORNIA
2719 N. Air Fresno Drive
Fresno, CA 93727-1547
Tel: (209) 487-5189
TDD: (209) 487-5917

330 N. Brand Blvd.
Suite 1200
Glendale, CA 91203-2304
Tel: (213) 894-2956
TDD: (213) 894-6338

880 Front St.
Suite 4-S-29
San Diego, CA 92188-0270
Tel: (619) 557-7252
TDD: (619) 557-6998

211 Main St.
Fourth Floor
San Francisco, CA 94105-1988
Tel: (415) 744-6820
TDD: (415) 744-6778

901 W. Civic Center Drive
Suite 160
Santa Ana, CA 92703-2352
Tel: (714) 836-2494
TDD: (714) 836-2200

660 J St.
Room 215
Sacramento, CA 95814-2413
Tel: (916) 551-1426
TDD: None Listed

6477 Telephone Road
Suite 10
Ventura, CA 93003-4459
Tel: (805) 642-1866
TDD: None Listed

COLORADO
721 19th St.
Suite 426
Denver, CO 80202-2259
Tel: (303) 844-3984
TDD: (303) 844-5638

CONNECTICUT
330 Main St.
Second Floor
Hartford, CT 06106
Tel: (203) 240-4700
TDD: (203) 524-1611

DISTRICT OF COLUMBIA
1111 18th Street, N.W.
Sixth Floor
Washington, DC 20036
Tel: (202) 634-1500
TDD: (202) 634-6185

DELAWARE
920 N. King St.
Suite 412
Wilmington, DE 19801
Tel: (302) 573-6295
TDD: (302) 573-6644

FLORIDA
1320 S. Dixie Highway
Suite 501
Coral Gables, FL 33146-2911
Tel: (305) 536-5521
TDD: (305) 530-7110

7825 Baymeadows Way
Suite 100-B
Jacksonville, FL 32256-7504
Tel: (904) 443-1900
TDD: (904) 443-1909

501 E. Polk St.
Suite 104
Tampa, FL 33602-3945
Tel: (813) 228-2594
TDD: None Listed

5601 Corporate Way
Suite 402
West Palm Beach, FL 33407
Tel: (407) 689-3922
TDD: None Listed

GEORGIA
1720 Peachtree Road, NW
Sixth Floor
Atlanta, GA 30309
Tel: (404) 347-4749
TDD: (404) 347-0107

52 N. Main St.
Room 225
Statesboro, GA 30458
Tel: (912) 489-8719
TDD: None Listed

GUAM
238 Archbishop F.C. Flores St.
Room 508
Agana, GU 96910
Tel: (671) 472-7277
TDD: None Listed

HAWAII
300 Ala Moana Blvd.
Room 2213
Honolulu, HI 96850-4981
Tel: (808) 541-2990
TDD: (808) 541-3650

IDAHO
1020 Main St.
Suite 290
Boise, ID 83702-5745
Tel: (208) 334-1696
TDD: (208) 334-9637

ILLINOIS
500 W. Madison St.
Room 1250
Chicago, IL 60661-2511
Tel: (312) 353-4528
TDD: (312) 886-5108

511 W. Capitol St.
Suite 302
Springfield, IL 62704
Tel: (217) 492-4416
TDD: (217) 492-4418

INDIANA
429 N. Pennsylvania
Suite 100
Indianapolis, IN 46204-1873
Tel: (317) 226-7272
TDD: (317) 226-5338

IOWA
373 Collins Road, N.E.
Suite 100
Cedar Rapids, IA 52402-3147
Tel: (319) 393-8630
TDD: (319) 393-9610

210 Walnut St.
Room 749
Des Moines, IA 50309
Tel: (515) 284-4422
TDD: (515) 284-4233

KANSAS
100 E. English St.
Suite 510
Wichita, KS 67202
Tel: (316) 269-6273
TDD: (316) 269-6205

KENTUCKY
600 Dr. M.L. King Jr. Place
Room 188
Louisville, KY 40202
Tel: (502) 582-5971
TDD: (502) 582-6715

LOUISIANA
1661 Canal St.
Suite 2000
New Orleans, LA 70112
Tel: (504) 589-6685
TDD: (504) 589-2053

500 Fannin St.
Room 8A-08
Shreveport, LA 71101
Tel: (318) 676-3196
TDD: None Listed

MAINE
40 Western Ave.
Room 512
Augusta, ME 04330
Tel: (207) 622-8378
TDD: (207) 626-9147

MARYLAND
10 N. Calvert St.
Third Floor
Baltimore, MD 21202
Tel: (410) 962-4392
TDD: (410) 962-7458

MASSACHUSETTS
10 Causeway St.
Room 265
Boston, MA 02222-1093
Tel: (617) 565-5590
TDD: (617) 565-5797

1550 Main St.
Room 212
Springfield, MA 01103
Tel: (413) 785-0268
TDD: None Listed

MICHIGAN
477 Michigan Ave.
Room 515
Detroit, MI 48226
Tel: (313) 226-6075
TDD: (313) 226-2958

228 West Washington St.
Room 11
Marquette, MI 49885
Tel: (906) 225-1108
TDD: (906) 228-4126

MINNESOTA
100 N. Sixth St.
Suite 610
Minneapolis, MN 55403-1563
Tel: (612) 370-2324
TDD: (612) 777-2332

MISSISSIPPI
101 W. Capitol St.
Suite 400
Jackson, MS 39201
Tel: (601) 965-4378
TDD: (601) 965-5328

1 Hancock Plaza
Suite 1001
Gulfport, MS 39501-7758
Tel: (601) 863-4449
TDD: (601) 865-9926

MISSOURI
323 W. Eighth St.
Suite 501
Kansas City, MO 64105
Tel: (816) 374-6708
TDD: (816) 374-6764

815 Olive St.
Room 242
St. Louis, MO 63101
Tel: (314) 539-6600
TDD: (314) 539-6654

620 S. Glenstone St.
Suite 110
Springfield, MO 65802-3200
Tel: (417) 864-7670
TDD: (417) 864-8855

MONTANA
301 S. Park
Room 528
Helena, MT 59626
Tel: (406) 449-5381
TDD: (406) 449-5053

NEBRASKA
11145 Mill Valley Road
Omaha, NE 68154
Tel: (402) 221-4691
TDD: (402) 498-3611

NEVADA
301 E. Stewart St.
Room 301
Las Vegas, NV 89125-2527
Tel: (702) 388-6611
TDD: None Listed

50 S. Virginia St.
Room 238
Reno, NV 89505-3216
Tel: (702) 784-5268
TDD: None Listed

NEW HAMPSHIRE
143 N. Main St.
Suite 202
Concord, NH 03302-1257
Tel: (603) 225-1400
TDD: (603) 225-1462

NEW JERSEY
60 Park Place
Fourth Floor
Newark, NJ 07102
Tel: (201) 645-2434
TDD: (201) 645-4653

2600 Mt. Ephraim Ave.
Camden, NJ 08104
Tel: (609) 757-5183
TDD: None Listed

NEW MEXICO
625 Silver Ave., S.W.
Suite 320
Albuquerque, NM 87102
Tel: (505) 766-1870
TDD: (505) 766-1883

NEW YORK
26 Federal Plaza
Room 3100
New York, NY 10278
Tel: (212) 264-2454
TDD: (212) 264-9147

100 S. Clinton St.
Room 1071
Syracuse, NY 13260
Tel: (315) 423-5383
TDD: (315) 423-5723

111 W. Huron St.
Room 1311
Buffalo, NY 14202
Tel: (716) 846-4301
TDD: (716) 846-3248

333 E. Water St.
4th Floor
Elmira, NY 14901
Tel: (607) 734-8130
TDD: (607) 734-0557

35 Pinelawn Road
Room 102E
Melville, NY 11747
Tel: (516) 454-0750
TDD: None Listed

100 State St.
Room 410
Rochester, NY 14614
Tel: (716) 263-6700
TDD: None Listed

Leo O'Brian Building
Room 815
Albany, NY 12207
Tel: (518) 472-6300
TDD: None Listed

NORTH CAROLINA
200 N. College St.
Charlotte, NC 28202
Tel: (704) 344-6563
TDD: (704) 344-6640

NORTH DAKOTA
657 Second Ave., N.
Room 218
Fargo, ND 58108-3086
Tel: (701) 239-5131
TDD: (701) 239-5657

OHIO
1240 E. Ninth St.
Room 317
Cleveland, OH 44199
Tel: (216) 522-4180
TDD: (216) 522-8350

2 Nationwide Plaza
Suite 1400
Columbus, OH 43215-2592
Tel: (614) 469-6860
TDD: (614) 469-6684

525 Vine St.
Suite 870
Cincinnati, OH 45202
Tel: (513) 684-2814
TDD: (513) 684-6920

OKLAHOMA
200 N.W. Fifth St.
Suite 670
Oklahoma City, OK 73102
Tel: (405) 231-4301
TDD: None Listed

OREGON
222 S.W. Columbia
Suite 500
Portland, OR 97201-6605
Tel: (503) 326-2682
TDD: (503) 326-2591

PENNSYLVANIA
475 Allendale Road
Suite 201
King Of Prussia, PA 19406
Tel: (215) 962-3804
TDD: (215) 962-3806

960 Penn Ave.
Fifth Floor
Pittsburgh, PA 15222
Tel: (412) 644-2780
TDD: (412) 644-5143

100 Chestnut St.
Room 309
Harrisburg, PA 17101
Tel: (717) 782-3840
TDD: (717) 782-3477

20 N. Pennsylvania Ave.
Room 2327
Wilkes-Barre, PA 18702
Tel: (717) 826-6497
TDD: (717) 821-4174

PUERTO RICO
Carlos Chardon Ave.
Room 691
Hato Rey, PR 00918
Tel: (809) 766-5572
TDD: (809) 766-5174

RHODE ISLAND
380 Westminster Mall
Fifth Floor
Providence, RI 02903
Tel: (401) 528-4561
TDD: (401) 528-4690

SOUTH CAROLINA
1835 Assembly St.
Room 358
Columbia, SC 29201
Tel: (803) 765-5376
TDD: (803) 253-3364

SOUTH DAKOTA
101 S. Main Ave.
Suite 101
Sioux Falls, SD 57102-0527
Tel: (605) 330-4231
TDD: (605) 331-3527

TENNESSEE
50 Vantage Way
Suite 201
Nashville, TN 37228-1500
Tel: (615) 736-5881
TDD: (615) 736-2499

TEXAS
4300 Amon Carter Blvd.
Suite 114
Fort Worth, TX 76155
Tel: (817) 885-6500
TDD: (817) 885-6552

10737 Gateway West
Suite 320
El Paso, TX 79935
Tel: (915) 540-5676
TDD: (915) 540-5196

222 E. Van Buren St.
Room 500
Harlingen, TX 78550
Tel: (512) 427-8533
TDD: (512) 423-0691

9301 Southwest Freeway
Suite 550
Houston, TX 77074-1591
Tel: (713) 773-6500
TDD: (713) 773-6568

1611 10th St.
Suite 200
Lubbock, TX 79401
Tel: (806) 743-7462
TDD: (806) 743-7474

7400 Blanco Road
Suite 200
San Antonio, TX 78216
Tel: (512)229-4535
TDD: (512)229-4555

606 N. Carancahua
Suite 1200
Corpus Christi, TX 78476
Tel: (512) 888-3331
TDD: (512) 888-3188

819 Taylor St.
Room 8A-27
Ft. Worth, TX 76102
Tel: (817) 334-3777
TDD: None Listed

300 E. Eighth St.
Room 520
Austin, TX 78701
Tel: (512) 482-5288
TDD: None Listed

505 E. Travis
Room 103
Marshall, TX 75670
Tel: (903) 935-5257
TDD: None Listed

UTAH
125 S. State St.
Room 2237
Salt Lake City, UT 84138-1195
Tel: (801) 524-5804
TDD: (801) 524-4040

VERMONT
87 State St.
Room 205
Montpelier, VT 05602
Tel: (802) 828-4422
TDD: (802) 828-4552

VIRGINIA
400 N. Eighth St.
Room 3015
Richmond, VA 23240
Tel: (804) 771-2400
TDD: (804) 771-8078

VIRGIN ISLANDS
4200 United Shopping Plaza
Suite 7
Christiansted
St. Croix, VI 00820-4487
Tel: (809) 778-5380
TDD: None Listed

Veterans Drive
Room 210
St. Thomas, VI 00802
Tel: (809) 774-8530
TDD: None Listed

WASHINGTON
915 Second Ave.
Room 1792
Seattle, WA 98174-1088
Tel: (206) 553-1420
TDD: (206) 553-6809

W. 601 First Ave.
10th Floor E.
Spokane, WA 99204-0317
Tel: (509) 353-2800
TDD: (509) 353-2424

WEST VIRGINIA
168 W. Main St.
Fifth Floor
Clarksburg, WV 26301
Tel: (304) 623-5631
TDD: (304) 623-5616

550 Eagan St.
Room 309
Charleston, WV 25301
Tel: (304) 347-5220
TDD: (304) 347-5438

WISCONSIN
212 E. Washington Ave.
Room 213
Madison, WI 53703
Tel: (608) 264-5261
TDD: (608) 264-5333

310 W. Wisconsin Ave.
Suite 400
Milwaukee, WI 53203
Tel: (414) 297-3941
TDD: (414) 297-1095

WYOMING
100 E. B St.
Room 4001
Casper, WY 82602-2839
Tel: (307) 261-5761
TDD: (307) 261-5806

Small Business Development Centers (SBDCs)

SBDCs, sponsored by SBA in partnership with state and local governments, the educational community and the private sector, provide high-quality, low-cost assistance, counseling and training to prospective and existing small business owners.

The following list of lead SBDCs is arranged by regions. To locate your region refer to the guide, "Small Business Administration Regional Structure" on page 222.

REGION I

State Director
Small Business Development Center
University of Southern Maine
96 Falmouth Street
Portland, ME 04103
Tel: 207-780-4420
Fax: 207-780-4810

State Director
Small Business Development Center
University of Massachusetts
School of Management
Amherst, MA 01003-4935
Tel: 413-545-6301
Fax: 413-545-1273

State Director
Small Business Development Center
University of Connecticut
Box U-41
368 Fairfield Road
Storrs, CT 06269-2041
Tel: 203-486-4135
Fax: 203-486-1576

State Director
Small Business Development Center
Bryant College
1150 Douglas Pike
Smithfield, RI 02917
Tel: 401-232-6111
Fax: 401-232-6416

State Director
Small Business Development Center
Vermont Technical College
P.O. Box 422
Randolph Center, VT 05060
Tel: 802-728-9101
Fax: 802-728-3026

State Director
Small Business Development Center
University of New Hampshire
108 McConnell Hall
Durham, NH 03824
Tel: 603-862-2200
Fax: 603-862-4468

REGION II

State Director
Small Business Development Center
Rutgers University
Ackerson Hall
180 University Street
Newark, NJ 07102
Tel: 201-648-5950
Fax: 201-648-1110

State Director
Small Business Development Center
State University of New York
SUNY Upstate
SUNY Plaza, S-523
Albany, NY 12246
Tel: 518-443-5398
Fax: 518-465-4992

State Director
Small Business Development Center
State University of New York
SUNY Downstate
SUNY Plaza, S-523
Albany, NY 12246
Tel: 518-443-5398
Fax: 518-465-4992

Director
Small Business Development Center
University of the Virgin Islands
8000 Nisky Center
Charlotte Amalie
St. Thomas, Virgin Islands 00802-5804
Tel: 809-776-3206
Fax: 809-775-3756

Director
Small Business Development Center
University of Puerto Rico
Box 5253—College Station
Building B
Mayaguez, PR 00681
Tel: 809-834-3590
Fax: 809-834-3790

REGION III

State Director
Small Business Development Center
University of Pennsylvania
The Wharton School
444 Vance Hall
Philadelphia, PA 19104
Tel: 215-898-1219
Fax: 215-573-2135

Acting Director
Small Business Development Center
Howard University
2600 6th Street, N.W.
Washington, D.C. 20059
Tel: 202-806-1550
Fax: 202-806-1777

State Director
Small Business Development Center
University of Delaware
Purnell Hall
Newark, DE 19711
Tel: 302-831-2747
Fax: 302-831-1423

State Director
Small Business Development Center
Governor's Office of Community and Industrial Development
1115 Virginia Street, East
Charleston, WV 25301
Tel: 304-558-2960
Fax: 304-558-0127

State Director
Small Business Development Center
Department of Economic and Employment Development
217 East Redwood Street
Baltimore, MD 21202
Tel: 410-333-6995
Fax: 410-333-4460

State Director
Small Business Development Center
Department of Economic Development
1021 East Cary Street
Richmond, VA 23206
Tel: 804-371-8258
Fax: 804-371-8185

REGION IV

State Director
Small Business Development Center
University of South Carolina
College of Business Administration
1710 College Street
Columbia, SC 29208
Tel: 803-777-4907
Fax: 803-777-4403

State Director
Small Business Development Center
University of West Florida
19 West Garden Street
Pensacola, FL 32501
Tel: 904-444-2060
Fax: 904-444-2070

State Director
Small Business Development Center
University of Alabama
1717 11th Avenue South
Birmingham, AL 35294
Tel: 205-934-7260
Fax: 205-934-7645

State Director
Small Business Development Center
University of Georgia
Chicopee Complex
1180 East Broad Street
Athens, GA 30602
Tel: 706-542-6762
Fax: 706-542-6776

State Director
Small Business Development Center
University of Kentucky
College of Business and Economics
225 Business and Economics Building
Lexington, KY 40506-0034
Tel: 606-257-7668
Fax: 606-258-1907

State Director
Small Business Development Center
University of Mississippi
Old Chemistry Building
University, MS 38677
Tel: 601-232-5001
Fax: 601-232-5650

State Director
Small Business Development Center
Memphis State University
South Campus
Getwell Road, Building #1
Memphis, TN 38152
Tel: 901-678-2500
Fax: 901-678-4072

State Director
Small Business Development Center
University of North Carolina
4509 Creedmoor Road
Raleigh, NC 27612
Tel: 919-571-4154
Fax: 919-571-4161

REGION V

State Director
Small Business Development Center
University of Wisconsin
432 North Lake Street
Madison, WI 53706
Tel: 608-263-7794
Fax: 608-262-3878

Acting State Director
Small Business Development Center
Department of Trade and Economic Development
500 Metro Square
121 Seventh Place East
St. Paul, MN 55101-2146
Tel: 612-297-5770
Fax: 612-296-1290

State Director
Small Business Development Center
Wayne State University
2727 Second Avenue
Detroit, MI 48201
Tel: 313-964-1798
Fax: 313-964-3648

State Director
Small Business Development Center
Department of Commerce and Community Affairs
620 East Adams Street
Springfield, IL 62701
Tel: 217-524-5856
Fax: 217-785-6328

State Director
Small Business Development Center
Economic Development Council
One North Capitol
Indianapolis, IN 46204
Tel: 317-264-6871
Fax: 317-264-3102

State Director
Small Business Development Center
Department of Development
77 South High Street
Columbus, OH 43226-1001
Tel: 614-466-2711
Fax: 614-466-0829

REGION VI

Acting State Director
Small Business Development Center
University of Arkansas
Little Rock Technology Center Building
100 South Main
Little Rock, AR 72201
Tel: 501-324-9043
Fax: 501-324-9049

State Director
Small Business Development Center
Northeast Louisiana University
College of Business Administration
700 University Avenue
Monroe, LA 71209
Tel: 318-342-5506
Fax: 318-342-5510

State Director
Small Business Development Center
SE Oklahoma State University
517 West University
Station A, Box 2584
Durant, OK 74701
Tel: 405-920-0277
Fax: 405-920-7071

Region Director
Small Business Development Center
University of Houston
1100 Louisiana
Houston, TX 77002
Tel: 713-752-8444
Fax: 713-756-1500

Region Director
South Texas-Border
Small Business Development Center
University of Texas at San Antonio
Cypress Tower
1222 North Main Street
San Antonio, TX 78212
Tel: 210-558-2450
Fax: 210-558-2464

Region Director
Northwest Texas
Small Business Development Center
Texas Tech University
2579 South Loop 289
Lubbock, TX 79423-1637
Tel: 806-745-3973
Fax: 806-745-6207

Region Director
North Texas
Small Business Development Center
Dallas County Community College
1402 Corinth Street
Dallas, TX 75215
Tel: 214-565-5833
Fax: 214-565-5815

State Director
Small Business Development Center
Santa Fe Community College
P.O. Box 4187
Santa Fe, NM 87502-4187
Tel: 505-438-1362
Fax: 505-438-1237

REGION VII

State Director
Small Business Development Center
University of Nebraska at Omaha
60th & Dodge Streets
Omaha, NE 68182
Tel: 402-554-2521
Fax: 402-554-3747

State Director
Small Business Development Center
Iowa State University
137 Lynn Avenue
Ames, IA 50010
Tel: 515-292-6351
Fax: 515-292-0020

State Director
Small Business Development Center
University of Missouri
University Place
Columbia, MO 65211
Tel: 314-882-0344
Fax: 314-884-4297

State Director
Small Business Development Center
Wichita State University
1845 Fairmount
Wichita, KS 67260-0148
Tel: 316-689-3193
Fax: 316-689-3647

REGION VIII

State Director
Small Business Development Center
University of Utah
102 West 500 South
Salt Lake City, UT 84101
Tel: 801-581-7905
Fax: 801-581-7814

State Director
Small Business Development Center
University of South Dakota
School of Business
414 East Clark
Vermillion, SD 57069
Tel: 605-677-5498
Fax: 605-677-5427

State Director
Small Business Development Center
University of North Dakota
Gamble Hall, University Station
Grand Forks, ND 58202-7308
Tel: 701-777-3700
Fax: 701-777-3225

State Director
Small Business Development Center
Department of Commerce
1424 Ninth Avenue
Helena, MT 59620
Tel: 406-444-4780
Fax: 406-444-2808

State Director
Small Business Development Center
Office of Business Development
1625 Broadway
Denver, CO 80202
Tel: 303-892-3809
Fax: 303-892-3848

REGION IX

State Director
Small Business Development Center
University of Nevada in Reno
College of Business Admin.
Reno, NV 89557-0100
Tel: 702-784-1717
Fax: 702-784-4337

State Director
Small Business Development Center
Maricopa County Community College
2411 West 14th Street
Tempe, AZ 85281-6941
Tel: 602-731-8720
Fax: 602-731-8637

State Director
Small Business Development Center
University of Hawaii at Hilo
523 West Lanikaula Street
Hilo, HI 96720
Tel: 808-933-3515
Fax: 808-933-3683

State Director
Small Business Development Center
California Trade and Commerce Agency
801 K Street
Sacramento, CA 95814
Tel: 916-324-5068
Fax: 916-322-5084

REGION X

State Director
Small Business Development Center
Washington State University
College of Business and Economics
245 Todd Hall
Pullman, WA 99164-4727
Tel: 509-335-1576
Fax: 509-335-0949

State Director
Small Business Development Center
Lane Community College
99 West 10th Avenue
Eugene, OR 97401
Tel: 503-726-2250
Fax: 503-345-6006

State Director
Small Business Development Center
Boise State University
1910 University Drive
Boise, ID 83725
Tel: 208-385-1640
Fax: 208-385-3877

State Director
Small Business Development Center
University of Alaska/Anchorage
430 West 7th Avenue
Anchorage, AK 99501
Tel: 907-274-7232
Fax: 907-274-9524

Returns on Various Types of Investments

*R. S. Salomon, Jr.**

Why I Like Financial Assets

In a reduced-inflation environment, stocks and bonds have racked up great long-term performance records. But is inflation on the comeback trail? Is now the time to cut back on financial assets and buy tangible assets? That thought is advanced in the Money Guide included in this issue of the magazine.

My advice: Don't overdo hard assets. This isn't the 1970s. Look at the table on page 249. Within any given year, the performance ranking of different assets can come out in any order. But over very long measurement periods, financial assets—bonds, stocks and even plain old cash—outperform such tangible assets as housing, farmland, oil and gold.

Despite their recent sharp runup, oil prices are down from a year ago while silver prices have rallied, but apart from these changes the one-year returns all fall within quite a narrow range. They don't change the long-term rankings.

This exercise proves two things. One is that how you allocate your portfolio among broad categories is probably more important than what preoccupies so many people, that is, *which* stocks or bonds or hard assets. The other point is that—since financial assets outperform over long periods—you should not abandon financial assets lightly.

There are many factors that determine whether financial or tangible assets will take the lead in any year, but none is as important as inflation. Investing in financial assets is all about confidence. A gold coin that you carry in your pocket is a store of value in itself, but a bond isn't. A bond isn't even worth the paper it's printed on if investors lose confidence in the future value of money.

Stocks fall somewhere between the two extremes of bonds on the one hand and hard assets on the other. Stocks represent ownership in business goodwill, inventories and real estate, and so can retain real value, even if inflation goes haywire and people are pushing around wheelbarrows of currency. But inflation also crimps profits, because corporations cannot pass through price increases as fast as their costs and taxes rise. Unexpected inflation is very damaging to all financial assets. It's what killed the stock market from 1973 well into the early 1980s.

This survey began in the late 1970s, when inflation was a very real concern. At that time the long-term returns of the three principal tangible asset categories—commodities, real estate and collectibles—were very impressive, and confidence in the value of money was approaching rock bottom. Yet, with hindsight, that would have been a good time to dump your diamonds, oil and farmland and buy stocks.

There are those who worry that we are headed into a replay of the 1970s, when hard assets beat out the other kind. I completely disagree and remain very optimistic about the likelihood that inflation will remain subdued. The world is awash in oil, even though prices have moved up recently in response to political events. Indeed, the 20-year return for black gold has been a meager 2.9%, not even equal to inflation. Wages are unlikely to accelerate dramatically anytime soon, and the prices of branded consumer products remain under pressure.

In addition, even though President Clinton's health care reform package stands absolutely no chance of passage in its current form, the threat of change has precipitated a significant slowdown in the rate of increase in prices of health care products and services. In fact, health care inflation now is running at the lowest rate of the postwar period.

There is another recent development that I would actually classify as deflationary. Florida Power & Light recently surprised investors by dramatically cutting its dividend. The company is not in distress, but management thinks it prudent to retain more earnings in the face of deregulation and the threat of increased competition. It seems likely that other utilities might follow suit, taking a sizable chunk of money out of investors' pockets in the process. If this scenario proves correct, the loss of income would reinforce consumers' price sensitivity. And competition in unexpected places, like utility rates, will keep a lid on the cost of living.

---

* Chairman and chief executive of Salomon Brothers Asset Management, Inc., and portfolio manager of Salomon Brothers Capital Fund, Inc., Research assistant: Caroline Davenport.

In the long race, stocks win

Assets	20 years rank	20 years return[1]	10 years rank	10 years return[1]	5 years rank	5 years return[1]	1 year rank	1 year return[1]
Stocks	1	13.1%	1	15.5%	2	10.4%	6	2.6%
Foreign exchange[2]	2	11.9	3	13.0	1	10.6	5	3.3
Bonds	3	10.2	2	14.1	3	9.9	10	0.7
Stamps	4	9.1	10	–0.9	11	1.1	8	1.9
3-month Treasury bills	5	8.3	4	6.7	4	5.6	4	4.3
Diamonds	6	7.9	5	5.9	9	1.4	11	0.0
Housing	7	6.3	6	4.1	6	2.9	9	1.8
Consumer Price Index	8	5.7	7	3.6	5	3.5	7	2.1
Farmland	9	4.6	9	–0.7	7	2.4	2	6.4
Gold	10	4.5	8	–0.2	10	1.3	3	4.7
Oil	11	2.9	12	–5.2	12	–1.9	12	–9.8
Silver	12	1.0	11	–4.9	8	1.9	1	31.1
Sotheby's common		NA		NA	13	–3.3	13	–11.4

[1]Average annual return. [2]Combines money-market returns with changes in exchange rates. NA: Not applicable.

Sources: Salomon Brothers Inc; diamonds, The Diamond Registry; basket of U.S. stamps, Scott Publishing Co.; oil, West Texas intermediate first nearby crude contract; housing, National Association of Realtors; farmland (excluding income), U.S. government statistics.

Even in a period that includes a bout of double-digit inflation, equities beat out collectibles and other hard assets.

If all this is true, then what has the Federal Reserve Board so worried? In my view, the Fed has moved to tighten monetary policy in response to excessive growth in the economy and, more recently, to the weakening in the U.S. dollar. Although the U.S. dollar has strengthened slightly over the past year, it has been going downhill since January. (Note: This year we have recalculated foreign currency returns to incorporate both changes in exchange rates and the yield on money-market investments.)

In sharp contrast to most other developed countries, the U.S. is both large and self-contained. Trade accounts for about 12% of gross national product here, as compared with roughly 30% or more in other mature economies. What that means is that many people in the U.S. are not terribly concerned with the relative value of the dollar. The reality is that their lives tend to revolve around domestically produced goods and services.

For investors in the capital markets, however, the value of the dollar is extremely important. If people do not want our money, it is a sign that confidence in the value of the dollar, and consequently confidence in the value of paper assets attached to the dollar, is slipping.

My view is that the U.S. dollar is significantly undervalued at present. As it begins to stabilize, it will help to restore confidence in paper assets in general.

The basket of assets that I track has remained relatively constant over time. In the past two years I have dropped old master paintings and Chinese ceramics, since Sotheby's has discontinued its performance indexes on these asset categories.

The loss of these categories is unfortunate. Collectibles are an intriguing piece of the investment puzzle, partly because the motivation of buyers in these markets defies simple analysis. Many people who buy old masters, for example, are not motivated principally by concerns about inflation, but rather by the desire to show off their wealth. Thus, the markets for high-priced collectibles tend to follow broader patterns of wealth creation—be it the Middle East in the 1970s or Wall Street in the 1980s. The last big buyers of art were the Japanese. Given the performance of the markets in Japan, it is easy to see why this group has lost interest in van Goghs.

Why did Sotheby's discontinue its indexes? There are a number of possible explanations. But it is worth noting that recent auctions have not gone particularly well, and declining indexes presumably do not constitute particularly good publicity. One is not even on safe ground saying that price declines provide buying opportunities in these markets. To a conspicuous consumer, high prices are more tempting than low ones.

In any event, we have decided to keep an eye on Sotheby's stock price as a proxy for the collectibles markets. The company came public in 1988, so there is not enough price history to include the long-term performance in our table. Over the past year the stock price has fallen by almost 7.7%—the worst one-year return after oil—reinforcing the impression created by the press that this has not been a block-buster year for collectibles.

So, for all these reasons, I continue to favor financial assets, with an emphasis on stocks over bonds. Stocks are more attractive because they look reasonably valued and the outlook for corporate earnings is good.

However, one tangible category—commercial real estate—looks interesting. In the past, inflation and tax incentives drove this market. As it turned out, these two factors ballooned the supply of property well beyond even the most optimistic demand scenarios. Today the tax incentives for commercial real estate development have disappeared, and inflation is subdued. The good news is that the economy is growing, and it looks as though vacancy rates are coming down for an old-fashioned reason: more demand than supply. As the fundamental picture improves, commercial real estate may provide some interesting investment opportunities.

Stock Market: U.S. and Foreign

Investment Returns on Stocks, Bonds, and Bills

Roger G. Ibbotson and Carl G. Gargula***

Our look at history consists of examining the returns of five capital market sectors. We measure total returns (capital gains plus income) on large company stocks, long-term corporate bonds, long-term government bonds, U.S. Treasury bills, and rates of inflation on consumer goods. Comparing the returns from the various sectors gives us insights into the returns available from taking risk and the relationships between capital market returns and inflation.

THE RISKS AND REWARDS

We display graphically the rewards and risks available from the U.S. capital markets over the past 68 years. Exhibit 1 shows the growth of an investment in large company stocks, long-term government bonds, and Treasury bills as well as the increase in the inflation index over the 68-year period. Each of the series is initiated at $1 at year-end 1925. The vertical scale is logarithmic so that equal distances represent equal percentage changes anywhere along the axis. The graph vividly portrays that despite setbacks such as that of October 1987, large company stocks were the big winner over the entire period. If $1 were invested in stocks at year-end 1925 and all dividends reinvested, the dollar investment would have grown to $800.08 by year-end 1993. This phenomenal growth was not without substantial risk, especially during the earlier portion of the period. In contrast, long-term government bonds (with a constant 20-year maturity) exhibited much less risk, but grew to only $28.03.

A virtually riskless strategy (for those with short-term time horizons) has been to buy U.S. Treasury bills. However, Treasury bills have had a marked tendency to track inflation, with the result that their real (inflation adjusted) return is near zero for the entire 1926–1993 period. Note that the tracking is only prevalent over the latter portion of the period. During periods of deflation (such as the late 1920s and early 1930s) the Treasury bill returns were near zero, but not negative, since no one intentionally buys securities with negative yields. Beginning in the early 1940s, the yields (returns) on Treasury bills were pegged by the government at low rates while high inflation was experienced. The government pegging ended with the U.S. Treasury-Federal Reserve Accord in March 1951.

We summarize the investment returns in Exhibit 2 by presenting the average annual returns over the 1926–1993 period. Large company stocks returned a compounded (geometric mean) total return of 10.3 percent per year. The annual compound return from capital appreciation alone was 5.4 percent. After adjusting for inflation, annual compounded total returns were 7.0 percent per year.

The average total return over any single year (arithmetic mean) for stocks was 12.3 percent, with positive returns recorded in more than two-thirds of the years (48 out of 68 years). The risk or degree of return fluctuation is measured by standard deviation as 20.5 percent. The frequency distribution (histogram) counts the number of years the returns fell in each 5 percent return increment. Note the wide variations in large company stock returns relative to the other capital market sectors. Annual stock returns ranged from 54.0 percent in 1933 to −43.3 percent in 1931.

A simple example illustrates the difference between geometric and arithmetic means. Suppose $1 was invested in a large company stock portfolio that experiences successive annual returns of +50 percent and −50 percent. At the end of the first year, the portfolio is worth $1.50. At the end of the second year, the portfolio is worth $0.75. The annual arithmetic mean is 0 percent, whereas the annual geometric mean (compounded return) is −13.4 percent. Naturally, it is the geometric mean that more directly measures the change in wealth over more than one period. On the other hand, the arithmetic mean is a better representation of typical performance over any single annual period.

The other capital market sectors also had returns commensurate with their risks. Long-term corporate bonds outperformed the default-free, long-term government bonds, which in turn outperformed the essentially riskless U.S. Treasury bills. Over the entire period the riskless U.S. Treasury bills had a return almost identical with the inflation rate. Thus, we again note that the real rate of inter-

* Professor, Yale School of Management, New Haven, Connecticut and President of Ibbotson Associates.

** Managing Director and General Counsel, Communications Resources Group, Ibbotson Associates.

EXHIBIT 1: WEALTH INDICES OF INVESTMENTS IN THE U.S. CAPITAL MARKETS, 1925–1993 (Year-End 1925 = $1.00)

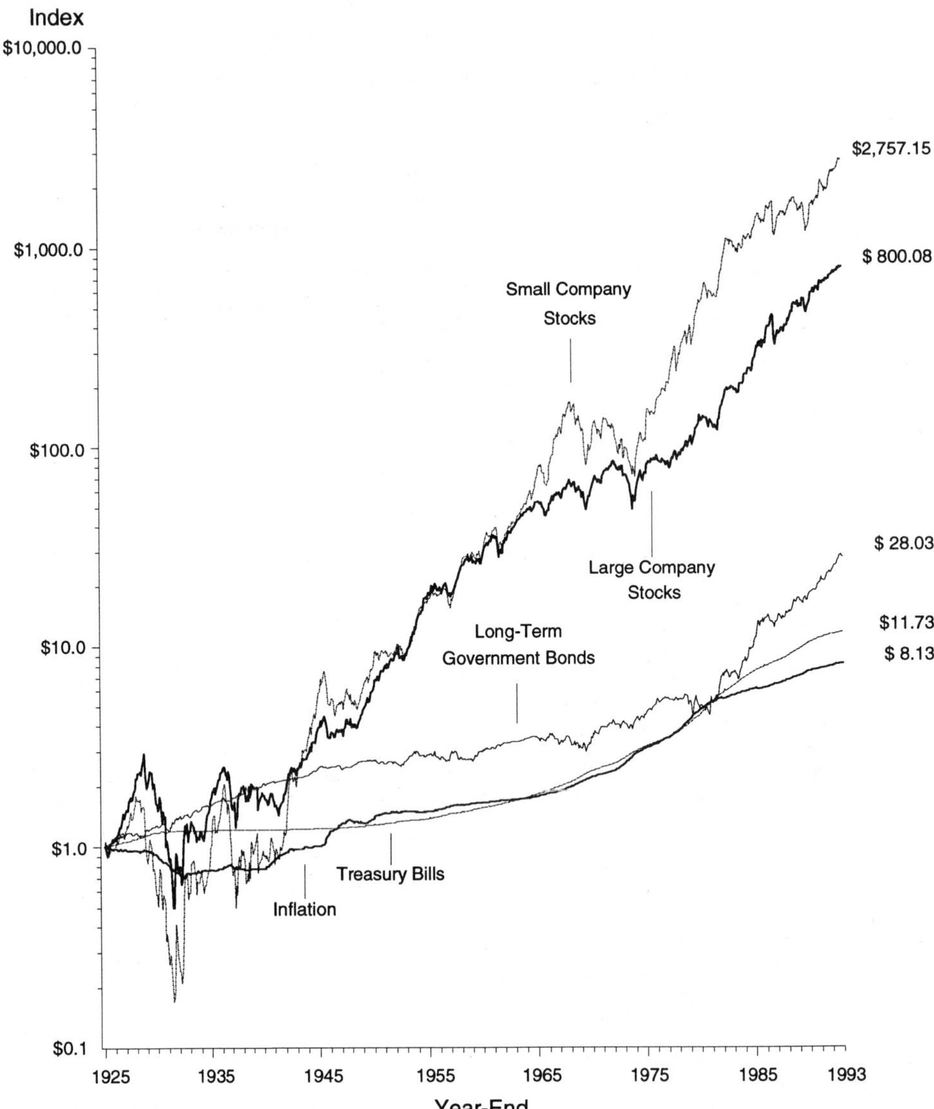

Source: *Stocks, Bonds, Bills, and Inflation: 1994 Yearbook,* published by Ibbotson Associates, Inc., 225 North Michigan Avenue, Suite 700, Chicago, IL. 60601-7676, telephone 312-616-1620. Used with permission. All rights reserved.

est (the inflation-adjusted riskless rate) has been on average very near 0 percent historically.

MEASUREMENT OF THE FIVE SERIES

The returns were computed by compounding monthly returns, with no adjustments made for transactions costs or taxes. We describe each of the five total return series which are listed annually in Exhibit 3. The index numbers in Exhibit 3 are dollar values of a $1 investment made on December 31, 1925. They can be converted to yearly returns by taking the ratio of a given year-end index value to the previous year-end value, then subtracting one (1). For example, the return for large company stocks for 1993 equals (800.078 ÷ 727.412) − 1 = .0999 = 9.99 percent.

Large Company Stocks

The total return index is based upon Standard & Poor's (S&P) Composite Index with

EXHIBIT 2: BASIC SERIES: SUMMARY STATISTICS OF ANNUAL TOTAL RETURNS, 1926–1993

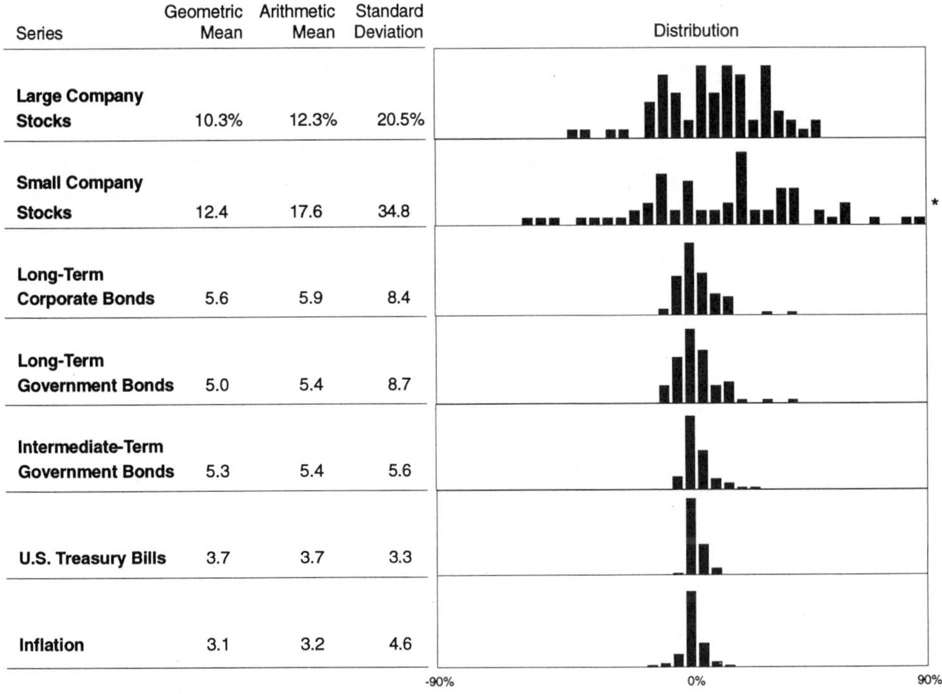

Series	Geometric Mean	Arithmetic Mean	Standard Deviation
Large Company Stocks	10.3%	12.3%	20.5%
Small Company Stocks	12.4	17.6	34.8
Long-Term Corporate Bonds	5.6	5.9	8.4
Long-Term Government Bonds	5.0	5.4	8.7
Intermediate-Term Government Bonds	5.3	5.4	5.6
U.S. Treasury Bills	3.7	3.7	3.3
Inflation	3.1	3.2	4.6

* The 1933 Small Company Stock Total Returns was 142.9 percent.

Source: *Stocks, Bonds, Bills and Inflation: 1994 Yearbook,* published by Ibbotson Associates, Inc., 225 North Michigan Avenue, Suite 700, Chicago, IL 60601-7676, telephone 312-616-1620. Used with permission.

dividends reinvested monthly. To the extent that the 500 stocks currently included in the S&P Composite Index (prior to March 1957, there were 90 stocks) are representative of all stocks in the United States, the market value weighting scheme allows the returns of the index to correspond to the aggregate stock market returns in the U.S. economy.

Long-Term Corporate Bonds

We measure the total returns of a corporate bond index with approximately 20 years to maturity. We use Salomon Brothers' High-Grade Long-Term Corporate Bond Index from its beginning in 1969 through 1993. For the period 1946–68 we backdate Salomon Brothers' index using Salomon Brothers' monthly yield data and similar methodology. For the period 1926–45 we compute returns using Standard & Poor's monthly high-grade corporate composite bond yield data, assuming a 4 percent coupon and a 20-year maturity.

Long-Term Government Bonds

To measure the total returns of long-term U.S. government bonds, we use the bond data obtained from the U.S. Government Bond File (constructed by Lawrence Fisher) at the Center for Research in Security Prices (CRSP) at the University of Chicago. We attempt to maintain a 20-year bond portfolio whose returns do not reflect the potential tax benefits, impaired negotiability, or the special redemption or call privileges frequently characterizing government bond prices and yields.

U.S. Treasury Bills

For the U.S. Treasury bill index, we again use the data in the CRSP U.S. Government Bond File. We measure one-month holding period returns for the shortest-term bills not less than one month in maturity. Since U.S. Treasury bills were not initiated until 1929, we use short-term coupon bonds whenever bill quotes are unavailable.

Consumer Price Index

We utilize the Consumer Price Index for All Urban Consumers (CPI-U), not seasonally adjusted, to measure inflation. The CPI-U, and its predecessor, the CPI (which we use prior to January 1978) is constructed by the Bureau of Labor Statistics, U.S. Department of Labor, Washington, D.C.

EXHIBIT 3: BASIC SERIES, INDICES OF YEAR-END CUMULATIVE WEALTH, 1925–1993 (December 1925 = $1.00)

Year	Large Stocks Total Returns	Large Stocks Capital Apprec	Small Stocks Total Returns	Long-Term Corp Bonds Total Returns	Long-Term Government Bonds Total Returns	Long-Term Government Bonds Capital Apprec	Intermediate-Term Government Bonds Total Returns	Intermediate-Term Government Bonds Capital Apprec	U.S. T-Bills Total Returns	Inflation
1925	1.000	1.000	1.000	1.000	1.000	1.000	1.000	1.000	1.000	1.000
1926	1.116	1.057	1.003	1.074	1.078	1.039	1.054	1.015	1.033	0.985
1927	1.535	1.384	1.224	1.154	1.174	1.095	1.101	1.025	1.065	0.965
1928	2.204	1.908	1.710	1.186	1.175	1.061	1.112	0.997	1.103	0.955
1929	2.018	1.681	0.832	1.225	1.215	1.059	1.178	1.014	1.155	0.957
1930	1.516	1.202	0.515	1.323	1.272	1.072	1.258	1.048	1.183	0.899
1931	0.859	0.636	0.259	1.299	1.204	0.982	1.228	0.991	1.196	0.814
1932	0.789	0.540	0.245	1.439	1.407	1.109	1.337	1.041	1.207	0.730
1933	1.214	0.792	0.594	1.588	1.406	1.074	1.361	1.031	1.211	0.734
1934	1.197	0.745	0.738	1.808	1.547	1.146	1.483	1.092	1.213	0.749
1935	1.767	1.053	1.035	1.982	1.624	1.171	1.587	1.146	1.215	0.771
1936	2.367	1.346	1.705	2.116	1.746	1.225	1.636	1.165	1.217	0.780
1937	1.538	0.827	0.716	2.174	1.750	1.195	1.661	1.165	1.221	0.804
1938	2.016	1.035	0.951	2.307	1.847	1.229	1.765	1.216	1.221	0.782
1939	2.008	0.979	0.954	2.399	1.957	1.272	1.845	1.255	1.221	0.778
1940	1.812	0.829	0.905	2.480	2.076	1.319	1.899	1.280	1.221	0.786
1941	1.602	0.681	0.823	2.548	2.096	1.306	1.909	1.278	1.222	0.862
1942	1.927	0.766	1.190	2.614	2.163	1.316	1.946	1.293	1.225	0.942
1943	2.427	0.915	2.242	2.688	2.208	1.311	2.000	1.309	1.229	0.972
1944	2.906	1.041	3.446	2.815	2.270	1.315	2.036	1.314	1.233	0.993
1945	3.965	1.361	5.983	2.930	2.514	1.424	2.082	1.327	1.237	1.015
1946	3.645	1.199	5.287	2.980	2.511	1.393	2.102	1.326	1.242	1.199
1947	3.853	1.199	5.335	2.911	2.445	1.328	2.122	1.322	1.248	1.307
1948	4.065	1.191	5.223	3.031	2.529	1.341	2.161	1.326	1.258	1.343
1949	4.829	1.313	6.254	3.132	2.692	1.396	2.211	1.338	1.272	1.318
1950	6.360	1.600	8.677	3.198	2.693	1.367	2.227	1.329	1.287	1.395
1951	7.888	1.863	9.355	3.112	2.587	1.282	2.235	1.307	1.306	1.477
1952	9.336	2.082	9.638	3.221	2.617	1.263	2.271	1.300	1.328	1.490
1953	9.244	1.944	9.013	3.331	2.713	1.271	2.345	1.308	1.352	1.499
1954	14.108	2.820	14.473	3.511	2.907	1.326	2.407	1.322	1.364	1.492
1955	18.561	3.564	17.431	3.527	2.870	1.272	2.392	1.281	1.385	1.497
1956	19.778	3.658	18.177	3.287	2.710	1.165	2.382	1.237	1.419	1.540
1957	17.646	3.134	15.529	3.573	2.912	1.209	2.568	1.287	1.464	1.587

1958	25.298	4.327	25.605	3.494	2.734	1.098	2.535	1.233	1.486	1.615
1959	28.322	4.694	29.804	3.460	2.673	1.030	2.525	1.177	1.530	1.639
1960	28.455	4.554	28.823	3.774	3.041	1.125	2.822	1.264	1.571	1.663
1961	36.106	5.607	38.072	3.956	3.070	1.093	2.874	1.243	1.604	1.674
1962	32.954	4.945	33.540	4.270	3.282	1.124	3.034	1.264	1.648	1.695
1963	40.469	5.879	41.444	4.364	3.322	1.093	3.084	1.237	1.700	1.723
1964	47.139	6.642	51.193	4.572	3.438	1.085	3.209	1.237	1.760	1.743
1965	53.008	7.244	72.567	4.552	3.462	1.048	3.242	1.199	1.829	1.777
1966	47.674	6.295	67.479	4.560	3.589	1.037	3.394	1.194	1.916	1.836
1967	59.104	7.560	123.870	4.335	3.259	0.896	3.428	1.148	1.997	1.892
1968	65.642	8.139	168.429	4.446	3.251	0.847	3.583	1.136	2.101	1.981
1969	60.059	7.210	126.233	4.086	3.086	0.755	3.557	1.054	2.239	2.102
1970	62.465	7.222	104.226	4.837	3.460	0.792	4.156	1.145	2.385	2.218
1971	71.406	8.001	121.423	5.370	3.917	0.844	4.519	1.177	2.490	2.292
1972	84.956	9.252	126.807	5.760	4.140	0.841	4.752	1.168	2.585	2.371
1973	72.500	7.645	87.618	5.825	4.094	0.777	4.971	1.142	2.764	2.579
1974	53.311	5.373	70.142	5.647	4.272	0.750	5.254	1.120	2.986	2.894
1975	73.144	7.068	107.189	6.474	4.665	0.755	5.665	1.121	3.159	3.097
1976	90.584	8.422	168.691	7.681	5.447	0.816	6.394	1.180	3.319	3.246
1977	84.077	7.453	211.500	7.813	5.410	0.752	6.484	1.119	3.489	3.466
1978	89.592	7.532	261.120	7.807	5.346	0.684	6.710	1.069	3.740	3.778
1979	106.113	8.459	374.614	7.481	5.280	0.617	6.985	1.015	4.128	4.281
1980	140.514	10.639	523.992	7.274	5.071	0.530	7.258	0.946	4.592	4.812
1981	133.616	9.605	596.717	7.185	5.166	0.476	7.944	0.903	5.267	5.242
1982	162.223	11.023	763.829	10.242	7.251	0.589	10.256	1.031	5.822	5.445
1983	198.745	12.926	1066.828	10.883	7.298	0.532	11.015	0.997	6.335	5.652
1984	211.199	13.106	995.680	12.718	8.427	0.544	12.560	1.009	6.959	5.875
1985	279.117	16.559	1241.234	16.546	11.037	0.641	15.113	1.100	7.496	6.097
1986	330.671	18.981	1326.275	19.829	13.745	0.737	17.401	1.177	7.958	6.166
1987	347.967	19.366	1202.966	19.776	13.372	0.658	17.906	1.121	8.393	6.438
1988	406.458	21.769	1478.135	21.893	14.665	0.661	18.999	1.096	8.926	6.722
1989	534.455	27.703	1628.590	25.447	17.322	0.718	21.524	1.143	9.673	7.034
1990	517.499	25.886	1277.449	27.173	18.392	0.699	23.618	1.155	10.429	7.464
1991	675.592	32.695	1847.629	32.577	21.942	0.769	27.270	1.240	11.012	7.693
1992	727.412	34.155	2279.039	35.637	23.709	0.772	29.230	1.248	11.398	7.916
1993	800.078	36.565	2757.147	40.336	28.034	0.855	32.516	1.317	11.728	8.133

Source: *Stocks, Bonds, Bills, and Inflation: 1994 Yearbook*, published by Ibbotson Associates, Inc., 225 North Michigan Avenue, Suite 700, Chicago, IL 60601-7676, telephone 312-616-1620. Used with permission.

The Constant Dollar Dow

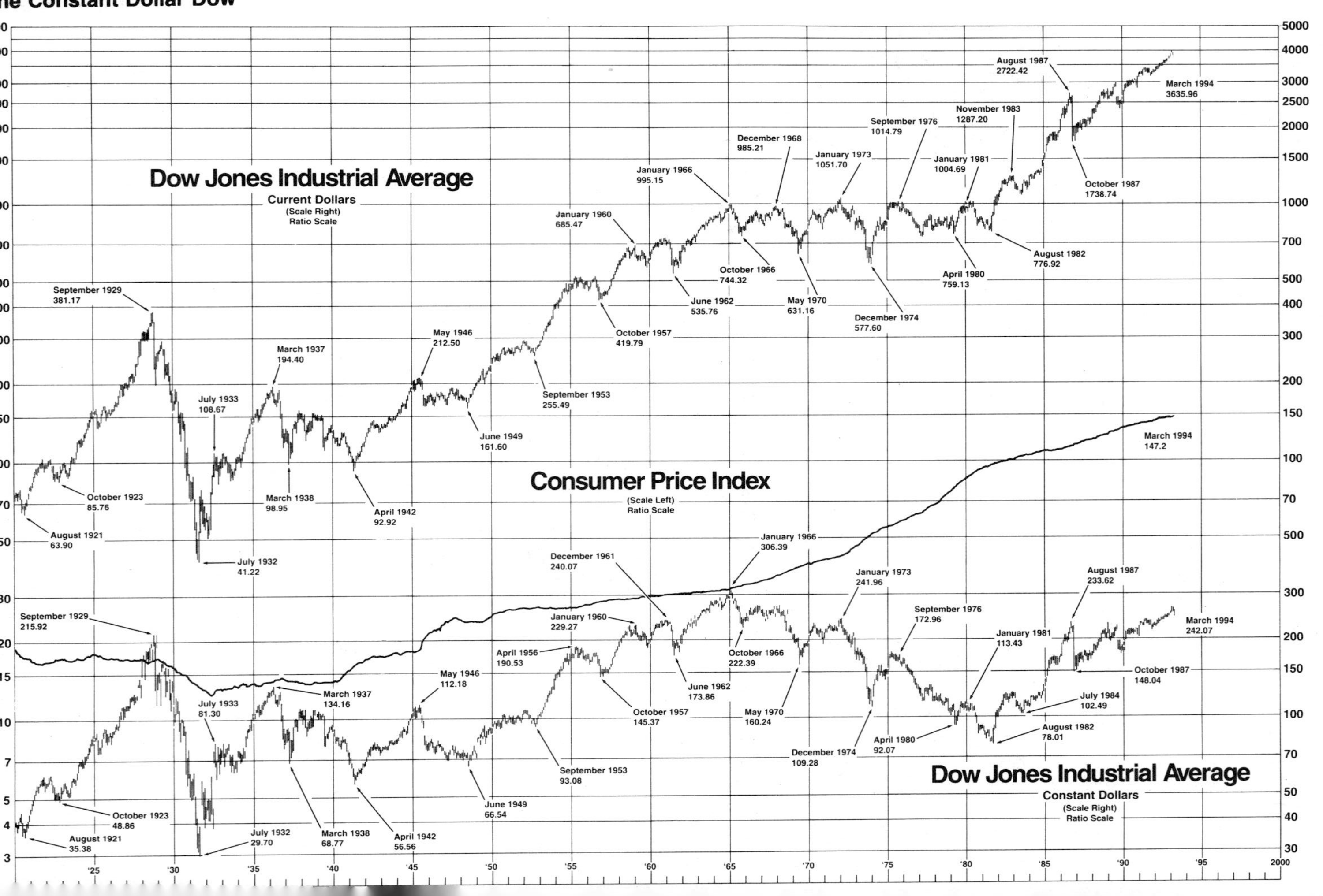

Cash dividends on NYSE-listed common stocks

	Common stocks		
	Number of issues listed at year-end	Number paying cash dividends during year	Estimated aggregate cash payments (millions)
1935	776	387	$1,336
1940	829	577	2,099
1945	881	746	2,275
1950	1,039	930	5,404
1951	1,054	961	5,467
1952	1,067	975	5,595
1953	1,069	964	5,874
1954	1,076	968	6,439
1955	1,076	982	7,488
1956	1,077	975	8,341
1957	1,098	991	8,807
1958	1,086	961	8,711
1959	1,092	953	9,337
1960	1,126	981	9,872
1961	1,145	981	10,430
1962	1,168	994	11,203
1963	1,194	1,032	12,096
1964	1,227	1,066	13,555
1965	1,254	1,111	15,302
1966	1,267	1,127	16,151
1967	1,255	1,116	16,866
1968	1,253	1,104	18,124
1969	1,290	1,121	19,404
1970	1,330	1,120	19,781
1971	1,399	1,132	20,256
1972	1,478	1,195	21,490
1973	1,536	1,276	23,627
1974	1,543	1,308	25,662
1975	1,531	1,273	26,901
1976	1,550	1,304	30,608
1977	1,549	1,360	36,270
1978	1,552	1,373	41,151
1979	1,536	1,359	46,937
1980	1,540	1,361	53,072
1981	1,534	1,337	60,628
1982	1,499	1,287	62,224
1983	1,518	1,259	67,102
1984	1,511	1,243	68,215
1985	1,503	1,206	74,237
1986	1,536	1,180	76,161
1987	1,606	1,219	84,377
1988	1,643	1,270	102,190
1989	1,683	1,303	101,778
1990	1,741	N/A	103,150 *
1991	1,860	N/A	123,385 *
1992	2,068	N/A	109,696 *
1993	2,331	N/A	120,206 *

* Estimate based on average annual yield of the NYSE Composite Index.

N/A - Not available.

Source: New York Stock Exchange *Fact Book*.

NYSE Composite Index (Dec. 31, 1965=50) (closing prices)

	High	Date	Low	Date	Year-end
1945	10.86	12/8	8.22	1/20	10.67
1950	12.01	12/30	9.85	1/14	12.01
1951	13.89	9/14, 10/6, 10/13	12.28	1/6	13.60
1952	14.49	12/26	13.31	10/24	14.49
1953	14.65	1/2	12.62	9/18	13.60
1954	19.40	12/31	13.70	1/8	19.40
1955	23.71	12/9, 12/30	19.05	1/7, 1/14	23.71
1956	25.90	8/3	22.55	1/20	24.35
1957	26.30	7/12	20.92	12/20	21.11
1958	28.85	12/24	21.45	1/10	28.85
1959	32.39	7/31	28.94	2/6	32.15
1960	31.99	1/8	28.38	10/21	30.94
1961	38.60	12/8, 12/15	31.17	1/6	38.39
1962	38.02	3/16	28.20	6/22	33.81
1963	39.92	12/27	34.41	1/4, 3/1	39.92
1964	46.49	11/18, 11/20	40.47	1/3	45.65
1965	50.00	12/31	43.64	6/28	50.00
1966	51.06	2/9	39.37	10/7	43.72
1967	54.16	10/9	43.74	1/3	53.83
1968	61.27	11/29	48.70	3/5	58.90
1969	59.32	5/14	49.31	7/29	51.53
1970	52.36	1/5	37.69	5/26	50.23
1971	57.76	4/28	49.60	11/23	56.43
1972	65.14	12/11	56.23	1/3	64.48
1973	65.48	1/11	49.05	12/5	51.82
1974	53.37	3/13	32.89	10/3	36.13
1975	51.24	7/15	37.06	1/2	47.64
1976	57.88	12/31	48.04	1/2	57.88
1977	57.69	1/3	49.78	11/2	52.50
1978	60.38	9/11, 9/12	48.37	3/6	53.62
1979	63.39	10/5	53.88	2/27	61.95
1980	81.02	11/28	55.30	3/27	77.86
1981	79.14	1/6	64.96	9/25	71.11
1982	82.35	11/9	58.80	8/12	81.03
1983	99.63	10/10	79.79	1/3	95.18
1984	98.12	11/6	85.13	7/24	96.38
1985	121.90	12/16	94.60	1/4	121.58
1986	145.75	9/4	117.75	1/22	138.58
1987	187.99	8/25	125.91	12/4	138.23
1988	159.42	10/21	136.72	1/20	156.26
1989	199.34	10/9	154.98	1/3	195.04
1990	201.13	7/16	162.20	10/11	180.49
1991	229.44	12/31	170.97	1/9	229.44
1992	242.08	12/18	217.92	4/8	240.21
1993	260.67	12/29	236.21	1/8	259.08

Series records

High	260.67	12/29/93	Low	4.64	4/25/42

Source: New York Stock Exchange *Fact Book*.

NYSE Program trading participation in NYSE volume, 1993

	Total program trading as % of NYSE volume	Buy programs as % of NYSE volume	Sell programs as % of NYSE volume	Total program trading as % of twice (TTV) NYSE volume
January	9.4 %	5.1 %	4.3 %	4.7 %
February	12.8	7.6	5.2	6.4
March	14.2	7.4	6.8	7.1
April	10.5	5.9	4.6	5.2
May	12.1	5.1	7.0	6.0
June	13.8	8.4	5.4	6.9
July	12.7	6.9	5.8	6.4
August	11.5	6.4	5.1	5.8
September	14.9	8.3	6.6	7.5
October	9.7	5.5	4.2	4.8
November	9.7	4.6	5.1	4.9
December	12.0	6.4	5.6	6.0
1993	**11.9 %**	**6.5 %**	**5.4 %**	**6.0 %**
1992	11.5	5.8	5.7	5.8
1991	11.0	5.9	5.1	5.5
1990	10.7	5.2	5.5	5.3
1989	9.9	5.4	4.5	5.0

Note: Starting June 13, 1991 percentages include Crossing Session II volume.

Source: New York Stock Exchange *Fact Book.*

Compounded growth rates in NYSE Composite Index (percent)

	Initial year*															Index at year end
	'78	**'79**	**'80**	**'81**	**'82**	**'83**	**'84**	**'85**	**'86**	**'87**	**'88**	**'89**	**'90**	**'91**	**'92**	
'78																**53.62**
'79	15.5															**61.95**
'80	20.5	25.7														**77.86**
'81	9.9	7.1	-8.7													**71.11**
'82	10.9	9.4	2.0	14.0												**81.03**
'83	12.2	11.3	6.9	15.7	17.5											**95.18**
'84	10.3	9.2	5.5	10.7	9.1	1.3										**96.38**
'85	12.4	11.9	9.3	14.3	14.5	13.0	26.1									**121.58**
'86	12.6	12.2	10.1	14.3	14.4	13.3	19.9	14.0								**138.58**
'87	11.1	10.6	8.5	11.7	11.3	9.8	12.8	6.6	-0.3							**138.23**
'88	11.3	10.8	9.1	11.9	11.6	10.4	12.8	8.7	6.2	13.0						**156.26**
'89	12.5	12.2	10.7	13.4	13.4	12.7	15.1	12.5	12.1	18.8	24.8					**195.04**
'90	10.6	10.2	8.8	10.9	10.5	9.6	11.0	8.2	6.8	9.3	7.5	-7.5				**180.49**
'91	11.8	11.5	10.3	12.4	12.3	11.6	13.2	11.2	10.6	13.5	13.7	8.5	27.1			**229.44**
'92	11.3	11.0	9.8	11.7	11.5	10.8	12.1	10.2	9.6	11.7	11.3	7.2	15.4	4.7		**240.21**
'93	11.1	10.8	9.7	11.4	11.1	10.5	11.6	9.9	9.4	11.0	10.6	7.4	12.8	6.3	7.9	**259.08**

*Index figures taken at year end.

The table on this page presents annual growth rates in the NYSE Composite Index from 1978–93. Growth rate is a term referring to the average rate of increase or decrease, compounded annually, between two periods.

To obtain the growth rate, for example, between 1982 and 1993, go down the vertical column under 1982 to the horizontal row opposite 1993, which shows an 11.1% rate. This means that stock prices, as measured by the NYSE Composite Index, increased at a yearly rate of 11.1%, compounded annually, between the ends of those years. Stock prices showed an increase of 7.9% in 1993.

The price appreciation on stocks is only a partial measure of the return on money invested in stock. To compute a total return, it is necessary to add the dividends received each year—a calculation not included in this table.

Source: New York Stock Exchange *Fact Book.*

NYSE Composite Index — yield and P/E ratio

End of period	Yield ◆	Price/ earnings ratio ★	End of period	Yield ◆	Price/ earnings ratio ★
1993			**1984**		
December	2.5 %	23.4	**December**	4.5 %	10.4
September	2.9	23.8	**September**	4.5	10.6
June	3.0	22.8	**June**	4.9	10.1
March	2.8	23.3	**March**	4.5	11.6
1992			**1983**		
December	3.0	22.7	**December**	4.4	13.0
September	2.9	25.4	**September**	4.2	13.9
June	2.9	26.3	**June**	4.1	13.9
March	2.6	27.1	**March**	4.9	14.7
1991			**1982**		
December	2.4	25.8	**December**	5.2	14.7
September	3.4	19.7	**September**	6.1	12.5
June	3.4	17.6	**June**	7.0	11.3
March	3.6	17.1	**March**	7.2	10.3
1990			**1981**		
December	3.7	14.8	**December**	6.7	11.3
September	4.5	13.6	**September**	7.1	9.9
June	3.5	15.5	**June**	6.0	11.9
March	3.7	14.9	**March**	5.7	12.5
1989			**1980**		
December	3.2	15.0	**December**	5.4	13.1
September	3.4	14.2	**September**	5.7	12.7
June	3.5	13.3	**June**	6.0	9.8
March	3.9	12.5	**March**	6.8	9.4
1988			**1979**		
December	3.6	12.7	**December**	6.2	10.1
September	3.7	13.1	**September**	6.0	9.9
June	3.4	15.4	**June**	6.4	9.9
March	3.9	15.4	**March**	5.7	10.5
1987			**1978**		
December	3.4	15.5	**December**	5.9	10.3
September	2.9	22.0	**September**	5.3	10.9
June	2.7	21.1	**June**	5.5	11.8
March	2.8	20.2	**March**	6.0	10.7
1986			**1977**		
December	3.4	16.1	**December**	5.7	11.6
September	3.3	16.6	**September**	5.5	11.3
June	3.3	16.6	**June**	5.3	12.7
March	3.5	15.5	**March**	5.2	12.6
1985			**1976**		
December	3.6	13.5	**December**	4.6	14.3
September	4.2	10.7	**September**	4.6	13.4
June	4.2	12.6	**June**	4.3	14.1
March	4.4	11.3	**March**	4.2	15.2

◆ Latest quarterly dividend divided by closing index value at end of period.

★ Latest closing index value divided by trailing 12 months of earnings.

Source: New York Stock Exchange *Fact Book.*

NASDAQ Index Performance: 10 Years

Year	Value	Composite	Industrial	Bank	Other Finance	Insurance	Transportation	Utility[a]
1993	High	787.42 10/15	809.72 11/12	725.65 10/15	921.28 10/13	956.91 10/12	746.26 12/31	205.94 10/14
	Low	645.87 4/26	660.17 4/26	530.03 1/05	775.76 1/08	787.80 1/08	624.44 2/23	126.05 1/04
	Close	776.8	805.84	689.43	892.64	920.59	746.26	185.02
	% Chg.	14.75	11.16	29.37	13.16	14.51	17.69	44.9
1992	High	676.95 12/31	741.92 2/12	532.93 12/31	788.81 12/31	803.91 12/31	634.1 12/31	127.73 12/31
	Low	547.84 6/26	581.6 6/26	352.81 1/01	558.38 1/01	589.03 4/08	530.06 7/20	106.14 10/05
	Close	676.95	724.94	532.93	788.81	803.91	634.1	127.73
	% Chg.	15.5	8.4	52.0	40.7	33.7	11.0	16.6
1991	High	586.34 12/31	668.95 12/31	350.56 12/31	560.79 12/31	601.09 12/31	571.39 12/31	109.52 12/31
	Low	355.75 1/14	387.47 1/14	246.07 1/15	340.72 1/14	434.23 1/14	405.00 1/15	77.85 1/14
	Close	586.34	668.95	350.56	560.79	601.09	571.39	109.52
	% Chg.	56.8	64.7	37.5	56.2	33.0	37.0	30.3
1990	High	469.60 7/16	510.61 7/16	400.19 1/08	512.55 1/03	554.21 1/04	509.93 1/03	128.66 1/02
	Low	325.44 10/16	344.11 10/16	235.25 11/01	323.14 10/30	379.36 10/17	360.34 10/16	76.95 10/17
	Close	373.84	406.05	254.91	359.13	451.84	417.07	84.03
	% Chg.	-17.8	-9.4	-34.8	-29.0	-17.2	-16.3	-34.5
1989	High	485.73 10/09	472.42 10/09	491.16 8/25	567.23 10/09	561.34 12/05	498.20 12/29	137.18 10/09
	Low	378.56 1/03	374.93 1/03	375.38 12/19	457.79T1/03	424.74 1/03	394.62 1/03	87.13 1/03
	Close	454.82	447.99	391.02	505.64	546.01	498.20	128.25
	% Chg.	19.3	18.2	-10.2	10.1	27.2	25.9	47.1
1988	High	396.11 7/05	413.09 7/05	464.91 8/05	477.88 10/10	435.80 10/10	403.68 11/02	87.18 12/30
	Low	331.97 1/12	334.85 1/20	396.44 1/04	410.75 1/13	339.41 1/26	320.91 2/09	60.83 1/12
	Close	381.38	378.95	435.31	459.34	429.14	395.81	87.18
	% Chg.	15.4	11.8	11.4	12.9	22.2	24.0	41.0
1987	High	455.26 8/26	488.92 10/05	526.64 3/20	542.04 3/20	475.78 8/21	436.53 8/21	76.83 8/21
	Low	291.88 10/28	288.30 10/28	366.75 12/07	382.43 12/07	333.66 10/28	276.03 10/28	52.45 10/28
	Close	330.47	338.94	390.66	406.96	351.06	319.21	61.81
	% Chg.	-5.3	-3.0	-5.3	-11.7	-13.1	-8.5	12.4
1986	High	411.16 7/03	414.45 7/03	457.59 7/03	553.42 7/03	467.05 3/19	365.81 6/20	63.13 7/03
	Low	323.01 1/09	326.56 1/09	346.35 1/09	424.52 1/02	381.59 1/09	288.13 1/09	51.49 1/09
	Close	348.83	349.33	412.53	460.64	404.14	348.84	54.99
	% Chg.	7.4	5.8	18.1	8.8	5.8	19.6	4.8
1985	High	325.16 12/16	330.17 12/31	350.08 12/23	423.52 12/16	385.45 12/17	296.91 12/13	52.86 12/20
	Low	245.91 1/02	258.85 1/02	230.23 1/02	298.20 1/02	276.33 1/08	236.20 1/04	40.86 1/02
	Close	324.93	330.17	349.36	423.49	382.07	291.59	52.46
	% Chg.	31.4	26.6	52.0	41.8	35.0	21.9	26.4
1984	High	287.90 1/06	336.16 1/06	229.77 12/31	298.62 12/31	283.91 12/26	290.70 1/09	48.81 1/06
	Low	225.30 7/25	250.18 7/25	33.81 6/01	252.34 5/30	226.87 7/19	194.33 7/25	33.81 7/26
	Close	247.35	260.73	229.77	298.62	283.11	239.29	41.52
	% Chg.	-11.2	-19.4	12.8	7.6	9.9	-14.8	-11.4
1983	High	328.91 6/24	408.42 6/24	203.75 12/30	284.39 9/26	68.09 5/10	293.76 11/30	68.09 6/16
	Low	230.59 1/03	270.55 1/03	155.68 1/12	206.86 1/04	217.33 1/24	257.12 1/04	44.73 10/12
	Close	278.60	323.68	203.75	277.53	257.63	280.80	46.87
	% Chg.	19.9	18.3	30.3	33.7	13.8	43.6	-5.9

Note: The Nasdaq Composite Index and its subindexes started on February 5, 1971, when Nasdaq itself began operation. The Industrial Index, also begun in February 1971, is Nasdaq's largest subindex, with 3,318 issues represented in its calculation.

a. Index reset to a base of 200 on November 1, 1993. Rebased using factor of 5.74805.

Source: *1994 NASDAQ FACT BOOK & COMPANY DIRECTORY,* published by the National Association of Securities Dealers, Inc., 1735 K Street, N.W., Washington, D.C. 20006-1500.

Ten-Year Comparisons of NASDAQ, NYSE, and Amex

	Companies			Issues			Share Volume (millions)		
Year	Nasdaq	NYSE	Amex	Nasdaq	NYSE	Amex	Nasdaq	NYSE	Amex
1993	**4,611**	2,362	869	**5,393**	2,927	1,010	**66,540**	66,923	4,582
1992	**4,113**	2,089	814	**4,764**	2,658	942	**48,455**	51,376	3,600
1991	**4,094**	1,885	860	**4,684**	2,426	1,058	**41,311**	45,266	3,367
1990	**4,132**	1,769	859	**4,706**	2,284	1,063	**33,380**	39,665	3,329
1989	**4,293**	1,719	859	**4,963**	2,241	1,069	**33,530**	41,699	3,125
1988	**4,451**	1,681	896	**5,144**	2,234	1,101	**31,070**	40,850	2,515
1987	**4,706**	1,647	869	**5,537**	2,244	1,077	**37,890**	47,801	3,506
1986	**4,417**	1,573	796	**5,189**	2,257	957	**28,737**	35,680	2,979
1985	**4,136**	1,540	783	**4,784**	2,298	940	**20,699**	27,511	2,101
1984	**4,097**	1,543	792	**4,728**	2,319	930	**15,159**	23,071	1,545

Source: *1994 NASDAQ FACT BOOK & COMPANY DIRECTORY,* published by the National Association of Securities Dealers, Inc., 1735 K Street, N.W., Washington, D.C. 20006-1500.

OPEN–END INVESTMENT COMPANIES

Millions of dollars

Item	1992	1993	1993			1994				
			Oct.	Nov.	Dec.	Jan.	Feb.	Mar.	Apr.[r]	May
1 **Sales of own shares**[2]	**647,055**	↑	**74,490**	**72,865**	**89,775**	**98,679**	**78,032**	**87,381**	**71,164**	**65,218**
2 Redemptions of own shares	447,140		47,168	51,306	62,764	61,829	56,235	73,395	61,925	55,148
3 Net sales[3]	199,915		27,322	21,559	27,011	36,849	21,797	13,986	9,239	10,070
4 **Assets**[4]	**1,056,310**	n.a.	**1,411,628**	**1,416,841**	**1,510,047**	**1,572,907**	**1,561,705**	**1,500,745**	**1,510,827**	**1,529,547**
5 Cash[5]	73,999		104,301	103,352	100,209	110,022	113,975	112,399	118,221	120,107
6 Other	982,311	↓	1,307,327	1,303,489	1,409,838	1,462,879	1,447,730	1,388,347	1,392,606	1,409,440

1. Data on sales and redemptions exclude money market mutual funds but include limited-maturity municipal bond funds. Data on asset positions exclude both money market mutual funds and limited-maturity municipal bond funds.

2. Includes reinvestment of net income dividends. Excludes reinvestment of capital gains distributions and share issue of conversions from one fund to another in the same group.

3. Excludes sales and redemptions resulting from transfers of shares into or out of money market mutual funds within the same fund family.

4. Market value at end of period, less current liabilities.

5. Includes all U.S. Treasury securities and other short-term debt securities.

SOURCE. Investment Company Institute. Data based on reports of membership, which comprises substantially all open–end investment companies registered with the Securities and Exchange Commission. Data reflect underwritings of new companies.

Source: *Federal Reserve Bulletin*, Board of Governors of the Federal Reserve System.

THE MAJOR MARKET AVERAGES

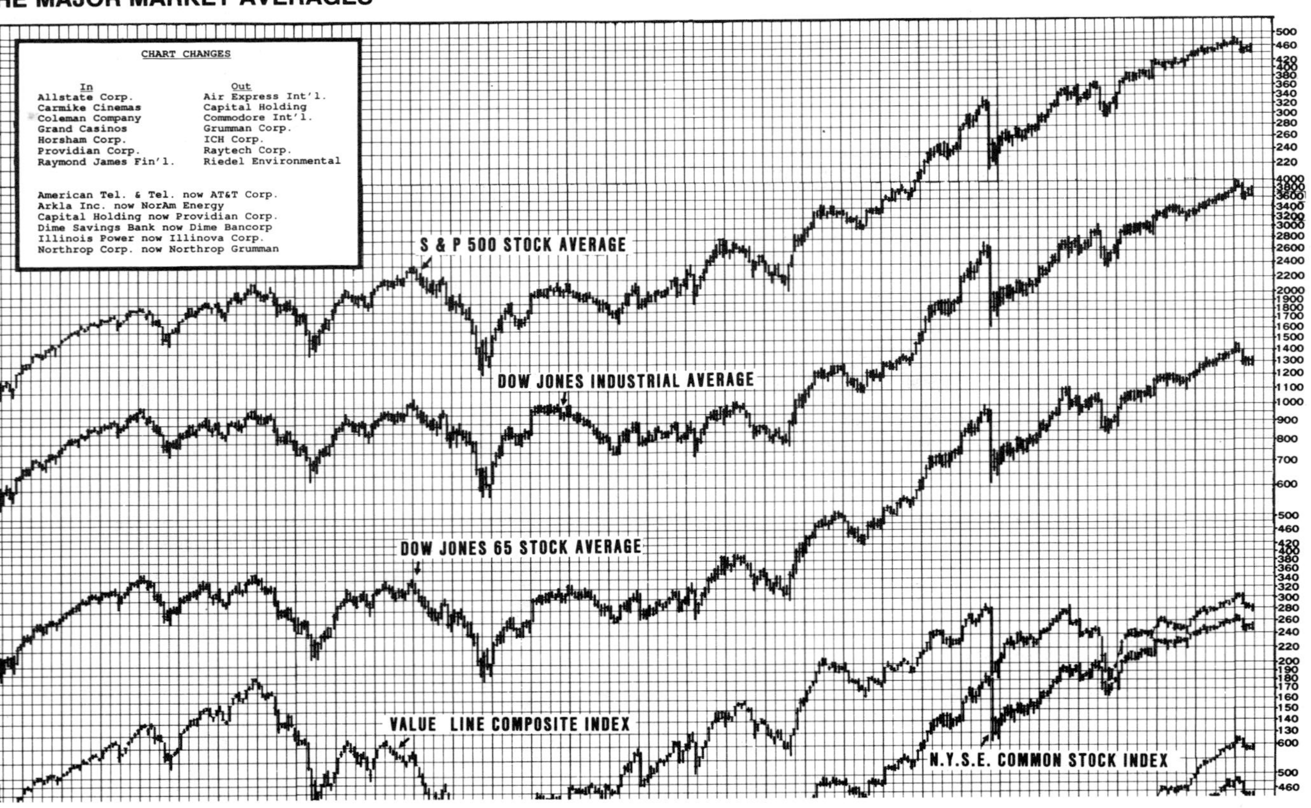
CHART CHANGES
In
Allstate Corp.
Carmike Cinemas
Coleman Company
Grand Casinos
Horsham Corp.
Providian Corp.
Raymond James Fin'l.
Out
Air Express Int'l.
Capital Holding
Commodore Int'l.
Grumman Corp.
ICH Corp.
Raytech Corp.
Riedel Environmental
American Tel. & Tel. now AT&T Corp.
Arkla Inc. now NorAm Energy
Capital Holding now Providian Corp.
Dime Savings Bank now Dime Bancorp
Illinois Power now Illinova Corp.
Northrop Corp. now Northrop Grumman
S & P 500 STOCK AVERAGE
DOW JONES INDUSTRIAL AVERAGE
DOW JONES 65 STOCK AVERAGE
VALUE LINE COMPOSITE INDEX
N.Y.S.E. COMMON STOCK INDEX

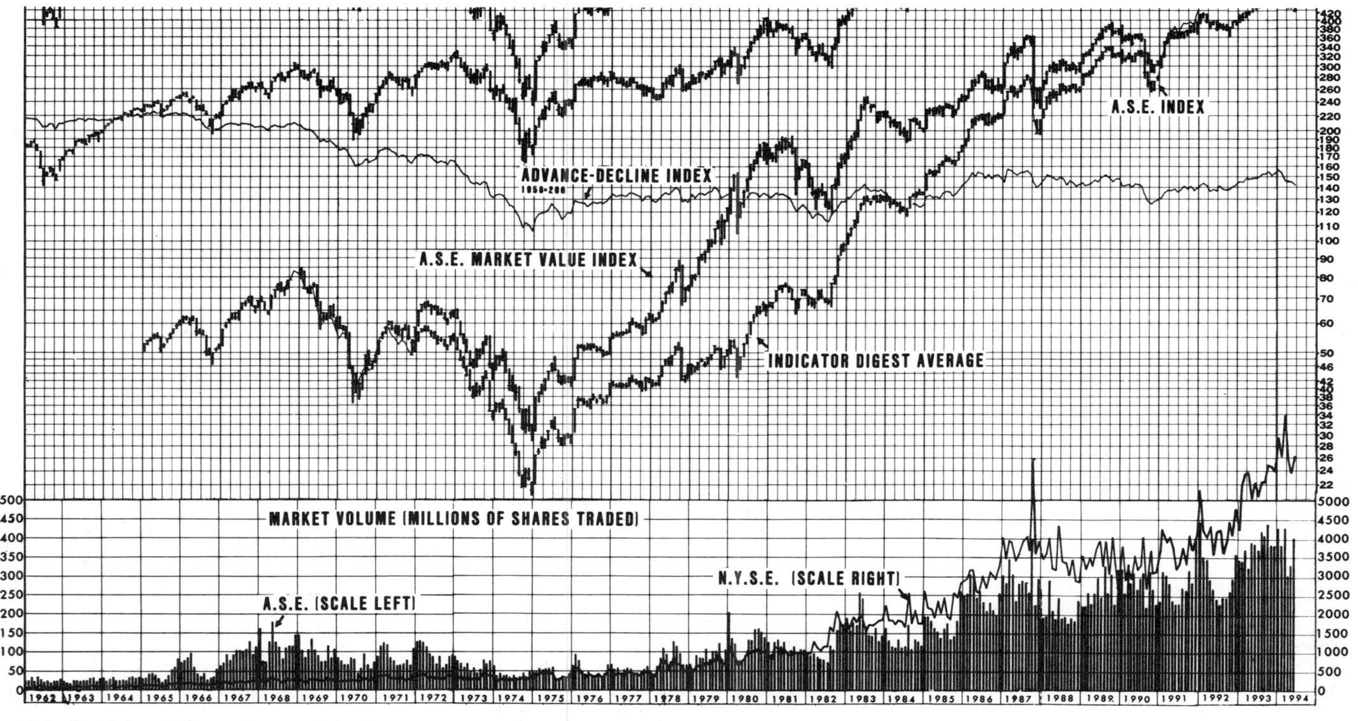

Data in this edition are complete through June 30, 1994; issuance date July 7, 1994.

Source: Chart Courtesy of Securities Research Company, a division of Babson-United Investment Advisors, Inc., 101 Prescott St., Wellesley Hills, MA 02181-3319.

QUARTERLY DOW JONES INDUSTRIAL STOCK AVERAGE

The table below lists the total earnings (losses) of the Dow Jones Industrial Average component stocks of record based on generally accepted accounting principles as reported by the company and adjusted by the Dow Divisor in effect at quarter end and the total dividends of the component stocks based upon the record date and adjusted by the Dow Divisor in effect at quarter end. N.A.-Not available. d-Indicates deficit/negative earnings for the quarter. r-Revised to reflect Woolworth Corp.'s restatement.

Year Ended	Quarter Ended	Clos. Avg.	Qtrly Chg.	% Chg.	Qtrly Earns	12-Mth Earns	P/E Ratio	Qtrly Divs	12-Mth Divs	Divs Yield	Payout Ratio
1994	June 30	3624.96	− 11.00	− 0.30	N.A.	N.A.	N.A.	25.66	101.31	2.79	N.A.
	Mar. 31	3635.96	− 118.13	− 2.89	47.47	150.22	24.2	25.67	100.71	2.76	.6704
1993	Dec. 31	3754.09	+ 198.97	+ 5.59	r40.42	r146.84	r25.6	25.18	99.66	2.65	r.6786
	Sept. 30	3555.12	+ 39.04	+ 1.11	r43.73	r104.52	r34.0	24.80	100.61	2.83	r.9625
	June 30	3516.08	+ 80.97	+ 2.36	r18.60	r84.65	r41.5	25.06	101.84	2.90	r1.2030
	Mar. 31	3435.11	+ 134.00	+ 4.06	r44.09	r113.43	r30.3	24.62	102.29	2.98	r.9017
1992	Dec. 31	3301.11	+ 29.45	+ 0.90	d1.90	108.25	30.5	26.13	100.72	3.05	.9304
	Sept. 30	3271.66	− 46.86	− 1.41	23.86	84.35	38.8	26.03	97.99	3.00	1.1617
	June 30	3318.52	+ 83.05	+ 2.57	47.38	71.60	46.3	25.51	95.52	2.88	1.3341
	Mar. 31	3235.47	+ 66.64	+ 2.10	38.91	60.62	53.4	23.05	93.28	2.88	1.5388
1991	Dec. 31	3168.83	+ 152.06	+ 5.04	d25.80	49.27	64.3	23.40	95.18	3.00	1.9318
	Sept. 30	3016.77	+ 110.02	+ 3.78	11.11	100.91	29.9	23.56	97.58	3.23	.9670
	June 28	2906.75	− 7.11	− 0.24	36.40	131.42	22.1	23.27	99.37	3.42	.7561
	Mar. 28	2913.86	+ 280.20	+ 10.64	27.56	154.17	18.9	24.95	102.32	3.51	.6637
1990	Dec. 31	2633.66	+ 181.18	+ 7.39	25.84	172.05	15.3	25.80	103.70	3.94	.6027
	Sept. 28	2452.48	− 428.21	− 14.86	41.62	193.17	12.7	25.35	101.40	4.13	.5249
	June 29	2880.69	+ 173.48	+ 6.41	59.15	207.78	13.9	26.22	104.75	3.64	.5041
	Mar. 30	2707.21	− 45.99	− 1.67	45.44	205.60	13.2	26.33	106.67	3.94	.5188
1989	Dec. 29	2753.20	+ 60.38	+ 1.69	46.96	221.48	12.4	23.50	103.00	3.74	.4651
	Sept. 29	2692.82	+ 252.76	+ 10.35	56.23	225.48	11.9	28.70	100.29	3.72	.4447
	June 30	2440.06	+ 146.44	+ 6.38	56.97	226.52	10.8	28.14	92.13	3.77	.4067
	Mar. 31	2293.62	+ 125.05	+ 5.77	61.32	229.75	10.0	22.66	84.17	3.67	.3663
1988	Dec. 30	2168.57	+ 55.66	+ 2.63	50.96	215.46	10.1	20.79	79.53	3.67	.3691
	Sept. 30	2112.91	− 28.80	− 1.34	57.27	181.04	11.7	20.54	76.41	3.62	.4221
	June 30	2141.71	+ 153.65	+ 7.73	60.20	168.54	12.7	20.18	73.92	3.45	.4386
	Mar. 31	1988.06	+ 49.23	+ 2.54	47.03	144.45	13.8	18.02	71.85	3.61	.4974
1987	Dec. 31	1938.83	− 657.45	− 25.32	16.54	133.05	14.6	17.67	71.20	3.67	.5351
	Sept. 30	2596.28	+ 177.75	+ 7.34	44.77	137.99	18.8	18.05	70.62	2.72	.5117
	June 30	2418.53	+ 113.84	+ 4.94	36.11	126.23	19.2	18.11	69.36	2.87	.5494
	Mar. 31	2304.69	+ 408.74	+ 21.56	35.63	126.49	18.2	17.37	68.19	2.96	.5391
1986	Dec. 31	1895.95	+ 128.37	+ 7.26	21.48	115.59	16.4	17.09	67.04	3.54	.5800
	Sept. 30	1767.58	− 125.14	− 6.61	33.01	118.80	14.9	16.79	67.14	3.80	.5652
	June 30	1892.72	+ 74.11	+ 4.08	36.37	103.39	18.3	16.94	65.37	3.45	.6323
	Mar. 31	1818.61	+ 271.94	+ 17.58	24.73	96.43	18.9	16.22	63.38	3.49	.6573
1985	Dec. 31	1546.67	+ 218.04	+ 16.41	24.69	96.11	16.1	17.19	62.03	4.01	.6454
	Sept. 30	1328.63	− 6.83	− 0.51	17.60	90.78	14.6	15.02	61.83	4.65	.6811
	June 28	1335.46	+ 68.68	+ 5.14	29.41	102.26	13.1	14.95	61.53	4.61	.6017
	Mar. 29	1266.78	+ 55.21	+ 4.56	24.41	107.87	11.7	14.87	61.56	4.86	.5707
1984	Dec. 31	1211.57	+ 4.86	+ 0.40	19.36	113.58	10.7	16.99	60.63	5.00	.5338
	Sept. 28	1206.71	+ 74.31	+ 6.56	29.08	108.11	11.2	14.72	58.41	4.84	.5403
	June 29	1132.40	− 32.49	− 2.79	35.02	102.07	11.1	14.98	57.67	5.09	.5650
	Mar. 30	1164.89	− 93.75	− 7.45	30.12	87.38	13.3	13.94	56.39	4.84	.6453
1983	Dec. 30	1258.64	+ 25.51	+ 2.07	13.89	72.45	17.4	14.77	56.33	4.47	.7775
	Sept. 30	1233.13	+ 11.17	+ 0.91	23.04	56.12	22.0	13.98	54.59	4.43	.9727
	June 30	1221.96	+ 91.93	+ 8.13	20.33	11.59	105.4	13.70	54.05	4.42	4.6635
	Mar. 31	1130.03	+ 83.49	+ 7.98	15.19	9.52	118.7	13.88	54.10	4.79	5.6828
1982	Dec. 31	1046.54	+ 150.29	+ 16.77	d2.44	9.15	114.4	13.03	54.14	5.17	5.9169
	Sept. 30	896.25	+ 84.32	+ 10.38	d21.49	35.15	25.5	13.44	55.55	6.20	1.5804
	June 30	811.93	− 10.84	− 1.32	18.26	79.90	10.2	13.75	55.84	6.88	.6989
	Mar. 31	822.77	− 52.23	− 5.97	14.82	97.13	8.5	13.92	56.28	6.84	.5794
1981	Dec. 31	875.00	+ 25.02	+ 2.94	23.56	113.71	7.7	14.44	56.22	6.42	.4944
	Sept. 30	849.98	− 126.90	− 12.99	23.26	123.32	6.9	13.73	56.18	6.61	.4539
	June 30	976.88	− 26.99	− 2.69	35.49	128.91	7.6	14.19	55.98	5.73	.4266
	Mar. 31	1003.87	+ 39.88	+ 4.14	31.40	123.60	8.1	13.86	54.99	5.48	.4449

Source: Reprinted by permission of Barron's *National Business and Financial Weekly*,

Stock Market Averages by Industry Group

The charts in this quarterly publication provide the investor with easy-to-read factual portrayals of both the market record and the underlying investment record of a large number of listed stocks which are traded on the New York and American Stock Exchanges. They represent a broadly diversified list of industrial, transportation, and utility enterprises. Each chart depicts the latest 12 years of monthly PRICE RANGES, RATIO-CATOR (relative performance), and TRADING VOLUMES plotted against the running background of per share EARNINGS and DIVIDEND trends. All data have been fully adjusted for all stock dividends and splits and are drawn on uniform semi-logarithmic (ratio) scale grids. The charted trends reflect relative, or percentage changes. Thus, in this scale, the vertical linear distance for a 100% move is the same any place on the chart–irrespective of whether the rise is from $5 to $10, $20 to $40 etc. This permits an accurate comparison from one chart to any other with the exception of those charts that have a special scale reduction. However, the comparability still exists within each of those charts.

These long-range charts complement the graphs found in the weekly-plotted and monthly published SRC Red Book of 5-Trend SECURITY CHARTS, which provide the latest short-term trends of the stocks charted herein.

These definitions apply to pages 268–283.

All Capitalization figures are based on company's *latest annual* report.

Bonds include other long term debt.

Stocks included in the Dow-Jones Averages are designated by a star "★" placed *before the heading.*

Unless prefaced by a "•" for American Stock Exchange issues, all stocks charted are traded on the New York Stock Exchange.

Earnings and Dividends are read from the left-hand scale of each chart.

Earnings Lines—on a per share 12 months ended basis—are represented by the solid black line. Dots show whether company issues quarterly, semi-annual or only annual earnings reports. Earnings off the range of the charts, and deficits are shown by typed notations.

Dividend Lines—representing the annual rate of interim dividend payments—are shown by the dashed lines. The small circles show the month in which dividend payments are made. Dividends off the range of the charts as well as extra or irregular payments of each year are shown in typed figures.

Monthly Price Ranges represented by the solid vertical bars show the highest and lowest point of each month's transactions. Crossbars indicate the month's closing price.

Price Scale—The price ranges are always read from the scale at the right side of each chart. This scale is equal to 15 times the Earnings and Dividend scale at the left, so when the Price Range bars and the Earnings line coincide, it shows the price is at 15 times earnings. When the price is above the earnings line, the ratio of price to earnings is greater than 15 times earnings; when below, it is less.

Monthly Ratio-Cator: The plottings for this line are obtained by dividing the closing price of the stock by the closing price of the Dow-Jones Industrial Average for the same day. The resulting percentage is then multiplied by a factor of 750 to bring the line closer to the price bars for easier comparison. This line is plotted and read from the right scale. The plotting indicates whether the stock has kept pace, outperformed, or lagged the general market as represented by the DJIA.

Moving Average: This line represents the average of closing prices for the most recent 48-month period. Since our database starts in 1978, the majority of the moving averages begin in 1982. For those companies with shorter records the line begins when there is 48-months of price history.

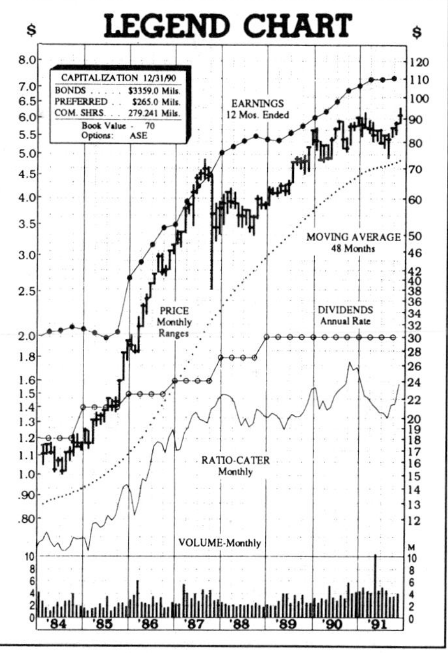

Volume: The number of shares traded each month is shown by vertical bars at the bottom of each chart on an arithmetic scale. Thousands are indicated by a T at the top of the right volume scale and millions by an M.

Source: Chart Courtesy of Securities Research Company, a division of Babson-United Investment Advisors, Inc., 101 Prescott St., Wellesley Hills, MA 02181-3319.

STOCK MARKET AVERAGES BY INDUSTRY GROUP

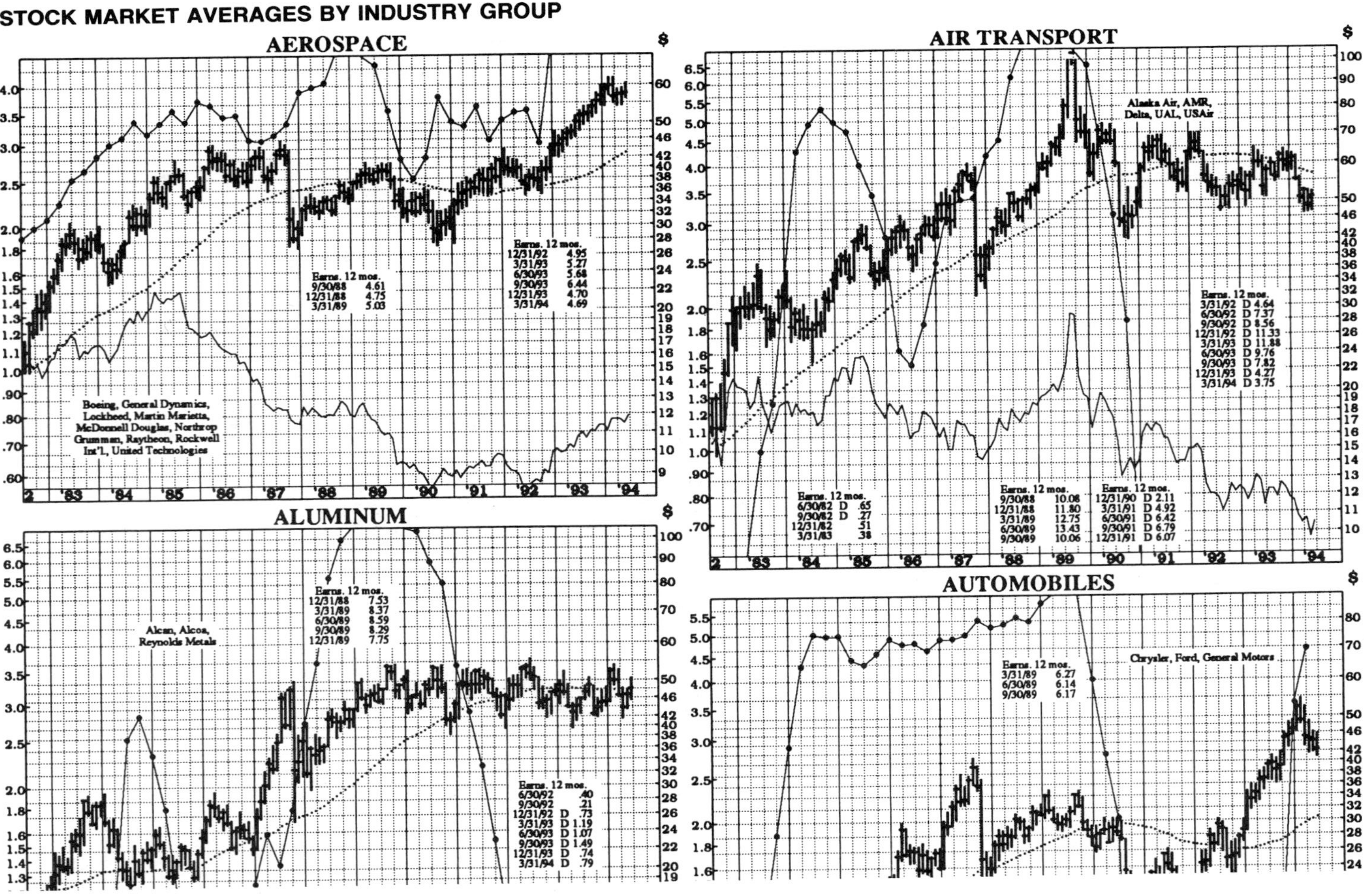

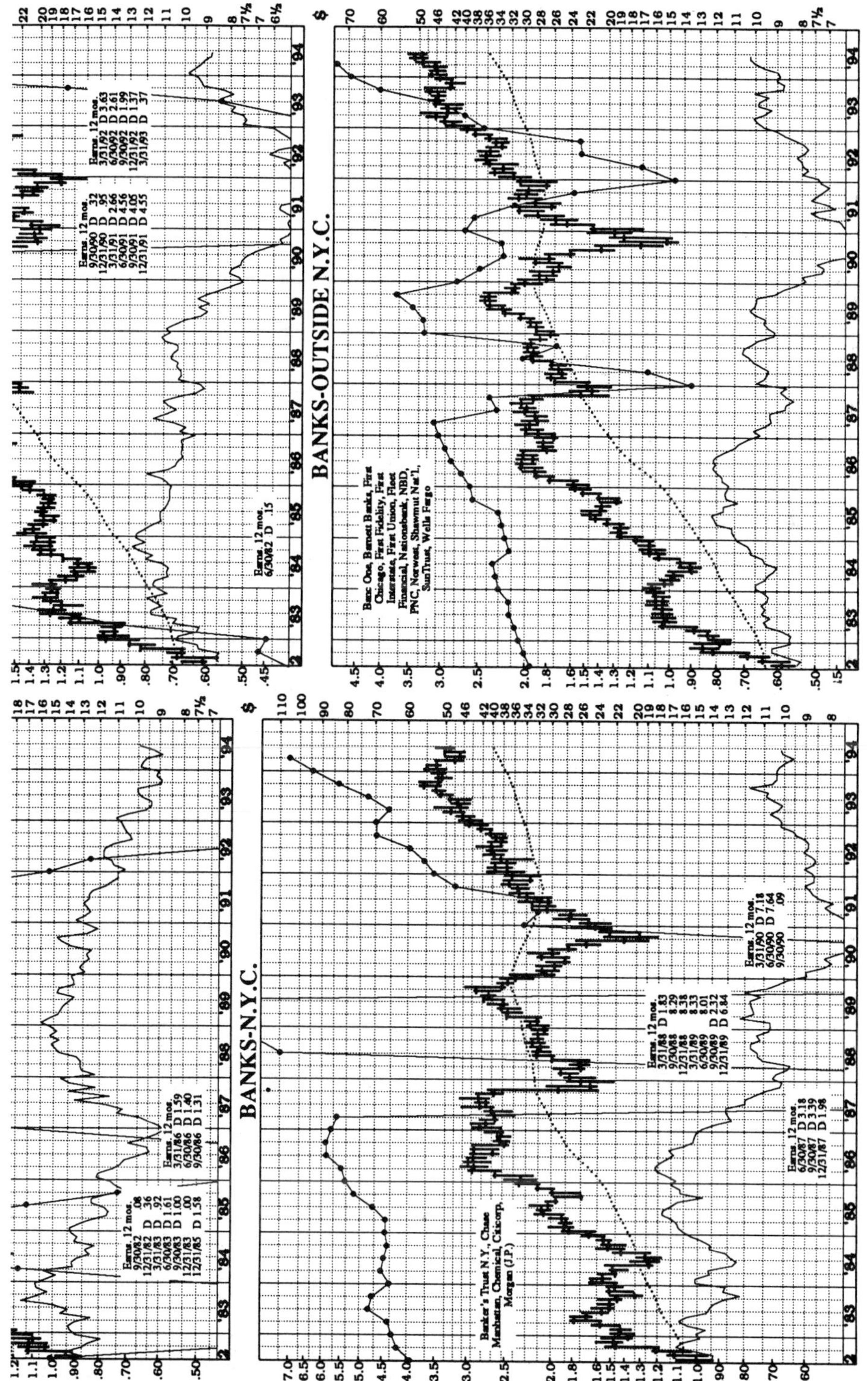
BANKS-N.Y.C.
Banker's Trust N.Y., Chase Manhattan, Chemical, Citicorp, Morgan (J.P.)
BANKS-OUTSIDE N.Y.C.
Banc One, Barnett Banks, First Chicago, First Fidelity, First Interstate, First Union, Fleet Financial, Nationsbank, NBD, PNC, Norwest, Shawmut Nat'l, SunTrust, Wells Fargo

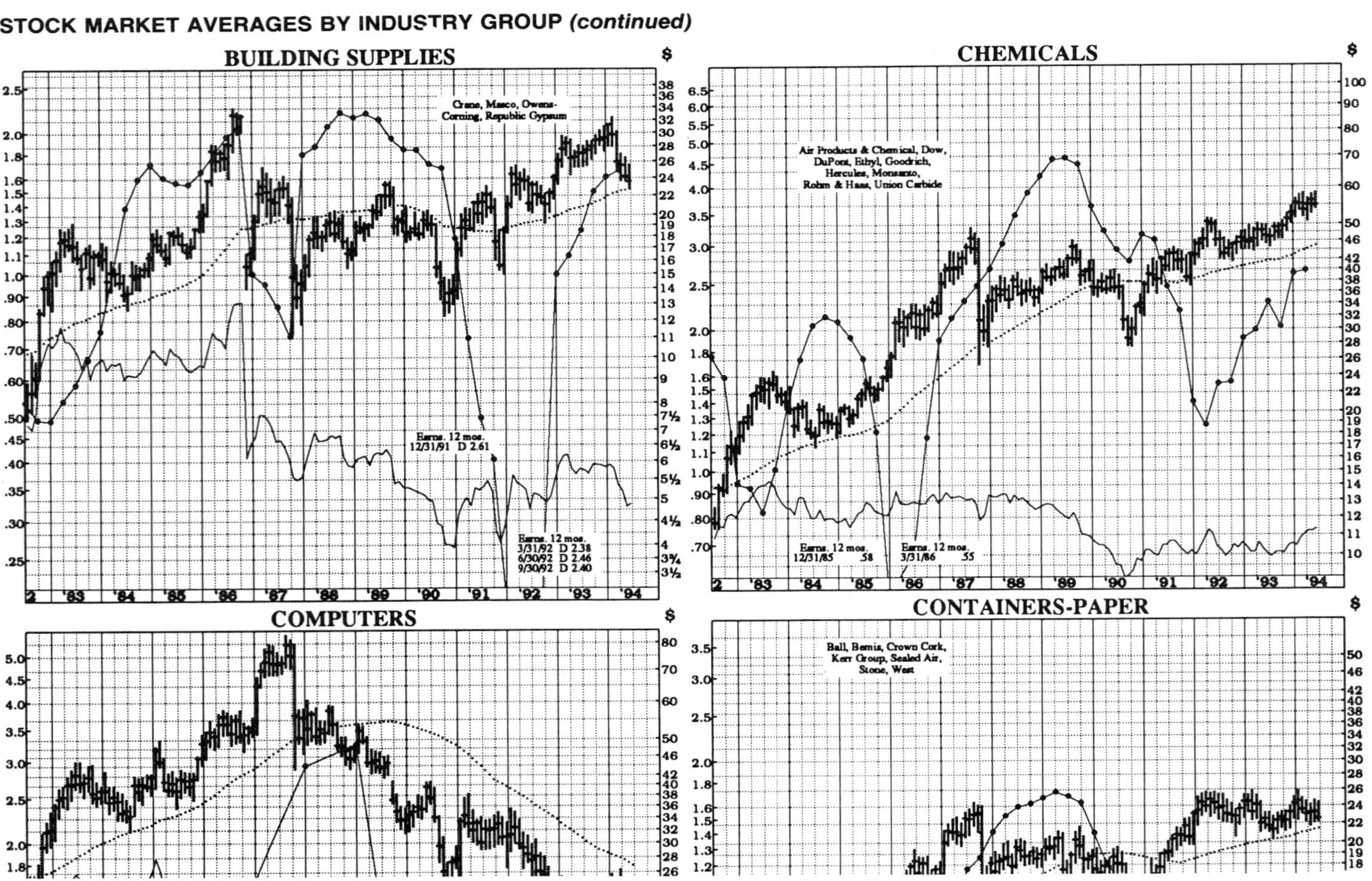
STOCK MARKET AVERAGES BY INDUSTRY GROUP (continued)
BUILDING SUPPLIES
Crane, Masco, Owens-Corning, Republic Gypsum
Earns. 12 mos. 12/31/91 D 2.61
Earns. 12 mos. 3/31/92 D 2.38 6/30/92 D 2.46 9/30/92 D 2.40
CHEMICALS
Air Products & Chemical, Dow, DuPont, Ethyl, Goodrich, Hercules, Monsanto, Rohm & Haas, Union Carbide
Earns. 12 mos. 12/31/85 .58
Earns. 12 mos. 3/31/86 .55
COMPUTERS
CONTAINERS-PAPER
Ball, Bemis, Crown Cork, Kerr Group, Sealed Air, Stone, West
'83 '84 '85 '86 '87 '88 '89 '90 '91 '92 '93 '94
$

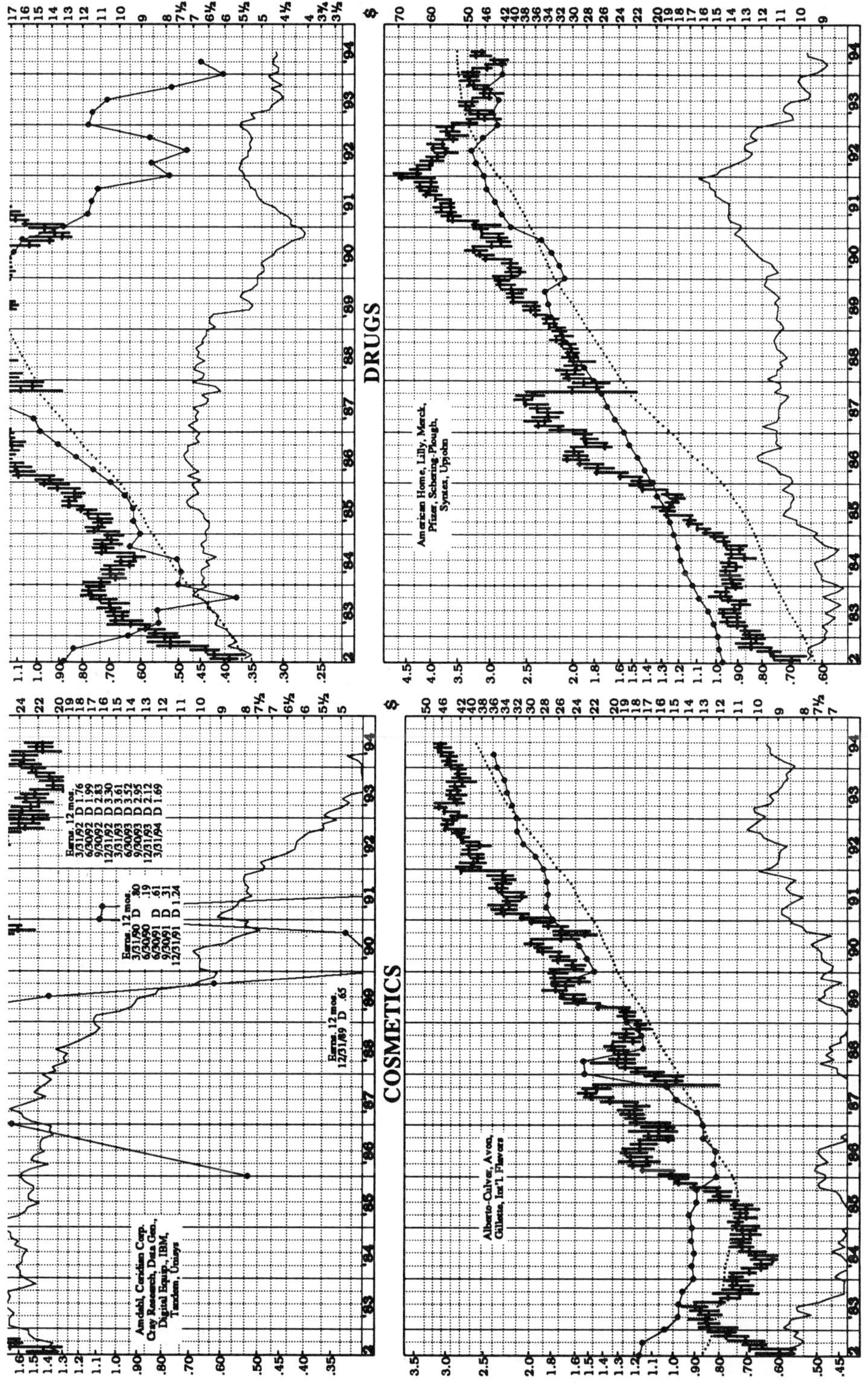
Amdahl, Ceridian Corp.
Cray Research, Data Gen.,
Digital Equip., IBM,
Tandem, Unisys
Earns. 12 mos.
12/31/89 D .65
Earns. 12 mos.
3/31/90 D .80
6/30/90 .19
6/30/91 D .61
9/30/91 D .31
12/31/91 D 1.24
Earns. 12 mos.
3/31/92 D 1.76
6/30/92 D 1.99
9/30/92 D 2.83
12/31/92 D 3.30
3/31/93 D 3.61
6/30/93 D 3.52
9/30/93 D 2.95
12/31/93 D 2.12
3/31/94 D 1.69
COSMETICS
Alberto-Culver, Avon,
Gillette, Int'l. Flavors
DRUGS
American Home, Lilly, Merck,
Pfizer, Schering-Plough,
Syntex, Upjohn
$
'83 '84 '85 '86 '87 '88 '89 '90 '91 '92 '93 '94

STOCK MARKET AVERAGES BY INDUSTRY GROUP (*continued*)

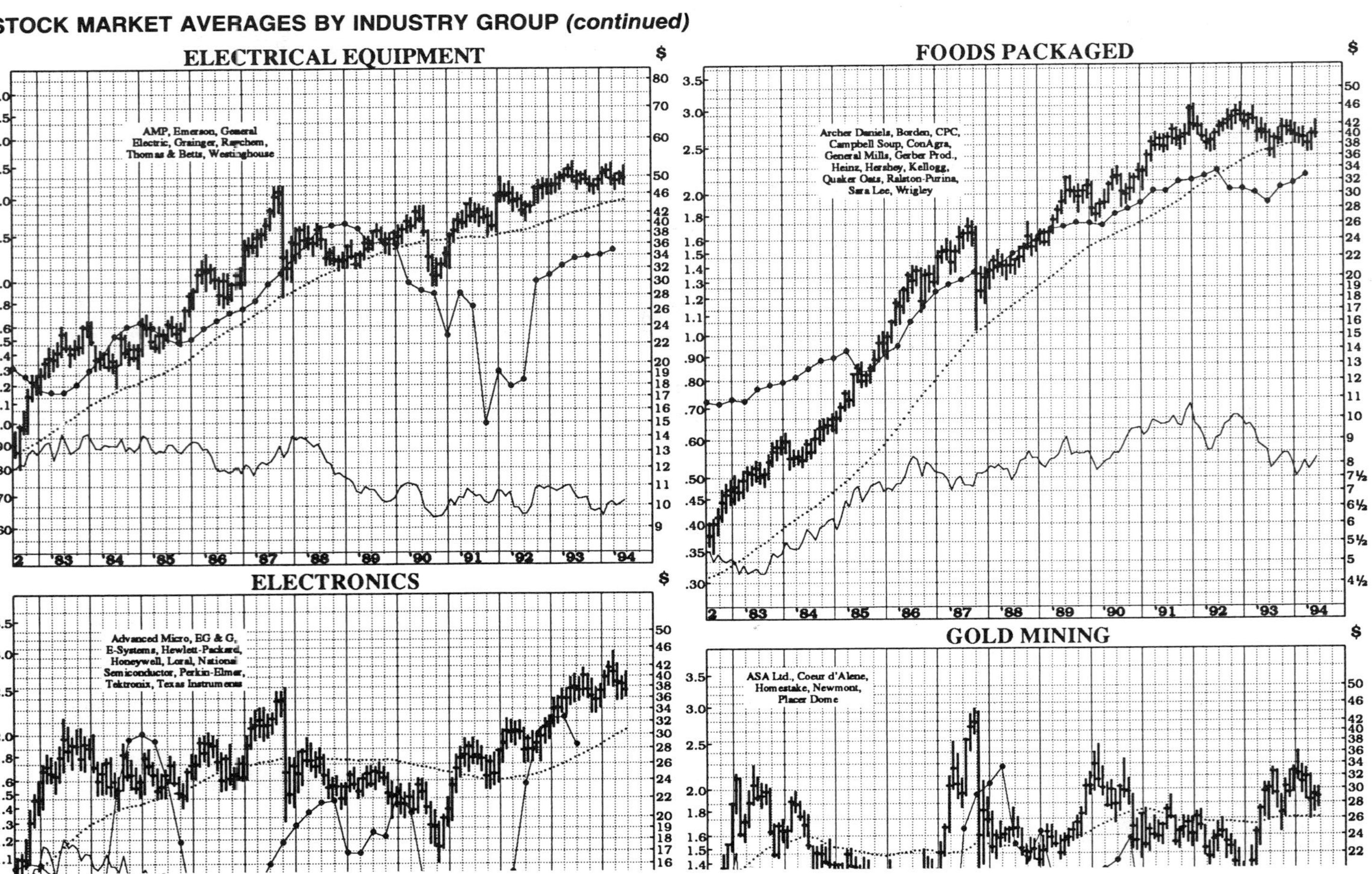
ELECTRICAL EQUIPMENT
AMP, Emerson, General Electric, Grainger, Raychem, Thomas & Betts, Westinghouse
ELECTRONICS
Advanced Micro, EG & G, E-Systems, Hewlett-Packard, Honeywell, Loral, National Semiconductor, Perkin-Elmer, Tektronix, Texas Instruments
FOODS PACKAGED
Archer Daniels, Borden, CPC, Campbell Soup, ConAgra, General Mills, Gerber Prod., Heinz, Hershey, Kellogg, Quaker Oats, Ralston-Purina, Sara Lee, Wrigley
GOLD MINING
ASA Ltd., Coeur d'Alene, Homestake, Newmont, Placer Dome
'83 '84 '85 '86 '87 '88 '89 '90 '91 '92 '93 '94
$

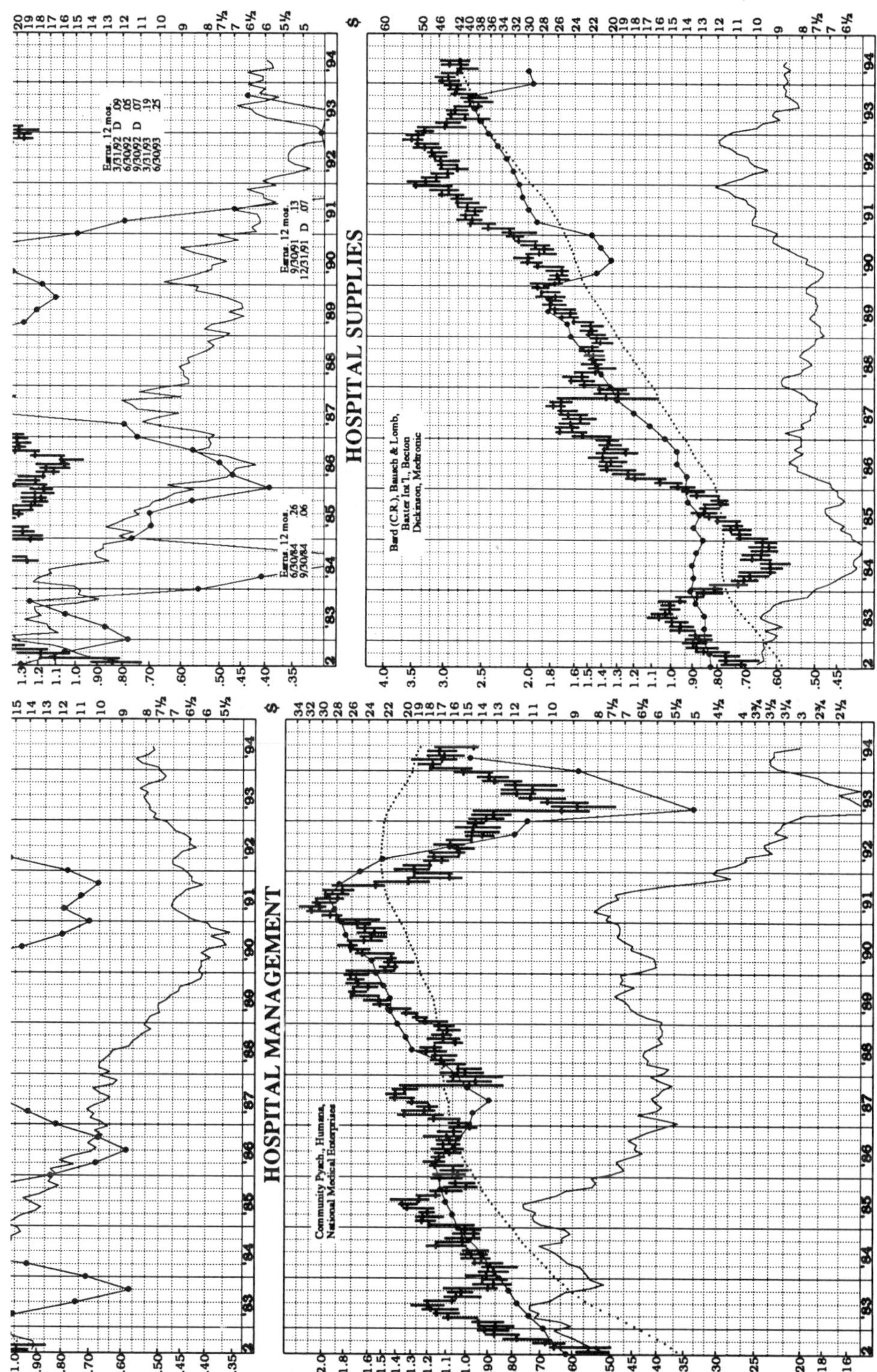
HOSPITAL MANAGEMENT
Community Psych, Humana, National Medical Enterprises
HOSPITAL SUPPLIES
Bard (C.R.), Bausch & Lomb, Baxter Int'l, Becton Dickinson, Medtronic

STOCK MARKET AVERAGES BY INDUSTRY GROUP *(continued)*

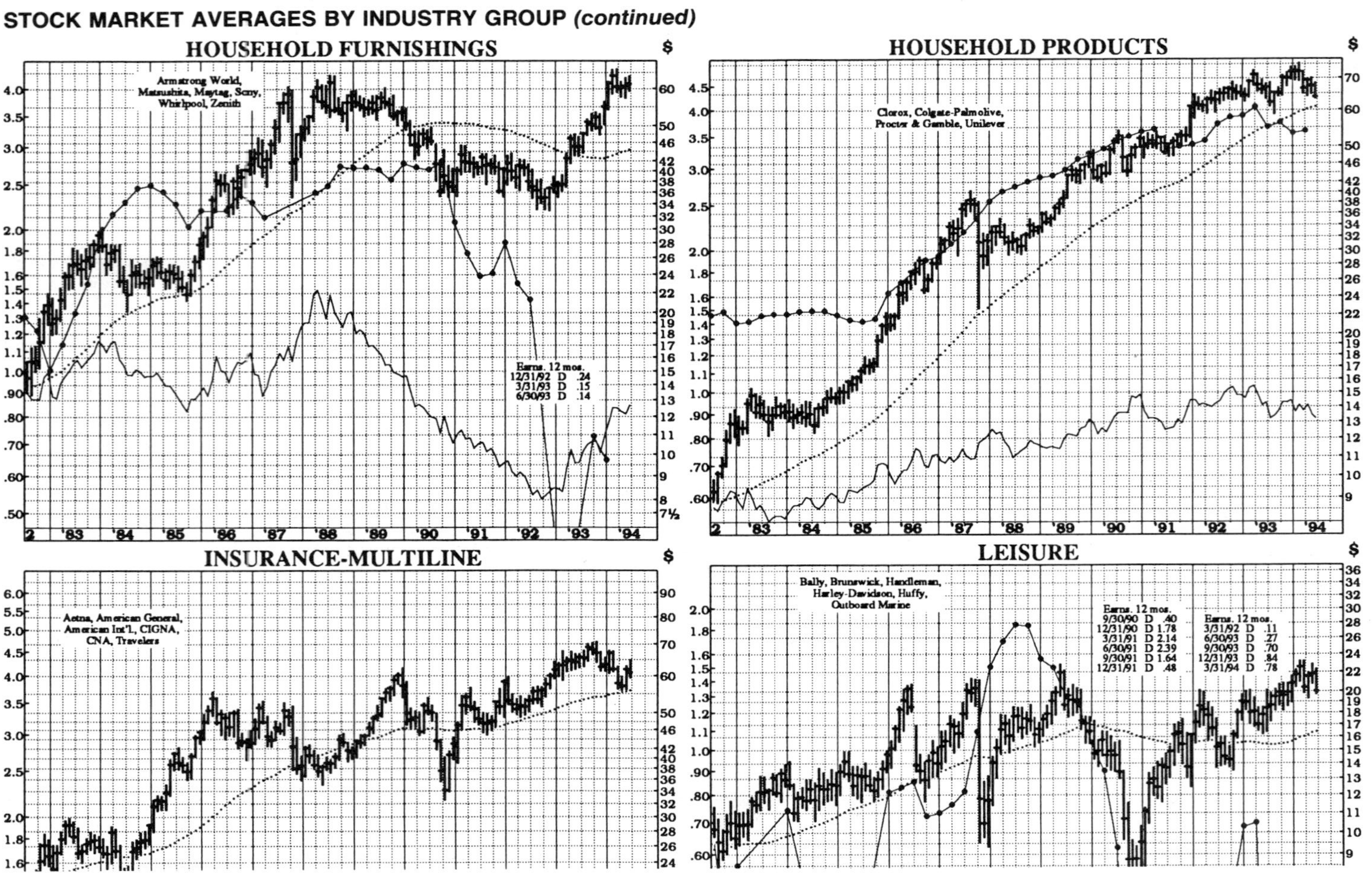

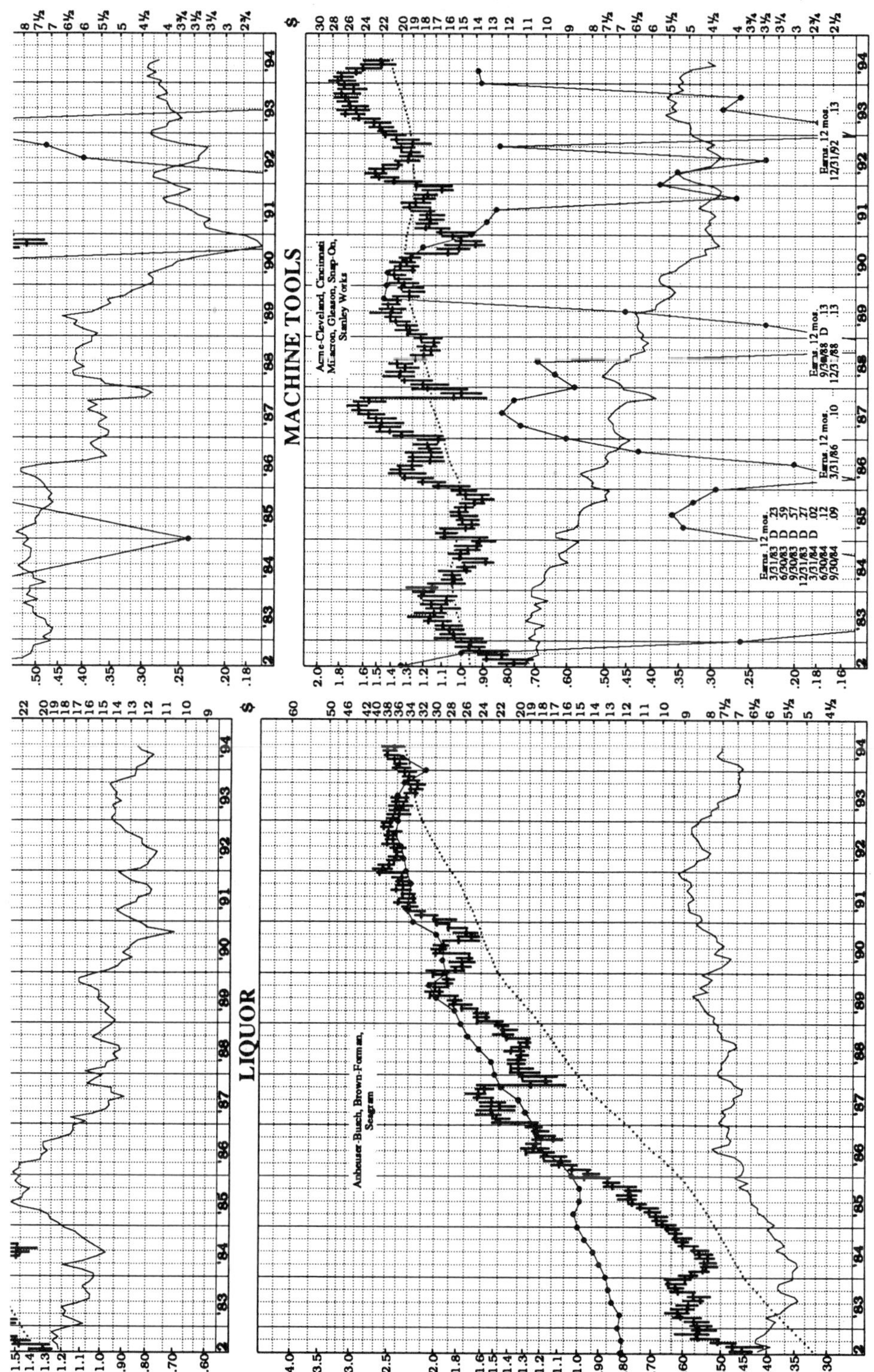
MACHINE TOOLS
Acme-Cleveland, Cincinnati Milacron, Gleason, Snap-On, Stanley Works
Earns. 12 mos.
3/31/83 D .23
6/30/83 D .59
9/30/83 D .57
12/31/83 D .77
3/31/84 D .02
6/30/84 .12
9/30/84 .09
Earns. 12 mos.
3/31/86 .10
Earns. 12 mos.
9/30/88 D .13
12/31/88 .13
Earns. 12 mos.
12/31/92 .13
LIQUOR
Anheuser-Busch, Brown-Forman, Seagram

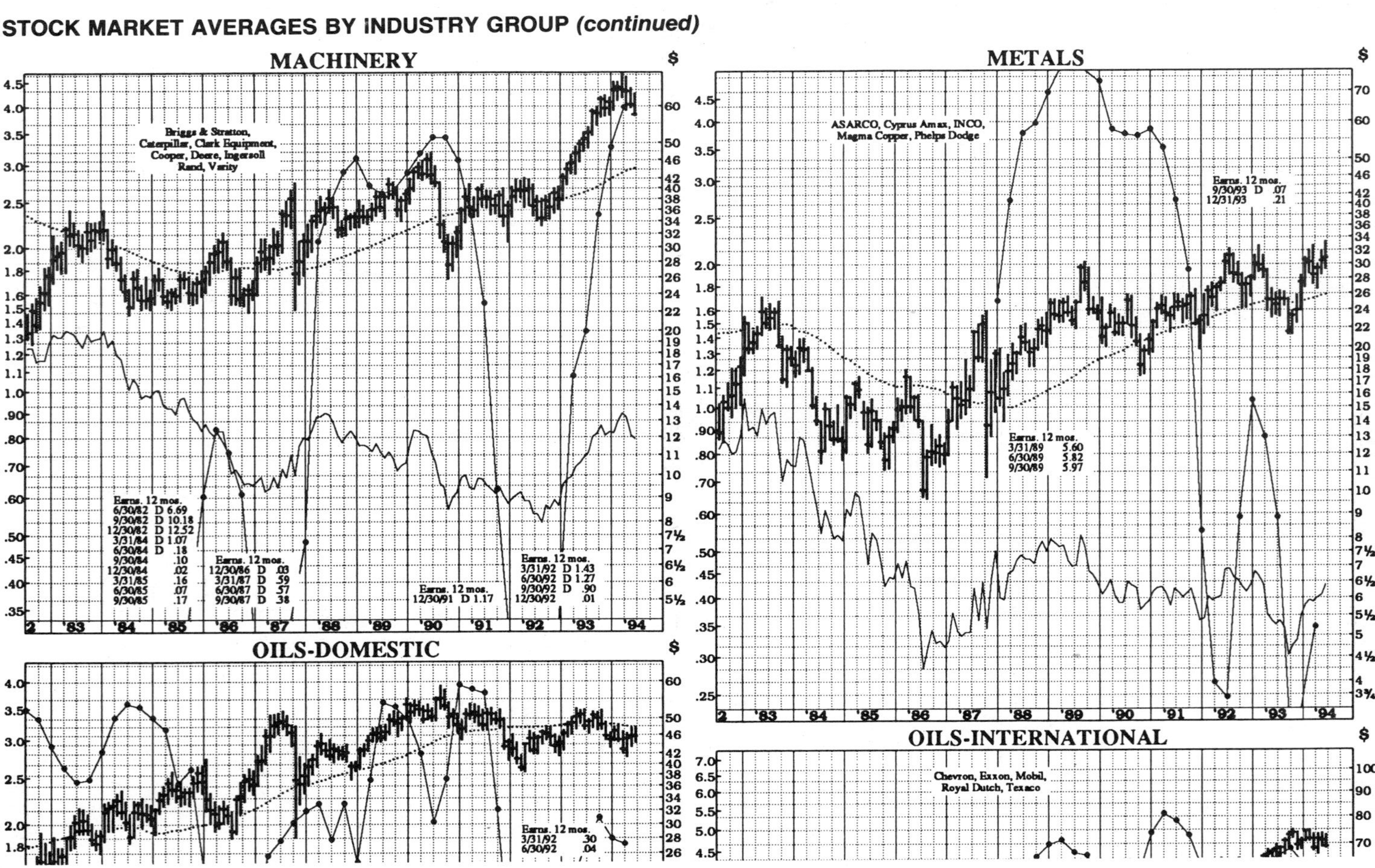
STOCK MARKET AVERAGES BY INDUSTRY GROUP (continued)
MACHINERY
Briggs & Stratton, Caterpillar, Clark Equipment, Cooper, Deere, Ingersoll Rand, Varity
Earns. 12 mos.
6/30/82 D 6.69
9/30/82 D 10.18
12/30/82 D 12.52
3/31/84 D 1.07
6/30/84 D .18
9/30/84 .10
12/30/84 .02
3/31/85 .16
6/30/85 .07
9/30/85 .17
Earns. 12 mos.
12/30/86 D .03
3/31/87 D .59
6/30/87 D .57
9/30/87 D .38
Earns. 12 mos.
12/30/91 D 1.17
Earns. 12 mos.
3/31/92 D 1.43
6/30/92 D 1.27
9/30/92 D .90
12/30/92 .01
OILS-DOMESTIC
Earns. 12 mos.
3/31/92 .30
6/30/92 .04
METALS
ASARCO, Cyprus Amax, INCO, Magma Copper, Phelps Dodge
Earns. 12 mos.
9/30/93 D .07
12/31/93 .21
Earns. 12 mos.
3/31/89 5.60
6/30/89 5.82
9/30/89 5.97
OILS-INTERNATIONAL
Chevron, Exxon, Mobil, Royal Dutch, Texaco

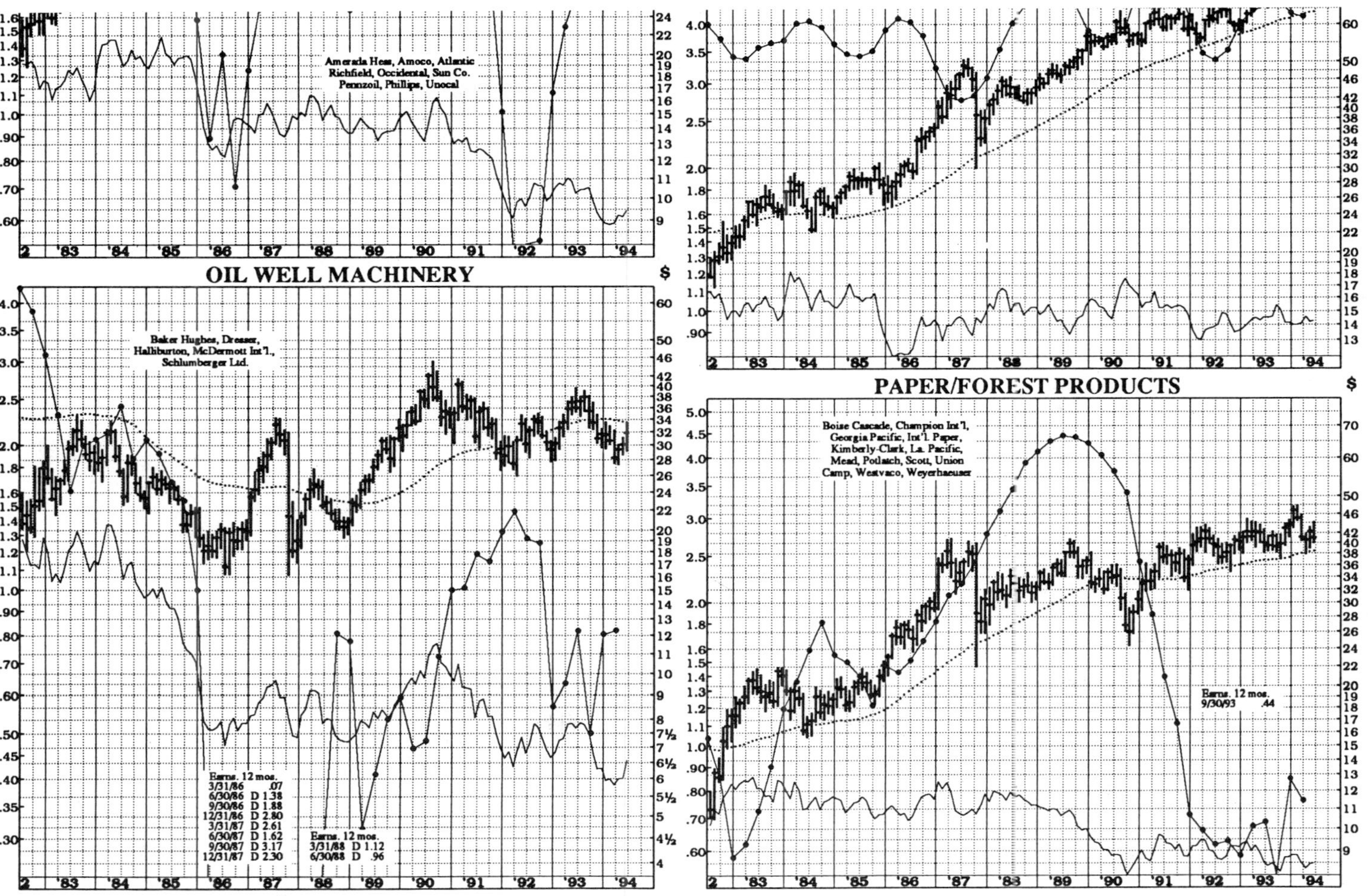
Amerada Hess, Amoco, Atlantic Richfield, Occidental, Sun Co. Pennzoil, Phillips, Unocal
OIL WELL MACHINERY
Baker Hughes, Dresser, Halliburton, McDermott Int'l., Schlumberger Ltd.
Earns. 12 mos. 3/31/86 .07 6/30/86 D 1.38 9/30/86 D 1.88 12/31/86 D 2.80 3/31/87 D 2.61 6/30/87 D 1.62 9/30/87 D 3.17 12/31/87 D 2.30
Earns. 12 mos. 3/31/88 D 1.12 6/30/88 D .96
PAPER/FOREST PRODUCTS
Boise Cascade, Champion Int'l, Georgia Pacific, Int'l. Paper, Kimberly-Clark, La. Pacific, Mead, Potlatch, Scott, Union Camp, Westvaco, Weyerhaeuser
Earns. 12 mos. 9/30/93 .44

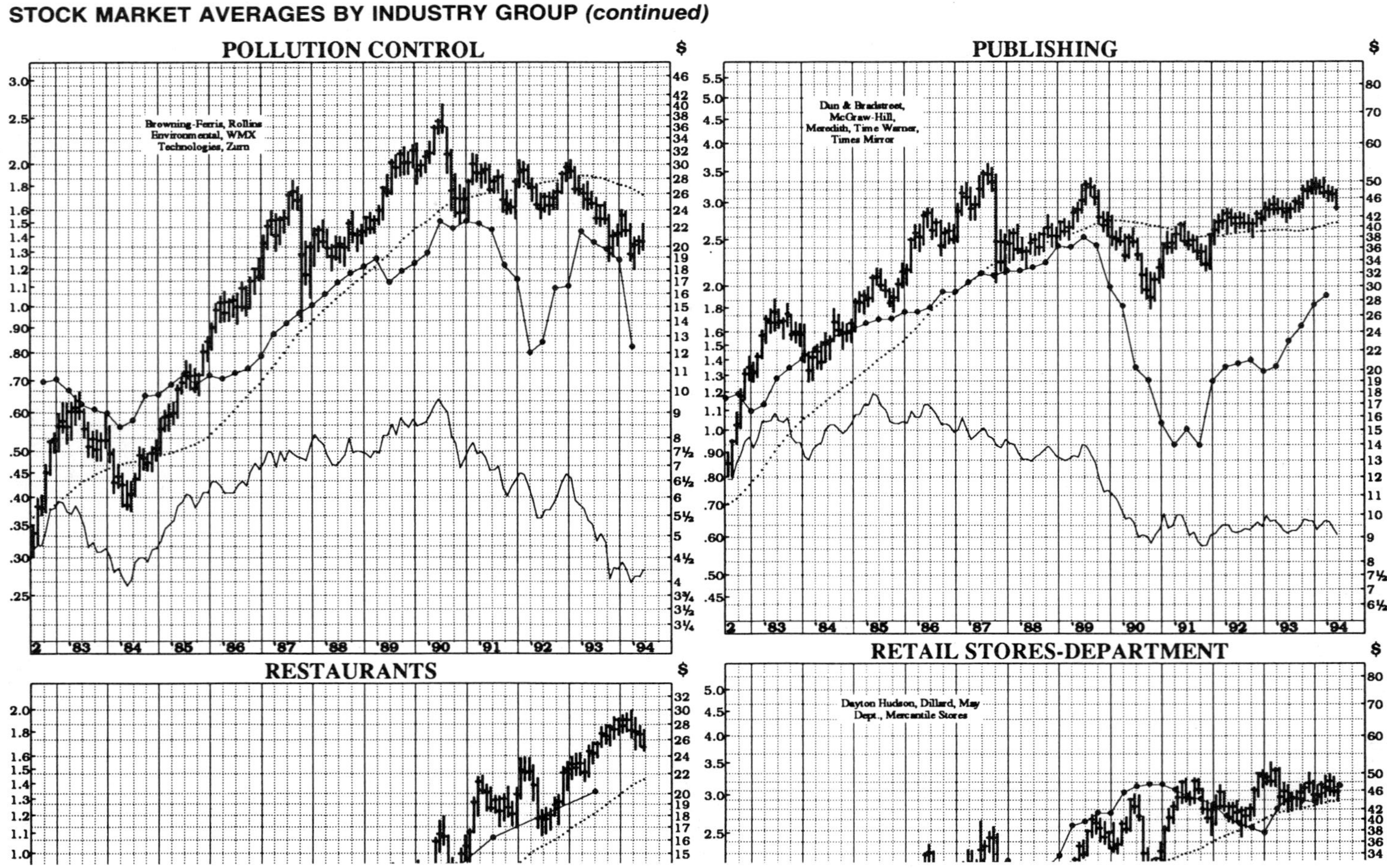
STOCK MARKET AVERAGES BY INDUSTRY GROUP (continued)
POLLUTION CONTROL
Browning-Ferris, Rollins Environmental, WMX Technologies, Zurn
PUBLISHING
Dun & Bradstreet, McGraw-Hill, Meredith, Time Warner, Times Mirror
RESTAURANTS
RETAIL STORES-DEPARTMENT
Dayton Hudson, Dillard, May Dept., Mercantile Stores

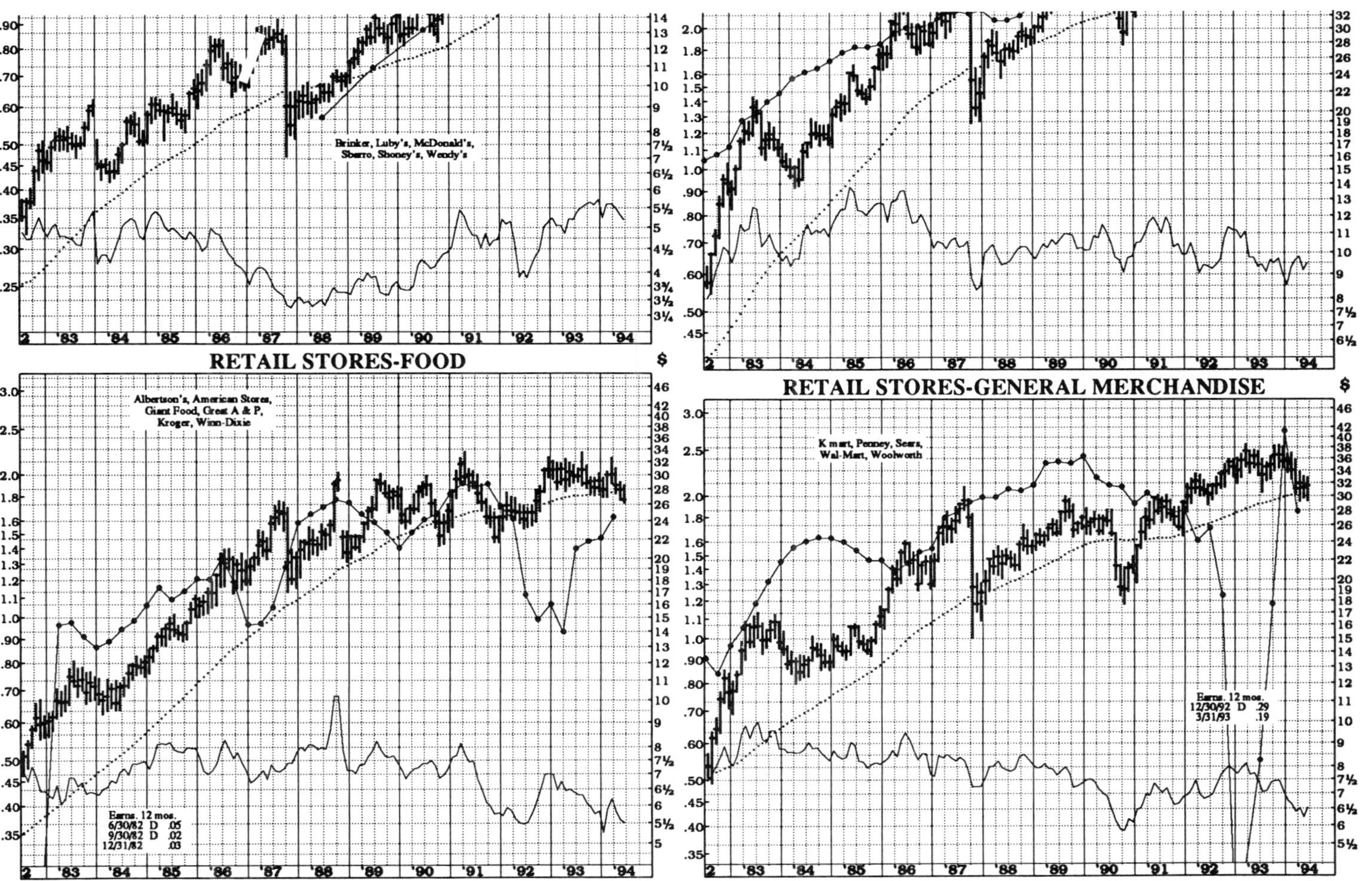
Brinker, Luby's, McDonald's,
Sbarro, Shoney's, Wendy's
RETAIL STORES-FOOD
Albertson's, American Stores,
Giant Food, Great A & P,
Kroger, Winn-Dixie
Earns. 12 mos.
6/30/82 D .05
9/30/82 D .02
12/31/82 .03
RETAIL STORES-GENERAL MERCHANDISE
K mart, Penney, Sears,
Wal-Mart, Woolworth
Earns. 12 mos.
12/30/92 D .29
3/31/93 .19

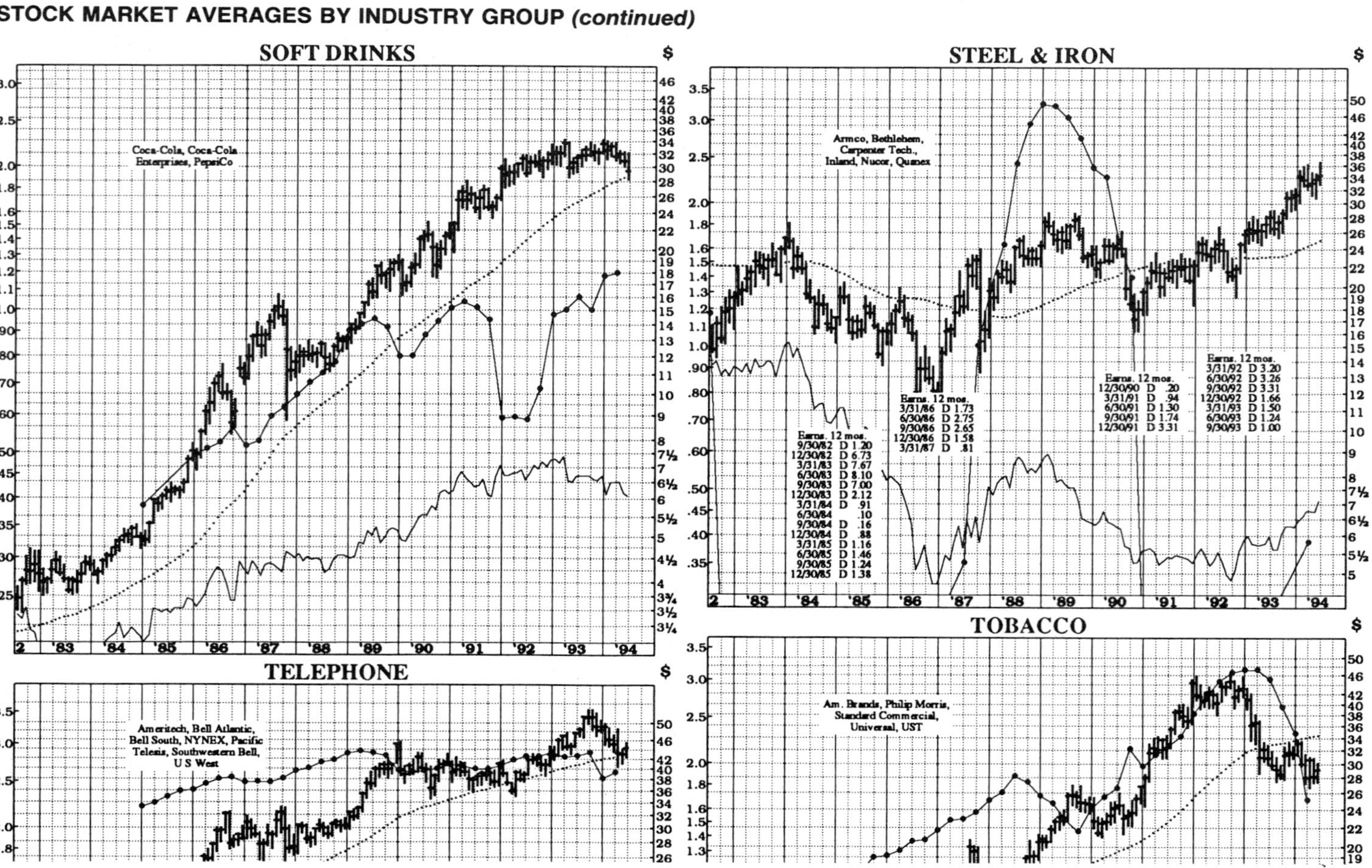
STOCK MARKET AVERAGES BY INDUSTRY GROUP (continued)
SOFT DRINKS
Coca-Cola, Coca-Cola Enterprises, PepsiCo
STEEL & IRON
Armco, Bethlehem, Carpenter Tech., Inland, Nucor, Quanex
Earns. 12 mos.
9/30/82 D 1.20
12/30/82 D 6.73
3/31/83 D 7.67
6/30/83 D 8.10
9/30/83 D 7.00
12/30/83 D 2.12
3/31/84 D .91
6/30/84 .10
9/30/84 D .16
12/30/84 D .88
3/31/85 D 1.16
6/30/85 D 1.46
9/30/85 D 1.24
12/30/85 D 1.38
Earns. 12 mos.
3/31/86 D 1.73
6/30/86 D 2.75
9/30/86 D 2.65
12/30/86 D 1.58
3/31/87 D .81
Earns. 12 mos.
12/30/90 D .20
3/31/91 D .94
6/30/91 D 1.30
9/30/91 D 1.74
12/30/91 D 3.31
Earns. 12 mos.
3/31/92 D 3.20
6/30/92 D 3.26
9/30/92 D 3.31
12/30/92 D 1.66
3/31/93 D 1.50
6/30/93 D 1.24
9/30/93 D 1.00
TELEPHONE
Ameritech, Bell Atlantic, Bell South, NYNEX, Pacific Telesis, Southwestern Bell, U S West
TOBACCO
Am. Brands, Philip Morris, Standard Commercial, Universal, UST
'83 '84 '85 '86 '87 '88 '89 '90 '91 '92 '93 '94
$

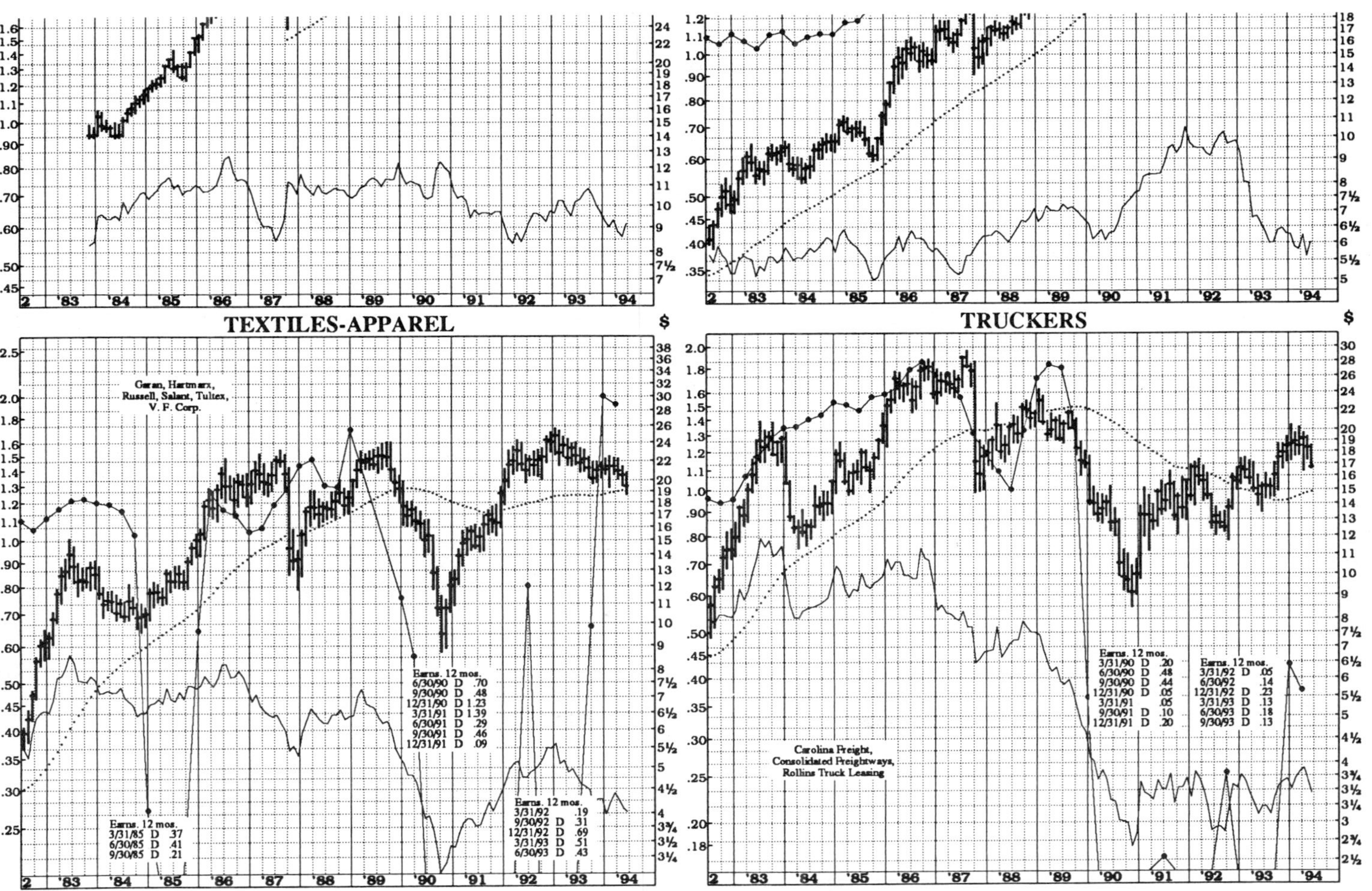
TEXTILES-APPAREL
Garan, Hartmarx, Russell, Salant, Tultex, V. F. Corp.
Earns. 12 mos.
3/31/85 D .37
6/30/85 D .41
9/30/85 D .21
Earns. 12 mos.
6/30/90 D .70
9/30/90 D .48
12/31/90 D 1.23
3/31/91 D 1.39
6/30/91 D .29
9/30/91 D .46
12/31/91 D .09
Earns. 12 mos.
3/31/92 .19
9/30/92 D .31
12/31/92 D .69
3/31/93 D .51
6/30/93 D .43
TRUCKERS
Carolina Freight, Consolidated Freightways, Rollins Truck Leasing
Earns. 12 mos.
3/31/90 D .20
6/30/90 D .48
9/30/90 D .44
12/31/90 D .05
3/31/91 .05
9/30/91 D .10
12/31/91 D .20
Earns. 12 mos.
3/31/92 D .05
6/30/92 .14
12/31/92 D .23
3/31/93 D .13
6/30/93 D .18
9/30/93 D .13

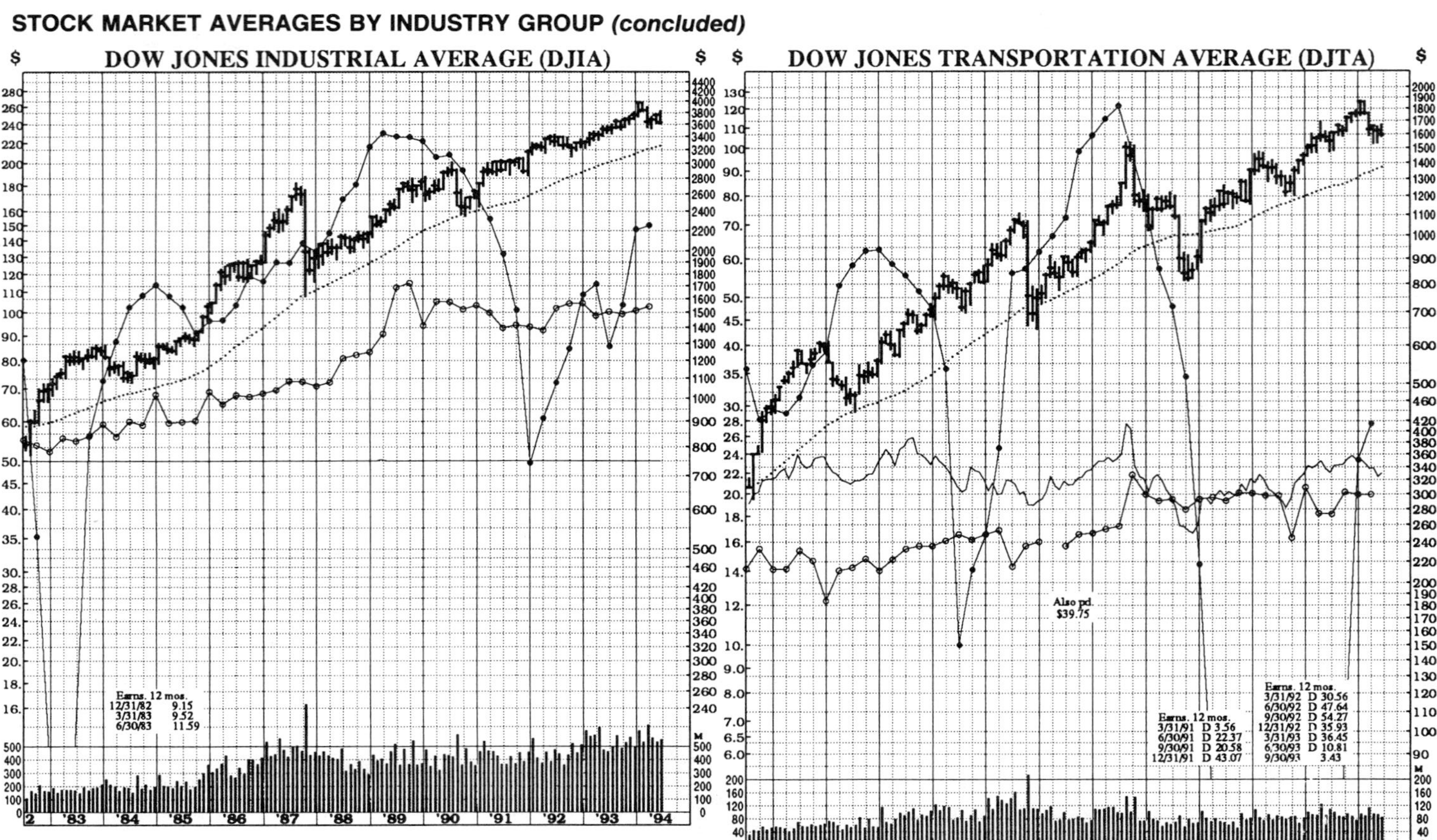
STOCK MARKET AVERAGES BY INDUSTRY GROUP (concluded)
DOW JONES INDUSTRIAL AVERAGE (DJIA)
Earns. 12 mos.
12/31/82 9.15
3/31/83 9.52
6/30/83 11.59
DOW JONES TRANSPORTATION AVERAGE (DJTA)
Also pd. $39.75
Earns. 12 mos.
3/31/91 D 3.56
6/30/91 D 22.37
9/30/91 D 20.58
12/31/91 D 43.07
Earns. 12 mos.
3/31/92 D 30.56
6/30/92 D 47.64
9/30/92 D 54.27
12/31/92 D 35.93
3/31/93 D 36.45
6/30/93 D 10.81
9/30/93 3.43

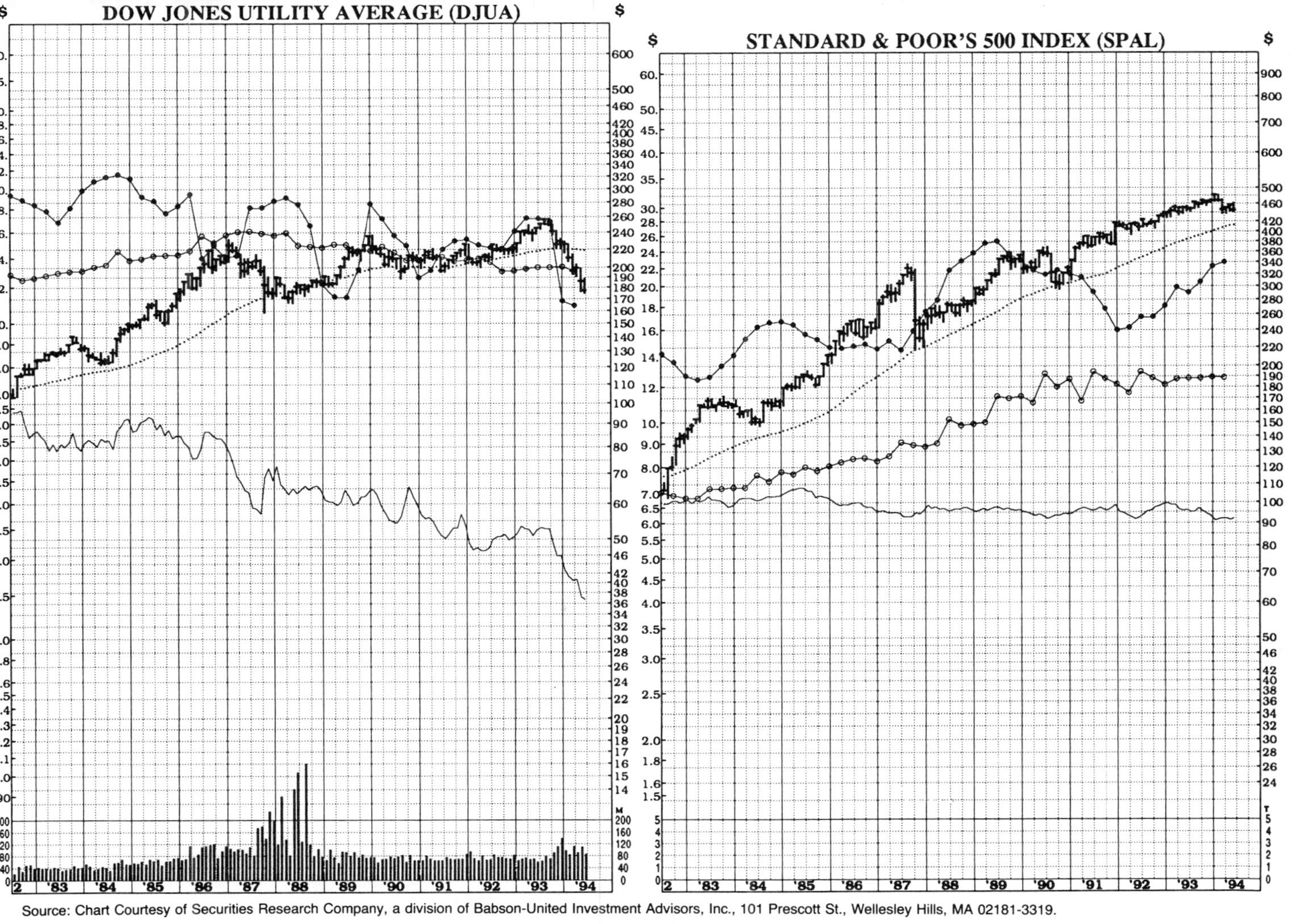

Source: Chart Courtesy of Securities Research Company, a division of Babson-United Investment Advisors, Inc., 101 Prescott St., Wellesley Hills, MA 02181-3319.

Components—Dow Jones 65 Stock Averages

The Dow Jones Stock Averages are compiled by using the New York Stock Exchange only closing prices and adjusting by the then current appropriate divisor. The divisors appear under the Dow Jones Half-Hourly Averages. A list of the stocks on which these averages are based follows:

Industrials

Allied Sig.	Du Pont	Minn M&M
Alum Co	Eastman	Morgan (J.P.)
Amer Exp	Exxon	Philip Morris
AT&T	Gen Electric	Proc Gamb
Beth Steel	Gen Motors	Sears
Boeing	Goodyear	Texaco
Caterpillar	IBM	Union Carbide
Chevron	Int'l Paper	United Tech
Coca-Cola	McDonald's	Westinghouse
Disney (Walt)	Merck	Woolworth

Transportation

AMR Corp.	Cons Rail	Santa Fe
Airbrn Freigt	CSX Corp.	Southwest Airl
Alaska Air	Delta Air	UAL Corp.
Amer Pres	Fed Express	Union Pac
Burlington	Norfolk So	USAir
Caro Freight	Roadway Svcs	Xtra Corp.
Cons Freight	Ryder System	

Utilities

Am El Power	Cons N Gas	Panhandle
Noram Energy	Detroit Edis	Peoples En
Centerior	Houston Ind	Peco Energy
Comwlth Edis	Niag Mohawk	Pub Serv E
Cons Edison	Pacific G&E	SCEcorp

Source: Reprinted by permission of Barrons *National Business and Financial Weekly,*

NEW SECURITY ISSUES U.S. Corporations
Millions of dollars

Type of issue, offering, or issuer	1991	1992	1993	1993						1994	
				July	Aug.	Sept.	Oct.	Nov.	Dec.	Jan.[r]	Feb.
1 **All issues**[1]	**465,246**	**559,729**	n.a.	**47,628**[r]	**52,955**[r]	**64,530**[r]	**56,143**[r]	**54,808**[r]	**44,313**[r]	**55,448**	**47,778**
2 **Bonds**[2]	**389,822**	**471,404**	n.a.	**38,032**[r]	**43,688**[r]	**53,837**[r]	**45,608**[r]	**43,214**[r]	**33,782**[r]	**49,411**	**39,037**
By type of offering											
3 Public, domestic	286,930	377,960	488,895	37,392	40,447	49,132[r]	42,645[r]	39,525[r]	32,201[r]	44,161	31,761
4 Private placement, domestic[3]	74,930	65,853	n.a.	n.a.	n.a.	n.a.	n.a.	n.a.	n.a.	n.a.	n.a.
5 Sold abroad	27,962	27,591	41,533	640[r]	3,241[r]	4,705[r]	2,963[r]	3,689[r]	1,582[r]	5,250	7,276
By industry group											
6 Manufacturing	86,628	82,058	67,411	2,498	6,132	4,036[r]	3,273	3,334[r]	3,068	4,585	3,411
7 Commercial and miscellaneous	36,666	43,043	37,873	4,735[r]	2,331	2,378[r]	6,306[r]	3,078	2,525[r]	2,869	2,445
8 Transportation	13,598	9,979	8,234	611	723	288	1,416	648[r]	895[r]	693	100
9 Public utility	23,944	48,055	52,742	5,797	3,474	5,163	2,585	1,763	2,336	2,566	1,853
10 Communication	9,431	15,394	29,040	2,331	2,979	2,237	2,991	1,015	2,001	2,495	2,212
11 Real estate and financial	219,555	272,875	335,127	22,060[r]	28,049[r]	39,735[r]	29,039[r]	33,376[r]	22,958[r]	36,203	29,016
12 **Stocks**[2]	**75,424**	**88,325**	n.a.[r]	**9,596**	**9,267**	**10,693**	**10,535**	**11,594**	**10,531**	**6,037**	**8,741**
By type of offering											
13 Public preferred	17,085	21,339	20,533	1,913	3,319	1,358	2,549	1,385	650	1,592	1,198
14 Common	48,230	57,118	90,559	7,683	5,948	9,336	7,987	10,209	9,881	4,444	7,543
15 Private placement[3]	10,109	9,867	n.a.	n.a.	n.a.	n.a.	n.a.	n.a.	n.a.	n.a.	n.a.
By industry group											
16 Manufacturing	24,111	22,723	22,271	1,618	1,961	2,274	2,121	2,169	2,267	1,564	1,807
17 Commercial and miscellaneous	19,418	20,231	25,761	2,525	1,457	2,242	1,842	3,061	1,970	1,516	1,682
18 Transportation	2,439	2,595	2,237	114	466	153	128	221	162	78	703
19 Public utility	3,474	6,532	7,050	495	582	908	1,103	371	129	293	203
20 Communication	475	2,366	3,439	n.a.	115	248	18	1,074	1,603	n.a.	120
21 Real estate and financial	25,507	33,879	49,889	4,844	4,675	4,666	5,323	4,486	4,381	2,584	4,064

1. Figures represent gross proceeds of issues maturing in more than one year; they are the principal amount or number of units calculated by multiplying by the offering price. Figures exclude secondary offerings, employee stock plans, investment companies other than closed-end, intracorporate transactions, equities sold abroad, and Yankee bonds. Stock data include ownership securities issued by limited partnerships.

2. Monthly data cover only public offerings.
3. Monthly data are not available.

SOURCES. IDD Information Services, Inc., Securities Data Company, and the Board of Governors of the Federal Reserve System.

Source: *Federal Reserve Bulletin,* Board of Governors of the Federal Reserve System.

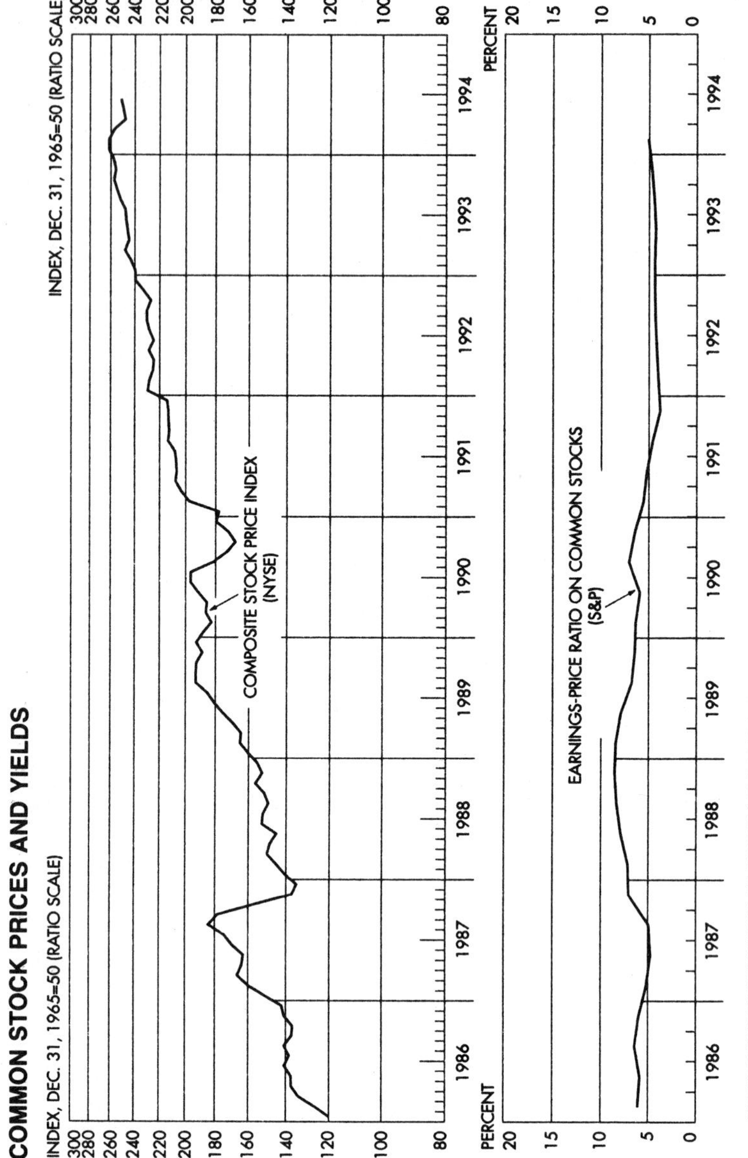
COMMON STOCK PRICES AND YIELDS
INDEX, DEC. 31, 1965=50 (RATIO SCALE)
300
280
260
240
220
200
180
160
140
120
100
80
COMPOSITE STOCK PRICE INDEX
(NYSE)
PERCENT
20
15
10
5
0
EARNINGS-PRICE RATIO ON COMMON STOCKS
(S&P)
1986
1987
1988
1989
1990
1991
1992
1993
1994
SOURCES: NEW YORK STOCK EXCHANGE AND STANDARD & POOR'S CORPORATION
COUNCIL OF ECONOMIC ADVISERS

Period	Common stock prices [1]							Common stock yields (percent) [6]	
	New York Stock Exchange indexes (Dec. 31, 1965=50, except as noted) [2]					Dow-Jones industrial average [4]	Standard & Poor's composite index (1941–43=10) [5]	Dividend-price ratio	Earnings-price ratio
	Composite	Industrial	Transportation	Utility [3]	Finance				
1984	92.46	108.01	85.63	92.89	89.28	1,178.48	160.46	4.64	10.02
1985	108.09	123.79	104.11	113.49	114.21	1,328.23	186.84	4.25	8.12
1986	136.00	155.85	119.87	142.72	147.20	1,792.76	236.34	3.49	6.09
1987	161.70	195.31	140.39	148.59	146.48	2,275.99	286.83	3.08	5.48
1988	149.91	180.95	134.12	143.53	127.26	2,060.82	265.79	3.64	8.01
1989	180.02	216.23	175.28	174.87	151.88	2,508.91	322.84	3.45	7.41
1990	183.46	225.78	158.62	181.20	133.26	2,678.94	334.59	3.61	6.47
1991	206.33	258.14	173.99	185.32	150.82	2,929.33	376.18	3.24	4.79
1992	229.01	284.62	201.09	198.91	179.26	3,284.29	415.74	2.99	4.22
1993	249.58	299.99	242.49	228.90	216.42	3,522.06	451.41	2.78	4.46
1993: June	247.16	298.78	234.30	226.53	209.75	3,513.81	448.06	2.81	4.29
July	247.85	295.34	238.30	232.55	218.94	3,529.43	447.29	2.81	
Aug	251.93	298.83	250.82	237.44	224.96	3,597.01	454.13	2.76	
Sept	254.86	300.92	248.15	244.21	229.35	3,592.29	459.24	2.73	4.45
Oct	257.53	306.61	254.04	240.97	228.18	3,625.81	463.90	2.72	
Nov	255.93	310.84	262.96	230.12	214.08	3,674.70	462.89	2.72	
Dec	257.73	313.22	268.11	229.95	216.00	3,744.10	465.95	2.72	4.69
1994: Jan	262.11	320.92	278.29	225.15	218.71	3,868.36	472.99	2.69	
Feb	261.97	322.41	276.67	220.85	217.12	3,905.62	471.58	2.70	
Mar	257.32	318.08	265.68	215.45	211.02	3,816.98	463.81	2.78	5.08
Apr	247.97	304.48	250.43	210.08	208.12	3,661.48	447.23	2.90	
May	249.56	307.58	244.75	205.77	211.30	3,707.99	450.90	2.89	
June	251.21	308.66	246.64	206.54	215.89	3,737.58	454.83	2.84	
Week ended:									
1994: June 4	253.13	311.00	249.43	207.55	217.91	3,762.60	457.98	2.85	
11	253.53	310.68	246.66	210.00	219.34	3,760.09	458.14	2.83	
18	254.26	312.16	250.04	208.97	219.22	3,795.30	460.49	2.81	
25	248.66	306.15	245.21	203.63	212.39	3,702.13	450.47	2.85	
July 2 [p]	246.03	302.95	242.17	201.88	209.79	3,661.79	446.32	2.88	

[1] Average of daily closing prices.
[2] Includes all the stocks (more than 2,000 in 1992) listed on the NYSE.
[3] Dec. 31, 1965=100. Effective April 27, 1993 the NYSE doubled the value of the utility index to facilitate trading of options and futures on the index. All indexes shown here reflect the doubling.
[4] Includes 30 stocks.
[5] Includes 500 stocks.
[6] Standard & Poor's series. Dividend-price ratios based on Wednesday closing prices. Earnings-price ratios based on prices at end of quarter.

NOTE.—All data relate to stocks listed on the New York Stock Exchange (NYSE).

Sources: New York Stock Exchange, Dow-Jones & Company, Inc., and Standard & Poor's Corporation.

Source: *Economic Indicators,* Council of Economic Advisers.

A Guide to SEC Corporate Filings

SEC DISCLOSURE STATUTE

The purpose of the Federal securities laws is to provide disclosure of material financial and other information on companies seeking to raise capital through the public offering of their securities, as well as companies whose securities are already publicly held. This enables investors to evaluate the securities of these companies on an informed and realistic basis.

The Securities Act of 1933 is a *disclosure* statute. It generally requires that, before securities may be offered to the public, a registration statement must be filed with the Commission disclosing prescribed categories of information. Before the sale of securities can begin, the registration statement must become "effective," and investors must be furnished a prospectus containing the most significant information in the registration statement.

The Securities Exchange Act of 1934 deals in large part with securities already outstanding and requires the registration of securities listed on a national securities exchange, as well as Over-the-Counter securities in which there is a substantial public interest. Issuers of registered securities must file annual and other periodic reports designed to provide a public file of current material information.

The Exchange Act also requires disclosure of material information to holders of registered securities in solicitations of proxies for the election of directors or approval of corporate action at a shareholder's meeting, or in attempt to acquire control of a company through a tender offer or other planned stock acquisitions. It provides that insiders of companies whose equity securities are registered must report their holdings and transactions in all equity securities of their companies.

The Securities Act of 1933	The Securities Exchange Act of 1934	The Investment Act of 1940
S-1	Form 3	N-1A
S-2	Form 4	N-2
S-3	Form 8	N-5
S-4	8-K	N-14
S-6	10-C	
S-8	10-K	
S-11	10-Q	
S-18	20-F	
F-1	13F	
F-2	13D	
F-3	13E-3	
F-4	13E-4	
F-6	13G	
	14D-1	
	14D-9	
	Proxy Statement	

Source: A *Guide to SEC Corporate Filings*, Disclosure, Inc., 5161 River Road, Bethesda, MD 20816. Provided by Disclosure. To order copies of any SEC filings, call 800–638–8241.

PERIODIC ANNUAL REPORTS

10-K

This report provides a comprehensive overview of the registrant. The report must be filed within 90 days after close of company's fiscal year and contains the following items of disclosure:

Items Reported

COVER PAGE

Lists Fiscal Year End, State or other jurisdiction of incorporation or organization, Title of each class of securities and the exchange on which it is registered and the number of shares outstanding of each of the issuer's classes of common stock, as of the latest practicable date (date is commonly the filing date, NOT the time period covered in the document).

Part I

1. **Business.** Identifies principal products and services of the company, principal markets and methods of distribution and, if "material," competitive factors, backlog and expectation of fulfillment, availability of raw materials, importance of patents, licenses, and franchises, estimated cost of research, number of employees, and effects of compliance with environmental laws.

   If there is more than one line of business, a statement is included for each of the last three years. The statement includes total sales and net income for each line which, during either of the last two fiscal years, accounted for 10 percent or more of total sales or pretax income.
2. **Properties.** Location and character of principal plants, mines, and other important properties and if held in fee or leased.
3. **Legal Proceedings.** Brief description of material legal proceedings pending.
4. **Submission of Matters to a Vote of Secu-**

rity Holders. Information relating to the convening of a meeting of shareholders, whether annual or special, and the matters voted upon.

Part II

5. **Market for the Registrant's Common Stock and Related Security Holder Matters.** Includes principal market in which voting securities are traded with high and low sales prices (in the absence thereof, the range of bid and asked quotations for each quarterly period during the past two years) and the dividends paid during the past two years. In addition to the frequency and amount of dividends paid, this item contains a discussion concerning future dividends.
6. **Selected Financial Data.** These are five-year selected data including net sales and operating revenue; income or loss from continuing operations, both total and per common share; total assets; long-term obligations including redeemable preferred stock; and cash dividend declared per common share. The data also includes additional items that could enhance understanding of trends in financial condition and results of operations. Further, the effects of inflation and changing prices should be reflected in the five-year summary.
7. **Management's Discussion and Analysis of Financial Condition and Results of Operations.** Under broad guidelines, this includes: liquidity, capital resources and results of operations; trends that are favorable or unfavorable as well as significant events or uncertainties; causes of any material changes in the financial statements as a whole; limited data concerning subsidiaries; and discussion of effects of inflation and changing prices.
8. **Financial Statements and Supplementary Data.** Two-year audited balance sheets as well as three-year audited statements of income and cash flow statement.
9. **Changes in and disagreements with Accountants on Accounting and Financial Disclosure.**

Part III*

10. **Directors and Executive Officers.** Name, office, term of office and specific background data on each.
11. **Remuneration of Directors and Officers.** List of each director and highest paid officers with aggregate annual remuneration exceeding $40,000. Also includes total paid all officers and directors as a group.
12. **Security Ownership of Certain Beneficial Owners and Management.** Identification of owners of 5 percent or more of registrant's stock in addition to listing the amount and percent of each class of stock held by officers and directors.
13. **Certain Relationships and Related Transactions.**

* Disclosure normally made via a proxy statement may in some cases be made using Part III of Form 10-K.

Part IV

14. **Exhibits, Financial Statement Schedules and Reports on Form 8-K.** Complete, audited annual financial information and a list of exhibits filed. Also, any unscheduled material events or corporate changes filed in an 8-K during the year.

Form 10-K Schedules (when applicable)

- **I.** Investments other than investments in affiliates
- **II.** Receivables from related parties and underwriters, promoters and employees other than affiliates
- **III.** Condensed financial information
- **IV.** Indebtedness of affiliates (not current)
- **V.** Property, plant and equipment
- **VI.** Accumulated depreciation, depletion and amortization of property, plant and equipment
- **VII.** Guarantees of securities of other issuers
- **VIII.** Valuation and qualifying accounts
- **IX.** Short-term borrowings
- **X.** Supplementary income statement information
- **XI.** Supplementary profit and loss information
- **XII.** Income from dividends (equity in net profit and loss of affiliates)

Annual Report to Shareholders

The Annual Report to Shareholders is the principal document used by most major companies to communicate directly with shareholders. Since it is not a required, official SEC filing, companies have considerable discretion in determining what types of information this report will contain and how it is to be presented.

In addition to financial information, the Annual Report to Shareholders often provides non-financial details of the business which are not reported elsewhere. These may include marketing plans and forecasts of future programs and plans.

20-F

Annual Report/Registration Statement filed by certain foreign issuers of securities trading in the United States. Form 20-F must be filed 6 months after close of fiscal year.

Part I

1. Description of Business
2. Description of Property
3. Material Legal Proceedings
4. Control of Registrant
5. Nature of Trading Market
6. Exchange Controls and Other Limitations Affecting Security Holders
7. Taxation
8. Selected Financial Data
9. Management Discussion and Analysis
10. Directors and Officers
11. Compensation of Directors and Officers
12. Options to Purchase Securities from Registrant or Subsidiaries
13. Interests of Management in Certain Transactions

Part II

14. Description of Securities to be Registered

Part III

15. Defaults upon Senior Securities
16. Changes in Securities and Changes in Security for Registered Securities

Part IV

17.
18. } Financial Statements and Exhibits
19.

10-Q

This is the quarterly financial report filed by most companies, which, although unaudited, provides a continuing view of a company's financial position during the year. The 10-Q report must be filed within 45 days after close of fiscal year quarter.

Items Reported

COVER PAGE

Lists time period represented, State of incorporation, former name, address and fiscal year if changed since last report, whether the registrant filed any 1934 Act reports during the past 12 months and has been subject to such filing requirements for the past 90 days, whether the registrant has filed all documents and reports required under the Securities Exchange Act of 1934 subsequent to the distribution of securities, and the number of shares outstanding of each of the company's classes of common stock as of the last practicable date (date is commonly the filing date, NOT the time period covered in the document).

Part I

FINANCIAL STATEMENTS

1. Quarterly Financial Statements
2. Management Discussion and Analysis of material changes in the amount of revenue and expense items in relation to previous quarters, including the effect of any changes in accounting principles.

Part II

1. **Legal Proceedings.** Brief description of material legal proceedings pending; when civil rights or environmental statutes are involved, proceedings must be disclosed.
2. **Changes in Securities.** Material changes in the rights of holders of any class of registered security.
3. **Defaults upon Senior Securities.** Material defaults in the payment of principal, interest, sinking fund or purchase fund installment, dividend, or other material default not cured within 30 days.
4. **Submission of Matters to a Vote of Security Holders.** Information relating to the convening of a meeting of shareholders, whether annual or special, and the matters voted upon, with particular emphasis on the election of directors.
5. **Other Materially Important Events.** Information on any other item of interest to shareholders not already provided for in this form or reported in an 8-K.
6. **Exhibits and Reports on Form 8-K.** Any unscheduled material events or corporate changes reported in an 8-K during the prior quarter.

CORPORATE CHANGES AND VOTING MATTERS

8-K

This is a report of unscheduled material events or corporate changes deemed of importance to the shareholders or to the SEC. Items 1–3 and 8 must be reported in an 8-K within 15 days of the event. Items 4 and 6 must be filed within 5 business days after the event, and Item 5 is optional, meaning there is no mandatory time for filing.

1. Changes in Control of Registrant.
2. Acquisition or Disposition of Assets.
3. Bankruptcy or Receivership.
4. Changes in Registrant's Certifying Accountant.
5. Other Materially Important Events.
6. Resignation of Registrant's Directors.
7. Financial Statements and Exhibits.
8. Change in Fiscal Year.

10-C

Over-the-Counter companies use this form to report changes in name and amount of NASDAQ-listed securities. It is similar in purpose to the 8-K and must be filed within 10 days after the change.

Proxy Statement

A proxy statement provides official notification to designated classes of shareholders of matters to be brought to a vote at a shareholders' meeting. Proxy votes may be solicited for changing the company officers, or many other matters. Disclosures normally made via a proxy statement may in some cases be made using Part III of Form 10-K.

TENDER OFFER/ACQUISITION REPORTS

13-D

Filing required by 5% (or more) equity owners within ten days of acquisition event.

1. Security and issuer
2. Identity and background of person filing the statement
3. Source and amount of funds or other consideration
4. Purpose of the transaction
5. Interest in securities of the issuer
6. Contracts, arrangements or relationships with respect to securities of the issuer
7. Material to be filed as exhibits which may include but is not limited to:
   - Acquisition Agreements
   - Financing Arrangements
   - Contracts, Guarantees and other Agreements

14D-1

Tender offer filing made with the SEC at the time an offer is made to holders of equity securities of the target company, if acceptance of the offer would give the bidder over 5% ownership of the subject securities.

1. Security and subject company
2. Identity and background information
3. Past contacts, transactions or negotiations with subject company
4. Source and amount of funds or other consideration
5. Purpose of the tender offer and plans or proposals of the bidder
6. Interest in securities of the subject company
7. Contracts, arrangements or relationships with respect to the subject company's securities
8. Persons retained, employed or to be compensated
9. Financial statements of certain bidders
10. Additional information
11. Material to be filed as exhibits which may include but is not limited to:
    - Tender Offer Material
    - Loan Agreements
    - Contracts and Other Agreements
    - Legal Opinion on Tax Consequences
    - Prospectus

14D-9

A solicitation/recommendation statement that must be submitted to equity holders and filed with the SEC by the management of a company subject to a tender offer within ten days of the making of the tender offer.

1. Security and subject company
2. Tender offer of the bidder
3. Identity and background
4. The solicitation or recommendation
5. Persons retained, employed or to be compensated
6. Recent transactions and intent with respect to securities
7. Certain negotiations and transactions by the subject company
8. Additional information
9. Material to be filed as exhibits

13E-3

Transaction statement pursuant to the Securities Exchange Act of 1934 with respect to a public company or affiliate going private.

1. Issuer and class of security subject to the transaction
2. Identity and background of the individuals
3. Past contacts, transactions or negotiations
4. Terms of the transaction

5. Plans or proposals of the issuer or affiliate
6. Source and amount of funds or other considerations
7. Purpose, alternatives, reasons and effects
8. Fairness of the transaction
9. Reports, opinions, appraisals and certain negotiations
10. Interest in securities of the issuer
11. Contracts, arrangements or relationships with respect to the issuer's securities
12. Present intention and recommendation of certain persons with regard to the transaction
13. Other provisions of the transaction
14. Financial information
15. Persons and assets employed, retained or utilized
16. Additional information
17. Material to be filed as exhibits
    - Loan Agreements
    - Fairness Opinions and Appraisals
    - Contracts and Other Agreements
    - Disclosure Materials Sent to Security Holders
    - Statement of Appraisal Rights and Procedures

13E-4

Issuer tender offer statement pursuant to the Securities Exchange Act of 1934.

1. Security and issuer
2. Source and amount of funds
3. Purpose of the tender offer and plans or proposals of the issuer or affiliate
4. Interest in securities of the issuer
5. Contracts, arrangements or relationships with respect to the issuer's securities
6. Person retained, employed or to be compensated
7. Financial information
8. Additional information
9. Material to be filed as exhibits
    - Tender Offer Material
    - Loan Agreement
    - Contracts and Other Agreements
    - Legal Opinion on Tax Consequences
    - Prospectus, if applicable

SECURITY HOLDINGS BY INSIDERS AND INSTITUTIONS

13-F

A quarterly report of equity holdings required of all institutions with equity assets of $100 million or more. This includes banks, insurance companies, investment companies, investment advisors and large internally managed endowments, foundations and pension funds. The report must be filed within 45 days after close of fiscal quarter.

13-G

An annual filing which must be filed by all reporting persons (primarily institutions) meeting the 5 percent equity ownership rule within 45 days after the end of each calendar year.

1. Name and address of issuer
2. Identification of reporting person
3. 13D-1 or 13D-2 applicability
4. Amount of shares beneficially owned:
    - Percent of Class Outstanding
    - Sole or Shared Power to Vote
    - Sole or Shared Power to Dispose
5. Ownership of 5 percent or less of a class of stock
6. Ownership of more than 5 percent on behalf of another person
7. Identification of subsidiary which acquired the security being reported on by the parent holding company (if applicable)
8. Identification and classification of members of the group (if applicable)
9. Notice of dissolution of group (if applicable)
10. Certification

Form 3

Initial statement which identifies holdings of registrant's securities owned by directors, officers and 10 percent shareholders. A Form 3 must be filed within 10 days after the event.

Form 4

Amendment to Form 3 reporting a sale or acquisition of registrant's securities. A Form 4 must be filed by the 10th day of the month following the month in which the transaction occurred.

REGISTRATION OF SECURITIES

Registration Statements

Registration statements are of two principal types: (1) "offering" registrations filed under the Securities Act of 1933, and (2) "trading" registrations filed under the Securities Exchange Act of 1934.

"Offering" registrations are used to register securities before they are offered to investors. Part I of the registration, a preliminary prospectus or "red herring," contains preliminary information that will be in the final prospectus. Included in Part I (or incorporated by reference) in many registration statements are:

- Description of Securities to be Registered
- Use of Proceeds
- Risk Factors
- Determination of Offering Price
- Potential Dilution
- Selling Security Holders
- Plan of Distribution
- Interests of Named Experts and Counsel
- Information with Respect to the Registrant (description of business, legal proceedings, market price and dividends on common equity, financial statements, Management Discussion and Analysis, changes in and disagreements with accountants, directors and executive officers, security ownership of certain beneficial owners and management and certain relationships and related transactions).

Part II of the registration contains information not required in the prospectus. This includes:

- Expenses of Issuance and Distribution
- Indemnification of Directors and Officers
- Recent Sales of Unregistered Securities, Undertakings, Exhibits and Financial Statement Schedules

"Offering" registration statements vary in purpose and content according to the type of organization issuing stock:

S-1 Companies reporting under the 1934 Act for less than 3 years. Permits no incorporation by reference and requires complete disclosure in the prospectus.

S-2 Companies reporting under the 1934 Act for 3 or more years but not meeting the minimum voting stock requirement. Reference to 1934 Act reports permits incorporation and presentation of financial information in the prospectus or in an Annual Report to Shareholders delivered with the prospectus.

S-3 Companies reporting under the 1934 Act for 3 or more years and having at least $150 million of voting stock held by non-affiliates, or as an alternative test, $100 million of voting stock coupled with an annual trading volume of 3 million shares. Allows minimal disclosure in the prospectus and maximum incorporation by reference of 1934 Act reports.

S-4 Registration used in certain business combinations or reorganizations.

S-6 Filed by unit investment trusts registered under the Investment Act of 1940 on Form N-8B-2.

S-8 Registration used to register securities to be offered to employees under stock option and various other employee benefit plans.

S-11 Filed by real estate companies, primarily limited partnerships and investment trusts.

S-18 Short form initial registration of up to $7.5 million in securities.

SE Non-electronically filed exhibits made by registrants filing with the EDGAR Project.

N-1A Filed by open-end management investment companies.

N-2 Filed by closed-end management investment companies.

N-5 Registration of small business investment companies.

N-14 Registration of the securities of management investment and business development companies to be issued in business combinations under the Investment Act of 1940.

F-1 Registration of securities by foreign private issuers eligible to use Form 20-F, for which no other form is prescribed.

F-2 Registration of securities by foreign private issuers meeting certain 1934 Act filing requirements.

F-3 Registration of securities by foreign private issuers offered pursuant to certain types of transactions, subject to the 1934 Act filing requirements for the preceding 3 years.

F-4 Registration of securities issued in business combinations involving foreign private registrants.

F-6 Registration of depository shares evidenced by the American Depository Receipts (ADRs).

"Trading" registrations are filed to permit trading among investors on a securities exchange or in the Over-the-Counter market. These Registration Statements do not include a prospectus. Registration statements which serve to register securities for trading fall into three categories:

Quick Reference Chart to Contents of SEC Filings

REPORT CONTENTS	10-K	20-F	10-Q	8-K	10-C	6-K	Proxy Statements	Prospectus	Registration Statements: '34 Act F-10	Registration Statements: '34 Act 8-A 8-B	Registration Statements: '33 Act "S" Type	ARS	Listing Application
Auditor													
☐ Name	■	■	░				▨	■	■		■	■	░
☐ Opinion	■	■	░						■			■	
☐ Changes				■			░						
Compensation Plans													
☐ Equity	░		░				▨	▨	■		▨		░
☐ Monetary	░		░				■	▨	■		▨		░
Company Information													
☐ Nature of Business	■	■				▨		■	■		■	░	░
☐ History	▨	■					░	■	▨		■	░	░
☐ Organization and Change	▨	▨		■	░	▨	░	■		▨	■	░	
Debt Structure	■					▨		■	■		■	■	
Depreciation & Other Schedules	■	■				▨		■	■		■		
Dilution Factors	■	■		▨		▨		■	■		■	■	
Directors, Officers, Insiders													
☐ Identification	▨	■				▨	■	■	■		■	▨	
☐ Background	░	░	░	░	░	░	■	■	░		■	░	
☐ Holdings	░	■		░			■	■	■		■		
☐ Compensation	░	■		░			■	■	■		■		
Earnings Per Share	■	■	■			▨			■			■	
Financial Information													
☐ Annual Audited	■	■							■		■	■	
☐ Interim Audited		■					░	░			░		
☐ Interim Unaudited	░		■	░		▨		▨			▨		
Foreign Operations	■						░	■	■		■	░	▨
Labor Contracts	░	░		░					▨		▨		
Legal Agreements	▨	░		░					▨		▨		
Legal Counsel				░			░	■			■		░
Loan Agreements	▨			░			░		▨		▨		
Plants and Properties	■	▨		░				▨	■		▨	░	
Product-Line Breakout	■							■			■	░	
Securities Structure	■	■			░			■	■		■		
Subsidiaries	■	■					░		■		■		
Underwriting				░				■			■		
Unregistered Securities	░			░			░	░			■		
Block Movements	░			▨			░		■				░

TENDER OFFER/ACQUISITION REPORTS	13D	13G	14D-1	14D-9	13E-3	13E-4
Name of Issuer (Subject Company)	■	■	■	■	■	■
Filing Person (or Company)	■	■	■	■	■	■
Amount of Shares Owned	■	■				
Percent of Class Outstanding	■	■				
Financial Statements of Bidder			▨		▨	▨
Purpose of Tender Offer			■	■	■	■
Source and Amount of Funds	■		■		■	
Identity and Background Information			■	■	■	
Persons Retained, Employed or to be Compensated	░		■	■	■	■
Exhibits	▨		▨	▨	▨	▨

■ *always included* ▨ *frequently included* ░ *special circumstances*

(1) **Form 10** may be used by companies during the first two years they are subject to the 1934 Act filing requirements. It is a combination registration statement and annual report with information content similar to that of SEC required 10-Ks.

(2) **Form 8-A** is used by 1934 Act registrants wishing to register additional securities or classes thereof.

(3) **Form 8-B** is used by "successor issuers" (usually companies which have changed their name or state of incorporation) as notification that previously registered securities are to be traded under a new corporate identification.

Prospectus

When the sale of securities as proposed in an "offering" registration statement is approved by the SEC, any changes required by the SEC are incorporated into the prospectus. This document must be made available to investors before the sale of the security is initiated. It also contains the actual offering price, which may have been changed after the registration statement was approved.

Form 8 (Amendment)

Form 8 is used to amend or supplement any 1934 Act report previously submitted. 1933 Act registration statements are amended by filing an amended registration statement (pre-effective amendment) or by the prospectus itself, as previously noted.

Listing Application

Like the Annual Report to Shareholders, a listing application is not an official SEC filing. It is filed by the company with the NYSE, AMEX or other stock exchange to document proposed new listings. Usually a Form 8-A registration is filed with the SEC at about the same time.

How to Read the New York Stock Exchange and American Stock Exchange Quotations

(1)	(2)	(3)	(4)	(5)	(6)	(7)	(8)	(9)	(10)	(11)	(12)
52 Weeks					Yld		Vol				Net
Hi	Lo	Stock	Sym	Div	%	P-E	100s	Hi	Lo	Close	Chg
42¾	23⅝	WestPtPepri	WPM		...	13	47	30¼	29⅝	30¼ +	⅝
18¾	15¾	WestcstEngy	g WE	.80	5.0	15	9	15⅞	15¾	15⅞ +	⅛
17¼	3⅞	WestnCoNA	WSN		...	...	1026	4¼	4⅛	4¼ −	⅛

The composite quotations take into account prices paid for a stock on the New York or American Exchanges, plus those prices paid on regional exchanges, Over-the-Counter (OTC) and elsewhere, as shown in the example from the Wall Street Journal. The stock market quotations are explained below:

(1) The highest price per share paid in the past 52 weeks in terms of ⅛ of a dollar, i.e., 10⅛ means $10.125.
(2) The lowest price paid per share in the last 52 weeks.
(3) The name of the company in abbreviated form.
(4) The Stock Exchange symbol used to identify the stock.
(5) The regular annual dividend paid. Special or extra dividends are specified by letters given in the footnotes in the Explanatory Notes shown below.
(6) The yield, that is, the annual dividend divided by the current price of the stock expressed in percent. For example, a stock that sells for $20.00 per share and pays a dividend of $2.00 per share has a yield of 10 percent (2/20).
(7) The P/E ratio is the current price of the stock divided by the company's last reported annual earnings per share. The P/E ratio is generally high for companies which are thought to have a relatively large and persistent earning's growth rate. The average P/E ratio for the Dow Jones stocks varied from 9.8 to 39.5 during the last five years.
(8) The number of shares sold on the day reported in 100s of shares.
(9) The highest price paid per share on the day reported.
(10) The lowest price paid per share on the day reported.
(11) The last price paid per share on the day reported.
(12) The change in the closing price from the previous day's closing price.

EXPLANATORY NOTES

The following explanations apply to New York and American exchange listed issues and the National Association of Securities Dealers Automated Quotations system's over-the-counter securities. Exchange prices are composite quotations that include trades on the Midwest, Pacific, Philadelphia, Boston and Cincinnati exchanges and reported by the NASD and Instinet.

Boldfaced quotations highlight those issues whose price changed by 5% or more from their previous closing price.

Underlined quotations are those stocks with large changes in volume, per exchange, compared with the issue's average trading volume. The calculation includes common stocks of $5 a share or more with an average volume over 65 trading days of at least 5,000 shares. The underlined quotations are for the 40 largest volume percentage leaders on the NYSE and the NASD's National Market System. It includes the 20 largest volume percentage gainers on the Amex.

The 52-week high and low columns show the highest and lowest price of the issue during the preceding 52 weeks plus the current week, but not the latest trading day. These ranges are adjusted to reflect stock payouts of 1% or more, and cash dividends of 10% or more.

Dividend rates, unless noted, are annual disbursements based on the last quarterly, semiannual, or annual declaration. Special or extra dividends, special situations or payments not designated as regular are identified by footnotes.

Yield is defined as the dividends paid by a company on its securities, expressed as a percentage of price.

The P/E ratio is determined by dividing the price of a share of stock by its company's earnings per share of that stock. These earnings are the primary per-share earnings reported by the company for the most recent four quarters. Extraordinary items are usually excluded.

Sales figures are the unofficial daily total of shares traded, quoted in hundreds (two zeros omitted).

Exchange ticker symbols are shown for all New York and American exchange common stocks, and Dow Jones News/Retrieval symbols are listed for Class A and Class B shares listed on both markets. Nasdaq symbols are listed for all Nasdaq NMS issues. A more detailed explanation of Nasdaq ticker symbols appears with the NMS listings.

FOOTNOTES: ▲—New 52-week high. ▼—New 52-week low. **a**—Extra dividend or extras in addition to the regular dividend. **b**—Indicates annual rate of the cash dividend and that a stock dividend was paid. **c**—Liquidating dividend. **e**—Indicates a dividend was declared or paid in the preceding 12 months, but that there isn't a regular rate. **g**—Indicates the dividend and earnings are expressed in Canadian money. The stock trades in U.S. dollars. No yield or P/E ratio is shown. **h**—Indicates a temporary exception to Nasdaq qualifications. **i**—Indicates amount declared or paid after a stock dividend or split. **j**—Indicates dividend was paid this year, and that at the last dividend meeting a dividend was omitted or deferred. **k**—Indicates dividend declared or paid this year on cumulative issues with dividends in arrears. **n**—Newly issued in the past 52 weeks. The high-low range begins with the start of trading and doesn't cover the entire period. **pf**—Preferred. **pp**—Holder owes installment(s) of purchase price. **pr**—Preference. **r**—Indicates a cash dividend declared or paid in the preceding 12 months, plus a stock dividend. **rt**—Rights. **s**—Stock split or stock dividend amounting to 25% or more in the past 52 weeks. The high-low price is adjusted from the old stock. Dividend calculations begin with the date the split was paid or the stock dividend occurred. **t**—Paid in stock in the preceding 12 months, estimated cash value on ex-dividend or ex-distribution date, except Nasdaq listings where payments are in stock. **un**—Units. **v**—Trading halted on primary market. **vj**—In bankruptcy or receivership or being reorganized under the Bankruptcy Code, or securities assumed by such companies. **wd**—When distributed. **wi**—When issued. **wt**—Warrants. **ww**—With warrants. **x**—Ex-dividend or ex-rights. **xw**—Without warrants. **y**—Ex-dividend and sales in full, not in hundreds. **z**—Sales in full, not in hundreds.

How to Read Over-the-Counter NASDAQ Listings

The notation is the same as that for the New York and American Stock Exchanges on page 296.

(1)	(2)	(3)	(4)	(5)	(6)	(7)	(8)	(9)	(10)	(11)	(12)
52 Weeks					Yld		Vol				Net
Hi	Lo	Stock	Sym	Div	%	P-E	100s	Hi	Lo	Close	Chg
4¾	1⅛	HuntrEnvr	HESI		. . .	. . .	158	4⅛	3⅞	4⅛ +	¼
22	14⅜	HuntgBcshr	HBAN	.80b	3.8	11	1231	21¾	21	21¼ −	¼
14¾	7¼	Hurco	HURC	.20	1.8	28	66	11¾	10¾	11 −	¾
32½	8¼	HutchTech	HTCH		. . .	21	282	28	27¼	27¼ −	¾
8⅜	3⅞	HycorBio	HYBD		. . .	675	265	6⅞	6½	6¾ −	1/16
3½	1/16	HycorBio wt			. . .	. . .	10	3	2¾	3 −	⅛
6⅞	4	HydeAthl	HYDE		. . .	19	62	5½	4¾	5 +	¼

NASDAQ SYMBOL EXPLANATION

All securities listed in the Nasdaq system are identified by a four letter or five letter symbol. The fifth letter indicates the issues that aren't common or capital shares, or are subject to restrictions or special conditions. Below is a rundown of fifth letter identifiers and a description of what they represent:

A—Class A. **B**—Class B. **C**—Exempt from Nasdaq listing qualifications for a limited period. **D**—New issue. **E**—Delinquent in required filings with SEC, as determined by the NASD. **F**—Foreign. **G**—First convertible bond. **H**—Second convertible bond, same company. **I**—Third convertible bond, same company. **J**—Voting. **K**—Non-voting. **L**—Miscellaneous situations, including second class units, third class of warrants or sixth class of preferred stock. **M**—Fourth preferred, same company. **N**—Third preferred, same company. **O**—Second preferred, same company. **P**—First preferred, same company. **Q**—In bankruptcy proceedings. **R**—Rights. **S**—Shares of beneficial interest. **T**—With warrants or rights. **U**—Units. **V**—When issued and when distributed. **W**—Warrants. **Y**—American Depository Receipt (ADR). **Z**—Miscellaneous situations, including second class of warrants, fifth class of preferred stock and any unit, receipt or certificate representing a limited partnership interest.

Source: Reprinted by permission of THE WALL STREET JOURNAL,

The Ex-dividend Explained

The ex-dividend status of a stock is indicated by an *x* in the newspaper quotation or *xd* on the ticker tape. This is an abbreviation for *without dividend.*

A stock that is purchased during the ex-dividend period will not pay a previously declared dividend to its new owner. The ex-dividend period spans four business days before the so-called record date—the date a dividend issuing corporation uses to tally its shareowners. An ex-dividend stock buyer is not entitled to a dividend because his name is not recorded with the dividend issuing corporation until after the record date.

The New York Stock Exchange requires that the buyer in every transaction be recorded with the issuing corporation on the fifth business day following a trade. A stock buyer, therefore, must purchase his shares at least five business days before the record date in order for the corporation to record his name in time for him to receive his dividend. A purchase one day later disqualifies a buyer from a dividend because the transfer of ownership cannot be completed by the record date. Therefore, on the fourth business day prior to the record date, a stock is sold ex-dividend.

In our example below, the corporation's Board has decided to pay a 50‰ dividend to shareholders of record on Monday, the 10th. A person buying shares up to the close of business on Monday, the 3rd, would be eligible for the dividend because normal settlement (5 business days) will be made on Monday the 10th. On Tuesday, the 4th, however, the stock would begin selling ex-dividend because a stock purchaser as of that date could not settle till after the record date.

On the ex-dividend date, the Exchange specialist will reduce all open buy orders and open sell stop orders by the amount of the dividend. This is done to more equitably reflect the stock's value since purchasers of stock on or after the ex-dividend date are ineligible for a dividend.

EX-DIVIDEND EXPLANATION

Any Month	Date	Calendar Day	Status
	3	Monday	With/Dividend
	4	Tuesday	Ex-Dividend (Without Dividend)
	5	Wednesday	" "
	6	Thursday	" "
	7	Friday	" "
	8	Saturday	Not a trading day
	9	Sunday	Not a trading day
	10	Monday	Record Date/Business Day
	11	Tuesday	Business Day

Source: *Taking The Mystery Out of Ex-Dividend,* The New York Stock Exchange, Inc.

Margin Accounts Explained

Stocks may be purchased by paying the purchase price in full (plus commissions and taxes) or on a margin account. With the margin account, the investors put up part of the purchase price in cash or securities, and the broker lends the remainder. The margin investor must pay the usual commissions as well as interest on the broker's loan. The stocks purchased on margin are held by the broker as collateral on the loan. Dividends are applied to the margin account and help offset the interest payments.

Margin (M) is defined as the market value (V) of the securities less the broker's loan (L), divided by the market value of the securities. The ratio is expressed as a percentage:

$$M = \frac{V - L}{V} \times 100$$

Example: You buy 100 shares of a stock at $20 per share at a total cost (V) of $2,000. You put up $1,200 in cash and borrow (L) $800 from the broker. The margin at the time of purchase is

$$M = \frac{\$2,000 - \$800}{\$2,000} \times 100 = 60\%$$

The margin at the time of purchase is called *initial margin.* The smallest allowed value of initial margin (set by the Federal Reserve) is currently 50%. Thus, with the above stock, if you buy 100 shares at $20 per share on 50% initial margin, you put up $1,000 (.5 × $2,000), and the broker's loan is $1,000.

After the purchase there is a *maintenance margin* (set by the Exchange) below which the margin is not permitted to decrease. The maintenance margin on the New York Stock Exchange is 25%. Some brokers, however, require a higher maintenance margin of about 30%. Thus, if the 100 shares of stocks discussed above decrease in price from $20 to $13 per share, then the margin is

$$M = \left(\frac{\$1,300 - \$1,000}{\$1,300}\right) \times 100 = 23\%$$

The margin of 23% is now below the maintenance margin of 25% set by the Exchange. The securities are said to be *under margined,* and a call for additional cash (or securities) is issued by the broker in order to bring up the margin to 25%. If the investor does not meet the call for additional cash (margin call) within a specified time, the stocks in the margin account are immediately sold.

MARGIN REQUIREMENTS (percent of market value and effective date)

	Mar. 11, 1968	June 8, 1968	May 6, 1970	Dec. 6, 1971	Nov. 24, 1972	Jan. 3, 1974
Margin stocks	70	80	65	55	65	50
Convertible bonds	50	60	50	50	50	50
Short sales	70	80	65	55	65	50

Note: Regulations G, T, and U of the Federal Reserve Board of Governors, prescribed in accordance with the Securities Exchange Act of 1934, limit the amount of credit to purchase and carry margin stocks that may be extended on securities as collateral by prescribing a maximum loan value, which is a specified percentage of the market value of the collateral at the time the credit is extended. Margin requirements are the difference between the market value (100 percent) and the maximum loan value. The term "margin stocks" is defined in the corresponding regulation.

Source: *Federal Reserve Bulletin.*

Short Selling Explained

Short selling provides an opportunity to profit from a decline in the price of a stock. If you believe that a stock is due for a substantial decline, you arrange to have your broker borrow the stock from another investor who owns the shares. The borrowed stock is then sold. This cash is held as collateral against the borrowed shares. When (and if) the stock price declines, you purchase the stock at the market price and use it to replace the borrowed shares. The broker arranges the return of your cash collateral less the cost of the repurchased stock. Your profit per share is the price received on the sale of the stock less the purchase price.

There are certain cash outlays and costs associated with the short sale. Generally there is no charge for borrowing the stock, although occasionally stock lenders may charge a premium over the market price. You must deposit $2,000 or the required initial margin, whichever is the greater, at the time the stock is borrowed. Thus, if you borrow 100 shares of a stock priced at $50 per share and the margin required is 50%, you must put up $2,500 (.5 × $50 × 100) in cash or securities. The margin deposit is returned when you close out the short sale. You pay commission when the stock is sold and when it is repurchased. In addition, you must pay the stock lender any dividends which are declared during the period you are short the stock. It is well to remember that if cash is used for the deposit, there is a loss of the interest which you would have obtained if the cash had been invested.

The dividend payments and interest loss can be reduced or eliminated if you short stocks which pay little or no dividends and use interest-bearing securities (such as T-bills or negotiable certificates of deposit) as the margin deposit.

An increase in the price of the stock can result in substantial losses since you may be forced to repurchase at a higher price than you sold. If there are many short sellers seeking to purchase the stock in order to close out their position, prices may be driven to very high levels.

The short sale cannot be executed while the stock price is declining on the exchange. According to the rules of the SEC, the stock must undergo an increase in price prior to the execution of a short sale.

Mutual Fund Reporting Regulations

The new SEC regulations concerning mutual fund reporting practices which went into effect May 1988 require that an easy-to-read table giving all fund charges must appear near the front of all prospectuses. Included must be such items as front end and back end loads, 12b–1 plans to recover marketing and distribution costs, and sales loads imposed on reinvested dividends applied everytime the find reinvest dividends. Typically, fund expense ratios (annual operating expenses to assets) range from .7% to 1%.

Advertisements that contain yields must calculate yields (capital gains plus dividends) on a consistent basis prescribed by the SEC, taking into account any front end sales charges. To put the yield figure into perspective, ads must provide one, five and ten year total return information.

Fund fees are now shown in the newspaper listing by means of the following letters after the fund's name:

r	indicates a back end load or redemption fee
p	indicates a 12b–1 plan is in effect
t	indicates both a back end and a 12b–1 fee
N.L.	indicates there is no front end or back end load

How to Read Mutual Fund Quotations

The following tables provide explanations of the mutal fund quotations appearing in *The Wall Street Journal*. Note that the performance data provided by Lipper Analytical Services differ depending on the day of the week that the quotation appears. Thus, in the example shown, performance data are given for Wednesday with returns for 13 weeks, 3 years, and YTD (year to date).

The Monday edition of the *Journal* provides information on a fund's initial charges and expenses. The ranking of a fund's total return for each category of investment objective over the longest time period given in the day's quotation is assigned a letter from A (top 20%) to E (bottom 20%).

Extensive mutual fund quotations are also given in the *Investor's Business Daily*. The latter also provides toll free phone numbers and dollar size of the fund families. Rankings of a fund's total return are provided for performance over the prior three year period versus all other mutual funds ranging from A+ for the top 5%, A for the top 10%, B+ for the top 20%, to E below the top 70%. Note that the rankings are against all mutual funds, whereas in *The Wall Street Journal* funds are ranked against other funds with the same investment objective as defined in the table included here.

What These Listings Provide...

		NASD DATA			LIPPER ANALYTICAL DATA			
Monday	Inv. Obj.	NAV	Offer Price	NAV Chg.	%Ret YTD	Max Initl Chrg.	Total Exp Ratio	..
Tuesday	Inv. Obj.	NAV	Offer Price	NAV Chg.	—% Total Return— YTD	4 wk	1 yr	Rank
WEDNESDAY	**Inv. Obj.**	**NAV**	**Offer Price**	**NAV Chg.**	**—% Total Return— YTD**	**13 wk**	**3 yr**	**Rank**
Thursday	Inv. Obj.	NAV	Offer Price	NAV Chg.	—% Total Return— YTD	26 wk	4 yr	Rank
Friday	Inv. Obj.	NAV	Offer Price	NAV Chg.	—% Total Return— YTD	39 wk	5 yr	Rank

EXPLANATORY NOTES

Mutual fund data are supplied by two organizations. The daily Net Asset Value (NAV), Offer Price and Net Change calculations are supplied by the National Association of Securities Dealers (NASD) through Nasdaq, its automated quotation system. Performance and cost data are supplied by Lipper Analytical Services Inc.

Daily price data are entered into Nasdaq by the fund, its management company or agent. Performance and cost calculations are percentages provided by Lipper Analytical Services, based on prospectuses filed with the Securities and Exchange Commission, fund reports, financial reporting services and other sources believed to be authoritative, accurate and timely. Though verified, the data cannot be guaranteed by Lipper or its data sources and should be double-checked with the funds before making any investment decisions.

Performance figures are on a total return basis without regard to sales, deferred sales or redemption charges.

INVESTMENT OBJECTIVE (Inv. Obj.) – Based on stated investment goals outlined in the prospectus. The Journal assembled 10 groups based on classifications used by Lipper Analytical in the daily Mutual Fund Scorecard and other calculations. A detailed breakdown of classifications appears at the bottom of this page.

NET ASSET VALUE (NAV) – Per share value prepared by the fund, based on closing quotes unless noted, and supplied to the NASD by 5:30 p.m. Eastern time.

OFFER PRICE – Net asset value plus sales commission, if any.

NAV CHG. – Gain or loss, based on the previous NAV quotation.

% TOTAL RETURN – Performance calculations, as percentages, assuming reinvestment of all distributions. Sales charges aren't reflected. For funds declaring dividends daily, calculations are based on the most current data supplied by the fund within publication deadlines. A YEAR TO DATE (YTD) change is listed daily, with results ranging from 4 weeks to 5 years offered throughout the week. See chart on this page for specific schedule.

MAXIMUM INITIAL SALES COMMISSION (Max Initl Chrg) – Based on prospectus; the sales charge may be modified or suspended temporarily by the fund, but any percentage change requires formal notification to the shareholders.

TOTAL EXPENSE RATIO (Total Exp Ratio) -- Based on the fund's annual report, the ratio is total operating expenses for the fiscal year divided by the fund's average net assets. It includes all asset based charges such as advisory fees, other non-advisory fees and distribution expenses (12b-1).

RANKING (R) – Funds are grouped by investment objectives defined by The Wall Street Journal and ranked on longest time period listed each day. Percentages are annualized for periods greater than one year. Performance measurement begins at either the closest Thursday or month-end for periods of more than one year. Gains of 100% or more are shown as a whole number, not carried out one decimal place. A=top 20%; B=next 20%; C=middle 20%; D=next 20%; E=bottom 20%.

QUOTATIONS FOOTNOTES

e-Ex-distribution. **f**-Previous day's quotation. **s**-Stock split or dividend. **x**-Ex–dividend.

p-Distribution costs apply, 12b-1 plan. **r**-Redemption charge may apply. **t**–Footnotes p and r apply.

NA-Not available due to incomplete price, performance or cost data. **NE**-Deleted by Lipper editor; data in question. **NL**-No Load (sales commission). **NN**-Fund doesn't wish to be tracked. **NS**-Fund didn't exist at start of period.

k-Recalculated by Lipper, using updated data. **n**-No valid comparison with other funds because of expense structure.

Source: Reprinted by permission of *The Wall Street Journal*,

Example of the Mutual Fund format in The Wall Street Journal.

	Inv. Obj.	NAV	Offer Price	NAV Chg.	-% Total Return- YTD	13 wks	3 yrs	R
SIBdA	...	20.16	20.16	−0.02	NA	NA	NA	..
SmCoInA	...	10.44	10.44	+0.03	NA	NA	NA	..
Benham Group:								
AdjGov	BST	10.04	NL	+0.01	+0.4	+1.2	NS	..
CaTFI	MUN	11.00	NL	...	+1.6	+4.2	+8.6	E
CatfIn	MUN	10.01	NL	...	+1.2	+6.4	+10.0	B
CaTFS	MUN	10.23	NL	+0.01	+0.9	+2.9	NS	..
CatfH	MUN	9.13	NL	−0.01	+0.6	+4.3	+8.9	D
CatfL	MUN	11.26	NL	...	+1.0	+5.5	+9.7	B
EqGro	STK	11.82	NL	+0.02	+1.2	+7.8	NS	..
EurBd	WBD	9.96	NL	−0.02	0.0	−3.1	NS	..
GNMA	BND	10.87	NL	...	+1.4	+3.1	+11.9	B
GoldIn	SEC	7.47	NL	+0.09	−1.1	−5.9	−15.2	E

Source: Reprinted by permission of *The Wall Street Journal*,

MUTUAL FUND OBJECTIVES

Categories used by the Wall Street Journal, based on classifications developed by Lipper Analytical Services Inc., and fund groups included in each:

STOCK FUNDS

General U.S. (STK): Capital Appreciation; Growth and Income; Growth; Equity Income; Option Income.

Small Company (SML): Small Company Growth.

Sector (SEC): Health/Biotechnology; Natural Resources; Environmental; Science & Technology; Speciality & Miscellaneous; Utility; Financial Services; Real Estate; Gold Oriented.

World (WOR): Global; Small Company Global; International; European Region; Pacific Region; Japanese; Latin American; Canadian.

BOND FUNDS

Short Term (BST): Adjustable Rate Preferred; Adjustable Rate Mortgage; Short U.S. Treasury; Short U.S. Government; Short Investment Grade.

Intermediate & Long Term (BND): Intermediate U.S. Treasury; Intermediate U.S. Government; General U.S. Treasury; General U.S. Government; GNMA; U.S. Mortgage; Corporate Debt A-Rated; Corporate Debt BBB-Rated; Intermediate Investment Grade; General Bond; Flexible Income; Target Maturity.

High Yield (BHI): High Current Yield.

World (WBD): Short World Multi-Market; Short World Single-Market; General World Income.

Municipal Bonds, All Maturities (MUN): Short Municipal Debt; General Municipal Debt; Intermediate Municipal Debt; Insured Municipal Debt; High Yield Municipal Debt; Single-State Municipals; Single-State Insured Municipals; Single-State Intermediated Municipals.

STOCK & BOND FUNDS

Blended Funds (S&B): Flexible Portfolio; Global Flexible Portfolio; Balanced; Balanced Target Maturity; Convertible Securities; Income.

Source: Reprinted by permission of *The Wall Street Journal*,

Top 50 No- and Low-Load Mutual Funds *(Based on Five- and 10-Year Performance)*

What $10,000 Grew to in 5 years (1989 - 1993)*

Fidelity Select Biotechnology	$ 37,338
CGM Capital Development Fund (c)	36,004
Twentieth Century Giftrust Investors	35,765
Thomson Opportunity Fund/Class B	35,592
Berger One Hundred Fund	34,776
Twentieth Century Ultra Investors	34,443
INVESCO Strategic—Financial Services	33,225
T Rowe Price Science & Technology	32,801
Kaufmann Fund	32,538
Fidelity Contrafund	32,437
MFS Emerging Growth Fund/Class B	32,148
INVESCO Strategic—Technology	31,877
INVESCO Strategic—Leisure	31,485
Fidelity Select Home Finance	30,702
INVESCO Strategic—Health Sciences	30,396
Fidelity Select Medical Delivery	29,929
Fidelity Select Software & Computer	29,651
Fidelity Blue Chip Growth Fund	28,855
Fidelity Select Technology	28,746
Fidelity Select Retailing	28,538
Brandywine Fund	28,282
Fidelity Select Electronics	27,870
Keystone Custodian Series/S-4	27,659
Fidelity Select Health Care	27,508
Fidelity Select Regional Banks	27,505
Wasatch Aggressive Equity Fund	27,489
Fidelity Select Brokerage & Invmt Mgmt	27,353
Fidelity Growth Company Fund	27,297
John Hancock Freedom Regional Bank/Class B	27,118
Janus Twenty Fund (c)	27,081
Legg Mason Special Investment Trust	26,511
Fidelity Select Computers	25,995
INVESCO Dynamics Fund	25,851
Special Portfolios—Stock	25,696
Founders Special Fund	25,645
Fidelity Select Automotive	25,566
T Rowe Price New America Growth	25,387
Strong Discovery Fund	25,349
Founders Frontier Fund	25,317
Vanguard Specialized Ports—Health Care	25,005
Acorn Fund (c)	24,962
Fidelity Select Transportation	24,859
Fidelity Select Telecommunications	24,689
Janus Fund	24,583
Fidelity Select Financial Services	24,509
Founders Growth Fund	24,454
Fidelity Convertible Securities	24,452
Fidelity Magellan Fund	24,178
Janus Venture Fund (c)	23,940
SteinRoe Special Fund	23,899

What $10,000 Grew to in 10 years (1984 - 1992)*

Twentieth Century Giftrust Investors	$ 73,624
CGM Capital Development Fund (c)	71,709
Fidelity Select Health Care	57,231
Fidelity Magellan Fund	54,167
Acorn Fund (c)	52,102
Fidelity Contrafund	50,862
T Rowe Price International Stock	49,621
Evergreen Limited Market Fund	49,412
Berger One Hundred Fund	49,352
CGM Mutual Fund	46,988
Twentieth Century Ultra Investors	46,967
Fidelity Growth Company Fund	46,543
Scudder International Fund	45,838
INVESCO Industrial Fund	45,630
Vanguard/Trustees' Equity—International	44,915
Mutual Qualified Fund (c)	44,372
Fidelity Retirement Growth	44,210
SteinRoe Special Fund	44,028
Fidelity Select Utilities	43,944
Fidelity Select Financial Services	43,917
Mutual Shares Fund (c)	43,412
Sequoia Fund (c)	42,811
IAI Regional Fund	42,139
Vanguard/Windsor Fund (c)	42,087
Scudder Capital Growth Fund	42,061
Century Shares Trust	41,954
SAFECO Equity Fund	41,769
SoGen International Fund	41,355
SIT "New Beginning" Growth Fund	41,353
Selected American Shares	41,347
Lexington Corporate Leaders Trust	41,327
Janus Fund	41,307
State Farm Balanced Fund	41,079
Dodge & Cox Stock Fund	41,040
Neuberger & Berman Manhattan Fund	40,870
Special Portfolios—Stock	40,845
Elfun Trusts	40,463
Neuberger & Berman Guardian Fund	40,305
Mutual Beacon Fund	39,632
Fidelity Puritan Fund	39,206
Vanguard Index Trust—500 Portfolio	39,120
Nicholas II	39,071
Founders Growth Fund	38,703
Neuberger & Berman Partners Fund	38,689
Scudder Japan Fund	38,117
Twentieth Century Growth Investors	37,951
Dodge & Cox Balanced Fund	37,872
Retmt Planning Fund of America—Growth	37,798
Alliance Bond—Corpt Bond Port/Class A	37,448
Nicholas Fund	37,432

* *Does not take into account sales commissions or income taxes that would have to be paid. Includes reinvestment of all dividends and capital gains.*
(c) Fund closed to new investors.

Source: IBC/*Donoghue's Mutual Funds Almanac.*

Top 10 No- and Low-Load Mutual Funds Listed by Fund Type

Taxable Bond Funds

Funds	1993 Annual % Gain	Assets ($ Millions) as of 11/30/93
Benham Target Maturities Trust—2020	35.6%	$ 56.2
Alliance Bond—Corpt Bond Port/Class A	31.1	232.7
Benham Target Maturities Trust—2015	30.5	89.0
Benham Target Maturities Trust—2010	26.3	70.6
Keystone Custodian Series/B-4	26.2	951.7
Fidelity Capital & Income	24.9	2,569.2
PaineWebber Fxd Incm—High Incm Cl A	22.8	347.7
Loomis Sayles Bond Fund	22.2	55.9
Fidelity Spartan High Income Fund	21.9	640.3
T Rowe Price High Yield Fund	21.8	1,582.2

Balanced Funds

Funds	1993 Annual % Gain	Assets ($ Millions) as of 11/30/93
USAA Cornerstone Fund	23.8%	$ 708.0
CGM Mutual Fund	21.8	851.7
Fidelity Puritan Fund	21.4	8,278.9
Fidelity Balanced Fund	19.3	4,211.9
Westwood Balanced Fund/Institutional Class	16.8	2.0
Payson Balanced Fund	16.0	8.5
Dodge & Cox Balanced Fund	16.0	446.0
The Parnassus Income Fund—Balanced	15.9	9.0
Evergreen Foundation Fund	15.7	202.8
American AAdvantage Balanced Fund	14.8	518.0

Tax-Exempt Bond Funds

Funds	1993 Annual % Gain	Assets ($ Millions) as of 11/30/93
Fundamental CA Municipal Fund	16.9%	$ 15.5
Evergreen Insured National Tax-Free Fund	16.0	34.9
Overland Express Municipal Income Fund	15.0	95.4
Fidelity Spartan FL Municipal Income	14.9	447.2
California Municipal Income/Fortress	14.9	12.5
Merrill Lynch MA Municipal Bond/Class A	14.8	7.8
California Tax-Free Income Fund	14.8	279.9
Rochester Fund Municipals	14.6	1,668.9
Piper Jaffray National Tax-Exempt Fund	14.6	78.7
Merrill Lynch OH Municipal Bond/Class A	14.5	8.9

Growth & Income Funds

Funds	1993 Annual % Gain	Assets ($ Millions) as of 11/30/93
SAFECO Equity Fund	30.9%	$ 148.9
Henlopen Fund	29.9	1.5
Fidelity Asset Manager: Growth	26.3	1,241.0
Franklin Balance Sheet Investment	25.6	18.2
Merrill Lynch Phoenix Fund/Class B	24.7	228.7
Northeast Investors Trust	23.6	476.7
Berger One Hundred & One Fund	23.6	112.9
Strong Total Return Fund	23.4	608.8
Fidelity Asset Manager	23.3	7,238.0
Mutual Beacon Fund	22.9	933.7

Growth Funds

Funds	1993 Annual % Gain	Assets ($ Millions) as of 11/30/93
Montgomery Emerging Markets Fund	58.7%	$ 311.5
Fidelity Select Brokerage & Invmt Mgmt	49.3	147.4
Fidelity Select Industrial Equipment	43.3	71.7
Oak Hall Equity Fund	42.1	15.3
Fidelity Select Leisure	39.6	118.3
Templeton Capital Accumulation	39.4	19.1
Fidelity Select Broadcast & Media	38.0	96.7
Thomson Opportunity Fund/Class B	36.2	618.2
INVESCO Strategic—Leisure	35.7	283.2
Fidelity Select Automotive	35.4	102.2

International Bond Funds

Funds	1993 Annual % Gain	Assets ($ Millions) as of 11/30/93
Bull & Bear Global Income Fund	25.0%	$ 59.9
Fidelity Global Bond Fund	21.9	558.7
Warburg, Pincus Global Fixed Income	19.6	56.3
T Rowe Price International Bond	19.4	708.1
Franklin Global Government Income	18.2	187.8
Alliance N American Govt Incm Tr/Cl A	17.3	223.2
Alliance N American Govt Incm Tr/Cl B	16.5	1,064.1
PIMCO Foreign	16.1	334.9
Prudential Intmd Global Income/Class A	16.0	342.6
Scudder International Bond Fund	15.8	1,264.2

International Stock Funds

Funds	1993 Annual % Gain	Assets ($ Millions) as of 11/30/93
Merrill Lynch Dragon Fund/Class A	87.2%	$ 186.3
Merrill Lynch Dragon Fund/Class B	85.8	601.6
T Rowe Price New Asia Fund	78.8	1,164.7
Scudder Latin America Fund	74.3	202.1
Fidelity Pacific Basin Fund	63.9	408.6
Lexington Worldwide Emerging Markets	63.4	57.9
Scudder Pacific Opportunities	60.1	167.0
Oakmark International Fund	53.6	612.4
Warburg, Pincus Instit Intl Equity	52.4	90.3
Evergreen Global Real Estate Equity	52.0	103.2

Precious Metals/Gold Funds

Funds	1993 Annual % Gain	Assets ($ Millions) as of 11/30/93
United Services Gold Shares Fund	123.9%	$ 240.6
Fidelity Select Precious Metals & Minerals	111.6	316.6
Keystone Precious Metals Holdings	101.9	150.5
Blanchard Precious Metals Fund	100.4	51.8
Vanguard Splzd—Gold & Precious Metals	93.4	409.8
United Services World Gold Fund	89.8	119.8
Thomson Precious Metals/Class B	89.5	23.9
Bull & Bear Gold Investors	87.6	41.0
Lexington Goldfund	87.0	90.6
Benham Gold Equities Index Fund	81.2	440.4

Annual Percentage Gain includes reinvestment of income and capital gain distribution.

Source: IBC/*Donoghue's Mutual Funds Almanac.*

HOW TO READ OUR LISTINGS

The total just keeps growing and growing. This edition of the *Barron's*/Lipper Mutual Fund Quarterly includes 5,201 funds, up 240 from the first quarter's level and an increase of 1,375 over the past 12 months. In three years, the number of new listings has doubled–but with help from high technology and plenty of overtime, we now bring you the results about one month sooner, less than two weeks after the end of the quarter. We've replaced our old-fashioned footnotes with graphic icons, to improve ease of use. The significance of the symbols:

- ◪ **means the fund's availability is limited. AHA Investment Funds, for example, are open only to participants in the American Hospital Associations Investment Program.**
- ☒ **means the fund is closed to new investors. So complain all you want, but you can't buy CGM Capital Development or Acorn Fund.**
- ▮||| **means the fund is open only to institutions.**
- ☼ **means the fund is designed for retirement plans.**
- ✋ **means the fund has waived some fees.**
- ★ **means something unusual is going on that may affect the fund's performance or operations. Check the footnotes for details.**

WITH THE AVERAGE EQUITY fund losing 2.6% in the second quarter, it's understandable if you have no great desire to check the results for your holdings. But a look anyway. Though most funds were bashed by sliding stock prices, some managed to beat the averages. A few even posted substantial gains: Japanese equity funds, for example, leaped 9.5% on average. And no matter how small, new or obscure your fund is, you'll find it in our listings.

The stock and taxable bond funds, listed alphabetically, begin on page 307. Tax-exempt funds begin on page 389. If you can't find your fund, check the list of name changes, mergers and liquidations on page 418. There, you'll also find a list of new funds.

Beside every fund's name is its objective, defined below. The third column shows the fund's total net assets on May 31, in millions of dollars. The fourth column shows its net asset value at quarter's end, figured by dividing the total net assets by the number of shares outstanding. It tells you what you would have had to pay for a share, excluding any sales charge.

The most important part – performance – comes next. These columns tell you how much you'd have as of June 30 if you invested a net $10,000 at the beginning of one of the three periods shown. The result is total return: The amount an investment makes, including dividend payments and share-price appreciation, assuming you reinvest them in fund shares.

Total return doesn't incorporate sales charges, because that would skew the performance results and make it hard for people who already own a fund to compare it to other funds. To compare your fund with its rivals, begin with the five benchmarks at the top of page 307. Performance data for every fund category Lipper tracks and for major market indexes appear on page F20.[1]

The next column is dividend yield, which tells how much a fund paid out in cash dividends over the past 12 months.

For more info about a fund, you can dial one of the listed phone numbers.

Front-end fees represent the maximum a fund will charge for sales. Redemption fees often decline the longer you stay in the fund; again, our table lists the max. Annual 12b-1 fees generally reflect what funds charged during their last fiscal year; for young funds, we show the most they can hit you with. Sometimes, when funds convince Lipper they're really charging a different fee, that's the number we've used. The 12b-1 column includes "service" fees. All annual fees, by the way, are included in funds' expenses, and affect total return.

Finally, we tell you who the fund's portfolio manager is, and how long he or she has been in charge. If the captain is really a committee, that's reflected too.

–Leslie P. Norton

DEBT AND EQUITY FUNDS

Balanced: Goal is preserving principal; fund maintains a 60%/40% or so ratio of stocks to bonds.

(continued)

[1] This page number refers to *Barron's National Business and Financial Weekly*, July 11, 1994.

Source: Lipper Analytical Services, Inc. Reprinted by permission of *Barron's National Business and Financial Weekly*,

PERFORMANCE OF MUTUAL FUNDS *(continued)*

Balanced Target: Invests to provide a guaranteed return of principal at maturity. Some assets are in zero-coupon Treasury bonds, the remainder are in long-term growth stocks.

Canadian: Invests primarily in securities traded in Canadian markets.

Capital Appreciation: Seeks maximum capital appreciation through strategies such as high turnover, leveraging, buying unregistered shares or options.

Convertibles: Invests primarily in convertible bonds and/or preferred stock.

Emerging Markets: Invests at least 65% of assets in securities of emerging markets.

Environmental: Invests at least 65% of assets in stocks of companies engaged in contributing to a cleaner and healthier environment, such as waste-management companies.

Equity Income: Normally has more than 60% of its assets in equities and seeks high income.

European Region: Focuses on one European stock market, or several.

Financial Services: Invests at least 65% of assets in stocks of financial-service companies.

Fixed Income: Typically has more than 75% of assets in fixed-income securities, such as bonds, preferred stocks, money-market instruments.

Flexible: Aims for high total return by allocating its portfolio among a wide range of asset classes.

Global: At least 25% of its portfolio is in non-U.S. securities.

Global Flexible: Similar to flexible; invests at least 25% of assets in securities traded outside the U.S.

Global Small-Company: Invests at least a quarter of its assets outside the U.S.; limits 65% of its holdings on the basis of market cap.

Gold: Has at least 65% of its assets in gold-mining or gold-oriented mining finance shares, gold coins or bullion.

Growth: Invests in companies whose long-term earnings are expected to grow faster than those of the stocks in the major market indexes.

Growth & Income: Seeks earnings growth as well as dividend income.

Health/Biotech: At least 65% invested in health-care, medical and biotech stocks.

Income: Seeks high current income through stocks, bonds and money-market instruments.

International: Invests in securities traded primarily outside the U.S.

Japanese: Concentrates on securities trading in Tokyo.

Latin American: Invests primarily in securities in Mexico, Brazil, Chile and other Latin American countries.

MidCap: Invests in companies with market caps or revenues between $800 million and the average market cap of the Wilshire 4500 Index. (That's the Wilshire 5000, excluding the stocks in the S&P 500.)

Natural Resource: Usually invests more than 65% of its equity holdings in natural-resource stocks.

Pacific Region: Concentrates on stocks trading in one or more of the Pacific Basin markets.

Real Estate: At least 65% of assets in REITs and other real-estate securities.

S&P 500 Index: Designed to replicate the performance of the Standard & Poor's 500 Index on a reinvested basis; passively managed, with adviser fee no higher than 0.5%.

Small-Company Growth: Limits investments in companies on the basis of their size.

Specialty: Limits its investments to a specific industry, or falls outside other classifications.

Science & Technology: Minimum 65% invested in science and technology stocks.

Questions? Complaints?

Queries about the data in these pages should be directed to:

Mutual Fund Profiles Dept.
Lipper Analytical Services
47 Maple St., Summit, N.J. 07901, (908) 273-2772

Utility: Utilities comprise at least 65% of its equity portfolio.

World Fixed-Income: May own common and preferred, but invests primarily in U.S. and foreign debt.

MUNICIPAL BOND FUNDS

General Muni: Puts at least 65% of its assets in municipal bonds carrying the top four credit ratings.

Insured Muni: At least 65% of its holdings have been insured for timely payment of interest.

Intermediate Muni: Its tax-exempt debt holdings have an average maturity of five to 10 years.

High-Yield Muni: Can put 50%-plus of assets in low-rated credits.

Short Muni: Invests in tax-exempt debt maturing, on average, in less than five years.

Single-State Muni: Limits investments to securities exempt from taxation in a particular state. States with only a few such funds are lumped together in the Single State category; the following state funds are identified separately: Arizona; California; Colorado; Connecticut; Florida; Georgia; Kansas; Kentucky; Louisiana; Maryland; Massachusetts; Michigan; Minnesota; Missouri; New Jersey; New York; North Carolina; Ohio; Oregon; Pennsylvania; South Carolina; Texas; Virginia. ■

BARRON'S LIPPER FUND LISTINGS

BENCHMARKS

How a $10,000 investment would have fared in the average fund

Objective	3/31/94 - 6/30/94	6/30/93 - 6/30/94	6/30/89 - 6/30/94
Growth & Income Funds	$9,959.27	$10,201.43	$15,785.66
Fixed Income Funds	9,874.14	9,928.09	14,577.94
Small-Company Growth Funds	9,425.49	10,257.73	17,312.33
Gold Oriented Funds	9,296.75	10,049.94	12,514.08
International Funds	10,091.82	12,010.33	15,539.07
Emerging Market Funds	9,439.41	12,711.38	17,275.00

DEBT AND EQUITY FUNDS

FUND NAME	OBJECTIVE	TOTAL NET ASSETS ($ MIL) 5/31/94	NET ASSET $ VALUE 6/30/94	PERFORMANCE (Return on initial $10,000 Investment) 3/31/94-6/30/94	6/30/93-6/30/94	6/30/89-6/30/94	DIVIDEND YIELD % 6/94	PHONE NUMBER 800	In-State	FEES Load	12b-1	Redemption	MANAGER	SINCE
AAL BOND ◪	Fixed Income	438.9	9.57	9,864.00	9,711.00	14,496.00	5.9	553-6319	414-734-5721	4.75	0.25	None	Duff & Phelps Inv. Co.	'87
AAL CAPITAL GROWTH ◪	Growth	874.7	14.03	9,932.00	9,664.00	15,592.00	3.2	553-6319	414-734-5721	4.75	0.25	None	Duff & Phelps Inv. Co.	'87
AAL SMALLER CO STK ◪	Midcap	144.2	8.96	8,582.00	☆	☆	0.0	553-6319	414-734-5721	4.75	0.25	None	Pilgrim Baxter Greig	'93
AAL TARGET 2001 ◪☒	Fixed Income	1.8	10.35	9,790.00	9,532.00	☆	6.4	553-6319	414-734-5721	4.75	0.10	None	Duff & Phelps Inv. Co.	'90
AAL TARGET 2006 ◪☒	Fixed Income	1.4	10.64	9,644.00	9,291.00	☆	6.8	553-6319	414-734-5721	4.75	0.10	None	Duff & Phelps Inv. Co.	'90
AAL UTILITIES ◪	Utility	26.2	9.42	9,577.00	☆	☆	0.0	553-6319	414-734-5721	4.75	0.25	None	Duff & Phelps Inv. Co.	'94
AARP BAL STOCK & BOND	Balanced	130.5	14.32	10,109.00	☆	☆	0.0	253-2277	617-439-4640	None	None	None	Hoffman/Hutchinson	'94/'94
AARP CAPITAL GROWTH	Growth	693.2	30.25	9,612.00	9,740.00	13,413.00	0.2	253-2277	617-439-4640	None	None	None	Aronoff/Cox	'89/'84
AARP GNMA	Fixed Income	5,876.9	14.85	9,940.00	9,811.00	14,379.00	6.4	253-2277	617-439-4640	None	None	None	Pruyne/Glen	'84/'85
AARP GROWTH & INC	Growth Income	2,098.6	32.51	10,344.00	10,728.00	16,810.00	3.3	253-2277	617-439-4640	None	None	None	Hoffman/Millard	'90/'85
AARP HIGH QUAL BOND	Fixed Income	592.0	15.27	9,836.00	9,806.00	14,470.00	5.6	253-2277	617-439-4640	None	None	None	Hutchinson/Thorne	'87/'84
ABT EMERGING GROWTH	Capital Appreciation	61.8	12.45	8,712.00	9,481.00	21,248.00	0.0	553-7838	407-655-7255	4.75	0.25	None	Harold Ireland	'83
ABT GROWTH & INCOME TR	Growth Income	67.0	10.21	10,065.00	9,539.00	12,384.00	2.1	553-7838	407-655-7255	4.75	0.25	None	Ted Wolff	'91
ABT UTILITY INCOME FD	Utility	116.9	11.01	9,699.00	8,564.00	13,790.00	4.9	553-7838	407-655-7255	4.75	0.25	None	Ted Wolff	'91
ACCESSOR GROWTH	Growth	18.4	13.63	10,075.00	10,597.00	☆	1.1	759-3504	206-224-7420	None	None	None	Doug Holmes	'92

(continued)

PERFORMANCE OF MUTUAL FUNDS *(continued)*

FUND NAME	OBJECTIVE	TOTAL NET ASSETS ($ MIL) 5/31/94	NET ASSET $ VALUE 6/30/94	PERFORMANCE (Return on initial $10,000 Investment) 3/31/94-6/30/94	6/30/93-6/30/94	6/30/89-6/30/94	DIVIDEND YIELD % 6/94	PHONE NUMBER 800	In-State	FEES Load	12b-1	Redemption	MANAGER	SINCE
ACCESSOR INSTL INV FXD	Fixed Income	34.0	11.64	9,932.00	☆	☆	0.0	759-3504	206-224-7420	None	None	None	Xavier Urpi	'94
ACCESSOR INT FXD-INC	Fixed Income	30.0	11.40	9,841.00	9,696.00	☆	5.1	759-3504	206-224-7420	None	None	None	Anne Beucler	'93
ACCESSOR MORTGAGE SEC	Fixed Income	32.5	11.61	9,882.00	9,950.00	☆	4.5	759-3504	206-224-7420	None	None	None	Keith Anderson	'92
ACCESSOR SHT-INT FXD-INC	Fixed Income	32.6	11.86	9,962.00	9,980.00	☆	3.8	759-3504	206-224-7420	None	None	None	John Axtell	'92
ACCESSOR SMALL CAP	Small Company Growth	19.4	13.64	9,591.00	10,071.00	☆	0.2	759-3504	206-224-7420	None	None	None	Nancy Feldkiercher	'92
ACCESSOR VALUE & INCOME	Growth Income	14.4	12.94	9,928.00	10,011.00	☆	1.8	759-3504	206-224-7420	None	None	None	Pat O'Connor	'92
ACORN FUND ☒	Small Company Growth	1,972.1	12.69	9,628.00	10,287.00	19,708.00	0.5	922-6769	312-634-9240	None	None	2.00	Ralph Wanger	'70
ACORN INV INTL ☒	International	1,394.2	15.55	9,811.00	12,036.00	☆	0.0	922-6769	312-634-9240	None	None	2.00	Ralph Wanger	'92
ADDISON CAPITAL	Growth Income	36.6	20.45	9,761.00	9,728.00	15,226.00	1.1	526-6397	215-665-6000	3.00	0.40	None	Cheston/Kelley/Thomas	'86/'90
ADV INNR CIR A&F LRG CAP	Growth Income	35.7	9.61	10,148.00	☆	☆	0.0	932-7781	215-989-6611	None	None	None	Aronson/Fogler	'93/'93
ADV INNR CIR CLVR CAP EQ	Growth	18.5	12.66	10,251.00	11,960.00	☆	0.5	932-7781	215-989-6611	None	None	None	Clover Capital Mgt. Inc	'91
ADV INNR CIR CLVR CAP FX	Fixed Income	8.7	9.35	9,928.00	10,050.00	☆	5.9	932-7781	215-989-6611	None	None	None	Clover Capital Mgt. Inc	'91
ADV INNR CIR JRK&VYL BAL	Flexible	30.6	12.59	9,914.00	10,720.00	☆	1.7	932-7781	215-989-6611	None	None	None	Jurika & Voyles, Inc.	'92
ADV INNR CIR PIN OAK	Small Company Growth	8.9	9.36	7,542.00	8,232.00	☆	0.0	932-7781	215-989-6611	None	None	None	Oak Associates	'92
ADV INNR CIR RLSTN G&I	Growth Income	14.1	10.46	10,023.00	☆	☆	1.0	932-7781	215-989-6611	None	None	None	Joseph Harrison	'93
ADV INNR CIR RLSTN GOVT	Fixed Income	6.4	9.16	9,824.00	☆	☆	4.8	932-7781	215-989-6611	None	None	None	Joseph Harrison	'93
ADV INNR CIR RLSTN MW GR	Growth	21.1	11.51	9,829.00	☆	☆	0.2	932-7781	215-989-6611	None	None	None	Norm Klopp	'93
ADV INNR CIR WHITE OAK	Growth	6.0	10.50	9,504.00	9,924.00	☆	0.3	932-7781	215-989-6611	None	None	None	Oak Associates	'92
ADVANCE CAP I BALANCED	Balanced	45.5	9.82	9,792.00	9,710.00	12,842.00	3.2	345-4783	810-350-8543	None	0.25	None	Multiple Managers	'87
ADVANCE CAP I BOND ☚	Fixed Income	4.3	9.84	9,744.00	9,730.00	14,512.00	7.3	345-4783	810-350-8543	None	0.25	None	Shoemaker/Cappelli	'87/'91
ADVANCE CAP I EQ UNVERSE	Growth Income	10.2	8.44	9,275.00	9,247.00	11,472.00	0.9	345-4783	810-350-8543	None	0.25	None	Multiple Managers	'87
ADVANCE CAP I LG TM INC ☚	Fixed Income	1.1	9.41	9,623.00	9,503.00	☆	7.6	345-4783	810-350-8543	None	0.25	None	Shoemaker/Cappelli	'92/'93
ADVANCE CAP I RETIRE INC	Fixed Income	60.6	9.52	9,691.00	9,700.00	☆	8.2	345-4783	810-350-8543	None	0.25	None	Shoemaker/Cappelli	'92/'93
ADVANTAGE GOVT SEC	Fixed Income	164.6	8.96	9,778.00	9,419.00	15,165.00	6.4	243-8115	203-525-1421	None	0.65	4.00	Margaret D. Patel	'88
ADVANTAGE GROWTH	Growth	81.4	15.78	9,676.00	9,842.00	15,704.00	0.3	243-8115	203-525-1421	None	0.95	4.00	Robert Thomas	'89
ADVANTAGE HIGH YIELD	Fixed Income	138.2	8.76	9,736.00	10,509.00	17,119.00	9.2	243-8115	203-525-1421	None	0.65	4.00	Patel/Crocker	'89/'93
ADVANTAGE INCOME	Income	80.9	12.13	9,887.00	9,961.00	15,366.00	4.0	243-8115	203-525-1421	None	0.75	4.00	Susann Stauffer	'86
ADVANTAGE SPECIAL	Small Company Growth	35.6	18.85	9,267.00	10,427.00	18,897.00	0.0	243-8115	203-525-1421	None	0.95	4.00	Robert Thomas	'89
ADVISORS FUND LP; A	Flexible	92.5	24.40	9,572.00	9,104.00	☆	0.0	None	212-720-9218	5.00	0.25	None	Team Managed	'90
AETNA AETNA FUND; ADV	Flexible	88.0	10.28	☆	☆	☆	0.0	238-6263	203-273-0121	None	0.50	1.00	John Kim	'94
AETNA AETNA FUND; SEL	Flexible	88.0	10.29	9,886.00	10,139.00	☆	2.6	238-6263	203-273-0121	None	None	None	John Kim	'94
AETNA ASIAN GROWTH; ADV	Pacific Region	27.1	8.16	☆	☆	☆	0.0	238-6263	203-273-0121	None	0.50	1.00	Anna Tong	'94
AETNA ASIAN GROWTH; SEL	Pacific Region	27.1	8.16	9,927.00	☆	☆	0.0	238-6263	203-273-0121	None	None	None	Anna Tong	'94
AETNA BOND; ADV	Fixed Income	48.6	9.68	☆	☆	☆	0.0	238-6263	203-273-0121	None	0.50	1.00	Jeanne Wong-Boehm	'94
AETNA BOND; SEL	Fixed Income	48.6	9.68	9,825.00	9,883.00	☆	5.9	238-6263	203-273-0121	None	None	None	Jeanne Wong-Boehm	'92
AETNA GOVT; ADV	Fixed Income	19.8	9.55	☆	☆	☆	0.0	238-6263	203-273-0121	None	0.50	1.00	Jeanne Wong-Boehm	'94
AETNA GOVT; SEL	Fixed Income	19.8	9.55	9,949.00	☆	☆	0.0	238-6263	203-273-0121	None	None	None	Jeanne Wong-Boehm	'94
AETNA GRO & INC; ADV	Growth Income	107.8	10.56	☆	☆	☆	0.0	238-6263	203-273-0121	None	0.50	1.00	Team Managed	'94
AETNA GRO & INC; SEL	Growth Income	107.8	10.57	9,953.00	10,146.00	☆	1.5	238-6263	203-273-0121	None	None	None	Team Managed	'92
AETNA GROWTH; SEL	Growth	25.4	9.90	9,659.00	☆	☆	0.0	238-6263	203-273-0121	None	None	None	Peter Canoni	'94
AETNA INTL GROWTH; SEL	International	50.5	11.12	10,100.00	11,560.00	☆	3.5	238-6263	203-273-0121	None	None	None	Douglas Thomson	'94
AETNA SMALL CO GRO; ADV	Small Company Growth	25.0	9.63	☆	☆	☆	0.0	238-6263	203-273-0121	None	0.50	1.00	Thomas Dibella	'94
AETNA SMALL CO GRO; SEL	Small Company Growth	25.0	9.65	9,583.00	☆	☆	0.0	238-6263	203-273-0121	None	None	None	Thomas Dibella	'94
AFFILIATED FUND	Growth Income	4,051.4	10.33	10,147.00	10,418.00	16,041.00	3.0	426-1130	212-848-1800	5.75	0.25	None	Thomas S. Henderson	'9[illegible]
AHA INV BALANCED ◪	Balanced	45.1	11.67	9,888.00	10,105.00	15,064.00	3.5	445-1341	708-295-5000	None	None	None	Avatar/Criterion/Cambiar	'88/'9[illegible]

AHA INV DVSD EQUITY ◪	Growth	23.1	13.90	9,998.00	10,498.00	15,812.00	1.9	445-1341	708-295-5000	None	None	None	Cambiar/Invt Research Co	'88/'91
AHA INV FULL MAT FXD INC ◪	Fixed Income	45.8	9.48	9,872.00	9,910.00	14,513.00	6.0	445-1341	708-295-5000	None	None	None	Bankers Tr/Criterion	'90/'88
AHA INV LTD MAT FXD INC ◪	Fixed Income	188.2	10.09	10,010.00	10,164.00	13,956.00	4.8	445-1341	708-295-5000	None	None	None	Patterson/Neuberger Berman	'88/'92
AIM EQ AGGRESS GRO ⊠	Small Company Growth	539.3	23.67	9,610.00	11,570.00	25,965.00	0.0	347-1919	713-626-1919	5.50	0.25	None	Schoolar/Kippes	'92/'92
AIM EQ CHARTER; INSTL	Growth Income	N/A	N/A	N/A	N/A	☆	0.0	347-1919	713-626-1919	None	None	None	Lerner/Sachnowitz	'91/'91
AIM EQ CHARTER; RTL	Growth Income	1,572.4	8.58	9,861.00	9,918.00	18,074.00	1.9	347-1919	713-626-1919	5.50	0.30	None	Lerner/Sachnowitz	'68/'91
AIM EQ CONSTELTN; RTL	Capital Appreciation	3,191.7	16.09	9,338.00	10,151.00	23,607.00	0.0	347-1919	713-626-1919	5.50	0.30	None	Schoolar/Barnard/Kippes	'87/'90
AIM EQ WEINGARTEN; INSTL	Growth	N/A	N/A	N/A	N/A	☆	0.0	347-1919	713-626-1919	None	None	None	Schoolar/Barnard	'91/'91
AIM EQ WEINGARTEN; RTL	Growth	4,043.4	16.15	9,562.00	9,863.00	16,984.00	0.7	347-1919	713-626-1919	5.50	0.30	None	Schoolar/Barnard	'87/'90
AIM INTL EQUITY	International	620.6	12.58	10,080.00	12,236.00	☆	0.1	347-1919	713-626-1919	5.50	0.30	None	Griffin/Rogge	'92/'92
AIM INV ADJ RATE; RTL	Fixed Income	61.0	9.63	9,990.00	10,149.00	☆	4.2	347-1919	713-626-1919	1.00	0.25	None	Kelley/Beauchamp/Walsh	'92/'92
AIM INV LTD TREAS; AIM	Fixed Income	338.9	9.92	10,008.00	10,167.00	13,815.00	3.8	347-1919	713-626-1919	1.00	0.15	None	Beauchamp/Walsh/Kelley	'87/'92
AIM INV LTD TREAS; INSTL	Fixed Income	179.9	9.92	10,014.00	10,186.00	13,935.00	4.0	347-1919	713-626-1919	None	None	None	Beauchamp/Walsh/Kelley	'87/'92
AIM SUMMIT FUND ★	Growth	705.9	8.91	9,469.00	9,695.00	16,943.00	1.0	347-1919	713-626-1919	8.50	None	None	Julian Lerner	'88
AIM BALANCED FUND; A	Balanced	30.7	14.97	9,784.00	10,016.00	17,611.00	2.3	347-1919	713-626-1919	4.75	0.25	None	Alley/Cody	'92/'92
AIM BALANCED FUND; B	Balanced	12.3	14.98	9,759.00	☆	☆	0.0	347-1919	713-626-1919	None	1.00	5.00	Alley/Cody	'93/'93
AIM GOVERNMENT SECS; A	Fixed Income	124.9	9.32	9,916.00	9,805.00	14,127.00	7.6	347-1919	713-626-1919	4.75	0.25	None	Kelley/Beauchamp/Walsh	'92/'92
AIM GOVERNMENT SECS; B	Fixed Income	15.3	9.32	9,906.00	☆	☆	0.0	347-1919	713-626-1919	None	1.00	5.00	Kelley/Beauchamp/Walsh	'93/'93
AIM GROWTH; A	Growth	129.5	10.04	9,078.00	9,328.00	13,629.00	0.0	347-1919	713-626-1919	5.50	0.25	None	Barnard/Smith	'92/'92
AIM GROWTH; B	Growth	23.8	9.98	9,056.00	☆	☆	0.0	347-1919	713-626-1919	None	1.00	5.00	Barnard/Smith	'93/'93
AIM HIGH YIELD; A	Fixed Income	567.2	9.49	9,926.00	10,505.00	17,197.00	10.2	347-1919	713-626-1919	4.75	0.25	None	Petersen/Pessarra	'82/'92
AIM HIGH YIELD; B	Fixed Income	99.9	9.48	9,906.00	☆	☆	0.0	347-1919	713-626-1919	None	1.00	5.00	Petersen/Pessarra	'93/'93
AIM INCOME; A	Fixed Income	214.7	7.45	9,730.00	9,551.00	14,437.00	8.0	347-1919	713-626-1919	4.75	0.25	None	Alley/Pessarra	'92/'93
AIM INCOME; B	Fixed Income	8.0	7.43	9,708.00	☆	☆	0.0	347-1919	713-626-1919	None	1.00	5.00	Alley/Pessarra	'93/'93
AIM UTILITIES; A	Utility	169.0	12.09	9,522.00	8,806.00	14,993.00	5.0	347-1919	713-626-1919	5.50	0.25	None	Alley/Cody	'92/'92
AIM UTILITIES; B	Utility	35.9	12.09	9,507.00	☆	☆	0.0	347-1919	713-626-1919	None	1.00	5.00	Alley/Cody	'93/'93
AIM VALUE; A	Growth	1,016.4	20.23	9,579.00	10,509.00	22,096.00	0.2	347-1919	713-626-1919	5.50	0.25	None	Cody/Dobberpuhl	'92/'92
AIM VALUE; B	Growth	290.8	20.17	9,559.00	☆	☆	0.0	347-1919	713-626-1919	None	1.00	5.00	Cody/Dobberpuhl	'93/'93
ALGER DEFINED ALLCAP ✪	Capital Appreciation	4.7	8.35	8,780.00	☆	☆	0.0	992-3863	201-547-3600	None	None	None	David Alger	'93
ALGER DEFINED GROWTH ✪	Growth	8.6	9.07	9,303.00	☆	☆	0.0	992-3863	201-547-3600	None	None	None	David Alger	'93
ALGER DEFINED MID CAP ✪	Midcap	5.7	9.41	9,410.00	☆	☆	0.0	992-3863	201-547-3600	None	None	None	David Alger	'93
ALGER DEFINED SM CAP ✪	Small Company Growth	8.0	9.21	9,524.00	☆	☆	0.0	992-3863	201-547-3600	None	None	None	David Alger	'93
ALGER BALANCED	Balanced	3.6	10.12	9,602.00	9,634.00	☆	0.0	992-3863	201-547-3600	None	0.75	5.00	David Alger	'92
ALGER GROWTH	Growth	65.8	18.77	9,348.00	10,428.00	20,625.00	0.0	992-3863	201-547-3600	None	0.75	5.00	David Alger	'86
ALGER INCOME & GROWTH	Growth Income	7.1	11.17	9,434.00	8,860.00	12,630.00	0.0	992-3863	201-547-3600	None	0.75	5.00	David Alger	'86
ALGER LEVERAGED ALLCAP	Growth	2.4	9.17	8,912.00	☆	☆	0.0	992-3863	201-547-3600	None	0.75	5.00	David Alger	'93
ALGER MIDCAP GROWTH	Growth	13.0	10.93	9,185.00	10,854.00	☆	0.0	992-3863	201-547-3600	None	0.75	5.00	David Alger	'93
ALGER SMALL CAPITAL	Small Company Growth	266.4	19.91	9,356.00	9,711.00	19,065.00	0.0	992-3863	201-547-3600	None	0.75	5.00	David Alger	'86
ALLIANCE BALANCED; A	Balanced	160.3	13.10	9,865.00	9,787.00	13,063.00	2.9	227-4618	201-319-4000	4.25	0.30	None	Bruce Calvert	'90
ALLIANCE BALANCED; B	Balanced	14.1	12.96	9,848.00	9,708.00	☆	2.3	227-4618	201-319-4000	None	1.00	4.00	Bruce Calvert	'91
ALLIANCE BALANCED; C	Balanced	6.4	12.97	9,856.00	9,715.00	☆	2.3	227-4618	201-319-4000	None	1.00	None	Bruce Calvert	'93
ALLIANCE BD CORP BD; A	Fixed Income	222.3	12.51	9,589.00	9,742.00	16,772.00	9.0	227-4618	201-319-4000	4.25	0.30	None	Wayne Lyski	'86
ALLIANCE BD CORP BD; B	Fixed Income	180.3	12.50	9,565.00	9,673.00	☆	8.3	227-4618	201-319-4000	None	1.00	3.00	Wayne Lyski	'93
ALLIANCE BD CORP BD; C	Fixed Income	52.5	12.50	9,565.00	9,673.00	☆	8.3	227-4618	201-319-4000	None	1.00	None	Wayne Lyski	'93
ALLIANCE BD US GOVT; A	Fixed Income	486.8	7.84	9,892.00	9,807.00	14,431.00	8.3	227-4618	201-319-4000	4.25	0.30	None	Paul DeNoon	'92
ALLIANCE BD US GOVT; B	Fixed Income	756.5	7.84	9,874.00	9,737.00	☆	7.6	227-4618	201-319-4000	None	1.00	3.00	Paul DeNoon	'92
ALLIANCE BD US GOVT; C	Fixed Income	238.0	7.83	9,861.00	9,725.00	☆	7.6	227-4618	201-319-4000	None	1.00	None	Paul DeNoon	'93
ALLIANCE COUNTERPT; A	Growth Income	46.3	16.42	9,868.00	9,985.00	14,057.00	0.0	227-4618	201-319-4000	4.25	0.30	None	Dutch Handke	'85
ALLIANCE COUNTERPT; B	Growth Income	0.4	16.25	9,843.00	9,894.00	☆	0.0	227-4618	201-319-4000	None	1.00	4.00	Dutch Handke	'93
ALLIANCE COUNTERPT; C	Growth Income	0.4	16.27	9,849.00	9,911.00	☆	0.0	227-4618	201-319-4000	None	1.00	None	Dutch Handke	'93

★ AIM SUMMIT--Contractual plan fund.

PERFORMANCE OF MUTUAL FUNDS *(continued)*

FUND NAME	OBJECTIVE	TOTAL NET ASSETS ($ MIL) 5/31/94	NET ASSET $ VALUE 6/30/94	PERFORMANCE (Return on initial $10,000 Investment) 3/31/94-6/30/94	6/30/93-6/30/94	6/30/89-6/30/94	DIVIDEND YIELD % 6/94	PHONE NUMBER 800	In-State	FEES Load	12b-1	Redemption	MANAGER	SINCE
ALLIANCE FUND; A	Growth	792.7	6.45	9,788.00	10,125.00	17,098.00	0.0	227-4618	201-319-4000	4.25	0.30	None	Harrison/Jenkel	'90/'85
ALLIANCE FUND; B	Growth	15.9	6.33	9,753.00	10,019.00	☆	0.0	227-4618	201-319-4000	None	1.00	4.00	Harrison/Jenkel	'91/'91
ALLIANCE FUND; C	Growth	6.1	6.34	9,754.00	10,034.00	☆	0.0	227-4618	201-319-4000	None	1.00	None	Harrison/Jenkel	'93/'93
ALLIANCE GLBL DOLLAR; A	World Income	8.8	8.46	9,674.00	☆	☆	0.0	227-4618	201-319-4000	4.25	0.30	None	Wayne Lyski	'94
ALLIANCE GLBL DOLLAR; B	World Income	33.2	8.47	9,665.00	☆	☆	0.0	227-4618	201-319-4000	None	1.00	3.00	Wayne Lyski	'94
ALLIANCE GLBL DOLLAR; C	World Income	8.4	8.47	9,666.00	☆	☆	0.0	227-4618	201-319-4000	None	1.00	None	Wayne Lyski	'94
ALLIANCE GLBL SM CAP; A	Global Small Company	63.2	10.93	9,596.00	10,469.00	10,324.00	0.0	227-4618	201-319-4000	4.25	0.30	None	Cook/Heisterberg/Rice	'92/'93
ALLIANCE GLBL SM CAP; B	Global Small Company	3.7	10.64	9,577.00	10,401.00	☆	0.0	227-4618	201-319-4000	None	1.00	4.00	Cook/Heisterberg/Rice	'92/'93
ALLIANCE GLBL SM CAP; C	Global Small Company	1.3	10.65	9,586.00	10,400.00	☆	0.0	227-4618	201-319-4000	None	1.00	None	Cook/Heisterberg/Rice	'93/'93
ALLIANCE GRO & INC; A	Growth Income	423.8	2.25	9,880.00	9,973.00	14,903.00	2.5	227-4618	201-319-4000	4.25	0.30	None	Tom Perkins	'90
ALLIANCE GRO & INC; B	Growth Income	95.7	2.24	9,857.00	9,891.00	☆	1.6	227-4618	201-319-4000	None	1.00	4.00	Tom Perkins	'91
ALLIANCE GRO & INC; C	Growth Income	17.5	2.24	9,857.00	9,911.00	☆	1.8	227-4618	201-319-4000	None	1.00	None	Tom Perkins	'93
ALLIANCE INC BUILDER; A	Specialty	0.1	9.61	9,894.00	☆	☆	0.0	227-4618	201-319-4000	4.25	0.30	None	Robert Sinche	'94
ALLIANCE INC BUILDER; B	Specialty	0.1	9.62	9,887.00	☆	☆	0.0	227-4618	201-319-4000	None	1.00	4.00	Robert Sinche	'94
ALLIANCE INC BUILDER; C	Specialty	76.1	9.61	9,877.00	9,820.00	☆	3.8	227-4618	201-319-4000	None	1.00	None	Sinche/Perkins	'91/'91
ALLIANCE INTL; A	International	200.4	18.38	10,378.00	11,868.00	12,987.00	0.0	227-4618	201-319-4000	4.25	0.30	None	A. Rama Krishna	'93
ALLIANCE INTL; B	International	27.6	17.90	10,359.00	11,765.00	☆	0.0	227-4618	201-319-4000	None	1.00	4.00	A. Rama Krishna	'93
ALLIANCE INTL; C	International	13.0	17.91	10,359.00	11,772.00	☆	0.0	227-4618	201-319-4000	None	1.00	None	A. Rama Krishna	'93
ALLIANCE MTGE INC; A	Fixed Income	717.9	8.45	9,837.00	9,648.00	15,021.00	7.6	227-4618	201-319-4000	4.25	0.30	None	Ullman/Young	'92/'92
ALLIANCE MTGE INC; B	Fixed Income	1,228.5	8.45	9,818.00	9,579.00	☆	6.8	227-4618	201-319-4000	None	1.00	3.00	Ullman/Young	'92/'92
ALLIANCE MTGE INC; C	Fixed Income	91.3	8.44	9,807.00	9,568.00	☆	6.9	227-4618	201-319-4000	None	1.00	None	Ullman/Young	'93/'93
ALLIANCE MTGE STR; A	Fixed Income	79.2	9.66	9,968.00	10,192.00	☆	5.5	227-4618	201-319-4000	4.25	0.30	None	Ullman/Young	'92/'92
ALLIANCE MTGE STR; B	Fixed Income	177.6	9.67	9,960.00	10,131.00	☆	4.8	227-4618	201-319-4000	None	1.00	3.00	Ullman/Young	'92/'92
ALLIANCE MTGE STR; C	Fixed Income	218.9	9.67	9,960.00	10,131.00	☆	4.8	227-4618	201-319-4000	None	1.00	None	Ullman/Young	'93/'93
ALLIANCE MU-MK INCOME	World Income	13.5	1.84	10,042.00	10,059.00	☆	3.9	227-4618	201-319-4000	None	0.90	1.00	Sinche/Peebles	'90/'92
ALLIANCE MU-MK STR; A	World Income	64.2	8.04	9,686.00	9,742.00	☆	8.3	227-4618	201-319-4000	4.25	0.30	None	Sinche/Bloom	'91/'91
ALLIANCE MU-MK STR; B	World Income	315.3	8.04	9,657.00	9,673.00	☆	7.5	227-4618	201-319-4000	None	1.00	3.00	Sinche/Bloom	'91/'91
ALLIANCE MU-MK STR; C	World Income	2.1	8.04	9,668.00	9,685.00	☆	7.5	227-4618	201-319-4000	None	1.00	None	Sinche/Bloom	'93/'93
ALLIANCE N AM GV INC; A	World Income	318.9	8.52	9,485.00	9,475.00	☆	12.1	227-4618	201-319-4000	4.25	0.30	None	Wayne Lyski	'92
ALLIANCE N AM GV INC; B	World Income	1,744.9	8.52	9,467.00	9,397.00	☆	11.3	227-4618	201-319-4000	None	1.00	3.00	Wayne Lyski	'92
ALLIANCE N AM GV INC; C	World Income	431.0	8.52	9,477.00	9,408.00	☆	11.3	227-4618	201-319-4000	None	1.00	None	Wayne Lyski	'93
ALLIANCE NEW EUROPE; A	European Region	86.1	12.06	9,877.00	11,709.00	☆	0.0	227-4618	201-319-4000	4.25	0.30	None	Perkins/Banz	'92/'93
ALLIANCE NEW EUROPE; B	European Region	28.9	11.83	9,858.00	11,621.00	☆	0.0	227-4618	201-319-4000	None	1.00	4.00	Perkins/Banz	'92/'93
ALLIANCE NEW EUROPE; C	European Region	11.6	11.84	9,867.00	11,631.00	☆	0.0	227-4618	201-319-4000	None	1.00	None	Perkins/Banz	'93/'93
ALLIANCE PORT BAL; A	Balanced	9.7	15.97	9,685.00	9,935.00	☆	1.5	227-4618	201-319-4000	4.25	0.30	None	Judith Taylor	'90
ALLIANCE PORT BAL; B	Balanced	44.0	13.86	9,665.00	9,863.00	15,265.00	0.9	227-4618	201-319-4000	None	1.00	4.00	Judith Taylor	'87
ALLIANCE PORT BAL; C	Balanced	4.3	13.87	9,672.00	☆	☆	0.0	227-4618	201-319-4000	None	1.00	None	Judith Taylor	'93
ALLIANCE PORT CONSV; A	Flexible	15.9	10.20	9,808.00	9,699.00	☆	2.7	227-4618	201-319-4000	4.25	0.30	None	Franklin Kennedy III	'92
ALLIANCE PORT CONSV; B	Flexible	30.8	10.30	9,783.00	9,634.00	☆	1.9	227-4618	201-319-4000	None	1.00	4.00	Franklin Kennedy III	'92
ALLIANCE PORT CONSV; C	Flexible	4.6	10.31	9,793.00	☆	☆	0.0	227-4618	201-319-4000	None	1.00	None	Franklin Kennedy III	'93
ALLIANCE PORT GR INV; A	Flexible	16.8	11.36	9,701.00	9,831.00	☆	0.9	227-4618	201-319-4000	4.25	0.30	None	Franklin Kennedy III	'92
ALLIANCE PORT GR INV; B	Flexible	33.3	11.39	9,694.00	9,776.00	☆	0.6	227-4618	201-319-4000	None	0.50	4.00	Franklin Kennedy III	'92
ALLIANCE PORT GR INV; C	Flexible	3.5	11.39	9,685.00	☆	☆	0.0	227-4618	201-319-4000	None	1.00	None	Franklin Kennedy III	'93
ALLIANCE PORT GROWTH; A	Growth	114.0	23.55	9,849.00	10,752.00	☆	0.0	227-4618	201-319-4000	4.25	0.30	None	Tyler Smith	'90
ALLIANCE PORT GROWTH; B	Growth	451.0	19.96	9,833.00	10,675.00	21,185.00	0.0	227-4618	201-319-4000	None	1.00	4.00	Tyler Smith	'87

ALLIANCE PORT GROWTH; C	Growth	73.7	19.97	9,833.00	☆	☆	0.0	227-4618	201-319-4000	None	1.00	None	Tyler Smith	'93
ALLIANCE PORT SH GOV; A	Fixed Income	2.0	9.66	9,902.00	9,933.00	☆	5.1	227-4618	201-319-4000	4.25	0.30	None	Paul DeNoon	'93
ALLIANCE PORT SH GOV; B	Fixed Income	6.3	9.77	9,875.00	9,885.00	☆	4.3	227-4618	201-319-4000	None	1.00	3.00	Paul DeNoon	'93
ALLIANCE PORT SH GOV; C	Fixed Income	7.9	9.76	9,875.00	☆	☆	0.0	227-4618	201-319-4000	None	1.00	None	Paul DeNoon	'93
ALLIANCE PREMIER GR; A	Growth	38.1	11.22	9,689.00	9,991.00	☆	0.0	227-4618	201-319-4000	4.25	0.30	None	Al Harrison	'92
ALLIANCE PREMIER GR; B	Growth	150.3	11.13	9,678.00	9,946.00	☆	0.0	227-4618	201-319-4000	None	1.00	4.00	Al Harrison	'92
ALLIANCE PREMIER GR; C	Growth	6.8	11.14	9,679.00	9,955.00	☆	0.0	227-4618	201-319-4000	None	1.00	None	Al Harrison	'93
ALLIANCE QUASAR; A	Small Company Growth	170.0	21.13	9,219.00	9,837.00	11,160.00	0.0	227-4618	201-319-4000	4.25	0.30	None	Cook/Rice	'92/'92
ALLIANCE QUASAR; B	Small Company Growth	13.9	20.49	9,197.00	9,749.00	☆	0.0	227-4618	201-319-4000	None	1.00	4.00	Cook/Rice	'92/'92
ALLIANCE QUASAR; C	Small Company Growth	1.4	20.50	9,201.00	9,758.00	☆	0.0	227-4618	201-319-4000	None	1.00	None	Cook/Rice	'93/'93
ALLIANCE SH-TM MU-MK; A	World Income	720.3	8.73	9,921.00	10,047.00	13,992.00	6.9	227-4618	201-319-4000	4.25	0.30	None	Sinche/Bloom	'89/'90
ALLIANCE SH-TM MU-MK; B	World Income	1,276.3	8.73	9,902.00	9,975.00	☆	6.1	227-4618	201-319-4000	None	1.00	3.00	Sinche/Bloom	'90/'90
ALLIANCE SH-TM MU-MK; C	World Income	11.0	8.73	9,902.00	9,975.00	☆	6.1	227-4618	201-319-4000	None	1.00	None	Sinche/Bloom	'93/'93
ALLIANCE TECHNOLOGY; A	Science & Technology	171.8	25.05	9,203.00	10,611.00	20,659.00	0.0	227-4618	201-319-4000	4.25	0.30	None	Anastos/Malone	'92/'92
ALLIANCE TECHNOLOGY; B	Science & Technology	6.9	24.84	9,186.00	10,539.00	☆	0.0	227-4618	201-319-4000	None	1.00	4.00	Anastos/Malone	'93/'93
ALLIANCE TECHNOLOGY; C	Science & Technology	2.6	24.84	9,183.00	10,543.00	☆	0.0	227-4618	201-319-4000	None	1.00	None	Anastos/Malone	'93/'93
ALLIANCE UTILITY INC; A	Utility	0.9	8.83	9,491.00	☆	☆	0.0	227-4618	201-319-4000	4.25	0.30	None	Susan Bridges	'93
ALLIANCE UTILITY INC; B	Utility	2.0	8.83	9,472.00	☆	☆	0.0	227-4618	201-319-4000	None	1.00	4.00	Susan Bridges	'93
ALLIANCE UTILITY INC; C	Utility	1.2	8.84	9,482.00	☆	☆	0.0	227-4618	201-319-4000	None	1.00	None	Susan Bridges	'93
ALLIANCE WORLD INCOME	World Income	108.4	1.87	10,102.00	10,191.00	☆	4.1	227-4618	201-319-4000	None	0.68	None	Sinche/Peebles	'90/'92
ALLMERICA GRO & INC	Growth Income	12.0	10.34	10,294.00	10,267.00	☆	2.2	828-0540	508-855-1000	4.50	0.25	None	Madelyn Wharton	'92
ALLMERICA GROWTH	Growth	9.1	10.77	10,000.00	10,068.00	☆	0.5	828-0540	508-855-1000	4.50	0.25	None	John Duggan	'92
ALLMERICA INV GRD INC	Fixed Income	12.4	9.33	9,853.00	9,698.00	☆	6.1	828-0540	508-855-1000	4.50	0.25	None	John Grant	'92
AMANA INCOME FUND	Equity Income	10.2	11.73	9,596.00	9,668.00	13,451.00	2.5	728-8762	206-734-9900	None	None	None	Nicholas Kaiser	'86
AMBASSADOR BALANCED; FID ▮lll	Balanced	47.7	9.42	9,546.00	9,504.00	☆	1.7	892-4366	None	None	None	None	Hill/Conrad/Chatain	'93/'93
AMBASSADOR BALANCED; INV	Balanced	0.4	9.42	9,549.00	9,497.00	☆	1.6	892-4366	None	None	None	None	Hill/Conrad/Chatain	'93/'93
AMBASSADOR BALANCED; RET	Balanced	0.3	9.42	9,549.00	9,497.00	☆	1.6	892-4366	None	3.75	0.25	None	Hill/Conrad/Chatain	'93/'93
AMBASSADOR BOND; FID ▮lll	Fixed Income	148.0	9.37	9,892.00	9,860.00	☆	6.2	892-4366	None	None	None	None	Stephen Chatain	'91
AMBASSADOR BOND; INV	Fixed Income	31.8	9.37	9,886.00	9,850.00	☆	6.1	892-4366	None	None	None	None	Stephen Chatain	'92
AMBASSADOR BOND; RET	Fixed Income	1.2	9.37	9,886.00	9,850.00	☆	6.1	892-4366	None	3.75	0.25	None	Stephen Chatain	'92
AMBASSADOR CORE GRO; FID ▮lll	Growth	73.7	15.22	9,460.00	9,266.00	☆	0.5	892-4366	None	None	None	None	Michael Hill	'93
AMBASSADOR CORE GRO; INV	Growth	108.1	15.21	9,459.00	9,259.00	14,417.00	0.5	892-4366	None	None	None	None	Michael Hill	'93
AMBASSADOR CORE GRO; RET	Growth	5.7	15.21	9,459.00	9,259.00	☆	0.5	892-4366	None	3.75	0.25	None	Michael Hill	'93
AMBASSADOR GRO STK; FID ▮lll	Growth	226.5	11.87	9,020.00	9,329.00	☆	0.1	892-4366	None	None	None	None	Ann Conrad	'91
AMBASSADOR GRO STK; INV	Growth	58.9	11.85	9,011.00	9,314.00	☆	0.1	892-4366	None	None	None	None	Ann Conrad	'92
AMBASSADOR GRO STK; RET	Growth	4.6	11.85	9,011.00	9,314.00	☆	0.1	892-4366	None	3.75	0.25	None	Ann Conrad	'92
AMBASSADOR INDEXED; FID ▮lll	S&P Index	92.2	11.50	10,029.00	10,103.00	☆	2.5	892-4366	None	None	None	None	Bruce George	'92
AMBASSADOR INDEXED; INV	S&P Index	0.9	11.50	10,023.00	10,096.00	☆	2.5	892-4366	None	None	None	None	Bruce George	'92
AMBASSADOR INDEXED; RET	S&P Index	0.4	11.50	10,023.00	10,096.00	☆	2.5	892-4366	None	3.75	0.25	None	Bruce George	'92
AMBASSADOR INT BD; FID ▮lll	Fixed Income	178.2	9.37	9,851.00	9,795.00	☆	6.3	892-4366	None	None	None	None	Napoleon Rodgers	'91
AMBASSADOR INT BD; INV	Fixed Income	106.2	9.37	9,895.00	9,835.00	☆	6.7	892-4366	None	None	None	None	Napoleon Rodgers	'92
AMBASSADOR INT BD; RET	Fixed Income	5.8	9.37	9,844.00	9,785.00	☆	6.2	892-4366	None	3.75	0.25	None	Napoleon Rodgers	'92
AMBASSADOR INTL; FID ▮lll	International	70.8	12.52	9,897.00	11,050.00	☆	0.0	892-4366	None	None	None	None	David Richardson	'93
AMBASSADOR INTL; INV	International	41.6	12.50	9,889.00	11,033.00	☆	0.0	892-4366	None	None	None	None	David Richardson	'93
AMBASSADOR INTL; RET	International	1.5	12.50	9,889.00	11,033.00	☆	0.0	892-4366	None	3.75	0.25	None	David Richardson	'93
AMBASSADOR SM CO; FID ▮lll	Small Company Growth	64.6	12.45	9,222.00	9,743.00	☆	0.0	892-4366	None	None	None	None	Stalzer/Harris	'92/'93
AMBASSADOR SM CO; INV	Small Company Growth	35.0	12.44	9,222.00	9,735.00	☆	0.0	892-4366	None	None	None	None	Stalzer/Harris	'92/'93
AMBASSADOR SM CO; RET	Small Company Growth	2.9	12.44	9,222.00	9,735.00	☆	0.0	892-4366	None	3.75	0.25	None	Stalzer/Harris	'92/'93
AMCAP FUND	Growth	2,932.6	11.63	9,836.00	10,361.00	16,084.00	0.9	421-4120	714-671-7000	5.75	0.25	None	Multiple Managers	'67
AMCORE VINTAGE EQUITY	Growth	132.6	10.08	10,067.00	10,123.00	☆	1.8	438-6375	None	4.25	0.25	None	Darrell Thompson	'92

PERFORMANCE OF MUTUAL FUNDS *(continued)*

FUND NAME	OBJECTIVE	TOTAL NET ASSETS ($ MIL) 5/31/94	NET ASSET $ VALUE 6/30/94	PERFORMANCE (Return on initial $10,000 Investment) 3/31/94-6/30/94	6/30/93-6/30/94	6/30/89-6/30/94	DIVIDEND YIELD % 6/94	PHONE NUMBER 800	In-State	FEES Load	12b-1	Redemption	MANAGER	SINCE
AMCORE VINTAGE FXD INC	Fixed Income	90.0	9.67	9,875.00	9,897.00	☆	5.8	438-6375	None	3.75	0.25	None	Dean Countryman	'92
AMELIA EARHART EAGLE EQ	Growth	0.3	11.56	9,682.00	11,231.00	☆	0.0	525-3863	919-972-9922	4.50	0.25	None	Jill H. Travis	'93
AMER AADV BALANCED ▮	Balanced	551.5	12.05	10,135.00	10,285.00	15,853.00	4.6	None	817-967-3509	None	None	None	Multiple Managers	'87
AMER AADV EQUITY ▮	Growth Income	491.6	13.59	10,218.00	10,565.00	16,292.00	3.0	None	817-967-3509	None	None	None	Multiple Managers	'87
AMER AADV INTL EQU ▮	International	152.6	11.94	9,917.00	11,984.00	☆	1.4	None	817-967-3509	None	None	None	Multiple Managers	'91
AMER AADV LTD TERM ▮	Fixed Income	201.9	9.74	9,980.00	10,186.00	14,308.00	5.3	None	817-967-3509	None	None	None	Fields/Mundy	'91/'91
AMER CAP COMSTOCK; A	Growth Income	920.6	15.32	9,887.00	9,976.00	15,727.00	1.8	421-5666	713-993-0500	5.75	0.25	None	David Reichert	'89
AMER CAP COMSTOCK; B	Growth Income	18.8	15.33	9,866.00	9,898.00	☆	0.9	421-5666	713-993-0500	None	1.00	5.00	David Reichert	'92
AMER CAP CORP BOND; A	Fixed Income	160.9	6.56	9,765.00	9,821.00	14,272.00	7.5	421-5666	713-993-0500	4.75	0.25	None	David R. Troth	'79
AMER CAP CORP BOND; B	Fixed Income	12.1	6.57	9,758.00	9,739.00	☆	6.5	421-5666	713-993-0500	None	1.00	4.00	David R. Troth	'92
AMER CAP EMERG GRO; A	Midcap	635.6	22.74	9,259.00	9,611.00	21,888.00	0.0	421-5666	713-993-0500	5.75	0.25	None	Gary Lewis	'89
AMER CAP EMERG GRO; B	Midcap	211.3	22.29	9,241.00	9,532.00	☆	0.0	421-5666	713-993-0500	None	1.00	5.00	Gary Lewis	'92
AMER CAP EMERG GRO; C	Midcap	19.0	22.56	9,242.00	☆	☆	0.0	421-5666	713-993-0500	None	1.00	1.00	Gary Lewis	'93
AMER CAP ENTERPRISE; A	Growth	749.1	11.54	9,784.00	10,033.00	16,943.00	0.4	421-5666	713-993-0500	5.75	0.25	None	Stephen Boyd	'89
AMER CAP ENTERPRISE; B	Growth	79.9	11.45	9,758.00	9,948.00	☆	0.0	421-5666	713-993-0500	None	1.00	5.00	Stephen Boyd	'91
AMER CAP ENTERPRISE; C	Growth	5.3	11.50	9,767.00	☆	☆	0.0	421-5666	713-993-0500	None	1.00	1.00	Stephen Boyd	'93
AMER CAP EQUITY INC; A	Equity Income	211.2	5.22	9,964.00	10,351.00	16,275.00	3.2	421-5666	713-993-0500	5.75	0.25	None	Jim Gilligan	'90
AMER CAP EQUITY INC; B	Equity Income	188.1	5.22	9,945.00	10,278.00	☆	2.4	421-5666	713-993-0500	None	1.00	5.00	Jim Gilligan	'92
AMER CAP EQUITY INC; C	Equity Income	21.8	5.22	9,945.00	☆	☆	2.4	421-5666	713-993-0500	None	1.00	1.00	Jim Gilligan	'93
AMER CAP EXCHANGE ☒	Growth	36.9	108.30	10,146.00	10,167.00	16,436.00	1.2	421-5666	713-993-0500	None	None	None	Stephen Boyd	'90
AMER CAP FED MTGE; A	Fixed Income	56.5	12.08	9,999.00	10,033.00	13,299.00	4.5	421-5666	713-993-0500	2.25	0.25	None	Jack Reynoldson	'91
AMER CAP FED MTGE; B ☒	Fixed Income	22.8	12.10	9,987.00	9,964.00	☆	3.7	421-5666	713-993-0500	None	1.00	3.00	Jack Reynoldson	'91
AMER CAP FED MTGE; C	Fixed Income	9.1	12.08	9,987.00	9,956.00	☆	3.7	421-5666	713-993-0500	None	1.00	1.00	Jack Reynoldson	'93
AMER CAP GOVERNMENT; A	Fixed Income	2,906.6	9.95	9,870.00	9,711.00	14,502.00	7.4	421-5666	713-993-0500	4.75	0.25	None	Jack Reynoldson	'88
AMER CAP GOVERNMENT; B	Fixed Income	321.6	9.95	9,849.00	9,634.00	☆	6.6	421-5666	713-993-0500	None	1.00	4.00	Jack Reynoldson	'91
AMER CAP GOVERNMENT; C	Fixed Income	38.5	9.94	9,849.00	9,634.00	☆	6.6	421-5666	713-993-0500	None	1.00	1.00	Jack Reynoldson	'93
AMER CAP GROW & INC; A	Growth Income	205.9	12.17	9,972.00	10,537.00	15,858.00	2.1	421-5666	713-993-0500	5.75	0.25	None	Jim Gilligan	'90
AMER CAP GROW & INC; B	Growth Income	10.8	12.18	9,948.00	☆	☆	0.0	421-5666	713-993-0500	None	1.00	5.00	Jim Gilligan	'93
AMER CAP HARBOR; A	Convertible Securities	403.6	13.68	9,710.00	9,822.00	14,889.00	4.2	421-5666	713-993-0500	5.75	0.25	None	James Behrman	'84
AMER CAP HARBOR; B	Convertible Securities	70.1	13.63	9,688.00	9,751.00	☆	3.4	421-5666	713-993-0500	None	1.00	5.00	James Behrman	'91
AMER CAP HIGH YIELD; A	Fixed Income	392.4	6.25	9,912.00	10,444.00	14,166.00	10.6	421-5666	713-993-0500	4.75	0.25	None	Ellis Bigelow	'89
AMER CAP HIGH YIELD; B	Fixed Income	64.9	6.26	9,893.00	10,367.00	☆	9.8	421-5666	713-993-0500	None	1.00	4.00	Ellis Bigelow	'92
AMER CAP HIGH YIELD; C	Fixed Income	13.1	6.24	9,893.00	☆	☆	0.0	421-5666	713-993-0500	None	1.00	1.00	Ellis Bigelow	'93
AMER CAP PACE; A	Growth	2,247.0	11.05	9,831.00	9,936.00	15,009.00	1.1	421-5666	713-993-0500	5.75	0.25	None	Alan Sachtleben	'92
AMER CAP PACE; B	Growth	36.5	10.96	9,803.00	9,854.00	☆	0.2	421-5666	713-993-0500	None	1.00	5.00	Alan Sachtleben	'92
AMER CAP TGT PORT '97 ☒	Fixed Income	17.9	13.07	9,879.00	9,820.00	☆	0.0	421-5666	713-993-0500	3.00	0.25	None	Jack Reynoldson	'90
AMER CAP US GOVT INC; A	Fixed Income	78.3	8.27	9,861.00	9,691.00	☆	8.4	421-5666	713-993-0500	4.75	0.25	None	Jack Reynoldson	'92
AMER CAP US GOVT INC; B	Fixed Income	239.2	8.27	9,840.00	9,614.00	☆	7.6	421-5666	713-993-0500	None	1.00	4.00	Jack Reynoldson	'92
AMER CAP US GOVT INC; C	Fixed Income	42.8	8.27	9,840.00	9,614.00	☆	7.6	421-5666	713-993-0500	None	1.00	1.00	Jack Reynoldson	'93
AMER CAP UTIL INCOME; A	Utility	7.5	8.46	9,745.00	☆	☆	0.0	421-5666	713-993-0500	4.75	0.25	None	Jim Gilligan	'93
AMER CAP UTIL INCOME; B	Utility	8.5	8.45	9,724.00	☆	☆	0.0	421-5666	713-993-0500	None	1.00	4.00	Jim Gilligan	'93
AMER CAP UTIL INCOME; C	Utility	1.3	8.45	9,724.00	☆	☆	0.0	421-5666	713-993-0500	None	1.00	1.00	Jim Gilligan	'93
AMER CAP WRLD GL EQ; A	Global	41.8	11.61	10,131.00	11,184.00	☆	0.0	421-5666	713-993-0500	5.75	0.25	None	New/Armist	'94/'91
AMER CAP WRLD GL EQ; B	Global	48.7	11.41	10,106.00	11,088.00	☆	0.0	421-5666	713-993-0500	None	1.00	5.00	New/Armist	'94/'91
AMER CAP WRLD GL EQ; C	Global	5.1	11.52	10,105.00	11,098.00	☆	0.0	421-5666	713-993-0500	None	1.00	1.00	New/Armist	'94/'93

AMER CAP WRLD GL GOV; A	World Income	62.6	8.18	9,772.00	9,953.00	☆	8.6	421-5666	713-993-0500	4.75	0.25	None	Reynoldson/McHenry	'91/'91
AMER CAP WRLD GL GOV; B	World Income	146.8	8.22	9,753.00	9,875.00	☆	7.7	421-5666	713-993-0500	None	1.00	4.00	Reynoldson/McHenry	'91/'91
AMER CAP WRLD GL GOV; C	World Income	23.5	8.17	9,751.00	9,886.00	☆	7.8	421-5666	713-993-0500	None	1.00	1.00	Reynoldson/McHenry	'93/'93
AMER FDS INC US GOVT	Fixed Income	1,394.7	13.14	9,853.00	9,731.00	14,752.00	7.7	421-4120	714-671-7000	4.75	0.30	None	Multiple Managers	'85
AMER PERFORM AGGR GROWTH	Small Company Growth	17.1	11.09	8,922.00	9,446.00	☆	0.0	762-7085	None	4.00	0.25	None	Joe Sing	'92
AMER PERFORM BOND	Fixed Income	22.7	9.29	9,911.00	9,928.00	☆	6.2	762-7085	None	4.00	0.25	None	James Huntzinger	'90
AMER PERFORM EQUITY	Growth	56.6	11.08	9,934.00	10,068.00	☆	1.1	762-7085	None	4.00	0.25	None	Grafton Potter	'90
AMER PERFORM INTMDT BOND	Fixed Income	56.8	10.19	9,922.00	9,932.00	☆	6.1	762-7085	None	3.00	0.25	None	James Huntzinger	'90
AMERICA'S UTILITY FUND	Utility	119.1	19.69	9,503.00	8,486.00	☆	4.6	487-3863	804-649-1315	None	None	None	Julie M. Cannell	'92
AMERICAN BALANCED FUND	Balanced	1,824.9	11.92	10,091.00	10,142.00	15,613.00	4.8	421-4120	714-671-7000	5.75	0.25	None	Multiple Managers	'75
AMERICAN GROWTH	Growth	67.5	9.25	9,914.00	10,895.00	18,638.00	0.5	525-2406	303-623-6137	5.75	None	None	Robert Brody	'58
AMERICAN HERITAGE FUND	Capital Appreciation	101.9	1.09	8,651.00	7,743.00	15,225.00	6.1	828-5050	212-397-3900	None	None	None	Heiko Thieme	'90
AMERICAN HIGH-INCOME TR	Fixed Income	803.5	14.16	9,956.00	10,294.00	16,950.00	8.5	421-4120	714-671-7000	4.75	0.30	None	Multiple Managers	'88
AMERICAN LEADERS; A	Growth Income	228.8	14.59	10,130.00	10,240.00	16,312.00	1.6	245-4770	412-288-1900	4.50	None	None	Peter R. Anderson	'91
AMERICAN LEADERS; C	Growth Income	12.4	14.60	10,139.00	10,169.00	☆	0.8	245-4770	412-288-1900	None	0.75	1.00	Peter R. Anderson	'93
AMERICAN LEADERS; FORT	Growth Income	16.6	14.56	10,106.00	☆	☆	0.0	245-4770	412-288-1900	1.00	None	1.00	Peter R. Anderson	'93
AMERICAN MUTUAL	Growth Income	5,195.8	21.11	10,119.00	10,216.00	15,911.00	3.9	421-4120	714-671-7000	5.75	0.25	None	Multiple Managers	'50
AMERICAN NATIONAL GROWTH	Growth	112.3	4.06	10,014.00	10,684.00	15,016.00	1.2	231-4639	409-763-2767	5.75	None	None	Gordon D. Dixon	'93
AMERICAN NATIONAL INCOME	Equity Income	117.1	20.70	10,052.00	10,443.00	16,329.00	2.6	231-4639	409-763-2767	5.75	None	None	David Zimansky	'91
AMSOUTH BALANCED	Balanced	232.3	11.57	10,084.00	10,282.00	☆	3.4	451-8379	205-326-4732	4.50	None	None	AmSouth Bank	'91
AMSOUTH BOND FUND	Fixed Income	73.9	10.47	9,890.00	9,872.00	14,593.00	6.7	451-8379	205-326-4732	3.00	None	None	AmSouth Bank	'88
AMSOUTH EQUITY FUND	Capital Appreciation	197.9	14.43	10,151.00	10,533.00	15,953.00	1.9	451-8379	205-326-4732	4.50	None	None	AmSouth Bank	'88
AMSOUTH GOVT INCOME	Fixed Income	15.7	9.43	10,001.00	☆	☆	0.0	451-8379	205-326-4732	3.00	None	None	AmSouth Bank	'93
AMSOUTH LTD MATURITY	Fixed Income	52.3	10.16	9,919.00	9,997.00	13,980.00	5.3	451-8379	205-326-4732	3.00	None	None	AmSouth Bank	'89
AMSOUTH REGIONAL EQUITY	Capital Appreciation	53.0	16.47	10,104.00	10,444.00	18,701.00	1.3	451-8379	205-326-4732	4.50	None	None	AmSouth Bank	'88
AMTRUST VALUE FUND	Growth	0.5	9.23	9,139.00	☆	☆	0.0	532-1146	512-578-7778	None	None	None	James Baker	'93
AMWAY MUTUAL FUND	Growth	63.3	7.02	9,474.00	9,708.00	17,005.00	1.9	346-2670	616-676-6288	3.00	None	None	Bruce Ebel	'88
ANALYSTS INV FXD INC	Fixed Income	1.1	13.15	9,795.00	☆	☆	0.0	None	513-984-3377	None	None	None	Lee Manzler	'93
ANALYSTS INV STOCK	Growth	2.1	15.23	9,663.00	☆	☆	0.0	None	513-984-3377	None	None	None	Lee Manzler	'93
ANALYTIC OPTIONED EQU	Equity Income	66.2	11.74	10,129.00	10,161.00	13,964.00	2.6	374-2633	714-833-0294	None	None	None	Chuck Dobson	'78
ANALYTIC ENHANCED EQUITY	Growth	1.3	9.83	10,133.00	10,260.00	☆	4.6	374-2633	714-833-0294	None	None	None	Steve Huntsinger	'93
ANALYTIC MASTER FXD INC	Fixed Income	5.7	9.63	9,976.00	10,052.00	☆	6.7	374-2633	714-833-0294	None	None	None	John Flom	'93
ANALYTIC SH-TERM GOVT	Fixed Income	24.9	9.69	9,989.00	10,100.00	☆	5.1	374-2633	714-833-0294	None	None	None	John Flom	'93
ANCHOR CAP ACCUM ☛	Midcap	14.0	19.39	9,823.00	9,500.00	13,520.00	0.4	None	610-458-9599	None	0.75	4.00	Paul Jaspard	'83
ANCHOR INTL BOND ☛	World Income	18.0	N/A	N/A	N/A	N/A	0.0	None	610-458-9599	None	None	4.00	Paul Jaspard	'88
API TRUST GROWTH FUND	Capital Appreciation	46.9	11.82	9,579.00	10,437.00	15,197.00	0.0	544-6060	804-846-1361	None	1.00	None	David Basten	'85
API TRUST TOTAL RETURN	Balanced	4.7	21.62	9,622.00	10,131.00	12,041.00	0.0	544-6060	804-846-1361	None	1.00	None	David Basten	'88
AQUINAS BALANCED	Balanced	29.6	9.34	9,887.00	☆	☆	0.0	423-6369	214-233-6655	None	None	None	Multiple Managers	'94
AQUINAS EQ GRO	Growth	8.1	8.95	9,471.00	☆	☆	0.0	423-6369	214-233-6655	None	None	None	Multiple Managers	'94
AQUINAS EQ INC	Equity Income	33.5	9.42	10,320.00	☆	☆	0.0	423-6369	214-233-6655	None	None	None	Multiple Managers	'94
AQUINAS FXD INC	Fixed Income	28.3	9.46	9,883.00	☆	☆	0.0	423-6369	214-233-6655	None	None	None	Multiple Managers	'94
ARBOR GOLDENOAK DVSFD; A ▮	Growth Income	26.2	9.94	9,696.00	10,304.00	☆	0.6	545-6331	None	None	None	None	Citizens Comm. & Savings	'93
ARBOR GOLDENOAK DVSFD; B ▮	Growth Income	0.2	9.93	9,699.00	10,270.00	☆	0.4	545-6331	None	5.75	0.25	None	Citizens Comm. & Savings	'93
ARBOR GOLDENOAK INTMDT; A ▮	Fixed Income	69.0	9.64	9,924.00	9,922.00	☆	4.9	545-6331	None	None	None	None	Citizens Comm. & Savings	'93
ARBOR GOLDENOAK INTMDT; B ▮	Fixed Income	0.3	9.64	9,917.00	9,902.00	☆	4.6	545-6331	None	4.50	0.25	None	Citizens Comm. & Savings	'93
ARBOR OVB CAP APP; A	Growth	60.8	9.09	9,279.00	☆	☆	0.0	545-6331	None	None	None	None	Dave Nolen	'93
ARBOR OVB CAP APP; B	Growth	0.3	9.07	9,265.00	☆	☆	0.0	545-6331	None	None	0.25	None	Dave Nolen	'93
ARBOR OVB EMRG GRO; A	Small Company Growth	33.3	7.97	8,515.00	☆	☆	0.0	545-6331	None	None	None	None	Dave Nolen	'93
ARBOR OVB EMRG GRO; B	Small Company Growth	0.7	7.96	8,513.00	☆	☆	0.0	545-6331	None	None	0.25	None	Dave Nolen	'93
ARBOR OVB GOVT SECS; A	Fixed Income	40.8	9.22	9,816.00	☆	☆	0.0	545-6331	None	None	None	None	Jay Thomas	'93

PERFORMANCE OF MUTUAL FUNDS (continued)

FUND NAME	OBJECTIVE	TOTAL NET ASSETS ($ MIL) 5/31/94	NET ASSET $ VALUE 6/30/94	PERFORMANCE (Return on initial $10,000 Investment) 3/31/94-6/30/94	6/30/93-6/30/94	6/30/89-6/30/94	DIVIDEND YIELD % 6/94	PHONE NUMBER 800	In-State	FEES Load	12b-1	Redemption	MANAGER	SINCE
ARBOR OVB GOVT SECS; B	Fixed Income	0.4	9.22	9,799.00	☆	☆	0.0	545-6331	None	None	0.25	None	Jay Thomas	'93
ARCH BALANCED; INSTL	Balanced	21.2	9.62	9,976.00	☆	☆	0.0	452-2724	617-722-7868	None	None	None	Jo Ann Dotson	'94
ARCH BALANCED; INV ★	Balanced	5.7	9.62	9,976.00	9,913.00	☆	3.1	452-2724	617-722-7868	4.50	0.30	None	Jo Ann Dotson	'93
ARCH BALANCED; TR ★	Balanced	63.9	9.62	9,975.00	9,912.00	☆	3.1	452-2724	617-722-7868	None	None	None	Jo Ann Dotson	'93
ARCH EMERGING GRO; INSTL	Small Company Growth	2.1	10.98	9,564.00	☆	☆	0.0	452-2724	617-722-7868	None	None	None	R. Anthony	'94
ARCH EMERGING GRO; INV	Small Company Growth	9.8	10.98	9,564.00	10,696.00	☆	0.0	452-2724	617-722-7868	4.50	None	None	R. Anthony	'92
ARCH EMERGING GRO; TR ▮	Small Company Growth	66.9	10.98	9,564.00	10,706.00	☆	0.0	452-2724	617-722-7868	None	None	None	R. Anthony	'92
ARCH GOVT & CORP; INSTL	Fixed Income	5.5	9.87	9,923.00	☆	☆	0.0	452-2724	617-722-7868	None	None	None	David Bethke	'94
ARCH GOVT & CORP; INV	Fixed Income	5.3	9.86	9,865.00	9,835.00	14,049.00	6.0	452-2724	617-722-7868	4.50	None	None	David Bethke	'88
ARCH GOVT & CORP; TR	Fixed Income	134.9	9.86	9,873.00	9,864.00	14,218.00	6.4	452-2724	617-722-7868	None	None	None	David Bethke	'93
ARCH GR & INC EQ; INSTL	Growth Income	19.0	12.55	10,040.00	☆	☆	0.0	452-2724	617-722-7868	None	None	None	Gene Gillespie	'94
ARCH GR & INC EQ; INV	Growth Income	16.8	12.55	10,040.00	10,105.00	16,248.00	1.6	452-2724	617-722-7868	4.50	None	None	Gene Gillespie	'88
ARCH GR & INC EQ; TR	Growth Income	222.8	12.56	10,049.00	10,108.00	16,264.00	1.6	452-2724	617-722-7868	None	None	None	Gene Gillespie	'86
ARCH INTL EQUITY; INSTL	International	0.1	10.09	☆	☆	☆	0.0	452-2724	617-722-7868	None	None	None	Dana Bruce	'94
ARCH INTL EQUITY; TR	International	12.3	10.09	☆	☆	☆	0.0	452-2724	617-722-7868	None	None	None	Dana Bruce	'94
ARCH US GOVT SEC; INV	Fixed Income	10.7	10.28	9,865.00	9,846.00	14,557.00	5.7	452-2724	617-722-7868	4.50	None	None	David Bethke	'88
ARCH US GOVT SEC; TR	Fixed Income	33.1	10.28	9,872.00	9,875.00	14,702.00	6.0	452-2724	617-722-7868	None	None	None	David Bethke	'88
ARK FDS CAPITAL GROWTH ☛	Growth	51.6	9.66	9,560.00	☆	☆	0.0	842-2265	None	None	None	None	First Natl Bk of Maryland	'93
ARK FDS GROWTH & INCOME ☛	Flexible	88.8	9.82	9,871.00	☆	☆	0.0	842-2265	None	None	None	None	First Natl Bk of Maryland	'93
ARK FDS INCOME ☛	Fixed Income	53.8	9.48	9,907.00	☆	☆	0.0	842-2265	None	None	None	None	First Natl Bk of Maryland	'93
ARMSTRONG ASSOCIATES	Growth	9.7	8.19	9,647.00	10,110.00	13,147.00	0.0	None	214-720-9101	None	None	None	C.K. Lawson	'68
ASIA HOUSE ASEAN	Pacific Region	1.2	9.98	9,970.00	☆	☆	0.0	923-8476	None	None	0.25	2.00	John Vail	'94
ASIA HOUSE FAR EAST	Pacific Region	1.7	10.11	10,060.00	☆	☆	0.0	923-8476	None	None	0.25	2.00	John Vail	'94
ASM FUND	Growth Income	20.4	9.35	9,989.00	10,308.00	☆	6.8	445-2763	813-963-3150	None	None	None	Steven H. Adler	'91
ASSET MGMT FINL ARM	Fixed Income	1,335.6	9.83	10,007.00	10,227.00	☆	4.2	527-3713	312-856-0715	None	0.25	None	Edward Sammons, Jr.	'91
ASSET MGMT FINL INT LIQ	Fixed Income	200.3	10.53	9,997.00	10,137.00	14,277.00	5.0	527-3713	312-856-0715	None	0.15	None	Edward Sammons, Jr.	'82
ASSET MGMT FINL INT MTGE	Fixed Income	220.6	9.42	9,922.00	9,966.00	14,371.00	5.8	527-3713	312-856-0715	None	0.15	None	Edward Sammons, Jr.	'86
ASSET MGMT FINL MTGE SEC	Fixed Income	66.5	10.41	9,945.00	9,904.00	14,639.00	7.1	527-3713	312-856-0715	None	0.15	None	Edward Sammons, Jr.	'84
ATLANTA GROWTH FUND	Specialty	6.6	10.60	9,797.00	9,980.00	☆	0.0	762-0227	404-875-1200	3.75	0.25	None	Shapiro/Astrop/Wedgewood	'92/'92
ATLAS BALANCED ☛	Balanced	8.9	9.41	9,956.00	☆	☆	0.0	933-2852	None	3.00	0.25	None	John Doney	'93
ATLAS GOVT & MTGE SEC ☛	Fixed Income	286.8	9.80	9,897.00	9,751.00	☆	7.3	933-2852	None	3.00	0.25	None	David Welch	'90
ATLAS GROWTH & INCOME ☛	Growth Income	68.4	13.04	9,550.00	9,797.00	☆	1.3	933-2852	None	3.00	0.25	None	John Wallace	'93
ATLAS STRATEGIC GROWTH ☛	Growth	6.1	9.92	10,102.00	☆	☆	0.0	933-2852	None	3.00	0.25	None	Robert Doll, Jr.	'93
ATLAS US TREAS INTMDT ☛	Fixed Income	10.7	9.48	9,952.00	9,890.00	☆	5.0	933-2852	None	3.00	0.25	None	Roberta Conger	'92
AVESTA TR BALANCED ✪	Balanced	27.0	16.73	9,853.00	9,761.00	13,942.00	0.0	392-3936	713-236-4865	None	None	None	Davis/Harper	'94/'91
AVESTA TR CORE EQUITY ✪	Capital Appreciation	16.0	10.10	9,902.00	10,090.00	☆	0.0	392-3936	713-236-4865	None	None	None	Theodore Davis	'93
AVESTA TR EQUITY GROWTH ✪	Growth	27.9	17.77	9,878.00	9,780.00	14,216.00	0.0	392-3936	713-236-4865	None	None	None	William Leszinski	'93
AVESTA TR EQUITY INCOME ✪	Equity Income	40.8	17.70	9,933.00	9,922.00	14,274.00	0.0	392-3936	713-236-4865	None	None	None	Robert Heintz	'88
AVESTA TR INCOME ✪	Fixed Income	64.1	15.26	9,807.00	9,714.00	13,625.00	0.0	392-3936	713-236-4865	None	None	None	H. Mitchell Harper	'91
AVESTA TR SH-INT GOVT ✪	Fixed Income	21.4	10.08	9,980.00	9,990.00	☆	0.0	392-3936	713-236-4865	None	None	None	Guy Barba	'93
AVESTA TR SMALL CAP ✪	Small Company Growth	10.5	9.55	9,381.00	9,646.00	☆	0.0	392-3936	713-236-4865	None	None	None	Juliet Ellis	'93
AVESTA TR US GOVT SECS ✪	Fixed Income	2.9	10.00	9,737.00	9,497.00	☆	0.0	392-3936	713-236-4865	None	None	None	John Miller	'93
AVONDALE TOTAL RETURN	Balanced	7.3	21.82	9,806.00	9,784.00	13,603.00	1.3	424-2295	817-761-3777	None	None	None	Herbert R. Smith, Inc.	'88
B STEARNS EMERG MKT DEBT	World Income	46.4	8.44	9,832.00	9,469.00	☆	9.3	766-4111	212-272-7519	4.50	0.25	None	Mark Arnold	'93
BABSON BOND PORTFOLIO L	Fixed Income	148.0	1.51	9,850.00	9,915.00	14,803.00	7.2	422-2766	816-471-5200	None	None	None	Edward L. Martin	'84

BABSON BOND PORTFOLIO S	Fixed Income	33.7	9.71	9,934.00	9,986.00	14,526.00	7.0	422-2766	816-471-5200	None	None	None	Edward L. Martin	'88
DAVID L BABSON GROWTH	Growth	234.5	11.78	9,990.00	10,380.00	14,041.00	1.6	422-2766	816-471-5200	None	None	None	David G. Kirk	'85
BABSON ENTERPRISE ⊠	Small Company Growth	189.6	16.03	9,932.00	10,659.00	17,899.00	0.3	422-2766	816-471-5200	None	None	None	Peter C. Schliemann	'85
BABSON ENTERPRISE II	Small Company Growth	35.6	16.56	9,634.00	10,810.00	☆	0.0	422-2766	816-471-5200	None	None	None	Schliemann/James	'91/'91
BABSON VALUE	Growth Income	60.2	25.24	10,124.00	11,653.00	17,035.00	1.8	422-2766	816-471-5200	None	None	None	Nick Whitridge	'84
BABSON-STEWART IVORY	International	47.0	16.41	10,284.00	12,193.00	16,629.00	0.2	422-2766	816-471-5200	None	None	None	John Wright	'88
BAIRD ADJ RATE INCOME	Fixed Income	210.7	9.66	9,847.00	10,159.00	☆	4.7	792-2473	414-765-3500	3.25	0.30	None	Jim Kochan	'92
BAIRD BLUE CHIP	Growth Income	60.1	18.32	10,200.00	10,227.00	15,992.00	1.1	792-2473	414-765-3500	5.75	0.45	None	Evans/Bosworth	'87/'87
BAIRD CAP DEVELOPMENT	Midcap	53.0	21.95	9,535.00	10,068.00	17,482.00	0.2	792-2473	414-765-3500	5.75	0.45	None	Kellner/Wilson	'86/'86
BAIRD QUALITY BOND	Fixed Income	8.2	9.20	9,726.00	9,803.00	☆	7.1	792-2473	414-765-3500	4.00	0.45	None	Jim Kochan	'92
BARON ASSET FUND	Small Company Growth	69.4	20.40	9,860.00	10,740.00	14,867.00	1.5	992-2766	212-759-7700	None	0.25	None	Ronald Baron	'87
BARTLETT CAP BASIC VALUE	Growth Income	96.2	14.97	10,101.00	10,575.00	14,169.00	1.5	800-4612	513-621-4612	None	None	None	Miller/Uible	'90/'93
BARTLETT CAP FIXED INC	Fixed Income	107.4	9.76	9,865.00	9,877.00	14,084.00	4.9	800-4612	513-621-4612	None	None	None	Dale H. Rabiner	'86
BARTLETT CAP SH TM BOND	Fixed Income	26.1	9.85	10,024.00	☆	☆	0.0	800-4612	513-621-4612	None	None	None	Dale H. Rabiner	'94
BARTLETT CAP VALUE INTL	International	57.3	12.19	9,807.00	11,976.00	☆	0.5	800-4612	513-621-4612	None	None	None	Madelynn M. Matlock	'89
BASCOM HILL BALANCED	Balanced	11.0	22.36	10,251.00	10,188.00	13,570.00	4.6	767-0300	608-273-2020	3.00	None	None	Frank Burgess	'86
BASCOM HILL INVESTORS	Growth Income	10.3	17.19	10,443.00	10,337.00	13,766.00	3.2	767-0300	608-273-2020	None	None	None	Frank Burgess	'78
BAYFUNDS BOND; INST	Fixed Income	62.4	9.61	9,896.00	☆	☆	0.0	229-3863	None	None	None	None	Rick Vincent	'93
BAYFUNDS BOND; INV	Fixed Income	6.3	9.61	9,890.00	9,959.00	☆	5.5	229-3863	None	None	None	None	Rick Vincent	'93
BAYFUNDS EQUITY; INST	Growth	87.2	10.15	9,739.00	☆	☆	0.0	229-3863	None	None	None	None	Gerri Carrol	'93
BAYFUNDS EQUITY; INV	Growth	31.1	10.15	9,732.00	9,833.00	☆	1.1	229-3863	None	None	None	None	Gerri Carrol	'93
BAYFUNDS SH TM YLD; INST	Fixed Income	82.6	9.41	9,699.00	☆	☆	0.0	229-3863	None	None	None	None	Eric Letendre	'93
BAYFUNDS SH TM YLD; INV	Fixed Income	61.1	9.41	9,693.00	9,881.00	☆	4.8	229-3863	None	None	None	None	Eric Letendre	'93
BB&T BALANCED; INV	Balanced	8.1	9.67	9,929.00	☆	☆	3.7	228-1872	614-899-4668	2.00	0.25	None	BB&T	'93
BB&T BALANCED; TR ▮	Balanced	32.6	9.66	9,935.00	☆	☆	3.9	228-1872	614-899-4668	None	None	None	BB&T	'93
BB&T GRO & INC; INV	Growth Income	7.6	10.82	9,924.00	10,258.00	☆	2.5	228-1872	614-899-4668	2.00	0.25	None	Branch Banking & Trust Co	'93
BB&T GRO & INC; TR ▮	Growth Income	83.6	10.84	9,939.00	10,272.00	☆	2.7	228-1872	614-899-4668	None	None	None	Branch Banking & Trust Co	'92
BB&T INTMDT GOVT; INV	Fixed Income	7.3	9.45	9,883.00	9,777.00	☆	6.3	228-1872	614-899-4668	2.00	0.25	None	Branch Banking & Trust Co	'93
BB&T INTMDT GOVT; TR ▮	Fixed Income	60.9	9.46	9,889.00	9,813.00	☆	6.6	228-1872	614-899-4668	None	None	None	Branch Banking & Trust Co	'92
BB&T SH-INTMDT GOVT; INV	Fixed Income	13.3	9.67	9,932.00	9,948.00	☆	5.3	228-1872	614-899-4668	2.00	0.20	None	Branch Banking & Trust Co	'93
BB&T SH-INTMDT GOVT; TR ▮	Fixed Income	37.0	9.68	9,948.00	9,975.00	☆	5.4	228-1872	614-899-4668	None	None	None	Branch Banking & Trust Co	'92
BBK GRP DIVERSA	Global Flexible	48.0	12.01	9,710.00	10,145.00	12,896.00	2.5	882-8383	415-571-5800	None	None	None	Team Managed	'86
BBK INTL INTL EQUITY	International	203.1	5.98	9,852.00	11,412.00	10,959.00	0.0	882-8383	415-571-5800	None	None	None	Richard Holbrook	'93
BBK INTL INTL FXD INC	World Income	148.2	8.33	9,016.00	8,589.00	☆	13.3	882-8383	415-571-5800	None	None	None	Arthur Micheletti	'92
BEACON HILL MUTUAL	Growth	4.4	27.17	9,902.00	9,435.00	12,599.00	0.0	343-0529	617-482-0795	None	None	None	David L. Stone	'64
BENCHMARK BALANCED; A	Balanced	23.5	9.59	9,725.00	☆	☆	2.1	None	None	None	None	None	N/A	N/A
BENCHMARK BOND; A	Fixed Income	225.7	18.85	9,795.00	9,839.00	☆	8.2	None	None	None	None	None	N/A	N/A
BENCHMARK BOND; C	Fixed Income	4.0	18.85	☆	☆	☆	0.0	None	None	None	None	None	N/A	N/A
BENCHMARK DVSD GRO; A	Growth	183.8	9.80	9,580.00	9,630.00	☆	0.5	None	None	None	None	None	N/A	N/A
BENCHMARK EQ INDEX; A	S&P Index	277.9	10.40	10,037.00	10,123.00	☆	2.5	None	None	None	None	None	N/A	N/A
BENCHMARK FOCUSED GR; A	Growth	45.1	9.62	9,441.00	☆	☆	0.1	None	None	None	None	None	N/A	N/A
BENCHMARK INTL BOND; A	World Income	25.7	20.30	10,064.00	☆	☆	0.0	None	None	None	None	None	N/A	N/A
BENCHMARK INTL GRO; A	International	102.9	10.32	10,382.00	☆	☆	0.0	None	None	None	None	None	N/A	N/A
BENCHMARK INTL GRO; C	International	2.8	10.33	☆	☆	☆	0.0	None	None	None	None	None	N/A	N/A
BENCHMARK SH INT BD; A	Fixed Income	108.2	19.69	9,992.00	10,142.00	☆	4.9	None	None	None	None	None	N/A	N/A
BENCHMARK SHORT DURATION	Fixed Income	177.3	9.99	10,067.00	10,320.00	☆	3.3	None	None	None	None	None	N/A	N/A
BENCHMARK SM CO IDX; A	Small Company Growth	75.3	10.66	9,621.00	10,413.00	☆	0.7	None	None	None	None	None	N/A	N/A
BENCHMARK SM CO IDX; C	Small Company Growth	3.3	10.64	☆	☆	☆	0.0	None	None	None	None	None	N/A	N/A
BENCHMARK TREAS IDX; A	Fixed Income	61.7	19.27	9,876.00	9,851.00	☆	5.5	None	None	None	None	None	N/A	N/A
BENCHMARK US GOVT SECS; A	Fixed Income	24.5	19.35	9,976.00	10,055.00	☆	4.5	None	None	None	None	None	N/A	N/A

★ ARCH BALANCED; INV & TR--Fund has been reclassified from Flexible Portfolio to Balanced.

PERFORMANCE OF MUTUAL FUNDS *(continued)*

FUND NAME	OBJECTIVE	TOTAL NET ASSETS ($ MIL) 5/31/94	NET ASSET $ VALUE 6/30/94	PERFORMANCE (Return on initial $10,000 Investment) 3/31/94-6/30/94	6/30/93-6/30/94	6/30/89-6/30/94	DIVIDEND YIELD % 6/94	PHONE NUMBER 800	In-State	FEES Load	12b-1	Redemption	MANAGER	SINCE
BENHAM EQ EQ GROWTH	Growth	96.1	11.60	10,139.00	10,137.00	☆	1.9	472-3389	415-965-4274	None	None	None	Steve Colton	'91
BENHAM EQ GOLD EQ INDEX	Gold	599.9	11.77	8,870.00	9,547.00	13,203.00	0.1	472-3389	415-965-4274	None	None	None	Bill Martin	'92
BENHAM EQ INC & GROWTH	Growth Income	230.8	14.27	10,052.00	9,960.00	☆	2.9	472-3389	415-965-4274	None	None	None	Steve Colton	'91
BENHAM EQ UTILITIES INC	Utility	164.0	9.06	9,905.00	9,103.00	☆	5.4	472-3389	415-965-4274	None	None	None	Steve Colton	'93
BENHAM GOVT ADJ RATE	Fixed Income	762.3	9.55	9,906.00	10,074.00	☆	5.3	472-3389	415-965-4274	None	None	None	Merk/Rankin	'91/'94
BENHAM GOVT GNMA	Fixed Income	1,057.9	10.14	9,957.00	9,895.00	14,871.00	6.4	472-3389	415-965-4274	None	None	None	Tyler/Colton	'87/'94
BENHAM GOVT LG TREAS/AGY	Fixed Income	18.3	8.91	9,654.00	9,446.00	☆	6.6	472-3389	415-965-4274	None	None	None	David W. Schroeder	'92
BENHAM GOVT SH TREAS/AGY	Fixed Income	29.3	9.75	9,998.00	10,107.00	☆	3.8	472-3389	415-965-4274	None	None	None	David W. Schroeder	'92
BENHAM GOVT TREAS NOTE	Fixed Income	323.6	9.98	9,926.00	9,919.00	14,462.00	4.8	472-3389	415-965-4274	None	None	None	David W. Schroeder	'90
BENHAM INTL EURO GOVT	World Income	247.7	10.62	10,084.00	10,771.00	☆	5.4	472-3389	415-965-4274	None	None	None	Tyler/Paul	'92/'92
BENHAM TARGET 1995	Fixed Income	79.2	94.06	10,000.00	10,138.00	15,127.00	0.0	472-3389	415-965-4274	None	None	None	David W. Schroeder	'90
BENHAM TARGET 2000	Fixed Income	258.8	66.77	9,819.00	9,604.00	15,600.00	0.0	472-3389	415-965-4274	None	None	None	David W. Schroeder	'90
BENHAM TARGET 2005	Fixed Income	100.1	45.69	9,746.00	9,399.00	15,717.00	0.0	472-3389	415-965-4274	None	None	None	David W. Schroeder	'90
BENHAM TARGET 2010	Fixed Income	48.4	32.25	9,510.00	9,201.00	15,134.00	0.0	472-3389	415-965-4274	None	None	None	David W. Schroeder	'90
BENHAM TARGET 2015	Fixed Income	56.9	23.48	9,277.00	9,140.00	14,396.00	0.0	472-3389	415-965-4274	None	None	None	David W. Schroeder	'90
BENHAM TARGET 2020	Fixed Income	58.5	16.05	9,219.00	9,104.00	☆	0.0	472-3389	415-965-4274	None	None	None	David W. Schroeder	'90
BERGER INV SMALL CO GR	Small Company Growth	147.7	2.36	9,328.00	☆	☆	0.0	333-1001	303-329-0200	None	0.25	None	William Keithler	'94
BERGER ONE HUNDRED	Growth	1,868.7	14.33	8,917.00	9,528.00	24,349.00	0.0	333-1001	303-329-0200	None	0.75	None	Berger/Linafelter	'74/'91
BERGER ONE HUNDRED & ONE	Growth Income	337.0	10.80	9,635.00	10,329.00	19,231.00	1.0	333-1001	303-329-0200	None	0.75	None	Berger/Linafelter	'74/'91
BERWYN FUND	Growth Income	53.8	17.29	9,579.00	10,733.00	16,612.00	0.0	824-2249	610-640-4330	None	None	1.00	Robert Killen	'84
BERWYN INCOME FUND	Income	39.2	11.24	9,800.00	10,441.00	17,677.00	5.8	824-2249	610-640-4330	None	None	None	Robert Killen	'87
BFM INSTL CORE FIXED INC	Fixed Income	11.4	9.36	9,904.00	9,933.00	☆	5.8	227-7236	None	None	None	None	Team Managed	'92
BFM INSTL SHORT DURATION	Fixed Income	38.2	9.71	10,020.00	10,231.00	☆	4.9	227-7236	None	None	None	None	Team Managed	'92
BHIRUD MID CAP GROWTH	Midcap	9.8	10.08	8,976.00	9,634.00	☆	0.9	845-8406	None	5.75	0.25	None	Suresh L. Bhirud	'92
BILTMORE BALANCED	Balanced	183.8	9.85	9,922.00	10,105.00	☆	3.2	462-7538	919-725-0036	4.50	None	None	Mercer	'93
BILTMORE EQUITY FUND	Growth Income	70.2	10.08	10,039.00	10,177.00	☆	1.8	462-7538	919-725-0036	4.50	None	None	Mercer	'93
BILTMORE EQUITY INDEX FD	S&P Index	167.9	10.02	10,025.00	10,106.00	☆	2.3	462-7538	919-725-0036	4.50	None	None	Tim Swanson	'93
BILTMORE FIXED INCOME	Fixed Income	138.9	9.21	9,857.00	9,763.00	☆	6.1	462-7538	919-725-0036	4.50	None	None	Tony Montione	'93
BILTMORE QUANT EQUITY	Growth	N/A	9.49	9,903.00	☆	☆	0.0	462-7538	919-725-0036	4.50	None	None	Cherry Stribling	'94
BILTMORE SH-TM FXD INC	Fixed Income	145.6	9.67	10,016.00	10,164.00	☆	4.9	462-7538	919-725-0036	4.50	None	None	Tony Montione	'93
BILTMORE SPECIAL VALUES	Small Company Growth	14.5	9.68	9,661.00	10,149.00	☆	0.4	462-7538	919-725-0036	4.50	None	None	Satterwhite	'93
BJB GLOBAL INCOME; A	World Income	45.3	11.15	9,637.00	9,664.00	☆	5.3	362-2863	None	4.00	0.25	None	Urs Schwytter	'92
BJB GLOBAL INCOME; B	World Income	0.1	11.15	9,625.00	☆	☆	0.0	362-2863	None	None	1.00	4.00	Urs Schwytter	'93
BJB INTL EQUITY; A	International	20.5	10.95	9,080.00	☆	☆	0.0	362-2863	None	4.00	0.25	None	Moriarty/Younes	'93/'93
BJB INTL EQUITY; B	International	0.1	10.95	9,080.00	☆	☆	0.0	362-2863	None	None	1.00	4.00	Moriarty/Younes	'93/'93
BLACKROCK GOVT INC; A	Fixed Income	73.8	9.30	9,984.00	10,135.00	☆	5.2	225-1852	None	3.00	0.10	None	Team Managed	'91
BLACKROCK GOVT INC; B	Fixed Income	4.0	9.30	9,963.00	10,028.00	☆	4.2	225-1852	None	None	1.00	1.00	Team Managed	'92
BLANCHARD PREC METALS	Gold	75.0	8.78	9,350.00	10,733.00	12,630.00	0.0	None	212-779-7979	None	0.75	None	Peter Cavelti	'88
BLANCHARD AMER EQUITY	Growth	14.0	9.06	9,597.00	9,447.00	☆	0.0	None	212-779-7979	None	0.50	None	Jeff Miller	'92
BLANCHARD EMRG MKTS	Emerging Markets	10.0	7.74	9,663.00	☆	☆	0.0	None	212-779-7979	None	0.50	None	James Fairweather	'94
BLANCHARD FLEX INCOME	Fixed Income	509.0	4.75	9,786.00	10,039.00	☆	7.6	None	212-779-7979	None	0.25	None	Jack Burks	'92
BLANCHARD GLBL GRO	Global Flexible	110.0	9.81	9,751.00	10,588.00	13,216.00	0.0	None	212-779-7979	None	0.75	None	Team Managed	'86
BLANCHARD SH-TERM BOND	Fixed Income	40.0	2.92	10,026.00	10,313.00	☆	5.6	None	212-779-7979	None	0.25	None	Jack Burks	'93
BLANCHARD SH-TM GLBL INC	World Income	507.0	1.76	9,886.00	9,934.00	☆	6.8	None	212-779-7979	None	0.25	None	McHenry/Abberly	'91/'93
BNY HAMILTON EQ INC	Equity Income	132.2	10.52	9,755.00	9,833.00	☆	2.9	426-9363	None	None	0.25	None	Robert G. Knott, Jr.	'92

BNY HAMILTON INTMDT GOVT	Fixed Income	69.1	9.35	9,828.00	9,657.00	☆	5.5	426-9363	None	None	0.25	None	Mark A. Hemenetz	'92
BOND FUND OF AMERICA	Fixed Income	5,003.2	13.19	9,856.00	9,888.00	15,443.00	8.0	421-4120	714-671-7000	4.75	0.25	None	Multiple Managers	'74
BOND PORT FOR ENDOWMENTS ◪	Fixed Income	44.6	16.62	9,849.00	9,800.00	15,504.00	7.8	421-4120	714-671-7000	None	None	None	Multiple Managers	'75
BRANDYWINE BLUE FUND	Growth	22.5	15.94	9,545.00	10,795.00	☆	0.0	338-1579	302-656-6200	None	None	None	Friess Associates	'91
BRANDYWINE FUND	Growth	1,956.3	23.44	9,399.00	10,689.00	22,260.00	0.0	338-1579	302-656-6200	None	None	None	Friess Associates	'85
BRIDGES INVESTMENT FD	Growth Income	18.2	17.36	10,051.00	10,211.00	14,951.00	3.5	None	402-397-4700	None	None	None	Edson L. Bridges II	'63
BRINSON GLOBAL	Global Flexible	266.1	10.43	9,981.00	10,077.00	☆	2.5	448-2430	312-220-7100	None	None	None	Gary P. Brinson	'92
BRINSON GLOBAL BOND	World Income	27.2	9.55	9,846.00	☆	☆	0.0	448-2430	312-220-7100	None	None	None	Brinson Partners Inc.	'93
BRINSON GLOBAL EQUITY	Global	20.9	9.49	10,193.00	☆	☆	0.0	448-2430	312-220-7100	None	None	None	Team Managed	'94
BRINSON NON-US EQUITY	International	75.1	9.69	10,189.00	☆	☆	0.0	448-2430	312-220-7100	None	None	None	Brinson Partners Inc.	'93
BRINSON US EQUITY FUND	Growth Income	6.2	9.65	10,287.00	☆	☆	0.0	448-2430	312-220-7100	None	None	None	Team Managed	'94
BROWN CAP BALANCED	Flexible	1.2	10.87	9,882.00	10,330.00	☆	0.5	525-3863	919-972-9922	4.00	0.20	None	Brown Capital Management	'92
BROWN CAP EQUITY	Capital Appreciation	0.8	11.30	9,843.00	10,440.00	☆	0.0	525-3863	919-972-9922	4.00	0.20	None	Brown Capital Management	'92
BROWN CAP SMALL COMPANY	Small Company Growth	1.8	10.04	9,392.00	9,839.00	☆	0.0	525-3863	919-972-9922	4.00	0.20	None	Brown Capital Management	'92
BRUCE FUND	Capital Appreciation	2.2	94.04	9,323.00	9,117.00	12,267.00	7.4	872-7823	312-236-9160	None	None	None	Robert Bruce	'83
BSR TR GROWTH & INCOME	Growth Income	19.6	11.94	10,006.00	10,193.00	☆	0.7	543-8721	513-629-2000	None	0.25	None	Brandon Reid	'91
BSR TR SH/INTMDT FXD INC	Fixed Income	40.3	10.22	9,924.00	10,001.00	☆	5.7	543-8721	513-629-2000	None	0.25	None	H. Dean Benner	'91
BT INSTL EQ 500 INDEX ☞	S&P Index	258.8	10.26	10,040.00	10,119.00	☆	2.4	545-1074	None	None	0.20	None	Frank Salerno	'93
BT INV CAPITAL APPREC ☞	Growth	21.5	10.71	9,378.00	10,171.00	☆	0.0	545-1074	None	None	0.20	None	Mary Lisanti	'93
BT INV CAPITAL GROWTH FD ☞	Growth	13.8	9.94	9,746.00	9,696.00	☆	1.1	545-1074	None	None	0.20	None	Paul Phillips	'92
BT INV INTL EQUITY FD ☞	International	48.5	13.25	9,672.00	11,969.00	☆	1.1	545-1074	None	None	0.20	None	Francis Ledwidge	'92
BT INV SH/INT US GOVT FD ☞	Fixed Income	14.2	9.81	10,010.00	10,171.00	☆	3.8	545-1074	None	None	0.20	None	Goodchild/Hudson	'92/'92
BT INV UTILITY FUND ☞	Utility	32.1	9.47	9,536.00	8,931.00	☆	4.4	545-1074	None	None	0.20	None	Murray Stahl	'92
BT PYRAMID INV EQ 500 ☞	S&P Index	171.8	10.20	10,040.00	10,111.00	☆	2.0	545-1074	None	None	0.20	None	Frank Salerno	'93
BT PYRAMID LTD GOVT SECS ☞	Fixed Income	22.8	9.81	10,015.00	10,200.00	☆	4.0	545-1074	None	None	0.20	None	Goodchild/Hudson	'92/'92
BULL&BEAR GOLD INVESTORS	Gold	56.2	15.71	9,368.00	9,308.00	12,096.00	0.0	847-4200	212-363-1100	None	1.00	None	Robert W. Radsch	'82
BULL&BEAR SPL EQUITIES	Capital Appreciation	49.5	17.89	8,839.00	8,034.00	11,830.00	0.0	847-4200	212-363-1100	None	1.00	None	Brett B. Sneed	'88
BULL&BEAR GLBL INC	World Income	46.6	8.25	9,585.00	9,488.00	13,661.00	8.7	847-4200	212-363-1100	None	0.50	None	C.Clifford McCarthy Jr.	'90
BULL&BEAR QUALITY GROWTH	Growth Income	4.6	13.06	9,739.00	☆	☆	0.0	847-4200	212-363-1100	None	1.00	None	Thomas B. Winmill	'93
BULL&BEAR US & OVERSEAS	Global	9.8	7.65	9,659.00	9,949.00	13,654.00	0.0	847-4200	212-363-1100	None	1.00	None	Robert W. Radsch	'87
BULL&BEAR US GOVT SEC	Fixed Income	18.0	14.63	9,825.00	9,817.00	14,318.00	4.4	847-4200	212-363-1100	None	0.25	None	C.Clifford McCarthy Jr.	'90
BURNHAM FUND; A	Growth Income	108.0	19.72	10,002.00	9,846.00	14,288.00	4.8	874-3863	212-262-3100	3.00	0.25	None	Burnham/Ferguson	'61/'75
BURNHAM FUND; B	Growth Income	0.4	19.69	10,012.00	☆	☆	0.0	874-3863	212-262-3100	None	1.00	1.25	Burnham/Ferguson	'93/'93
BURNHAM FUND; C	Growth Income	N/A	19.65	9,916.00	☆	☆	0.0	874-3863	212-262-3100	None	0.25	None	Burnham/Ferguson	'93/'93
C & O AGGRESSIVE GROWTH	Small Company Growth	23.8	12.27	10,066.00	11,043.00	☆	0.3	237-7073	404-239-0707	None	None	None	Orkin/Faulkenberry	'92/'92
CA INV TR II S&P 500	S&P Index	13.6	10.67	10,034.00	10,110.00	☆	2.7	225-8778	415-398-2727	None	None	None	Bank of America	'92
CA INV TR II S&P MIDCAP	Midcap	20.3	11.29	9,625.00	9,921.00	☆	2.0	225-8778	415-398-2727	None	None	None	Bank of America	'92
CA INV TR II US GOVT SEC	Fixed Income	31.2	10.23	9,776.00	9,714.00	15,599.00	6.7	225-8778	415-398-2727	None	None	None	Philip McClanahan	'85
CALDWELL FUND	Growth Income	4.0	N/A	N/A	N/A	N/A	0.0	338-9477	813-488-6772	None	None	None	Roland Caldwell	'85
CALDWELL GROWTH	Growth	1.6	N/A	N/A	N/A	☆	0.0	338-9477	813-488-6772	None	None	None	Roland Caldwell	'92
CALVERT FD INCOME; A	Fixed Income	47.8	15.98	9,761.00	9,614.00	14,622.00	7.4	368-2748	301-951-4820	3.75	0.25	None	Patterson/Gilkison	'82/'82
CALVERT FD US GOVT; A	Fixed Income	10.7	13.91	9,842.00	9,759.00	13,826.00	5.2	368-2748	301-951-4820	3.75	0.25	None	Van Order/Denzler	'93/'93
CALVERT SOCIAL INV BD; A	Fixed Income	61.4	15.75	9,861.00	9,853.00	14,798.00	6.2	368-2748	301-951-4820	3.75	0.35	None	Domenic Colasacco	'87
CALVERT SOCIAL INV EQ; A	Growth	82.5	19.99	9,528.00	9,614.00	13,102.00	1.4	368-2748	301-951-4820	4.75	0.35	None	Domenic Colasacco	'87
CALVERT SOCIAL INV GRO; A	Balanced	517.5	28.41	9,822.00	9,811.00	13,850.00	3.4	368-2748	301-951-4820	4.75	0.35	None	Colasacco/Trosko	'82/'86
CALVERT WRLD VAL GLBL; A	Global	122.7	17.57	9,876.00	11,871.00	☆	0.4	368-2748	301-951-4820	4.75	0.35	None	Murray Johnston Intl Ltd	'92
CALVERT-ARIEL APPREC; A	Midcap	215.8	21.70	9,963.00	10,700.00	☆	0.2	368-2748	301-951-4820	4.75	0.35	None	Eric McKissack	'89
CALVERT-ARIEL GROWTH ☒	Small Company Growth	198.1	28.41	9,941.00	10,553.00	13,819.00	1.0	368-2748	301-951-4820	4.75	0.35	None	John W. Rogers	'86
CAMBRIDGE CAP GROWTH; A	Growth	23.6	14.38	9,910.00	9,808.00	☆	0.3	382-0016	None	5.50	None	None	Cathy Dudley	'92
CAMBRIDGE CAP GROWTH; B	Growth	44.8	14.31	9,889.00	9,731.00	☆	0.0	382-0016	None	None	0.75	1.00	Cathy Dudley	'92

PERFORMANCE OF MUTUAL FUNDS *(continued)*

FUND NAME	OBJECTIVE	TOTAL NET ASSETS ($ MIL) 5/31/94	NET ASSET $ VALUE 6/30/94	PERFORMANCE (Return on initial $10,000 Investment) 3/31/94-6/30/94	6/30/93-6/30/94	6/30/89-6/30/94	DIVIDEND YIELD % 6/94	PHONE NUMBER 800	In-State	FEES Load	12b-1	Redemption	MANAGER	SINCE
CAMBRIDGE GOVT INC; A	Fixed Income	33.4	12.83	9,866.00	9,636.00	☆	6.8	382-0016	None	4.75	None	None	Gary Madich	'92
CAMBRIDGE GOVT INC; B	Fixed Income	90.2	12.85	9,852.00	9,585.00	☆	6.2	382-0016	None	None	0.50	1.00	Gary Madich	'92
CAMBRIDGE GROWTH; A	Growth	16.0	13.89	9,132.00	8,927.00	☆	0.0	382-0016	None	5.50	None	None	Lewis/Arends	'92/'93
CAMBRIDGE GROWTH; B	Growth	32.2	13.77	9,113.00	8,884.00	☆	0.0	382-0016	None	None	0.75	1.00	Lewis/Arends	'92/'93
CAMBRIDGE INC & GRO; A	Balanced	16.6	14.82	10,142.00	10,653.00	☆	1.9	382-0016	None	5.50	None	None	Kaplan/Wilmore	'93/'93
CAMBRIDGE INC & GRO; B	Balanced	41.4	14.83	10,115.00	10,577.00	☆	1.1	382-0016	None	None	0.75	1.00	Kaplan/Wilmore	'93/'93
CAMCO INTMDT TM	Fixed Income	0.1	9.95	10,034.00	10,318.00	☆	3.4	423-2345	610-832-1075	None	0.20	None	Daryl L. Hudson	'92
CAMCO SH TM	Fixed Income	0.1	10.00	10,041.00	10,211.00	☆	3.1	423-2345	610-832-1075	None	0.15	None	Daryl L. Hudson	'92
CAMCO TOTAL RETURN	Fixed Income	1.9	9.90	10,006.00	10,271.00	☆	3.1	423-2345	610-832-1075	None	0.20	None	Daryl L. Hudson	'92
CANANDAIGUA CIT BOND ✪	Fixed Income	0.4	9.95	9,891.00	9,793.00	☆	0.0	724-2621	716-394-4260	None	None	None	Gregory MacKay	'92
CANANDAIGUA CIT EQUITY ✪	Growth Income	5.4	10.66	9,972.00	10,380.00	☆	0.0	724-2621	716-394-4260	None	None	None	Robert Swartout	'92
CAPITAL EXCHANGE ⊠	Growth	89.0	163.98	9,896.00	10,357.00	16,577.00	1.5	225-6265	617-482-8260	None	None	None	Duncan Richardson	'87
CAPITAL INCOME BUILDER	Equity Income	3,333.9	31.57	9,905.00	10,315.00	17,246.00	5.1	421-4120	714-671-7000	5.75	0.30	None	Multiple Managers	'87
CAPITAL WORLD BOND	World Income	581.4	15.15	9,798.00	10,199.00	15,274.00	6.5	421-4120	714-671-7000	4.75	0.30	None	Multiple Managers	'87
CAPITAL WORLD GRO & INC	Global	2,390.5	17.18	9,913.00	11,528.00	☆	2.4	421-4120	714-671-7000	5.75	0.30	None	Multiple Managers	'93
CAPP-RUSH EMERG GRO	Small Company Growth	18.9	10.38	8,460.00	9,269.00	☆	0.0	621-7874	301-657-1517	None	None	None	Frank Cappiello	'92
CAPP-RUSH GOLD	Gold	6.6	9.52	9,093.00	☆	☆	0.0	621-7874	301-657-1517	None	None	None	Frank Cappiello	'94
CAPP-RUSH GROWTH	Growth	11.2	11.05	9,625.00	10,399.00	☆	0.0	621-7874	301-657-1517	None	None	None	Frank Cappiello	'92
CAPP-RUSH UTIL INC	Utility	9.5	8.39	9,202.00	8,182.00	☆	6.1	621-7874	301-657-1517	None	None	None	Frank Cappiello	'92
CAPSTONE FD OF SOUTHWEST	Capital Appreciation	6.2	15.04	8,894.00	8,656.00	13,606.00	0.0	262-6631	713-260-9000	4.75	0.35	None	Sharon Keith	'87
CAPSTONE GOVT INCOME FD	Fixed Income	108.8	4.80	10,021.00	10,140.00	11,605.00	2.0	262-6631	713-260-9000	None	0.20	None	Jaroski/Potter	'87/'91
CAPSTONE MED RESEARCH	Health/Biotechnology	12.9	17.11	9,386.00	10,099.00	21,548.00	0.8	262-6631	713-260-9000	4.75	0.25	None	Samuel D. Isaly	'89
CAPSTONE NEW ZEALAND	Pacific Region	3.2	10.85	9,748.00	11,343.00	☆	0.5	262-6631	713-260-9000	4.75	0.35	None	Rob Scharar	'91
CAPSTONE NIKKO JAPAN	Japanese	3.7	8.50	11,379.00	11,872.00	☆	0.0	262-6631	713-260-9000	4.75	0.35	None	Toshihiko Tsuyusaki	'91
CAPSTONE US TREND	Growth	92.3	12.46	9,564.00	9,394.00	14,111.00	1.1	262-6631	713-260-9000	4.75	0.35	None	Dan Watson	'86
CARDINAL FUND	Growth Income	254.6	12.27	9,882.00	10,178.00	15,205.00	2.5	848-7734	614-464-5511	6.00	None	None	John Schlater	'84
CARDINAL GOVT OBLIGATION	Fixed Income	180.4	8.07	9,953.00	9,955.00	14,230.00	8.1	848-7734	614-464-5511	4.50	None	None	John R. Carle	'86
CARDINAL AGGRESSIVE GRO	Capital Appreciation	9.4	8.96	9,314.00	8,990.00	☆	0.0	848-7734	614-464-5511	5.50	0.25	None	Timothy McCombs	'93
CARDINAL BALANCED FUND	Flexible	14.1	9.67	9,777.00	9,862.00	☆	1.8	848-7734	614-464-5511	5.50	0.25	None	Barry McMahon	'93
CARILLON INVST CAPITAL	Flexible	41.0	12.78	9,937.00	10,846.00	16,115.00	3.0	999-1840	513-595-2600	5.00	None	None	George L. Clucas	'88
CENTERLAND INTL EQ; ADMIN	International	47.3	15.20	9,987.00	11,786.00	14,233.00	0.0	323-9919	None	4.50	None	None	Team Managed	'87
CENTERLAND INTL EQ; CNTLD	International	278.1	15.24	9,993.00	☆	☆	0.0	323-9919	None	None	None	None	Team Managed	N/A
CENTURION GROWTH FUND	Growth	3.3	8.56	9,772.00	9,408.00	8,529.00	0.1	448-6984	614-766-6666	4.75	0.25	None	Robert Meeder, Sr.	'93
CENTURY SHARES TRUST	Financial Services	219.1	22.56	10,039.00	9,190.00	17,089.00	2.0	321-1928	617-482-3060	None	None	None	Allan W. Fulkerson	'76
CFS CALAMOS CONVERTIBLE	Convertible Securities	16.7	12.34	9,581.00	9,971.00	16,317.00	3.1	323-9943	708-245-7200	4.50	0.50	None	Calamos/Calamos	'85/'88
CFS CALAMOS GRO & INC	Convertible Securities	4.5	12.08	9,495.00	9,645.00	16,731.00	2.8	323-9943	708-245-7200	4.50	0.50	None	Calamos/Calamos	'88/'88
CFS CALAMOS GROWTH	Growth	2.1	13.94	9,949.00	10,033.00	☆	0.1	323-9943	708-245-7200	4.50	0.50	None	John Calamos	'90
CFS CALAMOS STRAT INCOME	Fixed Income	2.8	10.30	9,553.00	9,978.00	☆	3.1	323-9943	708-245-7200	4.50	0.50	None	John Calamos	'90
CG CAP MKTS BALANCED ◪	Balanced	13.5	8.17	9,948.00	10,113.00	☆	2.0	None	None	None	None	None	N/A	N/A
CG CAP MKTS INTL EQUITY ◪	International	517.8	10.40	10,277.00	12,312.00	☆	0.3	None	None	None	None	None	N/A	N/A
CG CAP MKTS INTL FXD	World Income	119.8	8.19	9,977.00	10,328.00	☆	7.9	None	None	None	None	None	N/A	N/A
CG CAP MKTS INTMDT FXD ◪	Fixed Income	216.0	7.87	9,900.00	9,921.00	☆	6.0	None	None	None	None	None	N/A	N/A
CG CAP MKTS LRG CAP GRO ◪	Growth	404.3	9.23	9,819.00	9,747.00	☆	0.0	None	None	None	None	None	N/A	N/A
CG CAP MKTS LRG CAP VAL ◪	Growth Income	752.3	8.87	10,068.00	10,108.00	☆	1.7	None	None	None	None	None	N/A	N/A
CG CAP MKTS MORTGAGE ◪	Fixed Income	117.6	7.63	9,919.00	9,859.00	☆	6.5	None	None	None	None	None	N/A	N/A

CG CAP MKTS SM CAP GRO ◪	Small Company Growth	153.5	10.99	8,935.00	10,319.00	☆	0.0	None	None	None	None	None	N/A	N/A
CG CAP MKTS SM CAP VAL ◪	Small Company Growth	299.1	8.53	9,617.00	9,331.00	☆	0.8	None	None	None	None	None	N/A	N/A
CG CAP MKTS TOT RTN FXD ◪	Fixed Income	95.8	7.82	9,790.00	9,695.00	☆	5.6	None	None	None	None	None	N/A	N/A
CGM CAP DEVELOPMENT ⊠	Growth	500.6	23.51	8,802.00	9,968.00	27,622.00	0.3	345-4048	617-859-7714	None	None	None	G. Kenneth Heebner	'76
CGM TR FIXED INCOME	Fixed Income	33.9	10.28	9,857.00	10,085.00	☆	6.7	345-4048	617-859-7714	None	None	None	Heebner/Saul	'93/'93
CGM TR MUTUAL FUND	Balanced	1,146.1	26.60	9,744.00	9,898.00	18,611.00	3.1	345-4048	617-859-7714	None	None	None	G. Kenneth Heebner	'80
CGM TR REALTY FUND	Real Estate	1.3	9.99	☆	☆	☆	0.0	345-4048	617-859-7714	None	None	None	G. Kenneth Heebner	'94
CHARTER CAP BLUE CHIP	Growth	8.5	12.90	10,023.00	10,445.00	13,790.00	0.0	None	414-257-1842	None	None	None	Toll/Mirek	'90/'93
CHESAPEAKE GROWTH FUND	Growth	134.5	12.21	9,119.00	11,067.00	☆	0.0	525-3863	919-972-9922	3.00	None	None	Gardner/Lewis Asset Mgt.	'93/'93
CHESTNUT ST EXCH LP ⊠▮lll	Growth	191.5	140.37	10,152.00	10,378.00	17,637.00	1.9	422-6538	None	None	None	None	Gayland Gee	'90
CHUBB INV GOVERNMENT SEC	Fixed Income	13.7	10.01	9,891.00	9,884.00	14,976.00	7.1	258-3648	603-226-5000	3.00	0.25	None	Ned Gerstman	'87
CHUBB INV GROWTH & INC	Growth Income	19.3	15.71	9,887.00	10,477.00	17,618.00	1.7	258-3648	603-226-5000	5.00	0.25	None	David Schafer	'93
CHUBB INV TOTAL RETURN	Balanced	17.1	14.02	9,918.00	10,352.00	17,086.00	2.8	258-3648	603-226-5000	5.00	0.25	None	O'Reilly/Schafer	'87/'93
CIGNA INSTL INTL STOCK	International	7.4	13.89	10,499.00	12,507.00	☆	0.8	528-6718	None	None	None	None	Lee Mickelburough	'94
CLIPPER FUND	Growth	248.5	47.75	10,023.00	10,228.00	15,593.00	1.5	776-5033	310-247-3940	None	None	None	Gipson/Sandler	'84/'94
CMSTOCK PRTNRS STRAT; A	Fixed Income	92.5	9.37	9,829.00	10,924.00	☆	7.8	334-6899	None	4.50	0.30	None	Team Managed	'92
CMSTOCK PRTNRS STRAT; O ⊠	Fixed Income	454.1	9.36	9,826.00	10,934.00	14,116.00	8.2	334-6899	None	4.50	None	None	Team Managed	'88
COHEN & STEERS REALTY	Real Estate	326.3	33.47	10,124.00	11,001.00	☆	4.4	437-9912	212-832-3232	None	None	None	Cohen/Steers	'91/'91
COLONIAL ADJ RATE; A	Fixed Income	17.1	9.66	9,970.00	10,110.00	☆	4.1	426-3750	617-426-3750	3.25	0.25	None	Leslie Finnemore	'92
COLONIAL ADJ RATE; B	Fixed Income	4.1	9.66	9,954.00	10,044.00	☆	3.5	426-3750	617-426-3750	None	0.90	4.00	Leslie Finnemore	'93
COLONIAL FED SEC; A	Fixed Income	1,409.2	10.20	9,840.00	9,611.00	14,428.00	7.7	426-3750	617-426-3750	4.75	0.25	None	Helen Peters	'92
COLONIAL FED SEC; B	Fixed Income	71.6	10.20	9,821.00	9,539.00	☆	6.9	426-3750	617-426-3750	None	1.00	5.00	Helen Peters	'92
COLONIAL FUND; A	Growth Income	545.4	7.81	9,857.00	10,187.00	15,490.00	2.0	426-3750	617-426-3750	5.75	0.35	None	Rie/Palmer	'93/'93
COLONIAL FUND; B	Growth Income	224.1	7.81	9,840.00	10,107.00	☆	1.1	426-3750	617-426-3750	None	1.00	5.00	Rie/Palmer	'93/'93
COLONIAL GLBL EQUITY; A	Global	8.0	11.96	9,892.00	11,709.00	☆	1.4	426-3750	617-426-3750	5.75	0.25	None	Palmer/Lanzendorf	'92/'92
COLONIAL GLBL EQUITY; B	Global	58.2	11.93	9,872.00	11,612.00	☆	0.7	426-3750	617-426-3750	None	1.00	5.00	Palmer/Lanzendorf	'92/'93
COLONIAL GROWTH; A	Growth	159.6	13.28	9,823.00	10,296.00	15,530.00	0.5	426-3750	617-426-3750	5.75	0.35	None	Rie/Lanzendorf	'86/'93
COLONIAL GROWTH; B	Growth	44.9	13.23	9,800.00	10,224.00	☆	0.0	426-3750	617-426-3750	None	1.00	5.00	Rie/Lanzendorf	'92/'93
COLONIAL HI YLD SEC; A	Fixed Income	395.4	6.61	9,936.00	10,664.00	16,933.00	9.8	426-3750	617-426-3750	4.75	0.25	None	Peters/Feingold	'93/'93
COLONIAL HI YLD SEC; B	Fixed Income	226.1	6.61	9,918.00	10,585.00	☆	9.0	426-3750	617-426-3750	None	1.00	5.00	Peters/Feingold	'92/'93
COLONIAL INCOME; A	Fixed Income	140.6	6.13	9,811.00	9,806.00	14,234.00	8.0	426-3750	617-426-3750	4.75	0.25	None	Carl C. Ericson	'91
COLONIAL INCOME; B	Fixed Income	21.0	6.13	9,792.00	9,733.00	☆	7.1	426-3750	617-426-3750	None	1.00	5.00	Carl C. Ericson	'92
COLONIAL INTL EQ INDEX	International	5.1	N/A	N/A	N/A	N/A	0.0	426-3750	617-426-3750	5.75	0.25	None	Lanzendorf/Palmer	'90/'93
COLONIAL INTL FD GRO; A	International	56.1	10.06	10,020.00	☆	☆	0.0	426-3750	617-426-3750	5.75	0.25	None	Simon Davies	'93
COLONIAL INTL FD GRO; B	International	88.1	10.02	10,000.00	☆	☆	0.0	426-3750	617-426-3750	None	1.00	5.00	Simon Davies	'93
COLONIAL NATURAL RES; A	Natural Resources	33.3	12.42	10,100.00	10,925.00	☆	0.9	426-3750	617-426-3750	5.75	0.25	None	Lanzendorf/Cordes	'93/'93
COLONIAL NATURAL RES; B	Natural Resources	13.1	12.40	10,076.00	10,836.00	☆	0.3	426-3750	617-426-3750	None	1.00	5.00	Lanzendorf/Cordes	'93/'93
COLONIAL SMALL STOCK; A	Small Company Growth	25.7	16.69	9,543.00	10,530.00	12,416.00	0.0	426-3750	617-426-3750	5.75	0.25	None	Lanzendorf/Haynie	'90/'93
COLONIAL SMALL STOCK; B	Small Company Growth	8.2	16.50	9,527.00	10,456.00	☆	0.0	426-3750	617-426-3750	None	1.00	5.00	Lanzendorf/Haynie	'92/'93
COLONIAL STRAT INC; A	Fixed Income	676.6	6.81	9,869.00	10,153.00	15,017.00	9.0	426-3750	617-426-3750	4.75	0.25	None	Carl C. Ericson	'91
COLONIAL STRAT INC; B	Fixed Income	613.9	6.81	9,851.00	10,078.00	☆	8.2	426-3750	617-426-3750	None	1.00	5.00	Carl C. Ericson	'92
COLONIAL US FD GRO; A	Growth	99.9	11.46	9,899.00	10,005.00	☆	1.2	426-3750	617-426-3750	5.75	0.25	None	State St Asset Mgt	'92
COLONIAL US FD GRO; B	Growth	151.0	11.40	9,881.00	9,929.00	☆	0.5	426-3750	617-426-3750	None	1.00	5.00	State St Asset Mgt	'92
COLONIAL US GOVT; A	Fixed Income	826.1	6.39	9,927.00	9,892.00	13,650.00	6.8	426-3750	617-426-3750	4.75	0.25	None	Leslie Finnemore	'87
COLONIAL US GOVT; B	Fixed Income	876.9	6.39	9,908.00	9,818.00	☆	6.0	426-3750	617-426-3750	None	1.00	5.00	Leslie Finnemore	'92
COLONIAL UTILITIES; A	Utility	417.0	11.71	9,565.00	8,633.00	14,507.00	5.8	426-3750	617-426-3750	4.75	0.25	None	J.E. Lennon	'92
COLONIAL UTILITIES; B	Utility	835.5	11.71	9,547.00	8,569.00	☆	4.9	426-3750	617-426-3750	None	1.00	5.00	J.E. Lennon	'92
COLUMBIA BALANCED	Balanced	228.5	17.12	9,965.00	10,182.00	☆	3.2	547-1707	503-222-3606	None	None	None	Mike Powers	'91
COLUMBIA COMMON STOCK	Growth Income	116.6	14.78	10,000.00	10,419.00	☆	1.5	547-1707	503-222-3606	None	None	None	Terry Chambers	'91
COLUMBIA FIXED INCOME	Fixed Income	261.5	12.50	9,895.00	9,831.00	15,139.00	6.4	547-1707	503-222-3606	None	None	None	Tom Thomsen	'83

PERFORMANCE OF MUTUAL FUNDS (continued)

FUND NAME	OBJECTIVE	TOTAL NET ASSETS ($ MIL) 5/31/94	NET ASSET $ VALUE 6/30/94	PERFORMANCE (Return on initial $10,000 Investment) 3/31/94-6/30/94	6/30/93-6/30/94	6/30/89-6/30/94	DIVIDEND YIELD % 6/94	PHONE NUMBER 800	In-State	FEES Load	12b-1	Redemption	MANAGER	SINCE
COLUMBIA GROWTH	Growth	584.8	24.85	9,753.00	10,194.00	17,185.00	0.7	547-1707	503-222-3606	None	None	None	Alec Macmillan	'92
COLUMBIA HIGH YIELD	Fixed Income	8.2	9.29	9,936.00	☆	☆	0.0	547-1707	503-222-3606	None	None	1.00	Tom Thomsen	'93
COLUMBIA INTL STOCK	International	115.3	13.19	10,217.00	12,587.00	☆	0.0	547-1707	503-222-3606	None	None	None	James McAlear	'92
COLUMBIA SPECIAL	Midcap	821.4	18.82	9,607.00	10,822.00	19,382.00	0.1	547-1707	503-222-3606	None	None	None	Alan Folkman	'85
COLUMBIA US GOVT SEC	Fixed Income	35.0	8.14	10,004.00	10,108.00	14,266.00	3.8	547-1707	503-222-3606	None	None	None	Tom Thomsen	'86
COMMON SENSE GOVERNMENT	Fixed Income	345.7	10.21	9,833.00	9,691.00	14,234.00	6.8	544-5445	404-381-1000	6.75	None	None	Jack Reynoldson	'88
COMMON SENSE GRO & INC	Growth Income	704.1	15.03	9,848.00	9,959.00	15,602.00	1.8	544-5445	404-381-1000	8.50	None	None	David Reichert	'90
COMMON SENSE GROWTH FUND	Growth	2,134.0	14.69	9,906.00	10,076.00	16,953.00	0.7	544-5445	404-381-1000	8.50	None	None	Stephen Boyd	'89
COMPASS CAP SMALL CAP	Small Company Growth	21.1	11.21	9,642.00	10,293.00	☆	0.7	451-8371	215-254-1000	3.75	None	None	Kenneth Fisher	'91
COMPASS CAP EQU INCOME	Equity Income	276.6	12.40	10,297.00	10,999.00	17,409.00	2.8	451-8371	215-254-1000	3.75	None	None	Wellington Mgmt. Co.	'93
COMPASS CAP FIX INCOME	Fixed Income	256.8	10.07	9,845.00	9,847.00	14,719.00	5.9	451-8371	215-254-1000	3.75	None	None	Bill Cavallos	'89
COMPASS CAP GROWTH	Growth	132.5	10.46	9,873.00	9,891.00	14,019.00	0.5	451-8371	215-254-1000	3.75	None	None	Wellington Mgmt. Co.	'93
COMPASS CAP INTL EQ	International	32.3	13.64	10,341.00	12,056.00	☆	0.2	451-8371	215-254-1000	3.75	None	None	Sir William Vincent	'91
COMPASS CAP INTL FIX INC	World Income	43.8	10.36	9,794.00	10,278.00	☆	9.6	451-8371	215-254-1000	3.75	None	None	Morgan Grenfell Asset Mgt	'91
COMPASS CAP SHT/INTMDT	Fixed Income	246.4	10.18	9,971.00	10,056.00	14,200.00	5.1	451-8371	215-254-1000	3.75	None	None	Bill Cavallos	'89
COMPOSITE BOND & STK; A	Balanced	197.5	11.26	9,921.00	9,997.00	14,267.00	3.8	543-8072	509-353-3550	4.50	0.25	None	Team Managed	'91
COMPOSITE BOND & STK; B	Balanced	1.7	11.27	9,921.00	☆	☆	0.0	543-8072	509-353-3550	None	1.00	3.00	Team Managed	'94
COMPOSITE GOVT SEC; A	Fixed Income	227.9	9.92	9,838.00	9,659.00	14,271.00	6.5	543-8072	509-353-3550	4.00	0.25	None	Team Managed	'92
COMPOSITE GOVT SEC; B	Fixed Income	0.6	9.92	9,822.00	☆	☆	0.0	543-8072	509-353-3550	None	1.00	3.00	Team Managed	'94
COMPOSITE GROWTH FD; A	Growth Income	96.6	12.01	10,037.00	10,375.00	14,226.00	1.4	543-8072	509-353-3550	4.50	0.25	None	Team Managed	'91
COMPOSITE GROWTH FD; B	Growth Income	0.4	12.00	10,017.00	☆	☆	0.0	543-8072	509-353-3550	None	1.00	3.00	Team Managed	'94
COMPOSITE INCOME FD; A	Fixed Income	96.5	8.55	9,858.00	9,781.00	14,590.00	7.0	543-8072	509-353-3550	4.00	0.25	None	Team Managed	'92
COMPOSITE INCOME FD; B	Fixed Income	0.8	8.56	9,845.00	☆	☆	0.0	543-8072	509-353-3550	None	1.00	3.00	Team Managed	'94
COMPOSITE NRTHWST 50; A	Growth	161.0	14.15	9,789.00	10,281.00	17,006.00	0.5	543-8072	509-353-3550	4.50	0.25	None	Team Managed	'88
COMPOSITE NRTHWST 50; B	Growth	0.9	14.15	9,772.00	☆	☆	0.0	543-8072	509-353-3550	None	1.00	3.00	Team Managed	'94
CONCORDE VALUE FUND	Growth Income	11.9	11.83	9,933.00	10,380.00	12,300.00	0.3	338-1579	214-387-8258	None	None.	None	Team Managed	'87
CONESTOGA EQUITY	Growth	48.8	14.14	9,886.00	10,151.00	☆	0.8	344-2716	None	4.00	None	None	Joe Stocke	'90
CONESTOGA INCOME FUND	Fixed Income	24.7	10.00	9,846.00	9,784.00	☆	4.9	344-2716	None	4.00	None	None	Dintino/Moyer	'90/'90
CONESTOGA LTD MATURITY	Fixed Income	21.9	10.36	9,955.00	9,989.00	☆	4.6	344-2716	None	4.00	None	None	Craig Moyer	'90
CONN MUTUAL GOVT ACCT	Fixed Income	73.9	10.05	9,854.00	9,728.00	14,580.00	6.6	322-2642	None	4.00	None	None	Steve Libera	'85
CONN MUTUAL GROWTH ACCT	Growth	68.8	14.39	9,804.00	10,363.00	18,658.00	1.5	322-2642	None	5.00	None	None	Peter Antos	'89
CONN MUTUAL INCOME ACCT	Fixed Income	48.1	9.40	9,975.00	10,112.00	14,342.00	7.0	322-2642	None	2.00	None	None	Steve Libera	'85
CONN MUTUAL TOT RTN ACCT	Balanced	185.9	13.70	9,867.00	10,181.00	17,085.00	3.5	322-2642	None	5.00	None	None	Peter Antos	'89
COPLEY FUND	Growth Income	77.2	19.17	9,628.00	8,916.00	14,634.00	0.0	None	508-674-8459	None	None	None	Irving Levine	'78
COREFUND BALANCED; A	Balanced	43.0	9.88	9,741.00	9,838.00	☆	3.6	355-2673	None	None	None	None	Steve Dalton	'93
COREFUND BALANCED; B	Balanced	2.3	9.89	9,734.00	9,814.00	☆	3.1	355-2673	None	4.50	0.25	None	Steve Dalton	'93
COREFUND EQUITY INDEX	S&P Index	76.1	20.54	10,073.00	10,055.00	15,539.00	2.7	355-2673	None	None	None	None	Larry Aasheim	'91
COREFUND GLOBAL BOND; A	World Income	25.2	9.06	9,619.00	☆	☆	0.0	355-2673	None	None	None	None	Pete Wilson	'93
COREFUND GLOBAL BOND; B	World Income	0.2	9.04	9,607.00	☆	☆	0.0	355-2673	None	4.50	0.25	None	Pete Wilson	'93
COREFUND GOVT INC; A	Fixed Income	9.2	9.52	9,917.00	9,822.00	☆	5.2	355-2673	None	None	None	None	Bill Lawarnie	'93
COREFUND GOVT INC; B	Fixed Income	1.6	9.51	9,902.00	9,799.00	☆	4.9	355-2673	None	4.50	0.25	None	Bill Lawarnie	'93
COREFUND GROWTH EQ; A	Growth	66.7	9.11	9,361.00	9,199.00	☆	0.5	355-2673	None	None	None	None	Tim Connors	'92
COREFUND GROWTH EQ; B	Growth	1.8	9.10	9,374.00	9,187.00	☆	0.5	355-2673	None	4.50	0.25	None	Tim Connors	'93
COREFUND INTL GROWTH; A	International	108.4	13.18	10,107.00	11,631.00	☆	0.9	355-2673	None	None	None	None	Martin Curie, Ltd.	'90
COREFUND INTL GROWTH; B	International	2.0	13.17	10,107.00	11,610.00	☆	0.8	355-2673	None	4.50	0.25	None	Martin Curie, Ltd.	'93

COREFUND INTMDT BD; A	Fixed Income	47.6	9.63	9,940.00	9,966.00	☆	4.4	355-2673	None	None	None	None	Leslie Jarrelman	'94
COREFUND INTMDT BD; B	Fixed Income	9.4	9.63	9,945.00	9,941.00	☆	4.2	355-2673	None	4.50	0.25	None	Leslie Jarrelman	'94
COREFUND VALUE EQ; A	Growth Income	21.0	12.60	9,637.00	9,865.00	☆	0.7	355-2673	None	None	None	None	Doug Pyle	'90
COREFUND VALUE EQ; B	Growth Income	5.0	12.60	9,613.00	9,831.00	☆	0.5	355-2673	None	4.50	0.25	None	Doug Pyle	'93
CORNERSTONE GROWTH ☛	Capital Appreciation	4.5	7.87	10,234.00	10,382.00	11,200.00	0.3	728-0670	404-240-0666	None	0.50	None	Cornerstone Capital	'92
CORP FUND ACCUM PROGRAM ◪	Fixed Income	95.1	19.73	9,868.00	9,716.00	14,555.00	6.0	None	609-282-2800	None	None	None	Jay Harbeck	'92
COVENANT PORTFOLIO	Growth Income	3.9	12.54	10,016.00	10,125.00	☆	0.2	275-2683	None	4.50	0.35	None	Godfried Hohenberg	'93
COWEN OPPTY; A	Small Company Growth	30.9	12.02	9,812.00	10,984.00	22,837.00	0.0	262-7116	212-495-6000	4.75	None	None	William Church	'88
COWEN INCOME+GROWTH; A	Equity Income	39.5	10.71	10,137.00	9,692.00	14,041.00	4.4	262-7116	212-495-6000	4.75	None	None	William Rechter	'86
CRABBE HUSON ASST ALLOC	Flexible	114.4	12.56	9,862.00	10,495.00	15,646.00	1.7	541-9732	503-295-0919	None	0.25	None	Richard Huson	'89
CRABBE HUSON EQUITY	Growth	79.3	15.58	9,905.00	11,057.00	19,315.00	0.5	541-9732	503-295-0919	None	0.25	None	Richard Huson	'89
CRABBE HUSON GOVT INCOME	Fixed Income	9.8	10.36	9,938.00	9,914.00	13,574.00	4.4	541-9732	503-295-0919	None	0.25	None	Jay Willoughby	'89
CRABBE HUSON INCOME	Fixed Income	5.7	9.84	9,920.00	9,874.00	13,766.00	4.6	541-9732	503-295-0919	None	0.25	None	Jay Willoughby	'89
CRABBE HUSON REAL ESTATE	Real Estate	16.8	10.30	☆	☆	☆	0.0	541-9732	503-295-0919	None	0.25	None	Jay Willoughby	'94
CRABBE HUSON SPECIAL	Midcap	79.9	12.68	9,922.00	12,165.00	23,262.00	0.0	541-9732	503-295-0919	None	0.25	None	James Crabbe	'87
CRESCENT FUND	Balanced	10.8	10.84	10,183.00	11,219.00	☆	1.2	424-2295	513-579-2210	None	None	None	Crescent Mgmt & Research	'93
CRESTFUNDS BOND; INV	Fixed Income	1.0	9.37	9,852.00	9,647.00	☆	5.4	451-5435	None	4.50	0.15	None	Boyce G. Reid	'94
CRESTFUNDS BOND; TR	Fixed Income	75.7	9.37	9,853.00	9,654.00	☆	5.6	451-5435	None	None	0.15	None	Boyce G. Reid	'92
CRESTFUNDS CAP APP; INV	Growth	1.0	9.31	9,366.00	9,749.00	☆	0.0	451-5435	None	4.50	0.15	None	David Halloran	'93
CRESTFUNDS CAP APP; TR	Growth	11.9	9.37	9,379.00	9,764.00	☆	0.0	451-5435	None	None	0.15	None	David Halloran	'93
CRESTFUNDS SH/INT; INV	Fixed Income	0.6	9.65	9,935.00	9,942.00	☆	4.9	451-5435	None	3.50	0.15	None	Boyce G. Reid	'94
CRESTFUNDS SH/INT; TR	Fixed Income	86.2	9.64	9,924.00	9,951.00	☆	5.1	451-5435	None	None	0.15	None	Boyce G. Reid	'92
CRESTFUNDS SPEC EQ; INV	Small Company Growth	2.7	10.46	9,373.00	10,017.00	☆	0.0	451-5435	None	4.50	0.15	None	Jeffery E. Markunas	'94
CRESTFUNDS SPEC EQ; TR	Small Company Growth	42.0	10.46	9,364.00	10,018.00	☆	0.1	451-5435	None	None	0.15	None	Jeffery E. Markunas	'94
CRESTFUNDS VALUE; INV	Growth Income	6.6	10.79	10,018.00	10,195.00	☆	1.2	451-5435	None	4.50	0.15	None	Jeffery E. Markunas	'93
CRESTFUNDS VALUE; TR	Growth Income	176.7	10.73	10,009.00	10,182.00	☆	1.4	451-5435	None	None	0.15	None	Jeffery E. Markunas	'92
CROWLEY GROWTH	Growth	5.0	10.24	10,020.00	10,378.00	☆	1.1	None	302-529-1717	2.00	None	None	Robert A. Crowley	'89
CROWLEY INCOME	Fixed Income	5.9	10.66	9,944.00	10,073.00	☆	6.2	None	302-529-1717	2.00	None	None	Robert A. Crowley	'89
CT&T GROWTH & INCOME	Growth Income	11.0	9.63	9,966.00	☆	☆	0.0	992-8151	None	None	0.25	None	Jerrold Stadden	'93
CT&T INTMDT FXD INC	Fixed Income	11.3	9.36	9,840.00	☆	☆	0.0	992-8151	None	None	0.25	None	Thomas Marthaler	'93
CUFUND ADJ RATE ▮ll	Fixed Income	183.5	9.95	10,058.00	10,319.00	☆	3.8	538-9683	610-989-6611	None	None	None	Emily Hollis	'92
CUFUND SHORT-TERM ▮ll	Fixed Income	41.7	9.60	9,956.00	10,018.00	☆	4.3	538-9683	610-989-6611	None	None	None	Emily Hollis	'92
CUNA US GOVT INCOME	Fixed Income	2.2	9.48	9,871.00	☆	☆	0.0	638-5660	410-547-2308	None	0.25	None	Peter Van Dyke	'93
CUTLER TR APPROVED LIST	Growth	17.1	9.78	10,061.00	9,893.00	☆	2.1	228-8537	503-770-9000	None	None	None	Kenneth R. Cutler	'92
CUTLER TR EQUITY INCOME	Equity Income	10.8	9.56	10,010.00	9,863.00	☆	2.7	228-8537	503-770-9000	None	None	None	Kenneth R. Cutler	'92
CUTLER TR GOVT SECS	Fixed Income	5.0	9.81	9,927.00	9,897.00	☆	4.7	228-8537	503-770-9000	None	None	None	Kenneth R. Cutler	'92
DEAN WITTER AMER VALUE	Growth	1,415.3	20.28	9,278.00	9,530.00	18,461.00	0.0	869-3863	212-392-2550	None	1.00	5.00	Anita Kolleeny	'87
DEAN WITTER CAP GROWTH	Growth	509.5	11.53	9,755.00	9,905.00	☆	0.0	869-3863	212-392-2550	None	1.00	5.00	Paul Vance	'90
DEAN WITTER CONVERT	Convertible Securities	194.1	10.27	9,623.00	10,372.00	13,780.00	3.7	869-3863	212-392-2550	None	1.00	5.00	Ronald Worobel	'92
DEAN WITTER DEV GRO	Small Company Growth	315.6	15.63	8,901.00	9,540.00	16,613.00	0.0	869-3863	212-392-2550	None	1.00	5.00	Ronald Worobel	'92
DEAN WITTER DIVID GRO	Growth Income	6,690.4	29.22	10,030.00	10,030.00	15,566.00	2.3	869-3863	212-392-2550	None	1.00	5.00	Paul Vance	'81
DEAN WITTER DVSD INC	Fixed Income	353.9	9.61	9,969.00	10,077.00	☆	7.8	869-3863	212-392-2550	None	0.85	5.00	Gupta/Avelar/Tran	'92/'92
DEAN WITTER EURO GROW	European Region	652.7	12.09	9,829.00	12,161.00	☆	0.0	869-3863	212-392-2550	None	1.00	5.00	Jeremy Lodwick	'94
DEAN WITTER FED SEC	Fixed Income	941.7	8.97	9,839.00	9,624.00	14,053.00	6.9	869-3863	212-392-2550	None	0.85	5.00	Rajesh Gupta	'87
DEAN WITTER GLBL DIV	Global	1,243.2	10.94	10,235.00	11,145.00	☆	0.9	869-3863	212-392-2550	None	1.00	5.00	Paul Vance	'93
DEAN WITTER GLBL SH-TM	World Income	219.3	8.77	10,040.00	9,982.00	☆	6.6	869-3863	212-392-2550	None	0.75	3.00	Vihn Tran	'90
DEAN WITTER HEALTH SCI	Health/Biotechnology	252.6	9.19	8,879.00	9,850.00	☆	0.0	869-3863	212-392-2550	None	1.00	5.00	Ronald Worobel	'92
DEAN WITTER HIGH YIELD ☒	Fixed Income	538.0	7.21	9,585.00	10,842.00	13,667.00	12.0	869-3863	212-392-2550	5.50	None	None	Peter Avelar	'90
DEAN WITTER INTMDT INC	Fixed Income	247.6	9.46	9,900.00	9,884.00	13,642.00	5.8	869-3863	212-392-2550	None	0.85	5.00	Rochelle Siegel	'89
DEAN WITTER MGD ASSETS	Flexible	282.4	10.52	10,122.00	10,386.00	15,042.00	1.9	869-3863	212-392-2550	None	1.00	5.00	Kenton Hinchliffe	'88

PERFORMANCE OF MUTUAL FUNDS *(continued)*

FUND NAME	OBJECTIVE	TOTAL NET ASSETS ($ MIL) 5/31/94	NET ASSET $ VALUE 6/30/94	PERFORMANCE (Return on initial $10,000 Investment) 3/31/94-6/30/94	6/30/93-6/30/94	6/30/89-6/30/94	DIVIDEND YIELD % 6/94	PHONE NUMBER 800	In-State	FEES Load	12b-1	Redemption	MANAGER	SINCE
DEAN WITTER NTRL RES	Natural Resources	141.8	11.18	10,329.00	10,340.00	14,086.00	0.7	869-3863	212-392-2550	None	1.00	5.00	Diane Lisa Sobin	'90
DEAN WITTER PACIFIC GR	Pacific Region	1,313.8	19.62	10,251.00	12,781.00	☆	0.0	869-3863	212-392-2550	None	1.00	5.00	Graham Bamping	'90
DEAN WITTER PREC MTLS	Gold	69.2	10.79	9,067.00	9,797.00	☆	0.0	869-3863	212-392-2550	None	1.00	5.00	Diane Lisa Sobin	'90
DEAN WITTER PREMIER INC	Fixed Income	54.7	8.79	9,978.00	9,867.00	☆	6.6	869-3863	212-392-2550	3.00	0.20	None	Scott Amero	'91
DW RET SRS AMER VALUE	Growth	4.9	9.68	9,622.00	9,642.00	☆	0.2	869-3863	212-392-2550	None	None	None	Anita Kolleeny	'93
DW RET SRS CAP GROWTH ✿	Growth	0.2	9.25	9,914.00	10,279.00	☆	0.5	869-3863	212-392-2550	None	None	None	Paul Vance	'93
DW RET SRS DIV GROWTH ✿	Growth Income	10.6	10.66	10,046.00	10,238.00	☆	2.1	869-3863	212-392-2550	None	None	None	Paul Vance	'93
DW RET SRS GLOBAL EQUITY ✿	Global	1.5	10.52	10,019.00	10,493.00	☆	0.5	869-3863	212-392-2550	None	None	None	Thomas Connelly	'93
DW RET SRS INTMDT INC ✿	Fixed Income	0.4	9.34	9,938.00	9,908.00	☆	6.4	869-3863	212-392-2550	None	None	None	Rochelle Siegel	'93
DW RET SRS STRATEGIST ✿	Flexible	1.1	9.49	9,896.00	9,667.00	☆	1.3	869-3863	212-392-2550	None	None	None	Mark Bavoso	'93
DW RET SRS US GOVT SECS ✿	Fixed Income	2.7	9.46	9,917.00	9,805.00	☆	4.5	869-3863	212-392-2550	None	None	None	Rajesh Gupta	'93
DW RET SRS UTILITIES ✿	Utility	3.0	9.96	9,852.00	9,271.00	☆	3.4	869-3863	212-392-2550	None	None	None	Edward Gaylor	'93
DW RET SRS VALUE ADDED ✿	Growth Income	5.0	10.47	9,952.00	10,568.00	☆	1.0	869-3863	212-392-2550	None	None	None	Kenton Hinchliffe	'93
DEAN WITTER SH-TM BOND	Fixed Income	45.0	9.53	10,041.00	☆	☆	0.0	869-3863	212-392-2550	None	None	None	Rochelle Siegel	'94
DEAN WITTER SH-TM TREAS	Fixed Income	516.8	9.85	9,949.00	9,964.00	☆	4.9	869-3863	212-392-2550	None	0.35	None	Rajesh Gupta	'91
DEAN WITTER STRATEGIST	Flexible	802.2	14.02	9,801.00	9,970.00	15,866.00	1.8	869-3863	212-392-2550	None	1.00	5.00	Mark Bavoso	'88
DEAN WITTER US GOVT	Fixed Income	10,430.2	8.63	9,891.00	9,725.00	13,670.00	6.9	869-3863	212-392-2550	None	0.75	5.00	Rajesh Gupta	'92
DEAN WITTER UTILITIES	Utility	3,311.1	12.53	9,629.00	9,054.00	14,441.00	4.9	869-3863	212-392-2550	None	1.00	5.00	Edward Gaylor	'88
DEAN WITTER VAL-ADD EQ	Growth Income	461.2	19.23	9,938.00	10,226.00	15,225.00	0.5	869-3863	212-392-2550	None	1.00	5.00	Kenton Hinchliffe	'93
DEAN WITTER WRLDWD INC	World Income	209.9	8.59	9,946.00	9,831.00	13,023.00	5.9	869-3863	212-392-2550	None	0.85	5.00	Vihn Tran	'89
DEAN WITTER WRLDWD INV	Global	541.6	18.08	9,945.00	11,831.00	15,529.00	0.0	869-3863	212-392-2550	None	1.00	5.00	Thomas Connelly	'83
DELAWARE DECATUR INCOME	Equity Income	1,458.1	15.93	10,229.00	10,433.00	14,018.00	4.5	523-4640	215-988-1333	5.75	None	None	J. B. Fields	'93
DELAWARE DECATUR TOT RET	Equity Income	426.1	12.47	10,244.00	10,390.00	14,919.00	3.2	523-4640	215-988-1333	5.75	0.30	None	J.B. Fields	'92
DELAWARE DELCAP; RET	Midcap	924.7	23.32	9,174.00	10,047.00	15,430.00	0.0	523-4640	215-988-1333	5.75	0.30	None	Edward N. Antoian	'86
DELAWARE DELCHESTER; RET	Fixed Income	987.9	6.61	9,891.00	10,398.00	16,136.00	11.2	523-4640	215-988-1333	4.75	0.30	None	Matlack/Nichols	'92/'92
DELAWARE FUND; RET	Balanced	469.2	17.66	9,989.00	10,228.00	15,796.00	3.3	523-4640	215-988-1333	5.75	0.30	None	Burwell/Dutton	'92/'88
DELAWARE INTL EQ; RET	International	51.9	12.07	10,126.00	11,819.00	☆	1.9	523-4640	215-988-1333	5.75	0.30	None	Clive A. Gillmore	'91
DELAWARE TREAS RSVS; RET	Fixed Income	965.4	9.27	9,885.00	9,854.00	13,988.00	7.1	523-4640	215-988-1333	3.00	0.15	None	Team Managed	'93
DELAWARE TREND; RET ★	Capital Appreciation	260.5	12.21	9,285.00	10,059.00	19,141.00	0.0	523-4640	215-988-1333	5.75	0.30	None	Edward N. Antoian	'84
DELAWARE US GOVT; RET	Fixed Income	223.8	7.94	9,736.00	9,528.00	14,031.00	9.0	523-4640	215-988-1333	4.75	0.30	None	Team Managed	'94
DELAWARE VALUE; RET	Capital Appreciation	176.8	19.65	9,752.00	10,440.00	18,091.00	0.2	523-4640	215-988-1333	5.75	0.30	None	Edward A. Trumpbour	'87
DEPOSITORS BOSTON ⊠	Growth	56.6	81.15	9,848.00	9,689.00	14,479.00	1.2	225-6265	617-482-8260	None	None	None	Thomas E. Faust, Jr.	'91
DFA GRP 1 YEAR FIXED INC ▮ll	Fixed Income	635.0	101.14	10,048.00	10,260.00	13,711.00	4.0	None	310-395-8005	None	None	None	Team Managed	'83
DFA GRP 5 YEAR GOVT ▮ll	Fixed Income	213.0	100.00	9,908.00	9,880.00	14,863.00	4.7	None	310-395-8005	None	None	None	Team Managed	'87
DFA GRP CONTL SMALL CO ▮ll	European Region	333.0	15.27	10,133.00	13,268.00	13,603.00	0.9	None	310-395-8005	None	None	None	Team Managed	'88
DFA GRP DFA/AEW RE SECS ▮ll	Real Estate	28.0	10.51	9,669.00	10,063.00	☆	2.2	None	310-395-8005	None	None	None	Team Managed	'93
DFA GRP GLOBAL FIXED INC ▮ll	World Income	125.0	97.30	9,771.00	9,903.00	☆	4.8	None	310-395-8005	None	None	None	Team Managed	'90
DFA GRP INTL HIGH BK-MKT ▮ll	International	92.0	11.74	10,510.00	12,188.00	☆	0.3	None	310-395-8005	None	None	None	Team Managed	'93
DFA GRP INTL VALUE	International	78.0	10.28	10,514.00	☆	☆	0.0	None	310-395-8005	None	None	None	David Price	'94
DFA GRP INTMDT GOVT ▮ll	Fixed Income	60.0	105.78	9,831.00	9,755.00	☆	6.6	None	310-395-8005	None	None	None	Team Managed	'90
DFA GRP JAPAN SMALL CO ▮ll	Japanese	315.0	29.47	11,387.00	11,110.00	11,389.00	0.1	None	310-395-8005	None	None	None	Team Managed	'86
DFA GRP LARGE CAP INTL ▮ll	International	48.0	12.56	10,415.00	11,230.00	☆	1.2	None	310-395-8005	None	None	None	Team Managed	'91
DFA GRP LARGE CAP VALUE ▮ll	Growth	133.0	9.93	9,879.00	9,749.00	☆	3.4	None	310-395-8005	None	None	None	Team Managed	'93
DFA GRP PAC RIM SMALL CO ▮ll	Pacific Region	182.0	16.23	9,982.00	12,440.00	☆	0.7	None	310-395-8005	None	None	None	Team Managed	'93
DFA GRP SMALL CAP VALUE ▮ll	Small Company Growth	225.0	11.28	9,912.00	11,447.00	☆	1.1	None	310-395-8005	None	None	None	Team Managed	'93

DFA GRP UK SMALL COMPANY ▮lll	European Region	209.0	23.23	9,732.00	11,308.00	11,740.00	1.8	None	310-395-8005	None	None	None	Team Managed	'86
DFA GRP US 6-10 SMALL CO ▮lll	Small Company Growth	128.0	10.98	9,674.00	10,306.00	☆	2.3	None	310-395-8005	None	None	None	Team Managed	'92
DFA GRP US 9-10 SMALL CO ▮lll	Small Company Growth	659.0	8.17	9,784.00	11,261.00	16,282.00	0.2	None	310-395-8005	None	None	None	Team Managed	'81
DFA GRP US LARGE CO ▮lll	Growth	43.0	13.33	10,043.00	10,127.00	☆	2.5	None	310-395-8005	None	None	None	Team Managed	'90
DG INV EQUITY	Growth	259.8	10.15	9,844.00	10,097.00	☆	1.4	344-2488	None	2.00	None	None	Ron Lindquist	'92
DG INV GOVT INCOME	Fixed Income	141.6	9.40	9,867.00	9,836.00	☆	5.6	344-2488	None	2.00	None	None	John Mark McKenzie	'92
DG INV LTD TM GOVT INC	Fixed Income	114.5	9.64	9,987.00	10,102.00	☆	5.1	344-2488	None	2.00	None	None	John Mark McKenzie	'92
DIAZ-VERSON AMERICAS EQ	Global	6.0	10.92	9,294.00	11,495.00	☆	0.0	343-5133	None	4.50	0.50	None	Salvador Diaz-Verson	'93
DIVERSIFICATION FUND ⊠	Growth	69.2	163.47	9,775.00	9,822.00	15,058.00	1.2	225-6265	617-482-8260	None	None	None	Robert S. Goodof	'87
DODGE & COX BALANCED	Balanced	629.6	44.85	9,991.00	10,301.00	16,878.00	3.7	None	415-434-0311	None	None	None	Team Managed	'31
DODGE & COX INCOME	Fixed Income	195.5	11.01	9,849.00	9,900.00	15,220.00	6.8	None	415-434-0311	None	None	None	Team Managed	'89
DODGE & COX STOCK	Growth Income	485.1	52.38	10,067.00	10,470.00	17,014.00	2.0	None	415-434-0311	None	None	None	Team Managed	'65
DOMINI SOCIAL EQUITY	Growth	30.3	11.82	9,963.00	10,022.00	☆	1.3	762-6814	None	None	0.25	None	Amy Domini	'91
DOMINION INSIGHT GROWTH	Growth	6.9	10.24	9,209.00	9,386.00	☆	0.0	880-1095	214-385-9595	3.50	None	None	Jim Collins	'92
DREMAN CONTRARIAN PORT	Growth Income	17.6	13.42	10,204.00	10,444.00	15,389.00	1.9	533-1608	201-332-8228	None	None	None	David N. Dreman	'88
DREMAN FIXED INCOME PORT	Fixed Income	4.8	9.66	9,959.00	10,012.00	14,051.00	5.5	533-1608	201-332-8228	None	None	None	William F Coughlin	'88
DREMAN HIGH RETURN PORT	Equity Income	30.7	15.54	10,203.00	10,530.00	18,969.00	1.5	533-1608	201-332-8228	None	None	None	David N. Dreman	'88
DREMAN SMALL CAP VALUE	Small Company Growth	5.3	10.80	10,218.00	10,398.00	☆	0.3	533-1608	201-332-8228	None	None	None	Holmes/Schuss	'93/'94
DREY-WILSH LG CO GRO	Growth	8.1	12.26	9,871.00	9,864.00	☆	1.9	373-9387	516-338-3300	None	None	1.00	Wilshire Associates Inc.	'92
DREY-WILSH LG CO VAL	Growth	12.5	13.30	9,970.00	9,600.00	☆	2.6	373-9387	516-338-3300	None	None	1.00	Wilshire Associates Inc.	'92
DREY-WILSH SM CO GRO	Small Company Growth	8.4	13.83	9,159.00	9,911.00	☆	0.5	373-9387	516-338-3300	None	None	1.00	Wilshire Associates Inc.	'92
DREY-WILSH SM CO VAL	Small Company Growth	23.9	13.75	10,000.00	9,957.00	☆	2.4	373-9387	516-338-3300	None	None	1.00	Wilshire Associates Inc.	'92
DREYFUS 100% TREA INT LP	Fixed Income	219.6	12.67	9,930.00	9,864.00	14,996.00	7.4	373-9387	516-338-3300	None	None	None	Barbara Kenworthy	'87
DREYFUS 100% TREA LNG LP	Fixed Income	157.2	14.07	9,817.00	9,684.00	15,389.00	7.3	373-9387	516-338-3300	None	None	None	Barbara Kenworthy	'87
DREYFUS 100% TREA SHT LP	Fixed Income	179.5	15.05	9,999.00	10,145.00	14,215.00	8.1	373-9387	516-338-3300	None	None	None	Barbara Kenworthy	'87
DREYFUS A BONDS PLUS	Fixed Income	565.8	13.84	9,791.00	9,796.00	14,986.00	6.8	373-9387	516-338-3300	None	None	None	Barbara Kenworthy	'85
DREYFUS APPRECIATION FD	Growth	224.0	14.21	10,050.00	10,119.00	15,232.00	1.7	373-9387	516-338-3300	None	0.20	None	Fayez Sarofim & Co.	'90
DREYFUS ASSET ALLOC; C	Flexible	51.9	12.44	10,048.00	☆	☆	1.0	373-9387	516-338-3300	None	0.50	None	Howard Stein	'93
DREYFUS BALANCED	Balanced	73.7	13.21	10,139.00	10,521.00	☆	3.1	373-9387	516-338-3300	None	None	None	Dreyfus Mgt. Inc.	'92
DREYFUS CAP VALUE; A	Capital Appreciation	424.9	11.73	9,686.00	10,083.00	11,049.00	2.1	373-9387	516-338-3300	4.50	None	None	Comstock Partners	'87
DREYFUS CAP VALUE; B	Capital Appreciation	94.4	11.56	9,657.00	9,994.00	☆	2.0	373-9387	516-338-3300	None	0.75	4.00	Comstock Partners	'93
DREYFUS CAPITAL GROWTH	Capital Appreciation	585.8	15.09	9,655.00	10,138.00	15,851.00	4.9	373-9387	516-338-3300	3.00	None	None	Howard Stein	'69
DREYFUS EDISON ELEC INDX	Utility	84.1	11.10	9,168.00	8,087.00	☆	5.9	373-9387	516-338-3300	None	None	None	Wells Fargo Nikko Adv.	'91
DREYFUS FOCUS LG CO GR	Growth	5.0	11.87	10,025.00	☆	☆	0.0	373-9387	516-338-3300	None	0.50	None	Howard Stein	'93
DREYFUS FOCUS LG CO VAL	Growth	5.1	12.15	9,975.00	☆	☆	0.0	373-9387	516-338-3300	None	0.50	None	Howard Stein	'93
DREYFUS FOCUS SM CO GR	Small Company Growth	4.7	11.47	9,671.00	☆	☆	0.0	373-9387	516-338-3300	None	0.50	None	Howard Stein	'93
DREYFUS FOCUS SM CO VAL	Small Company Growth	5.1	12.15	9,728.00	☆	☆	0.0	373-9387	516-338-3300	None	0.50	None	Howard Stein	'93
DREYFUS FUND	Growth Income	2,670.4	12.28	9,771.00	10,083.00	14,507.00	2.4	373-9387	516-338-3300	None	None	None	Wolodymyr Wronskyj	'86
DREYFUS GLOBAL BOND	World Income	10.7	12.19	9,895.00	☆	☆	0.0	373-9387	516-338-3300	None	0.25	None	Theodora Zemek	'94
DREYFUS GLOBAL GROWTH	Global Flexible	153.1	33.61	9,923.00	10,807.00	15,735.00	0.0	373-9387	516-338-3300	3.00	0.25	None	Stein/McDermott	'93/'93
DREYFUS GNMA	Fixed Income	1,580.8	14.32	9,942.00	9,894.00	14,562.00	6.8	373-9387	516-338-3300	None	0.20	None	Garitt Kono	'93
DREYFUS GRO OPPORTUNITY	Growth	413.1	10.03	9,892.00	9,946.00	13,499.00	0.0	373-9387	516-338-3300	None	None	None	Earnest Wiggins	'93
DREYFUS GROWTH & INCOME	Growth Income	1,658.4	15.97	9,711.00	10,560.00	☆	2.2	373-9387	516-338-3300	None	None	None	Richard Hoey	'92
DREYFUS INSTL SH TREAS; A	Fixed Income	47.6	1.97	10,124.00	☆	☆	0.0	373-9387	516-338-3300	None	None	None	Barbara Kenilworthy	'93
DREYFUS INSTL SH TREAS; B	Fixed Income	27.6	1.98	10,118.00	☆	☆	0.0	373-9387	516-338-3300	None	0.25	None	Barbara Kenilworthy	'93
DREYFUS INTL EQUITY	International	181.6	14.92	9,933.00	11,866.00	☆	0.4	373-9387	516-338-3300	None	0.50	None	M&G Investment Ltd	'93
DREYFUS INVSTRS GNMA FD	Fixed Income	45.6	14.57	9,995.00	10,024.00	14,593.00	7.4	373-9387	516-338-3300	None	None	None	Garitt Kono	'93
DREYFUS NEW LEADERS	Small Company Growth	358.2	32.95	9,913.00	10,750.00	17,931.00	0.2	373-9387	516-338-3300	None	0.25	1.00	Thomas Frank	'85
DREYFUS PREM GL INV; A	Global	76.9	15.32	10,000.00	11,089.00	☆	0.5	373-9387	516-338-3300	4.50	None	None	Stein/McDermott	'93/'93
DREYFUS PREM GL INV; B	Global	72.2	15.17	9,980.00	10,991.00	☆	0.3	373-9387	516-338-3300	None	0.75	4.00	Stein/McDermott	'93/'93

★ DELAWARE TREND; RET--Fund has been reclassified from Midcap to Capital Appreciation.

PERFORMANCE OF MUTUAL FUNDS *(continued)*

FUND NAME	OBJECTIVE	TOTAL NET ASSETS ($ MIL) 5/31/94	NET ASSET $ VALUE 6/30/94	PERFORMANCE (Return on initial $10,000 Investment) 3/31/94-6/30/94	6/30/93-6/30/94	6/30/89-6/30/94	DIVIDEND YIELD % 6/94	PHONE NUMBER 800	In-State	FEES Load	12b-1	Redemption	MANAGER	SINCE
DREYFUS PREM GNMA; A	Fixed Income	175.6	13.99	9,954.00	9,912.00	14,994.00	6.2	373-9387	516-338-3300	4.50	None	None	Garitt Kono	'93
DREYFUS PREM GNMA; B	Fixed Income	33.8	14.00	9,940.00	9,855.00	☆	5.6	373-9387	516-338-3300	None	0.50	3.00	Garitt Kono	'93
DREYFUS PREM GROWTH; A	Global	7.1	13.03	10,023.00	☆	☆	0.0	373-9387	516-338-3300	4.50	None	None	Fayez Sarofim & Co.	'93
DREYFUS PREM GROWTH; B	Global	8.0	12.94	10,008.00	☆	☆	0.0	373-9387	516-338-3300	None	0.75	4.00	Fayez Sarofim & Co.	'93
DREYFUS SHT-INTMDT GOVT	Fixed Income	521.1	10.88	9,993.00	10,101.00	14,823.00	7.1	373-9387	516-338-3300	None	None	None	Barbara Kenworthy	'87
DREYFUS SHT-TERM INCOME	Fixed Income	282.1	11.90	9,987.00	10,214.00	☆	7.1	373-9387	516-338-3300	None	0.20	None	Barbara Kenworthy	'92
DREYFUS STRAT GROWTH LP	Flexible	63.9	41.68	10,576.00	12,680.00	15,357.00	0.0	373-9387	516-338-3300	3.00	0.25	None	Howard Stein	'93
DREYFUS STRAT INCOME	Fixed Income	348.9	13.24	9,744.00	9,733.00	15,192.00	7.3	373-9387	516-338-3300	3.00	0.25	None	Barbara Kenworthy	'86
DREYFUS STRAT INVEST; A	Flexible	257.3	19.26	9,506.00	9,812.00	15,667.00	0.6	373-9387	516-338-3300	4.50	None	None	Richard C. Shields	'90
DREYFUS STRAT INVEST; B	Flexible	40.1	19.06	9,487.00	9,734.00	☆	0.5	373-9387	516-338-3300	None	0.75	4.00	Richard C. Shields	'93
DREYFUS THIRD CENTURY	Growth	390.4	7.58	9,475.00	9,671.00	15,281.00	0.5	373-9387	516-338-3300	None	None	None	Diane Coffey	'90
DUPREE INTMDT GOVT BOND	Fixed Income	8.4	9.65	9,625.00	9,667.00	☆	6.5	866-0614	606-254-7741	None	None	None	Bill Griggs	'92
EAGLE GROWTH SHARES	Growth	2.4	11.27	9,463.00	9,096.00	10,399.00	0.0	749-9933	407-395-2155	8.50	None	None	Donald Baxter	'87
EBI FDS EQUITY	Growth Income	79.2	57.74	10,032.00	10,355.00	15,525.00	0.6	972-9030	404-892-0666	None	1.00	None	Michael Harhai	'93
EBI FDS FLEX	Flexible	253.1	51.91	10,077.00	10,208.00	14,999.00	2.1	972-9030	404-892-0666	None	1.00	None	Edward Mitchell	'88
EBI FDS INCOME	Fixed Income	32.8	46.23	9,924.00	9,904.00	13,738.00	5.1	972-9030	404-892-0666	None	1.00	None	James Baker	'93
EBI FDS MULTIFLEX	Flexible	80.8	38.92	9,989.00	☆	☆	0.0	972-9030	404-892-0666	None	1.00	None	Kevin Means	'93
ECLIPSE BALANCED	Balanced	25.9	17.78	9,792.00	10,172.00	15,935.00	3.4	872-2710	404-631-0414	None	None	None	Wesley G. McCain	'89
ECLIPSE EQUITY FUND	Small Company Growth	193.6	12.34	9,384.00	10,317.00	14,947.00	0.6	872-2710	404-631-0414	None	None	None	Wesley G. McCain	'87
EHRENKRANTZ GROWTH	Growth	6.2	5.41	9,927.00	10,550.00	13,547.00	0.6	424-8570	212-407-0591	None	None	None	Ehrenkrantz/King/Nussbaum	'87/'87
ELFUN DIVERSIFIED FUND ◪	Balanced	56.3	13.62	10,007.00	10,195.00	15,334.00	3.4	242-0134	203-326-4040	None	None	None	MacDougall/Carlson	'88/'88
ELFUN GLOBAL FUND ◪	Global	112.6	16.47	9,940.00	12,059.00	17,318.00	0.7	242-0134	203-326-4040	None	None	None	Ralph R. Layman	'91
ELFUN INCOME FUND ◪	Fixed Income	188.6	10.96	9,908.00	9,921.00	14,902.00	6.3	242-0134	203-326-4040	None	None	None	Robert A. MacDougall	'84
ELFUN TRUSTS ◪	Growth	917.7	32.56	10,115.00	10,364.00	15,947.00	2.4	242-0134	203-326-4040	None	None	None	David Carlson	'88
ELITE GROUP GROWTH & INC	Growth Income	22.2	14.41	9,959.00	10,817.00	16,449.00	0.7	423-1068	206-624-5863	None	None	None	Richard McCormick	'87
ELITE GROUP INCOME	Fixed Income	11.9	9.64	9,889.00	9,911.00	13,888.00	6.1	423-1068	206-624-5863	None	None	None	William Church	'93
EMERALD EQUITY; A	Growth	23.7	10.93	9,714.00	9,757.00	☆	1.0	637-6336	None	4.50	0.25	None	Russell Creighton	'93
EMERALD EQUITY; B	Growth	1.1	10.91	9,694.00	☆	☆	0.0	637-6336	None	None	1.00	4.50	Russell Creighton	'94
EMERALD EQUITY; INSTL	Growth	214.6	10.96	9,729.00	☆	☆	0.0	637-6336	None	None	None	None	Russell Creighton	'94
EMERALD GOVT SECS; A	Fixed Income	53.1	10.00	9,868.00	9,905.00	☆	6.3	637-6336	None	4.50	0.25	None	Andrew Cantor	'91
EMERALD GOVT SECS; B	Fixed Income	1.0	10.01	9,859.00	☆	☆	0.0	637-6336	None	None	1.00	4.50	Andrew Cantor	'94
EMERALD GOVT SECS; INSTL	Fixed Income	72.9	10.00	9,884.00	☆	☆	0.0	637-6336	None	None	None	None	Andrew Cantor	'94
EMERALD SMALL CAP; A	Small Company Growth	1.0	8.92	9,074.00	☆	☆	0.0	637-6336	None	4.50	0.25	None	Dean McQuiddy	'94
EMERALD SMALL CAP; B	Small Company Growth	1.1	8.87	9,042.00	☆	☆	0.0	637-6336	None	None	1.00	4.50	Dean McQuiddy	'94
EMERALD SMALL CAP; INSTL	Small Company Growth	46.7	8.91	9,073.00	☆	☆	0.0	637-6336	None	None	None	None	Dean McQuiddy	'94
ENDOWMENTS INC ◪	Growth Income	53.1	16.68	10,158.00	10,093.00	16,014.00	3.8	421-4120	714-671-7000	None	None	None	Multiple Managers	'75
ENTERPRISE CAPITAL APPR	Capital Appreciation	100.3	28.74	9,664.00	9,846.00	18,888.00	0.0	432-4320	404-396-8118	4.75	0.45	None	Jeff Miller	'87
ENTERPRISE GOVT SEC	Fixed Income	101.5	11.04	9,484.00	9,547.00	14,211.00	8.0	432-4320	404-396-8118	4.75	0.45	None	Barach/Gundlach	'92/'92
ENTERPRISE GROWTH	Growth	88.9	7.75	9,580.00	10,769.00	16,652.00	0.1	432-4320	404-396-8118	4.75	0.45	None	Ron Canakaris	'80
ENTERPRISE GROWTH & INC	Growth Income	51.1	17.37	10,152.00	10,352.00	14,531.00	2.3	432-4320	404-396-8118	4.75	0.45	None	John Rock	'87
ENTERPRISE HIGH YLD BOND	Fixed Income	42.8	11.09	9,984.00	10,465.00	15,079.00	8.5	432-4320	404-396-8118	4.75	0.45	None	Jim Caywood	'87
ENTERPRISE INTL GROWTH	International	26.5	17.00	10,113.00	11,912.00	14,535.00	2.3	432-4320	404-396-8118	4.75	0.45	None	Thomas Maier	'92
ENTERPRISE SMALL COMPANY	Small Company Growth	18.7	5.15	9,626.00	☆	☆	0.0	432-4320	404-396-8118	4.75	0.45	None	Kenneth Fisher	'93
EUROPACIFIC GROWTH	International	6,968.4	21.01	9,902.00	12,076.00	19,084.00	1.0	421-4120	714-671-7000	5.75	0.25	None	Multiple Managers	'84
EV CLASSIC GOVT OBLIG ★	Fixed Income	N/A	9.31	9,867.00	☆	☆	0.0	225-6265	617-482-8260	None	1.00	None	Su Schiff	'93

EV CLASSIC INVESTORS ★	Balanced	N/A	9.58	9,851.00	☆	☆	0.0	225-6265	617-482-8260	None	1.00	None	Thomas E. Faust, Jr.	'93
EV CLASSIC TOTAL RETURN ★	Utility	N/A	8.51	9,358.00	☆	☆	0.0	225-6265	617-482-8260	None	1.00	None	Bragdon/Martin	'93/'93
EATON VANCE EQUITY-INC	Equity Income	36.3	10.20	9,640.00	9,128.00	11,698.00	4.2	225-6265	617-482-8260	None	1.00	6.00	Edwin W. Bragdon	'87
EATON VANCE GOVT SH TREA ★	Fixed Income	N/A	56.37	10,077.00	10,258.00	☆	0.0	225-6265	617-482-8260	None	0.25	None	Michael Terry	'91
EATON VANCE GROWTH	Growth	126.8	7.41	9,724.00	9,682.00	14,074.00	0.8	225-6265	617-482-8260	4.75	0.25	None	Peter Kiely	'90
EATON VANCE HIGH INC	Fixed Income	415.6	7.24	9,953.00	10,535.00	15,018.00	10.4	225-6265	617-482-8260	None	1.00	6.00	Hooker Talcott Jr.	'86
EATON VANCE INC OF BOSTN	Fixed Income	105.4	8.17	9,982.00	10,641.00	16,512.00	10.8	225-6265	617-482-8260	4.75	0.25	None	Hooker Talcott Jr.	'86
EATON VANCE INV GLBL	World Income	296.5	8.33	9,841.00	9,631.00	☆	7.7	225-6265	617-482-8260	None	1.00	3.00	Mark S. Venezia	'90
EV MRTHN GOVT OBLIG ★	Fixed Income	N/A	9.30	9,872.00	☆	☆	0.0	225-6265	617-482-8260	None	1.00	6.00	Su Schiff	'93
EV MRTHN GREATER CHINA ★	Pacific Region	N/A	11.48	9,948.00	11,640.00	☆	0.0	225-6265	617-482-8260	None	0.75	6.00	Robert Lloyd George, Mgt	'93
EV MRTHN INVESTORS ★	Balanced	N/A	9.45	9,845.00	☆	☆	0.0	225-6265	617-482-8260	None	0.75	6.00	Thomas E. Faust, Jr.	'93
EV MRTHN TOTAL RETURN ★	Utility	N/A	8.51	9,470.00	☆	☆	0.0	225-6265	617-482-8260	None	0.75	6.00	Bragdon/Martin	'93/'93
EATON VANCE NTRL RES	Natural Resources	10.7	13.42	10,190.00	10,395.00	14,151.00	0.0	225-6265	617-482-8260	None	1.00	6.00	Thomas E. Faust, Jr.	'90
EATON VANCE SPL EQUITIES	Growth	68.0	7.14	9,213.00	9,050.00	15,564.00	0.0	225-6265	617-482-8260	4.75	0.25	None	Clifford Krauss	'87
EATON VANCE STOCK FUND	Growth Income	94.3	11.94	10,001.00	10,129.00	15,072.00	2.0	225-6265	617-482-8260	4.75	0.25	None	Duncan Richardson	'94
EV TRAD CHINA GRO ★	Pacific Region	N/A	13.70	9,956.00	11,846.00	☆	0.0	225-6265	617-482-8260	4.75	0.50	None	Robert Lloyd George, Mgt	'92
EV TRAD GOVT OBLIG	Fixed Income	467.6	10.75	9,894.00	9,987.00	14,754.00	8.4	225-6265	617-482-8260	4.75	0.25	None	Su Schiff	'84
EV TRAD INVESTORS	Balanced	211.2	6.74	9,859.00	10,170.00	15,150.00	4.2	225-6265	617-482-8260	4.75	0.25	None	Thomas E. Faust, Jr.	'93
EV TRAD TOTAL RETURN	Utility	524.4	7.80	9,480.00	8,529.00	14,707.00	5.3	225-6265	617-482-8260	4.75	0.25	None	Edwin W. Bragdon	'81
EVERGREEN AMERICAN RET	Balanced	39.6	11.02	9,982.00	10,123.00	15,251.00	5.4	235-0064	914-694-2020	None	None	None	Irene O'Neill	'88
EVERGREEN FOUNDATION	Balanced	288.4	12.47	9,992.00	10,255.00	☆	2.4	235-0064	914-694-2020	None	None	None	Stephen Lieber	'90
EVERGREEN FUND	Growth	555.3	13.95	10,036.00	10,462.00	14,255.00	0.6	235-0064	914-694-2020	None	None	None	Stephen Lieber	'71
EVERGREEN FXD GOVT SECS	Fixed Income	8.9	9.00	9,787.00	9,599.00	☆	6.7	235-0064	914-694-2020	None	None	None	James Colby III	'93
EVERGREEN GLBL REAL EST	Real Estate	141.8	13.33	9,556.00	11,444.00	14,827.00	0.0	235-0064	914-694-2020	None	None	None	Sam Lieber	'89
EVERGREEN LIMITED MKT	Small Company Growth	93.6	20.55	9,712.00	10,454.00	16,190.00	0.0	235-0064	914-694-2020	None	None	None	Lieber/Wenger	'83/'93
EVERGREEN RET SM CAP EQ	Small Company Growth	2.5	9.74	9,886.00	☆	☆	0.0	235-0064	914-694-2020	None	None	None	Nola M. Falcone	'93
EVERGREEN TAX STRT FOUND	Balanced	7.4	10.15	10,156.00	☆	☆	0.0	235-0064	914-694-2020	None	None	None	Lieber/Colby	'93/'93
EVERGREEN TOTAL RETURN	Equity Income	1,055.7	17.83	9,925.00	9,632.00	13,741.00	5.9	235-0064	914-694-2020	None	None	None	Nola M. Falcone	'78
EVERGREEN US REAL ESTATE	Real Estate	8.3	10.07	9,281.00	☆	☆	0.0	235-0064	914-694-2020	None	None	None	Sam Lieber	'93
EVERGREEN VALUE TIMING	Growth Income	62.6	14.91	10,102.00	10,398.00	16,731.00	0.9	235-0064	914-694-2020	None	None	None	Edmund Nicklin	'86
EXCEL MIDAS GOLD SHARES	Gold	8.5	3.78	9,043.00	10,663.00	16,648.00	0.0	783-3444	619-485-9400	4.50	0.25	None	Kgeld Thygesen	'92
EXCEL VALUE FUND	Growth	0.6	3.79	9,499.00	7,996.00	7,080.00	0.0	783-3444	619-485-9400	4.50	0.25	None	Jack Heilbron	'91
EXCHANGE FUND BOSTON ⊠	Growth	64.5	191.79	9,771.00	9,914.00	13,972.00	1.4	225-6265	617-482-8260	None	None	None	Thomas E. Faust, Jr.	'91
EXECUTIVE INV BLUE CHIP	Growth Income	1.0	13.64	10,000.00	10,239.00	☆	1.6	423-4026	212-858-8000	4.75	0.50	None	Denise Burns	'90
EXECUTIVE INV HIGH YIELD	Fixed Income	14.8	7.39	9,878.00	10,425.00	14,729.00	10.2	423-4026	212-858-8000	4.75	0.50	None	George Ganter	'89
EXETER EQUITY TRUST	Growth	11.5	9.75	9,752.00	9,386.00	☆	1.1	525-3863	919-972-9922	4.75	0.25	None	Branch Cabell & Co	'91
EXETER FIXED INC TRUST	Fixed Income	1.7	9.46	9,846.00	9,848.00	☆	6.0	525-3863	919-972-9922	3.75	0.25	None	Richmond Capital Mgt.	'92
FAHNESTOCK HUD CAP APPRE	Growth	17.3	12.34	9,507.00	10,286.00	☆	0.0	221-5588	None	4.50	0.50	None	Howard Shawn	'91
FAIRMONT FUND	Capital Appreciation	21.5	24.03	10,174.00	12,003.00	15,574.00	0.0	262-9936	502-636-5633	None	None	None	Morton H. Sachs	'81
FAM VALUE	Growth Income	195.3	19.84	10,122.00	9,945.00	17,446.00	0.5	932-3271	518-234-7400	None	None	None	Thomas Putnam	'87
FASCIANO FUND	Midcap	16.9	17.34	9,994.00	10,331.00	15,944.00	0.0	848-6050	312-444-6050	None	None	None	Michael Fasciano	'88
FBL SERIES BLUE CHIP	Growth Income	6.5	18.04	10,061.00	10,265.00	15,580.00	0.8	247-4170	515-225-5586	None	0.50	5.00	Team Managed	'87
FBL SERIES GRO COM STK	Growth Income	63.2	13.03	9,871.00	10,289.00	17,542.00	4.4	247-4170	515-225-5586	None	0.50	5.00	Roger Grefe	'86
FBL SERIES HI GRADE BD	Fixed Income	7.4	10.00	9,867.00	10,105.00	14,708.00	6.5	247-4170	515-225-5586	None	0.50	5.00	Bob Rummelhart	'87
FBL SERIES HI YLD BD	Fixed Income	6.2	10.02	9,950.00	10,194.00	16,143.00	7.8	247-4170	515-225-5586	None	0.50	5.00	Bob Rummelhart	'87
FBL SERIES MANAGED	Flexible	18.1	11.63	9,874.00	10,021.00	15,986.00	4.0	247-4170	515-225-5586	None	0.50	5.00	Roger Grefe	'87
FBP CONTRARIAN BALANCED	Balanced	22.8	12.12	10,004.00	10,324.00	☆	2.6	543-8721	513-629-2000	None	None	None	Flippin Bruce & Porter	'89
FBP CONTRARIAN EQUITY	Growth	3.4	10.15	10,079.00	☆	☆	0.0	543-8721	513-629-2000	None	None	None	Flippin Bruce & Porter	'93
FEDERATED ARMS; INSTL	Fixed Income	1,630.2	9.65	9,943.00	10,132.00	13,870.00	4.6	245-4770	412-288-1900	None	None	None	Gary Madich	'87
FEDERATED ARMS; INT SV	Fixed Income	348.7	9.65	9,937.00	10,104.00	☆	4.3	245-4770	412-288-1900	None	0.25	None	Gary Madich	'92

★ EATON VANCE FUNDS--Fund does not disclose total net assets.

PERFORMANCE OF MUTUAL FUNDS (continued)

FUND NAME	OBJECTIVE	TOTAL NET ASSETS ($ MIL) 5/31/94	NET ASSET $ VALUE 6/30/94	PERFORMANCE (Return on initial $10,000 Investment) 3/31/94-6/30/94	6/30/93-6/30/94	6/30/89-6/30/94	DIVIDEND YIELD % 6/94	PHONE NUMBER 800	In-State	FEES Load	12b-1	Redemption	MANAGER	SINCE
FEDERATED EXCHANGE ⊠	Growth	86.0	69.90	10,098.00	10,115.00	15,723.00	1.2	245-4770	412-288-1900	None	None	None	Peter R. Anderson	'89
FEDERATED GNMA; INSTL	Fixed Income	1,697.6	10.78	9,926.00	9,780.00	14,617.00	7.5	245-4770	412-288-1900	None	None	None	Gary Madich	'87
FEDERATED GNMA; INT SV	Fixed Income	131.9	10.78	9,920.00	9,757.00	☆	7.3	245-4770	412-288-1900	None	0.25	None	Gary Madich	'92
FEDERATED GROWTH TRUST	Growth	427.4	21.05	9,454.00	9,414.00	14,399.00	0.8	245-4770	412-288-1900	None	None	None	Gregory M. Melvin	'87
FEDERATED HIGH YIELD TR	Fixed Income	332.9	8.80	10,003.00	10,338.00	16,625.00	9.6	245-4770	412-288-1900	None	None	None	Mark E. Durbiano	'84
FEDRTD IDX MAX; INSTL	S&P Index	428.0	11.28	10,036.00	10,104.00	☆	2.7	245-4770	412-288-1900	None	None	None	Peter R. Anderson	'90
FEDRTD IDX MAX; INSTL SVC	S&P Index	4.5	11.29	10,036.00	☆	☆	0.0	245-4770	412-288-1900	None	0.30	None	Peter R. Anderson	'93
FEDRTD IDX MID-CAP	Midcap	31.0	10.28	9,605.00	9,851.00	☆	1.9	245-4770	412-288-1900	None	None	None	Peter R. Anderson	'92
FEDRTD IDX MINI-CAP	Small Company Growth	87.5	10.99	9,619.00	10,307.00	☆	1.0	245-4770	412-288-1900	None	None	None	Peter R. Anderson	'92
FEDERATED INC; INSTL	Fixed Income	1,524.2	9.89	9,908.00	9,938.00	14,462.00	7.4	245-4770	412-288-1900	None	None	None	Gary Madich	'87
FEDERATED INC; INT SV	Fixed Income	50.7	9.89	9,902.00	9,912.00	☆	7.2	245-4770	412-288-1900	None	0.25	None	Gary Madich	'92
FEDERATED INT GOV; INSTL	Fixed Income	896.4	10.28	9,942.00	9,985.00	14,472.00	4.4	245-4770	412-288-1900	None	None	None	Susan M. Nason	'91
FEDERATED INT GOV; INT SV	Fixed Income	29.0	10.28	9,936.00	9,961.00	☆	4.1	245-4770	412-288-1900	None	0.25	None	Susan M. Nason	'92
FEDERATED INTMDT INC; SVC	Fixed Income	0.2	9.39	9,906.00	☆	☆	0.0	245-4770	412-288-1900	None	0.25	None	Randall S. Bauer	'93
FEDERATED S-I GOV; INSTL	Fixed Income	809.3	10.29	10,009.00	10,152.00	13,774.00	3.8	245-4770	412-288-1900	None	None	None	Susan M. Nason	'91
FEDERATED S-I GOV; INT SV	Fixed Income	40.3	10.29	10,003.00	10,127.00	☆	3.5	245-4770	412-288-1900	None	0.25	None	Susan M. Nason	'92
FEDERATED SHT INC; INSTL	Fixed Income	353.0	8.74	9,937.00	10,106.00	13,280.00	5.7	245-4770	412-288-1900	None	None	None	Randall S. Bauer	'86
FEDERATED SHT INC; INT SV	Fixed Income	39.9	8.74	9,930.00	10,081.00	☆	5.5	245-4770	412-288-1900	None	0.25	None	Randall S. Bauer	'92
FEDERATED STOCK TRUST	Growth Income	548.0	24.94	10,144.00	10,254.00	15,565.00	1.7	245-4770	412-288-1900	None	None	None	Peter R. Anderson	'82
FEDERATED US GOVT BOND	Fixed Income	101.7	9.58	9,774.00	9,603.00	14,710.00	5.5	245-4770	412-288-1900	None	None	None	Robert J. Ostrowski	'85
FFB LEXICON CAP APPREC ◪	Growth Income	146.5	10.81	9,800.00	9,825.00	☆	1.6	833-8974	None	None	None	None	Donald Demers	'93
FFB LEXICON FXD INC ◪	Fixed Income	92.9	9.86	9,848.00	9,826.00	☆	5.6	833-8974	None	None	None	None	Mander/Bescker	'91/'91
FFB LEXICON INTMDT GOVT ◪	Fixed Income	115.0	9.88	9,928.00	9,941.00	☆	5.5	833-8974	None	None	None	None	Robert Cheshire	'91
FFB LEXICON SELECT VALUE ◪	Growth	41.4	11.26	9,878.00	10,489.00	☆	2.0	833-8974	None	None	None	None	Tim O'Grady	'92
FFB LEXICON SMALL CO GRO ◪	Small Company Growth	23.7	10.70	9,252.00	9,734.00	☆	0.8	833-8974	None	None	None	None	Frank Sustersic	'92
FFB EQUITY	Capital Appreciation	5.5	9.95	9,679.00	9,345.00	14,641.00	3.5	437-8790	None	4.50	0.25	None	Richard Vivona	'93
FFTW AAA ASSET-BACKED	Fixed Income	4.1	9.68	9,989.00	☆	☆	0.0	762-4848	212-308-4848	None	None	None	Dave Marmon	'94
FFTW STABLE RETURN	Fixed Income	4.3	9.70	9,984.00	☆	☆	0.0	762-4848	212-308-4848	None	None	None	Stewart Russell	'94
FFTW US SH TM FXD INC	Fixed Income	191.5	9.94	10,079.00	10,287.00	☆	3.2	762-4848	212-308-4848	None	None	None	Marmon/Russell	'94/'94
FFTW WORLDWIDE FI HEDGED	World Income	17.6	9.56	10,114.00	10,197.00	☆	4.7	762-4848	212-308-4848	None	None	None	Liaquat Ahamed	'92
FFTW WORLDWIDE FXD INC	World Income	199.1	9.35	9,934.00	10,085.00	☆	4.8	762-4848	212-308-4848	None	None	None	Liaquat Ahamed	'92
FIDELITY ADV EQ GRO	Growth	696.0	27.33	9,603.00	10,073.00	☆	0.0	522-7297	None	4.75	0.75	None	Robert Stansky	'92
FIDELITY ADV EQ INC; A	Equity Income	74.5	15.21	10,344.00	10,678.00	☆	1.6	522-7297	None	4.75	0.75	None	Bettina Doulton	'93
FIDELITY ADV GLBL RES	Natural Resources	130.0	16.53	10,116.00	10,614.00	19,283.00	0.0	522-7297	None	4.75	0.75	None	Malcolm MacNaught	'87
FIDELITY ADV GOVT; A	Fixed Income	91.6	9.10	9,877.00	9,708.00	14,215.00	5.5	522-7297	None	4.75	0.25	None	Curt Hollingsworth	'92
FIDELITY ADV GROWTH OPP	Growth	3,365.5	25.10	10,040.00	11,019.00	20,924.00	0.3	522-7297	None	4.75	0.75	None	George Vanderheiden	'87
FIDELITY ADV HI YIELD; A	Fixed Income	624.6	11.30	9,932.00	10,599.00	20,407.00	7.8	522-7297	None	4.75	0.25	None	Margaret Eagle	'87
FIDELITY ADV INC & GRO	Balanced	2,735.6	14.48	9,771.00	10,077.00	17,425.00	3.0	522-7297	None	4.75	0.75	None	Robert Haber	'87
FIDELITY ADV INST EQ GRO	Growth	362.7	27.59	9,623.00	10,157.00	24,808.00	0.4	522-7297	None	None	None	None	Robert Stansky	'87
FIDELITY ADV INST EQ INC	Equity Income	175.5	15.29	10,369.00	10,774.00	15,904.00	2.2	522-7297	None	None	None	None	Bettina Doulton	'93
FIDELITY ADV INST LTD TM	Fixed Income	179.7	10.44	9,941.00	10,063.00	15,083.00	7.0	522-7297	None	None	None	None	Michael Gray	'87
FIDELITY ADV INST SH-IN2	Fixed Income	0.1	9.42	9,964.00	☆	☆	0.0	522-7297	None	None	0.25	None	Curt Hollingsworth	'94
FIDELITY ADV INST SH-INT	Fixed Income	386.3	9.42	9,971.00	9,982.00	14,199.00	5.7	522-7297	None	None	None	None	Curt Hollingsworth	'87
FIDELITY ADV LTD TM; A	Fixed Income	98.4	10.43	9,923.00	10,000.00	☆	6.5	522-7297	None	4.75	0.25	None	Michael Gray	'92
FIDELITY ADV OVERSEAS	International	473.0	13.71	10,156.00	12,056.00	☆	0.2	522-7297	None	4.75	0.75	None	John Hickling	'93

FIDELITY ADV SHT FXD INC	Fixed Income	833.2	9.50	9,928.00	10,056.00	14,289.00	6.6	522-7297	None	1.50	0.15	None	Donald Taylor	'89
FIDELITY ADV STRAT OPP; A	Capital Appreciation	357.9	19.65	10,103.00	10,415.00	16,547.00	2.1	522-7297	None	4.75	0.75	None	Daniel Frank	'86
FIDELITY ASSET MANAGER	Flexible	11,211.1	14.23	9,854.00	10,487.00	17,787.00	3.8	544-8888	None	None	None	None	Bob Beckwitt	'88
FIDELITY ASSET MGR GRO	Flexible	2,858.9	13.31	9,765.00	10,641.00	☆	0.7	544-8888	None	None	None	None	Bob Beckwitt	'91
FIDELITY ASSET MGR INC	Income	500.0	10.65	9,981.00	10,339.00	☆	4.5	544-8888	None	None	None	None	Bob Beckwitt	'92
FIDELITY BALANCED	Balanced	5,294.0	12.52	9,827.00	9,977.00	16,617.00	4.1	544-8888	None	None	None	None	Robert Haber	'88
FIDELITY BLUE CHIP GROW	Growth	1,906.0	24.52	10,066.00	11,211.00	25,010.00	0.0	544-8888	None	3.00	None	None	Michael Gordon	'93
FIDELITY CANADA	Canadian	171.8	16.50	9,423.00	9,343.00	13,291.00	0.0	544-8888	None	None	None	None	George Domolky	'87
FIDELITY CAPITAL & INC	Fixed Income	2,727.0	9.18	9,756.00	10,464.00	17,937.00	9.5	544-8888	None	None	None	1.50	Breazzano/Harmetz	'90/'90
FIDELITY CAPITAL APPREC	Capital Appreciation	1,910.4	16.04	9,804.00	10,803.00	14,889.00	0.6	544-8888	None	3.00	None	None	Thomas Sweeney	'86
FIDELITY CONGRESS ST ⊠	Growth Income	62.1	141.30	9,898.00	10,046.00	15,787.00	2.8	544-8888	None	None	None	None	Sandy Cushman	'92
FIDELITY CONTRAFUND	Growth	7,714.1	29.13	9,671.00	10,139.00	24,845.00	0.6	544-8888	None	3.00	None	None	Will Danoff	'90
FIDELITY CONVERTIBLE	Convertible Securities	910.2	15.16	9,789.00	10,098.00	19,901.00	5.0	544-8888	None	None	None	None	Andy Offit	'92
FIDELITY D-MARK PERFORM	World Income	6.9	15.68	10,638.00	11,256.00	☆	0.0	544-8888	None	0.40	None	None	Scott Kuldell	'94
FIDELITY DESTINY I ★	Growth	3,240.4	16.92	10,083.00	11,247.00	21,028.00	1.4	752-2347	None	8.24	None	None	George Vanderheiden	'80
FIDELITY DESTINY II ★	Growth	1,368.6	27.30	10,066.00	11,305.00	21,993.00	0.9	752-2347	None	8.24	None	None	George Vanderheiden	'85
FIDELITY DISCPLN EQU	Growth	890.2	17.80	9,944.00	10,532.00	19,340.00	1.2	544-8888	None	None	None	None	Brad Lewis	'88
FIDELITY DIVIDEND GROWTH	Growth	73.3	11.17	9,654.00	10,600.00	☆	0.1	544-8888	None	None	None	None	Fergus Shiel	'94
FIDELITY DVSD INTL	International	341.5	11.88	10,042.00	11,578.00	☆	0.1	544-8888	None	None	None	None	Greg Fraser	'91
FIDELITY EMERGING GROW	Small Company Growth	605.7	14.84	8,978.00	9,370.00	☆	0.0	544-8888	None	3.00	None	None	Larry Greenberg	'93
FIDELITY EMERGING MKTS	Emerging Markets	1,546.3	15.88	9,458.00	12,530.00	☆	0.3	544-8888	None	3.00	None	1.50	Richard Hazelwood	'93
FIDELITY EQUITY-INC	Equity Income	6,939.1	31.97	10,211.00	10,702.00	15,848.00	3.4	544-8888	None	None	None	None	Steve Peterson	'93
FIDELITY EQUITY-INC II	Equity Income	6,097.1	18.50	10,315.00	10,839.00	☆	2.4	544-8888	None	None	None	None	Brian Posner	'92
FIDELITY EUROPE	European Region	471.6	19.02	9,774.00	11,676.00	14,572.00	0.4	544-8888	None	3.00	None	None	Sally Walden	'92
FIDELITY EUROPE CAP APP	European Region	406.1	10.93	9,829.00	☆	☆	0.0	544-8888	None	None	None	None	Kevin McCarey	'93
FIDELITY EXCHANGE ⊠	Growth	181.8	96.88	10,076.00	9,975.00	15,655.00	2.4	544-8888	None	None	None	None	Sandy Cushman	'92
FIDELITY FIFTY	Capital Appreciation	50.4	10.17	9,883.00	☆	☆	0.0	544-8888	None	3.00	None	None	Scott Stewart	'93
FIDELITY FUND	Growth Income	1,622.3	18.60	9,983.00	10,535.00	16,257.00	2.0	544-8888	None	None	None	None	Beth Terrana	'93
FIDELITY GLOBAL BALANCED	Global Flexible	382.9	11.77	9,546.00	10,449.00	☆	2.3	544-8888	None	None	None	None	Robert Haber	'93
FIDELITY GLOBAL BOND	World Income	568.3	10.23	9,433.00	9,266.00	14,516.00	7.1	544-8888	None	None	None	None	Jonathan Kelly	'93
FIDELITY GOVT SECURITIES	Fixed Income	684.1	9.47	9,844.00	9,765.00	15,183.00	6.7	544-8888	None	None	None	None	Curt Hollingsworth	'90
FIDELITY GROWTH & INCOME	Growth Income	8,435.8	21.55	10,055.00	10,485.00	18,768.00	2.2	544-8888	None	3.00	None	None	Steven Kaye	'93
FIDELITY GROWTH COMPANY	Growth	2,764.8	26.91	9,597.00	9,989.00	20,690.00	0.3	544-8888	None	3.00	None	None	Robert Stansky	'87
FIDELITY INC GNMA	Fixed Income	773.3	10.21	9,895.00	9,790.00	14,391.00	5.6	544-8888	None	None	None	None	Bob Ives	'93
FIDELITY INC MORTGAGE	Fixed Income	347.7	10.46	10,092.00	10,207.00	14,822.00	5.6	544-8888	None	None	None	None	Kevin Grant	'93
FIDELITY INTERMEDIATE BD	Fixed Income	1,816.9	10.03	9,951.00	10,072.00	14,774.00	6.7	544-8888	None	None	None	None	Michael Gray	'87
FIDELITY INTL GRO & INC	International	1,481.2	17.31	10,070.00	11,210.00	15,688.00	0.4	544-8888	None	None	None	None	Rick Mace	'93
FIDELITY INV GRADE BOND	Fixed Income	923.5	7.07	9,886.00	9,979.00	15,555.00	7.3	544-8888	None	None	None	None	Michael Gray	'87
FIDELITY JAPAN	Japanese	443.8	14.90	11,153.00	11,844.00	☆	0.0	544-8888	None	None	None	1.00	John Hickling	'93
FIDELITY LATIN AMERICA	Latin American	715.7	13.16	8,886.00	12,382.00	☆	0.4	544-8888	None	3.00	None	1.50	Patti Satterthwaite	'93
FIDELITY LOW-PRICE	Midcap	2,120.3	17.23	9,908.00	11,260.00	☆	0.9	544-8888	None	3.00	None	1.50	Joel Tillinghast	'89
FIDELITY MAGELLAN FUND	Growth	34,344.7	63.94	9,551.00	10,135.00	18,929.00	0.9	544-8888	None	3.00	None	None	Jeff Vinik	'92
FIDELITY MARKET INDEX	S&P Index	290.2	32.99	10,037.00	10,106.00	☆	2.4	544-8888	None	None	None	0.50	Jennifer Farrelly	'94
FIDELITY MID-CAP STOCK	Midcap	21.8	9.69	9,908.00	☆	☆	0.0	544-8888	None	None	None	None	Jennifer Uhrig	'94
FIDELITY NC CASH MGT TRM	Fixed Income	71.5	9.85	10,059.00	10,226.00	13,349.00	3.2	544-8888	None	None	None	None	Duby/Stehman	'94/'94
FIDELITY NEW MILLENNIUM	Capital Appreciation	311.6	11.35	9,660.00	10,223.00	☆	0.1	544-8888	None	3.00	None	None	Neal Miller	'92
FIDELITY NEW MKTS INC	World Income	218.6	9.49	9,527.00	9,791.00	☆	7.1	544-8888	None	None	None	None	Rob Citrone	'93
FIDELITY OTC	Midcap	1,270.2	21.94	9,316.00	9,858.00	17,304.00	0.4	544-8888	None	3.00	None	None	Abigail Johnson	'94
FIDELITY OVERSEAS	International	2,008.2	28.19	10,068.00	12,015.00	15,554.00	1.5	544-8888	None	None	None	None	John Hickling	'93
FIDELITY PACIFIC BASIN	Pacific Region	493.6	19.01	10,538.00	13,255.00	14,619.00	0.7	544-8888	None	None	None	None	Simon Fraser	'93

★ FIDELITY DESTINY I and FIDELITY DESTINY II--Sold through a contractual plan.

PERFORMANCE OF MUTUAL FUNDS (continued)

FUND NAME	OBJECTIVE	TOTAL NET ASSETS ($ MIL) 5/31/94	NET ASSET $ VALUE 6/30/94	PERFORMANCE (Return on initial $10,000 Investment) 3/31/94-6/30/94	6/30/93-6/30/94	6/30/89-6/30/94	DIVIDEND YIELD % 6/94	PHONE NUMBER 800	In-State	FEES Load	12b-1	Redemption	MANAGER	SINCE
FIDELITY PURITAN	Equity Income	10,398.7	15.54	10,095.00	10,750.00	17,223.00	4.1	544-8888	None	None	None	None	Richard Fentin	'87
FIDELITY REAL ESTATE	Real Estate	544.2	13.66	10,048.00	10,341.00	18,033.00	4.6	544-8888	None	None	None	None	Barry Greenfield	'86
FIDELITY RETIREMENT GR	Capital Appreciation	2,946.2	17.38	9,937.00	10,909.00	19,507.00	0.8	544-8888	None	None	None	None	Harris Leviton	'92
FIDELITY SEL AIR TRANS	Specialty	7.4	14.00	9,231.00	10,129.00	13,876.00	0.0	544-8888	None	3.00	None	None	Brenda Reed	'92
FIDELITY SEL AMER GOLD	Gold	382.8	21.08	9,082.00	10,110.00	14,419.00	0.0	544-8888	None	3.00	None	None	Malcolm MacNaught	'85
FIDELITY SEL AUTOMOTIVE	Specialty	112.5	22.32	9,529.00	10,220.00	21,088.00	0.0	544-8888	None	3.00	None	None	Richard Patton	'93
FIDELITY SEL BIO TECH	Health/Biotechnology	400.8	23.01	9,271.00	9,131.00	25,025.00	0.0	544-8888	None	3.00	None	None	Karen Firestone	'92
FIDELITY SEL BROKERAGE	Financial Services	30.0	16.62	10,546.00	10,922.00	21,496.00	0.0	544-8888	None	3.00	None	None	Arieh Coll	'93
FIDELITY SEL CHEMICALS	Specialty	107.6	32.34	10,602.00	12,313.00	19,126.00	0.6	544-8888	None	3.00	None	None	Steve Wymer	'93
FIDELITY SEL CNSMR PRDCT	Specialty	7.4	13.36	9,423.00	9,968.00	☆	0.0	544-8888	None	3.00	None	None	Mary English	'94
FIDELITY SEL COMPUTER	Science & Technology	100.0	24.37	9,114.00	12,311.00	24,612.00	0.0	544-8888	None	3.00	None	None	Harry Lange	'92
FIDELITY SEL CONST&HOUSE	Specialty	48.7	17.11	9,218.00	10,820.00	17,945.00	0.0	544-8888	None	3.00	None	None	Katherine Collins	'92
FIDELITY SEL DEFENSE	Specialty	4.8	17.80	9,833.00	10,980.00	15,253.00	0.5	544-8888	None	3.00	None	None	Steve Binder	'92
FIDELITY SEL DVLP COMM	Science & Technology	165.8	15.53	9,124.00	9,876.00	☆	0.0	544-8888	None	3.00	None	None	Paul Antico	'93
FIDELITY SEL ELECTRONIC	Science & Technology	128.5	16.45	9,411.00	11,958.00	26,939.00	0.0	544-8888	None	3.00	None	None	Harry Lange	'94
FIDELITY SEL ENERGY	Natural Resources	113.0	17.10	10,821.00	10,098.00	13,917.00	0.2	544-8888	None	3.00	None	None	Bob Bertleson	'92
FIDELITY SEL ENERGY SER	Natural Resources	47.5	11.84	11,313.00	9,408.00	12,995.00	0.4	544-8888	None	3.00	None	None	Bill Mankivsky	'91
FIDELITY SEL ENVIRONMENT	Environmental	48.9	10.34	9,530.00	9,443.00	11,135.00	0.0	544-8888	None	3.00	None	None	Philip Barton	'93
FIDELITY SEL FINANCIAL	Financial Services	118.4	51.28	10,567.00	10,755.00	21,033.00	0.4	544-8888	None	3.00	None	None	Steve Binder	'93
FIDELITY SEL FOOD	Specialty	71.8	28.91	9,891.00	10,445.00	18,589.00	0.3	544-8888	None	3.00	None	None	Bill Mankivsky	'93
FIDELITY SEL HEALTH	Health/Biotechnology	551.3	63.88	10,814.00	11,450.00	23,517.00	0.3	544-8888	None	3.00	None	None	Charles Mangum	'92
FIDELITY SEL HOME FIN	Financial Services	194.5	26.25	11,208.00	13,326.00	27,766.00	0.0	544-8888	None	3.00	None	None	David Ellison	'85
FIDELITY SEL INDUS EQUIP	Specialty	116.6	17.73	9,209.00	10,733.00	16,725.00	0.0	544-8888	None	3.00	None	None	Albert Ruback	'91
FIDELITY SEL INDUS MAT	Specialty	144.0	21.79	10,371.00	12,013.00	17,320.00	0.2	544-8888	None	3.00	None	None	Louis Salemy	'92
FIDELITY SEL INSURANCE	Financial Services	8.0	19.45	10,514.00	9,780.00	18,586.00	0.1	544-8888	None	3.00	None	None	Robert Chow	'93
FIDELITY SEL LEISURE	Specialty	67.9	36.71	9,500.00	10,815.00	15,701.00	0.0	544-8888	None	3.00	None	None	Deborah Wheeler	'92
FIDELITY SEL MEDICAL	Health/Biotechnology	184.0	19.29	10,010.00	12,691.00	23,173.00	0.0	544-8888	None	3.00	None	None	Louis Salemy	'93
FIDELITY SEL MULTIMEDIA	Specialty	30.7	20.12	10,137.00	11,506.00	16,136.00	0.0	544-8888	None	3.00	None	None	Stephen Dufour	'93
FIDELITY SEL NAT GAS	Natural Resources	81.0	9.82	10,744.00	9,709.00	☆	0.0	544-8888	None	3.00	None	None	Michael Tempero	'94
FIDELITY SEL PAPER&FRS	Specialty	30.0	17.68	10,293.00	10,955.00	16,299.00	0.0	544-8888	None	3.00	None	None	Scott Offen	'93
FIDELITY SEL PREC MTLS	Gold	380.3	16.80	10,219.00	11,365.00	15,404.00	1.3	544-8888	None	3.00	None	None	Malcolm MacNaught	'81
FIDELITY SEL REGL BANKS	Financial Services	199.4	18.85	10,781.00	10,904.00	23,597.00	0.7	544-8888	None	3.00	None	None	Steve Binder	'90
FIDELITY SEL RETAILING	Specialty	92.8	23.69	9,713.00	10,513.00	22,344.00	0.0	544-8888	None	3.00	None	None	Jeff Feinberg	'94
FIDELITY SEL SOFTWARE	Science & Technology	144.8	21.00	8,253.00	8,335.00	22,300.00	0.0	544-8888	None	3.00	None	None	Arieh Coll	'91
FIDELITY SEL TECHNOLOGY	Science & Technology	189.3	34.89	8,983.00	10,092.00	24,699.00	0.0	544-8888	None	3.00	None	None	Harry Lange	'93
FIDELITY SEL TELECOMM	Science & Technology	397.2	35.52	10,111.00	10,542.00	18,765.00	0.4	544-8888	None	3.00	None	None	Davis Felman	'94
FIDELITY SEL TRANSPORT	Specialty	11.4	20.79	10,013.00	11,216.00	20,879.00	0.0	544-8888	None	3.00	None	None	Beso Sikharulidze	'93
FIDELITY SEL UTILITIES	Utility	232.1	34.74	10,051.00	9,339.00	16,616.00	2.8	544-8888	None	3.00	None	None	John Muresianu	'92
FIDELITY SH-INT GOVT FD	Fixed Income	134.2	9.38	9,961.00	9,911.00	☆	5.7	544-8888	None	None	None	None	Curt Hollingsworth	'91
FIDELITY SHORT WORLD	World Income	334.8	9.29	9,813.00	9,959.00	☆	7.7	544-8888	None	None	None	None	Scott Kuldell	'94
FIDELITY SHORT-TERM BOND	Fixed Income	1,955.4	8.95	9,886.00	10,034.00	14,267.00	6.9	544-8888	None	None	None	None	Donald Taylor	'89
FIDELITY SM CAP STOCK	Small Company Growth	652.3	9.82	9,406.00	9,876.00	☆	0.2	544-8888	None	3.00	None	None	Brad Lewis	'93
FIDELITY SOEAST ASIA	Pacific Region	739.2	12.62	10,064.00	12,505.00	☆	0.6	544-8888	None	3.00	None	1.50	Alan Liu	'93
FIDELITY SP SIT INITL ⊠	Capital Appreciation	18.8	19.87	10,112.00	10,476.00	16,983.00	2.5	544-8888	None	4.75	None	None	Daniel Frank	'83
FIDELITY SPARTAN GNMA	Fixed Income	422.2	9.53	9,901.00	9,818.00	☆	5.4	544-8888	None	None	None	None	Bob Ives	'93

FIDELITY SPARTAN GOV INC	Fixed Income	274.8	9.88	9,843.00	9,669.00	14,482.00	5.8	544-8888	None	None	None	None	Bob Ives	'93
FIDELITY SPARTAN HIINC	Fixed Income	639.8	11.59	9,927.00	10,806.00	☆	9.7	544-8888	None	None	None	1.00	David Glancy	'93
FIDELITY SPARTAN INV GRD	Fixed Income	109.8	9.66	9,830.00	9,793.00	☆	7.5	544-8888	None	None	None	None	Michael Gray	'92
FIDELITY SPARTAN LG GOVT	Fixed Income	57.5	10.39	9,509.00	9,088.00	☆	6.9	544-8888	None	None	None	None	Curt Hollingsworth	'93
FIDELITY SPARTAN LTD MAT	Fixed Income	1,069.3	9.56	9,938.00	9,990.00	14,050.00	5.5	544-8888	None	None	None	None	Curt Hollingsworth	'88
FIDELITY SPARTAN S-I GOV	Fixed Income	51.0	9.41	9,971.00	9,970.00	☆	6.6	544-8888	None	None	None	None	Curt Hollingsworth	'92
FIDELITY SPARTAN SH-TM	Fixed Income	913.3	9.33	9,855.00	10,003.00	☆	6.9	544-8888	None	None	None	None	Donald Taylor	'92
FIDELITY SPARTAN STRT	Fixed Income	21.6	9.08	10,045.00	☆	☆	0.0	544-8888	None	None	None	0.50	George Fischer	'93
FIDELITY STOCK SELECTOR	Growth	745.0	18.47	9,882.00	10,400.00	☆	1.3	544-8888	None	None	None	None	Brad Lewis	'90
FIDELITY STRLING PERFORM	World Income	3.4	14.32	10,499.00	10,751.00	☆	0.0	544-8888	None	0.40	None	None	Scott Kuldell	'94
FIDELITY TREND	Growth	1,268.5	54.31	9,796.00	9,985.00	16,518.00	0.5	544-8888	None	None	None	None	Alan Leifer	'87
FIDELITY US BOND INDEX ▥	Fixed Income	327.0	10.25	9,899.00	9,909.00	☆	7.0	544-8888	None	None	None	None	Christine Thompson	'90
FIDELITY US EQUITY INDEX	S&P Index	1,845.1	16.41	10,041.00	10,121.00	16,099.00	2.7	544-8888	None	None	None	None	Jay Weed	'88
FIDELITY UTIL INCOME	Utility	1,240.4	14.09	9,991.00	9,781.00	17,261.00	3.4	544-8888	None	None	None	None	John Muresianu	'92
FIDELITY VALUE FUND	Capital Appreciation	2,325.4	41.78	10,370.00	11,481.00	17,636.00	0.8	544-8888	None	None	None	None	Jeff Ubben	'92
FIDELITY WORLDWIDE	Global	578.0	13.39	10,121.00	11,997.00	☆	0.7	544-8888	None	None	None	None	Penelope Dobkin	'90
FIDELITY YEN PERFORM	World Income	3.0	17.11	10,446.00	10,961.00	☆	0.0	544-8888	None	0.40	None	None	Scott Kuldell	'94
FIDUCIARY CAPITAL GROWTH	Growth	34.4	18.35	9,823.00	10,151.00	15,402.00	0.3	338-1579	414-765-3500	None	None	None	Kellner/Wilson	'81/'81
FIDUCIARY EXCHANGE ⊠	Growth	54.2	137.19	9,701.00	9,625.00	15,499.00	1.2	225-6265	617-482-8260	None	None	None	Duncan Richardson	'87
FIDUCIARY TOTAL RETURN	Balanced	2.5	11.45	9,845.00	10,115.00	14,972.00	1.5	338-1579	414-765-3500	None	1.00	None	Kellner/Wilson	'86/'86
59 WALL ST EUROPEAN	European Region	99.0	29.15	9,798.00	11,366.00	☆	5.1	None	212-493-8100	None	None	None	Brown Brothers Harriman	'92
59 WALL ST PAC BASIN	Pacific Region	113.2	37.99	9,860.00	12,365.00	☆	1.9	None	212-493-8100	None	None	None	Brown Brothers Harriman	'92
59 WALL ST SMALL CO	Small Company Growth	40.2	11.09	9,304.00	9,694.00	☆	4.2	None	212-493-8100	None	None	None	Brown Brothers Harriman	'91
FINL HRZNS GOVT BOND	Fixed Income	75.4	10.32	9,844.00	9,737.00	14,985.00	5.4	533-5622	None	None	0.50	5.00	Wayne Frisbee	'89
FINL HRZNS GROWTH	Growth	6.3	13.74	9,892.00	10,205.00	14,193.00	0.3	533-5622	None	None	0.50	5.00	John Schaffner	'89
FIRST AMER ASST ALL; INST	Flexible	50.7	10.12	10,041.00	☆	☆	0.0	637-2548	612-973-4069	None	None	None	Cory Johnson	'94
FIRST AMER ASST ALL; RET	Flexible	0.8	10.12	10,030.00	10,071.00	☆	2.4	637-2548	612-973-4069	4.50	0.10	None	Cory Johnson	'92
FIRST AMER BALANCED; INST	Balanced	117.7	10.39	9,977.00	☆	☆	0.0	637-2548	612-973-4069	None	None	None	Jim Rovner	'94
FIRST AMER BALANCED; RET	Balanced	13.1	10.39	9,974.00	10,285.00	☆	3.2	637-2548	612-973-4069	4.50	0.10	None	Jim Rovner	'92
FIRST AMER DVSFD GR; RET	Growth Income	26.0	8.72	9,826.00	9,651.00	☆	1.2	637-2548	612-973-4069	4.50	0.25	None	Ron Heithoff	'92
FIRST AMER EQ INDEX; INST	Growth Income	155.8	10.26	10,052.00	☆	☆	0.0	637-2548	612-973-4069	None	None	None	Jim Rovner	'94
FIRST AMER EQ INDEX; RET	Growth Income	0.7	10.26	10,039.00	10,100.00	☆	2.3	637-2548	612-973-4069	4.50	0.10	None	Jim Rovner	'92
FIRST AMER EQTY INC; RET	Equity Income	24.1	9.73	10,078.00	10,323.00	☆	5.2	637-2548	612-973-4069	4.50	0.25	None	Scott Limper	'92
FIRST AMER FXD INC; INST	Fixed Income	53.6	10.51	9,907.00	☆	☆	0.0	637-2548	612-973-4069	None	None	None	Martin Jones	'94
FIRST AMER FXD INC; RET ✋	Fixed Income	8.7	10.52	9,917.00	10,001.00	14,608.00	5.6	637-2548	612-973-4069	3.75	0.25	None	Martin Jones	'87
FIRST AMER GOVT BD; INST	Fixed Income	3.9	9.04	9,942.00	☆	☆	0.0	637-2548	612-973-4069	None	None	None	Richard Stanley	'94
FIRST AMER GOVT BD; RET ✋	Fixed Income	2.1	9.04	9,942.00	9,996.00	13,533.00	4.0	637-2548	612-973-4069	3.00	0.25	None	Richard Stanley	'94
FIRST AMER INT TERM; INST	Fixed Income	57.4	9.62	9,961.00	☆	☆	0.0	637-2548	612-973-4069	None	None	None	Martin Jones	'94
FIRST AMER INT TERM; RET ✋	Fixed Income	3.1	9.62	9,961.00	10,010.00	☆	5.0	637-2548	612-973-4069	3.75	0.25	None	Martin Jones	'92
FIRST AMER LTD TERM; INST	Fixed Income	73.6	9.83	10,013.00	☆	☆	0.0	637-2548	612-973-4069	None	None	None	Martin Jones	'94
FIRST AMER LTD TERM; RET ✋	Fixed Income	13.0	9.83	10,013.00	10,199.00	☆	3.9	637-2548	612-973-4069	2.00	0.25	None	Martin Jones	'92
FIRST AMER MGD INC; RET	Fixed Income	63.1	9.57	10,059.00	10,281.00	☆	6.5	637-2548	612-973-4069	2.00	0.25	None	Graham Bentz	'92
FIRST AMER MTGE SEC; INST	Fixed Income	31.2	9.80	9,928.00	☆	☆	0.0	637-2548	612-973-4069	None	None	None	Martin Jones	'94
FIRST AMER MTGE SEC; RET ✋	Fixed Income	0.3	9.80	9,928.00	10,085.00	☆	5.7	637-2548	612-973-4069	3.75	0.25	None	Martin Jones	'92
FIRST AMER REGNL EQ; INST	Small Company Growth	79.0	11.60	9,744.00	☆	☆	0.0	637-2548	612-973-4069	None	None	None	Rick Rinkoff	'94
FIRST AMER REGNL EQ; RET	Small Company Growth	8.4	11.60	9,741.00	10,624.00	☆	0.6	637-2548	612-973-4069	4.50	0.10	None	Rick Rinkoff	'92
FIRST AMER SPEC EQU; INST	Capital Appreciation	104.6	15.71	9,967.00	☆	☆	0.0	637-2548	612-973-4069	None	None	None	Larry Smith	'94
FIRST AMER SPEC EQU; RET	Capital Appreciation	6.2	15.72	9,971.00	10,931.00	16,853.00	1.7	637-2548	612-973-4069	4.50	0.10	None	Larry Smith	'87
FIRST AMER STOCK; INST	Growth Income	131.5	15.97	10,018.00	☆	☆	0.0	637-2548	612-973-4069	None	None	None	Jim Doak	'94
FIRST AMER STOCK; RET	Growth Income	7.5	15.97	10,016.00	10,624.00	16,258.00	1.7	637-2548	612-973-4069	4.50	0.10	None	Jim Doak	'87

PERFORMANCE OF MUTUAL FUNDS *(continued)*

FUND NAME	OBJECTIVE	TOTAL NET ASSETS ($ MIL) 5/31/94	NET ASSET $ VALUE 6/30/94	PERFORMANCE (Return on initial $10,000 Investment) 3/31/94-6/30/94	6/30/93-6/30/94	6/30/89-6/30/94	DIVIDEND YIELD % 6/94	PHONE NUMBER 800	In-State	FEES Load	12b-1	Redemption	MANAGER	SINCE
FIRST BOS INSTL GOVT; A	Fixed Income	28.5	9.12	9,861.00	9,801.00	☆	4.9	545-5799	None	2.50	None	None	Bob Michele	'93
FIRST EAGLE FD OF AMER	Capital Appreciation	117.4	14.46	9,488.00	10,616.00	16,323.00	0.0	451-3623	212-943-9200	None	None	1.00	Levy/Cohen	'87/'89
FIRST EAGLE INTL FD	International	20.1	12.06	9,648.00	☆	☆	0.0	451-3623	212-943-9200	None	None	1.00	Raphael/Lerner	'94/'94
FIRST TOT EQ; I	Growth Income	83.1	10.53	10,105.00	☆	☆	0.0	442-1941	None	None	None	None	Pruett/Ratlif	'93/'93
FIRST TOT EQ; III	Growth Income	1.4	10.52	10,077.00	☆	☆	0.0	442-1941	None	None	0.75	None	Pruett/Ratlif	'93/'93
FIRST TOT FXD; I	Fixed Income	73.3	9.41	9,870.00	☆	☆	0.0	442-1941	None	None	None	None	Stephen T. Ashby	'93
FIRST TOT FXD; III	Fixed Income	0.9	9.40	9,824.00	☆	☆	0.0	442-1941	None	None	0.75	None	Stephen T. Ashby	'93
FIRST INV FD FOR INC	Fixed Income	411.4	3.93	9,975.00	10,524.00	14,372.00	10.3	423-4026	212-858-8000	6.25	0.30	None	Nancy Jones	'89
FIRST INV GLOBAL FUND	Global	212.5	5.95	10,051.00	11,105.00	15,015.00	0.2	423-4026	212-858-8000	6.25	0.30	None	Wellington Mgmt. Co.	'89
FIRST INV GOVT	Fixed Income	244.2	10.79	9,895.00	9,728.00	13,857.00	6.3	423-4026	212-858-8000	6.25	0.30	None	Larry Waldorf	'92
FIRST INV GOVT PLUS I	Balanced Target	1.4	11.01	9,666.00	9,148.00	14,580.00	5.9	423-4026	212-858-8000	8.00	None	None	Patricia Poitra	'86
FIRST INV HIGH YIELD	Fixed Income	179.6	5.04	9,962.00	10,583.00	13,843.00	9.5	423-4026	212-858-8000	6.25	0.30	None	George Ganter	'89
FIRST INV SRS BLUE CHIP	Growth Income	120.9	14.90	9,920.00	9,956.00	14,745.00	0.6	423-4026	212-858-8000	6.25	0.30	None	Denise Burns	'89
FIRST INV SRS INV GRADE	Fixed Income	45.0	9.48	9,860.00	9,788.00	☆	6.5	423-4026	212-858-8000	6.25	0.30	None	Nancy Jones	'91
FIRST INV SRS SP SITUAT	Small Company Growth	68.5	16.22	9,253.00	10,313.00	☆	0.0	423-4026	212-858-8000	6.25	0.30	None	Patricia Poitra	'90
FIRST INV SRS TOT RTN	Flexible	55.1	11.19	9,718.00	9,944.00	☆	2.1	423-4026	212-858-8000	6.25	0.30	None	Team Managed	'92
FIRST INV SRSII GR & INC	Growth Income	24.3	6.43	10,054.00	☆	☆	0.0	423-4026	212-858-8000	6.25	0.30	None	Wellington Mgmt. Co.	'93
FIRST INV SRSII MADE USA	Growth	9.3	10.88	9,535.00	9,010.00	☆	1.1	423-4026	212-858-8000	6.25	0.30	None	Denise Burns	'92
FIRST INV SRSII UTIL	Utility	61.6	5.08	9,809.00	9,188.00	☆	4.1	423-4026	212-858-8000	6.25	0.30	None	Margaret Haggerty	'93
FIRST MUTUAL FUND	Capital Appreciation	22.8	8.21	8,953.00	9,610.00	13,124.00	0.7	257-4414	None	None	0.25	None	David P. Como	'82
FIRST OMAHA EQUITY	Growth Income	129.0	10.48	10,190.00	10,334.00	☆	1.9	662-4203	None	None	0.25	None	Vicki Hohenstein	'92
FIRST OMAHA FXD INCOME	Fixed Income	61.5	9.58	9,789.00	9,770.00	☆	7.0	662-4203	None	None	0.25	None	Dick Chapman	'92
FIRST OMAHA SH-INTMDT	Fixed Income	22.1	9.62	9,921.00	9,978.00	☆	5.7	662-4203	None	None	0.25	None	Dick Chapman	'92
FRST PRAIRIE DVSFD; A	Income	48.9	12.26	10,022.00	10,037.00	15,773.00	5.7	821-1185	None	4.50	None	None	Arthur Krill	'86
FRST PRAIRIE DVSFD; B	Income	0.8	12.24	10,010.00	☆	☆	0.0	821-1185	None	None	0.75	4.00	Arthur Krill	'94
FRST PRAIRIE GVT INT; A	Fixed Income	0.1	7.80	9,958.00	10,034.00	☆	6.7	821-1185	None	3.00	None	None	Annette Furmanski-Cole	'93
FRST PRAIRIE GVT INT; B	Fixed Income	0.1	7.79	9,944.00	☆	☆	0.0	821-1185	None	None	0.50	3.00	Annette Furmanski-Cole	'94
1ST PRIORITY EQUITY; INV	Growth Income	6.5	10.09	9,897.00	10,193.00	☆	1.8	433-2829	205-326-7041	2.00	0.30	None	Charlie Murray	'92
1ST PRIORITY EQUITY; TR	Growth Income	152.3	10.09	9,904.00	10,225.00	☆	2.1	433-2829	205-326-7041	None	None	None	Charlie Murray	'92
1ST PRIORITY FXD INC; INV	Fixed Income	10.7	9.68	9,816.00	9,690.00	☆	4.9	433-2829	205-326-7041	2.00	0.30	None	Jerry Harris	'92
1ST PRIORITY FXD INC; TR	Fixed Income	165.2	9.68	9,823.00	9,720.00	☆	5.2	433-2829	205-326-7041	None	None	None	Jerry Harris	'92
1ST PRIORITY LTD GOVT	Fixed Income	47.3	9.69	9,985.00	☆	☆	0.0	433-2829	205-326-7041	2.00	None	None	John Haigler	'93
FIRST UN BAL; INV B	Balanced	41.6	11.47	9,947.00	10,162.00	☆	3.4	326-3241	704-374-4343	4.00	0.25	None	Dean Hawes	'91
FIRST UN BAL; INV C	Balanced	89.0	11.48	9,934.00	10,121.00	☆	2.9	326-3241	704-374-4343	None	0.75	4.00	Dean Hawes	'93
FIRST UN BAL; TR	Balanced	806.4	11.47	9,954.00	10,190.00	☆	3.7	326-3241	704-374-4343	None	None	None	Dean Hawes	'91
FIRST UN FXD INC; INV B	Fixed Income	22.1	9.79	9,915.00	9,918.00	14,286.00	6.5	326-3241	704-374-4343	4.00	0.10	None	Tom Ellis	'89
FIRST UN FXD INC; INV C	Fixed Income	13.7	9.81	9,888.00	9,852.00	☆	5.7	326-3241	704-374-4343	None	0.75	4.00	Tom Ellis	'93
FIRST UN FXD INC; TR	Fixed Income	363.5	9.79	9,909.00	9,937.00	☆	6.8	326-3241	704-374-4343	None	None	None	Tom Ellis	'91
FIRST UN MGD BD; TR	Fixed Income	106.5	9.61	9,863.00	9,763.00	☆	6.7	326-3241	704-374-4343	None	None	None	Glen Insley	'93
FIRST UN US GOVT; INV B	Fixed Income	31.1	9.33	9,883.00	9,785.00	☆	7.3	326-3241	704-374-4343	4.00	0.25	None	Rollin Williams	'93
FIRST UN US GOVT; INV C	Fixed Income	226.2	9.33	9,870.00	9,736.00	☆	6.7	326-3241	704-374-4343	None	0.75	4.00	Rollin Williams	'93
FIRST UN US GOVT; TR	Fixed Income	14.4	9.33	9,889.00	☆	☆	0.0	326-3241	704-374-4343	None	None	None	Rollin Williams	'93
FIRST UN UTILITY; INV B	Utility	3.3	9.11	10,048.00	☆	☆	0.0	326-3241	704-374-4343	4.00	0.25	None	Malcolm Trevillian	'94
FIRST UN UTILITY; INV C	Utility	24.5	9.11	10,024.00	☆	☆	0.0	326-3241	704-374-4343	None	0.75	4.00	Malcolm Trevillian	'94
FIRST UN UTILITY; TR	Utility	5.2	9.11	10,043.00	☆	☆	0.0	326-3241	704-374-4343	None	None	None	Malcolm Trevillian	'94

FIRST UN VALUE; INV B	Growth	189.9	17.13	10,145.00	10,362.00	15,600.00	2.8	326-3241	704-374-4343	4.00	0.25	None	Bill Davis	'91
FIRST UN VALUE; INV C	Growth	78.1	17.13	10,133.00	10,316.00	☆	2.3	326-3241	704-374-4343	None	0.75	4.00	Bill Davis	'93
FIRST UN VALUE; TR	Growth	498.9	17.12	10,146.00	10,388.00	☆	3.2	326-3241	704-374-4343	None	None	None	Bill Davis	'91
FLAG INV EMERGING GROWTH	Small Company Growth	24.6	10.72	8,860.00	9,054.00	10,112.00	0.0	645-3923	410-637-6819	4.50	0.25	None	Fred Meserve	'93
FLAG INV INTL; FLAG	International	15.4	13.00	10,046.00	12,593.00	12,774.00	6.5	645-3923	410-637-6819	4.50	0.25	None	Glenmede Trust/Williams	'93/'93
FLAG INV INTMDT-TM INC	Fixed Income	105.2	9.97	9,921.00	9,912.00	☆	6.2	645-3923	410-637-6819	1.50	0.25	None	Randolph/Corbin	'91/'91
FLAG INV QUAL GRO; FLAG	Growth	38.9	12.09	9,726.00	9,773.00	☆	0.7	645-3923	410-637-6819	4.50	0.25	None	Killebrow/Brandaleone	'89/'89
FLAG INV TPHONE INC; A	Equity Income	462.6	12.64	9,917.00	9,795.00	17,052.00	3.3	645-3923	410-637-6819	4.50	0.25	None	Behrens/Buppert	'84/'84
FLAG INV TPHONE INC; B	Equity Income	31.0	12.60	9,916.00	9,770.00	☆	3.3	645-3923	410-637-6819	1.50	0.60	1.00	Behrens/Buppert	'93/'93
FLAG INV VALUE BLDR; A	Balanced	134.5	11.09	9,946.00	10,123.00	☆	2.9	645-3923	410-637-6819	4.50	0.25	None	Buppert/Owen	'92/'92
FLAG INV VALUE BLDR; B	Balanced	11.5	11.09	9,937.00	10,087.00	☆	2.4	645-3923	410-637-6819	1.50	0.60	1.00	Buppert/Owen	'92/'92
FLAGSHIP UTILITY; A	Utility	28.2	9.69	9,875.00	9,317.00	☆	6.6	227-4648	513-461-0332	4.20	0.40	None	Bedford/Huber	'92/'92
FLAGSHIP UTILITY; C	Utility	5.2	9.69	9,861.00	☆	☆	6.0	227-4648	513-461-0332	None	None	1.00	Bedford/Huber	'93/'93
FLEX-FUNDS BOND	Fixed Income	12.5	19.25	9,973.00	10,019.00	14,123.00	3.8	325-3539	614-766-7000	None	0.20	None	Philip Voelker	'88
FLEX-FUNDS GROWTH	Flexible	24.3	13.04	9,797.00	10,202.00	14,080.00	0.8	325-3539	614-766-7000	None	0.20	None	Robert Meeder, Jr.	'92
FLEX-FUNDS MUIRFIELD	Flexible	80.3	5.34	10,066.00	10,590.00	16,441.00	1.0	325-3539	614-766-7000	None	0.20	None	Robert Meeder, Jr.	'88
FLEX-FUNDS SHT GLBL INC	World Income	8.0	9.34	10,006.00	10,082.00	☆	3.5	325-3539	614-766-7000	None	0.20	None	Joseph Zarr	'92
FMB DVSD EQ; CNSMR	Growth	5.2	11.16	10,109.00	10,082.00	☆	0.7	453-4234	None	4.00	0.10	None	Dan Van Timmeren	'93
FMB DVSD EQ; INSTL	Growth	39.8	11.16	10,109.00	10,082.00	☆	0.7	453-4234	None	None	None	None	Dan Van Timmeren	'93
FMB INTMDT GOVT; CNSMR	Fixed Income	10.8	9.90	9,902.00	9,961.00	☆	5.8	453-4234	None	3.00	0.10	None	Duane Carpenter	'91
FMB INTMDT GOVT; INSTL	Fixed Income	110.2	9.90	9,903.00	9,963.00	☆	5.8	453-4234	None	None	None	None	Duane Carpenter	'91
FONTAINE CAPITAL APPREC	Capital Appreciation	6.3	10.31	9,736.00	10,022.00	☆	1.3	247-1550	410-825-7890	None	None	None	Richard H. Fontaine	'89
FONTAINE GLBL GROWTH	Global	0.4	9.76	9,683.00	10,107.00	☆	1.1	247-1550	410-825-7890	None	None	None	Richard H. Fontaine	'92
FONTAINE GLBL INCOME	World Income	0.8	10.48	9,962.00	11,138.00	☆	1.0	247-1550	410-825-7890	None	None	None	Richard H. Fontaine	'92
FORTIS ADVTG ASSET ALLOC	Flexible	113.1	13.52	9,671.00	9,926.00	15,324.00	2.3	800-2638	612-738-4000	4.50	0.45	None	Poling/Ott	'88/'88
FORTIS ADVTG CAP APPREC	Small Company Growth	60.9	20.69	8,884.00	9,280.00	16,798.00	0.0	800-2638	612-738-4000	4.50	0.45	None	Stephen Poling	'88
FORTIS ADVTG GVT TOT RTN	Fixed Income	78.3	8.01	9,678.00	9,460.00	13,378.00	8.4	800-2638	612-738-4000	4.50	0.35	None	Dennis M. Ott	'86
FORTIS ADVTG HIGH YIELD	Fixed Income	94.4	8.35	9,857.00	10,828.00	16,152.00	10.9	800-2638	612-738-4000	4.50	0.35	None	Dennis M. Ott	'88
FORTIS EQU CAPITAL FD	Growth Income	234.4	16.48	9,728.00	10,051.00	16,007.00	0.7	800-2638	612-738-4000	4.75	0.25	None	Stephen Poling	'83
FORTIS FIDUCIARY FD	Growth	52.5	26.86	9,627.00	9,934.00	16,071.00	0.0	800-2638	612-738-4000	4.75	0.25	None	Stephen Poling	'83
FORTIS GROWTH FD	Capital Appreciation	530.3	23.71	8,775.00	8,887.00	16,831.00	0.0	800-2638	612-738-4000	4.75	0.25	None	Stephen Poling	'83
FORTIS INC US GOVT FD	Fixed Income	569.3	8.94	9,764.00	9,599.00	14,102.00	8.1	800-2638	612-738-4000	4.50	None	None	Dennis M. Ott	'85
FORTIS WRLDWIDE GL GRO	Global	47.3	13.33	9,494.00	10,068.00	☆	0.0	800-2638	612-738-4000	4.75	0.25	None	James Byrd	'91
FORTRESS ADJ RT GOVT	Fixed Income	703.7	9.59	9,947.00	10,116.00	☆	4.2	245-4770	412-288-1900	None	0.25	1.00	Gary Madich	'91
FORTRESS BOND FUND	Fixed Income	144.0	9.23	9,880.00	9,999.00	16,013.00	8.0	245-4770	412-288-1900	1.00	None	1.00	Mark E. Durbiano	'92
FORTRESS UTILITY	Utility	919.9	11.89	9,799.00	9,512.00	16,498.00	5.2	245-4770	412-288-1900	1.00	None	1.00	Christopher H. Wiles	'90
44 WALL STREET EQUITY	Capital Appreciation	8.8	5.87	9,186.00	10,560.00	17,115.00	0.0	543-2620	212-248-8080	None	None	None	Mark D. Beckerman	'88
FORUM INVESTORS BOND	Fixed Income	24.6	10.09	9,916.00	10,086.00	☆	8.1	None	207-879-0001	3.75	None	None	Forum Advisors	'89
FORUM PAYSON BALANCED	Balanced	11.9	11.26	9,701.00	9,987.00	☆	3.2	None	207-879-0001	None	None	None	H.M. Payson & Co.	'93
FORUM PAYSON VALUE	Growth Income	5.5	11.73	9,719.00	10,564.00	☆	1.6	None	207-879-0001	None	None	None	H.M. Payson & Co.	'93
FOUNDERS BALANCED	Balanced	95.9	8.73	9,955.00	10,935.00	16,160.00	1.7	525-2440	303-394-4404	None	0.25	None	Patrick S. Adams	'93
FOUNDERS BLUE CHIP FUND	Growth Income	314.2	6.26	9,720.00	10,518.00	16,050.00	0.4	525-2440	303-394-4404	None	0.25	None	Patrick S. Adams	'93
FOUNDERS DISCOVERY FUND	Small Company Growth	170.4	18.01	8,911.00	9,233.00	☆	0.0	525-2440	303-394-4404	None	0.25	None	Michael K. Haines	'89
FOUNDERS FRONTIER FUND	Small Company Growth	239.1	24.44	9,293.00	9,897.00	17,021.00	0.0	525-2440	303-394-4404	None	0.25	None	Michael K. Haines	'87
FOUNDERS GOVERNMENT SEC ☛	Fixed Income	25.4	9.08	9,746.00	9,561.00	13,396.00	5.4	525-2440	303-394-4404	None	0.25	None	Montgomery C. Cleworth	'93
FOUNDERS GROWTH FUND	Growth	330.5	11.02	8,974.00	9,710.00	17,166.00	0.0	525-2440	303-394-4404	None	0.25	None	Edward Keely	'93
FOUNDERS OPPTY BOND	Fixed Income	5.3	8.84	9,695.00	☆	☆	0.0	525-2440	303-394-4404	None	0.25	None	Montgomery C. Cleworth	'93
FOUNDERS PASSPORT FUND	International	24.2	9.68	9,778.00	☆	☆	0.0	525-2440	303-394-4404	None	0.25	None	Michael W. Gerding	'93
FOUNDERS SPECIAL FUND	Capital Appreciation	319.1	6.77	9,136.00	9,799.00	18,182.00	0.0	525-2440	303-394-4404	None	0.25	None	Charles Hooper	'91
FOUNDERS WORLDWIDE GROW	Global	90.9	16.75	9,841.00	11,737.00	☆	0.0	525-2440	303-394-4404	None	0.25	None	Michael W. Gerding	'90

PERFORMANCE OF MUTUAL FUNDS *(continued)*

				PERFORMANCE (Return on initial $10,000 Investment)				PHONE NUMBER		FEES				
FUND NAME	OBJECTIVE	TOTAL NET ASSETS ($ MIL) 5/31/94	NET ASSET $ VALUE 6/30/94	3/31/94-6/30/94	6/30/93-6/30/94	6/30/89-6/30/94	DIVIDEND YIELD % 6/94	800	In-State	Load	12b-1	Redemption	MANAGER	SINCE
FOUNTAIN SQ BALANCED	Balanced	64.6	9.46	9,916.00	9,899.00	☆	2.9	654-5372	513-579-5452	4.50	None	None	Atteberry/Folker	'93/'93
FOUNTAIN SQ MID CAP	Midcap	29.6	9.86	9,756.00	10,236.00	☆	0.7	654-5372	513-579-5452	4.50	None	None	Lyle Fiore	'93
FOUNTAIN SQ QUALITY BD	Fixed Income	48.9	9.43	9,832.00	9,725.00	☆	6.2	654-5372	513-579-5452	4.50	None	None	Tom Atteberry	'93
FOUNTAIN SQ QUALITY GRO	Growth	73.6	9.44	9,951.00	9,947.00	☆	1.5	654-5372	513-579-5452	4.50	None	None	Steve Folker	'93
FOUNTAIN SQ US GOVT SECS	Fixed Income	31.6	9.58	9,918.00	9,911.00	☆	5.9	654-5372	513-579-5452	4.50	None	None	Tom Atteberry	'93
FPA CAPITAL	Growth	169.0	18.86	9,772.00	11,026.00	20,607.00	0.2	982-4372	310-996-5425	6.50	None	None	Robert L. Rodriguez	'84
FPA NEW INCOME	Fixed Income	113.9	10.57	9,935.00	10,261.00	16,125.00	6.5	982-4372	310-996-5425	4.50	None	None	Robert L. Rodriguez	'84
FPA PARAMOUNT ⊠	Growth Income	339.0	13.48	10,235.00	10,966.00	17,997.00	1.8	982-4372	310-996-5425	6.50	None	None	William M. Sams	'81
FPA PERENNIAL FUND	Growth Income	62.1	21.47	10,042.00	10,099.00	15,287.00	2.1	982-4372	310-996-5425	6.50	None	None	Christopher Linden	'84
FRANKLIN AGE HI INC	Fixed Income	1,816.3	2.68	9,987.00	10,334.00	15,639.00	10.0	342-5236	415-312-3200	4.00	None	None	Wiskemann/Molumphy	'72/'91
FRANKLIN BALANCE SHEET	Capital Appreciation	77.4	21.95	10,266.00	11,480.00	☆	1.3	342-5236	415-312-3200	1.50	0.50	None	Lippman/Baughman	'90/'90
FRANKLIN CA GROWTH FUND	Growth	4.9	11.12	9,652.00	11,443.00	☆	1.1	342-5236	415-312-3200	4.50	0.25	None	Conrad Herrmann	'93
FRANKLIN CUST DYNATECH	Science & Technology	66.2	9.16	9,612.00	9,884.00	16,538.00	1.3	342-5236	415-312-3200	4.50	None	None	R. Johnson	'68
FRANKLIN CUST GROWTH	Growth	525.3	14.21	10,305.00	10,350.00	15,235.00	2.1	342-5236	415-312-3200	4.50	None	None	Jerry Palmeieri	'48
FRANKLIN CUST INCOME	Income	4,546.1	2.21	9,846.00	10,048.00	17,403.00	8.1	342-5236	415-312-3200	4.25	None	None	Matt Avery	'90
FRANKLIN CUST US GOVT	Fixed Income	12,556.6	6.58	9,894.00	9,775.00	14,580.00	8.1	342-5236	415-312-3200	4.25	None	None	Jack Lemein	'70
FRANKLIN CUST UTILITIES	Utility	2,785.2	8.26	9,267.00	8,409.00	14,484.00	6.3	342-5236	415-312-3200	4.25	None	None	Johnson/Edwards	'87/'91
FRANKLIN EQUITY FUND	Growth	293.8	6.53	9,849.00	10,230.00	13,100.00	1.5	342-5236	415-312-3200	4.00	None	None	Conrad Herrmann	'93
FRANKLIN GLOBAL HEALTH	Health/Biotechnology	6.1	9.92	9,546.00	10,857.00	☆	0.6	342-5236	415-312-3200	4.50	0.25	None	R. Johnson	'92
FRANKLIN GOLD FUND	Gold	409.9	14.51	9,672.00	10,342.00	13,924.00	1.3	342-5236	415-312-3200	4.00	None	None	Wiskemann/Christensen	'72/'88
FRANKLIN INTL INTL EQU	International	49.5	12.95	9,826.00	12,543.00	☆	1.7	342-5236	415-312-3200	4.50	0.25	None	Templeton Invt Council	'93
FRANKLIN INTL PAC GROWTH	Pacific Region	53.9	14.89	10,285.00	12,856.00	☆	1.3	342-5236	415-312-3200	4.50	0.25	None	Templeton Invt Council	'93
FRANKLIN INV ADJ RATE	Fixed Income	39.2	9.78	10,048.00	10,148.00	☆	4.3	342-5236	415-312-3200	2.25	0.25	None	Leman/Coffey	'91/'91
FRANKLIN INV ADJ US GOVT	Fixed Income	916.9	9.40	10,011.00	9,848.00	13,155.00	3.3	342-5236	415-312-3200	2.25	0.25	None	Leman/Coffey	'87/'90
FRANKLIN INV CONV SEC	Convertible Securities	61.2	12.01	9,874.00	10,654.00	17,522.00	5.3	342-5236	415-312-3200	4.00	None	None	Jamieson/Nori	'87/'92
FRANKLIN INV EQUITY INC	Equity Income	74.4	13.62	10,182.00	10,359.00	16,519.00	5.4	342-5236	415-312-3200	4.00	None	None	Frank Felicelli	'88
FRANKLIN INV GLOBAL GOVT	World Income	205.4	8.09	9,566.00	9,640.00	13,591.00	8.0	342-5236	415-312-3200	4.00	None	None	Kohli/Jamieson	'88/'93
FRANKLIN INV SH-INT USG	Fixed Income	245.1	10.11	9,963.00	9,968.00	14,269.00	4.6	342-5236	415-312-3200	2.25	None	None	Jack Lemein	'87
FRANKLIN MGD CORP QUAL	Income	32.1	23.90	9,977.00	10,184.00	15,878.00	4.0	342-5236	415-312-3200	1.50	0.25	None	W. Lippman	'87
FRANKLIN MGD INV GRADE	Fixed Income	29.9	8.84	9,966.00	10,042.00	14,630.00	4.8	342-5236	415-312-3200	4.00	0.25	None	W. Lippman	'87
FRANKLIN MGD RISING DIV	Growth Income	274.7	14.33	10,127.00	9,564.00	14,451.00	1.7	342-5236	415-312-3200	4.00	0.50	None	W. Lippman	'87
FRANKLIN PREMIER RET	Flexible	24.5	6.11	10,024.00	10,710.00	15,509.00	2.7	342-5236	415-312-3200	4.00	None	None	Costa/Wiskemann	'87/'72
FRANKLIN PRT TX-AD HY	Fixed Income	76.5	8.23	9,934.00	10,208.00	16,183.00	9.3	342-5236	415-312-3200	4.00	None	None	Martin Wiskemann	'87
FRANKLIN PRT TX-AD INTL	World Income	22.7	10.79	9,932.00	10,441.00	15,658.00	7.6	342-5236	415-312-3200	4.00	None	None	Bill Kohli	'90
FRANKLIN PRT TX-AD USG	Fixed Income	538.1	10.01	9,880.00	9,688.00	14,604.00	7.1	342-5236	415-312-3200	4.00	None	None	Jack Lemein	'87
FRANKLIN REAL ESTATE SEC	Real Estate	7.6	10.88	10,187.00	☆	☆	0.0	342-5236	415-312-3200	4.50	0.25	None	Avery/Willoughby	'93/'93
FRANKLIN SM CAP GROWTH	Small Company Growth	25.5	11.50	9,337.00	11,222.00	☆	0.2	342-5236	415-312-3200	4.50	0.25	None	Ed Jamieson	'92
FRANKLIN STRAT MTGE	Fixed Income	5.2	9.50	9,941.00	9,917.00	☆	5.5	342-5236	415-312-3200	4.25	None	None	Roger Bayston	'93
FRANKLIN STRAT GLBL UTIL	Utility	125.7	11.61	9,728.00	10,658.00	☆	2.6	342-5236	415-312-3200	4.50	0.25	None	S. Edwards	'92
FRANKLIN/TEMP GERMAN GVT	World Income	12.4	12.80	10,507.00	11,110.00	☆	4.6	342-5236	415-312-3200	3.00	0.25	None	Templeton Invt Council	'93
FRANKLIN/TEMP GL CURR	World Income	50.9	14.09	10,322.00	10,619.00	15,437.00	4.2	342-5236	415-312-3200	3.00	0.45	None	Templeton Invt Council	'93
FRANKLIN/TEMP HARD CURR	World Income	49.1	13.41	10,567.00	11,080.00	☆	3.5	342-5236	415-312-3200	3.00	0.45	None	Templeton Invt Council	'93
FRANKLIN/TEMP HIGH INC	World Income	18.2	11.35	10,249.00	10,304.00	☆	4.9	342-5236	415-312-3200	3.00	0.45	None	Templeton Invt Council	'93
FREMONT BOND	Fixed Income	12.2	9.45	9,881.00	9,848.00	☆	5.6	548-4539	415-768-9000	None	None	None	William Gross	'94
FREMONT GLOBAL	Global Flexible	334.0	12.81	9,969.00	10,648.00	14,890.00	1.8	548-4539	415-768-9000	None	None	None	Rhodes/Redo/Landini	'88/'88

FREMONT GROWTH	Growth	32.6	10.39	9,811.00	9,796.00	☆	1.5	548-4539	415-768-9000	None	None	None	Pang/Sit	'92/'92
FREMONT INTL GROWTH	International	26.2	9.08	9,848.00	☆	☆	0.0	548-4539	415-768-9000	None	None	None	Andrew B. Kim	'94
FRONTIER EQUITY FUND	Growth	0.9	6.46	8,489.00	7,797.00	☆	0.0	231-2901	414-691-1196	8.00	None	None	James Fay	'93
FUND FOR US GOVT SEC; A	Fixed Income	1,649.2	7.70	9,934.00	9,808.00	13,889.00	7.8	245-4770	412-288-1900	4.50	None	None	Gary Madich	'87
FUND FOR US GOVT SEC; C	Fixed Income	102.1	7.70	9,912.00	9,723.00	☆	6.9	245-4770	412-288-1900	None	0.75	1.00	Gary Madich	'93
FUNDAMENTAL INVESTORS	Growth Income	2,233.4	17.46	10,022.00	10,604.00	17,160.00	2.3	421-4120	714-671-7000	5.75	0.25	None	Multiple Managers	'78
FUNDAMENTAL GOVT STRAT	Fixed Income	34.1	1.54	8,618.00	8,426.00	☆	10.5	322-6864	212-635-3005	None	0.25	None	Team Managed	'92
FUNDTRUST AGGRESSIVE GRO	Capital Appreciation	36.4	14.80	9,763.00	10,409.00	15,725.00	1.3	638-1896	212-644-1400	1.50	0.50	None	Michael Hirsch	'84
FUNDTRUST GROWTH FUND	Growth	32.2	13.55	9,956.00	10,506.00	15,053.00	1.1	638-1896	212-644-1400	1.50	0.50	None	Michael Hirsch	'84
FUNDTRUST GROWTH&INCOME	Growth Income	51.1	15.46	10,092.00	10,340.00	14,544.00	2.8	638-1896	212-644-1400	1.50	0.50	None	Michael Hirsch	'84
FUNDTRUST INCOME FUND	Fixed Income	72.9	9.73	9,847.00	9,887.00	13,971.00	6.8	638-1896	212-644-1400	1.50	0.50	None	Michael Hirsch	'84
FUNDTRUST MGD TOT RETURN	Flexible	17.2	11.04	9,973.00	10,148.00	14,091.00	3.4	638-1896	212-644-1400	1.50	0.50	None	Michael Hirsch	'88
FXD INC LTD; FORT	Fixed Income	15.6	9.71	9,930.00	☆	☆	0.0	245-4770	412-288-1900	1.00	0.15	1.00	Deborah Cunningham	'93
FXD INC LTD; INV	Fixed Income	231.2	9.71	9,928.00	10,094.00	☆	5.9	245-4770	412-288-1900	1.00	0.25	None	Deborah Cunningham	'92
GABELLI ASSET	Growth	994.2	22.36	9,881.00	10,518.00	15,427.00	0.7	422-3554	914-921-5100	None	0.13	None	Mario J. Gabelli	'86
GABELLI EQ EQ INCOME	Equity Income	50.2	11.08	9,920.00	10,261.00	☆	2.5	422-3554	914-921-5100	4.50	0.25	None	Mario J. Gabelli	'92
GABELLI EQ SM CAP GRO	Small Company Growth	206.0	16.33	9,743.00	10,626.00	☆	0.0	422-3554	914-921-5100	4.50	0.25	None	Mario J. Gabelli	'91
GABELLI GL CONVERTIBLE	Convertible Securities	7.8	10.37	9,990.00	☆	☆	0.0	422-3554	914-921-5100	None	0.25	None	Hartswell Woodson III	'94
GABELLI GL COUCH POTATO	Global	19.1	9.97	10,071.00	☆	☆	0.0	422-3554	914-921-5100	None	0.25	None	Mario J. Gabelli	'94
GABELLI GL GL TELECOM	Global	131.8	9.62	9,938.00	☆	☆	0.0	422-3554	914-921-5100	None	0.25	None	Salvatore Muoio	'93
GABELLI GROWTH	Growth	557.3	21.23	9,694.00	10,038.00	15,739.00	0.4	422-3554	914-921-5100	None	0.18	None	Team Managed	'94
GABELLI INV ABC FUND	Growth	26.9	10.11	9,990.00	10,888.00	☆	2.8	422-3554	914-921-5100	2.00	0.25	None	Mario J. Gabelli	'93
GABELLI VALUE FUND	Capital Appreciation	457.1	11.55	10,158.00	11,312.00	☆	0.4	422-3554	914-921-5100	5.50	0.25	None	Mario J. Gabelli	'89
GABELLI CONVERTIBLE SEC	Convertible Securities	118.5	11.39	9,870.00	10,355.00	☆	4.8	422-3554	914-921-5100	None	None	None	Mario J. Gabelli	'89
GALAXY ASSET ALLOC; RTL	Flexible	143.4	10.40	9,824.00	9,809.00	☆	2.3	628-0414	None	None	None	None	Fred Thompson	'91
GALAXY EQUITY GROWTH; RTL	Growth	429.5	13.28	9,989.00	10,043.00	☆	1.2	628-0414	None	None	None	None	Bob Armknecht	'90
GALAXY EQUITY INCOME; RTL	Equity Income	138.7	12.23	10,167.00	10,211.00	☆	2.3	628-0414	None	None	None	None	Edward Klieziewicz	'90
GALAXY EQUITY VALUE; RTL	Growth Income	221.5	12.50	9,967.00	10,405.00	15,076.00	1.3	628-0414	None	None	None	None	G. Jay Evans	'92
GALAXY HI QUAL BOND; RTL	Fixed Income	156.9	9.87	9,727.00	9,705.00	☆	6.5	628-0414	None	None	None	None	Ken Thomae	'90
GALAXY INTL EQU; RTL	International	95.6	12.68	10,177.00	11,994.00	☆	0.1	628-0414	None	None	None	None	James Knauf	'91
GALAXY INTMDT BOND; RTL	Fixed Income	350.0	9.79	9,831.00	9,487.00	13,469.00	6.2	628-0414	None	None	None	None	Bruce R. Barton	'92
GALAXY SHT-TM BOND; RTL	Fixed Income	84.9	9.82	9,934.00	10,063.00	☆	4.4	628-0414	None	None	None	None	Ken Thomae	'91
GALAXY SM CO EQUITY; RTL	Small Company Growth	85.8	11.00	9,167.00	10,125.00	☆	0.0	628-0414	None	None	None	None	Steve Barbaro	'91
GAM EUROPE	European Region	21.8	87.06	9,837.00	11,419.00	☆	0.0	426-4685	212-407-4700	5.00	None	None	Bennett/Crerar	'93/'93
GAM GLOBAL	Global	22.2	150.27	9,930.00	13,181.00	16,910.00	0.4	426-4685	212-407-4700	5.00	None	None	John Horseman	'90
GAM INTERNATIONAL	International	106.7	198.94	10,097.00	13,688.00	22,055.00	0.5	426-4685	212-407-4700	5.00	None	None	John Horseman	'90
GAM NORTH AMERICA	Capital Appreciation	1.9	85.20	10,040.00	9,704.00	☆	1.8	426-4685	212-407-4700	5.00	None	None	Fayez Sarofim & Co.	'90
GAM PACIFIC BASIN	Pacific Region	44.5	194.77	10,904.00	13,292.00	22,532.00	0.0	426-4685	212-407-4700	5.00	None	None	Bunker/Kirkby	'87/'87
GATEWAY INDEX PLUS FUND	Growth Income	178.9	15.51	10,137.00	10,261.00	16,158.00	1.8	354-6339	513-248-2700	None	None	None	Peter W. Thayer	'77
GATEWAY MID CAP INDEX	Midcap	9.8	9.37	9,600.00	9,548.00	☆	1.2	354-6339	513-248-2700	None	None	None	Peter W. Thayer	'92
GATEWAY SM CAP INDEX	Small Company Growth	12.9	9.53	9,464.00	9,709.00	☆	0.4	354-6339	513-248-2700	None	None	None	Peter W. Thayer	'93
GE FXD INC; A	Fixed Income	25.7	11.38	9,906.00	☆	☆	0.0	242-0134	203-326-4040	4.25	0.50	None	Robert A. MacDougall	'93
GE FXD INC; B	Fixed Income	0.1	11.37	9,893.00	☆	☆	0.0	242-0134	203-326-4040	None	1.00	5.00	Robert A. MacDougall	'93
GE FXD INC; C	Fixed Income	12.0	11.38	9,912.00	9,876.00	☆	5.1	242-0134	203-326-4040	None	0.25	None	Robert A. MacDougall	'93
GE FXD INC; D ▮III	Fixed Income	2.7	11.38	9,918.00	☆	☆	0.0	242-0134	203-326-4040	None	None	None	Robert A. MacDougall	'93
GE GLBL EQTY; A	Global	0.2	18.52	9,883.00	☆	☆	0.0	242-0134	203-326-4040	4.75	0.50	None	Ralph R. Layman	'93
GE GLBL EQTY; B	Global	0.1	18.53	9,883.00	☆	☆	0.0	242-0134	203-326-4040	None	1.00	5.00	Ralph R. Layman	'93
GE GLBL EQTY; C	Global	17.5	18.57	9,893.00	11,791.00	☆	0.0	242-0134	203-326-4040	None	0.25	None	Ralph R. Layman	'93
GE GLBL EQTY; D ▮III	Global	9.4	18.61	9,904.00	☆	☆	0.0	242-0134	203-326-4040	None	None	None	Ralph R. Layman	'93
GE INTL EQTY; A	International	0.1	14.63	10,000.00	☆	☆	0.0	242-0134	203-326-4040	4.75	0.50	None	Ralph R. Layman	'94

PERFORMANCE OF MUTUAL FUNDS *(continued)*

FUND NAME	OBJECTIVE	TOTAL NET ASSETS ($ MIL) 5/31/94	NET ASSET $ VALUE 6/30/94	PERFORMANCE (Return on initial $10,000 Investment) 3/31/94-6/30/94	6/30/93-6/30/94	6/30/89-6/30/94	DIVIDEND YIELD % 6/94	PHONE NUMBER 800	In-State	FEES Load	12b-1	Redemption	MANAGER	SINCE
GE INTL EQTY; B	International	0.1	14.61	9,986.00	☆	☆	0.0	242-0134	203-326-4040	None	1.00	5.00	Ralph R. Layman	'94
GE INTL EQTY; C ◪	International	0.1	14.64	10,000.00	☆	☆	0.0	242-0134	203-326-4040	None	0.25	None	Ralph R. Layman	'94
GE INTL EQTY; D ▮	International	25.9	14.66	10,014.00	☆	☆	0.0	242-0134	203-326-4040	None	None	None	Ralph R. Layman	'94
GE SH-TM GOVT; A	Fixed Income	0.1	11.75	9,998.00	☆	☆	0.0	242-0134	203-326-4040	2.50	0.50	None	Robert A. MacDougall	'94
GE SH-TM GOVT; B	Fixed Income	0.1	11.76	9,998.00	☆	☆	0.0	242-0134	203-326-4040	None	0.85	3.00	Robert A. MacDougall	'94
GE SH-TM GOVT; C	Fixed Income	0.1	11.76	10,008.00	☆	☆	0.0	242-0134	203-326-4040	None	0.25	None	Robert A. MacDougall	'94
GE SH-TM GOVT; D	Fixed Income	7.8	11.76	10,019.00	☆	☆	0.0	242-0134	203-326-4040	None	None	None	Robert A. MacDougall	'94
GE STRAT INV; A	Balanced	0.8	15.27	10,013.00	☆	☆	0.0	242-0134	203-326-4040	4.75	0.50	None	Carlson/MacDougall	'93/'93
GE STRAT INV; B	Balanced	0.1	15.20	9,967.00	☆	☆	0.0	242-0134	203-326-4040	None	1.00	5.00	Carlson/MacDougall	'93/'93
GE STRAT INV; C	Balanced	12.4	15.26	9,980.00	10,024.00	☆	1.7	242-0134	203-326-4040	None	0.25	None	Carlson/MacDougall	'93/'93
GE STRAT INV; D ▮	Balanced	11.7	15.28	9,987.00	☆	☆	0.0	242-0134	203-326-4040	None	None	None	Carlson/MacDougall	'93/'93
GE US EQUITY; A	Growth Income	25.0	15.52	10,019.00	☆	☆	0.0	242-0134	203-326-4040	4.75	0.50	None	Eugene Bolton	'93
GE US EQUITY; B	Growth Income	0.1	15.47	9,987.00	☆	☆	0.0	242-0134	203-326-4040	None	1.00	5.00	Eugene Bolton	'93
GE US EQUITY; C	Growth Income	14.8	15.53	10,013.00	10,032.00	☆	1.3	242-0134	203-326-4040	None	0.25	None	Eugene Bolton	'93
GE US EQUITY; D ▮	Growth Income	81.5	15.55	10,019.00	☆	☆	0.0	242-0134	203-326-4040	None	None	None	Eugene Bolton	'93
GE S&S PRGRM LG-TM INTST ◪	Fixed Income	2,875.2	10.89	9,914.00	9,917.00	15,004.00	6.5	242-0134	203-326-4040	None	None	None	Robert A. MacDougall	'87
GE S&S PRGRM MUTUAL FUND ◪	Growth Income	1,738.3	35.39	10,025.00	10,046.00	16,171.00	2.8	242-0134	203-326-4040	None	None	None	Eugene Bolton	'90
GENERAL SECURITIES	Capital Appreciation	27.0	12.34	10,024.00	10,358.00	16,451.00	1.1	393-9990	312-368-5410	None	None	None	Jack Robinson	'51
GIBRALTAR EQUITY GROWTH	Growth Income	0.9	12.07	9,885.00	9,489.00	11,792.00	0.0	None	215-525-6102	None	None	None	Norman McAvoy	'90
GIBRALTAR US GOVT	Fixed Income	1.3	9.84	9,981.00	10,238.00	☆	4.1	None	215-525-6102	4.50	0.25	None	Joseph Waltman	'92
GINTEL ERISA	Growth Income	42.3	24.40	9,686.00	8,793.00	11,593.00	8.4	243-5808	203-622-6400	None	None	None	Gintel/Godman	'82/'92
GINTEL FUND	Growth	114.6	13.06	9,554.00	8,863.00	13,338.00	3.8	243-5808	203-622-6400	None	None	None	Gintel/Godman	'81/'92
GIT EQUITY EQUITY INCOME	Equity Income	3.6	15.45	10,056.00	9,899.00	13,966.00	2.5	336-3063	703-528-6500	None	None	None	Charles Tennes	'93
GIT EQUITY SELECT GROWTH	Growth	4.6	16.87	9,526.00	9,409.00	12,983.00	0.0	336-3063	703-528-6500	None	None	None	Charles Tennes	'93
GIT EQUITY SPEC GROWTH	Midcap	35.3	19.15	9,809.00	10,910.00	13,552.00	0.8	336-3063	703-528-6500	None	None	None	Richard Carney	'83
GIT EQUITY WORLDWIDE GRO	International	4.3	10.71	9,679.00	12,349.00	☆	0.4	336-3063	703-528-6500	None	None	None	Charles Tennes	'93
GIT INCOME GOVERNMENT	Fixed Income	7.9	9.51	9,887.00	9,839.00	14,170.00	3.6	336-3063	703-528-6500	None	None	None	John Edwards	'89
GIT INCOME MAXIMUM INC	Fixed Income	7.6	7.05	9,864.00	10,141.00	14,048.00	8.5	336-3063	703-528-6500	None	None	None	John Edwards	'88
GLENMEDE EQUITY FUND	Growth	61.2	12.58	9,834.00	9,913.00	☆	2.5	441-7379	None	None	None	None	John Church	'93
GLENMEDE INSTL INTERNATL	International	15.8	12.94	10,276.00	12,237.00	☆	0.9	441-7379	None	None	None	None	Andrew B. Williams	'92
GLENMEDE INTERNATIONAL	International	261.5	13.63	10,328.00	12,326.00	17,387.00	1.9	441-7379	None	None	None	None	Andrew B. Williams	'88
GLENMEDE INTL FIXED INC	World Income	15.9	10.75	10,238.00	10,916.00	☆	4.3	441-7379	None	None	None	None	Sheryl Durham	'93
GLENMEDE INTMDT GOVT	Fixed Income	398.4	10.01	9,894.00	9,851.00	14,819.00	6.1	441-7379	None	None	None	None	Sheryl Durham	'93
GLENMEDE MODEL EQUITY	Growth	18.9	10.44	9,633.00	10,761.00	☆	2.0	441-7379	None	None	None	None	Andrew B. Williams	'93
GLENMEDE SMALL CAP EQU	Small Company Growth	89.8	13.51	9,751.00	10,671.00	☆	0.9	441-7379	None	None	None	None	Williams/Mancuso	'92/'93
GLOBAL UTILITY FUND; A	Utility	135.6	13.34	9,760.00	10,222.00	☆	3.4	225-1852	None	5.25	0.20	None	William Hicks	'91
GLOBAL UTILITY FUND; B	Utility	286.7	13.34	9,740.00	10,139.00	☆	2.6	225-1852	None	None	1.00	5.00	William Hicks	'91
GOLDEN RNBOW A JAMES ADV	Growth Income	194.2	16.67	9,790.00	9,851.00	☆	3.9	227-4648	513-461-0332	None	0.20	None	Team Managed	'91
GOLDMAN SACHS EQ CAP GRO	Growth	862.5	15.45	9,891.00	10,863.00	☆	0.2	526-7384	212-902-0800	5.50	0.25	None	Team Managed	'92
GOLDMAN SACHS EQ G&I	Growth Income	75.2	15.76	10,060.00	11,144.00	☆	1.4	526-7384	212-902-0800	5.50	0.25	None	Team Managed	'93
GOLDMAN SACHS EQ INTL	International	323.6	16.08	9,509.00	10,720.00	☆	0.0	526-7384	212-902-0800	5.50	0.25	None	Team Managed	'92
GOLDMAN SACHS EQ SEL EQU	Growth	92.0	15.03	10,020.00	10,588.00	☆	1.1	526-7384	212-902-0800	5.50	0.25	None	Team Managed	'91
GOLDMAN SACHS EQ SM CAP	Small Company Growth	341.6	19.40	9,681.00	11,095.00	☆	0.2	526-7384	212-902-0800	5.50	0.25	None	Team Managed	'92
GOLDMAN SACHS ADJ AGY; IN ▮	Fixed Income	1,323.2	9.81	10,011.00	10,208.00	☆	4.2	526-7384	212-902-0800	None	None	None	Team Managed	'91
GOLDMAN SACHS ADJ MTGE	Fixed Income	18.4	4.87	10,054.00	10,448.00	☆	4.8	526-7384	212-902-0800	1.50	0.25	None	Team Managed	'93

GOLDMAN SACHS CORE; INSTL	Fixed Income	24.4	9.40	9,878.00	☆	☆	0.0	526-7384	212-902-0800	None	None	None	Team Managed	'94
GOLDMAN SACHS GLBL INC	World Income	599.7	13.70	9,802.00	9,949.00	☆	7.0	526-7384	212-902-0800	4.50	0.25	None	Team Managed	'91
GOLDMAN SACHS GOV AGENCY	Fixed Income	72.3	9.71	9,899.00	10,062.00	☆	4.4	526-7384	212-902-0800	None	None	None	Team Managed	'92
GOLDMAN SACHS GOVT INC	Fixed Income	12.6	13.74	9,924.00	9,901.00	☆	5.6	526-7384	212-902-0800	4.50	0.25	None	Team Managed	'93
GOVERNMENT INCOME SEC	Fixed Income	3,224.6	8.55	9,942.00	9,829.00	13,947.00	7.7	245-4770	412-288-1900	1.00	None	1.00	Gary Madich	'87
GOVERNMENT STREET BOND	Fixed Income	26.0	20.40	9,928.00	9,914.00	☆	6.3	543-8721	513-629-2000	None	None	None	T. Leavell & Assoc.	'91
GOVERNMENT STREET EQUITY	Growth	28.5	21.90	9,700.00	9,819.00	☆	1.4	543-8721	513-629-2000	None	None	None	T. Leavell & Assoc.	'91
GOVETT DEVELOP MKTS BOND	World Income	6.4	7.95	10,230.00	☆	☆	0.0	634-6838	415-274-2700	4.95	0.35	None	Simon Osborne	'93
GOVETT EMERGING MKTS	Emerging Markets	73.0	15.43	9,578.00	12,841.00	☆	0.0	634-6838	415-274-2700	4.95	0.50	None	Rachael Maunder	'92
GOVETT GLBL GOVT INC	World Income	79.3	8.79	9,577.00	9,811.00	☆	10.0	634-6838	415-274-2700	4.95	0.35	None	Simon Osborne	'92
GOVETT INTL EQUITY	International	32.6	12.64	10,202.00	11,961.00	☆	0.0	634-6838	415-274-2700	4.95	0.50	None	Gareth Watts	'92
GOVETT LATIN AMERICA	Latin American	8.4	8.33	9,035.00	☆	☆	0.0	634-6838	415-274-2700	4.95	0.50	None	Carolyn Lane	'94
GOVETT PACIFIC STRATEGY	Pacific Region	19.5	8.97	10,170.00	☆	☆	0.0	634-6838	415-274-2700	4.95	0.50	None	Peter Robson	'93
GOVETT SMALLER COMPANIES	Small Company Growth	32.6	15.75	9,962.00	12,382.00	☆	0.0	634-6838	415-274-2700	4.95	0.50	None	Garett Van Wagoner	'93
GRADISON GR TR ESTAB VAL	Growth	254.3	21.26	9,650.00	10,280.00	15,143.00	0.9	869-5999	513-579-5700	None	0.50	None	William Leugers	'83
GRADISON GR TR OPPTY VAL	Small Company Growth	84.6	17.32	9,884.00	10,256.00	15,887.00	0.5	869-5999	513-579-5700	None	0.50	None	William Leugers	'83
GRADISON-MCDONALD GOVT	Fixed Income	238.7	12.40	9,898.00	9,779.00	14,352.00	5.7	869-5999	513-579-5700	2.00	0.25	None	Michael Link	'87
GREEN CENTURY BALANCED	Balanced	3.2	9.68	9,821.00	9,617.00	☆	0.8	934-7336	None	None	0.50	None	Team Managed	'92
GREENFIELD FUND	Flexible	0.7	N/A	N/A	N/A	N/A	0.0	None	212-986-2600	None	None	1.00	R.F. Nichols Jr.	'81
GREENSPRING FUND	Growth Income	37.0	14.27	10,007.00	10,723.00	15,593.00	2.7	366-3863	410-823-5353	None	None	None	C. Carlson	'87
GRIFFIN BOND; A	Fixed Income	6.2	8.57	9,827.00	☆	☆	0.0	676-4450	None	4.50	0.25	None	Bruce Salvog	'93
GRIFFIN GRO & INC; A	Growth Income	11.2	10.79	10,103.00	☆	☆	0.0	676-4450	None	4.50	0.25	None	Paul Dow	'93
GRIFFIN US GOVT INC; A	Fixed Income	16.8	8.83	9,971.00	☆	☆	0.0	676-4450	None	4.50	0.25	None	Scott King	'93
GROWTH FD OF WASHINGTON	Growth	38.7	14.89	10,054.00	10,066.00	13,257.00	0.9	348-4782	None	4.75	0.25	None	Prabha S. Carpenter	'86
GROWTH FUND OF AMERICA	Growth	5,078.5	25.41	9,743.00	10,468.00	16,283.00	0.5	421-4120	714-671-7000	5.75	0.25	None	Multiple Managers	'73
GS SHT-TERM GOVT AGCY	Fixed Income	224.9	9.71	10,004.00	10,084.00	13,786.00	5.5	526-7384	212-902-0800	None	None	None	Team Managed	'93
GT AMERICA GROWTH; A	Growth	138.1	18.59	10,293.00	12,849.00	20,310.00	0.0	824-1580	415-392-6181	4.75	0.35	None	Team Managed	'91
GT AMERICA GROWTH; B	Growth	15.8	18.44	10,279.00	12,757.00	☆	0.0	824-1580	415-392-6181	None	1.00	5.00	Team Managed	'93
GT EUROPE GROWTH; A	European Region	776.1	10.16	9,658.00	10,877.00	11,600.00	0.8	824-1580	415-392-6181	4.75	0.35	None	Team Managed	'93
GT EUROPE GROWTH; B	European Region	84.0	10.08	9,637.00	10,802.00	☆	0.8	824-1580	415-392-6181	None	1.00	5.00	Team Managed	'93
GT GLOBAL EMERG MKTS; A	Emerging Markets	286.9	15.17	9,422.00	12,722.00	☆	0.1	824-1580	415-392-6181	4.75	0.50	None	Team Managed	'92
GT GLOBAL EMERG MKTS; B	Emerging Markets	190.8	15.10	9,408.00	12,666.00	☆	0.0	824-1580	415-392-6181	None	1.00	5.00	Team Managed	'93
GT GLOBAL GOVT INC; A	World Income	603.8	8.76	9,601.00	9,732.00	14,901.00	14.1	824-1580	415-392-6181	4.75	0.35	None	Team Managed	'89
GT GLOBAL GOVT INC; B	World Income	283.8	8.76	9,585.00	9,666.00	☆	13.3	824-1580	415-392-6181	None	1.00	5.00	Team Managed	'92
GT GLOBAL GRO & INC; A	Global	305.9	5.95	9,949.00	10,843.00	☆	4.1	824-1580	415-392-6181	4.75	0.35	None	Team Managed	'91
GT GLOBAL GRO & INC; B	Global	315.9	5.96	9,933.00	10,775.00	☆	3.5	824-1580	415-392-6181	None	1.00	5.00	Team Managed	'92
GT GLOBAL HIGH INC; A	World Income	198.2	11.81	10,125.00	9,979.00	☆	12.6	824-1580	415-392-6181	4.75	0.35	None	Team Managed	'92
GT GLOBAL HIGH INC; B	World Income	197.6	11.80	10,107.00	9,924.00	☆	11.9	824-1580	415-392-6181	None	1.00	5.00	Team Managed	'92
GT GLOBAL HLTH CARE; A	Health/Biotechnology	387.3	17.11	9,406.00	10,158.00	☆	0.4	824-1580	415-392-6181	4.75	0.50	None	Team Managed	'89
GT GLOBAL HLTH CARE; B	Health/Biotechnology	27.5	17.02	9,398.00	10,103.00	☆	0.2	824-1580	415-392-6181	None	1.00	5.00	Team Managed	'93
GT GLOBAL PACIFIC GR; A	Pacific Region	446.6	13.08	10,062.00	11,286.00	15,652.00	0.0	824-1580	415-392-6181	4.75	0.35	None	Team Managed	'87
GT GLOBAL PACIFIC GR; B	Pacific Region	107.9	12.98	10,046.00	11,211.00	☆	0.0	824-1580	415-392-6181	None	1.00	5.00	Team Managed	'93
GT GLOBAL STRAT INC; A	World Income	300.1	10.73	9,992.00	9,847.00	15,812.00	9.9	824-1580	415-392-6181	4.75	0.35	None	Team Managed	'92
GT GLOBAL STRAT INC; B	World Income	478.3	10.73	9,975.00	9,785.00	☆	9.2	824-1580	415-392-6181	None	1.00	5.00	Team Managed	'92
GT GLOBAL TELECOMM; A	Global	1,488.8	16.09	9,853.00	11,684.00	☆	0.5	824-1580	415-392-6181	4.75	0.50	None	Team Managed	'92
GT GLOBAL TELECOMM; B	Global	956.9	15.99	9,840.00	11,620.00	☆	0.5	824-1580	415-392-6181	None	1.00	5.00	Team Managed	'93
GT INTL GROWTH; A	International	473.6	10.46	10,000.00	11,482.00	14,494.00	0.0	824-1580	415-392-6181	4.75	0.35	None	Team Managed	'87
GT INTL GROWTH; B	International	58.9	10.38	9,981.00	11,407.00	☆	0.0	824-1580	415-392-6181	None	1.00	5.00	Team Managed	'93
GT JAPAN GROWTH; A	Japanese	125.9	13.75	10,675.00	12,603.00	12,047.00	0.0	824-1580	415-392-6181	4.75	0.35	None	Team Managed	'91
GT JAPAN GROWTH; B	Japanese	21.9	13.65	10,639.00	12,511.00	☆	0.0	824-1580	415-392-6181	None	1.00	5.00	Team Managed	'93

PERFORMANCE OF MUTUAL FUNDS (continued)

FUND NAME	OBJECTIVE	TOTAL NET ASSETS ($ MIL) 5/31/94	NET ASSET $ VALUE 6/30/94	PERFORMANCE (Return on initial $10,000 Investment) 3/31/94-6/30/94	6/30/93-6/30/94	6/30/89-6/30/94	DIVIDEND YIELD % 6/94	PHONE NUMBER 800	In-State	FEES Load	12b-1	Redemption	MANAGER	SINCE
GT LATIN AMER GROWTH; A	Latin American	244.7	20.52	8,669.00	12,505.00	☆	1.0	824-1580	415-392-6181	4.75	0.50	None	Team Managed	'91
GT LATIN AMER GROWTH; B	Latin American	136.1	20.43	8,657.00	12,448.00	☆	0.9	824-1580	415-392-6181	None	1.00	5.00	Team Managed	'93
GT WORLDWIDE GROWTH; A	Global	197.0	16.53	9,940.00	10,835.00	15,765.00	0.0	824-1580	415-392-6181	4.75	0:35	None	Team Managed	'87
GT WORLDWIDE GROWTH; B	Global	43.3	16.40	9,927.00	10,765.00	☆	0.5	824-1580	415-392-6181	None	1.00	5.00	Team Managed	'93
GUARDIAN ASSET ALLOC	Flexible	55.3	10.44	9,694.00	10,004.00	☆	1.8	221-3253	None	4.50	0.25	None	Frank J. Jones	'93
GUARDIAN BAIL GIFF INTL	International	31.4	13.22	10,115.00	11,921.00	☆	0.0	221-3253	None	4.50	0.25	None	R. Robin Menzies	'93
GUARDIAN INV QUAL BOND	Fixed Income	20.0	9.35	9,816.00	9,729.00	☆	4.9	221-3253	None	4.50	0.25	None	Michelle Babakian	'93
GUARDIAN PARK AVENUE FD	Growth	604.4	27.48	9,881.00	10,164.00	17,638.00	0.7	221-3253	None	4.50	0.15	None	Charles E. Albers	'72
GUARDIAN US GOVT SECS FD	Fixed Income	27.1	9.69	9,797.00	9,704.00	14,490.00	4.8	221-3253	None	4.50	0.25	None	Michelle Babakian	'89
ALEX HAMILTON EQTY G & I	Growth Income	4.9	9.53	10,136.00	☆	☆	0.0	801-2142	None	4.50	0.25	None	Mike Donelly	'94
ALEX HAMILTON GOVT INC	Fixed Income	4.9	9.22	9,919.00	☆	☆	0.0	801-2142	None	4.50	0.25	None	Kathy Mavs	'94
J HANCOCK DISCOVERY; A	Small Company Growth	3.7	8.54	9,553.00	9,456.00	☆	0.0	225-5291	None	5.00	0.30	None	Chapman/Hazard	'92/'93
J HANCOCK DISCOVERY; B	Small Company Growth	29.0	8.33	9,531.00	9,385.00	☆	0.0	225-5291	None	None	1.00	5.00	Chapman/Hazard	'91/'91
J HANCOCK DIVERSIFIED	Growth Income	66.6	12.43	9,973.00	10,240.00	☆	1.9	225-5291	None	None	0.50	None	Paul McManus	'91
J HANCOCK FR AV&T; A	Science & Technology	68.1	10.01	9,303.00	9,382.00	12,733.00	0.0	225-5291	None	5.00	0.30	None	Barry Gordon	'73
J HANCOCK FR AV&T; B	Science & Technology	0.1	9.98	9,284.00	☆	☆	0.0	225-5291	None	None	1.00	5.00	Barry Gordon	'94
J HANCOCK FR ENVIRO; A	Environmental	13.2	8.09	9,608.00	9,677.00	☆	0.0	225-5291	None	5.00	0.30	None	Beckwith/Wills/Behar	'89/'89
J HANCOCK FR ENVIRO; B	Environmental	0.7	7.99	9,603.00	9,627.00	☆	0.0	225-5291	None	None	1.00	5.00	Beckwith/Wills/Behar	'92/'92
J HANCOCK FR GL TECH; A	Science & Technology	46.5	16.17	9,084.00	10,525.00	14,950.00	0.0	225-5291	None	5.00	0.30	None	Barry Gordon	'83
J HANCOCK FR GL TECH; B	Science & Technology	4.1	16.09	9,060.00	☆	☆	0.0	225-5291	None	None	0.75	5.00	Barry Gordon	'94
J HANCOCK FR GLB INC; A	World Income	9.8	8.80	9,898.00	10,059.00	☆	7.9	225-5291	None	4.50	0.30	None	Robert Kowit	'92
J HANCOCK FR GLB INC; B	World Income	136.0	8.79	9,871.00	9,997.00	13,208.00	7.3	225-5291	None	None	1.00	5.00	Robert Kowit	'90
J HANCOCK FR GLBL RX; A	Health/Biotechnology	18.2	14.72	9,328.00	10,729.00	☆	0.0	225-5291	None	5.00	0.30	None	Benjamin Williams	'92
J HANCOCK FR GLBL RX; B	Health/Biotechnology	0.4	14.69	9,309.00	☆	☆	0.0	225-5291	None	None	1.00	5.00	Benjamin Williams	'94
J HANCOCK FR GLD&GOV; A	Gold	18.3	14.67	9,503.00	9,436.00	☆	4.9	225-5291	None	5.00	0.30	None	Anne McDonley	'93
J HANCOCK FR GLD&GOV; B	Gold	48.0	14.63	9,490.00	9,366.00	13,050.00	4.3	225-5291	None	None	1.00	5.00	Anne McDonley	'93
J HANCOCK FR GLOBAL; A	Global	95.7	12.89	9,946.00	11,766.00	☆	0.0	225-5291	None	5.00	0.30	None	Beckwith/Wills/Behar	'93/'94
J HANCOCK FR GLOBAL; B	Global	27.5	12.72	9,937.00	11,710.00	15,053.00	0.0	225-5291	None	None	1.00	5.00	Beckwith/Wills/Behar	'93/'94
J HANCOCK FR GLOBAL; C	Global	0.5	12.97	9,962.00	11,826.00	☆	0.0	225-5291	None	None	None	None	Beckwith/Wills/Behar	'93/'94
J HANCOCK FR INTL; A	International	3.1	8.09	10,176.00	☆	☆	0.0	225-5291	None	5.00	0.30	None	Team Managed	'94
J HANCOCK FR INTL; B	International	2.7	8.07	10,151.00	☆	☆	0.0	225-5291	None	None	1.00	5.00	Team Managed	'94
J HANCOCK FR PAC BSN; A	Pacific Region	45.8	14.93	10,304.00	12,633.00	17,996.00	0.0	225-5291	None	5.00	0.30	None	Beckwith/Wills/Behar	'93/'94
J HANCOCK FR PAC BSN; B	Pacific Region	4.8	14.91	10,297.00	☆	☆	0.0	225-5291	None	None	1.00	5.00	Beckwith/Wills/Behar	'94/'94
J HANCOCK FR REG BNK; A	Financial Services	153.4	22.11	10,825.00	11,761.00	☆	1.3	225-5291	None	5.00	0.30	None	Jim Schmidt	'92
J HANCOCK FR REG BNK; B	Financial Services	291.9	22.01	10,805.00	11,682.00	25,911.00	0.8	225-5291	None	None	1.00	5.00	Jim Schmidt	'85
J HANCOCK GROWTH; A	Growth	147.8	14.78	9,217.00	9,320.00	14,511.00	0.0	225-5291	None	5.00	0.30	None	Robert Freedman	'93
J HANCOCK GROWTH; B	Growth	2.1	14.77	9,211.00	☆	☆	0.0	225-5291	None	None	1.00	5.00	Robert Freedman	'94
J HANCOCK GROWTH; C	Growth	1.2	14.86	9,233.00	9,357.00	☆	0.0	225-5291	None	None	None	None	Robert Freedman	'93
J HANCOCK LTD GOVT; A	Fixed Income	249.6	8.55	9,969.00	10,055.00	13,980.00	5.2	225-5291	None	3.00	0.30	None	Anne McDonley	'94
J HANCOCK LTD GOVT; B	Fixed Income	3.9	8.55	9,951.00	☆	☆	0.0	225-5291	None	None	1.00	3.00	Anne McDonley	'94
J HANCOCK S-T STRAT; A	Fixed Income	8.6	8.50	10,043.00	10,311.00	☆	10.2	225-5291	None	3.00	0.30	None	Kowit/Cavanaugh	'92/'93
J HANCOCK S-T STRAT; B	Fixed Income	104.6	8.49	10,027.00	10,126.00	☆	8.2	225-5291	None	None	1.00	3.00	Kowit/Cavanaugh	'91/'93
J HANCOCK SOVER ACHV; A	Growth	24.1	11.55	9,813.00	10,154.00	☆	0.5	225-5291	None	5.00	0.30	None	Team Managed	'92
J HANCOCK SOVER ACHV; B	Growth	97.5	11.48	9,804.00	10,121.00	13,580.00	0.1	225-5291	None	None	1.00	5.00	Team Managed	'92
J HANCOCK SOVER BAL; A	Balanced	63.1	10.04	9,921.00	10,139.00	☆	6.4	225-5291	None	5.00	0.30	None	Team Managed	'92

J HANCOCK SOVER BAL; B	Balanced	81.5	10.03	9,902.00	10,068.00	☆	5.6	225-5291	None	None	1.00	5.00	Team Managed	'92
J HANCOCK SOVER BOND; A	Fixed Income	1,390.5	14.28	9,868.00	9,870.00	14,916.00	8.4	225-5291	None	4.50	0.30	None	Ho/Evans	'88/'88
J HANCOCK SOVER BOND; B	Fixed Income	22.1	14.28	9,848.00	☆	☆	0.0	225-5291	None	None	1.00	5.00	Ho/Evans	'93/'93
J HANCOCK SOVER BOND; C ▮	Fixed Income	0.9	14.28	9,876.00	9,909.00	☆	8.9	225-5291	None	None	None	None	Ho/Evans	'93/'93
J HANCOCK SOVER GOVT; A	Fixed Income	335.3	9.52	9,798.00	9,714.00	☆	6.8	225-5291	None	4.50	0.30	None	Anne C. Hodsdon	'92
J HANCOCK SOVER GOVT; B	Fixed Income	214.7	9.51	9,787.00	9,681.00	14,320.00	6.5	225-5291	None	None	1.00	5.00	Anne C. Hodsdon	'92
J HANCOCK SOVER INV; A	Growth Income	1,162.9	14.18	9,910.00	9,946.00	16,364.00	3.0	225-5291	None	5.00	0.30	None	Team Managed	'79
J HANCOCK SOVER INV; B	Growth Income	66.0	14.16	9,885.00	☆	☆	0.0	225-5291	None	None	1.00	5.00	Team Managed	'94
J HANCOCK SOVER INV; C ▮	Growth Income	12.9	14.20	9,918.00	9,979.00	☆	3.2	225-5291	None	None	None	None	Team Managed	'93
J HANCOCK SPEC EQ; A ⊠	Small Company Growth	264.2	13.47	9,176.00	9,486.00	24,156.00	0.0	225-5291	None	5.00	0.30	None	Michael DiCarlo	'88
J HANCOCK SPEC EQ; B ⊠	Small Company Growth	144.7	13.37	9,164.00	9,429.00	☆	0.0	225-5291	None	None	1.00	5.00	Michael DiCarlo	'93
J HANCOCK SPEC EQ; C ⊠	Small Company Growth	6.0	13.51	9,190.00	☆	☆	0.0	225-5291	None	None	None	None	Michael DiCarlo	'93
J HANCOCK SPEC OPPTY; A	Capital Appreciation	85.7	7.49	9,339.00	☆	☆	0.0	225-5291	None	5.00	0.30	None	Michael DiCarlo	'93
J HANCOCK SPEC OPPTY; B	Capital Appreciation	121.2	7.45	9,312.00	☆	☆	0.0	225-5291	None	None	1.00	5.00	Michael DiCarlo	'93
J HANCOCK SPEC VALUE; A	Growth Income	1.5	8.62	10,199.00	☆	☆	0.0	225-5291	None	5.00	0.30	None	Team Managed	'94
J HANCOCK SPEC VALUE; B	Growth Income	0.3	8.61	10,180.00	☆	☆	0.0	225-5291	None	None	1.00	5.00	Team Managed	'94
J HANCOCK STRAT INC; A	Fixed Income	335.3	7.07	9,859.00	10,185.00	13,549.00	10.2	225-5291	None	4.50	0.30	None	Frederick L. Cavanaugh	'86
J HANCOCK STRAT INC; B	Fixed Income	77.7	7.07	9,855.00	☆	☆	0.0	225-5291	None	None	1.00	5.00	Frederick L. Cavanaugh	'93
J HANCOCK UTILITIES; A	Utility	0.8	8.02	9,721.00	☆	☆	0.0	225-5291	None	5.00	0.30	None	Andrew St. Pierre	'94
J HANCOCK UTILITIES; B	Utility	0.4	8.00	9,697.00	☆	☆	0.0	225-5291	None	None	1.00	5.00	Andrew St. Pierre	'94
HANOVER BLUE CHIP; INV	Growth Income	47.9	9.80	9,903.00	9,916.00	☆	1.4	821-2371	None	3.00	None	None	Steve Duff	'93
HANOVER GOVT SECS; INV	Fixed Income	76.0	9.48	9,853.00	9,833.00	☆	4.9	821-2371	None	3.00	None	None	Pam Wooster	'93
HANOVER SH-TM GOVT; INV	Fixed Income	26.9	9.60	9,989.00	10,098.00	☆	3.9	821-2371	None	1.50	None	None	Guy Barba	'93
HANOVER SM CAP GRO; INV	Small Company Growth	18.2	9.24	9,259.00	9,121.00	☆	0.0	821-2371	None	3.00	None	None	Francis Lane	'93
HARBOR BOND	Fixed Income	163.5	10.48	9,857.00	9,924.00	15,823.00	5.9	422-1050	419-247-2477	None	None	None	William Gross	'87
HARBOR CAPITAL APPREC	Growth	172.4	15.14	9,522.00	10,245.00	18,895.00	0.2	422-1050	419-247-2477	None	None	None	Spiros Segalas	'90
HARBOR GROWTH	Growth	175.4	11.97	9,403.00	9,574.00	14,255.00	0.2	422-1050	419-247-2477	None	None	None	Arthur E. Nicholas	'93
HARBOR INTERNATIONAL ⊠	International	2,649.2	23.69	10,064.00	12,124.00	18,446.00	0.9	422-1050	419-247-2477	None	None	None	Hakan Castegren	'87
HARBOR INTL GROWTH	International	55.5	10.11	9,768.00	☆	☆	0.0	422-1050	419-247-2477	None	None	None	Howard B. Moss	'93
HARBOR SHORT DURATION	Fixed Income	110.1	8.89	10,040.00	10,203.00	☆	15.6	422-1050	419-247-2477	None	None	None	Adnan Akant	'92
HARBOR VALUE	Growth Income	58.9	12.79	10,338.00	10,187.00	14,228.00	2.5	422-1050	419-247-2477	None	None	None	John Strauss	'87
HARRIS INSIGHT CONVERT	Convertible Securities	4.8	9.27	9,805.00	10,208.00	13,125.00	6.3	982-8782	302-792-6400	4.50	0.25	None	Mary Ann Gassner	'92
HARRIS INSIGHT EQUITY	Growth Income	49.2	12.22	9,812.00	10,015.00	16,249.00	1.8	982-8782	302-792-6400	4.50	0.25	None	Cindy Galor	'92
HARRIS INSIGHT MGD FI	Fixed Income	72.2	9.84	9,930.00	9,976.00	☆	5.3	982-8782	302-792-6400	4.50	0.25	None	Michael Larson	'93
HARTWELL EMRG GRO; A	Small Company Growth	119.1	18.23	8,351.00	7,587.00	16,295.00	0.0	343-2898	617-621-6100	5.75	0.25	None	John M. Hartwell	'68
HARTWELL EMRG GRO; B	Small Company Growth	2.9	18.10	8,329.00	☆	☆	0.0	343-2898	617-621-6100	None	1.00	3.00	John M. Hartwell	'93
HARTWELL EMRG GRO; C	Small Company Growth	1.2	18.14	8,340.00	☆	☆	0.0	343-2898	617-621-6100	None	1.00	1.00	John M. Hartwell	'93
HARTWELL GROWTH; A	Capital Appreciation	21.3	19.35	8,852.00	9,139.00	13,442.00	0.0	343-2898	617-621-6100	5.75	0.25	None	William Miller	'84
HARTWELL GROWTH; B	Capital Appreciation	0.3	19.25	8,851.00	☆	☆	0.0	343-2898	617-621-6100	None	1.00	3.00	William Miller	'93
HARTWELL GROWTH; C	Capital Appreciation	0.2	19.16	8,829.00	☆	☆	0.0	343-2898	617-621-6100	None	1.00	1.00	William Miller	'93
HAWTHORNE INV BOND	Fixed Income	N/A	10.42	10,010.00	10,203.00	☆	4.6	272-4548	617-227-4800	None	None	None	Charles G. Dyer	'93
HAWTHORNE INV SEA FUND	Growth	N/A	9.40	9,875.00	9,767.00	☆	2.8	272-4548	617-227-4800	None	None	None	Charles G. Dyer	'90
HEARTLAND US GOVT SECS	Fixed Income	75.7	9.32	9,615.00	9,603.00	15,965.00	6.1	432-7856	414-347-7777	None	0.25	None	Retzer/Nasgovitz	'89/'87
HEARTLAND VALUE	Small Company Growth	248.6	23.65	9,858.00	11,425.00	20,540.00	0.0	432-7856	414-347-7777	None	0.25	None	Nasgovitz/Denison	'85/'88
HEARTLAND VALUE & INC	Growth Income	9.4	9.89	9,593.00	☆	☆	0.0	432-7856	414-347-7777	None	0.25	None	William Nasgovitz	'93
HENLOPEN FUND	Growth	7.0	11.67	9,503.00	10,488.00	☆	0.0	338-1579	302-654-3131	None	None	None	Michael Hershey	'92
HERCULES EURO VALUE	European Region	16.3	9.88	9,850.00	☆	☆	0.0	584-1317	612-342-1100	None	0.50	None	Pictet Intl Mgmt	'93
HERCULES GLOBAL SH-TM	World Income	2.3	9.91	9,975.00	☆	☆	0.0	584-1317	612-342-1100	None	0.25	None	Salomon Bros. Asset Mgt	'93
HERCULES LATIN AMER VAL	Latin American	28.9	9.14	8,393.00	☆	☆	0.0	584-1317	612-342-1100	None	0.50	None	Bankers Trust Company	'93
HERCULES N AMER GR & INC	Growth	17.2	9.46	9,793.00	☆	☆	0.0	584-1317	612-342-1100	None	0.50	None	Multiple Managers	'93

PERFORMANCE OF MUTUAL FUNDS (continued)

FUND NAME	OBJECTIVE	TOTAL NET ASSETS ($ MIL) 5/31/94	NET ASSET $ VALUE 6/30/94	PERFORMANCE (Return on initial $10,000 Investment) 3/31/94-6/30/94	6/30/93-6/30/94	6/30/89-6/30/94	DIVIDEND YIELD % 6/94	PHONE NUMBER 800	PHONE NUMBER In-State	FEES Load	FEES 12b-1	FEES Redemption	MANAGER	SINCE
HERCULES PAC BASIN VALUE	Pacific Region	38.8	10.68	10,574.00	☆	☆	0.0	584-1317	612-342-1100	None	0.50	None	Edinburgh Fund Managers	'93
HERCULES WORLD BOND	World Income	33.6	9.35	9,698.00	☆	☆	0.0	584-1317	612-342-1100	None	0.30	None	Salomon Bros. Asset Mgt	'93
HERITAGE CAPITAL APPREC	Capital Appreciation	72.2	14.37	10,105.00	10,706.00	14,578.00	1.8	421-4184	813-573-8143	4.00	0.50	None	Herb Ehlers	'85
HERITAGE INC DIVERSIFIED	Fixed Income	38.7	9.78	9,777.00	9,828.00	☆	7.7	421-4184	813-573-8143	4.00	0.35	None	Blount/Ross	'93/'90
HERITAGE INC INSTL GOVT	Fixed Income	5.2	9.84	9,987.00	☆	☆	0.0	421-4184	813-573-8143	None	0.25	None	Peter Wallace	'93
HERITAGE INC LTD MAT GOV	Fixed Income	50.4	9.16	9,941.00	9,964.00	☆	3.9	421-4184	813-573-8143	None	0.35	None	Ross/Wallace	'90/'93
HERITAGE INCOME-GROWTH	Equity Income	33.1	11.07	9,994.00	10,392.00	14,558.00	4.2	421-4184	813-573-8143	4.00	0.25	None	Lou Kirschbaum	'90
HERITAGE SMALL CAP STK	Small Company Growth	41.1	15.23	9,567.00	10,650.00	☆	0.0	421-4184	813-573-8143	4.75	0.25	None	Awad/Henwood	'93/'93
HIGHMARK BALANCED	Balanced	25.3	9.56	10,010.00	☆	☆	0.0	433-6884	None	4.50	None	None	Merus Capital Mgmt	'93
HIGHMARK BOND	Fixed Income	64.4	10.00	9,859.00	9,598.00	14,114.00	6.4	433-6884	None	3.00	None	None	Jack Montgomery	'94
HIGHMARK GOVT BOND	Fixed Income	5.4	9.39	9,939.00	☆	☆	0.0	433-6884	None	3.00	None	None	William Howard	'93
HIGHMARK GROWTH	Growth	14.8	9.44	9,590.00	☆	☆	0.0	433-6884	None	4.50	None	None	Merus Capital Mgmt	'93
HIGHMARK INC & GRO	Growth Income	5.1	9.65	10,141.00	☆	☆	0.0	433-6884	None	4.50	None	None	Merus Capital Mgmt	'93
HIGHMARK INCOME EQUITY	Equity Income	212.0	11.62	10,284.00	10,279.00	15,381.00	3.3	433-6884	None	4.50	None	None	Merus Capital Mgmt	'88
HILLIARD LYONS GROWTH	Growth	22.4	15.15	9,987.00	9,911.00	☆	0.8	444-1854	502-588-8400	4.75	0.25	None	Samuel C. Harvey	'92
HODGES FUND	Capital Appreciation	8.7	9.79	9,290.00	9,520.00	☆	0.1	388-8512	214-954-1177	2.50	0.50	None	Hodges Capital Mgt	'92
HOMESTATE PA GROWTH	Growth	9.9	12.37	9,841.00	11,386.00	☆	0.5	232-0224	717-396-7864	5.00	0.35	None	Kenneth G. Mertz II	'92
HOMESTEAD SHORT-TERM BD	Fixed Income	47.7	5.03	9,980.00	10,129.00	☆	4.7	258-3030	None	None	None	None	Peter Morris	'91
HOMESTEAD VALUE	Growth Income	72.4	14.62	10,310.00	10,862.00	☆	1.6	258-3030	None	None	None	None	Peter Morris	'90
HOUSEHLD PRSNL EQ INC	Equity Income	5.6	9.79	9,771.00	☆	☆	0.0	231-0180	312-368-5410	None	0.25	None	Roger Weissenberg	'93
HOUSEHLD PRSNL FXD INC	Fixed Income	5.1	9.18	9,816.00	☆	☆	0.0	231-0180	312-368-5410	None	0.25	None	Paul Fricke	'93
HOUSEHLD PRSNL GROWTH EQ	Growth	5.4	9.82	9,646.00	☆	☆	0.0	231-0180	312-368-5410	None	0.25	None	Steve Maraffio	'93
HOUSEHLD PRSNL SH-TM INC	Fixed Income	5.2	9.57	9,881.00	☆	☆	0.0	231-0180	312-368-5410	None	0.25	None	Paul Fricke	'93
HYPRN II HYPRN SHDUR 2	Fixed Income	59.8	9.17	9,947.00	9,998.00	☆	3.6	497-3746	212-980-8400	None	1.00	3.00	L. David Ricci	'93
HYPRN HYPRN SH DUR I	Fixed Income	32.2	8.88	9,964.00	10,065.00	☆	4.5	497-3746	212-980-8400	3.00	0.25	None	L. David Ricci	'93
IAA TRUST ASSET ALLOC	Fixed Income	8.7	11.08	9,991.00	10,071.00	14,390.00	3.1	245-2100	610-834-3500	3.00	0.25	None	John Jacobs	'78
IAA TRUST GROWTH	Growth	61.5	15.16	9,755.00	9,758.00	13,897.00	1.5	245-2100	610-834-3500	3.00	0.25	None	Gregory Turner	'79
IAI BOND FUND	Fixed Income	94.4	8.86	9,785.00	9,722.00	14,839.00	6.5	945-3863	612-376-2700	None	0.19	None	Larry R. Hill	'84
IAI INTERNATIONAL FUND	International	146.3	13.29	10,294.00	12,345.00	15,812.00	0.7	945-3863	612-376-2700	None	0.24	None	Roy Gillson	'90
IAI INV I INSTL BOND	Fixed Income	86.4	9.05	9,799.00	☆	☆	0.0	945-3863	612-376-2700	None	None	None	Larry R. Hill	'93
IAI INV II GROWTH	Growth	12.7	9.47	9,773.00	☆	☆	0.0	945-3863	612-376-2700	None	0.04	None	Team Managed	'93
IAI INV VII GRO & INC	Capital Appreciation	118.9	12.95	9,794.00	10,114.00	14,505.00	0.5	945-3863	612-376-2700	None	0.20	None	Carlin/McCallister	'91/'93
IAI REGIONAL FUND	Growth	569.1	19.39	9,729.00	10,008.00	16,495.00	0.8	945-3863	612-376-2700	None	0.25	None	Julian P. Carlin	'80
IAI RESERVE FUND	Fixed Income	93.2	9.94	10,065.00	10,242.00	13,098.00	3.7	945-3863	612-376-2700	None	0.05	None	Tim Palmer	'91
IAI VALUE FUND	Growth	34.0	10.77	9,936.00	10,815.00	15,113.00	0.3	945-3863	612-376-2700	None	0.02	None	Douglas Platt	'91
IAI BALANCED FUND	Balanced	50.3	9.64	9,813.00	9,648.00	☆	3.2	945-3863	612-376-2700	None	0.07	None	Simenstead/Diedrich	'93/'93
IAI EMERGING GROWTH FUND	Small Company Growth	230.1	12.40	8,634.00	9,234.00	☆	0.0	945-3863	612-376-2700	None	0.24	None	Rick Leggott	'91
IAI GOVERNMENT FUND	Fixed Income	37.6	9.78	9,928.00	9,893.00	☆	4.5	945-3863	612-376-2700	None	0.12	None	Scott Bettin	'91
IAI MIDCAP GROWTH FUND	Midcap	58.8	13.04	9,742.00	11,310.00	☆	0.0	945-3863	612-376-2700	None	0.08	None	Suzanne Zak	'93
IBM FDS LARGE CO INDEX	S&P Index	145.9	14.33	10,042.00	10,106.00	☆	2.5	426-9876	None	None	None	None	IBM Credit Invt Mgt	'90
IBM FDS SMALL CO INDEX	Small Company Growth	254.2	16.89	9,657.00	9,946.00	☆	1.4	426-9876	None	None	None	None	IBM Credit Invt Mgt	'90
IBM FDS TREAS INDEX	Fixed Income	129.1	10.09	9,865.00	9,817.00	☆	5.6	426-9876	None	None	None	None	IBM Credit Invt Mgt	'91
IBM FDS UTILITY INDEX	Utility	65.2	9.82	9,951.00	9,071.00	☆	4.6	426-9876	None	None	None	None	IBM Credit Invt Mgt	'93
IDEX FUND	Growth	301.0	17.10	9,474.00	9,569.00	17,421.00	0.2	624-4339	813-587-1800	8.50	None	None	Thomas F. Marsico	'86
IDEX FUND 3 ☒	Growth	164.0	13.98	9,405.00	9,537.00	17,400.00	0.2	624-4339	813-587-1800	8.50	None	None	Thomas F. Marsico	'87

IDEX II FLEX INC; A	Fixed Income	23.4	8.95	9,822.00	10,138.00	14,340.00	6.6	624-4339	813-587-1800	4.75	0.35	None	Ronald V. Speaker	'87
IDEX II FLEX INC; C	Fixed Income	0.5	8.95	9,819.00	☆	☆	0.0	624-4339	813-587-1800	None	0.90	None	Ronald V. Speaker	'93
IDEX II GLOBAL; A	Global	68.5	15.05	9,856.00	12,118.00	☆	0.0	624-4339	813-587-1800	5.50	0.35	None	Helen Young-Hayes	'92
IDEX II GLOBAL; C	Global	2.6	14.90	9,777.00	☆	☆	0.0	624-4339	813-587-1800	None	0.90	None	Helen Young-Hayes	'93
IDEX II GROWTH; A	Growth	461.5	16.34	9,461.00	9,453.00	17,283.00	0.0	624-4339	813-587-1800	5.50	0.35	None	Thomas F. Marsico	'86
IDEX II GROWTH; C	Growth	2.7	16.27	9,448.00	☆	☆	0.0	624-4339	813-587-1800	None	0.90	None	Thomas F. Marsico	'93
IDEX II INCOME PLUS; A	Fixed Income	66.3	9.95	9,852.00	9,972.00	15,985.00	7.5	624-4339	813-587-1800	4.75	0.35	None	David Halfpap	'89
IDEX II INCOME PLUS; C	Fixed Income	1.9	9.94	9,822.00	☆	☆	0.0	624-4339	813-587-1800	None	0.90	None	David Halfpap	'93
IDS BLUE CHIP ADVNTG	Growth Income	139.0	6.13	10,016.00	10,344.00	☆	1.6	328-8300	612-671-3733	5.00	None	None	Steve Merrell	'93
IDS BOND FUND	Fixed Income	2,243.5	4.89	9,779.00	9,959.00	15,547.00	8.2	328-8300	612-671-3733	5.00	None	None	Frederick C. Quirsfeld	'85
IDS DISCOVERY FUND	Midcap	518.2	10.19	8,954.00	9,336.00	17,473.00	0.0	328-8300	612-671-3733	5.00	None	None	Ray Hirsch	'88
IDS DVSD EQUITY INCM	Equity Income	808.9	7.42	9,917.00	10,721.00	☆	3.6	328-8300	612-671-3733	5.00	None	None	Richard Lazarchic	'90
IDS EQUITY PLUS FUND	Growth Income	611.8	10.37	9,694.00	9,780.00	16,950.00	0.9	328-8300	612-671-3733	5.00	None	None	Joseph M. Barsky III	'83
IDS EXTRA INCOME	Fixed Income	1,689.1	4.17	9,722.00	10,318.00	15,779.00	10.3	328-8300	612-671-3733	5.00	None	None	John A. Utter	'83
IDS FEDERAL INCOME	Fixed Income	1,029.7	4.85	9,976.00	9,955.00	14,176.00	5.9	328-8300	612-671-3733	5.00	None	None	James Synder	'93
IDS GLOBAL BOND	World Income	427.0	5.70	9,889.00	10,083.00	16,641.00	6.6	328-8300	612-671-3733	5.00	None	None	Ray S. Goodner	'89
IDS GLOBAL GROWTH	Global	526.4	6.47	9,878.00	11,843.00	☆	0.4	328-8300	612-671-3733	5.00	None	None	Edward Korff	'90
IDS GROWTH FUND	Growth	964.2	16.68	9,794.00	10,196.00	18,922.00	0.0	328-8300	612-671-3733	5.00	None	None	Mary J. Malevich	'92
IDS INTERNATIONAL	International	659.3	10.32	10,310.00	11,888.00	15,698.00	0.9	328-8300	612-671-3733	5.00	None	None	Peter L. Lamaison	'84
IDS MANAGED RETIREMENT	Flexible	2,082.6	10.89	9,851.00	10,307.00	19,234.00	1.2	328-8300	612-671-3733	5.00	None	None	Richard Lazarchic	'93
IDS MUTUAL	Balanced	2,933.3	11.81	10,082.00	10,260.00	15,511.00	4.5	328-8300	612-671-3733	5.00	None	None	Medcalf/Labenski	'83/'87
IDS NEW DIMENSIONS	Growth	4,003.6	13.45	9,697.00	10,164.00	20,613.00	0.5	328-8300	612-671-3733	5.00	None	None	Gordon Fines	'91
IDS PRECIOUS METALS	Gold	72.7	7.82	9,265.00	10,041.00	12,789.00	0.5	328-8300	612-671-3733	5.00	None	None	Richard Warden	'91
IDS PROGRESSIVE FUND	Capital Appreciation	264.4	6.55	9,879.00	10,526.00	13,330.00	1.5	328-8300	612-671-3733	5.00	None	None	Michael W. Garbisch	'91
IDS SELECTIVE FUND	Fixed Income	1,548.7	8.82	9,832.00	9,825.00	15,232.00	6.9	328-8300	612-671-3733	5.00	None	None	Ray S. Goodner	'85
IDS STOCK FUND	Growth Income	2,198.1	18.71	9,994.00	10,621.00	17,742.00	2.9	328-8300	612-671-3733	5.00	None	None	Joseph M. Barsky III	'93
IDS STR AGGR EQUITY	Capital Appreciation	650.1	13.28	9,229.00	9,543.00	15,387.00	0.0	328-8300	612-671-3733	None	1.00	5.00	Ray Hirsch	'90
IDS STR SHRT-TRM INC	Fixed Income	212.7	0.98	9,882.00	9,931.00	13,035.00	4.0	328-8300	612-671-3733	None	1.00	5.00	James Synder	'93
IDS STR WRLDWD GROW	International	251.1	5.52	10,279.00	11,670.00	13,416.00	0.0	328-8300	612-671-3733	None	1.00	5.00	Peter L. Lamaison	'91
IDS STRATEGY EQUITY	Growth Income	1,102.9	9.10	9,978.00	10,359.00	16,143.00	1.8	328-8300	612-671-3733	None	1.00	5.00	Tom Medcalf	'89
IDS STRATEGY INCOME	Fixed Income	715.9	5.98	9,762.00	9,832.00	14,982.00	6.9	328-8300	612-671-3733	None	1.00	5.00	John A. Utter	'91
IDS UTILITIES INCOME	Utility	669.2	6.23	9,885.00	9,837.00	16,673.00	4.9	328-8300	612-671-3733	5.00	None	None	Richard Warden	'93
IFT FR INST ADJ RATE	Fixed Income	31.8	9.77	10,053.00	10,171.00	☆	4.5	342-5236	415-312-3200	None	None	None	Leman/Coffey	'92/'92
IFT FR INST ADJ USG	Fixed Income	64.6	9.40	10,020.00	9,891.00	☆	3.8	342-5236	415-312-3200	None	None	None	Leman/Coffey	'91/'91
INCOME FUND OF AMERICA	Equity Income	10,367.8	13.44	10,066.00	10,072.00	15,688.00	6.1	421-4120	714-671-7000	5.75	0.25	None	Multiple Managers	73
INDEPND CAP BALANCED	Balanced	3.2	9.09	9,666.00	☆	☆	0.0	950-4243	None	4.50	0.35	None	Sherman/Secord/Angers	'93/'93
INDEPND CAP OPPORTUNIT	Capital Appreciation	27.6	10.59	9,725.00	9,971.00	☆	0.2	950-4243	None	4.50	0.50	None	Secord/Angers	'94/'94
INDEPND CAP SHT-INT GOVT	Fixed Income	20.8	9.65	9,978.00	10,076.00	☆	5.1	950-4243	None	1.50	0.25	None	Peter Sherman	'93
INDEPND CAP SM CAP STOCK	Small Company Growth	1.0	9.64	9,573.00	☆	☆	0.0	950-4243	None	4.50	0.30	None	Paul G. Secord	'93
INDEPND CAP TOT RTN BOND	Fixed Income	32.0	9.45	9,962.00	9,816.00	☆	5.5	950-4243	None	4.50	0.30	None	Peter Sherman	'90
INDEPND CAP TOT RTN GRO	Growth	27.7	11.05	9,239.00	9,409.00	☆	0.0	950-4243	None	4.50	0.40	None	Paul G. Secord	'93
INDEPND ONE US GOVT; TR	Fixed Income	71.4	9.72	9,887.00	9,907.00	☆	5.7	934-3883	None	None	None	None	Kerry Baker	'93
INFINITY BEA SH DUR; CLT	Fixed Income	108.7	4.94	10,041.00	10,325.00	☆	4.6	852-9730	None	None	None	None	Gordon Bennett	'92
INFINITY BEA SH DUR; SVC	Fixed Income	9.3	4.93	10,008.00	10,257.00	☆	4.1	852-9730	None	None	0.25	None	Gordon Bennett	'92
INSTL INTL FOREIGN EQU	International	766.4	13.66	10,111.00	12,302.00	☆	0.7	638-5660	410-547-2308	None	None	None	Martin G. Wade	'89
INSTL INVSTRS CAP APPREC	Growth Income	42.8	132.65	9,780.00	10,554.00	15,315.00	1.2	631-6364	212-551-1920	None	None	None	McCabe/Trautman	'93/'93
INSTL INVSTRS TX-ADV INC	Income	17.8	100.73	10,050.00	10,185.00	14,370.00	2.1	631-6364	212-551-1920	None	None	None	Trautman/Keasler	'93/'93
INTERMEDIATE BD FD AMER	Fixed Income	1,687.9	13.32	9,908.00	9,847.00	14,356.00	7.1	421-4120	714-671-7000	4.75	0.30	None	Multiple Managers	'88
INTL SRS INTL EQ; A	International	245.9	18.59	10,109.00	12,190.00	14,060.00	0.4	245-4770	412-288-1900	4.50	None	None	Randall S. Bauer	'92
INTL SRS INTL EQ; C	International	6.3	18.43	10,088.00	12,071.00	☆	0.2	245-4770	412-288-1900	None	0.75	1.00	Randall S. Bauer	'93

PERFORMANCE OF MUTUAL FUNDS (continued)

FUND NAME	OBJECTIVE	TOTAL NET ASSETS ($ MIL) 5/31/94	NET ASSET $ VALUE 6/30/94	PERFORMANCE (Return on initial $10,000 Investment) 3/31/94-6/30/94	6/30/93-6/30/94	6/30/89-6/30/94	DIVIDEND YIELD % 6/94	PHONE NUMBER 800	In-State	FEES Load	12b-1	Redemption	MANAGER	SINCE
INTL SRS INTL INC; A	World Income	239.1	10.13	9,563.00	10,466.00	☆	7.9	245-4770	412-288-1900	4.50	0.25	None	Randall S. Bauer	'91
INTL SRS INTL INC; C	World Income	8.7	10.12	9,544.00	10,400.00	☆	7.2	245-4770	412-288-1900	None	0.75	1.00	Randall S. Bauer	'93
INVESCO DVSFD SMALL CO	Small Company Growth	12.3	9.61	9,816.00	☆	☆	0.0	525-8085	303-930-6300	None	None	None	Kevin Means	'93
INVESCO DYNAMICS	Midcap	274.1	9.70	9,497.00	10,352.00	21,349.00	0.0	525-8085	303-930-6300	None	0.25	None	Tim Miller	'93
INVESCO EMERGING GROWTH	Small Company Growth	176.5	11.39	9,844.00	11,195.00	☆	0.0	525-8085	303-930-6300	None	0.25	None	Doug Pratt	'93
INVESCO GROWTH FUND	Growth Income	485.5	5.03	9,534.00	10,010.00	17,773.00	0.5	525-8085	303-930-6300	None	0.25	None	R. Dalton Sim	'88
INVESCO INC HIGH YIELD	Fixed Income	231.2	6.79	9,878.00	10,051.00	14,647.00	9.0	525-8085	303-930-6300	None	0.25	None	Jerry Paul	'94
INVESCO INC SELECT INC	Fixed Income	131.8	6.16	9,912.00	10,021.00	15,290.00	7.5	525-8085	303-930-6300	None	0.25	None	Jerry Paul	'94
INVESCO INC SH-TM BOND	Fixed Income	8.0	9.43	9,927.00	☆	☆	0.0	525-8085	303-930-6300	None	0.25	None	Richard Hinderlie	'94
INVESCO INC US GOVT SECS	Fixed Income	27.5	7.01	9,681.00	9,434.00	13,918.00	5.8	525-8085	303-930-6300	None	0.25	None	Richard Hinderlie	'94
INVESCO INDUST INCOME	Equity Income	3,966.6	11.32	9,863.00	10,324.00	19,130.00	4.2	525-8085	303-930-6300	None	0.25	None	Paul/Mayer	'94/'93
INVESCO INTL EUROPEAN	European Region	367.7	12.32	9,648.00	11,343.00	13,729.00	1.1	525-8085	303-930-6300	None	None	None	Chamberlain/Mill	'90/'86
INVESCO INTL INTL GROWTH	International	138.5	16.49	10,230.00	11,481.00	12,380.00	0.4	525-8085	303-930-6300	None	None	None	Davidson/Ehrman	'87/'93
INVESCO INTL PACIFIC	Pacific Region	303.5	16.51	10,749.00	12,614.00	13,586.00	0.3	525-8085	303-930-6300	None	None	None	Pickstone/Pratt	'93/'93
INVESCO MULT ASSET ALLO	Flexible	3.1	9.58	9,979.00	☆	☆	0.0	525-8085	303-930-6300	None	0.25	None	Kevin Means	'93
INVESCO MULT BALANCED	Balanced	3.4	10.28	10,198.00	☆	☆	0.0	525-8085	303-930-6300	None	0.25	None	Kelly/Paul	'94/'94
INVESCO STRAT ENERGY	Natural Resources	59.5	10.63	10,588.00	9,141.00	9,867.00	1.0	525-8085	303-930-6300	None	None	None	Tim Miller	'92
INVESCO STRAT ENVIRON	Environmental	45.3	6.35	9,230.00	9,248.00	☆	0.1	525-8085	303-930-6300	None	None	None	John Schroer	'93
INVESCO STRAT FINANCIAL	Financial Services	285.9	15.28	10,180.00	10,197.00	26,021.00	1.2	525-8085	303-930-6300	None	None	None	Doug Pratt	'92
INVESCO STRAT GOLD	Gold	307.1	5.73	8,389.00	9,363.00	12,074.00	0.0	525-8085	303-930-6300	None	None	None	Dan Leonard	'89
INVESCO STRAT HEALTH	Health/Biotechnology	461.4	31.31	9,247.00	9,896.00	22,439.00	0.0	525-8085	303-930-6300	None	None	None	Kurokawa/Schroer	'92/'94
INVESCO STRAT LEISURE	Specialty	261.6	20.80	9,463.00	10,967.00	22,229.00	0.0	525-8085	303-930-6300	None	None	None	Tim Miller	'92
INVESCO STRAT TECH	Science & Technology	255.9	21.62	9,583.00	10,210.00	26,994.00	0.0	525-8085	303-930-6300	None	None	None	Daniel B. Leonard	'85
INVESCO STRAT UTILITIES	Utility	135.3	9.52	9,678.00	9,399.00	15,827.00	3.6	525-8085	303-930-6300	None	None	None	Brian Kelly	'93
INVESCO VALUE EQUITY	Growth Income	101.0	16.89	10,055.00	10,504.00	15,688.00	1.9	525-8085	303-930-6300	None	None	None	Harhai/Irrgang	'93/'94
INVESCO VALUE INTMDT GVT	Fixed Income	34.7	12.13	9,951.00	10,026.00	14,660.00	5.8	525-8085	303-930-6300	None	None	None	Baker/ Jenkins	'93/'94
INVESCO VALUE TOTAL RET	Flexible	265.6	17.65	10,097.00	10,456.00	16,075.00	3.6	525-8085	303-930-6300	None	None	None	Mitchell/Griffin	'87/'94
INVESTMENT CO OF AMERICA	Growth Income	19,078.9	18.02	10,115.00	10,389.00	16,483.00	2.6	421-4120	714-671-7000	5.75	0.25	None	Multiple Managers	'34
INVESTORS RESEARCH	Capital Appreciation	37.0	4.50	9,978.00	10,024.00	14,325.00	1.2	732-1733	805-569-3253	5.75	0.25	None	Richard W. Arms, Jr.	'94
INVESTORS TR ADJ RT; A	Fixed Income	5.0	6.18	9,864.00	☆	☆	0.0	426-5520	206-625-1755	4.50	0.25	None	Delores Driscoll	'93
INVESTORS TR ADJ RT; B	Fixed Income	2.4	6.18	9,846.00	☆	☆	0.0	426-5520	206-625-1755	None	1.00	5.00	Delores Driscoll	'93
INVESTORS TR GOVT; A	Fixed Income	17.5	8.83	9,535.00	☆	☆	0.0	426-5520	206-625-1755	4.50	0.23	None	David W. Hoyle	'93
INVESTORS TR GOVT; B	Fixed Income	1,334.5	8.82	9,516.00	9,337.00	13,710.00	8.1	426-5520	206-625-1755	None	0.98	5.00	David W. Hoyle	'87
INVESTORS TR GROWTH; A ★	Growth	3.7	8.03	9,594.00	☆	☆	0.0	426-5520	206-625-1755	4.50	0.25	None	John Moore	'93
INVESTORS TR GROWTH; B ★	Growth	4.1	7.99	9,569.00	☆	☆	0.0	426-5520	206-625-1755	None	1.00	5.00	John Moore	'93
INVESTORS TR VALUE; A	Growth Income	3.0	7.12	10,022.00	☆	☆	0.0	426-5520	206-625-1755	4.50	0.25	None	Carl Faust	'93
INVESTORS TR VALUE; B	Growth Income	5.4	7.12	10,006.00	☆	☆	0.0	426-5520	206-625-1755	None	1.00	5.00	Carl Faust	'93
INVMNT SRS CAP GR; A	Capital Appreciation	10.8	11.94	9,345.00	9,563.00	☆	0.8	245-4770	412-288-1900	4.50	0.25	None	Gregory M. Melvin	'92
INVMNT SRS CAP GR; C	Capital Appreciation	0.7	11.92	9,329.00	9,485.00	☆	0.1	245-4770	412-288-1900	None	0.75	1.00	Gregory M. Melvin	'93
INVMNT SRS CAP GR; INVMNT	Capital Appreciation	9.3	11.94	9,358.00	9,588.00	☆	1.1	245-4770	412-288-1900	5.75	None	None	Gregory M. Melvin	'89
INVMNT SRS HI QUAL STOCK	Growth Income	41.1	13.74	10,117.00	10,168.00	15,796.00	0.8	245-4770	412-288-1900	5.75	None	None	Peter R. Anderson	'87
INVMNT SRS US GOVT BOND	Fixed Income	37.3	9.44	9,934.00	9,729.00	13,868.00	6.5	245-4770	412-288-1900	5.75	None	None	Kathy Foody-Malus	'90
ISRAEL GROWTH FUND	Emerging Markets	0.9	6.23	7,625.00	☆	☆	0.0	708-7228	None	None	0.75	None	Israel Growth Inv. Adv.	'94
IVY CHINA REGION; A	Pacific Region	12.7	9.40	9,883.00	☆	☆	0.0	456-5111	None	5.75	0.25	None	Trebbi-Longa/Landry	'93/'93
IVY CHINA REGION; B	Pacific Region	6.8	9.40	9,864.00	☆	☆	0.0	456-5111	None	None	1.00	5.00	Trebbi-Longa/Landry	'93/'93

IVY EMERGING GROWTH; A	Small Company Growth	15.0	15.40	8,773.00	10,535.00	☆	0.0	456-5111	None	5.75	0.25	None	James Broadfoot	'93
IVY EMERGING GROWTH; B	Small Company Growth	2.9	15.40	8,755.00	☆	☆	0.0	456-5111	None	None	1.00	5.00	James Broadfoot	'93
IVY GROWTH FUND; A	Growth	251.3	14.09	9,688.00	10,187.00	15,347.00	0.7	456-5111	None	5.75	0.25	None	Team Managed	'74
IVY GROWTH FUND; B	Growth	0.6	14.09	9,664.00	☆	☆	0.0	456-5111	None	None	1.00	5.00	Team Managed	'93
IVY GROWTH WITH INC; A	Growth Income	24.7	9.15	9,739.00	10,503.00	16,030.00	2.4	456-5111	None	5.75	0.25	None	Team Managed	'84
IVY GROWTH WITH INC; B	Growth Income	4.0	9.15	9,693.00	☆	☆	0.0	456-5111	None	None	1.00	5.00	Team Managed	'93
IVY INTL FUND; A	International	188.8	27.04	10,101.00	12,208.00	17,114.00	0.8	456-5111	None	5.75	0.25	None	Hakan Castegren	'86
IVY INTL FUND; B	International	15.1	27.04	10,078.00	☆	☆	0.0	456-5111	None	None	1.00	5.00	Hakan Castegren	'93
JACKSON NATL GROWTH	S&P Index	33.0	10.62	10,028.00	10,085.00	☆	2.2	888-3863	None	4.75	None	None	PPM America	'92
JACKSON NATL INCOME	Fixed Income	29.4	9.62	9,845.00	9,708.00	☆	6.1	888-3863	None	4.75	None	None	PPM America	'92
JACKSON NATL TOTAL RET	Flexible	34.7	10.48	10,029.00	10,136.00	☆	4.1	888-3863	None	4.75	None	None	PPM America	'92
JANUS BALANCED	Balanced	89.8	11.97	9,975.00	10,331.00	☆	2.1	525-8983	303-333-3863	None	None	None	James P. Craig	'93
JANUS ENTERPRISE	Midcap	252.7	20.47	9,752.00	10,565.00	☆	0.1	525-8983	303-333-3863	None	None	None	James P. Goff	'92
JANUS FLEXIBLE INCOME	Fixed Income	400.1	9.14	9,858.00	10,308.00	15,071.00	7.9	525-8983	303-333-3863	None	None	None	Ronald V. Speaker	'91
JANUS FUND	Capital Appreciation	9,346.7	18.66	9,883.00	10,153.00	18,450.00	2.0	525-8983	303-333-3863	None	None	None	James P. Craig	'86
JANUS GROWTH AND INCOME	Growth Income	493.3	13.71	9,621.00	9,667.00	☆	1.0	525-8983	303-333-3863	None	None	None	Thomas F. Marsico	'91
JANUS INTMDT GOVT SECS	Fixed Income	42.0	4.87	9,935.00	9,798.00	☆	4.7	525-8983	303-333-3863	None	None	None	Ronald V. Speaker	'91
JANUS MERCURY	Capital Appreciation	279.5	11.83	9,344.00	10,974.00	☆	0.0	525-8983	303-333-3863	None	None	None	Warren B. Lammert	'93
JANUS OVERSEAS	International	15.5	9.80	☆	☆	☆	0.0	525-8983	303-333-3863	None	None	None	Helen Hayes	'94
JANUS SHORT-TERM BOND	Fixed Income	55.4	2.90	10,017.00	10,208.00	☆	5.5	525-8983	303-333-3863	None	None	None	Ronald V. Speaker	'92
JANUS TWENTY ☒	Capital Appreciation	2,826.6	22.00	9,358.00	9,079.00	19,358.00	1.1	525-8983	303-333-3863	None	None	None	Thomas F. Marsico	'88
JANUS VENTURE ☒	Small Company Growth	1,431.0	46.07	9,721.00	9,808.00	18,402.00	1.1	525-8983	303-333-3863	None	None	None	Lammert/Goff	'93/'93
JANUS WORLDWIDE	Global	1,341.0	24.54	9,891.00	11,782.00	☆	1.1	525-8983	303-333-3863	None	None	None	Helen Hayes	'92
THE JAPAN FUND	Japanese	673.3	12.71	10,530.00	11,691.00	13,287.00	2.1	535-2726	617-439-4640	None	None	None	Allan/Kwak	'90/'89
JEFFERSON-PILOT CAP APP	Growth	35.4	15.89	9,742.00	9,874.00	15,865.00	0.7	458-4498	910-691-3448	4.50	None	None	W. Hardee Mills	'93
JEFFERSON-PILOT INV GRD	Fixed Income	22.4	9.14	9,808.00	9,659.00	13,899.00	5.3	458-4498	910-691-3448	4.50	None	None	Robert E. Whalen	'92
JENSEN PORTFOLIO	Growth Income	8.8	8.61	9,666.00	9,794.00	☆	1.4	221-4384	503-274-2044	None	None	None	Val E. Jensen	'92
JPM INSTL BOND	Fixed Income	86.3	9.38	9,892.00	☆	☆	0.0	521-5411	212-826-1303	None	None	None	Rip Reeves	'93
JPM INSTL DIVERSIFIED	Flexible	59.2	9.90	10,061.00	☆	☆	0.0	521-5411	212-826-1303	None	None	None	Gerald H. Osterberg	'93
JPM INSTL EMRG MKTS EQTY	Emerging Markets	90.1	10.81	9,695.00	☆	☆	0.0	521-5411	212-826-1303	None	None	None	Doug Dooley	'93
JPM INSTL INTL EQUITY	International	145.5	10.72	10,479.00	☆	☆	0.0	521-5411	212-826-1303	None	None	None	Paul Quinsee	'93
JPM INSTL SELECTED US EQ	Growth Income	47.6	10.60	10,019.00	☆	☆	0.0	521-5411	212-826-1303	None	None	None	Peterson/Riegel	'93/'93
JPM INSTL SH TM BOND	Fixed Income	44.0	9.69	9,998.00	☆	☆	0.0	521-5411	212-826-1303	None	None	None	Connie Plaehn	'93
JPM INSTL US SMALL CO	Small Company Growth	71.1	9.66	9,324.00	☆	☆	0.0	521-5411	212-826-1303	None	None	None	Otness/Kittler	'93/'93
KAUFMANN FUND	Small Company Growth	1,202.5	3.20	9,412.00	10,637.00	23,558.00	1.1	666-4943	212-344-2661	None	1.00	0.20	Utsch/Auriana	'86/'86
KEELEY SMALL CAP VALUE	Small Company Growth	3.3	9.67	9,603.00	☆	☆	0.0	533-5344	312-786-5050	4.50	0.25	None	John Keeley	'93
KEMPER ADJ RATE GOVT; A	Fixed Income	228.2	8.36	9,960.00	10,122.00	14,052.00	4.9	621-1048	312-781-1121	3.50	None	None	Beimford/Schumacher	'92/'91
KEMPER BLUE CHIP; A	Growth Income	164.6	11.71	9,599.00	9,316.00	15,512.00	1.6	621-1048	312-781-1121	5.75	None	None	James Neel	'90
KEMPER DVSFD INCOME; A	Fixed Income	477.1	5.88	9,938.00	10,493.00	17,964.00	9.2	621-1048	312-781-1121	4.50	None	None	McNamara/Resis	'89/'92
KEMPER ENVIRONMENTAL; A	Environmental	26.1	11.70	9,451.00	8,857.00	☆	0.0	621-1048	312-781-1121	5.75	None	None	Frank Korth	'90
KEMPER GLOBAL INCOME; A	World Income	86.6	8.64	9,978.00	10,073.00	☆	7.5	621-1048	312-781-1121	4.50	None	None	Johns/Beimford	'89/'93
KEMPER GROWTH FUND; A	Growth	1,676.9	12.23	9,265.00	9,175.00	17,257.00	0.0	621-1048	312-781-1121	5.75	None	None	C Beth Conter	'94
KEMPER HIGH YIELD; A	Fixed Income	2,316.9	7.87	9,944.00	10,508.00	16,474.00	9.8	621-1048	312-781-1121	4.50	None	None	McNamara/Resis	'90/'92
KEMPER INC&CAP PRES; A	Fixed Income	529.6	8.10	9,896.00	9,894.00	14,746.00	7.2	621-1048	312-781-1121	4.50	None	None	Harry Resis	'89
KEMPER INTL FUND; A	International	363.8	10.43	10,097.00	11,806.00	14,805.00	0.0	621-1048	312-781-1121	5.75	None	None	Dennis Ferro	'94
KEMPER PT SH GLBL; INL	World Income	67.2	6.92	9,894.00	9,696.00	☆	7.7	621-1048	312-781-1121	None	0.75	4.00	Johns/Beimford	'91/'93
KEMPER PT SH GLBL; PREM	World Income	3.2	6.94	9,915.00	9,776.00	☆	8.5	621-1048	312-781-1121	None	None	None	Johns/Beimford	'92/'93
KEMPER RETIRE SRS I ☒	Balanced Target	108.3	10.67	9,544.00	9,624.00	☆	3.6	621-1048	312-781-1121	5.00	None	None	James Neel	'94
KEMPER RETIRE SRS II ☒	Balanced Target	178.8	12.30	9,609.00	9,593.00	☆	4.6	621-1048	312-781-1121	5.00	None	None	James Neel	'94
KEMPER RETIRE SRS III ☒	Balanced Target	127.6	9.87	9,601.00	9,524.00	☆	3.8	621-1048	312-781-1121	5.00	None	None	James Neel	'94

★ INVESTORS TR GROWTH; A & B--Fund has been reclassified from Capital Appreciation to Growth.

PERFORMANCE OF MUTUAL FUNDS (continued)

FUND NAME	OBJECTIVE	TOTAL NET ASSETS ($ MIL) 5/31/94	NET ASSET $ VALUE 6/30/94	PERFORMANCE (Return on initial $10,000 Investment) 3/31/94-6/30/94	6/30/93-6/30/94	6/30/89-6/30/94	DIVIDEND YIELD % 6/94	PHONE NUMBER 800	In-State	FEES Load	12b-1	Redemption	MANAGER	SINCE
KEMPER RETIRE SRS IV ☒	Balanced Target	152.0	8.83	9,598.00	9,369.00	☆	1.7	621-1048	312-781-1121	5.00	None	None	James Neel	'94
KEMPER SH-INT GOVT; A	Fixed Income	13.1	8.10	9,981.00	10,002.00	☆	5.7	621-1048	312-781-1121	None	None	None	Beimford/Schumacher	'92/'92
KEMPER SH-INT GOVT; B	Fixed Income	258.6	8.06	9,949.00	9,902.00	13,260.00	5.0	621-1048	312-781-1121	None	0.75	4.00	Beimford/Schumacher	'92/'91
KEMPER SH-TM GLBL; A	World Income	69.0	6.95	9,921.00	9,776.00	☆	8.1	621-1048	312-781-1121	3.50	None	None	Johns/Beimford	'90/'93
KEMPER SM CAP EQTY; A	Midcap	474.5	5.31	9,171.00	10,001.00	18,186.00	0.0	621-1048	312-781-1121	5.75	None	None	C. Beth Cotner	'87
KEMPER TECHNOLOGY FD; A	Science & Technology	590.1	9.41	9,289.00	9,976.00	16,685.00	0.0	621-1048	312-781-1121	5.75	None	None	Goers/Korth	'91/'94
KEMPER TOTAL RETURN; A	Balanced	1,750.1	8.84	9,455.00	9,601.00	15,820.00	2.2	621-1048	312-781-1121	5.75	None	None	C Beth Conter	'86
KEMPER US GOVT SEC; A	Fixed Income	5,526.4	8.59	9,926.00	9,882.00	14,487.00	7.5	621-1048	312-781-1121	4.50	None	None	Beimford/Schumacher	'81/'91
KEMPER US MTGE; A	Fixed Income	1,999.8	6.92	9,890.00	9,809.00	☆	7.5	621-1048	312-781-1121	4.50	None	None	Beimford/Schumacher	'92/'92
KEMPER US MTGE; B	Fixed Income	2,363.7	6.91	9,869.00	9,730.00	13,717.00	6.7	621-1048	312-781-1121	None	0.75	4.00	Beimford/Schumacher	'92/'91
KENILWORTH FUND	Growth	3.0	9.35	9,492.00	☆	☆	0.5	None	312-236-5388	None	None	None	B. Padmanabha Pai	'93
KENT FDS EXP MKT EQ; INST	Small Company Growth	293.3	11.94	9,838.00	10,512.00	☆	0.9	343-2898	617-621-6100	None	None	None	Old Kent Bank	'92
KENT FDS EXP MKT EQ; INV	Small Company Growth	6.8	11.92	9,765.00	10,483.00	☆	0.9	343-2898	617-621-6100	4.00	0.25	None	Old Kent Bank	'92
KENT FDS FIXED INC; INST	Fixed Income	584.3	9.55	9,890.00	9,848.00	☆	5.2	343-2898	617-621-6100	None	None	None	Old Kent Bank	'92
KENT FDS FIXED INC; INV	Fixed Income	7.4	9.57	9,900.00	9,827.00	☆	5.2	343-2898	617-621-6100	4.00	0.25	None	Old Kent Bank	'92
KENT FDS INDEX EQ; INST	S&P Index	302.5	10.53	10,021.00	10,081.00	☆	2.3	343-2898	617-621-6100	None	None	None	Old Kent Bank	'92
KENT FDS INDEX EQ; INV	S&P Index	4.2	10.55	10,021.00	10,069.00	☆	2.3	343-2898	617-621-6100	4.00	0.25	None	Old Kent Bank	'92
KENT FDS INTL EQ; INST	International	194.4	13.52	10,305.00	11,680.00	☆	0.9	343-2898	617-621-6100	None	None	None	Old Kent Bank	'92
KENT FDS INTL EQ; INV	International	5.2	13.47	10,275.00	11,659.00	☆	0.8	343-2898	617-621-6100	4.00	0.25	None	Old Kent Bank	'92
KENT FDS LTD MAT; INST	Fixed Income	187.5	9.75	10,015.00	10,178.00	☆	4.0	343-2898	617-621-6100	None	None	None	Old Kent Bank	'92
KENT FDS LTD MAT; INV	Fixed Income	1.5	9.75	10,015.00	10,155.00	☆	3.9	343-2898	617-621-6100	4.00	0.25	None	Old Kent Bank	'92
KENT FDS VALUE PLUS; INST	Growth	252.7	10.23	9,968.00	9,975.00	☆	2.9	343-2898	617-621-6100	None	None	None	Old Kent Bank	'92
KENT FDS VALUE PLUS; INV	Growth	6.3	10.19	9,988.00	9,966.00	☆	2.9	343-2898	617-621-6100	4.00	0.25	None	Old Kent Bank	'92
KEYSTONE AM CAP P&I	Fixed Income	33.3	9.66	9,991.00	10,203.00	☆	4.2	343-2898	617-621-6100	3.00	0.25	None	Christopher Conkey	'91
KEYSTONE AM CAP P&I2; B	Fixed Income	109.0	9.69	9,977.00	10,128.00	☆	3.5	343-2898	617-621-6100	None	1.00	3.00	Christopher Conkey	'91
KEYSTONE AM CAP P&I2; C	Fixed Income	4.2	9.67	9,976.00	10,120.00	☆	3.5	343-2898	617-621-6100	None	1.00	1.00	Christopher Conkey	'93
KEYSTONE AM EQ INC; A	Equity Income	25.4	12.02	10,125.00	10,147.00	15,627.00	1.9	343-2898	617-621-6100	5.75	0.25	None	Walter McCormick	'87
KEYSTONE AM EQ INC; B	Equity Income	6.0	12.03	10,113.00	10,076.00	☆	1.1	343-2898	617-621-6100	None	1.00	3.00	Walter McCormick	'93
KEYSTONE AM EQ INC; C	Equity Income	5.9	12.04	10,113.00	10,069.00	☆	1.1	343-2898	617-621-6100	None	1.00	1.00	Walter McCormick	'93
KEYSTONE AM GLBL OPP; A	Global Small Company	61.8	17.95	9,487.00	11,256.00	20,937.00	0.0	343-2898	617-621-6100	5.75	0.25	None	Roland W. Gillis	'91
KEYSTONE AM GLBL OPP; B	Global Small Company	95.3	17.78	9,473.00	11,178.00	☆	0.0	343-2898	617-621-6100	None	1.00	3.00	Roland W. Gillis	'93
KEYSTONE AM GLBL OPP; C	Global Small Company	34.9	17.83	9,469.00	11,202.00	☆	0.0	343-2898	617-621-6100	None	1.00	1.00	Roland W. Gillis	'93
KEYSTONE AM GOVT SEC; A	Fixed Income	39.7	9.36	9,822.00	9,827.00	14,550.00	7.0	343-2898	617-621-6100	4.75	0.25	None	Christopher Conkey	'88
KEYSTONE AM GOVT SEC; B	Fixed Income	14.9	9.36	9,804.00	9,755.00	☆	6.2	343-2898	617-621-6100	None	1.00	3.00	Christopher Conkey	'93
KEYSTONE AM GOVT SEC; C	Fixed Income	18.3	9.36	9,793.00	9,745.00	☆	6.2	343-2898	617-621-6100	None	1.00	1.00	Christopher Conkey	'93
KEYSTONE AM INT BD; A	Fixed Income	16.1	8.77	9,855.00	9,883.00	14,517.00	6.9	343-2898	617-621-6100	4.75	0.25	None	Christopher Conkey	'88
KEYSTONE AM INT BD; B	Fixed Income	17.3	8.78	9,847.00	9,807.00	☆	6.1	343-2898	617-621-6100	None	1.00	3.00	Christopher Conkey	'93
KEYSTONE AM INT BD; C	Fixed Income	13.4	8.78	9,847.00	9,817.00	☆	6.1	343-2898	617-621-6100	None	1.00	1.00	Christopher Conkey	'93
KEYSTONE AM OMEGA; A	Capital Appreciation	89.7	15.48	9,439.00	9,971.00	19,565.00	0.0	343-2898	617-621-6100	5.75	0.25	None	Maureen E. Cullinane	'89
KEYSTONE AM OMEGA; B	Capital Appreciation	17.3	15.36	9,423.00	☆	☆	0.0	343-2898	617-621-6100	None	1.00	3.00	Maureen E. Cullinane	'93
KEYSTONE AM OMEGA; C	Capital Appreciation	7.0	15.39	9,424.00	☆	☆	0.0	343-2898	617-621-6100	None	1.00	1.00	Maureen E. Cullinane	'93
KEYSTONE AM STR INC; A	Fixed Income	105.3	7.42	9,680.00	10,337.00	15,034.00	9.2	343-2898	617-621-6100	4.75	0.25	None	Keller/Gunn/Conkey	'87/'87
KEYSTONE AM STR INC; B	Fixed Income	158.5	7.44	9,662.00	10,259.00	☆	8.4	343-2898	617-621-6100	None	1.00	3.00	Keller/Gunn/Conkey	'93/'93
KEYSTONE AM STR INC; C	Fixed Income	59.5	7.44	9,662.00	10,260.00	☆	8.4	343-2898	617-621-6100	None	1.00	1.00	Keller/Gunn/Conkey	'93/'93
KEYSTONE AM WORLD BD; A	World Income	7.0	8.54	9,539.00	9,746.00	14,513.00	7.0	343-2898	617-621-6100	4.75	0.25	None	Gilman Gunn	'92

KEYSTONE AM WORLD BD; B	World Income	3.3	8.57	9,529.00	☆	☆	0.0	343-2898	617-621-6100	None	1.00	3.00	Gilman Gunn	'93
KEYSTONE AM WORLD BD; C	World Income	1.7	8.53	9,496.00	☆	☆	0.0	343-2898	617-621-6100	None	1.00	1.00	Gilman Gunn	'93
KEYSTONE AUSSIE INCOME	World Income	7.9	9.02	9,845.00	10,466.00	☆	5.5	343-2898	617-621-6100	4.75	0.25	None	David Manor	'89
KEYSTONE B-1	Fixed Income	374.0	14.74	9,798.00	9,688.00	13,601.00	6.8	343-2898	617-621-6100	None	1.00	4.00	Barbara McCue	'86
KEYSTONE B-2	Fixed Income	858.1	15.25	9,699.00	9,847.00	13,699.00	8.0	343-2898	617-621-6100	None	1.00	4.00	Kristine R. Cloyes	'85
KEYSTONE B-4	Fixed Income	830.8	4.74	9,420.00	10,186.00	14,142.00	9.5	343-2898	617-621-6100	None	1.00	4.00	Donald Keller	'89
KEYSTONE FUND AMER; A	Global	23.5	9.40	8,918.00	☆	☆	0.0	343-2898	617-621-6100	5.75	0.25	None	Gilman Gunn	'93
KEYSTONE FUND AMER; B	Global	142.4	9.36	8,906.00	☆	☆	0.0	343-2898	617-621-6100	None	1.00	3.00	Gilman Gunn	'93
KEYSTONE FUND AMER; C	Global	16.3	9.37	8,907.00	☆	☆	0.0	343-2898	617-621-6100	None	1.00	1.00	Gilman Gunn	'93
KEYSTONE INSTL ADJ RATE	Fixed Income	22.6	9.68	9,971.00	10,218.00	☆	4.7	343-2898	617-621-6100	None	None	None	Christopher Conkey	'91
KEYSTONE INTERNATIONAL	International	155.3	7.41	9,711.00	11,288.00	12,581.00	0.4	343-2898	617-621-6100	None	1.00	4.00	Gilman Gunn	'91
KEYSTONE K-1	Income	1,421.7	9.26	9,956.00	9,884.00	14,167.00	3.9	343-2898	617-621-6100	None	1.00	4.00	McCormick/McCue	'84/'84
KEYSTONE K-2	Growth	377.8	7.76	9,580.00	10,283.00	16,821.00	0.0	343-2898	617-621-6100	None	1.00	4.00	Walter McCormick	'89
KEYSTONE PREC METALS	Gold	206.0	22.77	9,275.00	10,475.00	14,414.00	0.2	343-2898	617-621-6100	None	1.00	4.00	Pirnie/Thorne	'79/'74
KEYSTONE S-1	Growth Income	207.5	22.01	9,866.00	9,792.00	14,270.00	1.2	343-2898	617-621-6100	None	1.00	4.00	Maureen E. Cullinane	'89
KEYSTONE S-3	Growth	251.8	8.87	9,715.00	9,941.00	15,044.00	0.3	343-2898	617-621-6100	None	1.00	4.00	Jill Lyndon	'87
KEYSTONE S-4	Small Company Growth	1,005.6	6.63	8,958.00	9,971.00	20,530.00	0.0	343-2898	617-621-6100	None	1.00	4.00	Roland W. Gillis	'86
KIDDER EQUITY INCOME; A	Equity Income	81.2	22.77	9,894.00	9,429.00	15,239.00	1.5	528-7778	212-656-1640	5.75	0.50	None	Thomas A. Masi	'94
KIDDER EQUITY INCOME; B	Equity Income	1.7	22.67	9,882.00	9,381.00	☆	1.4	528-7778	212-656-1640	None	1.00	None	Thomas A. Masi	'94
KIDDER EQUITY INCOME; C	Equity Income	4.5	22.74	9,903.00	9,473.00	☆	2.2	528-7778	212-656-1640	None	None	None	Thomas A. Masi	'94
KIDDER GOVT INCOME; A	Fixed Income	63.6	13.81	9,819.00	9,675.00	13,525.00	5.0	528-7778	212-656-1640	2.25	0.50	None	John F. Green	'93
KIDDER GOVT INCOME; B	Fixed Income	1.6	13.80	9,813.00	9,646.00	☆	4.7	528-7778	212-656-1640	None	0.75	None	John F. Green	'93
KIDDER GOVT INCOME; C	Fixed Income	4.1	13.80	9,831.00	9,717.00	☆	5.5	528-7778	212-656-1640	None	None	None	John F. Green	'93
KIDDER INV II EMERG; A	Emerging Markets	47.8	10.80	9,791.00	☆	☆	0.0	528-7778	212-656-1640	5.75	0.25	None	Antoine W. Van Agtmael	'94
KIDDER INV II EMERG; B	Emerging Markets	27.6	10.76	9,773.00	☆	☆	0.0	528-7778	212-656-1640	None	1.00	1.00	Antoine W. Van Agtmael	'94
KIDDER INV II EMERG; C	Emerging Markets	15.8	10.81	9,801.00	☆	☆	0.0	528-7778	212-656-1640	None	None	None	Antoine W. Van Agtmael	'94
KIDDER INV III SM CP; A	Small Company Growth	33.1	9.86	8,703.00	☆	☆	0.0	528-7778	212-656-1640	5.75	0.25	None	Owen T. Barry III	'93
KIDDER INV III SM CP; B	Small Company Growth	16.7	9.81	8,689.00	☆	☆	0.0	528-7778	212-656-1640	None	1.00	None	Owen T. Barry III	'93
KIDDER INV III SM CP; C	Small Company Growth	6.2	9.88	8,713.00	☆	☆	0.0	528-7778	212-656-1640	None	None	None	Owen T. Barry III	'93
KIDDER INV ADJ RATE; A	Fixed Income	91.9	11.85	9,959.00	10,204.00	☆	4.0	528-7778	212-656-1640	2.25	0.25	None	John F. Green	'92
KIDDER INV ADJ RATE; B	Fixed Income	9.2	11.85	9,947.00	10,154.00	☆	3.4	528-7778	212-656-1640	None	0.75	None	John F. Green	'93
KIDDER INV ADJ RATE; C	Fixed Income	17.9	11.86	9,965.00	10,239.00	☆	4.1	528-7778	212-656-1640	None	None	None	John F. Green	'93
KIDDER INV ASST ALLO; A	Flexible	1.9	12.84	10,005.00	10,014.00	☆	1.8	528-7778	212-656-1640	5.75	0.25	None	Thomas A. Masi	'94
KIDDER INV ASST ALLO; B	Flexible	68.9	12.86	9,986.00	9,935.00	☆	1.0	528-7778	212-656-1640	None	1.00	1.00	Thomas A. Masi	'94
KIDDER INV ASST ALLO; C	Flexible	3.8	12.86	10,017.00	10,042.00	☆	2.1	528-7778	212-656-1640	None	None	None	Thomas A. Masi	'94
KIDDER INV GLBL EQ; A	Global	188.4	15.88	9,919.00	11,873.00	☆	0.0	528-7778	212-656-1640	5.75	0.25	None	Ralph R. Layman	'91
KIDDER INV GLBL EQ; B	Global	30.6	15.74	9,906.00	11,778.00	☆	0.0	528-7778	212-656-1640	None	1.00	None	Ralph R. Layman	'93
KIDDER INV GLBL EQ; C	Global	27.8	15.92	9,925.00	11,894.00	☆	0.0	528-7778	212-656-1640	None	None	None	Ralph R. Layman	'93
KIDDER INV GLBL FXD; A	World Income	173.6	12.07	10,063.00	10,354.00	☆	5.2	528-7778	212-656-1640	2.25	0.25	None	Kenneth A. Windheim	'92
KIDDER INV GLBL FXD; B	World Income	28.3	12.07	10,051.00	10,303.00	☆	4.7	528-7778	212-656-1640	None	0.75	None	Kenneth A. Windheim	'93
KIDDER INV GLBL FXD; C	World Income	20.7	12.07	10,069.00	10,372.00	☆	5.5	528-7778	212-656-1640	None	None	None	Kenneth A. Windheim	'93
KIDDER INV INTMDT; A	Fixed Income	39.9	11.56	9,861.00	9,744.00	☆	5.0	528-7778	212-656-1640	2.25	0.25	None	Robert A. MacDougall	'92
KIDDER INV INTMDT; B	Fixed Income	3.5	11.56	9,849.00	9,685.00	☆	4.4	528-7778	212-656-1640	None	0.75	None	Robert A. MacDougall	'93
KIDDER INV INTMDT; C	Fixed Income	1.8	11.56	9,876.00	9,756.00	☆	5.2	528-7778	212-656-1640	None	None	None	Robert A. MacDougall	'93
LANDMARK FXD INTMDT INC	Fixed Income	53.2	9.16	9,841.00	9,780.00	☆	5.5	223-4447	212-564-3456	4.00	0.20	None	Mark Lindbloom	'93
LANDMARK FXD US GOVT INC	Fixed Income	69.0	9.48	9,944.00	9,960.00	14,004.00	4.5	223-4447	212-564-3456	1.50	0.20	None	Tom Halley	'88
LANDMARK I BALANCED	Balanced	246.1	13.46	9,956.00	9,971.00	14,118.00	2.6	223-4447	212-564-3456	4.75	0.20	None	Lindbloom/Hyde	'93/'92
LANDMARK II EQUITY	Growth	194.2	14.06	10,089.00	10,341.00	14,165.00	0.6	223-4447	212-564-3456	4.75	0.20	None	Dwight Hyde	'92
LANDMARK INTL EQUITY	International	32.1	11.84	9,801.00	10,994.00	☆	0.0	223-4447	212-564-3456	3.50	0.15	None	Henry de Vismes	'91
LAUREL FDS AST MGR; INV	S&P Index	N/A	N/A	N/A	N/A	☆	0.0	225-5267	None	None	0.09	None	Rich Wilk	'94

PERFORMANCE OF MUTUAL FUNDS (continued)

FUND NAME	OBJECTIVE	TOTAL NET ASSETS ($ MIL) 5/31/94	NET ASSET $ VALUE 6/30/94	PERFORMANCE (Return on initial $10,000 Investment) 3/31/94-6/30/94	6/30/93-6/30/94	6/30/89-6/30/94	DIVIDEND YIELD % 6/94	PHONE NUMBER 800	In-State	FEES Load	12b-1	Redemption	MANAGER	SINCE
LAUREL FDS BALANCED; TR	Balanced	74.6	9.67	10,021.00	☆	☆	0.0	235-4331	412-364-1746	None	None	None	Carroll/Gala	'93/'93
LAUREL FDS BD INDEX; TR	Fixed Income	4.8	9.31	9,868.00	☆	☆	0.0	235-4331	412-364-1746	None	None	None	Laurie Carroll	'93
LAUREL FDS CAP APP; INSTL	Growth	69.6	27.47	10,041.00	10,686.00	☆	1.2	221-7930	None	None	0.15	None	Guy Scott	'93
LAUREL FDS CAP APP; INV	Growth	341.2	27.47	10,038.00	10,679.00	13,925.00	1.1	225-5267	None	None	0.14	None	Guy Scott	'91
LAUREL FDS EUROPEAN; TR	European Region	9.7	11.61	9,856.00	10,907.00	14,229.00	1.0	235-4331	412-364-1746	None	None	None	Catherine Adibi	'90
LAUREL FDS INTMDT INC; TR	Fixed Income	93.2	10.33	9,921.00	9,916.00	☆	4.8	235-4331	412-364-1746	None	None	None	Laurie Carroll	'91
LAUREL FDS INTMDT; INV	Fixed Income	20.4	12.22	9,772.00	9,739.00	13,819.00	5.8	225-5267	None	None	0.15	None	Almond Goduti	'90
LAUREL FDS MGD INC; INV	Fixed Income	84.4	10.41	9,697.00	9,963.00	14,531.00	6.6	225-5267	None	None	0.06	None	Goduti/Leach/MacBride	'89/'89
LAUREL FDS MGD INC; TR	Fixed Income	12.8	10.41	9,703.00	9,993.00	☆	6.9	221-7930	None	None	None	None	Goduti/Leach/MacBride	'93/'93
LAUREL FDS MIDCAP STK; TR	Midcap	16.8	9.39	9,550.00	☆	☆	0.0	235-4331	412-364-1746	None	None	None	John O'Toole	'93
LAUREL FDS S&P 500; TR	S&P Index	116.7	9.79	10,013.00	☆	☆	0.0	235-4331	412-364-1746	None	None	None	John O'Toole	'93
LAUREL FDS SH-TM BOND	Fixed Income	12.5	9.90	10,053.00	☆	☆	0.0	235-4331	412-364-1746	None	None	None	Laurie Carroll	'93
LAUREL FDS SPEC GRO; INV	Growth	84.2	15.89	9,737.00	9,251.00	16,597.00	0.0	225-5267	None	None	0.25	None	Guy Scott	'90
LAUREL FDS SPEC GRO; TR	Growth	12.0	16.01	9,738.00	9,292.00	☆	0.0	221-7930	None	None	None	None	Guy Scott	'93
LAUREL FDS STOCK; TR	Growth Income	212.7	17.43	9,924.00	10,108.00	17,813.00	1.5	235-4331	412-364-1746	None	None	None	Burt Mullins	'87
LAUREL INV ASSET ALL; INV	Flexible	15.0	14.42	9,850.00	9,880.00	15,468.00	1.4	225-5267	None	None	0.10	None	Edgar Peters	'88
LAUREL INV CONTR; INV	Growth	3.5	15.64	9,836.00	9,935.00	16,319.00	0.0	225-5267	None	None	0.20	None	Guy Scott	'91
LAUREL INV INTL; INV	International	5.7	13.25	10,091.00	11,315.00	12,022.00	0.0	225-5267	None	None	0.07	None	Bruce Clarke	'90
LAUREL INV SHTM; INV	Fixed Income	2.4	11.85	9,985.00	9,996.00	13,744.00	5.7	225-5267	None	None	0.12	None	Roberta Shea	'89
LAZARD BOND	Fixed Income	18.3	9.58	9,818.00	9,833.00	☆	6.0	228-0203	212-632-6000	None	None	None	Haim/O'Grady	'91/'91
LAZARD EQUITY	Capital Appreciation	63.0	13.82	10,048.00	10,866.00	16,147.00	1.1	228-0203	212-632-6000	None	None	None	Gullquist/Rome	'87/'91
LAZARD INTL EQUITY	International	765.8	12.64	10,088.00	12,423.00	☆	0.2	228-0203	212-632-6000	None	None	None	John Reinsberg	'92
LAZARD INTL FXD INC	World Income	19.6	10.52	10,158.00	10,799.00	☆	5.0	228-0203	212-632-6000	None	None	None	Haim/Handler	'91/'92
LAZARD INTL SMALL CAP	International	63.8	10.71	9,597.00	☆	☆	0.0	228-0203	212-632-6000	None	None	None	John Reinsberg	'93
LAZARD SMALL CAP	Small Company Growth	383.3	14.93	9,901.00	11,131.00	☆	0.1	228-0203	212-632-6000	None	None	None	Alexanderson/Rome/Purcell	'91/'91
LAZARD SPECIAL EQUITY	Capital Appreciation	86.4	15.39	9,704.00	10,376.00	15,721.00	0.9	228-0203	212-632-6000	None	None	None	Charles Dreifus	'86
LAZARD STRATEGIC YIELD	World Income	46.1	9.42	9,782.00	10,103.00	☆	7.1	228-0203	212-632-6000	None	None	None	Haim/Handler/Ramos	'91/'93
LEEB INV PERSONAL FIN	Growth	47.4	10.29	9,692.00	9,788.00	☆	1.8	543-8721	513-629-2000	None	None	None	Stephen Leeb	'92
LEGG MASON AM LEAD CO TR	Growth	57.1	9.66	9,969.00	☆	☆	0.0	822-5544	410-539-0000	None	1.00	None	J. Eric Leo	'93
LEGG MASON GL GLBL GOVT	World Income	156.7	9.77	10,042.00	10,394.00	☆	5.5	822-5544	410-539-0000	None	0.75	None	Keith Gardner	'93
LEGG MASON INC GOVT INT	Fixed Income	275.2	9.95	9,933.00	9,994.00	14,469.00	5.2	822-5544	410-539-0000	None	0.50	None	Stephen A. Walsh	'91
LEGG MASON INC HIGH YLD	Fixed Income	40.2	14.25	9,875.00	☆	☆	0.0	822-5544	410-539-0000	None	0.50	None	Trudy Whitehead	'94
LEGG MASON INC INV GRADE	Fixed Income	66.1	9.60	9,787.00	9,781.00	14,461.00	6.1	822-5544	410-539-0000	None	0.50	None	Kent S. Engel	'87
LEGG MASON SPECIAL INV	Midcap	595.5	19.74	9,260.00	10,497.00	18,812.00	0.0	822-5544	410-539-0000	None	1.00	None	William H. Miller III	'85
LEGG MASON TOTAL RETURN	Growth Income	199.4	13.04	10,002.00	10,469.00	15,255.00	2.3	822-5544	410-539-0000	None	1.00	None	Miller/Dennin	'90/'92
LEGG MASON VALUE TRUST	Growth	961.3	18.18	9,848.00	10,486.00	14,066.00	0.6	822-5544	410-539-0000	None	0.95	None	William H. Miller III	'82
LEPERCQ-ISTEL TR L-I FD	Growth Income	15.7	14.37	10,055.00	10,233.00	13,677.00	2.8	338-1579	212-698-0749	None	1.00	None	Hanson/Ngudu	'93/'93
LEXINGTON CONVERTIBLE	Convertible Securities	7.5	13.33	9,809.00	10,428.00	16,297.00	0.0	526-0056	201-845-7300	None	0.25	None	Richard Russell	'88
LEXINGTON CORP LEADERS	Growth Income	156.3	10.44	10,115.00	10,038.00	16,115.00	0.4	526-0056	201-845-7300	None	None	None	Lexington Mgmt	'88
LEXINGTON GLOBAL	Global	82.4	13.87	10,176.00	11,721.00	15,039.00	0.4	526-0056	201-845-7300	None	None	None	Saler/Stack	'94/'94
LEXINGTON GNMA INCOME	Fixed Income	152.5	7.79	9,916.00	9,909.00	14,661.00	7.1	526-0056	201-845-7300	None	None	None	Denis P. Jamison	'81
LEXINGTON GOLDFUND	Gold	149.8	6.14	9,579.00	10,091.00	12,176.00	0.3	526-0056	201-845-7300	None	0.25	None	William S. Stack	'94
LEXINGTON GROWTH & INC	Growth Income	133.7	15.52	9,936.00	10,180.00	15,033.00	1.2	526-0056	201-845-7300	None	0.25	None	William S. Stack	'91
LEXINGTON INTERNATIONAL	International	15.0	10.66	10,360.00	☆	☆	0.0	526-0056	201-845-7300	None	0.25	None	Richard Saler	'94
LEXINGTON SH-INTMDT GOVT	Fixed Income	6.2	9.68	9,934.00	☆	☆	0.0	526-0056	201-845-7300	None	None	None	Denis P. Jamison	'93

LEXINGTON STRAT INVMENTS	Gold	73.8	2.48	10,877.00	10,926.00	8,808.00	1.5	526-0056	201-845-7300	5.75	None	None	William S. Stack	'94
LEXINGTON STRAT SILVER	Specialty	53.7	3.92	9,053.00	11,136.00	10,289.00	0.0	526-0056	201-845-7300	5.75	None	None	William S. Stack	'94
LEXINGTON WRLDWD EMERG	Emerging Markets	283.7	12.08	9,861.00	12,860.00	17,275.00	0.0	526-0056	201-845-7300	None	None	None	Stack/Saler	'91/'94
LIBERTY EQTY INC; A	Equity Income	93.2	11.00	10,039.00	10,298.00	15,476.00	3.9	245-4770	412-288-1900	4.50	0.50	None	Christopher H. Wiles	'91
LIBERTY EQTY INC; C	Equity Income	27.8	11.00	10,021.00	10,221.00	☆	3.1	245-4770	412-288-1900	None	0.75	1.00	Christopher H. Wiles	'93
LIBERTY EQTY INC; FORT	Equity Income	26.5	11.00	10,033.00	☆	☆	0.0	245-4770	412-288-1900	1.00	None	1.00	Christopher H. Wiles	'93
LIBERTY FINL GRO & INC ☛	Growth Income	31.4	10.47	10,017.00	10,382.00	☆	2.7	872-5426	617-722-6000	4.50	0.30	None	Robert A. Christensen	'92
LIBERTY FINL US GOVT	Fixed Income	798.0	8.75	9,958.00	9,854.00	14,363.00	7.3	872-5426	617-722-6000	4.50	0.30	None	Michael T. Kennedy	'92
LIBERTY FINL UTILITIES ☛	Utility	284.5	10.59	9,725.00	9,635.00	☆	4.9	872-5426	617-722-6000	4.50	0.30	None	Robert A. Christensen	'91
LIBERTY HIGH INCOME; A	Fixed Income	438.5	10.76	10,023.00	10,421.00	17,794.00	9.7	245-4770	412-288-1900	4.50	None	None	Mark E. Durbiano	'89
LIBERTY HIGH INCOME; C	Fixed Income	25.1	10.75	9,995.00	10,327.00	☆	8.9	245-4770	412-288-1900	None	0.75	1.00	Mark E. Durbiano	'93
LIBERTY HIGH INCOME; SEL	Fixed Income	0.9	10.75	9,993.00	☆	☆	0.0	245-4770	412-288-1900	None	None	None	Mark E. Durbiano	'94
LIBERTY UTILITY; A	Utility	820.3	10.70	9,810.00	9,503.00	16,266.00	5.4	245-4770	412-288-1900	4.50	None	None	Christopher H. Wiles	'90
LIBERTY UTILITY; C	Utility	63.8	10.71	9,801.00	9,453.00	☆	4.6	245-4770	412-288-1900	None	0.75	1.00	Christopher H. Wiles	'93
LINCOLN ADV CORP INC; A	Fixed Income	9.4	9.02	9,791.00	☆	☆	0.0	923-8476	219-455-3361	4.50	0.35	None	Dave Berry	'93
LINCOLN ADV CORP INC; B	Fixed Income	0.1	9.96	☆	☆	☆	0.0	923-8476	219-455-3361	None	1.00	5.00	Dave Berry	'94
LINCOLN ADV CORP INC; D ✪	Fixed Income	0.4	9.06	9,808.00	☆	☆	0.0	923-8476	219-455-3361	None	None	None	Dave Berry	'94
LINCOLN ADV ENTRPRSE; A	Midcap	9.7	8.23	8,645.00	☆	☆	0.0	923-8476	219-455-3361	5.50	0.35	None	Ed Petner	'93
LINCOLN ADV ENTRPRSE; B	Midcap	0.1	8.79	☆	☆	☆	0.0	923-8476	219-455-3361	None	1.00	5.00	Ed Petner	'94
LINCOLN ADV ENTRPRSE; C	Midcap	0.1	8.98	☆	☆	☆	0.0	923-8476	219-455-3361	None	1.00	None	Ed Petner	'94
LINCOLN ADV ENTRPRSE; D ✪	Midcap	0.1	8.24	8,655.00	☆	☆	0.0	923-8476	219-455-3361	None	None	None	Ed Petner	'94
LINCOLN ADV GOVT INC; A	Fixed Income	9.6	9.33	9,874.00	☆	☆	0.0	923-8476	219-455-3361	4.50	0.35	None	Dave Berry	'93
LINCOLN ADV GOVT INC; D ✪	Fixed Income	0.2	9.34	9,885.00	☆	☆	0.0	923-8476	219-455-3361	None	None	None	Dave Berry	'94
LINCOLN ADV GRO&INC; A	Growth Income	10.3	9.56	9,696.00	☆	☆	0.0	923-8476	219-455-3361	5.50	0.35	None	Bob McFarland	'93
LINCOLN ADV GRO&INC; B	Growth Income	0.1	9.32	9,693.00	☆	☆	0.0	923-8476	219-455-3361	None	1.00	5.00	Bob McFarland	'94
LINCOLN ADV GRO&INC; C	Growth Income	0.1	9.78	☆	☆	☆	0.0	923-8476	219-455-3361	None	1.00	None	Bob McFarland	'94
LINCOLN ADV GRO&INC; D ✪	Growth Income	1.2	9.57	9,716.00	☆	☆	0.0	923-8476	219-455-3361	None	None	None	Bob McFarland	'94
LINCOLN ADV NEW PAC; A	Pacific Region	10.6	9.76	10,295.00	☆	☆	0.0	923-8476	219-455-3361	5.50	0.35	None	Peter Robson	'93
LINCOLN ADV NEW PAC; B	Pacific Region	0.1	10.15	10,273.00	☆	☆	0.0	923-8476	219-455-3361	None	1.00	5.00	Peter Robson	'94
LINCOLN ADV NEW PAC; D ✪	Pacific Region	0.1	9.77	10,295.00	☆	☆	0.0	923-8476	219-455-3361	None	None	None	Peter Robson	'94
LINCOLN ADV US GRO; A	Growth	10.0	9.27	9,626.00	☆	☆	0.0	923-8476	219-455-3361	5.50	0.35	None	Paula Blacher	'93
LINCOLN ADV US GRO; B	Growth	0.1	9.27	9,636.00	☆	☆	0.0	923-8476	219-455-3361	None	1.00	5.00	Paula Blacher	'94
LINCOLN ADV US GRO; C	Growth	0.1	9.66	☆	☆	☆	0.0	923-8476	219-455-3361	None	1.00	None	Paula Blacher	'94
LINCOLN ADV US GRO; D ✪	Growth	0.5	9.27	9,626.00	☆	☆	0.0	923-8476	219-455-3361	None	None	None	Paula Blacher	'94
LINCOLN ADV WRLD GRO; A	International	10.8	10.80	10,286.00	☆	☆	0.0	923-8476	219-455-3361	5.50	0.35	None	Walter Scott	'93
LINCOLN ADV WRLD GRO; B	International	0.1	10.26	10,270.00	☆	☆	0.0	923-8476	219-455-3361	None	1.00	5.00	Walter Scott	'94
LINCOLN ADV WRLD GRO; C	International	0.1	10.28	☆	☆	☆	0.0	923-8476	219-455-3361	None	1.00	None	Walter Scott	'94
LINCOLN ADV WRLD GRO; D ✪	International	0.1	10.82	10,295.00	☆	☆	0.0	923-8476	219-455-3361	None	None	None	Walter Scott	'94
LINDNER DIVIDEND	Equity Income	1,552.1	25.66	9,929.00	10,149.00	16,652.00	5.7	None	314-727-5305	None	None	2.00	Eric Ernest Ryback	'82
LINDNER FUND	Growth	1,556.1	22.42	9,778.00	10,483.00	15,241.00	2.0	None	314-727-5305	None	None	2.00	Lange/Ryback/Callahan	'77/'82
LINDNER INV BULWARK	Capital Appreciation	24.1	7.17	10,170.00	☆	☆	0.0	None	314-727-5305	None	None	2.00	Ryback/Callahan	'94/'94
LINDNER INV L/R SM CAP	Small Company Growth	5.1	4.79	9,736.00	☆	☆	0.0	None	314-727-5305	None	None	2.00	Eric Ernest Ryback	'94
LINDNER INV UTILITY	Utility	11.5	10.02	9,607.00	☆	☆	0.0	None	314-727-5305	None	None	2.00	Eric Ernest Ryback	'93
LMH FUND	Growth Income	6.0	17.78	10,074.00	9,756.00	10,647.00	1.3	847-6002	203-226-4768	None	None	None	Heine/Wayne	'83/'91
LOOMIS SAYLES BOND	Fixed Income	84.3	10.70	9,712.00	10,313.00	☆	7.6	633-3330	617-482-2450	None	None	None	Daniel J. Fuss	'91
LOOMIS SAYLES GLBL BOND	World Income	29.1	9.85	9,373.00	9,842.00	☆	5.0	633-3330	617-482-2450	None	None	None	John de Beer	'91
LOOMIS SAYLES GRO & INC	Growth Income	25.1	12.31	10,000.00	10,551.00	☆	1.0	633-3330	617-482-2450	None	None	None	Jeffrey W. Wardlow	'91
LOOMIS SAYLES GROWTH	Growth	31.9	12.03	9,616.00	9,584.00	☆	0.0	633-3330	617-482-2450	None	None	None	Jerome A. Castellini	'91
LOOMIS SAYLES INTL EQU	International	66.4	12.70	9,837.00	12,205.00	☆	0.8	633-3330	617-482-2450	None	None	None	Frank E. Jedlicka	'91
LOOMIS SAYLES SH-TM BOND	Fixed Income	16.3	9.62	10,025.00	10,200.00	☆	6.3	633-3330	617-482-2450	None	None	None	John Hyll	'92

PERFORMANCE OF MUTUAL FUNDS *(continued)*

FUND NAME	OBJECTIVE	TOTAL NET ASSETS ($ MIL) 5/31/94	NET ASSET $ VALUE 6/30/94	PERFORMANCE (Return on initial $10,000 Investment) 3/31/94-6/30/94	6/30/93-6/30/94	6/30/89-6/30/94	DIVIDEND YIELD % 6/94	PHONE NUMBER 800	In-State	FEES Load	12b-1	Redemption	MANAGER	SINCE
LOOMIS SAYLES SMALL CAP	Small Company Growth	79.9	12.73	9,507.00	10,334.00	☆	0.0	633-3330	617-482-2450	None	None	None	Friedman/Petherick	'91/'93
LOOMIS SAYLES US GOVT	Fixed Income	17.4	9.55	9,725.00	9,639.00	☆	6.4	633-3330	617-482-2450	None	None	None	Kent P. Newmark	'91
LORD ABBETT BOND-DEB	Fixed Income	998.6	9.27	9,832.00	10,307.00	16,513.00	9.5	426-1130	212-848-1800	4.75	0.25	None	Morais A. Taylor	'92
LORD ABBETT DEVEL GROWTH	Midcap	126.6	9.11	9,193.00	10,334.00	16,017.00	0.0	426-1130	212-848-1800	5.75	0.25	None	John Gibbons	'89
LORD ABBETT EQU 1990 ☒	Balanced Target	53.0	13.83	10,080.00	10,336.00	☆	0.0	426-1130	212-848-1800	5.50	0.25	None	John Walsh	'90
LORD ABBETT FUNDMNTL VAL	Growth Income	33.2	12.51	10,064.00	10,255.00	16,194.00	1.5	426-1130	212-848-1800	5.75	0.25	None	Thomas Hudson	'92
LORD ABBETT GLBL EQUITY	Global	82.3	12.47	10,122.00	11,196.00	14,563.00	1.2	426-1130	212-848-1800	5.75	0.25	None	E. Wayne Nordberg	'88
LORD ABBETT GLBL INCOME	World Income	273.4	8.22	9,939.00	9,850.00	15,479.00	9.4	426-1130	212-848-1800	4.75	0.25	None	Zane Brown	'92
LORD ABBETT INV LTD DUR	Fixed Income	10.3	4.51	9,884.00	☆	☆	0.0	426-1130	212-848-1800	3.00	0.25	None	David Seito	'93
LORD ABBETT US GOVT	Fixed Income	3,527.2	2.69	9,827.00	9,701.00	14,844.00	9.1	426-1130	212-848-1800	4.75	0.25	None	Robert S. Dow	'92
LORD ABBETT VALUE APPREC	Growth	197.8	11.22	9,938.00	10,230.00	16,317.00	1.4	426-1130	212-848-1800	5.75	0.25	None	Denise Higgins	'90
LUTHERAN BRO FUND ◪	Growth Income	525.8	16.64	9,858.00	9,654.00	15,525.00	1.7	328-4552	612-339-8091	5.00	None	None	Scott Vergin	'92
LUTHERAN BRO HI YLD ◪	Fixed Income	477.7	9.15	9,891.00	10,449.00	16,424.00	8.9	328-4552	612-339-8091	5.00	None	None	Tom Haag	'92
LUTHERAN BRO INCOME ◪	Fixed Income	947.2	8.21	9,819.00	9,681.00	14,291.00	7.0	328-4552	612-339-8091	5.00	None	None	Charles E. Heeren	'86
LUTHERAN BRO OPPTY GRO ◪	Small Company Growth	74.8	9.08	9,126.00	9,956.00	☆	0.0	328-4552	612-339-8091	5.00	None	None	Dave Himebrook	'93
M STANLEY INSTL ACTIVE	International	176.5	11.73	10,209.00	11,413.00	☆	1.6	548-7786	617-557-8000	None	None	None	Paul Jackson	'93
M STANLEY INSTL ASIAN EQ	Pacific Region	251.8	21.03	10,442.00	13,864.00	☆	0.4	548-7786	617-557-8000	None	None	None	Kan Wah Chin	'91
M STANLEY INSTL BALANCED	Balanced	25.8	9.21	10,055.00	10,239.00	☆	5.1	548-7786	617-557-8000	None	None	None	Crowe/Sexauer	'92/'91
M STANLEY INSTL EMG DEBT	World Income	88.2	8.15	10,149.00	☆	☆	0.0	548-7786	617-557-8000	None	None	None	Paul Ghaffari	'94
M STANLEY INSTL EMRG GRO	Small Company Growth	103.6	14.23	9,163.00	9,767.00	☆	0.0	548-7786	617-557-8000	None	None	None	Dennis Sherva	'89
M STANLEY INSTL EMRG MKT	Emerging Markets	765.3	16.21	9,408.00	13,793.00	☆	0.0	548-7786	617-557-8000	None	None	None	Dhar/Biggs	'92/'93
M STANLEY INSTL EQ GR	Growth	85.5	11.40	9,853.00	10,411.00	☆	1.7	548-7786	617-557-8000	None	None	None	Feuerman/Bovich	'93/'93
M STANLEY INSTL EURO EQ	European Region	11.6	13.87	10,191.00	13,475.00	☆	0.6	548-7786	617-557-8000	None	None	None	Robert Sargent	'93
M STANLEY INSTL FXD INC	Fixed Income	206.9	9.98	9,882.00	9,782.00	☆	5.1	548-7786	617-557-8000	None	None	None	Nadosy/Knox	'93/'91
M STANLEY INSTL GLBL EQ	Global	40.6	13.30	9,963.00	12,837.00	☆	1.1	548-7786	617-557-8000	None	None	None	Michael Cowan	'93
M STANLEY INSTL GLBL FXD	World Income	125.4	10.39	9,630.00	9,951.00	☆	6.5	548-7786	617-557-8000	None	None	None	Coughlan/Smith	'91/'91
M STANLEY INSTL GOLD	Gold	17.8	8.89	8,971.00	☆	☆	0.0	548-7786	617-557-8000	None	None	None	Peter Palmeddo	'94
M STANLEY INSTL HI YLD	Fixed Income	98.7	10.24	9,857.00	10,525.00	☆	8.9	548-7786	617-557-8000	None	None	None	Robert Angevine	'92
M STANLEY INSTL INT EQ	International	1,191.3	14.93	10,191.00	13,133.00	☆	1.4	548-7786	617-557-8000	None	None	None	Dominic Caldecott	'89
M STANLEY INSTL INTL SM	International	118.2	16.30	10,093.00	12,654.00	☆	0.2	548-7786	617-557-8000	None	None	None	Margaret Naylor	'92
M STANLEY INSTL JAPANESE	Japanese	35.1	10.41	☆	☆	☆	0.0	548-7786	617-557-8000	None	None	None	Dominic Caldecott	'94
M STANLEY INSTL REAL YLD	World Income	39.9	9.16	9,514.00	☆	☆	0.0	548-7786	617-557-8000	None	None	None	Lucy Pereria	'93
M STANLEY INSTL SM CAP	Small Company Growth	35.7	10.55	9,841.00	10,389.00	☆	2.3	548-7786	617-557-8000	None	None	None	Crowe/Stadlinger	'93/'93
M STANLEY INSTL VALUE EQ	Growth Income	69.3	11.76	10,244.00	10,700.00	☆	3.0	548-7786	617-557-8000	None	None	None	Crowe/Stadlinger	'92/'93
M STANLEY AMER VALUE; A	Small Company Growth	9.7	11.70	9,785.00	☆	☆	0.0	548-7786	617-482-9300	4.75	0.25	None	Crowe/Stadlinger	'93/'93
M STANLEY AMER VALUE; B	Small Company Growth	7.3	11.69	9,783.00	☆	☆	0.0	548-7786	617-482-9300	None	1.00	1.00	Crowe/Stadlinger	'93/'93
M STANLEY ASIAN GRO; A	Pacific Region	143.1	15.50	10,361.00	12,917.00	☆	0.0	548-7786	617-482-9300	4.75	0.25	None	James Cheng	'93
M STANLEY ASIAN GRO; B	Pacific Region	118.9	15.40	10,336.00	12,833.00	☆	0.0	548-7786	617-482-9300	None	1.00	1.00	James Cheng	'93
M STANLEY GL EQ ALLO; A	Global	33.7	11.99	10,135.00	10,902.00	☆	0.2	548-7786	617-482-9300	4.75	0.25	None	Stephen Bott	'93
M STANLEY GL EQ ALLO; B	Global	29.9	11.90	10,128.00	10,834.00	☆	0.0	548-7786	617-482-9300	None	1.00	1.00	Stephen Bott	'93
M STANLEY GL FXD INC; A	World Income	10.5	9.53	9,700.00	10,042.00	☆	6.3	548-7786	617-482-9300	4.75	0.25	None	Smith/Coughlin	'93/'93
M STANLEY GL FXD INC; B	World Income	5.6	9.54	9,689.00	9,976.00	☆	5.6	548-7786	617-482-9300	None	1.00	1.00	Smith/Coughlin	'93/'93
M STANLEY WORLDWIDE; A	World Income	6.6	12.16	☆	☆	☆	0.0	548-7786	617-482-9300	4.75	0.25	None	Robert Angevine	'94
M STANLEY WORLDWIDE; B	World Income	5.9	12.16	☆	☆	☆	0.0	548-7786	617-482-9300	None	1.00	1.00	Robert Angevine	'94
MACKENZIE ADJ US GOVT; A	Fixed Income	12.4	9.71	10,045.00	10,132.00	☆	3.5	456-5111	None	1.00	0.25	None	Dan Johnedis	'93

MACKENZIE AMERICAN FUND	Growth	38.5	11.28	9,622.00	9,939.00	12,357.00	0.0	456-5111	None	5.75	0.25	None	Rohr/Christ	'85/'85
MACKENZIE CANADA FUND	Canadian	36.0	9.85	9,712.00	10,106.00	10,766.00	0.0	456-5111	None	5.75	0.25	None	Sturm/Christ	'87/'87
MACKENZIE FIXED INCOME	Fixed Income	120.5	9.38	9,776.00	9,984.00	14,684.00	6.6	456-5111	None	4.75	0.25	None	Ferris/Johnedis	'93/'93
MACKENZIE GLOBAL FUND	Global	17.9	11.52	9,979.00	11,672.00	☆	0.2	456-5111	None	5.75	0.25	None	Landry/Trebbi-Longa	'91/'91
MACKENZIE N AMERICAN	Flexible	33.8	6.40	9,760.00	9,923.00	13,025.00	6.3	456-5111	None	5.75	0.25	None	Ferris/Johnedis	'89/'93
MADISON BOND FUND	Fixed Income	8.3	20.39	9,889.00	9,914.00	☆	5.2	767-0300	608-273-2020	2.50	0.25	2.00	Frank Burgess	'90
MAINSTAY CAPITAL APPRE	Capital Appreciation	415.1	18.09	9,383.00	10,000.00	21,985.00	0.0	522-4202	None	None	1.00	5.00	Team Managed	'91
MAINSTAY CONVERTIBLE	Convertible Securities	128.2	12.37	9,690.00	10,900.00	19,389.00	2.8	522-4202	None	None	1.00	5.00	Team Managed	'91
MAINSTAY EQUITY INDEX	S&P Index	60.9	13.49	10,030.00	10,052.00	☆	0.0	522-4202	None	5.50	None	None	James Mehling	'92
MAINSTAY GLOBAL	Global	41.2	11.30	9,965.00	11,144.00	11,992.00	0.0	522-4202	None	None	1.00	5.00	Stokes/Tapley	'91/'91
MAINSTAY GOVT	Fixed Income	1,143.9	8.01	9,891.00	9,859.00	13,314.00	7.5	522-4202	None	None	1.00	5.00	Team Managed	'86
MAINSTAY HI YLD CORP	Fixed Income	1,008.2	7.75	9,910.00	10,968.00	16,644.00	8.7	522-4202	None	None	1.00	5.00	Team Managed	'91
MAINSTAY NAT RES/GOLD	Natural Resources	20.4	10.05	9,599.00	9,941.00	11,700.00	0.0	522-4202	None	None	1.00	5.00	Stokes/Tapley	'91/'91
MAINSTAY TOTAL RETURN	Balanced	597.1	14.42	9,584.00	9,951.00	16,299.00	2.5	522-4202	None	None	1.00	5.00	Team Managed	'91
MAINSTAY VALUE	Growth Income	392.0	15.39	10,040.00	10,617.00	18,952.00	0.3	522-4202	None	None	1.00	5.00	Team Managed	'86
MAIRS & POWER GROWTH	Growth	39.7	38.15	10,277.00	10,673.00	19,959.00	1.2	None	612-222-8478	None	None	None	George A. Mairs III	'80
MANAGERS BALANCED	Balanced	1.7	10.99	9,583.00	9,755.00	13,799.00	2.4	835-3879	203-857-5321	None	None	None	Multiple Managers	'87
MANAGERS BOND	Fixed Income	38.0	20.10	9,695.00	9,785.00	15,227.00	7.3	835-3879	203-857-5321	None	None	None	Multiple Managers	'84
MANAGERS CAPITAL APPREC	Capital Appreciation	81.5	23.84	9,747.00	10,514.00	16,867.00	0.2	835-3879	203-857-5321	None	None	None	Multiple Managers	'84
MANAGERS INCOME EQUITY	Equity Income	42.8	27.01	10,307.00	10,397.00	14,534.00	2.9	835-3879	203-857-5321	None	None	None	Multiple Managers	'84
MANAGERS INTL EQUITY	International	79.0	35.90	10,116.00	12,164.00	17,909.00	0.9	835-3879	203-857-5321	None	None	None	Multiple Managers	'85
MANAGERS INTMDT MTGE	Fixed Income	150.8	15.34	8,570.00	7,841.00	13,124.00	10.8	835-3879	203-857-5321	None	None	None	Multiple Managers	'86
MANAGERS SH & INT BD	Fixed Income	91.6	19.24	9,523.00	9,676.00	14,216.00	6.9	835-3879	203-857-5321	None	None	None	Multiple Managers	'84
MANAGERS SHORT GOVT	Fixed Income	44.0	17.32	9,441.00	9,438.00	12,265.00	8.0	835-3879	203-857-5321	None	None	None	Multiple Managers	'87
MANAGERS SPECIAL EQUITY	Small Company Growth	102.7	36.23	9,679.00	10,260.00	17,026.00	0.0	835-3879	203-857-5321	None	None	None	Multiple Managers	'84
MARINER FDS GOVT SECS	Fixed Income	12.4	9.42	9,898.00	☆	☆	0.0	634-2536	212-503-6826	4.75	0.12	None	David Fox	'94
MARINER FIXED INCOME FD	Fixed Income	88.6	9.58	9,910.00	10,019.00	☆	6.4	634-2536	212-503-6826	4.75	0.06	None	David Fox	'94
MARINER NORTH AMERICA	Global	10.5	11.04	9,485.00	10,443.00	☆	0.1	634-2536	212-503-6826	5.00	0.23	None	William Paynter-Bryant	'92
MARINER SH-TM FXD INC	Fixed Income	18.4	9.65	10,004.00	10,181.00	☆	5.2	634-2536	212-503-6826	2.00	0.10	None	David Fox	'94
MARINER SMALL CAP	Small Company Growth	22.8	10.53	8,969.00	9,543.00	☆	0.0	634-2536	212-503-6826	5.00	0.10	None	Joseph Sing	'93
MARINER TOTAL RETURN EQ	Growth Income	76.7	12.32	10,000.00	10,149.00	15,923.00	2.7	634-2536	212-503-6826	5.00	0.06	None	Leo Grohowski	'87
MARK TWAIN EQUITY	Growth	29.3	9.50	9,968.00	9,840.00	☆	0.6	None	314-889-0715	3.50	None	None	Carlo Enloe	'93
MARK TWAIN FXD INCOME	Fixed Income	35.2	9.48	9,755.00	9,595.00	☆	6.2	None	314-889-0715	3.50	None	None	Carlo Enloe	'93
MARKETWATCH EQUITY	Growth Income	113.2	9.81	10,146.00	9,728.00	☆	1.6	232-9091	None	4.50	0.25	None	Team Managed	'93
MARKETWATCH FLEX INC	Fixed Income	27.8	9.71	9,972.00	9,983.00	☆	3.3	232-9091	None	4.50	0.25	None	Team Managed	'93
MARKETWATCH INT FXD INC	Fixed Income	65.3	9.45	9,880.00	9,750.00	☆	4.4	232-9091	None	4.50	0.25	None	Team Managed	'93
MARQUIS GOVT SEC; A	Fixed Income	99.5	9.47	9,938.00	☆	☆	0.0	462-9511	None	3.50	None	None	Not Available	N/A
MARQUIS GOVT SEC; B	Fixed Income	0.1	9.51	9,921.00	☆	☆	0.0	462-9511	None	None	0.75	3.50	Not Available	N/A
MARQUIS GRO & INC; A	Flexible	65.9	9.50	9,926.00	☆	☆	0.0	462-9511	None	3.50	None	None	Not Available	N/A
MARQUIS GRO & INC; B	Flexible	0.7	9.55	9,905.00	☆	☆	0.0	462-9511	None	None	0.75	3.50	Not Available	N/A
MARQUIS VALUE EQTY; A	Growth	40.8	9.36	9,933.00	☆	☆	0.0	462-9511	None	3.50	None	None	Not Available	N/A
MARQUIS VALUE EQTY; B	Growth	0.2	9.40	9,916.00	☆	☆	0.0	462-9511	None	None	0.75	3.50	Not Available	N/A
MARSHALL BALANCED	Balanced	23.5	9.33	9,736.00	☆	☆	0.0	236-8560	414-287-8500	None	None	None	Charles Mehlhouse	'93
MARSHALL EQUITY INCOME	Equity Income	36.6	9.44	10,093.00	☆	☆	0.0	236-8560	414-287-8500	None	None	None	Bruce Hudson	'93
MARSHALL GOVT INC	Fixed Income	60.3	9.18	9,873.00	9,760.00	☆	7.3	236-8560	414-287-8500	None	None	None	Larry Pavelec	'93
MARSHALL INTMDT BD	Fixed Income	298.7	9.32	9,862.00	9,815.00	☆	6.9	236-8560	414-287-8500	None	None	None	Larry Pavelec	'93
MARSHALL MID-CAP STOCK	Midcap	36.1	8.90	9,329.00	☆	☆	0.0	236-8560	414-287-8500	None	None	None	Charles Mehlhouse	'93
MARSHALL SHORT-TERM INC	Fixed Income	101.3	9.71	10,017.00	10,198.00	☆	4.4	236-8560	414-287-8500	None	None	None	Larry Pavelec	'93
MARSHALL STOCK	Growth Income	225.9	9.43	9,608.00	9,644.00	☆	0.8	236-8560	414-287-8500	None	None	None	Charles Mehlhouse	'93
MARSHALL VALUE EQUITY	Growth Income	65.9	10.01	10,260.00	☆	☆	0.0	236-8560	414-287-8500	None	None	None	Charles Mehlhouse	'93

PERFORMANCE OF MUTUAL FUNDS *(continued)*

FUND NAME	OBJECTIVE	TOTAL NET ASSETS ($ MIL) 5/31/94	NET ASSET $ VALUE 6/30/94	PERFORMANCE (Return on initial $10,000 Investment) 3/31/94-6/30/94	6/30/93-6/30/94	6/30/89-6/30/94	DIVIDEND YIELD % 6/94	PHONE NUMBER 800	In-State	FEES Load	12b-1	Redemption	MANAGER	SINCE
MAS BALANCED	Balanced	306.4	11.12	9,919.00	10,114.00	☆	3.6	354-8185	610-940-5000	None	None	None	Team Managed	'92
MAS EMERGING GRO	Midcap	317.8	14.96	9,139.00	10,070.00	☆	0.1	354-8185	610-940-5000	None	None	None	Team Managed	'90
MAS EQUITY	Growth	1,199.9	20.42	10,074.00	10,298.00	17,447.00	1.8	354-8185	610-940-5000	None	None	None	Team Managed	'84
MAS FXD INC	Fixed Income	1,065.4	11.02	9,735.00	9,900.00	15,616.00	7.6	354-8185	610-940-5000	None	None	None	Team Managed	'84
MAS FXD INC II	Fixed Income	128.1	10.55	9,751.00	9,878.00	☆	7.0	354-8185	610-940-5000	None	None	None	Team Managed	'90
MAS GLBL FXD INC	World Income	40.3	10.15	9,827.00	10,338.00	☆	3.8	354-8185	610-940-5000	None	None	None	Team Managed	'93
MAS HIGH YIELD	Fixed Income	146.8	8.92	9,857.00	10,458.00	16,437.00	8.1	354-8185	610-940-5000	None	None	None	Team Managed	'89
MAS INTL EQUITY	International	1,132.1	14.19	9,875.00	11,638.00	16,353.00	1.4	354-8185	610-940-5000	None	None	None	Team Managed	'88
MAS LTD DUR FXD	Fixed Income	91.0	10.30	9,991.00	10,081.00	☆	3.4	354-8185	610-940-5000	None	None	None	Team Managed	'92
MAS MTGE SECS	Fixed Income	127.4	10.03	9,892.00	9,984.00	☆	4.7	354-8185	610-940-5000	None	None	None	Team Managed	'92
MAS SEL EQUITY	Growth	29.0	16.97	9,953.00	10,174.00	17,465.00	1.8	354-8185	610-940-5000	None	None	None	Team Managed	'88
MAS SEL FXD INC	Fixed Income	36.0	10.00	9,804.00	10,054.00	16,032.00	9.4	354-8185	610-940-5000	None	None	None	Team Managed	'87
MAS SMALL CAP	Small Company Growth	261.2	16.67	9,876.00	11,180.00	20,509.00	1.4	354-8185	610-940-5000	None	None	None	Team Managed	'86
MAS SPEC PURP FXD	Fixed Income	338.4	11.61	9,740.00	9,947.00	☆	6.9	354-8185	610-940-5000	None	None	None	Team Managed	'92
MAS VALUE	Growth Income	999.6	12.18	10,141.00	10,746.00	17,822.00	2.3	354-8185	610-940-5000	None	None	None	Team Managed	'84
MASS INVESTORS GRO; A	Growth	1,018.6	9.87	9,445.00	9,607.00	16,220.00	0.0	225-2606	617-954-5000	5.75	0.35	None	Gerry Bennett	'93
MASS INVESTORS GRO; B	Growth	9.7	9.78	9,422.00	☆	☆	0.0	225-2606	617-954-5000	None	1.00	4.00	Gerry Bennett	'93
MASS INVESTORS TRUST; A	Growth Income	1,616.7	11.11	9,947.00	10,293.00	17,067.00	3.1	225-2606	617-954-5000	5.75	0.35	None	Jeffrey Shames	'92
MASS INVESTORS TRUST; B	Growth Income	40.0	11.08	9,931.00	☆	☆	0.0	225-2606	617-954-5000	None	1.00	4.00	Jeffrey Shames	'93
MATHERS FUND	Growth	360.4	14.40	9,789.00	9,662.00	12,600.00	1.6	962-3863	708-295-7400	None	None	None	Henry G. Van der Eb, Jr	'75
MATRIX GROWTH FUND	Growth	14.2	13.52	9,769.00	9,683.00	15,821.00	0.4	877-3344	513-621-2875	None	None	None	Peter Williams	'88
MAXUS EQUITY	Flexible	15.3	13.16	9,887.00	10,641.00	☆	0.8	446-2987	216-292-3434	None	0.50	None	Richard Barone	'89
MAXUS INCOME FUND	Fixed Income	37.2	10.22	9,991.00	9,813.00	13,933.00	6.4	446-2987	216-292-3434	None	0.50	None	Richard Barone	'85
MAXUS LAUREATE FUND	Capital Appreciation	2.6	9.60	9,816.00	10,252.00	☆	0.0	446-2987	216-292-3434	None	0.50	None	Robert Beausoleil	'93
MEGY FD INCOME	World Income	0.3	11.50	10,061.00	11,826.00	☆	0.3	933-8637	407-832-7733	2.87	0.50	1.00	Hector Megy	'91
MENTOR GROWTH	Midcap	185.0	12.68	9,421.00	10,434.00	16,663.00	0.0	472-0090	804-782-3207	None	0.75	5.00	Price/Ziglar/Drummond	'85/'91
MENTOR STRATEGY FUND	Flexible	159.1	11.29	9,464.00	☆	☆	0.0	472-0090	804-782-3207	None	0.75	5.00	Hays/Graves	'93/'94
MERGER FUND	Capital Appreciation	N/A	13.44	10,267.00	11,315.00	15,194.00	0.2	343-8959	None	None	0.25	None	Green/Smith	'89/'89
MERIDIAN FUND	Midcap	193.2	24.27	9,759.00	10,348.00	20,524.00	0.1	446-6662	415-461-6237	None	None	None	Richard Aster Jr	'84
MERRILL ADJ RATE SEC; A	Fixed Income	23.0	9.50	9,916.00	10,095.00	☆	3.8	None	609-282-2800	3.00	0.25	None	Maunz/Hewson	'91/'91
MERRILL ADJ RATE SEC; B	Fixed Income	374.4	9.51	9,914.00	10,046.00	☆	3.3	None	609-282-2800	None	0.75	3.00	Maunz/Hewson	'91/'91
MERRILL AMERICAS INC; A	World Income	19.9	8.81	9,793.00	☆	☆	0.0	None	609-282-2800	3.00	0.25	None	Paolo Valle	'93
MERRILL AMERICAS INC; B	World Income	116.2	8.81	9,781.00	☆	☆	0.0	None	609-282-2800	None	0.75	3.00	Paolo Valle	'93
MERRILL BASIC VALUE; A	Growth Income	2,308.3	23.17	10,105.00	10,568.00	15,527.00	2.9	None	609-282-2800	6.50	None	None	Paul F. Hoffmann	'77
MERRILL BASIC VALUE; B	Growth Income	1,749.7	22.87	10,075.00	10,461.00	14,751.00	2.0	None	609-282-2800	None	1.00	4.00	Paul F. Hoffmann	'88
MERRILL BL INV & RET; A	Balanced	40.8	11.36	9,734.00	10,176.00	14,800.00	3.3	None	609-282-2800	6.50	None	None	Denis Cummings	'91
MERRILL BL INV & RET; B	Balanced	747.7	11.41	9,711.00	10,071.00	14,066.00	2.1	None	609-282-2800	None	1.00	4.00	Denis Cummings	'91
MERRILL CAPITAL; A	Growth Income	2,342.5	27.82	10,131.00	10,590.00	16,395.00	3.4	None	609-282-2800	6.50	None	None	Ernest S. Watts	'83
MERRILL CAPITAL; B	Growth Income	3,234.1	27.33	10,107.00	10,483.00	15,583.00	2.5	None	609-282-2800	None	1.00	4.00	Ernest S. Watts	'88
MERRILL CONSULTS INTL	International	247.8	12.76	10,241.00	11,975.00	☆	0.4	None	609-282-2800	None	1.00	None	James Boller	'92
MERRILL CORP HI INC; A	Fixed Income	888.3	7.80	9,877.00	10,426.00	18,328.00	9.6	None	609-282-2800	4.00	None	None	Vincent T. Lathbury III	'82
MERRILL CORP HI INC; B	Fixed Income	2,236.9	7.80	9,859.00	10,342.00	17,615.00	8.8	None	609-282-2800	None	0.75	4.00	Vincent T. Lathbury III	'88
MERRILL CORP INTMDT; A	Fixed Income	177.6	11.03	9,909.00	9,883.00	14,983.00	6.6	None	609-282-2800	2.00	None	None	Jay Harbeck	'92
MERRILL CORP INTMDT; B	Fixed Income	145.9	11.03	9,897.00	9,833.00	☆	6.1	None	609-282-2800	None	0.50	2.00	Jay Harbeck	'92
MERRILL CORP INV GRD; A	Fixed Income	379.8	10.96	9,875.00	9,796.00	14,959.00	6.9	None	609-282-2800	4.00	None	None	Jay Harbeck	'92

MERRILL CORP INV GRD; B	Fixed Income	501.3	10.96	9,857.00	9,725.00	14,408.00	6.1	None	609-282-2800	None	0.75	4.00	Jay Harbeck	'92
MERRILL DEVLOP CAP MKT	Emerging Markets	420.5	14.61	9,229.00	12,873.00	☆	0.5	None	609-282-2800	6.50	None	None	Grace Pineda	'89
MERRILL DRAGON FUND; A	Pacific Region	257.9	15.49	10,272.00	12,993.00	☆	0.5	None	609-282-2800	6.50	0.25	None	Kara Tan Bhala	'92
MERRILL DRAGON FUND; B	Pacific Region	856.8	15.40	10,246.00	12,892.00	☆	0.0	None	609-282-2800	None	1.00	4.00	Kara Tan Bhala	'92
MERRILL EUROFUND; A	European Region	269.2	14.84	9,867.00	12,295.00	16,985.00	0.0	None	609-282-2800	6.50	None	None	Adrian Holmes	'93
MERRILL EUROFUND; B	European Region	1,178.3	14.26	9,841.00	12,167.00	16,141.00	0.0	None	609-282-2800	None	1.00	4.00	Adrian Holmes	'93
MERRILL FD TOMORROW; A	Growth	10.0	13.99	9,530.00	9,798.00	13,966.00	1.1	None	609-282-2800	6.50	None	None	Vincent P. Dileo	'88
MERRILL FD TOMORROW; B	Growth	338.2	13.85	9,506.00	9,703.00	13,262.00	0.5	None	609-282-2800	None	1.00	4.00	Vincent P. Dileo	'84
MERRILL FDMNTL GRO; A	Growth	8.1	9.37	9,670.00	9,957.00	☆	0.0	None	609-282-2800	6.50	0.25	None	Lawrence Fuller	'92
MERRILL FDMNTL GRO; B	Growth	45.8	9.26	9,646.00	9,883.00	☆	0.0	None	609-282-2800	None	1.00	1.00	Lawrence Fuller	'92
MERRILL FEDERAL SEC; A	Fixed Income	1,436.3	9.34	9,888.00	9,794.00	14,440.00	5.5	None	609-282-2800	4.00	0.25	None	Maunz/Hewson	'89/'92
MERRILL FEDERAL SEC; B	Fixed Income	1,618.4	9.34	9,876.00	9,748.00	13,838.00	5.0	None	609-282-2800	None	0.75	4.00	Maunz/Hewson	'91/'92
MERRILL GL INV & RET; A	World Income	102.8	9.16	9,732.00	9,864.00	17,013.00	6.2	None	609-282-2800	4.00	None	None	Robert Parish	'93
MERRILL GL INV & RET; B	World Income	812.6	9.16	9,714.00	9,780.00	16,377.00	5.4	None	609-282-2800	None	0.75	4.00	Robert Parish	'93
MERRILL GLBL ALLOC; A	Global Flexible	1,260.6	13.23	9,992.00	10,816.00	19,814.00	3.8	None	609-282-2800	6.50	None	None	Bryan Ison	'89
MERRILL GLBL ALLOC; B	Global Flexible	6,034.0	13.05	9,969.00	10,710.00	18,847.00	2.8	None	609-282-2800	None	1.00	4.00	Bryan Ison	'89
MERRILL GLBL CONV; A ▮	Convertible Securities	5.7	10.72	9,996.00	10,405.00	14,413.00	2.9	None	609-282-2800	4.00	None	None	Harry Dewdney	'88
MERRILL GLBL CONV; B	Convertible Securities	37.4	10.76	9,971.00	10,307.00	13,688.00	2.0	None	609-282-2800	None	1.00	4.00	Harry Dewdney	'88
MERRILL GLBL HOLDNGS; A	Global	334.0	13.01	9,939.00	11,377.00	15,947.00	2.8	None	609-282-2800	6.50	None	None	Frederick P. Ives	'85
MERRILL GLBL HOLDNGS; B	Global	51.4	12.74	9,914.00	11,255.00	15,150.00	1.7	None	609-282-2800	None	1.00	4.00	Frederick P. Ives	'88
MERRILL GLBL UTILITY; A	Utility	73.7	12.26	9,759.00	9,903.00	☆	3.4	None	609-282-2800	6.50	None	None	Walter D. Rogers	'90
MERRILL GLBL UTILITY; B	Utility	576.5	12.21	9,746.00	9,833.00	☆	2.7	None	609-282-2800	None	0.75	4.00	Walter D. Rogers	'90
MERRILL GR INV & RET; A	Growth Income	326.5	17.76	9,972.00	11,383.00	19,751.00	0.0	None	609-282-2800	6.50	None	None	Stephen C. Johnes	'88
MERRILL GR INV & RET; B	Growth Income	1,251.2	16.82	9,947.00	11,258.00	18,763.00	0.0	None	609-282-2800	None	1.00	4.00	Stephen C. Johnes	'87
MERRILL HEALTHCARE; A	Health/Biotechnology	68.2	3.57	9,154.00	9,684.00	☆	0.4	None	609-282-2800	6.50	None	None	Jordan Schreiber	'92
MERRILL HEALTHCARE; B	Health/Biotechnology	62.9	3.26	9,106.00	9,588.00	☆	0.0	None	609-282-2800	None	1.00	4.00	Jordan Schreiber	'92
MERRILL INSTL INTMDT	Fixed Income	106.7	9.72	9,934.00	9,957.00	14,454.00	5.5	None	609-282-2800	None	0.15	None	Jay Harbeck	'92
MERRILL INTL EQUITY; A	International	208.0	11.36	10,161.00	☆	☆	0.0	None	609-282-2800	6.50	0.25	None	Albert/Pineda/Silverman	'93/'93
MERRILL INTL EQUITY; B	International	844.3	11.28	10,144.00	☆	☆	0.0	None	609-282-2800	None	1.00	4.00	Albert/Pineda/Silverman	'93/'93
MERRILL LATIN AMER; A ☒	Latin American	171.6	14.78	8,985.00	13,339.00	☆	0.7	None	609-282-2800	6.50	0.25	None	Grace Pineda	'91
MERRILL LATIN AMER; B ☒	Latin American	722.0	14.71	8,964.00	13,235.00	☆	0.3	None	609-282-2800	None	1.00	4.00	Grace Pineda	'91
MERRILL NATURAL RES; A	Natural Resources	17.4	15.23	10,133.00	10,939.00	14,045.00	0.9	None	609-282-2800	6.50	None	None	Peter Lehman	'94
MERRILL NATURAL RES; B	Natural Resources	221.6	15.13	10,107.00	10,830.00	13,344.00	0.3	None	609-282-2800	None	1.00	4.00	Peter Lehman	'94
MERRILL PACIFIC; A	Pacific Region	579.5	23.29	10,572.00	12,020.00	18,325.00	0.1	None	609-282-2800	6.50	None	None	Stephen I. Silverman	'83
MERRILL PACIFIC; B	Pacific Region	737.2	22.30	10,544.00	11,893.00	17,425.00	0.0	None	609-282-2800	None	1.00	4.00	Stephen I. Silverman	'88
MERRILL PHOENIX; A	Growth Income	246.9	12.95	9,825.00	10,749.00	17,737.00	2.0	None	609-282-2800	6.50	None	None	Robert J. Martorelli	'86
MERRILL PHOENIX; B	Growth Income	337.3	12.68	9,799.00	10,633.00	16,852.00	0.8	None	609-282-2800	None	1.00	4.00	Robert J. Martorelli	'88
MERRILL SH-TM GLBL; A	World Income	67.8	8.20	9,906.00	10,032.00	☆	6.9	None	609-282-2800	3.00	0.25	None	Alex Bouzakis	'92
MERRILL SH-TM GLBL; B	World Income	1,098.8	8.19	9,882.00	9,967.00	☆	6.3	None	609-282-2800	None	0.75	3.00	Alex Bouzakis	'92
MERRILL SPEC VALUE; A	Growth	82.9	15.71	9,893.00	11,049.00	14,209.00	0.0	None	609-282-2800	6.50	None	None	Dennis Stattman	'89
MERRILL SPEC VALUE; B	Growth	129.0	15.28	9,864.00	10,935.00	13,497.00	0.0	None	609-282-2800	None	1.00	4.00	Dennis Stattman	'89
MERRILL STRAT DIV; A	Equity Income	22.5	12.48	10,306.00	10,015.00	14,076.00	3.6	None	609-282-2800	6.50	None	None	Walter D. Rogers	'88
MERRILL STRAT DIV; B	Equity Income	174.6	12.45	10,279.00	9,916.00	13,378.00	2.5	None	609-282-2800	None	1.00	4.00	Walter D. Rogers	'87
MERRILL TECHNOLOGY; A	Science & Technology	195.2	5.49	10,619.00	13,308.00	☆	0.0	None	609-282-2800	6.50	None	None	Jim Renck	'92
MERRILL TECHNOLOGY; B	Science & Technology	282.4	5.38	10,591.00	13,168.00	☆	0.0	None	609-282-2800	None	1.00	4.00	Jim Renck	'92
MERRILL UTILITY INC; A	Utility	3.6	8.13	9,446.00	☆	☆	0.0	None	609-282-2800	6.50	None	None	Walter D. Rogers	'93
MERRILL UTILITY INC; B	Utility	25.7	8.13	9,427.00	☆	☆	0.0	None	609-282-2800	None	0.75	4.00	Walter D. Rogers	'93
MERRILL WORLD INC; A	World Income	393.5	8.52	9,806.00	10,084.00	16,595.00	8.3	None	609-282-2800	4.00	None	None	Parish/Lathbury	'93/'88
MERRILL WORLD INC; B	World Income	1,862.1	8.51	9,777.00	9,997.00	☆	7.5	None	609-282-2800	None	0.75	4.00	Parish/Lathbury	'93/'91
MERRIMAN ASSET ALLOC	Global Flexible	31.5	10.91	9,702.00	10,342.00	14,040.00	0.9	423-4893	206-285-8877	None	None	None	Merriman/Notaro	'89/'89

PERFORMANCE OF MUTUAL FUNDS *(continued)*

FUND NAME	OBJECTIVE	TOTAL NET ASSETS ($ MIL) 5/31/94	NET ASSET $ VALUE 6/30/94	PERFORMANCE (Return on initial $10,000 Investment) 3/31/94-6/30/94	6/30/93-6/30/94	6/30/89-6/30/94	DIVIDEND YIELD % 6/94	PHONE NUMBER 800	In-State	FEES Load	12b-1	Redemption	MANAGER	SINCE
MERRIMAN CAP APPREC	Growth	27.8	10.63	9,824.00	10,097.00	13,527.00	0.7	423-4893	206-285-8877	None	None	None	Merriman/Notaro	'89/'89
MERRIMAN FLEXIBLE BOND	Fixed Income	11.3	10.03	9,902.00	10,381.00	14,448.00	4.3	423-4893	206-285-8877	None	None	None	Merriman/Notaro	'88/'88
MERRIMAN GROWTH & INCOME	Growth Income	12.1	10.87	9,964.00	10,269.00	13,067.00	0.8	423-4893	206-285-8877	None	None	None	Merriman/Notaro	'88/'88
MERRIMAN LVGD GROWTH	Capital Appreciation	5.7	10.28	9,828.00	10,151.00	☆	0.3	423-4893	206-285-8877	None	None	None	Merriman/Notaro	'92/'92
METLIFE PORT INTL EQ; A	International	10.8	10.56	10,242.00	☆	☆	0.0	882-3302	617-348-2000	4.50	0.25	None	Steve Bamford	'94
METLIFE PORT INTL EQ; B	International	6.9	10.54	10,233.00	☆	☆	0.0	882-3302	617-348-2000	None	1.00	5.00	Steve Bamford	'94
METLIFE PORT INTL EQ; C	International	49.6	10.58	10,262.00	12,892.00	☆	0.5	882-3302	617-348-2000	None	None	None	Steve Bamford	'92
METLIFE PORT INTL EQ; D	International	0.8	10.53	10,223.00	☆	☆	0.0	882-3302	617-348-2000	None	1.00	1.00	Steve Bamford	'94
METLIFE PORT INTL FI; A	World Income	0.8	8.17	10,160.00	☆	☆	0.0	882-3302	617-348-2000	4.50	0.25	None	Nick Sanjana	'94
METLIFE PORT INTL FI; B	World Income	1.0	8.15	10,143.00	☆	☆	0.0	882-3302	617-348-2000	None	1.00	5.00	Nick Sanjana	'94
METLIFE PORT INTL FI; C	World Income	22.6	8.18	10,174.00	10,855.00	☆	5.3	882-3302	617-348-2000	None	None	None	Nick Sanjana	'92
METLIFE PORT INTL FI; D	World Income	0.5	8.16	10,154.00	☆	☆	0.0	882-3302	617-348-2000	None	1.00	1.00	Nick Sanjana	'94
METLIFE SS CAP APP; A	Capital Appreciation	246.2	9.11	9,174.00	9,972.00	19,839.00	0.0	882-3302	617-348-2000	4.50	0.50	None	Fredrick R. Kobrick	'86
METLIFE SS CAP APP; B	Capital Appreciation	49.2	9.05	9,160.00	9,917.00	☆	0.0	882-3302	617-348-2000	None	1.00	5.00	Fredrick R. Kobrick	'93
METLIFE SS CAP APP; C	Capital Appreciation	65.8	9.16	9,188.00	10,025.00	☆	0.0	882-3302	617-348-2000	None	None	None	Fredrick R. Kobrick	'93
METLIFE SS CAP APP; D	Capital Appreciation	2.4	9.07	9,171.00	9,939.00	☆	0.0	882-3302	617-348-2000	None	1.00	1.00	Fredrick R. Kobrick	'93
METLIFE SS EQ INC; A	Equity Income	41.2	10.87	9,638.00	10,430.00	15,168.00	2.4	882-3302	617-348-2000	4.50	0.50	None	Bartlett R. Geer	'92
METLIFE SS EQ INC; B	Equity Income	10.1	10.86	9,626.00	10,381.00	☆	1.9	882-3302	617-348-2000	None	1.00	5.00	Bartlett R. Geer	'93
METLIFE SS EQ INC; C	Equity Income	20.5	10.86	9,642.00	10,486.00	☆	2.9	882-3302	617-348-2000	None	None	None	Bartlett R. Geer	'93
METLIFE SS EQ INC; D	Equity Income	1.2	10.86	9,626.00	10,379.00	☆	1.9	882-3302	617-348-2000	None	1.00	1.00	Bartlett R. Geer	'93
METLIFE SS EQ INVMT; A	Growth Income	31.1	12.43	9,818.00	10,093.00	15,723.00	0.0	882-3302	617-348-2000	4.50	0.50	None	Peter Bennett	'89
METLIFE SS EQ INVMT; B	Growth Income	4.0	12.35	9,809.00	10,037.00	☆	0.0	882-3302	617-348-2000	None	1.00	5.00	Peter Bennett	'93
METLIFE SS EQ INVMT; C	Growth Income	32.0	12.48	9,827.00	10,141.00	☆	0.0	882-3302	617-348-2000	None	None	None	Peter Bennett	'93
METLIFE SS EQ INVMT; D	Growth Income	0.6	12.36	9,810.00	10,045.00	☆	0.0	882-3302	617-348-2000	None	1.00	1.00	Peter Bennett	'93
METLIFE SS GOVT SEC, A	Fixed Income	95.0	6.93	9,862.00	9,882.00	14,687.00	6.2	882-3302	617-348-2000	4.50	0.25	None	Jack Kallis	'87
METLIFE SS GOVT SEC; B	Fixed Income	14.2	6.93	9,844.00	9,810.00	☆	5.4	882-3302	617-348-2000	None	1.00	5.00	Jack Kallis	'93
METLIFE SS GOVT SEC; C	Fixed Income	0.3	6.94	9,869.00	9,923.00	☆	6.5	882-3302	617-348-2000	None	None	None	Jack Kallis	'93
METLIFE SS GOVT SEC; D	Fixed Income	1.5	6.94	9,844.00	9,821.00	☆	5.4	882-3302	617-348-2000	None	1.00	1.00	Jack Kallis	'93
METLIFE SS HIGH INC; A	Fixed Income	636.6	6.18	9,931.00	10,842.00	16,062.00	9.9	882-3302	617-348-2000	4.50	0.25	None	Bartlett R. Geer	'87
METLIFE SS HIGH INC; B	Fixed Income	74.1	6.16	9,897.00	10,747.00	☆	9.1	882-3302	617-348-2000	None	1.00	5.00	Bartlett R. Geer	'93
METLIFE SS HIGH INC; C	Fixed Income	1.1	6.16	9,920.00	10,853.00	☆	10.1	882-3302	617-348-2000	None	None	None	Bartlett R. Geer	'93
METLIFE SS HIGH INC; D	Fixed Income	2.9	6.17	9,912.00	10,755.00	☆	9.2	882-3302	617-348-2000	None	1.00	1.00	Bartlett R. Geer	'93
METLIFE SS MGD ASSTS; A	Flexible	176.1	8.49	9,704.00	10,272.00	15,504.00	2.5	882-3302	617-348-2000	4.50	0.25	None	Michael Yogg	'91
METLIFE SS MGD ASSTS; B	Flexible	106.8	8.47	9,688.00	10,191.00	☆	1.9	882-3302	617-348-2000	None	1.00	5.00	Michael Yogg	'93
METLIFE SS MGD ASSTS; C	Flexible	23.4	8.49	9,699.00	10,296.00	☆	2.8	882-3302	617-348-2000	None	None	None	Michael Yogg	'93
METLIFE SS MGD ASSTS; D	Flexible	9.2	8.48	9,688.00	10,200.00	☆	1.9	882-3302	617-348-2000	None	1.00	1.00	Michael Yogg	'93
METLIFE SS MODERATE; C	Balanced	28.3	8.95	9,858.00	☆	☆	0.0	882-3302	617-348-2000	None	None	None	Michael Yogg	'94
MFS BOND; A	Fixed Income	450.6	12.44	9,773.00	9,839.00	15,152.00	9.0	225-2606	617-954-5000	4.75	0.35	None	Geoff Kurinsky	'86
MFS BOND; B	Fixed Income	37.3	12.42	9,756.00	☆	☆	0.0	225-2606	617-954-5000	None	1.00	4.00	Geoff Kurinsky	'93
MFS BOND; C	Fixed Income	8.0	12.41	9,757.00	☆	☆	0.0	225-2606	617-954-5000	None	1.00	None	Geoff Kurinsky	'94
MFS CAP GROWTH; A	Capital Appreciation	1.0	13.64	9,985.00	☆	☆	0.0	225-2606	617-954-5000	5.75	0.35	None	Kevin Parke	'93
MFS CAP GROWTH; B	Capital Appreciation	422.5	13.59	9,956.00	10,226.00	15,915.00	0.0	225-2606	617-954-5000	None	1.00	4.00	Kevin Parke	'88
MFS EMERG GRO; A ⊠	Midcap	431.9	16.82	9,097.00	☆	☆	0.0	225-2606	617-954-5000	5.75	0.35	None	John Ballen	'93
MFS EMERG GRO; B ⊠	Midcap	734.0	16.73	9,078.00	10,335.00	25,711.00	0.0	225-2606	617-954-5000	None	1.00	4.00	John Ballen	'87
MFS EMERGING EQUITIES ▮lll	Small Company Growth	29.4	11.73	9,317.00	11,741.00	☆	1.8	225-2606	617-954-5000	None	None	None	Chris Felipe	'93

MFS GOLD & NATL RES; A	Gold	2.9	6.23	9,162.00	☆	☆	0.0	225-2606	617-954-5000	5.75	0.35	None	Redmond Patriquin	'93
MFS GOLD & NATL RES; B	Gold	30.9	6.16	9,139.00	9,290.00	11,341.00	0.0	225-2606	617-954-5000	None	1.00	4.00	Redmond Patriquin	'88
MFS GOVT LTD MAT; A	Fixed Income	294.5	8.61	9,999.00	9,953.00	13,181.00	5.8	225-2606	617-954-5000	2.50	0.35	None	Steve Nothern	'88
MFS GOVT LTD MAT; B	Fixed Income	21.5	8.60	9,977.00	☆	☆	0.0	225-2606	617-954-5000	None	1.00	4.00	Steve Nothern	'93
MFS GOVT MTGE; A	Fixed Income	435.6	6.43	9,936.00	9,842.00	13,585.00	7.0	225-2606	617-954-5000	4.75	0.35	None	James Calmas	'93
MFS GOVT MTGE; B	Fixed Income	1,285.5	6.42	9,904.00	☆	☆	0.0	225-2606	617-954-5000	None	1.00	4.00	James Calmas	'93
MFS GOVT SEC; A	Fixed Income	347.0	9.25	9,896.00	9,806.00	14,431.00	7.3	225-2606	617-954-5000	4.75	0.35	None	Steve Nothern	'86
MFS GOVT SEC; B	Fixed Income	102.4	9.24	9,877.00	☆	☆	0.0	225-2606	617-954-5000	None	1.00	4.00	Steve Nothern	'93
MFS GROWTH OPPTY; A	Growth	632.2	10.51	9,633.00	9,656.00	14,472.00	0.4	225-2606	617-954-5000	5.75	0.35	None	Paul McMahon	'92
MFS GROWTH OPPTY; B	Growth	2.4	10.45	9,622.00	☆	☆	0.0	225-2606	617-954-5000	None	1.00	4.00	Paul McMahon	'93
MFS HIGH INCOME; A	Fixed Income	532.5	4.99	9,773.00	10,171.00	15,224.00	9.0	225-2606	617-954-5000	4.75	0.35	None	Joan Batchelder	'83
MFS HIGH INCOME; B	Fixed Income	283.0	4.99	9,752.00	☆	☆	0.0	225-2606	617-954-5000	None	1.00	4.00	Joan Batchelder	'93
MFS HIGH INCOME; C	Fixed Income	2.3	4.99	9,753.00	☆	☆	0.0	225-2606	617-954-5000	None	1.00	None	Joan Batchelder	'94
MFS INTMDT INCOME; A	Fixed Income	1.4	8.15	9,728.00	☆	☆	0.0	225-2606	617-954-5000	4.75	0.35	None	Steve Nothern	'93
MFS INTMDT INCOME; B	Fixed Income	361.6	8.15	9,728.00	9,634.00	12,991.00	5.3	225-2606	617-954-5000	None	1.00	4.00	Steve Nothern	'88
MFS LTD MAT; A	Fixed Income	101.6	7.08	9,965.00	10,133.00	☆	6.1	225-2606	617-954-5000	2.50	0.35	None	Geoff Kurinsky	'92
MFS LTD MAT; B	Fixed Income	13.1	7.08	9,958.00	☆	☆	0.0	225-2606	617-954-5000	None	1.00	4.00	Geoff Kurinsky	'93
MFS MGD SECTORS; A	Specialty	119.9	12.25	9,967.00	☆	☆	0.0	225-2606	617-954-5000	5.75	0.35	None	Ken Enright	'93
MFS MGD SECTORS; B	Specialty	209.6	12.21	9,951.00	9,809.00	15,260.00	0.0	225-2606	617-954-5000	None	1.00	4.00	Ken Enright	'93
MFS OTC FUND; A	Small Company Growth	13.4	7.45	8,965.00	☆	☆	0.0	225-2606	617-954-5000	5.75	0.35	None	John Ballen	'93
MFS OTC FUND; B	Small Company Growth	23.4	7.38	8,945.00	☆	☆	0.0	225-2606	617-954-5000	None	1.00	4.00	John Ballen	'93
MFS RESEARCH; A	Growth Income	298.9	12.73	9,800.00	10,721.00	17,715.00	0.3	225-2606	617-954-5000	5.75	0.35	None	Bill McAdams	'93
MFS RESEARCH; B	Growth Income	12.8	12.68	9,784.00	☆	☆	0.0	225-2606	617-954-5000	None	1.00	4.00	Bill McAdams	'93
MFS RESEARCH; C	Growth Income	2.7	12.68	9,784.00	☆	☆	0.0	225-2606	617-954-5000	None	1.00	None	Bill McAdams	'94
MFS STRATEGIC INCOME; A	Fixed Income	47.2	7.52	9,808.00	9,793.00	13,970.00	5.9	225-2606	617-954-5000	4.75	0.35	None	James Swanson	'92
MFS STRATEGIC INCOME; B	Fixed Income	2.9	7.50	9,787.00	☆	☆	0.0	225-2606	617-954-5000	None	1.00	4.00	James Swanson	'93
MFS TOTAL RETURN; A	Balanced	1,799.3	12.66	9,972.00	10,128.00	15,919.00	4.4	225-2606	617-954-5000	4.75	0.35	None	Richard Dahlberg	'84
MFS TOTAL RETURN; B	Balanced	771.8	12.66	9,953.00	☆	☆	0.0	225-2606	617-954-5000	None	1.00	4.00	Richard Dahlberg	'93
MFS UNION STD EQUITY	Growth	11.8	9.24	9,778.00	☆	☆	0.0	225-2606	617-954-5000	None	0.25	None	Nancy Dougherty	'94
MFS UTILITIES; A	Utility	43.6	6.89	9,705.00	9,916.00	☆	5.1	225-2606	617-954-5000	4.75	0.35	None	Maura Shaughnhessy	'92
MFS UTILITIES; B	Utility	17.5	6.88	9,678.00	☆	☆	0.0	225-2606	617-954-5000	None	1.00	4.00	Maura Shaughnhessy	'93
MFS UTILITIES; C	Utility	1.7	6.89	9,681.00	☆	☆	0.0	225-2606	617-954-5000	None	1.00	None	Maura Shaughnhessy	'94
MFS VALUE; A	Capital Appreciation	143.9	9.40	9,681.00	10,579.00	16,389.00	0.3	225-2606	617-954-5000	5.75	0.35	None	John Brennan	'91
MFS VALUE; B	Capital Appreciation	8.5	9.33	9,648.00	☆	☆	0.0	225-2606	617-954-5000	None	1.00	4.00	John Brennan	'93
MFS WORLD EQUITY; A	Global	10.6	16.06	9,871.00	☆	☆	0.0	225-2606	617-954-5000	5.75	0.35	None	David Mannheim	'93
MFS WORLD EQUITY; B	Global	168.9	15.96	9,846.00	11,328.00	15,444.00	0.1	225-2606	617-954-5000	None	1.00	4.00	David Mannheim	'92
MFS WORLD EQUITY; C	Global	1.5	15.97	9,852.00	☆	☆	0.0	225-2606	617-954-5000	None	1.00	None	David Mannheim	'94
MFS WORLD GOVTS; A	World Income	397.9	11.13	9,830.00	9,913.00	15,881.00	10.2	225-2606	617-954-5000	4.75	0.35	None	Leslie Nanberg	'84
MFS WORLD GOVTS; B	World Income	63.3	11.10	9,811.00	☆	☆	0.0	225-2606	617-954-5000	None	1.00	4.00	Leslie Nanberg	'93
MFS WORLD GOVTS; C	World Income	8.0	11.09	9,694.00	☆	☆	0.0	225-2606	617-954-5000	None	1.00	None	Leslie Nanberg	'94
MFS WORLD GROWTH; A	Global	101.8	15.98	9,852.00	☆	☆	0.0	225-2606	617-954-5000	5.75	0.35	None	John Ballen	'93
MFS WORLD GROWTH; B	Global	175.9	15.90	9,833.00	☆	☆	0.0	225-2606	617-954-5000	None	1.00	4.00	John Ballen	'93
MFS WORLD GROWTH; C	Global	7.5	15.91	9,833.00	☆	☆	0.0	225-2606	617-954-5000	None	1.00	None	John Ballen	'94
MFS WORLD TOT RTN; A	Global Flexible	90.7	10.41	9,938.00	10,882.00	☆	4.0	225-2606	617-954-5000	4.75	0.35	None	Frederick Simmons	'91
MFS WORLD TOT RTN; B	Global Flexible	36.6	10.40	9,923.00	☆	☆	0.0	225-2606	617-954-5000	None	1.00	4.00	Frederick Simmons	'93
MFS WORLD TOT RTN; C	Global Flexible	7.4	10.39	9,927.00	☆	☆	0.0	225-2606	617-954-5000	None	1.00	None	Frederick Simmons	'94
MFS WRLDWDE FXD INC	World Income	40.9	9.64	9,867.00	9,943.00	☆	8.9	225-2606	617-954-5000	None	None	None	Chris Felipe	'92
MIDWEST INC ADJ GOVT SEC	Fixed Income	56.0	9.91	10,032.00	10,294.00	☆	3.9	543-8721	513-629-2000	1.00	0.25	None	Tavares/Goetz	'93/'93
MIDWEST INC INTMDT GOVT	Fixed Income	72.0	10.31	9,812.00	9,615.00	14,137.00	5.3	543-8721	513-629-2000	1.00	0.25	None	Bruce Chaiken	'93
MIDWEST STRT FINL EQ; A	Capital Appreciation	3.6	8.87	9,616.00	☆	☆	0.0	543-8721	513-629-2000	4.00	0.25	None	Thomas Mench	'93

PERFORMANCE OF MUTUAL FUNDS (continued)

FUND NAME	OBJECTIVE	TOTAL NET ASSETS ($ MIL) 5/31/94	NET ASSET $ VALUE 6/30/94	PERFORMANCE (Return on initial $10,000 Investment) 3/31/94-6/30/94	6/30/93-6/30/94	6/30/89-6/30/94	DIVIDEND YIELD % 6/94	PHONE NUMBER 800	In-State	FEES Load	12b-1	Redemption	MANAGER	SINCE
MIDWEST STRT FINL EQ; C	Capital Appreciation	5.7	8.87	9,596.00	9,307.00	☆	0.5	543-8721	513-629-2000	1.00	1.00	None	Thomas Mench	'93
MIDWEST STRT GOVT LG MAT	Fixed Income	7.0	7.56	9,613.00	9,521.00	☆	6.3	543-8721	513-629-2000	1.00	0.25	None	Thomas Mench	'91
MIDWEST STRT GOVT SEC	Fixed Income	38.5	9.32	9,605.00	9,386.00	13,556.00	6.6	543-8721	513-629-2000	1.00	0.25	None	Bruce Chaiken	'92
MIDWEST STRT TOT RTN; A	Fixed Income	29.8	8.56	9,676.00	9,372.00	13,260.00	4.3	543-8721	513-629-2000	4.00	0.25	None	Thomas Mench	'88
MIDWEST STRT UTIL; A	Utility	41.3	10.33	9,917.00	9,564.00	☆	3.6	543-8721	513-629-2000	4.00	0.25	None	Thomas Mench	'89
MIDWEST STRT UTIL; C	Utility	1.8	10.33	9,909.00	☆	☆	0.0	543-8721	513-629-2000	1.00	1.00	None	Thomas Mench	'93
MIM MUTUAL AFA EQU INC	Equity Income	3.0	10.13	10,022.00	9,375.00	☆	1.6	233-1240	216-642-3000	None	0.70	None	AFA Financial, Inc.	'91
MIM MUTUAL BOND INCOME	Income	2.5	8.98	10,056.00	9,789.00	11,993.00	1.0	233-1240	216-642-3000	None	0.70	None	Harvey M. Salkin	'86
MIM MUTUAL STOCK APPREC	Capital Appreciation	52.2	13.36	9,064.00	8,774.00	20,265.00	0.0	233-1240	216-642-3000	None	0.70	None	Martin A. Weisberg	'94
MIM MUTUAL STOCK GROWTH	Growth	8.0	10.10	9,300.00	9,241.00	10,551.00	0.0	233-1240	216-642-3000	None	0.70	None	Martin A. Weisberg	'93
MIM MUTUAL STOCK INCOME	Growth Income	6.2	9.80	9,839.00	9,670.00	11,426.00	0.1	233-1240	216-642-3000	None	0.70	None	Harvey M. Salkin	'86
MIMLIC ASSET ALLOCATION	Flexible	55.2	12.85	9,735.00	9,632.00	14,941.00	2.1	443-3677	None	5.00	0.35	None	Thomas Gunderson	'89
MIMLIC FIXED INCOME SEC	Fixed Income	14.0	9.61	9,861.00	9,679.00	14,361.00	6.0	443-3677	None	5.00	0.30	None	Wayne Schmidt	'91
MIMLIC INVESTORS I	Growth Income	30.1	16.14	9,659.00	9,728.00	15,416.00	0.1	443-3677	None	5.00	0.30	None	Jim Tatera	'85
MIMLIC MORTGAGE	Fixed Income	27.5	9.77	9,929.00	9,742.00	14,531.00	6.0	443-3677	None	5.00	0.30	None	Kent Weber	'90
MINERVA EQUITY	Growth	10.1	9.72	10,045.00	☆	☆	0.0	393-9998	None	None	None	None	Katsunari Yamaguchi	'93
MINERVA FIXED INCOME	Fixed Income	2.9	9.18	9,801.00	☆	☆	0.0	393-9998	None	None	None	None	Akihito Sakata	'93
MMA PRAXIS GROWTH	Growth Income	14.3	9.64	10,033.00	☆	☆	0.0	977-2947	614-897-4600	None	0.05	5.00	Keith Yonder	'93
MMA PRAXIS INTMDT INC	Fixed Income	15.5	9.35	9,879.00	☆	☆	0.0	977-2947	614-897-4600	None	0.05	5.00	Delmar King	'93
MONETTA FUND ⊠	Growth Income	439.1	14.31	9,458.00	9,838.00	17,538.00	0.0	666-3882	708-462-9800	None	None	None	Robert S. Bacarella	'86
MONETTA INTMDT BOND	Fixed Income	2.9	9.77	9,914.00	10,091.00	☆	5.7	666-3882	708-462-9800	None	None	None	Alogna/Grossman	'93/'93
MONETTA MID-CAP EQUITY	Midcap	11.1	12.14	9,728.00	11,034.00	☆	0.1	666-3882	708-462-9800	None	None	None	John M. Alogna	'93
MONITOR FIXED INC; INV	Fixed Income	2.3	20.28	9,836.00	9,699.00	☆	6.3	253-0412	614-463-5580	2.00	0.25	None	Stephen Geis	'91
MONITOR FIXED INC; TR	Fixed Income	112.9	20.28	9,844.00	9,725.00	☆	6.6	253-0412	614-463-5580	None	None	None	Stephen Geis	'89
MONITOR GROWTH; INV	Growth	3.5	25.13	10,009.00	10,037.00	☆	1.4	253-0412	614-463-5580	4.00	0.25	None	Douglas Epp	'94
MONITOR GROWTH; TR	Growth	100.5	25.13	10,016.00	10,062.00	☆	1.6	253-0412	614-463-5580	None	None	None	Douglas Epp	'94
MONITOR INC EQUITY; TR	Equity Income	124.2	21.64	9,931.00	10,037.00	☆	3.5	253-0412	614-463-5580	None	None	None	James Buskirk	'89
MONITOR MTGE SEC; INV	Fixed Income	5.8	7.52	8,644.00	8,197.00	☆	19.5	253-0412	614-463-5580	2.00	0.25	None	Mark Goldstein	'94
MONITOR MTGE SEC; TR	Fixed Income	67.4	7.51	8,639.00	8,209.00	☆	19.9	253-0412	614-463-5580	None	None	None	Mark Goldstein	'94
MONITOR SHT/INT FXD; TR	Fixed Income	129.3	19.62	9,944.00	10,038.00	☆	.6.3	253-0412	614-463-5580	None	None	None	Stephen Geis	'89
MONITREND GOLD FUND	Gold	2.0	7.86	7,558.00	6,184.00	4,949.00	0.0	251-1970	615-298-1000	4.50	0.99	None	Johann DeVilliers	'91
MONITREND GOVERNMENT	Fixed Income	1.0	13.10	9,903.00	9,812.00	12,223.00	5.7	251-1970	615-298-1000	4.75	0.10	None	Pacific Income Advisors	'92
MONITREND GROWTH FUND	Growth	0.8	10.68	8,260.00	8,551.00	☆	0.0	251-1970	615-298-1000	4.75	0.99	None	Robert Bender	'92
MONITREND SUMMATION FUND	Growth Income	1.8	16.60	9,776.00	9,218.00	9,630.00	0.2	251-1970	615-298-1000	4.50	0.99	None	Team Managed	'93
MNTGMRY FIN SH DUR GOVT	Fixed Income	1.0	98.17	9,996.00	☆	☆	5.1	572-3863	415-627-2400	None	None	None	William Stevens	'93
MONTGOMERY II STRAT US	Flexible	1.3	12.24	10,200.00	☆	☆	0.0	572-3863	415-627-2400	None	None	None	Stevens/Honour/Pratt	'94/'94
MONTGOMERY INSTL EMERG	Emerging Markets	130.6	43.72	9,705.00	☆	☆	0.0	572-3863	415-627-2400	None	None	0.75	Jimenez/Sudweeks	'93/'93
MONTGOMERY EMERG MKTS	Emerging Markets	674.8	13.68	9,675.00	12,610.00	☆	0.1	572-3863	415-627-2400	None	None	None	Jimenez/Sudweeks	'92/'92
MONTGOMERY GLBL COMMUN	Global	252.8	14.20	9,423.00	11,406.00	☆	0.0	572-3863	415-627-2400	None	None	None	Castro/Boich	'93/'93
MONTGOMERY GLBL OPPTY	Global	13.0	12.93	9,363.00	☆	☆	0.0	572-3863	415-627-2400	None	None	None	Castro/Boich	'93/'93
MONTGOMERY GROWTH	Growth	116.4	15.27	10,214.00	☆	☆	0.0	572-3863	415-627-2400	None	None	None	Roger W. Honous	'93
MONTGOMERY INTL SM CAP ★	International	39.7	12.03	8,984.00	☆	☆	0.0	572-3863	415-627-2400	None	None	None	Castro/Boich	'93/'93
MONTGOMERY INTMDT DUR	Fixed Income	1.7	9.54	9,940.00	☆	☆	0.0	572-3863	415-627-2400	None	None	None	William Stevens	'94
MONTGOMERY SHORT DUR	Fixed Income	22.2	9.80	9,997.00	10,231.00	☆	6.1	572-3863	415-627-2400	None	None	None	Midanek/Stevens	'92/'92
MONTGOMERY SMALL CAP ⊠	Small Company Growth	219.7	15.15	8,980.00	9,841.00	☆	0.0	572-3863	415-627-2400	None	None	None	Stuart O. Roberts	'90

MORAN EQUITY FUND	Growth	N/A	12.70	10,176.00	10,296.00	☆	1.3	772-6672	203-869-5100	3.00	0.25	None	Frederick Moran	'90
MORGAN GRENFELL EMERG EQ	Emerging Markets	46.6	8.86	9,620.00	☆	☆	0.0	932-7781	215-989-6611	None	None	None	Lamb/Getley	'94/'94
MORGAN GRENFELL FXD INC	Fixed Income	201.0	10.05	10,052.00	10,126.00	☆	6.3	932-7781	215-989-6611	None	None	None	David Baldt	'92
MORGAN GRENFELL GLBL FXD	World Income	29.7	9.76	9,889.00	☆	☆	0.0	932-7781	215-989-6611	None	None	None	Kelson/Hall	'93/'93
MORGAN GRENFELL INTL FXD	World Income	10.6	9.85	9,782.00	☆	☆	0.0	932-7781	215-989-6611	None	None	None	Kelson/Hall	'94/'94
MORGAN GRENFELL INTL SM	International	64.1	10.69	10,152.00	☆	☆	0.0	932-7781	215-989-6611	None	None	None	Bamping/Freeze	'93/'93
MORGAN KEEGAN SOUTHERN	Growth	40.7	12.96	9,886.00	10,042.00	14,325.00	0.5	366-7426	901-524-4100	3.00	0.50	None	Timothy Johnson	'90
MSB FUND	Growth Income	38.6	16.10	9,793.00	10,478.00	15,449.00	1.0	631-6364	212-551-1920	None	None	None	McCabe/Trautman	'93/'93
MUHLENKAMP FUND	Flexible	16.0	16.93	9,901.00	10,006.00	16,680.00	0.6	860-3863	412-935-5520	None	None	None	Ronald Muhlenkamp	'88
MUNDER MULTI-SEASON; A	Growth	2.8	10.08	9,720.00	☆	☆	0.0	239-3334	None	5.50	0.25	None	Munder/Barr	'93/'93
MUNDER MULTI-SEASON; B	Growth	49.0	10.01	9,700.00	9,852.00	☆	0.0	239-3334	None	None	1.00	5.00	Munder/Barr	'93/'93
MUNDER MULTI-SEASON; C	Growth	3.2	10.11	9,721.00	☆	☆	0.0	239-3334	None	None	None	None	Munder/Barr	'93/'93
MUNDER MULTI-SEASON; D	Growth	1.5	10.02	9,700.00	☆	☆	0.0	239-3334	None	None	1.00	1.00	Munder/Barr	'93/'93
MUTUAL BENEFIT FUND	Growth Income	48.2	17.89	9,950.00	10,278.00	15,234.00	1.9	323-4726	401-751-8600	4.75	None	None	Markston Inv. Mgt.	'81
MUTUAL BEACON	Growth Income	1,443.3	31.97	10,198.00	11,355.00	17,324.00	1.1	448-3863	201-912-2100	None	None	None	Michael F. Price	'85
MUTUAL DISCOVERY ⊠	Small Company Growth	707.2	13.49	10,022.00	12,190.00	☆	0.7	448-3863	201-912-2100	None	None	None	Michael F. Price	'92
MUTUAL QUALIFIED	Growth Income	1,558.7	27.08	10,188.00	11,235.00	16,824.00	1.3	448-3863	201-912-2100	None	None	None	Michael F. Price	'80
MUTUAL SHARES	Growth Income	3,561.5	80.38	10,217.00	10,993.00	16,299.00	1.7	448-3863	201-912-2100	None	None	None	Michael F. Price	'75
N&B ADV MGT TR BALANCED ✪	Flexible	174.9	13.97	9,575.00	9,813.00	13,987.00	1.6	877-9700	212-476-8800	None	None	None	Havell/Goldstein	'89/'94
N&B EQ NYCDC SOC RESP	Growth	64.2	9.79	10,093.00	☆	☆	0.0	877-9700	212-476-8800	None	None	None	Prindle/Haboucha	'94/'94
N&B GENESIS FUND	Small Company Growth	126.9	7.87	9,899.00	10,367.00	14,874.00	0.1	877-9700	212-476-8800	None	None	None	Milman/Vale	'88/'94
N&B GENESIS TRUST	Small Company Growth	2.3	10.08	9,912.00	10,431.00	14,964.00	0.0	877-9700	212-476-8800	None	None	None	Milman/Vale	'93/'94
N&B GUARDIAN FUND	Growth Income	2,190.2	18.22	10,127.00	10,674.00	18,358.00	1.6	877-9700	212-476-8800	None	None	None	Simons/Marx	'82/'88
N&B GUARDIAN TRUST	Growth Income	20.7	10.52	10,135.00	10,678.00	18,367.00	0.7	877-9700	212-476-8800	None	None	None	Simons/Marx	'93/'93
N&B INC GOVT INC FUND	Fixed Income	11.0	9.42	9,878.00	☆	☆	0.0	877-9700	212-476-8800	None	None	None	Havell/White	'93/'93
N&B INC GOVT INC TRUST	Fixed Income	0.1	9.31	9,885.00	☆	☆	0.0	877-9700	212-476-8800	None	None	None	Havell/White	'93/'93
N&B INC LTD MAT FUND	Fixed Income	317.2	9.94	9,973.00	10,066.00	14,071.00	5.6	877-9700	212-476-8800	None	None	None	Havell/Weinblatt	'86/'93
N&B INC LTD MAT TRUST	Fixed Income	0.6	9.50	9,976.00	10,083.00	14,094.00	5.6	877-9700	212-476-8800	None	None	None	Havell/Weinblatt	'93/'93
N&B INC ULTRA FUND	Fixed Income	106.6	9.48	10,038.00	10,184.00	13,028.00	3.6	877-9700	212-476-8800	None	None	None	Havell/Giuliano	'86/'86
N&B INC ULTRA TRUST	Fixed Income	1.0	9.81	10,040.00	10,197.00	13,045.00	3.6	877-9700	212-476-8800	None	None	None	Havell/Giuliano	'93/'93
N&B MANHATTAN FUND	Capital Appreciation	498.5	10.16	9,416.00	9,831.00	15,641.00	0.2	877-9700	212-476-8800	None	None	None	Mark Goldstein	'92
N&B MANHATTAN TRUST	Capital Appreciation	8.8	9.34	9,387.00	9,844.00	15,663.00	0.1	877-9700	212-476-8800	None	None	None	Mark Goldstein	'93
N&B PARTNERS FUND	Growth	1,277.2	19.52	9,904.00	10,346.00	16,218.00	0.5	877-9700	212-476-8800	None	None	None	Kassen/Wittington	'90/'93
N&B PARTNERS TRUST	Growth	2.5	9.65	9,908.00	10,353.00	16,227.00	0.1	877-9700	212-476-8800	None	None	None	Kassen/Wittington	'93/'93
N&B SEL SCTRS FUND	Growth	611.6	22.72	10,179.00	10,803.00	18,242.00	1.1	877-9700	212-476-8800	None	None	None	Marx/Simons	'88/'88
N&B SEL SCTRS TRUST	Growth	0.7	10.57	10,193.00	11,115.00	18,769.00	0.2	877-9700	212-476-8800	None	None	None	Marx/Simons	'93/'93
NATIONAL INDUSTRIES	Growth Income	31.5	12.12	9,926.00	9,952.00	14,584.00	0.5	367-7814	303-220-8500	None	None	None	Richard Barrett	'84
NATIONS ADJ RT; INV A	Fixed Income	16.7	9.66	9,975.00	10,110.00	☆	4.8	321-7854	None	3.25	0.15	None	John Swaim	'92
NATIONS ADJ RT; INV C	Fixed Income	3.6	9.66	9,972.00	10,061.00	☆	4.3	321-7854	None	None	0.75	None	John Swaim	'92
NATIONS ADJ RT; INV N	Fixed Income	4.7	9.66	9,968.00	10,076.00	☆	4.4	321-7854	None	None	0.50	4.00	John Swaim	'93
NATIONS ADJ RT; TR A	Fixed Income	46.1	9.66	9,980.00	10,127.00	☆	4.9	321-7854	None	None	None	None	John Swaim	'92
NATIONS BALANCED; INV A	Balanced	5.1	10.22	9,681.00	9,634.00	☆	2.2	321-7854	None	5.75	0.25	None	Steve Hoeft	'92
NATIONS BALANCED; INV C	Balanced	1.1	10.19	9,661.00	9,563.00	☆	1.4	321-7854	None	None	0.75	None	Steve Hoeft	'92
NATIONS BALANCED; INV N	Balanced	51.2	10.21	9,669.00	9,585.00	☆	1.9	321-7854	None	None	0.75	5.00	Steve Hoeft	'93
NATIONS BALANCED; TR A	Balanced	190.4	10.23	9,687.00	9,655.00	☆	2.4	321-7854	None	None	None	None	Steve Hoeft	'92
NATIONS CAP GRO; INV A	Growth	11.1	10.76	9,697.00	10,040.00	☆	0.5	321-7854	None	5.75	0.25	None	Edwin Riley	'92
NATIONS CAP GRO; INV C	Growth	2.5	10.71	9,684.00	9,966.00	☆	0.0	321-7854	None	None	0.75	None	Edwin Riley	'92
NATIONS CAP GRO; INV N	Growth	18.5	10.74	9,684.00	9,966.00	☆	0.0	321-7854	None	None	0.75	5.00	Edwin Riley	'93
NATIONS CAP GRO; TR A	Growth	683.0	10.77	9,703.00	10,062.00	☆	0.7	321-7854	None	None	None	None	Edwin Riley	'92
NATIONS DVSD INC; INV A	Fixed Income	11.5	9.92	9,842.00	10,004.00	☆	7.1	321-7854	None	4.75	0.15	None	Mark Ahnrud	'92

★ MONTGOMERY INTL SM CAP--Fund has been reclassified from Global Small Company to International.

PERFORMANCE OF MUTUAL FUNDS (continued)

FUND NAME	OBJECTIVE	TOTAL NET ASSETS ($ MIL) 5/31/94	NET ASSET $ VALUE 6/30/94	PERFORMANCE (Return on initial $10,000 Investment) 3/31/94-6/30/94	6/30/93-6/30/94	6/30/89-6/30/94	DIVIDEND YIELD % 6/94	PHONE NUMBER 800	In-State	FEES Load	12b-1	Redemption	MANAGER	SINCE
NATIONS DVSD INC; INV C	Fixed Income	3.0	9.92	9,831.00	9,948.00	☆	6.5	321-7854	None	None	0.75	None	Mark Ahnrud	'92
NATIONS DVSD INC; INV N	Fixed Income	41.4	9.92	9,831.00	9,948.00	☆	6.5	321-7854	None	None	0.75	5.00	Mark Ahnrud	'93
NATIONS DVSD INC; TR A	Fixed Income	27.4	9.92	9,848.00	10,022.00	☆	7.3	321-7854	None	None	None	None	Mark Ahnrud	'92
NATIONS EMERG GR; INV A	Small Company Growth	2.7	10.08	9,342.00	9,985.00	☆	0.0	321-7854	None	5.75	0.25	None	Edward Smiley	'92
NATIONS EMERG GR; INV C	Small Company Growth	0.4	9.97	9,318.00	9,906.00	☆	0.0	321-7854	None	None	0.75	None	Edward Smiley	'92
NATIONS EMERG GR; INV N	Small Company Growth	10.4	10.01	9,320.00	9,906.00	☆	0.0	321-7854	None	None	0.75	5.00	Edward Smiley	'93
NATIONS EMERG GR; TR A	Small Company Growth	148.3	10.12	9,344.00	10,015.00	☆	0.0	321-7854	None	None	None	None	Edward Smiley	'92
NATIONS EQ INDEX; TR A	S&P Index	98.9	9.59	10,030.00	☆	☆	0.0	321-7854	None	None	None	None	Greg Golden	'93
NATIONS EQU INC; INV A	Equity Income	33.7	11.24	10,182.00	10,381.00	☆	3.0	321-7854	None	5.75	0.25	None	Eric Williams	'91
NATIONS EQU INC; INV C	Equity Income	4.2	11.31	10,162.00	10,301.00	☆	1.8	321-7854	None	None	0.75	None	Eric Williams	'92
NATIONS EQU INC; INV N	Equity Income	46.0	11.25	10,171.00	10,335.00	☆	2.7	321-7854	None	None	0.75	5.00	Eric Williams	'93
NATIONS EQU INC; TR A	Equity Income	224.8	11.26	10,188.00	10,407.00	☆	3.3	321-7854	None	None	None	None	Eric Williams	'91
NATIONS GOVT SEC; INV A	Fixed Income	14.0	9.64	9,820.00	9,755.00	☆	6.4	321-7854	None	4.75	0.15	None	William Brown	'92
NATIONS GOVT SEC; INV C	Fixed Income	5.2	9.64	9,808.00	9,699.00	☆	5.8	321-7854	None	None	0.75	None	William Brown	'92
NATIONS GOVT SEC; INV N	Fixed Income	56.3	9.64	9,811.00	9,708.00	☆	5.9	321-7854	None	None	0.65	5.00	William Brown	'93
NATIONS GOVT SEC; TR A	Fixed Income	44.5	9.64	9,826.00	9,772.00	☆	6.6	321-7854	None	None	None	None	William Brown	'92
NATIONS INTL EQU; INV A	International	3.2	11.96	10,234.00	11,806.00	☆	0.3	321-7854	None	5.75	0.25	None	Richard Williams	'92
NATIONS INTL EQU; INV C	International	0.3	11.81	10,192.00	11,696.00	☆	0.0	321-7854	None	None	0.75	None	Richard Williams	'92
NATIONS INTL EQU; INV N	International	17.3	11.91	10,207.00	11,702.00	☆	0.1	321-7854	None	None	0.75	5.00	Richard Williams	'93
NATIONS INTL EQU; TR A	International	378.1	12.02	10,239.00	11,845.00	☆	0.4	321-7854	None	None	None	None	Richard Williams	'91
NATIONS MGD BOND; INV A	Fixed Income	6.4	9.91	9,870.00	9,867.00	☆	5.5	321-7854	None	3.25	0.15	None	Mark Ahnrud	'93
NATIONS MGD BOND; INV C	Fixed Income	0.2	9.91	9,863.00	9,815.00	☆	4.9	321-7854	None	None	0.75	None	Mark Ahnrud	'93
NATIONS MGD BOND; TR A	Fixed Income	190.3	9.91	9,875.00	9,883.00	☆	5.7	321-7854	None	None	None	None	Mark Ahnrud	'93
NATIONS MTGE SEC; TR A	Fixed Income	75.9	9.26	9,807.00	9,749.00	☆	6.9	321-7854	None	None	None	None	John Swaim	'93
NATIONS S-I GOVT; INV A	Fixed Income	111.4	4.03	9,894.00	9,950.00	☆	5.5	321-7854	None	3.25	0.15	None	William Brown	'92
NATIONS S-I GOVT; INV C	Fixed Income	22.2	4.03	9,891.00	9,899.00	☆	5.0	321-7854	None	None	0.75	None	William Brown	'92
NATIONS S-I GOVT; INV N	Fixed Income	11.7	4.03	9,884.00	9,908.00	☆	5.1	321-7854	None	None	0.60	4.00	William Brown	'93
NATIONS S-I GOVT; TR A	Fixed Income	475.1	4.03	9,899.00	9,968.00	☆	5.7	321-7854	None	None	None	None	William Brown	'92
NATIONS SHTM INC; INV A	Fixed Income	4.7	9.63	9,956.00	10,091.00	☆	4.9	321-7854	None	1.50	0.25	None	Greg Cobb	'94
NATIONS SHTM INC; INV C	Fixed Income	12.9	9.63	9,952.00	10,066.00	☆	4.6	321-7854	None	None	0.50	None	Greg Cobb	'94
NATIONS SHTM INC; INV N	Fixed Income	26.7	9.63	9,952.00	10,077.00	☆	4.7	321-7854	None	None	0.35	None	Greg Cobb	'94
NATIONS SHTM INC; TR A	Fixed Income	193.0	9.63	9,960.00	10,113.00	☆	5.1	321-7854	None	None	None	None	Greg Cobb	'94
NATIONS SPECIAL EQ; TR A	Growth	8.3	12.48	9,279.00	10,084.00	☆	3.6	321-7854	None	None	None	None	Gil Knight	'92
NATIONS STR INC; INV A	Fixed Income	1.3	9.55	9,874.00	9,868.00	☆	5.3	321-7854	None	3.25	0.15	None	Mark Ahnrud	'93
NATIONS STR INC; INV C	Fixed Income	0.1	9.55	9,867.00	9,816.00	☆	4.7	321-7854	None	None	0.75	None	Mark Ahnrud	'93
NATIONS STR INC; INV N	Fixed Income	2.0	9.55	9,864.00	9,820.00	☆	4.8	321-7854	None	None	0.65	5.00	Mark Ahnrud	'93
NATIONS STR INC; TR A	Fixed Income	555.7	9.55	9,879.00	9,884.00	☆	5.5	321-7854	None	None	None	None	Mark Ahnrud	'93
NATIONS VALUE; INV A	Growth Income	35.8	13.10	9,919.00	10,462.00	☆	1.5	321-7854	None	5.75	0.25	None	Sharon Herrmann	'89
NATIONS VALUE; INV C	Growth Income	3.7	13.03	9,900.00	10,385.00	☆	0.8	321-7854	None	None	0.75	None	Sharon Herrmann	'92
NATIONS VALUE; INV N	Growth Income	27.6	13.09	9,917.00	10,415.00	☆	1.2	321-7854	None	None	0.75	5.00	Sharon Herrmann	'93
NATIONS VALUE; TR A	Growth Income	842.8	13.10	9,918.00	10,477.00	☆	1.7	321-7854	None	None	None	None	Sharon Herrmann	'93
NATIONWIDE II GOVT INC	Fixed Income	39.1	9.47	9,853.00	9,861.00	☆	5.5	848-0920	614-249-7855	None	0.20	5.00	Wayne Frisbee	'92
NATIONWIDE BOND	Fixed Income	137.5	8.82	9,745.00	9,540.00	14,419.00	7.5	848-0920	614-249-7855	4.50	None	None	Mike Groseclose	'80
NATIONWIDE FUND	Growth Income	697.9	15.18	9,935.00	10,277.00	15,903.00	2.3	848-0920	614-249-7855	4.50	None	None	Charles Bath	'85
NATIONWIDE GROWTH	Growth	440.5	10.55	9,965.00	10,315.00	14,935.00	1.7	848-0920	614-249-7855	4.50	None	None	John Schaffner	'81

NCC EQUITY; INSTL	Growth	90.4	13.34	10,081.00	10,017.00	☆	1.5	622-3863	None	None	0.01	None	Gerald Gray	'89
NCC EQUITY; RETAIL	Growth	7.5	13.36	10,081.00	9,993.00	☆	1.2	622-3863	None	3.75	0.01	None	Gerald Gray	'89
NCC FXD INC; INSTL	Fixed Income	95.6	10.17	9,848.00	9,736.00	☆	6.4	622-3863	None	None	0.01	None	Larry Kekst	'89
NCC FXD INC; RETAIL	Fixed Income	5.5	10.22	9,834.00	9,745.00	☆	6.1	622-3863	None	3.75	0.01	None	Larry Kekst	'91
NEW ALTERNATIVES FUND	Environmental	29.6	28.49	9,734.00	9,761.00	12,831.00	1.0	None	516-423-7373	4.75	None	None	Schoenwald/Schoenwald	'82/'82
NEW ECONOMY FUND	Growth	2,315.6	14.22	9,753.00	10,403.00	17,473.00	0.8	421-4120	714-671-7000	5.75	0.25	None	Multiple Managers	'83
NEW ENGLAND ADJ RATE; A	Fixed Income	612.8	7.32	10,004.00	10,136.00	☆	4.0	343-7104	None	1.00	0.25	None	Scott Nicholson	'91
NEW ENGLAND ADJ RATE; B	Fixed Income	1.4	7.32	9,986.00	☆	☆	0.0	343-7104	None	None	1.00	4.00	Scott Nicholson	'93
NEW ENGLAND BALANCED; A	Balanced	186.8	11.56	9,962.00	10,365.00	14,646.00	2.6	343-7104	None	5.75	0.25	None	Ramos/Beck	'90/'90
NEW ENGLAND BALANCED; B	Balanced	13.6	11.53	9,943.00	☆	☆	0.0	343-7104	None	None	1.00	4.00	Ramos/Beck	'93/'93
NEW ENGLAND BOND INC; A	Fixed Income	164.5	11.17	9,784.00	9,768.00	15,018.00	6.4	343-7104	None	4.50	0.25	None	Catherine Bunting	'89
NEW ENGLAND BOND INC; B	Fixed Income	6.3	11.17	9,765.00	☆	☆	0.0	343-7104	None	None	1.00	4.00	Catherine Bunting	'93
NEW ENGLAND CAP GRO; A	Growth	100.7	13.82	9,518.00	9,479.00	☆	0.0	343-7104	None	5.75	0.25	None	Hurckes/Pape	'92/'92
NEW ENGLAND CAP GRO; B	Growth	12.4	13.75	9,502.00	☆	☆	0.0	343-7104	None	None	1.00	4.00	Hurckes/Pape	'93/'93
NEW ENGLAND GL GOVT; A	World Income	20.2	11.22	9,887.00	9,923.00	14,399.00	6.3	343-7104	None	4.50	0.25	None	Andrea Burke	'91
NEW ENGLAND GL GOVT; B	World Income	1.1	11.21	9,860.00	☆	☆	0.0	343-7104	None	None	1.00	4.00	Andrea Burke	'93
NEW ENGLAND GOVT SEC; A	Fixed Income	170.3	10.82	9,804.00	9,742.00	14,003.00	6.8	343-7104	None	4.50	0.25	None	Back Bay Advisors	'93
NEW ENGLAND GOVT SEC; B	Fixed Income	2.4	10.82	9,794.00	☆	☆	0.0	343-7104	None	None	1.00	4.00	Back Bay Advisors	'93
NEW ENGLAND GR OPPTY; A	Growth Income	107.6	12.15	10,050.00	10,057.00	15,933.00	1.8	343-7104	None	5.75	0.35	None	Charles Glueck	'88
NEW ENGLAND GR OPPTY; B	Growth Income	3.6	12.14	10,057.00	☆	☆	0.0	343-7104	None	None	1.00	4.00	Charles Glueck	'93
NEW ENGLAND GROWTH ⊠	Growth	1,124.5	9.78	9,823.00	10,082.00	17,824.00	0.2	343-7104	None	6.50	0.25	None	G. Kenneth Heebner	'76
NEW ENGLAND HIGH INC; A	Fixed Income	33.4	9.55	9,920.00	10,419.00	15,386.00	9.2	343-7104	None	4.50	0.35	None	Charles Glueck	'88
NEW ENGLAND HIGH INC; B	Fixed Income	2.8	9.54	9,904.00	☆	☆	0.0	343-7104	None	None	1.00	4.00	Charles Glueck	'93
NEW ENGLAND INTL EQ; A	International	134.5	16.12	10,536.00	11,915.00	☆	0.7	343-7104	None	5.75	0.25	None	Nick Carn	'92
NEW ENGLAND INTL EQ; B	International	24.0	16.03	10,525.00	☆	☆	0.0	343-7104	None	None	1.00	4.00	Nick Carn	'93
NEW ENGLAND INTL EQ; C	International	30.3	16.20	10,561.00	☆	☆	0.0	343-7104	None	None	None	None	Nick Carn	'93
NEW ENGLAND LTD GOVT; A	Fixed Income	492.6	11.85	9,934.00	9,967.00	14,456.00	6.4	343-7104	None	3.00	0.35	None	Back Bay Advisors	'93
NEW ENGLAND LTD GOVT; B	Fixed Income	9.7	11.84	9,917.00	☆	☆	0.0	343-7104	None	None	1.00	4.00	Back Bay Advisors	'93
NEW ENGLAND VALUE; A	Growth Income	197.7	7.63	10,095.00	10,678.00	16,201.00	0.8	343-7104	None	5.75	0.25	None	Ramos/McMurtrie/Mills	'93/'93
NEW ENGLAND VALUE; B	Growth Income	7.4	7.60	10,061.00	☆	☆	0.0	343-7104	None	None	1.00	4.00	Ramos/McMurtrie/Mills	'93/'93
NEW PERSPECTIVE FUND	Global	5,722.7	14.59	9,938.00	11,652.00	17,895.00	1.4	421-4120	714-671-7000	5.75	0.25	None	Multiple Managers	'73
NEW YORK VENTURE	Growth	1,058.4	11.71	10,130.00	10,447.00	19,494.00	1.3	279-0279	505-983-4335	4.75	0.25	None	Shelby M.C. Davis	'69
NICH-APP BALANCED INSTL	Balanced	0.2	11.10	9,550.00	☆	☆	0.0	551-8045	619-687-8000	None	None	None	John Wylie	'93
NICH-APP BALANCED; A	Balanced	6.2	12.68	9,386.00	9,314.00	☆	1.2	551-8045	619-687-8000	5.25	0.25	None	John Wylie	'93
NICH-APP BALANCED; B	Balanced	16.5	12.70	9,391.00	9,266.00	☆	0.6	551-8045	619-687-8000	None	0.75	1.00	John Wylie	'93
NICH-APP CORE GR INSTL	Growth	79.6	11.95	9,424.00	9,261.00	☆	0.0	551-8045	619-687-8000	None	None	None	John Marshall, Jr.	'93
NICH-APP CORE GR; A	Growth	68.9	12.47	9,411.00	9,213.00	☆	0.0	551-8045	619-687-8000	5.25	0.25	None	John Marshall, Jr.	'93
NICH-APP CORE GR; B	Growth	147.7	12.38	9,393.00	9,152.00	☆	0.0	551-8045	619-687-8000	None	0.75	1.00	John Marshall, Jr.	'93
NICH-APP EMERG GR INSTL	Small Company Growth	164.9	10.54	9,262.00	☆	☆	0.0	551-8045	619-687-8000	None	None	None	Catherine Avery	'93
NICH-APP EMERG GR; A	Small Company Growth	103.0	11.19	9,248.00	☆	☆	0.0	551-8045	619-687-8000	5.25	0.25	None	Catherine Avery	'93
NICH-APP EMERG GR; B	Small Company Growth	139.1	11.15	9,238.00	☆	☆	0.0	551-8045	619-687-8000	None	0.75	1.00	Catherine Avery	'93
NICH-APP GOVT INCOME; A	Fixed Income	0.9	12.31	9,914.00	10,058.00	☆	2.5	551-8045	619-687-8000	4.75	0.25	None	John Wylie	'93
NICH-APP GOVT INCOME; B	Fixed Income	7.0	12.33	9,889.00	9,982.00	☆	2.2	551-8045	619-687-8000	None	0.50	1.00	John Wylie	'93
NICH-APP GR EQUITY; A	Midcap	91.6	11.65	9,388.00	9,405.00	18,972.00	0.0	225-1852	None	5.25	None	None	Jack Marshall	'91
NICH-APP GR EQUITY; B	Midcap	260.3	11.27	9,360.00	9,321.00	☆	0.0	225-1852	None	None	None	5.00	Jack Marshall	'91
NICH-APP INC & GR INSTL	Equity Income	18.4	12.65	9,544.00	10,515.00	☆	3.7	551-8045	619-687-8000	None	None	None	John Wylie	'93
NICH-APP INC & GR; A	Equity Income	36.1	13.38	9,525.00	10,421.00	☆	2.7	551-8045	619-687-8000	5.25	0.25	None	John Wylie	'93
NICH-APP INC & GR; B	Equity Income	71.4	13.49	9,513.00	10,382.00	☆	2.2	551-8045	619-687-8000	None	0.75	1.00	John Wylie	'93
NICH-APP WRLDWD GR INSTL	Global	4.2	12.93	9,833.00	☆	☆	0.0	551-8045	619-687-8000	None	None	None	Art Nicholas	'93
NICH-APP WRLDWD GR; A	Global	20.6	14.68	9,826.00	11,155.00	☆	0.0	551-8045	619-687-8000	5.25	0.25	None	Art Nicholas	'93

PERFORMANCE OF MUTUAL FUNDS (continued)

FUND NAME	OBJECTIVE	TOTAL NET ASSETS ($ MIL) 5/31/94	NET ASSET $ VALUE 6/30/94	PERFORMANCE (Return on initial $10,000 Investment) 3/31/94-6/30/94	6/30/93-6/30/94	6/30/89-6/30/94	DIVIDEND YIELD % 6/94	PHONE NUMBER 800	In-State	FEES Load	12b-1	Redemption	MANAGER	SINCE
NICH-APP WRLDWD GR; B	Global	69.8	14.57	9,805.00	11,080.00	☆	0.0	551-8045	619-687-8000	None	0.75	1.00	Art Nicholas	'93
NICHOLAS EQUITY INCOME	Equity Income	7.6	10.05	10,045.00	☆	☆	0.0	None	414-272-6133	None	None	None	Albert O. Nicholas	'93
NICHOLAS FUND	Growth	2,982.0	49.36	10,079.00	10,084.00	16,488.00	1.5	None	414-272-6133	None	None	None	Albert O. Nicholas	'69
NICHOLAS II	Midcap	629.4	25.46	9,965.00	10,300.00	15,312.00	1.0	None	414-272-6133	None	None	None	David O. Nicholas	'93
NICHOLAS INCOME	Fixed Income	151.3	3.39	10,040.00	10,311.00	14,890.00	8.6	None	414-272-6133	None	None	None	Albert O. Nicholas	'77
NICHOLAS LTD EDITION ⊠	Small Company Growth	156.7	17.64	9,655.00	10,230.00	18,113.00	0.5	None	414-272-6133	None	None	None	David O. Nicholas	'93
NOMURA PACIFIC BASIN	Pacific Region	58.3	18.11	10,815.00	12,127.00	15,723.00	1.5	833-0018	212-509-7893	None	None	None	Takeo Nakamura	'85
NORTH AM GOVT BD; ISI	World Income	93.1	9.21	9,851.00	9,819.00	☆	9.0	645-3923	410-637-6819	3.00	0.40	None	R. Alan Medaugh	'93
NORTHEAST INV GROWTH	Growth	36.3	23.87	9,933.00	9,856.00	15,676.00	0.8	225-6704	617-523-3588	None	None	None	William A. Oates	'80
NORTHEAST INV TRUST	Fixed Income	553.7	10.14	10,040.00	11,216.00	16,720.00	9.9	225-6704	617-523-3588	None	None	None	Ernest E. Monrad	'60
NORTHERN FDS FXD INCOME	Fixed Income	63.4	9.72	☆	☆	☆	0.0	595-9111	414-271-5885	None	None	None	Michael Lannan	'94
NORTHERN FDS GROWTH EQTY	Growth	73.1	9.95	☆	☆	☆	0.0	595-9111	414-271-5885	None	None	None	Karen Adams	'94
NORTHERN FDS INCOME EQTY	Equity Income	26.6	9.76	☆	☆	☆	0.0	595-9111	414-271-5885	None	None	None	William Hyatt	'94
NORTHERN FDS INTL EQTY	International	51.6	10.20	☆	☆	☆	0.0	595-9111	414-271-5885	None	None	None	Robert Lafleur	'94
NORTHERN FDS INTL FXD	World Income	5.5	9.94	☆	☆	☆	0.0	595-9111	414-271-5885	None	None	None	Michael Lannan	'94
NORTHERN FDS INTL GRO EQ	International	72.7	• 10.33	☆	☆	☆	0.0	595-9111	414-271-5885	None	None	None	Robert Lafleur	'94
NORTHERN FDS SELECT EQTY	Growth	4.9	9.66	☆	☆	☆	0.0	595-9111	414-271-5885	None	None	None	Robert Streed	'94
NORTHERN FDS SMALL CAP	Small Company Growth	39.4	9.66	☆	☆	☆	0.0	595-9111	414-271-5885	None	None	None	Susan French	'94
NORTHERN FDS US GOVT	Fixed Income	104.3	9.83	☆	☆	☆	0.0	595-9111	414-271-5885	None	None	None	Michael Lannan	'94
NORTHSTAR HI YLD; A	Fixed Income	48.3	4.72	9,790.00	☆	☆	0.0	595-7827	203-863-6200	4.75	0.30	None	Thomas Ole Dial	'93
NORTHSTAR HI YLD; B	Fixed Income	13.0	4.72	9,772.00	☆	☆	0.0	595-7827	203-863-6200	None	1.00	5.00	Thomas Ole Dial	'94
NORTHSTAR INC & GRO; A	Balanced	61.2	9.74	9,891.00	☆	☆	0.0	595-7827	203-863-6200	4.75	0.30	None	Myosogland/Wadsworth	'93/'93
NORTHSTAR INC & GRO; B	Balanced	13.8	9.74	9,883.00	☆	☆	0.0	595-7827	203-863-6200	None	1.00	5.00	Myosogland/Wadsworth	'94/'94
NORTHSTAR MULT-SECT; A	Fixed Income	26.5	4.56	9,681.00	☆	☆	0.0	595-7827	203-863-6200	4.75	0.30	None	Dial/Dzwill	'93/'93
NORTHSTAR MULT-SECT; B	Fixed Income	8.1	4.56	9,663.00	☆	☆	0.0	595-7827	203-863-6200	None	1.00	5.00	Dial/Dzwill	'94/'94
NORTHWEST NORTHWEST GRO	Growth	1.3	6.01	9,232.00	9,289.00	13,366.00	0.2	728-8762	206-734-9900	None	None	None	Nicholas Kaiser	'90
NORWEST ADJ US GOVT; A ★	Fixed Income	79.4	9.63	9,844.00	9,993.00	☆	5.0	338-1348	612-667-8833	1.50	None	0.50	Roger Adams	'92
NORWEST ADJ US GOVT; B	Fixed Income	0.4	9.59	9,825.00	☆	☆	0.0	338-1348	612-667-8833	None	0.75	1.50	Roger Adams	'93
NORWEST ADJ US GOVT; TR	Fixed Income	25.7	9.63	9,834.00	☆	☆	0.0	338-1348	612-667-8833	None	None	None	Roger Adams	'93
NORWEST CONTR STK; A	Growth Income	0.1	9.69	10,040.00	☆	☆	0.0	338-1348	612-667-8833	4.50	None	None	James C. Peery	'93
NORWEST CONTR STK; B	Growth Income	0.1	9.67	10,022.00	☆	☆	0.0	338-1348	612-667-8833	None	0.75	4.00	James C. Peery	'93
NORWEST CONTR STK; TR	Growth Income	4.5	9.68	10,040.00	☆	☆	0.0	338-1348	612-667-8833	None	None	None	James C. Peery	'93
NORWEST GOVT INC; A ★	Fixed Income	20.9	8.93	9,626.00	9,656.00	14,723.00	7.5	338-1348	612-667-8833	3.25	None	None	Mark Karstom	'88
NORWEST GOVT INC; B	Fixed Income	9.7	8.92	9,607.00	☆	☆	0.0	338-1348	612-667-8833	None	0.75	3.00	Mark Karstom	'93
NORWEST GOVT INC; TR	Fixed Income	120.8	8.93	9,626.00	☆	☆	0.0	338-1348	612-667-8833	None	None	None	Mark Karstom	'93
NORWEST INC STOCK; A ★	Growth Income	11.7	9.32	10,190.00	9,814.00	☆	3.0	338-1348	612-667-8833	4.50	None	None	Dave Roberts	'93
NORWEST INC STOCK; B	Growth Income	0.8	9.31	10,178.00	☆	☆	0.0	338-1348	612-667-8833	None	0.75	4.00	Dave Roberts	'93
NORWEST INC STOCK; TR	Growth Income	15.2	9.33	10,190.00	☆	☆	0.0	338-1348	612-667-8833	None	None	None	Dave Roberts	'93
NORWEST INCOME; A ★	Fixed Income	6.2	9.43	9,661.00	9,667.00	14,976.00	7.3	338-1348	612-667-8833	3.25	None	None	Mark Karstom	'87
NORWEST INCOME; B	Fixed Income	2.6	9.42	9,653.00	☆	☆	0.0	338-1348	612-667-8833	None	0.75	3.00	Mark Karstom	'93
NORWEST INCOME; TR	Fixed Income	93.7	9.42	9,670.00	☆	☆	0.0	338-1348	612-667-8833	None	None	None	Mark Karstom	'93
NORWEST SMALL CO; A	Small Company Growth	0.3	9.46	9,803.00	☆	☆	0.0	338-1348	612-667-8833	4.50	None	None	Kirk McCown	'93
NORWEST SMALL CO; B	Small Company Growth	0.2	9.44	9,795.00	☆	☆	0.0	338-1348	612-667-8833	None	0.75	4.00	Kirk McCown	'93
NORWEST SMALL CO; TR	Small Company Growth	9.3	9.42	9,802.00	☆	☆	0.0	338-1348	612-667-8833	None	None	None	Kirk McCown	'93
NORWEST TOT RT BD; A	Fixed Income	0.2	9.48	9,941.00	☆	☆	0.0	338-1348	612-667-8833	4.50	None	None	David B. Kinney	'93

NORWEST TOT RT BD; B	Fixed Income	0.2	9.49	9,923.00	☆	☆	0.0	338-1348	612-667-8833	None	0.75	3.00	David B. Kinney	'93
NORWEST TOT RT BD; TR	Fixed Income	11.7	9.48	9,941.00	☆	☆	0.0	338-1348	612-667-8833	None	None	None	David B. Kinney	'93
NORWEST VALUGROWTH; A ★	Growth	12.9	16.57	9,583.00	9,848.00	16,513.00	1.1	338-1348	612-667-8833	4.00	None	None	David Beeck	'88
NORWEST VALUGROWTH; B	Growth	2.2	16.50	9,575.00	☆	☆	0.0	338-1348	612-667-8833	None	0.75	4.00	David Beeck	'93
NORWEST VALUGROWTH; TR	Growth	113.1	16.56	9,599.00	☆	☆	0.0	338-1348	612-667-8833	None	None	None	David Beeck	'93
NOTTINGHAM II CAP VALUE	Balanced	6.3	10.22	9,845.00	10,166.00	☆	0.8	525-3863	919-972-9922	4.50	0.35	None	Capital Invstmnt Counsel	'91
NOTTINGHAM II HATTRS UTL	Utility	2.8	9.83	9,753.00	9,157.00	☆	2.1	525-3863	919-972-9922	None	0.75	None	Hatteras Cap. Mgmt	'91
NOTTINGHAM II INVSTK FXD	Fixed Income	17.5	9.66	9,883.00	9,731.00	☆	6.3	525-3863	919-972-9922	None	None	None	Investek Cap. Mgmt.	'91
NTH AM FDS ASSET ALLOC; C	Flexible	93.3	10.91	9,864.00	10,222.00	☆	1.7	334-0575	203-698-0068	None	1.00	None	Goldman Sachs Asset Mgt.	'92
NTH AM FDS GLBL GRO; C	Global	91.7	14.42	10,205.00	11,666.00	☆	0.0	334-0575	203-698-0068	None	1.00	None	Walter Oechsle	'90
NTH AM FDS GOVT SECS; A	Fixed Income	129.4	9.62	9,975.00	9,989.00	☆	4.8	334-0575	203-698-0068	4.75	0.35	None	Salomon Bros. Asset Mgt	'91
NTH AM FDS GR & INC; C	Growth Income	43.1	12.26	10,027.00	10,214.00	☆	1.0	334-0575	203-698-0068	None	1.00	None	Wellington Mgmt. Co.	'91
NTH AM FDS GROWTH; C	Growth	70.8	14.41	9,877.00	10,655.00	☆	0.2	334-0575	203-698-0068	None	1.00	None	Goldman Sachs Asset Mgt.	'91
NTH AM FDS INV QUAL; A	Fixed Income	13.1	9.93	9,848.00	9,584.00	☆	5.8	334-0575	203-698-0068	4.75	0.35	None	Wellington Mgmt. Co.	'91
NTH AM FDS STRAT INC; A	Fixed Income	16.3	9.09	9,982.00	☆	☆	0.0	334-0575	203-698-0068	4.75	0.35	None	Salomon Bros. Asset Mgt	'93
NY LIFE INSTL BOND	Fixed Income	213.5	9.58	9,866.00	9,858.00	☆	7.5	695-2126	None	None	None	None	Ravi Akhoury	'91
NY LIFE INSTL EAFE INDEX	International	71.7	13.07	10,498.00	11,639.00	☆	0.4	695-2126	None	None	None	None	James Mehling	'92
NY LIFE INSTL GROWTH EQ	Growth	265.0	13.21	9,303.00	10,041.00	☆	0.0	695-2126	None	None	None	None	Spelman/Carryl	'92/'92
NY LIFE INSTL INDEXED BD	Fixed Income	166.2	10.62	9,879.00	9,832.00	☆	6.2	695-2126	None	None	None	None	James Mehling	'91
NY LIFE INSTL INDEXED EQ	S&P Index	236.3	13.35	10,030.00	10,086.00	☆	2.2	695-2126	None	None	None	None	James Mehling	'92
NY LIFE INSTL MULTI-ASST	Flexible	256.5	11.29	9,982.00	10,034.00	☆	3.5	695-2126	None	None	None	None	James Mehling	'92
NY LIFE INSTL SH-TM BD	Fixed Income	114.5	10.26	10,000.00	10,131.00	☆	7.0	695-2126	None	None	None	None	Ravi Akhoury	'91
NY LIFE INSTL VALUE EQ	Growth Income	348.4	12.48	10,048.00	10,791.00	☆	1.3	695-2126	None	None	None	None	Laplaige/Kolefas	'91/'91
OAK HALL EQUITY	Capital Appreciation	36.6	12.55	9,174.00	9,501.00	☆	0.0	625-4255	207-879-0001	None	0.20	None	John Hathaway	'92
OAK VALUE FUND	Growth	7.0	11.61	10,175.00	11,408.00	☆	0.0	525-3863	919-972-9922	None	None	None	David R. Carr	'93
OAKMARK	Growth	1,362.1	23.60	10,292.00	11,608.00	☆	1.0	625-6275	312-621-0600	None	None	None	Robert Sanborn	'91
OAKMARK INTERNATIONAL	International	1,454.4	13.76	9,405.00	11,667.00	☆	0.6	625-6275	312-621-0600	None	None	None	David Herro	'92
OBERWEIS EMERGING GROWTH	Small Company Growth	87.8	18.16	8,714.00	9,114.00	19,583.00	0.0	323-6166	708-897-7100	None	0.50	None	James Oberweis	'87
OFFITBANK EMERGING MKTS	World Income	23.7	9.75	10,038.00	☆	☆	0.0	None	None	None	None	None	N/A	N/A
OFFITBANK HIGH YIELD	Fixed Income	153.9	9.51	10,060.00	☆	☆	0.0	None	None	None	None	None	N/A	N/A
OLD DOMINION INVESTRS TR	Equity Income	6.8	19.28	10,439.00	10,446.00	13,305.00	2.0	441-6580	804-539-2396	4.00	0.25	None	Birdsong/Hollingsworth	'64/'93
OLD WESTBURY INTL FUND ▮▮▮✵	International	81.3	9.68	9,632.00	☆	☆	0.0	934-7336	None	4.50	0.35	None	John Trott	'93
OLYMPIC TR BALANCED INC	Balanced	36.1	15.71	10,063.00	10,366.00	15,283.00	5.9	346-7301	213-362-8900	None	None	None	Roger DeBard	'85
OLYMPIC TR EQUITY INC	Equity Income	88.3	15.07	10,033.00	10,340.00	14,674.00	3.0	346-7301	213-362-8900	None	None	None	George Wiley	'87
OLYMPIC TR INTERNATIONAL	International	26.2	16.79	9,878.00	11,671.00	☆	0.8	346-7301	213-362-8900	None	None	None	Bouwer/Ketterer	'90/'90
OLYMPIC TR LOW DURATION	Fixed Income	45.9	9.93	10,078.00	10,897.00	☆	7.7	346-7301	213-362-8900	None	None	None	Rivelle/Landmann	'93/'93
OLYMPIC TR SH-TM INV	Fixed Income	10.4	10.21	10,121.00	10,746.00	☆	5.1	346-7301	213-362-8900	None	None	None	Rivelle/Landmann	'93/'93
OLYMPIC TR SMALL CAPITAL	Small Company Growth	13.3	19.53	9,692.00	10,377.00	18,829.00	1.0	346-7301	213-362-8900	None	None	None	Davis/Hitchman	'88/'94
OMNI INVESTMENT	Capital Appreciation	16.1	148.27	10,361.00	12,140.00	15,492.00	0.2	223-9790	312-922-0431	None	None	None	Robert Perkins	'85
111 CORCORAN BOND FD	Fixed Income	97.8	9.54	9,858.00	9,821.00	☆	6.6	422-2080	919-683-7277	4.50	None	None	Jim Agnew	'92
ONE FUND GROWTH	Growth	5.4	11.67	9,667.00	10,285.00	☆	1.0	578-8078	None	5.00	0.25	None	Steve Williams	'92
ONE FUND INC & GRO	Growth Income	7.6	10.65	9,905.00	10,196.00	☆	3.1	578-8078	None	5.00	0.25	None	Steve Williams	'92
ONE FUND INCOME	Fixed Income	4.6	9.39	9,795.00	9,667.00	☆	6.5	578-8078	None	3.00	0.25	None	Michael Boedeker	'92
ONE FUND INTERNATIONAL	International	10.0	13.32	9,934.00	13,955.00	☆	0.4	578-8078	None	5.00	0.25	None	Jean-Marie Eveillard	'93
ONE GROUP ASSET ALLO; A	Flexible	1.6	9.65	9,832.00	9,881.00	☆	2.7	338-4345	None	4.50	0.25	None	Bank One	'93

★ NORWEST ADJ US GOVT; A--The maximum load is currently reduced to 1.50%.
★ NORWEST GOVT INC; A--The maximum load is currently reduced to 3.25%.
★ NORWEST INC STOCK; A--The maximum load is currently reduced to 4.00%.
★ NORWEST INCOME; A--The maximum load is currently reduced to 3.25%.
★ NORWEST VALUGROWTH; A--The maximum load is currently reduced to 4.00%.

FUND NAME	OBJECTIVE	TOTAL NET ASSETS ($ MIL) 5/31/94	NET ASSET $ VALUE 6/30/94	PERFORMANCE (Return on initial $10,000 Investment) 3/31/94-6/30/94	6/30/93-6/30/94	6/30/89-6/30/94	DIVIDEND YIELD % 6/94	PHONE NUMBER 800	In-State	FEES Load	12b-1	Redemption	MANAGER	SINCE
ONE GROUP ASSET ALLO; FID	Flexible	44.2	9.64	9,838.00	9,897.00	☆	3.0	338-4345	None	None	None	None	Bank One	'93
ONE GROUP BLUE CHIP; A	Growth Income	4.2	12.52	9,978.00	9,839.00	☆	1.5	338-4345	None	4.50	0.25	None	Scott Andrews	'92
ONE GROUP BLUE CHIP; FID	Growth Income	89.9	12.53	9,991.00	9,868.00	☆	1.7	338-4345	None	None	None	None	Scott Andrews	'90
ONE GROUP DISC VAL; A	Growth	10.3	11.95	9,781.00	10,418.00	☆	1.8	338-4345	None	4.50	0.25	None	Terrence Pavlic	'92
ONE GROUP DISC VAL; FID	Growth	425.3	11.90	9,747.00	10,403.00	14,463.00	2.1	338-4345	None	None	None	None	Terrence Pavlic	'92
ONE GROUP EQ INDEX; A	S&P Index	1.3	11.59	10,007.00	10,056.00	☆	2.3	338-4345	None	4.50	0.15	None	Mark Pelligrino	'92
ONE GROUP EQ INDEX; FID	S&P Index	155.3	11.59	10,012.00	10,062.00	☆	2.5	338-4345	None	None	None	None	Mark Pelligrino	'91
ONE GROUP GOVT ARM; A	Fixed Income	19.5	9.84	10,007.00	10,194.00	☆	3.9	338-4345	None	3.00	0.25	None	Bank One	'93
ONE GROUP GOVT ARM; FID	Fixed Income	150.9	9.85	10,018.00	10,217.00	☆	4.0	338-4345	None	None	None	None	Bank One	'93
ONE GROUP GOVT BOND; A	Fixed Income	1.7	9.35	9,832.00	9,684.00	☆	5.3	338-4345	None	4.50	0.25	None	Bank One	'93
ONE GROUP GOVT BOND; FID	Fixed Income	203.4	9.35	9,858.00	9,725.00	☆	5.5	338-4345	None	None	None	None	Bank One	'93
ONE GROUP INCOME EQ; A	Equity Income	12.4	13.20	10,222.00	10,295.00	☆	3.0	338-4345	None	4.50	0.25	None	Ralph Patek	'92
ONE GROUP INCOME EQ; FID	Equity Income	207.3	13.22	10,236.00	10,325.00	15,690.00	3.2	338-4345	None	None	None	None	Ralph Patek	'87
ONE GROUP INCOME; A	Fixed Income	5.5	9.24	9,880.00	9,765.00	☆	5.6	338-4345	None	4.50	0.25	None	Thomas Wilson	'92
ONE GROUP INCOME; FID	Fixed Income	562.6	9.23	9,887.00	9,778.00	14,323.00	5.9	338-4345	None	None	None	None	Thomas Wilson	'89
ONE GROUP INTL EQ; A	International	2.3	13.52	10,150.00	11,483.00	☆	0.1	338-4345	None	4.50	0.25	None	Bank One	'93
ONE GROUP INTL EQ; FID	International	135.8	13.49	10,158.00	11,544.00	☆	0.8	338-4345	None	None	None	None	Bank One	'92
ONE GROUP INTMDT FXD; FID	Fixed Income	92.2	9.72	9,907.00	9,925.00	☆	6.2	338-4345	None	None	None	None	Jim Sexton	'92
ONE GROUP LG CO GRO; FID	Growth Income	134.3	11.32	10,234.00	10,856.00	☆	2.2	338-4345	None	None	None	None	Lynn Yturri	'92
ONE GROUP LG CO VAL; A	Growth Income	0.7	11.41	9,994.00	10,198.00	☆	1.4	338-4345	None	4.50	0.25	None	Mark Pelligrino	'92
ONE GROUP LG CO VAL; FID	Growth Income	168.8	11.34	9,991.00	10,157.00	☆	1.6	338-4345	None	None	None	None	Mark Pelligrino	'91
ONE GROUP LTD VOL BD; A	Fixed Income	15.5	10.32	9,965.00	10,049.00	☆	5.2	338-4345	None	3.00	0.25	None	Tim Holihen	'92
ONE GROUP LTD VOL BD; FID	Fixed Income	448.9	10.33	9,971.00	10,079.00	☆	5.4	338-4345	None	None	None	None	Tim Holihen	'90
ONE GROUP S-T GLOBAL; A	World Income	0.2	8.73	9,790.00	9,430.00	☆	7.4	338-4345	None	4.50	None	None	Bank One	'93
ONE GROUP S-T GLOBAL; FID	World Income	39.1	8.72	9,795.00	9,433.00	☆	7.6	338-4345	None	None	None	None	Bank One	'93
ONE GROUP SMALL CO; A	Midcap	8.2	15.93	9,599.00	9,948.00	☆	0.2	338-4345	None	4.50	0.25	None	Richard R. Jandrain	'92
ONE GROUP SMALL CO; FID	Midcap	394.9	15.96	9,602.00	9,984.00	18,501.00	0.4	338-4345	None	None	None	None	Richard R. Jandrain	'89
OPPENHEIMER ASST ALL; A	Flexible	268.1	12.33	9,905.00	10,357.00	14,757.00	3.4	525-7048	303-671-3200	5.75	0.25	None	Team Managed	'91
OPPENHEIMER CHMPN HY; A	Fixed Income	138.6	12.50	10,052.00	10,618.00	18,956.00	8.7	525-7048	303-671-3200	4.75	0.25	None	Ralph Stellmacher	'87
OPPENHEIMER DISCVRY; A	Small Company Growth	558.6	32.76	9,012.00	9,561.00	18,132.00	0.0	525-7048	303-671-3200	5.75	0.25	None	Paul LaRocca	'94
OPPENHEIMER EQ INC; A	Equity Income	1,806.7	9.44	10,031.00	10,065.00	14,654.00	5.0	525-7048	303-671-3200	5.75	0.25	None	John Doney	'92
OPPENHEIMER FUND; A	Growth	243.1	10.55	9,832.00	10,584.00	15,795.00	0.3	525-7048	303-671-3200	5.75	0.25	None	Richard Rubinstein	'92
OPPENHEIMER GL G&I; A	Global Flexible	127.2	14.54	9,905.00	11,855.00	☆	2.0	525-7048	303-671-3200	5.75	0.25	None	Wilby/Steinmetz	'91/'90
OPPENHEIMER GLBL ENVIRN	Environmental	32.7	9.74	9,374.00	9,905.00	☆	0.2	525-7048	303-671-3200	5.75	0.25	None	John Wallace	'91
OPPENHEIMER GLBL FD; A	Global	1,781.0	35.47	9,880.00	12,582.00	17,663.00	0.7	525-7048	303-671-3200	5.75	0.25	None	Bill Wilby	'92
OPPENHEIMER GLBL FD; B	Global	124.4	35.24	9,855.00	☆	☆	0.0	525-7048	303-671-3200	None	0.25	5.00	Bill Wilby	'93
OPPENHEIMER GLD & SP MIN	Gold	186.0	13.28	9,432.00	10,825.00	12,267.00	0.4	525-7048	303-671-3200	5.75	0.25	None	Bill Wilby	'92
OPPENHEIMER GLO BIO-TECH	Health/Biotechnology	172.9	18.11	8,661.00	8,459.00	16,906.00	0.0	525-7048	303-671-3200	5.75	0.25	None	Sandra Panem	'92
OPPENHEIMER HI YLD; A	Fixed Income	1,021.6	13.63	9,993.00	10,627.00	16,604.00	10.3	525-7048	303-671-3200	4.75	0.25	None	Ralph Stellmacher	'88
OPPENHEIMER HI YLD; B	Fixed Income	78.1	13.57	9,975.00	10,531.00	☆	9.6	525-7048	303-671-3200	None	0.25	5.00	Ralph Stellmacher	'93
OPPENHEIMER INV GRD; A	Fixed Income	101.5	10.31	9,860.00	9,788.00	14,455.00	6.5	525-7048	303-671-3200	4.75	0.25	None	Mary Wilson	'91
OPPENHEIMER INV GRD; B	Fixed Income	2.7	10.31	9,851.00	9,692.00	☆	5.7	525-7048	303-671-3200	None	0.25	5.00	Mary Wilson	'93
OPPENHEIMER LTD GOVT; A	Fixed Income	195.7	10.51	9,917.00	10,168.00	14,953.00	6.7	525-7048	303-671-3200	3.50	0.25	None	Arthur Steinmetz	'90
OPPENHEIMER MAIN I&G; A	Growth Income	662.5	20.40	9,478.00	11,445.00	28,159.00	1.7	525-7048	303-671-3200	5.75	0.25	None	John Wallace	'92
OPPENHEIMER MTGE INC; A	Fixed Income	85.0	13.27	9,934.00	10,024.00	14,430.00	7.1	525-7048	303-671-3200	4.75	0.25	None	Eva A. Zeff	'92

OPPENHEIMER MTGE INC; B	Fixed Income	2.4	13.26	9,900.00	9,928.00	☆	6.3	525-7048	303-671-3200	None	0.25	5.00	Eva A. Zeff	'93
OPPENHEIMER SPECIAL; A	Growth	692.4	26.65	9,838.00	10,027.00	16,757.00	0.6	525-7048	303-671-3200	5.75	0.25	None	Robert Doll, Jr.	'87
OPPENHEIMER SPECIAL; B	Growth	8.6	26.44	9,829.00	☆	☆	0.0	525-7048	303-671-3200	None	0.25	5.00	Robert Doll, Jr.	'93
OPPENHEIMER STR I&G; A	Fixed Income	45.0	4.86	9,993.00	9,787.00	☆	4.5	525-7048	303-671-3200	4.75	0.25	None	Steinmertz/Negri/Johnson	'92/'92
OPPENHEIMER STR I&G; B	Fixed Income	15.7	4.85	9,975.00	9,705.00	☆	3.7	525-7048	303-671-3200	None	0.25	5.00	Steinmertz/Negri/Johnson	'92/'92
OPPENHEIMER STR INC; A	Fixed Income	3,144.1	4.80	9,950.00	10,372.00	☆	9.6	525-7048	303-671-3200	4.75	0.25	None	Steinmertz/Negri	'89/'89
OPPENHEIMER STR INC; B	Fixed Income	1,425.0	4.81	9,952.00	10,290.00	☆	8.8	525-7048	303-671-3200	None	0.25	5.00	Steinmertz/Negri	'92/'92
OPPENHEIMER STR INV; A	Fixed Income	27.1	4.77	9,893.00	10,000.00	☆	7.2	525-7048	303-671-3200	4.75	0.25	None	Steinmertz/Negri	'92/'92
OPPENHEIMER STR INV; B	Fixed Income	14.4	4.76	9,857.00	9,906.00	☆	6.4	525-7048	303-671-3200	None	0.25	5.00	Steinmertz/Negri	'92/'92
OPPENHEIMER STR SHRT; A	Fixed Income	29.6	4.60	9,945.00	10,145.00	☆	6.6	525-7048	303-671-3200	3.50	0.25	None	Steinmertz/Negri	'92/'92
OPPENHEIMER STR SHRT; B	Fixed Income	7.3	4.59	9,925.00	10,033.00	☆	5.7	525-7048	303-671-3200	None	0.25	4.00	Steinmertz/Negri	'92/'92
OPPENHEIMER TARGET	Capital Appreciation	327.5	24.36	9,725.00	9,914.00	15,943.00	0.5	525-7048	303-671-3200	5.75	0.25	None	Doll/Johnson	'88/'92
OPPENHEIMER TIME	Capital Appreciation	346.1	15.45	8,905.00	9,660.00	13,986.00	0.0	525-7048	303-671-3200	5.75	0.25	None	Jay Tracey	'91
OPPENHEIMER TOT RET; A	Growth Income	1,257.3	7.84	9,450.00	9,990.00	17,797.00	2.5	525-7048	303-671-3200	5.75	0.25	None	John Wallace	'90
OPPENHEIMER TOT RET; B	Growth Income	354.2	7.80	9,440.00	9,921.00	☆	1.7	525-7048	303-671-3200	None	0.25	5.00	John Wallace	'93
OPPENHEIMER US GOVT; A	Fixed Income	315.4	9.20	9,900.00	9,881.00	14,253.00	7.0	525-7048	303-671-3200	4.75	0.25	None	Arthur Steinmetz	'87
OPPENHEIMER VALUE; A	Growth Income	89.9	14.20	10,237.00	10,309.00	16,057.00	1.9	525-7048	303-671-3200	5.75	0.25	None	David Salerno	'91
OPPENHEIMER VALUE; B	Growth Income	7.0	14.14	10,199.00	10,227.00	☆	1.3	525-7048	303-671-3200	None	0.25	5.00	David Salerno	'93
ORI GROWTH FUND	Growth	1.9	9.82	9,247.00	☆	☆	0.0	407-7298	None	None	None	None	David Klaskin	'94
OVERLAND ASSET ALLOC; A	Flexible	51.1	11.28	9,937.00	10,038.00	15,776.00	2.1	552-9612	None	4.50	0.25	None	Janic Derringer	'88
OVERLAND DIV INC; A	Equity Income	2.2	10.28	10,145.00	10,455.00	☆	3.3	552-9612	None	4.50	0.25	None	Wisniewski/Bissell	'93/'93
OVERLAND GRO & INC; A	Growth Income	15.7	15.53	9,873.00	10,280.00	☆	1.5	552-9612	None	4.50	0.25	None	Wisniewski/Bissell	'90/'90
OVERLAND SH-TM GOVT	Fixed Income	21.9	50.79	9,957.00	10,110.00	☆	2.4	552-9612	None	3.00	0.25	None	Glessman/Kraschel	'92/'93
OVERLAND STRAT GRO; A	Capital Appreciation	27.2	11.75	9,348.00	10,224.00	☆	0.0	552-9612	None	4.50	0.25	None	Hickman/Bissell	'93/'93
OVERLAND US GOVT INC; A	Fixed Income	48.2	10.01	9,843.00	9,792.00	15,310.00	7.2	552-9612	None	4.50	0.05	None	Single/Niedermeyer	'88/'88
OVERLAND VAR RT GOVT; A	Fixed Income	1,795.6	9.64	9,877.00	10,021.00	☆	4.3	552-9612	None	3.00	0.25	None	Single/Glessman	'90/'92
P HZN AGG GRO	Capital Appreciation	142.2	22.43	9,272.00	8,948.00	17,861.00	0.0	332-3863	619-456-9197	4.50	None	None	Jeff Mallet	'90
P HZN ASSET ALLOCATION	Flexible	1.8	14.12	9,871.00	☆	☆	0.0	332-3863	619-456-9197	4.50	None	None	Helton/Vielaber	'94/'94
P HZN CAP INC	Convertible Securities	206.4	13.93	9,696.00	10,329.00	19,969.00	3.9	332-3863	619-456-9197	4.50	None	None	William Hensel	'87
P HZN US GOVT SEC	Fixed Income	124.6	9.31	9,877.00	9,713.00	14,581.00	6.4	332-3863	619-456-9197	4.50	None	None	Michael Kagawa	'92
PACIFIC ADV BALANCED	Balanced	0.2	8.47	9,953.00	9,442.00	☆	0.1	282-6693	818-796-6693	5.75	0.25	None	Pacific Global Inv Mgmt	'93
PACIFIC ADV GOVT SECS	Fixed Income	1.9	8.79	9,977.00	9,846.00	☆	1.1	282-6693	818-796-6693	4.75	0.25	None	Spectrum Asset Mgmt.	'93
PACIFIC ADV INCOME	Income	0.5	9.08	10,044.00	10,168.00	☆	1.0	282-6693	818-796-6693	4.75	0.25	None	MMG Money Manangement	'93
PACIFIC ADV SMALL CAP	Small Company Growth	2.7	11.11	9,627.00	11,222.00	☆	0.0	282-6693	818-796-6693	5.75	0.25	None	First Wilshire Securities	'93
PACIFIC CAP GROWTH STOCK	Growth	53.3	9.59	10,089.00	☆	☆	0.0	452-2724	617-722-7868	4.00	None	None	Chris Labelle	'93
PACIFIC CAP SH INT TREAS	Fixed Income	3.3	9.42	9,884.00	☆	☆	0.0	452-2724	617-722-7868	4.00	None	None	Chuck Tovstein	'93
PACIFIC CAP US TREAS SEC	Fixed Income	59.1	8.85	9,740.00	☆	☆	0.0	452-2724	617-722-7868	4.00	None	None	Chuck Tovstein	'93
PACIFICA ASSET PRES	Fixed Income	117.6	10.05	10,054.00	10,262.00	☆	4.2	662-8417	None	None	0.11	None	Mark Romano	'90
PACIFICA BALANCED	Balanced	115.6	11.54	9,890.00	10,410.00	☆	3.7	662-8417	None	4.50	0.34	None	Sanchez/Bowden/Romano	'90/'90
PACIFICA EQUITY VALUE	Growth	161.0	12.00	9,930.00	10,952.00	☆	1.8	662-8417	None	4.50	0.33	None	Sanchez/Bowden	'90/'90
PACIFICA GOVT INCOME	Fixed Income	149.5	9.59	9,727.00	9,637.00	☆	6.9	662-8417	None	4.50	0.50	None	Mark Romano	'90
PAINEWBR ASST ALLOC; A	Flexible	197.0	10.19	9,404.00	9,853.00	☆	1.4	647-1568	None	4.50	0.25	None	Whitney Merrill	'92
PAINEWBR ASST ALLOC; B	Flexible	68.2	10.24	9,389.00	9,774.00	13,480.00	0.6	647-1568	None	None	1.00	5.00	Whitney Merrill	'92
PAINEWBR ASST ALLOC; D	Flexible	12.0	10.17	9,392.00	9,786.00	☆	0.8	647-1568	None	None	1.00	None	Whitney Merrill	'92
PAINEWBR ATLAS GL GR; A	Global	203.9	14.25	9,140.00	10,477.00	12,728.00	0.3	647-1568	None	4.50	0.25	None	Frank Jennings	'92
PAINEWBR ATLAS GL GR; B	Global	153.6	13.98	9,119.00	10,392.00	☆	0.0	647-1568	None	None	1.00	5.00	Frank Jennings	'92
PAINEWBR ATLAS GL GR; D	Global	73.4	14.06	9,118.00	10,394.00	☆	0.1	647-1568	None	None	1.00	None	Frank Jennings	'92
PAINEWBR BL CHIP GR; A	Growth	55.6	14.50	9,804.00	10,061.00	☆	0.0	647-1568	None	4.50	0.25	None	Karen Levy Finkel	'91
PAINEWBR BL CHIP GR; B	Growth	38.9	14.11	9,785.00	9,980.00	13,839.00	0.0	647-1568	None	None	1.00	5.00	Karen Levy Finkel	'86
PAINEWBR BL CHIP GR; D	Growth	3.7	14.27	9,787.00	9,987.00	☆	0.0	647-1568	None	None	1.00	None	Karen Levy Finkel	'92

PERFORMANCE OF MUTUAL FUNDS (continued)

FUND NAME	OBJECTIVE	TOTAL NET ASSETS ($ MIL) 5/31/94	NET ASSET $ VALUE 6/30/94	PERFORMANCE (Return on initial $10,000 Investment) 3/31/94-6/30/94	6/30/93-6/30/94	6/30/89-6/30/94	DIVIDEND YIELD % 6/94	PHONE NUMBER 800	In-State	FEES Load	12b-1	Redemption	MANAGER	SINCE
PAINEWBR CAP APPREC; A ★	Midcap	58.9	10.99	9,433.00	10,233.00	☆	0.0	647-1568	None	4.50	0.25	None	Todger Anderson	'92
PAINEWBR CAP APPREC; B ★	Midcap	133.4	11.32	9,418.00	10,152.00	☆	0.0	647-1568	None	None	1.00	5.00	Todger Anderson	'92
PAINEWBR CAP APPREC; D ★	Midcap	28.6	10.83	9,417.00	10,159.00	☆	0.0	647-1568	None	None	1.00	None	Todger Anderson	'92
PAINEWBR DIVIDEND GR; A	Growth Income	235.4	19.19	9,665.00	9,539.00	13,387.00	1.5	647-1568	None	4.50	0.25	None	Ellen Harris	'94
PAINEWBR DIVIDEND GR; B	Growth Income	303.3	19.12	9,648.00	9,468.00	☆	0.6	647-1568	None	None	1.00	5.00	Ellen Harris	'94
PAINEWBR DIVIDEND GR; D	Growth Income	39.1	19.17	9,648.00	9,467.00	☆	0.6	647-1568	None	None	1.00	None	Ellen Harris	'94
PAINEWBR EUROPE GR; A	European Region	93.7	8.95	9,342.00	11,024.00	☆	0.2	647-1568	None	4.50	0.25	None	Lauren Young	'94
PAINEWBR EUROPE GR; B	European Region	44.4	8.79	9,311.00	10,940.00	☆	0.0	647-1568	None	None	1.00	5.00	Lauren Young	'94
PAINEWBR EUROPE GR; D	European Region	20.2	8.84	9,315.00	10,948.00	☆	0.0	647-1568	None	None	1.00	None	Lauren Young	'94
PAINEWBR GL GR&INC; A	Global Flexible	66.0	10.07	9,324.00	10,501.00	13,822.00	1.6	647-1568	None	4.50	0.25	None	Frank Jennings	'92
PAINEWBR GL GR&INC; B	Global Flexible	34.2	9.95	9,316.00	10,420.00	☆	1.4	647-1568	None	None	1.00	5.00	Frank Jennings	'92
PAINEWBR GL GR&INC; D	Global Flexible	12.3	9.96	9,308.00	10,417.00	☆	1.5	647-1568	None	None	1.00	None	Frank Jennings	'92
PAINEWBR GLOB ENGY; A	Natural Resources	12.6	11.30	10,273.00	9,834.00	☆	0.8	647-1568	None	4.50	0.25	None	William Furth	'91
PAINEWBR GLOB ENGY; B	Natural Resources	19.7	11.32	10,254.00	9,749.00	13,546.00	0.0	647-1568	None	None	1.00	5.00	William Furth	'87
PAINEWBR GLOB ENGY; D	Natural Resources	0.9	11.23	10,256.00	9,759.00	☆	0.0	647-1568	None	None	1.00	None	William Furth	'92
PAINEWBR GLOBAL INC; A	World Income	691.1	10.16	9,772.00	10,036.00	☆	7.0	647-1568	None	4.00	0.25	None	Waugh/Fachler	'91/'91
PAINEWBR GLOBAL INC; B	World Income	908.6	10.12	9,751.00	9,952.00	15,264.00	6.3	647-1568	None	None	1.00	5.00	Waugh/Fachler	'89/'87
PAINEWBR GLOBAL INC; D	World Income	116.9	10.14	9,758.00	9,978.00	☆	6.5	647-1568	None	None	0.75	None	Waugh/Fachler	'92/'92
PAINEWBR GROWTH; A	Growth	138.2	18.55	9,435.00	10,078.00	16,631.00	0.0	647-1568	None	4.50	0.25	None	Ellen Harris	'85
PAINEWBR GROWTH; B	Growth	92.2	18.10	9,417.00	9,998.00	☆	0.0	647-1568	None	None	1.00	5.00	Ellen Harris	'91
PAINEWBR GROWTH; D	Growth	27.3	18.22	9,421.00	9,993.00	☆	0.0	647-1568	None	None	1.00	None	Ellen Harris	'92
PAINEWBR HIGH INCOME; A	Fixed Income	338.5	8.10	9,474.00	10,418.00	18,582.00	11.0	647-1568	None	4.00	0.25	None	Evan Steen	'91
PAINEWBR HIGH INCOME; B	Fixed Income	302.8	8.09	9,446.00	10,343.00	☆	10.2	647-1568	None	None	1.00	5.00	Evan Steen	'91
PAINEWBR HIGH INCOME; D	Fixed Income	174.9	8.11	9,455.00	10,369.00	☆	10.5	647-1568	None	None	0.75	None	Evan Steen	'92
PAINEWBR INVEST GR; A	Fixed Income	312.2	9.93	9,679.00	9,675.00	15,101.00	7.9	647-1568	None	4.00	0.25	None	Mary King	'93
PAINEWBR INVEST GR; B	Fixed Income	77.9	9.93	9,661.00	9,613.00	☆	7.1	647-1568	None	None	1.00	5.00	Mary King	'91
PAINEWBR INVEST GR; D	Fixed Income	59.4	9.93	9,674.00	9,631.00	☆	7.4	647-1568	None	None	0.75	None	Mary King	'92
PAINEWBR REG FINL GR; A	Financial Services	51.4	18.18	10,745.00	10,793.00	24,195.00	0.0	647-1568	None	4.50	0.25	None	Karen Levy Finkel	'86
PAINEWBR REG FINL GR; B	Financial Services	12.4	17.91	10,718.00	10,712.00	☆	0.0	647-1568	None	None	1.00	5.00	Karen Levy Finkel	'91
PAINEWBR REG FINL GR; D	Financial Services	5.1	18.18	10,880.00	10,874.00	☆	0.0	647-1568	None	None	1.00	None	Karen Levy Finkel	'92
PAINEWBR S/T GOVT; A	Fixed Income	307.8	2.25	9,265.00	9,470.00	☆	5.5	647-1568	None	3.00	0.25	None	Ed Rosenzweig	'93
PAINEWBR S/T GOVT; B	Fixed Income	28.3	2.25	9,248.00	9,399.00	☆	4.7	647-1568	None	None	1.00	3.00	Ed Rosenzweig	'93
PAINEWBR S/T GOVT; D	Fixed Income	701.6	2.25	9,254.00	9,423.00	☆	5.0	647-1568	None	None	0.75	None	Ed Rosenzweig	'93
PAINEWBR SEC SM CAP; A	Small Company Growth	23.4	10.16	9,779.00	10,080.00	☆	1.4	647-1568	None	4.50	0.25	None	Charles M. Royce	'93
PAINEWBR SEC SM CAP; B	Small Company Growth	54.3	10.12	9,759.00	10,018.00	☆	0.8	647-1568	None	None	1.00	5.00	Charles M. Royce	'93
PAINEWBR SEC SM CAP; D	Small Company Growth	18.8	10.11	9,759.00	10,013.00	☆	0.8	647-1568	None	None	1.00	None	Charles M. Royce	'93
PAINEWBR US GOVT; A	Fixed Income	539.3	8.91	9,530.00	9,377.00	13,745.00	7.0	647-1568	None	4.00	0.25	None	Ed Rosenzweig	'93
PAINEWBR US GOVT; B	Fixed Income	129.2	8.91	9,502.00	9,307.00	☆	6.1	647-1568	None	None	1.00	5.00	Ed Rosenzweig	'93
PAINEWBR US GOVT; D	Fixed Income	99.4	8.91	9,519.00	9,342.00	☆	6.4	647-1568	None	None	0.75	None	Ed Rosenzweig	'93
PAINEWBR UTILITY INC; A	Utility	14.5	8.41	9,608.00	☆	☆	0.0	647-1568	None	4.50	0.25	None	William Furth	'93
PAINEWBR UTILITY INC; B	Utility	42.3	8.41	9,589.00	☆	☆	0.0	647-1568	None	None	1.00	5.00	William Furth	'93
PAINEWBR UTILITY INC; D	Utility	16.6	8.40	9,578.00	☆	☆	0.0	647-1568	None	None	1.00	None	William Furth	'93
PANAGORA ASSET ALLOC	Flexible	2.9	9.84	10,018.00	10,061.00	☆	1.1	423-6041	617-439-6300	None	None	None	Kathy Lino	'93
PANAGORA GLOBAL	Global Flexible	42.0	10.44	10,126.00	10,923.00	☆	3.7	423-6041	617-439-6300	None	None	None	James Rullo	'93
PANAGORA INTL EQUITY	International	15.0	10.73	10,066.00	11,044.00	☆	2.3	423-6041	617-439-6300	None	None	None	James Rullo	'93

PAPP AMERICA-ABROAD	Growth	10.2	10.95	9,928.00	10,561.00	☆	0.9	421-4004	602-956-0980	None	None	None	L. Roy Papp	'91
L ROY PAPP STOCK FUND	Growth	38.1	14.11	9,678.00	9,897.00	☆	1.0	421-4004	602-956-0980	None	None	None	L. Roy Papp	'89
PARAGON GULF SOUTH GRO	Small Company Growth	81.0	15.35	9,546.00	10,367.00	☆	0.0	None	504-332-5968	4.50	None	None	Don Allred	'91
PARAGON INTMDT-TERM BOND	Fixed Income	316.7	9.86	9,827.00	9,729.00	☆	6.7	None	504-332-5968	4.50	None	None	Keith Mooney	'89
PARAGON SHORT-TERM GOVT	Fixed Income	162.1	9.99	9,987.00	10,067.00	☆	5.0	None	504-332-5968	4.50	None	None	Keith Mooney	'89
PARAGON VALUE EQUITY INC	Equity Income	103.5	11.69	10,014.00	10,248.00	☆	2.6	None	504-332-5968	4.50	None	None	Richard Chauvin, Jr.	'89
PARAGON VALUE GROWTH	Growth Income	177.4	14.03	9,652.00	9,989.00	☆	1.4	None	504-332-5968	4.50	None	None	Don Allred	'89
PARIBAS INSTL QUANT EQ	Growth	3.1	7.71	9,897.00	9,639.00	16,257.00	0.0	233-1137	212-841-3200	None	1.00	4.00	Paribas Asset Mgmt	'86
PARIBAS INSTL QUANTUS "	Flexible	77.8	10.32	9,636.00	9,601.00	14,830.00	0.6	233-1137	212-841-3200	None	None	None	Paribas Asset Mgmt	'86
PARKSTONE BALANCED; A ☛	Balanced	12.1	10.67	9,602.00	9,837.00	☆	2.4	451-8377	None	4.50	0.10	None	First of Amer Invt Corp	'93
PARKSTONE BALANCED; INSTL	Balanced	53.8	10.67	9,604.00	9,856.00	☆	2.5	451-8377	None	None	None	None	First of Amer Invt Corp	'92
PARKSTONE BOND; A ☛	Fixed Income	18.4	9.30	9,872.00	9,838.00	☆	6.0	451-8377	None	4.00	0.10	None	First of Amer Invt Corp	'93
PARKSTONE BOND; INSTL	Fixed Income	475.7	9.29	9,882.00	9,844.00	14,528.00	6.1	451-8377	None	None	None	None	First of Amer Invt Corp	'88
PARKSTONE EQUITY; A ☛	Growth	37.7	14.69	9,262.00	9,743.00	☆	0.0	451-8377	None	4.50	0.10	None	First of Amer Invt Corp	'93
PARKSTONE EQUITY; INSTL	Growth	579.9	14.70	9,263.00	9,756.00	16,209.00	0.0	451-8377	None	None	None	None	First of Amer Invt Corp	'88
PARKSTONE GOVT INC; A ☛	Fixed Income	53.8	9.41	9,973.00	10,094.00	☆	7.8	451-8377	None	4.00	0.10	None	First of Amer Invt Corp	'93
PARKSTONE GOVT INC; INSTL	Fixed Income	100.8	9.41	9,971.00	10,104.00	☆	7.9	451-8377	None	None	None	None	First of Amer Invt Corp	'92
PARKSTONE HI INC; A ☛	Equity Income	78.7	13.50	9,637.00	9,837.00	☆	2.7	451-8377	None	4.50	0.10	None	First of Amer Invt Corp	'93
PARKSTONE HI INC; INSTL	Equity Income	373.3	13.50	9,639.00	9,847.00	15,941.00	2.8	451-8377	None	None	None	None	First of Amer Invt Corp	'88
PARKSTONE INT GOVT; A	Fixed Income	36.7	9.62	9,917.00	9,910.00	☆	6.0	451-8377	None	4.00	0.10	None	First of Amer Invt Corp	'93
PARKSTONE INT GOVT; INSTL	Fixed Income	279.3	9.62	9,925.00	9,920.00	14,166.00	6.1	451-8377	None	None	None	None	First of Amer Invt Corp	'88
PARKSTONE INTL DSC; A ☛	International	35.5	13.18	9,895.00	11,499.00	☆	0.1	451-8377	None	4.50	0.10	None	Ivory & Sime	'93
PARKSTONE INTL DSC; INSTL	International	257.2	13.24	9,888.00	11,512.00	☆	0.1	451-8377	None	None	None	None	Ivory & Sime	'92
PARKSTONE LTD MAT; A ☛	Fixed Income	25.4	9.57	9,964.00	10,032.00	☆	6.4	451-8377	None	3.00	0.10	None	First of Amer Invt Corp	'93
PARKSTONE LTD MAT; INSTL	Fixed Income	155.9	9.57	9,962.00	10,043.00	13,926.00	6.5	451-8377	None	None	None	None	First of Amer Invt Corp	'88
PARKSTONE SM CAP; A ☛	Small Company Growth	44.7	19.75	9,085.00	9,945.00	☆	0.0	451-8377	None	4.50	0.10	None	First of Amer Invt Corp	'93
PARKSTONE SM CAP; INSTL	Small Company Growth	286.0	19.83	9,084.00	9,985.00	19,663.00	0.0	451-8377	None	None	None	None	First of Amer Invt Corp	'88
PARNASSUS FUND	Growth	118.4	31.02	9,409.00	10,822.00	17,587.00	0.8	999-3505	415-362-3505	3.50	None	None	Jerome L. Dodson	'85
PARNASSUS BALANCED	Balanced	16.2	15.43	9,607.00	9,267.00	☆	7.4	999-3505	415-362-3505	None	None	None	Jerome L. Dodson	'92
PARNASSUS FXD INC	Fixed Income	4.7	14.27	9,557.00	9,528.00	☆	6.8	999-3505	415-362-3505	None	None	None	Jerome L. Dodson	'92
PASADENA BALANCED; A	Balanced	67.7	20.36	9,869.00	9,689.00	15,406.00	1.6	648-8050	818-351-9686	5.50	None	None	Roger Engemann	'87
PASADENA GROWTH; A	Growth	442.5	14.62	9,721.00	9,626.00	15,431.00	0.0	648-8050	818-351-9686	5.50	None	None	Roger Engemann	'86
PASADENA NIFTY FIFTY; A	Growth	109.7	16.16	9,926.00	9,872.00	☆	0.0	648-8050	818-351-9686	5.50	None	None	Roger Engemann	'90
PAUZE/SWANSON GOV TOTAL	Fixed Income	10.9	9.25	9,842.00	☆	☆	0.0	873-8637	210-308-1234	None	0.25	None	Philip Pauze	'94
PAX WORLD FUND	Balanced	398.3	13.13	10,061.00	9,662.00	14,293.00	3.8	767-1729	603-431-8022	None	0.12	None	Anthony S. Brown	'71
PBHG EMERGING GROWTH	Small Company Growth	47.7	11.21	9,166.00	12,008.00	☆	0.0	932-7781	215-989-6611	None	None	None	Pilgrim/Baxter	'93/'9
PBHG GROWTH FUND	Capital Appreciation	414.7	12.82	8,739.00	10,444.00	24,395.00	0.0	809-8008	None	None	None	None	Gary Pilgrim	'85
PDC&J PERFORMANCE	Capital Appreciation	19.1	17.15	9,767.00	10,213.00	16,491.00	0.5	None	513-223-0600	None	None	None	Johnson/Carlson	'84/'8
PDC&J PRESERVATION	Fixed Income	15.4	10.96	9,901.00	9,879.00	14,278.00	6.1	None	513-223-0600	None	None	None	Johnson/Carlson	'85/'8
PEACHTREE BOND	Fixed Income	76.4	9.42	9,883.00	☆	☆	0.0	282-6680	None	2.50	None	None	Mark Johnston	'94
PEACHTREE EQUITY	Growth Income	80.4	9.39	9,884.00	☆	☆	0.0	282-6680	None	3.75	None	None	Shelton Prince	'94
PELICAN FUND	Growth	96.3	11.49	9,965.00	10,165.00	☆	2.9	447-3167	617-330-7512	None	None	None	Richard Mayo	'89
PENN SQUARE MUTUAL	Growth Income	240.7	10.45	10,001.00	10,465.00	16,083.00	1.7	523-8440	610-670-1031	4.75	0.12	None	James E. Jordan, Jr	'86
PENNSYLVANIA MUTUAL ⊠	Small Company Growth	888.3	8.04	9,781.00	10,350.00	15,027.00	1.3	221-4268	212-355-7311	None	None	1.00	Charles M. Royce	'7
PEOPLES INDEX FUND	S&P Index	286.2	15.35	10,026.00	10,090.00	☆	2.0	373-9387	516-338-3300	None	None	1.00	Wells Fargo Nikko Adv.	'90
PEOPLES S&P MIDCAP	Midcap	72.3	15.91	9,625.00	9,954.00	☆	1.7	373-9387	516-338-3300	None	None	1.00	Woodbridge Cap Mgt Inc	'9
PERFORM EQUITY; CNSMR	Growth	5.3	11.06	9,894.00	9,874.00	☆	1.8	524-2276	None	4.70	0.10	None	C. Windham	'92
PERFORM EQUITY; INSTL	Growth	93.9	11.06	9,900.00	9,898.00	☆	2.1	524-2276	None	None	None	None	C. Windham	'92
PERFORM INT GVT; CNSMR	Fixed Income	3.4	9.79	9,849.00	9,753.00	☆	5.5	524-2276	None	2.00	0.10	None	P. Farnsley	'92
PERFORM INT GVT; INSTL	Fixed Income	158.4	9.79	9,855.00	9,777.00	☆	5.8	524-2276	None	None	None	None	P. Farnsley	'92

★ PAINEWBR CAP APPREC; A, B & D--Fund has been reclassified from Small Company Growth to Midcap.

PERFORMANCE OF MUTUAL FUNDS (continued)

FUND NAME	OBJECTIVE	TOTAL NET ASSETS ($ MIL) 5/31/94	NET ASSET $ VALUE 6/30/94	PERFORMANCE (Return on initial $10,000 Investment) 3/31/94-6/30/94	6/30/93-6/30/94	6/30/89-6/30/94	DIVIDEND YIELD % 6/94	PHONE NUMBER 800	In-State	FEES Load	12b-1	Redemption	MANAGER	SINCE
PERFORM SHT GVT; CNSMR	Fixed Income	0.6	9.76	9,986.00	10,084.00	☆	3.8	524-2276	None	2.00	0.10	None	Robert H. Spaulding	'92
PERFORM SHT GVT; INSTL	Fixed Income	111.7	9.76	9,992.00	10,109.00	☆	4.1	524-2276	None	None	None	None	Robert H. Spaulding	'92
PERKINS OPPORTUNITY FUND	Capital Appreciation	3.4	17.89	9,019.00	11,368.00	☆	0.0	424-2295	612-473-8367	4.75	0.25	None	Richard W. Perkins	'93
PERMANENT PORT AGGR GR	Capital Appreciation	6.6	28.89	9,547.00	10,120.00	☆	0.1	531-5142	707-778-1000	None	None	None	Terry Coxon	'90
PERMANENT PORT PERMANENT	Global Flexible	77.3	16.58	9,713.00	10,025.00	12,263.00	1.5	531-5142	707-778-1000	None	None	None	Terry Coxon	'82
PERMANENT PORT TREASURY	Fixed Income	126.6	65.52	10,075.00	10,250.00	12,499.00	1.7	531-5142	707-778-1000	None	0.25	None	Terry Coxon	'87
PERMANENT PORT VERSATILE	Fixed Income	28.7	54.75	10,018.00	10,218.00	☆	1.3	531-5142	707-778-1000	None	None	None	Terry Coxon	'91
PERRITT CAPITAL GROWTH	Small Company Growth	6.7	11.44	9,293.00	9,883.00	12,101.00	0.0	326-6941	312-649-6940	None	None	None	Gerald W. Perritt	'88
PFAMCO BALANCED	Flexible	133.2	10.09	9,967.00	9,885.00	☆	3.3	800-7674	714-640-3462	None	None	None	PIMCO/Parametric/PFAMCO	'92/'92
PFAMCO CAPITAL APPREC	Capital Appreciation	131.3	12.78	9,748.00	10,053.00	☆	0.9	800-7674	714-640-3462	None	None	None	Cadence Cap Mgmt Corp.	'91
PFAMCO DVSFD LOW P/E	Growth Income	18.1	11.05	9,652.00	10,248.00	☆	2.0	800-7674	714-640-3462	None	None	None	NFJ Investment Grp Inc	'91
PFAMCO EMERGING MKTS	Emerging Markets	36.3	13.96	9,674.00	14,242.00	☆	0.2	800-7674	714-640-3462	None	None	None	Blairlogie Capital Mgmt	'93
PFAMCO ENHANCED EQUITY	Growth Income	60.5	11.39	10,006.00	9,855.00	☆	2.0	800-7674	714-640-3462	None	None	None	Parametric Port. Assoc	'91
PFAMCO EQUITY INCOME	Equity Income	82.3	11.22	9,998.00	9,974.00	☆	3.4	800-7674	714-640-3462	None	None	None	NFJ Investment Grp Inc	'91
PFAMCO INTL ACTIVE	International	15.8	11.54	10,539.00	12,044.00	☆	0.4	800-7674	714-640-3462	None	None	None	Blairlogie Capital Mgmt	'93
PFAMCO INTL EQUITY	International	62.5	9.46	10,184.00	11,205.00	☆	0.7	800-7674	714-640-3462	None	None	None	Parametric Port. Assoc	'90
PFAMCO MGD BOND & INCOME	Fixed Income	355.1	9.51	9,890.00	9,875.00	☆	5.9	800-7674	714-640-3462	None	None	None	Pacific Investment Mgt Co	'91
PFAMCO MICRO CAP GRO	Small Company Growth	23.7	10.95	9,522.00	10,976.00	☆	0.1	800-7674	714-640-3462	None	None	None	Cadence Cap Mgmt Corp.	'93
PFAMCO MID CAP GROWTH	Midcap	109.4	13.09	9,527.00	9,903.00	☆	0.5	800-7674	714-640-3462	None	None	None	Cadence Cap Mgmt Corp.	'91
PFAMCO SMALL CAP GRO ☒	Small Company Growth	45.0	17.73	9,652.00	10,275.00	☆	0.0	800-7674	714-640-3462	None	None	None	Cadence Cap Mgmt Corp.	'91
PFAMCO SMALL CAP VALUE	Small Company Growth	33.5	12.08	9,620.00	10,242.00	☆	2.1	800-7674	714-640-3462	None	None	None	NFJ Investment Grp Inc	'91
PFAMCO UTILITY STK; INST	Utility	23.2	8.58	9,650.00	☆	☆	0.0	800-7674	714-640-3462	None	None	None	Pacific Fin'l Asset Mgmt	'94
PHILADELPHIA FUND	Growth Income	83.6	6.32	9,859.00	9,970.00	12,346.00	2.0	749-9933	407-395-2155	None	0.50	None	Donald Baxter	'87
PHILLIPS CAPITAL INV	Growth	5.7	13.77	10,022.00	10,338.00	15,146.00	1.4	None	214-458-2448	None	None	1.00	Guy F. Phillips Jr.	'89
PHOENIX ASSET RSV; A	Fixed Income	9.2	4.66	9,952.00	10,179.00	☆	6.2	243-4361	203-253-1000	2.25	0.25	None	David Albrycht	'93
PHOENIX ASSET RSV; B	Fixed Income	5.9	4.66	9,940.00	10,132.00	☆	5.8	243-4361	203-253-1000	None	0.75	2.00	David Albrycht	'93
PHOENIX BALANCED FD	Balanced	2,827.8	15.02	9,869.00	9,798.00	16,225.00	3.2	243-4361	203-253-1000	4.75	0.25	None	Patricia Bannan	'86
PHOENIX CAPITAL APPREC	Growth	431.5	17.32	9,786.00	10,167.00	☆	0.6	243-4361	203-253-1000	4.75	0.25	None	Cathy Dudley	'89
PHOENIX CONVERTIBLE FD	Convertible Securities	236.5	17.47	10,000.00	10,184.00	15,670.00	3.9	243-4361	203-253-1000	4.75	0.25	None	John Hamlin	'92
PHOENIX ENDOWMENT EQTY ◪★	Growth	5.9	9.69	9,531.00	10,013.00	☆	1.4	243-4361	203-253-1000	None	None	None	Tom Melvin	'93
PHOENIX ENDOWMENT FXD ◪	Fixed Income	1.8	9.28	9,860.00	9,805.00	☆	6.5	243-4361	203-253-1000	None	None	None	David Albrycht	'93
PHOENIX EQUITY OPP	Growth Income	185.8	7.15	9,801.00	9,669.00	15,220.00	0.8	243-4361	203-253-1000	4.75	0.25	None	Robert Milnamow	'93
PHOENIX GROWTH FD	Growth	2,215.5	20.09	9,897.00	10,002.00	16,171.00	1.2	243-4361	203-253-1000	4.75	0.25	None	Cathy Dudley	'90
PHOENIX HIGH YIELD FD	Fixed Income	577.0	8.35	9,720.00	10,303.00	15,830.00	9.2	243-4361	203-253-1000	4.75	0.25	None	Curtis Barrows	'85
PHOENIX INC & GRO; A	Balanced	531.3	9.25	9,978.00	10,066.00	15,902.00	4.6	243-4361	203-253-1000	4.75	0.25	None	John Hamlin	'93
PHOENIX INC & GRO; B	Balanced	389.2	9.25	9,957.00	9,997.00	☆	3.9	243-4361	203-253-1000	None	1.00	5.00	John Hamlin	'93
PHOENIX INTERNATIONAL	International	158.8	12.50	10,040.00	12,601.00	☆	0.0	243-4361	203-253-1000	4.75	0.25	None	Jeanne Dorey	'93
PHOENIX MULTI-SECT; A	Fixed Income	191.2	12.22	9,800.00	9,805.00	☆	8.1	243-4361	203-253-1000	4.75	0.25	None	Michael Haylon	'93
PHOENIX MULTI-SECT; B	Fixed Income	168.8	12.20	9,780.00	9,746.00	☆	7.4	243-4361	203-253-1000	None	1.00	5.00	Michael Haylon	'93
PHOENIX STOCK FD	Capital Appreciation	143.4	13.00	9,916.00	10,224.00	15,536.00	1.6	243-4361	203-253-1000	4.75	0.25	None	Michael Matty	'90
PHOENIX TOTAL RETURN	Flexible	349.1	14.99	9,927.00	10,186.00	17,166.00	0.3	243-4361	203-253-1000	4.75	0.25	None	Robert Milnamow	'89
PHOENIX US GOVT SEC FD	Fixed Income	288.2	9.05	9,867.00	9,750.00	14,399.00	6.8	243-4361	203-253-1000	4.75	0.25	None	Christopher J. Kelleher	'90
PHOENIX WORLDWIDE OPP	Global	120.2	10.17	9,779.00	12,746.00	14,493.00	0.3	243-4361	203-253-1000	4.75	0.25	None	Jeanne Dorey	'93
PIC ENDEAVOR GROWTH	Growth	73.3	10.51	9,687.00	9,669.00	☆	0.1	576-8229	818-449-8500	None	None	None	Provident Invt Counsel	'92
PIC INSTL BALANCED	Balanced	9.2	10.43	9,720.00	9,501.00	☆	1.8	576-8229	818-449-8500	None	None	None	Provident Invt Counsel	'92

PIC INSTL GROWTH	Growth	80.5	10.59	9,680.00	9,636.00	☆	0.0	576-8229	818-449-8500	None	None	None	Provident Invt Counsel	'92
PIERPONT BOND FUND	Fixed Income	95.5	9.80	9,887.00	9,905.00	14,655.00	5.1	521-5411	212-826-1303	None	None	None	Rip Reeves	'93
PIERPONT CAP APPREC	Small Company Growth	204.4	20.62	9,330.00	9,706.00	15,705.00	0.4	521-5411	212-826-1303	None	None	None	Chip Otness	'93
PIERPONT EQUITY	Growth Income	231.5	18.80	10,011.00	10,513.00	18,383.00	1.0	521-5411	212-826-1303	None	None	None	William Peterson	'93
PIERPONT INTL EQUITY	International	196.5	11.40	10,468.00	11,447.00	☆	1.1	521-5411	212-826-1303	None	None	None	Paul Quinsee	'93
PILGRIM CORP UTILITIES ★	Utility	5.9	6.79	9,682.00	8,092.00	6,866.00	5.9	334-3444	310-551-0833	3.00	0.25	None	Howard N. Kornblue	'91
PILGRIM GL SH MU-MK ★	World Income	20.6	6.77	10,148.00	10,389.00	6,396.00	6.1	334-3444	310-551-0833	3.00	0.30	None	S.G. Warburg & Co.	'92
PILGRIM GL SH MU-MK II	World Income	5.9	7.46	10,022.00	9,934.00	☆	6.0	334-3444	310-551-0833	None	0.75	4.00	S.G. Warburg & Co.	'92
PILGRIM GNMA	Fixed Income	62.8	12.73	9,900.00	9,750.00	13,581.00	7.1	334-3444	310-551-0833	3.00	0.25	None	Rob Womack	'93
PILGRIM INSTL ALL-AM; B	World Income	15.5	6.56	9,941.00	☆	☆	0.0	334-3444	310-551-0833	None	1.00	4.00	Team Managed	'93
PILGRIM INSTL ALL-AM; C	World Income	5.0	6.55	9,926.00	☆	☆	0.0	334-3444	310-551-0833	None	1.00	1.50	Team Managed	'93
PILGRIM MAGNACAP	Growth Income	195.3	12.36	10,266.00	10,913.00	15,832.00	1.2	334-3444	310-551-0833	5.00	0.30	None	Howard N. Kornblue	'89
PILGRIM ADJ GOVT I ⊠	Fixed Income	454.3	6.77	9,831.00	9,835.00	☆	5.4	334-3444	310-551-0833	None	1.00	4.00	Brian Carrico	'91
PILGRIM ADJ GOVT I-A	Fixed Income	284.6	6.81	9,847.00	9,849.00	☆	5.2	334-3444	310-551-0833	None	1.00	4.00	Brian Carrico	'92
PILGRIM ADJ GOVT II	Fixed Income	22.8	6.90	9,865.00	9,925.00	☆	5.2	334-3444	310-551-0833	3.00	0.25	None	Brian Carrico	'91
PILGRIM ADJ GOVT III	Fixed Income	9.3	6.90	9,881.00	9,956.00	☆	5.4	334-3444	310-551-0833	5.00	None	None	Brian Carrico	'91
PILGRIM ADJ GOVT IV	Fixed Income	36.7	6.97	9,853.00	9,928.00	☆	5.1	334-3444	310-551-0833	None	0.60	0.25	Brian Carrico	'93
PILGRIM ADJ RT I ⊠	Fixed Income	78.4	6.94	9,900.00	10,219.00	☆	6.3	334-3444	310-551-0833	None	1.00	4.00	Brian Carrico	'91
PILGRIM ADJ RT I-A	Fixed Income	209.7	6.97	9,901.00	10,230.00	☆	6.3	334-3444	310-551-0833	None	1.00	4.00	Brian Carrico	'92
PILGRIM ADJ RT II	Fixed Income	40.4	7.09	9,917.00	10,294.00	☆	6.0	334-3444	310-551-0833	3.00	0.25	None	Brian Carrico	'91
PILGRIM ADJ RT III	Fixed Income	27.9	7.05	9,919.00	10,302.00	☆	6.2	334-3444	310-551-0833	5.00	None	None	Brian Carrico	'91
PILGRIM ADJ RT IV	Fixed Income	176.9	7.17	9,921.00	10,307.00	☆	5.8	334-3444	310-551-0833	None	0.60	0.25	Brian Carrico	'93
PILGRIM HIGH YIELD	Fixed Income	16.7	6.15	10,003.00	10,431.00	15,629.00	8.7	334-3444	310-551-0833	3.00	0.25	None	Randolph Birkman	'93
PILLAR BALANCED GRO; A ▮lll	Flexible	27.3	10.08	9,870.00	9,809.00	☆	3.6	932-7782	None	None	None	None	Fernando Garip	'92
PILLAR BALANCED GRO; B	Flexible	8.1	10.09	9,863.00	9,785.00	☆	3.4	932-7782	None	4.00	0.25	None	Fernando Garip	'92
PILLAR EQUITY AGGR GRO; A ▮lll	Small Company Growth	36.2	11.40	9,486.00	10,436.00	☆	1.0	932-7782	None	None	None	None	John Gustafson	'92
PILLAR EQUITY AGGR GRO; B	Small Company Growth	4.0	11.39	9,481.00	10,415.00	☆	0.8	932-7782	None	4.00	0.25	None	John Gustafson	'92
PILLAR EQUITY GRO; A ▮lll	Growth	67.9	10.27	9,839.00	9,978.00	☆	1.9	932-7782	None	None	None	None	Pete Fusco	'93
PILLAR EQUITY GRO; B	Growth	3.1	10.29	9,834.00	9,955.00	☆	1.6	932-7782	None	4.00	0.25	None	Pete Fusco	'93
PILLAR EQUITY INC; A ▮lll	Income	37.8	10.59	10,117.00	9,952.00	☆	2.8	932-7782	None	None	None	None	Richard Bodenstein	'92
PILLAR EQUITY INC; B	Income	5.6	10.60	10,110.00	9,930.00	☆	2.5	932-7782	None	4.00	0.25	None	Richard Bodenstein	'92
PILLAR FIXED INC; A ▮lll	Fixed Income	104.6	9.77	9,818.00	9,638.00	☆	6.0	932-7782	None	None	None	None	Bob Lowe	'92
PILLAR FIXED INC; B	Fixed Income	6.6	9.76	9,802.00	9,609.00	☆	5.7	932-7782	None	4.00	0.25	None	Bob Lowe	'92
PILLAR INT-TERM GOVT; A ▮lll	Fixed Income	32.6	9.78	9,828.00	9,694.00	☆	5.1	932-7782	None	None	None	None	Frances Tendall	'92
PILLAR INT-TERM GOVT; B	Fixed Income	3.0	9.78	9,822.00	9,670.00	☆	4.8	932-7782	None	4.00	0.25	None	Frances Tendall	'92
PILLAR SHORT-TERM; A ▮lll	Fixed Income	29.2	9.95	10,063.00	10,241.00	☆	3.0	932-7782	None	None	None	None	Bob Lowe	'92
PILLAR SHORT-TERM; B	Fixed Income	0.5	9.97	10,057.00	10,225.00	☆	2.7	932-7782	None	1.00	0.25	None	Bob Lowe	'92
PIMCO FOREIGN ✪	World Income	461.4	9.61	9,581.00	9,998.00	☆	5.6	927-4648	714-760-4880	None	None	None	John Hague	'92
PIMCO GLOBAL FUND ✪	World Income	54.4	9.76	10,023.00	☆	☆	0.0	927-4648	714-760-4880	None	None	None	John Hague	'93
PIMCO GROWTH STOCK ✪	Capital Appreciation	23.1	13.47	10,014.00	10,165.00	16,622.00	1.4	927-4648	714-760-4880	None	None	None	Ben Ehlert	'87
PIMCO HIGH YIELD ✪	Fixed Income	224.3	10.30	9,999.00	10,580.00	☆	8.6	927-4648	714-760-4880	None	None	None	Ben Trosky	'92
PIMCO LONG-TERM US GOVT ✪	Fixed Income	28.2	9.58	9,743.00	9,557.00	☆	5.6	927-4648	714-760-4880	None	None	None	Frank Rabinovitch	'91
PIMCO LOW DURATION ✪	Fixed Income	2,225.9	9.87	9,977.00	10,269.00	14,896.00	6.1	927-4648	714-760-4880	None	None	None	William Gross	'87
PIMCO LOW DURATION II ✪	Fixed Income	151.1	9.75	9,959.00	10,108.00	☆	5.8	927-4648	714-760-4880	None	None	None	William Gross	'91
PIMCO SHORT-TERM ✪	Fixed Income	107.3	9.88	10,077.00	10,321.00	13,216.00	4.6	927-4648	714-760-4880	None	None	None	Dave Edington	'87
PIMCO STOCK PLUS ✪	Growth Income	15.6	9.50	10,096.00	10,196.00	☆	4.1	927-4648	714-760-4880	None	None	None	Dave Edington	'93
PIMCO TOTAL RETURN ✪	Fixed Income	5,304.6	9.91	9,819.00	9,938.00	15,905.00	6.0	927-4648	714-760-4880	None	None	None	William Gross	'87
PIMCO TOTAL RETURN III ✪	Fixed Income	93.3	8.89	9,829.00	10,057.00	☆	6.3	927-4648	714-760-4880	None	None	None	William Gross	'91
PINNACLE FUND	Growth	14.6	19.89	9,576.00	9,716.00	15,048.00	0.5	None	317-633-4080	None	None	None	Heartland Cap. Mgmt	'85
PIONEER AMERICA	Fixed Income	78.9	10.39	9,811.00	9,704.00	14,331.00	5.9	225-6292	617-742-7825	4.50	0.25	None	Sherman Russ	'93

★ PHOENIX ENDOWMENT EQTY--Fund has been reclassified from Capital Appreciation to Growth.
★ PILGRIM CORP UTILITIES--On 6/4/93, the fund's NAV was reduced by $0.73 as a result of the RTC takeover of one of its holdings, Western Federal S&L Assoc.
★ PILGRIM GL SH MU-MK--On 6/4/93, the fund's NAV was reduced by $0.73 as a result of the RTC takeover of one of its holdings, Western Federal S&L Assoc.

PERFORMANCE OF MUTUAL FUNDS *(continued)*

FUND NAME	OBJECTIVE	TOTAL NET ASSETS ($ MIL) 5/31/94	NET ASSET $ VALUE 6/30/94	PERFORMANCE (Return on initial $10,000 Investment) 3/31/94-6/30/94	6/30/93-6/30/94	6/30/89-6/30/94	DIVIDEND YIELD % 6/94	PHONE NUMBER 800	In-State	FEES Load	12b-1	Redemption	MANAGER	SINCE
PIONEER BOND FUND	Fixed Income	107.0	9.04	9,834.00	9,874.00	14,688.00	7.4	225-6292	617-742-7825	4.50	0.25	None	Sherman Russ	'87
PIONEER CAPITAL GROWTH	Growth	274.2	15.41	10,085.00	11,388.00	☆	0.0	225-6292	617-742-7825	5.75	0.25	None	Warren Isabelle	'90
PIONEER EQUITY-INCOME	Equity Income	163.7	15.85	10,221.00	10,240.00	☆	3.3	225-6292	617-742-7825	5.75	0.25	None	John Carey	'90
PIONEER EUROPE	European Region	56.4	18.07	9,962.00	11,774.00	☆	1.7	225-6292	617-742-7825	5.75	0.25	None	Patrick Smith	'93
PIONEER FUND	Growth Income	2,041.6	22.44	10,025.00	10,402.00	15,079.00	2.1	225-6292	617-742-7825	5.75	0.25	None	John Carey	'86
PIONEER GOLD SHARES	Gold	23.8	7.40	9,170.00	9,920.00	☆	0.0	225-6292	617-742-7825	5.75	0.25	None	David Tripple	'90
PIONEER GROWTH SHARES ★	Growth	121.9	10.28	8,720.00	8,743.00	15,207.00	0.0	225-6292	617-742-7825	5.75	0.25	None	Warren Isabelle	'93
PIONEER II	Growth Income	4,390.7	18.31	10,119.00	10,528.00	14,601.00	1.7	225-6292	617-742-7825	5.75	0.25	None	Tripple/Boggan/Kurland	'80/'91
PIONEER INCOME	Income	279.7	9.44	9,844.00	9,880.00	14,779.00	6.7	225-6292	617-742-7825	4.50	0.25	None	Carey/Russ	'93/'93
PIONEER INTL GROWTH	International	221.7	21.00	9,818.00	13,305.00	☆	0.1	225-6292	617-742-7825	5.75	0.25	None	Norman Kurland	'93
PIONEER SH-TM INC TR	Fixed Income	71.2	3.84	9,974.00	10,192.00	☆	5.6	225-6292	617-742-7825	2.50	0.25	None	Richard Schlanger	'92
PIONEER THREE	Growth Income	1,005.6	18.94	9,494.00	10,202.00	16,030.00	1.3	225-6292	617-742-7825	5.75	0.25	None	Robert W. Benson	'86
PIONEER US GOVT TRUST	Fixed Income	102.4	9.71	9,881.00	9,786.00	14,245.00	6.8	225-6292	617-742-7825	4.50	0.25	None	Sherman Russ	'94
PIONEER WNTHRP REAL EST	Real Estate	27.2	12.02	9,883.00	☆	☆	0.0	225-6292	617-742-7825	5.75	0.25	None	Robert W. Benson	'93
PIPER GLBL PAC-EURO GRO	International	165.8	15.02	10,330.00	12,698.00	☆	0.0	866-7778	612-342-6402	4.00	0.32	None	Team Managed	'90
PIPER INSTL ENHANCED 500	Growth Income	19.0	9.82	9,898.00	9,962.00	☆	2.3	866-7778	612-342-6402	None	None	None	Tony Elavia	'93
PIPER INSTL GOVT ADJ	Fixed Income	37.1	9.46	9,770.00	9,906.00	☆	5.3	866-7778	612-342-6402	1.00	None	None	Griffin/McGlinch/Rinkey	'93/'93
PIPER JAFFRAY BALANCED	Balanced	49.7	11.66	9,999.00	9,961.00	15,088.00	3.0	866-7778	612-342-6402	4.00	0.32	None	Rinkey/Elavia/Dow	'87/'89
PIPER JAFFRAY EMERG GR	Midcap	214.9	17.78	9,184.00	9,950.00	☆	0.0	866-7778	612-342-6402	4.00	0.32	None	Multiple Managers	'94
PIPER JAFFRAY GOVT INC	Fixed Income	136.4	8.60	9,638.00	9,343.00	14,114.00	8.1	866-7778	612-342-6402	4.00	0.32	None	Rinkey/Griffin/Stone	'87/'87
PIPER JAFFRAY GRO & INC	Growth Income	80.2	9.95	10,018.00	10,121.00	☆	2.4	866-7778	612-342-6402	4.00	0.32	None	Dow/Schonberg/Elavia	'94/'94
PIPER JAFFRAY INSTL GOVT	Fixed Income	614.0	8.23	8,123.00	7,620.00	13,193.00	12.5	866-7778	612-342-6402	1.50	0.23	None	Bruntjen/Goldstein	'88/'88
PIPER JAFFRAY SECTOR	Capital Appreciation	83.9	16.50	9,677.00	10,252.00	19,282.00	0.2	866-7778	612-342-6402	4.00	0.32	None	Ed Nicoski	'87
PIPER JAFFRAY VALUE FUND	Growth	210.1	18.23	9,870.00	9,906.00	17,801.00	0.6	866-7778	612-342-6402	4.00	0.32	None	Beissel/Shrewsbury/Dow	'87/'87
PIPER TR INTMDT DURATION	Fixed Income	41.5	9.40	9,871.00	☆	☆	0.0	866-7778	612-342-6402	None	None	None	Rinkey/Wagner	'94/'94
PIPER TR SHORT DURATION	Fixed Income	115.6	9.67	9,931.00	☆	☆	0.0	866-7778	612-342-6402	None	None	None	Griffin/McGlinch/Rinkey	'94/'94
PNC BALANCED; INSTL	Flexible	17.4	11.92	9,884.00	☆	☆	0.0	422-6538	None	None	None	None	Gayland Gee	'93
PNC BALANCED; INV	Flexible	61.7	11.92	9,882.00	10,082.00	☆	2.3	422-6538	None	4.50	0.40	None	Gayland Gee	'90
PNC BALANCED; SERV ▮	Flexible	58.0	11.92	9,878.00	☆	☆	0.0	422-6538	None	None	None	None	Gayland Gee	'93
PNC CORE EQUITY; INSTL	Growth	45.2	9.62	10,055.00	☆	☆	0.0	422-6538	None	None	None	None	John Bye	'93
PNC CORE EQUITY; INV	Growth	0.3	9.63	10,057.00	☆	☆	0.0	422-6538	None	4.50	0.40	None	John Bye	'93
PNC CORE EQUITY; SERV ▮	Growth	27.1	9.62	10,050.00	☆	☆	0.0	422-6538	None	None	None	None	John Bye	'93
PNC GROWTH EQUITY; INSTL	Growth	91.1	9.70	9,381.00	☆	☆	0.0	422-6538	None	None	None	None	Mike Clark	'93
PNC GROWTH EQUITY; INV	Growth	4.5	9.68	9,371.00	9,321.00	☆	0.0	422-6538	None	4.50	0.40	None	Mike Clark	'92
PNC GROWTH EQUITY; SERV ▮	Growth	23.5	9.69	9,380.00	☆	☆	0.0	422-6538	None	None	None	None	Mike Clark	'93
PNC INDEX EQUITY; INSTL	S&P Index	168.2	10.53	10,041.00	☆	☆	0.0	422-6538	None	None	None	None	Francis X. Morris	'93
PNC INDEX EQUITY; INV	S&P Index	2.2	10.53	10,051.00	10,069.00	☆	2.6	422-6538	None	4.50	0.40	None	Francis X. Morris	'92
PNC INDEX EQUITY; SERV ▮	S&P Index	22.4	10.53	10,045.00	☆	☆	0.0	422-6538	None	None	None	None	Francis X. Morris	'93
PNC INTL EQUITY; INSTL	International	228.3	13.05	10,038.00	☆	☆	0.0	422-6538	None	None	None	None	Herve Van Caloen	'93
PNC INTL EQUITY; INV	International	11.9	13.01	10,015.00	11,707.00	☆	0.7	422-6538	None	4.50	0.40	None	Herve Van Caloen	'92
PNC INTL EQUITY; SERV ▮	International	52.5	13.04	10,038.00	☆	☆	0.0	422-6538	None	None	None	None	Herve Van Caloen	'93
PNC INTMDT BOND; INSTL	Fixed Income	48.3	9.12	9,916.00	☆	☆	0.0	422-6538	None	None	None	None	Beth Wagner	'93
PNC INTMDT BOND; SERV ▮	Fixed Income	33.6	9.12	9,910.00	☆	☆	0.0	422-6538	None	None	None	None	Beth Wagner	'93
PNC INTMDT GOVT; INSTL	Fixed Income	135.3	9.73	9,877.00	☆	☆	0.0	422-6538	None	None	None	None	William C. Lowry	'94
PNC INTMDT GOVT; INV	Fixed Income	8.5	9.73	9,871.00	9,821.00	☆	5.4	422-6538	None	4.50	0.25	None	William C. Lowry	'94

PNC INTMDT GOVT; SERV ▮	Fixed Income	38.9	9.73	9,871.00	☆	☆	0.0	422-6538	None	None	None	None	William C. Lowry	'94
PNC MGD INCOME; INSTL	Fixed Income	372.3	9.93	9,819.00	☆	☆	0.0	422-6538	None	None	None	None	Beth Wagner	'94
PNC MGD INCOME; INV	Fixed Income	10.2	9.93	9,808.00	9,721.00	☆	6.2	422-6538	None	4.50	0.45	None	Beth Wagner	'94
PNC MGD INCOME; SERV ▮	Fixed Income	42.8	9.93	9,815.00	☆	☆	0.0	422-6538	None	None	None	None	Beth Wagner	'94
PNC SH-TM BOND; INSTL	Fixed Income	32.1	9.66	9,975.00	☆	☆	0.0	422-6538	None	None	None	None	Beth Wagner	'93
PNC SH-TM BOND; INV	Fixed Income	0.1	9.66	9,969.00	☆	☆	0.0	422-6538	None	4.50	0.25	None	Beth Wagner	'93
PNC SH-TM BOND; SERV ▮	Fixed Income	6.1	9.66	9,970.00	☆	☆	0.0	422-6538	None	None	None	None	Beth Wagner	'93
PNC SM CAP GRO EQ; INSTL	Small Company Growth	31.0	9.16	9,299.00	☆	☆	0.0	422-6538	None	None	None	None	John Bye	'93
PNC SM CAP GRO EQ; INV	Small Company Growth	1.1	9.14	9,289.00	☆	☆	0.0	422-6538	None	4.50	0.40	None	John Bye	'93
PNC SM CAP GRO EQ; SERV ▮	Small Company Growth	14.1	9.14	9,279.00	☆	☆	0.0	422-6538	None	None	None	None	John Bye	'93
PNC SM CAP VAL EQ; INSTL	Small Company Growth	158.1	12.93	9,810.00	☆	☆	0.0	422-6538	None	None	None	None	Edwin B. Powell	'93
PNC SM CAP VAL EQ; INV	Small Company Growth	15.2	12.90	9,795.00	10,872.00	☆	0.1	422-6538	None	4.50	0.40	None	Edwin B. Powell	'92
PNC SM CAP VAL EQ; SERV	Small Company Growth	36.2	12.91	9,795.00	☆	☆	0.0	422-6538	None	None	None	None	Edwin B. Powell	'93
PNC VALUE EQUITY; INSTL	Capital Appreciation	546.1	11.27	10,147.00	☆	☆	0.0	422-6538	None	None	None	None	Edwin B. Powell	'93
PNC VALUE EQUITY; INV	Capital Appreciation	8.9	11.26	10,129.00	10,510.00	☆	2.0	422-6538	None	4.50	0.40	None	Edwin B. Powell	'92
PNC VALUE EQUITY; SERV ▮	Capital Appreciation	80.5	11.27	10,141.00	☆	☆	0.0	422-6538	None	None	None	None	Edwin B. Powell	'93
PORT DVSD INV FX INC; SHS	Fixed Income	31.7	9.57	9,843.00	9,837.00	14,638.00	6.3	821-7432	None	None	None	None	Bruce Repasy	'91
PORTICO FDS BALANCED	Balanced	90.7	20.93	9,535.00	9,891.00	☆	2.1	982-8909	414-287-3710	None	0.25	None	Wear/Westman	'94/'92
PORTICO FDS BOND IMMDEX	Fixed Income	250.6	25.92	9,898.00	9,889.00	☆	6.3	982-8909	414-287-3710	None	0.25	None	Stanek/Westman	'89/'92
PORTICO FDS EQUITY INDEX	S&P Index	78.0	31.36	10,037.00	10,095.00	☆	2.4	982-8909	414-287-3710	None	0.25	None	Tranchita	'92
PORTICO FDS GRO & INCOME	Growth Income	162.3	22.39	10,100.00	10,014.00	☆	2.0	982-8909	414-287-3710	None	0.25	None	Marian Zentmyer	'93
PORTICO FDS INT BD MKT	Fixed Income	74.1	9.77	9,939.00	10,001.00	☆	5.0	982-8909	414-287-3710	None	0.25	None	Stanek/Westman	'93/'93
PORTICO FDS MIDCORE GRO ★	Midcap	105.9	20.04	9,406.00	10,241.00	☆	0.4	982-8909	414-287-3710	None	None	None	Bart Wear	'92
PORTICO FDS SH-TM BD MKT	Fixed Income	125.1	10.08	10,000.00	10,171.00	☆	5.4	982-8909	414-287-3710	None	0.25	None	Stanek/Tranchita	'89/'93
PORTICO FDS SPECIAL GRO	Small Company Growth	350.4	29.70	9,271.00	10,029.00	☆	0.2	982-8909	414-287-3710	None	0.25	None	Harkness/Docter	'89/'89
PRA REAL ESTATE	Real Estate	124.8	9.45	9,965.00	10,653.00	13,351.00	4.4	435-1405	302-651-8448	None	None	None	Michael T. Oliver	'89
PREFERRED ASSET ALLOC	Flexible	59.2	10.27	9,898.00	9,873.00	☆	2.9	662-4769	309-675-5123	None	None	None	Mellon/PanAgora	'92/'92
PREFERRED FXD INC	Fixed Income	45.3	9.80	9,924.00	9,954.00	☆	4.7	662-4769	309-675-5123	None	None	None	J.P. Morgan Inv Mgt Inc	'92
PREFERRED GROWTH	Growth	179.6	12.46	9,375.00	10,034.00	☆	0.0	662-4769	309-675-5123	None	None	None	Jennison Assoc Cap Corp	'92
PREFERRED INTL	International	98.5	12.02	9,983.00	12,666.00	☆	0.6	662-4769	309-675-5123	None	None	None	Mercator Asset Mgt, Inc	'92
PREFERRED SHT-TM GOVT	Fixed Income	30.1	9.77	9,986.00	10,086.00	☆	3.8	662-4769	309-675-5123	None	None	None	Caterpillar Inv Mgt Ltd	'92
PREFERRED VALUE	Growth Income	122.7	11.33	10,053.00	10,061.00	☆	1.4	662-4769	309-675-5123	None	None	None	Oppenheimer Capital	'92
T ROWE PRICE ADJ RATE	Fixed Income	187.5	4.64	9,920.00	10,109.00	☆	4.8	638-5660	410-547-2308	None	None	None	Peter Van Dyke	'91
T ROWE PRICE BALANCED	Balanced	355.8	11.22	9,886.00	10,211.00	16,418.00	3.4	638-5660	410-547-2308	None	None	None	Richard T. Whitney	'91
T ROWE PRICE BLUE CHIP	Growth	30.8	10.84	9,891.00	11,026.00	☆	0.5	638-5660	410-547-2308	None	None	None	Thomas Broadus	'93
T ROWE PRICE CAP APPREC	Capital Appreciation	568.5	12.59	10,024.00	10,712.00	16,099.00	1.4	638-5660	410-547-2308	None	None	None	Richard P. Howard	'89
T ROWE PRICE DIV GROWTH	Growth Income	46.5	11.06	10,081.00	10,617.00	☆	2.6	638-5660	410-547-2308	None	None	None	Bill Stromberg	'92
T ROWE PRICE EQU INCOME	Equity Income	2,933.4	16.09	10,195.00	10,554.00	15,433.00	3.4	638-5660	410-547-2308	None	None	None	Brian C. Rogers	'89
T ROWE PRICE GNMA	Fixed Income	802.3	9.05	9,886.00	9,792.00	14,485.00	7.4	638-5660	410-547-2308	None	None	None	Peter Van Dyke	'87
T ROWE PRICE GRO & INC	Growth Income	1,189.6	15.79	10,108.00	10,145.00	15,295.00	3.0	638-5660	410-547-2308	None	None	None	Stephen W. Boesel	'87
T ROWE PRICE GROWTH STK	Growth	1,991.8	19.67	10,041.00	10,701.00	16,915.00	0.7	638-5660	410-547-2308	None	None	None	M. David Testa	'84
T ROWE PRICE HIGH YLD	Fixed Income	1,241.3	8.17	9,647.00	9,858.00	14,156.00	9.6	638-5660	410-547-2308	None	None	1.00	Richard Swingle	'84
T ROWE PRICE INDEX EQU ✪	S&P Index	198.4	12.80	10,031.00	10,103.00	☆	2.4	638-5660	410-547-2308	None	None	None	Richard T. Whitney	'90
T ROWE PRICE INTL ASIA	Pacific Region	2,019.5	8.93	10,079.00	12,419.00	☆	0.4	638-5660	410-547-2308	None	None	None	Martin G. Wade	'90
T ROWE PRICE INTL BOND	World Income	737.7	9.79	10,030.00	10,577.00	17,615.00	6.5	638-5660	410-547-2308	None	None	None	David Boardman	'88
T ROWE PRICE INTL DISC	International	473.5	16.99	9,953.00	12,431.00	17,193.00	0.4	638-5660	410-547-2308	None	None	2.00	Martin G. Wade	'89
T ROWE PRICE INTL EU STK	European Region	334.9	11.74	9,824.00	11,837.00	☆	0.3	638-5660	410-547-2308	None	None	None	Martin G. Wade	'90
T ROWE PRICE INTL GL GVT	World Income	43.4	9.49	9,966.00	10,005.00	☆	5.5	638-5660	410-547-2308	None	None	None	David Boardman	'90
T ROWE PRICE INTL JAPAN	Japanese	157.6	12.24	10,890.00	12,105.00	☆	0.0	638-5660	410-547-2308	None	None	None	Martin G. Wade	'93
T ROWE PRICE INTL LAT	Latin American	136.4	8.51	9,092.00	☆	☆	0.0	638-5660	410-547-2308	None	None	2.00	Martin G. Wade	'93

★ PIONEER GROWTH SHARES--Fund has been reclassified from Midcap to Growth.
★ PORTICO MIDCORE GRO--Fund has been reclassified from Growth to Midcap.

PERFORMANCE OF MUTUAL FUNDS *(continued)*

FUND NAME	OBJECTIVE	TOTAL NET ASSETS ($ MIL) 5/31/94	NET ASSET $ VALUE 6/30/94	PERFORMANCE (Return on initial $10,000 Investment) 3/31/94-6/30/94	6/30/93-6/30/94	6/30/89-6/30/94	DIVIDEND YIELD % 6/94	PHONE NUMBER 800	In-State	FEES Load	12b-1	Redemption	MANAGER	SINCE
T ROWE PRICE INTL SH GL	**World Income**	**86.6**	**4.51**	**9,877.00**	**9,971.00**	☆	**6.9**	**638-5660**	**410-547-2308**	**None**	**None**	**None**	**David Boardman**	**'92**
T ROWE PRICE INTL STOCK	**International**	**5,240.3**	**11.97**	**10,084.00**	**12,213.00**	**16,823.00**	**0.8**	**638-5660**	**410-547-2308**	**None**	**None**	**None**	**Testa/Wade**	**'80/'80**
T ROWE PRICE MID-CAP GRO	**Midcap**	**85.8**	**14.30**	**9,835.00**	**10,816.00**	☆	**0.0**	**638-5660**	**410-547-2308**	**None**	**None**	**None**	**Brian Berghuis**	**'92**
T ROWE PRICE NEW AMER GR	**Growth**	**620.4**	**25.25**	**9,532.00**	**10,214.00**	**17,913.00**	**0.0**	**638-5660**	**410-547-2308**	**None**	**None**	**None**	**John H. Laporte**	**'85**
T ROWE PRICE NEW ERA	**Natural Resources**	**853.8**	**20.46**	**10,194.00**	**10,737.00**	**13,886.00**	**1.8**	**638-5660**	**410-547-2308**	**None**	**None**	**None**	**George A. Roche**	**'79**
T ROWE PRICE NEW HORIZON	Small Company Growth	1,588.8	14.58	9,370.00	10,625.00	18,079.00	0.0	638-5660	410-547-2308	None	None	None	John H. Laporte	'87
T ROWE PRICE NEW INCOME	Fixed Income	1,375.1	8.59	9,885.00	9,948.00	14,615.00	6.3	638-5660	410-547-2308	None	None	None	Charles P. Smith	'86
T ROWE PRICE OTC	Small Company Growth	190.7	14.78	9,906.00	10,722.00	14,681.00	0.0	638-5660	410-547-2308	None	None	None	Greg A. McCrickard	'92
T ROWE PRICE SCI & TECH	Science & Technology	577.9	17.14	9,215.00	10,343.00	24,590.00	0.0	638-5660	410-547-2308	None	None	None	Laporte/Morris	'87/'91
T ROWE PRICE SH-TERM BD	Fixed Income	601.9	4.83	9,929.00	10,027.00	13,886.00	5.9	638-5660	410-547-2308	None	None	None	Veena A. Kutler	'91
T ROWE PRICE SM CAP ☒	Small Company Growth	446.1	14.38	9,863.00	10,810.00	18,319.00	0.7	638-5660	410-547-2308	None	None	None	Preston G. Athey	'88
T ROWE PRICE SPCTRM GRO	Growth Income	750.2	11.45	9,965.00	10,866.00	☆	1.4	638-5660	410-547-2308	None	None	None	Van Dyke/Notzon	'90/'90
T ROWE PRICE SPCTRM INC	Fixed Income	613.6	10.40	9,918.00	10,083.00	☆	6.5	638-5660	410-547-2308	None	None	None	Van Dyke/Notzon	'90/'90
T ROWE PRICE SUM GNMA	Fixed Income	16.1	9.37	9,852.00	☆	☆	0.0	638-5660	410-547-2308	None	None	None	Peter Van Dyke	'93
T ROWE PRICE SUM LTD BD	Fixed Income	17.9	4.68	9,790.00	☆	☆	0.0	638-5660	410-547-2308	None	None	None	Veena A. Kutler	'93
T ROWE PRICE TREAS INTMD	Fixed Income	181.2	5.09	9,927.00	9,941.00	☆	5.7	638-5660	410-547-2308	None	None	None	Smith/Kutler	'89/'89
T ROWE PRICE TREAS LONG	Fixed Income	54.2	9.67	9,773.00	9,613.00	☆	6.9	638-5660	410-547-2308	None	None	None	Peter Van Dyke	'89
PRIMARY INC INCOME	Income	3.7	11.08	9,957.00	9,980.00	☆	4.5	443-6544	414-271-7870	None	None	None	David Aushwitz	'89
PRIMARY INC US GOVT	Fixed Income	1.3	9.74	9,855.00	9,832.00	☆	5.2	443-6544	414-271-7870	None	None	None	James T. Dean, Jr.	'89
PRIMARY TREND	Growth Income	21.8	10.98	10,055.00	9,972.00	12,625.00	0.7	443-6544	414-271-7870	None	None	None	David Aushwitz	'89
PRINCIPAL PRES BALANCED	Balanced	15.8	9.83	9,990.00	9,837.00	☆	3.4	826-4600	414-334-5521	4.50	0.25	None	Ralph Patek	'93
PRINCIPAL PRES DIV ACHVR	Growth Income	21.8	13.08	10,222.00	9,814.00	14,406.00	1.2	826-4600	414-334-5521	4.50	0.25	None	R. Douglas Ziegler	'92
PRINCIPAL PRES GOVT	Fixed Income	49.9	9.18	9,865.00	9,690.00	14,569.00	6.7	826-4600	414-334-5521	4.50	0.25	None	Vern Van Vooren	'89
PRINCIPAL PRES S&P 100 +	Growth Income	40.4	14.34	9,998.00	9,987.00	15,457.00	1.6	826-4600	414-334-5521	4.50	0.25	None	William Zink	'93
PRINCIPAL SP MKT INTL	International	16.2	12.05	9,950.00	12,167.00	☆	0.8	247-4123	515-247-5711	None	None	None	Opsal/Dau	'93/'93
PRINCIPAL SP MKT MBS	Fixed Income	25.5	9.31	9,864.00	9,760.00	☆	6.5	247-4123	515-247-5711	None	None	None	Schafer/Alexander	'93/'93
PRINCOR BLUE CHIP FUND	Growth Income	25.4	11.51	10,106.00	9,904.00	☆	2.3	247-4123	515-247-5711	5.00	0.25	None	Williams/White	'91/'94
PRINCOR BOND FUND	Fixed Income	90.8	10.49	9,829.00	9,843.00	14,830.00	7.5	247-4123	515-247-5711	5.00	0.25	None	Brattebo/Dyslin	'87/'93
PRINCOR CAPITAL ACCUM	Growth Income	264.7	19.63	10,087.00	10,033.00	14,246.00	2.1	247-4123	515-247-5711	5.00	0.15	None	White/Green	'69/'92
PRINCOR EMERGING GROWTH	Midcap	77.1	23.67	9,925.00	10,849.00	18,885.00	0.2	247-4123	515-247-5711	5.00	0.25	None	Hamilton/Craven	'87/'93
PRINCOR GOVT SEC INCOME	Fixed Income	261.1	10.52	9,842.00	9,602.00	14,647.00	6.6	247-4123	515-247-5711	5.00	0.20	None	Schafer/Alexander	'85/'93
PRINCOR GROWTH FUND	Growth	101.0	29.10	9,891.00	10,796.00	19,921.00	1.3	247-4123	515-247-5711	5.00	0.25	None	Hamilton/Craven	'87/'93
PRINCOR HIGH YIELD FUND	Fixed Income	19.9	7.86	9,998.00	10,009.00	13,363.00	8.5	247-4123	515-247-5711	5.00	0.25	None	Hovey/Denkinger	'87/'93
PRINCOR MANAGED FUND	Balanced	49.8	12.24	9,989.00	10,034.00	14,762.00	3.4	247-4123	515-247-5711	5.00	0.25	None	Vogel/Green	'93/'93
PRINCOR UTILITIES FUND	Utility	57.2	9.27	9,558.00	8,432.00	☆	4.6	247-4123	515-247-5711	5.00	0.25	None	Green/Vogel	'93/'93
PRINCOR WORLD FD	International	102.7	7.00	9,943.00	12,137.00	16,709.00	0.3	247-4123	515-247-5711	5.00	0.25	None	Opsal/Dau	'93/'93
PROGRESSIVE AGGR GRO ☒	Capital Appreciation	0.5	9.51	10,000.00	12,303.00	12,089.00	0.0	543-2620	212-248-8080	4.00	None	None	Mark D. Beckerman	'94
PROGRESSIVE ENVIRONMNT ☒	Environmental	2.3	4.31	9,229.00	8,850.00	☆	0.0	543-2620	212-248-8080	4.50	None	None	Mark D. Beckerman	'94
PROGRESSIVE VALUE ☒	Growth	1.0	9.72	9,492.00	10,308.00	8,574.00	0.0	543-2620	212-248-8080	4.00	None	None	Mark D. Beckerman	'94
PRUDENT SPECULATOR FUND	Small Company Growth	2.9	6.53	9,355.00	10,159.00	8,731.00	0.0	444-4778	213-252-9000	None	0.25	None	Ed Bernstein	'89
PRUDENTIAL ADJ RATE; A	Fixed Income	103.6	9.50	9,986.00	10,061.00	☆	4.2	225-1852	None	1.00	0.50	None	Kay Willcox	'92
PRUDENTIAL ADJ RATE; B	Fixed Income	3.3	9.53	9,986.00	10,060.00	☆	4.2	225-1852	None	None	1.00	1.00	Kay Willcox	'92
PRUDENTIAL EQU INC; A	Equity Income	137.4	13.43	10,081.00	10,356.00	☆	2.4	225-1852	None	5.25	0.20	None	Warren Spitz	'90
PRUDENTIAL EQU INC; B	Equity Income	829.1	13.41	10,063.00	10,283.00	16,151.00	1.7	225-1852	None	None	1.00	5.00	Warren Spitz	'87
PRUDENTIAL EQUITY; A	Growth	250.1	13.48	10,052.00	10,565.00	☆	1.6	225-1852	None	5.25	0.20	None	Tom Jackson	'90

PRUDENTIAL EQUITY; B	Growth	1,894.9	13.44	10,037.00	10,486.00	17,984.00	0.8	225-1852		None	None	1.00	5.00	Tom Jackson	'82
PRUDENTIAL FLX CONSV; A	Flexible	34.4	10.91	9,999.00	10,097.00	☆	3.4	225-1852		None	5.25	0.20	None	McHugh/Guidone	'90/'93
PRUDENTIAL FLX CONSV; B	Flexible	438.5	10.89	9,990.00	10,020.00	15,566.00	2.6	225-1852		None	None	1.00	5.00	McHugh/Guidone	'89/'93
PRUDENTIAL FLX STRAT; A	Flexible	31.9	11.37	9,913.00	10,102.00	☆	2.0	225-1852		None	5.25	0.20	None	Smith/Gleason/Bushe	'93/'90
PRUDENTIAL FLX STRAT; B	Flexible	354.2	11.32	9,895.00	10,034.00	14,952.00	1.5	225-1852		None	None	1.00	5.00	Smith/Gleason/Bushe	'93/'90
PRUDENTIAL GL GENSIS; A	Global Small Company	29.2	18.54	9,968.00	12,998.00	☆	0.8	225-1852		None	5.25	0.20	None	Dan Duane	'90
PRUDENTIAL GL GENSIS; B	Global Small Company	174.5	18.00	9,945.00	12,898.00	15,984.00	0.3	225-1852		None	None	1.00	5.00	Dan Duane	'88
PRUDENTIAL GL NT RES; A	Natural Resources	6.5	12.25	10,057.00	10,149.00	☆	0.0	225-1852		None	5.25	0.20	None	Leigh Goehring	'90
PRUDENTIAL GL NT RES; B	Natural Resources	64.2	11.99	10,042.00	10,067.00	13,071.00	0.0	225-1852		None	None	1.00	5.00	Leigh Goehring	'87
PRUDENTIAL GLOBAL; A	Global	57.0	13.68	10,007.00	12,470.00	☆	0.0	225-1852		None	5.25	0.20	None	Dan Duane	'91
PRUDENTIAL GLOBAL; B	Global	355.9	13.37	9,985.00	12,380.00	14,197.00	0.0	225-1852		None	None	0.89	5.00	Dan Duane	'84
PRUDENTIAL GNMA; A	Fixed Income	9.9	13.89	9,928.00	9,796.00	☆	7.2	225-1852		None	4.50	0.15	None	Kay Willcox	'90
PRUDENTIAL GNMA; B	Fixed Income	281.0	13.85	9,907.00	9,733.00	13,504.00	6.6	225-1852		None	None	0.75	5.00	Kay Willcox	'82
PRUDENTIAL GOVT PLUS; A	Fixed Income	46.7	8.58	9,857.00	9,688.00	☆	6.8	225-1852		None	4.50	0.15	None	Marty Lawlor	'90
PRUDENTIAL GOVT PLUS; B	Fixed Income	1,933.4	8.58	9,838.00	9,612.00	13,674.00	6.0	225-1852		None	None	1.00	5.00	Marty Lawlor	'85
PRUDENTIAL GOVT INTMDT	Fixed Income	304.0	9.41	9,912.00	9,898.00	14,061.00	7.4	225-1852		None	None	0.21	None	Kay Willcox	'92
PRUDENTIAL GR OPPTY; A	Small Company Growth	97.1	11.70	9,824.00	10,362.00	☆	0.0	225-1852		None	5.25	0.20	None	Bob Fetch	'90
PRUDENTIAL GR OPPTY; B	Small Company Growth	398.3	11.33	9,810.00	10,286.00	17,120.00	0.0	225-1852		None	None	1.00	5.00	Bob Fetch	'81
PRUDENTIAL GROWTH; A	Growth	4.0	13.04	9,729.00	9,685.00	☆	0.0	225-1852		None	5.25	0.20	None	Greg Smith	'90
PRUDENTIAL GROWTH; B	Growth	180.8	12.90	9,705.00	9,616.00	12,201.00	0.0	225-1852		None	None	1.00	5.00	Greg Smith	'83
PRUDENTIAL HI YLD; A	Fixed Income	163.4	8.14	9,952.00	10,410.00	☆	10.5	225-1852		None	4.50	0.10	None	Lars Berkman	'90
PRUDENTIAL HI YLD; B	Fixed Income	3,545.3	8.13	9,939.00	10,352.00	15,002.00	9.9	225-1852		None	None	0.75	5.00	Lars Berkman	'79
PRUDENTIAL INCOMVRT; A	Specialty	14.9	11.44	9,854.00	9,944.00	☆	3.8	225-1852		None	5.25	0.20	None	Anne Moseley-Cox	'90
PRUDENTIAL INCOMVRT; B	Specialty	270.3	11.44	9,837.00	9,862.00	13,562.00	3.0	225-1852		None	None	1.00	5.00	Anne Moseley-Cox	'85
PRUDENTIAL INSTL ACT BAL	Balanced	73.1	10.68	9,898.00	10,189.00	☆	1.3	824-7513		None	None	None	None	Jennison Assoc Cap Corp	'93
PRUDENTIAL INSTL BAL	Flexible	48.4	10.81	9,908.00	10,023.00	☆	2.1	824-7513		None	None	None	None	Prudential Invstmnt Corp	'93
PRUDENTIAL INSTL GROWTH	Growth	80.8	11.11	9,439.00	9,718.00	☆	0.1	824-7513		None	None	None	None	Jennison Assoc Cap Corp	'93
PRUDENTIAL INSTL INCOME	Fixed Income	38.2	9.48	9,879.00	9,852.00	☆	5.4	824-7513		None	None	None	None	Prudential Invstmnt Corp	'93
PRUDENTIAL INSTL INTL ST	International	78.3	14.14	9,937.00	12,252.00	☆	0.2	824-7513		None	None	None	None	Mercator Asset Mgt, Inc	'93
PRUDENTIAL INSTL STK IDX	S&P Index	42.9	10.76	10,056.00	10,102.00	☆	1.7	824-7513		None	None	None	None	Prudential Invstmnt Corp	'93
PRUDENTIAL INT GL; A	World Income	265.9	7.70	9,807.00	9,877.00	13,586.00	7.2	225-1852		None	3.00	0.25	None	Jeff Brummette	'93
PRUDENTIAL INT GL; B	World Income	33.4	7.71	9,793.00	9,808.00	☆	6.6	225-1852		None	None	0.15	3.00	Jeff Brummette	'93
PRUDENTIAL MULTI-SEC; A	Capital Appreciation	52.8	12.98	9,939.00	10,562.00	☆	1.6	225-1852		None	5.25	0.20	None	Hamacher/Smith	'92/'92
PRUDENTIAL MULTI-SEC; B	Capital Appreciation	128.8	12.91	9,916.00	10,477.00	☆	0.7	225-1852		None	None	1.00	5.00	Hamacher/Smith	'92/'92
PRUDENTIAL PAC GR; A	Pacific Region	98.1	16.65	10,079.00	12,561.00	☆	0.4	225-1852		None	5.25	0.20	None	Dan Duane	'92
PRUDENTIAL PAC GR; B	Pacific Region	431.4	16.43	10,067.00	12,477.00	☆	0.2	225-1852		None	None	1.00	5.00	Dan Duane	'92
PRUDENTIAL S GL AST; A	World Income	70.9	1.83	10,061.00	9,994.00	☆	4.9	225-1852		None	0.99	0.15	None	Jeff Brummette	'91
PRUDENTIAL SHT GLBL; A	World Income	34.0	8.75	9,928.00	9,842.00	☆	6.5	225-1852		None	3.00	0.30	None	Jeff Brummette	'90
PRUDENTIAL SHT GLBL; B	World Income	262.8	8.75	9,906.00	9,763.00	☆	5.6	225-1852		None	None	1.00	3.00	Jeff Brummette	'90
PRUDENTIAL STRUC MAT; A	Fixed Income	107.6	11.25	9,950.00	10,035.00	☆	6.0	225-1852		None	3.25	0.10	None	Annamarie Carlucci	'93
PRUDENTIAL STRUC MAT; B	Fixed Income	137.3	11.24	9,924.00	9,952.00	☆	5.3	225-1852		None	None	0.85	3.00	Annamarie Carlucci	'93
PRUDENTIAL US GOVT; A	Fixed Income	7.0	9.44	9,806.00	9,672.00	☆	6.5	225-1852		None	4.50	0.15	None	Annamarie Carlucci	'90
PRUDENTIAL US GOVT; B	Fixed Income	140.8	9.45	9,787.00	9,598.00	13,442.00	5.7	225-1852		None	None	1.00	5.00	Annamarie Carlucci	'86
PRUDENTIAL UTILITY; A	Utility	294.3	8.79	9,699.00	9,417.00	☆	3.3	225-1852		None	5.25	0.20	None	Warren Spitz	'90
PRUDENTIAL UTILITY; B	Utility	4,164.9	8.76	9,676.00	9,333.00	14,783.00	2.5	225-1852		None	None	1.00	5.00	Warren Spitz	'84
PUTNAM ADJ RT GOVT; A	Fixed Income	140.1	10.18	9,918.00	9,913.00	12,451.00	4.5	225-1581	617-292-1000	3.25		0.25	None	Jeffrey Saef	'94
PUTNAM ADJ RT GOVT; B	Fixed Income	42.5	10.17	9,912.00	9,863.00	☆	3.9	225-1581	617-292-1000	None		0.85	3.00	Jeffrey Saef	'94
PUTNAM AMERICAN GOVT INC	Fixed Income	2,630.7	8.29	9,885.00	9,690.00	13,176.00	8.0	225-1581	617-292-1000	4.75		0.25	None	Taubes/Senter	'92/'92
PUTNAM ASIA PAC GRO; A	Pacific Region	117.2	14.37	10,527.00	13,755.00	☆	0.0	225-1581	617-292-1000	5.75		0.25	None	David Thomas	'91
PUTNAM ASIA PAC GRO; B	Pacific Region	78.7	14.29	10,515.00	13,691.00	☆	0.0	225-1581	617-292-1000	None		1.00	5.00	David Thomas	'93

PERFORMANCE OF MUTUAL FUNDS (continued)

FUND NAME	OBJECTIVE	TOTAL NET ASSETS ($ MIL) 5/31/94	NET ASSET $ VALUE 6/30/94	PERFORMANCE (Return on initial $10,000 Investment) 3/31/94-6/30/94	6/30/93-6/30/94	6/30/89-6/30/94	DIVIDEND YIELD % 6/94	PHONE NUMBER 800	In-State	FEES Load	12b-1	Redemption	MANAGER	SINCE
PUTNAM ASST BALANCED; A	Flexible	26.6	8.10	9,890.00	☆	☆	0.0	225-1581	617-292-1000	5.75	0.25	None	Karman/Coburn	'94/'94
PUTNAM ASST BALANCED; B	Flexible	37.8	8.08	9,878.00	☆	☆	0.0	225-1581	617-292-1000	None	1.00	5.00	Karman/Coburn	'94/'94
PUTNAM ASST CONSV; A	Flexible	13.6	8.14	9,855.00	☆	☆	0.0	225-1581	617-292-1000	5.75	0.25	None	Karman/Coburn	'94/'94
PUTNAM ASST CONSV; B	Flexible	20.5	8.12	9,831.00	☆	☆	0.0	225-1581	617-292-1000	None	1.00	5.00	Karman/Coburn	'94/'94
PUTNAM ASST GROWTH; A	Flexible	19.9	8.06	9,890.00	☆	☆	0.0	225-1581	617-292-1000	5.75	0.25	None	Karman/Coburn	'94/'94
PUTNAM ASST GROWTH; B	Flexible	21.7	8.04	9,877.00	☆	☆	0.0	225-1581	617-292-1000	None	1.00	5.00	Karman/Coburn	'94/'94
PUTNAM BALANCED GOVT; A	Fixed Income	60.1	4.67	9,897.00	9,879.00	☆	5.7	225-1581	617-292-1000	3.25	0.25	None	Christopher Ray	'93
PUTNAM BALANCED GOVT; B	Fixed Income	24.0	4.67	9,902.00	9,817.00	☆	5.0	225-1581	617-292-1000	None	1.00	3.00	Christopher Ray	'93
PUTNAM CAP APPREC ◪	Growth	3.1	10.26	9,809.00	12,230.00	☆	0.4	225-1581	617-292-1000	5.75	None	None	Gerald Zukowski	'93
PUTNAM CAP GROWTH ◪	Growth Income	2.2	8.86	9,726.00	10,507.00	☆	1.0	225-1581	617-292-1000	5.75	None	None	James Giblin	'93
PUTNAM CONV INC-GRO; A	Convertible Securities	684.4	18.57	9,898.00	10,386.00	16,643.00	5.1	225-1581	617-292-1000	5.75	0.25	None	Mullin/Pohl	'92/'92
PUTNAM CONV INC-GRO; B	Convertible Securities	22.5	18.49	9,871.00	☆	☆	0.0	225-1581	617-292-1000	None	1.00	5.00	Mullin/Pohl	'93/'93
PUTNAM CORPORATE ASSET	Equity Income	131.0	41.34	9,919.00	10,083.00	15,169.00	7.0	225-1581	617-292-1000	2.50	None	None	Sheldon N. Simon	'92
PUTNAM DIVIDEND GRO; A	Growth Income	47.2	9.43	10,051.00	10,169.00	☆	2.9	225-1581	617-292-1000	5.75	0.25	None	Michael Mach	'91
PUTNAM DIVIDEND GRO; B	Growth Income	7.5	9.40	10,034.00	☆	☆	0.0	225-1581	617-292-1000	None	1.00	5.00	Michael Mach	'93
PUTNAM DVSFD INCOME; A	Fixed Income	1,492.4	11.85	9,788.00	10,153.00	16,308.00	7.6	225-1581	617-292-1000	4.75	0.25	None	Leichter/Daly/Saef	'89/'89
PUTNAM DVSFD INCOME; B	Fixed Income	1,492.4	11.81	9,769.00	10,071.00	☆	6.9	225-1581	617-292-1000	None	1.00	5.00	Leichter/Daly/Saef	'93/'93
PUTNAM ENERGY-RES; A	Natural Resources	119.7	13.86	10,390.00	8,796.00	13,853.00	0.5	225-1581	617-292-1000	5.75	0.25	None	Douglas Terreson	'92
PUTNAM ENERGY-RES; B	Natural Resources	6.0	13.80	10,360.00	☆	☆	0.0	225-1581	617-292-1000	None	1.00	5.00	Douglas Terreson	'94
PUTNAM EQUITY INCOME; A	Equity Income	315.9	8.43	10,202.00	10,475.00	14,192.00	3.8	225-1581	617-292-1000	5.75	0.25	None	Bousa/Taubes	'92/'93
PUTNAM EQUITY INCOME; B	Equity Income	23.1	8.42	10,174.00	☆	☆	0.0	225-1581	617-292-1000	None	1.00	5.00	Bousa/Taubes	'93/'93
PUTNAM EUROPE GROWTH; A	European Region	68.7	11.64	9,890.00	11,945.00	☆	1.0	225-1581	617-292-1000	5.75	0.25	None	Justin Scott	'90
PUTNAM EUROPE GROWTH; B	European Region	23.2	11.63	9,873.00	☆	☆	0.0	225-1581	617-292-1000	None	1.00	5.00	Justin Scott	'94
PUTNAM FEDERAL INCOME	Fixed Income	501.6	9.47	9,807.00	9,597.00	13,934.00	7.9	225-1581	617-292-1000	4.75	0.25	None	Taubes/Senter	'92/'92
GEORGE PUTNAM BOSTON; A	Balanced	893.7	13.23	10,122.00	10,145.00	15,670.00	4.4	225-1581	617-292-1000	5.75	0.25	None	Bousa/Taubes	'93/'93
GEORGE PUTNAM BOSTON; B	Balanced	143.2	13.18	10,105.00	10,071.00	☆	3.8	225-1581	617-292-1000	None	1.00	5.00	Bousa/Taubes	'93/'93
PUTNAM GLOBAL GOVT; A	World Income	501.6	13.48	9,595.00	9,632.00	15,829.00	6.6	225-1581	617-292-1000	4.75	0.25	None	Daly/Turner	'89/'92
PUTNAM GLOBAL GOVT; B	World Income	16.7	13.46	9,573.00	☆	☆	0.0	225-1581	617-292-1000	None	1.00	5.00	Daly/Turner	'94/'94
PUTNAM GLOBAL GROWTH; A	Global	1,291.0	9.37	10,043.00	11,482.00	16,170.00	0.0	225-1581	617-292-1000	5.75	0.25	None	Regan/Zukowski	'88/'93
PUTNAM GLOBAL GROWTH; B	Global	620.8	9.23	10,044.00	11,409.00	☆	0.0	225-1581	617-292-1000	None	1.00	5.00	Regan/Zukowski	'92/'93
PUTNAM GRO & INC; A	Growth Income	5,620.1	13.09	10,176.00	10,351.00	16,587.00	3.4	225-1581	617-292-1000	5.75	0.25	None	King/Kreisel/Giblin	'93/'93
PUTNAM GRO & INC; B	Growth Income	2,814.3	13.01	10,167.00	10,280.00	☆	2.8	225-1581	617-292-1000	None	1.00	5.00	King/Kreisel/Giblin	'93/'93
PUTNAM GROWTH FUND; A	Growth	4.8	9.43	9,662.00	10,812.00	☆	0.0	225-1581	617-292-1000	5.75	0.10	None	Chuck Swanberg	'93
PUTNAM HIGH YIELD ADVTG	Fixed Income	707.2	9.79	9,867.00	10,536.00	17,069.00	10.8	225-1581	617-292-1000	4.75	0.25	None	Jin Ho	'87
PUTNAM HIGH YIELD; A	Fixed Income	3,007.4	12.41	9,895.00	10,482.00	16,819.00	10.6	225-1581	617-292-1000	4.75	0.25	None	D'Alelio/Ho	'85/'86
PUTNAM HIGH YIELD; B	Fixed Income	498.2	12.38	9,884.00	10,404.00	☆	9.9	225-1581	617-292-1000	None	1.00	5.00	D'Alelio/Ho	'93/'93
PUTNAM HLTH SCIENCES; A	Health/Biotechnology	723.9	25.66	10,276.00	10,317.00	18,181.00	0.9	225-1581	617-292-1000	5.75	0.25	None	Joanne Soja	'93
PUTNAM HLTH SCIENCES; B	Health/Biotechnology	44.2	25.43	10,258.00	10,236.00	☆	0.7	225-1581	617-292-1000	None	1.00	5.00	Joanne Soja	'93
PUTNAM INCOME; A	Fixed Income	777.0	6.66	9,838.00	9,887.00	15,097.00	8.1	225-1581	617-292-1000	4.75	0.25	None	Geissinger/Bankart/Daly	'90/'89
PUTNAM INCOME; B	Fixed Income	157.3	6.64	9,820.00	9,808.00	☆	7.4	225-1581	617-292-1000	None	1.00	5.00	Geissinger/Bankart/Daly	'93/'93
PUTNAM INVESTORS; A	Growth	799.1	7.63	9,720.00	10,032.00	17,025.00	0.6	225-1581	617-292-1000	5.75	0.25	None	Cobb/Ainley/Santos	'88/'94
PUTNAM INVESTORS; B	Growth	18.5	7.56	9,705.00	9,937.00	☆	0.3	225-1581	617-292-1000	None	1.00	5.00	Cobb/Ainley/Santos	'93/'94
PUTNAM MANAGED INC; A	Income	479.3	8.58	10,015.00	10,127.00	15,347.00	6.3	225-1581	617-292-1000	5.75	0.25	None	Edward Bousa	'92
PUTNAM MANAGED INC; B	Income	2.2	8.57	10,015.00	☆	☆	0.0	225-1581	617-292-1000	None	1.00	5.00	Edward Bousa	'94
PUTNAM NEW OPPTY; A ★	Growth	657.5	21.89	9,271.00	10,704.00	☆	0.0	225-1581	617-292-1000	5.75	0.25	None	Daniel Miller	'90

PUTNAM NEW OPPTY; B ★	Growth	319.1	21.69	9,253.00	10,623.00	☆	0.0	225-1581	617-292-1000	None	1.00	5.00	Daniel Miller	'93
PUTNAM OTC EMERG GRO; A	Small Company Growth	416.3	9.94	9,178.00	10,421.00	18,056.00	0.0	225-1581	617-292-1000	5.75	0.25	None	Daniel Miller	'92
PUTNAM OTC EMERG GRO; B	Small Company Growth	36.7	9.86	9,172.00	☆	☆	0.0	225-1581	617-292-1000	None	1.00	5.00	Daniel Miller	'93
PUTNAM OVERSEAS GRO	International	3.3	11.83	10,120.00	12,581.00	☆	0.0	225-1581	617-292-1000	5.75	0.25	None	Justin Scott	'91
PUTNAM RSRCH ANLYSTS; A ◪	Capital Appreciation	3.0	9.06	9,587.00	10,120.00	☆	0.0	225-1581	617-292-1000	5.75	0.25	None	Richard Frucci	'92
PUTNAM US GOVT INC; A	Fixed Income	3,497.0	12.49	9,904.00	9,748.00	13,961.00	7.9	225-1581	617-292-1000	4.75	0.25	None	Michael Martino	'94
PUTNAM US GOVT INC; B	Fixed Income	1,884.5	12.45	9,885.00	9,675.00	☆	7.2	225-1581	617-292-1000	None	1.00	5.00	Michael Martino	'94
PUTNAM UTIL GR & INC; A ◪	Utility	572.8	8.82	9,806.00	9,378.00	☆	5.1	225-1581	617-292-1000	5.75	0.25	None	Sheldon N. Simon	'90
PUTNAM UTIL GR & INC; B	Utility	521.6	8.79	9,786.00	9,300.00	☆	4.4	225-1581	617-292-1000	None	1.00	5.00	Sheldon N. Simon	'92
PUTNAM VISTA; A ★	Growth	628.4	6.87	9,398.00	10,024.00	17,711.00	0.3	225-1581	617-292-1000	5.75	0.25	None	Jennifer Silver	'91
PUTNAM VISTA; B ★	Growth	118.9	6.81	9,380.00	9,936.00	☆	0.1	225-1581	617-292-1000	None	1.00	5.00	Jennifer Silver	'93
PUTNAM VOYAGER; A	Capital Appreciation	3,027.4	10.86	9,662.00	10,389.00	19,063.00	0.0	225-1581	617-292-1000	5.75	0.25	None	Matthew A. Weatherbie	'83
PUTNAM VOYAGER; B	Capital Appreciation	846.1	10.65	9,638.00	10,308.00	☆	0.0	225-1581	617-292-1000	None	1.00	5.00	Matthew A. Weatherbie	'92
QUANT BOS FRN G&I; SHS	International	28.3	10.68	10,491.00	12,694.00	12,158.00	1.3	331-1244	617-259-1144	None	0.50	1.00	Davis/Umstead	'87/'94
QUANT BOS GR & INC; A	Growth Income	3.9	13.82	9,971.00	10,054.00	☆	1.6	331-1244	617-259-1144	None	None	None	Stonberg/Esielonis	'91/'93
QUANT BOS GR & INC; SHS	Growth Income	35.5	13.79	9,949.00	9,996.00	16,529.00	1.0	331-1244	617-259-1144	None	0.50	1.00	Stonberg/Esielonis	'85/'93
QUANT BOS NUMERIC; A	Small Company Growth	28.8	14.24	9,205.00	10,356.00	☆	0.0	331-1244	617-259-1144	None	None	None	John C. Bogle, Jr.	'93
QUANT BOS NUMERIC; SHS	Small Company Growth	42.6	14.10	9,198.00	10,301.00	☆	0.0	331-1244	617-259-1144	None	0.50	1.00	John C. Bogle, Jr.	'92
QUEST FOR VALUE FUND; A	Capital Appreciation	237.2	11.90	10,154.00	10,137.00	16,767.00	0.3	232-3863	None	5.50	0.50	None	Eileen Rominger	'89
QUEST FOR VALUE FUND; B	Capital Appreciation	9.3	11.87	10,145.00	☆	☆	0.0	232-3863	None	None	1.00	5.00	Eileen Rominger	'93
QUEST FOR VALUE FUND; C ✿	Capital Appreciation	1.9	11.86	10,137.00	☆	☆	0.0	232-3863	None	None	1.00	1.00	Eileen Rominger	'93
QUEST VALUE GLBL EQ; A	Global	149.1	14.09	10,188.00	11,354.00	☆	0.2	232-3863	None	5.50	0.50	None	R.J. Glasebrook II	'90
QUEST VALUE GLBL EQ; B	Global	5.6	14.03	10,174.00	☆	☆	0.0	232-3863	None	None	1.00	5.00	R.J. Glasebrook II	'93
QUEST VALUE GLBL EQ; C ✿	Global	0.9	14.03	10,174.00	☆	☆	0.0	232-3863	None	None	1.00	1.00	R.J. Glasebrook II	'93
QUEST VALUE GLBL INC; A	World Income	17.7	8.51	9,777.00	9,746.00	☆	6.9	232-3863	None	3.00	0.25	None	Robert J. Bluestone	'91
QUEST VALUE GLBL INC; B	World Income	1.1	8.53	9,758.00	☆	☆	0.0	232-3863	None	None	1.00	5.00	Robert J. Bluestone	'93
QUEST VALUE GLBL INC; C ✿	World Income	0.2	8.53	9,759.00	☆	☆	0.0	232-3863	None	None	1.00	1.00	Robert J. Bluestone	'93
QUEST VALUE GOVT INC; A	Fixed Income	143.1	10.98	9,860.00	9,726.00	14,232.00	5.1	232-3863	None	4.75	0.30	None	Robert J. Bluestone	'88
QUEST VALUE GOVT INC; B	Fixed Income	4.9	10.97	9,854.00	☆	☆	0.0	232-3863	None	None	1.00	5.00	Robert J. Bluestone	'93
QUEST VALUE GOVT INC; C ✿	Fixed Income	1.0	10.97	9,846.00	☆	☆	0.0	232-3863	None	None	1.00	1.00	Robert J. Bluestone	'93
QUEST VALUE GR & INC; A	Growth Income	28.9	9.75	10,249.00	10,710.00	☆	3.0	232-3863	None	4.75	0.40	None	Colin Glinsman	'92
QUEST VALUE GR & INC; B	Growth Income	1.6	9.74	10,236.00	☆	☆	0.0	232-3863	None	None	1.00	5.00	Colin Glinsman	'93
QUEST VALUE GR & INC; C ✿	Growth Income	0.3	9.75	10,235.00	☆	☆	0.0	232-3863	None	None	1.00	1.00	Colin Glinsman	'93
QUEST VALUE INV QUAL; A	Fixed Income	51.1	9.98	9,651.00	9,587.00	☆	6.6	232-3863	None	4.75	0.40	None	Robert J. Bluestone	'90
QUEST VALUE INV QUAL; B	Fixed Income	4.6	9.98	9,636.00	☆	☆	0.0	232-3863	None	None	1.00	5.00	Robert J. Bluestone	'93
QUEST VALUE INV QUAL; C ✿	Fixed Income	2.2	9.98	9,637.00	☆	☆	0.0	232-3863	None	None	1.00	1.00	Robert J. Bluestone	'93
QUEST VALUE OPPTY; A	Flexible	134.4	18.67	10,366.00	10,555.00	19,796.00	1.7	232-3863	None	5.50	0.50	None	R.J. Glasebrook II	'89
QUEST VALUE OPPTY; B	Flexible	15.0	18.61	10,350.00	☆	☆	0.0	232-3863	None	None	1.00	5.00	R.J. Glasebrook II	'93
QUEST VALUE OPPTY; C ✿	Flexible	2.4	18.61	10,356.00	☆	☆	0.0	232-3863	None	None	1.00	1.00	R.J. Glasebrook II	'93
QUEST VALUE SM CAP; A	Small Company Growth	116.6	15.52	9,568.00	10,035.00	18,105.00	0.0	232-3863	None	5.50	0.50	None	Jenny Beth Jones	'89
QUEST VALUE SM CAP; B	Small Company Growth	10.8	15.46	9,561.00	☆	☆	0.0	232-3863	None	None	1.00	5.00	Jenny Beth Jones	'93
QUEST VALUE SM CAP; C ✿	Small Company Growth	1.3	15.47	9,567.00	☆	☆	0.0	232-3863	None	None	1.00	1.00	Jenny Beth Jones	'93
RAINBOW FUND	Capital Appreciation	1.7	4.96	9,502.00	9,710.00	10,867.00	0.0	None	212-983-2980	None	None	None	Robert M. Furman	'74
RBB BALANCED	Balanced	0.8	10.48	10,153.00	10,527.00	16,422.00	4.2	888-9723	212-878-0600	4.75	0.40	None	Gayland Gee	'92
RBB BEA; EMERG MARKETS ◪	Emerging Markets	96.5	20.56	9,423.00	12,704.00	☆	0.5	888-9723	212-878-0600	None	None	1.50	Emilio Bassini	'93
RBB BEA; INTL EQ ◪	International	585.6	19.21	10,100.00	11,619.00	☆	0.3	888-9723	212-878-0600	None	None	1.00	Emilio Bassini	'92
RBB BEA; STRAT FXD INC ◪	Fixed Income	138.9	15.54	9,918.00	10,323.00	☆	9.2	888-9723	212-878-0600	None	None	0.50	BEA Associates	'93
RBB GOVT SECS	Fixed Income	55.5	9.65	9,880.00	9,797.00	☆	8.0	888-9723	212-878-0600	4.75	0.40	None	Robert Morgan	'92
RBRTSN STEPH CONTRARIAN	Growth	640.5	11.85	9,564.00	11,618.00	☆	0.0	766-3863	415-781-9700	None	0.75	None	Paul Stephens	'93
RBRTSN STEPH EMERGING GR	Small Company Growth	168.6	16.87	9,114.00	11,523.00	21,134.00	0.0	766-3863	415-781-9700	None	0.25	None	Robert Czepiel	'87

★ PUTNAM NEW OPPTY; A & B--Fund has been reclassified from Midcap to Growth.

★ PUTNAM VISTA; A & B--Fund has been reclassified from Midcap to Growth.

PERFORMANCE OF MUTUAL FUNDS (continued)

FUND NAME	OBJECTIVE	TOTAL NET ASSETS ($ MIL) 5/31/94	NET ASSET $ VALUE 6/30/94	PERFORMANCE (Return on initial $10,000 Investment) 3/31/94-6/30/94	6/30/93-6/30/94	6/30/89-6/30/94	DIVIDEND YIELD % 6/94	PHONE NUMBER 800	In-State	FEES Load	12b-1	Redemption	MANAGER	SINCE
RBRTSN STEPH VALUE PLUS	Small Company Growth	45.1	12.96	9,565.00	11,115.00	☆	0.0	766-3863	415-781-9700	None	None	None	Ron Elijah	'92
RCM FUND	Growth	44.0	19.57	9,505.00	☆	☆	0.0	None	810-644-2701	None	None	None	George P. Schwartz	'93
REA-GRAHAM BALANCED	Global Flexible	17.3	13.05	9,886.00	9,652.00	11,406.00	0.6	433-1998	310-208-2282	4.75	0.35	None	Rea/Rea	'82/'82
REGIS ACADIAN EMRG MKTS	Emerging Markets	4.4	11.29	8,705.00	11,580.00	☆	0.0	638-7983	617-557-8000	None	None	None	Team Managed	'93
REGIS ACADIAN INTL EQ	International	2.3	12.02	10,256.00	11,514.00	☆	0.0	638-7983	617-557-8000	None	None	None	Team Managed	'93
REGIS C&B BALANCED	Balanced	31.9	11.78	10,043.00	10,115.00	☆	3.9	638-7983	617-557-8000	None	None	None	Thompson/Medveckis	'89/'89
REGIS C&B EQUITY	Growth	202.7	12.72	10,168.00	10,355.00	☆	2.3	638-7983	617-557-8000	None	None	None	Thompson/Medveckis	'90/'90
REGIS DSI DISCIP VALUE	Equity Income	43.3	10.68	10,171.00	10,507.00	☆	1.9	638-7983	617-557-8000	None	None	None	Ronald L. McCullough	'89
REGIS DSI LTD MAT BOND	Fixed Income	29.4	9.50	9,969.00	9,861.00	☆	6.0	638-7983	617-557-8000	None	None	None	Michael H. Porreca	'89
REGIS FMA SMALL COMPANY	Small Company Growth	20.2	11.14	9,393.00	10,548.00	☆	0.2	638-7983	617-557-8000	None	None	None	Patricia Falkowski	'92
REGIS FMA SPECTRUM	Flexible	16.9	10.15	9,912.00	10,048.00	☆	1.1	638-7983	617-557-8000	None	None	None	Patricia Falkowski	'90
REGIS ICM BALANCED	Balanced	0.2	9.94	10,102.00	☆	☆	0.0	638-7983	617-557-8000	None	None	None	McCleary/Nelson	'93/'93
REGIS ICM EQUITY	Growth Income	2.6	9.97	10,101.00	☆	☆	0.0	638-7983	617-557-8000	None	None	None	David Nelson	'93
REGIS ICM FIXED INCOME	Fixed Income	13.5	9.80	9,811.00	9,859.00	☆	4.6	638-7983	617-557-8000	None	None	None	John Evans	'92
REGIS ICM SMALL COMPANY	Small Company Growth	101.6	15.68	9,637.00	10,303.00	20,760.00	0.4	638-7983	617-557-8000	None	None	None	Robert D. McDorman, Jr.	'89
REGIS SAMI PRFD STK INC	Utility	79.0	9.47	9,804.00	10,082.00	☆	6.3	638-7983	617-557-8000	None	None	None	Scott T. Fleming	'92
REGIS SIRACH FIXED INC	Fixed Income	12.0	9.43	9,804.00	☆	☆	0.0	638-7983	617-557-8000	None	None	None	Stephen Romano	'93
REGIS SIRACH GROWTH	Growth	85.3	9.31	9,698.00	☆	☆	0.0	638-7983	617-557-8000	None	None	None	George Kauffman	'93
REGIS SIRACH SH-TM RSVS	Fixed Income	21.5	10.09	10,080.00	☆	☆	0.0	638-7983	617-557-8000	None	None	None	Stephen Romano	'93
REGIS SIRACH SPEC EQ	Small Company Growth	486.9	15.01	9,271.00	9,765.00	☆	0.0	638-7983	617-557-8000	None	None	None	Harvey Bateman	'89
REGIS SIRACH STRAT BAL	Balanced	100.2	9.30	9,728.00	☆	☆	0.0	638-7983	617-557-8000	None	None	None	George Kauffman	'93
REGIS STRLG PTNR BAL	Balanced	54.9	11.04	9,727.00	10,174.00	☆	2.8	638-7983	617-557-8000	None	None	None	Paul Ersham	'91
REGIS STRLG PTNR EQ	Equity Income	21.9	12.03	9,555.00	10,296.00	☆	1.2	638-7983	617-557-8000	None	None	None	Paul Ersham	'91
REGIS STRLG PTNR SHT FXD	Fixed Income	23.2	9.80	9,991.00	10,160.00	☆	5.0	638-7983	617-557-8000	None	None	None	Dave Ralston	'92
REGIS TS&W EQUITY	Growth Income	35.0	10.54	10,038.00	10,083.00	☆	1.5	638-7983	617-557-8000	None	None	None	Whitworth/Ferwerda	'92/'92
REGIS TS&W FIXED INCOME	Fixed Income	30.6	9.73	9,807.00	9,674.00	☆	4.7	638-7983	617-557-8000	None	None	None	Charles Gomer	'92
REGIS TS&W INTL EQUITY	International	39.4	13.16	10,023.00	12,335.00	☆	0.4	638-7983	617-557-8000	None	None	None	G.D. Rothenberg	'92
REICH & TANG EQUITY	Midcap	91.2	17.14	9,971.00	10,474.00	15,408.00	1.3	221-3079	212-476-5055	None	None	None	Robert Hoerle	'85
REICH & TANG GOVT SEC	Fixed Income	18.7	N/A	N/A	N/A	N/A	0.0	221-3079	212-476-5055	None	None	None	Molly Flewharty	'88
REMBRANDT BALANCED; INV	Flexible	2.5	9.54	9,937.00	9,987.00	☆	2.6	443-4725	None	4.50	0.30	None	Cerney/Rumas/Gidley	'93/'93
REMBRANDT BALANCED; TR	Flexible	54.6	9.54	9,943.00	10,002.00	☆	2.9	443-4725	None	None	None	None	Cerney/Rumas/Gidley	'93/'93
REMBRANDT GLBL FXD; INV	World Income	0.1	10.13	9,902.00	10,248.00	☆	5.5	443-4725	None	4.50	0.25	None	Hellen/Crijns	'93/'93
REMBRANDT GLBL FXD; TR	World Income	16.4	10.15	9,922.00	10,283.00	☆	5.7	443-4725	None	None	None	None	Hellen/Crijns	'93/'93
REMBRANDT GROWTH; INV	Growth	1.2	9.82	9,871.00	9,771.00	☆	1.3	443-4725	None	4.50	0.30	None	Bonetti/Dibble/Ellefson	'93/'93
REMBRANDT GROWTH; TR	Growth	98.6	9.81	9,878.00	9,803.00	☆	1.6	443-4725	None	None	None	None	Bonetti/Dibble/Ellefson	'93/'93
REMBRANDT INTL EQ; INV	International	1.0	12.82	10,248.00	11,731.00	☆	0.0	443-4725	None	4.50	0.30	None	Gijs Dorrasteijn	'93
REMBRANDT INTL EQ; TR	International	29.6	12.86	10,263.00	11,756.00	☆	0.0	443-4725	None	None	None	None	Gijs Dorrasteijn	'93
REMBRANDT SH/INT GVT; INV	Fixed Income	0.1	9.53	9,913.00	9,820.00	☆	4.3	443-4725	None	4.50	0.25	None	Gidley/Pratt	'93/'93
REMBRANDT SH/INT GVT; TR	Fixed Income	100.9	9.54	9,920.00	9,853.00	☆	4.5	443-4725	None	None	None	None	Gidley/Pratt	'93/'93
REMBRANDT SMALL CAP; INV	Small Company Growth	0.2	9.34	9,331.00	9,930.00	☆	0.1	443-4725	None	4.50	0.30	None	Barbara Knapp	'93
REMBRANDT SMALL CAP; TR	Small Company Growth	43.7	9.34	9,346.00	9,971.00	☆	0.3	443-4725	None	None	None	None	Barbara Knapp	'93
REMBRANDT TXBL FXD; INV	Fixed Income	0.5	9.55	9,845.00	9,814.00	☆	4.7	443-4725	None	4.50	0.25	None	Gidley/Pratt	'93/'93
REMBRANDT TXBL FXD; TR	Fixed Income	105.0	9.54	9,851.00	9,855.00	☆	4.9	443-4725	None	None	None	None	Gidley/Pratt	'93/'93
REMBRANDT VALUE; INV	Growth	0.6	9.99	10,318.00	10,027.00	☆	2.8	443-4725	None	4.50	0.30	None	Corney/Rumas	'93/'93
REMBRANDT VALUE; TR	Growth	49.7	9.98	10,315.00	10,049.00	☆	3.1	443-4725	None	None	None	None	Corney/Rumas	'93/'93

RET SYS CORE EQUITY	Growth Income	3.4	11.76	9,751.00	10,103.00	☆	1.2	772-3615	212-503-0160	None	0.20	None	Retirement System Inv.	'91
RET SYS EMERG GROWTH EQ	Small Company Growth	1.6	12.40	9,561.00	11,135.00	☆	0.0	772-3615	212-503-0160	None	0.20	None	Putnam	'91
RET SYS INT FXD-INC	Fixed Income	3.0	10.58	9,880.00	9,889.00	☆	4.8	772-3615	212-503-0160	None	0.20	None	Retirement System Inv.	'91
RETIRE PLAN AMER BOND	Fixed Income	42.1	6.00	9,964.00	9,949.00	13,209.00	8.4	279-0279	505-983-4335	None	1.00	4.00	B. Clark Stamper	'90
RETIRE PLAN AMER CV SEC	Convertible Securities	45.7	16.41	9,869.00	10,106.00	☆	3.1	279-0279	505-983-4335	4.75	0.25	None	Shelby M.C. Davis	'92
RETIRE PLAN AMER GL VAL	Financial Services	51.3	11.13	10,127.00	10,150.00	☆	0.7	279-0279	505-983-4335	4.75	0.25	None	Shelby M.C. Davis	'91
RETIRE PLAN AMER GRO	Growth	64.1	14.24	10,007.00	11,126.00	15,947.00	0.4	279-0279	505-983-4335	None	1.00	4.00	Graham Tanaka	'87
RETIRE PLAN AMER RE SECS	Real Estate	16.3	15.62	10,265.00	☆	☆	0.0	279-0279	505-983-4335	4.75	0.25	None	Shelby M.C. Davis	'94
REYNOLDS BLUE CHIP GRO	Growth Income	28.7	13.63	9,715.00	9,414.00	13,561.00	1.0	338-1579	415-461-7860	None	None	None	Frederick L. Reynolds	'88
REYNOLDS OPPORTUNITY	Growth	5.1	8.85	9,124.00	9,385.00	☆	0.0	338-1579	415-461-7860	None	None	None	Frederick L. Reynolds	'92
REYNOLDS US GOVT BOND	Fixed Income	4.9	9.73	9,869.00	9,730.00	☆	5.7	338-1579	415-461-7860	None	None	None	Frederick L. Reynolds	'92
RIGHTIME BLUE CHIP FUND	Growth Income	227.2	32.86	10,040.00	10,439.00	16,035.00	0.7	242-1421	215-887-8111	4.75	0.50	None	Rights/Soslow/Houser	'87/'88
RIGHTIME FUND	Growth Income	154.3	35.26	9,930.00	10,496.00	15,881.00	0.0	242-1421	215-887-8111	None	0.75	None	Rights/Soslow/Houser	'85/'88
RIGHTIME GOVERNMENT SEC	Fixed Income	28.0	13.01	9,992.00	9,876.00	11,687.00	5.0	242-1421	215-887-8111	4.75	0.25	None	Rights/Soslow/Houser	'86/'86
RIGHTIME MIDCAP FUND	Midcap	65.1	28.26	10,039.00	10,248.00	☆	0.0	242-1421	215-887-8111	4.75	0.50	None	Rights/Soslow/Houser	'92/'92
RIGHTIME SOC AWARENESS	Growth	7.9	26.69	10,038.00	9,811.00	☆	0.0	242-1421	215-887-8111	4.75	0.50	None	Rights/Soslow/Houser	'90/'90
RIMCO BOND	Fixed Income	47.4	9.34	9,864.00	9,856.00	☆	5.5	934-3883	202-835-4280	3.50	None	None	Roger Marshall	'92
RIMCO STOCK	Growth Income	59.2	11.67	10,040.00	10,708.00	☆	1.4	934-3883	202-835-4280	3.50	None	None	Philip Tasho	'92
RIVERFRONT INCOME EQUITY ☚	Equity Income	N/A	10.45	10,412.00	10,740.00	☆	3.0	424-2295	None	4.50	0.25	None	SunBank	'92
RIVERFRONT US GOVT INC ☚	Fixed Income	N/A	9.15	9,818.00	9,636.00	☆	5.7	424-2295	None	4.50	0.25	None	Provident Bank	'92
RIVERSIDE CAP EQUITY ★	Growth	79.5	12.67	9,953.00	11,177.00	☆	0.5	662-4203	None	3.00	0.25	None	John Ray	'91
RIVERSIDE CAP FXD INC	Fixed Income	41.8	9.43	9,820.00	9,780.00	☆	5.9	662-4203	None	3.00	0.25	None	Alfred Jordan	'91
ROCHESTER BOND FD FOR GR	Convertible Securities	102.2	12.71	9,754.00	11,074.00	19,091.00	5.2	None	716-383-1708	3.25	0.75	None	Michael S. Rosen	'86
ROCKWOOD GROWTH	Capital Appreciation	0.7	15.30	9,846.00	9,659.00	10,164.00	0.0	None	208-522-5593	None	None	None	Ross H. Farmer	'86
ROD SQ INTL SEC INTL EQ	International	25.7	12.76	10,265.00	11,908.00	13,168.00	0.0	336-9970	302-651-8418	4.00	0.03	None	Multiple Managers	'87
ROD SQ MULTI-MGR GRO&INC	Growth Income	6.3	8.60	9,696.00	9,936.00	15,474.00	0.7	336-9970	302-651-8418	4.00	0.06	None	Multiple Managers	'87
ROD SQ MULTI-MGR GROWTH	Growth	67.5	15.63	9,911.00	10,572.00	16,359.00	0.0	336-9970	302-651-8418	4.00	0.02	None	Multiple Managers	'87
ROD SQ STRAT DVSD INC	Fixed Income	38.2	12.60	9,919.00	9,942.00	☆	5.6	336-9970	302-651-8418	3.50	0.03	None	Clayton Albright	'94
ROYCE FD EQUITY INCOME	Equity Income	87.0	5.32	9,835.00	10,128.00	☆	3.4	221-4268	212-355-7311	None	None	1.00	Charles M. Royce	'90
ROYCE FD OTC	Small Company Growth	21.4	6.41	9,831.00	11,161.00	☆	0.0	221-4268	212-355-7311	None	0.25	1.00	Charles M. Royce	'92
ROYCE FD PREMIER	Small Company Growth	138.6	6.39	9,892.00	10,916.00	☆	0.3	221-4268	212-355-7311	None	None	1.00	Charles M. Royce	'92
ROYCE FD VALUE ☚	Small Company Growth	174.9	9.37	9,771.00	10,243.00	14,299.00	0.5	221-4268	212-355-7311	None	0.69	1.00	Charles M. Royce	'82
RSI TR ACTIVELY MGD BD ✹	Fixed Income	135.7	26.00	9,834.00	9,771.00	14,847.00	0.0	772-3615	212-503-0160	None	None	None	Retirement System Inv.	'90
RSI TR CORE EQUITY ✹	Growth Income	136.5	33.83	9,971.00	10,077.00	15,485.00	0.0	772-3615	212-503-0160	None	None	None	Retirement System Inv.	'83
RSI TR EMERG GROWTH EQ ✹	Small Company Growth	45.3	31.59	9,149.00	10,263.00	17,371.00	0.0	772-3615	212-503-0160	None	None	None	Friess/Putnam	'90/'90
RSI TR INTERNATL EQUITY ✹	International	26.4	37.79	10,325.00	11,791.00	13,633.00	0.0	772-3615	212-503-0160	None	None	None	Morgan Grenfell Inv.	'84
RSI TR INTMDT-TERM BOND ✹	Fixed Income	90.1	25.24	9,906.00	9,886.00	14,528.00	0.0	772-3615	212-503-0160	None	None	None	Retirement System Inv.	'83
RSI TR SHORT-TERM INVEST ✹	Fixed Income	30.7	18.19	10,078.00	10,254.00	12,749.00	0.0	772-3615	212-503-0160	None	None	None	Retirement System Inv.	'90
RSI TR VALUE EQUITY ✹	Growth Income	34.5	25.19	9,886.00	9,832.00	12,948.00	0.0	772-3615	212-503-0160	None	None	None	NFJ Investment Grp Inc	'92
RUSHMORE AMER GAS INDEX	Natural Resources	206.0	10.79	9,838.00	8,930.00	13,000.00	3.9	621-7874	301-657-1517	None	None	None	Team Managed	'92
RUSHMORE USG INT TERM	Fixed Income	15.4	8.86	9,773.00	9,484.00	14,296.00	5.8	621-7874	301-657-1517	None	None	None	Team Managed	'92
RUSHMORE USG LONG TERM	Fixed Income	27.4	9.00	9,644.00	9,292.00	13,967.00	6.2	621-7874	301-657-1517	None	None	None	Team Managed	'92
RYDEX NOVA FUND	Capital Appreciation	31.1	9.77	9,949.00	☆	☆	0.0	820-0888	301-652-4402	None	None	None	Skip Viragh	'93
RYDEX OTC FUND	Capital Appreciation	0.3	8.76	8,994.00	☆	☆	0.0	820-0888	301-652-4402	None	None	None	Terry Apple	'94
RYDEX PRECIOUS METALS	Gold	17.5	8.34	8,042.00	☆	☆	0.0	820-0888	301-652-4402	None	None	None	Apple/Byrum	'93/'93
RYDEX URSA FUND	Capital Appreciation	98.8	10.54	10,343.00	☆	☆	0.0	820-0888	301-652-4402	None	None	None	Skip Viragh	'94
RYDEX US GOVT BOND FUND	Fixed Income	0.1	8.42	9,563.00	☆	☆	0.0	820-0888	301-652-4402	None	None	None	Mike Byrum	'94
S BERNSTEIN GOVT SH DUR	Fixed Income	178.5	12.40	10,000.00	10,146.00	13,874.00	3.5	None	212-756-4097	None	None	None	Investment Policy Group	'89
S BERNSTEIN INTL VALUE	International	1,091.9	16.66	10,060.00	11,726.00	☆	0.1	None	212-756-4097	None	None	None	Investment Policy Group	'92
S BERNSTEIN INTMDT DUR	Fixed Income	781.2	12.71	9,885.00	9,947.00	15,024.00	5.5	None	212-756-4097	None	None	None	Investment Policy Group	'89

★ RIVERSIDE CAP EQUITY--Fund has been reclassified from Midcap to Growth.

PERFORMANCE OF MUTUAL FUNDS (*continued*)

FUND NAME	OBJECTIVE	TOTAL NET ASSETS ($ MIL) 5/31/94	NET ASSET $ VALUE 6/30/94	PERFORMANCE (Return on initial $10,000 Investment) 3/31/94-6/30/94	6/30/93-6/30/94	6/30/89-6/30/94	DIVIDEND YIELD % 6/94	PHONE NUMBER 800	In-State	FEES Load	12b-1	Redemption	MANAGER	SINCE
S BERNSTEIN SH DUR PLUS	Fixed Income	542.0	12.40	10,024.00	10,172.00	14,194.00	4.4	None	212-756-4097	None	None	None	Investment Policy Group	'88
SAFECO COMMON EQUITY	Growth Income	271.3	13.30	10,238.00	11,511.00	19,641.00	1.5	426-6730	206-545-5530	None	None	None	Doug Johnson	'84
SAFECO COMMON GROWTH	Growth	168.7	18.34	9,592.00	10,865.00	15,923.00	0.0	426-6730	206-545-5530	None	None	None	Thomas Maguire	'89
SAFECO COMMON INCOME	Equity Income	190.7	16.86	9,974.00	10,114.00	14,233.00	4.7	426-6730	206-545-5530	None	None	None	Arley N. Hudson	'78
SAFECO COMMON NORTHWEST	Growth	38.9	12.26	9,870.00	10,345.00	☆	0.4	426-6730	206-545-5530	None	None	None	Charles Driggs	'92
SAFECO TR GNMA	Fixed Income	50.2	9.14	9,903.00	9,700.00	14,280.00	6.7	426-6730	206-545-5530	None	None	None	Paul Stevenson	'88
SAFECO TR HIGH-YLD BOND	Fixed Income	30.1	8.73	10,053.00	10,353.00	15,418.00	9.6	426-6730	206-545-5530	None	None	None	Ron Spaulding	'88
SAFECO TR INTMDT US TRES	Fixed Income	13.6	9.82	9,914.00	9,803.00	14,288.00	5.4	426-6730	206-545-5530	None	None	None	Ron Spaulding	'88
SAGAMORE BOND	Fixed Income	4.3	10.17	9,806.00	9,685.00	☆	6.2	273-3936	317-692-3900	2.75	0.25	None	Ramsey/Lynch/Donaldson	'91/'91
SAGAMORE GROWTH	Growth	13.2	10.52	9,895.00	9,435.00	☆	1.1	273-3936	317-692-3900	2.75	0.50	None	Ramsey/Lynch/Donaldson	'91/'91
SAGAMORE TOTAL RETURN	Balanced	10.9	10.49	9,834.00	9,797.00	☆	3.5	273-3936	317-692-3900	2.75	0.38	None	Ramsey/Lynch/Donaldson	'91/'91
SALOMON BROS CAPITAL	Capital Appreciation	105.2	16.96	9,070.00	9,460.00	13,847.00	0.1	725-6666	212-783-1301	None	None	None	Robert S. Salomon, Jr.	'90
SALOMON BROS INVESTORS	Growth Income	368.3	14.48	9,837.00	10,228.00	15,560.00	1.9	725-6666	212-783-1301	None	None	None	Fleischmann/White	'92/'92
SALOMON BROS OPPORTUNITY	Capital Appreciation	114.4	29.90	10,136.00	10,406.00	14,410.00	2.1	725-6666	212-783-1301	None	None	None	Irving Brilliant	'79
SAM SMALL-CAP FUND	Small Company Growth	87.2	13.18	9,627.00	10,576.00	12,055.00	0.0	445-9469	901-761-2474	None	None	None	Hawkins/Cates	'91/'94
SAM VALUE TRUST	Growth	478.6	18.40	10,496.00	12,166.00	19,829.00	0.5	445-9469	901-761-2474	None	None	None	Hawkins/Cates	'87/'94
SBSF FDS CAPITAL GROWTH	Midcap	4.3	7.29	9,605.00	☆	☆	0.0	422-7273	212-903-1200	None	0.25	None	Charles G. Crane	'93
SBSF FDS CONVERTIBLE SEC	Convertible Securities	57.4	11.33	9,812.00	10,274.00	16,044.00	5.2	422-7273	212-903-1200	None	0.25	None	Louis R. Benzak	'88
SBSF FDS SBSF FUND	Growth	118.9	14.96	9,914.00	10,575.00	16,393.00	1.3	422-7273	212-903-1200	None	0.25	None	Louis R. Benzak	'83
SCHAFER VALUE FUND	Growth Income	47.3	35.57	9,919.00	10,903.00	20,186.00	0.5	343-0481	212-644-1800	None	None	None	David Schafer	'85
SCHOONER FUND	Small Company Growth	3.9	25.06	9,972.00	10,071.00	☆	0.5	776-5033	310-247-3940	None	None	None	Gipson/Gray	'93/'94
SCHRODER CAP INTL EQUITY	International	417.3	22.05	10,180.00	12,660.00	15,942.00	0.4	344-8332	212-841-3848	None	0.25	None	Mark J. Smith	'89
SCHRODER CAP US EQUITY	Growth	19.4	8.20	9,868.00	10,268.00	17,532.00	0.6	344-8332	212-841-3848	None	None	None	Fariba Talebi	'91
SCHRODER CAP US SMALL CO	Small Company Growth	12.7	11.06	9,928.00	☆	☆	0.0	344-8332	212-841-3848	None	0.50	None	Ira L. Unschuld	'93
SCHWAB CAP INTL IDX	International	124.4	10.43	10,327.00	☆	☆	0.0	266-5623	None	None	None	0.75	Dimensional Fund Adv	'93
SCHWAB CAP SM-CAP IDX	Small Company Growth	57.7	9.32	9,539.00	☆	☆	0.0	266-5623	None	None	None	0.50	Dimensional Fund Adv	'93
SCHWAB INV 1000	Growth Income	526.9	12.16	9,959.00	10,024.00	☆	2.1	266-5623	None	None	None	0.50	Dimensional Fund Adv	'91
SCHWAB INV LONG-TM GOVT	Fixed Income	5.7	9.25	9,812.00	9,721.00	☆	6.6	266-5623	None	None	None	None	Regan/Ward	'93/'93
SCHWAB INV SHORT/INTMDT	Fixed Income	207.2	9.79	9,890.00	9,893.00	☆	5.5	266-5623	None	None	None	None	Regan/Ward	'91/'91
SCM PORTFOLIO FUND	Flexible	0.8	10.07	9,931.00	9,813.00	12,454.00	2.8	None	404-834-5839	None	None	1.00	Stephen McCutcheon	'89
SCOTTISH WIDOWS INTL	International	41.3	14.58	10,034.00	12,378.00	☆	0.0	243-8115	203-525-1421	5.50	0.25	None	Allan McKenzie	'90
SCUDDER BALANCED	Balanced	63.9	11.49	9,852.00	9,946.00	☆	2.4	225-2470	617-439-4640	None	None	None	Ward/Beaty/Hutchison	'93/'93
SCUDDER CAP GROWTH	Growth	1,329.6	18.57	9,562.00	9,840.00	14,048.00	0.0	225-2470	617-439-4640	None	None	None	Aronoff/Cox/Gadsen	'89/'84
SCUDDER DEVELOPMENT	Midcap	626.6	27.58	8,695.00	8,704.00	17,034.00	0.0	225-2470	617-439-4640	None	None	None	McKay/Chin	'88/'93
SCUDDER EMRG MKTS INCOME	World Income	70.4	10.65	9,884.00	☆	☆	0.0	225-2470	617-439-4640	None	None	None	Lincoln Rathnam	'93
SCUDDER GLBL SMALLCO	Global Small Company	248.5	15.54	9,817.00	11,044.00	☆	1.1	225-2470	617-439-4640	None	None	None	Moran/Franklin	'91/'91
SCUDDER GLOBAL FUND	Global	1,114.8	23.97	9,971.00	11,324.00	16,667.00	1.0	225-2470	617-439-4640	None	None	None	Holzer/Bratt	'86/'86
SCUDDER GNMA FUND	Fixed Income	506.9	13.97	9,899.00	9,677.00	14,382.00	7.2	225-2470	617-439-4640	None	None	None	Glen/Pruyne	'85/'85
SCUDDER GOLD FUND	Gold	140.9	12.64	9,166.00	10,626.00	12,292.00	1.9	225-2470	617-439-4640	None	None	None	Donald/Wallace	'88/'88
SCUDDER GROWTH & INC	Growth Income	1,796.5	17.00	10,314.00	10,764.00	16,923.00	2.7	225-2470	617-439-4640	None	None	None	Hoffman/Millard/Thorndike	'90/'87
SCUDDER INCOME FUND	Fixed Income	503.0	12.73	9,809.00	9,819.00	15,050.00	6.5	225-2470	617-439-4640	None	None	None	Hutchinson/Thorne	'86/'90
SCUDDER INTRN'L BOND	World Income	1,283.9	11.97	9,528.00	9,718.00	18,876.00	7.5	225-2470	617-439-4640	None	None	None	Teitelbaum/Greshin	'93/'88
SCUDDER INTRN'L- STK	International	2,305.0	42.64	10,183.00	11,927.00	15,784.00	0.8	225-2470	617-439-4640	None	None	None	Franklin/Bratt/Cheng	'76/'89
SCUDDER LATIN AMERICA	Latin American	623.4	19.90	9,234.00	13,588.00	☆	0.3	225-2470	617-439-4640	None	None	2.00	Games/Truscott/Cornell	'92/'92
SCUDDER MANAGED INT GOV	Fixed Income	22.4	9.40	9,911.00	9,844.00	☆	5.5	225-2470	617-439-4640	None	None	None	Glen/Pruyne	'93/'93

SCUDDER PACIFIC OPPTY	Pacific Region	427.3	15.89	10,278.00	11,987.00	☆	0.5	225-2470	617-439-4640	None	None	None	Allan/Bratt/Cornell	'94/'92
SCUDDER QUALITY GROW	Growth	112.6	15.10	9,889.00	10,041.00	☆	0.5	225-2470	617-439-4640	None	None	None	Ward/Beaty/Shields	'91/'91
SCUDDER SHRT TRM BND	Fixed Income	2,718.4	11.37	9,921.00	10,059.00	14,722.00	6.7	225-2470	617-439-4640	None	None	None	Poor/Gootkind/Dolan	'84/'89
SCUDDER ST GLBL INC	World Income	702.8	10.96	10,046.00	9,963.00	☆	8.1	225-2470	617-439-4640	None	None	None	Craddock/Teitelbaum	'91/'93
SCUDDER VALUE FUND	Growth	33.8	12.44	9,968.00	9,912.00	☆	0.9	225-2470	617-439-4640	None	None	None	Hall/Wallace	'92/'92
SCUDDER ZERO CP 2000	Fixed Income	23.5	11.30	9,775.00	9,528.00	15,160.00	6.7	225-2470	617-439-4640	None	None	None	Thorne/Heisler/Ross	'86/'88
SEAFIRST ASSET ALLOC ◪ ✪	Flexible	155.0	13.24	9,932.00	10,054.00	15,057.00	3.2	323-9919	None	None	None	None	Team Managed	'88
SEAFIRST BLUE CHIP FUND ✪	Growth	140.1	16.86	9,965.00	10,335.00	15,878.00	1.3	323-9919	None	None	None	None	Chris Helton	'93
SEAFIRST BOND FUND ✪	Fixed Income	67.3	10.55	9,900.00	9,857.00	14,245.00	5.4	323-9919	None	None	None	None	Steve Vielhaber	'94
SECOND FID EXCHANGE ☒	Growth	64.1	122.15	9,847.00	9,983.00	14,241.00	1.4	225-6265	617-482-8260	None	None	None	Robert S. Goodof	'87
SECURITY EQ EQUITY; A	Growth	363.1	5.30	9,833.00	10,312.00	16,988.00	2.0	888-2461	913-295-3127	5.75	None	None	Terry Millberger	'81
SECURITY EQ GLOBAL; A	Global	17.9	10.61	10,241.00	☆	☆	0.0	888-2461	913-295-3127	5.75	None	None	Stack/Saler	'94/'94
SECURITY GRO & INC; A	Growth Income	70.7	6.78	9,372.00	9,383.00	13,082.00	2.2	888-2461	913-295-3127	5.75	None	None	John Cleland	'66
SECURITY INC CORP BOND	Fixed Income	99.1	6.92	9,650.00	9,455.00	14,403.00	6.8	888-2461	913-295-3127	4.75	0.25	None	Jane Tedder	'85
SECURITY INC US GOVT	Fixed Income	8.7	4.52	9,759.00	9,648.00	14,374.00	6.3	888-2461	913-295-3127	4.75	0.25	None	Jane Tedder	'85
SECURITY ULTRA; A	Capital Appreciation	55.7	6.28	9,101.00	9,412.00	12,195.00	0.0	888-2461	913-295-3127	5.75	None	None	Ron Niedziela	'87
SEI DAILY CORP DAILY; A	Fixed Income	45.6	1.97	10,046.00	☆	☆	0.0	342-5734	610-254-1000	None	0.06	None	John Keough	'93
SEI DAILY GNMA; A ▮	Fixed Income	241.6	9.24	9,909.00	9,652.00	14,694.00	6.6	342-5734	610-254-1000	None	0.06	None	Paul Kaplan	'87
SEI DAILY INT GOVT; A ▮	Fixed Income	339.1	9.53	9,909.00	9,896.00	14,356.00	5.2	342-5734	610-254-1000	None	0.06	None	Paul Kaplan	'87
SEI DAILY SHT-TM GOVT; A ▮	Fixed Income	113.1	9.77	9,998.00	10,104.00	13,827.00	4.0	342-5734	610-254-1000	None	0.05	None	Paul Kaplan	'87
SEI DAILY SHT-TM GOVT; B ▮	Fixed Income	0.1	9.75	9,988.00	10,048.00	☆	3.8	342-5734	610-254-1000	None	0.36	None	Paul Kaplan	'90
SEI DAILY SHT-TM MTGE; A ▮	Fixed Income	5.4	9.74	9,973.00	10,134.00	☆	3.3	342-5734	610-254-1000	None	0.13	None	Seth Wolberg	'93
SEI INDEX BOND ▮	Fixed Income	53.4	9.84	9,895.00	9,857.00	14,441.00	5.7	342-5734	610-254-1000	None	0.05	None	Paul Greff	'93
SEI INDEX S&P 500 ▮	S&P Index	440.6	15.03	10,032.00	10,107.00	16,149.00	2.8	342-5734	610-254-1000	None	0.04	None	Todd Johnson	'94
SEI INSTL BALANCED; A	Flexible	52.7	11.21	9,578.00	9,593.00	☆	2.0	342-5734	610-254-1000	None	0.13	None	Anthony Gray	'92
SEI INSTL BOND; A	Fixed Income	108.0	10.17	9,767.00	9,591.00	14,855.00	5.8	342-5734	610-254-1000	None	0.09	None	Paul Rapponetti	'87
SEI INSTL CAP APPREC; A	Growth	815.2	14.76	9,676.00	9,820.00	17,120.00	1.8	342-5734	610-254-1000	None	0.09	None	Anthony Gray	'88
SEI INSTL CAPITAL GROWTH	Capital Appreciation	140.9	10.94	9,588.00	10,119.00	☆	1.7	342-5734	610-254-1000	None	0.01	None	Anthony Gray	'90
SEI INSTL EQU INC; A	Equity Income	421.9	13.60	10,289.00	10,319.00	15,542.00	3.5	342-5734	610-254-1000	None	0.09	None	John Brown	'88
SEI INSTL INTMDT BD; A	Fixed Income	309.4	9.77	9,839.00	9,675.00	13,998.00	5.6	342-5734	610-254-1000	None	0.08	None	Western Asset Mgmt.	'94
SEI INSTL MID-CAP; A	Midcap	99.2	10.46	9,373.00	9,673.00	☆	0.2	342-5734	610-254-1000	None	0.12	None	Nicholas Applegate Mgmt.	'93
SEI INSTL SM CAP GR; A	Small Company Growth	270.7	12.23	8,769.00	9,602.00	☆	0.0	342-5734	610-254-1000	None	0.14	None	Multiple Managers	'92
SEI INSTL VALUE; A	Growth Income	130.2	10.36	9,987.00	9,540.00	13,283.00	2.7	342-5734	610-254-1000	None	0.08	None	Robert Milne	'92
SEI INTL INTL EQTY; A ▮	International	514.3	10.71	10,181.00	10,974.00	☆	1.0	342-5734	610-254-1000	None	0.30	None	Richard Carr	'91
SEI INTL INTL FXD INC; A ▮	World Income	30.3	10.45	10,185.00	☆	☆	0.0	342-5734	610-254-1000	None	0.30	None	Gerri Boyle	'93
SELECTED AMERICAN SHARES	Growth Income	462.3	13.90	9,977.00	9,975.00	15,189.00	2.0	279-0279	505-983-4335	None	0.25	None	Shelby M.C. Davis	'93
SELECTED CAP GOVT INC	Fixed Income	9.2	8.74	9,998.00	9,963.00	14,059.00	5.7	279-0279	505-983-4335	None	0.25	None	B. Clark Stamper	'93
SELECTED SPECIAL SHARES	Small Company Growth	48.3	9.54	9,795.00	10,083.00	14,277.00	0.0	279-0279	505-983-4335	None	0.25	None	Shelby M.C. Davis	'93
SELIGMAN CAPITAL; A	Capital Appreciation	173.9	13.67	8,842.00	9,008.00	18,066.00	0.0	221-7844	212-850-1864	4.75	0.25	None	Loris D. Muzzatti	'88
SELIGMAN CAPITAL; D	Capital Appreciation	3.1	13.56	8,857.00	8,941.00	☆	0.0	221-7844	212-850-1864	None	1.00	1.00	Loris D. Muzzatti	'93
SELIGMAN COMMON STK; A	Growth Income	536.3	12.74	10,053.00	10,258.00	17,300.00	2.9	221-7844	212-850-1864	4.75	0.25	None	Charles C. Smith	'91
SELIGMAN COMMON STK; D	Growth Income	9.3	12.72	10,023.00	10,151.00	☆	2.0	221-7844	212-850-1864	None	1.00	1.00	Charles C. Smith	'93
SELIGMAN COMMUNICATN; A	Science & Technology	135.3	12.94	9,230.00	11,462.00	23,468.00	0.0	221-7844	212-850-1864	4.75	0.25	None	Paul Wick	'90
SELIGMAN COMMUNICATN; D	Science & Technology	31.5	12.76	9,206.00	11,308.00	☆	0.0	221-7844	212-850-1864	None	1.00	1.00	Paul Wick	'93
SELIGMAN FRONTIER; A	Small Company Growth	48.5	10.09	9,334.00	10,831.00	20,629.00	0.0	221-7844	212-850-1864	4.75	0.25	None	Paul Wick	'91
SELIGMAN FRONTIER; D	Small Company Growth	5.3	9.92	9,288.00	10,665.00	☆	0.0	221-7844	212-850-1864	None	1.00	1.00	Paul Wick	'93
SELIGMAN GROWTH; A	Growth	552.1	4.80	9,467.00	10,081.00	16,183.00	0.0	221-7844	212-850-1864	4.75	0.25	None	David Watts	'92
SELIGMAN GROWTH; D	Growth	1.6	4.67	9,359.00	9,795.00	☆	0.0	221-7844	212-850-1864	None	1.00	1.00	David Watts	'93
SELIGMAN HEND GL EMG; A	Global Small Company	38.0	10.38	9,549.00	11,671.00	☆	0.0	221-7844	212-850-1864	4.75	0.25	None	Iain Clark	'92
SELIGMAN HEND GL EMG; D	Global Small Company	30.0	10.30	9,537.00	11,581.00	☆	0.0	221-7844	212-850-1864	None	1.00	1.00	Iain Clark	'93

PERFORMANCE OF MUTUAL FUNDS (continued)

FUND NAME	OBJECTIVE	TOTAL NET ASSETS ($ MIL) 5/31/94	NET ASSET $ VALUE 6/30/94	PERFORMANCE (Return on initial $10,000 Investment) 3/31/94-6/30/94	6/30/93-6/30/94	6/30/89-6/30/94	DIVIDEND YIELD % 6/94	PHONE NUMBER 800	In-State	FEES Load	12b-1	Redemption	MANAGER	SINCE
SELIGMAN HEND GL INT; A	International	54.5	16.63	10,323.00	12,112.00	☆	0.1	221-7844	212-850-1864	4.75	0.25	None	Iain Clark	'92
SELIGMAN HEND GL INT; D	International	13.2	16.55	10,299.00	☆	☆	0.0	221-7844	212-850-1864	None	1.00	1.00	Iain Clark	'93
SELIGMAN HI INC BOND; A	Fixed Income	58.3	6.58	9,976.00	10,606.00	16,885.00	9.7	221-7844	212-850-1864	4.75	0.25	None	Dan Charleston	'89
SELIGMAN HI INC BOND; D	Fixed Income	6.4	6.59	9,951.00	☆	☆	0.0	221-7844	212-850-1864	None	1.00	1.00	Dan Charleston	'93
SELIGMAN HI INC GOVT; A	Fixed Income	61.4	6.71	9,830.00	9,831.00	13,849.00	7.0	221-7844	212-850-1864	4.75	0.25	None	Lenord Lovito	'94
SELIGMAN HI INC GOVT; D	Fixed Income	5.6	6.72	9,805.00	☆	☆	0.0	221-7844	212-850-1864	None	1.00	1.00	Lenord Lovito	'94
SELIGMAN INCOME; A	Income	311.3	13.41	9,839.00	10,037.00	16,024.00	5.3	221-7844	212-850-1864	4.75	0.25	None	Charles C. Smith	'91
SELIGMAN INCOME; D	Income	66.4	13.39	9,825.00	9,960.00	☆	4.7	221-7844	212-850-1864	None	1.00	1.00	Charles C. Smith	'93
SENTINEL BALANCED	Balanced	230.7	14.33	9,959.00	9,924.00	15,078.00	3.7	233-4332	802-229-3761	5.00	0.30	None	Rodney A. Buck	'82
SENTINEL BOND	Fixed Income	81.7	6.04	9,864.00	9,763.00	15,049.00	6.3	233-4332	802-229-3761	5.00	0.20	None	Richard D. Temple	'85
SENTINEL COMMON STOCK	Growth Income	865.6	28.17	10,093.00	10,049.00	15,832.00	2.7	233-4332	802-229-3761	5.00	0.30	None	Christopher E. Martin	'85
SENTINEL EMERGING GROWTH	Small Company Growth	95.6	5.27	9,652.00	10,105.00	☆	0.0	233-4332	802-229-3761	5.00	0.30	None	Louis E. Conrad II	'93
SENTINEL GOVERNMENT SEC	Fixed Income	119.0	9.56	9,866.00	9,703.00	14,653.00	5.8	233-4332	802-229-3761	5.00	0.20	None	David M. Brownlee	'93
SENTINEL GROWTH	Growth	51.1	15.78	9,455.00	9,354.00	13,888.00	0.2	233-4332	802-229-3761	5.00	0.30	None	Robert L. Lee	'93
SENTINEL WORLD FUND	International	33.1	12.77	10,151.00	11,882.00	☆	0.2	233-4332	802-229-3761	5.00	0.30	None	Sandor Cseh	'93
SENTRY FUND	Growth	76.9	14.57	10,094.00	10,444.00	16,836.00	1.5	533-7827	None	None	None	None	Keith Ringberg	'77
SEQUOIA FUND ☒	Growth	1,563.9	54.91	10,282.00	10,215.00	17,668.00	0.9	None	212-832-5280	None	None	None	Ruane/Cuniff	'70/'70
SEVEN SEAS EMERG MKTS	Emerging Markets	18.7	9.24	9,487.00	☆	☆	0.0	647-7327	617-542-9049	None	0.25	None	Rob Furdak	'94
SEVEN SEAS GROWTH & INC	Growth Income	23.3	9.65	9,917.00	☆	☆	0.0	647-7327	617-542-9049	None	0.25	None	Brent Dixon	'93
SEVEN SEAS INTMDT FUND	Fixed Income	19.2	9.24	9,897.00	☆	☆	0.0	647-7327	617-542-9049	None	0.25	None	Dudley Hall	'93
SEVEN SEAS MATRIX EQUITY	Growth	122.2	11.24	9,882.00	10,151.00	☆	2.4	647-7327	617-542-9049	None	0.25	None	Doug Holmes	'92
SEVEN SEAS S&P 500 INDEX	S&P Index	328.1	10.14	10,039.00	10,131.00	☆	3.2	647-7327	617-542-9049	None	0.25	None	Ann Eisenberg	'92
SEVEN SEAS S&P MIDCAP	Midcap	30.8	10.94	9,633.00	9,926.00	☆	2.0	647-7327	617-542-9049	None	0.25	None	Lynn Blake	'92
SEVEN SEAS S-T GOVT	Fixed Income	23.1	9.64	9,997.00	10,119.00	☆	4.[illegible]	647-7327	617-542-9049	None	0.25	None	John Reohr	'94
SEVEN SEAS YIELD PLUS	Fixed Income	1,252.3	9.98	10,080.00	10,328.00	☆	3.6	647-7327	617-542-9049	None	0.25	None	Mark Reilly	'94
1784 ASSET ALLOC	Flexible	6.9	9.59	9,955.00	9,828.00	☆	2.2	355-2673	None	None	0.25	None	Ablin/Clausen	'93/'93
1784 GOVT MED TM	Fixed Income	89.8	9.32	9,885.00	9,791.00	☆	6.4	355-2673	None	None	0.25	None	Jack Ablin	'93
1784 GRO & INC	Growth Income	121.6	10.16	9,637.00	10,460.00	☆	1.3	355-2673	None	None	0.25	None	Eugene Takach	'93
SHADOW STOCK	Small Company Growth	32.8	9.67	9,518.00	10,430.00	14,322.00	0.5	422-2766	816-471-5200	None	None	None	Schliemann/Whitridge	'87/'87
SHAWMUT FXD INCOME; INV	Fixed Income	10.0	9.51	9,842.00	9,692.00	☆	5.8	742-9688	508-626-7877	2.00	0.25	None	Max Brenninkmeyer	'93
SHAWMUT FXD INCOME; TR	Fixed Income	88.4	9.51	9,838.00	9,715.00	☆	6.1	742-9688	508-626-7877	None	None	None	Max Brenninkmeyer	'92
SHAWMUT GRO & INC EQ; INV	Growth Income	19.6	10.51	10,301.00	10,614.00	☆	1.8	742-9688	508-626-7877	4.00	0.25	None	Brendan Henebry	'93
SHAWMUT GRO & INC EQ; TR	Growth Income	156.2	10.51	10,309.00	10,642.00	☆	2.1	742-9688	508-626-7877	None	None	None	Brendan Henebry	'92
SHAWMUT GROW EQTY; INV	Growth	5.6	9.58	9,590.00	9,830.00	☆	0.4	742-9688	508-626-7877	4.00	0.25	None	Brad Bruce	'93
SHAWMUT GROW EQTY; TR	Growth	17.9	9.58	9,597.00	9,819.00	☆	0.3	742-9688	508-626-7877	None	None	None	Brad Bruce	'93
SHAWMUT INTMDT GOVT; INV	Fixed Income	13.3	9.51	9,863.00	9,781.00	☆	5.3	742-9688	508-626-7877	2.00	0.25	None	Glen Insley	'93
SHAWMUT INTMDT GOVT; TR	Fixed Income	62.5	9.51	9,869.00	9,805.00	☆	5.5	742-9688	508-626-7877	None	None	None	Glen Insley	'92
SHAWMUT LTD TM INC INV	Fixed Income	8.3	9.54	9,946.00	☆	☆	0.0	742-9688	508-626-7877	2.00	0.25	None	Duke/Spencer	'93/'93
SHAWMUT LTD TM INC; TR	Fixed Income	59.1	9.54	9,952.00	9,982.00	☆	5.1	742-9688	508-626-7877	None	None	None	Duke/Spencer	'92/'92
SHAWMUT SMALL CAP EQ; INV	Small Company Growth	18.5	10.37	9,792.00	10,599.00	☆	0.0	742-9688	508-626-7877	4.00	0.25	None	Peter Larson	'93
SHAWMUT SMALL CAP EQ; TR	Small Company Growth	97.7	10.38	9,806.00	10,618.00	☆	0.1	742-9688	508-626-7877	None	None	None	Peter Larson	'92
SIERRA CORP INCOME; A	Fixed Income	475.2	9.88	9,605.00	9,472.00	☆	8.6	222-5852	818-725-4620	4.50	0.25	None	James Goldberg	'90
SIERRA EMERGING GROWTH; A	Midcap	128.8	13.02	9,408.00	10,340.00	☆	0.0	222-5852	818-725-4620	4.50	0.25	None	James P. Goff	'93
SIERRA GROWTH & INCOME; A	Growth Income	127.0	11.30	10,027.00	10,667.00	☆	1.0	222-5852	818-725-4620	4.50	0.25	None	William M. Reigel	'93
SIERRA GROWTH; A	Growth	125.7	10.73	9,140.00	10,009.00	☆	0.0	222-5852	818-725-4620	5.75	0.25	None	Warren B. Lammert	'93

SIERRA INTL GROWTH; A	International	123.7	10.74	10,170.00	11,239.00	☆	0.2	222-5852	818-725-4620	4.50	0.25	None	Doug Dooley	'90
SIERRA SH TM HI QUAL; A	Fixed Income	21.4	2.39	9,976.00	☆	☆	0.0	222-5852	818-725-4620	3.50	0.25	None	Thomas M. Poor	'93
SIERRA SHT GLBL GOVT; A	World Income	229.6	2.34	9,985.00	10,108.00	☆	6.8	222-5852	818-725-4620	3.50	0.25	None	Margaret Craddock	'92
SIERRA US GOVT; A	Fixed Income	690.2	9.45	9,744.00	9,541.00	☆	7.7	222-5852	818-725-4620	4.50	0.25	None	Robert L. Davidson	'89
SIFE TRUST FUND	Financial Services	453.2	4.06	10,685.00	10,939.00	18,486.00	2.5	524-7433	510-937-3964	6.25	None	None	Marchese/Sloan/Edgar	'84/'91
SIG SELECT GOVT; INV	Fixed Income	117.3	9.92	9,902.00	9,792.00	☆	6.1	444-7123	None	None	0.25	2.00	E. Christian Goetz	'91
SIG SELECT GOVT; TR	Fixed Income	108.3	9.92	9,909.00	9,816.00	☆	6.3	444-7123	None	None	None	None	E. Christian Goetz	'91
SIG SELECT VALUE; INV	Growth Income	26.4	11.56	9,820.00	9,634.00	☆	1.5	444-7123	None	None	0.25	2.00	Kevin M. Lewis	'93
SIG SELECT VALUE; TR	Growth Income	85.4	11.56	9,826.00	9,655.00	☆	1.7	444-7123	None	None	None	None	Kevin M. Lewis	'93
SIT BALANCED	Balanced	1.2	9.55	9,932.00	☆	☆	0.0	332-5580	612-334-5888	None	None	None	Sit/Rogers	'93/'93
SIT BOND FUND	Fixed Income	3.3	9.46	9,924.00	☆	☆	0.0	332-5580	612-334-5888	None	None	None	Brilley/Rogers	'93/'93
SIT GROWTH	Midcap	303.3	11.08	9,210.00	9,538.00	17,019.00	0.2	332-5580	612-334-5888	None	None	None	Sit/Anderson	'82/'85
SIT GROWTH & INCOME	Growth Income	36.0	23.89	10,016.00	9,942.00	15,159.00	1.0	332-5580	612-334-5888	None	None	None	Mitchelson/Sit	'82/'82
SIT INTERNATIONAL GROWTH	International	63.9	14.90	10,171.00	12,551.00	☆	0.6	332-5580	612-334-5888	None	None	None	Kim/Sit	'91/'91
SIT US GOVERNMENT	Fixed Income	36.3	10.34	9,998.00	10,265.00	14,836.00	6.0	332-5580	612-334-5888	None	None	None	Brilley/Sit	'87/'91
SKYLINE EUROPE	European Region	25.0	9.61	9,118.00	9,477.00	☆	0.0	458-5222	312-670-6035	None	None	None	David Donnelly	'93
SKYLINE SPECIAL EQ ☒	Small Company Growth	213.0	17.09	9,666.00	10,844.00	23,851.00	0.0	458-5222	312-670-6035	None	None	None	William Dutton	'87
SKYLINE SPECIAL EQ II	Midcap	69.0	10.41	9,802.00	10,568.00	☆	1.2	458-5222	312-670-6035	None	None	None	Kenneth S. Kailin	'93
SM BARNEY WLD GLBL; A	World Income	89.3	11.74	9,708.00	10,121.00	☆	6.8	544-7835	212-698-5349	4.00	0.25	None	Team Managed	'91
SM BARNEY WLD GLBL; B	World Income	6.4	11.74	9,696.00	10,086.00	☆	6.5	544-7835	212-698-5349	None	0.70	1.00	Team Managed	'93
SM BARNEY WLD GLBL; C	World Income	3.2	11.74	9,710.00	10,127.00	☆	6.9	544-7835	212-698-5349	None	0.15	1.50	Team Managed	'93
SM BARNEY WLD INTL; A	International	476.4	17.27	9,920.00	12,597.00	21,007.00	0.0	544-7835	212-698-5349	4.50	0.25	None	Mauritis Edersheim	'86
SM BARNEY WLD INTL; B	International	225.1	17.08	9,896.00	12,513.00	☆	0.0	544-7835	212-698-5349	None	1.00	1.00	Mauritis Edersheim	'93
SM BARNEY WLD INTL; C	International	53.8	17.26	9,920.00	12,589.00	☆	0.0	544-7835	212-698-5349	None	0.25	1.50	Mauritis Edersheim	'93
SM BARNEY CAP APP; A	Capital Appreciation	58.9	12.63	8,894.00	9,132.00	☆	0.0	544-7835	212-698-5349	4.50	0.25	None	Thomas F. Narisco	'92
SM BARNEY CAP APP; B	Capital Appreciation	84.2	12.48	8,876.00	9,063.00	☆	0.0	544-7835	212-698-5349	None	1.00	1.00	Thomas F. Narisco	'92
SM BARNEY CAP APP; C	Capital Appreciation	13.9	12.63	8,894.00	9,172.00	☆	0.0	544-7835	212-698-5349	None	0.25	1.50	Thomas F. Narisco	'92
SM BARNEY INC & GRO; A	Growth Income	691.6	12.58	10,053.00	10,142.00	15,033.00	3.1	544-7835	212-698-5349	4.50	0.25	None	Bruce Sargent	'74
SM BARNEY INC & GRO; B	Growth Income	28.1	12.59	10,035.00	10,076.00	☆	2.4	544-7835	212-698-5349	None	1.00	1.00	Bruce Sargent	'92
SM BARNEY INC & GRO; C	Growth Income	3.1	12.58	10,053.00	10,150.00	☆	3.1	544-7835	212-698-5349	None	0.25	1.50	Bruce Sargent	'93
SM BARNEY INC RET; A	Fixed Income	42.3	9.46	10,046.00	10,208.00	14,013.00	4.4	544-7835	212-698-5349	1.50	None	None	Patrick Sheehan	'92
SM BARNEY INC RET; B	Fixed Income	3.2	9.46	10,037.00	10,172.00	☆	4.1	544-7835	212-698-5349	None	0.35	1.00	Patrick Sheehan	'92
SM BARNEY INC RET; C	Fixed Income	6.5	9.46	10,032.00	10,198.00	☆	4.3	544-7835	212-698-5349	None	0.15	1.50	Patrick Sheehan	'93
SM BARNEY MTHLY GOVT; A	Fixed Income	49.5	12.07	9,918.00	9,837.00	14,809.00	7.3	544-7835	212-698-5349	4.00	None	None	Patrick Sheehan	'92
SM BARNEY MTHLY GOVT; B	Fixed Income	3.4	12.06	9,892.00	9,766.00	☆	6.6	544-7835	212-698-5349	None	0.70	1.00	Patrick Sheehan	'92
SM BARNEY SH-TM TRES; A	Fixed Income	168.9	4.00	9,963.00	9,999.00	☆	4.5	544-7835	212-698-5349	None	0.35	None	Patrick Sheehan	'92
SM BARNEY US GOVT; A	Fixed Income	424.7	12.77	9,921.00	9,831.00	14,844.00	8.1	544-7835	212-698-5349	4.00	None	None	Patrick Sheehan	'92
SM BARNEY US GOVT; B	Fixed Income	22.9	12.76	9,896.00	9,761.00	☆	7.4	544-7835	212-698-5349	None	0.70	1.00	Patrick Sheehan	'92
SM BARNEY US GOVT; C	Fixed Income	14.5	12.78	9,917.00	9,823.00	☆	8.0	544-7835	212-698-5349	None	0.15	1.50	Patrick Sheehan	'93
SM BARNEY UTILITY; A	Utility	85.4	11.74	9,625.00	9,097.00	☆	6.8	544-7835	212-698-5349	4.50	0.25	None	Phil Miller	'90
SM BARNEY UTILITY; B	Utility	8.7	11.74	9,612.00	9,033.00	☆	6.0	544-7835	212-698-5349	None	1.00	1.00	Phil Miller	'92
SM BARNEY UTILITY; C	Utility	0.4	11.73	9,624.00	9,095.00	☆	6.8	544-7835	212-698-5349	None	0.25	1.50	Phil Miller	'93
SM BREEDEN INST INT GVT/	Fixed Income	12.8	9.71	9,934.00	9,984.00	☆	5.2	221-3138	None	None	None	None	Daniel C. Dektar	'92
SM BREEDEN INSTL SH GVT/	Fixed Income	272.8	9.90	10,082.00	10,308.00	☆	4.6	221-3138	None	None	None	None	Daniel C. Dektar	'92
SM BREEDEN INTMDT GOVT	Fixed Income	6.7	9.62	9,905.00	9,964.00	☆	5.2	221-3138	None	3.50	0.25	None	Daniel C. Dektar	'92
SM BREEDEN SHORT GOVT	Fixed Income	227.0	9.83	10,070.00	10,280.00	☆	5.1	221-3138	None	2.75	0.25	None	Daniel C. Dektar	'92
SM BRNY/SHRSN 1996 ☒	Balanced Target	79.5	9.43	10,011.00	10,135.00	15,389.00	5.1	None	212-720-9218	5.00	None	None	Williamson/Cohen	'89/'89
SM BRNY/SHRSN 1998 ☒	Balanced Target	115.0	7.81	9,936.00	9,920.00	☆	5.8	None	212-720-9218	5.00	None	None	Williamson/Cohen	'91/'91
SM BRNY/SHRSN 2000 ☒	Balanced Target	80.5	7.63	9,695.00	10,018.00	☆	4.4	None	212-720-9218	5.00	None	None	Richard Freeman	'91
SM BRNY/SHRSN ADJ RT; A	Fixed Income	284.7	9.78	10,004.00	10,159.00	☆	3.9	None	212-720-9218	None	0.75	None	Blackrock Financial Mgt	'92

PERFORMANCE OF MUTUAL FUNDS (continued)

FUND NAME	OBJECTIVE	TOTAL NET ASSETS ($ MIL) 5/31/94	NET ASSET $ VALUE 6/30/94	PERFORMANCE (Return on initial $10,000 Investment) 3/31/94-6/30/94	6/30/93-6/30/94	6/30/89-6/30/94	DIVIDEND YIELD % 6/94	PHONE NUMBER 800	In-State	FEES Load	12b-1	Redemption	MANAGER	SINCE
SM BRNY/SHRSN ADJ RT; B	Fixed Income	8.5	9.78	10,004.00	10,159.00	☆	3.9	None	212-720-9218	None	0.75	5.00	Blackrock Financial Mgt	'92
SM BRNY/SHRSN AGGR; A	Capital Appreciation	170.6	23.78	9,336.00	10,785.00	16,603.00	0.0	None	212-720-9218	5.00	0.25	None	Freeman/Fried	'83/'86
SM BRNY/SHRSN AGGR; B	Capital Appreciation	41.5	23.50	9,318.00	10,706.00	☆	0.0	None	212-720-9218	None	1.00	5.00	Freeman/Fried	'92/'92
SM BRNY/SHRSN APPREC; A	Growth	1,444.7	10.79	10,084.00	10,334.00	16,075.00	1.4	None	212-720-9218	5.00	0.25	None	Williamson/Cohen	'79/'79
SM BRNY/SHRSN APPREC; B	Growth	1,259.4	10.74	10,066.00	10,262.00	☆	0.7	None	212-720-9218	None	1.00	5.00	Williamson/Cohen	'92/'92
SM BRNY/SHRSN CONVRT; A	Convertible Securities	2.4	14.31	9,832.00	10,111.00	☆	5.1	None	212-720-9218	5.00	0.25	None	Levande/Swab	'92/'92
SM BRNY/SHRSN CONVRT; B	Convertible Securities	84.9	14.31	9,820.00	10,063.00	14,058.00	4.6	None	212-720-9218	None	0.75	5.00	Levande/Swab	'90/'86
SM BRNY/SHRSN DVSD; A	Fixed Income	76.4	7.77	9,833.00	10,139.00	☆	8.6	None	212-720-9218	4.50	0.25	None	Wells/Stein	'94/'94
SM BRNY/SHRSN DVSD; B	Fixed Income	2,493.4	7.77	9,820.00	10,088.00	☆	8.1	None	212-720-9218	None	0.75	4.50	Wells/Stein	'94/'94
SM BRNY/SHRSN EURO; A	European Region	2.2	14.11	9,972.00	11,652.00	☆	0.0	None	212-720-9218	5.00	0.25	None	Team Managed	'94
SM BRNY/SHRSN EURO; B	European Region	38.1	13.99	9,957.00	11,552.00	13,165.00	0.0	None	212-720-9218	None	1.00	5.00	Team Managed	'94
SM BRNY/SHRSN FDMNTL; A	Growth	156.7	7.97	10,231.00	10,777.00	17,488.00	1.0	None	212-720-9218	5.00	0.25	None	John Goode	'90
SM BRNY/SHRSN FDMNTL; B	Growth	394.8	7.95	10,219.00	10,705.00	☆	0.2	None	212-720-9218	None	1.00	5.00	John Goode	'92
SM BRNY/SHRSN GL BD; A	World Income	2.6	15.09	9,793.00	9,880.00	☆	6.5	None	212-720-9218	4.50	0.25	None	Wells/Stein	'94/'94
SM BRNY/SHRSN GL BD; B	World Income	68.2	15.09	9,780.00	9,829.00	14,871.00	6.0	None	212-720-9218	None	0.75	4.50	Wells/Stein	'94/'94
SM BRNY/SHRSN GL OPP; A	Global	35.0	29.05	9,966.00	11,079.00	12,451.00	0.1	None	212-720-9218	5.00	0.25	None	Team Managed	'94
SM BRNY/SHRSN GL OPP; B	Global	64.9	28.68	9,945.00	10,982.00	☆	0.0	None	212-720-9218	None	1.00	5.00	Team Managed	'94
SM BRNY/SHRSN GOVT; A	Fixed Income	7.4	9.33	9,886.00	9,889.00	☆	7.5	None	212-720-9218	4.50	0.25	None	James Conroy	'92
SM BRNY/SHRSN GOVT; B	Fixed Income	730.5	9.33	9,873.00	9,850.00	14,510.00	7.0	None	212-720-9218	None	0.75	4.50	James Conroy	'84
SM BRNY/SHRSN GR&INC; A	Growth Income	7.4	9.56	9,930.00	10,086.00	☆	2.4	None	212-720-9218	5.00	0.25	None	Gerken/Novello	'92/'92
SM BRNY/SHRSN GR&INC; B	Growth Income	199.1	9.58	9,917.00	10,022.00	☆	1.5	None	212-720-9218	None	0.75	5.00	Gerken/Novello	'92/'92
SM BRNY/SHRSN HI INC; A	Fixed Income	227.1	11.27	9,931.00	10,315.00	☆	9.9	None	212-720-9218	4.50	0.25	None	John Bianchi	'92
SM BRNY/SHRSN HI INC; B	Fixed Income	500.2	11.27	9,918.00	10,263.00	14,828.00	9.4	None	212-720-9218	None	0.75	4.50	John Bianchi	'88
SM BRNY/SHRSN INV GD; A	Fixed Income	12.0	11.30	9,592.00	9,490.00	☆	7.8	None	212-720-9218	4.50	0.25	None	George Mueller, Jr.	'92
SM BRNY/SHRSN INV GD; B	Fixed Income	405.8	11.30	9,580.00	9,437.00	15,095.00	7.2	None	212-720-9218	None	0.75	4.50	George Mueller, Jr.	'85
SM BRNY/SHRSN LTD TRES	Fixed Income	44.3	7.27	9,855.00	9,648.00	☆	4.5	None	212-720-9218	1.25	0.15	1.00	James Conroy	'91
SM BRNY/SHRSN METALS; A	Gold	21.0	19.31	9,213.00	10,326.00	12,587.00	0.0	None	212-720-9218	5.00	0.25	None	Ailsing O'Duffy	'90
SM BRNY/SHRSN METALS; B	Gold	55.6	19.08	9,200.00	10,253.00	☆	0.0	None	212-720-9218	None	1.00	5.00	Ailsing O'Duffy	'92
SM BRNY/SHRSN MGD GV; A	Fixed Income	378.0	12.33	9,964.00	9,950.00	15,028.00	6.4	None	212-720-9218	4.50	0.25	None	James Conroy	'90
SM BRNY/SHRSN MGD GV; B	Fixed Income	394.7	12.33	9,950.00	9,901.00	☆	5.9	None	212-720-9218	None	0.75	4.50	James Conroy	'92
SM BRNY/SHRSN SECTOR; A	Capital Appreciation	2.2	14.19	9,485.00	9,702.00	☆	0.8	None	212-720-9218	5.00	0.25	None	Elaine M. Garzarelli	'92
SM BRNY/SHRSN SECTOR; B	Capital Appreciation	102.5	14.14	9,439.00	9,626.00	13,781.00	0.1	None	212-720-9218	None	1.00	5.00	Elaine M. Garzarelli	'87
SM BRNY/SHRSN SHORT; A	World Income	40.6	6.26	9,911.00	9,698.00	☆	5.6	None	212-720-9218	3.00	0.25	None	Alan Brown	'90
SM BRNY/SHRSN SHORT; B	World Income	19.1	6.26	9,895.00	9,634.00	☆	4.9	None	212-720-9218	None	0.75	3.00	Alan Brown	'92
SM BRNY/SHRSN SP EQ; A ★	Small Company Growth	43.7	17.11	9,184.00	9,688.00	☆	0.0	None	212-720-9218	5.00	0.25	None	George Novello	'92
SM BRNY/SHRSN SP EQ; B ★	Small Company Growth	146.9	16.92	9,166.00	9,613.00	14,266.00	0.0	None	212-720-9218	None	1.00	5.00	George Novello	'90
SM BRNY/SHRSN STRAT; A	Flexible	6.7	16.50	10,012.00	10,448.00	☆	3.3	None	212-720-9218	5.00	0.25	None	William Carter	'92
SM BRNY/SHRSN STRAT; B	Flexible	317.7	16.51	9,947.00	10,319.00	15,801.00	2.0	None	212-720-9218	None	1.00	5.00	William Carter	'87
SM BRNY/SHRSN TEL GR; A	Science & Technology	76.2	11.50	9,939.00	10,036.00	16,385.00	0.0	None	212-720-9218	5.00	0.25	None	Guy Scott	'91
SM BRNY/SHRSN TEL GR; B	Science & Technology	190.5	11.37	9,921.00	9,966.00	☆	0.0	None	212-720-9218	None	1.00	5.00	Guy Scott	'92
SM BRNY/SHRSN TEL INC ☒	Specialty	67.8	106.48	10,649.00	10,605.00	16,504.00	4.0	None	212-720-9218	None	None	None	Guy Scott	'91
SM BRNY/SHRSN TOT RT; A	Growth Income	63.6	15.44	10,192.00	10,789.00	☆	7.7	None	212-720-9218	5.00	0.25	None	John Fullerton	'92
SM BRNY/SHRSN TOT RT; B	Growth Income	1,625.6	15.44	10,179.00	10,737.00	17,538.00	7.2	None	212-720-9218	None	0.75	5.00	John Fullerton	'85
SM BRNY/SHRSN UTIL; A	Utility	43.1	12.92	9,541.00	8,957.00	☆	6.8	None	212-720-9218	5.00	0.25	None	Levande/Mueller	'92/'92
SM BRNY/SHRSN UTIL; B	Utility	1,895.2	12.92	9,525.00	8,907.00	14,419.00	6.2	None	212-720-9218	None	0.75	5.00	Levande/Mueller	'88/'88

SM BRNY/SHRSN WORLD; A	World Income	59.5	1.68	9,982.00	9,752.00	☆	4.0	None	212-720-9218	None	0.90	None	Alan Brown	'91
SM BRNY/SHRSN WORLD; B	World Income	0.1	1.68	9,982.00	9,754.00	☆	4.0	None	212-720-9218	None	0.90	5.00	Alan Brown	'93
SM&R AMER NATL GOVT INC	Fixed Income	20.5	10.13	9,870.00	10,071.00	☆	5.4	231-4639	409-763-2767	4.50	None	None	Terry E. Frank	'93
SM&R AMER NATL PRIMARY	Fixed Income	15.8	1.00	10,078.00	10,274.00	☆	2.7	231-4639	409-763-2767	None	None	None	Vera M. Young	'92
SMALLCAP WORLD FUND	Global Small Company	3,143.0	21.97	9,611.00	11,233.00	☆	0.3	421-4120	714-671-7000	5.75	0.30	None	Multiple Managers	'90
SMITH HAYES SMALL CAP	Small Company Growth	7.2	11.59	9,674.00	10,121.00	☆	0.0	None	None	None	None	None	N/A	N/A
SOCIETY RIT BALANCED	Balanced	38.0	17.54	10,011.00	9,871.00	14,702.00	0.0	689-7097	216-689-7097	None	None	None	Michael Cobb	'87
SOCIETY RIT US GOVT	Fixed Income	16.0	17.33	9,858.00	9,676.00	14,430.00	0.0	689-7097	216-689-7097	None	None	None	Paul Lehman	'87
SOCIETY BALANCED	Balanced	102.8	9.46	10,026.00	☆	☆	0.0	362-5365	None	4.00	None	None	Aveni/Heine	'93/'94
SOCIETY DVSD STOCK	Growth	248.0	11.87	10,207.00	10,524.00	☆	1.8	362-5365	None	4.00	None	None	Larry Babin	'89
SOCIETY GROWTH STOCK	Growth	67.4	9.63	10,008.00	☆	☆	0.0	362-5365	None	4.00	None	None	Martha Kelly	'93
SOCIETY INTL GROWTH	International	60.1	12.50	10,154.00	11,973.00	☆	0.0	362-5365	None	4.00	None	None	Clay Finley	'91
SOCIETY INTMDT INCOME	Fixed Income	105.6	9.42	9,925.00	☆	☆	0.0	362-5365	None	2.00	None	None	Michael Bercher	'93
SOCIETY INVMT QUAL BOND	Fixed Income	107.5	9.29	9,881.00	☆	☆	0.0	362-5365	None	2.00	None	None	Richard Heine	'93
SOCIETY LTD TM INCOME	Fixed Income	85.4	9.99	9,964.00	10,047.00	☆	5.4	362-5365	None	2.00	None	None	Michael Bercher	'89
SOCIETY OH REGIONAL STK	Capital Appreciation	32.5	13.99	9,967.00	10,742.00	☆	1.2	362-5365	None	4.00	None	None	Lynn Hamilton	'89
SOCIETY SPEC GRO STOCK	Midcap	27.0	8.66	9,064.00	☆	☆	0.0	362-5365	None	4.00	None	None	Robert Gray	'93
SOCIETY SPEC VALUE STOCK	Growth Income	92.2	9.97	9,849.00	☆	☆	0.0	362-5365	None	4.00	None	None	Anthony Aveni	'93
SOCIETY STOCK INDEX	S&P Index	75.3	9.57	10,033.00	☆	☆	0.0	362-5365	None	4.00	None	None	Denise Coyne	'93
SOCIETY US GOVT INCOME	Fixed Income	165.2	10.53	9,935.00	9,875.00	☆	6.2	362-5365	None	2.00	None	None	Paul Lehman	'93
SOCIETY VALUE STOCK	Growth Income	173.6	9.69	10,185.00	☆	☆	0.0	362-5365	None	4.00	None	None	Judith Jones	'93
SOGEN INTERNATIONAL ⊠	Global	1,807.4	23.10	9,906.00	11,357.00	17,652.00	2.0	334-2143	212-399-1141	3.75	0.25	None	Jean-Marie Eveillard	'79
SOGEN GOLD FUND	Gold	23.8	10.94	9,580.00	☆	☆	0.0	334-2143	212-399-1141	3.75	0.25	None	Jean-Marie Eveillard	'93
SOGEN OVERSEAS FUND	International	211.8	11.57	10,026.00	☆	☆	0.0	334-2143	212-399-1141	3.75	0.25	None	Jean-Marie Eveillard	'93
SOUND SHORE	Growth	60.5	16.15	9,903.00	10,505.00	16,261.00	1.2	551-1980	207-879-0001	None	None	None	Kane/Burn	'85/'85
SOUTHTRUST VULCAN BOND	Fixed Income	32.5	9.89	9,859.00	9,788.00	☆	6.5	239-7470	None	4.00	None	None	Dave Howell	'93
SOUTHTRUST VULCAN STK	Growth	37.8	9.95	9,853.00	9,710.00	☆	1.9	239-7470	None	4.50	None	None	Bob Hardin	'93
SPECIAL PORTFOLIOS CASH ✪	Fixed Income	26.1	9.46	10,052.00	10,291.00	☆	6.8	800-2638	612-738-4000	None	None	None	Poling/Ott	'89/'89
SPECIAL PORTFOLIOS STOCK ✪	Capital Appreciation	73.0	30.48	8,830.00	9,022.00	17,498.00	0.0	800-2638	612-738-4000	None	None	None	Stephen Poling	'83
SS RESEARCH CAPITAL; A	Capital Appreciation	18.4	8.84	9,305.00	10,424.00	☆	0.0	882-3302	617-348-2000	4.50	0.25	None	Fredrick R. Kobrick	'93
SS RESEARCH CAPITAL; B	Capital Appreciation	56.3	8.77	9,300.00	10,367.00	☆	0.0	882-3302	617-348-2000	None	1.00	5.00	Fredrick R. Kobrick	'93
SS RESEARCH CAPITAL; C	Capital Appreciation	22.8	8.89	9,319.00	10,458.00	21,322.00	0.0	882-3302	617-348-2000	None	None	None	Fredrick R. Kobrick	'86
SS RESEARCH CAPITAL; D	Capital Appreciation	30.4	8.78	9,301.00	10,368.00	☆	0.0	882-3302	617-348-2000	None	1.00	1.00	Fredrick R. Kobrick	'93
SS RESEARCH GL ENGY; A	Natural Resources	29.8	11.84	11,117.00	8,764.00	☆	0.0	882-3302	617-348-2000	4.50	0.50	None	Dan Rice	'90
SS RESEARCH GL ENGY; B	Natural Resources	6.1	11.78	11,103.00	8,719.00	☆	0.0	882-3302	617-348-2000	None	1.00	5.00	Dan Rice	'93
SS RESEARCH GL ENGY; C	Natural Resources	0.9	11.90	11,132.00	8,802.00	☆	0.0	882-3302	617-348-2000	None	None	None	Dan Rice	'93
SS RESEARCH GL ENGY; D	Natural Resources	1.9	11.77	11,104.00	8,712.00	☆	0.0	882-3302	617-348-2000	None	1.00	1.00	Dan Rice	'93
SS RESEARCH GOVT INC; A	Fixed Income	714.3	11.95	9,882.00	9,949.00	14,972.00	6.7	882-3302	617-348-2000	4.50	0.25	None	Jack Kallis	'87
SS RESEARCH GOVT INC; B	Fixed Income	47.9	11.93	9,863.00	9,868.00	☆	5.9	882-3302	617-348-2000	None	1.00	5.00	Jack Kallis	'93
SS RESEARCH GOVT INC; C	Fixed Income	0.2	11.94	9,880.00	9,966.00	☆	7.0	882-3302	617-348-2000	None	None	None	Jack Kallis	'93
SS RESEARCH GOVT INC; D	Fixed Income	15.2	11.93	9,863.00	9,868.00	☆	5.9	882-3302	617-348-2000	None	1.00	1.00	Jack Kallis	'93
SS RESEARCH GROWTH; A	Growth	0.7	8.03	9,817.00	10,115.00	☆	0.7	882-3302	617-348-2000	4.50	0.25	None	Peter Woodworth	'93
SS RESEARCH GROWTH; B	Growth	1.3	7.98	9,803.00	10,038.00	☆	0.3	882-3302	617-348-2000	None	1.00	5.00	Peter Woodworth	'93
SS RESEARCH GROWTH; C	Growth	235.0	8.04	9,829.00	10,134.00	15,211.00	0.9	882-3302	617-348-2000	None	None	None	Peter Woodworth	'93
SS RESEARCH GROWTH; D	Growth	0.4	7.98	9,803.00	10,039.00	☆	0.3	882-3302	617-348-2000	None	1.00	1.00	Peter Woodworth	'93
SS RESEARCH SM CAP; A	Small Company Growth	15.3	8.04	8,894.00	☆	☆	0.0	882-3302	617-348-2000	4.50	0.25	None	Charles Glovsky	'94
SS RESEARCH SM CAP; B	Small Company Growth	22.6	8.01	8,880.00	☆	☆	0.0	882-3302	617-348-2000	None	1.00	5.00	Charles Glovsky	'94
SS RESEARCH SM CAP; C	Small Company Growth	3.5	8.07	8,907.00	☆	☆	0.0	882-3302	617-348-2000	None	None	None	Charles Glovsky	'93
SS RESEARCH SM CAP; D	Small Company Growth	9.1	8.01	8,870.00	☆	☆	0.0	882-3302	617-348-2000	None	1.00	1.00	Charles Glovsky	'94
STAGECOACH INST ASST ALL	Flexible	210.8	9.51	9,843.00	☆	☆	0.0	776-0179	None	None	None	None	Wells Fargo Nikko Adv.	'93

★ SM BRNY/SHRSN SP EQ; A & B--Fund has been reclassified from Midcap to Small Company Growth.

PERFORMANCE OF MUTUAL FUNDS (continued)

FUND NAME	OBJECTIVE	TOTAL NET ASSETS ($ MIL) 5/31/94	NET ASSET $ VALUE 6/30/94	PERFORMANCE (Return on initial $10,000 Investment) 3/31/94-6/30/94	6/30/93-6/30/94	6/30/89-6/30/94	DIVIDEND YIELD % 6/94	PHONE NUMBER 800	In-State	FEES Load	12b-1	Redemption	MANAGER	SINCE
STAGECOACH INST BD INDEX	Fixed Income	15.7	9.20	9,838.00	☆	☆	0.0	776-0179	None	None	None	None	Wells Fargo Nikko Adv.	'93
STAGECOACH INST GROW STK	Growth	48.4	10.02	9,543.00	☆	☆	0.0	776-0179	None	None	None	None	Jon Hickman	'93
STAGECOACH INST S&P 500	S&P Index	159.6	9.93	10,001.00	☆	☆	0.0	776-0179	None	None	None	None	Wells Fargo Nikko Adv.	'93
STAGECOACH INST SH-INT	Fixed Income	7.1	9.23	9,914.00	☆	☆	0.0	776-0179	None	None	None	None	Thomas/Glessman	'93/'93
STAGECOACH INST TRES ALL	Fixed Income	49.6	9.01	9,823.00	☆	☆	0.0	776-0179	None	None	None	None	Wells Fargo Nikko Adv.	'93
STAGECOACH ASSET ALLOC	Flexible	1,079.5	17.37	9,837.00	9,912.00	16,135.00	4.0	222-8222	None	4.50	0.05	None	Janic Derringer	'87
STAGECOACH CORP STOCK	S&P Index	252.8	31.44	10,020.00	10,044.00	15,410.00	1.9	222-8222	None	None	0.05	None	Hom/Gashman	'84/'84
STAGECOACH DVSD INCOME	Income	37.6	10.72	10,144.00	10,475.00	☆	3.0	222-8222	None	4.50	0.05	None	Wisniewski/Bissell	'92/'92
STAGECOACH GINNIE MAE	Fixed Income	247.6	10.46	9,863.00	9,800.00	☆	7.6	222-8222	None	4.50	0.05	None	Single/Niedermeyer	'91/'93
STAGECOACH GOVT ALLOC	Fixed Income	213.4	14.22	9,814.00	9,822.00	14,949.00	6.6	222-8222	None	4.50	0.05	None	Janic Derringer	'93
STAGECOACH GROWTH & INC	Growth Income	117.5	13.95	9,884.00	10,300.00	☆	1.5	222-8222	None	4.50	0.05	None	Wisniewski/Bissell	'90/'90
STAGECOACH VAR RATE GOVT	Fixed Income	28.8	10.43	9,956.00	10,084.00	☆	4.2	222-8222	None	3.00	0.05	None	Single/Glessman	'91/'92
STAND AYER WOOD EQUITY	Growth	81.3	28.87	9,686.00	10,328.00	☆	1.1	729-0066	617-350-6100	None	None	None	David H. Cameron	'91
STAND AYER WOOD FXD INC	Fixed Income	1,382.5	19.32	9,812.00	9,860.00	15,492.00	7.5	729-0066	617-350-6100	None	None	None	Caleb Aldrich	'93
STAND AYER WOOD GL FXD	World Income	136.6	18.07	9,643.00	☆	☆	0.0	729-0066	617-350-6100	None	None	None	Richard S. Wood	'93
STAND AYER WOOD INTL EQU	International	105.1	24.69	9,994.00	11,766.00	14,022.00	2.6	729-0066	617-350-6100	None	None	None	Clayson/Schoeck	'88/'93
STAND AYER WOOD INTL FXD	World Income	1,137.7	21.41	9,551.00	9,960.00	☆	6.3	729-0066	617-350-6100	None	None	None	Richard S. Wood	'91
STAND AYER WOOD SEC	Fixed Income	74.6	18.98	9,918.00	9,936.00	☆	7.9	729-0066	617-350-6100	None	None	None	Sweeney/Driscoll	'89/'89
STAND AYER WOOD SML CAP	Small Company Growth	86.1	43.94	9,563.00	11,368.00	19,945.00	0.0	729-0066	617-350-6100	None	None	None	Nicholas S. Battelle	'88
STAND AYER WOOD STAR	Fixed Income	320.2	19.35	10,006.00	10,210.00	13,615.00	5.3	729-0066	617-350-6100	None	None	None	Jennifer Pline	'93
STAR RELATIVE VALUE	Growth	63.0	11.33	9,901.00	10,467.00	☆	1.9	677-3863	513-632-5547	4.50	None	None	Joseph Belew	'91
STAR STELLAR; INV	Global Flexible	50.3	11.12	9,942.00	10,333.00	☆	2.0	677-3863	513-632-5547	4.50	0.25	None	Kirk Mentzer	'93
STAR STELLAR; TR	Global Flexible	47.2	11.12	☆	☆	☆	0.0	677-3863	513-632-5547	None	None	None	Kirk Mentzer	'94
STAR US GOVT INC	Fixed Income	49.6	9.47	9,868.00	9,808.00	☆	5.8	677-3863	513-632-5547	3.50	None	None	Kirk Mentzer	'93
STARBURST GOVT INC; INV	Fixed Income	74.7	9.66	9,960.00	9,874.00	☆	5.7	239-6669	205-558-6702	2.50	0.25	None	Dan Davidson	'92
STATE BOND COMMON STOCK	Growth	43.6	7.60	10,093.00	10,186.00	15,940.00	1.0	437-6663	612-835-0097	4.75	0.25	None	Keith Martens	'84
STATE BOND DIVERSIFIED	Growth Income	38.2	8.93	10,216.00	10,348.00	15,663.00	3.2	437-6663	612-835-0097	4.75	0.25	None	Keith Martens	'84
STATE BOND PROGRESS	Growth	8.8	N/A	N/A	N/A	N/A	0.0	437-6663	612-835-0097	4.75	0.25	None	Keith Martens	'84
STATE BOND US GOVT SEC	Fixed Income	14.0	4.84	9,873.00	9,670.00	14,190.00	6.5	437-6663	612-835-0097	5.00	0.25	None	Keith Martens	'85
STATE FARM BALANCED ◪	Balanced	348.2	29.83	9,932.00	10,103.00	18,395.00	3.0	None	309-766-2029	None	None	None	Kurt Moser	'91
STATE FARM GROWTH ◪	Growth	728.1	21.11	9,738.00	9,794.00	16,880.00	2.1	None	309-766-2029	None	None	None	Kurt Moser	'91
STATE FARM INTERIM ◪	Fixed Income	101.0	9.99	9,974.00	10,047.00	14,354.00	7.2	None	309-766-2029	None	None	None	Kurt Moser	'91
STATE ST MSTR INVEST; A	Growth Income	88.5	8.15	9,885.00	9,990.00	☆	1.5	882-3302	617-348-2000	4.50	0.25	None	Peter Bennett	'93
STATE ST MSTR INVEST; B	Growth Income	96.9	8.13	9,868.00	9,914.00	☆	0.8	882-3302	617-348-2000	None	1.00	5.00	Peter Bennett	'93
STATE ST MSTR INVEST; C	Growth Income	698.4	8.16	9,879.00	10,002.00	16,143.00	1.8	882-3302	617-348-2000	None	None	None	Peter Bennett	'88
STATE ST MSTR INVEST; D	Growth Income	12.3	8.14	9,855.00	9,909.00	☆	0.8	882-3302	617-348-2000	None	1.00	1.00	Peter Bennett	'93
STEADMAN AMER INDUSTRY ⊠	Capital Appreciation	2.1	1.21	8,582.00	8,288.00	5,426.00	0.0	424-8570	202-223-1000	None	None	None	Team Managed	N/A
STEADMAN ASSOCIATED FD	Equity Income	6.6	0.68	8,831.00	8,395.00	9,315.00	0.0	424-8570	202-223-1000	None	None	None	Team Managed	N/A
STEADMAN INVESTMENT ⊠	Growth	2.8	1.11	8,952.00	7,762.00	8,043.00	0.0	424-8570	202-223-1000	None	None	None	Team Managed	N/A
STEADMAN TECH & GROWTH ⊠	Growth	1.2	1.90	8,225.00	7,063.00	5,080.00	0.0	424-8570	202-223-1000	None	None	None	Team Managed	N/A
STEINROE CAPITAL OPP	Capital Appreciation	162.5	28.71	9,367.00	10,540.00	14,683.00	0.0	338-2550	None	None	None	None	Dunn/Santella	'91/'91
STEINROE GOVT INC	Fixed Income	48.3	9.48	9,868.00	9,774.00	14,273.00	5.9	338-2550	None	None	None	None	Michael T. Kennedy	'88
STEINROE INCOME FD	Fixed Income	156.2	9.36	9,875.00	9,931.00	14,700.00	7.4	338-2550	None	None	None	None	Ann Henderson	'90
STEINROE INTERNATIONAL	International	59.2	9.99	10,236.00	☆	☆	0.0	338-2550	None	None	None	None	Rockefeller Group	'94
STEINROE INTMDT BOND	Fixed Income	293.5	8.44	9,920.00	9,953.00	14,600.00	6.5	338-2550	None	None	None	None	Michael T. Kennedy	'88

STEINROE LTD MATURITY	Fixed Income	30.3	9.61	9,941.00	10,066.00	☆	4.9	338-2550	None	None	None	None	Lisa Wilhelm	'93
STEINROE PRIME EQTY	Growth Income	122.2	14.09	10,028.00	10,611.00	17,431.00	1.1	338-2550	None	None	None	None	Ralph Segall	'87
STEINROE SPECIAL FD	Growth	1,192.2	22.24	9,933.00	10,223.00	17,959.00	0.9	338-2550	None	None	None	None	Dunn/Peterson	'91/'91
STEINROE STOCK FUND	Growth	337.3	22.31	9,708.00	9,838.00	17,073.00	0.5	338-2550	None	None	None	None	Capital Management Grp	'91
STEINROE TOTAL RETRN	Equity Income	223.2	25.14	9,853.00	10,139.00	15,883.00	4.7	338-2550	None	None	None	None	Robert A. Christensen	'81
STEPSTONE BALANCED; INSTL	Flexible	160.1	11.26	9,903.00	10,096.00	☆	3.4	634-1100	213-236-5698	None	None	None	Carl J. Colombo	'91
STEPSTONE BALANCED; INVST	Flexible	8.1	11.26	9,903.00	10,096.00	☆	3.4	634-1100	213-236-5698	4.50	None	None	Carl J. Colombo	'92
STEPSTONE BLUE; INSTL	Growth	28.2	9.11	9,769.00	☆	☆	0.0	634-1100	213-236-5698	None	None	None	Harold C. Elliott	'94
STEPSTONE CV SECS; INSTL	Convertible Securities	6.6	9.25	9,770.00	☆	☆	0.0	634-1100	213-236-5698	None	None	None	Harold C. Elliott	'94
STEPSTONE EMRG GRO; INSTL	Small Company Growth	14.1	8.86	9,365.00	☆	☆	0.0	634-1100	213-236-5698	None	None	None	Seth Shalov	'94
STEPSTONE GRO EQU; INSTL	Growth	139.0	13.42	9,498.00	10,061.00	☆	0.5	634-1100	213-236-5698	None	None	None	Clyde Powers	'91
STEPSTONE GRO EQU; INVST	Growth	1.4	13.44	9,492.00	10,054.00	☆	0.5	634-1100	213-236-5698	4.50	None	None	Clyde Powers	'92
STEPSTONE GVT SECS; INSTL	Fixed Income	28.1	9.15	9,861.00	☆	☆	0.0	634-1100	213-236-5698	None	None	None	Stephen Blocklin	'94
STEPSTONE INT-TM; INSTL	Fixed Income	117.4	9.88	9,828.00	9,817.00	☆	5.8	634-1100	213-236-5698	None	None	None	Jim Atkinson	'91
STEPSTONE INT-TM; INVST	Fixed Income	8.6	9.88	9,828.00	9,817.00	☆	5.8	634-1100	213-236-5698	3.00	None	None	Jim Atkinson	'92
STEPSTONE LTD GOVT; INSTL	Fixed Income	38.2	9.64	9,928.00	10,029.00	☆	3.8	634-1100	213-236-5698	None	None	None	Martin Standish	'93
STEPSTONE LTD GOVT; INVST	Fixed Income	2.1	9.65	9,928.00	☆	☆	0.0	634-1100	213-236-5698	None	None	None	Martin Standish	'93
STEPSTONE VALUE; INSTL	Growth Income	143.1	13.17	9,982.00	10,254.00	☆	2.2	634-1100	213-236-5698	None	None	None	Richard H. Earnest	'91
STEPSTONE VALUE; INVST	Growth Income	10.1	13.17	9,982.00	10,307.00	☆	2.3	634-1100	213-236-5698	4.50	None	None	Richard H. Earnest	'92
STI CLASSIC AGGR GRO; INV	Small Company Growth	3.0	9.47	9,614.00	☆	☆	0.0	428-6970	None	3.75	0.40	None	Thomas Edgar	'94
STI CLASSIC AGGR GRO; TR	Small Company Growth	53.2	9.47	9,634.00	☆	☆	0.0	428-6970	None	None	None	None	Thomas Edgar	'94
STI CLASSIC BALANCED; INV	Balanced	2.3	9.49	9,788.00	☆	☆	0.0	428-6970	None	3.75	0.25	None	Tony Gray/Earl Denney	'94/'94
STI CLASSIC BALANCED; TR	Balanced	90.4	9.43	9,828.00	☆	☆	0.0	428-6970	None	None	None	None	Tony Gray/Earl Denney	'93/'93
STI CLASSIC CAP GRO; INV	Growth	170.7	11.45	9,660.00	9,801.00	☆	0.5	428-6970	None	3.75	0.49	None	Anthony Gray	'92
STI CLASSIC CAP GRO; TR	Growth	878.2	11.45	9,677.00	9,863.00	☆	1.2	428-6970	None	None	None	None	Anthony Gray	'92
STI CLASSIC INV GRD; INV	Fixed Income	35.6	9.83	9,864.00	9,871.00	☆	4.6	428-6970	None	3.75	0.30	None	Earl Denney	'92
STI CLASSIC INV GRD; TR	Fixed Income	459.3	9.82	9,873.00	9,899.00	☆	5.1	428-6970	None	None	None	None	Earl Denney	'92
STI CLASSIC SUNBELT; INV	Growth	15.9	9.28	9,567.00	☆	☆	0.0	428-6970	None	3.75	0.40	None	James Foster	'94
STI CLASSIC VAL INC; INV	Equity Income	60.6	10.31	10,417.00	10,821.00	☆	2.5	428-6970	None	3.75	0.30	None	Gregory DePrince	'93
STI CLASSIC VAL INC; TR	Equity Income	565.0	10.32	10,431.00	10,883.00	☆	2.9	428-6970	None	None	None	None	Gregory DePrince	'93
STOCK & BOND FUND; A	Balanced	123.7	15.91	9,968.00	10,048.00	14,078.00	3.3	245-4770	412-288-1900	None	None	None	Mike Donnelly	'89
STOCK & BOND FUND; C	Balanced	1.0	15.89	9,951.00	9,949.00	☆	2.4	245-4770	412-288-1900	None	0.75	1.00	Mike Donnelly	'93
STRATTON GROWTH FUND	Growth Income	25.5	20.57	10,368.00	10,596.00	14,605.00	2.4	634-5726	215-941-0255	None	None	None	Stratton/Affleck	'72/'79
STRATTON MONTHLY DIV	Utility	136.7	24.30	9,274.00	8,357.00	13,853.00	8.0	634-5726	215-941-0255	None	None	None	Stratton/Heffernan	'80/'80
STRATTON SMALL-CAP YIELD	Small Company Growth	8.4	25.81	9,995.00	10,392.00	☆	2.0	634-5726	215-941-0255	None	None	None	Stratton/Reichel	'93/'93
STRONG ADVANTAGE	Fixed Income	613.9	10.03	10,038.00	10,457.00	14,388.00	5.4	368-1030	414-359-1400	None	None	None	Jeff Koch	'91
STRONG AMER UTILITIES	Utility	33.7	9.53	10,127.00	☆	☆	4.5	368-1030	414-359-1400	None	None	None	W.H. Reaves	'93
STRONG ASIA PACIFIC	Pacific Region	57.7	9.84	10,218.00	☆	☆	0.0	368-1030	414-359-1400	None	None	None	Anthony L.T. Cragg	'93
STRONG COMMON STOCK ⊠★	Growth	787.5	17.19	9,971.00	10,913.00	☆	0.1	368-1030	414-359-1400	None	None	None	Weiss/Murphy/Carlson	'91/'91
STRONG DISCOVERY FUND	Capital Appreciation	357.5	15.67	9,425.00	10,481.00	17,649.00	1.8	368-1030	414-359-1400	None	None	None	Richard S. Strong	'87
STRONG GOVERNMENT	Fixed Income	246.9	9.85	9,807.00	9,912.00	15,070.00	6.1	368-1030	414-359-1400	None	None	None	Brad Tank	'90
STRONG GROWTH	Growth	41.9	10.53	9,776.00	☆	☆	0.0	368-1030	414-359-1400	None	None	None	Ronald C. Ognar	'93
STRONG INCOME	Fixed Income	123.6	9.47	9,860.00	10,191.00	12,303.00	7.5	368-1030	414-359-1400	None	None	None	Jeff Koch	'92
STRONG INTL BOND	World Income	1.3	10.56	10,560.00	☆	☆	0.0	368-1030	414-359-1400	None	None	None	Shirish Maleker	'94
STRONG INTL STOCK	International	257.5	13.81	10,192.00	12,916.00	☆	0.2	368-1030	414-359-1400	None	None	None	Anthony L.T. Cragg	'93
STRONG INVESTMENT	Flexible	257.5	17.92	9,815.00	10,248.00	14,375.00	3.5	368-1030	414-359-1400	None	None	None	Tank/Stephens/Mueller	'93/'93
STRONG OPPORTUNITY	Growth	577.0	27.80	10,185.00	11,081.00	16,243.00	0.1	368-1030	414-359-1400	None	None	None	Murphy/Weiss/Carlson	'91/'91
STRONG SH-TM GLBL BD	World Income	2.3	10.18	10,180.00	☆	☆	0.0	368-1030	414-359-1400	None	None	None	Shirish Maleker	'94
STRONG SHORT-TERM BOND	Fixed Income	1,378.9	9.72	9,869.00	10,142.00	14,017.00	6.6	368-1030	414-359-1400	None	None	None	Brad Tank	'90
STRONG TOTAL RETURN	Growth Income	621.8	22.94	9,782.00	10,498.00	13,164.00	1.0	368-1030	414-359-1400	None	None	None	Ronald C. Ognar	'93

★ STRONG COMMON STOCK--Fund has been reclassified from Midcap to Growth.

PERFORMANCE OF MUTUAL FUNDS (continued)

FUND NAME	OBJECTIVE	TOTAL NET ASSETS ($ MIL) 5/31/94	NET ASSET $ VALUE 6/30/94	PERFORMANCE (Return on initial $10,000 Investment) 3/31/94-6/30/94	6/30/93-6/30/94	6/30/89-6/30/94	DIVIDEND YIELD % 6/94	PHONE NUMBER 800	In-State	FEES Load	12b-1	Redemption	MANAGER	SINCE
SUNAMER BALANCED; A	Balanced	53.9	14.20	9,939.00	☆	☆	0.0	858-8850	212-551-5125	5.75	0.35	None	Stan Feeley	'93
SUNAMER BALANCED; B	Balanced	195.4	14.14	9,931.00	9,975.00	15,139.00	1.5	858-8850	212-551-5125	None	1.00	4.00	Stan Feeley	'93
SUNAMER BLUE CHIP; A	Growth	1.9	14.73	9,939.00	☆	☆	0.0	858-8850	212-551-5125	5.75	0.25	None	Stan Feeley	'93
SUNAMER BLUE CHIP; B	Growth	82.0	14.67	9,926.00	9,876.00	11,597.00	0.0	858-8850	212-551-5125	None	1.00	4.00	Stan Feeley	'92
SUNAMER DVSD INC; A	Fixed Income	14.4	4.59	9,792.00	☆	☆	0.0	858-8850	212-551-5125	4.75	0.35	None	Leary/Dudley	'93/'93
SUNAMER DVSD INC; B	Fixed Income	178.0	4.60	9,791.00	9,829.00	☆	8.4	858-8850	212-551-5125	None	1.00	4.00	Leary/Dudley	'92/'92
SUNAMER FED SECS; A	Fixed Income	0.6	9.97	9,893.00	☆	☆	0.0	858-8850	212-551-5125	4.75	0.35	None	Christopher Leary	'93
SUNAMER FED SECS; B	Fixed Income	75.7	9.98	9,887.00	9,693.00	13,700.00	5.1	858-8850	212-551-5125	None	1.00	4.00	Christopher Leary	'93
SUNAMER HIGH INC; A	Fixed Income	34.8	7.60	9,694.00	10,126.00	15,789.00	10.5	858-8850	212-551-5125	4.75	0.35	None	Charles Dudley	'90
SUNAMER HIGH INC; B	Fixed Income	149.6	7.61	9,700.00	☆	☆	0.0	858-8850	212-551-5125	None	1.00	4.00	Charles Dudley	'93
SUNAMER MID-CAP GRO; A	Growth	34.1	13.05	9,348.00	9,282.00	14,862.00	0.0	858-8850	212-551-5125	5.75	0.35	None	Dudley/Snell	'93/'91
SUNAMER SMALL CO GRO; A	Small Company Growth	35.1	15.40	9,205.00	9,352.00	14,050.00	0.0	858-8850	212-551-5125	5.75	0.35	None	Audrey Snell	'91
SUNAMER SMALL CO GRO; B	Small Company Growth	43.0	15.33	9,196.00	☆	☆	0.0	858-8850	212-551-5125	None	1.00	4.00	Audrey Snell	'93
SUNAMER US GOVT SEC; A	Fixed Income	73.4	8.22	9,923.00	☆	☆	0.0	858-8850	212-551-5125	4.75	0.35	None	Christopher Leary	'93
SUNAMER US GOVT SEC; B	Fixed Income	809.2	8.22	9,906.00	9,929.00	13,421.00	5.7	858-8850	212-551-5125	None	1.00	4.00	Christopher Leary	'93
SUNBURST SHRT-INT GOVT	Fixed Income	12.2	9.50	9,902.00	☆	☆	0.0	467-2506	None	2.50	None	None	James Plunkett	'93
SWISSKEY SBC SH-TM WORLD	World Income	48.1	9.45	9,885.00	9,930.00	☆	5.1	762-6814	None	None	0.35	None	Fabio Salvoldeli	'92
SWISSKEY SBC WORLD GRO	Global	31.2	16.14	10,183.00	11,705.00	☆	0.3	762-6814	None	4.80	0.35	None	Miller/Grimm	'92/'92
T U & P BALANCED	Balanced	19.0	13.02	9,871.00	10,086.00	14,388.00	2.0	999-0887	608-831-1300	None	None	None	Thompson, Plumb & Assoc.	'87
T U & P BOND	Fixed Income	9.7	10.01	9,911.00	9,868.00	☆	4.4	999-0887	608-831-1300	None	None	None	Thompson, Plumb & Assoc.	'92
T U & P GROWTH	Growth	5.5	19.15	9,701.00	9,672.00	☆	0.0	999-0887	608-831-1300	None	None	None	Thompson, Plumb & Assoc.	'92
TARGET INTL EQ	International	177.0	13.30	10,045.00	12,512.00	☆	0.0	225-1852	None	None	None	None	Lazard Freres Asset Mgt.	'93
TARGET INTMDT-TERM BOND	Fixed Income	69.6	9.80	9,948.00	10,089.00	☆	5.3	225-1852	None	None	None	None	Pacific Investment Mgt Co	'93
TARGET LARGE CAP GROWTH	Growth	130.2	9.35	9,863.00	9,917.00	☆	0.5	225-1852	None	None	None	None	Roger Engemann Mgmt. Co.	'93
TARGET LARGE CAP VALUE	Growth Income	129.2	9.79	10,020.00	9,955.00	☆	1.1	225-1852	None	None	None	None	INVESCO MIM Inc.	'93
TARGET MTGE BACKED SECS	Fixed Income	69.0	9.68	9,949.00	9,988.00	☆	6.2	225-1852	None	None	None	None	Wellington Mgmt. Co.	'93
TARGET SMALL CAP GROWTH	Small Company Growth	89.1	10.73	9,078.00	9,840.00	☆	0.1	225-1852	None	None	None	None	Nicholas Applegate Mgmt.	'93
TARGET SMALL CAP VALUE	Small Company Growth	87.1	11.71	9,383.00	9,869.00	☆	0.0	225-1852	None	None	None	None	Oak Hall Cap Adv Inc	'93
TARGET TOTAL RETURN BOND	Fixed Income	31.2	9.65	9,937.00	9,928.00	☆	5.6	225-1852	None	None	None	None	Pacific Investment Mgt Co	'93
TCW/DW BALANCED	Balanced	150.1	9.18	9,699.00	☆	☆	0.0	869-3863	212-392-2550	None	1.00	None	James Tilton	'93
TCW/DW CORE EQUITY	Growth	728.5	11.46	9,471.00	9,888.00	☆	0.0	869-3863	212-392-2550	None	1.00	5.00	James Tilton	'92
TCW/DW INCOME & GROWTH	Fixed Income	64.7	9.95	9,779.00	10,262.00	☆	5.4	869-3863	212-392-2550	None	0.75	None	Howard Marks	'93
TCW/DW LATIN AMER GR	Latin American	350.2	11.32	8,722.00	11,998.00	☆	0.0	869-3863	212-392-2550	None	1.00	5.00	Philip Wargnier	'92
TCW/DW NTH AMER GOVT INC	World Income	2,087.0	9.22	9,728.00	9,762.00	☆	7.8	869-3863	212-392-2550	None	0.75	None	Philip Barach	'92
TCW/DW NTH AMER INT INC	World Income	1.7	9.86	☆	☆	☆	0.0	869-3863	212-392-2550	None	0.75	None	James Goldberg	'94
TCW/DW SMALL CAP GRO	Small Company Growth	58.1	8.39	8,850.00	☆	☆	0.0	869-3863	212-392-2550	None	1.00	5.00	Annette Longnon Geddes	'93
TEMPLETON AMERICAN TR	Growth	36.2	13.30	10,000.00	10,725.00	☆	0.3	237-0738	813-823-8712	None	0.25	5.00	Gary Motyl	'92
TEMPLETON CAP ACCUMULATR ★	Global Flexible	32.0	14.91	9,927.00	12,082.00	☆	0.9	237-0738	813-823-8712	None	None	None	Gary Motyl	'93
TEMPLETON DEVELP MRKTS	Emerging Markets	1,751.8	13.72	9,436.00	12,345.00	☆	0.3	237-0738	813-823-8712	5.75	0.25	None	Mark Mobius	'91
TEMPLETON FDS FOREIGN	International	4,293.8	9.40	9,968.00	12,069.00	18,938.00	1.4	237-0738	813-823-8712	5.75	0.25.	None	Mark G. Holowesko	'87
TEMPLETON FDS WORLD	Global	5,099.0	15.72	10,070.00	11,894.00	16,563.00	1.7	237-0738	813-823-8712	5.75	0.25	None	Mark G. Holowesko	'87
TEMPLETON GLOBAL OPP	Global	469.2	12.52	9,835.00	11,498.00	☆	0.9	237-0738	813-823-8712	5.75	0.25	None	Howard Leonard	'93
TEMPLETON GROWTH	Global	5,029.3	17.51	10,040.00	11,756.00	18,330.00	1.6	237-0738	813-823-8712	5.75	0.25	None	Mark G. Holowesko	'87
TEMPLETON INC INCOME	World Income	203.4	8.96	9,762.00	9,779.00	14,274.00	8.0	237-0738	813-823-8712	4.50	0.25	None	Samuel J. Forester, Jr.	'90
TEMPLETON REAL ESTATE TR	Real Estate	117.2	12.99	9,644.00	10,923.00	☆	1.7	237-0738	813-823-8712	5.75	0.25	None	Jeffrey Everett	'92

TEMPLETON SMALL CO GROW	Global Small Company	1,366.9	7.69	9,637.00	11,227.00	16,103.00	0.9	237-0738	813-823-8712	5.75	0.25	None	Dan Jacobs	'92
THE NEW USA FUND	Growth	208.3	11.07	9,437.00	9,305.00	☆	0.0	222-2872	310-448-6856	5.00	0.60	None	David Ryan	'92
THIRD AVENUE VALUE FUND	Specialty	154.8	16.93	9,895.00	10,296.00	☆	1.3	443-1021	212-888-6685	4.50	None	None	Martin J. Whitman	'90
THOMSON EQUITY INC; A	Equity Income	13.4	11.73	9,655.00	10,477.00	☆	2.8	227-7337	203-352-4946	5.50	0.25	None	Team Managed	'91
THOMSON EQUITY INC; B	Equity Income	164.3	11.71	9,643.00	10,403.00	13,823.00	2.0	227-7337	203-352-4946	None	1.00	1.00	Team Managed	'90
THOMSON GOVERNMENT; A	Fixed Income	18.5	8.85	9,847.00	9,816.00	☆	6.8	227-7337	203-352-4946	4.75	0.25	None	Team Managed	'92
THOMSON GOVERNMENT; B	Fixed Income	414.9	8.81	9,826.00	9,728.00	13,427.00	6.0	227-7337	203-352-4946	None	1.00	1.00	Team Managed	'92
THOMSON GROWTH; A	Growth	96.6	20.88	9,789.00	10,169.00	☆	0.0	227-7337	203-352-4946	5.50	0.25	None	Team Managed	'91
THOMSON GROWTH; B	Growth	1,057.3	20.46	9,771.00	10,095.00	16,898.00	0.0	227-7337	203-352-4946	None	1.00	1.00	Team Managed	'86
THOMSON INCOME; A	Fixed Income	4.7	7.60	9,781.00	9,586.00	☆	9.3	227-7337	203-352-4946	4.75	0.25	None	Team Managed	'92
THOMSON INCOME; B	Fixed Income	197.5	7.55	9,761.00	9,485.00	12,479.00	8.5	227-7337	203-352-4946	None	1.00	1.00	Team Managed	'92
THOMSON INTL; A	International	23.1	12.42	10,139.00	11,368.00	☆	0.0	227-7337	203-352-4946	5.50	0.25	None	Team Managed	'92
THOMSON INTL; B	International	278.2	12.10	10,126.00	11,283.00	14,371.00	0.0	227-7337	203-352-4946	None	1.00	1.00	Team Managed	'92
THOMSON OPPORTUNITY; A ⊠	Capital Appreciation	90.5	24.72	8,662.00	9,310.00	☆	0.0	227-7337	203-352-4946	5.50	0.25	None	Team Managed	'91
THOMSON OPPORTUNITY; B ⊠	Capital Appreciation	535.8	24.05	8,645.00	9,237.00	23,931.00	0.0	227-7337	203-352-4946	None	1.00	1.00	Team Managed	'86
THOMSON PREC MTLS; A	Gold	7.7	12.07	9,467.00	10,532.00	☆	0.0	227-7337	203-352-4946	5.50	0.25	None	Team Managed	'91
THOMSON PREC MTLS; B	Gold	51.2	11.76	9,453.00	10,453.00	12,895.00	0.0	227-7337	203-352-4946	None	1.00	1.00	Team Managed	'88
THOMSON SH-INT GOVT; A	Fixed Income	6.4	9.45	10,020.00	10,087.00	☆	5.1	227-7337	203-352-4946	3.00	0.25	None	Team Managed	'92
THOMSON SH-INT GOVT; B	Fixed Income	103.7	9.45	10,007.00	10,037.00	☆	4.6	227-7337	203-352-4946	None	0.75	1.00	Team Managed	'92
THOMSON TARGET FUND; A	Midcap	73.0	11.85	9,666.00	10,475.00	☆	0.0	227-7337	203-352-4946	5.50	0.25	None	Team Managed	'92
THOMSON TARGET FUND; B	Midcap	479.3	11.71	9,646.00	10,388.00	☆	0.0	227-7337	203-352-4946	None	1.00	1.00	Team Managed	'92
THORNBURG LTD TERM INC	Fixed Income	21.8	11.84	9,958.00	10,101.00	☆	5.7	847-0200	505-984-0200	2.50	0.17	None	Steven Bohlin	'92
THORNBURG LTD US GOVT	Fixed Income	188.1	12.15	9,935.00	9,940.00	14,264.00	5.4	847-0200	505-984-0200	2.50	0.19	None	Steven Bohlin	'87
TIFI EMERGING MARKETS	Emerging Markets	479.3	11.39	9,230.00	11,482.00	☆	0.4	237-0738	813-823-8712	None	None	None	Dr. J. Mark Mobius	'93
TIFI FOREIGN EQ (SAF)	International	65.8	10.59	9,860.00	12,343.00	☆	2.9	237-0738	813-823-8712	None	None	None	James Chaney	'93
TIFI FOREIGN EQUITY ▮▮▮✪	International	757.0	12.91	9,855.00	12,033.00	☆	0.7	237-0738	813-823-8712	None	None	None	James Chaney	'93
TIFI GLOBAL FXD INC	World Income	0.7	9.43	9,895.00	9,674.00	☆	1.7	237-0738	813-823-8712	None	None	None	Tom Latta	'93
TIFI GROWTH	Global	195.1	11.44	9,974.00	11,672.00	☆	1.4	237-0738	813-823-8712	None	None	None	James Chaney	'93
TOCQUEVILLE ASIA-PAC	International	4.4	11.46	10,088.00	12,179.00	☆	0.0	697-3863	212-698-0851	None	0.25	None	Navellou/Seguier	'91/'93
TOCQUEVILLE TOCQ FUND	Growth	29.8	13.32	10,294.00	11,047.00	17,248.00	1.0	697-3863	212-698-0851	None	0.25	None	Sicart/Kleinschmidt	'87/'91
TORCHMARK GOVT SECS	Fixed Income	1.4	9.19	9,811.00	9,539.00	☆	5.8	733-3863	913-236-2050	None	0.25	None	John E. Sundeen	'93
TORRAY FUND	Flexible	21.5	14.16	10,328.00	10,437.00	☆	0.9	None	301-493-4600	None	None	None	Robert E. Torray	'90
TOT RTN TREAS; INV A	Fixed Income	185.7	9.42	9,833.00	9,817.00	14,557.00	7.0	645-3923	410-637-6819	4.50	0.25	None	R. Alan Medaugh	'88
TOT RTN TREAS; INV B ⊠	Fixed Income	2.2	9.37	9,822.00	9,780.00	☆	7.0	645-3923	410-637-6819	1.50	0.60	1.00	R. Alan Medaugh	'92
TOT RTN TREAS; ISI	Fixed Income	218.2	9.42	9,833.00	9,817.00	14,557.00	7.0	645-3923	410-637-6819	4.45	0.25	None	R. Alan Medaugh	'88
TOWER CAPITAL APPREC	Growth Income	133.6	12.95	9,908.00	10,103.00	16,063.00	1.8	999-0124	504-533-5180	3.00	0.25	None	Paul Mangus	'91
TOWER TOTAL RETURN BOND	Fixed Income	74.6	9.58	9,879.00	9,819.00	☆	6.2	999-0124	504-533-5180	3.00	0.25	None	John Hall	'92
TOWER US GOVT INCOME	Fixed Income	70.0	9.87	9,892.00	9,851.00	14,234.00	7.0	999-0124	504-533-5180	3.00	None	None	Jeff Tanguis	'92
TR CREDIT UN 1996 ◪⊠	Fixed Income	127.3	9.50	9,968.00	☆	☆	5.6	526-7384	212-902-0800	None	None	0.50	Team Managed	'93
TR CREDIT UN F 1997 ◪⊠	Fixed Income	97.6	9.57	9,948.00	☆	☆	0.0	526-7384	212-902-0800	None	None	0.50	Team Managed	'94
TR CREDIT UN GOVT ◪	Fixed Income	617.2	9.79	10,021.00	10,244.00	☆	4.2	526-7384	212-902-0800	None	None	None	Team Managed	'93
TR CREDIT UN MTGE SEC ◪	Fixed Income	297.4	9.62	9,979.00	10,105.00	☆	6.2	526-7384	212-902-0800	None	None	None	Team Managed	'93
TR FED SEC INT GOVT; SHS	Fixed Income	4.9	10.14	9,962.00	9,952.00	14,557.00	6.3	821-7432	None	None	None	None	Bruce Repasy	'88
TR FED SEC SHT GOVT; SHS	Fixed Income	6.7	9.40	9,962.00	10,103.00	14,159.00	5.3	821-7432	None	None	None	None	Bruce Repasy	'88
TRADEMARK EQUITY FUND	Growth	137.1	10.45	10,367.00	10,445.00	☆	1.7	245-0242	None	None	None	None	Jacqueline Tytus	'93
TRADEMARK GOVT INCOME	Fixed Income	98.8	9.20	9,833.00	9,643.00	☆	6.3	245-0242	None	None	None	None	Clarence Lee Jr.	'93
TRADEMARK SH-INTMDT GOVT	Fixed Income	47.4	9.31	9,922.00	9,874.00	☆	6.1	245-0242	None	None	None	None	Clarence Lee Jr.	'93
TRANSAM BD ADJ GOVT; A	Fixed Income	19.8	9.80	10,012.00	10,142.00	☆	4.1	472-3863	713-751-2800	3.50	None	None	Team Managed	'91
TRANSAM BD ADJ GOVT; B	Fixed Income	11.3	9.80	9,995.00	10,077.00	☆	3.4	472-3863	713-751-2800	None	0.90	3.00	Team Managed	'91
TRANSAM BD GOVT SEC	Fixed Income	587.3	7.62	9,845.00	9,752.00	14,323.00	8.2	472-3863	713-751-2800	4.75	0.25	None	Team Managed	'84

★ TEMPLETON CAP ACCUMULATR--Sold only on a contractual plan.

PERFORMANCE OF MUTUAL FUNDS (continued)

FUND NAME	OBJECTIVE	TOTAL NET ASSETS ($ MIL) 5/31/94	NET ASSET $ VALUE 6/30/94	PERFORMANCE (Return on initial $10,000 Investment) 3/31/94-6/30/94	6/30/93-6/30/94	6/30/89-6/30/94	DIVIDEND YIELD % 6/94	PHONE NUMBER 800	In-State	FEES Load	12b-1	Redemption	MANAGER	SINCE
TRANSAM BD INTMDT GOVT	Fixed Income	9.7	9.40	9,878.00	9,750.00	14,071.00	6.8	472-3863	713-751-2800	4.75	None	1.00	Team Managed	'86
TRANSAM BD INV QUAL; A	Fixed Income	91.7	8.37	9,787.00	9,695.00	14,292.00	8.2	472-3863	713-751-2800	4.75	0.25	None	Team Managed	'80
TRANSAM BD INV QUAL; B	Fixed Income	6.4	8.37	9,767.00	9,618.00	☆	7.3	472-3863	713-751-2800	None	1.00	5.00	Team Managed	'93
TRANSAM BD US GOVT; A	Fixed Income	21.8	7.72	9,862.00	9,747.00	13,855.00	7.8	472-3863	713-751-2800	4.75	0.25	None	Team Managed	'85
TRANSAM CAP GROWTH; A ★	Growth	77.2	11.06	9,163.00	9,805.00	13,821.00	0.0	472-3863	713-751-2800	5.75	0.25	None	Ben A. Hock, Jr.	'93
TRANSAM CAP GROWTH; B ★	Growth	13.1	10.97	9,157.00	9,725.00	☆	0.0	472-3863	713-751-2800	None	1.00	5.00	Ben A. Hock, Jr.	'93
TRANSAM INV GR & INC; A	Growth Income	119.1	10.75	9,762.00	9,495.00	15,862.00	3.5	472-3863	713-751-2800	5.75	0.25	None	Jeffrey Talley	'92
TRANSAM INV GR & INC; B	Growth Income	109.1	10.78	9,744.00	9,410.00	☆	2.7	472-3863	713-751-2800	None	1.00	5.00	Jeffrey Talley	'92
TRANSAM INV INSTL SECS	Fixed Income	3.1	25.15	10,020.00	10,243.00	☆	1.8	472-3863	713-751-2800	None	0.25	None	Team Managed	'93
TRANSAM SPEC EMER GR; A	Small Company Growth	118.8	23.46	9,310.00	10,073.00	☆	0.0	472-3863	713-751-2800	5.75	0.25	None	Edgar Larsen	'91
TRANSAM SPEC EMER GR; B	Small Company Growth	259.5	22.84	9,288.00	9,996.00	19,945.00	0.0	472-3863	713-751-2800	None	1.00	5.00	Edgar Larsen	'87
TRANSAM SPEC GOVT INC	Fixed Income	259.3	8.99	9,810.00	9,706.00	13,608.00	7.5	472-3863	713-751-2800	None	1.00	5.00	Team Managed	'88
TRANSAM SPEC HI YLD; A	Fixed Income	8.9	7.73	9,914.00	10,614.00	☆	10.6	472-3863	713-751-2800	4.75	0.25	None	Team Managed	'93
TRANSAM SPEC HI YLD; B	Fixed Income	157.0	7.73	9,896.00	10,533.00	16,064.00	9.7	472-3863	713-751-2800	None	1.00	5.00	Team Managed	'87
TRANSAM SPEC NATRL RES	Natural Resources	29.0	14.59	9,858.00	9,932.00	13,735.00	0.0	472-3863	713-751-2800	None	1.00	5.00	B. J. Willingham	'94
TRENT EQUITY FUND	Capital Appreciation	5.1	10.75	9,340.00	10,174.00	☆	0.0	328-7368	910-282-9302	None	None	None	Trent Capital Mgmt	'94
TRIFLEX FUND	Balanced	20.0	14.86	10,021.00	10,264.00	14,120.00	2.7	231-4639	409-763-2767	5.75	None	None	William R. Berger	'93
TRUST CO OF SO GROWTH	Growth	2.7	10.06	9,608.00	9,849.00	☆	0.1	525-3863	919-972-9922	None	None	None	Gupton/Smith	'93/'93
TURNER GROWTH EQUITY	Capital Appreciation	85.4	11.56	9,581.00	9,792.00	☆	0.8	932-7781	215-989-6611	None	None	None	Turner Invest. Partners	'92
TWEEDY BROWNE GLBL VALUE	Global Small Company	364.6	12.21	9,959.00	12,234.00	☆	0.0	432-4789	212-916-0600	None	None	None	Team Managed	'93
TWEEDY BROWNE VALUE	Growth Income	19.9	9.82	10,113.00	☆	☆	0.0	432-4789	212-916-0600	None	None	None	Multiple Managers	'93
TWEN CENTURY PR MGD BD	Fixed Income	7.9	9.37	9,864.00	9,768.00	☆	5.3	345-2021	816-531-5575	None	None	None	Bud Hoops	'93
TWEN CENTURY WRLD EMRG	Emerging Markets	48.7	5.38	☆	☆	☆	0.0	345-2021	816-531-5575	None	None	2.00	Tyson/Koanski	'94/'94
TWEN CENTURY WRLD INTL	International	1,217.8	7.52	10,135.00	12,309.00	☆	0.0	345-2021	816-531-5575	None	None	None	Kopinski/Tyson	'91/'91
TWEN CENTURY BALANCED	Balanced	680.6	15.29	9,776.00	10,021.00	16,637.00	2.6	345-2021	816-531-5575	None	None	None	Team Managed	'88
TWEN CENTURY GIFTRUST	Small Company Growth	181.5	15.85	9,548.00	11,210.00	25,496.00	0.0	345-2021	816-531-5575	None	None	None	Team Managed	'83
TWEN CENTURY GROWTH	Growth	4,414.2	21.36	9,574.00	10,118.00	17,427.00	0.3	345-2021	816-531-5575	None	None	None	Team Managed	'58
TWEN CENTURY HERITAGE	Growth	871.8	9.76	9,578.00	10,141.00	17,108.00	0.7	345-2021	816-531-5575	None	None	None	Team Managed	'87
TWEN CENTURY INTMDT BD	Fixed Income	3.2	9.63	9,942.00	☆	☆	0.0	345-2021	816-531-5575	None	None	None	Hoops/Gahagan/Kirby	'94/'94
TWEN CENTURY LIMITED BD	Fixed Income	3.7	9.76	9,970.00	☆	☆	0.0	345-2021	816-531-5575	None	None	None	Hoops/Gahagan/Kirby	'94/'94
TWEN CENTURY LNG-TM BD	Fixed Income	130.9	9.12	9,836.00	9,790.00	14,346.00	6.1	345-2021	816-531-5575	None	None	None	Team Managed	'87
TWEN CENTURY SELECT	Growth Income	4,403.8	36.09	9,639.00	9,571.00	15,389.00	1.1	345-2021	816-531-5575	None	None	None	Team Managed	'58
TWEN CENTURY ULTRA INV	Midcap	9,261.0	19.26	9,171.00	9,630.00	23,773.00	0.0	345-2021	816-531-5575	None	None	None	Team Managed	'87
TWEN CENTURY US GOVT INT	Fixed Income	3.5	9.68	9,947.00	☆	☆	0.0	345-2021	816-531-5575	None	None	None	Hoops/Gahagan/Kirby	'94/'94
TWEN CENTURY US GOVT SHT	Fixed Income	426.9	9.33	9,976.00	10,006.00	13,346.00	3.8	345-2021	816-531-5575	None	None	None	Team Managed	'82
TWEN CENTURY VALUE	Growth Income	101.0	5.04	10,185.00	☆	☆	0.0	345-2021	816-531-5575	None	None	None	Zuger/Davidson	'93/'93
TWEN CENTURY VISTA INV	Midcap	663.2	8.73	9,151.00	8,801.00	15,555.00	0.0	345-2021	816-531-5575	None	None	None	Team Managed	'83
UNITED MISSOURI BK BOND	Fixed Income	82.9	10.75	9,904.00	9,877.00	14,257.00	5.7	422-2766	816-471-5200	None	None	None	George Root	'82
UNITED MISSOURI BK HRTLD	Small Company Growth	26.5	9.29	9,990.00	10,480.00	13,574.00	1.8	422-2766	816-471-5200	None	None	None	David Anderson	'91
UNITED MISSOURI BK STOCK	Growth	118.3	15.42	10,101.00	10,535.00	15,340.00	2.2	422-2766	816-471-5200	None	None	None	David Anderson	'82
UNITED CONTL INCOME	Balanced	420.4	20.51	9,998.00	10,344.00	15,977.00	3.3	None	913-236-2000	5.75	0.25	None	Cynthia Prince-Fox	'93
UNITED GOLD & GOVERNMENT	Gold	44.2	8.99	9,414.00	10,524.00	12,777.00	0.4	None	913-236-2000	5.75	0.25	None	Michael L. Avery	'94
UNITED GOVERNMENT SECS	Fixed Income	168.5	5.09	9,874.00	9,800.00	14,709.00	5.9	None	913-236-2000	4.25	0.25	None	John E. Sundeen	'91
UNITED HIGH INCOME	Fixed Income	975.0	8.96	9,955.00	10,374.00	13,822.00	8.9	None	913-236-2000	5.75	0.25	None	Louise D. Rieke	'90
UNITED HIGH INCOME II	Fixed Income	371.0	4.05	9,971.00	10,406.00	15,150.00	8.7	None	913-236-2000	5.75	0.25	None	Louise D. Rieke	'92

UNITED INTL GROWTH	International	585.4	8.98	9,955.00	13,332.00	17,187.00	0.5	None	913-236-2000	5.75	0.25	None	Mark Yockey	'90
UNITED NEW CONCEPTS	Small Company Growth	220.6	10.19	9,314.00	9,942.00	21,154.00	0.0	None	913-236-2000	5.75	0.25	None	Mark G. Seferovich	'89
UNITED RETIREMENT SHARES	Growth Income	459.4	7.64	9,973.00	10,503.00	16,695.00	2.3	None	913-236-2000	5.75	0.25	None	James D. Wineland	'88
UNITED VANGUARD FUND	Growth	954.6	6.90	9,677.00	10,677.00	14,367.00	0.3	None	913-236-2000	5.75	0.25	None	James D. Wineland	'92
UNITED ACCUMULATIVE	Growth	1,008.2	6.98	9,970.00	10,184.00	14,850.00	1.2	None	913-236-2000	5.75	0.25	None	Antonio Intagliata	'79
UNITED BOND	Fixed Income	566.8	5.83	9,810.00	9,742.00	14,487.00	6.6	None	913-236-2000	5.75	0.25	None	James C. Cusser	'92
UNITED INCOME	Equity Income	3,143.2	24.01	9,852.00	10,571.00	16,994.00	1.5	None	913-236-2000	5.75	0.25	None	Russell E. Thompson	'79
UNITED SCIENCE & TECH	Science & Technology	431.9	13.32	9,142.00	9,773.00	16,031.00	0.0	None	913-236-2000	5.75	0.25	None	Abel Garcia	'84
UNIVERSAL CAPITAL GROWTH	Capital Appreciation	4.8	10.70	9,177.00	9,881.00	☆	0.0	223-9100	708-932-3000	4.75	0.50	None	Dreher/Biscan	'91/'91
US LARGE STOCK FUND	Growth Income	81.6	4.94	9,980.00	10,021.00	☆	1.2	223-3332	212-908-9500	None	None	None	Joseph N. Pappo	'93
US ALL AMERICAN EQUITY ★	Growth Income	10.6	19.52	9,751.00	9,832.00	12,966.00	2.3	873-8637	210-308-1234	None	None	None	Batterymarch, Inc.	'93
US CHINA REGION OPPTY	Pacific Region	6.3	7.75	9,628.00	☆	☆	0.0	873-8637	210-308-1234	None	None	1.00	Batterymarch, Inc.	'94
US EUROPEAN INCOME	Global Flexible	2.8	4.32	9,954.00	10,671.00	7,009.00	2.8	873-8637	210-308-1234	None	None	None	Ralph Aldis	'91
US GLOBAL RESOURCES	Natural Resources	23.2	5.74	9,273.00	9,626.00	10,504.00	0.2	873-8637	210-308-1234	None	None	None	Ralph Aldis	'92
US GOLD SHARES	Gold	258.4	2.48	10,458.00	10,185.00	7,669.00	2.4	873-8637	210-308-1234	None	None	None	Victor Flores	'92
US GROWTH FUND	Capital Appreciation	3.7	5.37	9,624.00	10,100.00	11,003.00	0.0	873-8637	210-308-1234	None	None	None	Frank Holmes	'93
US INCOME FUND	Utility	12.4	12.56	9,783.00	9,417.00	13,938.00	2.7	873-8637	210-308-1234	None	None	None	Frank Holmes	'93
US INTMDT TREASURY	Fixed Income	4.1	10.16	9,847.00	9,732.00	☆	6.7	873-8637	210-308-1234	None	None	None	Allen Parker	'92
US REAL ESTATE	Real Estate	15.7	9.86	9,640.00	9,229.00	11,446.00	2.7	873-8637	210-308-1234	None	None	None	Allen Parker	'87
US SPECIAL TERM GOVT	Fixed Income	18.0	9.87	10,018.00	10,269.00	☆	4.1	873-8637	210-308-1234	None	None	None	Allen Parker	'93
US WORLD GOLD	Gold	226.8	15.63	9,014.00	10,713.00	13,570.00	0.0	873-8637	210-308-1234	None	None	None	Victor Flores	'90
USAA INV TR BALANCED	Balanced	128.1	12.17	10,099.00	10,216.00	14,460.00	4.5	382-8722	None	None	None	None	John W. Saunders, Jr.	'89
USAA INV TR CORNERSTONE	Global Flexible	814.3	22.89	10,000.00	10,602.00	15,190.00	2.6	382-8722	None	None	None	None	Harry W. Miller	'90
USAA INV TR GNMA	Fixed Income	259.8	9.79	9,993.00	9,967.00	☆	7.6	382-8722	None	None	None	None	Carl W. Shirley	'91
USAA INV TR GOLD	Gold	172.3	8.44	9,184.00	9,174.00	10,917.00	0.1	382-8722	None	None	None	None	Mark Johnson	'94
USAA INV TR INTL	International	184.1	16.21	10,201.00	12,413.00	17,047.00	0.0	382-8722	None	None	None	None	David Peebles	'88
USAA INV TR WORLD GROWTH	Global	143.0	12.52	10,008.00	11,387.00	☆	0.1	382-8722	None	None	None	None	David Peebles	'92
USAA MUTUAL AGGR GROWTH	Small Company Growth	256.2	17.13	9,059.00	9,510.00	13,392.00	0.1	382-8722	None	None	None	None	William Fries	'94
USAA MUTUAL GRO & INC	Growth Income	128.0	9.96	10,091.00	10,168.00	☆	1.8	382-8722	None	None	None	None	R. David Ullom	'93
USAA MUTUAL GROWTH FUND	Growth	596.3	17.09	10,154.00	9,976.00	16,299.00	0.9	382-8722	None	None	None	None	David Parsons	'94
USAA MUTUAL INCOME FUND	Fixed Income	1,721.5	11.40	9,796.00	9,475.00	15,094.00	8.2	382-8722	None	None	None	None	John W. Saunders, Jr.	'85
USAA MUTUAL INCOME STOCK	Equity Income	1,173.9	13.18	10,000.00	9,867.00	16,134.00	6.9	382-8722	None	None	None	None	Harry W. Miller	'89
USAA MUTUAL SH-TM BOND	Fixed Income	46.3	9.70	9,977.00	10,103.00	☆	4.5	382-8722	None	None	None	None	Paul Lundmark	'93
USAFFINITY GOVT INC	Fixed Income	2.6	9.30	9,859.00	9,638.00	☆	6.7	800-3030	617-262-9200	4.50	0.35	None	D. Vandervort	'93
USAFFINITY GREEN	Environmental	1.8	9.40	8,910.00	9,520.00	☆	0.0	800-3030	617-262-9200	4.50	0.35	None	M. Meyer	'94
USAFFINITY GROWTH	Growth	6.0	11.15	9,587.00	9,832.00	☆	0.0	800-3030	617-262-9200	4.50	0.35	None	R. Turner	'92
USAFFINITY GROWTH & INC	Growth Income	3.2	10.31	10,200.00	9,944.00	☆	2.6	800-3030	617-262-9200	4.50	0.35	None	Tengler/Spare	'92/'92
UST MSTR AGING OF AMER	Growth	11.9	6.80	9,743.00	9,811.00	☆	0.6	233-1136	619-456-9394	4.50	None	None	Roger F. Schaefer	'92
UST MSTR BUS & INDUST	Growth	17.6	9.32	9,738.00	11,761.00	☆	0.9	233-1136	619-456-9394	4.50	None	None	David J. Williams	'92
UST MSTR COMMUN & ENTER	Growth	21.6	8.25	9,582.00	10,770.00	☆	0.4	233-1136	619-456-9394	4.50	None	None	John J. Apruzese	'92
UST MSTR EARLY LIFE	Small Company Growth	28.1	8.08	9,455.00	10,243.00	☆	0.0	233-1136	619-456-9394	4.50	None	None	Timothy W. Evnin	'92
UST MSTR EMERGING AMER	Latin American	38.3	8.30	9,153.00	11,743.00	☆	0.6	233-1136	619-456-9394	4.50	None	None	Harry C. Rowney	'92
UST MSTR ENVIRONMENTAL	Environmental	4.3	6.02	9,647.00	9,472.00	☆	0.1	233-1136	619-456-9394	4.50	None	None	Victor Sapuppo	'92
UST MSTR EQUITY	Growth	120.1	18.53	9,800.00	10,211.00	15,994.00	0.4	233-1136	619-456-9394	4.50	None	None	Laird Grant	'89
UST MSTR GLBL COMPETITOR	Growth	11.7	7.47	9,731.00	10,217.00	☆	0.8	233-1136	619-456-9394	4.50	None	None	Wendy S. Popowich	'92
UST MSTR INC & GROWTH	Growth Income	99.8	11.52	9,905.00	10,432.00	15,006.00	2.7	233-1136	619-456-9394	4.50	None	None	Richard L. Bayles	'90
UST MSTR INT-TM MGD; ORIG	Fixed Income	42.6	6.70	9,954.00	9,771.00	☆	4.8	233-1136	619-456-9394	4.50	None	None	Henry Milkewicz	'94
UST MSTR INTL	International	56.3	10.38	10,138.00	11,816.00	13,895.00	1.4	233-1136	619-456-9394	4.50	None	None	Harry C. Rowney	'87
UST MSTR L-T SPPLY ENERG	Natural Resources	7.8	7.86	10,245.00	9,609.00	☆	1.2	233-1136	619-456-9394	4.50	None	None	Richard L. Bayles	'92
UST MSTR MGD INC	Fixed Income	110.3	8.32	9,834.00	9,688.00	14,900.00	5.2	233-1136	619-456-9394	4.50	None	None	Henry Milkewicz	'86

★ TRANSAM CAP GRO; A & B--Fund has been reclassified from Capital Appreciation to Growth.

★ US ALL AMERICAN EQUITY--Fund has been reclassified from S&P 500 Index to Growth & Income.

PERFORMANCE OF MUTUAL FUNDS (continued)

FUND NAME	OBJECTIVE	TOTAL NET ASSETS ($ MIL) 5/31/94	NET ASSET $ VALUE 6/30/94	PERFORMANCE (Return on initial $10,000 Investment) 3/31/94-6/30/94	6/30/93-6/30/94	6/30/89-6/30/94	DIVIDEND YIELD % 6/94	PHONE NUMBER 800	In-State	FEES Load	12b-1	Redemption	MANAGER	SINCE
UST MSTR PACIFIC/ASIA	Pacific Region	51.1	9.42	10,189.00	12,836.00	☆	1.1	233-1136	619-456-9394	4.50	None	None	Harry C. Rowney	'92
UST MSTR PAN EUROPEAN	European Region	38.0	7.85	9,837.00	11,145.00	☆	0.5	233-1136	619-456-9394	4.50	None	None	Harry C. Rowney	'92
UST MSTR PRODUCTIVITY	Growth	15.9	6.98	8,979.00	9,729.00	☆	0.2	233-1136	619-456-9394	4.50	None	None	Ronald C. Steele	'92
UST MSTR SH-TM GOVT; ORIG	Fixed Income	24.9	6.89	10,031.00	10,151.00	☆	3.6	233-1136	619-456-9394	4.50	None	None	Charles E. Rabus	'92
VALLEY FORGE FD	Growth	10.7	9.71	10,104.00	10,398.00	14,285.00	1.5	548-1942	610-688-6839	None	None	None	Bernard B. Klawans	'72
VALUE LINE AGGR INCOME	Fixed Income	31.9	7.27	9,766.00	10,400.00	15,487.00	9.3	223-0818	212-907-1500	None	None	None	Team Managed	'86
VALUE LINE ARM	Fixed Income	35.2	9.00	9,304.00	9,440.00	☆	5.6	223-0818	212-907-1500	None	None	None	Team Managed	'92
VALUE LINE ASSET ALLOC	Flexible	19.3	10.23	9,499.00	☆	☆	0.0	223-0818	212-907-1500	None	0.25	None	Team Managed	'93
VALUE LINE CONVERTIBLE	Convertible Securities	48.9	11.98	9,656.00	9,981.00	15,892.00	5.5	223-0818	212-907-1500	None	None	None	Team Managed	'85
VALUE LINE FUND	Growth Income	290.3	16.15	9,439.00	9,137.00	17,115.00	0.3	223-0818	212-907-1500	None	None	None	Team Managed	'50
VALUE LINE INCOME	Equity Income	142.7	6.28	9,943.00	9,492.00	14,917.00	3.0	223-0818	212-907-1500	None	None	None	Team Managed	'52
VALUE LINE LVGE GROWTH	Capital Appreciation	268.6	22.07	9,444.00	9,630.00	16,722.00	0.3	223-0818	212-907-1500	None	None	None	Team Managed	'72
VALUE LINE SM-CAP GRO	Small Company Growth	10.3	11.47	9,720.00	11,159.00	☆	0.3	223-0818	212-907-1500	None	0.25	None	Team Managed	'93
VALUE LINE SPECIAL SIT	Midcap	80.5	14.46	8,948.00	9,560.00	12,316.00	0.0	223-0818	212-907-1500	None	None	None	Team Managed	'56
VALUE LINE US GOVT SEC	Fixed Income	394.9	11.11	9,443.00	9,398.00	14,288.00	8.3	223-0818	212-907-1500	None	None	None	Team Managed	'81
VALUESTAR SH-INT BD; INV	Fixed Income	30.5	9.83	9,975.00	☆	☆	0.0	824-3741	None	3.00	None	None	Donald Turk	'94
VAN ECK ASIA DYNASTY; A	Pacific Region	104.0	12.51	10,032.00	11,969.00	☆	0.0	221-2220	212-687-5201	4.75	0.50	None	Peter Soo	'93
VAN ECK ASIA DYNASTY; B	Pacific Region	36.7	12.45	10,024.00	☆	☆	0.0	221-2220	212-687-5201	None	1.00	6.00	Peter Soo	'93
VAN ECK GLBL BAL; A	Global Flexible	14.3	9.18	9,946.00	☆	☆	0.0	221-2220	212-687-5201	4.75	0.50	None	Brian Hopkinson/S-H Lau	'93/'93
VAN ECK GLBL BAL; B	Global Flexible	4.9	9.14	9,935.00	☆	☆	0.0	221-2220	212-687-5201	None	1.00	6.00	Brian Hopkinson/S-H Lau	'93/'93
VAN ECK GOLD/RESOURCES	Gold	225.0	5.64	9,053.00	9,674.00	12,937.00	0.0	221-2220	212-687-5201	5.75	0.25	None	L. Palermo	'92
VAN ECK INTL INV GOLD	Gold	623.9	14.47	9,959.00	10,521.00	14,423.00	1.0	221-2220	212-687-5201	5.75	None	None	Harry Bingham	'84
VAN ECK WORLD INCOME; A	World Income	167.2	8.13	9,815.00	9,637.00	14,755.00	7.7	221-2220	212-687-5201	4.75	0.25	None	David Kenerson	'87
VAN ECK WORLD TRENDS	Global	27.8	14.46	10,091.00	11,473.00	13,519.00	0.0	221-2220	212-687-5201	4.75	0.25	None	David Kenerson	'85
VANCE SANDERS EXCHANGE ☒	Growth	181.1	236.72	9,979.00	9,914.00	15,358.00	1.3	225-6265	617-482-8260	None	None	None	Thomas E. Faust, Jr.	'91
VANGUARD ADM INT TREAS	Fixed Income	309.9	9.73	9,908.00	9,776.00	☆	5.7	662-7447	215-669-1000	None	None	None	Ian A. MacKinnon	'92
VANGUARD ADM LG TM TREAS	Fixed Income	104.4	9.45	9,739.00	9,578.00	☆	7.1	662-7447	215-669-1000	None	None	None	Ian A. MacKinnon	'92
VANGUARD ADM SH TM TREAS	Fixed Income	275.2	9.86	9,992.00	10,082.00	☆	4.6	662-7447	215-669-1000	None	None	None	Ian A. MacKinnon	'92
VANGUARD ASSET ALLOC	Flexible	1,204.9	13.45	9,896.00	9,936.00	15,875.00	3.5	662-7447	215-669-1000	None	None	None	Thomas Hazuka	'88
VANGUARD BALANCED INDEX	Balanced	386.0	10.27	9,903.00	9,976.00	☆	3.8	662-7447	215-669-1000	None	None	None	George U. Sauter	'92
VANGUARD BD INDX INTMDT	Fixed Income	42.0	9.46	9,871.00	☆	☆	0.0	662-7447	215-669-1000	None	None	None	Ian A. MacKinnon	'94
VANGUARD BD INDX LONG	Fixed Income	4.7	9.21	9,724.00	☆	☆	0.0	662-7447	215-669-1000	None	None	None	Ian A. MacKinnon	'94
VANGUARD BD INDX SHORT	Fixed Income	57.4	9.73	9,970.00	☆	☆	0.0	662-7447	215-669-1000	None	None	None	Ian A. MacKinnon	'94
VANGUARD BD INDX TOTAL	Fixed Income	1,681.5	9.39	9,899.00	9,875.00	14,834.00	6.5	662-7447	215-669-1000	None	None	None	Ian A. MacKinnon	'86
VANGUARD CONVERTIBLE	Convertible Securities	190.8	10.89	9,648.00	10,050.00	16,127.00	4.7	662-7447	215-669-1000	None	None	None	Rohit M. Desai	'86
VANGUARD EQUITY INCOME	Equity Income	908.0	12.74	10,196.00	9,906.00	14,386.00	4.7	662-7447	215-669-1000	None	None	None	Roger Newell	'88
VANGUARD EXPLORER FUND	Small Company Growth	951.4	41.95	9,595.00	10,617.00	16,826.00	0.3	662-7447	215-669-1000	None	None	None	Abrams/Granahan	'94/'90
VANGUARD FXD GNMA PORT	Fixed Income	6,164.5	9.78	9,964.00	9,880.00	14,946.00	6.5	662-7447	215-669-1000	None	None	None	Paul Kaplan	'94
VANGUARD FXD HI YLD	Fixed Income	2,129.7	7.37	9,924.00	10,183.00	15,315.00	9.3	662-7447	215-669-1000	None	None	1.00	Earl E. McEvoy	'84
VANGUARD FXD INTMDT CORP	Fixed Income	98.6	9.22	9,882.00	☆	☆	0.0	662-7447	215-669-1000	None	None	None	Ian A. MacKinnon	'93
VANGUARD FXD INTMDT TREA	Fixed Income	875.9	9.91	9,892.00	9,756.00	☆	5.8	662-7447	215-669-1000	None	None	None	Ian A. MacKinnon	'91
VANGUARD FXD LG-TM CORP	Fixed Income	2,736.1	8.28	9,769.00	9,727.00	15,715.00	7.3	662-7447	215-669-1000	None	None	None	Earl E. McEvoy	'94
VANGUARD FXD LG-TM TREAS	Fixed Income	690.9	9.37	9,745.00	9,589.00	14,881.00	7.0	662-7447	215-669-1000	None	None	None	Ian A. MacKinnon	'86
VANGUARD FXD SHT-TM CORP	Fixed Income	3,346.2	10.51	10,006.00	10,141.00	14,687.00	5.6	662-7447	215-669-1000	None	None	None	Ian A. MacKinnon	'82
VANGUARD FXD SHT-TM FED	Fixed Income	1,696.9	9.92	9,954.00	10,069.00	14,334.00	5.1	662-7447	215-669-1000	None	None	None	Ian A. MacKinnon	'87

VANGUARD FXD SHT-TM TREA	Fixed Income	666.2	9.99	9,987.00	10,071.00	☆	4.8	662-7447	215-669-1000	None	None	None	Ian A. MacKinnon	'91
VANGUARD INDEX 500 PORT	S&P Index	8,604.1	41.81	10,040.00	10,124.00	16,183.00	2.7	662-7447	215-669-1000	None	None	None	George U. Sauter	'87
VANGUARD INDEX EXTND MKT	Midcap	941.5	18.19	9,732.00	10,239.00	15,693.00	1.3	662-7447	215-669-1000	None	None	None	George U. Sauter	'87
VANGUARD INDEX S&P GRO	Growth Income	57.7	9.64	9,989.00	9,953.00	☆	2.2	662-7447	215-669-1000	None	None	None	George U. Sauter	'92
VANGUARD INDEX S&P VALUE	Growth Income	288.5	11.20	10,079.00	10,277.00	☆	3.4	662-7447	215-669-1000	None	None	None	George U. Sauter	'92
VANGUARD INDEX TOT STOCK	Growth	637.9	11.04	9,910.00	10,079.00	☆	2.4	662-7447	215-669-1000	None	None	None	George U. Sauter	'92
VANGUARD INSTL INDEX FD	S&P Index	2,971.8	42.20	10,042.00	10,134.00	☆	2.8	662-7447	215-669-1000	None	None	None	George U. Sauter	'90
VANGUARD INTL IDX EMRG	Emerging Markets	12.2	10.57	☆	☆	☆	0.0	662-7447	215-669-1000	None	None	1.00	Gus Sauter	'94
VANGUARD INTL IDX EURO	European Region	674.8	11.54	9,948.00	11,591.00	☆	1.7	662-7447	215-669-1000	None	None	None	George U. Sauter	'90
VANGUARD INTL IDX PAC	Pacific Region	648.3	12.07	11,053.00	11,754.00	☆	0.5	662-7447	215-669-1000	None	None	None	George U. Sauter	'90
VANGUARD PREFERRED STK	Fixed Income	341.4	8.66	9,765.00	9,799.00	15,734.00	6.2	662-7447	215-669-1000	None	None	None	Earl E. McEvoy	'82
VANGUARD PRIMECAP	Growth	1,037.3	18.44	10,082.00	10,994.00	18,064.00	0.4	662-7447	215-669-1000	None	None	None	Howard B. Schow	'84
VANGUARD QUANTITATIVE	Growth Income	561.7	15.14	9,933.00	10,032.00	16,691.00	2.4	662-7447	215-669-1000	None	None	None	John Nagorniak	'86
VANGUARD SMALL CAP STK	Small Company Growth	547.7	14.84	9,661.00	10,545.00	15,707.00	1.2	662-7447	215-669-1000	None	None	None	George U. Sauter	'89
VANGUARD SPL ENERGY	Natural Resources	403.3	15.70	10,776.00	10,135.00	16,518.00	1.9	662-7447	215-669-1000	None	None	1.00	Ernst Von Metzsch	'84
VANGUARD SPL GOLD	Gold	627.6	12.65	9,906.00	10,785.00	15,107.00	2.1	662-7447	215-669-1000	None	None	1.00	David Hutchins	'87
VANGUARD SPL HEALTH	Health/Biotechnology	591.1	32.81	10,040.00	10,887.00	20,791.00	2.3	662-7447	215-669-1000	None	None	1.00	Edward Owens	'84
VANGUARD SPL UTILITIES	Utility	618.1	10.14	9,780.00	9,252.00	☆	5.7	662-7447	215-669-1000	None	None	None	John R. Ryan	'92
VANGUARD STAR	Balanced	3,780.3	12.89	10,105.00	10,228.00	15,093.00	3.6	662-7447	215-669-1000	None	None	None	The Vanguard Group	'85
VANGUARD WELLESLEY INC	Income	6,085.2	17.71	9,965.00	9,919.00	16,085.00	6.4	662-7447	215-669-1000	None	None	None	Ryan/McEvoy	'87/'82
VANGUARD WELLINGTON FUND	Balanced	8,414.3	19.51	10,148.00	10,239.00	15,401.00	4.7	662-7447	215-669-1000	None	None	None	Bajakian/Kaplan	'72/'94
VANGUARD WINDSOR ⊠	Growth Income	10,952.8	13.98	10,379.00	11,022.00	15,492.00	2.6	662-7447	215-669-1000	None	None	None	John C. Neff	'64
VANGUARD WINDSOR II	Growth Income	7,957.7	16.51	10,262.00	10,354.00	15,640.00	3.0	662-7447	215-669-1000	None	None	None	Multiple Managers	'85
VANGUARD WORLD INTL GRO	International	2,684.0	13.54	10,203.00	12,546.00	15,600.00	0.8	662-7447	215-669-1000	None	None	None	Richard R. Foulkes	'81
VANGUARD WORLD US GROWTH	Growth	1,848.4	14.58	10,048.00	10,151.00	17,696.00	1.4	662-7447	215-669-1000	None	None	None	J. Parker Hall, III	'87
VANGUARD/MORGAN GROWTH	Growth	1,082.5	11.07	9,685.00	9,733.00	15,297.00	1.5	662-7447	215-669-1000	None	None	None	Multiple Managers	'93
VANGUARD/TRUST EQ INTL	International	1,101.5	32.80	10,365.00	11,800.00	14,928.00	2.6	662-7447	215-669-1000	None	None	None	Jarrod Wilcox	'91
VANGUARD/TRUST EQ US	Growth Income	128.5	28.57	9,477.00	9,814.00	13,863.00	1.2	662-7447	215-669-1000	None	None	None	John Geewax	'92
VANKAMP ADJ RT GOVT; A	Fixed Income	7.2	9.41	9,995.00	10,108.00	☆	5.2	225-2222	708-684-6503	3.00	0.30	None	Laura Alter	'92
VANKAMP ADJ RT GOVT; B	Fixed Income	27.1	9.42	9,976.00	10,036.00	☆	4.4	225-2222	708-684-6503	None	1.00	3.00	Laura Alter	'92
VANKAMP ADJ RT GOVT; C	Fixed Income	4.0	9.40	9,955.00	☆	☆	0.0	225-2222	708-684-6503	None	1.00	1.00	Laura Alter	'93
VANKAMP GRO & INC; A	Growth Income	48.0	17.70	9,620.00	9,764.00	14,523.00	0.9	225-2222	708-684-6503	4.65	0.30	None	Dan Smith	'92
VANKAMP GRO & INC; B	Growth Income	24.4	17.68	9,598.00	9,666.00	☆	0.3	225-2222	708-684-6503	None	1.00	4.00	Dan Smith	'92
VANKAMP GRO & INC; C	Growth Income	0.5	17.69	9,593.00	☆	☆	0.0	225-2222	708-684-6503	None	1.00	1.00	Dan Smith	'93
VANKAMP GRO & INC; D	Growth Income	0.1	17.62	9,618.00	☆	☆	0.0	225-2222	708-684-6503	None	0.30	0.75	Dan Smith	'94
VANKAMP HIGH YIELD; A	Fixed Income	242.5	9.64	9,875.00	10,291.00	14,303.00	10.9	225-2222	708-684-6503	4.65	0.30	None	Kevin G. Mathews	'87
VANKAMP HIGH YIELD; B	Fixed Income	31.4	9.64	9,855.00	10,211.00	☆	10.1	225-2222	708-684-6503	None	1.00	4.00	Kevin G. Mathews	'93
VANKAMP HIGH YIELD; C	Fixed Income	1.1	9.64	9,855.00	☆	☆	0.0	225-2222	708-684-6503	None	1.00	1.00	Kevin G. Mathews	'93
VANKAMP HIGH YIELD; D	Fixed Income	0.1	9.65	9,867.00	☆	☆	0.0	225-2222	708-684-6503	None	0.30	0.75	Kevin G. Mathews	'94
VANKAMP SHORT GLBL; A	World Income	156.1	8.16	9,766.00	9,651.00	☆	8.1	225-2222	708-684-6503	3.00	0.30	None	Tom Slefinger	'90
VANKAMP SHORT GLBL; B	World Income	288.1	8.16	9,747.00	9,590.00	☆	7.3	225-2222	708-684-6503	None	1.00	3.00	Tom Slefinger	'91
VANKAMP SHORT GLBL; C	World Income	0.2	8.17	9,747.00	☆	☆	0.0	225-2222	708-684-6503	None	1.00	1.00	Tom Slefinger	'93
VANKAMP SHORT GLBL; D	World Income	0.1	8.17	9,777.00	☆	☆	0.0	225-2222	708-684-6503	None	0.30	0.75	Tom Slefinger	'94
VANKAMP STRAT INC; A ✪	Fixed Income	24.4	11.98	9,638.00	☆	☆	0.0	225-2222	708-684-6503	4.65	0.30	None	Peter Hegel	'93
VANKAMP STRAT INC; B ✪	Fixed Income	45.1	11.97	9,616.00	☆	☆	0.0	225-2222	708-684-6503	None	1.00	4.00	Peter Hegel	'93
VANKAMP STRAT INC; C ✪	Fixed Income	2.1	11.97	9,616.00	☆	☆	0.0	225-2222	708-684-6503	None	1.00	1.00	Peter Hegel	'93
VANKAMP US GOVT; A	Fixed Income	3,268.5	14.26	9,891.00	9,626.00	14,477.00	8.7	225-2222	708-684-6503	4.65	0.30	None	J. Doyle	'84
VANKAMP US GOVT; B	Fixed Income	473.7	14.25	9,867.00	9,548.00	☆	7.8	225-2222	708-684-6503	None	1.00	4.00	J. Doyle	'92
VANKAMP US GOVT; C	Fixed Income	12.0	14.22	9,860.00	☆	☆	0.0	225-2222	708-684-6503	None	1.00	1.00	J. Doyle	'93
VANKAMP US GOVT; D	Fixed Income	0.1	14.26	9,886.00	☆	☆	0.0	225-2222	708-684-6503	None	0.30	0.75	J. Doyle	'94

PERFORMANCE OF MUTUAL FUNDS (continued)

FUND NAME	OBJECTIVE	TOTAL NET ASSETS ($ MIL) 5/31/94	NET ASSET $ VALUE 6/30/94	PERFORMANCE (Return on initial $10,000 Investment) 3/31/94-6/30/94	6/30/93-6/30/94	6/30/89-6/30/94	DIVIDEND YIELD % 6/94	PHONE NUMBER 800	In-State	FEES Load	12b-1	Redemption	MANAGER	SINCE
VANKAMP UTILITY; A	Utility	52.3	12.91	9,707.00	☆	☆	0.0	225-2222	708-684-6503	4.65	0.30	None	Dan Smith	'93
VANKAMP UTILITY; B	Utility	85.1	12.88	9,684.00	☆	☆	0.0	225-2222	708-684-6503	None	1.00	4.00	Dan Smith	'93
VANKAMP UTILITY; C	Utility	1.1	12.87	9,691.00	☆	☆	0.0	225-2222	708-684-6503	None	1.00	1.00	Dan Smith	'93
VANKAMP UTILITY; D	Utility	0.1	12.92	9,700.00	☆	☆	0.0	225-2222	708-684-6503	None	0.30	0.75	Dan Smith	'94
VENTURE INCOME (+) PLUS	Fixed Income	63.8	4.95	9,903.00	10,583.00	13,193.00	11.8	279-0279	505-983-4335	4.75	0.25	None	B. Clark Stamper	'90
VICTORY AGGR GROWTH	Small Company Growth	30.3	8.94	9,420.00	☆	☆	0.0	832-1373	None	4.75	None	None	C. Lee Liscom	'94
VICTORY CORP BOND	Fixed Income	60.5	9.23	9,857.00	9,726.00	☆	5.6	832-1373	None	4.75	None	None	Timothy J. Brothers	'93
VICTORY EQUITY	Growth	125.8	9.98	9,681.00	9,860.00	☆	0.9	832-1373	None	4.75	None	None	C. Lee Liscom	'93
VICTORY EQUITY INCOME	Equity Income	0.4	9.60	10,021.00	☆	☆	0.0	832-1373	None	4.75	None	None	C. Lee Liscom	'94
VICTORY FD FOR INCOME	Fixed Income	36.2	9.67	9,933.00	9,963.00	14,577.00	7.6	832-1373	None	2.00	None	None	Robert Hennes	'87
VICTORY GOVT BOND	Fixed Income	120.7	9.38	9,901.00	9,783.00	☆	5.2	832-1373	None	4.75	None	None	Peter A. Farrell	'93
VICTORY INTERNATIONAL	International	35.7	9.98	10,234.00	☆	☆	0.0	832-1373	None	4.75	None	None	David McCraw	'94
VICTORY SHORT-TERM GOVT	Fixed Income	37.2	9.59	9,936.00	10,037.00	☆	4.0	832-1373	None	2.00	None	None	Susan H. Bailey	'93
VISION GRO & INC	Growth Income	24.7	9.64	9,787.00	☆	☆	0.0	836-2211	716-842-4488	4.50	None	None	Harbor Capital Management	'93
VISION US GOVT SECS	Fixed Income	25.2	9.01	9,719.00	☆	☆	0.0	836-2211	716-842-4488	4.50	None	None	M. Evanco	'93
VISTA BALANCED; A	Balanced	20.1	10.82	9,997.00	10,142.00	☆	3.4	348-4782	None	4.50	0.25	None	Adams/Nelson	'92/'92
VISTA BALANCED; B	Balanced	1.9	10.77	9,967.00	☆	☆	0.0	348-4782	None	None	0.75	5.00	Adams/Nelson	'93/'93
VISTA BOND ☛	Fixed Income	55.4	10.28	9,891.00	9,883.00	☆	6.4	348-4782	None	None	0.23	None	Mark Buonaugurio	'91
VISTA CAPITAL GR; A	Midcap	394.7	30.33	9,700.00	10,534.00	22,633.00	0.1	348-4782	None	4.75	0.25	None	Tincher/Klassen	'91/'93
VISTA CAPITAL GR; B ★	Midcap	41.7	30.24	9,687.00	☆	☆	0.0	348-4782	None	None	0.75	5.00	Tincher/Klassen	'93/'93
VISTA EQUITY ☛	Growth	90.7	12.51	10,042.00	10,306.00	☆	2.3	348-4782	None	None	0.15	None	Mark Tincher	'94
VISTA EQUITY INCOME	Equity Income	12.1	11.80	9,982.00	☆	☆	0.0	348-4782	None	4.50	0.05	None	Mark Tincher	'93
VISTA GLBL FXD INC; A	World Income	2.3	10.04	9,934.00	10,252.00	☆	3.7	348-4782	None	4.50	0.25	None	Madis Senner	'92
VISTA GLBL FXD INC; B	World Income	0.2	10.05	9,943.00	☆	☆	0.0	348-4782	None	None	0.75	5.00	Madis Senner	'93
VISTA GOVT INCOME; A	Fixed Income	116.0	10.87	9,846.00	9,800.00	14,501.00	5.6	348-4782	None	4.50	0.05	None	Tom Nelson	'92
VISTA GOVT INCOME; B	Fixed Income	4.0	10.87	9,833.00	☆	☆	0.0	348-4782	None	None	0.75	5.00	Tom Nelson	'93
VISTA GRO & INC; A	Growth Income	1,193.8	29.21	9,861.00	9,931.00	24,294.00	1.3	348-4782	None	4.75	0.25	None	Mark Tincher	'91
VISTA GRO & INC; B	Growth Income	88.0	29.11	9,851.00	☆	☆	0.0	348-4782	None	None	0.75	5.00	Mark Tincher	'93
VISTA IEEE BALANCED FUND	Balanced	8.3	9.21	9,786.00	☆	☆	0.0	348-4782	None	None	0.25	None	Frederick Muller	'93
VISTA INTL EQUITY; A	International	33.1	11.88	9,917.00	11,090.00	☆	0.0	348-4782	None	4.75	0.25	None	Joseph DeSantis	'93
VISTA INTL EQUITY; B	International	4.2	11.84	9,908.00	☆	☆	0.0	348-4782	None	None	0.75	5.00	Joseph DeSantis	'93
VISTA SH-TM BD ☛	Fixed Income	54.9	9.95	10,055.00	10,245.00	☆	4.8	348-4782	None	None	0.21	None	Linda Struble	'90
VOLUMETRIC FUND	Growth	11.4	14.03	9,518.00	9,440.00	13,923.00	0.2	541-3863	914-623-7637	None	None	None	Gabriel Gibs	'86
VOYAGEUR FD US GOVT SEC	Fixed Income	136.7	9.76	9,827.00	9,605.00	15,179.00	7.9	553-2143	612-376-7000	4.75	0.25	None	Wyatt/Vandenberg	'90/'93
VOYAGEUR GROWTH STOCK	Growth	28.5	17.12	9,873.00	9,753.00	15,827.00	0.4	553-2143	612-376-7000	4.75	0.25	None	James C. King	'90
WADDELL & REED GL INC	World Income	10.2	9.27	9,989.00	10,028.00	☆	3.7	None	913-236-2000	None	1.00	3.00	John E. Sundeen	'92
WADDELL & REED GROWTH	Growth	50.6	13.22	9,389.00	10,771.00	☆	0.0	None	913-236-2000	None	1.00	3.00	Mark G. Seferovich	'92
WADDELL & REED LTD-TM	Fixed Income	11.5	9.67	9,919.00	9,887.00	☆	3.6	None	913-236-2000	None	1.00	3.00	W. Patrick Sterner	'92
WADDELL & REED TOT RTN	Growth Income	72.5	11.75	9,800.00	10,362.00	☆	0.0	None	913-236-2000	None	1.00	3.00	Russell E. Thompson	'92
WADE FUND	Growth	0.5	30.56	9,993.00	9,923.00	15,100.00	0.0	None	901-682-4613	None	None	None	Maury Wade	'73
WALL STREET FUND	Growth	10.8	6.85	9,049.00	9,928.00	13,700.00	0.0	443-4693	212-207-1660	4.00	None	None	Robert Morse	'84
WASATCH AGGRESSIVE EQU	Small Company Growth	38.0	18.13	9,502.00	10,626.00	21,590.00	0.0	551-1700	801-533-0778	None	None	None	Samuel S. Stewart Jr.	'87
WASATCH GROWTH ★	Growth	12.6	13.67	9,434.00	9,830.00	17,366.00	0.0	551-1700	801-533-0778	None	None	None	Samuel S. Stewart Jr.	'87
WASATCH INCOME	Fixed Income	3.4	10.04	10,010.00	10,198.00	14,229.00	0.2	551-1700	801-533-0778	None	None	None	Samuel S. Stewart Jr.	'87
WASATCH MID-CAP ★	Midcap	1.0	9.86	9,676.00	9,508.00	☆	0.0	551-1700	801-533-0778	None	None	None	Samuel S. Stewart Jr.	'92

WASHINGTON MUTUAL INV	Growth Income	12,719.9	17.05	10,261.00	10,099.00	15,769.00	3.3	421-4120	714-671-7000	5.75	0.25	None	Multiple Managers	'52
WAYNE HUMMER GROWTH FUND	Growth	90.2	20.91	9,880.00	9,940.00	16,366.00	1.4	621-4477	312-431-1700	None	None	None	Alan Bird	'83
WAYNE HUMMER INCOME FUND	Fixed Income	31.7	14.63	9,845.00	9,989.00	☆	6.5	621-4477	312-431-1700	None	None	None	David Poitras	'92
WEITZ PARTNERS VALUE	Growth Income	53.0	9.35	10,108.00	☆	☆	0.0	232-4161	402-391-1980	None	None	None	Wallace Weitz	'94
WEITZ FIXED INCOME	Fixed Income	20.4	10.55	9,904.00	9,926.00	13,967.00	5.2	232-4161	402-391-1980	None	None	None	Weitz/Hayes	'88/'88
WEITZ HICKORY	Growth	2.6	11.36	9,514.00	10,845.00	☆	2.5	232-4161	402-391-1980	None	None	None	Richard Lawson	'93
WEITZ VALUE	Growth Income	111.1	15.55	10,089.00	10,422.00	16,336.00	0.2	232-4161	402-391-1980	None	None	None	Wallace Weitz	'86
WESTCORE BALANCED; INSTL	Flexible	52.4	17.70	9,946.00	9,903.00	☆	3.0	392-2673	303-623-2577	None	None	None	Fish/Cahill	'91/'91
WESTCORE BALANCED; RET	Flexible	3.2	17.68	9,941.00	☆	☆	0.0	392-2673	303-623-2577	4.50	0.35	None	Fish/Cahill	'93/'93
WESTCORE BASIC VAL; INSTL	Growth Income	78.6	20.44	9,987.00	10,014.00	13,214.00	2.8	392-2673	303-623-2577	None	None	None	Charlie Fish	'87
WESTCORE BASIC VAL; RET	Growth Income	0.7	20.44	9,981.00	☆	☆	0.0	392-2673	303-623-2577	4.50	0.35	None	Charlie Fish	'93
WESTCORE BOND PLUS	Fixed Income	58.2	14.25	9,897.00	9,868.00	14,684.00	6.0	392-2673	303-623-2577	4.50	None	None	Warren Hastings III	'90
WESTCORE EQ INCOME; INSTL	Equity Income	42.7	10.31	9,965.00	9,749.00	15,495.00	4.8	392-2673	303-623-2577	None	None	None	Larry Luchini	'88
WESTCORE EQ INCOME; RET	Equity Income	4.0	10.31	9,951.00	☆	☆	0.0	392-2673	303-623-2577	4.50	0.35	None	Larry Luchini	'93
WESTCORE GNMA; INSTL	Fixed Income	34.3	15.15	9,903.00	9,793.00	14,360.00	6.5	392-2673	303-623-2577	None	None	None	Warren Hastings III	'90
WESTCORE GNMA; RET	Fixed Income	8.5	15.14	9,894.00	☆	☆	0.0	392-2673	303-623-2577	4.50	0.30	None	Warren Hastings III	'93
WESTCORE GROWTH; INSTL	Growth	3.7	14.92	9,915.00	☆	☆	0.0	392-2673	303-623-2577	None	None	None	Peter Glidden	'93
WESTCORE GROWTH; RET	Growth	0.1	14.92	9,915.00	☆	☆	0.0	392-2673	303-623-2577	4.50	0.35	None	Peter Glidden	'93
WESTCORE INT-TM BD; INSTL	Fixed Income	89.0	9.95	9,883.00	9,845.00	14,367.00	5.3	392-2673	303-623-2577	None	None	None	John Cormey	'92
WESTCORE INT-TM BD; RET	Fixed Income	1.9	9.95	9,872.00	☆	☆	0.0	392-2673	303-623-2577	4.50	0.30	None	John Cormey	'93
WESTCORE LONG-TERM BOND	Fixed Income	26.9	9.11	9,717.00	9,592.00	15,322.00	6.3	392-2673	303-623-2577	4.50	None	None	John Cormey	'92
WESTCORE MIDCO GRO; INSTL	Midcap	335.5	15.24	9,495.00	10,304.00	21,517.00	0.0	392-2673	303-623-2577	None	None	None	Todger Anderson	'86
WESTCORE MIDCO GRO; RET	Midcap	16.2	15.25	9,490.00	☆	☆	0.0	392-2673	303-623-2577	4.50	0.35	None	Todger Anderson	'93
WESTCORE MODERN VAL EQU	Growth Income	36.7	12.50	10,083.00	10,040.00	15,915.00	2.5	392-2673	303-623-2577	4.50	None	None	Varilyn Schock	'91
WESTCORE SH-TM GOV; INSTL	Fixed Income	46.3	15.30	9,992.00	10,115.00	13,868.00	3.8	392-2673	303-623-2577	None	None	None	Warren Hastings III	'90
WESTCORE SH-TM GOV; RET	Fixed Income	8.1	15.30	9,995.00	☆	☆	0.0	392-2673	303-623-2577	2.00	0.25	None	Warren Hastings III	'93
WESTON NEW CENTURY CAP	Flexible	37.8	11.59	9,940.00	10,679.00	15,386.00	1.9	None	617-239-0445	None	0.25	None	Douglas Biggar	'89
WESTON NEW CENTURY I	Income	22.1	10.84	9,927.00	10,398.00	14,489.00	4.1	None	617-239-0445	None	0.25	None	Douglas Biggar	'89
WESTWOOD BALANCED; INSTL	Balanced	18.9	6.95	9,919.00	10,934.00	☆	2.8	253-4510	None	4.00	None	None	Byrne/Fraze	'91/'91
WESTWOOD EQUITY; INSTL	Capital Appreciation	8.1	5.26	9,962.00	11,159.00	15,424.00	0.9	253-4510	None	4.00	None	None	Susan Byrne	'87
WESTWOOD INTMDT BD; INSTL	Fixed Income	8.2	9.59	9,817.00	9,742.00	☆	4.6	253-4510	None	4.00	None	None	Patricia Fraze	'91
WILLIAM PENN QUALITY INC	Fixed Income	28.5	9.89	9,814.00	10,038.00	15,557.00	8.8	523-8440	610-670-1031	4.75	0.25	None	Miller Anderson & Sherr.	'87
WILLIAM PENN US GOVT	Fixed Income	47.0	10.00	9,883.00	9,839.00	15,058.00	8.3	523-8440	610-670-1031	4.75	0.25	None	Miller Anderson & Sherr.	'87
WINTHROP FOCUS AGG GRO	Midcap	119.6	15.25	9,858.00	11,348.00	18,568.00	0.2	225-8011	212-504-4000	None	0.50	4.00	Engle/Vogel	'89/'93
WINTHROP FOCUS FIX INC	Fixed Income	36.6	9.83	9,893.00	9,858.00	14,842.00	5.8	225-8011	212-504-4000	None	0.25	4.00	Cathy Jameson	'86
WINTHROP FOCUS GRO&INC	Growth Income	57.9	13.02	10,065.00	10,674.00	15,799.00	1.6	225-8011	212-504-4000	None	0.50	4.00	James Engle	'86
WINTHROP FOCUS GROWTH	Growth	52.3	10.44	9,952.00	10,539.00	14,978.00	0.0	225-8011	212-504-4000	None	0.50	4.00	Engle/Vogel	'89/'93
WM BLAIR GROWTH SHARES	Growth	151.6	9.46	10,194.00	11,124.00	19,360.00	0.4	742-7272	312-364-8000	None	None	None	Barber/Fuller	'93/'93
WM BLAIR INCOME	Fixed Income	170.3	10.07	9,890.00	9,993.00	☆	5.7	742-7272	312-364-8000	None	None	None	Bentley M. Myer	'91
WM BLAIR INTL GROWTH SHS	International	55.8	13.62	10,089.00	12,264.00	☆	0.0	742-7272	312-364-8000	None	None	None	Framlington Overseas Mgmt	'92
WOMENS EQUITY MUTUAL FD	Capital Appreciation	0.7	9.98	9,690.00	☆	☆	0.0	424-2295	415-296-9135	None	None	None	Pro-Conscience Funds	'93
WOOD ISLAND GROWTH FUND	Growth	5.1	14.64	9,832.00	10,483.00	15,989.00	0.4	None	415-461-3850	None	None	None	Siebel/Kirk	'84/'84
WOOD ISLAND TOTAL RETURN	Flexible	1.9	8.96	9,912.00	10,048.00	14,738.00	1.2	None	415-461-3850	None	None	None	Siebel/Kirk	'83/'83
WOODWARD BOND; RTL	Fixed Income	516.9	9.50	9,769.00	9,763.00	☆	7.3	688-3350	None	4.50	0.35	None	Douglas Swanson	'91
WOODWARD EQ INDEX; RTL	S&P Index	330.7	10.61	10,040.00	10,107.00	☆	2.7	688-3350	None	None	0.35	None	F. Richard Neumann	'92
WOODWARD GRO/VAL; RTL	Growth Income	542.9	11.00	10,196.00	10,631.00	☆	1.7	688-3350	None	4.50	0.35	None	George Abel	'91
WOODWARD INTMDT BD; RTL	Fixed Income	412.9	9.70	9,803.00	9,784.00	☆	5.4	688-3350	None	4.50	0.35	None	Douglas Swanson	'91
WOODWARD INTRINSIC; RTL	Growth Income	214.4	10.54	10,026.00	10,420.00	☆	3.0	688-3350	None	4.50	0.35	None	Christopher Gassen	'91
WOODWARD OPPTY; RTL	Small Company Growth	484.0	13.76	9,737.00	10,730.00	☆	0.6	688-3350	None	4.50	0.35	None	Ronald L. Doyle	'91
WORKING ASSETS CIT BAL	Balanced	44.6	10.64	9,944.00	9,585.00	☆	1.8	223-7010	415-989-3200	4.00	0.35	None	Seneca/Little	'93/'93

★ VISTA CAPITAL GR; B--Fund has been reclassified from Growth to Midcap.
★ WASATCH GROWTH--Fund has been reclassified from Midcap to Growth.

★ WASATCH MID-CAP--Fund has been reclassified from Growth to Midcap.

PERFORMANCE OF MUTUAL FUNDS (continued)

FUND NAME	OBJECTIVE	TOTAL NET ASSETS ($ MIL) 5/31/94	NET ASSET $ VALUE 6/30/94	PERFORMANCE (Return on initial $10,000 Investment) 3/31/94-6/30/94	6/30/93-6/30/94	6/30/89-6/30/94	DIVIDEND YIELD % 6/94	PHONE NUMBER 800	In-State	FEES Load	12b-1	Redemption	MANAGER	SINCE
WORKING ASSETS CIT EMERG	Midcap	3.1	9.93	10,051.00	☆	☆	0.0	223-7010	415-989-3200	4.00	0.35	None	Ron Jacks	'94
WORKING ASSETS CIT GL EQ	Global	5.0	9.80	9,800.00	☆	☆	0.0	223-7010	415-989-3200	4.00	0.35	None	Lilia Clemente	'94
WORKING ASSETS CIT GRO	Growth	51.6	11.05	10,009.00	9,694.00	☆	0.0	223-7010	415-989-3200	4.00	0.35	None	Seneca/Little	'93/'93
WORKING ASSETS CIT INC	Fixed Income	24.0	10.04	9,907.00	10,000.00	☆	5.6	223-7010	415-989-3200	2.00	0.35	None	Gail Seneca	'93
WORLD APPRECIATION FUND	Environmental	N/A	N/A	N/A	N/A	☆	0.0	421-4120	714-671-7000	None	None	None	Multiple Managers	'90
WORLD INV UTILITY; A	Utility	1.3	9.65	☆	☆	☆	0.0	245-4770	412-288-1900	4.50	None	None	Christopher H. Wiles	'94
WORLD INV UTILITY; FORT	Utility	0.4	9.65	☆	☆	☆	0.0	245-4770	412-288-1900	1.00	0.25	1.00	Christopher H. Wiles	'94
WPG FUNDS TR DVD INCOME	Equity Income	23.9	12.07	9,535.00	9,105.00	13,686.00	4.6	223-3332	212-908-9500	None	None	None	Nelson Schaenen, Jr.	'89
WPG FUNDS TR GOVT SEC	Fixed Income	313.8	9.24	9,532.00	9,421.00	14,095.00	7.7	223-3332	212-908-9500	None	0.05	None	David W. Hoyle	'86
WPG FUNDS TR QUANT EQ	Growth Income	60.0	5.33	9,963.00	9,981.00	☆	1.5	223-3332	212-908-9500	None	None	None	Joseph N. Pappo	'93
WPG GROWTH	Small Company Growth	171.2	98.10	8,729.00	9,237.00	15,377.00	0.3	223-3332	212-908-9500	None	None	None	John P. Callaghan	'93
WPG GROWTH & INCOME	Growth Income	65.4	21.97	9,679.00	9,783.00	16,038.00	3.9	223-3332	212-908-9500	None	None	None	A. Roy Knutsen	'92
WPG INTERNATIONAL	International	17.5	11.40	10,142.00	12,025.00	12,064.00	0.0	223-3332	212-908-9500	None	None	None	Raymond Haines	'94
WPG TUDOR FUND	Capital Appreciation	175.4	19.77	8,978.00	9,379.00	15,060.00	0.0	223-3332	212-908-9500	None	None	None	Melville Straus	'73
WRBG PINCUS CAP APP; COM	Growth	155.4	13.22	9,962.00	10,110.00	15,042.00	0.4	257-5614	212-878-0600	None	None	None	Andrew H. Massie	'89
WRBG PINCUS CAP APP; SR 2	Growth	11.3	13.18	9,955.00	10,060.00	☆	0.2	257-5614	212-878-0600	None	0.50	None	Andrew H. Massie	'91
WRBG PINCUS EMER GR; COM	Small Company Growth	198.4	20.01	9,457.00	9,969.00	16,779.00	0.0	257-5614	212-878-0600	None	None	None	Dater/Lurito	'88/'93
WRBG PINCUS EMER GR; SR 2	Small Company Growth	47.9	19.74	9,440.00	9,920.00	☆	0.0	257-5614	212-878-0600	None	0.50	None	Dater/Lurito	'91/'93
WRBG PINCUS FXD INC	Fixed Income	83.9	9.67	9,860.00	10,065.00	14,154.00	6.1	257-5614	212-878-0600	None	None	None	Christensen/Van Daven	'92/'92
WRBG PINCUS GL FXD; COM	World Income	86.9	10.43	9,767.00	10,130.00	☆	5.7	257-5614	212-878-0600	None	None	None	Christensen/Bhandari	'90/'93
WRBG PINCUS GRO & INC	Growth Income	227.7	13.45	9,621.00	10,827.00	19,908.00	0.5	257-5614	212-878-0600	None	None	None	Anthony G. Orphanos	'92
WRBG PINCUS INSTL INT EQ	International	223.6	15.40	10,448.00	13,372.00	☆	1.1	257-5614	212-878-0600	None	None	None	Richard King	'92
WRBG PINCUS INTL EQ; COM	International	899.3	19.36	10,400.00	13,170.00	20,930.00	0.3	257-5614	212-878-0600	None	None	None	Richard King	'89
WRBG PINCUS INTL EQ; SR 2	International	129.7	19.27	10,413.00	13,143.00	☆	0.2	257-5614	212-878-0600	None	0.50	None	Richard King	'91
WRBG PINCUS INTMDT GOVT	Fixed Income	43.7	9.78	9,903.00	9,930.00	14,765.00	5.5	257-5614	212-878-0600	None	None	None	Christensen/Van Daven	'89/'92
WRIGHT EQ INTL BLUE CHIP	International	184.1	13.12	9,985.00	11,621.00	☆	0.5	232-0013	203-333-6666	None	0.20	None	Team Managed	'89
WRIGHT EQ JR BLUE CHIP	Small Company Growth	62.1	11.16	9,625.00	10,343.00	13,615.00	0.8	232-0013	203-333-6666	None	0.20	None	Team Managed	'85
WRIGHT EQ QUAL CORE EQU	Growth Income	84.5	12.02	9,958.00	9,925.00	15,090.00	1.3	232-0013	203-333-6666	None	0.20	None	Team Managed	'85
WRIGHT EQ SEL BLUE CHIP	Growth Income	186.9	14.06	9,818.00	9,899.00	14,421.00	1.1	232-0013	203-333-6666	None	0.20	None	Team Managed	'83
WRIGHT EQUI DUTCH	European Region	8.4	10.63	10,066.00	12,360.00	☆	0.0	888-9471	203-333-6666	None	0.25	None	Team Managed	'90
WRIGHT EQUI HONG KONG	Pacific Region	22.1	16.22	9,649.00	11,522.00	☆	0.9	888-9471	203-333-6666	None	0.25	None	Team Managed	'90
WRIGHT EQUI ITALIAN	European Region	2.5	5.57	9,330.00	11,253.00	☆	0.0	888-9471	203-333-6666	None	0.25	None	Team Managed	'90
WRIGHT EQUI SPANISH	European Region	13.2	6.47	9,715.00	11,512.00	☆	0.0	888-9471	203-333-6666	None	0.25	None	Team Managed	'90
WRIGHT INC CURRENT INC	Fixed Income	101.4	9.94	9,870.00	9,673.00	14,453.00	7.0	232-0013	203-333-6666	None	0.20	None	Team Managed	'87
WRIGHT INC GOVT OBLIG	Fixed Income	20.5	12.60	9,674.00	9,404.00	14,649.00	7.0	232-0013	203-333-6666	None	0.20	None	Team Managed	'83
WRIGHT INC NEAR TERM BD	Fixed Income	292.6	10.17	9,910.00	9,831.00	14,123.00	6.1	232-0013	203-333-6666	None	0.20	None	Team Managed	'83
WRIGHT INC TOTAL RETURN	Fixed Income	190.1	11.79	9,806.00	9,565.00	14,112.00	6.4	232-0013	203-333-6666	None	0.20	None	Team Managed	'83
WRLD FDS NEWPORT TIGER	Pacific Region	387.9	10.73	10,603.00	12,769.00	22,002.00	0.4	527-9500	804-285-8211	5.00	None	None	John Mussey	'89
WRLD FDS VNTBEL EUROPAC	International	148.8	16.28	9,963.00	12,100.00	15,345.00	1.0	527-9500	804-285-8211	None	None	None	Fabrizio Pierallini	'94
WRLD FDS VNTBEL US VALUE	Growth Income	34.5	11.51	10,332.00	10,382.00	☆	1.3	527-9500	804-285-8211	None	None	None	Ed Walczak	'90
WSIS WERTHEIM EQTY VALUE	Growth	2.8	9.47	10,021.00	☆	☆	0.0	464-3108	212-492-6000	None	None	None	J Richard Walton	'94
WSIS WERTHEIM HI YLD INC	Fixed Income	3.1	9.07	9,755.00	☆	☆	0.0	464-3108	212-492-6000	None	None	None	Kenneth Malamed	'94
WSIS WERTHEIM INV GR INC	Fixed Income	1.1	9.33	9,788.00	☆	☆	0.0	464-3108	212-492-6000	None	None	None	Kenneth Malamed	'94
WSIS WERTHEIM SH-TM INV	Fixed Income	2.5	9.90	10,047.00	☆	☆	0.0	464-3108	212-492-6000	None	None	None	Not Available	'94
WSIS WERTHEIM SMALL CAP	Small Company Growth	4.2	9.46	9,793.00	☆	☆	0.0	464-3108	212-492-6000	None	None	None	Nancy Tooke	'94

YACKTMAN FUND	Growth	156.3	9.34	10,110.00	10,310.00	☆	2.0	525-8258	None	None	0.15	None	Donald Yacktman	'92
YAMAICHI FDS GLOBAL FUND	Global	32.8	9.03	10,089.00	11,508.00	13,165.00	1.0	327-6143	212-432-8670	4.75	None	None	Edward Burke	'89
ZSA ASSET ALLOCATION	Flexible	15.6	10.40	9,472.00	9,213.00	☆	1.3	525-3863	919-972-9922	None	0.35	None	Zaske, Sarafa & Assoc.	'92
ZSA EQUITY	Capital Appreciation	4.0	9.94	9,360.00	8,955.00	☆	0.0	525-3863	919-972-9922	None	0.35	None	Zaske, Sarafa & Assoc.	'92
ZWEIG SR TR APPREC; A	Small Company Growth	230.5	14.14	9,847.00	10,499.00	☆	0.4	272-2700	212-635-9800	5.50	0.30	None	David Katzen	'91
ZWEIG SR TR APPREC; C	Small Company Growth	135.2	14.01	9,832.00	10,415.00	☆	0.0	272-2700	212-635-9800	None	1.00	1.25	David Katzen	'92
ZWEIG SR TR GOVT SEC; A	Fixed Income	54.6	9.87	9,891.00	10,049.00	13,897.00	4.8	272-2700	212-635-9800	4.75	0.30	None	Timothy Clark	'92
ZWEIG SR TR GOVT SEC; C	Fixed Income	23.7	9.85	9,886.00	10,009.00	☆	4.4	272-2700	212-635-9800	None	0.75	1.25	Timothy Clark	'92
ZWEIG SR TR MGD ASST; A	Flexible	150.0	11.99	9,893.00	10,332.00	☆	1.4	272-2700	212-635-9800	5.50	0.30	None	Timothy Clark	'93
ZWEIG SR TR MGD ASST; C	Flexible	587.8	11.96	9,876.00	10,265.00	☆	0.8	272-2700	212-635-9800	None	1.00	1.25	Timothy Clark	'93
ZWEIG SR TR PRIORITY; A	Capital Appreciation	51.0	12.11	9,806.00	9,903.00	16,026.00	0.2	272-2700	212-635-9800	5.50	0.30	None	Joe Kalish	'89
ZWEIG SR TR PRIORITY; C	Capital Appreciation	20.0	11.99	9,796.00	9,835.00	☆	0.0	272-2700	212-635-9800	None	1.00	1.25	Joe Kalish	'92
ZWEIG SR TR STRATEGY; A	Growth	429.3	12.42	9,904.00	10,464.00	☆	0.8	272-2700	212-635-9800	5.50	0.30	None	David Katzen	'89
ZWEIG SR TR STRATEGY; C	Growth	260.5	12.41	9,888.00	10,385.00	☆	0.3	272-2700	212-635-9800	None	1.00	1.25	David Katzen	'92

MUNICIPAL BOND FUNDS

FUND NAME	OBJECTIVE	TOTAL NET ASSETS ($ MIL) 5/31/94	NET ASSET $ VALUE 6/30/94	PERFORMANCE (Return on initial $10,000 Investment) 3/31/94-6/30/94	6/30/93-6/30/94	6/30/89-6/30/94	DIVIDEND YIELD % 6/94	PHONE NUMBER 800	In-State	FEES Load	12b-1	Redemption	MANAGER	SINCE
AAL MUNICIPAL BOND ◪	General Muni	372.5	10.50	10,020.00	9,939.00	14,006.00	5.1	553-6319	414-734-5721	4.75	0.25	None	Duff & Phelps Inv. Co.	'87
AARP INS TF GEN BOND	Insured Muni	2,002.8	17.16	10,077.00	9,913.00	14,290.00	5.0	253-2277	617-439-4640	None	None	None	Carleton/Condon	'88/'89
ABT FL HIGH INCOME MUNI	Florida Muni	73.2	10.11	10,201.00	10,274.00	☆	6.7	553-7838	407-655-7255	4.75	0.25	None	Steven Eldredge	'92
ABT FL LTD TM TAX-FREE	Florida Muni	2.9	11.45	10,171.00	☆	☆	0.0	553-7838	407-655-7255	3.00	0.25	None	Steven Eldredge	'94
ABT FL TAX-FREE FUND	Florida Muni	197.5	10.72	10,073.00	10,006.00	14,443.00	6.0	553-7838	407-655-7255	4.75	0.25	None	Steven Eldredge	'89
ACCESSOR MUNI INTMDT FXD	Intermediate Muni	13.5	11.29	10,037.00	☆	☆	0.0	759-3504	206-224-7420	None	None	None	Michael Powers	'94
ADVANTAGE MUNI NATL	General Muni	28.7	9.23	10,119.00	☆	☆	5.6	243-8115	203-525-1421	None	0.50	4.00	Margaret D. Patel	'93
ADVANTAGE MUNI NY	New York Muni	13.3	9.07	10,062.00	☆	☆	5.5	243-8115	203-525-1421	None	0.50	4.00	Margaret D. Patel	'93
ADVANTAGE MUNI PA	Pennsylvania Muni	13.4	9.22	10,148.00	☆	☆	5.4	243-8115	203-525-1421	None	0.50	4.00	Margaret D. Patel	'93
AETNA TAX-FREE; ADV	General Muni	27.3	9.23	☆	☆	☆	0.0	238-6263	203-273-0121	None	0.50	1.00	Neil Grabowski	'94
AETNA TAX-FREE; SEL	General Muni	27.3	9.23	10,075.00	☆	☆	0.0	238-6263	203-273-0121	None	None	None	Neil Grabowski	'94
AIM TXFR INTMDT; AIM	Intermediate Muni	100.6	10.61	10,104.00	10,215.00	14,078.00	4.5	347-1919	713-626-1919	1.00	None	None	Berry/Turman	'88/'87
AIM TXFR TX-EX BD OF CT	Connecticut Muni	41.0	10.63	10,079.00	10,118.00	☆	5.5	347-1919	713-626-1919	4.75	0.25	None	Berry/Turman	'92/'92
AIM MUNICIPAL BOND; A	General Muni	278.4	8.09	10,099.00	10,105.00	14,458.00	5.9	347-1919	713-626-1919	4.75	0.25	None	Berry/Turman	'92/'92
AIM MUNICIPAL BOND; B	General Muni	5.3	8.09	10,078.00	☆	☆	0.0	347-1919	713-626-1919	None	1.00	5.00	Berry/Turman	'93/'93
ALABAMA TAX FREE BOND	Single State Muni	10.4	9.91	10,065.00	10,123.00	☆	4.4	543-8721	513-629-2000	None	None	None	T. Leavell & Assoc.	'93
ALLIANCE MUNI II FL; A	Florida Muni	7.1	9.01	10,051.00	9,565.00	☆	6.3	227-4618	201-319-4000	4.25	0.30	None	Susan G. Peabody	'93
ALLIANCE MUNI II FL; B	Florida Muni	16.4	9.01	10,032.00	9,496.00	☆	5.5	227-4618	201-319-4000	None	1.00	3.00	Susan G. Peabody	'93
ALLIANCE MUNI II FL; C	Florida Muni	50.3	9.01	10,032.00	9,496.00	☆	5.5	227-4618	201-319-4000	None	1.00	None	Susan G. Peabody	'93
ALLIANCE MUNI II MA; A	Massachusetts Muni	0.5	10.16	10,312.00	☆	☆	0.0	227-4618	201-319-4000	4.25	0.30	None	Peabody/Mather	'94/'94

PERFORMANCE OF MUTUAL FUNDS (continued)

FUND NAME	OBJECTIVE	TOTAL NET ASSETS ($ MIL) 5/31/94	NET ASSET $ VALUE 6/30/94	PERFORMANCE (Return on initial $10,000 Investment) 3/31/94-6/30/94	6/30/93-6/30/94	6/30/89-6/30/94	DIVIDEND YIELD % 6/94	PHONE NUMBER 800	In-State	FEES Load	12b-1	Redemption	MANAGER	SINCE
ALLIANCE MUNI II MA; B	Massachusetts Muni	0.6	10.16	10,294.00	☆	☆	0.0	227-4618	201-319-4000	None	1.00	3.00	Peabody/Mather	'94/'94
ALLIANCE MUNI II MA; C	Massachusetts Muni	0.1	10.16	10,294.00	☆	☆	0.0	227-4618	201-319-4000	None	1.00	None	Peabody/Mather	'94/'94
ALLIANCE MUNI II MI; A	Michigan Muni	1.0	9.52	10,209.00	☆	☆	0.0	227-4618	201-319-4000	4.25	0.30	None	Peabody/Mather	'94/'94
ALLIANCE MUNI II MI; B	Michigan Muni	1.3	9.52	10,191.00	☆	☆	0.0	227-4618	201-319-4000	None	1.00	3.00	Peabody/Mather	'94/'94
ALLIANCE MUNI II MI; C	Michigan Muni	2.1	9.52	10,191.00	☆	☆	0.0	227-4618	201-319-4000	None	1.00	None	Peabody/Mather	'94/'94
ALLIANCE MUNI II MN; A	Minnesota Muni	2.0	9.28	10,160.00	9,825.00	☆	6.1	227-4618	201-319-4000	4.25	0.30	None	Susan G. Peabody	'93
ALLIANCE MUNI II MN; B	Minnesota Muni	6.0	9.28	10,151.00	9,755.00	☆	5.3	227-4618	201-319-4000	None	1.00	3.00	Susan G. Peabody	'93
ALLIANCE MUNI II MN; C	Minnesota Muni	10.6	9.28	10,140.00	9,755.00	☆	5.3	227-4618	201-319-4000	None	1.00	None	Susan G. Peabody	'93
ALLIANCE MUNI II NJ; A	New Jersey Muni	8.6	9.13	10,008.00	9,636.00	☆	6.2	227-4618	201-319-4000	4.25	0.30	None	Peabody/Oliver	'93/'94
ALLIANCE MUNI II NJ; B	New Jersey Muni	28.1	9.13	9,988.00	9,567.00	☆	5.4	227-4618	201-319-4000	None	1.00	3.00	Peabody/Oliver	'93/'94
ALLIANCE MUNI II NJ; C	New Jersey Muni	27.9	9.13	9,988.00	9,567.00	☆	5.4	227-4618	201-319-4000	None	1.00	None	Peabody/Oliver	'93/'94
ALLIANCE MUNI II OH; A	Ohio Muni	2.3	9.19	10,115.00	9,738.00	☆	6.1	227-4618	201-319-4000	4.25	0.30	None	Peabody/Oliver	'93/'94
ALLIANCE MUNI II OH; B	Ohio Muni	18.2	9.19	10,096.00	9,667.00	☆	5.4	227-4618	201-319-4000	None	1.00	3.00	Peabody/Oliver	'93/'94
ALLIANCE MUNI II OH; C	Ohio Muni	26.6	9.19	10,096.00	9,667.00	☆	5.4	227-4618	201-319-4000	None	1.00	None	Peabody/Oliver	'93/'94
ALLIANCE MUNI II PA; A	Pennsylvania Muni	6.6	9.28	10,129.00	9,857.00	☆	6.2	227-4618	201-319-4000	4.25	0.30	None	Peabody/Oliver	'93/'94
ALLIANCE MUNI II PA; B	Pennsylvania Muni	21.9	9.28	10,110.00	9,786.00	☆	5.5	227-4618	201-319-4000	None	1.00	3.00	Peabody/Oliver	'93/'94
ALLIANCE MUNI II PA; C	Pennsylvania Muni	20.2	9.28	10,110.00	9,786.00	☆	5.5	227-4618	201-319-4000	None	1.00	None	Peabody/Oliver	'93/'94
ALLIANCE MUNI CA; A	California Muni	508.0	9.87	10,058.00	9,813.00	14,185.00	6.0	227-4618	201-319-4000	4.25	0.30	None	Susan G. Peabody	'86
ALLIANCE MUNI CA; B	California Muni	162.1	9.88	10,049.00	9,752.00	☆	5.3	227-4618	201-319-4000	None	1.00	3.00	Susan G. Peabody	'93
ALLIANCE MUNI CA; C	California Muni	119.8	9.88	10,049.00	9,752.00	☆	5.3	227-4618	201-319-4000	None	1.00	None	Susan G. Peabody	'93
ALLIANCE MUNI INS CA; A	California Muni	106.6	12.37	10,010.00	9,633.00	13,811.00	5.5	227-4618	201-319-4000	4.25	0.30	None	Susan G. Peabody	'86
ALLIANCE MUNI INS CA; B	California Muni	26.0	12.37	9,989.00	9,556.00	☆	4.7	227-4618	201-319-4000	None	1.00	3.00	Susan G. Peabody	'93
ALLIANCE MUNI INS CA; C	California Muni	14.9	12.37	9,989.00	9,556.00	☆	4.7	227-4618	201-319-4000	None	1.00	None	Susan G. Peabody	'93
ALLIANCE MUNI INS NA; A	Insured Muni	170.0	9.46	10,058.00	9,783.00	14,217.00	5.7	227-4618	201-319-4000	4.25	0.30	None	Susan G. Peabody	'86
ALLIANCE MUNI INS NA; B	Insured Muni	54.7	9.46	10,038.00	9,719.00	☆	4.9	227-4618	201-319-4000	None	1.00	3.00	Susan G. Peabody	'93
ALLIANCE MUNI INS NA; C	Insured Muni	29.1	9.46	10,038.00	9,719.00	☆	4.9	227-4618	201-319-4000	None	1.00	None	Susan G. Peabody	'93
ALLIANCE MUNI NATL; A	General Muni	370.7	9.83	10,041.00	9,775.00	14,466.00	6.1	227-4618	201-319-4000	4.25	0.30	None	Susan G. Peabody	'86
ALLIANCE MUNI NATL; B	General Muni	260.8	9.83	10,021.00	9,704.00	☆	5.3	227-4618	201-319-4000	None	1.00	3.00	Susan G. Peabody	'93
ALLIANCE MUNI NATL; C	General Muni	159.6	9.83	10,021.00	9,713.00	☆	5.3	227-4618	201-319-4000	None	1.00	None	Susan G. Peabody	'93
ALLIANCE MUNI NY; A	New York Muni	200.3	9.21	10,053.00	9,736.00	14,335.00	6.1	227-4618	201-319-4000	4.25	0.30	None	Peabody/Oliver	'86/'94
ALLIANCE MUNI NY; B	New York Muni	79.4	9.21	10,033.00	9,675.00	☆	5.3	227-4618	201-319-4000	None	1.00	3.00	Peabody/Oliver	'93/'94
ALLIANCE MUNI NY; C	New York Muni	38.2	9.21	10,033.00	9,675.00	☆	5.3	227-4618	201-319-4000	None	0.75	None	Peabody/Oliver	'93/'94
AMBASSADOR MI TX-FR; FID	Michigan Muni	2.2	9.19	10,088.00	☆	☆	0.0	892-4366	None	None	None	None	Wendy Harries	'94
AMBASSADOR MI TX-FR; INV	Michigan Muni	16.1	9.19	10,082.00	☆	☆	0.0	892-4366	None	None	None	None	Wendy Harries	'94
AMBASSADOR MI TX-FR; RET	Michigan Muni	0.2	9.19	10,082.00	☆	☆	0.0	892-4366	None	3.75	0.25	None	Wendy Harries	'94
AMBASSADOR TX-FR INT; FID	Short-Term Muni	3.1	10.12	10,100.00	10,057.00	☆	4.6	892-4366	None	None	None	None	Wendy Harries	'92
AMBASSADOR TX-FR INT; INV	Short-Term Muni	103.9	10.12	10,089.00	10,042.00	13,488.00	4.5	892-4366	None	None	None	None	Wendy Harries	'92
AMBASSADOR TX-FR INT; RET	Short-Term Muni	4.9	10.12	10,089.00	10,042.00	☆	4.5	892-4366	None	3.75	0.25	None	Wendy Harries	'92
AMCORE VINTAGE INT TX-FR	Intermediate Muni	33.0	9.86	10,055.00	10,028.00	☆	4.3	438-6375	None	3.75	0.25	None	Dean Countryman	'93
AMER CAP MUNI BOND; A	General Muni	315.9	9.89	10,053.00	10,070.00	14,290.00	5.9	421-5666	713-993-0500	4.75	0.25	None	Bob Evans	'88
AMER CAP MUNI BOND; B	General Muni	34.3	9.89	10,022.00	9,959.00	☆	5.0	421-5666	713-993-0500	None	1.00	4.00	Bob Evans	'92
AMER CAP MUNI BOND; C	General Muni	6.5	9.90	10,022.00	☆	☆	0.0	421-5666	713-993-0500	None	1.00	1.00	Bob Evans	'93
AMER CAP TEXAS MUNI; A	Texas Muni	14.3	9.71	10,056.00	10,125.00	☆	5.7	421-5666	713-993-0500	4.75	0.25	None	Bob Evans	'92
AMER CAP TEXAS MUNI; B	Texas Muni	8.8	9.71	10,035.00	10,041.00	☆	4.8	421-5666	713-993-0500	None	1.00	4.00	Bob Evans	'92
AMER CAP TX-EX HI YD; A	High-Yield Muni	426.3	10.76	10,152.00	10,249.00	14,347.00	7.3	421-5666	713-993-0500	4.75	0.25	None	Wayne Godlin	'91

AMER CAP TX-EX HI YD; B	High-Yield Muni	145.4	10.75	10,123.00	10,163.00	☆	6.5	421-5666	713-993-0500	None	1.00	4.00	Wayne Godlin	'92
AMER CAP TX-EX INS; A	Insured Muni	72.5	11.03	10,045.00	10,080.00	13,660.00	5.6	421-5666	713-993-0500	4.75	0.25	None	Bob Evans	'89
AMER CAP TX-EX INS; B	Insured Muni	38.4	11.03	10,035.00	10,007.00	☆	4.9	421-5666	713-993-0500	None	1.00	4.00	Bob Evans	'92
AMER FDS TX-EX SR I MD	Maryland Muni	74.2	14.84	10,052.00	9,981.00	13,813.00	5.1	421-4120	714-671-7000	4.75	0.25	None	Multiple Managers	'86
AMER FDS TX-EX SR I VA	Virginia Muni	93.1	15.31	10,033.00	10,004.00	13,945.00	5.3	421-4120	714-671-7000	4.75	0.25	None	Multiple Managers	'86
AMER FDS TX-EX SR II CA	California Muni	221.3	15.24	10,104.00	10,058.00	14,093.00	5.5	421-4120	714-671-7000	4.75	0.25	None	Multiple Managers	'86
AMER PERFORM INTMDT TXFR	Intermediate Muni	18.2	10.30	10,101.00	10,195.00	☆	5.3	762-7085	None	3.00	0.25	None	Bill Bequette	'92
ARBOR OVB WV TX-EX; A	Single State Muni	24.6	9.44	10,033.00	☆	☆	0.0	545-6331	None	None	None	None	Jay Thomas	'93
ARBOR OVB WV TX-EX; B	Single State Muni	1.7	9.43	10,016.00	☆	☆	0.0	545-6331	None	None	0.25	None	Jay Thomas	'93
ARCH TX-EX MO; INV	Missouri Muni	27.9	11.00	10,088.00	9,940.00	☆	5.0	452-2724	617-722-7868	4.50	0.10	None	Peter Merzian	'93
ARCH TX-EX MO; TR	Missouri Muni	47.7	11.00	10,093.00	9,960.00	14,115.00	5.2	452-2724	617-722-7868	None	None	None	Peter Merzian	'93
ATLAS CA INS INTMDT ✋	California Muni	27.1	9.91	10,033.00	10,113.00	☆	4.4	933-2852	None	3.00	0.25	None	Andrew Windmueller	'93
ATLAS CA MUNI BOND ✋	California Muni	187.8	10.74	10,071.00	10,015.00	☆	5.6	933-2852	None	3.00	0.25	None	Andrew Windmueller	'91
ATLAS NATL INS INTMDT ✋	Intermediate Muni	16.3	9.91	10,075.00	10,156.00	☆	4.4	933-2852	None	3.00	0.25	None	Andrew Windmueller	'93
ATLAS NATL MUNI BOND ✋	General Muni	55.4	10.76	10,069.00	9,998.00	☆	5.6	933-2852	None	3.00	0.25	None	Andrew Windmueller	'91
BABSON TX-FR INC LONG	General Muni	29.8	8.52	10,050.00	9,824.00	13,972.00	4.9	422-2766	816-471-5200	None	None	None	Joel Vernick	'86
BABSON TX-FR INC SHORT	Short-Term Muni	28.9	10.62	10,089.00	10,071.00	13,438.00	4.3	422-2766	816-471-5200	None	None	None	Joel Vernick	'86
BB&T NC INTMDT TX-FR; INV	Single State Muni	12.8	9.81	10,071.00	10,030.00	☆	3.8	228-1872	614-899-4668	2.00	0.15	None	Branch Banking & Trust Co	'93
BB&T NC INTMDT TX-FR; TR ▮	Single State Muni	25.0	9.81	10,075.00	10,044.00	☆	4.0	228-1872	614-899-4668	None	None	None	Branch Banking & Trust Co	'92
BENHAM CA TX-FR HIGH YLD	California Muni	105.0	8.96	10,078.00	10,101.00	14,370.00	6.3	472-3389	415-965-4274	None	None	None	Steve Permut	'88
BENHAM CA TX-FR INSURED	California Muni	190.6	9.55	10,074.00	9,872.00	14,146.00	5.5	472-3389	415-965-4274	None	None	None	David MacEwen	'91
BENHAM CA TX-FR INTMDT	California Muni	445.8	10.75	10,078.00	10,098.00	14,051.00	5.0	472-3389	415-965-4274	None	None	None	David MacEwen	'91
BENHAM CA TX-FR LONG	California Muni	276.4	10.73	10,061.00	9,949.00	14,320.00	5.8	472-3389	415-965-4274	None	None	None	David MacEwen	'91
BENHAM CA TX-FR SHT-TM	California Muni	122.1	10.08	10,056.00	10,175.00	☆	3.7	472-3389	415-965-4274	None	None	None	David MacEwen	'92
BENHAM MUNI AZ INTMDT	Single State Muni	4.4	10.06	☆	☆	☆	0.0	472-3389	415-965-4274	None	None	None	David MacEwen	'94
BENHAM MUNI FL INTMDT	Florida Muni	3.9	10.03	☆	☆	☆	0.0	472-3389	415-965-4274	None	None	None	David MacEwen	'94
BENHAM MUNI NATL TF INT	Intermediate Muni	70.6	10.53	10,080.00	10,112.00	14,228.00	4.9	472-3389	415-965-4274	None	None	None	David MacEwen	'91
BENHAM MUNI NATL TF LONG	General Muni	57.6	11.14	10,063.00	9,910.00	14,596.00	5.5	472-3389	415-965-4274	None	None	None	David MacEwen	'91
BILTMORE SC MUNI	South Carolina Muni	82.4	10.54	10,076.00	10,118.00	☆	5.4	462-7538	919-725-0036	4.50	None	None	Michael J. Peters	'93
BLANCHARD FLEX TAX-FREE ✋	General Muni	25.0	4.77	10,048.00	☆	☆	0.0	None	212-779-7979	None	0.25	None	Ken McCauley	'93
BNY HAMILTON INTMDT NY	New York Muni	53.2	9.92	10,077.00	10,065.00	☆	3.9	426-9363	None	None	0.25	None	Colleen M. Frey	'92
BT INV INTMDT TAX FREE ✋	Intermediate Muni	29.7	9.99	10,055.00	10,065.00	☆	4.1	545-1074	None	None	0.20	None	Gary Pollack	'92
BULL&BEAR MUNI INCOME	General Muni	18.8	15.77	9,866.00	9,482.00	13,118.00	4.6	847-4200	212-363-1100	None	0.50	None	C.Clifford McCarthy Jr.	'90
CA INV TR CA INS TX-FR	California Muni	17.9	10.13	10,121.00	10,076.00	☆	4.5	225-8778	415-398-2727	None	None	None	Philip McClanahan	'92
CA INV TR CA TX-FR INC	California Muni	224.6	11.99	10,044.00	9,818.00	14,349.00	5.5	225-8778	415-398-2727	None	None	None	Philip McClanahan	'85
CALVERT MUNI AZ INTMDT	Single State Muni	2.1	4.84	10,084.00	☆	☆	0.0	368-2748	301-951-4820	2.75	None	None	Reno Martini	'93
CALVERT MUNI CA INTMDT	California Muni	40.8	10.10	10,075.00	10,185.00	☆	5.0	368-2748	301-951-4820	2.75	0.25	None	Reno Martini	'92
CALVERT MUNI FL INTMDT	Florida Muni	2.9	4.80	10,129.00	☆	☆	0.0	368-2748	301-951-4820	2.75	None	None	Reno Martini	'93
CALVERT MUNI INTMDT MUNI	Intermediate Muni	44.6	10.03	10,096.00	10,343.00	☆	4.9	368-2748	301-951-4820	2.75	0.25	None	Reno Martini	'92
CALVERT MUNI MD INTMDT	Single State Muni	8.4	4.78	10,035.00	☆	☆	0.0	368-2748	301-951-4820	2.75	None	None	Reno Martini	'93
CALVERT MUNI MI INTMDT	Michigan Muni	8.2	4.87	10,101.00	☆	☆	0.0	368-2748	301-951-4820	2.75	None	None	Reno Martini	'93
CALVERT MUNI NY INTMDT	New York Muni	2.8	4.86	10,102.00	☆	☆	0.0	368-2748	301-951-4820	2.75	None	None	Reno Martini	'93
CALVERT MUNI PA INTMDT	Pennsylvania Muni	1.5	4.79	10,145.00	☆	☆	0.0	368-2748	301-951-4820	2.75	None	None	Reno Martini	'93
CALVERT MUNI VA INTMDT	Single State Muni	6.0	4.85	10,099.00	☆	☆	0.0	368-2748	301-951-4820	2.75	None	None	Reno Martini	'93
CALVERT TX-FR RSVS LONG	General Muni	49.3	16.11	10,011.00	10,110.00	13,932.00	5.7	368-2748	301-951-4820	3.75	0.35	None	Reno Martini	'83
CALVERT TX-FR RSVS LTD	Short-Term Muni	654.5	10.66	10,067.00	10,311.00	12,929.00	3.5	368-2748	301-951-4820	2.00	None	None	Reno Martini	'81
CALVERT TX-FR RSVS VT	Single State Muni	67.6	15.72	10,038.00	10,093.00	☆	5.3	368-2748	301-951-4820	3.75	0.35	None	Reno Martini	'91
CAMBRIDGE MUNI INC; A	General Muni	26.4	14.52	10,054.00	9,904.00	☆	5.7	382-0016	None	4.75	None	None	William Grady	'93
CAMBRIDGE MUNI INC; B	General Muni	50.1	14.54	10,041.00	9,852.00	☆	5.1	382-0016	None	None	0.50	1.00	William Grady	'93
CARNEGIE TX EX OH MUNI	Ohio Muni	12.8	9.48	10,041.00	10,147.00	13,879.00	5.8	321-2322	216-781-4440	4.50	None	None	Roy Wallace	'86

PERFORMANCE OF MUTUAL FUNDS *(continued)*

FUND NAME	OBJECTIVE	TOTAL NET ASSETS ($ MIL) 5/31/94	NET ASSET $ VALUE 6/30/94	PERFORMANCE (Return on initial $10,000 Investment) 3/31/94-6/30/94	6/30/93-6/30/94	6/30/89-6/30/94	DIVIDEND YIELD % 6/94	PHONE NUMBER 800	In-State	FEES Load	12b-1	Redemption	MANAGER	SINCE
CASCADES TX-FR TR OF OR	Oregon Muni	322.2	10.27	10,058.00	10,024.00	13,940.00	5.5	872-6734	212-697-6666	4.00	None	None	Edward Potts	'86
CG CAP MKTS MUNI BOND ◪	General Muni	62.1	7.95	10,008.00	9,635.00	☆	5.0	None	None	None	None	None	N/A	N/A
CGM TR AMERICAN TAX FREE	General Muni	11.4	9.21	10,091.00	☆	☆	0.0	345-4048	617-859-7714	None	None	None	Janice H. Saul	'93
CHUBB INV TAX EXEMPT FD	General Muni	15.9	11.70	10,027.00	9,983.00	14,091.00	5.0	258-3648	603-226-5000	3.00	0.25	None	Frederick Gaertner	'89
CHURCHILL TX-FR FD OF KY	Kentucky Muni	243.9	10.30	10,097.00	10,083.00	14,389.00	5.9	872-5859	212-697-6666	4.00	None	None	T. Radford Hazelip	'87
COLONIAL CA TAX-EX; A	California Muni	342.1	6.99	10,033.00	9,840.00	13,686.00	6.0	426-3750	617-426-3750	4.75	None	None	William Loring	'86
COLONIAL CA TAX-EX; B	California Muni	103.3	6.99	10,014.00	9,766.00	☆	5.2	426-3750	617-426-3750	None	0.75	5.00	William Loring	'92
COLONIAL CT TAX-EX; A	Connecticut Muni	84.9	7.21	10,077.00	9,861.00	☆	5.7	426-3750	617-426-3750	4.75	None	None	Jeffrey Augustine	'91
COLONIAL CT TAX-EX; B	Connecticut Muni	72.1	7.21	10,058.00	9,788.00	☆	5.0	426-3750	617-426-3750	None	0.75	5.00	Jeffrey Augustine	'92
COLONIAL FL TAX-EX; A	Florida Muni	24.4	7.21	10,171.00	9,853.00	☆	5.7	426-3750	617-426-3750	4.75	None	None	Jeffrey Augustine	'93
COLONIAL FL TAX-EX; B	Florida Muni	32.3	7.21	10,152.00	9,780.00	☆	4.9	426-3750	617-426-3750	None	0.75	5.00	Jeffrey Augustine	'93
COLONIAL HY MUNI; B ☒	High-Yield Muni	115.3	9.74	10,066.00	10,044.00	☆	6.2	426-3750	617-426-3750	None	1.00	5.00	Bonny Boatman	'92
COLONIAL INT TAX-EX; A	Intermediate Muni	17.6	7.53	10,188.00	10,174.00	☆	4.8	426-3750	617-426-3750	3.25	0.20	None	William Loring	'93
COLONIAL INT TAX-EX; B	Intermediate Muni	13.5	7.53	10,171.00	10,115.00	☆	4.1	426-3750	617-426-3750	None	0.85	4.00	William Loring	'93
COLONIAL MA TAX-EX; A	Massachusetts Muni	205.8	7.52	10,095.00	10,018.00	14,540.00	6.0	426-3750	617-426-3750	4.75	None	None	Jeffrey Augustine	'88
COLONIAL MA TAX-EX; B	Massachusetts Muni	53.1	7.52	10,076.00	9,944.00	☆	5.2	426-3750	617-426-3750	None	0.75	5.00	Jeffrey Augustine	'92
COLONIAL MI TAX-EX; A	Michigan Muni	43.0	6.76	10,144.00	10,004.00	13,908.00	5.8	426-3750	617-426-3750	4.75	None	None	Brian Hartford	'93
COLONIAL MI TAX-EX; B	Michigan Muni	15.2	6.76	10,125.00	9,930.00	☆	5.0	426-3750	617-426-3750	None	0.75	5.00	Brian Hartford	'93
COLONIAL MN TAX-EX; A	Minnesota Muni	40.7	6.95	10,078.00	10,052.00	13,765.00	6.0	426-3750	617-426-3750	4.75	None	None	Brian Hartford	'93
COLONIAL MN TAX-EX; B	Minnesota Muni	12.5	6.95	10,059.00	9,977.00	☆	5.2	426-3750	617-426-3750	None	0.75	5.00	Brian Hartford	'93
COLONIAL NC TAX-EX; A	North Carolina Muni	16.3	6.79	10,175.00	☆	☆	0.0	426-3750	617-426-3750	4.75	None	None	Jeffrey Augustine	'93
COLONIAL NC TAX-EX; B	North Carolina Muni	13.2	6.79	10,156.00	☆	☆	0.0	426-3750	617-426-3750	None	0.75	5.00	Jeffrey Augustine	'93
COLONIAL NY TAX-EX; A	New York Muni	59.5	6.82	10,047.00	9,833.00	13,941.00	6.0	426-3750	617-426-3750	4.75	None	None	Jeffrey Augustine	'87
COLONIAL NY TAX-EX; B	New York Muni	45.0	6.82	10,028.00	9,760.00	☆	5.2	426-3750	617-426-3750	None	0.75	5.00	Jeffrey Augustine	'92
COLONIAL OH TAX-EX; A	Ohio Muni	75.7	7.05	10,142.00	9,924.00	13,963.00	5.7	426-3750	617-426-3750	4.75	None	None	Brian Hartford	'93
COLONIAL OH TAX-EX; B	Ohio Muni	53.3	7.05	10,123.00	9,851.00	☆	4.9	426-3750	617-426-3750	None	0.75	5.00	Brian Hartford	'93
COLONIAL SH-TM TAX-EX; A	Short-Term Muni	13.2	7.46	10,073.00	10,179.00	☆	2.9	426-3750	617-426-3750	1.00	0.10	None	William Loring	'93
COLONIAL TAX-EX INS; A	Insured Muni	224.4	7.92	10,085.00	9,902.00	13,910.00	5.5	426-3750	617-426-3750	4.75	0.25	None	William Loring	'87
COLONIAL TAX-EX INS; B	Insured Muni	50.4	7.92	10,066.00	9,828.00	☆	4.7	426-3750	617-426-3750	None	1.00	5.00	William Loring	'92
COLONIAL TAX-EX; A	General Muni	3,172.8	13.01	10,044.00	9,921.00	13,937.00	6.2	426-3750	617-426-3750	4.75	0.25	None	Hardie/Boatman	'84/'93
COLONIAL TAX-EX; B	General Muni	474.6	13.01	10,025.00	9,847.00	☆	5.4	426-3750	617-426-3750	None	1.00	5.00	Hardie/Boatman	'92/'93
COLUMBIA MUNI BOND	Oregon Muni	378.7	11.85	10,075.00	9,944.00	13,807.00	5.4	547-1707	503-222-3606	None	None	None	Tom Thomsen	'84
COMMON SENSE MUNI BOND	General Muni	108.5	13.21	10,043.00	10,056.00	14,107.00	5.4	544-5445	404-381-1000	4.75	None	None	Bob Evans	'88
COMPASS CAP MUNI BOND	Intermediate Muni	36.3	10.30	10,128.00	9,939.00	☆	4.9	451-8371	215-254-1000	3.75	None	None	Bob Cembor	'93
COMPASS CAP NJ MUNI BD	New Jersey Muni	106.2	10.81	10,109.00	9,992.00	☆	4.8	451-8371	215-254-1000	3.75	None	None	Bob Cembor	'93
COMPASS CAP PA MUNI BD	Pennsylvania Muni	18.9	9.47	10,096.00	☆	☆	0.0	451-8371	215-254-1000	3.75	None	None	Mary Ellen Durkosh	'93
COMPOSITE TX-EX BD; A	General Muni	239.5	7.39	10,063.00	9,859.00	14,130.00	5.2	543-8072	509-353-3550	4.00	0.25	None	Team Managed	'92
COMPOSITE TX-EX BD; B	General Muni	0.7	7.39	10,030.00	☆	☆	0.0	543-8072	509-353-3550	None	1.00	3.00	Team Managed	'94
CONESTOGA PA TAX-FREE	Pennsylvania Muni	7.8	9.83	10,050.00	9,995.00	☆	4.5	344-2716	None	4.00	None	None	Craig Moyer	'92
COREFUND INTMDT MUNI; A	Intermediate Muni	1.1	9.68	10,101.00	9,971.00	☆	4.0	355-2673	None	None	None	None	Joe Baxter	'93
COREFUND INTMDT MUNI; B	Intermediate Muni	1.3	9.67	10,085.00	9,946.00	☆	3.8	355-2673	None	4.50	0.25	None	Joe Baxter	'93
CRESTFUNDS VA MUNI; INV	Virginia Muni	7.2	9.68	10,120.00	9,841.00	☆	4.6	451-5435	None	4.50	None	None	Boyce G. Reid	'94
CRESTFUNDS VA MUNI; TR	Virginia Muni	44.8	9.69	10,131.00	9,829.00	☆	4.6	451-5435	None	None	0.15	None	Boyce G. Reid	'94
CT&T INTMDT MUNI	Intermediate Muni	10.2	9.68	10,099.00	☆	☆	0.0	992-8151	None	None	0.25	None	Lois Pasquale	'93
CUNA TX-FR INTMDT-TERM	Intermediate Muni	2.2	9.63	10,101.00	☆	☆	0.0	638-5660	410-547-2308	None	0.25	None	Peter Van Dyke	'93

DEAN WITTER CAL TAX FR	California Muni	1,111.9	12.32	10,017.00	9,882.00	13,644.00	5.3	869-3863	212-392-2550	None	0.75	5.00	James Willison	'84
DEAN WITTER LTD MUNI TR	Intermediate Muni	145.6	9.54	10,037.00	☆	☆	0.0	869-3863	212-392-2550	None	None	None	Katherine H. Stromberg	'93
DEAN WITTER MUNI AZ	Arizona Muni	56.3	10.00	10,075.00	9,853.00	☆	5.6	869-3863	212-392-2550	4.00	0.15	None	James Willison	'91
DEAN WITTER MUNI CA	California Muni	128.8	10.00	10,004.00	9,721.00	☆	5.9	869-3863	212-392-2550	4.00	0.15	None	James Willison	'91
DEAN WITTER MUNI FL	Florida Muni	81.7	10.24	10,115.00	9,931.00	☆	5.6	869-3863	212-392-2550	4.00	0.15	None	James Willison	'91
DEAN WITTER MUNI MA	Massachusetts Muni	18.0	10.21	10,076.00	9,889.00	☆	5.7	869-3863	212-392-2550	4.00	0.15	None	James Willison	'91
DEAN WITTER MUNI MI	Michigan Muni	21.3	10.09	10,059.00	9,848.00	☆	5.7	869-3863	212-392-2550	4.00	0.15	None	James Willison	'91
DEAN WITTER MUNI MN	Minnesota Muni	12.0	9.98	10,125.00	9,884.00	☆	5.6	869-3863	212-392-2550	4.00	0.15	None	James Willison	'91
DEAN WITTER MUNI NJ	New Jersey Muni	51.1	10.09	10,039.00	9,793.00	☆	5.7	869-3863	212-392-2550	4.00	0.15	None	James Willison	'91
DEAN WITTER MUNI NY	New York Muni	15.2	10.17	10,041.00	9,783.00	☆	6.0	869-3863	212-392-2550	4.00	0.15	None	James Willison	'91
DEAN WITTER MUNI OH	Ohio Muni	26.2	10.08	10,046.00	9,853.00	☆	5.6	869-3863	212-392-2550	4.00	0.15	None	James Willison	'91
DEAN WITTER MUNI PA	Pennsylvania Muni	52.2	10.14	10,088.00	9,787.00	☆	5.7	869-3863	212-392-2550	4.00	0.15	None	James Willison	'91
DEAN WITTER NY TXFR IN	New York Muni	230.2	11.30	10,003.00	9,753.00	13,762.00	5.3	869-3863	212-392-2550	None	0.75	5.00	James Willison	'85
DW SELECT MUNI REINVEST	General Muni	92.5	11.82	10,052.00	9,903.00	13,974.00	5.6	869-3863	212-392-2550	None	None	None	James Willison	'83
DEAN WITTER TAX-EXEMPT	General Muni	1,461.2	11.43	10,061.00	9,898.00	14,203.00	6.4	869-3863	212-392-2550	4.00	None	None	James Willison	'80
DELAWARE TX-FR INSURED	Insured Muni	90.7	10.95	10,042.00	10,093.00	13,942.00	5.7	523-4640	215-988-1333	4.75	0.30	None	Patrick P. Coyne	'94
DELAWARE TX-FR INTMDT	Intermediate Muni	27.8	10.24	10,127.00	10,335.00	☆	5.1	523-4640	215-988-1333	3.00	0.30	None	Patrick P. Coyne	'93
DELAWARE TX-FR PA	Pennsylvania Muni	1,002.8	8.26	10,028.00	10,106.00	14,337.00	5.9	523-4640	215-988-1333	4.75	0.30	None	J. Michael Pokorny	'80
DELAWARE TX-FR USA	General Muni	733.5	12.01	10,057.00	10,204.00	14,331.00	6.0	523-4640	215-988-1333	4.75	0.30	None	J. Michael Pokorny	'84
DG INV MUNI INC	General Muni	36.3	9.98	10,037.00	9,881.00	☆	4.8	344-2488	None	2.00	None	None	John Mark McKenzie	'92
DREYFUS BASIC INT MUNI	Intermediate Muni	4.3	12.48	☆	☆	☆	0.0	373-9387	516-338-3300	None	None	None	Karen Hand	'94
DREYFUS BASIC MUNI BOND	General Muni	4.3	12.61	☆	☆	☆	0.0	373-9387	516-338-3300	None	None	None	Karen Hand	'94
DREYFUS CA INTMDT MUNI	California Muni	282.7	13.04	10,097.00	10,129.00	☆	5.4	373-9387	516-338-3300	None	None	None	Lawrence Troutman	'92
DREYFUS CA TAX EX BOND	California Muni	1,654.3	14.43	10,028.00	9,952.00	13,765.00	5.8	373-9387	516-338-3300	None	None	None	Lawrence Troutman	'86
DREYFUS CT INTMDT MUNI	Single State Muni	139.5	12.91	10,073.00	10,110.00	☆	5.3	373-9387	516-338-3300	None	None	None	Stephen Kris	'92
DREYFUS FL INTMDT MUNI	Florida Muni	459.8	13.00	10,096.00	10,133.00	☆	5.2	373-9387	516-338-3300	None	None	None	Stephen Kris	'92
DREYFUS GEN CA MUNI BD	California Muni	352.8	13.04	10,039.00	9,908.00	☆	6.0	373-9387	516-338-3300	None	None	None	Paul Disdier	'89
DREYFUS GEN MUNI BOND	General Muni	1,021.8	14.48	10,024.00	9,845.00	14,784.00	6.0	373-9387	516-338-3300	None	0.20	None	Paul Disdier	'88
DREYFUS GEN NY MUNI BD	New York Muni	338.6	19.53	10,051.00	9,948.00	14,955.00	5.8	373-9387	516-338-3300	None	0.20	None	Monica Wieboldt	'88
DREYFUS INSURED MUNI BD	Insured Muni	251.3	17.34	10,043.00	9,729.00	13,856.00	5.6	373-9387	516-338-3300	None	0.20	None	Lawrence Troutman	'85
DREYFUS INTMDT MUNI	Intermediate Muni	1,744.1	13.74	10,107.00	10,116.00	14,388.00	5.5	373-9387	516-338-3300	None	None	None	Monica Wieboldt	'85
DREYFUS MA INTMDT MUNI	Massachusetts Muni	83.9	12.84	10,067.00	10,084.00	☆	5.1	373-9387	516-338-3300	None	None	None	Lawrence Troutman	'92
DREYFUS MA TAX EX BOND	Massachusetts Muni	167.8	15.83	10,051.00	9,955.00	14,104.00	5.7	373-9387	516-338-3300	None	None	None	Lawrence Troutman	'86
DREYFUS MUNICIPAL BOND	General Muni	4,067.5	12.26	10,044.00	9,888.00	14,169.00	6.1	373-9387	516-338-3300	None	None	None	Richard Moynihan	'76
DREYFUS NJ INTMDT MUNI	Single State Muni	238.4	13.04	10,095.00	10,063.00	☆	5.2	373-9387	516-338-3300	None	None	None	Stephen Kris	'92
DREYFUS NJ MUNI BOND	New Jersey Muni	638.0	12.98	10,056.00	9,955.00	14,585.00	6.0	373-9387	516-338-3300	None	0.25	None	Samuel Weinstock	'87
DREYFUS NY INS TAX EX BD	New York Muni	172.9	11.10	10,016.00	9,819.00	13,956.00	5.3	373-9387	516-338-3300	None	0.25	None	Susan Byrne	'91
DREYFUS NY INTMDT TAX EX	New York Muni	391.0	17.63	10,111.00	10,130.00	14,371.00	5.0	373-9387	516-338-3300	None	0.25	None	Monica Wieboldt	'87
DREYFUS NY TAX EX BOND	New York Muni	1,947.1	14.90	10,041.00	9,902.00	14,198.00	5.8	373-9387	516-338-3300	None	None	None	Monica Wieboldt	'85
DREYFUS PA INTMDT MUNI	Pennsylvania Muni	18.4	12.45	10,130.00	☆	☆	0.0	373-9387	516-338-3300	None	None	None	Monica Wieboldt	'93
DREYFUS PREM CA INS; B	California Muni	2.4	11.31	10,028.00	☆	☆	0.0	373-9387	516-338-3300	None	0.50	3.00	Stephen Kris	'93
DREYFUS PREM CA MUNI; A	California Muni	217.3	12.55	10,055.00	9,997.00	14,493.00	5.9	373-9387	516-338-3300	4.50	None	None	Paul Disdier	'88
DREYFUS PREM CA MUNI; B	California Muni	19.0	12.56	10,041.00	9,949.00	☆	5.3	373-9387	516-338-3300	None	0.50	3.00	Paul Disdier	'93
DREYFUS PREM INS CA; A	California Muni	1.3	11.31	10,050.00	☆	☆	0.0	373-9387	516-338-3300	4.50	None	None	Stephen Kris	'93
DREYFUS PREM MUNI BD; A	General Muni	542.4	13.73	10,050.00	9,962.00	14,953.00	6.3	373-9387	516-338-3300	4.50	None	None	Samuel Weinstock	'87
DREYFUS PREM MUNI BD; B	General Muni	97.1	13.73	10,035.00	9,896.00	☆	5.7	373-9387	516-338-3300	None	0.50	3.00	Samuel Weinstock	'93
DREYFUS PREM MUNI AZ; A	Arizona Muni	12.6	12.48	10,040.00	9,877.00	☆	6.0	373-9387	516-338-3300	4.50	None	None	Stephen Kris	'92
DREYFUS PREM MUNI AZ; B	Arizona Muni	6.9	12.49	10,028.00	9,828.00	☆	5.4	373-9387	516-338-3300	None	0.50	3.00	Stephen Kris	'93
DREYFUS PREM MUNI CT; A	Connecticut Muni	362.7	11.77	10,090.00	9,953.00	14,353.00	5.7	373-9387	516-338-3300	4.50	None	None	Samuel Weinstock	'87
DREYFUS PREM MUNI CT; B	Connecticut Muni	33.4	11.76	10,075.00	9,889.00	☆	5.1	373-9387	516-338-3300	None	0.50	3.00	Samuel Weinstock	'93

PERFORMANCE OF MUTUAL FUNDS *(continued)*

FUND NAME	OBJECTIVE	TOTAL NET ASSETS ($ MIL) 5/31/94	NET ASSET $ VALUE 6/30/94	PERFORMANCE (Return on initial $10,000 Investment) 3/31/94-6/30/94	6/30/93-6/30/94	6/30/89-6/30/94	DIVIDEND YIELD % 6/94	PHONE NUMBER 800	In-State	FEES Load	12b-1	Redemption	MANAGER	SINCE
DREYFUS PREM MUNI FL; A	Florida Muni	285.5	14.43	10,139.00	10,038.00	14,873.00	5.8	373-9387	516-338-3300	4.50	None	None	Paul Disdier	'88
DREYFUS PREM MUNI FL; B	Florida Muni	23.0	14.43	10,131.00	9,979.00	☆	5.2	373-9387	516-338-3300	None	0.50	3.00	Paul Disdier	'93
DREYFUS PREM MUNI GA; A	Georgia Muni	10.2	12.58	10,049.00	9,837.00	☆	5.8	373-9387	516-338-3300	4.50	None	None	Stephen Kris	'92
DREYFUS PREM MUNI GA; B	Georgia Muni	17.3	12.59	10,044.00	9,788.00	☆	5.2	373-9387	516-338-3300	None	0.50	3.00	Stephen Kris	'93
DREYFUS PREM MUNI MA; A	Massachusetts Muni	76.6	11.58	10,047.00	10,015.00	14,557.00	6.1	373-9387	516-338-3300	4.50	None	None	Samuel Weinstock	'87
DREYFUS PREM MUNI MA; B	Massachusetts Muni	3.8	11.57	10,024.00	9,951.00	☆	5.5	373-9387	516-338-3300	None	0.50	3.00	Samuel Weinstock	'93
DREYFUS PREM MUNI MD; A	Maryland Muni	332.3	12.42	10,059.00	9,923.00	14,482.00	5.8	373-9387	516-338-3300	4.50	None	None	Paul Disdier	'88
DREYFUS PREM MUNI MD; B	Maryland Muni	31.2	12.42	10,044.00	9,865.00	☆	5.2	373-9387	516-338-3300	None	0.50	3.00	Paul Disdier	'93
DREYFUS PREM MUNI MI; A	Michigan Muni	187.0	15.22	10,102.00	10,120.00	14,782.00	5.8	373-9387	516-338-3300	4.50	None	None	Paul Disdier	'88
DREYFUS PREM MUNI MI; B	Michigan Muni	14.5	15.22	10,087.00	10,067.00	☆	5.2	373-9387	516-338-3300	None	0.50	3.00	Paul Disdier	'93
DREYFUS PREM MUNI MN; A	Minnesota Muni	155.9	14.68	10,098.00	10,030.00	14,520.00	5.8	373-9387	516-338-3300	4.50	None	None	Paul Disdier	'88
DREYFUS PREM MUNI MN; B	Minnesota Muni	21.5	14.70	10,084.00	9,971.00	☆	5.2	373-9387	516-338-3300	None	0.50	3.00	Paul Disdier	'93
DREYFUS PREM MUNI NC; A	North Carolina Muni	68.3	12.65	10,035.00	9,771.00	☆	5.7	373-9387	516-338-3300	4.50	None	None	Samuel Weinstock	'91
DREYFUS PREM MUNI NC; B	North Carolina Muni	39.6	12.64	10,020.00	9,717.00	☆	5.1	373-9387	516-338-3300	None	0.50	3.00	Samuel Weinstock	'93
DREYFUS PREM MUNI OH; A	Ohio Muni	292.7	12.68	10,087.00	10,106.00	14,848.00	5.8	373-9387	516-338-3300	4.50	None	None	Paul Disdier	'88
DREYFUS PREM MUNI OH; B	Ohio Muni	28.2	12.68	10,065.00	10,047.00	☆	5.2	373-9387	516-338-3300	None	0.50	3.00	Paul Disdier	'93
DREYFUS PREM MUNI PA; A	Pennsylvania Muni	236.4	15.93	10,078.00	9,986.00	14,917.00	5.9	373-9387	516-338-3300	4.50	None	None	Paul Disdier	'88
DREYFUS PREM MUNI PA; B	Pennsylvania Muni	61.1	15.93	10,064.00	9,929.00	☆	5.3	373-9387	516-338-3300	None	0.50	3.00	Paul Disdier	'93
DREYFUS PREM MUNI TX; A	Texas Muni	76.4	20.37	10,130.00	10,030.00	15,036.00	5.9	373-9387	516-338-3300	4.50	None	None	Paul Disdier	'88
DREYFUS PREM MUNI TX; B	Texas Muni	16.3	20.37	10,115.00	9,981.00	☆	5.4	373-9387	516-338-3300	None	0.50	3.00	Paul Disdier	'93
DREYFUS PREM MUNI VA; A	Virginia Muni	66.1	15.88	10,016.00	9,823.00	☆	6.1	373-9387	516-338-3300	4.50	None	None	Samuel Weinstock	'91
DREYFUS PREM MUNI VA; B	Virginia Muni	25.8	15.88	10,002.00	9,768.00	☆	5.5	373-9387	516-338-3300	None	0.50	3.00	Samuel Weinstock	'93
DREYFUS PREM NY MUNI; A	New York Muni	162.1	14.06	10,073.00	9,980.00	14,825.00	5.4	373-9387	516-338-3300	4.50	None	None	Paul Disdier	'88
DREYFUS PREM NY MUNI; B	New York Muni	56.1	14.06	10,059.00	9,907.00	☆	4.7	373-9387	516-338-3300	None	0.50	3.00	Paul Disdier	'93
DREYFUS SHT-INT MUNI	Short-Term Muni	574.8	12.97	10,070.00	10,230.00	13,513.00	4.4	373-9387	516-338-3300	None	0.10	None	Samuel Weinstock	'87
DUPREE KY TX-FR INC	Kentucky Muni	260.0	7.21	9,918.00	10,077.00	14,614.00	5.7	866-0614	606-254-7741	None	None	None	Bill Griggs	'89
DUPREE KY TX-FR SHT-MED	Single State Muni	69.9	5.17	10,022.00	10,172.00	13,330.00	4.0	866-0614	606-254-7741	None	None	None	Bill Griggs	'87
DUPREE TN TX-FR INC	Tennessee Muni	0.7	9.51	9,888.00	☆	☆	0.0	866-0614	606-254-7741	None	None	None	William Griggs II	'93
ELFUN TAX-EX INCOME FUND ◪	General Muni	1,222.9	11.32	10,015.00	9,883.00	14,007.00	6.0	242-0134	203-326-4040	None	None	None	Robert R. Kaelin	'84
EMERALD FL TX-EX; A	Florida Muni	144.1	10.52	10,084.00	9,873.00	☆	5.2	637-6336	None	4.50	0.25	None	Doug Byrne	'91
EMERALD FL TX-EX; B	Florida Muni	3.6	10.52	10,075.00	☆	☆	0.0	637-6336	None	None	1.00	4.50	Doug Byrne	'94
EMERALD FL TX-EX; INSTL	Florida Muni	36.2	10.53	10,107.00	☆	☆	0.0	637-6336	None	None	None	None	Doug Byrne	'94
EMPIRE BUILDER TAX FR BD	New York Muni	105.7	17.48	10,128.00	10,019.00	14,004.00	4.9	847-5886	212-309-8400	4.25	None	None	James Vaccacio	'87
ENTERPRISE TAX-EX INCOME	General Muni	39.3	13.31	10,081.00	9,899.00	13,733.00	5.1	432-4320	404-396-8118	4.75	0.45	None	Gerald Barth	'92
EV CLASSIC AL TAX FREE	Single State Muni	N/A	9.19	10,082.00	☆	☆	0.0	225-6265	617-482-8260	None	0.95	None	Timothy Browse	'93
EV CLASSIC AZ TAX FREE	Arizona Muni	N/A	9.22	10,039.00	☆	☆	0.0	225-6265	617-482-8260	None	0.95	None	Cynthia J. Clemson	'93
EV CLASSIC CA LTD MAT	California Muni	N/A	9.53	10,065.00	☆	☆	0.0	225-6265	617-482-8260	None	0.90	None	Raymond E. Hender	'93
EV CLASSIC CA MUNICIPALS	California Muni	N/A	9.16	9,942.00	☆	☆	0.0	225-6265	617-482-8260	None	1.00	None	Robert MacIntosh	'93
EV CLASSIC CO TAX FREE	Colorado Muni	N/A	9.01	10,023.00	☆	☆	0.0	225-6265	617-482-8260	None	0.95	None	Cynthia J. Clemson	'93
EV CLASSIC CT LTD MAT	Single State Muni	N/A	9.42	10,019.00	☆	☆	0.0	225-6265	617-482-8260	None	0.90	None	Raymond E. Hender	'93
EV CLASSIC CT TAX FREE	Connecticut Muni	N/A	9.11	9,989.00	☆	☆	0.0	225-6265	617-482-8260	None	0.95	None	Nicole Anderes	'94
EV CLASSIC FL LTD MAT	Florida Muni	N/A	9.48	10,108.00	☆	☆	0.0	225-6265	617-482-8260	None	0.90	None	Raymond E. Hender	'93
EV CLASSIC FL TAX FREE	Florida Muni	N/A	9.10	9,991.00	☆	☆	0.0	225-6265	617-482-8260	None	0.95	None	Thomas J. Fetter	'93
EV CLASSIC GA TAX FREE	Georgia Muni	N/A	9.11	9,981.00	☆	☆	0.0	225-6265	617-482-8260	None	0.95	None	David Reilly	'93
EV CLASSIC KY TAX FREE	Kentucky Muni	N/A	9.08	10,027.00	☆	☆	0.0	225-6265	617-482-8260	None	0.95	None	Timothy Browse	'93

EV CLASSIC MA LTD MAT	Massachusetts Muni	N/A	9.51	10,099.00	☆	☆	0.0	225-6265	617-482-8260	None	0.90	None	Raymond E. Hender	'93
EV CLASSIC MA TAX FREE	Massachusetts Muni	N/A	9.10	9,963.00	☆	☆	0.0	225-6265	617-482-8260	None	0.95	None	Robert MacIntosh	'93
EV CLASSIC MD TAX FREE	Maryland Muni	N/A	9.05	10,005.00	☆	☆	0.0	225-6265	617-482-8260	None	0.95	None	Timothy Browse	'93
EV CLASSIC MI LTD MAT	Michigan Muni	N/A	9.49	10,108.00	☆	☆	0.0	225-6265	617-482-8260	None	0.90	None	Raymond E. Hender	'93
EV CLASSIC MI TAX FREE	Michigan Muni	N/A	9.08	10,006.00	☆	☆	0.0	225-6265	617-482-8260	None	0.95	None	Timothy Browse	'93
EV CLASSIC MN TAX FREE	Minnesota Muni	N/A	9.25	10,044.00	☆	☆	0.0	225-6265	617-482-8260	None	0.95	None	Robert MacIntosh	'93
EV CLASSIC MO TAX FREE	Missouri Muni	N/A	9.16	10,050.00	☆	☆	0.0	225-6265	617-482-8260	None	0.95	None	Cynthia J. Clemson	'93
EV CLASSIC MS TAX FREE	Single State Muni	N/A	9.04	10,074.00	☆	☆	0.0	225-6265	617-482-8260	None	0.95	None	Cynthia J. Clemson	'93
EV CLASSIC NATL LTD MAT	Intermediate Muni	N/A	9.52	10,081.00	☆	☆	0.0	225-6265	617-482-8260	None	0.90	None	Raymond E. Hender	'93
EV CLASSIC NATL MUNI	High-Yield Muni	N/A	9.11	10,034.00	☆	☆	0.0	225-6265	617-482-8260	None	1.00	None	Thomas M. Metzold	'93
EV CLASSIC NC TAX FREE	North Carolina Muni	N/A	9.18	9,974.00	☆	☆	0.0	225-6265	617-482-8260	None	0.95	None	David Reilly	'93
EV CLASSIC NJ LTD MAT	Single State Muni	N/A	9.55	10,085.00	☆	☆	0.0	225-6265	617-482-8260	None	0.90	None	Raymond E. Hender	'93
EV CLASSIC NJ TAX FREE	New Jersey Muni	N/A	9.20	10,005.00	☆	☆	0.0	225-6265	617-482-8260	None	0.95	None	Robert MacIntosh	'93
EV CLASSIC NY LTD MAT	New York Muni	N/A	9.49	10,097.00	☆	☆	0.0	225-6265	617-482-8260	None	0.90	None	Raymond E. Hender	'93
EV CLASSIC NY TAX FREE	New York Muni	N/A	9.19	10,026.00	☆	☆	0.0	225-6265	617-482-8260	None	0.95	None	Nicole Anderes	'94
EV CLASSIC OH LTD MAT	Single State Muni	N/A	9.51	10,117.00	☆	☆	0.0	225-6265	617-482-8260	None	0.90	None	Raymond E. Hender	'93
EV CLASSIC OH TAX FREE	Ohio Muni	N/A	9.04	10,045.00	☆	☆	0.0	225-6265	617-482-8260	None	0.95	None	Thomas J. Fetter	'93
EV CLASSIC OR TAX FREE	Oregon Muni	N/A	9.12	10,002.00	☆	☆	0.0	225-6265	617-482-8260	None	0.95	None	Cynthia J. Clemson	'93
EV CLASSIC PA LTD MAT	Pennsylvania Muni	N/A	9.52	10,110.00	☆	☆	0.0	225-6265	617-482-8260	None	0.90	None	Raymond E. Hender	'93
EV CLASSIC PA TAX FREE	Pennsylvania Muni	N/A	9.08	10,002.00	☆	☆	0.0	225-6265	617-482-8260	None	0.95	None	David Reilly	'93
EV CLASSIC RI TAX FREE	Single State Muni	N/A	9.01	10,100.00	☆	☆	0.0	225-6265	617-482-8260	None	0.95	None	Nicole Anderes	'94
EV CLASSIC TN TAX FREE	Tennessee Muni	N/A	9.08	9,994.00	☆	☆	0.0	225-6265	617-482-8260	None	0.95	None	Cynthia J. Clemson	'93
EV CLASSIC TX TAX FREE	Texas Muni	N/A	9.06	10,051.00	☆	☆	0.0	225-6265	617-482-8260	None	0.95	None	Timothy Browse	'93
EV CLASSIC VA TAX FREE	Virginia Muni	N/A	9.10	9,978.00	☆	☆	0.0	225-6265	617-482-8260	None	0.95	None	David Reilly	'93
EV CLASSIC WV TAX FREE	Single State Muni	N/A	9.05	9,955.00	☆	☆	0.0	225-6265	617-482-8260	None	0.95	None	Timothy Browse	'93
EV MRTHN AL TAX FREE ★	Single State Muni	N/A	10.07	10,049.00	9,776.00	☆	5.6	225-6265	617-482-8260	None	0.95	6.00	Timothy Browse	'92
EV MRTHN AR TAX FREE ★	Single State Muni	N/A	9.97	10,127.00	9,818.00	☆	5.6	225-6265	617-482-8260	None	0.95	6.00	Timothy Browse	'92
EV MRTHN AZ TAX FREE ★	Arizona Muni	N/A	10.23	10,024.00	9,758.00	☆	5.6	225-6265	617-482-8260	None	0.95	6.00	Cynthia J. Clemson	'93
EV MRTHN CA LTD ★	California Muni	N/A	9.99	10,050.00	9,991.00	☆	4.7	225-6265	617-482-8260	None	0.75	3.00	Raymond E. Hender	'92
EV MRTHN CA MUNI	California Muni	454.5	9.37	9,939.00	9,719.00	12,999.00	6.0	225-6265	617-482-8260	None	1.00	6.00	Robert MacIntosh	'91
EV MRTHN CO TAX FREE ★	Colorado Muni	N/A	9.83	10,025.00	9,697.00	☆	5.8	225-6265	617-482-8260	None	0.95	6.00	Cynthia J. Clemson	'92
EV MRTHN CT TAX FREE ★	Connecticut Muni	N/A	9.90	9,983.00	9,665.00	☆	5.7	225-6265	617-482-8260	None	0.95	6.00	Nicole Anderes	'94
EV MRTHN FL LTD ★	Florida Muni	N/A	10.06	10,110.00	10,042.00	☆	4.7	225-6265	617-482-8260	None	0.75	3.00	Raymond E. Hender	'92
EV MRTHN FL TAX FREE ★	Florida Muni	N/A	10.41	10,012.00	9,696.00	☆	5.8	225-6265	617-482-8260	None	0.95	6.00	Thomas J. Fetter	'90
EV MRTHN GA TAX FREE ★	Georgia Muni	N/A	9.68	9,992.00	9,690.00	☆	5.5	225-6265	617-482-8260	None	0.95	6.00	David Reilly	'92
EV MRTHN KY TAX FREE ★	Kentucky Muni	N/A	9.71	10,026.00	9,671.00	☆	5.6	225-6265	617-482-8260	None	0.95	6.00	Timothy Browse	'92
EV MRTHN LA TAX FREE ★	Louisiana Muni	N/A	9.90	10,085.00	9,704.00	☆	5.8	225-6265	617-482-8260	None	0.95	6.00	Nicole Anderes	'94
EV MRTHN MA LTD ★	Massachusetts Muni	N/A	9.93	10,082.00	10,029.00	☆	4.8	225-6265	617-482-8260	None	0.75	3.00	Raymond E. Hender	'92
EV MRTHN MA TAX FREE ★	Massachusetts Muni	N/A	10.11	9,962.00	9,725.00	☆	5.9	225-6265	617-482-8260	None	0.95	6.00	Robert MacIntosh	'91
EV MRTHN MD TAX FREE ★	Maryland Muni	N/A	9.90	10,018.00	9,621.00	☆	5.5	225-6265	617-482-8260	None	0.95	6.00	Timothy Browse	'92
EV MRTHN MI TAX FREE ★	Michigan Muni	N/A	10.05	10,040.00	9,707.00	☆	5.6	225-6265	617-482-8260	None	0.95	6.00	Timothy Browse	'92
EV MRTHN MN TAX FREE ★	Minnesota Muni	N/A	9.91	10,043.00	9,750.00	☆	5.7	225-6265	617-482-8260	None	0.95	6.00	Robert MacIntosh	'91
EV MRTHN MO TAX FREE ★	Missouri Muni	N/A	10.12	10,061.00	9,685.00	☆	5.6	225-6265	617-482-8260	None	0.95	6.00	Cynthia J. Clemson	'92
EV MRTHN MS TAX FREE ★	Single State Muni	N/A	9.23	10,090.00	9,758.00	☆	5.9	225-6265	617-482-8260	None	0.95	6.00	Cynthia J. Clemson	'93
EV MRTHN NATL LTD ★	Intermediate Muni	N/A	10.12	10,075.00	10,059.00	☆	4.9	225-6265	617-482-8260	None	0.75	3.00	Raymond E. Hender	'92
EV MRTHN NATL MUNI	High-Yield Muni	2,169.3	9.56	10,052.00	9,890.00	13,979.00	6.7	225-6265	617-482-8260	None	1.00	6.00	Thomas M. Metzold	'94
EV MRTHN NC TAX FREE ★	North Carolina Muni	N/A	9.86	9,998.00	9,681.00	☆	5.6	225-6265	617-482-8260	None	0.95	6.00	Nicole Anderes	'94
EV MRTHN NJ LTD ★	Single State Muni	N/A	10.00	10,079.00	9,981.00	☆	4.7	225-6265	617-482-8260	None	0.75	3.00	Raymond E. Hender	'92
EV MRTHN NJ TAX FREE ★	New Jersey Muni	N/A	10.30	10,001.00	9,748.00	☆	5.9	225-6265	617-482-8260	None	0.95	6.00	Robert MacIntosh	'91
EV MRTHN NY LTD ★	New York Muni	N/A	10.04	10,110.00	10,021.00	☆	4.7	225-6265	617-482-8260	None	0.75	3.00	Raymond E. Hender	'92

★ EATON VANCE FUNDS--Fund does not disclose total net assets.

PERFORMANCE OF MUTUAL FUNDS (continued)

FUND NAME	OBJECTIVE	TOTAL NET ASSETS ($ MIL) 5/31/94	NET ASSET $ VALUE 6/30/94	PERFORMANCE (Return on initial $10,000 Investment) 3/31/94-6/30/94	6/30/93-6/30/94	6/30/89-6/30/94	DIVIDEND YIELD % 6/94	PHONE NUMBER 800	In-State	FEES Load	12b-1	Redemption	MANAGER	SINCE
EV MRTHN NY TAX FREE ★	New York Muni	N/A	10.60	10,025.00	9,756.00	☆	5.8	225-6265	617-482-8260	None	0.95	6.00	Nicole Anderes	'94
EV MRTHN OH TAX FREE ★	Ohio Muni	N/A	10.19	10,055.00	9,778.00	☆	5.7	225-6265	617-482-8260	None	0.95	6.00	Thomas J. Fetter	'91
EV MRTHN OR TAX FREE ★	Oregon Muni	N/A	9.97	10,007.00	9,687.00	☆	5.4	225-6265	617-482-8260	None	0.95	6.00	Cynthia J. Clemson	'91
EV MRTHN PA LTD ★	Pennsylvania Muni	N/A	10.08	10,092.00	10,035.00	☆	4.8	225-6265	617-482-8260	None	0.75	3.00	Raymond E. Hender	'92
EV MRTHN PA TAX FREE ★	Pennsylvania Muni	N/A	10.22	10,028.00	9,786.00	☆	5.9	225-6265	617-482-8260	None	0.95	6.00	David Reilly	'91
EV MRTHN RI TAX FREE ★	Single State Muni	N/A	9.23	10,094.00	9,766.00	☆	5.9	225-6265	617-482-8260	None	0.95	6.00	Nicole Anderes	'94
EV MRTHN SC TAX FREE ★	South Carolina Muni	N/A	9.82	10,036.00	9,724.00	☆	5.5	225-6265	617-482-8260	None	0.95	6.00	David Reilly	'92
EV MRTHN TN TAX FREE ★	Tennessee Muni	N/A	9.85	10,029.00	9,710.00	☆	5.5	225-6265	617-482-8260	None	0.95	6.00	Cynthia J. Clemson	'93
EV MRTHN TX TAX FREE ★	Texas Muni	N/A	10.03	10,072.00	9,777.00	☆	6.1	225-6265	617-482-8260	None	0.95	6.00	Timothy Browse	'92
EV MRTHN VA TAX FREE ★	Virginia Muni	N/A	10.02	9,953.00	9,720.00	☆	5.7	225-6265	617-482-8260	None	0.95	6.00	David Reilly	'92
EV MRTHN WV TAX FREE ★	Single State Muni	N/A	9.21	10,014.00	9,732.00	☆	5.8	225-6265	617-482-8260	None	0.95	6.00	Timothy Browse	'93
EATON VANCE MUNI BOND LP	General Muni	104.3	9.70	10,087.00	9,883.00	14,588.00	6.3	225-6265	617-482-8260	4.75	None	None	Thomas J. Fetter	'87
EATON VANCE CT LTD ★	Single State Muni	N/A	9.64	10,054.00	10,038.00	☆	4.6	225-6265	617-482-8260	None	0.90	3.00	Raymond E. Hender	'93
EATON VANCE MI LTD ★	Michigan Muni	N/A	9.63	10,089.00	10,027.00	☆	4.8	225-6265	617-482-8260	None	0.90	3.00	Raymond E. Hender	'93
EATON VANCE OH LTD ★	Single State Muni	N/A	9.72	10,098.00	10,067.00	☆	4.8	225-6265	617-482-8260	None	0.90	3.00	Raymond E. Hender	'93
EVERGREEN MUNI INS NATL	Insured Muni	39.7	9.83	10,056.00	9,828.00	☆	5.5	235-0064	914-694-2020	None	None	None	James Colby III	'92
EVERGREEN MUNI SH-INT CA	California Muni	28.5	10.04	10,064.00	10,176.00	☆	4.3	235-0064	914-694-2020	None	None	None	Steven Shachat	'92
EVERGREEN MUNI SHT-INT	Short-Term Muni	55.2	10.18	10,061.00	10,135.00	☆	4.7	235-0064	914-694-2020	None	None	None	Steven Shachat	'91
EXECUTIVE INV INS TAX EX	Insured Muni	10.1	12.88	10,184.00	10,157.00	☆	5.5	423-4026	212-858-8000	4.75	0.50	None	Clark Wagner	'91
FD T-F INV RUSHMORE MD	Maryland Muni	53.2	10.48	10,059.00	9,957.00	13,317.00	5.4	621-7874	301-657-1517	None	None	None	Dan Gillespie	'91
FD T-F INV RUSHMORE VA	Virginia Muni	32.1	10.73	10,042.00	9,979.00	13,772.00	5.4	621-7874	301-657-1517	None	None	None	Dan Gillespie	'91
FFB NJ TAX-FREE	New Jersey Muni	40.5	10.46	10,099.00	9,964.00	☆	5.4	437-8790	None	4.50	0.25	None	Jocelyn Turner	'92
FIDELITY ADV HI MUNI; A	High-Yield Muni	552.8	11.61	10,089.00	9,923.00	15,494.00	5.9	522-7297	None	4.75	0.25	None	Peter Allegrini	'92
FIDELITY ADV INST LTD TX	Intermediate Muni	13.9	9.89	10,112.00	9,980.00	13,609.00	5.0	522-7297	None	None	None	None	John Haley Jr.	'85
FIDELITY ADV LTD TXEX; A	Intermediate Muni	56.6	9.89	10,106.00	9,943.00	☆	4.7	522-7297	None	4.75	0.25	None	John Haley Jr.	'92
FIDELITY ADV SH-INT TXEX	Short-Term Muni	9.1	9.95	10,063.00	☆	☆	0.0	522-7297	None	1.50	0.15	None	David Murphy	'94
FIDELITY AGGRESSIVE TX	High-Yield Muni	870.0	11.34	10,090.00	10,054.00	14,605.00	6.7	544-8888	None	None	None	1.00	Anne Punzak	'85
FIDELITY CA TX FR HI YLD	California Muni	517.5	11.11	10,008.00	9,824.00	13,946.00	6.2	544-8888	None	None	None	None	John Haley Jr.	'85
FIDELITY CA TX FR INSURD	California Muni	243.1	9.78	10,018.00	9,671.00	13,919.00	5.7	544-8888	None	None	None	None	John Haley Jr.	'86
FIDELITY HIGH YLD TAX-FR	High-Yield Muni	1,911.5	11.87	10,057.00	9,941.00	14,344.00	6.3	544-8888	None	None	None	None	Anne Punzak	'93
FIDELITY INSURED TAX FR	Insured Muni	394.1	11.12	10,048.00	9,802.00	14,053.00	5.6	544-8888	None	None	None	None	Gary Wickwire	'93
FIDELITY LTD TERM MUNI	Intermediate Muni	1,015.6	9.29	10,093.00	10,047.00	14,268.00	5.5	544-8888	None	None	None	None	David Murphy	'89
FIDELITY MA TX-FR HI YLD	Massachusetts Muni	1,159.7	11.12	10,085.00	10,055.00	14,524.00	6.3	544-8888	None	None	None	None	Gary Wickwire	'83
FIDELITY MI TX-FR HI YLD	Michigan Muni	504.3	11.28	10,071.00	9,978.00	14,306.00	6.1	544-8888	None	None	None	None	Peter Allegrini	'85
FIDELITY MN TX-FR	Minnesota Muni	314.9	10.59	10,100.00	9,992.00	13,815.00	6.0	544-8888	None	None	None	None	Steven Harvey	'93
FIDELITY MUNICIPAL BOND	General Muni	1,136.2	7.92	10,067.00	9,849.00	14,194.00	5.8	544-8888	None	None	None	None	Gary Swayze	'85
FIDELITY NY TX-FR HI YLD	New York Muni	431.1	11.65	10,066.00	9,827.00	14,088.00	5.8	544-8888	None	None	None	None	Norman Lind	'93
FIDELITY NY TX-FR INSURD	New York Muni	358.8	11.14	10,086.00	9,822.00	14,086.00	5.7	544-8888	None	None	None	None	David Murphy	'92
FIDELITY OH TX-FR HI YLD	Ohio Muni	398.9	11.09	10,129.00	10,062.00	14,404.00	5.9	544-8888	None	None	None	None	Peter Allegrini	'85
FIDELITY SPARTAN AGGR	High-Yield Muni	46.5	9.66	10,113.00	10,074.00	☆	6.3	544-8888	None	None	None	1.00	Anne Punzak	'93
FIDELITY SPARTAN CA HY	California Muni	469.6	10.00	10,010.00	9,827.00	☆	6.0	544-8888	None	None	None	0.50	John Haley Jr.	'89
FIDELITY SPARTAN CA INT	California Muni	33.7	9.39	10,089.00	☆	☆	0.0	544-8888	None	None	None	None	David Murphy	'93
FIDELITY SPARTAN CT HY	Connecticut Muni	383.9	10.69	10,083.00	9,938.00	14,074.00	6.0	544-8888	None	None	None	0.50	Peter Allegrini	'87
FIDELITY SPARTAN FL	Florida Muni	390.9	10.43	10,102.00	9,992.00	☆	5.6	544-8888	None	None	None	0.50	Anne Punzak	'92
FIDELITY SPARTAN IN MUNI	Intermediate Muni	256.0	9.74	10,132.00	10,124.00	☆	5.3	544-8888	None	None	None	None	David Murphy	'93

FIDELITY SPARTAN MD	Maryland Muni	40.7	9.55	10,132.00	9,918.00	☆	5.7	544-8888	None	None	None	0.50	Steven Harvey	'93
FIDELITY SPARTAN MUNI	General Muni	696.6	9.95	10,072.00	9,909.00	☆	6.0	544-8888	None	None	None	0.50	Norman Lind	'90
FIDELITY SPARTAN NJ HY	New Jersey Muni	368.7	10.88	10,118.00	9,927.00	14,405.00	5.8	544-8888	None	None	None	0.50	David Murphy	'91
FIDELITY SPARTAN NY HY	New York Muni	363.7	10.12	10,001.00	9,768.00	☆	6.0	544-8888	None	None	None	0.50	Norman Lind	'93
FIDELITY SPARTAN NY INT	New York Muni	27.7	9.46	10,190.00	☆	☆	0.0	544-8888	None	None	None	None	David Murphy	'93
FIDELITY SPARTAN PA HY	Pennsylvania Muni	270.8	10.25	10,148.00	10,102.00	14,707.00	6.3	544-8888	None	None	None	0.50	Steven Harvey	'93
FIDELITY SPARTAN S-I MUN	Short-Term Muni	1,079.8	9.79	10,114.00	10,195.00	13,521.00	4.6	544-8888	None	None	None	None	David Murphy	'89
59 WALL ST TX FR SH/INT	Short-Term Muni	70.9	10.11	10,034.00	10,161.00	☆	3.4	None	212-493-8100	None	None	None	Brown Brothers Harriman	'92
FINL HRZNS MUNI BOND	General Muni	28.3	10.24	9,971.00	9,552.00	13,625.00	4.9	533-5622	None	None	0.50	5.00	Randy Baney	'89
FIRST AMER CO INT; INST	Single State Muni	0.6	10.20	☆	☆	☆	0.0	637-2548	612-973-4069	None	None	None	Richard Stanley	'94
FIRST AMER CO INT; RET	Single State Muni	0.4	10.20	☆	☆	☆	0.0	637-2548	612-973-4069	3.00	0.25	None	Richard Stanley	'94
FIRST AMER LTD TXFR; RET	Short-Term Muni	17.6	9.83	9,911.00	10,044.00	☆	2.3	637-2548	612-973-4069	2.00	0.25	None	Scott Limper	'92
FIRST AMER MUNI BD; INST	Intermediate Muni	2.0	10.33	10,126.00	☆	☆	0.0	637-2548	612-973-4069	None	None	None	Richard Stanley	'94
FIRST AMER MUNI BD; RET	Intermediate Muni	1.1	10.34	10,136.00	10,081.00	13,244.00	4.1	637-2548	612-973-4069	3.00	0.25	None	Richard Stanley	'94
FIRST INV INSURED TAX EX	Insured Muni	1,396.7	9.75	10,041.00	9,859.00	13,569.00	5.9	423-4026	212-858-8000	6.25	0.30	None	Clark Wagner	'91
FIRST INV MULTI INS AZ	Arizona Muni	8.6	12.07	10,080.00	9,993.00	☆	5.6	423-4026	212-858-8000	6.25	0.30	None	Clark Wagner	'91
FIRST INV MULTI INS CA	California Muni	16.2	11.21	10,053.00	9,948.00	14,361.00	5.3	423-4026	212-858-8000	6.25	0.30	None	Clark Wagner	'91
FIRST INV MULTI INS CO	Colorado Muni	3.0	11.60	10,111.00	9,974.00	☆	5.3	423-4026	212-858-8000	6.25	0.30	None	Clark Wagner	'92
FIRST INV MULTI INS CT	Connecticut Muni	16.3	12.02	10,074.00	9,882.00	☆	5.0	423-4026	212-858-8000	6.25	0.30	None	Clark Wagner	'91
FIRST INV MULTI INS FL	Florida Muni	21.2	12.15	10,064.00	9,982.00	☆	5.3	423-4026	212-858-8000	6.25	0.30	None	Clark Wagner	'91
FIRST INV MULTI INS GA	Georgia Muni	1.6	11.62	10,089.00	10,085.00	☆	5.1	423-4026	212-858-8000	6.25	0.30	None	Clark Wagner	'92
FIRST INV MULTI INS MA	Massachusetts Muni	22.0	11.41	10,034.00	9,952.00	14,323.00	5.7	423-4026	212-858-8000	6.25	0.30	None	Clark Wagner	'91
FIRST INV MULTI INS MD	Maryland Muni	6.7	12.13	10,053.00	9,943.00	☆	5.4	423-4026	212-858-8000	6.25	0.30	None	Clark Wagner	'91
FIRST INV MULTI INS MI	Michigan Muni	30.2	11.88	10,042.00	9,926.00	14,609.00	5.3	423-4026	212-858-8000	6.25	0.30	None	Clark Wagner	'91
FIRST INV MULTI INS MN	Minnesota Muni	7.7	10.87	10,045.00	9,927.00	14,060.00	5.6	423-4026	212-858-8000	6.25	0.30	None	Clark Wagner	'91
FIRST INV MULTI INS MO	Missouri Muni	1.6	11.54	10,112.00	9,939.00	☆	5.3	423-4026	212-858-8000	6.25	0.30	None	Clark Wagner	'92
FIRST INV MULTI INS NC	North Carolina Muni	4.6	11.26	10,103.00	9,899.00	☆	5.3	423-4026	212-858-8000	6.25	0.30	None	Clark Wagner	'92
FIRST INV MULTI INS NJ	New Jersey Muni	60.9	12.52	10,050.00	9,947.00	14,420.00	5.4	423-4026	212-858-8000	6.25	0.30	None	Clark Wagner	'91
FIRST INV MULTI INS OH	Ohio Muni	19.2	11.71	10,075.00	9,950.00	14,500.00	5.3	423-4026	212-858-8000	6.25	0.30	None	Clark Wagner	'91
FIRST INV MULTI INS OR	Oregon Muni	4.2	11.25	10,083.00	9,881.00	☆	5.2	423-4026	212-858-8000	6.25	0.30	None	Clark Wagner	'92
FIRST INV MULTI INS PA	Pennsylvania Muni	34.5	12.17	10,080.00	10,012.00	☆	5.3	423-4026	212-858-8000	6.25	0.30	None	Clark Wagner	'91
FIRST INV MULTI INS VA	Virginia Muni	23.7	12.03	10,036.00	9,903.00	☆	5.2	423-4026	212-858-8000	6.25	0.30	None	Clark Wagner	'91
FIRST INV NY INS TAX FR	New York Muni	202.7	14.23	10,059.00	9,967.00	13,852.00	5.5	423-4026	212-858-8000	6.25	0.30	None	Clark Wagner	'91
FIRST INV SRS INS INT TE	Intermediate Muni	4.4	5.53	10,120.00	☆	☆	0.0	423-4026	212-858-8000	3.50	0.30	None	Clark Wagner	'93
FIRST PACIFIC HAWAII	Single State Muni	53.4	10.69	10,075.00	10,008.00	14,014.00	5.2	None	808-599-2400	None	0.06	None	Terry Lee	'91
FRST PRAIRIE MUN INS; A	Insured Muni	8.6	11.77	10,115.00	10,146.00	14,696.00	4.8	821-1185	None	4.50	None	None	John Erickson	'88
FRST PRAIRIE MUN INS; B	Insured Muni	0.1	11.78	10,109.00	☆	☆	0.0	821-1185	None	None	0.50	3.00	John Erickson	'94
FRST PRAIRIE MUN INT; A	Intermediate Muni	27.3	11.81	10,095.00	10,222.00	14,517.00	4.7	821-1185	None	3.00	None	None	John Erickson	'88
FRST PRAIRIE MUN INT; B	Intermediate Muni	0.1	11.81	10,073.00	☆	☆	0.0	821-1185	None	None	0.50	3.00	John Erickson	'94
FIRST UN FL MUNI; INV B	Florida Muni	8.6	9.24	9,956.00	☆	☆	5.0	326-3241	704-374-4343	4.00	0.25	None	Bob Drye	'93
FIRST UN FL MUNI; INV C	Florida Muni	24.0	9.24	9,943.00	☆	☆	4.5	326-3241	704-374-4343	None	0.75	4.00	Bob Drye	'93
FIRST UN FL MUNI; TR	Florida Muni	1.5	9.24	9,962.00	☆	☆	0.0	326-3241	704-374-4343	None	None	None	Bob Drye	'94
FIRST UN GA MUNI; INV B	Georgia Muni	1.3	9.06	9,987.00	☆	☆	4.8	326-3241	704-374-4343	4.00	0.25	None	Rick Marrone	'93
FIRST UN GA MUNI; INV C	Georgia Muni	6.0	9.06	9,975.00	☆	☆	4.3	326-3241	704-374-4343	None	0.75	4.00	Rick Marrone	'93
FIRST UN HI GRD; INV B	Insured Muni	78.4	10.21	9,942.00	9,889.00	☆	5.2	326-3241	704-374-4343	4.00	0.25	None	Bob Drye	'92
FIRST UN HI GRD; INV C	Insured Muni	38.9	10.21	9,929.00	9,839.00	☆	4.7	326-3241	704-374-4343	None	0.75	4.00	Bob Drye	'93
FIRST UN HI GRD; TR	Insured Muni	3.3	10.21	9,948.00	☆	☆	0.0	326-3241	704-374-4343	None	None	None	Bob Drye	'94
FIRST UN NC MUNI; INV B	North Carolina Muni	9.4	9.48	9,898.00	9,658.00	☆	5.4	326-3241	704-374-4343	4.00	0.25	None	Rick Marrone	'93
FIRST UN NC MUNI; INV C	North Carolina Muni	47.0	9.48	9,885.00	9,610.00	☆	4.8	326-3241	704-374-4343	None	0.75	4.00	Rick Marrone	'93
FIRST UN SC MUNI; INV B	South Carolina Muni	0.1	9.03	10,001.00	☆	☆	0.0	326-3241	704-374-4343	4.00	0.25	None	Bob Drye	'94

★ EATON VANCE FUNDS--Fund does not disclose total net assets.

PERFORMANCE OF MUTUAL FUNDS *(continued)*

FUND NAME	OBJECTIVE	TOTAL NET ASSETS ($ MIL) 5/31/94	NET ASSET $ VALUE 6/30/94	PERFORMANCE (Return on initial $10,000 Investment) 3/31/94-6/30/94	6/30/93-6/30/94	6/30/89-6/30/94	DIVIDEND YIELD % 6/94	PHONE NUMBER 800	In-State	FEES Load	12b-1	Redemption	MANAGER	SINCE
FIRST UN SC MUNI; INV C	South Carolina Muni	1.4	9.03	9,989.00	☆	☆	0.0	326-3241	704-374-4343	None	0.75	4.00	Bob Drye	'94
FIRST UN VA MUNI; INV B	Virginia Muni	1.6	9.15	10,006.00	☆	☆	4.7	326-3241	704-374-4343	4.00	0.25	None	Chuck Jeanne	'93
FIRST UN VA MUNI; INV C	Virginia Muni	3.0	9.15	9,994.00	☆	☆	4.2	326-3241	704-374-4343	None	0.75	4.00	Chuck Jeanne	'93
FIRST UN VA MUNI; TR	Virginia Muni	0.1	9.15	10,012.00	☆	☆	0.0	326-3241	704-374-4343	None	None	None	Chuck Jeanne	'94
FLAG INV MD INTMDT	Single State Muni	11.2	9.45	10,063.00	☆	☆	0.0	645-3923	410-637-6819	1.50	0.25	None	Randolph/Corbin	'93/'93
FLAGSHIP PA TRI TX EX; A	Pennsylvania Muni	42.3	9.95	10,051.00	10,015.00	14,166.00	6.1	227-4648	513-461-0332	4.20	0.40	None	Michael Davern	'92
FLAGSHIP TXEX AMER; A	General Muni	159.8	10.50	10,112.00	10,031.00	15,203.00	6.1	227-4648	513-461-0332	4.20	0.40	None	Robert Ashbaugh	'88
FLAGSHIP TXEX AMER; C	General Muni	40.0	10.49	10,098.00	9,967.00	☆	5.6	227-4648	513-461-0332	None	0.95	1.00	Robert Ashbaugh	'93
FLAGSHIP TXEX AZ DBL; A	Arizona Muni	82.7	10.31	10,072.00	9,936.00	14,381.00	5.8	227-4648	513-461-0332	4.20	0.40	None	Jan Terbrueggen	'92
FLAGSHIP TXEX CO DBL	Colorado Muni	35.8	9.51	10,086.00	9,968.00	14,194.00	6.1	227-4648	513-461-0332	4.20	0.40	None	Jan Terbrueggen	'92
FLAGSHIP TXEX CT DBL	Connecticut Muni	202.6	10.06	10,056.00	9,922.00	14,045.00	5.9	227-4648	513-461-0332	4.20	0.40	None	Rick Huber	'92
FLAGSHIP TXEX FL DBL	Florida Muni	372.2	10.26	10,055.00	9,954.00	☆	5.9	227-4648	513-461-0332	4.20	0.40	None	Robert Ashbaugh	'90
FLAGSHIP TXEX GA DBL; A	Georgia Muni	123.0	10.12	10,083.00	9,943.00	13,893.00	5.9	227-4648	513-461-0332	4.20	0.40	None	Michael Davern	'92
FLAGSHIP TXEX INTMDT	Intermediate Muni	35.9	10.08	10,098.00	10,202.00	☆	5.2	227-4648	513-461-0332	3.00	0.40	None	Michael Davern	'92
FLAGSHIP TXEX KS TRI	Kansas Muni	80.0	9.68	10,059.00	9,741.00	☆	5.8	227-4648	513-461-0332	4.20	0.40	None	Michael Davern	'92
FLAGSHIP TXEX KY TRI	Kentucky Muni	369.2	10.54	10,081.00	9,951.00	14,448.00	6.0	227-4648	513-461-0332	4.20	0.40	None	Ashbaugh/Huber	'87/'93
FLAGSHIP TXEX LA DBL; A	Louisiana Muni	66.8	10.37	10,086.00	9,924.00	☆	5.9	227-4648	513-461-0332	4.20	0.40	None	Jan Terbrueggen	'92
FLAGSHIP TXEX LTD TERM	Short-Term Muni	705.6	10.55	10,090.00	10,232.00	14,180.00	4.9	227-4648	513-461-0332	2.50	0.40	None	Robert Ashbaugh	'91
FLAGSHIP TXEX MI TRI; A	Michigan Muni	242.7	11.21	10,083.00	9,963.00	14,226.00	5.9	227-4648	513-461-0332	4.20	0.40	None	Michael Davern	'87
FLAGSHIP TXEX MI TRI; C	Michigan Muni	30.0	11.20	10,069.00	9,900.00	☆	5.3	227-4648	513-461-0332	None	0.95	1.00	Michael Davern	'93
FLAGSHIP TXEX MO DBL; A	Missouri Muni	187.4	10.39	10,067.00	9,979.00	14,490.00	5.9	227-4648	513-461-0332	4.20	0.40	None	Michael Davern	'92
FLAGSHIP TXEX NC TRI	North Carolina Muni	196.1	9.96	10,022.00	9,879.00	13,938.00	5.8	227-4648	513-461-0332	4.20	0.40	None	Robert Ashbaugh	'87
FLAGSHIP TXEX NJ DBL	New Jersey Muni	4.9	9.66	10,136.00	10,020.00	☆	5.9	227-4648	513-461-0332	4.20	0.40	None	Rick Huber	'92
FLAGSHIP TXEX NJ INTMDT	Single State Muni	9.3	9.95	10,161.00	10,144.00	☆	5.3	227-4648	513-461-0332	3.00	0.40	None	Rick Huber	'92
FLAGSHIP TXEX NM DBL	Single State Muni	51.2	9.53	10,063.00	9,886.00	☆	5.6	227-4648	513-461-0332	4.20	0.40	None	Jan Terbrueggen	'92
FLAGSHIP TXEX NY	New York Muni	48.5	10.28	10,064.00	10,003.00	☆	6.2	227-4648	513-461-0332	4.20	0.40	None	Rick Huber	'92
FLAGSHIP TXEX OH DBL; A	Ohio Muni	445.3	11.11	10,070.00	10,002.00	14,199.00	5.8	227-4648	513-461-0332	4.20	0.40	None	Robert Ashbaugh	'87
FLAGSHIP TXEX OH DBL; C	Ohio Muni	25.7	11.11	10,065.00	☆	☆	0.0	227-4648	513-461-0332	None	0.95	1.00	Robert Ashbaugh	'93
FLAGSHIP TXEX SC DBL; A	South Carolina Muni	6.3	9.12	10,115.00	☆	☆	4.5	227-4648	513-461-0332	4.20	0.40	None	Robert Ashbaugh	'93
FLAGSHIP TXEX TN DBL	Tennessee Muni	236.1	10.67	10,056.00	9,922.00	14,069.00	5.8	227-4648	513-461-0332	4.20	0.40	None	Robert Ashbaugh	'87
FLAGSHIP TXEX VA DBL	Virginia Muni	107.5	10.21	10,047.00	9,978.00	14,365.00	5.9	227-4648	513-461-0332	4.20	0.40	None	Rick Huber	'92
FMB MI BD; CNSMR	Michigan Muni	14.0	10.25	10,094.00	10,145.00	☆	4.6	453-4234	None	3.00	0.10	None	Dan Van Timmeren	'91
FMB MI BD; INSTL	Michigan Muni	15.3	10.25	10,094.00	10,145.00	☆	4.6	453-4234	None	None	None	None	Dan Van Timmeren	'91
FORTIS TAX-FREE MN	Minnesota Muni	55.3	10.15	10,142.00	10,064.00	14,097.00	5.7	800-2638	612-738-4000	4.50	None	None	Dennis M. Ott	'86
FORTIS TAX-FREE NATL	General Muni	77.5	10.46	10,070.00	9,951.00	14,278.00	5.6	800-2638	612-738-4000	4.50	None	None	Dennis M. Ott	'86
FORTIS TAX-FREE NY	New York Muni	13.4	10.81	10,061.00	10,063.00	14,250.00	5.7	800-2638	612-738-4000	4.50	None	None	Dennis M. Ott	'88
FORTRESS MUNI INC FD	General Muni	477.2	10.46	10,096.00	9,929.00	14,050.00	5.8	245-4770	412-288-1900	1.00	None	1.00	James Roberge	'93
FORUM MAINE MUNI	Single State Muni	27.3	10.32	10,071.00	10,128.00	☆	5.0	None	207-879-0001	3.75	None	None	Forum Advisors	'91
FORUM NH BOND FUND	Single State Muni	3.8	9.92	10,080.00	10,159.00	☆	5.1	None	207-879-0001	3.75	None	None	Forum Advisors	'92
FORUM TAXSAVER BOND	General Muni	16.5	10.26	10,046.00	10,293.00	☆	5.4	None	207-879-0001	3.75	None	None	Forum Advisors	'89
FOUNTAIN SQ OH TX FR	Ohio Muni	22.2	9.65	10,085.00	10,011.00	☆	4.0	654-5372	513-579-5452	4.50	0.35	None	Carla Sanders	'93
FRANKLIN CA TF INC	California Muni	13,356.7	7.07	10,087.00	10,125.00	14,190.00	6.4	342-5236	415-312-3200	4.00	None	None	B. Schroer	'77
FRANKLIN CA TF INS	California Muni	1,468.7	11.74	10,064.00	10,085.00	14,175.00	5.8	342-5236	415-312-3200	4.00	None	None	Don Duerson	'85
FRANKLIN CA TF INTMDT	California Muni	96.1	10.20	10,109.00	10,165.00	☆	5.2	342-5236	415-312-3200	2.25	0.05	None	Jeff Handy	'92
FRANKLIN FED TF INC	General Muni	6,857.8	11.72	10,056.00	10,093.00	14,517.00	6.7	342-5236	415-312-3200	4.25	None	None	A. Jennings	'83

FRANKLIN MUNI CA HI YLD	California Muni	31.9	9.58	10,018.00	10,048.00	☆	6.4	342-5236	415-312-3200	4.50	0.10	None	Andrew Jennings, Sr.	'93
FRANKLIN MUNI HI	Single State Muni	27.0	10.24	10,105.00	9,873.00	☆	5.9	342-5236	415-312-3200	4.50	0.10	None	Jennings/Amoroso	'92/'92
FRANKLIN MUNI WA	Washington Muni	4.3	9.41	10,123.00	9,725.00	☆	5.5	342-5236	415-312-3200	4.50	0.10	None	Shelia Amoroso	'93
FRANKLIN NY TF INC	New York Muni	4,606.3	11.63	10,086.00	10,152.00	14,768.00	6.5	342-5236	415-312-3200	4.00	None	None	John Pinkham	'90
FRANKLIN NY TF INS	New York Muni	250.3	10.68	10,079.00	9,983.00	☆	5.5	342-5236	415-312-3200	4.00	None	None	Don Duerson	'91
FRANKLIN NY TF INTMDT	New York Muni	40.0	10.08	10,180.00	10,153.00	☆	5.3	342-5236	415-312-3200	2.25	0.05	None	John Pinkham	'92
FRANKLIN TF AL	Single State Muni	171.5	11.26	10,071.00	10,139.00	14,271.00	5.8	342-5236	415-312-3200	4.00	None	None	Pomeroy/Amoroso	'87/'92
FRANKLIN TF AZ	Arizona Muni	758.9	11.07	10,069.00	10,100.00	14,344.00	5.9	342-5236	415-312-3200	4.25	None	None	Shelia Amoroso	'87
FRANKLIN TF AZ INSURED	Arizona Muni	14.2	9.56	10,096.00	9,779.00	☆	5.3	342-5236	415-312-3200	4.50	0.10	None	Don Duerson	'93
FRANKLIN TF CO	Colorado Muni	193.6	11.27	10,020.00	10,046.00	14,392.00	5.9	342-5236	415-312-3200	4.25	None	None	Shelia Amoroso	'87
FRANKLIN TF CT	Connecticut Muni	155.3	10.65	10,020.00	10,040.00	13,843.00	5.8	342-5236	415-312-3200	4.25	None	None	John Pinkham	'88
FRANKLIN TF FED INTMDT	Intermediate Muni	74.4	10.40	10,106.00	10,266.00	☆	5.2	342-5236	415-312-3200	2.25	None	None	Jeff Handy	'92
FRANKLIN TF FL	Florida Muni	1,302.4	11.29	10,092.00	10,170.00	14,499.00	6.0	342-5236	415-312-3200	4.50	None	None	Jennings/Amoroso	'87/'92
FRANKLIN TF FL INSURED	Florida Muni	35.2	9.30	10,053.00	9,660.00	☆	5.5	342-5236	415-312-3200	4.50	0.10	None	Don Duerson	'93
FRANKLIN TF GA	Georgia Muni	117.6	11.45	10,064.00	10,092.00	14,344.00	5.8	342-5236	415-312-3200	4.00	None	None	Pomeroy/Amoroso	'87/'92
FRANKLIN TF HI YLD	High-Yield Muni	3,269.5	10.76	10,087.00	10,342.00	14,658.00	7.1	342-5236	415-312-3200	4.25	None	None	A. Jennings	'86
FRANKLIN TF IN	Single State Muni	46.7	11.43	10,072.00	10,096.00	14,627.00	5.8	342-5236	415-312-3200	4.25	None	None	S. Wong	'87
FRANKLIN TF INSURED	Insured Muni	1,763.2	11.90	10,074.00	10,129.00	14,374.00	6.1	342-5236	415-312-3200	4.25	None	None	Don Duerson	'85
FRANKLIN TF KY	Kentucky Muni	29.7	10.43	10,093.00	9,896.00	☆	6.3	342-5236	415-312-3200	4.00	None	None	Shelia Amoroso	'91
FRANKLIN TF LA	Louisiana Muni	110.5	10.99	10,052.00	10,008.00	14,299.00	5.9	342-5236	415-312-3200	4.00	None	None	S. Wong	'87
FRANKLIN TF MA INS	Massachusetts Muni	292.4	11.26	10,056.00	10,094.00	14,119.00	6.0	342-5236	415-312-3200	4.25	None	None	Don Duerson	'85
FRANKLIN TF MD	Maryland Muni	151.7	10.78	10,056.00	10,045.00	14,193.00	5.8	342-5236	415-312-3200	4.00	None	None	Pomeroy/Johnson	'88/'92
FRANKLIN TF MI INS	Michigan Muni	1,030.3	11.71	10,076.00	10,110.00	14,245.00	5.9	342-5236	415-312-3200	4.25	None	None	Don Duerson	'85
FRANKLIN TF MN INS	Minnesota Muni	488.3	11.83	10,072.00	10,081.00	14,023.00	5.9	342-5236	415-312-3200	4.25	None	None	Don Duerson	'85
FRANKLIN TF MO	Missouri Muni	224.5	11.37	10,073.00	10,153.00	14,509.00	5.8	342-5236	415-312-3200	4.00	None	None	Shelia Amoroso	'87
FRANKLIN TF NC	North Carolina Muni	213.9	11.30	10,052.00	10,006.00	14,141.00	5.8	342-5236	415-312-3200	4.00	None	None	S. Wong	'87
FRANKLIN TF NJ	New Jersey Muni	543.1	11.21	10,038.00	9,987.00	14,214.00	6.0	342-5236	415-312-3200	4.25	None	None	S. Wong	'88
FRANKLIN TF OH INS	Ohio Muni	663.8	11.83	10,086.00	10,053.00	14,246.00	5.9	342-5236	415-312-3200	4.25	None	None	Don Duerson	'85
FRANKLIN TF OR	Oregon Muni	360.3	11.12	10,037.00	10,005.00	14,004.00	5.7	342-5236	415-312-3200	4.25	None	None	Shelia Amoroso	'87
FRANKLIN TF P RICO	Single State Muni	171.9	11.25	10,052.00	10,089.00	14,287.00	6.1	342-5236	415-312-3200	4.25	None	None	Shelia Amoroso	'85
FRANKLIN TF PA	Pennsylvania Muni	592.0	10.12	10,060.00	10,137.00	14,388.00	6.2	342-5236	415-312-3200	4.25	None	None	S. Wong	'86
FRANKLIN TF TX	Texas Muni	141.5	11.29	10,109.00	10,243.00	14,462.00	6.0	342-5236	415-312-3200	4.00	None	None	S. Wong	'87
FRANKLIN TF VA	Virginia Muni	255.9	11.24	10,035.00	10,097.00	14,398.00	5.9	342-5236	415-312-3200	4.00	None	None	S. Wong	'87
FREMONT CA INTMDT	California Muni	63.7	10.43	10,040.00	10,042.00	☆	5.1	548-4539	415-768-9000	None	None	None	William M. Feeney	'90
FUNDAMENTAL CALIF MUNI	California Muni	14.2	7.97	9,590.00	9,296.00	12,577.00	7.3	322-6864	212-635-3005	None	0.50	None	Lance Brofman	'84
FUNDAMENTAL HI-YLD MUNI	High-Yield Muni	1.1	6.36	9,615.00	9,383.00	10,172.00	7.0	322-6864	212-635-3005	None	0.50	None	David Wieder	'87
FUNDAMENTAL NY MUNI	New York Muni	201.6	1.02	9,578.00	9,390.00	13,144.00	6.2	322-6864	212-635-3005	None	0.50	None	Lance Brofman	'81
FXD INC LTD MUNI; FORT	Short-Term Muni	11.6	9.76	10,125.00	☆	☆	0.0	245-4770	412-288-1900	1.00	0.15	1.00	Mary Jo Ochson	'93
FXD INC LTD MUNI; INV	Short-Term Muni	36.8	9.76	10,119.00	☆	☆	0.0	245-4770	412-288-1900	1.00	0.25	None	Mary Jo Ochson	'93
FXD INC MULTI	General Muni	6.4	9.26	10,098.00	9,605.00	☆	6.4	245-4770	412-288-1900	None	0.75	3.00	Jonathan C. Conley	'93
GALAXY CT MUNI BOND; RTL	Connecticut Muni	25.2	9.54	10,112.00	9,841.00	☆	4.8	628-0414	None	None	None	None	Steve Woodruff	'93
GALAXY MA MUNI BOND; RTL	Massachusetts Muni	23.2	9.41	10,095.00	9,827.00	☆	5.2	628-0414	None	None	None	None	Dave Lindsay	'93
GALAXY NY MUNI BOND; RTL	New York Muni	70.4	10.26	10,122.00	9,871.00	☆	4.7	628-0414	None	None	None	None	Maria C. Schwenzer	'91
GALAXY TAX-EXEMPT BD; RTL	General Muni	135.5	10.30	10,083.00	9,921.00	☆	5.2	628-0414	None	None	None	None	Mary McGoldrick	'91
GE TX-EX; A	General Muni	0.1	11.41	10,052.00	☆	☆	0.0	242-0134	203-326-4040	4.25	0.50	None	Robert R. Kaelin	'93
GE TX-EX; B	General Muni	0.1	11.41	10,039.00	☆	☆	0.0	242-0134	203-326-4040	None	1.00	5.00	Robert R. Kaelin	'93
GE TX-EX; C	General Muni	7.1	11.41	10,058.00	9,853.00	☆	4.5	242-0134	203-326-4040	None	0.25	None	Robert R. Kaelin	'93
GE TX-EX; D	General Muni	5.0	11.41	10,064.00	☆	☆	0.0	242-0134	203-326-4040	None	None	None	Robert R. Kaelin	'93
GIT TAX-FREE ARIZONA	Arizona Muni	12.5	9.78	10,011.00	9,668.00	☆	4.5	336-3063	703-528-6500	None	None	None	Ricardo Fontanilla	'91
GIT TAX-FREE MARYLAND	Maryland Muni	3.0	9.44	10,105.00	9,734.00	☆	4.9	336-3063	703-528-6500	None	None	None	Ricardo Fontanilla	'93

PERFORMANCE OF MUTUAL FUNDS (continued)

FUND NAME	OBJECTIVE	TOTAL NET ASSETS ($ MIL) 5/31/94	NET ASSET $ VALUE 6/30/94	PERFORMANCE (Return on initial $10,000 Investment) 3/31/94-6/30/94	6/30/93-6/30/94	6/30/89-6/30/94	DIVIDEND YIELD % 6/94	PHONE NUMBER 800	In-State	FEES Load	12b-1	Redemption	MANAGER	SINCE
GIT TAX-FREE MISSOURI	Missouri Muni	12.6	9.87	10,040.00	9,742.00	☆	4.4	336-3063	703-528-6500	None	None	None	Ricardo Fontanilla	'91
GIT TAX-FREE NATIONAL	High-Yield Muni	35.4	9.90	10,019.00	9,666.00	13,374.00	4.3	336-3063	703-528-6500	None	None	None	Ricardo Fontanilla	'91
GIT TAX-FREE VIRGINIA	Virginia Muni	36.5	10.72	10,009.00	9,717.00	13,483.00	4.5	336-3063	703-528-6500	None	None	None	Ricardo Fontanilla	'91
GLENMEDE MUNI INTMDT	Intermediate Muni	38.8	10.03	10,033.00	10,068.00	☆	5.0	441-7379	None	None	None	None	Mary Ann B. Wirts	'92
GLENMEDE NJ MUNI	New Jersey Muni	3.2	9.49	10,047.00	☆	☆	0.0	441-7379	None	None	None	None	Mary Ann B. Wirts	'93
GOLDMAN SACHS CA MUNI	California Muni	9.7	12.89	9,985.00	☆	☆	0.0	526-7384	212-902-0800	4.50	0.25	None	Mark Muller	'94
GOLDMAN SACHS MUNI INC	General Muni	48.1	13.47	10,088.00	☆	☆	0.0	526-7384	212-902-0800	4.50	0.25	None	Mark Muller	'93
GOLDMAN SACHS SH DUR	Short-Term Muni	110.5	9.87	10,051.00	10,100.00	☆	3.6	526-7384	212-902-0800	None	None	None	Team Managed	'92
GRADISON-MCDONALD MUN OH	Ohio Muni	78.6	12.46	10,060.00	9,854.00	☆	5.2	869-5999	513-579-5700	2.00	0.25	None	Steve Dilbone	'92
GREAT HALL MN INSURED	Minnesota Muni	36.4	9.73	9,994.00	9,894.00	13,880.00	5.2	934-6674	612-371-7970	4.50	0.30	None	Hippen/Kanzenbach	'86/'86
GREAT HALL NATIONAL	High-Yield Muni	72.1	10.05	10,066.00	10,148.00	14,632.00	6.2	934-6674	612-371-7970	4.50	0.30	None	Hippen/Kanzenbach	'86/'86
GRIFFIN CA TAX-FREE; A	California Muni	11.4	7.62	10,022.00	☆	☆	0.0	676-4450	None	4.50	0.25	None	Scott King	'93
GRIFFIN MUNI BOND; A	General Muni	2.2	8.67	10,072.00	☆	☆	0.0	676-4450	None	4.50	0.25	None	Ronald Reuss	'93
GUARDIAN TAX-EXEMPT FUND	General Muni	18.2	9.18	9,969.00	9,544.00	☆	4.1	221-3253	None	4.50	0.25	None	Alex Grant	'93
ALEX HAMILTON MUNI INC	General Muni	4.8	9.22	10,096.00	☆	☆	0.0	801-2142	None	4.50	0.25	None	James Roberge	'94
J HANCOCK MGD TAX; A	General Muni	19.4	11.17	10,105.00	10,000.00	☆	5.9	225-5291	None	4.50	0.30	None	Frank Lucibella	'93
J HANCOCK MGD TAX; B	General Muni	236.2	11.17	10,078.00	9,938.00	14,063.00	5.2	225-5291	None	None	1.00	5.00	Frank Lucibella	'93
J HANCOCK TX-EXEMPT; A	General Muni	505.6	10.38	10,076.00	9,931.00	14,120.00	5.7	225-5291	None	4.50	0.30	None	Frank Lucibella	'88
J HANCOCK TX-EXEMPT; B	General Muni	1.8	10.37	10,028.00	☆	☆	0.0	225-5291	None	None	1.00	5.00	Frank Lucibella	'94
J HANCOCK TX-EX SRS CA	California Muni	46.0	11.23	10,064.00	9,913.00	14,071.00	5.5	225-5291	None	4.50	0.30	None	Diane Sales-Singer	'93
J HANCOCK TX-EX SRS MA	Massachusetts Muni	52.5	11.42	10,127.00	9,955.00	14,188.00	5.5	225-5291	None	4.50	0.30	None	Diane Sales-Singer	'93
J HANCOCK TX-EX SRS NY	New York Muni	54.4	11.61	10,059.00	9,963.00	14,404.00	5.5	225-5291	None	4.50	0.30	None	Diane Sales-Singer	'93
HANIFEN,IMHOFF COL BD TX	Colorado Muni	39.6	9.07	10,155.00	10,692.00	13,734.00	7.2	525-9989	303-291-5414	4.75	None	None	Fred Kelly Jr.	'90
HAWAIIAN TX-FR TR	Single State Muni	649.5	11.09	10,049.00	10,007.00	13,869.00	5.7	228-4227	212-697-6666	4.00	0.20	None	Lorene Okimoto	'91
HEARTLAND NE TAX FREE	Single State Muni	13.8	8.61	9,848.00	☆	☆	0.0	432-7856	414-347-7777	None	None	None	Patrick Retzer	'93
HEARTLAND WI TAX FREE	Single State Muni	111.2	9.61	9,894.00	9,875.00	☆	5.2	432-7856	414-347-7777	None	None	None	Patrick Retzer	'92
HOUGH FL TXFR SHORT TERM	Short-Term Muni	11.3	9.85	10,070.00	☆	☆	0.0	557-7555	813-825-7730	None	0.25	None	Team Managed	'93
HOUSEHLD PRSNL TX-EX INC	Intermediate Muni	5.4	9.79	10,061.00	☆	☆	0.0	231-0180	312-368-5410	None	0.25	None	Paul Fricke	'94
IAI TAX FREE FUND	General Muni	7.9	10.14	10,063.00	9,835.00	☆	5.7	945-3863	612-376-2700	None	None	None	Steve Coleman	'92
IBM FDS MUNICIPAL BOND	Intermediate Muni	32.1	9.84	10,062.00	10,106.00	☆	4.5	426-9876	None	None	None	None	IBM Credit Invt Mgt	'93
IDEX II TAX-EXEMPT; A	General Muni	30.0	11.15	10,089.00	10,132.00	13,759.00	4.8	624-4339	813-587-1800	4.75	0.35	None	Rachel Dennis	'85
IDEX II TAX-EXEMPT; C	General Muni	0.2	11.15	10,082.00	☆	☆	0.0	624-4339	813-587-1800	None	0.60	None	Rachel Dennis	'93
IDS CA TAX-EXEMPT	California Muni	259.0	5.13	10,012.00	10,035.00	14,006.00	6.0	328-8300	612-671-3733	5.00	None	None	Paul Hylle	'93
IDS HIGH YLD TAX-EXEMPT	High-Yield Muni	6,378.1	4.43	10,074.00	9,936.00	13,947.00	6.7	328-8300	612-671-3733	5.00	None	None	Kurt Larson	'79
IDS INSURED TAX-EXEMPT	Insured Muni	531.2	5.35	10,065.00	10,024.00	14,385.00	5.6	328-8300	612-671-3733	5.00	None	None	Paul Hylle	'93
IDS MA TAX-EXEMPT	Massachusetts Muni	72.6	5.24	10,104.00	10,074.00	14,147.00	5.7	328-8300	612-671-3733	5.00	None	None	Paul Hylle	'93
IDS MI TAX-EXEMPT	Michigan Muni	77.0	5.35	10,068.00	10,095.00	14,234.00	5.7	328-8300	612-671-3733	5.00	None	None	Paul Hylle	'93
IDS MN TAX-EXEMPT	Minnesota Muni	410.1	5.16	10,092.00	10,045.00	13,964.00	6.0	328-8300	612-671-3733	5.00	None	None	Paul Hylle	'93
IDS NY TAX-EXEMPT	New York Muni	120.9	5.12	10,069.00	10,010.00	14,280.00	5.9	328-8300	612-671-3733	5.00	None	None	Paul Hylle	'93
IDS OH TAX-EXEMPT	Ohio Muni	72.6	5.26	10,087.00	9,953.00	14,117.00	5.7	328-8300	612-671-3733	5.00	None	None	Paul Hylle	'93
IDS TAX-EXEMPT BOND	General Muni	1,196.8	3.81	10,070.00	9,922.00	13,755.00	6.0	328-8300	612-671-3733	5.00	None	None	Terry Seierstad	'93
INDEPND CAP MUNI BOND	General Muni	4.7	10.54	10,068.00	9,864.00	☆	5.1	950-4243	None	4.50	0.30	None	Peter Sherman	'90
INDEPND CAP NY MUNI	New York Muni	5.7	11.12	10,118.00	9,941.00	☆	5.2	950-4243	None	4.50	0.30	None	Peter Sherman	'90
INSIGHT INSTL LTD MUNI	Short-Term Muni	0.9	9.67	☆	☆	☆	0.0	245-4770	412-288-1900	None	None	None	Jonathan C. Conley	'94
INTMDT MUNI TR OH; INSTL	Single State Muni	3.2	9.46	10,096.00	☆	☆	0.0	245-4770	412-288-1900	None	None	None	Scott Albrecht	'93

INTMDT MUNI TR PA; INSTL	Pennsylvania Muni	2.9	9.75	10,025.00	☆	☆	0.0	245-4770	412-288-1900	None	None	None	Scott Albrecht	'93
INTMDT MUNI TR; INSTL	Intermediate Muni	306.5	10.43	10,087.00	10,078.00	14,019.00	5.0	245-4770	412-288-1900	None	None	None	Jonathan C. Conley	'85
INTMDT MUNI TR; INSTL SV	Intermediate Muni	1.5	10.43	10,080.00	☆	☆	0.0	245-4770	412-288-1900	None	0.25	None	Jonathan C. Conley	'93
INTMDT TX FR FD VERMONT	Single State Muni	0.3	19.34	10,121.00	☆	☆	0.0	675-3333	802-773-0674	None	None	None	Mark Bennett	'93
INVESCO TAX-FR LG-TM	General Muni	297.3	15.29	10,065.00	9,884.00	14,315.00	5.4	525-8085	303-930-6300	None	0.25	None	William B. Veronda	'84
INVESCO TAX-FR INTMDT BD	Intermediate Muni	5.0	9.52	10,080.00	☆	☆	0.0	525-8085	303-930-6300	None	0.25	None	William B. Veronda	'93
INVESTORS TR TX FR; A	Intermediate Muni	14.7	10.82	10,072.00	☆	☆	0.0	426-5520	206-625-1755	4.50	0.25	None	Barbara Brinkley	'93
INVESTORS TR TX FR; B	Intermediate Muni	4.5	10.83	10,061.00	☆	☆	0.0	426-5520	206-625-1755	None	1.00	5.00	Barbara Brinkley	'93
JACKSON NATL TAX-EXEMPT	General Muni	29.6	10.11	10,084.00	10,060.00	☆	4.7	888-3863	None	4.75	None	None	PPM America	'92
JANUS FEDERAL TAX-EXEMPT	General Muni	27.4	6.69	10,074.00	9,858.00	☆	5.2	525-8983	303-333-3863	None	None	None	Ronald V. Speaker	'93
KEMPER MUNI BOND; A	General Muni	3,916.7	9.83	10,090.00	9,999.00	14,616.00	5.8	621-1048	312-781-1121	4.50	None	None	Beimford/Mier	'83/'91
KEMPER TX-FR INC CA; A	California Muni	1,190.7	7.16	10,040.00	10,005.00	14,242.00	5.4	621-1048	312-781-1121	4.50	None	None	Beimford/Mier	'83/'89
KEMPER TX-FR INC FL; A	Florida Muni	126.4	10.02	10,121.00	10,057.00	☆	5.2	621-1048	312-781-1121	4.50	None	None	Beimford/Mier	'91/'91
KEMPER TX-FR INC NY; A	New York Muni	344.3	10.67	10,081.00	10,083.00	14,768.00	5.5	621-1048	312-781-1121	4.50	None	None	Beimford/Mier	'85/'89
KEMPER TX-FR INC OH; A	Ohio Muni	20.5	9.44	10,187.00	10,155.00	☆	5.6	621-1048	312-781-1121	4.50	None	None	Beimford/Mier	'93/'93
KEMPER TX-FR INC TX; A	Texas Muni	14.7	10.05	10,171.00	10,208.00	☆	5.7	621-1048	312-781-1121	4.50	None	None	Beimford/Mier	'91/'91
KENT FDS MED TX EX; INST	Intermediate Muni	247.9	9.95	10,090.00	10,043.00	☆	3.6	343-2898	617-621-6100	None	None	None	Old Kent Bank	'92
KENT FDS MED TX EX; INV	Intermediate Muni	3.9	9.96	10,100.00	10,031.00	☆	3.6	343-2898	617-621-6100	4.00	0.25	None	Old Kent Bank	'92
KENT FDS MI LTD BD; INST	Michigan Muni	87.9	9.86	10,133.00	10,216.00	☆	3.7	343-2898	617-621-6100	None	None	None	Old Kent Bank	'93
KENT FDS MI LTD BD; INV	Michigan Muni	0.5	9.86	10,122.00	10,195.00	☆	3.7	343-2898	617-621-6100	4.00	0.25	None	Old Kent Bank	'93
KEYSTONE AM TXFR INC; A	General Muni	111.3	9.50	10,021.00	9,753.00	13,540.00	6.0	343-2898	617-621-6100	4.75	0.25	None	Betsy Blacher	'88
KEYSTONE AM TXFR INC; B	General Muni	27.5	9.48	10,010.00	9,680.00	☆	5.6	343-2898	617-621-6100	None	0.75	3.00	Betsy Blacher	'93
KEYSTONE AM TXFR INC; C	General Muni	27.6	9.48	10,000.00	9,689.00	☆	5.6	343-2898	617-621-6100	None	0.75	1.00	Betsy Blacher	'93
KEYSTONE AM TXFR2 CA; A	California Muni	2.3	9.24	10,056.00	☆	☆	0.0	343-2898	617-621-6100	4.75	0.15	None	Betsy Blacher	'94
KEYSTONE AM TXFR2 CA; B	California Muni	8.4	9.26	10,045.00	☆	☆	0.0	343-2898	617-621-6100	None	0.90	3.00	Betsy Blacher	'94
KEYSTONE AM TXFR2 CA; C	California Muni	0.3	9.27	10,042.00	☆	☆	0.0	343-2898	617-621-6100	None	1.00	1.00	Betsy Blacher	'94
KEYSTONE AM TXFR2 MO; A	Missouri Muni	0.6	9.37	10,079.00	☆	☆	0.0	343-2898	617-621-6100	4.75	0.15	None	Betsy Blacher	'94
KEYSTONE AM TXFR2 MO; B	Missouri Muni	7.9	9.34	10,058.00	☆	☆	0.0	343-2898	617-621-6100	None	0.90	3.00	Betsy Blacher	'94
KEYSTONE AM TXFR2 MO; C	Missouri Muni	1.0	9.35	10,065.00	☆	☆	0.0	343-2898	617-621-6100	None	1.00	1.00	Betsy Blacher	'94
KEYSTONE AM TXFR FL; A	Florida Muni	46.5	10.20	10,058.00	9,785.00	☆	6.0	343-2898	617-621-6100	4.75	0.15	None	Betsy Blacher	'90
KEYSTONE AM TXFR FL; B	Florida Muni	28.3	10.16	10,039.00	9,708.00	☆	5.6	343-2898	617-621-6100	None	1.00	3.00	Betsy Blacher	'93
KEYSTONE AM TXFR FL; C	Florida Muni	13.8	10.17	10,036.00	9,707.00	☆	5.5	343-2898	617-621-6100	None	1.00	1.00	Betsy Blacher	'93
KEYSTONE AM TXFR MA; A	Massachusetts Muni	1.8	9.07	10,038.00	☆	☆	0.0	343-2898	617-621-6100	4.75	0.15	None	Betsy Blacher	'94
KEYSTONE AM TXFR MA; B	Massachusetts Muni	3.1	9.07	10,016.00	☆	☆	0.0	343-2898	617-621-6100	None	0.90	3.00	Betsy Blacher	'94
KEYSTONE AM TXFR MA; C	Massachusetts Muni	1.6	9.07	10,014.00	☆	☆	0.0	343-2898	617-621-6100	None	1.00	1.00	Betsy Blacher	'94
KEYSTONE AM TXFR NY; A	New York Muni	1.5	9.33	10,153.00	☆	☆	0.0	343-2898	617-621-6100	4.75	0.15	None	Betsy Blacher	'94
KEYSTONE AM TXFR NY; B	New York Muni	4.3	9.31	10,131.00	☆	☆	0.0	343-2898	617-621-6100	None	0.90	3.00	Betsy Blacher	'94
KEYSTONE AM TXFR NY; C	New York Muni	0.7	9.30	10,128.00	☆	☆	0.0	343-2898	617-621-6100	None	1.00	1.00	Betsy Blacher	'94
KEYSTONE AM TXFR PA; A	Pennsylvania Muni	31.7	10.92	10,060.00	9,931.00	☆	5.8	343-2898	617-621-6100	4.75	0.15	None	Betsy Blacher	'90
KEYSTONE AM TXFR PA; B	Pennsylvania Muni	24.8	10.87	10,042.00	9,858.00	☆	5.5	343-2898	617-621-6100	None	0.90	3.00	Betsy Blacher	'93
KEYSTONE AM TXFR PA; C	Pennsylvania Muni	9.2	10.89	10,039.00	9,857.00	☆	5.3	343-2898	617-621-6100	None	1.00	1.00	Betsy Blacher	'93
KEYSTONE AM TXFR TX; A	Texas Muni	2.2	10.08	10,078.00	9,893.00	☆	5.6	343-2898	617-621-6100	4.75	0.15	None	Betsy Blacher	'92
KEYSTONE AM TXFR TX; B	Texas Muni	1.7	10.01	10,058.00	9,756.00	☆	5.1	343-2898	617-621-6100	None	1.00	3.00	Betsy Blacher	'93
KEYSTONE AM TXFR TX; C	Texas Muni	0.8	9.98	10,066.00	9,745.00	☆	5.0	343-2898	617-621-6100	None	1.00	1.00	Betsy Blacher	'93
KEYSTONE TAX EXEMPT TR	General Muni	759.5	10.32	10,012.00	9,802.00	13,382.00	5.6	343-2898	617-621-6100	None	1.00	4.00	Betsy Blacher	'88
KEYSTONE TAX FREE FUND	General Muni	1,382.2	7.42	10,019.00	9,785.00	13,687.00	5.8	343-2898	617-621-6100	None	1.00	4.00	Betsy Blacher	'88
KIDDER INV II MUNI; A	General Muni	17.6	10.84	10,097.00	☆	☆	0.0	528-7778	212-656-1640	2.25	0.25	None	Robert R. Kaelin	'93
KIDDER INV II MUNI; B	General Muni	5.5	10.84	10,084.00	☆	☆	0.0	528-7778	212-656-1640	None	0.75	None	Robert R. Kaelin	'93
KIDDER INV II MUNI; C	General Muni	1.2	10.84	10,099.00	☆	☆	0.0	528-7778	212-656-1640	None	None	None	Robert R. Kaelin	'93
LANDMARK TX FR NY INC	New York Muni	107.1	10.55	9,980.00	9,789.00	13,867.00	5.3	223-4447	212-564-3456	4.00	0.20	None	Frank Flammino	'92

PERFORMANCE OF MUTUAL FUNDS (continued)

FUND NAME	OBJECTIVE	TOTAL NET ASSETS ($ MIL) 5/31/94	NET ASSET $ VALUE 6/30/94	PERFORMANCE (Return on initial $10,000 Investment) 3/31/94-6/30/94	6/30/93-6/30/94	6/30/89-6/30/94	DIVIDEND YIELD % 6/94	PHONE NUMBER 800	In-State	FEES Load	12b-1	Redemption	MANAGER	SINCE
LAUREL TF BOND; INV	Intermediate Muni	24.1	11.66	10,101.00	10,096.00	14,224.00	4.6	225-5267	None	None	0.06	None	Andrew Windmueller	'86
LAUREL TF BOND; TR	Intermediate Muni	13.5	11.66	10,107.00	10,106.00	☆	4.7	221-7930	None	None	None	None	Andrew Windmueller	'93
LAUREL TF CA BD; INV	California Muni	10.1	12.61	10,107.00	10,178.00	14,267.00	4.8	225-5267	None	None	0.03	None	Andrew Windmueller	'88
LAUREL TF CA BD; TR	California Muni	10.9	12.61	10,113.00	10,188.00	☆	4.9	221-7930	None	None	None	None	Andrew Windmueller	'93
LAUREL TF MA BD; INV	Massachusetts Muni	22.2	11.74	10,100.00	10,137.00	14,264.00	4.5	225-5267	None	None	0.05	None	Andrew Windmueller	'86
LAUREL TF MA BD; TR	Massachusetts Muni	14.7	11.74	10,107.00	10,151.00	☆	4.7	221-7930	None	None	None	None	Andrew Windmueller	'93
LAUREL TF NY BD; INV	New York Muni	4.3	12.59	10,109.00	10,125.00	14,020.00	4.9	225-5267	None	None	0.09	None	Andrew Windmueller	'88
LAUREL TF NY BD; TR	New York Muni	2.5	12.59	10,115.00	10,148.00	☆	5.1	221-7930	None	None	None	None	Andrew Windmueller	'93
LEAHI TR TAX FREE INCOME	General Muni	44.4	13.34	10,047.00	9,989.00	14,201.00	5.2	None	808-522-7777	None	0.25	None	Leahi Management Co.	'87
LEBENTHAL NY MUNI ☙	New York Muni	79.1	7.41	10,043.00	9,807.00	☆	5.6	221-5822	212-425-6116	4.50	0.25	None	Thomas G. Moles	'91
LEGG MASON TX FR PA	Pennsylvania Muni	63.5	15.72	10,083.00	10,058.00	☆	5.4	822-5544	410-539-0000	2.75	0.25	None	Victoria M. Schwatka	'91
LEGG MASON TX-FR INTMDT	Intermediate Muni	53.6	14.91	10,084.00	10,204.00	☆	4.7	822-5544	410-539-0000	2.00	0.25	None	Victoria M. Schwatka	'92
LEGG MASON TX-FR MD	Maryland Muni	146.7	15.63	10,088.00	10,103.00	☆	5.3	822-5544	410-539-0000	2.75	0.25	None	Victoria M. Schwatka	'91
LEXINGTON TX EX NATL	General Muni	12.7	10.08	10,095.00	9,737.00	13,411.00	5.2	526-0056	201-845-7300	None	None	None	Denis P. Jamison	'86
LIBERTY FINL INS MUNI ☙	Insured Muni	50.3	10.29	10,122.00	9,968.00	☆	4.9	872-5426	617-722-6000	4.50	0.30	None	M. Jane McCart	'91
LIBERTY FINL TAX-FR BOND ☙	General Muni	259.3	10.20	10,082.00	10,043.00	14,295.00	5.6	872-5426	617-722-6000	4.50	0.30	None	M. Jane McCart	'92
LIBERTY MUNI SECS; A	General Muni	741.3	11.00	10,074.00	9,986.00	14,188.00	5.9	245-4770	412-288-1900	4.50	None	None	Jonathan C. Conley	'84
LIBERTY MUNI SECS; C	General Muni	22.9	11.00	10,052.00	9,893.00	☆	4.9	245-4770	412-288-1900	None	0.75	1.00	Jonathan C. Conley	'93
LIBERTY MUNI SECS; SEL	General Muni	0.6	11.00	9,945.00	☆	☆	0.0	245-4770	412-288-1900	None	None	None	Jonathan C. Conley	'94
LINCOLN ADV TXFR INC; A	General Muni	9.6	9.21	10,081.00	☆	☆	0.0	923-8476	219-455-3361	4.50	0.35	None	Phil Byrde	'93
LINCOLN ADV TXFR INC; B	General Muni	0.1	9.95	☆	☆	☆	0.0	923-8476	219-455-3361	None	1.00	5.00	Phil Byrde	'94
LOOMIS SAYLES MUNI	General Muni	5.6	10.79	10,128.00	9,965.00	☆	4.7	633-3330	617-482-2450	None	None	None	Martha F. Hodgman	'93
LORD ABBETT CA TX-FR INC	California Muni	329.3	10.30	9,964.00	9,678.00	14,362.00	6.1	426-1130	212-848-1800	4.75	0.25	None	Barbara Grummel	'91
LORD ABBETT TX-FR CT	Connecticut Muni	105.6	9.81	9,969.00	9,785.00	☆	6.1	426-1130	212-848-1800	4.75	0.25	None	Phil Fang	'91
LORD ABBETT TX-FR FL	Florida Muni	191.4	4.67	10,004.00	9,745.00	☆	6.2	426-1130	212-848-1800	4.75	0.25	None	Barbara Grummel	'91
LORD ABBETT TX-FR HI	Single State Muni	93.3	4.77	10,004.00	9,789.00	☆	6.0	426-1130	212-848-1800	4.75	0.25	None	Phil Fang	'91
LORD ABBETT TX-FR MI	Michigan Muni	44.6	4.73	10,003.00	9,874.00	☆	6.2	426-1130	212-848-1800	4.75	None	None	Phil Fang	'92
LORD ABBETT TX-FR MO	Missouri Muni	118.2	4.96	9,987.00	9,819.00	☆	6.0	426-1130	212-848-1800	4.75	0.25	None	Barbara Grummel	'91
LORD ABBETT TX-FR NATL	General Muni	668.4	10.73	9,974.00	9,737.00	14,255.00	6.1	426-1130	212-848-1800	4.75	0.25	None	John Mousseau	'91
LORD ABBETT TX-FR NJ	New Jersey Muni	187.3	5.01	10,049.00	9,913.00	☆	6.0	426-1130	212-848-1800	4.75	0.25	None	John Mousseau	'91
LORD ABBETT TX-FR NY	New York Muni	352.2	10.70	9,898.00	9,711.00	14,179.00	6.0	426-1130	212-848-1800	4.75	0.25	None	Barbara Grummel	'91
LORD ABBETT TX-FR PA	Pennsylvania Muni	85.7	4.82	10,024.00	9,853.00	☆	6.1	426-1130	212-848-1800	4.75	0.15	None	Phil Fang	'92
LORD ABBETT TX-FR TX	Texas Muni	105.9	9.69	10,042.00	9,847.00	14,499.00	6.2	426-1130	212-848-1800	4.75	0.25	None	Barbara Grummel	'91
LORD ABBETT TX-FR WA	Washington Muni	80.9	4.76	10,004.00	9,725.00	☆	6.2	426-1130	212-848-1800	4.75	0.25	None	Barbara Grummel	'92
LTD TM TXEX BOND OF AMER	Intermediate Muni	185.5	14.01	10,117.00	☆	☆	0.0	421-4120	714-671-7000	4.75	0.25	None	Multiple Managers	'93
LUTHERAN BRO MUNI BOND ◪	General Muni	612.4	8.13	10,065.00	9,912.00	14,370.00	5.7	328-4552	612-339-8091	5.00	None	None	Janet Grangaard	'94
MACKENZIE CA MUNICIPAL	California Muni	41.7	9.91	10,082.00	10,067.00	13,818.00	5.8	456-5111	None	4.75	0.25	None	Dan Johnedis	'93
MACKENZIE LTD MUNICIPAL	Intermediate Muni	156.5	10.02	10,063.00	10,144.00	☆	6.0	456-5111	None	3.00	0.25	None	Dan Johnedis	'93
MACKENZIE NATL MUNICIPAL	General Muni	37.7	9.60	10,055.00	10,066.00	13,757.00	5.8	456-5111	None	4.75	0.25	None	Dan Johnedis	'93
MACKENZIE NY MUNICIPAL	New York Muni	42.4	9.50	10,020.00	10,047.00	13,980.00	5.7	456-5111	None	4.75	0.25	None	Dan Johnedis	'93
MAINSTAY CA	California Muni	17.7	9.48	10,104.00	9,999.00	☆	5.4	522-4202	None	4.50	None	None	Team Managed	'91
MAINSTAY NY	New York Muni	18.0	9.54	10,091.00	10,014.00	☆	6.0	522-4202	None	4.50	None	None	Team Managed	'91
MAINSTAY TAX FREE BD	General Muni	541.5	9.62	10,085.00	9,887.00	13,511.00	5.6	522-4202	None	None	0.50	5.00	Team Managed	'86
MANAGERS MUNI BOND	General Muni	16.2	22.52	10,066.00	9,876.00	13,707.00	5.4	835-3879	203-857-5321	None	None	None	Multiple Managers	'84
MANAGERS SHORT MUNI	Short-Term Muni	4.7	19.68	10,025.00	10,177.00	12,421.00	3.6	835-3879	203-857-5321	None	None	None	Multiple Managers	'84

MARINER NY TAX FREE BD	New York Muni	59.6	10.75	10,027.00	9,923.00	14,679.00	5.1	634-2536	212-503-6826	4.75	0.25	None	Lucia Dunbar	'90
MARK TWAIN MUNI INCOME	General Muni	24.5	9.92	10,057.00	10,059.00	☆	4.9	None	314-889-0715	3.50	None	None	Larry Kaestner	'93
MARKETWATCH VA MUNI	Virginia Muni	42.4	9.69	9,986.00	9,778.00	☆	3.9	232-9091	None	4.50	0.25	None	Team Managed	'93
MARSHALL INTMDT TX FR	Intermediate Muni	27.2	9.64	10,098.00	☆	☆	0.0	236-8560	414-287-8500	None	None	None	John D. Boritzke	'94
MARSHALL SHRT TAX FREE	Short-Term Muni	19.7	9.90	10,090.00	☆	☆	0.0	236-8560	414-287-8500	None	None	None	John D. Boritzke	'94
MAS MUNI FXD INC	General Muni	38.9	10.11	10,058.00	9,822.00	☆	5.9	354-8185	610-940-5000	None	None	None	Team Managed	'92
MAS PA MUNI FXD	Pennsylvania Muni	23.3	10.20	10,038.00	9,803.00	☆	5.9	354-8185	610-940-5000	None	None	None	Team Managed	'92
MERRILL CA MUNI BOND; A	California Muni	60.1	11.16	10,080.00	9,908.00	14,142.00	5.9	None	609-282-2800	4.00	None	None	Walter O'Conner	'91
MERRILL CA MUNI BOND; B	California Muni	739.3	11.16	10,068.00	9,851.00	13,785.00	5.4	None	609-282-2800	None	0.50	4.00	Walter O'Conner	'91
MERRILL CA MUNI INS; A	California Muni	16.2	9.38	10,143.00	9,917.00	☆	5.4	None	609-282-2800	4.00	None	None	Walter O'Conner	'93
MERRILL CA MUNI INS; B	California Muni	74.1	9.38	10,131.00	9,867.00	☆	4.9	None	609-282-2800	None	0.50	4.00	Walter O'Conner	'93
MERRILL MULTI LTD AZ; A	Single State Muni	2.3	9.94	10,105.00	☆	☆	0.0	None	609-282-2800	1.00	None	None	Helen Marie Sheehan	'93
MERRILL MULTI LTD AZ; B	Single State Muni	5.6	9.94	10,097.00	☆	☆	0.0	None	609-282-2800	None	0.35	1.00	Helen Marie Sheehan	'93
MERRILL MULTI LTD CA; A	California Muni	3.5	9.83	10,114.00	☆	☆	0.0	None	609-282-2800	1.00	None	None	Edward Andrews	'93
MERRILL MULTI LTD CA; B	California Muni	11.1	9.83	10,106.00	☆	☆	0.0	None	609-282-2800	None	0.35	1.00	Edward Andrews	'93
MERRILL MULTI LTD FL; A	Florida Muni	16.3	9.83	10,114.00	☆	☆	0.0	None	609-282-2800	1.00	None	None	Edward Andrews	'93
MERRILL MULTI LTD FL; B	Florida Muni	18.1	9.83	10,105.00	☆	☆	0.0	None	609-282-2800	None	0.35	1.00	Edward Andrews	'93
MERRILL MULTI LTD MA; A	Massachusetts Muni	7.1	9.93	10,111.00	☆	☆	0.0	None	609-282-2800	1.00	None	None	Peter Hayes	'93
MERRILL MULTI LTD MA; B	Massachusetts Muni	8.4	9.93	10,102.00	☆	☆	0.0	None	609-282-2800	None	0.35	1.00	Peter Hayes	'93
MERRILL MULTI LTD MI; A	Michigan Muni	3.6	9.85	10,103.00	☆	☆	0.0	None	609-282-2800	1.00	None	None	Edward Andrews	'93
MERRILL MULTI LTD MI; B	Michigan Muni	2.3	9.85	10,095.00	☆	☆	0.0	None	609-282-2800	None	0.35	1.00	Edward Andrews	'93
MERRILL MULTI LTD NJ; A	Single State Muni	6.4	9.90	10,098.00	☆	☆	0.0	None	609-282-2800	1.00	None	None	Helen Marie Sheehan	'93
MERRILL MULTI LTD NJ; B	Single State Muni	7.9	9.90	10,080.00	☆	☆	0.0	None	609-282-2800	None	0.35	1.00	Helen Marie Sheehan	'93
MERRILL MULTI LTD NY; A	New York Muni	4.8	9.87	10,145.00	☆	☆	0.0	None	609-282-2800	1.00	None	None	Edward Andrews	'93
MERRILL MULTI LTD NY; B	New York Muni	9.8	9.87	10,137.00	☆	☆	0.0	None	609-282-2800	None	0.35	1.00	Edward Andrews	'93
MERRILL MULTI LTD PA; A	Pennsylvania Muni	1.0	9.91	10,088.00	☆	☆	0.0	None	609-282-2800	1.00	None	None	Helen Marie Sheehan	'93
MERRILL MULTI LTD PA; B	Pennsylvania Muni	9.7	9.91	10,080.00	☆	☆	0.0	None	609-282-2800	None	0.35	1.00	Helen Marie Sheehan	'93
MERRILL MULTI MUN AZ; A	Arizona Muni	18.8	10.24	10,126.00	9,962.00	☆	5.6	None	609-282-2800	4.00	None	None	Walter O'Conner	'91
MERRILL MULTI MUN AZ; B	Arizona Muni	81.4	10.24	10,114.00	9,912.00	☆	5.1	None	609-282-2800	None	0.50	4.00	Walter O'Conner	'91
MERRILL MULTI MUN CO; A	Colorado Muni	10.6	9.22	10,049.00	☆	☆	0.0	None	609-282-2800	4.00	None	None	Hugh Hurley	'93
MERRILL MULTI MUN CO; B	Colorado Muni	14.3	9.22	10,048.00	☆	☆	0.0	None	609-282-2800	None	0.50	4.00	Hugh Hurley	'93
MERRILL MULTI MUN FL; A	Florida Muni	69.6	9.73	10,155.00	9,797.00	☆	5.5	None	609-282-2800	4.00	None	None	Michael Rubashkin	'93
MERRILL MULTI MUN FL; B	Florida Muni	224.1	9.73	10,143.00	9,747.00	☆	5.0	None	609-282-2800	None	0.50	4.00	Michael Rubashkin	'93
MERRILL MULTI MUN MA; A	Massachusetts Muni	8.1	10.28	10,135.00	9,880.00	☆	5.7	None	609-282-2800	4.00	None	None	Roberta Roffo	'93
MERRILL MULTI MUN MA; B	Massachusetts Muni	75.0	10.28	10,123.00	9,830.00	☆	5.1	None	609-282-2800	None	0.50	4.00	Roberta Roffo	'93
MERRILL MULTI MUN MD; A	Maryland Muni	1.5	9.04	10,071.00	☆	☆	0.0	None	609-282-2800	4.00	None	None	Michael Rubashkin	'93
MERRILL MULTI MUN MD; B	Maryland Muni	13.5	9.04	10,059.00	☆	☆	0.0	None	609-282-2800	None	0.50	4.00	Michael Rubashkin	'93
MERRILL MULTI MUN MI; A	Michigan Muni	15.5	9.67	10,130.00	9,881.00	☆	5.5	None	609-282-2800	4.00	None	None	Fred Stuebe	'93
MERRILL MULTI MUN MI; B	Michigan Muni	57.6	9.67	10,117.00	9,831.00	☆	5.0	None	609-282-2800	None	0.50	4.00	Fred Stuebe	'93
MERRILL MULTI MUN MN; A	Minnesota Muni	8.7	10.19	10,129.00	10,041.00	☆	5.4	None	609-282-2800	4.00	None	None	Hugh Hurley	'93
MERRILL MULTI MUN MN; B	Minnesota Muni	56.5	10.19	10,117.00	9,989.00	☆	4.9	None	609-282-2800	None	0.50	4.00	Hugh Hurley	'93
MERRILL MULTI MUN NC; A	North Carolina Muni	10.8	10.00	10,067.00	9,894.00	☆	5.4	None	609-282-2800	4.00	None	None	Hugh Hurley	'93
MERRILL MULTI MUN NC; B	North Carolina Muni	49.8	10.00	10,055.00	9,845.00	☆	4.9	None	609-282-2800	None	0.50	4.00	Hugh Hurley	'93
MERRILL MULTI MUN NJ; A	New Jersey Muni	45.8	10.49	10,074.00	9,844.00	☆	5.6	None	609-282-2800	4.00	None	None	Mike Petty	'93
MERRILL MULTI MUN NJ; B	New Jersey Muni	179.7	10.49	10,060.00	9,792.00	☆	5.0	None	609-282-2800	None	0.50	4.00	Mike Petty	'93
MERRILL MULTI MUN NM; A	Single State Muni	6.4	10.12	☆	☆	☆	0.0	None	609-282-2800	4.00	None	None	Vincent Giordano	'94
MERRILL MULTI MUN NM; B	Single State Muni	7.1	10.12	☆	☆	☆	0.0	None	609-282-2800	None	0.50	4.00	Vincent Giordano	'94
MERRILL MULTI MUN NY; A	New York Muni	30.9	11.01	10,029.00	9,783.00	14,235.00	5.9	None	609-282-2800	4.00	None	None	Michael Rubashkin	'93
MERRILL MULTI MUN NY; B	New York Muni	678.6	11.02	10,026.00	9,743.00	13,868.00	5.3	None	609-282-2800	None	0.50	4.00	Michael Rubashkin	'93
MERRILL MULTI MUN OH; A	Ohio Muni	9.4	10.34	10,097.00	9,903.00	☆	5.4	None	609-282-2800	4.00	None	None	Hugh Hurley	'93

PERFORMANCE OF MUTUAL FUNDS (continued)

FUND NAME	OBJECTIVE	TOTAL NET ASSETS ($ MIL) 5/31/94	NET ASSET $ VALUE 6/30/94	PERFORMANCE (Return on initial $10,000 Investment) 3/31/94-6/30/94	6/30/93-6/30/94	6/30/89-6/30/94	DIVIDEND YIELD % 6/94	PHONE NUMBER 800	In-State	FEES Load	12b-1	Redemption	MANAGER	SINCE
MERRILL MULTI MUN OH; B	Ohio Muni	64.6	10.34	10,085.00	9,856.00	☆	4.9	None	609-282-2800	None	0.50	4.00	Hugh Hurley	'93
MERRILL MULTI MUN OR; A	Oregon Muni	6.7	9.24	9,972.00	☆	☆	0.0	None	609-282-2800	4.00	None	None	Michael Rubashkin	'93
MERRILL MULTI MUN OR; B	Oregon Muni	25.0	9.24	9,960.00	☆	☆	0.0	None	609-282-2800	None	0.50	4.00	Michael Rubashkin	'93
MERRILL MULTI MUN PA; A	Pennsylvania Muni	28.4	10.84	10,095.00	10,037.00	☆	5.6	None	609-282-2800	4.00	None	None	William Petty	'90
MERRILL MULTI MUN PA; B	Pennsylvania Muni	130.4	10.84	10,083.00	9,987.00	☆	5.0	None	609-282-2800	None	0.50	4.00	William Petty	'90
MERRILL MULTI MUN TX; A	Texas Muni	13.2	10.36	10,128.00	10,051.00	☆	5.7	None	609-282-2800	4.00	None	None	Roberta Roffo	'93
MERRILL MULTI MUN TX; B	Texas Muni	78.1	10.36	10,116.00	10,000.00	☆	5.2	None	609-282-2800	None	0.50	4.00	Roberta Roffo	'93
MERRILL MUNI SRS INT; A	Intermediate Muni	34.5	9.85	10,139.00	10,153.00	14,108.00	5.5	None	609-282-2800	2.00	None	None	Vincent Giordano	'88
MERRILL MUNI SRS INT; B	Intermediate Muni	154.9	9.85	10,119.00	10,109.00	13,874.00	5.0	None	609-282-2800	None	0.30	2.00	Vincent Giordano	'88
MERRILL MUNI INS; A	Insured Muni	2,019.4	7.88	10,074.00	9,897.00	14,335.00	5.9	None	609-282-2800	4.00	None	None	Ken Jacob	'84
MERRILL MUNI INS; B	Insured Muni	883.2	7.87	10,043.00	9,821.00	13,803.00	5.1	None	609-282-2800	None	0.75	4.00	Ken Jacob	'88
MERRILL MUNI LTD MAT; A	Short-Term Muni	808.0	9.87	10,060.00	10,228.00	13,008.00	3.7	None	609-282-2800	0.75	None	None	Peter Hayes	'89
MERRILL MUNI LTD MAT; B	Short-Term Muni	149.9	9.87	10,052.00	10,196.00	☆	3.4	None	609-282-2800	None	0.35	1.00	Peter Hayes	'92
MERRILL MUNI NATL; A	General Muni	1,226.8	10.08	10,112.00	9,948.00	14,372.00	6.0	None	609-282-2800	4.00	None	None	Ken Jacob	'84
MERRILL MUNI NATL; B	General Muni	464.6	10.07	10,084.00	9,863.00	13,843.00	5.2	None	609-282-2800	None	0.75	4.00	Ken Jacob	'88
METLIFE SS TX-EX; A	General Muni	274.2	7.76	10,033.00	9,820.00	13,904.00	4.9	882-3302	617-348-2000	4.50	0.25	None	Susan Drake	'90
METLIFE SS TX-EX; B	General Muni	34.9	7.76	10,014.00	9,750.00	☆	4.2	882-3302	617-348-2000	None	1.00	5.00	Susan Drake	'93
METLIFE SS TX-EX; C	General Muni	0.4	7.75	10,039.00	9,847.00	☆	5.2	882-3302	617-348-2000	None	None	None	Susan Drake	'93
METLIFE SS TX-EX; D	General Muni	1.0	7.76	10,014.00	9,750.00	☆	4.2	882-3302	617-348-2000	None	1.00	1.00	Susan Drake	'93
MFS AL MUNI BOND; A	Single State Muni	84.3	10.25	10,137.00	10,109.00	☆	5.2	225-2606	617-954-5000	4.75	0.35	None	Geoff Schechter	'93
MFS AL MUNI BOND; B	Single State Muni	3.3	10.25	10,117.00	☆	☆	0.0	225-2606	617-954-5000	None	1.00	4.00	Geoff Schechter	'93
MFS AR MUNI BOND; A ☛	Single State Muni	199.1	9.73	10,188.00	10,042.00	☆	5.5	225-2606	617-954-5000	4.75	0.35	None	Cindy Brown	'92
MFS AR MUNI BOND; B	Single State Muni	6.5	9.72	10,150.00	☆	☆	0.0	225-2606	617-954-5000	None	1.00	4.00	Cindy Brown	'93
MFS CA MUNI BOND; A ☛	California Muni	310.0	5.39	9,996.00	9,812.00	14,250.00	5.8	225-2606	617-954-5000	4.75	0.35	None	David Smith	'93
MFS CA MUNI BOND; B	California Muni	23.5	5.40	9,988.00	☆	☆	0.0	225-2606	617-954-5000	None	1.00	4.00	David Smith	'93
MFS CA MUNI BOND; C	California Muni	2.4	5.40	9,971.00	☆	☆	0.0	225-2606	617-954-5000	None	1.00	None	David Smith	'94
MFS FL MUNI BOND; A ☛	Florida Muni	106.6	9.54	10,099.00	9,819.00	☆	5.8	225-2606	617-954-5000	4.75	0.35	None	Geoff Schechter	'93
MFS FL MUNI BOND; B	Florida Muni	9.2	9.53	10,071.00	☆	☆	0.0	225-2606	617-954-5000	None	1.00	4.00	Geoff Schechter	'93
MFS GA MUNI BOND; A	Georgia Muni	85.4	10.31	10,099.00	9,944.00	14,142.00	5.4	225-2606	617-954-5000	4.75	0.35	None	David Smith	'92
MFS GA MUNI BOND; B	Georgia Muni	7.1	10.31	10,078.00	☆	☆	0.0	225-2606	617-954-5000	None	1.00	4.00	David Smith	'93
MFS LA MUNI BOND; A ☛	Louisiana Muni	14.1	9.19	10,149.00	9,972.00	☆	5.9	225-2606	617-954-5000	4.75	0.35	None	Geoff Schechter	'93
MFS LA MUNI BOND; B	Louisiana Muni	1.9	9.20	10,124.00	☆	☆	0.0	225-2606	617-954-5000	None	1.00	4.00	Geoff Schechter	'93
MFS MA MUNI BOND; A	Massachusetts Muni	276.0	10.81	10,093.00	9,996.00	14,138.00	6.0	225-2606	617-954-5000	4.75	0.35	None	David Smith	'93
MFS MA MUNI BOND; B	Massachusetts Muni	5.5	10.82	10,084.00	☆	☆	0.0	225-2606	617-954-5000	None	1.00	4.00	David Smith	'93
MFS MD MUNI BOND; A	Maryland Muni	160.4	10.84	10,099.00	9,849.00	13,604.00	5.6	225-2606	617-954-5000	4.75	0.35	None	David Smith	'92
MFS MD MUNI BOND; B	Maryland Muni	7.8	10.83	10,081.00	☆	☆	0.0	225-2606	617-954-5000	None	1.00	4.00	David Smith	'93
MFS MS MUNI BOND; A ☛	Single State Muni	82.1	9.15	10,135.00	9,964.00	☆	6.0	225-2606	617-954-5000	4.75	0.35	None	Geoff Schechter	'93
MFS MS MUNI BOND; B	Single State Muni	7.3	9.16	10,121.00	☆	☆	0.0	225-2606	617-954-5000	None	1.00	4.00	Geoff Schechter	'93
MFS MUNI BOND; A	General Muni	2,048.3	10.58	10,084.00	9,926.00	14,393.00	5.7	225-2606	617-954-5000	4.75	None	None	Robert Dennis	'84
MFS MUNI BOND; B	General Muni	39.1	10.57	10,056.00	☆	☆	0.0	225-2606	617-954-5000	None	0.75	4.00	Robert Dennis	'93
MFS MUNI HIGH INCOME; A ☒	High-Yield Muni	789.3	8.84	10,082.00	10,125.00	13,745.00	7.8	225-2606	617-954-5000	4.75	None	None	Cindy Brown	'93
MFS MUNI HIGH INCOME; B	High-Yield Muni	0.1	8.84	10,050.00	☆	☆	0.0	225-2606	617-954-5000	None	1.00	4.00	Cindy Brown	'93
MFS MUNI INCOME; A	General Muni	6.0	8.53	10,115.00	☆	☆	0.0	225-2606	617-954-5000	4.75	0.35	None	David Smith	'93
MFS MUNI INCOME; B	General Muni	471.3	8.54	10,099.00	9,990.00	13,558.00	4.9	225-2606	617-954-5000	None	1.00	4.00	David Smith	'93
MFS MUNI INCOME; C	General Muni	8.1	8.54	10,101.00	☆	☆	0.0	225-2606	617-954-5000	None	1.00	None	David Smith	'94

MFS MUNI LTD MAT; A	Short-Term Muni	84.3	7.45	10,095.00	10,127.00	☆	3.9	225-2606	617-954-5000	2.50	0.35	None	Robert Dennis	'92
MFS MUNI LTD MAT; B	Short-Term Muni	8.4	7.45	10,088.00	☆	☆	0.0	225-2606	617-954-5000	None	1.00	4.00	Robert Dennis	'93
MFS NC MUNI BOND; A	North Carolina Muni	462.0	11.35	10,106.00	9,932.00	13,726.00	5.4	225-2606	617-954-5000	4.75	0.35	None	Geoff Schechter	'93
MFS NC MUNI BOND; B	North Carolina Muni	19.1	11.35	10,096.00	☆	☆	0.0	225-2606	617-954-5000	None	1.00	4.00	Geoff Schechter	'93
MFS NC MUNI BOND; C	North Carolina Muni	8.1	11.34	10,089.00	☆	☆	0.0	225-2606	617-954-5000	None	1.00	None	Geoff Schechter	'94
MFS NY MUNI BOND; A	New York Muni	163.4	10.41	10,098.00	10,000.00	14,679.00	5.5	225-2606	617-954-5000	4.75	0.35	None	Geoff Schechter	'93
MFS NY MUNI BOND; B	New York Muni	7.5	10.41	10,077.00	☆	☆	0.0	225-2606	617-954-5000	None	1.00	4.00	Geoff Schechter	'93
MFS PA MUNI BOND; A ▮Ⅲ	Pennsylvania Muni	15.1	9.18	10,218.00	9,980.00	☆	5.8	225-2606	617-954-5000	4.75	0.35	None	Geoff Schechter	'93
MFS PA MUNI BOND; B	Pennsylvania Muni	5.4	9.18	10,193.00	☆	☆	0.0	225-2606	617-954-5000	None	1.00	4.00	Geoff Schechter	'93
MFS SC MUNI BOND; A	South Carolina Muni	177.1	11.71	10,125.00	9,981.00	13,934.00	5.3	225-2606	617-954-5000	4.75	0.35	None	David Smith	'92
MFS SC MUNI BOND; B	South Carolina Muni	10.6	11.71	10,115.00	☆	☆	0.0	225-2606	617-954-5000	None	1.00	4.00	David Smith	'93
MFS TN MUNI BOND; A	Tennessee Muni	121.1	10.22	10,106.00	10,086.00	13,969.00	5.6	225-2606	617-954-5000	4.75	0.35	None	David Smith	'92
MFS TN MUNI BOND; B	Tennessee Muni	6.5	10.22	10,088.00	☆	☆	0.0	225-2606	617-954-5000	None	1.00	4.00	David Smith	'93
MFS TX MUNI BOND; A ☛	Texas Muni	18.7	9.78	10,114.00	9,959.00	☆	6.3	225-2606	617-954-5000	4.75	0.35	None	David Smith	'92
MFS TX MUNI BOND; B	Texas Muni	1.5	9.78	10,078.00	☆	☆	0.0	225-2606	617-954-5000	None	1.00	4.00	David Smith	'93
MFS VA MUNI BOND; A	Virginia Muni	445.3	11.05	10,093.00	9,896.00	13,856.00	5.7	225-2606	617-954-5000	4.75	0.35	None	David Smith	'93
MFS VA MUNI BOND; B	Virginia Muni	16.2	11.05	10,084.00	☆	☆	0.0	225-2606	617-954-5000	None	1.00	4.00	David Smith	'93
MFS VA MUNI BOND; C	Virginia Muni	1.5	11.05	10,086.00	☆	☆	0.0	225-2606	617-954-5000	None	1.00	None	David Smith	'94
MFS WA MUNI BOND; A ☛	Washington Muni	16.7	9.37	10,246.00	9,993.00	☆	6.0	225-2606	617-954-5000	4.75	0.35	None	David Smith	'92
MFS WA MUNI BOND; B	Washington Muni	2.1	9.37	10,220.00	☆	☆	0.0	225-2606	617-954-5000	None	1.00	4.00	David Smith	'93
MFS WV MUNI BOND; A	Single State Muni	130.8	11.16	10,125.00	10,032.00	14,162.00	5.6	225-2606	617-954-5000	4.75	0.35	None	Cindy Brown	'92
MFS WV MUNI BOND; B	Single State Muni	6.3	11.15	10,098.00	☆	☆	0.0	225-2606	617-954-5000	None	1.00	4.00	Cindy Brown	'93
MGD MUNI; FLAG INV	General Muni	51.3	10.21	10,064.00	9,879.00	☆	5.6	645-3923	410-637-6819	4.50	0.25	None	R. Alan Medaugh	'90
MGD MUNI; FLAG INV B	General Muni	2.3	10.16	10,053.00	9,847.00	☆	5.6	645-3923	410-637-6819	1.50	0.60	1.00	R. Alan Medaugh	'92
MGD MUNI; ISI	General Muni	87.0	10.21	10,064.00	9,879.00	☆	5.6	645-3923	410-637-6819	4.45	0.25	None	R. Alan Medaugh	'90
MIDWEST TX FR INTMDT	Intermediate Muni	109.4	10.69	10,082.00	10,166.00	13,984.00	4.5	543-8721	513-629-2000	1.00	0.25	None	John Goetz	'86
MIDWEST TX FR OH INS; A	Ohio Muni	80.5	11.74	10,050.00	9,955.00	14,195.00	5.1	543-8721	513-629-2000	4.00	0.25	None	John Goetz	'86
MIDWEST TX FR OH INS; C	Ohio Muni	1.8	11.74	10,038.00	☆	☆	0.0	543-8721	513-629-2000	1.00	0.25	None	John Goetz	'93
MONITOR OH TAX-FR; INV	Single State Muni	2.6	21.08	10,041.00	10,083.00	☆	4.2	253-0412	614-463-5580	2.00	0.25	None	William Doughty	'91
MONITOR OH TAX-FR; TR	Single State Muni	56.5	21.08	10,053.00	10,111.00	13,424.00	4.5	253-0412	614-463-5580	None	None	None	William Doughty	'88
MONTGOMERY CA SHRT DUR	California Muni	9.8	11.79	10,084.00	☆	☆	3.5	572-3863	415-627-2400	None	None	None	William Stevens	'93
MORGAN GRENFELL MUNI	Intermediate Muni	157.8	10.51	10,142.00	10,265.00	☆	5.7	932-7781	215-989-6611	None	None	None	David Baldt	'91
MUIR CA TAX FREE BOND	California Muni	17.5	15.43	10,127.00	9,821.00	☆	6.1	223-7010	415-989-3200	2.00	None	None	Kieschnick/Seneca	'91/'91
MUNI FD CAL INTMDT; INTER	California Muni	19.0	10.19	10,100.00	10,084.00	13,998.00	5.2	821-7432	None	None	None	None	Don Simmons	'93
MUNI FD TEMP INTMDT; SHS	Intermediate Muni	20.7	10.70	10,088.00	10,045.00	13,901.00	4.8	821-7432	None	None	None	None	Don Simmons	'92
MUNI SECS INC CA; FORT	California Muni	15.5	9.83	9,968.00	9,671.00	☆	5.9	245-4770	412-288-1900	1.00	0.50	1.00	Jonathan C. Conley	'92
MUNI SECS INC FL	Florida Muni	9.9	9.24	10,122.00	9,630.00	☆	6.2	245-4770	412-288-1900	None	0.75	3.00	James Roberge	'93
MUNI SECS INC MI	Michigan Muni	56.6	10.47	10,088.00	10,090.00	☆	5.0	245-4770	412-288-1900	3.00	None	None	Jonathan C. Conley	'91
MUNI SECS INC NJ	New Jersey Muni	10.1	9.28	10,068.00	9,690.00	☆	6.0	245-4770	412-288-1900	None	0.75	3.00	James Roberge	'93
MUNI SECS INC NY; FORT	New York Muni	22.9	9.92	10,021.00	9,741.00	☆	5.8	245-4770	412-288-1900	1.00	0.50	1.00	Jonathan C. Conley	'92
MUNI SECS INC OH; FORT	Ohio Muni	78.1	10.86	10,083.00	9,940.00	☆	5.1	245-4770	412-288-1900	1.00	0.40	1.00	Jonathan C. Conley	'90
MUNI SECS INC OH; TR	Ohio Muni	6.6	10.86	10,093.00	9,980.00	☆	5.5	245-4770	412-288-1900	None	None	None	Jonathan C. Conley	'92
MUNI SECS INC PA; INC	Pennsylvania Muni	8.3	10.72	10,033.00	☆	☆	0.0	245-4770	412-288-1900	None	0.75	3.00	Jonathan C. Conley	'93
MUNI SECS INC PA; INV	Pennsylvania Muni	69.7	10.79	10,052.00	9,852.00	☆	5.5	245-4770	412-288-1900	3.00	None	None	Jonathan C. Conley	'90
MUNI SECS INC PA; TR	Pennsylvania Muni	18.3	10.79	10,057.00	9,870.00	☆	5.7	245-4770	412-288-1900	None	None	None	Jonathan C. Conley	'92
MUNI SECS INC TX	Texas Muni	10.3	9.32	10,080.00	9,636.00	☆	6.2	245-4770	412-288-1900	None	0.75	3.00	James Roberge	'93
N&B INC MUNI SECURITIES	Intermediate Muni	72.0	10.48	10,082.00	10,077.00	13,767.00	4.3	877-9700	212-476-8800	None	None	None	Havell/Flahive	'87/'93
NARRAGANSETT INS TX-FREE	Single State Muni	31.3	9.44	10,118.00	9,889.00	☆	5.7	453-6864	212-697-6666	4.00	0.15	None	Salvtore DiSanto	'92
NATIONS FL INT; INV A	Florida Muni	2.4	10.07	10,073.00	10,066.00	☆	4.3	321-7854	None	3.25	0.15	None	Michele M. Poirier	'92
NATIONS FL INT; INV C	Florida Muni	0.7	10.07	10,065.00	10,015.00	☆	3.7	321-7854	None	None	0.75	None	Michele M. Poirier	'92

PERFORMANCE OF MUTUAL FUNDS *(continued)*

FUND NAME	OBJECTIVE	TOTAL NET ASSETS ($ MIL) 5/31/94	NET ASSET $ VALUE 6/30/94	PERFORMANCE (Return on initial $10,000 Investment) 3/31/94-6/30/94	6/30/93-6/30/94	6/30/89-6/30/94	DIVIDEND YIELD % 6/94	PHONE NUMBER 800	In-State	FEES Load	12b-1	Redemption	MANAGER	SINCE
NATIONS FL INT; INV N	Florida Muni	4.9	10.07	10,065.00	10,033.00	☆	3.9	321-7854	None	None	0.50	4.00	Michele M. Poirier	'93
NATIONS FL INT; TR A	Florida Muni	45.0	10.07	10,077.00	10,083.00	☆	4.4	321-7854	None	None	None	None	Michele M. Poirier	'92
NATIONS FL MUNI; INV A	Florida Muni	1.0	8.99	10,072.00	☆	☆	0.0	321-7854	None	4.25	0.15	None	Michele M. Poirier	'93
NATIONS FL MUNI; INV N	Florida Muni	19.7	8.99	10,062.00	☆	☆	0.0	321-7854	None	None	0.75	5.00	Michele M. Poirier	'93
NATIONS FL MUNI; TR A	Florida Muni	2.1	8.99	10,080.00	☆	☆	0.0	321-7854	None	None	None	None	Michele M. Poirier	'93
NATIONS GA INT; INV A	Single State Muni	13.4	10.29	10,072.00	10,028.00	☆	4.6	321-7854	None	3.25	0.15	None	Michele M. Poirier	'92
NATIONS GA INT; INV C	Single State Muni	3.0	10.29	10,064.00	9,976.00	☆	4.0	321-7854	None	None	0.75	None	Michele M. Poirier	'92
NATIONS GA INT; INV N	Single State Muni	6.5	10.29	10,064.00	9,995.00	☆	4.2	321-7854	None	None	0.50	4.00	Michele M. Poirier	'93
NATIONS GA INT; TR A	Single State Muni	33.0	10.29	10,077.00	10,045.00	☆	4.7	321-7854	None	None	None	None	Michele M. Poirier	'92
NATIONS GA MUNI; INV A	Georgia Muni	0.1	9.07	10,077.00	☆	☆	0.0	321-7854	None	4.25	0.15	None	Michele M. Poirier	'93
NATIONS GA MUNI; INV N	Georgia Muni	9.5	9.07	10,064.00	☆	☆	0.0	321-7854	None	None	0.75	5.00	Michele M. Poirier	'93
NATIONS GA MUNI; TR A	Georgia Muni	0.1	9.07	10,082.00	☆	☆	0.0	321-7854	None	None	None	None	Michele M. Poirier	'94
NATIONS INT MUNI; INV A	Intermediate Muni	0.1	9.68	10,048.00	☆	☆	0.0	321-7854	None	3.25	0.15	None	Lestyan/Poirier	'93/'93
NATIONS INT MUNI; INV N	Intermediate Muni	0.8	9.68	10,044.00	☆	☆	0.0	321-7854	None	None	0.50	4.00	Lestyan/Poirier	'93/'93
NATIONS INT MUNI; TR A	Intermediate Muni	37.4	9.68	10,056.00	☆	☆	0.0	321-7854	None	None	None	None	Lestyan/Poirier	'93/'93
NATIONS MD INT; INV A	Single State Muni	25.4	10.48	10,073.00	10,015.00	☆	4.7	321-7854	None	3.25	0.15	None	Cynthia Seibert	'90
NATIONS MD INT; INV C	Single State Muni	3.4	10.48	10,066.00	9,962.00	☆	4.1	321-7854	None	None	0.75	None	Cynthia Seibert	'92
NATIONS MD INT; INV N	Single State Muni	4.1	10.48	10,066.00	9,980.00	☆	4.3	321-7854	None	None	0.50	4.00	Cynthia Seibert	'93
NATIONS MD INT; TR A	Single State Muni	65.5	10.48	10,078.00	10,031.00	☆	4.8	321-7854	None	None	None	None	Cynthia Seibert	'90
NATIONS MD MUNI; INV A	Maryland Muni	0.1	8.98	10,041.00	☆	☆	0.0	321-7854	None	4.25	0.15	None	Melinda Lestyan	'93
NATIONS MD MUNI; INV N	Maryland Muni	3.5	8.98	10,027.00	☆	☆	0.0	321-7854	None	None	0.75	5.00	Melinda Lestyan	'93
NATIONS MUNI INC INV A	General Muni	26.4	10.34	10,079.00	9,864.00	☆	5.4	321-7854	None	4.25	0.15	None	Michele M. Poirier	'92
NATIONS MUNI INC; INV C	General Muni	3.8	10.34	10,065.00	9,806.00	☆	4.7	321-7854	None	None	0.75	None	Michele M. Poirier	'92
NATIONS MUNI INC; INV N	General Muni	18.1	10.34	10,065.00	9,806.00	☆	4.7	321-7854	None	None	0.75	5.00	Michele M. Poirier	'93
NATIONS MUNI INC; TR A	General Muni	73.2	10.34	10,084.00	9,881.00	☆	5.5	321-7854	None	None	None	None	Michele M. Poirier	'92
NATIONS NC INT; INV A	Single State Muni	11.0	9.97	10,050.00	10,006.00	☆	4.2	321-7854	None	3.25	0.15	None	Michele M. Poirier	'92
NATIONS NC INT; INV C	Single State Muni	1.6	9.97	10,042.00	9,954.00	☆	3.7	321-7854	None	None	0.75	None	Michele M. Poirier	'92
NATIONS NC INT; INV N	Single State Muni	5.1	9.97	10,043.00	9,972.00	☆	3.9	321-7854	None	None	0.50	4.00	Michele M. Poirier	'93
NATIONS NC INT; TR A	Single State Muni	12.8	9.97	10,055.00	10,023.00	☆	4.4	321-7854	None	None	None	None	Michele M. Poirier	'92
NATIONS NC MUNI; INV A	North Carolina Muni	1.1	9.03	10,009.00	☆	☆	0.0	321-7854	None	4.25	0.15	None	Michele M. Poirier	'93
NATIONS NC MUNI; INV N	North Carolina Muni	20.7	9.03	9,995.00	☆	☆	0.0	321-7854	None	None	0.75	5.00	Michele M. Poirier	'93
NATIONS NC MUNI; TR A	North Carolina Muni	0.2	9.03	10,013.00	☆	☆	0.0	321-7854	None	None	None	None	Michele M. Poirier	'94
NATIONS SC INT; INV A	Single State Muni	20.7	10.17	10,054.00	10,082.00	☆	4.6	321-7854	None	3.25	0.15	None	Michele M. Poirier	'92
NATIONS SC INT; INV C	Single State Muni	7.9	10.17	10,047.00	10,029.00	☆	4.1	321-7854	None	None	0.75	None	Michele M. Poirier	'92
NATIONS SC INT; INV N	Single State Muni	5.7	10.17	10,047.00	10,048.00	☆	4.3	321-7854	None	None	0.50	4.00	Michele M. Poirier	'93
NATIONS SC INT; TR A	Single State Muni	55.4	10.17	10,059.00	10,097.00	☆	4.8	321-7854	None	None	None	None	Michele M. Poirier	'92
NATIONS SC MUNI; INV A	South Carolina Muni	0.1	9.26	10,041.00	☆	☆	0.0	321-7854	None	4.25	0.15	None	Michele M. Poirier	'93
NATIONS SC MUNI; INV N	South Carolina Muni	7.6	9.26	10,028.00	☆	☆	0.0	321-7854	None	None	0.75	5.00	Michele M. Poirier	'93
NATIONS SC MUNI; TR A	South Carolina Muni	0.2	9.26	10,046.00	☆	☆	0.0	321-7854	None	None	None	None	Michele M. Poirier	'93
NATIONS SHTM MUNI; INV A	Short-Term Muni	0.3	9.82	10,055.00	☆	☆	0.0	321-7854	None	1.50	0.15	None	Lestyan/Poirier	'93/'93
NATIONS SHTM MUNI; INV N	Short-Term Muni	18.2	9.82	10,052.00	☆	☆	0.0	321-7854	None	None	0.35	None	Lestyan/Poirier	'93/'93
NATIONS SHTM MUNI; TR A	Short-Term Muni	29.0	9.82	10,060.00	☆	☆	0.0	321-7854	None	None	None	None	Lestyan/Poirier	'93/'93
NATIONS TN INT; INV A	Single State Muni	12.3	9.75	10,064.00	10,059.00	☆	4.5	321-7854	None	3.25	0.15	None	Melinda Lestyan	'93
NATIONS TN INT; INV N	Single State Muni	2.8	9.75	10,057.00	10,022.00	☆	4.1	321-7854	None	None	0.50	4.00	Melinda Lestyan	'93
NATIONS TN INT; TR A	Single State Muni	3.5	9.75	10,069.00	10,074.00	☆	4.6	321-7854	None	None	None	None	Melinda Lestyan	'93

NATIONS TN MUNI; INV A	Tennessee Muni	0.1	9.15	10,063.00	☆	☆	0.0	321-7854	None	4.25	0.15	None	Melinda Lestyan	'93
NATIONS TN MUNI; INV N	Tennessee Muni	4.4	9.15	10,050.00	☆	☆	0.0	321-7854	None	None	0.75	5.00	Melinda Lestyan	'93
NATIONS TX INT; INV A	Single State Muni	1.6	9.91	10,102.00	10,056.00	☆	4.3	321-7854	None	3.25	0.15	None	Melinda Lestyan	'93
NATIONS TX INT; INV N	Single State Muni	2.4	9.91	10,094.00	10,023.00	☆	3.9	321-7854	None	None	0.50	4.00	Melinda Lestyan	'93
NATIONS TX INT; TR A	Single State Muni	32.3	9.91	10,106.00	10,073.00	☆	4.4	321-7854	None	None	None	None	Melinda Lestyan	'93
NATIONS TX MUNI; INV A	Texas Muni	0.1	9.02	10,052.00	☆	☆	0.0	321-7854	None	4.25	0.15	None	Melinda Lestyan	'93
NATIONS TX MUNI; INV N	Texas Muni	10.5	9.02	10,038.00	☆	☆	0.0	321-7854	None	None	0.75	5.00	Melinda Lestyan	'93
NATIONS TX MUNI; TR A	Texas Muni	1.6	9.02	10,057.00	☆	☆	0.0	321-7854	None	None	None	None	Melinda Lestyan	'94
NATIONS VA INT; INV A	Single State Muni	92.1	10.41	10,063.00	10,022.00	☆	4.7	321-7854	None	3.25	0.15	None	Cynthia Seibert	'89
NATIONS VA INT; INV C	Single State Muni	9.7	10.41	10,056.00	9,969.00	☆	4.2	321-7854	None	None	0.75	None	Cynthia Seibert	'92
NATIONS VA INT; INV N	Single State Muni	9.3	10.41	10,056.00	9,988.00	☆	4.4	321-7854	None	None	0.50	4.00	Cynthia Seibert	'93
NATIONS VA INT; TR A	Single State Muni	181.9	10.41	10,068.00	10,038.00	☆	4.9	321-7854	None	None	None	None	Cynthia Seibert	'89
NATIONS VA MUNI; INV A	Virginia Muni	0.1	8.91	10,018.00	☆	☆	0.0	321-7854	None	4.25	0.15	None	Melinda Lestyan	'93
NATIONS VA MUNI; INV N	Virginia Muni	12.4	8.91	10,005.00	☆	☆	0.0	321-7854	None	None	0.75	5.00	Melinda Lestyan	'93
NATIONS VA MUNI; TR A	Virginia Muni	0.6	8.91	10,023.00	☆	☆	0.0	321-7854	None	None	None	None	Melinda Lestyan	'94
NATIONWIDE II TX-FR	General Muni	248.8	9.75	9,955.00	9,729.00	13,893.00	5.4	848-0920	614-249-7855	None	0.20	5.00	Alpha Benson	'86
NCC OH; INSTL	Single State Muni	62.8	10.48	10,135.00	10,048.00	☆	4.9	622-3863	None	None	0.01	None	Stephen P. Carpenter	'90
NCC OH; RETAIL	Single State Muni	2.7	10.44	10,135.00	10,047.00	☆	4.9	622-3863	None	3.00	0.01	None	Stephen P. Carpenter	'91
ND TAX-FREE FUND	Single State Muni	90.7	9.21	10,012.00	10,158.00	13,379.00	5.5	562-6637	701-852-5292	None	0.25	4.00	W. Dan Korgel	'89
NEW ENGLAND INT CA; A	California Muni	36.7	7.36	10,060.00	10,196.00	☆	5.2	343-7104	None	2.50	0.25	None	James Welch	'93
NEW ENGLAND INT CA; B	California Muni	5.2	7.36	10,055.00	☆	☆	0.0	343-7104	None	None	1.00	4.00	James Welch	'93
NEW ENGLAND INT NY; A	New York Muni	20.5	7.32	10,128.00	10,128.00	☆	5.2	343-7104	None	2.50	0.25	None	James Welch	'93
NEW ENGLAND INT NY; B	New York Muni	1.2	7.31	10,109.00	☆	☆	0.0	343-7104	None	None	1.00	4.00	James Welch	'93
NEW ENGLAND MA TX FR; A	Massachusetts Muni	120.7	15.80	10,027.00	9,817.00	13,883.00	5.8	343-7104	None	4.25	0.35	None	Nathan Wentworth	'88
NEW ENGLAND MA TX FR; B	Massachusetts Muni	3.2	15.77	9,996.00	☆	☆	0.0	343-7104	None	None	1.00	4.00	Nathan Wentworth	'93
NEW ENGLAND TXEX INC; A	General Muni	207.6	7.21	10,067.00	9,856.00	14,045.00	5.1	343-7104	None	4.50	0.25	None	Nathan Wentworth	'86
NEW ENGLAND TXEX INC; B	General Muni	6.8	7.21	10,061.00	☆	☆	0.0	343-7104	None	None	1.00	4.00	Nathan Wentworth	'93
NORTH CAROLINA TX FR BD	North Carolina Muni	3.6	9.93	10,041.00	10,051.00	☆	4.2	525-3863	919-972-9922	None	None	None	Boys,Arnold & Co.,Inc.	'93
NORTHERN FDS INTMDT TXEX	Intermediate Muni	251.5	9.96	☆	☆	☆	0.0	595-9111	414-271-5885	None	None	None	Eric Boeckmann	'94
NORTHERN FDS TAX EXEMPT	General Muni	142.5	9.91	☆	☆	☆	0.0	595-9111	414-271-5885	None	None	None	Peter Flood	'94
NORTHWEST IDAHO TAX-EX	Single State Muni	7.0	4.97	9,838.00	10,066.00	13,242.00	5.0	728-8762	206-734-9900	None	None	None	Vern Clemenson	'87
NORTHWEST WA TAX-EX	Washington Muni	1.8	4.72	9,788.00	9,978.00	☆	5.1	728-8762	206-734-9900	None	None	None	Vern Clemenson	'93
NORWEST AZ TAX-FREE; A	Arizona Muni	2.7	9.40	10,107.00	☆	☆	0.0	338-1348	612-667-8833	4.50	None	None	Margie Grace	'93
NORWEST AZ TAX-FREE; B	Arizona Muni	0.2	9.40	10,078.00	☆	☆	0.0	338-1348	612-667-8833	None	0.75	3.00	Margie Grace	'93
NORWEST AZ TAX-FREE; TR	Arizona Muni	0.1	9.39	10,096.00	☆	☆	0.0	338-1348	612-667-8833	None	None	None	Margie Grace	'93
NORWEST CO TAX-FREE; A ★	Colorado Muni	31.7	9.58	10,056.00	9,986.00	☆	5.3	338-1348	612-667-8833	3.25	None	None	Margie Grace	'93
NORWEST CO TAX-FREE; B	Colorado Muni	4.5	9.59	10,028.00	☆	☆	0.0	338-1348	612-667-8833	None	0.75	3.00	Margie Grace	'93
NORWEST CO TAX-FREE; TR	Colorado Muni	15.2	9.58	10,046.00	☆	☆	0.0	338-1348	612-667-8833	None	None	None	Margie Grace	'93
NORWEST MN TAX-FREE; A ★	Single State Muni	10.0	10.04	10,050.00	9,974.00	13,547.00	5.2	338-1348	612-667-8833	4.50	None	None	Pat Hovanetz	'88
NORWEST MN TAX-FREE; B	Single State Muni	2.5	10.04	10,032.00	☆	☆	0.0	338-1348	612-667-8833	None	0.75	3.00	Pat Hovanetz	'93
NORWEST MN TAX-FREE; TR	Single State Muni	0.9	10.05	10,050.00	☆	☆	0.0	338-1348	612-667-8833	None	None	None	Pat Hovanetz	'93
NORWEST TAX-FR INC; A ★	General Muni	34.4	9.52	10,131.00	9,974.00	☆	6.1	338-1348	612-667-8833	3.25	None	None	Bill Jackson	'93
NORWEST TAX-FR INC; B	General Muni	2.7	9.52	10,113.00	☆	☆	0.0	338-1348	612-667-8833	None	0.75	3.00	Bill Jackson	'93
NORWEST TAX-FR INC; TR	General Muni	102.1	9.52	10,131.00	☆	☆	0.0	338-1348	612-667-8833	None	None	None	Bill Jackson	'93
NTH AM FDS CA MUNI; A	California Muni	4.0	9.09	9,974.00	☆	☆	0.0	334-0575	203-698-0068	4.75	0.15	None	Lori Cohane	'94
NTH AM FDS CA MUNI; B	California Muni	0.4	9.09	☆	☆	☆	0.0	334-0575	203-698-0068	None	1.00	5.00	Lori Cohane	'94
NTH AM FDS CA MUNI; C	California Muni	0.3	9.09	☆	☆	☆	0.0	334-0575	203-698-0068	None	1.00	None	Lori Cohane	'94
NTH AM FDS NATL MUNI; A	General Muni	8.5	9.26	10,094.00	☆	☆	0.0	334-0575	203-698-0068	4.75	0.15	None	Lori Cohane	'93
NTH AM FDS NATL MUNI; B	General Muni	0.7	9.26	☆	☆	☆	0.0	334-0575	203-698-0068	None	1.00	5.00	Lori Cohane	'94
NTH AM FDS NATL MUNI; C	General Muni	0.9	9.26	☆	☆	☆	0.0	334-0575	203-698-0068	None	1.00	None	Lori Cohane	'94

★ NORWEST CO TAX-FREE; A--The maximum load is currently reduced to 3.25%.

★ NORWEST MN TAX-FREE; A--The maximum load is currently reduced to 3.25%.

★ NORWEST TAX-FR INC; A--The maximum load is currently reduced to 3.25%.

PERFORMANCE OF MUTUAL FUNDS (continued)

FUND NAME	OBJECTIVE	TOTAL NET ASSETS ($ MIL) 5/31/94	NET ASSET $ VALUE 6/30/94	PERFORMANCE (Return on initial $10,000 Investment) 3/31/94-6/30/94	6/30/93-6/30/94	6/30/89-6/30/94	DIVIDEND YIELD % 6/94	PHONE NUMBER 800	In-State	FEES Load	12b-1	Redemption	MANAGER	SINCE
NUVEEN AZ VALUE	Arizona Muni	15.7	9.91	10,095.00	9,964.00	☆	5.3	621-7227	312-917-7810	4.75	None	None	Steve Krupa	'92
NUVEEN CA INSURED VALUE	California Muni	199.0	10.07	10,087.00	9,848.00	14,170.00	5.5	621-7227	312-917-7810	4.75	None	None	Steve Krupa	'91
NUVEEN CA VALUE	California Muni	208.2	10.09	10,048.00	9,854.00	14,012.00	5.9	621-7227	312-917-7810	4.75	None	None	Steve Krupa	'91
NUVEEN FL VALUE	Florida Muni	48.6	9.78	10,098.00	9,885.00	☆	5.2	621-7227	312-917-7810	4.75	None	None	Tom Futrell	'92
NUVEEN INSURED MUNI BOND	Insured Muni	725.3	10.20	10,092.00	9,918.00	14,627.00	5.6	621-7227	312-917-7810	4.75	None	None	William Norris	'87
NUVEEN MA INSURED VALUE	Massachusetts Muni	55.9	9.93	10,087.00	9,984.00	14,201.00	5.4	621-7227	312-917-7810	4.75	None	None	Steve Peterson	'93
NUVEEN MA VALUE	Massachusetts Muni	70.6	9.46	10,088.00	10,025.00	14,350.00	5.7	621-7227	312-917-7810	4.75	None	None	Steve Peterson	'93
NUVEEN MD VALUE	Maryland Muni	46.4	9.75	10,079.00	9,892.00	☆	5.1	621-7227	312-917-7810	4.75	None	None	Ted Neild	'92
NUVEEN MI VALUE	Michigan Muni	26.4	9.99	10,063.00	9,969.00	☆	5.3	621-7227	312-917-7810	4.75	None	None	Ted Neild	'92
NUVEEN MUNI BOND	General Muni	2,635.4	8.96	10,107.00	10,110.00	14,134.00	5.7	621-7227	312-917-7810	4.75	None	None	Thomas Spalding	'77
NUVEEN NJ VALUE	New Jersey Muni	36.6	9.94	10,121.00	10,193.00	☆	5.1	621-7227	312-917-7810	4.75	None	None	Steve Peterson	'92
NUVEEN NY INSURED VALUE	New York Muni	368.2	10.05	10,077.00	9,899.00	14,471.00	5.4	621-7227	312-917-7810	4.75	None	None	William Norris	'87
NUVEEN NY VALUE	New York Muni	142.8	10.13	10,062.00	10,020.00	14,547.00	5.7	621-7227	312-917-7810	4.75	None	None	William Norris	'87
NUVEEN OH VALUE	Ohio Muni	161.1	10.06	10,081.00	9,982.00	14,547.00	5.6	621-7227	312-917-7810	4.75	None	None	William Norris	'87
NUVEEN PA VALUE	Pennsylvania Muni	48.8	9.80	10,095.00	9,849.00	☆	5.5	621-7227	312-917-7810	4.75	None	None	Tom O'Shaughnessy	'92
NUVEEN VA VALUE	Virginia Muni	54.8	9.85	10,024.00	9,926.00	☆	5.4	621-7227	312-917-7810	4.75	None	None	Bill Fitzgerald	'92
111 CORCORAN NC MUNI	North Carolina Muni	45.8	10.02	10,036.00	9,963.00	☆	4.6	422-2080	919-683-7277	4.50	None	None	Jim Agnew	'92
ONE GROUP INT TX-FR; A	Intermediate Muni	5.5	10.48	10,085.00	9,967.00	☆	4.9	338-4345	None	4.50	0.25	None	Mike Graham	'92
ONE GROUP INT TX-FR; FID	Intermediate Muni	182.5	10.49	10,100.00	9,989.00	☆	5.1	338-4345	None	None	None	None	Mike Graham	'90
ONE GROUP OH MUNI BD; A	Ohio Muni	14.7	10.61	10,090.00	9,995.00	☆	4.8	338-4345	None	4.50	0.25	None	Roberta Olsen	'92
ONE GROUP OH MUNI BD; FID	Ohio Muni	93.4	10.58	10,077.00	10,007.00	☆	5.0	338-4345	None	None	None	None	Roberta Olsen	'91
ONE GROUP TX-FR BD; A	General Muni	10.7	9.69	10,044.00	10,133.00	☆	5.5	338-4345	None	4.50	0.25	None	Patrick Morrissey	'93
ONE GROUP TX-FR BD; FID	General Muni	147.1	9.66	10,050.00	10,138.00	☆	5.8	338-4345	None	None	None	None	Patrick Morrissey	'93
OPPENHEIMER CA TX-EX; A	California Muni	249.9	10.01	9,994.00	9,868.00	14,193.00	6.2	525-7048	303-671-3200	4.75	0.25	None	Robert Patterson	'88
OPPENHEIMER FL TX-EX; A	Florida Muni	9.7	10.67	9,974.00	☆	☆	0.0	525-7048	303-671-3200	4.75	0.25	None	Robert Patterson	'93
OPPENHEIMER FL TX-EX; B	Florida Muni	7.4	10.69	9,955.00	☆	☆	0.0	525-7048	303-671-3200	None	0.75	5.00	Robert Patterson	'93
OPPENHEIMER MAIN CA; A	California Muni	80.0	11.82	10,021.00	9,940.00	☆	6.4	525-7048	303-671-3200	4.75	None	None	Robert Patterson	'90
OPPENHEIMER MAIN CA; B	California Muni	1.0	11.80	9,994.00	☆	☆	0.0	525-7048	303-671-3200	None	0.75	5.00	Robert Patterson	'93
OPPENHEIMER NY TX-EX; A	New York Muni	715.2	12.16	9,993.00	9,886.00	14,280.00	6.0	525-7048	303-671-3200	4.75	0.25	None	Robert Patterson	'85
OPPENHEIMER NY TX-EX; B	New York Muni	67.2	12.16	9,974.00	9,800.00	☆	5.1	525-7048	303-671-3200	None	0.25	5.00	Robert Patterson	'93
OPPENHEIMER PA TX-EX; A	Pennsylvania Muni	63.0	11.66	9,861.00	9,800.00	☆	5.9	525-7048	303-671-3200	4.75	0.15	None	Robert Patterson	'89
OPPENHEIMER PA TX-EX; B	Pennsylvania Muni	6.9	11.66	9,843.00	9,729.00	☆	5.1	525-7048	303-671-3200	None	0.75	5.00	Robert Patterson	'93
OPPENHEIMER TX-FR BD; A	General Muni	588.1	9.42	9,940.00	9,829.00	14,186.00	6.1	525-7048	303-671-3200	4.75	0.25	None	Robert Patterson	'85
OPPENHEIMER TXEX INS; A	Insured Muni	66.8	16.32	9,991.00	9,791.00	14,130.00	5.5	525-7048	303-671-3200	4.75	0.25	None	Robert Patterson	'92
OPPENHEIMER TXEX INT; A	Intermediate Muni	80.7	14.34	10,104.00	10,049.00	14,220.00	5.2	525-7048	303-671-3200	3.50	0.25	None	Robert Patterson	'92
OREGON MUNICIPAL BOND	Single State Muni	29.9	12.19	10,087.00	10,058.00	13,658.00	4.4	541-9732	503-295-0919	None	0.25	None	Jay Willoughby	'84
OVERLAND CA TX-FR BD; A	California Muni	325.3	10.76	10,064.00	10,097.00	14,588.00	5.9	552-9612	None	4.50	0.05	None	Wines/Klug	'88/'88
OVERLAND MUNI INCOME; A	General Muni	94.7	10.25	9,990.00	9,796.00	☆	6.0	552-9612	None	3.00	0.25	None	Wines/Sabrell	'91/'91
P HZN CA TX-EX BOND	California Muni	225.0	7.08	10,049.00	9,926.00	14,195.00	5.3	332-3863	619-456-9197	4.50	None	None	Kim Michalski	'84
P HZN NATL MUNI BOND	General Muni	1.6	9.50	10,093.00	☆	☆	0.0	332-3863	619-456-9197	4.50	None	None	Kim Michalski	'94
PACIFICA CA TAX-FREE	California Muni	202.6	10.48	10,071.00	9,912.00	☆	5.1	662-8417	None	4.50	0.11	None	Kelli Chaux	'90
PACIFICA SH TM CA TAX-FR	California Muni	29.8	9.98	10,152.00	10,240.00	☆	3.8	662-8417	None	None	0.06	None	Kelli Chaux	'93
PAINEWBR CALIF TX-FR; A	California Muni	205.7	10.67	9,992.00	9,786.00	13,694.00	5.5	647-1568	None	4.00	0.25	None	Gregory Serbe	'85
PAINEWBR CALIF TX-FR; B	California Muni	38.5	10.68	9,983.00	9,712.00	☆	4.7	647-1568	None	None	1.00	5.00	Gregory Serbe	'91
PAINEWBR CALIF TX-FR; D	California Muni	43.0	10.66	9,980.00	9,736.00	☆	4.9	647-1568	None	None	0.75	None	Gregory Serbe	'92

PAINEWBR MUNI HI INC; A	High-Yield Muni	75.0	10.07	10,050.00	9,845.00	14,239.00	5.8	647-1568	None	4.00	0.25	None	Gregory Serbe	'87
PAINEWBR MUNI HI INC; B	High-Yield Muni	30.1	10.06	10,021.00	9,761.00	☆	5.0	647-1568	None	None	1.00	5.00	Gregory Serbe	'91
PAINEWBR MUNI HI INC; D	High-Yield Muni	32.8	10.06	10,027.00	9,786.00	☆	5.3	647-1568	None	None	0.75	None	Gregory Serbe	'92
PAINEWBR NATL TX-FR; A	General Muni	400.1	11.24	10,007.00	9,823.00	13,985.00	5.6	647-1568	None	4.00	0.25	None	Gregory Serbe	'84
PAINEWBR NATL TX-FR; B	General Muni	66.8	11.24	9,989.00	9,751.00	☆	4.8	647-1568	None	None	1.00	5.00	Gregory Serbe	'91
PAINEWBR NATL TX-FR; D	General Muni	156.2	11.24	9,996.00	9,776.00	☆	5.1	647-1568	None	None	0.75	None	Gregory Serbe	'92
PAINEWBR NY TX-FR; A	New York Muni	39.1	10.31	10,010.00	9,790.00	14,240.00	5.4	647-1568	None	4.00	0.25	None	Gregory Serbe	'88
PAINEWBR NY TX-FR; B	New York Muni	18.4	10.31	9,992.00	9,715.00	☆	4.6	647-1568	None	None	1.00	5.00	Gregory Serbe	'91
PAINEWBR NY TX-FR; D	New York Muni	30.6	10.31	9,998.00	9,739.00	☆	4.9	647-1568	None	None	0.75	None	Gregory Serbe	'92
PARAGON LA TAX-FREE	Louisiana Muni	202.5	10.39	10,125.00	10,101.00	☆	5.1	None	504-332-5968	4.50	None	None	Keith Mooney	'89
PARKSTONE MI MUNI; A	Michigan Muni	42.9	10.53	10,055.00	10,092.00	☆	4.3	451-8377	None	4.00	0.10	None	First of Amer Invt Corp	'93
PARKSTONE MI MUNI; INSTL	Michigan Muni	181.6	10.53	10,061.00	10,102.00	☆	4.4	451-8377	None	None	None	None	First of Amer Invt Corp	'90
PARKSTONE MUNI; A	Intermediate Muni	12.5	10.29	10,058.00	10,071.00	☆	3.8	451-8377	None	4.00	0.10	None	First of Amer Invt Corp	'93
PARKSTONE MUNI; INSTL	Intermediate Muni	151.1	10.29	10,057.00	10,081.00	13,536.00	3.9	451-8377	None	None	None	None	First of Amer Invt Corp	'88
PARNASSUS CA TX-FR	California Muni	3.8	14.91	10,058.00	9,972.00	☆	5.1	999-3505	415-362-3505	None	None	None	David Pogran	'92
PHOENIX CA TAX EXEMPT	California Muni	130.1	12.92	10,052.00	10,000.00	13,932.00	5.7	243-4361	203-253-1000	4.75	0.25	None	James Wehr	'93
PHOENIX TAX-EXEMPT BOND	General Muni	158.0	10.77	10,056.00	9,921.00	14,687.00	6.1	243-4361	203-253-1000	4.75	0.25	None	James Wehr	'88
PIERPONT TAX EXEMPT BOND	Intermediate Muni	409.3	11.35	10,069.00	10,129.00	14,038.00	4.5	521-5411	212-826-1303	None	None	None	Ebby Jerry	'92
PILLAR NJ MUNI; A	New Jersey Muni	25.8	10.23	10,107.00	10,036.00	☆	4.7	932-7782	None	None	None	None	Charlene Palmer	'92
PILLAR NJ MUNI; B	New Jersey Muni	25.2	10.23	10,101.00	10,019.00	☆	4.5	932-7782	None	1.00	0.25	None	Charlene Palmer	'92
PIONEER CA DOUBLE TX-FR	California Muni	6.0	10.37	9,939.00	9,632.00	☆	5.8	225-6292	617-742-7825	3.50	0.15	None	Kathy McClaskey	'93
PIONEER INTMDT TAX-FR	Intermediate Muni	85.4	10.01	10,045.00	9,939.00	13,980.00	5.3	225-6292	617-742-7825	3.50	0.25	None	Kathy McClaskey	'86
PIONEER MA DOUBLE TX-FR	Massachusetts Muni	3.7	10.47	10,053.00	9,754.00	☆	5.6	225-6292	617-742-7825	3.50	0.15	None	Kathy McClaskey	'93
PIONEER NY TRIPLE TX-FR	New York Muni	4.1	10.53	10,007.00	9,798.00	☆	5.5	225-6292	617-742-7825	3.50	0.15	None	Kathy McClaskey	'93
PIONEER TAX-FREE INCOME	General Muni	496.5	11.71	10,076.00	9,953.00	14,507.00	5.5	225-6292	617-742-7825	4.50	0.25	None	Mark Winter	'86
PIPER JAFFRAY MINN TX-EX	Minnesota Muni	172.8	10.41	10,046.00	9,982.00	14,025.00	5.8	866-7778	612-342-6402	4.00	0.23	None	Reuss/White	'88/'88
PIPER JAFFRAY NATL TX-EX	General Muni	71.7	10.32	10,038.00	9,754.00	14,198.00	5.4	866-7778	612-342-6402	4.00	0.23	None	Reuss/White	'88/'88
PLANTERS TN TAX-FREE BD	Tennessee Muni	38.5	10.10	10,116.00	☆	☆	0.0	242-0242	None	4.00	None	None	Robert Eason	'93
PNC OH TX-FR INC; INSTL	Ohio Muni	2.3	9.68	10,094.00	☆	☆	0.0	422-6538	None	None	None	None	Kimberly A. Burford	'93
PNC OH TX-FR INC; INV	Ohio Muni	3.7	9.68	10,094.00	9,888.00	☆	5.4	422-6538	None	4.50	0.45	None	Kimberly A. Burford	'93
PNC OH TX-FR INC; SERV	Ohio Muni	1.4	9.68	10,088.00	☆	☆	0.0	422-6538	None	None	None	None	Kimberly A. Burford	'93
PNC PA TX-FR INC; INSTL	Pennsylvania Muni	0.5	9.90	10,125.00	☆	☆	0.0	422-6538	None	None	None	None	Douglas Gaydor	'93
PNC PA TX-FR INC; INV	Pennsylvania Muni	47.3	9.90	10,125.00	9,964.00	☆	5.4	422-6538	None	4.50	0.45	None	Douglas Gaydor	'93
PNC PA TX-FR INC; SERV	Pennsylvania Muni	10.5	9.90	10,119.00	☆	☆	0.0	422-6538	None	None	None	None	Douglas Gaydor	'93
PNC TX-FR INCOME; INSTL	General Muni	0.8	10.14	10,137.00	☆	☆	0.0	422-6538	None	None	None	None	W. Donald Simmons	'93
PNC TX-FR INCOME; INV	General Muni	7.3	10.14	10,126.00	9,891.00	☆	4.8	422-6538	None	4.50	0.45	None	W. Donald Simmons	'90
PNC TX-FR INCOME; SERV	General Muni	0.8	10.14	10,132.00	☆	☆	0.0	422-6538	None	None	None	None	W. Donald Simmons	'93
PORTICO FDS TX-EX INTMDT	Intermediate Muni	29.2	9.91	10,080.00	10,198.00	☆	4.0	982-8909	414-287-3710	None	None	None	Elfe/Pierson	'93/'93
T ROWE PRICE CA TX-FR BD	California Muni	138.8	9.85	10,071.00	9,939.00	14,125.00	5.5	638-5660	410-547-2308	None	None	None	Mary J. Miller	'90
T ROWE PRICE SUM MUN INC	General Muni	5.9	9.34	10,039.00	☆	☆	0.0	638-5660	410-547-2308	None	None	None	William T. Reynolds	'93
T ROWE PRICE SUM MUN INT	Intermediate Muni	12.1	9.74	10,130.00	☆	☆	0.0	638-5660	410-547-2308	None	None	None	Mary J. Miller	'93
T ROWE PRICE TX FR SH-IN	Short-Term Muni	504.4	5.24	10,059.00	10,201.00	13,247.00	4.1	638-5660	410-547-2308	None	None	None	Mary J. Miller	'89
T ROWE PRICE TX-FR INC	General Muni	1,374.5	9.10	10,061.00	9,926.00	14,321.00	5.7	638-5660	410-547-2308	None	None	None	William T. Reynolds	'90
T ROWE PRICE TX-FR INS	Intermediate Muni	90.8	10.27	10,125.00	10,215.00	☆	4.5	638-5660	410-547-2308	None	None	None	William T. Reynolds	'92
T ROWE PRICE TX-FR FL IN	Florida Muni	37.3	10.01	10,089.00	10,168.00	☆	4.0	638-5660	410-547-2308	None	None	None	William T. Reynolds	'93
T ROWE PRICE TX-FR GA BD	Georgia Muni	20.6	9.73	10,091.00	9,993.00	☆	4.9	638-5660	410-547-2308	None	None	None	Mary J. Miller	'93
T ROWE PRICE TX-FR HI YD	High-Yield Muni	880.9	11.62	10,071.00	10,107.00	14,769.00	6.2	638-5660	410-547-2308	None	None	None	C. Stephen Wolfe	'93
T ROWE PRICE TX-FR MD BD	Maryland Muni	747.6	9.89	10,065.00	9,958.00	14,206.00	5.7	638-5660	410-547-2308	None	None	None	Mary J. Miller	'90
T ROWE PRICE TX-FR NJ BD	New Jersey Muni	58.9	10.53	10,051.00	9,880.00	☆	5.2	638-5660	410-547-2308	None	None	None	William T. Reynolds	'91
T ROWE PRICE TX-FR NY BD	New York Muni	120.4	10.29	10,038.00	9,941.00	14,384.00	5.6	638-5660	410-547-2308	None	None	None	William T. Reynolds	'86

PERFORMANCE OF MUTUAL FUNDS (continued)

FUND NAME	OBJECTIVE	TOTAL NET ASSETS ($ MIL) 5/31/94	NET ASSET $ VALUE 6/30/94	PERFORMANCE (Return on initial $10,000 Investment) 3/31/94-6/30/94	6/30/93-6/30/94	6/30/89-6/30/94	DIVIDEND YIELD % 6/94	PHONE NUMBER 800	In-State	FEES Load	12b-1	Redemption	MANAGER	SINCE
T ROWE PRICE TX-FR SH MD	Short-Term Muni	77.8	5.03	10,059.00	10,217.00	☆	3.2	638-5660	410-547-2308	None	None	None	Mary J. Miller	'93
T ROWE PRICE TX-FR VA BD	Virginia Muni	155.9	10.42	10,071.00	9,938.00	☆	5.3	638-5660	410-547-2308	None	None	None	Mary J. Miller	'91
PRINCIPAL PRES INS TX-EX	Insured Muni	19.2	9.67	10,094.00	9,894.00	13,755.00	5.1	826-4600	414-334-5521	4.50	0.25	None	Vern Van Vooren	'86
PRINCIPAL PRES TAX-EX	General Muni	61.6	8.70	10,106.00	9,988.00	14,267.00	5.3	826-4600	414-334-5521	4.50	0.25	None	Vern Van Vooren	'84
PRINCOR TAX-EX BOND	General Muni	180.0	11.36	10,043.00	9,770.00	13,986.00	5.6	247-4123	515-247-5711	5.00	0.24	None	Garrett/Windsor	'91/'92
PRUDENTIAL BD HI YLD; A	High-Yield Muni	54.6	10.69	10,104.00	10,111.00	☆	6.7	225-1852	None	4.50	0.10	None	Liz Forsyth	'90
PRUDENTIAL BD HI YLD; B	High-Yield Muni	1,097.3	10.69	10,085.00	10,069.00	13,961.00	6.3	225-1852	None	None	0.50	5.00	Liz Forsyth	'87
PRUDENTIAL BD INS; A	Insured Muni	30.8	10.66	10,079.00	9,894.00	☆	5.4	225-1852	None	4.50	0.10	None	Liz Forsyth	'93
PRUDENTIAL BD INS; B	Insured Muni	738.0	10.66	10,060.00	9,845.00	13,829.00	4.9	225-1852	None	None	0.50	5.00	Liz Forsyth	'93
PRUDENTIAL BD MODIFD; A	Intermediate Muni	6.0	10.65	10,081.00	10,127.00	☆	4.8	225-1852	None	4.50	0.10	None	Marie Conti	'90
PRUDENTIAL BD MODIFD; B	Intermediate Muni	66.1	10.66	10,068.00	10,096.00	13,965.00	4.4	225-1852	None	None	0.50	5.00	Marie Conti	'87
PRUDENTIAL CA MUNI INC	California Muni	186.5	10.05	10,145.00	10,257.00	☆	6.5	225-1852	None	4.50	0.06	None	Webman/Smith	'90/'93
PRUDENTIAL MUNI AZ; A	Arizona Muni	7.4	11.46	10,027.00	9,943.00	☆	5.7	225-1852	None	4.50	0.10	None	Webman/Smith	'90/'93
PRUDENTIAL MUNI AZ; B	Arizona Muni	52.6	11.46	10,020.00	9,903.00	13,900.00	5.3	225-1852	None	None	0.50	5.00	Webman/Smith	'84/'93
PRUDENTIAL MUNI CA; A	California Muni	11.6	11.20	10,075.00	9,940.00	☆	5.9	225-1852	None	4.50	0.10	None	Webman/Smith	'90/'93
PRUDENTIAL MUNI CA; B	California Muni	191.9	11.19	10,068.00	9,899.00	13,703.00	5.4	225-1852	None	None	0.50	5.00	Webman/Smith	'84/'93
PRUDENTIAL MUNI FL; A	Florida Muni	140.0	9.82	10,082.00	9,888.00	☆	6.0	225-1852	None	4.50	None	None	Webman/Conti	'91/'93
PRUDENTIAL MUNI FL; D	Florida Muni	10.5	9.82	10,064.00	☆	☆	0.0	225-1852	None	None	0.75	1.00	Webman/Conti	'93/'93
PRUDENTIAL MUNI GA; A	Georgia Muni	1.2	11.08	10,072.00	9,890.00	☆	5.3	225-1852	None	4.50	0.10	None	Webman/Conti	'90/'93
PRUDENTIAL MUNI GA; B	Georgia Muni	20.1	11.08	10,058.00	9,858.00	13,679.00	4.8	225-1852	None	None	0.50	5.00	Webman/Conti	'84/'93
PRUDENTIAL MUNI MA; A	Massachusetts Muni	2.4	11.24	10,064.00	9,966.00	☆	5.9	225-1852	None	4.50	0.10	None	Webman/Rocklage	'90/'93
PRUDENTIAL MUNI MA; B	Massachusetts Muni	57.1	11.24	10,058.00	9,927.00	13,827.00	5.5	225-1852	None	None	0.50	5.00	Webman/Rocklage	'84/'93
PRUDENTIAL MUNI MD; A	Maryland Muni	2.8	10.56	10,067.00	9,856.00	☆	5.5	225-1852	None	4.50	0.10	None	Webman/Conti	'90/'93
PRUDENTIAL MUNI MD; B	Maryland Muni	52.5	10.57	10,053.00	9,817.00	13,543.00	5.1	225-1852	None	None	0.50	5.00	Webman/Conti	'85/'93
PRUDENTIAL MUNI MI; A	Michigan Muni	4.7	11.65	10,091.00	9,965.00	☆	5.5	225-1852	None	4.50	0.10	None	Webman/Smith	'90/'93
PRUDENTIAL MUNI MI; B	Michigan Muni	71.7	11.65	10,077.00	9,925.00	13,845.00	5.1	225-1852	None	None	0.50	5.00	Webman/Smith	'84/'93
PRUDENTIAL MUNI MN; A	Minnesota Muni	1.4	11.49	10,064.00	9,967.00	☆	5.1	225-1852	None	4.50	0.10	None	Webman/Smith	'90/'93
PRUDENTIAL MUNI MN; B	Minnesota Muni	25.3	11.49	10,041.00	9,919.00	13,253.00	4.7	225-1852	None	None	0.50	5.00	Webman/Smith	'84/'93
PRUDENTIAL MUNI NC; A	North Carolina Muni	2.1	10.92	10,037.00	9,860.00	☆	5.6	225-1852	None	4.50	0.10	None	Webman/Conti	'90/'93
PRUDENTIAL MUNI NC; B	North Carolina Muni	71.0	10.93	10,032.00	9,821.00	13,605.00	5.1	225-1852	None	None	0.50	5.00	Webman/Conti	'85/'93
PRUDENTIAL MUNI NJ; A	New Jersey Muni	15.0	10.70	10,038.00	9,906.00	☆	5.7	225-1852	None	4.50	0.10	None	Webman/Rocklage	'90/'93
PRUDENTIAL MUNI NJ; B	New Jersey Muni	328.5	10.70	10,023.00	9,867.00	14,158.00	5.3	225-1852	None	None	0.50	5.00	Webman/Rocklage	'88/'93
PRUDENTIAL MUNI NY; A	New York Muni	13.6	11.61	10,028.00	9,913.00	☆	5.8	225-1852	None	4.50	0.10	None	Webman/Rocklage	'90/'93
PRUDENTIAL MUNI NY; B	New York Muni	336.5	11.62	10,022.00	9,882.00	13,986.00	5.3	225-1852	None	None	0.50	5.00	Webman/Rocklage	'84/'93
PRUDENTIAL MUNI OH; A	Ohio Muni	4.6	11.61	10,088.00	10,009.00	☆	5.7	225-1852	None	4.50	0.10	None	Webman/Smith	'90/'93
PRUDENTIAL MUNI OH; B	Ohio Muni	117.0	11.61	10,065.00	9,969.00	13,957.00	5.3	225-1852	None	None	0.50	5.00	Webman/Smith	'84/'93
PRUDENTIAL MUNI PA; A	Pennsylvania Muni	10.4	10.32	10,044.00	9,944.00	☆	5.8	225-1852	None	4.50	0.10	None	Webman/Rocklage	'90/'93
PRUDENTIAL MUNI PA; B	Pennsylvania Muni	260.5	10.31	10,020.00	9,903.00	13,964.00	5.4	225-1852	None	None	0.50	5.00	Webman/Rocklage	'87/'93
PRUDENTIAL NATL MUNI; A	General Muni	14.0	14.92	10,048.00	9,886.00	☆	5.7	225-1852	None	4.50	0.10	None	Patricia Dolan	'90
PRUDENTIAL NATL MUNI; B	General Muni	757.8	14.95	10,042.00	9,843.00	13,984.00	5.2	225-1852	None	None	0.50	5.00	Patricia Dolan	'80
PUTNAM AZ TAX EX INC; A	Arizona Muni	144.1	8.77	10,033.00	9,919.00	☆	5.8	225-1581	617-292-1000	4.75	0.20	None	Howard Manning	'93
PUTNAM AZ TAX EX INC; B	Arizona Muni	13.5	8.77	10,019.00	☆	☆	0.0	225-1581	617-292-1000	None	0.95	5.00	Howard Manning	'93
PUTNAM CA TXEX INC; A	California Muni	3,349.6	8.13	10,010.00	9,909.00	14,186.00	6.3	225-1581	617-292-1000	4.75	0.20	None	William H. Reeves	'86
PUTNAM CA TXEX INC; B	California Muni	325.7	8.12	9,994.00	9,830.00	☆	5.6	225-1581	617-292-1000	None	0.80	5.00	William H. Reeves	'93
PUTNAM FL TXEX INC; A	Florida Muni	280.6	8.77	10,070.00	9,810.00	☆	5.7	225-1581	617-292-1000	4.75	0.20	None	Richard P. Wyke	'90

PUTNAM FL TXEX INC; B	Florida Muni	36.1	8.77	10,066.00	9,755.00	☆	5.0	225-1581	617-292-1000	None	0.80	5.00	Richard P. Wyke	'93
PUTNAM MA TAX EX II; A	Massachusetts Muni	244.4	8.97	10,022.00	9,975.00	☆	6.0	225-1581	617-292-1000	4.75	0.25	None	Triet N. Nguyen	'89
PUTNAM MA TAX EX II; B	Massachusetts Muni	23.0	8.97	10,017.00	☆	☆	0.0	225-1581	617-292-1000	None	0.95	5.00	Triet N. Nguyen	'93
PUTNAM MI TAX EX II; A	Michigan Muni	128.9	8.82	10,039.00	9,984.00	☆	5.9	225-1581	617-292-1000	4.75	0.20	None	Howard Manning	'93
PUTNAM MI TAX EX II; B	Michigan Muni	10.2	8.81	10,013.00	☆	☆	0.0	225-1581	617-292-1000	None	0.95	5.00	Howard Manning	'93
PUTNAM MN TAX EX II; A	Minnesota Muni	95.6	8.72	10,082.00	10,064.00	☆	5.8	225-1581	617-292-1000	4.75	0.20	None	Howard Manning	'93
PUTNAM MN TAX EX II; B	Minnesota Muni	8.8	8.71	10,079.00	☆	☆	0.0	225-1581	617-292-1000	None	0.95	5.00	Howard Manning	'93
PUTNAM MUNI INCOME; A	General Muni	855.1	8.68	10,089.00	9,978.00	14,897.00	6.2	225-1581	617-292-1000	4.75	0.25	None	Richard P. Wyke	'93
PUTNAM MUNI INCOME; B	General Muni	385.3	8.67	10,063.00	9,917.00	☆	5.5	225-1581	617-292-1000	None	0.85	5.00	Richard P. Wyke	'93
PUTNAM NJ TXEX INC; A	New Jersey Muni	248.3	8.75	10,069.00	9,906.00	☆	5.8	225-1581	617-292-1000	4.75	0.20	None	Tom Goggins	'93
PUTNAM NJ TXEX INC; B	New Jersey Muni	42.6	8.75	10,054.00	9,841.00	☆	5.1	225-1581	617-292-1000	None	0.80	5.00	Tom Goggins	'93
PUTNAM NY TX EX OPPT; A	New York Muni	174.6	8.58	10,082.00	10,103.00	☆	6.4	225-1581	617-292-1000	4.75	0.20	None	David J. Eurkus	'90
PUTNAM NY TX EX OPPT; B	New York Muni	3.2	8.58	10,076.00	☆	☆	0.0	225-1581	617-292-1000	None	0.95	5.00	David J. Eurkus	'94
PUTNAM NY TXEX INC; A	New York Muni	2,150.5	8.69	10,070.00	9,880.00	14,333.00	5.8	225-1581	617-292-1000	4.75	0.20	None	David J. Eurkus	'83
PUTNAM NY TXEX INC; B	New York Muni	175.2	8.67	10,057.00	9,813.00	☆	5.3	225-1581	617-292-1000	None	0.80	5.00	David J. Eurkus	'93
PUTNAM OH TAX EX II; A	Ohio Muni	193.9	8.71	10,017.00	9,989.00	☆	6.0	225-1581	617-292-1000	4.75	0.20	None	Tom Goggins	'93
PUTNAM OH TAX EX II; B	Ohio Muni	17.9	8.70	9,990.00	☆	☆	0.0	225-1581	617-292-1000	None	0.95	5.00	Tom Goggins	'93
PUTNAM PA TAX EX INC; A	Pennsylvania Muni	169.1	8.94	10,061.00	10,096.00	☆	5.9	225-1581	617-292-1000	4.75	0.20	None	Richard P. Wyke	'89
PUTNAM PA TAX EX INC; B	Pennsylvania Muni	19.7	8.93	10,045.00	☆	☆	0.0	225-1581	617-292-1000	None	0.95	5.00	Richard P. Wyke	'93
PUTNAM TX-FR INC HY; A	High-Yield Muni	341.8	14.10	10,045.00	☆	☆	0.0	225-1581	617-292-1000	4.75	0.20	None	Triet N. Nguyen	'93
PUTNAM TX-FR INC HY; B	High-Yield Muni	1,492.2	14.10	10,031.00	10,018.00	14,094.00	6.1	225-1581	617-292-1000	None	0.75	5.00	Triet N. Nguyen	'88
PUTNAM TX-FR INC INS; A	Insured Muni	142.6	14.49	10,047.00	☆	☆	0.0	225-1581	617-292-1000	4.75	0.20	None	Richard P. Wyke	'93
PUTNAM TX-FR INC INS; B	Insured Muni	430.7	14.50	10,032.00	9,809.00	13,589.00	5.0	225-1581	617-292-1000	None	1.00	5.00	Richard P. Wyke	'88
PUTNAM TXEX INC; A	General Muni	2,306.1	8.65	10,033.00	9,807.00	14,340.00	6.1	225-1581	617-292-1000	4.75	0.20	None	David J. Eurkus	'83
PUTNAM TXEX INC; B	General Muni	199.0	8.64	10,006.00	9,741.00	☆	5.5	225-1581	617-292-1000	None	0.80	5.00	David J. Eurkus	'93
QUEST VALUE CA	California Muni	30.3	10.42	10,011.00	9,937.00	☆	5.5	232-3863	None	4.75	0.25	None	Robert J. Bluestone	'90
QUEST VALUE NATL	General Muni	93.7	10.52	10,085.00	9,998.00	☆	5.8	232-3863	None	4.75	0.25	None	Robert J. Bluestone	'90
QUEST VALUE NY	New York Muni	32.2	10.67	10,077.00	9,942.00	☆	5.5	232-3863	None	4.75	0.25	None	Robert J. Bluestone	'90
RANSON MGD KANSAS	Kansas Muni	122.5	11.97	9,943.00	10,018.00	☆	5.5	345-2363	316-262-4955	4.25	0.25	None	Ranson/Meitzner	'90/'90
RANSON MGD KANSAS INS	Kansas Muni	30.8	11.92	10,041.00	10,108.00	☆	4.5	345-2363	316-262-4955	3.40	None	None	Ranson/Meitzner	'92/'92
RANSON MGD NEBRASKA	Single State Muni	6.5	10.73	10,037.00	☆	☆	0.0	345-2363	316-262-4955	4.25	None	None	Ranson/Meitzner	'93/'93
RBB TAX-FREE	General Muni	5.5	10.26	10,129.00	10,018.00	14,496.00	5.9	888-9723	212-878-0600	4.75	0.40	None	W. Donald Simmons	'88
REMBRANDT TX-EX FXD; INV	General Muni	0.8	9.54	10,085.00	9,884.00	☆	4.2	443-4725	None	4.50	0.25	None	Gidley/Pratt	'93/'93
REMBRANDT TX-EX FXD; TR	General Muni	61.5	9.56	10,091.00	9,919.00	☆	4.5	443-4725	None	None	None	None	Gidley/Pratt	'93/'93
RIVERSIDE CAP TN MUNI	Tennessee Muni	20.2	9.81	10,076.00	9,900.00	☆	4.9	662-4203	None	3.00	0.25	None	Alfred Jordan	'92
ROCHESTER FD MUNICIPALS	New York Muni	1,848.8	17.34	9,986.00	9,860.00	15,128.00	6.6	None	716-383-1708	4.00	0.25	None	Ronald H. Fielding	'83
ROCHESTER LTD TM NY	New York Muni	489.5	3.22	10,121.00	10,301.00	☆	4.9	None	716-383-1708	2.00	0.25	None	Ronald H. Fielding	'91
S BERNSTEIN CA MUNI	California Muni	169.1	13.13	10,032.00	10,068.00	☆	4.6	None	212-756-4097	None	None	None	Investment Policy Group	'90
S BERNSTEIN DIV MUNI	Intermediate Muni	523.6	13.06	10,032.00	10,098.00	13,712.00	4.7	None	212-756-4097	None	None	None	Investment Policy Group	'89
S BERNSTEIN NY MUNI	New York Muni	391.2	13.08	10,060.00	10,099.00	13,783.00	4.9	None	212-756-4097	None	None	None	Investment Policy Group	'89
SAFECO CA TX-FR INCOME	California Muni	77.4	11.21	9,961.00	9,787.00	14,210.00	5.7	426-6730	206-545-5530	None	None	None	Stephen C. Bauer	'83
SAFECO INSURED MUNI BOND	Insured Muni	3.4	9.62	10,002.00	9,486.00	☆	4.5	426-6730	206-545-5530	None	None	None	Stephen C. Bauer	'93
SAFECO INTMDT MUNI BOND	Intermediate Muni	11.1	10.11	10,084.00	10,103.00	☆	4.1	426-6730	206-545-5530	None	None	None	Stephen C. Bauer	'93
SAFECO MUNICIPAL BOND	General Muni	501.0	13.07	10,018.00	9,754.00	14,361.00	5.9	426-6730	206-545-5530	None	None	None	Stephen C. Bauer	'81
SAFECO WA MUNI BOND	Washington Muni	3.0	9.81	10,015.00	9,664.00	☆	4.6	426-6730	206-545-5530	None	None	None	Stephen C. Bauer	'93
SALOMON BROS NY MUNI BD	New York Muni	8.1	9.50	10,024.00	9,710.00	☆	5.8	725-6666	212-783-1301	None	None	None	Lori Cohane	'94
SCHWAB INV CA LT TXFR BD	California Muni	106.7	10.25	10,055.00	9,814.00	☆	5.4	266-5623	None	None	None	None	Keighley/Ward	'92/'92
SCHWAB INV CA SH/INTMDT	California Muni	51.0	9.83	10,071.00	10,124.00	☆	3.7	266-5623	None	None	None	None	Keighley/Ward	'93/'93
SCHWAB INV LT TXFR BD	General Muni	45.6	9.82	10,074.00	9,989.00	☆	5.3	266-5623	None	None	None	None	Keighley/Ward	'92/'92
SCHWAB INV SH/INT TX-FR	Short-Term Muni	67.1	9.87	10,092.00	10,181.00	☆	3.8	266-5623	None	None	None	None	Keighley/Ward	'93/'93

PERFORMANCE OF MUTUAL FUNDS *(continued)*

FUND NAME	OBJECTIVE	TOTAL NET ASSETS ($ MIL) 5/31/94	NET ASSET $ VALUE 6/30/94	PERFORMANCE (Return on initial $10,000 Investment) 3/31/94-6/30/94	6/30/93-6/30/94	6/30/89-6/30/94	DIVIDEND YIELD % 6/94	PHONE NUMBER 800	In-State	FEES Load	12b-1	Redemption	MANAGER	SINCE
SCUDDER CAL TXFREE	California Muni	318.2	9.89	10,083.00	9,860.00	14,529.00	5.2	225-2470	617-439-4640	None	None	None	Ragus/Carleton	'89/'83
SCUDDER HI YLD TXFR	High-Yield Muni	300.7	11.52	10,082.00	9,934.00	14,764.00	5.7	225-2470	617-439-4640	None	None	None	Condon/Manning	'87/'87
SCUDDER LTD TERM TX FR	Short-Term Muni	30.7	11.84	10,185.00	☆	☆	0.0	225-2470	617-439-4640	None	None	None	Carleton/Patton	'94/'94
SCUDDER MASS LTD TX FREE	Short-Term Muni	21.3	11.74	10,075.00	☆	☆	0.0	225-2470	617-439-4640	None	None	None	Condon/Meany	'94/'94
SCUDDER MASS TX FREE	Massachusetts Muni	324.9	13.08	10,091.00	10,033.00	14,701.00	6.1	225-2470	617-439-4640	None	None	None	Condon/Meany	'89/'91
SCUDDER MED TRM TXFR	Intermediate Muni	882.6	10.72	10,110.00	10,156.00	14,397.00	5.3	225-2470	617-439-4640	None	None	None	Carleton/Patton	'86/'87
SCUDDER MGD MUNI BOND	General Muni	814.4	8.35	10,076.00	9,921.00	14,490.00	5.4	225-2470	617-439-4640	None	None	None	Carleton/Condon	'86/'87
SCUDDER NY TXFREE	New York Muni	212.3	10.25	10,109.00	9,862.00	14,494.00	5.1	225-2470	617-439-4640	None	None	None	Ragus/Carleton	'90/'86
SCUDDER OHIO TXFREE	Ohio Muni	79.6	12.57	10,083.00	9,964.00	14,342.00	5.6	225-2470	617-439-4640	None	None	None	Manning/Condon	'87/'88
SCUDDER PENN TXFREE	Pennsylvania Muni	72.8	12.91	10,087.00	9,993.00	14,373.00	5.8	225-2470	617-439-4640	None	None	None	Manning/Condon	'87/'87
SECURITY TAX-EXEMPT FUND	General Muni	29.1	9.47	10,074.00	9,822.00	13,687.00	4.9	888-2461	913-295-3127	4.75	None	None	Jane Tedder	'84
SEI TX EX INT-TM MUNI ▮lll	Intermediate Muni	143.9	10.27	10,101.00	10,072.00	☆	4.7	342-5734	610-254-1000	None	0.08	None	Blake Miller	'93
SEI TX EX KS; A ▮lll	Kansas Muni	61.0	10.39	10,127.00	10,141.00	☆	5.6	342-5734	610-254-1000	None	None	None	Richard Winton	'94
SEI TX EX MA INTMDT ▮lll	Massachusetts Muni	11.1	10.02	10,147.00	10,122.00	☆	4.2	342-5734	610-254-1000	None	0.17	None	Joe Solido	'94
SEI TX EX PA MUNI; A ▮lll	Pennsylvania Muni	161.6	10.47	10,109.00	10,132.00	☆	5.1	342-5734	610-254-1000	None	0.06	None	Karen O'Leary	'94
SELIGMAN NJ TXEX; A	New Jersey Muni	77.0	7.48	10,050.00	9,881.00	14,187.00	5.5	221-7844	212-850-1864	4.75	0.25	None	Thomas G. Moles	'88
SELIGMAN NJ TXEX; D	New Jersey Muni	0.9	7.55	10,123.00	☆	☆	0.0	221-7844	212-850-1864	None	1.00	1.00	Thomas G. Moles	'94
SELIGMAN PA TXEX PA; A	Pennsylvania Muni	36.5	7.63	10,044.00	9,859.00	14,085.00	5.1	221-7844	212-850-1864	4.75	0.25	None	Thomas G. Moles	'86
SELIGMAN PA TXEX PA; D	Pennsylvania Muni	0.1	7.63	10,011.00	☆	☆	0.0	221-7844	212-850-1864	None	1.00	1.00	Thomas G. Moles	'94
SELIGMAN TXEX CA HY; A	California Muni	48.7	6.34	10,047.00	10,196.00	14,316.00	5.9	221-7844	212-850-1864	4.75	0.25	None	Thomas G. Moles	'84
SELIGMAN TXEX CA QLT; A	California Muni	103.2	6.46	10,007.00	9,752.00	13,906.00	5.4	221-7844	212-850-1864	4.75	0.25	None	Thomas G. Moles	'84
SELIGMAN TXEX CO; A	Colorado Muni	61.6	7.17	10,081.00	9,997.00	13,599.00	5.3	221-7844	212-850-1864	4.75	0.25	None	Thomas G. Moles	'86
SELIGMAN TXEX CO; D	Colorado Muni	0.2	7.17	10,058.00	☆	☆	0.0	221-7844	212-850-1864	None	1.00	1.00	Thomas G. Moles	'94
SELIGMAN TXEX FL; A	Florida Muni	51.4	7.43	10,069.00	9,936.00	14,221.00	5.8	221-7844	212-850-1864	4.75	0.25	None	Thomas G. Moles	'86
SELIGMAN TXEX FL; D	Florida Muni	0.1	7.43	10,049.00	☆	☆	0.0	221-7844	212-850-1864	None	1.00	1.00	Thomas G. Moles	'94
SELIGMAN TXEX GA; A	Georgia Muni	64.5	7.57	10,052.00	9,886.00	13,989.00	5.5	221-7844	212-850-1864	4.75	0.25	None	Thomas G. Moles	'87
SELIGMAN TXEX GA; D	Georgia Muni	0.7	7.57	10,029.00	☆	☆	0.0	221-7844	212-850-1864	None	1.00	1.00	Thomas G. Moles	'94
SELIGMAN TXEX LA; A	Louisiana Muni	63.6	8.04	10,034.00	9,900.00	14,031.00	5.5	221-7844	212-850-1864	4.75	0.25	None	Thomas G. Moles	'85
SELIGMAN TXEX LA; D	Louisiana Muni	0.5	8.03	9,998.00	☆	☆	0.0	221-7844	212-850-1864	None	1.00	1.00	Thomas G. Moles	'94
SELIGMAN TXEX MA; A	Massachusetts Muni	124.7	7.74	10,073.00	9,981.00	14,206.00	5.7	221-7844	212-850-1864	4.75	0.25	None	Thomas G. Moles	'84
SELIGMAN TXEX MA; D	Massachusetts Muni	1.0	7.73	10,036.00	☆	☆	0.0	221-7844	212-850-1864	None	1.00	1.00	Thomas G. Moles	'94
SELIGMAN TXEX MD; A	Maryland Muni	59.0	7.81	10,066.00	9,953.00	13,982.00	5.4	221-7844	212-850-1864	4.75	0.25	None	Thomas G. Moles	'85
SELIGMAN TXEX MD; D	Maryland Muni	0.2	7.81	10,043.00	☆	☆	0.0	221-7844	212-850-1864	None	1.00	1.00	Thomas G. Moles	'94
SELIGMAN TXEX MI; A	Michigan Muni	154.8	8.36	10,048.00	9,974.00	14,282.00	5.5	221-7844	212-850-1864	4.75	0.25	None	Thomas G. Moles	'84
SELIGMAN TXEX MI; D	Michigan Muni	0.4	8.36	10,025.00	☆	☆	0.0	221-7844	212-850-1864	None	1.00	1.00	Thomas G. Moles	'94
SELIGMAN TXEX MN; A	Minnesota Muni	137.1	7.75	10,062.00	10,234.00	14,073.00	5.9	221-7844	212-850-1864	4.75	0.25	None	Thomas G. Moles	'84
SELIGMAN TXEX MN; D	Minnesota Muni	1.0	7.75	10,039.00	☆	☆	0.0	221-7844	212-850-1864	None	1.00	1.00	Thomas G. Moles	'94
SELIGMAN TXEX MO; A	Missouri Muni	53.5	7.49	10,048.00	9,829.00	13,831.00	5.4	221-7844	212-850-1864	4.75	0.25	None	Thomas G. Moles	'86
SELIGMAN TXEX MO; D	Missouri Muni	0.4	7.49	10,025.00	☆	☆	0.0	221-7844	212-850-1864	None	1.00	1.00	Thomas G. Moles	'94
SELIGMAN TXEX NATL; A	General Muni	119.3	7.33	10,052.00	9,649.00	13,835.00	5.6	221-7844	212-850-1864	4.75	0.25	None	Thomas G. Moles	'84
SELIGMAN TXEX NATL; D	General Muni	0.4	7.32	10,028.00	☆	☆	0.0	221-7844	212-850-1864	None	1.00	1.00	Thomas G. Moles	'94
SELIGMAN TXEX NC; A	North Carolina Muni	40.3	7.40	10,022.00	9,793.00	☆	5.6	221-7844	212-850-1864	4.75	0.25	None	Thomas G. Moles	'90
SELIGMAN TXEX NC; D	North Carolina Muni	0.9	7.40	10,005.00	☆	☆	0.0	221-7844	212-850-1864	None	1.00	1.00	Thomas G. Moles	'94
SELIGMAN TXEX NY; A	New York Muni	94.5	7.78	10,058.00	9,807.00	14,091.00	5.5	221-7844	212-850-1864	4.75	0.25	None	Thomas G. Moles	'84
SELIGMAN TXEX NY; D	New York Muni	0.4	7.78	10,022.00	☆	☆	0.0	221-7844	212-850-1864	None	1.00	1.00	Thomas G. Moles	'94

SELIGMAN TXEX OH; A	Ohio Muni	177.2	8.00	10,095.00	10,002.00	14,249.00	5.5	221-7844	212-850-1864	4.75	0.25	None	Thomas G. Moles	'84
SELIGMAN TXEX OH; D	Ohio Muni	0.3	8.02	10,085.00	☆	☆	0.0	221-7844	212-850-1864	None	1.00	1.00	Thomas G. Moles	'94
SELIGMAN TXEX OR; A	Oregon Muni	60.4	7.50	10,078.00	10,036.00	13,994.00	5.4	221-7844	212-850-1864	4.75	0.25	None	Thomas G. Moles	'86
SELIGMAN TXEX OR; D	Oregon Muni	0.4	7.49	10,042.00	☆	☆	0.0	221-7844	212-850-1864	None	1.00	1.00	Thomas G. Moles	'94
SELIGMAN TXEX SC; A	South Carolina Muni	118.8	7.71	10,051.00	9,865.00	13,962.00	5.3	221-7844	212-850-1864	4.75	0.25	None	Thomas G. Moles	'87
SELIGMAN TXEX SC; D	South Carolina Muni	1.1	7.70	10,028.00	☆	☆	0.0	221-7844	212-850-1864	None	1.00	1.00	Thomas G. Moles	'94
SENTINEL PA TAX-FREE	Pennsylvania Muni	32.8	12.85	10,037.00	9,968.00	13,792.00	5.1	233-4332	802-229-3761	5.00	0.20	None	Kenneth J. Hart	'93
SENTINEL TAX-FREE INCOME	General Muni	107.0	12.97	10,059.00	10,001.00	☆	5.2	233-4332	802-229-3761	5.00	0.20	None	Kenneth J. Hart	'90
1784 MA TX-EX INC	Massachusetts Muni	49.0	9.70	10,083.00	10,050.00	☆	5.3	355-2673	None	None	0.25	None	Susan Sanderson	'93
1784 TX-EX MED TM	Intermediate Muni	33.9	9.82	10,145.00	10,171.00	☆	5.2	355-2673	None	None	0.25	None	David H. Thompson	'93
SHAWMUT CT INT MUNI; INV	Single State Muni	8.7	9.61	10,030.00	9,747.00	☆	4.1	742-9688	508-626-7877	2.00	None	None	Bob Gleeson	'93
SHAWMUT MA INT MUNI; INV	Massachusetts Muni	6.2	9.61	10,054.00	9,925.00	☆	4.2	742-9688	508-626-7877	2.00	None	None	P L Bank	'93
SHORT-TM MUNI; INST SVC	Short-Term Muni	32.5	10.15	10,052.00	☆	☆	0.0	245-4770	412-288-1900	None	0.25	None	Jonathan C. Conley	'93
SHORT-TM MUNI; INSTL	Short-Term Muni	327.8	10.15	10,058.00	10,176.00	12,909.00	4.0	245-4770	412-288-1900	None	None	None	Jonathan C. Conley	'84
SIERRA CA MUNICIPAL; A	California Muni	523.3	10.38	10,004.00	9,795.00	☆	5.9	222-5852	818-725-4620	4.50	0.25	None	Joseph Piraro	'91
SIERRA FL INSURED MUNI; A	Florida Muni	38.0	9.40	10,099.00	9,842.00	☆	5.4	222-5852	818-725-4620	4.50	0.25	None	William Grady	'93
SIERRA NATL MUNICIPAL; A	General Muni	360.8	10.85	10,013.00	9,909.00	☆	5.9	222-5852	818-725-4620	4.50	0.25	None	David Johnson	'90
SIG SELECT MD MUNI; INV	Single State Muni	36.9	10.29	10,049.00	9,923.00	☆	4.4	444-7123	None	None	0.25	2.00	Elizabeth D. Swartz	'92
SIG SELECT MD MUNI; TR	Single State Muni	11.1	10.29	10,056.00	9,947.00	☆	4.6	444-7123	None	None	None	None	Elizabeth D. Swartz	'92
SIG SELECT VA MUNI; INV	Single State Muni	77.2	10.38	10,021.00	9,951.00	☆	4.4	444-7123	None	None	0.25	2.00	Elizabeth D. Swartz	'92
SIG SELECT VA MUNI; TR	Single State Muni	37.3	10.38	10,027.00	9,974.00	☆	4.7	444-7123	None	None	None	None	Elizabeth D. Swartz	'92
SIT MN TAX-FREE INCOME	Minnesota Muni	20.6	9.86	10,211.00	☆	☆	0.0	332-5580	612-334-5888	None	None	None	Brilley/Sit	'93/'93
SIT TX-FR INCOME	General Muni	294.7	9.66	10,177.00	10,298.00	14,299.00	5.9	332-5580	612-334-5888	None	None	None	Brilley/Sit	'88/'91
SM BARNEY MUNI CA L; A	California Muni	7.1	6.39	10,096.00	10,185.00	☆	5.1	544-7835	212-698-5349	2.00	None	None	Peter Coffey	'93
SM BARNEY MUNI CA L; B	California Muni	2.2	6.39	10,075.00	10,138.00	☆	4.7	544-7835	212-698-5349	None	0.35	1.00	Peter Coffey	'93
SM BARNEY MUNI CA L; C	California Muni	0.5	6.40	10,108.00	10,171.00	☆	4.9	544-7835	212-698-5349	None	0.15	1.50	Peter Coffey	'93
SM BARNEY MUNI CA; A	California Muni	165.4	12.14	10,048.00	9,954.00	14,530.00	6.3	544-7835	212-698-5349	4.00	None	None	Peter Coffey	'87
SM BARNEY MUNI CA; B	California Muni	6.8	12.13	10,029.00	9,883.00	☆	5.5	544-7835	212-698-5349	None	0.70	1.00	Peter Coffey	'93
SM BARNEY MUNI CA; C	California Muni	10.0	12.15	10,044.00	9,947.00	☆	6.1	544-7835	212-698-5349	None	0.15	1.50	Peter Coffey	'93
SM BARNEY MUNI FL L; A	Florida Muni	13.1	6.43	10,111.00	10,200.00	☆	5.1	544-7835	212-698-5349	2.00	None	None	Peter Coffey	'93
SM BARNEY MUNI FL L; B	Florida Muni	3.9	6.43	10,118.00	10,165.00	☆	4.7	544-7835	212-698-5349	None	0.35	1.00	Peter Coffey	'93
SM BARNEY MUNI FL L; C	Florida Muni	5.5	6.43	10,123.00	10,186.00	☆	4.9	544-7835	212-698-5349	None	0.15	1.50	Peter Coffey	'93
SM BARNEY MUNI FL; A	Florida Muni	103.0	12.71	10,063.00	10,000.00	☆	6.0	544-7835	212-698-5349	4.00	None	None	Peter Coffey	'91
SM BARNEY MUNI FL; B	Florida Muni	2.7	12.70	10,044.00	9,930.00	☆	5.3	544-7835	212-698-5349	None	0.70	1.00	Peter Coffey	'93
SM BARNEY MUNI LTD; A	Intermediate Muni	273.8	6.51	10,081.00	10,182.00	14,191.00	5.8	544-7835	212-698-5349	2.00	None	None	Peter Coffey	'88
SM BARNEY MUNI LTD; B	Intermediate Muni	27.2	6.50	10,072.00	10,132.00	☆	5.4	544-7835	212-698-5349	None	0.35	1.00	Peter Coffey	'93
SM BARNEY MUNI LTD; C	Intermediate Muni	19.4	6.51	10,078.00	10,152.00	☆	5.6	544-7835	212-698-5349	None	0.15	1.50	Peter Coffey	'93
SM BARNEY MUNI NATL; A	General Muni	409.5	13.20	10,046.00	10,013.00	14,913.00	6.5	544-7835	212-698-5349	4.00	None	None	Peter Coffey	'86
SM BARNEY MUNI NATL; B	General Muni	19.0	13.19	10,035.00	9,943.00	☆	5.7	544-7835	212-698-5349	None	0.70	1.00	Peter Coffey	'93
SM BARNEY MUNI NATL; C	General Muni	9.4	13.20	10,050.00	9,998.00	☆	6.3	544-7835	212-698-5349	None	0.15	1.50	Peter Coffey	'93
SM BARNEY MUNI NJ; A	New Jersey Muni	66.6	13.11	10,057.00	9,907.00	☆	6.0	544-7835	212-698-5349	4.00	None	None	Peter Coffey	'90
SM BARNEY MUNI NJ; B	New Jersey Muni	3.3	13.10	10,039.00	9,838.00	☆	5.3	544-7835	212-698-5349	None	0.70	1.00	Peter Coffey	'93
SM BARNEY MUNI NJ; C	New Jersey Muni	2.3	13.10	10,061.00	9,900.00	☆	5.9	544-7835	212-698-5349	None	0.15	1.50	Peter Coffey	'93
SM BARNEY MUNI NY; A	New York Muni	70.3	12.72	10,066.00	9,984.00	14,698.00	6.2	544-7835	212-698-5349	4.00	None	None	Peter Coffey	'87
SM BARNEY MUNI NY; B	New York Muni	5.8	12.71	10,048.00	9,914.00	☆	5.4	544-7835	212-698-5349	None	0.70	1.00	Peter Coffey	'93
SM BRNY/SHRSN AZ; A	Arizona Muni	44.6	9.76	10,118.00	9,948.00	14,296.00	5.6	None	212-720-9218	4.50	0.15	None	Larry McDermott	'87
SM BRNY/SHRSN AZ; B	Arizona Muni	19.3	9.76	10,104.00	9,902.00	☆	5.2	None	212-720-9218	None	0.65	4.50	Larry McDermott	'92
SM BRNY/SHRSN CA; A	California Muni	406.1	15.34	10,098.00	10,096.00	14,392.00	5.7	None	212-720-9218	4.50	0.15	None	Deane/Fare	'84/'84
SM BRNY/SHRSN CA; B	California Muni	113.6	15.34	10,085.00	10,050.00	☆	5.3	None	212-720-9218	None	0.65	4.50	Deane/Fare	'92/'92
SM BRNY/SHRSN FL; A	Florida Muni	15.0	9.59	10,082.00	9,820.00	☆	5.5	None	212-720-9218	4.50	0.15	None	Larry McDermott	'92

PERFORMANCE OF MUTUAL FUNDS (continued)

FUND NAME	OBJECTIVE	TOTAL NET ASSETS ($ MIL) 5/31/94	NET ASSET $ VALUE 6/30/94	PERFORMANCE (Return on initial $10,000 Investment) 3/31/94-6/30/94	6/30/93-6/30/94	6/30/89-6/30/94	DIVIDEND YIELD % 6/94	PHONE NUMBER 800	In-State	FEES Load	12b-1	Redemption	MANAGER	SINCE
SM BRNY/SHRSN FL; B	Florida Muni	36.8	9.59	10,070.00	9,774.00	☆	5.0	None	212-720-9218	None	0.65	4.50	Larry McDermott	'92
SM BRNY/SHRSN INT CA	California Muni	32.4	8.12	10,108.00	10,046.00	☆	4.7	None	212-720-9218	1.25	0.15	1.00	Joseph Deane	'91
SM BRNY/SHRSN INT NY	New York Muni	69.8	8.16	10,147.00	10,037.00	☆	4.8	None	212-720-9218	1.25	0.15	1.00	Larry McDermott	'91
SM BRNY/SHRSN LTD MUNI	Short-Term Muni	94.2	8.06	10,080.00	10,179.00	☆	4.2	None	212-720-9218	1.25	0.15	1.00	Larry McDermott	'91
SM BRNY/SHRSN MA; A	Massachusetts Muni	30.4	12.16	10,030.00	9,735.00	13,948.00	6.1	None	212-720-9218	4.50	0.15	None	Larry McDermott	'87
SM BRNY/SHRSN MA; B	Massachusetts Muni	24.4	12.16	10,018.00	9,677.00	☆	5.4	None	212-720-9218	None	0.65	4.50	Larry McDermott	'92
SM BRNY/SHRSN MGD MU; A	General Muni	1,789.4	15.37	10,049.00	10,134.00	15,305.00	6.0	None	212-720-9218	4.50	0.15	None	Joseph Deane	'88
SM BRNY/SHRSN MGD MU; B	General Muni	405.9	15.37	10,036.00	10,083.00	☆	5.5	None	212-720-9218	None	0.65	4.50	Joseph Deane	'92
SM BRNY/SHRSN NJ; A	New Jersey Muni	119.7	12.49	10,093.00	9,906.00	14,604.00	5.8	None	212-720-9218	4.50	0.15	None	Larry McDermott	'88
SM BRNY/SHRSN NJ; B	New Jersey Muni	51.4	12.49	10,079.00	9,851.00	☆	5.2	None	212-720-9218	None	0.65	4.50	Larry McDermott	'92
SM BRNY/SHRSN NY; A	New York Muni	526.9	16.29	10,060.00	9,891.00	14,104.00	6.2	None	212-720-9218	4.50	0.15	None	Larry McDermott	'84
SM BRNY/SHRSN NY; B	New York Muni	152.0	16.29	10,045.00	9,837.00	☆	5.6	None	212-720-9218	None	0.65	4.50	Larry McDermott	'92
SM BRNY/SHRSN TX-EX; A	General Muni	18.7	17.04	10,075.00	9,961.00	☆	6.5	None	212-720-9218	4.50	0.15	None	Larry McDermott	'92
SM BRNY/SHRSN TX-EX; B	General Muni	1,078.7	17.04	10,062.00	9,904.00	13,806.00	5.9	None	212-720-9218	None	0.65	4.50	Larry McDermott	'85
SM&R AMER NATL TAX FREE	General Muni	7.2	9.46	9,959.00	☆	☆	0.0	231-4639	409-763-2767	4.50	None	None	Terry E. Frank	'93
SOCIETY OH TAX-FREE BOND	Ohio Muni	56.9	10.62	10,115.00	10,081.00	☆	4.7	362-5365	None	2.00	None	None	Robert Moore	'91
SS RESEARCH CAL TAX; A	California Muni	6.2	7.70	10,035.00	9,785.00	☆	5.0	882-3302	617-348-2000	4.50	0.25	None	Paul Clifford	'93
SS RESEARCH CAL TAX; B	California Muni	2.9	7.70	10,003.00	9,715.00	☆	4.2	882-3302	617-348-2000	None	1.00	5.00	Paul Clifford	'93
SS RESEARCH CAL TAX; C	California Muni	24.4	7.71	10,041.00	9,822.00	☆	5.3	882-3302	617-348-2000	None	None	None	Paul Clifford	'93
SS RESEARCH CAL TAX; D	California Muni	0.8	7.71	10,016.00	9,725.00	☆	4.2	882-3302	617-348-2000	None	1.00	1.00	Paul Clifford	'93
SS RESEARCH FL TAX; A	Florida Muni	3.9	9.23	10,164.00	☆	☆	0.0	882-3302	617-348-2000	4.50	0.25	None	Drake/Clifford	'93/'93
SS RESEARCH FL TAX; B	Florida Muni	2.8	9.23	10,156.00	☆	☆	0.0	882-3302	617-348-2000	None	1.00	5.00	Drake/Clifford	'93/'93
SS RESEARCH FL TAX; C	Florida Muni	3.4	9.23	10,171.00	☆	☆	0.0	882-3302	617-348-2000	None	None	None	Drake/Clifford	'93/'93
SS RESEARCH FL TAX; D	Florida Muni	1.2	9.23	10,156.00	☆	☆	0.0	882-3302	617-348-2000	None	1.00	1.00	Drake/Clifford	'93/'93
SS RESEARCH NY TAX; A	New York Muni	18.5	7.84	10,060.00	9,938.00	☆	5.0	882-3302	617-348-2000	4.50	0.25	None	Paul Clifford	'93
SS RESEARCH NY TAX; B	New York Muni	10.3	7.84	10,028.00	9,864.00	☆	4.2	882-3302	617-348-2000	None	1.00	5.00	Paul Clifford	'93
SS RESEARCH NY TAX; C	New York Muni	48.7	7.85	10,066.00	9,962.00	☆	5.2	882-3302	617-348-2000	None	None	None	Paul Clifford	'93
SS RESEARCH NY TAX; D	New York Muni	0.9	7.85	10,041.00	9,863.00	☆	4.1	882-3302	617-348-2000	None	1.00	1.00	Paul Clifford	'93
SS RESEARCH PA TAX; A	Pennsylvania Muni	6.1	9.21	10,088.00	☆	☆	0.0	882-3302	617-348-2000	4.50	0.25	None	Drake/Clifford	'93/'93
SS RESEARCH PA TAX; B	Pennsylvania Muni	4.5	9.21	10,069.00	☆	☆	0.0	882-3302	617-348-2000	None	1.00	5.00	Drake/Clifford	'93/'93
SS RESEARCH PA TAX; C	Pennsylvania Muni	3.4	9.22	10,094.00	☆	☆	0.0	882-3302	617-348-2000	None	None	None	Drake/Clifford	'93/'93
SS RESEARCH PA TAX; D	Pennsylvania Muni	1.2	9.21	10,070.00	☆	☆	0.0	882-3302	617-348-2000	None	1.00	1.00	Drake/Clifford	'93/'93
STAGECOACH CA TX FR BD	California Muni	425.8	10.27	10,067.00	9,862.00	☆	5.4	222-8222	None	4.50	0.05	None	Wines/Klug	'92/'92
STAGECOACH CA TX FR INC	California Muni	59.7	10.02	10,053.00	10,181.00	☆	4.0	222-8222	None	3.00	0.05	None	Milner/Wines	'92/'93
STAND AYER WOOD INT TAX	Intermediate Muni	29.7	20.46	10,167.00	10,188.00	☆	4.6	729-0066	617-350-6100	None	None	None	Furman/Kubiak	'92/'92
STAND AYER WOOD MA TX-EX	Massachusetts Muni	29.7	20.15	10,100.00	10,092.00	☆	4.6	729-0066	617-350-6100	None	None	None	Furman/Kubiak	'92/'92
STARBURST MUNI INCOME	General Muni	32.8	10.24	10,078.00	10,128.00	☆	4.4	239-6669	205-558-6702	2.50	0.15	None	Dan Davidson	'91
STATE BOND TAX EXEMPT FD	General Muni	81.3	10.58	10,106.00	10,154.00	14,054.00	5.6	437-6663	612-835-0097	4.50	0.25	None	Keith Martens	'84
STATE BOND TAX-FR INC MN	Minnesota Muni	16.5	10.45	10,085.00	10,075.00	13,685.00	5.4	437-6663	612-835-0097	4.50	0.25	None	Keith Martens	'88
STATE FARM MUNICIPAL ◪	General Muni	277.6	8.21	10,085.00	10,144.00	14,291.00	5.9	None	309-766-2029	None	None	None	Kurt Moser	'91
STEINROE HI-YLD MUNI	High-Yield Muni	310.7	11.06	10,202.00	10,095.00	13,896.00	6.0	338-2550	None	None	None	None	Jim Grabovac	'91
STEINROE INTMDT MUNI	Intermediate Muni	240.9	11.00	10,120.00	10,116.00	14,326.00	4.8	338-2550	None	None	None	None	Joanne Costopoulos	'91
STEINROE MGD MUNI	General Muni	698.7	8.70	10,086.00	9,971.00	14,305.00	5.7	338-2550	None	None	None	None	M. Jane McCart	'91
STEPSTONE CA TX FR; INSTL	California Muni	20.9	9.15	10,078.00	☆	☆	0.0	634-1100	213-236-5698	None	None	None	Clark Steinman	'93
STEPSTONE CA TX FR; INVST	California Muni	5.2	9.14	10,078.00	☆	☆	0.0	634-1100	213-236-5698	3.00	None	None	Clark Steinman	'93

STI CLASSIC FL; INV	Florida Muni	2.3	9.68	10,060.00	☆	☆	0.0	428-6970	None	3.75	0.15	None	Ron Schwartz	'94
STI CLASSIC GA; INV	Georgia Muni	3.3	9.35	10,115.00	☆	☆	0.0	428-6970	None	3.75	0.15	None	Gay Cash	'94
STI CLASSIC INV TX; INV	Intermediate Muni	46.1	10.67	10,161.00	10,325.00	☆	3.1	428-6970	None	3.75	0.30	None	Ron Schwartz	'92
STI CLASSIC TN; INV	Tennessee Muni	1.1	9.12	10,089.00	☆	☆	0.0	428-6970	None	3.75	0.15	None	Ainsley Moses	'94
STRONG HIGH YIELD MUNI	High-Yield Muni	73.1	9.66	10,162.00	☆	☆	0.0	368-1030	414-359-1400	None	None	None	Conlin/Bourbulas	'93/'93
STRONG INS MUNI BD	Insured Muni	49.7	10.48	10,099.00	9,794.00	☆	5.1	368-1030	414-359-1400	None	None	None	Conlin/Bourbulas	'91/'91
STRONG MUNICIPAL BOND	General Muni	348.7	9.52	10,073.00	9,988.00	14,567.00	5.9	368-1030	414-359-1400	None	None	None	Conlin/Bourbulas	'91/'91
STRONG SH-TM MUNI BD	Short-Term Muni	196.6	10.03	10,077.00	10,183.00	☆	4.2	368-1030	414-359-1400	None	None	None	G. Nolan Smith	'92
SUNAMER TAX EX INS; A	Insured Muni	163.0	11.86	10,047.00	9,831.00	13,179.00	5.4	858-8850	212-551-5125	4.75	0.35	None	John Keough	'85
SUNAMER TAX EX INS; B	Insured Muni	23.2	11.87	10,040.00	☆	☆	0.0	858-8850	212-551-5125	None	1.00	4.00	John Keough	'93
TAX FREE FUND OF VERMONT	Single State Muni	5.9	9.52	10,143.00	10,076.00	☆	5.6	675-3333	802-773-0674	None	None	None	John Pearson	'91
TAX-EXEMPT BD FD AMERICA	General Muni	1,369.2	11.54	10,093.00	10,010.00	14,223.00	5.8	421-4120	714-671-7000	4.75	0.25	None	Multiple Managers	'79
TAX-FREE FUND FOR UT	Single State Muni	26.3	9.32	10,102.00	9,892.00	☆	6.0	882-4937	212-697-6666	4.00	0.20	None	Sterling Jensen	'92
TAX-FREE FUND OF CO	Colorado Muni	213.1	10.13	10,144.00	10,082.00	14,308.00	5.5	872-2652	212-697-6666	4.00	None	None	Christopher Johns	'87
TAX-FREE TRUST OF AZ	Arizona Muni	373.6	10.16	10,080.00	9,972.00	14,204.00	5.6	437-1020	212-697-6666	4.00	None	None	Todd Curtis	'86
THOMSON TAX EXEMPT; A	General Muni	2.9	11.31	10,031.00	9,742.00	☆	5.2	227-7337	203-352-4946	4.75	0.25	None	Team Managed	'92
THOMSON TAX EXEMPT; B	General Muni	75.5	11.31	10,021.00	9,677.00	13,191.00	4.4	227-7337	203-352-4946	None	1.00	1.00	Team Managed	'92
THORNBURG INT MUNI NATL	Intermediate Muni	203.8	12.82	10,101.00	10,264.00	☆	5.2	847-0200	505-984-0200	3.50	0.23	None	Brian McMahon	'91
THORNBURG INT MUNI NM	Single State Muni	139.6	12.75	10,064.00	10,196.00	☆	4.8	847-0200	505-984-0200	3.50	0.22	None	Brian McMahon	'91
THORNBURG LTD MUNI CA	California Muni	106.7	12.57	10,109.00	10,237.00	13,679.00	4.6	847-0200	505-984-0200	2.50	0.12	None	Brian McMahon	'87
THORNBURG LTD MUNI NATL	Short-Term Muni	953.6	13.27	10,088.00	10,226.00	13,876.00	4.7	847-0200	505-984-0200	2.50	0.12	None	Brian McMahon	'84
TORCHMARK INS TAX-FREE	Insured Muni	2.2	9.42	10,091.00	9,733.00	☆	4.9	733-3863	913-236-2050	None	0.25	None	John Holiday	'93
TOWER LA MUNI INCOME	Louisiana Muni	80.3	10.70	10,071.00	9,931.00	14,305.00	5.5	999-0124	504-533-5180	3.00	None	None	Jeff Tanguis	'88
TRADEMARK KY MUNI BOND	Single State Muni	58.4	9.74	10,069.00	10,028.00	☆	4.4	245-0242	None	None	None	None	Catherin Hart Gooch	'93
TRANSAM CA TX-FR INC; A	California Muni	271.9	9.89	10,036.00	9,832.00	☆	5.9	472-3863	713-751-2800	4.75	0.15	None	Team Managed	'89
TRANSAM CA TX-FR INC; B	California Muni	80.1	9.89	10,017.00	9,759.00	☆	5.1	472-3863	713-751-2800	None	0.90	5.00	Team Managed	'91
TRANSAM SPEC HY TXFR; B	High-Yield Muni	148.9	9.24	10,111.00	10,146.00	13,965.00	6.6	472-3863	713-751-2800	None	1.00	5.00	Team Managed	'86
TRANSAM TAX-FREE BD; A	General Muni	136.4	9.98	10,071.00	9,847.00	☆	5.7	472-3863	713-751-2800	4.75	0.15	None	Team Managed	'90
TRANSAM TAX-FREE BD; B	General Muni	75.4	9.98	10,052.00	9,773.00	☆	4.9	472-3863	713-751-2800	None	0.90	5.00	Team Managed	'91
TWEN CENTURY TX-EX INT	Intermediate Muni	86.6	10.17	10,116.00	10,143.00	13,811.00	4.6	345-2021	816-531-5575	None	None	None	Team Managed	'87
TWEN CENTURY TX-EX LNG	General Muni	57.3	10.03	10,067.00	9,988.00	14,046.00	5.1	345-2021	816-531-5575	None	None	None	Team Managed	'87
TWEN CENTURY TX-EX SHT	Short-Term Muni	58.2	9.97	10,100.00	10,288.00	☆	3.5	345-2021	816-531-5575	None	None	None	Laurie S. Kirby	'93
UNITED MUNICIPAL BOND	General Muni	980.5	6.95	10,047.00	9,886.00	14,634.00	5.4	None	913-236-2000	4.25	0.25	None	John Holliday	'80
UNITED MUNICIPAL HI INC	High-Yield Muni	338.7	5.16	10,144.00	10,308.00	15,148.00	6.6	None	913-236-2000	4.25	0.25	None	John Holliday	'86
US NEAR TERM TAX FREE	Short-Term Muni	8.5	10.39	10,067.00	10,203.00	☆	4.9	873-8637	210-308-1234	None	None	None	Allen Parker	'91
US TAX FREE FUND	General Muni	17.9	11.40	10,087.00	10,075.00	13,754.00	6.5	873-8637	210-308-1234	None	None	None	Allen Parker	'87
USAA STATE TAX-FR FL	Florida Muni	29.7	8.97	10,122.00	☆	☆	0.0	382-8722	None	None	None	None	David G. Miller	'94
USAA TX EX CA BOND	California Muni	380.8	9.94	10,053.00	9,719.00	☆	5.8	382-8722	None	None	None	None	David G. Miller	'94
USAA TX EX INTMDT-TERM	Intermediate Muni	1,541.1	12.42	10,110.00	10,108.00	14,305.00	5.5	382-8722	None	None	None	None	Clifford A. Gladson	'93
USAA TX EX LONG-TERM	General Muni	1,853.5	12.93	10,000.00	9,861.00	14,263.00	6.0	382-8722	None	None	None	None	Kenneth Willman	'82
USAA TX EX NY BOND	New York Muni	55.5	10.73	10,047.00	9,795.00	☆	5.6	382-8722	None	None	None	None	Kenneth Willman	'90
USAA TX EX SHORT-TERM	Short-Term Muni	933.5	10.46	10,089.00	10,226.00	13,138.00	4.3	382-8722	None	None	None	None	Clifford A. Gladson	'94
USAA TX EX VA BOND	Virginia Muni	234.2	10.56	10,000.00	9,916.00	☆	5.8	382-8722	None	None	None	None	Clifford A. Gladson	'94
USAFFINITY TX-FREE MUNI	General Muni	1.9	9.93	10,107.00	9,812.00	☆	5.8	800-3030	617-262-9200	4.50	0.35	None	Klingart/Sanford	'93/'93
UST MSTR TX-EX INTMDT	Intermediate Muni	275.3	8.65	10,106.00	10,112.00	14,109.00	3.9	233-1136	619-456-9394	4.50	None	None	Mike G. Crofton	'91
UST MSTR TX-EX LONG	General Muni	83.0	8.73	10,059.00	9,934.00	14,876.00	4.5	233-1136	619-456-9394	4.50	None	None	Kenneth M. McAlley	'86
UST MSTR TX-EX NY INT	New York Muni	101.8	8.02	10,003.00	9,962.00	☆	3.8	233-1136	619-456-9394	4.50	None	None	Mike G. Crofton	'91
UST MSTR TX-EX SH-TM SEC	Short-Term Muni	51.1	6.97	10,066.00	10,182.00	☆	3.0	233-1136	619-456-9394	4.50	None	None	Mike G. Crofton	'92
VALUE LINE NY TX EX TR	New York Muni	41.3	9.84	10,010.00	9,879.00	14,341.00	5.5	223-0818	212-907-1500	None	None	None	Team Managed	'87
VALUE LINE TX EX HI YLD	General Muni	250.2	10.31	10,059.00	9,806.00	13,902.00	5.6	223-0818	212-907-1500	None	None	None	Team Managed	'84

PERFORMANCE OF MUTUAL FUNDS *(continued)*

FUND NAME	OBJECTIVE	TOTAL NET ASSETS ($ MIL) 5/31/94	NET ASSET $ VALUE 6/30/94	PERFORMANCE (Return on initial $10,000 Investment) 3/31/94-6/30/94	6/30/93-6/30/94	6/30/89-6/30/94	DIVIDEND YIELD % 6/94	PHONE NUMBER 800	In-State	FEES Load	12b-1	Redemption	MANAGER	SINCE
VALUESTAR TN TX EX; INV	Tennessee Muni	83.5	9.72	10,052.00	☆	☆	0.0	824-3741	None	3.00	None	None	James Niggins	'94
VANGUARD CA TX-FR INS IN	California Muni	57.0	9.99	10,196.00	☆	☆	0.0	662-7447	215-669-1000	None	None	None	Ian MacKinnon	'94
VANGUARD CA TX-FR INS LG	California Muni	929.0	10.54	10,132.00	9,965.00	14,352.00	5.6	662-7447	215-669-1000	None	None	None	Ian A. MacKinnon	'86
VANGUARD FL INS TX-FR	Florida Muni	291.9	10.26	10,174.00	10,056.00	☆	5.3	662-7447	215-669-1000	None	None	None	Ian A. MacKinnon	'92
VANGUARD MUNI HIGH YIELD	High-Yield Muni	1,765.8	10.27	10,120.00	10,032.00	14,877.00	6.1	662-7447	215-669-1000	None	None	None	Ian A. MacKinnon	'81
VANGUARD MUNI INS LG-TM	Insured Muni	1,940.4	11.85	10,129.00	9,972.00	14,567.00	5.9	662-7447	215-669-1000	None	None	None	Ian A. MacKinnon	'84
VANGUARD MUNI INTMDT-TM	Intermediate Muni	4,978.2	12.92	10,133.00	10,253.00	14,854.00	5.3	662-7447	215-669-1000	None	None	None	Ian A. MacKinnon	'81
VANGUARD MUNI LIMITED-TM	Short-Term Muni	1,797.1	10.55	10,079.00	10,232.00	13,739.00	4.3	662-7447	215-669-1000	None	None	None	Ian A. MacKinnon	'87
VANGUARD MUNI LONG-TM	General Muni	1,001.0	10.44	10,115.00	9,975.00	14,809.00	5.8	662-7447	215-669-1000	None	None	None	Ian A. MacKinnon	'81
VANGUARD MUNI SHORT-TM	Short-Term Muni	1,522.2	15.46	10,067.00	10,237.00	12,920.00	3.5	662-7447	215-669-1000	None	None	None	Ian A. MacKinnon	'81
VANGUARD NJ TX-FR INS LG	New Jersey Muni	700.1	11.07	10,131.00	9,968.00	14,576.00	5.6	662-7447	215-669-1000	None	None	None	Ian A. MacKinnon	'88
VANGUARD NY INS TAX-FR	New York Muni	759.7	10.36	10,142.00	9,989.00	14,638.00	5.7	662-7447	215-669-1000	None	None	None	Ian A. MacKinnon	'86
VANGUARD OH TX-FR INSURE	Ohio Muni	162.0	10.98	10,118.00	10,031.00	☆	5.4	662-7447	215-669-1000	None	None	None	Ian A. MacKinnon	'90
VANGUARD PA TX-FR INS LG	Pennsylvania Muni	1,430.5	10.70	10,116.00	10,068.00	14,786.00	5.8	662-7447	215-669-1000	None	None	None	Ian A. MacKinnon	'86
VANKAMP CA INSURED; A	California Muni	144.9	16.52	10,041.00	9,746.00	14,117.00	5.7	225-2222	708-684-6503	3.00	0.30	None	Joe Piraro	'92
VANKAMP CA INSURED; B	California Muni	18.2	16.52	10,031.00	9,667.00	☆	4.8	225-2222	708-684-6503	None	1.00	3.00	Joe Piraro	'93
VANKAMP CA INSURED; C	California Muni	4.6	16.50	10,025.00	☆	☆	0.0	225-2222	708-684-6503	None	1.00	1.00	Joe Piraro	'93
VANKAMP INS TAX FREE; A	Insured Muni	1,165.2	18.34	10,111.00	9,922.00	14,260.00	5.9	225-2222	708-684-6503	4.65	0.30	None	Joe Piraro	'92
VANKAMP INS TAX FREE; B	Insured Muni	27.5	18.31	10,088.00	9,832.00	☆	5.0	225-2222	708-684-6503	None	1.00	4.00	Joe Piraro	'93
VANKAMP INS TAX FREE; C	Insured Muni	4.9	18.32	10,088.00	☆	☆	0.0	225-2222	708-684-6503	None	1.00	1.00	Joe Piraro	'93
VANKAMP INS TAX FREE; D	Insured Muni	0.1	18.33	10,102.00	☆	☆	0.0	225-2222	708-684-6503	None	0.30	0.75	Joe Piraro	'94
VANKAMP LTD TM MUNI; A	General Muni	15.7	9.67	10,183.00	10,339.00	☆	5.2	225-2222	708-684-6503	3.00	0.30	None	Robert Waas	'93
VANKAMP LTD TM MUNI; B	General Muni	17.8	9.66	10,165.00	10,255.00	☆	4.5	225-2222	708-684-6503	None	1.00	3.00	Robert Waas	'93
VANKAMP LTD TM MUNI; C	General Muni	3.0	9.65	10,154.00	☆	☆	0.0	225-2222	708-684-6503	None	1.00	1.00	Robert Waas	'93
VANKAMP MUNI INC; A	General Muni	550.7	14.81	10,129.00	9,852.00	☆	6.1	225-2222	708-684-6503	4.65	0.30	None	David Johnson	'90
VANKAMP MUNI INC; B	General Muni	167.4	14.79	10,116.00	9,784.00	☆	5.4	225-2222	708-684-6503	None	1.00	4.00	David Johnson	'92
VANKAMP MUNI INC; C	General Muni	4.2	14.81	10,109.00	☆	☆	0.0	225-2222	708-684-6503	None	1.00	1.00	David Johnson	'93
VANKAMP MUNI INC; D	General Muni	0.1	14.82	10,134.00	☆	☆	0.0	225-2222	708-684-6503	None	0.30	0.75	David Johnson	'94
VANKAMP PA TAX FREE; A	Pennsylvania Muni	217.1	16.67	10,115.00	9,933.00	14,681.00	6.0	225-2222	708-684-6503	4.65	0.30	None	William Grady	'92
VANKAMP PA TAX FREE; B	Pennsylvania Muni	34.5	16.66	10,095.00	9,863.00	☆	5.2	225-2222	708-684-6503	None	1.00	4.00	William Grady	'93
VANKAMP PA TAX FREE; C	Pennsylvania Muni	2.7	16.66	10,101.00	☆	☆	0.0	225-2222	708-684-6503	None	1.00	1.00	William Grady	'93
VANKAMP PA TAX FREE; D	Pennsylvania Muni	0.1	16.67	10,114.00	☆	☆	0.0	225-2222	708-684-6503	None	0.30	0.75	William Grady	'94
VANKAMP TX FR HIGH; A	High-Yield Muni	623.6	14.36	10,072.00	10,352.00	12,750.00	7.3	225-2222	708-684-6503	4.65	0.30	None	David Johnson	'89
VANKAMP TX FR HIGH; B	High-Yield Muni	86.3	14.36	10,050.00	10,261.00	☆	6.5	225-2222	708-684-6503	None	1.00	4.00	David Johnson	'93
VANKAMP TX FR HIGH; C	High-Yield Muni	7.8	14.35	10,051.00	☆	☆	0.0	225-2222	708-684-6503	None	1.00	1.00	David Johnson	'93
VANKAMP TX FR HIGH; D	High-Yield Muni	2.1	14.35	10,064.00	☆	☆	0.0	225-2222	708-684-6503	None	0.30	0.75	David Johnson	'94
VENTURE MUN (+) PLUS	High-Yield Muni	179.4	9.17	10,165.00	10,412.00	14,174.00	6.7	279-0279	505-983-4335	None	1.00	4.00	B. Clark Stamper	'90

VICTORY NATL MUNI BD	Intermediate Muni	0.5	9.60	10,111.00	☆	☆	0.0	832-1373	None	4.75	None	None	Deborah A. Christopher	'94
VICTORY NY TAX-FREE	New York Muni	21.1	12.72	10,014.00	10,146.00	☆	5.5	832-1373	None	4.75	None	None	Robert Hennes	'91
VISION NY TX-FR	New York Muni	26.2	9.56	10,063.00	☆	☆	0.0	836-2211	716-842-4488	4.50	None	None	M. Evanco	'93
VISTA CA INTMDT TAX FREE	California Muni	39.0	9.61	10,083.00	☆	☆	0.0	348-4782	None	4.50	0.20	None	Pamela Hunter	'93
VISTA NY INCOME; A	New York Muni	107.7	11.15	10,070.00	9,945.00	14,704.00	5.0	348-4782	None	4.50	0.05	None	Pamela Hunter	'87
VISTA NY INCOME; B	New York Muni	4.8	11.14	10,068.00	☆	☆	0.0	348-4782	None	None	0.75	5.00	Pamela Hunter	'93
VISTA TX FR INCOME; A	General Muni	96.4	11.55	10,067.00	9,887.00	15,386.00	5.1	348-4782	None	4.50	0.17	None	Pamela Hunter	'87
VISTA TX FR INCOME; B	General Muni	8.5	11.51	10,053.00	☆	☆	0.0	348-4782	None	None	0.75	5.00	Pamela Hunter	'93
VLC TR OCEAN STATE TX-EX	Single State Muni	42.8	10.33	10,006.00	10,162.00	14,675.00	5.8	992-2207	401-421-1411	4.00	None	None	Samuel Hallowell	'92
VOYAGEUR AZ INSURED	Arizona Muni	263.4	10.39	9,949.00	9,850.00	☆	5.9	553-2143	612-376-7000	4.75	None	None	McCullagh/Dougall	'91/'93
VOYAGEUR CA INSURED	California Muni	22.7	9.89	9,799.00	9,640.00	☆	6.1	553-2143	612-376-7000	4.75	0.25	None	McCullagh/Dougall	'92/'93
VOYAGEUR CO TAX FREE	Colorado Muni	417.7	10.13	9,908.00	9,911.00	14,421.00	5.9	553-2143	612-376-7000	3.90	None	None	McCullagh/Dougall	'87/'93
VOYAGEUR FL INSURED	Florida Muni	295.8	10.07	9,856.00	9,768.00	☆	6.0	553-2143	612-376-7000	4.75	None	None	McCullagh/Dougall	'92/'93
VOYAGEUR IA TAX FREE	Single State Muni	38.3	9.21	9,976.00	☆	☆	0.0	553-2143	612-376-7000	3.75	None	None	Howell/Greenshields	'93/'93
VOYAGEUR KS TAX FREE	Kansas Muni	4.9	10.00	9,853.00	10,014.00	☆	5.9	553-2143	612-376-7000	4.75	None	None	Howell/Greenshields	'92/'92
VOYAGEUR MN INSURED	Minnesota Muni	317.6	10.15	9,961.00	9,986.00	14,329.00	5.7	553-2143	612-376-7000	4.75	0.25	None	Howell/Greenshields	'90/'93
VOYAGEUR MN INTMDT TX FR	Single State Muni	81.6	10.72	10,093.00	10,159.00	13,575.00	4.3	553-2143	612-376-7000	2.75	0.15	None	Howell/Greenshields	'90/'93
VOYAGEUR MN TAX FREE	Minnesota Muni	454.6	11.91	10,005.00	10,008.00	14,214.00	5.8	553-2143	612-376-7000	4.75	0.25	None	Howell/Greenshields	'90/'93
VOYAGEUR MO INSURED	Missouri Muni	34.6	9.77	9,910.00	9,860.00	☆	6.0	553-2143	612-376-7000	4.75	None	None	Howell/Greenshields	'92/'92
VOYAGEUR NATL INSURED	Insured Muni	30.1	9.78	9,893.00	9,788.00	☆	6.1	553-2143	612-376-7000	4.75	0.25	None	McCullagh/Howell	'92/'93
VOYAGEUR ND TAX FREE	Single State Muni	36.1	10.28	9,899.00	9,940.00	☆	5.9	553-2143	612-376-7000	4.75	None	None	McCullagh/Howell	'91/'91
VOYAGEUR NM TAX FREE	Single State Muni	21.8	10.16	9,950.00	10,009.00	☆	5.7	553-2143	612-376-7000	3.75	None	None	McCullagh/Dougall	'92/'93
VOYAGEUR OR INSURED	Oregon Muni	10.9	9.34	9,880.00	☆	☆	0.0	553-2143	612-376-7000	4.75	None	None	Howell/Greenshields	'93/'93
VOYAGEUR UT TAX FREE	Single State Muni	4.3	10.32	9,933.00	10,116.00	☆	6.0	553-2143	612-376-7000	3.75	None	None	McCullagh/Dougall	'92/'93
VOYAGEUR WA INSURED	Washington Muni	1.4	9.73	9,910.00	☆	☆	0.0	553-2143	612-376-7000	4.75	None	None	Howell/Greenshields	'93/'93
VOYAGEUR WI TAX FREE	Single State Muni	11.6	9.21	9,840.00	☆	☆	0.0	553-2143	612-376-7000	3.75	None	None	McCullagh/Howell	'93/'93
WADDELL & REED MUNI BD	General Muni	25.0	10.06	10,041.00	9,749.00	☆	3.9	None	913-236-2000	None	1.00	3.00	John Holliday	'92
WESTCORE AZ INT TX-FR	Single State Muni	25.1	10.40	10,085.00	10,133.00	☆	4.8	392-2673	303-623-2577	3.75	None	None	Jack Berryman	'92
WESTCORE CA INTMDT; INSTL	California Muni	3.8	9.81	10,058.00	9,983.00	☆	4.5	392-2673	303-623-2577	None	None	None	Gerry Wagner	'93
WESTCORE CA INTMDT; RET	California Muni	0.9	9.81	10,038.00	☆	☆	0.0	392-2673	303-623-2577	3.50	0.20	None	Gerry Wagner	'93
WESTCORE CO TX-EX	Single State Muni	10.3	10.42	10,086.00	10,121.00	☆	5.1	392-2673	303-623-2577	4.50	None	None	Bob Lindig	'91
WESTCORE OREGON TX-EX FD	Oregon Muni	53.8	15.91	9,968.00	9,952.00	13,831.00	5.3	392-2673	303-623-2577	4.50	None	None	Mary Gail Walton	'93
WESTCORE QUALITY TX EX	Intermediate Muni	13.6	14.87	10,109.00	10,097.00	☆	4.3	392-2673	303-623-2577	3.50	None	None	Mary Gail Walton	'93
WILLIAM PENN PA TAX-FREE	Pennsylvania Muni	91.0	10.79	10,018.00	10,084.00	14,283.00	5.5	523-8440	610-670-1031	4.75	0.25	None	Miller Anderson & Sherr.	'87
WINTHROP FOCUS MUNI TR	Intermediate Muni	33.8	9.66	10,150.00	☆	☆	0.0	225-8011	212-504-4000	None	0.25	4.00	Marybeth Leithead	'93
WOODWARD MI BD; RTL	Michigan Muni	44.4	9.84	10,072.00	9,988.00	☆	5.3	688-3350	None	4.50	0.35	None	Robert Grabowski	'93
WOODWARD MUNI BD; RTL	General Muni	62.5	9.95	10,091.00	10,071.00	☆	5.2	688-3350	None	4.50	0.35	None	Robert Grabowski	'93
WPG FUNDS TR INTMDT MUNI	Intermediate Muni	15.9	9.69	10,106.00	☆	☆	4.1	223-3332	212-908-9500	None	None	None	Schwarz/Miller	'93/'93
WRBG PINCUS NY MUNI BOND	New York Muni	72.4	10.19	10,165.00	10,231.00	13,955.00	4.5	257-5614	212-878-0600	None	None	None	Christensen/Parente	'92/'92
WRIGHT INC INS TAX FREE	Insured Muni	14.1	11.43	10,021.00	10,005.00	13,746.00	4.9	232-0013	203-333-6666	None	0.20	None	Team Managed	'85

(continued)

NAME CHANGES • NEW FUNDS • MERGERS • LIQUIDATIONS

Name Changes

FROM	TO
ADV INNR CIR PB EMRG GRO	PBHG EMRG GROWTH
ALLIANCE MU-MK INC & GRO	ALLIANCE INC BUILDR; C
BOSTON CO	LAUREL
BOULEVARD	FIRST AMER
CAPITOL FDS SPECIAL EQ; A	NATIONS SPEC EQ; TR A
CFS CALAMOS SM/MD CAP CV	CFS CALAMOS GRO & INC
COMPOSITE	COMPOSITE; A
COWEN	COWEN; A
DELA DECATUR I	DELA DECATUR INC
DELA DECATUR II	DELA DECATUR TOT RET
DREYFUS GLBL INV; A&B	DREYFUS PR GL INV; A&B
FIDELITY INV TR	FIDELITY
FIDELITY SEL BRDCST	FIDELITY SEL MULTIMED
FT SERIES	INTL SRS
GRADISON-MCDONALD EST	GRADISON GR TR EST VAL
GRADISON-MCDONALD OPP	GRAD'SN GR TR OPP VAL
GT PACIF GRO; A&B	GT GLOB PACIF GRO; A&B
INVESTORS PREF	VICTORY
J HANCOCK FR GLOBAL RX	J HAN'K FR GLBL RX; A
J HANCOCK FR PAC BASIN	J HAN'K FR PAC BSN; A
J HANCOCK STRAT UT; A&B	J HAN'K UTILITIES; A&B
JP GROWTH FUND	JEFFERSON-PIL CAP APP
JP INCOME FUND	JEFFERSON-PIL INV GRD
KEMPER ADJ RATE US GOV	KEMPER ADJ RATE GOV; A
KEMPER BLUE CHIP FUND	KEMPER BLUE CHIP; A
KEMPER DIVERSIFIED INC	KEMPER DVSFD INC; A
KEMPER ENVIRONMENTAL	KEMPER ENVIRON; A
KEMPER GLOBAL INCOME	KEMPER GLOBAL INC; A
KEMPER GROWTH	KEMPER GROWTH; A
KEMPER HIGH YIELD	KEMPER HIGH YIELD; A
KEMPER INC&CAP PRES	KEMP'R INC&CAP PRES; A
KEMPER INT'L FD	KEMPER INT'L FUND; A

FROM	TO
KEMPER MUNICIPAL BOND	KEMPER MUNI BOND; A
KEMPER PT GOVT; INL	KEMPER US MTGE; B
KEMPER PT GOVT; PREM	KEMPER US MTGE; A
KEMPER PT S-I GOVT; INL	KEMPER SH-INT GOVT; B
KEMPER PT S-I GOVT; PREM	KEMPER SH-INT GOVT; A
KEMPER SH-TM GLBL INC	KEMPER SH-TM GLBL; A
KEMPER SMALL CAP EQUITY	KEMPER SM CAP EQTY; A
KEMPER TAX-FREE INC	KEMPER TX-FR INC; A
KEMPER TECHNOLOGY	KEMPER TECHNOLOGY; A
KEMPER TOTAL RETURN	KEMPER TOTAL RET; A
KEMPER US GOVT SEC	KEMPER US GOVT SEC; A
LAUREL FDS	LAUREL FDS; TR
LOSANTIVILLE STELLAR	STAR STELLAR; INV
MAXUS PRISM FUND	MAXUS LAUREATE FUND
METLIFE SS BAL; C	METLIFE SS MOD; C
MFS INC & OPPTY; A&B	MFS STRATEGIC INC; A&B
NICH-APP BALANCED QUAL	NICH-APP BAL INSTL
NICH-APP CORE GR QUAL	NICH-APP CORE GR INSTL
NICH-APP EMRG GR QUAL	NICH-APP EMRG GR INST
NICH-APP INC & GR QUAL	NICH-APP INC & GR INSTL
NICH-APP WRLDWDGR QUAL	NICH-APP WW GR INST
NOTTINGHAM GOV	GOV STREET
NTH AM FDS GOVT SECS; C	NTH AM FDS GOV SECS; A
OPPENHEIMER GOV SEC; A	OPPENHEIM'R LTD GOV; A
OPPENHEIMER US GOV TR	OPPENHEIMER US GOV; A
SAFECO EQUITY	SAFECO COMMON EQUITY
SAFECO GROWTH	SAFECO COMMON GRO
SAFECO INCOME	SAFECO COMMON INC
SAFECO NORTHWEST	SAFECO COMMON NW
SEI CASH + ARM; A	SEI DAILY SHT-TM MTG; A
SEI CASH + CORP DAILY; A	SEI DAILY CORP DAILY; A
SEI CASH + GNMA; A	SEI DAILY GNMA; A
SEI CASH + INTMDT GOV; A	SEI DAILY INT GOV; A
SEI CASH + SH-TM GOV; A&B	SEI DLY SHT-TM GOV; A&B
SEI INTL INT'L	SEI INTL INTL EQTY; A

FROM	TO
SEI TX EX PA MUNI	SEI TX EX PA MUNI; A
SHAWMUT CT INTMUNI	SHAW'T CT INTMUN; INV
SHAWMUT FXD INCOME	SHAWMUT FXD INC; TR
SHAWMUT GRO & INC EQ	SHAWM'T GRO&INC EQ; TR
SHAWMUT GROWTH EQUITY	SHAWMUT GRO EQTY; TR
SHAWMUT INT GOV INC	SHAWMUT INT GOV; TR
SHAWMUT LTD TM INC	SHAW'T LTD TM INC; TR
SHAWMUT MA INT MUN	SHAW'T MA INT MUN; INV
SHAWMUT SMALL CAP EQ	SHAWMUT SM CAP EQ; TR
SIERRA SHT TM HIGH QUAL	SIERRA SH TM HI QUAL; A
STEADMAN OCEANO	STEADMAN TECH & GRO
SUNAMER EQ EMG GRO; A&B	SUN'R SM CO GRO; A&B
SUNAMER EQ GRO; A	SUNAMER MID-CAP GRO;A
SUNAMER EQ VALUE; B	SUNAMER BLUE CHIP; B
SWRW GROWTH PLUS	MATRIX GROWTH
TNE	NEW ENGLAND
TOCQUEVILLE EURPAC	TOCQUEVILLE ASIA-PAC
TR FOR TRAK	CG CAP MKTS
TRANSAM BD GOV INC	TRANSAM BD US GOV; A
TWENTIETH CENT	TWEN CENTURY
TX COMMERCE RIT	AVESTA TR
UST MSTR TX-EX INT; ORIG	UST MSTR TX-EX INTMDT
UST MSTR MGD INC; ORIG	UST MSTR MGD INC
VAN ECK INTL INVESTORS	VAN ECK INTL INV GOLD
VAN ECK WORLD INC	VAN ECK WORLD INC; A
VANGUARD TOT BD MKT	VANGUARD BD INDX TOT
WELLSFUNDS	STAGECOACH INST
ZSA GROWTH & INCOME	ZSA ASSET ALLOCATION
ZWEIG SR TR APPREC; B	ZWEIG SR TR APPREC; C
ZWEIG SR TR GOVT SEC; B	ZWEIG SR TR GOVT SEC; C
ZWEIG SR TR MGD ASST; B	ZWEIG SR TR MGD ASST; C
ZWEIG SR TR PRIORITY; B	ZWEIG SR TR PRIORITY; C
ZWEIG SR TR STRATEGY; B	ZWEIG SR TR STRAT; C

New Funds Added

1ST PRIORITY LTD GOV
AAL &FUNDS UTILITIES
AARP BAL STOCK & BOND
AETNA AETNA FUND; ADV
AETNA ASN GRO; ADV,SEL
AETNA BOND; ADV
AETNA GOV; ADV,SEL
AETNA GRO & INC; ADV
AETNA GROWTH; SEL
AETNA SM CO GR; ADV,SEL
AETNA TX-FREE; ADV,SEL
ALEX HAMILTON EQ G&I
ALEX HAMILTON GOV I
ALEX HAMILTON MUNI I
ALLIANCE GLB DLR; A,B,C
ALLIANCE I BUILDER; A,B
ALL'CE MUN II MA; A,B,C
ALL'CE MUN II MI; A,B,C
AMER CAP HI YIELD; C
AMER CAP MUNI BOND; C
ARCH BAL; INSTL
ARCH EMERG GRO; INST
ARCH GOV&CORP; INST
ARCH GR & INC EQ; INST
ARCH INTL EQ; INSTL,TR
ASIA HOUSE ASEAN
ASIA HOUSE FAR EAST
BARTLETT CP SH TM BD
BENCHMARK BOND; C
BENCHMARK INTL BD; A
BENCHMARK INT GRO; A,C
BENCHMARK SM CO IDX; C
BENHAM MUNI AZ INT
BENHAM MUNI FL INT
BILTMORE QUANT EQ
BLANCHARD EMRG MKTS
BRINSON GLOBAL EQUITY
BRINSON US EQUITY
CAPP-RUSH GOLD
CGM TR REALTY FUND
COMPASS CAP PA MUNI BD
COMPOSITE BND & STK; B
COMPOSITE GOV SEC; B
COMPOSITE GROWTH; B
COMPOSITE INCOME; B
COMPOSITE NW 50; B
COMPOSITE TX-EX BD; B
COREFUND GLB BD;A,B
CRABBE HUSON REAL EST
CUNA TX-FR INT-TERM
DFA GRP INTL VALUE
DREYFUS BASIC INT MUN
DREYFUS BASIC MUN BD
DREYFUS GLOBAL BD
DUPREE TN TX-FR INC
FEDERATED INT INC; SVC
FIDEL'Y ADV SH-INT TXEX
FIDELITY EURO CAP APP
FIDELITY MID-CAP STOCK
FIDEL'Y SPARTAN CA INT
FIDEL'Y SPARTAN NY INT
1ST AM CO INT; INST,RET
1ST EAGLE INTL FD
1ST UN FL MUNI; TR
1ST UN HI GRD; TR
1ST UN SC M; INV B,C
1ST UN US GOV; TR
1ST UN UTIL; INV B,C
1ST UN UTILITY; TR
1ST UN VA MUNI; TR
FOUNTAIN SQ OH TX FR
FREMONT INTL GROWTH
FRST PRAIRIE DVSFD; B
FRST PRAIRIE GVT INT; B
FRST PRAIRIE MUN INS; B
FRST PRAIRIE MUN INT; B
GE INTL EQ; A,B,C,D
GE SH-TM GOV; A,B,C,D
GOVETT LATIN AMERICA
GRIFFIN BOND; A
GRIFFIN CA TAX-FREE; A
GRIFFIN GRO & INC; A
GRIFFIN MUNI; A
GRIFFIN US GOV INC; A
HERITAGE INC INST GOV
HOUGH FL TXFR SHT TRM
IAI INV I INSTL BOND
INSIGHT INSTL LTD MUNI
INTM MUNI TR OH; INST
INTMDT MUNI TR PA; INST
J HANCOCK FR GLB RX; B
J HANCOCK FR PAC BSN; B
J HANCOCK TX-EXEMPT; B
JANUS OVERSEAS
JPM INSTL BOND
JPM INSTL DIVERSIFIED
JPM INSL EMRG MKTS EQ
JPM INSTL INTL EQUITY
JPM INSTL SELECT US EQ
JPM INSTL SH TM BOND
JPM INSTL US SM CO
KENILWORTH FUND
KEYST AM TXFR2 CA; A,B,C
KEYST AMTXFR2 MO; A,B,C
KEYST AM TXFR MA; A,B,C
KEYST AM TXFR NY; A,B,C
LEGG MASON INC HI YLD
LIBERTY EQTY INC FORT
LIBERTY HIGH INC; SEL
LIBERTY MUNI SECS; SEL
LINCOLN ADV CP INC; B
LINCOLN ADV ENTPR; B,C
LINCOLN ADV G&I; B,C
LINCOLN ADV NEW PAC; B
LINCOLN ADV TXFR I; B
LINCOLN ADV US GRO; B,C
LINCN ADV WLD GR; B,C
M STANLEY INST JAP'ESE
M STANLEY WW A,B
MARQUIS GOV SEC; A,B
MARQUIS GRO & INC; A,B
MARQUIS VALUE EQ; A,B
MARSHALL INT TX FR
MARSHALL SHT TAX FREE
MAS GLB FXD I
MERRL MULT M NM;A,B
METLFE PR INT EQ; A,B,D
METLFE PRT INT FI; A,B,D
MFS EMERG EQS
MFS WW FXD INC
MINERVA EQUITY
MINERVA FIXED INCOME
MONTGOMERY II STRT US
MONTGOMERY INT DUR
MORGAN GRENF INT FX
N&B ADV MGT TR BAL
N&B EQ NYCDC SOC RESP
NORTHERN FXD INC
NORTHERN GRO EQ
NORTHERN INC EQ
NORTHERN INT EQ
NORTHERN INTL FXD
NORTHERN INT GR EQ
NORTHERN INT TXEX
NORTHERN SEL EQ
NORTHERN SM CAP
NORTHERN TX EX
NORTHERN US GOV
N AM FDS CA MUN; A,B,C
N AM FDS NAT MUN; A,B,C
OFFITBANK EMERG MKTS
OFFITBANK HIGH YIELD
P HZN ASSET ALLOC
P HZN NATL MUNI BD
PAUZE/SWANSON GOV TOT
PEACHTREE BOND
PEACHTREE EQUITY
PLANTERS TN TX-FR BD
PNC CORE EQUITY; INV
PNC SH-TM BOND; INV
PNC SM CAP VAL EQ; SERV
RANSON MGD NEBRASKA
RYDEX OTC FUND
RYDEX PRECIOUS MET
RYDEX URSA FUND
RYDEX US GOV BD
SBSF FDS CAPITAL GRO
SCHWAB CAP INTL IDX
SCHWAB CAP SM-CAP IDX
SCUDDER EMRG MKTS I
SCUDDER LTD TRM TX FR
SCUDDER MNGD INT GOV
SCUDDER MA LTD TX FR
SECURITY EQ GLOBAL; A
SEI INTL INTL FXD INC; A
SEVEN SEAS EMRG MKTS
SHAWMUT FXD INC; INV
SHAWMUT G&I EQ; INV
SHAWMUT GROW EQ; INV
SHAWMUT INTM GOV; INV
SHAWMUT LTD TM I INV
SHAWMUT SM CAP EQ; INV
SM&R AMER NATL TAX FR
SMITH HAYES SMALL CAP
SS RESE SM CAP; A,B,D
STAND AYR WOOD INT TX
STAR STELLAR; TR
STEINROE INTL
STEPSTONE BAL; INVST
STEPSTNE CA TXFR; INST
STEPSTONE CA TX FR; INV
STEPSTONE GRO EQ; INV
STEPSTONE INT-TM; INV
STEPSTONE VALUE; INV
STRONG INTL BOND
STRONG SH-TM GLBL BD
SUNAMER BAL; A
SUNAMER BLUE CHIP; A
SUNAMER DVSD INC; A
SUNAMER HIGH INC; B
SUNAMER TAX EX INS; B
SUNBURST SHRT-INT GOV
TARGET INTL EQ
TARGET INT-TERM BD
TARGET LARGE CAP GRO
TARGET LARGE CAP VAL
TARGET MTG BACKD SEC
TARGET SMALL CAP GRO
TARGET SMALL CAP VAL
TARGET TOTAL RET BD
TCW/DW N AMER INT INC
TWEN CENT WRLD EMRG
TWEN CENT INT BD
TWEN CENT LTD BD
TWEN CENT US GOV INT
US CHINA REGION OPPTY
VAL'STR SH-INT BD; INV
VALUESTR TN TXEX; INV
VANGUARD CA TXFR INS I
VANGUARD INTL IDX EMG
VANKAMP GRO & INC; D
VANKAMP HIGH YIELD; D
VANKAMP INS TAX FR; D
VANKAMP MUNI INC; D
VANKAMP PA TAX FREE; D
VANKAMP SHORT GLBL; D
VANKAMP TX FR HIGH; D
VANKAMP US GOV; D

(continued)

PERFORMANCE OF MUTUAL FUNDS *(concluded)*

VANKAMP UTILITY; D	WORKG ASSETS CIT GL EQ
VICTORY AGGR GROWTH	WORLD INV UTILI; A
VICTORY EQUITY INCOME	WORLD INV UTIL; FORT
VICTORY INTERNATIONAL	WSIS WERTHEIM EQ VAL
VICTORY NATL MUNI BD	WSIS WERTHEIM HI YLD I
VISION GRO & INC	WSIS WERTHEIM INV GR I
VISTA IEEE BAL FUND	WSIS WERTHEIM SH-T INV
WORKG ASSETS CIT EMG	WSIS WERTHEIM SM CAP

Mergers

ALLIANCE GLBL CANADIAN	ALLIANCE INTL; A
BOSTON CO INV ASST; INST	LAUREL INV AS ALL; INV
BOSTON CO INV CONT; INST	LAUREL CONTRN; INV
BOSTON CO INV INTL; INST	LAUREL INV INTL; INV
BOSTON CO INV SHTM; INST	LAUREL INV SHTM; INV
BOSTON CO INTMDT; INST	LAUREL INTMDT; INV
BOSTON CO MGD INC; INST	LAUREL MGD INC; INV
BOSTON CO SPEC GRO; INST	LAUREL SPEC GRO; INV
BOSTON CO TF BOND; INST	LAUREL TF BOND; INV
BOSTON CO TF CA BD; INST	LAUREL TF CA BD; INV
BOSTON CO TF MA BD; INST	LAUREL TF MA BD; INV
BOSTON CO TF NY BD; INST	LAUREL TF NY BD; INV
CAPITOL EQUITY; A	NATIONS VALUE; TR A
CAPITOL FXD INC; A	NATIONS STR INC; TR A
CAPITOL MD TX-FR; A	NATIONS MD INT; TR A
CAPITOL MD TX-FR; B	NATIONS MD MUNI; INV A
DEAN WITTER EQ INC	DEAN WITTER VAL ADD EQ
HIGHMARK GRO EQ	HIGHMARK GROWTH
KEMPER PT DVSFD; INL	KEMPER DVSFD INC; B*
KEMPER PT DVSFD; PREM	KEMPER DVSFD INC
KEMPER PT GROWTH; INL	KEMPER GROWTH; B*
KEMPER PT GROWTH; PREM	KEMPER GROWTH
KEMPER PT HI YLD; INL	KEMPER HIGH YLD; B*
KEMPER PT HI YLD; PREM	KEMPER HIGH YIELD
KEMPER PT SM CP; INL	KEMPER SMALL CAP; B*
KEMPER PT SM CP PREM	KEMPER SM CAP EQ
KEMPER PT TOT RTN; INL	KEMPER TOT RET; B*
KEMPER PT TOT RTN; PREM	KEMPER TOT RTN
PAINEWBR INC; A	PAINWBR INVST GRD; A
PAINEWBR INC; B	PAINWBR INVST GRD; B
PAINEWBR INC; D	PAINWBR INVST GRD; D
PUTNAM TX TAX EX INC	PUTNAM TXEX INC; A
RIGHTIME GROWTH	RIGHTIME BLUE CHIP
SKYLINE MONTHLY INC	VANKAMP HI YLD; A
TRANSAM SPEC BLUE CHIP	TRANSAM INV GR&INC; A
VANGUARD SPL SERV	VANGUARD/MORGAN GRO
VANGUARD SPL TECH	VANGUARD EXPLORER

*-Not yet tracked

Liquidations

ACCESSOR EQ MKT
COLONIAL INTL EQ IND
EQUITY STRATEGIES
GATEWAY GOVT BD PLUS
LAUREL AST MGR; INV
MFS SELECT VALUE
MARINER EURO INDEX; A
MIDWEST STR TOT RTN; C
N&B PROF INV GRO
PRUDENTIAL S-T GL AST;B
VICTORY NY MUNICIPAL

Source: Lipper Analytical Services, Inc. Reprinted by permission of *Barron's National Business and Financial Weekly,*

A Guide to Mutual Fund Investing[1]

Sumner Levine

The essentials of good mutual fund investing are not very complicated and are summarized in the following.

1. *Determine Your Goals*

Begin by estimating the amount of cash you will need and when you will need it. Are you investing to purchase a home, to send the kids to college, for retirement—all of these and more? Your estimate must, of course, include the effects of inflation. How to calculate the effects of inflation on costs and hence the future purchasing power of your investments is explained below. The worksheet (Exhibit 1) given below should be helpful in formulating your thoughts.

2. *List Your Current Investments and Estimate Your Savings*

Take inventory of your current cash and investments by identifying and evaluating such items as:

bonds
certificates of deposit
checking accounts
money market funds
mutual funds
savings accounts
stocks

Also list your current and anticipated incomes, including those from salaries, self employment, rentals, royalties, trusts, social security, pensions, and other retirement plans. How much do you expect to save each year?

Using the above information and assuming plausible rates of return, estimate the future resources you expect to have available to meet your goals. The calculation is described below (see *Estimating The Future Value Of Your Investments*).

3. *Understand The Risk-Return Characteristics of Investments*

Different types of investments exhibit different risk return characteristics as shown in the Basic Series Exhibit on page 239. Risk refers to the extent by which the price of an investment fluctuates and is measured by the standard deviation (SD). The larger the SD, the greater the risk. For example, funds consisting of small company growth stocks with an SD of 35.3% are considerably riskier than, say, a Government bond fund with an SD of 8.6%. It is also evident from the Basic Series Exhibit that the greater the risk the greater the return. Over long time periods the greater return provided by more risky investments offsets the fluctuation in value associated with the risk. However, over relatively short time intervals investors in risky assets may experience substantial losses. Hence, it is generally best to reserve investments in riskier (aggressive) assets to money that will not be needed for several years (say, five years or more).

4. *Determine Your Risk Tolerance*

Your risk tolerance and hence the extent to which you elect to expose your portfolio to aggressive investments depend on several considerations. These include where you are in your career cycle (starting out, preparing for retirement, etc.), the number and age of your dependents, and your psychological makeup. The Worksheet provides some helpful guidance in these regards. Generally, as investors approach retirement age, investments are shifted from the more aggressive (riskier) assets to those that are less so, as discussed in the following.

5. *Select a Diversified Investment Portfolio Consistent With Your Risk Tolerance*

The importance of investment diversification in reducing risk for a given return is now well established. No one knows what type of investment will flourish or decline in the future so that a portfolio should have a broad exposure to different types of investments to reduce risk. An important requirement for effective diversification is that the investments composing your portfolio should tend to fluctuate (in price) oppositely to one another—or, at least, independently of one another. Hopefully as one investment decreases another will increase in value. In practice, diversification is achieved by including in your portfolio funds with different investment philosophies; for example, aggressive, growth, growth-income, fixed income, and foreign equity funds (see page 305 for definitions).

As discussed, the proportion of each fund type in your portfolio will depend on your risk tolerance. Since most investors are risk adverse the proportion of aggressive (riskier) funds in most portfolios is usually smaller than that of the more conservative funds. The shift

[1] The material in this section is for informational purposes only. Any portfolio decisions you make should be discussed with your tax and financial advisers.

EXHIBIT 1

YOUR INVESTMENT PROFILE

Before you launch your investment plan, make a realistic analysis of your financial circumstances and your feelings about risk. Answering the following questions will give you a starting point.

Do you have a sufficient financial "safety net" in place?

- ❏ Do you have 3 to 6 months' salary in a liquid investment that can be converted to cash easily, in case of an emergency?
- ❏ Do you have adequate insurance coverage for yourself and your family?

How will your personal circumstances affect your investing approach? How aggressively—or conservatively—you pursue your investing goals will depend on such factors as:

Your age ____________
Number of dependents ____________
Your current net worth ____________
Your annual income ____________
Amount you have to invest ____________

Your investing experience: ❏ None ❏ Limited ❏ Good ❏ Extensive

What specific investing goals do you have?	**How long do you have to achieve them?**
❏ College savings for your children	____________
❏ Home purchase	____________
❏ Retirement savings	____________
❏ Business investment	____________
❏ Wealth building	____________
❏ Other	____________

What is your primary investment objective?

❏ Maximum growth ❏ Growth ❏ Income ❏ Preservation of principal/safety

Should you consider tax-advantaged investments?

Are you in a tax bracket where you could keep more of your earnings if invested in tax-free investments? (Consult your tax advisor if you're unsure.)

How do you feel about investment risk?

For example, which of these descriptions fit you best:

- ❏ You want maximum investment growth. You're willing to risk the loss of some—or even most—of your principal in exchange for the chance to receive higher returns on your money.
- ❏ You seek high returns but not at the expense of too much risk. You're investing primarily for growth, but want to keep some portion of your money in more "secure" investments.
- ❏ You want good investment returns but only moderate exposure to risk. You're willing to accept slower growth of your investments in exchange for somewhat less portfolio risk.
- ❏ You want your returns to keep pace with inflation but keep risk to a minimum. You're still looking out for the future, but you have a low tolerance for risk and would limit your "growth investments."
- ❏ You want to safeguard your principal at all costs. You're extremely averse to risk and don't want to take any more chances than necessary to maintain the value of your portfolio and/or receive the steady income it generates.

Source: The Charles Schwab Guide to *Investing Made Easy*, Charles Schwab & Co., Inc.

into more conservative investments is usually more pronounced as the investor approaches retirement. Representative portfolios illustrating this point are shown below:

	Amount (%)
EARLY TO MID-CAREER	
Aggressive Growth	15–20
Growth	50–30
Fixed Income (Bond) Funds	25–35
International	10–15
PRE-RETIREMENT	
Aggressive Growth	10–
Growth	35–30
Fixed Income	45–50
International	10–
RETIREMENT	
Growth	30–35
Fixed Income	50–45
International	10–
Money Market	10–

For those in the higher tax brackets, tax free (municipal) funds should be considered. Investors with a greater risk tolerance might prefer a somewhat different allocation: for example, a greater proportion in aggressive growth funds. As a rule of thumb, the percentage of your portfolio in equity funds is given by 100 minus your age. Thus, a 65 year old would have 35% in equities.

Selection of funds for inclusion in the portfolio can be made by examining the year to year return of funds with different investment philosophies and picking those with a consistently superior performance (say, among the top 20% over the last 5 years). A simpler and perhaps a more satisfactory approach is to refer to a good service such as Morningstar, which specializes in evaluating fund performance. Several helpful references for selecting funds are given below. Be sure that the same management which achieved the superior performance is still in place. If a management change has occurred then it might be prudent to defer inclusion until the new management has proven itself.

As to the choice between a load fund (which charges a fee for purchasing and/or selling the fund) or a no-load fund, our preference is for a no-load fund since there is no evidence that load funds, as a group, out perform no-load funds. With a no-load fund the full amount of your investment goes to work for you at the outset.

Another item to check is the annual expense ratio charged by the fund. This should be at least consistent (or preferably lower) with that of other funds of the same type.

There are no hard and fast rules concerning the number of funds to own. The number will depend on your need for diversification, the size of your assets, and your tolerance for the paper work involved in keeping tax records and monitoring performance. Typically, a modest portfolio, of say, $50,000.00 to $100,000.00 might consist of two aggressive growth funds, two international equity funds, one conservative growth fund or growth-income fund, and a fixed income fund, giving a total of six funds. Larger portfolios of about one million dollars or more might consist of fifteen to twenty funds.

6. *Time Average Your Purchases*

The market constantly fluctuates; sometime it is up, sometime down. A simple way to average out this effect is to make constant dollar purchases on a monthly basis. Thus every month a fixed amount, say $200.00 is invested. To take inflation into account, the monthly purchase might be increased by the inflation rate. If the inflation rate is, say 4%, the $200.00 purchase would become $208.00.

A second approach to time averaging requires the value of your portfolio to increase by a fixed amount, say $200.00 per month. The amount of your monthly investment contribution would be the difference between the target value you set and the actual increase. Thus, if the value of the portfolio increased $100.00, then you would invest $100.00 assuming a target value of $200.00. If your portfolio increased $200.00 or more, you add nothing.

Another version of this approach requires that you sell shares for portfolio increases over $200.00 and reinvest the cash at a later time when the gain is less than $200.00. However, this approach usually incurs large capital gains taxes.

With this approach, if your portfolio lost money, say $20.00, you would contribute $220.00 to achieve a net increase of $200.00. In this way, you invest more in a weak market and less in a strong one.

7. *Monitor Your Portfolio and Keep Abreast of Developments*

The performance of your portfolio should be reviewed at least twice a year and preferably more often. Determine how well your funds have performed relative to others of the same type. Check to see if there has been a change in investment manager or philosophy.

The total returns on your portfolio should also be calculated. This is done by multiplying the return of each fund over the period in question by the fractional amount of the fund in the portfolio. Add up the results for all the funds to obtain the over all portfolio return.

Alas, the vicissitudes of the Government are such that even the most prudent investor cannot anticipate the changes in the tax law and it is essential therefore to keep informed by reading the financial press and consulting with your tax adviser.

INFORMATION SOURCES

The following is a selected list of information sources to help you evaluate and monitor funds.

1. *The Wall Street Journal*

Probably the most complete daily source of information. For details see page 300.

2. *Morningstar Mutual Funds*

An excellent detailed source of information. This loose leaf service provides updates every two weeks. Over 1240 funds are followed. Try your library or take a trial subscription. Also publishes a newsletter on closed-end funds (i.e., funds traded on one of the Stock Exchanges).

Screening thousands of mutual funds to identify those that meet certain return, risk, expense, or style criteria is greatly facilitated with the Morningstar floppy disk service. Considerable data on the characteristics of individual funds are provided, including performance graphs. However, the information provided by the disks is not as extensive as that given in the published version of the Morningstar service. Monthly and quarterly updates are available.

Morningstar
53 West Jackson Boulevard
Chicago, IL 60604
Telephone: 800-876-5005

3. Value Line publishes a *Mutual Fund Survey* which includes several hundred more funds than the Morningstar directory. The coverage is comparable to that of Morningstar.

Value Line Mutual Fund Survey
220 East 42nd Street
New York, NY 10017-5891
Telephone: 800-284-7607

4. *Mutual Fund Buyer's Guide*

This inexpensive monthly publication is a compact information source on safety ratings, performance, fees, asset size, and more. Covers over 1500 funds.

The Institute for Econometric Research
3471 N. Federal
Fort Lauderdale, FL 33306
Telephone: 800-442-9000

5. *No-Load Fund Investor*

A monthly publication covering 664 no-load and low-load funds. Contains information on returns, risk, asset size, and gives fund fixed diversification suggestions. Also available is the useful publication *Handbook For No-Load Fund Investors.*

The No-Load Fund Investor, Inc.
P.O. Box 283
Hastings-on-Hudson, NY 10706
Telephone: 800-252-2042

6. *Barron's*

This well-known weekly provides information on 52 week high and low prices, latest dividend payouts, and 12 month payouts. Quarterly reports are published on most funds summarizing extensive data provided by the Lipper organization. Available on most news stands and by subscription.

Barron's
200 Burnett Road
Chicopee, MA 01020

HELPFUL CALCULATIONS

How Inflation Affects Future Costs

Estimating future cash needs is an important aspect of investment planning. The effect of inflation on future costs can be calculated from the expression.

$F = P\ (1 + I)^n$
F is the cost n years from now
P is the present cost
I is the estimated inflation rate

Example:

You want to estimate the cost ten years from now for sending your child to college. The present cost is $6000.00 per year and you estimate the inflation of college costs to be about 6% per year.

Here P = $6000.00 per year
$I = .06$
$n = 10$ years
so that your future cost estimate is
$F = 6.000\ (1.06) = \$10{,}745/\text{yr}$

Estimating the Portfolio Return Required to Maintain Current Purchasing Power

The return on your portfolio will be decreased by income taxes and the purchasing power of your investment will be reduced by inflation. It is often important to know the before tax return which will just maintain the current purchasing power of your portfolio.

The appropriate expression for the calculation is

$$i = \frac{I}{1 - t}$$

Where

i is the before tax return
t is your income tax bracket
I is the inflation rate

Example:

You want to determine the rate of return on your portfolio required to maintain the current purchasing power of the assets. You are in the 35% tax bracket (Federal and State) and you estimate future inflation to be 4% per year.

The required before tax return is

$$i = \frac{.04}{1 - .35} = 6.15\%$$

Under these assumptions this return will just maintain the purchasing power of your investments over time. The purchasing power will increase if the investment return is greater and decrease if it is less than the calculated rate.

Return Required to Maintain Purchasing Power When Funds Are Withdrawn

In the above example it was assumed that no funds were withdrawn from the portfolio. We now assume that a percentage of the portfolio is withdrawn for, say, living expenses.

The before tax return required to maintain the purchasing power of the remaining portfolio is given by

$$i = \frac{I + w}{1 - t}$$

Where w is the percentage of the portfolio withdrawn.

Example:

Assume the same tax brackets and inflation rate as in the above example. You desire to withdraw 5% of the portfolio each year for living expenses. The required before tax return (i) is

$$i = \frac{.04 + .05}{1 - .35} = 13.8\%$$

At the calculated rate the purchasing power of the remaining portfolio will be preserved. If the rate of return is smaller, the purchasing power will decrease.

Estimating the Future Value of Your Investments

You often want to know how much your portfolio will grow if you invest a fixed amount each month (or other period) and the funds generated by the portfolio investments are reinvested.

The required expression for the size of the portfolio n months from now

$$F = P\,(1 + i)^n + A\left[\frac{(1 + i)^n - 1}{i}\right]$$

Where

P is the current value of the portfolio
A is the fixed amount invested each period (month, year, etc.)
n is the number of months from now at which it is desired to evaluate the portfolio
i is the after tax return per month (the annual after tax return divided by twelve)

Example:

Your current portfolio is valued at \$50,000.00. You want to know how much the portfolio will grow 10 years from now if you deposit \$200.00 per month over that time period. You assume a before tax return of 12% per year. If you are in the 35% tax bracket, your after tax return will be 7.8% [12 (1 − .35)] per year. The *monthly return* is just the annual return divided by 12 or .65% per month. Ten years corresponds to 120 months so that at ten years the portfolio will have grown to

$$F = 50{,}000(1.0065)^{120}\left[\frac{(1.0065)^{120} - 1}{1.0065}\right]$$

$$F = \$144{,}982$$

Calculations of this type are helpful in forming realistic expectations of portfolio growth possibilities.

Maximum Amount that Can Be Withdrawn Annually from a Portfolio During Retirement

You are now retired and have accumulated a portfolio valued at P dollars. It is invested at a return of i (after income taxes). You want to know the maximum amount you can withdraw each year over your remaining life so that nothing will remain at the end.

The appropriate expression is

$$A = P\left[\frac{i(1 + i)^n}{(1 + i)^n - 1}\right]$$

Where

A is the maximum amount that can be withdrawn each year over n years
P is the value of the portfolio at retirement
i is the after tax return
n is the number of years you expect to live after retirement

Example:

You are retired at the age of 68 with a portfolio of \$500,000.00. Life expectancy tables indicate that your remaining expected life is about 13 years. You estimate your after tax return to be about 6.5%. What is the most you can withdraw each year so that nothing remains when you have lived your expected life?

EXHIBIT 2: Table for Determining the Longevity of Retirement Savings

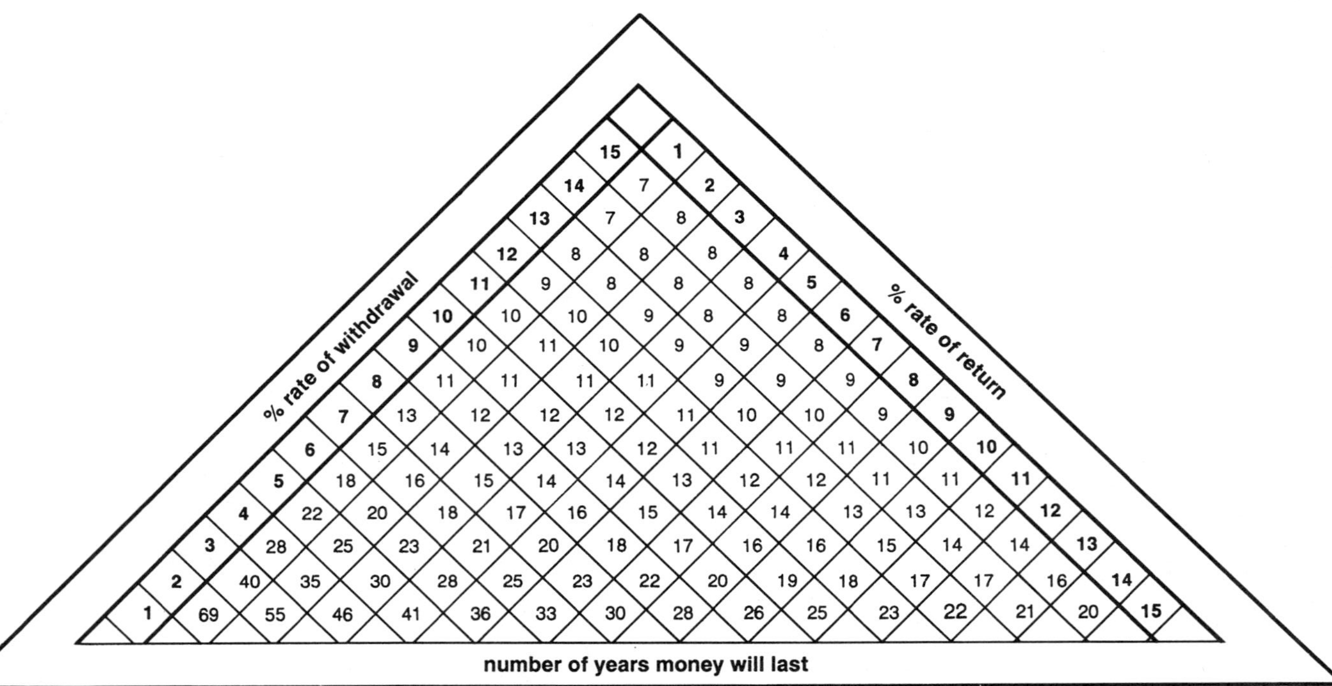

Number of years money will last

% rate of withdrawal \ % rate of return	1	2	3	4	5	6	7	8	9	10	11	12	13	14	15
1															
2	69														
3	40	55													
4	28	35	46												
5	22	25	30	41											
6	18	20	23	28	36										
7	15	16	18	21	25	33									
8	13	14	15	17	20	23	30								
9	11	12	13	14	16	18	22	28							
10	10	11	12	13	14	15	17	20	26						
11	10	11	11	12	12	13	14	16	19	25					
12	9	10	10	11	11	11	12	14	16	18	23				
13	8	8	9	9	9	10	11	12	13	15	17	22			
14	7	8	8	8	9	9	10	11	11	13	14	17	21		
15	7	8	8	8	8	8	9	9	10	11	12	14	16	20	

Source: *The Handbook For No-Load Fund Investors*, Sheldon Jacobs, The No-Load Fund Investor, Inc., P.O. Box 318, Irvington-on-Hudson, New York 10533.

$$A = \frac{500{,}000(.065)(1.065)^{13}}{(1.065)^{13} - 1} = \$58{,}151$$

How Long Will My Savings Last

You want to determine how long your investment savings will last given the after tax rate of return on your investments and a withdrawal rate.

The expression to use is:

$$n = -\frac{\ln\left(1 - \frac{Pi}{A}\right)}{\ln(1 + i)}$$

Where

ln designates the logarithm
n is the years required to use up all of your investment
P = the size of your investment when you start to withdraw
A = the amount to be withdrawn each year
i = the after tax rate of return

An alternative approach is to use Exhibit 2 based on the above equation. Find the rate of withdrawal on the left side and the rate of return on the right. The intersection of the two rows gives the number of years the money will last.

Example:

At retirement your investment savings are \$200,000.00 and you want to start withdrawing \$20,000.00 each year. You estimate an after tax return of 7%. How long will your savings last?

Here

$$i = .07$$
$$A = \$20{,}000.$$
$$P = \$200{,}000.$$

Therefore

$$n = -\frac{\ln\left(1 - \frac{200{,}000}{20{,}000} \times .07\right)}{\ln(1.07)} = 17.7 \text{ years}$$

Note if the withdrawal rate (A/P) is less than the rate of return (i), your savings will last indefinitely.

How to Check up on Your Investment Advisor

If you are considering investing with a firm that you know little about, check out the firm's background in the following three areas:

Disciplinary history records can be obtained from the National Association of Securities Dealers 800-289-9999. Also check the State regulator of the State in which the firm is located. To obtain the regulator's phone number call 202-737-0900.

For information about financial planners contact the Institute of Certified Financial Planners at 303-751-7600 or the International Association for Financial Planning at 404-395-1605.

Credit background information can be obtained, for a fee, from Dun and Bradstreet at (800-362-2255).

Litigation information, past or pending, is available from the State or Federal court house where the company has its headquarters. Mead Data Central will do a search, for a fee, of newspapers and periodicals. Telephone: 800-843-6476.

Investing in Foreign Securities

Sumner N. Levine

How to Invest Internationally

Interest in international investing has grown rapidly in recent years. One reason is apparent: the size of the non-U.S. securities markets has expanded from about 35% of the total in 1970 to about 62% in 1991. It is evident that focusing exclusively on the U.S. market eliminates nearly two-thirds of the available opportunities—many of which may be very attractive.

Another reason for including foreign securities in investment portfolios is the possible risk reduction resulting from country diversification. The securities markets of most countries are only weakly interdependent. Frequently when one market is decreasing in value, that of another country is increasing. The net effect of increasing markets in a portfolio is to offset effects of the decreasing markets. For example, from mid-1991 to mid-1992, the Tokyo stock market fell 27%. However, over the same 52-week period, the Mexican market rose 81%. Clearly, including Mexican equities in a portfolio equally weighted with Japanese securities would have resulted in a net increase in portfolio value. It should be mentioned that while most markets intend to be only weakly interrelated much of the time, certain events with global impact (such as the Persian Gulf War) can cause all major markets to move together. The extent and duration of such co-movements will, of course, differ from country to country.

A quantitative measure of the extent by which two markets move together is the correlation coefficient. Two perfectly related markets are assigned a correlation coefficient of one. If the two markets are totally unrelated in their movements, the correlation coefficient has a value of zero. Some coefficients with the U.S. market over the period 1970–1989 are given in Table 1.

TABLE 1

Canada	.82
France	.45
Germany	.44
Italy	.32
Japan	.46
Netherlands	.67
United Kingdom	.59

Source: Ennis, Knupp & Associates.

Problems with International Investing

Investors should be aware of certain problems often associated with international investing. These are briefly summarized below. Further details may be found in the references given at the end of this article:

- difficulty of obtaining high quality financial information about companies in a timely manner
- language problems
- political instability
- unfamiliar financial reporting practices
- currency risks resulting from fluctuations in conversion rates
- possible restrictions on repatriating foreign earnings
- high brokerage and other transaction fees
- leveling of withholding and other taxes on gains and dividends
- delays in the delivery of stock certificates and settlements
- smaller markets may present liquidity problems
- lax oversight and regulation of many foreign markets
- dividends and interest may only be paid semiannually or even annually

How to Invest

Foreign securities may be purchased in several ways as discussed in the following.

ADRs

Several hundred foreign issues are traded as stocks or American Depository Receipts (ADRs) on the New York and American Exchanges or over the counter (OTC), and so may be purchased through the usual channels.

ADRS are receipts issued by American banks for foreign stock. The actual foreign stock certificates are held by a custodial foreign bank. It is important to note that an ADR may not represent just one foreign stock certificate. Depending on the stock, an ADR may represent several foreign stock certificates or only a fraction of a stock certificate.

Most people are unaware that there are two kinds of ADRs, sponsored and unsponsored, with different investment implications. With a sponsored ADR, a foreign company approaches a U.S. bank to issue an ADR in the U.S. Unsponsored ADRs are set up by

Source: *The Business One Irwin International Almanac: Business and Investments*, edited by Sumner N. Levine and Caroline Levine, **IRWIN** Professional Publishing, Burr Ridge, Illinois.

a U.S. broker who approaches a U.S. bank with evidence of a market sufficient to warrant the issuance of an ADR. The U.S. bank then contacts the foreign company for a "no objection" letter. Stock certificates are then purchased and deposited in a foreign bank. The difference between the two types of ADRs from the viewpoint of the investor is that holders of sponsored ADRs are assured of receiving the full amount of the dividend and annual reports. Since unsponsored ADRs are set up on the initiative of a broker and not the company, the cost of distributing the dividend is taken out of the dividend by the bank, and annual reports are usually sent only on request.

Reports must be filed with the SEC for all companies listed on the exchanges or quoted on the NASDAQ. However, for those ADRs quoted on the OTC "pink sheets," SEC filings are not required, and information may be difficult to find.

Investors should also be aware that many ADRs are very thinly traded with wide spreads between the bid and ask prices.

Open-End Funds

A second approach to investing—particularly for investors with limited resources—is that of buying open-ended mutual funds. With mutual funds, investors are buying access to the expertise of the fund managers as well as all the other substantial resources often available to mutual funds.

Two categories of funds invest in foreign securities. Global funds have a portfolio that includes securities from both the U.S. and non-U.S. countries. International funds hold only non-U.S. securities. These include country funds which hold securities of companies within a given country and regional funds with portfolios consisting of companies within a geographic region (i.e., South America, etc.).

Load funds can be purchased through the management company or sponsoring broker. No-load funds must be purchased through the management company.

Closed-End Funds

Purchasing closed-end funds is yet another way for investors to participate in the foreign securities market. These funds are all traded on the exchanges so that buying them only requires a phone call to your broker. Since closed-end funds often trade at a discount from their net asset value, it is best to avoid purchasing them at a premium.

Fund Evaluation Services

Many open- and closed-end funds are evaluated by the *Morningstar Services* (53 West Jackson Boulevard, Chicago, IL. 60604-3608, phone 800-876-5005). The *No-Load Fund Investor* (P.O. Box 283, Hastings-on-the-Hudson, N.Y. 10706, phone 800-252-2042) and the *CDA/Weisenberger Financial Service* (1355 Piccard Drive, Rockville, MD. 20850 (phone 301-590-1398) emphasize open-end funds. A service focusing on closed-end funds is provided by Thomas J. Herzfeld Advisors (The Herzfeld Building, Miami, Florida).

Direct Purchase

Finally, foreign securities can be purchased directly through several large U.S. brokerage firms (Merrill Lynch, Goldman Sacks, Morgan Stanley, etc.); U.S. branches of foreign banks or foreign brokerage houses.

Many foreign banks and brokerage houses make available company research reports to their clients.

For information on foreign securities consult the following:

The Wall Street Journal
The Asian Wall Street Journal
Dow Jones & Company
22 Cortlandt Street
New York, NY 10007

The Asian Wall Street Journal, a weekly, is particularly helpful for the Asian region, including stock market coverage.

Barron's
World Financial Center
200 Liberty Street
New York, NY 10281

The weekly *International Trader* section is of special interest.

Capital International Perspectives
3 Place Des Bergues
1201 Geneva, Switzerland

Capital International Perspectives is a leading monthly publication dealing with international investments.

Datastream International
299 Park Avenue
New York, NY 10171
Tel: 212-593-6500

Provides comprehensive online financial and market information worldwide.

Disclosure
5161 River Road
Bethesda, MD 20816
Tel: 301-951-1300

This service also provides annual reports and filings on foreign firms. The *Worldscope* service provides company financial information in published and compact disk formats.

This service is available online through Dow Jones Retrieval.

Contact: Wright Investor Service
P.O. Box 428
Bridgeport, CT 06601
Tel: 203-333-6666

The Financial Times
Bracken House
10 Cannon Street
London EC4P 4BY, England

The Financial Times provides comprehensive coverage of European businesses and securities markets and is published daily.

Moody's Investor Services, International Manual
Moody's Investor Services
99 Church Street
New York, NY 10007
Tel: 212-553-0300

The International Manual provides financial information on about 5,000 major foreign corporations.

Reuters, based in London, is one of the largest international news agencies. Online services include Newsline which gives current international news, and Company News Year which provides access to one year of news items concerning specific companies.

Contact: Reuters Information Services
1700 Broadway
New York, NY 10019

For Further Reading

General Texts:

1. N. Berryessa and E. Kirzner. *Global Investing*. Business One Irwin, Homewood, Illinois (1988).
2. R. Keyes and D. Miller. *The Global Investor*. Longman, Chicago, Illinois (1990).
3. J. Lederman and K. Park. *The Global Equity Market*. Probus, Chicago, Illinois (1991).
4. Ibid., *The Global Bond Market*. Probus, Chicago, Illinois (1991).
5. S. Levine. *Global Investing*. HarperCollins, New York, New York (1992).
6. S. Levine and C. Levine (eds.). *International Almanac: Business and Investments*. Business One Irwin, Homewood, Illinois.
7. G. Warfield. *How to Buy Foreign Stocks*. Harper Row, New York, New York (1985).

Directories:

8. S. Allen and S. O'Connor. *Guide to World Equity Markets*. Euromoney London (annual).
9. *Handbook of World Stock and Commodity Exchanges*. Bossil Blackwell, Oxford (annual).

PERFORMANCES OF FOREIGN SECURITIES MARKETS

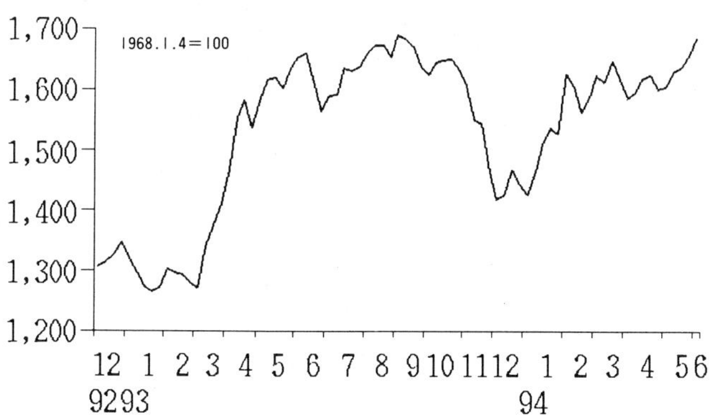

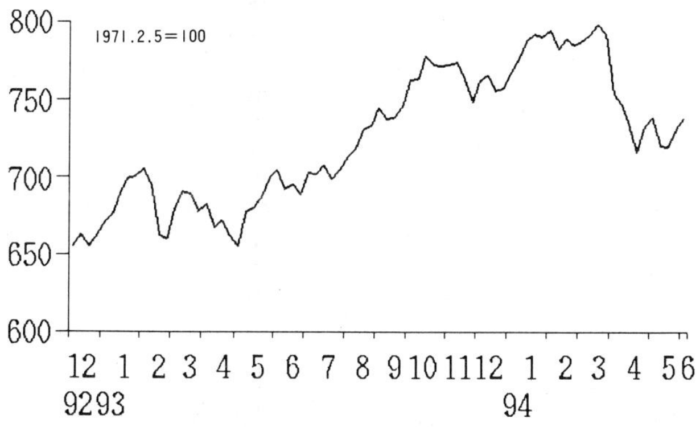

Source: *Investors Guide*, July 1994. Daiwa Securities Co., Ltd.

(continued)

PERFORMANCES OF FOREIGN SECURITIES MARKETS *(concluded)*

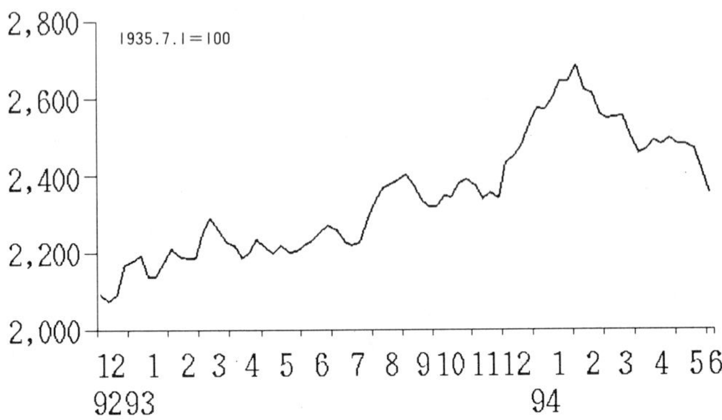

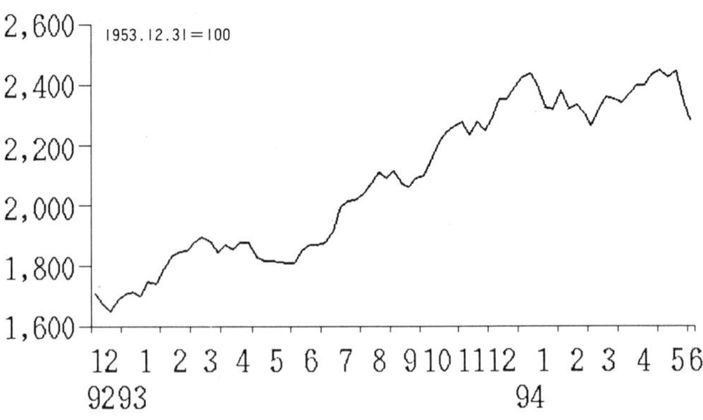

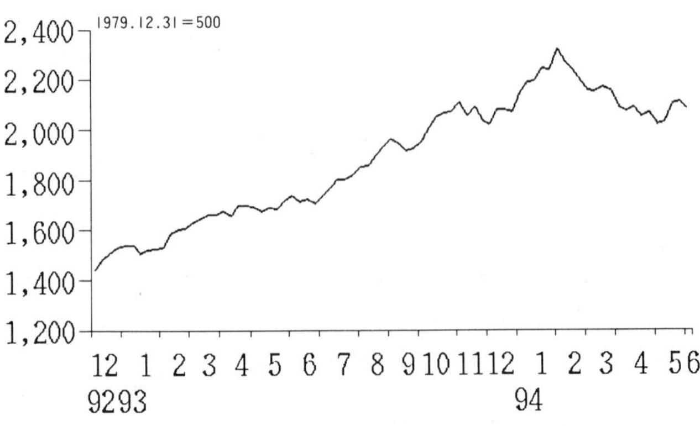

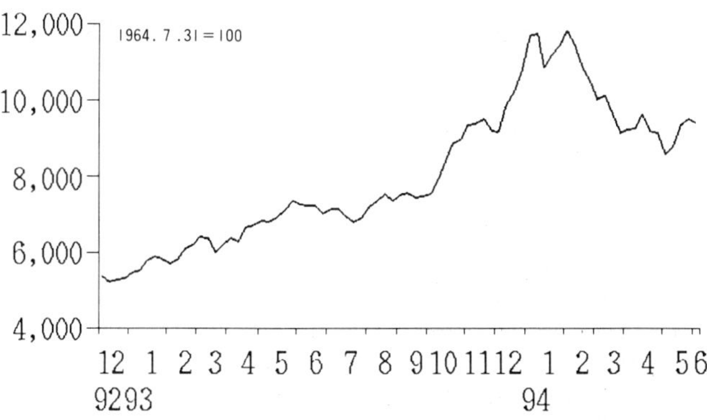

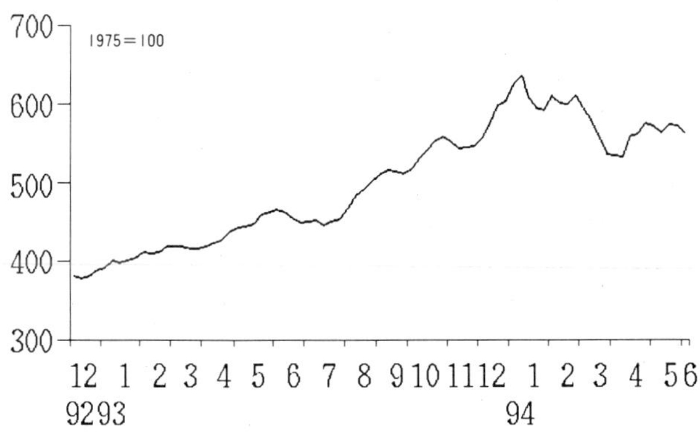

Source: *Investors Guide*, July 1994. Daiwa Securities Co., Ltd.

Stocks of Non-U.S. Corporate Issuers, December 31, 1993 (NYSE)

Country	Company	Symbol	Date Admitted
Argentina	Banco Frances del Rio de la Plata*	BFR	11/24/93
	BAESA - Buenos Aires Embotelladora, S.A.*	BAE	5/5/93
	YPF Sociedad Anonima*	YPF	6/29/93
Australia	Australia and New Zealand Banking Group Ltd. (PFD)	ANZPR	3/2/93
	Broken Hill Proprietary Company Limited*	BHP	5/28/87
	Coles Myer Ltd.*	CM	10/31/88
	FAI Insurances Limited*	FAI	9/28/88
	National Australia Bank Limited*	NAB	6/24/88
	News Corporation Ltd.*	NWS	5/20/86
	Orbital Engine Corporation Limited*	OE	12/4/91
	Western Mining Corp. Holdings Ltd.*	WMC	1/2/90
	Westpac Banking Corporation*	WBK	3/17/89
	Westpac Banking Corporation* (PFD)	WBKPR	11/17/89
Bermuda	ACE Limited	ACL	3/25/93
	Sphere Drake Holdings Limited	SD	9/22/93
Brazil	Aracruz Celulose, S.A.*	ARA	5/27/92
British W.I.	Club Med, Inc.	CMI	9/25/84
Canada	Abitibi-Price Inc.	ABY	7/1/87
	Alcan Aluminum Ltd.	AL	5/31/50
	American Barrick Resources Corp.	ABX	2/25/87
	BCE Inc.	BCE	8/18/76
	Campbell Resources Inc.	CCH	6/13/83
	Canadian Pacific Limited	CP	1/24/1883
	Cineplex Odeon Corporation	CPX	5/14/87
	Domtar Inc.	DTC	9/22/87
	Glamis Gold Ltd.	GLG	1/20/93
	Horsham Corporation	HSM	1/15/90
	Inco Limited	N	12/20/28
	InterTAN Inc.	ITN	11/1/88
	LAC Minerals Ltd.	LAC	7/30/85
	Laidlaw Inc. (Class A)	LDWA	12/10/90
	Laidlaw Inc. (Class B)	LDWB	12/10/90
	Magna International Inc.	MGA	10/9/92
	Mitel Corporation	MLT	5/18/81
	Moore Corporation Limited	MCL	11/13/80
	Northern Telecom Limited	NT	11/10/75
	Northgate Exploration Limited	NGX	2/3/70
	NOVA Corporation of Alberta	NVA	6/13/88
	Placer Dome Inc.	PDG	8/13/87
	Potash Corporation of Saskatchewan Inc.	POT	11/2/89
	Premdor Inc.	PI	4/2/93
	Ranger Oil Limited	RGO	1/28/83
	Seagram Company Ltd.	VO	12/2/35
	TransCanada Pipelines Limited	TRP	5/30/85
	United Dominion Industries Limited	UDI	12/6/83
	Westcoast Energy Inc.	WE	8/15/64

Country	Company	Symbol	Date Admitted
Cayman Is.	Elf Overseas Ltd. Ser. A (PFD)	EOLPRA	2/11/93
	Elf Overseas Ltd. Ser. B (PFD)	EOLPRB	2/11/93
	Espirito Santo Overseas (PFD)	ESBPRA	12/17/93
	Extecapital Ltd. (PFD)	BEXPR	12/23/92
	NewsCorp. Cayman Islands Ltd.* (PFD)	NWSPR	5/20/86
	NewsCorp Overseas Ltd., Ser. A (PFD)	NOPPRA	8/30/93
	Santander Finance Ltd. (PFD)	BSFPRA	11/4/93
Chile	Compania de Telefonos de Chile, S.A.*	CTC	7/20/90
	Enersis, S.A.*	ENI	10/20/93
	Madeco, S.A.*	MAD	5/28/93
	MASISA - Maderas y Sinteticos Sociedad Anonima*	MYS	6/17/93
	Sociedad Quimica y Minera de Chile, S.A.*	SQM	9/21/93
Denmark	Novo-Nordisk A/S*	NVO	7/9/81
France	Alcatel Alsthom Compagnie Générale d'Electricité*	ALA	5/20/92
	Rhone-Poulenc, S.A.* Ord. A	RP	1/26/93
	Rhone-Poulenc Overseas (PFD)	RPOPRA	7/13/93
	Rhone-Poulenc, S.A.* 1/4A (PFD)	RPPRA	11/10/89
	Societe National Elf Aquitaine*	ELF	6/14/91
	TOTAL*	TOT	10/25/91
Germany	Daimler - Benz AG*	DAI	10/5/93
Hong Kong	Amway Asia Pacific Ltd.	AAP	12/15/93
	Brilliance China Automotive Holdings Limited	CBA	10/9/92
	China Tire Holdings Limited	TIR	7/15/93
	Ek Chor China Motorcycle Co., Ltd.	EKC	6/29/93
	Hong Kong Telecommunications Ltd.*	HKT	12/8/88
	Tommy Hilfiger Corporation	TOM	9/23/92
Ireland	Allied Irish Banks PLC*	AIB	9/12/89
	Allied Irish Banks PLC* (PFD)	AIBPR	9/12/89
Israel	Elscint Limited	ELT	9/20/84
	Tadiran Limited	TAD	8/6/92
Italy	Benetton Group, S.p.A.*	BNG	6/9/89
	Fiat, S.p.A.* 5 Ord.	FIA	2/14/89
	Fiat, S.p.A.* 5 (PFD)	FIAPR	2/14/89
	Fiat, S.p.A.* 5 Svg. (PFD)	FIAPRA	2/14/89
	Fila Holdings, S.p.A.*	FLH	5/27/93
	Industrie Natuzzi, S.p.A.*	NTZ	5/13/93
	Luxottica Group, S.p.A.*	LUX	1/24/90
	Montedison, S.p.A.*	MNT	7/16/87
	Montedison, S.p.A.* (PFD)	MNTPR	7/16/87
Japan	Hitachi, Ltd.*	HIT	4/14/82
	Honda Motor Co., Ltd.*	HMC	2/11/77
	Kubota Corporation*	KUB	11/9/76
	Kyocera Corporation*	KYO	5/23/80
	Matsushita Electric Industrial Co., Ltd.*	MC	12/13/71
	Mitsubishi Bank Ltd.*	MBK	9/19/89
	Pioneer Electronic Corporation*	PIO	12/13/76
	Sony Corporation*	SNE	9/17/70
	TDK Corporation*	TDK	5/15/82

(continued)

Stocks of Non-U.S. Corporate Issuers, December 31, 1993 (NYSE) *(concluded)*

Country	Company	Symbol	Date Admitted
Liberia	Royal Caribbean Cruises Ltd.	RCL	4/28/93
Luxembourg	Espirito Santo Financial Holdings, S.A.*	ESF	6/30/93
Mexico	Bufete Industrial, S.A.*	GBI	11/4/93
	Coca-Cola Femsa, S.A. de C.V.*	KOF	9/14/93
	Consorcio G Grupo Dina, S.A. de C.V.*	DIN	3/31/93
	Empresas ICA Sociedad Controladora, S.A. de C.V.*	ICA	4/9/92
	Grupo Casa Autrey, S.A. de C.V.*	ATY	12/7/93
	Grupo Financiero Serfin, S.A. de C.V.*	SFN	12/1/93
	Grupo Mexicano de Desarrollo, S.A. de C.V.* (Ser. B)	GMDB	12/14/93
	Grupo Mexicano de Desarrollo, S.A. de C.V.* (Ser. L)	GMD	12/14/93
	Grupo Radio Central, S.A. de C.V.*	RC	7/1/93
	Grupo Televisa, S.A.***	TV	12/14/93
	Grupo Tribasa, S.A. de C.V.*	GTR	9/22/93
	Telefonos de Mexico, S.A. de C.V.*	TMX	5/14/91
	Transportacion Maritima Mexicana, S.A. de C.V.* (Ser. L)	TMM	6/10/92
	Transportacion Maritima Mexicana, S.A. de C.V.* Ord.	TMMA	6/10/92
	Vitro, S.A.*	VTO	11/19/91
Netherlands	AEGON N.V.**	AEG	11/5/91
	Elsag Bailey Process Automation N.V.	EBY	11/19/93
	KLM Royal Dutch Airlines**	KLM	5/22/57
	Koninklijke Ahold N.V.*	AHO	11/15/93
	Philips N.V.**	PHG	4/14/87
	Polygram N.V.**	PLG	12/14/89
	Royal Dutch Petroleum Co.**	RD	7/20/54
	Unilever N.V.**	UN	12/12/61
Netherlands Antilles	Schlumberger Limited	SLB	2/2/62
	Singer Company N.V.	SEW	8/2/91
New Zealand	Fletcher Challenge Ltd.*	FLC	12/13/93
	Fletcher Challenge Ltd. Forest Division Shares*	FFS	12/13/93
	Telecom Corporation of New Zealand Ltd.*	NZT	7/17/91
Norway	A/S Eksportfinans (PFD)	EKPPR	1/14/93
	Hafslund Nycomed AS*	HN	6/24/92
	Norsk Hydro a.s.*	NHY	6/25/86
Panama	Banco Latinoamericano de Exportaciones, S.A.	BLX	9/24/92
	Panamerican Beverages, Inc.	PB	9/22/93
People's Rep. of China	Shanghai Petrochemical Company, Ltd.*	SHI	7/26/93
Philippines	Benguet Corporation	BE	6/27/49
Portugal	Banco Comercial Portugues, S.A.*	BPC	6/12/92
South Africa	ASA Limited	ASA	12/8/58
Spain	ARGENTARIA - Corporacion Bancaria de Espana, S.A.*	AGR	5/12/93
	Banco Bilbao Vizcaya, S.A.*	BBV	12/14/88
	Banco Bilbao Vizcaya Int. (Gibraltar)* (PFD)	BVGPR	12/12/91
	Banco Bilbao Vizcaya Int. (Gibraltar)* (PFD)	BVGPRB	12/15/92
	Banco Bilbao Vizcaya Int. (Gibraltar)* (PFD)	BVGPRC	7/1/93
	Banco Central, S.A.*	BCM	7/20/83
	Banco de Santander, S.A.*	STD	7/30/87
	Empresa Nacional de Electricidad, S.A.*	ELE	6/1/88
	Repsol, S.A.*	REP	5/11/89
	Telefonica de Espana, S.A.*	TEF	6/12/87

Country	Company	Symbol	Date Admitted
Sweden	Aktiebolaget Svensk Exportkredit (PFD)	SEPPR	9/20/93
United Kingdom	Attwoods PLC*	A	4/12/91
	Automated Security (Holdings) PLC*	ASI	7/22/92
	Barclays Bank PLC* (PFD)	BCBPR	5/5/93
	Barclays Bank PLC* (PFD)	BCBPRA	6/26/89
	Barclays Bank PLC* (PFD)	BCBPRB	8/7/89
	Barclays Bank PLC* (PFD)	BCBPRC	7/23/90
	Barclays Bank PLC* (PFD)	BCBPRD	3/28/91
	Barclays Bank PLC*	BCS	9/9/86
	Bass PLC*	BAS	2/8/90
	BET Public Limited Company*	BEP	8/6/87
	British Airways PLC*	BAB	2/11/87
	British Gas PLC*	BRG	12/8/86
	British Petroleum Co. PLC*	BP	3/23/70
	British Steel PLC*	BST	12/5/88
	British Telecommunications PLC*	BTY	12/3/84
	Cable and Wireless Public Limited Co.*	CWP	9/27/89
	Carlton Communications PLC (PFD)	CCMPR	10/19/93
	English China Clays PLC*	ENC	4/30/92
	Enterprise Oil PLC*	ETP	10/16/92
	Enterprise Oil PLC Ser. A* (PFD)	ETPPR	7/20/92
	Enterprise Oil PLC Ser. B* (PFD)	ETPPRB	10/12/92
	Glaxo Holdings PLC*	GLX	6/10/87
	Grand Metropolitan PLC*	GRM	3/13/91
	Hanson PLC*	HAN	11/3/86
	Huntingdon International Holdings PLC*	HTD	2/16/89
	Imperial Chemical Industries PLC*	ICI	11/1/83
	Lasmo PLC*	LSO	6/8/93
	Lasmo PLC Ser. A*	LSOPRA	7/12/93
	Midland Bank PLC* (PFD)	MIBPRA	11/4/93
	National Westminster Bank PLC*	NW	10/22/86
	National Westminster Bank PLC* (PFD)	NWPRA	10/25/91
	National Westminster Bank PLC* (PFD)	NWPRB	6/14/93
	National Westminster Bank PLC (PFD)	NWXPRA	11/29/93
	Royal Bank of Scotland Group PLC*	RBSPR	10/16/89
	Royal Bank of Scotland Group PLC* (PFD)	RBSPRB	8/12/91
	Royal Bank of Scotland Group PLC* (PFD)	RBSPRC	9/28/92
	RTZ Corporation PLC*	RTZ	6/28/90
	Saatchi & Saatchi Company PLC*	SAA	12/8/87
	Shell Transport & Trading Co., PLC**	SC	3/13/57
	SmithKline Beecham PLC* (Class A)	SBH	7/27/89
	SmithKline Beecham PLC* (Class B)	SBE	7/27/89
	Tiphook PLC*	TPH	10/1/91
	Unilever PLC*	UL	12/12/61
	Vodafone Group PLC*	VOD	10/26/88
	Willis Corroon PLC*	WCG	10/9/90
	Wellcome PLC*	WEL	7/27/92
	Waste Management International PLC*	WME	4/7/92
	Zeneca Group PLC*	ZEN	5/12/93
Venezuela	Corimon C.A.*	CRM	3/23/93

* American Depositary Receipts/Shares

** NY Shares and/or Guilder Shares

*** Global Depositary Shares

Source: New York Stock Exchange *Fact Book*.

TOPIX (Tokyo Stock Price Index)

(Jan. 4, 1968=100)

	Year-end	High		Low	
		Index	Date	Index	Date
1950	11.57	13.24	Aug. 21	9.59	July 3
1951	16.94	17.11	Oct. 20	11.58	Jan. 4
1952	33.35	33.55	Nov. 22	17.07	Jan. 8
1953	33.30	42.18	Feb. 4	28.46	Apr. 1
1954	30.27	33.22	Jan. 11	26.79	Nov. 13
1955	39.06	39.06	Dec. 28	30.00	Mar. 28
1956	51.21	52.95	Dec. 6	38.81	Jan. 25
1957	43.40	54.82	Jan. 21	43.18	Dec. 27
1958	60.95	60.95	Dec. 27	43.48	Jan. 4
1959	80.00	90.14	Nov. 30	61.11	Jan. 9
1960	109.18	112.53	Nov. 15	79.46	Jan. 4
1961	101.66	126.59	July 14	90.86	Dec. 19
1962	99.67	111.45	Feb. 14	83.39	Oct. 30
1963	92.87	122.96	May 10	91.21	Dec. 18
1964	90.68	103.77	July 3	87.94	Nov. 11
1965	105.68	105.68	Dec. 28	81.29	July 15
1966	111.41	114.51	Mar. 24	105.21	Jan. 19
1967	100.89	117.60	May 31	99.17	Dec. 11
1968	131.31	142.95	Oct. 2	100.00	Jan. 4
1969	179.30	179.30	Dec. 27	132.62	Jan. 4
1970	148.35	185.70	Apr. 8	147.08	Dec. 9
1971	199.45	209.00	Aug. 14	148.05	Jan. 6
1972	401.70	401.70	Dec. 28	199.93	Jan. 4
1973	306.44	422.48	Jan. 24	284.69	Dec. 18
1974	278.34	342.47	June 5	251.96	Oct. 9
1975	323.43	333.11	July 2	268.24	Jan. 10
1976	383.88	383.88	Dec. 28	326.28	Jan. 5
1977	364.08	390.93	Sept. 29	350.49	Nov. 24
1978	449.55	452.60	Dec. 13	364.04	Jan. 4
1979	459.61	465.24	Sept. 29	435.13	July 13
1980	494.10	497.96	Oct. 20	449.01	Mar. 10
1981	570.31	603.92	Aug. 17	495.79	Jan. 5
1982	593.72	593.72	Dec. 28	511.52	Aug. 17
1983	731.82	731.82	Dec. 28	574.51	Jan. 25
1984	913.37	913.37	Dec. 28	735.45	Jan. 4
1985	1,049.40	1,058.35	July 27	916.93	Jan. 4
1986	1,556.37	1,583.35	Aug. 20	1,025.85	Jan. 21
1987	1,725.83	2,258.56	June 11	1,557.46	Jan. 13
1988	2,357.03	2,357.03	Dec. 28	1,690.44	Jan. 4
1989	2,881.37	2,884.80	Dec. 18	2,364.33	Mar. 27
1990	1,733.83	2,867.70	Jan. 4	1,523.43	Oct. 1
1991	1,714.68	2,028.85	Mar. 18	1,638.06	Dec. 24
1992	1,307.66	1,763.43	Jan. 6	1,102.50	Aug. 18
1993	1,439.31	1,698.67	Sept. 3	1,250.06	Jan. 25

Source: Tokyo Stock Exchange *1994 Fact Book.*

TOKYO STOCK EXCHANGE (TOPIX): 30 Most Active Stocks (Volume and Value), 1993

Rank	Stocks	Volume (mils. of shares)	Rank	Stocks	Value (¥ bils.)
1	NIPPON STEEL	1,514	1	NIPPON TELEGRAPH AND TELEPHONE	2,894
2	NEC	979	2	The Tokyo Electric Power	1,085
3	Sumitomo Metal Mining	922	3	The Nomura Securities	943
4	Mitsubishi Heavy Industries	904	4	JR East	934
5	FUJITSU	903	5	SONY	927
6	NIKKATSU	903	6	NEC	900
7	ISUZU MOTORS	827	7	Sumitomo Metal Mining	891
8	Hitachi	789	8	The Sumitomo Bank	799
9	NKK	681	9	The Mitsubishi Bank	753
10	TOSHIBA	651	10	SEGA ENTERPRISES	686
11	Mitsui Mining and Smelting	621	11	KYOCERA	682
12	Kawasaki Steel	603	12	FUJITSU	682
13	Japan Energy	575	13	Hitachi	652
14	Sumitomo Metal Industries	572	14	The Industrial Bank of Japan	628
15	NIPPON OIL	518	15	Mitsubishi Heavy Industries	589
16	ITOCHU	502	16	Matsushita Electric Industries	588
17	The Nomura Securities	488	17	The Sanwa Bank	578
18	TOKYO GAS	476	18	The Dai-Ichi Kangyo Bank	564
19	Fujikura	458	19	Sharp	537
20	Oki Electric Industries	452	20	NIPPON STEEL	534
21	Hitachi Zosen	443	21	TOYOTA MOTOR	533
22	Matsushita Electric Industries	441	22	SANKYO	521
23	Nippon Yusen	428	23	The Fuji Bank	488
24	NIPPON EXPRESS	427	24	CANON	459
25	Keisei Electric Railway	421	25	Keisei Electric Railway	458
26	The Furukawa Electric	413	26	The Tokio Marine and Fire Insurance	448
27	RICOH	413	27	Ito-Yokado	445
28	Sharp	410	28	TOSHIBA	443
29	Kawasaki Heavy Industries	403	29	NIPPON EXPRESS	417
30	Marubeni	391	30	The Nikko Securities	414

Total Trading Volume of the 30 stocks (A)	18,542	A/B	Total Trading Value of the 30 stocks (C)	21,486	C/D
Total Trading Volume of all stocks (B)	86,934	21.3%	Total Trading Value of all stocks (D)	86,889	24.7%

Source: Tokyo Stock Exchange *1994 Fact Book.*

TOKYO STOCK EXCHANGE (TOPIX): Yields and Dividends

	All 1st Section Stocks	1st Section Dividend-Paying Stocks		
	Weighted Average Yields (%)	Average Dividend per Share (¥)	Total Amount of Dividends (¥ mil.)	Simple Average Yields (%)
1951	...	10.69	28,264	11.91
1952	...	12.88	41,311	9.85
1953	...	11.17	52,414	7.44
1954	...	9.89	60,499	9.44
1955	...	8.70	69,734	7.96
1956	...	8.27	85,109	6.68
1957	...	7.71	113,006	7.14
1958	...	7.14	122,938	6.66
1959	4.68	6.76	138,102	4.54
1960	4.27	6.71	174,225	3.93
1961	4.47	6.63	230,781	3.24
1962	5.82	6.47	307,253	3.86
1963	5.08	6.26	348,900	4.24
1964	6.01	6.26	391,501	5.69
1965	6.01	6.08	409,041	5.92
1966	4.76	5.92	407,890	4.44
1967	4.96	5.97	456,892	4.74
1968	5.00	6.09	506,603	4.36
1969	4.19	6.28	569,413	3.37
1970	4.30	6.55	647,271	3.52
1971	4.01	6.65	710,819	3.41
1972	2.42	6.55	717,714	2.24
1973	2.02	6.75	849,748	2.09
1974	2.55	6.88	912,452	2.53
1975	2.54	6.51	881,019	2.31
1976	2.27	6.25	995,343	1.91
1977	2.16	6.34	1,040,454	1.82
1978	2.00	6.45	1,090,007	1.60
1979	1.87	6.49	1,191,842	1.57
1980	1.79	6.58	1,200,537	1.63
1981	1.65	6.69	1,498,879	1.55
1982	1.80	6.80	1,525,765	1.68
1983	1.55	6.88	1,594,659	1.39
1984	1.24	7.11	1,709,559	1.09
1985	1.05	7.25	1,829,277	0.99
1986	0.83	7.33	1,850,248	0.78
1987	0.56	7.36	2,042,359	0.63
1988	0.52	7.52	2,298,464	0.55
1989	0.46	7.78	2,495,041	0.47
1990	0.61	8.04	2,825,580	0.52
1991	0.73	8.21	2,761,480	0.64
1992	0.99	8.21	2,297,172	0.90
1993	0.86	8.16	2,572,525	0.82

Note: Total amount of dividends for 1993 is that of the sum from Jan. to Nov.

Source: Tokyo Stock Exchange *1994 Fact Book.*

TOPIX: Average Compound Annual Rates of Return on Common Stocks (1st Section)

(%)

To	From 1983	1984	1985	1986	1987	1988	1989	1990	1991	1992
1984	29.4									
1985	28.2	27.0								
1986	32.0	33.4	40.1							
1987	35.4	37.5	43.1	46.2						
1988	31.0	31.4	32.9	29.4	14.6					
1989	29.5	29.6	30.2	27.1	18.5	22.4				
1990	21.8	20.5	19.3	14.6	5.7	1.4	–15.9			
1991	17.0	15.4	13.5	8.9	1.1	–3.0	–13.6	–11.3		
1992	11.4	9.4	7.1	2.4	–4.7	–9.0	–17.5	–18.3	–24.8	
1993(P)	11.6	9.7	7.8	3.8	–2.0	–5.0	–10.8	–9.0	–7.9	12.8

Source: Japan Securities Research Institute

Note: The Tokyo Stock Exchange is divided into three sections. Sections 1 and 2 are made up of Japanese companies. Section 3, known as the foreign section is comprised of non-Japanese stocks.

Source: Tokyo Stock Exchange *1994 Fact Book.*

DOLLAR VOLUME OF EQUITY TRADING IN MAJOR WORLD MARKETS: 1993

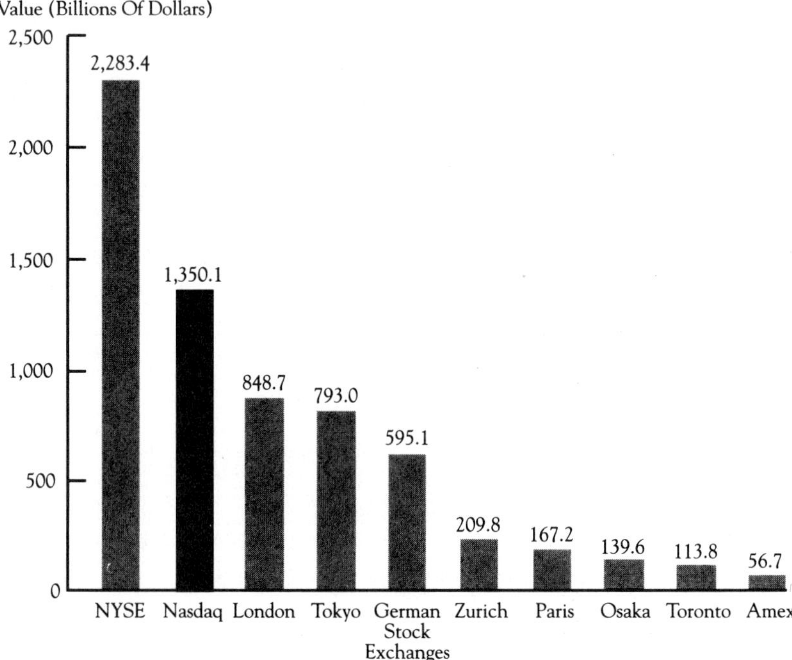

Source: *1994 NASDAQ FACT BOOK & COMPANY DIRECTORY,* published by the National Association of Securities Dealers, Inc., 1735 K Street N.W., Washington, D.C. 20006-1500.

FOREIGN COMPANIES AND ADR ISSUERS—NASDAQ, NYSE, AND AMEX: 1993

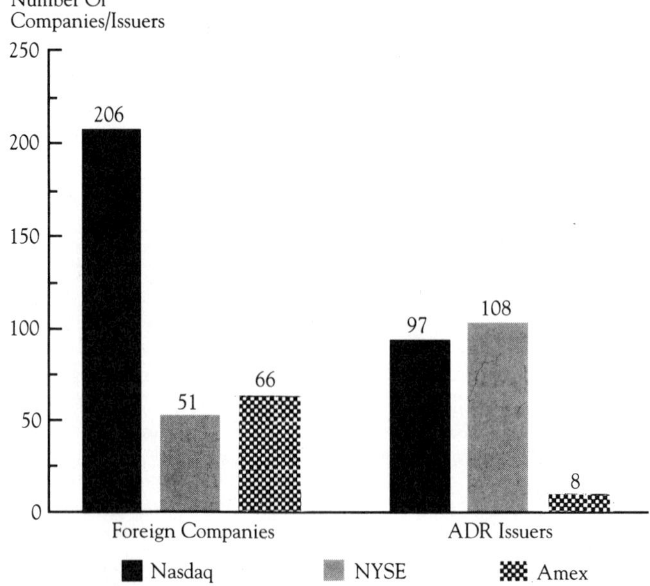

Source: *1994 NASDAQ FACT BOOK & COMPANY DIRECTORY,* published by the National Association of Securities Dealers, Inc., 1735 K Street N.W., Washington, D.C. 20006-1500.

Securities Markets: Notable Dates

1792 Original brokers' agreement subscribed to by 24 brokers (May 17).
1817 Constitution and the name "New York Stock Exchange Board" adopted (March 8).
1830 Dullest day in history of exchange—31 shares traded (March 16).
1840s Outdoor trading in unlisted securities begins at Wall and Hanover Streets, moves to Wall and Broad, then shifts south along Broad Street.*
1863 Name changed to "New York Stock Exchange" (NYSE) (January 29).
1867 Stock tickers first introduced (November 15).
1868 Membership made salable (October 23).
1869 Exchange required registering of securities by listed companies to prevent their over-issuance (February 1).
NYSE and Open Board of Brokers adopted plan of consolidation (May 8).
Gold speculation resulted in "Black Friday" (September 24).
1871 Continuous markets in stocks established.
1873 NYSE closed September 18–29.
Failure of Jay Cooke & Co. and others (September 18).
Trading hours set at 10 A.M. to 3 P.M.; Saturdays, 10 A.M. to noon (December 1).
1878 First telephones introduced in the exchange (November 13).
1881 Annunciator board installed for paging members (January 29).
1885 Unlisted Securities Department established (March 25).
1886 First million-share day—1,200,000 shares traded (December 15).
1895 Exchange recommended that companies listed or traded publish and distribute to stockholders annual statements showing income and balance sheet (January 23).
Exchange occupied new building with present trading floor at 18 Broad Street (April 23).
Call money loaned as high as 125%, following suspension of payments by Knickerbocker Trust Company on previous day. This period was generally known as panic of 1907 (October 23).
1908 E. S. Mendels forms New York Curb Agency in first departure from informal trading.*
1910 Unlisted Securities Department abolished (March 31).
1911 Trading rules established with formation of New York Curb Market Association.*
1914 Exchange closed from July 31 through December 11—World War I.
1915 Stock prices quoted in dollars as against percent of par value (October 13).
1919 Separate ticker system installed for bonds (January 2).
1920 Stock Clearing Corporation established (April 26).
1921 New York Curb Market association moves indoors at 86 Trinity Place; name shortened to New York Curb Market and ticker service initiated (June 21).*
1924 Sliding scale of commission rates adopted.
1927 Start of ten-share unit of trading for inactive stocks (January 3).
1929 Stock market crash; 16,410,000 shares traded (October 29).
New York Curb Market modifies its name to New York Curb Exchange.*
1930 Faster ticker—500 characters per minute—installed (September 2).
1931 Exchange building expanded; Telephone Quotation Department formed to send stock quotes to member firm offices.*
1933 Exchange announced formal adoption of rule requiring independent audit of statements of listed companies (January 6).
New York Stock Exchange closed for bank holiday, March 4–14.
Securities Act of 1933 enacted. Its two basic purposes: to provide full disclosure to investors and to prohibit fraud in connection with the sale of securities (May 27).
1934 Enactment of Securities Exchange Act of 1934 (June 6).
1938 First salaried president elected—Wm. McChesney Martin, Jr. (June 30).
1946 Listed stocks outnumber unlisted stocks for first time since the 1934 act imposed restrictions on unlisted trading.*
1952 Trading hours changed: weekdays, 10 A.M. to 3:30 P.M. Closed Saturdays (September 29).
1953 Name of New York Curb Exchange

* Refers to American Exchange (AMEX).

† Applies to both the New York Stock Exchange and the American Exchange.

Sources: New York Stock Exchange *Fact Book*, American Stock Exchange *Data Book* and *The Wall Street Journal*.

changed to American Stock Exchange.*

1958 First member corporation—Woodcock, Hess & Co. (June 4).

Mary C. Roebling becomes first woman governor.*

1962 Committee system of administration replaced by expanded paid staff reporting to president. Specialist system strengthened, surveillance of trading increased, listing and delisting standards introduced, and board restructured to give greater representation to commission and out-of-town brokers.*

1964 New member classification—Registered Trader (August 3).

New ticker—900 characters per minute—put into service (December 1).†

Am-Quote computerized telephone-quotation service was completed as first step in major automation program.*

1965 Fully automated quotation service introduced (March 8).

Electronic Systems Center created (October 15).

First women, Phyllis S. Peterson and Julia Montgomery Walsh, elected to regular membership.*

1966 New NYSE Composite Index inaugurated (July 14).

AMEX Price Change Index System introduced; computer complex installed for ticker, surveillance, and compared-clearance operations.*

1967 First woman member admitted—Muriel F. Siebert (December 28).

1968 Ticker speed increased to maximum 900 characters per minute; transmission begun to six European countries. Trading floor modernized; line capacity for communications doubled. Visitors gallery expanded.*

1969 Central Certificate Service fully activated (February 26).

1970 Public ownership of member firms approved (March 26).

Securities Investor Protection Corporation Act signed (December 30).

1971 New York Stock Exchange Incorporated (February 18).

First negotiated commission rates effective (April 5).

First member organization listed—Merrill Lynch (July 27).

AMEX incorporates and marks 50th anniversary of move indoors; Listed Company Advisory Committee formed, composed of nine chief executives of AMEX-listed companies.

1972 NYSE reorganization, based on Martin Report, approved (January 20).

Board of Directors, with ten public members, replaced Board of Governors (July 13).

Securities Industry Automation Corporation established with AMEX to consolidate facilities of both exchanges (July 17).*

First salaried chairman took office—James J. Needham (August 28).

Board of Governors reorganized to include ten public and ten industry representatives plus full-time salaried chairman as chief executive officer.*

1973 Depository Trust Company succeeded Central Certificate Service (May 11).

Chicago Board of Options Exchange opened with trading in 16 classes of call options (April 26).

AMEX formally adopts affirmative action employment plan; Market Value Index System introduced to replace Price Change Index.

1974 Trading hours extended to 4 P.M. (October 1).

Consolidated tape begun; 15 stocks reported (October 18).

1975 Fixed commission system abolished (April 30).

Full consolidated tape begun (June 16).

AMEX trades call options.

Trading begins in call options and odd lots of U.S. government instruments.*

1976 New data line installed, handling 36,000 characters per minute (January 19).

Specialists began handling odd lots in their stocks (May 24).

Varo, Inc.—first stock traded on both NYSE and AMEX (August 23).

Competition between specialists begun (October 11).

1977 Independent audit committee on listed companies' boards required (January 6).

Competitive Trader category for members approved (January 19).

National Securities Clearing Corporation (NSCC) began merging the clearing operations of the Stock Clearing Corporation of NYSE with American Stock Exchange Clearing Corporation and National Clearing Corporation of the NASD (January 20).

Foreign broker/dealers permitted to obtain membership (February 3).

Full Automated Bond System in effect (July 27).

1978 First 60 million share day in history (63,493,000 shares) (April 17).
Intermarket Trading System (ITS) began.
Registered Competitive Market-Maker category for members approved (May 2).
First 65 million share day in history (66,370,000 shares) (August 3).
Trading in Ginnie Maes inaugurated on the AMEX Commodities Exchange (ACE) (September 12).
AMEX reached an index high of 176.87 (September 13).

1979 Trading began at pilot post on the exchange floor. First stage in a $12-million upgrading of exchange facilities (January 29).
Board of Directors of NYSE approved plan for the creation of the New York Futures Exchange, a wholly owned subsidiary of NYSE. Futures contracts in seven financial instruments will be traded on the NYSE (March 1).
New York Commodities Exchange and NYSE terminated merger talks (March 15).
81,619,000 shares were traded on the NYSE, making it the heaviest trade day in exchange history (October 10).

1980 American Stock Exchange reached an all-time daily stock volume record of 14,980,680 shares sold (January 15).
NYSE volume of 67,752,000 shares traded was second largest volume on record to date (January 16).
NYSE Futures Exchange opened (August 7).
Option seat on the American Stock Exchange sold at an all-time high of $160,000 (December 24).
NYSE index reached an all time high of 81.02 (November 28).

1981 First 90 million share day in the history of the Exchange, 92,881,000 (January 7).
The New York Stock Exchange subsidiary, the New York Futures Exchange, started trading futures in Domestic Bank Certificates of Deposit.

1982 A new AMEX subsidiary, The American Gold Coin Exchange (AGCE), began trading in the Canadian Maple Leaf (January 21).
Trading in NYSE Composite Index Futures began on the New York Futures Exchange (May 6).
Trading started through experimental linkage between ITS operated by NYSE and six other exchanges and Computer Assisted Execution Service (CAES) operated by NASD, in 30 stocks exempted from exchange off-board trading rules under SEC Rule 19c-3. (May 17).
Record advance of 38.81 points reached in NYSE trading as measured by Dow Jones Industrial Average (August 17).
First 100 million share day (132,681,120 shares. (August 18).
Trading in Interest Rate Options on U.S. Treasury Bills & Notes started in May on the AMEX.
Trading soared to an all time high of 147,081,070 shares on the NYSE (October 7).
All time options high of 340,550 contracts were traded on the AMEX (October 7).
Dow Jones Industrial Average plunged 36.33 points, the largest one-day loss since the record plunge of 38.33 points on October 28, 1929 (October 25).

1983 Trading in options on NYSE Common Stock Index Futures started on New York Futures Exchange (January 28).
NYSE started trading options on the NYSE Common Stock Index (September 23).
Dow Jones Industrial Average reached an all time high of 1260.77 (September 26).
New shares of common stocks of seven regional telephone companies and shares of the "new" AT&T began trading on a "when issued" basis. Divestiture of AT&T effective January 1, 1984 (November 21).
AMEX stock trading went over the two billion share mark for the first time.*
The AMEX list of stock options increased by four index options, two on specific industry groups, one on the AMEX Market Value Index.*

1984 Largest NYSE trading day of 159,999,031 shares traded (January 5).
CBOT (Chicago Board of Trade) began trading a futures contract on the Major Market Index (July 23).
Trading began in NYSE Double Index Options (July 23).
NYSE volume soared to a record 236,565,110 shares traded (August 3).
NYSE opened on Presidential Election Day for first time ever.
Super DOT 250 (electronic order-

routing system) launched on NYSE (November 16).

1985 For the first time the NYSE index went over 100, closing at 101.12 (January 21).

19,091,950 shares were traded on the AMEX, the highest single day volume ever (February 6).

Ronald Reagan visited the NYSE, the first President to do so while in office (March 28).

Trading in options on gold bullion started on AMEX (April 26).

50 billionth share listed in NYSE (May 30).

NYSE began trading options in three over-the-counter stocks (June 3).

NYSE reached an all time index high of 113.49 (July 17).

Amex and Toronto Stock Exchange linked together as part of the first two-way electronic hookup between primary equity markets in different countries (September 24).

Instinet Corporation and the AMEX reached an agreement enabling European institutional investors to have access to the AMEX options market via Reuter's electronic terminals.

The opening trading time on both the NYSE and AMEX went from 10:00 A.M. to 9:30 A.M. (September 30).

The Dow Jones Industrial Average reached an all-time high of 1368.50 (October 16).

Options traded on two listed stocks on the NYSE (October 21).

Tokyo Stock Exchange admitted its first foreign member firms (December 1).

A daily record of 119,969 contracts traded on the AMEX Major Markets Index Option (December 13).

1986 The Dow Jones Industrial Average for the first time closed above 1600 at 1600.69 (February 6).

The Dow Jones Industrial Average for the first time closed above 1700 at 1713.99. (February 27).

The Dow Jones Industrial Average for the first time closed above 1800 at 1804.24 (March 20).

NYSE began trading the NYSE Beta Index Option (May 22).

NYSE Board of Directors expanded to 24 outside directors: 12 public members and 12 industry members (June 5).

New York Futures Exchange (NYFE) began trading the Commodity Research Bureau (CRB) index futures contract (June 12).

The Dow Jones Industrial Average for the first time closed above 1900 at 1903.54 (July 1).

The Directors of the NYSE voted to abandon the one-share-one-vote rule which gives common shareholders equal voting rights (July 3).

The Dow Jones Industrials nose-dived a record 86.61 points on a record volume of 237,600,000 shares traded (September 11).

$600,000.00 (the highest price ever) was paid for membership in the NYSE (December 1).

1987 The Dow Jones industrials passed the 2000 mark, closing at 2000.25 (January 8).

The Dow Jones Industrials closed above 2300 for the first time, up 33.95 points to 2333.52 (March 20).

The Dow Jones Industrials climbed above 2400 for the first time to close at 2405.54 (April 7).

Foreign currency warrants began trading (June 11).

The Chicago Board of Trade and the Chicago Board Options Exchange agreed to permit members of both exchanges to trade financial futures and options contracts side by side (June 25).

For the first time the Dow Jones Industrials closed over 2500 at 2510.04 (July 16).

AMEX Market Value closed at the all-time high of 365.0 (August 13).

A gain of 15.14 points brought the Dow Jones Industrials above 2700 points for the first time with the market closing at 2700.52 (August 17).

Dow Jones industrial average set a record at 2722.42 (August 25).

New York Futures Exchange began to trade the Russell 2000 and Russell 3000® Stock Index futures contracts (September 10).

A price of $1,150,000 was paid for a member of the NYSE, the highest ever (September 21).

The stock market 'crashed' with the Dow Jones Industrials down 508.00 points or 22% to close at 1738.74 on a record volume of 604.3 shares. Other record declines were: Dow Jones transportations off 164.78; utilities off 29.16; the S & P 500 stock index off 57.86; the AMEX index down 41.05, the NYSE down 30.51, and the NASDAQ composite of over-the-counter stocks off 46.12 (October 19).

A record volume of 608,148,710 shares

traded on the NYSE and 43,432,760 on the AMEX (October 20).

The Dow Jones Industrials rocketed 186.84 points, the highest ever, on a volume of 449,350,000 shares (October 21).

The AMEX Market Value Index registered its largest increase ever, 23.81 (October 21).

1988 343,949,330 shares were traded on the NYSE, making it the highest volume day to date since the 'crash' of 1987 (June 17).

The SEC approved a series of initiatives by the NYSE and the Chicago Mercantile Exchange to coordinate procedures between the equities and futures markets, including coordinated circuit breakers; a joint effort against front-running; inter-exchange communications; and shared audit trail and surveillance information (October 19).

The NYSE opened an office in London to assist European companies in gaining access to the U.S. capital markets and listing on the NYSE (November 7).

1989 Dow Jones industrials established a record high of 2734.64 (August 25).

The Dow Jones industrials plunged 190.58 points to 2569.26 (October 13).

The NYSE launched a new trading vehicle, the Exchange Stock Portfolio, which enables the trading of a standardized basket of stocks in a single execution (October 26).

The NYSE created a blue-ribbon panel to study market volatility and investor confidence (December 7).

The DJIA peaked to a record 2810.12 (December 29).

1990 The Dow Jones industrials closed above 2900 for the first time (June 4).

NYSE Market Volatility and Investor Confidence Panel released a study recommending initiatives for reducing market volatility and enhancing investor confidence.

The NYSE implemented a new rule requiring Trade Date + 1 (T+1) for the completion of transactions effected on the NYSE (August 6).

NYSE approved two crossing sessions which will extend trading hours to 5:15 P.M. (September 11).

1991 For the first time the Dow Jones industrials closed above 3,000 at 3,0004.46 on a volume of 246.9 million shares (April 17).

Dow Jones industrials rose to a record 3035.33 (June 4).

NYSE extended trading hours to 5:15 P.M. with two crossing sessions (June 13).

1992 For the first time the Dow Jones industrials closed over 3400 to reach a high of 3413.21 (June 1).

Globex, an after hours electronic system for trading options and futures on the Chicago Board of Trade and the Chicago Mercantile Exchange went into operation (June 25).

The New York Stock Exchange's "clean cross" rule allows large institutional investors to bypass floor trades by "crossing" trades of 25,000 shares or more between customers while ignoring orders placed at the same price by investors on the floor. A broker will have to accept a floor order if it is at a better price (October 26).

AMEX launched Emerging Company Marketplace.*

1993 Dow Jones Industrials plunged 82.94 to 3309.49, the biggest one day decline since November 15, 1991 (February 16).

The NASDAQ Composite Index had its worst decline since October 26, 1987 and closed at 665.39 (February 16).

The Dow Jones Industrials soared 55.65 points to reach a record of 3500.03 on the ninth heaviest trading day on the "Big Board" to date (May 19).

The Dow Jones Industrial Average hit a record high of 3604.83 (August 18).

The AMEX Market Value Index hit a record high of 484.28 (November 2).*

The Dow Jones Industrial Average closed above the 3700 mark at 3710.77 for the first time (November 17).

1994 The Dow Jones Industrial Average broke through the 3800 level and closed at 3803.88 (January 7).

Closing above the 3900 level for the first time, the Dow Jones Industrial Average reached 3914.48 (January 23).

Investment and Financial Terms

Accelerated Cost Recovery System (ACRS) A system that specifies the allowable depreciation recovery period for different types of assets. The normal recovery period is generally shorter than that allowed before the passage of the 1981 Economic Recovery Tax Act.*

Accruals Recurring continuous short-term liabilities. Examples are accrued wages and accrued interest.

Accrued interest Interest accrued on a bond since the last interest payment was made. The buyer of the bond pays the market price plus accrued interest. Exceptions include bonds that are in default and income bonds. (See: *Flat income bond.*)†

Acquisition The acquiring of control of one corporation by another. In "unfriendly" takeover attempts, the potential buying company may offer a price well above current market values, new securities and other inducements to stockholders. The management of the subject company might ask for a better price or try to join up with a third company. (See: *Merger, Proxy.*)††

Ad valorem tax A tax based on the value (or assessed value) of property.**

Aging of accounts receivable Analyzing accounts by the amount of time they have been on the books.*

American Depository Receipt (ADR) Issued by American banks, an ADR is a certificate which serves as a proxy for a foreign stock deposited in a foreign bank. For all practical purposes, trading an ADR is equivalent to trading the foreign stock. Hundreds of ADRs are traded on U.S. stock exchange.

Amortization Accounting for expenses or charges as applicable rather than as paid. Includes such practices as depreciation, depletion, write-off of intangibles, prepaid expenses, and deferred charges.†

Annual report The formal financial statement issued yearly by a corporation. The annual report shows assets, liabilities, earnings—how the company stood at the close of the business year, how it fared profit-wise during the year and other information of interest to shareowners.†

Arbitrage A technique employed to take advantage of differences in price. If, for example, ABC stock can be bought in New York for $10 a share and sold in London at $10.50, an arbitrageur may simultaneously purchase ABC stock here and sell the same amount in London, making a profit of 50 cents a share, less expenses. Arbitrage may also involve the purchase of rights to subscribe to a security, or the purchase of a convertible security—and the sale at or about the same time of the security obtainable through exercise of the rights or of the security obtainable through conversion.

Arrearage Overdue payment; frequently omitted dividend on preferred stock.

Assessed valuation The valuation placed on property for purposes of taxation.**

Asset-based public offerings Public offerings backed by receivables as collateral. Essentially, a firm factors (sells) its receivables in the securities markets.*

Assets Everything a corporation owns or due to it: Cash, investments, money due it, materials and inventories, which are called current assets; buildings and machinery, which are known as fixed assets; and patents and good will, called intangible assets. (See: *Liabilities.*)†

Asset utilization ratios A group of ratios that measures the speed at which the firm is turning over or utilizing its assets. We measure inventory turnover, fixed asset turnover, total asset turnover, and the average time it takes to collect accounts receivable.*

Assignment The liquidation of assets without going through formal court procedures. In order to affect an assignment, creditors must agree on liquidation values and the relative priority of claims.*

Assignment Notice to an option writer that an option holder has exercised the option and that the writer will now be required to deliver (receive) under the terms of the contract.††

Ask (See: *Bid and asked.*)†

Auction market The system of trading securities through brokers or agents on an exchange such as the New York Stock Exchange. Buyers compete with other buyers

---

* Entries from *Foundations of Financial Management.*

† Entries from *The Language of Investing Glossary.*

** Entries from *Tax-Exempt Securities & the Investor.*

†† Entries from the *Glossary.*

¶ Entries from the Federal Reserve *Glossary.*

Source: *Foundations of Financial Management,* 5th edition by Stanley B. Block and Geoffrey A. Hirt, Irwin, Homewood, IL 1989.

The *Language of Investing Glossary* published by the New York Stock Exchange, Inc.

The *Glossary* published by the New York Stock Exchange.

Tax-Exempt Securities & the Investor published by the Securities Industry Association.

The *Glossary* published by the Board of Governors of the Federal Reserve System.

while sellers compete with other sellers for the most advantageous price.††

Auditor's report Often called the accountant's opinion, it is the statement of the accounting firm's work and its opinion of the corporation's financial statements, especially if they conform to the normal and generally accepted practices of accountancy.††

Automated clearinghouse (ACH) An ACH transfers information between one financial institution and another and from account to account via computer tape. There are approximately 30 regional clearinghouses throughout the United States that claim the membership of over 10,000 financial institutions.*

Average collection period The average amount of time accounts receivable have been on the books. It may be computed by dividing accounts receivable by average daily credit sales.*

Averages Various ways of measuring the trend of securities prices, one of the most popular of which is the Dow-Jones average of 30 industrial stocks listed on the New York Stock Exchange. The prices of the 30 stocks are totaled and then divided by a divisor which is intended to compensate for past stock splits and stock dividends and which is changed from time to time. As a result point changes in the average have only the vaguest relationship to dollar price changes in stocks included in the average. (See: *NYSE composite index*.)††

Balance of payments The term refers to a system of government accounts that catalogs the flow of economic transactions between countries.*

Balance sheet A condensed financial statement showing the nature and amount of a company's assets, liabilities and capital on a given date. In dollar amounts the balance sheet shows what the company owned, what it owed, and the ownership interest in the company of its stockholders. (See: *Assets, Earnings report*.)†

Bankers acceptance Bankers acceptances are negotiable time drafts, or bills of exchange, that have been accepted by a bank which, by accepting, assumes the obligation to pay the holder of the draft the face amount of the instrument on the maturity date specified. They are used primarily to finance the export, import, shipment, or storage of goods.¶

Bankruptcy The market value of a firm's assets are less than its liabilities, and the firm has a negative net worth. The term is also used to describe in-court procedures associated with the reorganization or liquidation of a firm.*

Basis book A book of mathematical tables used to convert yields to equivalent dollar prices.**

Basis point One gradation on a 100-point scale representing one percent; used especially in expressing variations in the yields of bonds. Fixed income yields vary often and slightly within one percent and the basis point scale easily expresses these changes in hundredths of one percent. For example, the difference between 12.83% and 12.88% is 5 basis points.††

Basis price The price expressed in yield or percentage of return on the investment.**

Bear market A declining market. (See: *Bull market*.)†

Bearer bond A bond which does not have the owner's name registered on the books of the issuer and which is payable to the holder. (See: *Coupon bond, Registered bond*.)†

Bearer security A security that has no identification as to owner. It is presumed to be owned, therefore, by the bearer or the person who holds it. Bearer securities are freely and easily negotiable since ownership can be quickly transferred from seller to buyer.**

Beta A measure of the volatility of returns on an individual stock relative to the market. Stocks with a beta of 1.0 are said to have risk equal to that of the market (equal volatility). Stocks with betas greater than 1.0 have more risk than the market, while those with betas of less than 1.0 have less risk than the market.*

Bid and asked Often referred to as a quotation or quote. The bid is the highest price anyone has declared that he wants to pay for a security at a given time, the asked is the lowest price anyone will take at the same time. (See: *Quote*.)†

Blanket inventory liens A secured borrowing arrangement in which the lender has a general claim against the inventory of the borrower.*

Block A large holding or transaction of stock—popularly considered to be 10,000 shares or more.†

Blue chip A company known nationally for the quality and wide acceptance of its products or services, and for its ability to make money and pay dividends.†

Blue-sky laws A popular name for laws various states have enacted to protect the public against securities frauds. The term is believed to have originated when a judge ruled that a particular stock had about the same value as a patch of blue sky.†

Board room A room for registered representatives and customers in a broker's office where opening, high, low, and last prices of leading stocks used to be posted on a board throughout the market day. Today such price displays are normally electronically controlled although most board rooms have replaced the board with the ticker and/or individual quotation machines.†

Bond Basically an IOU or promissory note of a corporation, usually issued in multiples of $1,000 or $5,000, although $100 and $500 denominations are not unknown. A bond is evidence of a debt on which the issuing company usually promises to pay the bondholders a specified amount of interest for a specified length of time, and to repay the loan on the expiration date. In every case a bond represents debt—its holder is a creditor of the corporation and not a part owner as is the shareholder. (See: *Collateral*, *Convertible security*, *Debenture*, *General Mortgage Bond*, *Income Bond*.)††

Bond ratings Bonds are rated according to risk by Standard & Poor's and Moody's Investor Service. A bond that is rated Aaa by Moody's has the lowest risk, while a bond with a C rating has the highest risk. Coupon rates are greatly influenced by a corporation's bond rating.*

Book A notebook the specialist in a stock uses to keep a record of the buy and sell orders at specified prices, in sequence of receipt, which are left with him by other brokers. (See *Specialist*.)†

Book value (See: *Net worth*.)

Break-even analysis A numerical and graphical technique that is used to determine at what point the firm will break even (revenue = cost). To compute the break-even point, we divide fixed costs by price minus variable cost per unit.*

Broker An agent, who handles the public's orders to buy and sell securities, commodities, or other property. For this service a commission is charged. (See: *Commission broker*, *Dealer*.)†

Brokers' loans Money borrowed by brokers from banks or other brokers for a variety of uses. It may be used by specialists and to help finance inventories of stock they deal in; by brokerage firms to finance the underwriting of new issues of corporate and municipal securities; to help finance a firm's own investments; and to help finance the purchase of securities for customers who prefer to use the broker's credit when they buy securities. (See: *Margin*.)†

Bull market An advancing market. (See: *Bear market*.)†

Call (1) The right (option) to buy a share of stock at a specified price within a given time period (see options). (2) The redemption of a bond or preferred stock before its normal maturity.

Call feature Used for bonds and some preferred stock. A call allows the corporation to retire securities before maturity by forcing the bondholders to sell bonds back to it at a set price. The call provisions are included in the bond indenture.*

Call premium The premium paid by a corporation to call in a bond issue before the maturity date.*

Callable A bond issue, all or part of which may be redeemed by the issuing corporation under definite conditions before maturity. The term also applies to preferred shares which may be redeemed by the issuing corporation.†

Capital Sources of long-term financing that are available to the business firm.*

Capital asset pricing model A model that relates the risk-return trade offs of individual assets to market returns. A security is presumed to receive a risk-free rate of return plus a premium for risk.*

Capital gain or capital loss Profit or loss from the sale of a capital asset. A capital gain, under current federal income tax laws, may be either short-term (12 months or less) or long-term (more than 12 months). A short-term capital gain is taxed at the reporting individual's full income tax rate. A long-term capital gain is subject to a lower tax. The capital gains provisions of the tax law are complicated. You should consult your tax advisor for specific information.†

Capital lease A long-term, noncancelable lease that has many of the characteristics of debt. Under FASB *Statement No. 13*, the lease obligation must be shown directly on the balance sheet.*

Capital markets Competitive markets for equity securities or debt securities with maturities of more than one year. The best examples of capital market securities are common stock, bonds, and preferred stock.*

Capital rationing Occurs when a corporation has more dollars of capital budgeting projects with positive net present values than it has money to invest in them. Therefore, some projects that should be accepted are excluded because financial capital is rationed.*

Capital stock All shares representing ownership of a business, including preferred and common. (See: *Common stock*, *Preferred stock*.)†

Capitalization Total amount of the various

securities issued by a corporation. Capitalization may include bonds, debentures, preferred and common stock, and surplus. Bonds and debentures are usually carried on the books of the issuing company in terms of their par or face value. Preferred and common shares may be carried in terms of par or stated value. Stated value may be an arbitrary figure decided upon by the directors or may represent the amount received by the company from the sale of the securities at the time of issuance. (See: *Par*.)†

Carrying costs The cost to hold an asset, usually inventory. For inventory, carrying costs include such items as interest, warehousing costs, insurance, and material-handling expenses.*

Cash budget A series of monthly or quarterly budgets that indicate cash receipts, cash payments, and the borrowing requirements for meeting financial requirements. It is constructed from the pro forma income statement and other supportive schedules.*

Cash flow Reported net income of a corporation *plus* amounts charged off for depreciation, depletion, amortization, extraordinary charges to reserves, which are bookkeeping deductions and not paid out in actual dollars and cents. (See: *Amortization, Depreciation.*)††

Cash sale A transaction on the floor of the Stock Exchange which calls for delivery of the securities the same day. In "regular way" trades, the seller is to deliver on the fifth business day except for bonds, which is the next day.

Certificate The actual piece of paper which is evidence of ownership of stock in a corporation. Watermarked paper is finely engraved with delicate etchings to discourage forgery.††

Certificate of Deposit (CD) A money market instrument issued by banks. The time CD is characterized by its set date of maturity and interest rate and its wide acceptance among investors, companies and institutions as a highly negotiable short-term investment vehicle.††

CFTC The Commodity Futures Trading Commission, created by Congress in 1974 to regulate exchange trading in futures.††

Clientele effect The effect of investor preferences for dividends or capital gains. Investors tend to purchase securities that meet their needs.*

Coefficient of correlation The degree of associated movement between two or more variables. Variables that move in the same direction are said to be positively correlated, while negatively correlated variables move in opposite directions.*

Coefficient of variation A measure of risk determination that is computed by dividing the standard deviation for a series of numbers by the expected value. Generally, the larger the coefficient of variation, the greater the risk.*

Collateral trust bond A bond secured by collateral deposited with a trustee. The collateral is often the stocks or bonds of companies controlled by the issuing company but may be other securities.†

Combined leverage The total or combined impact of operating and financial leverage.

Commercial paper An unsecured promissory note that large corporations issue to investors. The minimum amount is usually $25,000.*

Commission The broker's basic fee for purchasing or selling securities or property as an agent.†

Commission broker An agent who executes the public's orders for the purchase or sale of securities or commodities.†

Commodities (See: *Futures*.)

Common equity The common stock or ownership capital of the firm. Common equity may be supplied through retained earnings or the sale of new common stock.*

Common stock Securities which represent an ownership interest in a corporation. If the company has also issued preferred stock, both common and preferred have ownership rights. Common stockholders assume the greater risk, but generally exercise the greater control and may gain the greater reward in the form of dividends and capital appreciation. The terms of common stock and capital stock are often used interchangeably when the company has no preferred stock.†

Common stock equivalent Warrants, options, and any convertible securities that pay less than two thirds of the average Aa bond yield at the time of issue.*

Common stockholder Holders of common stock are the owners of the company. Common stockholders elect the members of the board of directors, who in turn help select the top management.*

Compensating balances A bank requirement that business customers maintain a minimum average balance. The required amount is usually computed as a percentage of customer loans outstanding or as a percentage of the future loans to which the bank has committed itself.*

Competitive trader A member of the Exchange who trades in stocks on the Floor for an account in which he has an interest. Also known as a Registered Trader.†

Composition An out-of-court settlement in which creditors agree to accept a fractional settlement on their original claim.*

Compound sum The future value of a single amount or an annuity when compounded at a given interest rate for a specified time period.*

Conglomerate A corporation that has diversified its operations, usually by acquiring enterprises in widely varied industries.†

Consolidated balance sheet A balance sheet showing the financial condition of a corporation and its subsidiaries. (See: *Balance sheet.*)†

Consolidated tape The ticket tape reporting transactions in NYSE listed securities that take place on the NYSE or any of the participating regional stock exchanges and other markets. Similarly, transactions in AMEX-listed securities, and certain other securities listed on regional stock exchanges, are reported and identified on a separate tape.††

Consolidation The combination of two or more firms, generally of equal size and market power, to form an entirely new entity.*

Constant dollar accounting One of two methods of inflation-adjusted accounting that have been approved by the Financial Accounting Standards Board. Financial statements are adjusted to present prices, using the consumer price index. This is shown as supplemental information in the firm's annual report.*

Consumer price index An economic indicator published monthly by the U.S. Commerce Department. It measures the rate of inflation for consumer goods.*

Contribution margin The contribution to fixed costs from each unit of sales. The margin may be computed as price minus variable cost per unit.*

Conversion premium The market price of a convertible bond or preferred stock minus the security's conversion value.*

Conversion price The conversion ratio divided into the par value. The price of the common stock at which the security is convertible. An investor would usually not convert the security into common stock unless the market price were greater than the conversion price.*

Conversion ratio The number of shares of common stock an investor will receive if he exchanges a convertible bond or convertible preferred stock for common stock.*

Conversion value The conversion ratio multiplied by the market price per share of common stock.*

Convertible security A security that may be traded into the company for a different form or type of security. Convertible securities are usually bonds or preferred stock that may be exchanged for common stock.*

Corporate stock repurchase A corporation may repurchase its shares in the market as an alternative to paying a cash dividend. Earnings per share will go up, and if the price-earnings ratio remains the same, the stockholder will receive the same dollar benefit as through a cash dividend. Furthermore, the increase in stock price is a capital gain, whereas the cash dividend would be taxed as ordinary income. A corporation may also justify the repurchase of its stock because it is at a very low price or to maintain constant demand for the shares. Reacquired shares may be used for employee options or as part of a tender offer in a merger or acquisition. Firms may also reacquire part of their shares as a protective device against being taken over as a merger candidate.*

Corporation A form of ownership in which a separate, legal entity is created. A corporation may sue or be sued, engage in contracts and acquire property. It has a continual life and is not dependent on any one stockholder for maintaining its legal existence. A corporation is owned by stockholders who enjoy the privilege of limited liability. There is, however, the potential for double taxation in the corporate form of organization: the first time at the corporate level in the form of profits, and again at the stockholder level in the form of dividends.*

Correlation coefficient Measures the degree of relationship between two variables.*

Correspondent A securities firm, bank, or other financial organization which regularly performs services for another in a place or market to which the other does not have direct access. Securities firms may have correspondents in foreign countries or on exchanges of which they are not members. Correspondents are frequently linked by private wires. Member organizations of the N.Y.S.E. with offices in New York City may also act as correspondents for out-of-town member organizations which do not maintain New York City offices.†

Cost-benefit analysis A study of the incremental costs and benefits that can be derived from a given course of action.*

Cost of capital The cost of alternative sources of financing to the firm. (See: *Weighted average cost of capital.*)*

Cost of goods sold The cost specifically associated with units sold during the time period under study.*

Coupon bond Bond with interest coupons attached. The coupons are clipped as they come due and are presented by the holder for payment of interest. (See: *Bearer bond, Registered bond.*)†

Coupon rate The actual interest rate on the bond, usually payable in semiannual installments. The coupon rate normally stays constant during the life of the bond and indicates what the bondholder's annual dollar income will be.*

Coverage A term usually connected with revenue bonds. It is a ratio of net revenues pledged to principal and interest payments to debt service requirements. It is one of the factors used in evaluating the quality of an issue.**

Covered option An option position that is offset by an equal and opposite position in the underlying security.††

Covering Buying a security previously sold short. (See: *Short sale, Short covering.*)†

Credit terms The repayment provisions that are part of a credit arrangement. An example would be a 2/10, net 30 arrangement in which the customer may deduct 2 percent from the invoice price if payment takes place in the first ten days. Otherwise the full amount is due.*

Cumulative preferred A stock having a provision that if one or more dividends are omitted, the omitted dividends must be paid before dividends may be paid on the company's common stock.†

Cumulative voting A method of voting for corporate directors which enables the shareholder to multiply the number of his shares by the number of directorships being voted on and cast the total for one director or a selected group of directors. A 10-share holder normally casts 10 votes for each of, say 12 nominees to the board of directors. He thus has 120 votes. Under the cumulative voting principle he may do that or he may cast 120 (10 × 12) votes for only one nominee, 60 for two, 40 for three, or any other distribution he chooses. Cumulative voting is required under the corporate laws of some states, is permitted in most others.†

Currency futures contract A futures contract that may be used for hedging or speculation in foreign exchange.*

Current assets Those assets of a company which are reasonably expected to be realized in cash, or sold, or consumed during the normal operating cycle of the business. These include cash, U.S. government bonds, receivables and money due usually within one year, and inventories.†

Current cost accounting One of two methods of inflation-adjusted accounting approved by the Financial Accounting Standards Board in 1979. Financial statements are adjusted to the present, using current cost data rather than an index. This is shown as supplemental information in the firm's annual report.

Current liabilities Money owed and payable by a company, usually within one year.†

Current return (See: *Yield.*)

Current yield A relation stated as a percent of the annual interest to the actual market price of the bond.**

Day order An order to buy or sell which, if not executed expires at the end of the trading day on which it was entered.†

Dealer An individual or firm in the securities business who buys and sells stocks and bonds as a principal rather than as an agent. The dealer's profit or loss is the difference between the price paid and the price received for the same security. The dealer's confirmation must disclose to the customer that the principal has been acted upon. The same individual or firm may function, at different times, either as broker or dealer. (See: *NASD, Specialist.*)††

Debenture A long-term unsecured corporate bond. Debentures are usually issued by large, prestigious firms having excellent credit ratings in the financial community.*

Debit balance In a customer's margin account that portion of purchase price of stock, bonds, or commodities covered by credit extended by the broker to the margin customer.†

Debt limit The statutory or constitutional maximum debt that a municipality can legally incur.**

Debt service Refers to the payments required for interest and retirement of the principal amount of a debt.**

Debt utilization ratios A group of ratios that indicates to what extent debt is being used and the prudence with which it is being managed. Calculations include debt to total assets, times interest earned, and fixed charge coverage.*

Degree of financial leverage A measure of the impact of debt on the earnings capability of the firm. The percentage change in earnings per share is divided by the percentage change in earnings before interest and taxes at a given level of operation. Other algebraic statements are also used.*

Degree of operating leverage A measure of the impact of fixed costs on the operating earnings of the firm. The percentage change in operating income is divided by the percentage change in volume at a given level of operation. Other algebraic statements are also used.*

Denomination The face amount or par value of a security which the issuer promises to pay on the maturity date. Most municipal bonds are issued with a minimum denomination of $5,000, although a few older issues are available in $1,000 denominations.**

Depletion accounting Natural resources, such as metals, oil and gas, and timber, which conceivably can be reduced to zero over the years, present a special problem in capital management. Depletion is an accounting practice consisting of charges against earnings based upon the amount of the asset taken out of the total reserves in the period for which accounting is made. A bookkeeping entry, it does not represent any cash outlay nor are any funds earmarked for the purpose.†

Depository trust company (DTC) A central securities certificate depository through which members effect security deliveries between each other via computerized bookkeeping entries thereby reducing the physical movement of stock certificates.†

Depreciation Normally, charges against earnings to write off the cost, less salvage value, of an asset over its estimated useful life. It is a bookkeeping entry and does not represent any cash outlay nor are any funds earmarked for the purpose.†

Dilution of earnings This occurs when additional shares of stock are sold without creating an immediate increase in income. The result is a decline in earnings per share until earnings can be generated from the funds raised.*

Director Person elected by shareholders to establish company policies. The directors appoint the president, vice presidents, and all other operating officers. Directors decide, among other matters, if and when dividends shall be paid. (See: *Management, Proxy.*)†

Discount The amount by which a preferred stock or bond may sell below its par value. Also used as a verb to mean "takes into account" as the price of the stock has discounted the expected dividend cut. (See: *Premium.*)†

Discount rate [1]The interest rate at which future sums or annuities are discounted back to the present.*

The interest rate at which eligible depository institutions may borrow funds, usually for short periods, directly from the Federal Reserve Banks. The law requires the board of directors of each Reserve Bank to establish the discount rate every 14 days subject to the approval of the Board of Governors.¶

Discounted loan A loan in which the calculated interest payment is subtracted or discounted in advance. Because this lowers the amount of available funds, the effective interest rate is increased.*

Discretionary account An account in which the customer gives the broker or someone else discretion, which may be complete or within specific limits, either to the purchases, or sale of securities or commodities including selection, timing, amount, and price to be paid or received.†

Diversification Spreading investments among different companies in different fields. Another type of diversification is also offered by the securities of many individual companies because of the wide range of their activities. (See: *Investment trust.*)†

Dividend The payment designed by the board of directors to be distributed pro rata among the shares outstanding. On preferred shares, it is generally a fixed amount. On common shares, the dividend varies with the fortunes of the company and the amount of cash on hand, and may be omitted if business is poor or the directors determine to withhold earnings to invest in plant and equipment. Sometimes a company will pay a dividend out of past earnings even if it is not currently operating at a profit.†

Dividend information content This theory of dividends assumes that dividends provide information about the financial health and economic expectations of the company. If this is true, corporations must actively manage their dividends to provide the market with information.*

Dividend payment date The day on which a stockholder of record will receive his or her dividend.*

Dividend payout The percentage of dividends to earnings after taxes. It can be computed by dividing dividends per share by earnings per share.*

Dividend record date Stockholders owning the stock on the holder-of-record date are entitled to receive a dividend. In order to be listed as an owner on the corporate books, the investor must have bought the stock before it went ex-dividend.*

Dividend reinvestment plans Plans that provide the investor with an opportunity to buy additional shares of stock with the cash dividends paid by the company.*

Dividend valuation model A model for determining the value of a share of stock by taking the present value of an expected stream of future dividends.*

Dividend yield Dividends per share divided by market price per share. Dividend yield indicates the percentage return that a stockholder will receive on dividends alone.*

Dollar bond A bond that is quoted and traded in dollars rather than in terms of yield.**

Dollar cost averaging A system of buying securities at regular intervals with a fixed dollar amount. Under this system the investor buys by the dollars' worth rather than by the number of shares. If each investment is of the same number of dollars, payments buy more when the price is low and fewer when it rises. Thus temporary downswings in price benefit the investor if he continues periodic purchases in both good times and bad and the price at which the shares are sold is more than their average cost. (See: *Formula investing.*)†

Double-barrelled bond A bond secured by the pledge of two or more sources of repayment, e.g., secured by taxes as well as revenues.**

Double exemption Refers to securities that are exempt from state as well as Federal income taxes.**

Double taxation Short for *double taxation of dividends.* The federal government taxes corporate profits once as corporate income; any part of the remaining profits distributed as dividends to stockholders may be taxed again as income to the recipient stockholder.†

Dow theory A theory of market analysis based upon the performance of the Dow-Jones industrial and transportation stock price averages. The theory says that the market is in a basic upward trend if one of these averages advances above a previous important high, accompanied or followed by a similar advance in the other. When the averages both dip below previous important lows, this is regarded as confirmation of a basic downward trend. The theory does not attempt to predict how long either trend will continue, although it is widely misinterpreted as a method of forecasting future action.†

Down tick (See: *Up tick.*)

Dual trading Exists when one security, such as General Motors common stock, is traded on more than one stock exchange. This practice is quite common between NYSE-listed companies and regional exchanges.*

Dun & Bradstreet A credit-rating agency that publishes information on over 3 million business establishments through its *Reference Book.**

Du Pont System of Ratio Analysis An analysis of profitability that breaks down return on assets between the profit margin and asset turnover. The second, or modified, version shows how return on assets is translated into return on equity through the amount of debt that the firm has. Actually return on assets is divided by (1 − debt/assets) to arrive at return on equity.*

Earnings per share The earnings available to common stockholders divided by the number of common stock shares outstanding.*

Earnings report A statement—also called an *income statement*—issued by a company showing its earnings or losses over a given period. The earnings report lists the income earned, expenses, and the net result. (See: *Balance sheet.*)†

Economic indicators Hundreds of indicators exist. Each is a specialized series of data. The data are analyzed for their relationship to economic activity, and the indicator is classified as either a lagging indicator, a leading indicator, or a coincident indicator of economic activity.*

Economical ordering quantity (EOQ) The most efficient ordering quantity for the firm. The EOQ will allow the firm to minimize the total ordering and carrying costs associated with inventory.*

Efficient frontier A line drawn through the optimum point selections in a risk-return trade-off diagram. Each point represents the best possible trade-off between risk and return (the highest return at a given risk level or the lowest risk at a given return level).*

Efficient market hypothesis Hypothesis which suggests that markets adjust very quickly to new information and that it is very difficult for investors to select portfolios of securities that outperform the market.

Electronic funds transfer A system in which funds are moved between computer terminals without the use of written checks.*

Employment Act of 1946 An act which specifies the four goals that the Federal Reserve Board should strive to achieve: economic growth, stable prices, high employment, and a balance of trade.*

Equipment trust certificate A type of security, generally issued by a railroad, to pay for new equipment. Title to the equipment, such as a locomotive, is held by a trustee until the notes are paid off. An equipment trust certificate is usually secured by a first claim on the equipment.†

Equity The net worth of a business, consisting of capital stock, capital (or paid-in) surplus, earned surplus (or retained earnings), and occasionally, certain net worth reserves. *Common equity* is that part of the total net worth belonging to the common stockholders. *Total equity* would include preferred stockholders. The terms *common stock, net worth,* and *common equity* are frequently used interchangeably.†

Eurobonds Bonds payable or denominated in the borrower's currency, but sold outside the country of the borrower, usually by an international syndicate.*

Eurodollar loan A loan from a foreign bank denominated in dollars.*

Eurodollars U.S. dollars held on deposit by foreign banks and loaned out by those banks to anyone seeking dollars.*

Exchange acquisition A method of filling an order to buy a large block of stock on the floor of the exchange. Under certain circumstances, a member-broker can facilitate the purpose of a block by soliciting orders to sell. All orders to sell the security are lumped together and crossed with the buy order in the regular action market. The price to the buyer may be on a net basis or on a commission basis.†

Exchange distribution A method of selling large blocks of stock on the floor of the exchange. Under certain circumstances, a member-broker can facilitate the sale of a block of stock by soliciting and getting other member-brokers to solicit orders to buy. Individual buy orders are lumped together and crossed with the sell order in the regular auction market. A special commission is usually paid by the seller; ordinarily the buyer pays no commission.†

Ex-dividend A synonym for "without dividend." The buyer of a stock selling ex-dividend does not receive the recently declared dividend. Every dividend is payable on a fixed date to all shareholders recorded on the books of the company as of a previous date of record. For example, a dividend may be declared as payable to holders of record on the books of the company on a given Friday. Since five business days are allowed for delivery of stock in a "regular way" transaction on the New York Stock Exchange, the Exchange would declare the stock "ex-dividend" as of the opening of the market on the preceding Monday. That means anyone who bought it on and after Monday would not be entitled to that dividend. When stocks go ex-dividend, the stock tables include the symbol "x" following the name. (See: *Cash sale, Net change, Transfer.*)†

Ex-dividend date Four business days before the holder-of-record date. On the ex-dividend date the purchase of the stock no longer carries with it the right to receive the dividend previously declared.*

Expectations theory of interest rates This theory explains the shape of the term structure relative to expectations for future short-term interest rates. It is thought that long-term rates are an average of the expected short-term rates. Therefore, an upward-sloping yield curve would indicate that short-term rates will rise.*

Expected value A representative value from a probability distribution arrived at by multiplying each outcome by the associated probability and summing up the values.*

Export-Import Bank (Eximbank) An agency of the United States government that facilitates the financing of United States exports through its miscellaneous programs. In its direct loan program, the Eximbank lends money to foreign purchasers of U.S. products—such as aircraft, electrical equipment, heavy machinery, computers, and the like. The Eximbank also purchases eligible medium-term obligations of foreign buyers of U.S. goods at a discount from face value. In this discount program, private banks and other lenders are able to rediscount (sell at a lower price) promissory notes and drafts acquired from foreign customers of U.S. firms.*

Expropriation The action of a country in taking away or modifying the property rights of a corporation or individual.*

Ex-rights The situation in which the purchase of common stock during a rights offering no longer includes rights to purchase additional shares of common stock.*

Extension An out-of-court settlement in which creditors agree to allow the firm more time to meet its financial obligations. A new repayment schedule will be developed, subject to the acceptance of creditors.*

External corporate funds Corporate financing raised through sources outside of the firm. Bonds, common stock, and preferred stock fall in this category.*

External reorganization A reorganization under the formal bankruptcy laws in which a merger partner is found for the distressed firm. Ideally, the firm should be merged with a strong firm in its own industry, although this is not always possible.*

Factoring receivables Selling accounts receivable to a finance company or a bank.*

Federal budget deficit Government expenditures are greater than government tax revenues, and the government must borrow to balance revenues and expenditures. These deficits act as an economic stimulus.*

Federal budget surplus Government tax receipts are greater than government expenditures. A rarity during the last 20 years. These surpluses have a dampening effect on the economy.*

Federal National Mortgage Association A government agency that provides a secondary market in mortgages.*

Federal Reserve discount rate The rate of interest that the Fed charges on loans to the banking system. A monetary tool for management of the money supply.*

Federally sponsored agency securities Securities issued by federal agencies such as the Federal Land Bank and Federal Home Loan Board.*

Field warehousing An inventory financing arrangement in which collateralized inventory is stored on the premises of the borrower but is controlled by an independent warehousing company.*

FIFO A system of writing off inventory into cost of goods sold in which the items purchased first are written off first. Referred to as first-in, first-out.*

Financial Accounting Standards Board A privately supported rulemaking body for the accounting profession.*

Financial capital Common stock, preferred stock, bonds, and retained earnings. Financial capital appears on the corporate balance sheet under long-term liabilities and equity.*

Financial disclosure Presentation of financial information to the investment community.*

Financial futures market A market that allows for the trading of financial instruments related to a future point in time. A purchase or sale takes place in the present, with a reversal necessitated in the future to close out the position. If a purchase (sale) takes place initially, then a sale (purchase) will be necessary in the future. The market provides for futures contracts in Treasury bonds, Treasury bills, certificates of deposits, GNMA certificates, and many other instruments. Financial futures contracts may be executed on the Chicago Board of Trade, the Chicago Mercantile Exchange, the New York Futures Exchange, and other exchanges.*

Financial intermediary A financial institution such as a bank or a life insurance company that directs other people's money into such investments as government and corporate securities.*

Financial lease A long-term noncancelable lease. The financial lease has all the characteristics of long-term debt except that the lease payments are a combination of interest expense and amortization of the cost of the asset.*

Financial leverage A measure of the amount of debt used in the capital structure of the firm.*

Financial sweetener Usually refers to equity options, such as warrants or conversion privileges, attached to a debt security. The sweetener lowers the interest cost to the corporation.*

Fiscal policy The tax policies of the federal government and the spending associated with its tax revenues.*

Fixed costs Costs that remain relatively constant regardless of the volume of operations. Examples are rent, depreciation, property taxes, and executive salaries.*

Float The difference between the corporation's recorded cash balance on its books and the amount credited to the corporation by the bank.*

Floating rate bond The interest payment on the bond changes with market conditions rather than the price of the bond.*

Floating rate preferred stock The quarterly dividend on the preferred stock changes with market conditions. The market price is considerably less volatile than it is with regular preferred stock.*

Floor price Usually equal to the pure bond value. A convertible bond will not sell at less than its pure bond value even when its conversion value is below the pure bond value.*

Flotation cost The distribution cost of selling securities to the public. The cost includes the underwriter's spread and any associated fees.*

Forced conversion Occurs when a company calls a convertible security that has a conversion value greater than the call price. Investors will take the higher of the two values and convert the security to common stock rather than take a lower cash call price.*

Foreign Credit Insurance Association (FCIA) An agency established by a group of 60 U.S. insurance companies. It sells credit export insurance to interested exporters. The FCIA promises to pay for the exported merchandise if the foreign importer defaults on payment.*

Foreign exchange rate The relationship between the value of two or more currencies. For example, the exchange rate between U.S. dollars and French francs is stated as dollars per francs or francs per dollar.*

Foreign exchange risk A form of risk that refers to the possibility of experiencing a drop in revenue or an increase in cost in an international transaction due to a change in foreign exchange rates. Importers, exporters, investors, and multinational firms alike are exposed to this risk.*

Formula investing An investment technique. One formula calls for the shifting of funds from common shares to preferred shares or bonds as the market, on average, rises above a certain predetermined point—and the return of funds to common share investments as the market average declines. (See: *Dollar cost averaging.*)†

Founders' stock Stock owned by the original founders of a company. It often carries special voting rights that allow the founders to maintain voting privileges in excess of their proportionate ownership.*

Fourth market A market of stocks and bonds in which there is direct dealing between financial institutions, such as investment bankers, insurance companies, pension funds, and mutual funds.*

Free and open market A market in which supply and demand are freely expressed in terms of price. Contrasts with a controlled market in which supply, demand, and price may all be regulated.†

Fronting loan A parent company's loan to a foreign subsidiary is channeled through a financial intermediary, usually a large international bank. The bank fronts for the parent in extending the loan to the foreign affiliate.*

Fully diluted earnings per share Equals adjusted earnings after taxes divided by shares outstanding, plus common stock equivalents, plus all convertible securities.*

Fundamental research Analysis of industries and companies based on factors such as sales, assets, earnings, products or services, markets, and management. As supplied to the economy, fundamental research includes consideration of gross national product, interest rates, unemployment, inventories, savings, and so on. (See: *Technical research.*)†

Funded debt Usually long-term, interest-bearing bonds or debentures of a company. Could include long-term bank loans. Does *not* include short-term loans, preferred, or common stock.†

Futures contract A contract to buy or sell a commodity at some specified price in the future.*

General mortgage bond A bond which is secured by a blanket mortgage on the company's property, but which may be outranked by one or more other mortgages.†

General obligation bond A bond secured by the pledge of the issuer's full faith, credit and taxing power.**

Gilt-edged High-grade bond issued by a company which has demonstrated its ability to earn a comfortable profit over a period of years and pay its bondholders their interest without interruption.†

Give up A term with many different meanings. For one, a member of the exchange on the floor may act for a second member by executing an order for him with a third member. The first member tells the third member that he is acting on behalf of the second member and "gives up" the second member's name rather than his own.††

Going private The process by which all publicly owned shares of common stock are repurchased or retired, thereby eliminating listing fees, annual reports, and other expenses involved with publicly owned companies.*

Gold fix The setting of the price of gold by dealers (especially in a twice-daily London meeting at the central bank); the fix is the fundamental worldwide price for setting prices of gold bullion and gold-related contracts and products.††

Golden parachute Highly attractive termination payments made to current management in the event of a takeover of the company.*

Good delivery Certain basic qualifications must be met before a security sold on the exchange may be delivered. The security must be in proper form to comply with the contract of sale and to transfer title to the purchaser.†

Good 'til cancelled order (GTC) or open order An order to buy or sell which remains in effect until it is either executed or cancelled.†

Goodwill An intangible asset that reflects value above that generally recognized in the tangible assets of the firm.*

Government bonds Obligations of the U.S. government, regarded as the highest grade issues in existence.†

Growth stock Stock of a company with a record of growth in earnings at a relatively rapid rate.†

Guaranteed bond A bond which has interest or principal, or both, guaranteed by a company other than the issuer. Usually found in the railroad industry when large roads, leasing sections of trackage owned by small railroads, may guarantee the bonds of the smaller road.†

Guaranteed stock Usually preferred stock on which dividends are guaranteed by another company; under much the same circumstances as a bond is guaranteed.†

Hedge (See: *Arbitrage, Option, Short sale.*)

Hedging The purchase or sale of a derivative security (such as options or futures) in order to reduce or neutralize all or some portion of the risk of holding another security.††

Holding company A corporation which owns the securities of another, in most cases with voting control.†

Hurdle rate The minimum acceptable rate of return in a capital budgeting decision.*

Hypothecation The pledging of securities as collateral—for example, to secure the debit balance in a margin account.†

Inactive stock An issue traded on an exchange or in the over-the-counter market in which there is a relatively low volume of transactions. Volume may be no more than a few hundred shares a week or even less. On the New York Stock Exchange many inactive stocks are traded in 10-share units rather than the customary 100. (See: *Round lot.*)†

In-and-out Purchase and sale of the same security within a short period—a day, a week, even a month. An in-and-out trader is generally more interested in day-to-day price fluctuations than dividends or long-term growth.†

Income bond Generally income bonds promise to repay principal but to pay interest only when earned. In some cases unpaid interest on an income bond may accumulate as a claim against the corporation when the bond becomes due. An income bond may also be issued in lieu of preferred stock.†

Income statement A financial statement that measures the profitability of the firm over a period of time. All expenses are subtracted from sales to arrive at net income.*

Indenture A written agreement under which bonds and debentures are issued, setting forth maturity date, interest rate, and other terms.†

Independent broker Members on the floor of the NYSE who execute orders for other brokers having more business at that time than they can handle themselves, or for firms who do not have their Exchange member on the floor. Formerly known as *two-dollar brokers* from the time when these independent brokers received $2 per hundred shares for executing such orders. Their fees are paid by the commission brokers. (See: *Commission broker.*)†

Index A statistical yardstick expressed in terms of percentages of a base year or years. For instance, the Federal Reserve Board's index of industrial production is based on 1967 as 100. An index is not an average. (See: *Averages.*)†

Industrial revenue bond A security backed by private enterprises that have been financed by a municipal issue.**

Inflation The phenomenon of price increase with the passage of time.*

Inflation premium A premium to compensate the investor for the eroding effect of inflation on the value of the dollar. In the 1980s the inflation premium has been 3 to 4 percent. In the late 1970s it was in excess of 10 percent.*

Installment loan A borrowing arrangement in which a series of equal payments are used to pay off the loan.*

Institutional Investor An organization whose primary purpose is to invest its own assets or those held in trust by it for others. Includes pension funds, investment companies, insurance companies, universities, and banks.†

Interest Payments a borrower pays a lender for the use of his money. A corporation pays interest on its bonds to its bondholders. (See: *Bond, dividend.*)†

Interest factor *(IF)* The tabular value to insert into the various formulas. It is based on the number of periods (n) and the interest rate (i).*

Interest rate parity theory A theory based on the interplay between interest rate differentials and exchange rates. If one country has a higher interest rate than another country after adjustments for inflation, interest rates and foreign exchange rates will adjust until the foreign exchange rates and money market rates reach equilibrium (are properly balanced between the two countries).*

Intermarket Trading System (ITS) An electronic communications network now linking the trading floor of seven registered exchanges to foster competition among them in stocks listed on either the NYSE or AMEX and one or more regional exchanges. Through ITS, any broker or market-maker on the floor of any participating market can reach out to other participants for an execution whenever the nationwide quote shows a better price is available.††

Internal corporate funds Funds generated through the operations of the firm. The principal sources are retained earnings and cash flow added back from depreciation and other noncash deductions.*

Internal financing Funds made available for capital budgeting and working-capital expansion through the normal operations of the firm; internal financing is approximately equal to retained earnings plus depreciation.*

Internal rate of return (IRR) A discounted cash flow method for evaluating capital budgeting projects. The IRR is a discount rate which makes the present value of the cash inflows equal to the present value of the cash outflows.*

Internal reorganization A reorganization under the formal bankruptcy laws. New management may be brought in and a redesign of the capital structure may be implemented.*

International diversification Achieving diversification through many different foreign investments that are influenced by a variety of factors.*

International Finance Corporation (IFC) An affiliate of the World Bank established with the sole purpose of providing partial seed capital for private ventures around the world. Whenever a multinational company has difficulty raising equity capital due to lack of adequate private risk capital, the firm may explore the possibility of selling equity or debt (totaling up to 25 percent) to the International Finance Corporation.*

Intrinsic value The dollar amount of the difference between the exercise price of an option and the current cash value of the underlying security. Intrinsic value and time value are the two components of an option premium, or price.††

Inventory profits Profits generated as a result of an inflationary economy in which old inventory is sold at large profits because of increasing prices. This is particularly prevalent under FIFO accounting.*

Inverted yield curve A downward-sloping yield curve. Short-term rates are higher than long-term rates.*

Investment The use of money for the purpose of making more money, to gain income or increase capital, or both.††

Investment banker A financial organization that specializes in selling primary offerings of securities. Investment bankers can also perform other financial functions, such as advising clients, negotiating mergers and takeovers, and selling secondary offerings.*

Investment company A company or trust which uses its capital to invest in other companies. There are two principal types: the closed-end and the open-end, or mutual fund. Shares in closed-end investment companies, some of which are listed on the New York Stock Exchange, are readily transferable in the open market and are bought and sold like other shares. Capitalization of these companies remains the same unless action is taken to change, which is seldom. Open-end funds sell their own new shares to investors, stand ready to buy back their old shares, and are not listed. Open-end funds are so called because their capitalization is not fixed; they issue more shares as people want them.†

Investment counsel One whose principal business consists of acting as investment adviser and a substantial part of his business consists of rendering investment supervisory services.†

Investment tax credit (ITC) A percentage of the purchase price that may be deducted directly from tax obligations.

IRA Individual Retirement Account. A pension plan with major tax advantages. Any worker can begin an IRA by a cash contribution up to $2,000 annually which is not tax deductible; however, the investment return on which is tax deferred. (See: *Keogh Plan.*)

Issue Any of a company's securities, or the act of distributing such securities.†

Issuer A municipal unit that borrows money through the sale of bonds or notes.**

Keogh Plan Tax advantaged personal retirement program that can be established by a self-employed individual. Currently, annual contributions to a plan can be up to $15,000. Such contributions and reinvestments are not taxed as they accumulate but will be when withdrawn (presumably at retirement when taxable income may be less). (See: *IRA.*)††

Leading indicators The most commonly followed series of economic indicators (a series of the 12 leading indicators). These are used to help forecast economic activity.*

Lease A contractual arrangement between the owner of equipment (lessor) and the user of equipment (lessee) which calls for the lessee to pay the lessor an established lease payment. There are two kinds of leases, financial leases and operating leases.*

Legal list A list of investments selected by various states in which certain institutions and fiduciaries, such as insurance companies and banks, may invest. Legal lists are often restricted to high quality securities meeting certain specifications. (See: *Prudent man rule.*)††

Legal opinion An opinion concerning the legality of a bond issue usually written by a recognized law firm specializing in public borrowings.**

Letter of credit A credit letter normally issued by the importer's bank in which the bank promises to pay out the money for the merchandise when delivered.*

Level production Equal monthly production used to smooth out production schedules and employ manpower and equipment more efficiently and at a lower cost.*

Leverage The effect on a company when the company has bonds, preferred stock, or both outstanding. Example: If the earnings of a company with 1,000,000 common shares increases from $1,000,000 to $1,500,000—earnings per share would go from $1 to $1.50, or an increase of 50 percent. But if earnings of a company that had to pay $500,000 in bond interest increased that much—earnings per common share would jump from 50 cents to $1 a share, or 100 percent.††

Leveraged buy-out Existing management or an outsider makes an offer to "go private" by retiring all the shares of the company. The buying group borrows the necessary money, using the assets of the acquired firm as collateral. The buying group them repurchases all the shares and expects to retire the debt over time with the cash flow from operations or the sale of corporate assets.*

Liabilities All the claims against a corporation. Liabilities include accounts and wages and salaries payable, dividends declared payable, accrued taxes payable, fixed or long-term liabilities such as mortgage bonds, debentures, and bank loans. (See: *Assets, Balance sheet.*)†

LIBOR (See: *London Interbank Offered Rate.*)*

Life cycle curve A curve illustrating the growth phases of a firm. The dividend policy most likely to be employed during each phase is often illustrated.*

LIFO A system of writing off inventory into cost of goods sold in which the items purchased last are written off first. Referred to as last-in, first-out.*

Limit, limited order, or limited price order An order to buy or sell a stated amount of a security at a specified price, or at a better price, if obtainable after the order is represented in the Trading Crowd.†

Limited partnership A special form of partnership to limit liability for most of the partners. Under this arrangement, one or more partners are designated as general partners and have unlimited liability for the debts of the firm, while the other partners are designated as limited partners and are only liable for their initial contribution.*

Limited tax bond A bond secured by a pledge of a tax or group of taxes limited as to rate or amount.**

Liquidation The process of converting securities or other property into cash. The dissolution of a company, with cash remaining after sale of its assets and payment of all indebtedness being distributed to the shareholders.†

Liquidity The ability of the market in a particular security to absorb a reasonable amount of buying or selling at reasonable price changes. Liquidity is one of the most important characteristics of a good market.†

Liquidity ratios A group of ratios that allows one to measure the firm's ability to pay off short-term obligations as they come due. Primary attention is directed to the current ratio and the quick ratio.*

Listed stock The stock of a company which is traded on a securities exchange. The various stock exchanges have different standards for listing. Some of the guides used by the New York Stock Exchange for an original listing are national interest in the company, a minimum of 1.1-million shares publicly held among not less than 2,000 round-lot stockholders. The publicly held common shares should have a minimum aggregate market value of $18 million. The company should have net income in the latest year of over $2.5-million before federal income tax and $2-million in each of the preceding two years.††

Listing requirements Financial standards that corporations must meet before their common stock can be traded on a stock exchange. Listing requirements are not standard, but are set by each exchange. The requirements for the NYSE are the most stringent.*

Load The portion of the offering price of shares of open-end investment companies in excess of the value of the underlying assets which cover sales commissions and all other costs of distribution. The load is usually incurred only on purchase, there being, in most cases, no charge when the shares are sold (redeemed).†

Lockbox system A procedure used to expedite cash inflows to a business. Customers are requested to forward their checks to a post-office box in their geographic region, and a local bank picks up the checks and processes them for rapid collection. Funds are then wired to the corporate home office for immediate use.*

London Interbank Offered Rate (LIBOR) An interbank rate applicable for large deposits in the London market. It is a bench-mark rate just like the prime interest rate in the United States. Interest rates on Eurodollar loans are determined by adding premiums to this basic rate. Most often LIBOR is lower than the U.S. prime rate.*

Long Signifies ownership of securities: "I am long 100 U.S. Steel" means the speaker owns 100 shares. (See: *Short position, Short sale.*)†

Majority voting All directors must be elected by a vote of more than 50 percent. Minority shareholders are unable to achieve any representation on the board of directors.*

Management The board of directors, elected by the stockholders, and the officers of the corporation, appointed by the board of directors.†

Managing underwriter An investment banker who is responsible for the pricing, prospectus development, and legal work involved in the sale of a new issue of securities.*

Manipulation An illegal operation. Buying or selling a security for the purpose of creating a false or misleading appearance of active trading or for the purpose of raising or depressing the price to induce purchase or sale by others.†

Margin The amount paid by the customer when using a broker's credit to buy or sell a security. Under Federal Reserve regulations, the initial margin required since 1945 has ranged from the current rate 50 percent of the purchase price up to 100 percent. (See: *Brokers' loans, Equity, Margin call.*)††

Margin call A demand upon a customer to put up money or securities with the broker. The call is made when a purchase is made; also if a customer's equity in a margin account declines below a minimum standard set by the exchange or by the firm. (See: *Margin.*)†

Margin requirement A rule that specifies the amount of cash or equity that must be deposited with a brokerage firm or bank, with the balance of funds eligible for borrowing. Margin is set by the Board of Governors of the Federal Reserve Board. For example, margin of 60 percent would mean that a $10,000 purchase would allow the buyer to borrow $4,000 toward the purchase.*

Marginal corporate tax rate The rate that applies to each new dollar of taxable income. For a corporation, the rate in 1986 is 15 percent on the first $25,000, 18 percent on the second $25,000, 30 percent on the third 25,000, 40 percent on the fourth $25,000, and 46 percent on all larger amounts.*

Marginal cost of capital The cost of the last dollar of funds raised. It is assumed that each dollar is financed in proportion to the firm's optimum capital structure.*

Marginal principle of retained earnings The corporation must be able to earn a higher return on its retained earnings than a stockholder would receive after paying taxes on the distributed dividends.*

Market efficiency Markets are considered to be efficient when (1) prices adjust rapidly to new information; (2) there is a continuous market in which each successive trade is made at a price close to the previous price (the faster the price responds to new information and the smaller the differences in price changes, the more efficient the market); and (3) the market can absorb large dollar amounts of securities without destabilizing the prices.*

Market maker (See: *Dealer.*)

Market order An order to buy or sell a stated amount of a security at the most advantageous price obtainable after the order is represented in the trading crowd. (See: *Good 'til cancelled order, Limit order, Stop order.*)††

Market price In the case of a security, market price is usually considered the last reported price at which the stock or bond sold.†

Market risk premium A premium over and above the risk-free rate. It is represented by the difference between the market return (K_m) and the risk-free rate (R_f), and it may be multiplied by the beta coefficient to determine additional risk-adjusted return on a security.*

Market stabilization Intervention in the secondary markets by an investment banker to stabilize the price of a new security offering during the offering period. The purpose of market stabilization is to provide an orderly market for the distribution of the new issue.*

Market value maximization The concept of maximizing the wealth of shareholders. This calls for a recognition not only of earnings per share but also how they will be valued in the marketplace.*

Marketability The measure of the ease with which a security can be sold in the secondary market.**

Maturity The date on which a loan or a bond or debenture comes due and is to be paid off.†

Member corporation A securities brokerage firm, organized as a corporation, with at least one member of the New York Stock Exchange, who is an officer or an employee of the corporation.††

Member firm A securities brokerage firm organized as a partnership and having at least one general partner who is a member of the New York Stock Exchange, Inc. (See: *Member corporation.*)†

Member organization This term includes New York Stock Exchange Member Firm *and* Member Corporation. (See: *Member corporation, Member firm.*)†

Merger The combination of two or more companies in which the resulting firms maintain the identity of the acquiring company.*

Merger arbitrageur A specialist in merger investments who attempts to capitalize on the difference between the value offered and the current market value of the acquisition candidate.*

Merger premium The part of a buy-out or exchange offer which represents a value over and above the market value of the acquired firm.*

Minimum warrant value The market value of the common stock minus the option price of the warrant multiplied by the number of shares of the common stock that each warrant entitles the holder to purchase.*

Monetary policy Management by the Federal Reserve Board of the money supply and the resultant interest rates.*

Money market accounts Accounts at banks, savings and loans, and credit unions in which the depositor receives competitive money market rates on a typical minimum deposit of $1,000. These accounts may generally have three deposits and three withdrawals per month, and are not meant to be transaction accounts, but a place to keep minimum and excess cash balances. These accounts are insured by various appropriate governmental agencies up to $100,000.*

Money market funds A fund in which investors may purchase shares for as little as $500 or $1,000. The fund then reinvests the proceeds in high-yielding $100,000 bank CDs, $25,000–$100,000 commercial paper, and other large-denomination, high-yielding securities. Investors receive their pro rata portion of the interest proceeds daily as a credit to their shares.*

Money markets Competitive markets for securities with maturities of one year or less. The best examples of money market instruments would be Treasury bills, commercial paper, and negotiable certificates of deposit.*

Mortgage agreement A loan which requires real property (plant and equipment) as collateral.*

Mortgage bond A bond secured by a mortgage on a property. The value of the property may or may not equal the value of the bonds issued against it. (See: *Bond, Debenture.*)††

Multinational corporation A firm doing business across its national borders is considered a multinational enterprise. Some definitions require a minimum percentage (often 30 percent or more) of a firm's business activities to be carried on outside its national borders.*

Municipal bond A bond issued by a state or a political subdivision, such as county, city, town, or village. The term also designates bonds issued by state agencies and authorities. In general, interest paid on municipal bonds is exempt from federal income taxes and state and local income taxes within the state of issue.†

Municipal securities Securities issued by state and local government units. The income from these securities is exempt from federal income taxes.*

Mutual fund (See: *Investment company.*)

Mutually exclusive The selection of one choice precludes the selection of any competitive choice. For example, several machines can do an identical job in capital budgeting. If one machine is selected, the other machines will not be used.*

Naked option An option position that is *not* offset by an equal and opposite position in the underlying security.††

NASD The National Association of Securities Dealers, Inc. An association of brokers and dealers in the over-the-counter securities business.††

NASDAQ An automated information network which provides brokers and dealers with price quotations on securities traded over-the-counter. NASDAQ is an acronym for National Association of Securities Dealers Automated Quotations.†

National Market List The list of the best-known and most widely traded securities in the over-the-counter market.*

National market system A system mandated by the Securities Acts Amendments of 1975. The national market system that is envisioned will include computer processing and computerized competitive prices for all markets trading similar stocks. The exact form of the system is yet to be determined.*

Negotiable Refers to a security, title to which is transferable by delivery. (See: *Good delivery.*)†

Negotiable Order of Withdrawal account An interest earning account on which checks may be drawn. Withdrawals from NOW accounts may be subject to a 14-day or more notice requirement although such is rarely imposed. NOW accounts may be offered by commercial banks, mutual savings banks, and savings and loan associations and may be owned only by individuals and certain non-profit organizations and governmental units.¶

Net asset value Usually used in connection with investment companies to mean net asset value per share. An investment company computes its assets daily, or even twice daily, by totaling the market value of all securities owned. All liabilities are deducted, and the balance divided by the number of shares outstanding. The resulting figure is the net asset value per share. (See: *Assets, Investment company.*)††

Net change The change in the price of a security from the closing price on one day and the closing price on the following day on which the stock is traded. The net change is ordinarily the last figure on the stock price list. The mark + 1⅛ means up $1.125 a share from the last sale on the previous day the stock traded.†

Net debt Gross debt less sinking fund accumulations and all self-supporting debt.**

Net present value (NPV) The NPV equals the present value of the cash inflows minus the present value of the cash outflows with the cost of capital used as a discount rate. This method is used to evaluate capital budgeting projects. If the NPV is positive, a project should be accepted.*

Net present value profile A graphical presentation of the potential net present values of a project at different discount rates. It is very helpful in comparing the characteristics of two or more investments.*

Net trade credit A measure of the relationship between the firm's accounts receivable and accounts payable. If accounts receivable exceed accounts payable, the firm is a net provider of trade credit; otherwise, it is a net user.*

Net worth, or book value Stockholders' equity minus preferred stock ownership. Basically, net worth is the common stockholders' interest as represented by common stock par value, capital paid in excess of par, and retained earnings. If you take all the assets of the firm and subtract its liabilities and preferred stock, you arrive at net worth.*

New housing authority bonds A bond issued by a local public housing authority to finance public housing. It is backed by Federal funds and the solemn pledge of the U.S. Government that payment will be made in full.**

New issue A stock or bond sold by a corporation for the first time. Proceeds may be issued to retire outstanding securities of the company, for new plant or equipment, or for additional working capital, or to acquire a public ownership interest in the company for private owners.††

New issue market Market for new issues of municipal bonds and notes.**

New York Futures Exchange (NYFE) A subsidiary of the New York Stock Exchange devoted to the trading of futures products.††

New York Stock Exchange (NYSE) The largest organized securities market in the United States, founded in 1792. The Exchange itself does not buy, sell, own, or set the prices of securities traded there. The prices are determined by public supply and demand. The Exchange is a not-for-profit corporation of 1,366 individual members, governed by a Board of Directors consisting of 10 public representatives, 10 Exchange members or allied members and a full-time chairman, executive vice chairman and president.††

Nominal GNP GNP (gross national product) in current dollars without any adjustments for inflation.*

Nominal yield A return equal to the coupon rate.*

Noncumulative A type of preferred stock on which unpaid dividends do not accrue. Omitted dividends are, as a rule, gone forever. (See: *Cumulative preferred.*)††

Nonfinancial corporation A firm not in the banking or financial services industry. The term would primarily apply to manufacturing, wholesaling, and retail firms.*

Nonlinear break-even analysis Break-even analysis based on the assumption that cost and revenue relationships to quantity may vary at different levels of operation. Most of our analysis is based on *linear* break-even analysis.*

Normal recovery period The depreciation recovery period (3, 5, 10, 15 years) under the Accelerated Cost Recovery System of the 1981 Economic Recovery Tax Act.*

Normal yield curve An upward-sloping yield curve. Long-term interest rates are higher than short-term rates.*

Notes Short-term unsecured promises to pay specified amounts of money. For municipal notes maturities generally range from six to twelve months.**

NYSE composite index A composite index covering price movements of all common stocks listed on the "Big Board." It is based on the close of the market December 31, 1965 as 50.00 and is weighted according to the number of shares listed for each issue. The index is computed continuously and printed on the ticker tape each half hour. Point changes in the index are converted to dollars and cents so as to provide a meaningful measure of changes in the average price of listed stocks. The composite index is supplemented by separate indexes for four industry groups: industries, transportation, utilities, and finances. (See: *Averages.*)††

Odd lot An amount of stock less than the established 100-share unit. (See: *Round lot.*)††

Off-board This term may refer to transactions over-the-counter in unlisted securities, or to a transaction involving listed shares that is not executed on a national securities exchange.††

Offer The price at which a person is ready to sell. Opposed to bid, the price at which one is ready to buy. (See: *Bid and asked.*)†

Official statement Document prepared by or for the issuer that gives in detail the security and financial information about the issue.**

Open-end investment company (See: *Investment company.*)

Open interest In options and futures trading, the number of outstanding option contracts, at a given point in time, which have not been exercised and have not yet reached expiration.††

Open-market operations The purchase and sale of government securities in the open market by the Federal Reserve Board for its own account. The most common method for managing the money supply.*

Open order (See: *Good 'til cancelled order.*)

Operating lease A short-term, nonbinding obligation that is easily cancelable.*

Operating leverage A reflection of the extent to which fixed assets and fixed costs are utilized in the business firm.*

Optimum capital structure A capital structure that has the best possible mix of debt, preferred stock, and common equity. The optimum mix should provide the lowest possible cost of capital to the firm.*

Option A right to buy (call) or sell (put) a fixed amount of a given stock at a specified price within a limited period of time. The purchaser hopes that the stock's price will go up (a call) or down (a put) by an amount sufficient to provide a profit when the stock is sold. If the stock price holds steady or moves in the opposite direction, the price paid for the option is lost entirely. There are several other types of options available to the public but these are basically combinations of puts and calls. Individuals may write (sell) as well as purchase options. Options are also traded on stock indexes, futures, and debt instruments.††

Orders good until a specified time A market or limited price order which is to be represented in the Trading Crowd until a specified time, after which such order or the portion thereof not executed is to be treated as cancelled.†

Overbought An opinion as to price levels. May refer to a security which has had a sharp rise or to the market as a whole after a period of vigorous buying, which it may be argued, has left prices "too high."†

Overseas Private Investment Corporation (OPIC) A government agency that sells insurance policies to qualified firms. This agency insures against losses due to inconvertibility into dollars of amounts invested in a foreign country. Policies are also available from OPIC to insure against expropriation and against losses due to war or revolution.*

Oversold The reverse of overbought. A single security or a market which, it is believed, has declined to an unreasonable level.††

Over-the-counter A market for securities made up of securities dealers who may or may not be members of a securities exchange. The over-the-counter market is conducted over the telephone and deals mainly with stocks of companies without sufficient shares, stockholders, or earnings to warrant listing on an exchange. Over-the-counter dealers may act either as principals or as brokers for customers. The over-the-counter market is the principal market for bonds of all types. (See: *NASD, NASDAQ.*)††

Paper profit (LOSS) An unrealized profit or loss on a security still held. Paper profits and losses become realized profits only when the security is sold. (See: *Profit-taking.*)††

Par In the case of a common share, par means a dollar amount assigned to the share by the company's charter. Par value may also be used to compute the dollar amount of the common shares on the balance sheet. Par value has little relationship to the market value of common stock. Many companies issue no-par stock but give a stated per share value on the balance sheet. In the case of preferred stocks, it signifies the dollar value upon which dividends are figured. With bonds, par value is the face amount, usually $1,000.††

Parallel loan A U.S. firm that wishes to lend funds to a foreign affiliate (such as a Dutch affiliate) locates a foreign parent firm (such as a Dutch parent firm) that wishes to loan money to a U.S. affiliate. Avoiding the foreign exchange markets entirely, the U.S. parent lends dollars to the Dutch affiliate in the United States, while the Dutch parent lends guilders to the American affiliate in the Netherlands. At maturity, the two loans would each be repaid to the original lender. Notice that neither loan carries any foreign exchange risk in this arrangement.*

Participating preferred A preferred stock which is entitled to its stated dividend and, also, to additional dividends on a specified basis upon payment of dividends on the common stock.†

Partnership A form of ownership in which two or more partners are involved. Like the sole proprietorship, a partnership arrangement carries unlimited liability for the owners. However, there is only single taxation for the partners, an advantage over the corporate form of ownership.*

Passed dividend Omission of a regular or scheduled dividend.†

Payback A value that indicates the time period required to recoup an initial investment. The payback does not include the time-value-of-money concept.*

Paying agent Place where principal and interest is payable. Usually a designated bank or the treasurer's office of the issuer.**

Penny stocks Low-priced issues often highly speculative, selling at less than $1 a share. Frequently used as a term of disparagement, although a few penny stocks have developed into investment-caliber issues.†

Percent-of-sales method A method of determining future financial needs that is an alternative to the development of pro forma financial statements. We first determine the percentage relationship of various asset and liability accounts to sales, and then we show how that relationship changes as our volume of sales changes.*

Permanent current assets Current assets that will not be reduced or converted to cash within the normal operating cycle of the firm. Though from a strict accounting standpoint the assets should be removed from the current assets category, they generally are not.*

Perpetuity An investment without a maturity date.*

Planning horizon The length of time it takes to conceive, develop, and complete a project and to recover the cost of the project on a discounted cash flow basis.*

Pledging receivables Using accounts receivable as collateral for a loan. The firm usually may borrow 60 to 80 percent of the value of acceptable collateral.*

Point In the case of shares of stock, a point means $1. If ABC shares rises 3 points, each share has risen $3. In the case of bonds a point means $10, since a bond is quoted as a percentage of $1,000. A bond which rises 3 points gains 3 percent of $1,000, or $30 in value. An advance from 87 to 90 would mean an advance in dollar value from $870 to $900. In the case of market averages, the word point means merely that and no more. If, for example, the NYSE Composite Index rises from 90.25 to 91.25, it has risen a point. A point in this average, however, is not equivalent to $1. (See: *Index.*)††

Point-of-sales terminals Computer terminals in retail stores that either allow digital input or use optical scanners. The terminals may be used for inventory control or other purposes.*

Pooling of interests A method of financial recording for mergers in which the financial statements of the firms are combined, subject to minor adjustments, and goodwill is *not* created.*

Portfolio Holdings of securities by an individual or institution. A portfolio may contain bonds, preferred stocks, common stocks and other securities.††

Portfolio effect The impact of a given investment on the overall risk-return composition of the firm. A firm must consider not only the individual investment characteristics of a project, but also how the project relates to the entire portfolio of undertakings.*

Preemptive right The right of current common stockholders to maintain their ownership percentage on new issues of common stock.*

Preferred stock A class of stock with a claim on the company's earnings before payment may be made on the common stock and usually entitled to priority over common stock if the company liquidates. Usually entitled to dividends at a specified rate—when declared by the board of directors and before payment of a dividend on the common stock—depending upon the terms of the issue. (See: *Cumulative preferred, Participating preferred.*)†

Premium The amount by which a bond or preferred stock, may sell above its par value. For options, the price that the buyer pays the writer for an option contract ("option premium") is synonymous with "the price of an option." (See: *Discount.*)††

Present value The current or discounted value of a future sum or annuity. The value is discounted back at a given interest rate for a specified time period.*

Price-earnings ratio A popular way to compare stocks selling at various price levels. The PE ratio is the price of a share of stock divided by earnings per share for a twelve-month period. For example, a stock selling for $50 a share and earning $5 a share is said to be selling at a price-earnings ratio of 10.††

Primary distribution Also called primary offering. The original sale of a company's securities. (See: *Investment banker.*)††

Primary earnings per share Adjusted earnings after taxes divided by shares outstanding plus common stock equivalents.*

Primary market Market for new issues of securities.

Prime rate The lowest interest rate charged by commercial banks to their most creditworthy and largest corporate customers; other interest rates, such as personal, automobile, commercial and financing loans are often pegged to the prime.††

Principal The person for whom a broker

executes an order, or dealers buying or selling for their own accounts. The term *principal* may also refer to a person's capital or to the face amount of a bond.††

Private placement The sale of securities directly to a financial institution by a corporation. This eliminates the middleman and reduces the cost of issue to the corporation.*

Productivity The amount of physical output for each unit of productive input.¶

Profitability ratios A group of ratios that indicates the return on sales, total assets, and invested capital. Specifically, we compute the profit margin (net income to sales), return on assets, and return on equity.*

Profit-taking Selling stock which has appreciated in value since purchase, in order to realize the profit. The term is often used to explain a downturn in the market following a period of rising prices. (See: *Paper profit.*)††

Pro forma balance sheet A projection of future asset, liability, and stockholders' equity levels. Notes payable or cash is used as a plug or balancing figure for the statement.*

Pro forma financial statements A series of projected financial statements. Of major importance are the pro forma income statement, the pro forma balance sheet, and the cash budget.*

Pro forma income statement A projection of anticipated sales, expenses, and income.*

Prospectus The official selling circular that must be given to purchasers of new securities registered with the Securities and Exchange Commission. It highlights the much longer Registration Statement filed with the commission.††

Proxy Written authorization given by a shareholder to someone else to represent him and vote his shares at a shareholders' meeting.††

Proxy statement Information given to stockholders in conjunction with the solicitation of proxies.††

Prudent man rule An investment standard. In some states, the law requires that a fiduciary, such as a trustee, may invest the fund's money only in a list of securities designated by the state—the so-called legal list. In other states, the trustee may invest in a security if it is one that would be bought by a prudent man of discretion and intelligence, who is seeking a reasonable income and preservation of capital.††

Public Offering (See: *Primary distribution.*)

Public placement The sale of securities to the public through the investment banker-underwriter process. Public placements must be registered with the Securities and Exchange Commission.*

Public warehousing An inventory financing arrangement in which inventory, used as collateral, is stored with and controlled by an independent warehousing company.*

Purchase of assets A method of financial recording for mergers in which the difference between the purchase price and the adjusted book value is recognized as goodwill and amortized over a maximum time period of 40 years.*

Purchasing power parity theory A theory based on the interplay between inflation and exchange rates. A parity between the purchasing powers of two countries establishes the rate of exchange between the two currencies. Currency exchange rates, therefore, tend to vary inversely with their respective purchasing powers in order to provide the same or similar purchasing power.*

Pure bond value The value of the convertible bond if its present value is computed at a discount rate equal to interest rates on straight bonds of equal risk, without conversion privileges.*

Quote The highest bid to buy and the lowest offer to sell a security in a given market at a given time. If you ask your broker for a "quote" on a stock, he may come back with something like "45¼ to 45½." This means that $45.25 is the highest price any buyer wanted to pay at the time the quote was given on the floor of the exchange and that $45.50 was the lowest price which any seller would take at the same time. (See: *Bid and asked.*)††

Rally A brisk rise following a decline in the general price level of the market, or in an individual stock.†

Ratings Designations used by investors' services to give relative indications of quality.**

Real capital Long-term productive assets (plant and equipment).*

Real GNP GNP (gross national product) in current dollars adjusted for inflation.*

Real rate of return The rate of return that an investor demands for giving up the current use of his or her funds on a noninflation-adjusted basis. It is payment for forgoing current consumption. Historically, the real rate of return demanded by investors has been of the magnitude of 2 to 3 percent. However, throughout the 1980s the real rate of return has been much higher; that is, 5 to 7 percent.*

Record date The date on which you must be registered as a shareholder of a company in order to receive a declared dividend or, among other things, to vote on company affairs. (See: *Ex-dividend, Transfer.*)††

Redemption price The price at which a bond may be redeemed before maturity, at the option of the issuing company. Redemption value also applies to the price the company must pay to call in certain types of preferred stock. (See: *Callable.*)†

Red Herring (See: *Prospectus.*)

Refunding The process of retiring an old bond issue before maturity and replacing it with a new issue. Refunding will occur when interest rates have fallen and new bonds may be sold at lower interest rates.*

Registered bond A bond which is registered on the books of the issuing company in the name of the owner. It can be transferred only when endorsed by the registered owner. (See: *Bearer bond, Coupon bond.*)†

Registered representative The man or woman who serves the investor customers of a broker/dealer. In a New York Stock Exchange Member Organization, a Registered Representative must meet the requirements of the exchange as to background and knowledge of the securities business. Also known as an Account Executive or Customer's broker.††

Registrar Usually a trust company or bank charged with the responsibility of keeping a record of the owners of corporation's securities and preventing the issuance of more than the authorized amount. (See: *Transfer.*)††

Registration Before a public offering may be made of new securities by a company, or of outstanding securities by controlling stockholders—through the mails or in interstate commerce—the securities must be registered under the Securities Act of 1933. A statement is filed with the SEC by the issuer. It must disclose pertinent information relating to the company's operations, securities, management and purpose of the public offering.

Before a security may be admitted to dealings on a national securities exchange, it must be registered under the Securities Exchange Act of 1934. The application for registration must be filed with the exchange and the SEC by the company issuing the securities.††

Regional stock exchanges Organized exchanges outside of New York that list securities. Regional exchanges exist in San Francisco, Philadelphia, and a number of other U.S. cities.*

Regulation T The federal regulation governing the amount of credit which may be advanced by brokers and dealers to customers for the purchase of securities. (See: *Margin.*)†

Regulation U The federal regulation governing the amount of credit which may be advanced by a bank to its customers for the purchase of listed stocks. (See: *Margin.*)†

Reinvestment assumption An assumption must be made concerning the rate of return that can be earned on the cash flows generated by capital budgeting projects. The NPV method assumes the rate of reinvestment to be the cost of capital, while the IRR method assumes the rate to be the actual internal rate of return.*

REIT Real Estate Investment Trust, an organization similar to an investment company in some respects but concentrating its holdings in real estate investments. The yield is generally liberal since REIT's are required to distribute as much as 90 percent of their income. (See: *Investment company.*)†

Repatriation of earnings Returning earnings to the multinational parent company in the form of dividends.*

Replacement cost The cost of replacing the existing asset base at current prices as opposed to original cost.*

Replacement cost accounting Financial statements based on the present cost of replacing assets.*

Repurchase agreements When the Federal Reserve makes a repurchase agreement with a government securities dealer, it buys a security for immediate delivery with an agreement to sell the security back at the same price by a specific date (usually within 15 days) and receives interest at a specific rate. This arrangement allows the Federal Reserve to inject reserves into the banking system on a temporary basis to meet a temporary need and to withdraw these reserves as soon as that need has passed.¶

Required rate of return The rate of return that investors demand from an investment (securities) to compensate them for the amount of risk involved.*

Reserve requirements The amount of funds that commercial banks must hold in reserve for each dollar of deposits. Reserve requirements are set by the Federal Reserve Board and are different for savings and checking accounts. Low reserve requirements are stimulating; high reserve requirements are restrictive.*

Residual dividends This theory of dividend payout states that a corporation will retain as much earnings as it may profitably invest. If any income is left after investments, it will pay dividends. This theory assumes that dividends are a passive decision variable.*

Restructuring Redeploying the asset and liability structure of the firm. This can be accomplished through repurchasing shares with cash or borrowed funds, acquiring other firms, or selling off unprofitable or unwanted divisions.*

Revenue bond A bond payable from revenues derived from tolls, charges, or rents paid by users of the facility constructed from the proceeds of the bond issue.**

Rights When a company wants to raise more funds by issuing additional securities, it may give its stockholders the opportunity, ahead of others, to buy the new securities in proportion to the number of shares each owns. The piece of paper evidencing this privilege is called a right. Because the additional stock is usually offered to stockholders below the current market price, rights ordinarily have a market value of their own and are actively traded. In most cases they must be exercised within a relatively short period. Failure to exercise or sell rights may result in actual loss to the holder. (See: *Warrant.*)†

Rights offering A sale of new common stock through a preemptive rights offering. Usually one right will be issued for every share held. A certain number of rights may be used to buy shares of common stock from the company at a set price that is lower than the market price.*

Rights-on The situation in which the purchase of a share of common stock includes a right attached to the stock.*

Risk A measure of uncertainty about the outcome from a given event. The greater the variability of possible outcomes, on both the high side and the low side, the greater the risk.*

Risk-adjusted discount rate A discount rate used in the capital budgeting process that has been adjusted upward or downward from the basic cost of capital to reflect the risk dimension of a given project.*

Risk averse An aversion or dislike for risk. In order to induce most people to take larger risks, there must be increased potential for return.*

Risk-free rate of interest Rate of return on an asset that carries no risk. U.S. Treasury bills are often used to represent this measure, although longer-term government securities have also proved appropriate in some studies.*

Risk premium A premium associated with the special risks of an investment. Of primary interest are two types of risk, business risk and financial risk. Business risk relates to the inability of the firm to maintain its competitive position and sustain stability and growth in earnings. Financial risk relates to the inability of the firm to meet its debt obligations as they come due. The risk premium will also differ (be greater or less) for different types of investments (bonds, stocks, etc.).*

Risk-return trade-off function (See *Security market line.*)

Round lot A unit of trading or a multiple thereof. On the NYSE the unit of trading is generally 100 shares in stocks and $1,000 or $5,000 par value in the case of bonds. In some inactive stocks, the unit of trading is ten shares. (See: *Odd lot.*)††

Scale order An order to buy (or sell) a security which specifies the total amount to be bought (or sold) and the amount to be bought (or sold) at specified price variations.†

Seat A traditional figure-of-speech for a membership on an exchange.††

SEC The Securities and Exchange Commission, established by Congress to help protect investors. The SEC administers the Securities Act of 1933, the Securities Exchange Act of 1934, the Securities Act Amendments of 1975, the Trust Indenture Act, the Investment Company Act, the Investment Advisers Act, and the Public Utility Holding Company Act.†

Secondary offering The sale of a large block of stock in a publicly traded company, usually by estates, foundations, or large individual stockholders. Secondary offerings must be registered with the SEC and will usually be distributed by investment bankers.*

Secondary trading The buying and selling of publicly owned securities in secondary markets such as the New York Stock Exchange and the over-the-counter markets.*

Secured debt A general category of debt which indicates that the loan was obtained by pledging assets as collateral. Secured debt has many forms and usually offers some protective features to a given class of bondholders.*

Securities Act of 1933 An act that is sometimes referred to as the truth in securities act because it requires detailed financial disclosures before securities may be sold to the public.*

Securities Acts Amendments of 1975 The major feature of this act was to mandate a national securities market. (See: *National market system.*)*

Securities Exchange Act of 1934 Legislation that established the Securities and Exchange Commission (SEC) to supervise and regulate the securities markets.*

Security market line A line or equation that depicts the risk-related return of a security based on a risk-free rate plus a market premium related to the beta coefficient of the security.*

Self-liquidating assets Assets that are converted to cash within the normal operating cycle of the firm. An example is the purchase and sell-off of seasonal inventory.*

Semiannual compounding A compounding period of every six months. For example, a five-year investment in which interest is compounded semiannually would indicate an *n* value equal to 10 and an *i* value at one half the annual rate.*

Semivariable costs Costs that are partially fixed but still change somewhat as volume changes. Examples are utilities and "repairs and maintenance."*

Serial bond An issue which matures in part at periodic stated intervals.†

Settlement Conclusion of a securities transaction when a customer pays a broker/dealer for securities purchased or delivers securities sold and receives from the broker the proceeds of a sale. (See: *Cash sale.*)††

Shelf registration A process which permits large companies to file one comprehensive registration statement (under SEC Rule 415), which outlines the firm's plans for future long-term financing. Then, when market conditions appear to be appropriate, the firm can issue the securities without further SEC approval.*

Short covering Buying stock to return stock previously borrowed to make delivery on a short sale.†

Short position Stocks, options, or futures sold short and not covered as of a particular date. On the NYSE, a tabulation is issued once a month listing all issues on the Exchange in which there was a short position of 5,000 or more shares and issues in which the short position had changed by 2,000 or more shares in the preceding month. Short position also means the total amount of stock an individual has sold short and has not covered, as of a particular date.††

Short sale A transaction by a person who believes a security will decline and sells it, though the person does not own any. For instance: You instruct your broker to sell short 100 shares of XYZ. Your broker borrows the stock so delivery of the 100 shares can be made to the buyer. The money value of the shares borrowed is deposited by your broker with the lender. Sooner or later you must cover your short sale by buying the same amount of stock you borrowed for return to the lender. If you are able to buy XYZ at a lower price than you sold it for, your profit is the difference between the two prices—not counting commissions and taxes. But if you have to pay more for the stock than the price you received, that is the amount of your loss. Stock exchange and federal regulations govern and limit the conditions under which a short sale may be made on a national securities exchange. Sometimes people will sell short a stock they already own in order to protect a paper profit. This is known as selling short against the box.††

Simulation A method of dealing with uncertainty in which future outcomes are anticipated. The model may use random variables for inputs. By programming the computer to randomly select inputs from probability distributions, the outcomes generated by a simulation are distributed about a mean, and instead of generating one return or net present value, a range of outcomes with standard deviations is provided.*

Sinking fund Money regularly set aside by a company to redeem its bonds, debentures or preferred stock from time to time as specified in the indenture or charter.††

SIPC Securities Investor Protection Corporation, which provides funds for use, if necessary, to protect customers' cash and securities which may be on deposit with a SIPC member firm in the event the firm fails and is liquidated under the provisions of the SIPC Act. SIPC is not a government agency. It is a nonprofit membership corporation created, however, by an act of Congress.†

Special bid A method of filling an order to buy a large block of stock on the floor of the New York Stock Exchange. In a special bid, the bidder for the block of stock—a pension fund, for instance, will pay a special commission to the broker who represents him in making the purchase. The seller does not pay a commission. The special bid is made on the floor of the exchange at a fixed price which may not be below the last sale of the security or the current bid in the regular market, whichever is higher. Member firms may sell this stock for customers directly to the buyer's broker during trading hours.†

Special offering Opposite of special bid. A notice is printed on the ticker tape announcing the stock sale at a fixed price usually based on the last transaction in the regular auction market. If there are more buyers than stock, allotments are made. Only the seller pays the commission.†

Special tax bond A bond secured by a special tax, such as a gasoline tax.**

Specialist A member of the New York Stock Exchange, Inc., who has two functions: First, to maintain an orderly market in the securities registered to the specialist. In order to maintain an orderly market, the Exchange expects specialists to buy or sell for the own account, to a reasonable degree, when there is a temporary disparity between supply and demand. Second, the specialist acts as a broker's broker. When a commission broker on the Exchange floor receives a limit order, say, to buy at $50 a stock then selling at $60—he cannot wait at the post where the stock is traded to see if the price reaches the specified level. So he leaves the order with the specialist, who will try to execute it in the market if and when the stock declines to the specified price. At all times the specialist must put his customers' interests above his own. There are about 400 specialists on the NYSE. (See: *Limited order.*)††

Speculation The employment of funds by a speculator. Safety of principal is a secondary factor. (See: *Investment.*)†

Speculative warrant premium The market price of the warrant minus the warrant's intrinsic value.*

Speculator One who is willing to assume a relatively large risk in the hope of gain.††

Spin off The separation of a subsidiary or division of a corporation from its parent by issuing shares in a new corporate entity. Shareowners in the parent receive shares in the new company in proportion to their original holding and the total value remains approximately the same.††

Split The division of the outstanding shares of a corporation into a larger number of shares. A 3-for-1 split by a company with 1 million shares outstanding results in 3 million shares outstanding. Each holder of 100 shares before the 3-for-1 split would have 300 shares, although his proportionate equity in the company would remain the same; 100 parts of 1 million are the equivalent of 300 parts of 3 million. Ordinarily splits must be voted by directors and approved by shareholders. (See: *Stock dividend.*)

Spontaneous sources of funds Funds arising through the normal course of business, such as accounts payable generated from the purchase of goods for resale.*

Standard deviation A measure of the spread or dispersion of a series of numbers around the expected value. The standard deviation tells us how well the expected value represents a series of values.*

Step-up in conversion A feature that is sometimes written into the contract which allows the conversion ratio to decline in steps over time. This feature encourages early conversion when the conversion value is greater than the call price.*

Stock ahead Sometimes an investor who has entered an order to buy or sell a stock at a certain price will see transactions at that price reported on the ticker tape while his own order has not been executed. The reason is that other buy and sell orders at the same price came in to the specialist ahead of his and had priority. (See: *Book, Specialist.*)†

Stock dividend A dividend paid in securities rather than cash. The dividend may be additional shares of the issuing company, or shares of another company (usually a subsidiary) held by the company.††

Stock Index Futures Futures contracts based on market indexes, e.g., NYSE Composite Index Futures Contracts.††

Stock split A division of shares by a ratio set by the board of directors—2 for 1, 3 for 1, 3 for 2, and so on. Stock splits usually indicate that the company's stock has risen in price to a level that the directors feel limits the trading appeal of the stock. The par value is divided by the ratio set, and new shares are issued to the current stockholders of record to increase their shares to the stated level. For example, a two-for-one split would increase your holdings from one share to two shares.*

Stockholder of record A stockholder whose name is registered on the books of the issuing corporation.†

Stockholder wealth maximization Maximizing the wealth of the firm's shareholders through achieving the highest possible value for the firm in the marketplace. It is the overriding objective of the firm and should influence all decisions.*

Stockholders' equity The total ownership position of preferred and common stockholders.*

Stop limit order A stop order which becomes a limit order after the specified stop price has been reached. (See: *Limit order, Stop order.*)†

Stop order An order to buy at a price above or sell at a price below the current market. Stop buy orders are generally used to limit loss or protect unrealized profits on a short sale. Stop sell orders are generally used to protect unrealized profits or limit loss on a holding. A stop order becomes a market order when the stock sells at or beyond the specified price and, thus, may not necessarily be executed at that price.†

Stopped stock A service performed—in most cases by the specialist—for an order given him by a commission broker. Let's say XYZ just sold at $50 a share. Broker A comes along with an order to buy 100 shares at the market. The lowest offer is $50.50. Broker A believes he can do better for his client than $50.50, perhaps might get the stock at $50.25.

But he doesn't want to take a chance that he'll miss the market—that is, the next sale might be $50.50 and the following one even higher. So he asks the specialist if he will stop 100 at ½ ($50.50). The specialist agrees. The specialist guarantees Broker A he will get 100 shares at 50½ if the stock sells at that price. In the meantime, if the specialist or broker A succeeds in executing the order at $50.25, the stop is called off. (See: *Specialist.*)†

Street name Securities held in the name of a broker instead of his customer's name are said to be carried in a *street name*. This occurs when the securities have been bought on margin or when the customer wishes the security to be held by the broker.†

Subchapter S corporation A special corporate form of ownership in which profit is taxed as direct income to the stockholders and thus is only taxed once as would be true of a partnership. The stockholders still receive all the organizational benefits of a corporation, including limited liability. The Subchapter S designation can only apply to corporations with up to 35 stockholders.*

Subdivision Any legal and authorized political entity under a state's jurisdiction (county, city, water district, school district, etc.).**

Subordinated debenture An unsecured bond in which payment to the holder will take place only after designated senior debenture holders are satisfied.*

Swapping Selling one security and buying a similar one almost at the same time to take a loss, usually for tax purposes.††

Switch order or contingent order An order for the purchase (sale) of one stock and the sale (purchase) of another stock at a stipulated price difference.†

Switching Selling one security and buying another.†

Syndicate A group of investment bankers who together underwrite and distribute a new issue of securities or a large block of an outstanding issue.†

Synergy The recognition that the whole may be equal to more than the sum of the parts. The "2 + 2 = 5" effect.

Take-over The acquiring of one corporation by another—usually in a friendly merger but sometimes marked by a "proxy fight." In "unfriendly" take-over attempts, the potential buying company may offer a price well above current market values, new securities, and other inducements to stockholders. The management of the subject company might ask for a better price or fight the take-over or merger with another company. (See: *Proxy.*)†

Tax base The total resources available for taxation.**

Tax-exempt bond Another name for a municipal bond. The interest on a municipal bond is presently exempt from Federal income tax.**

Tax loss carry-forward A loss that can be carried forward for a number of years to offset future taxable income and perhaps be utilized by another firm in a merger or an acquisition.*

Tax shelter A medium or process intended to reduce or eliminate the tax burden of an individual. They range from such conventional ones as tax-exempt municipal securities and interest or dividend exclusion to sophisticated limited partnerships in real estate, cattle raising, equipment leasing, oil drilling, research and development activities and motion picture production.††

Technical insolvency A firm is unable to pay its bills as they come due.*

Technical research Analysis of the market and stocks based on supply and demand. The technician studies price movements, volume, and trends and patterns which are revealed by charting these factors, and attempts to assess the possible effect of current market action on future supply and demand for securities and individual issues. (See: *Fundamental research.*)†

Temporary current assets Current assets that will be reduced or converted to cash within the normal operating cycle of the firm.*

Tender offer A public offer to buy shares from existing stockholders of one public corporation by another company or other organization under specified terms good for a certain time period. Stockholders are asked to "tender" (surrender) their holdings for stated value, usually at a premium above current market price, subject to the tendering of a minimum and maximum number of shares.††

Term issue An issue that has a single maturity.**

Term loan An intermediate-length loan in which credit is generally extended from one to seven years. The loan is usually repaid in monthly or quarterly installments over its life rather than the one single period.*

Term structure of interest rates The relationship between interest rates and maturities for securities of equal risk. Usually government securities are used for the term structure.*

Terms of exchange The buy-out ratio or terms of trade in a merger or an acquisition.*

Thin market A market in which there are

comparatively few bids to buy or offers to sell, or both. The phrase may apply to a single security or to the entire stock market. In a thin market, price fluctuations between transactions are usually larger than when the market is liquid. A thin market in a particular stock may reflect lack of interest in that issue or a limited supply of or demand for stock in the market. (See: *Bid and asked, Liquidity, Offer.*)†

Third market Trading of stock exchange listed securities in the over-the-counter market by non-exchange-member brokers.††

Tight money A term to indicate time periods in which financing may be difficult to find and interest rates may be quite high by normal standards.*

Time order An order which becomes a market or limited price order at a specified time.†

Time value The part of an option premium that is in excess of the intrinsic value.††

Tips Supposedly "inside" information on corporation affairs.†

Trade credit Credit provided by sellers or suppliers in the normal course of business.*

Trader Individuals who buy and sell for their own accounts for short-term profit. Also, an employee of a broker/dealer or financial institution who specializes in handling purchases and sales of securities for the firm and/or its clients. (See: *Investor, Speculator.*)††

Trading market The secondary market for outstanding securities.*

Trading post One of 23 trading locations on the floor of the New York Stock Exchange at which stocks assigned to that location are bought and sold. About 75 stocks are traded at each post.†

Transaction exposure Foreign exchange gains and losses resulting from *actual* international transactions. These may be hedged through the foreign exchange market, the money market, or the currency futures market.*

Transfer This term may refer to two different operations. For one, the delivery of a stock certificate from the seller's broker to the buyer's broker and legal change of ownership, normally accomplished within a few days. For another, to record the change of ownership on the books of the corporation by the transfer agent. When the purchaser's name is recorded, dividends, notices of meetings, proxies, financial reports, and all pertinent literature sent by the issuer to its securities holders are mailed direct to the new owner. (See: *Registrar, Street name.*)††

Transfer agent A transfer agent keeps a record of the name of each registered shareowner, his or her address, the number of shares owned, and sees that certificates presented for transfer are properly cancelled and new certificates issued in the name of the new owner. (See: *Registrar.*)††

Translation exposure The foreign-located assets and liabilities of a multinational corporation, which are denominated in foreign currency units, and are exposed to losses and gains due to changing exchange rates. This is called accounting, or translation, exposure.*

Treasury bills Short-term U.S. Treasury securities issued in minimum denominations of $10,000 and usually having original maturities of 3, 6, or 12 months. Investors purchase bills at prices lower than the face value of the bills; the return to the investors is the difference between the price paid for the bills and the amount received when the bills are sold or when they mature. Treasury bills are the type of security used most frequently in open market operations.¶

Treasury bonds Long-term U.S. Treasury securities usually having initial maturities of more than 10 years and issued in denominations of $1,000 or more, depending on the specific issue. Bonds pay interest semiannually, with principal payable at maturity.¶

Treasury notes Intermediate-term coupon-bearing U.S. Treasury securities having initial maturities from 1 to 10 years and issued in denominations of $1,000 or more, depending on the maturity of the issue. Notes pay interest semiannually, and the principal is payable at maturity.¶

Treasury stock Stock issued by a company, but later reacquired. It may be held in the company's treasury indefinitely, reissued to the public, or retired. Treasury stock receives no dividends, and has no vote while held by the company.††

Trend analysis An analysis of performance that is made over a number of years in order to ascertain significant patterns.*

Trust receipt An instrument acknowledging that the borrower holds the inventory and proceeds for sale in trust for the lender.*

Two-step buy-out An acquisition plan in which the acquiring company attempts to gain control by offering a very high cash price for 51 percent of the shares of the target company. At the same time the acquiring company announces a second lower price that will be paid, either in cash, stock or bonds, at a subsequent point in time.*

Underwriter (See: *Investment banker.*)

Underwriting The process of selling securities and, at the same time, assuring the seller a specified price. Underwriting is done by investment bankers and represents a form of risk taking.*

Underwriting spread The difference between the price that a selling corporation receives for an issue of securities and the price at which the issue is sold to the public. The spread is the fee that investment bankers and others receive for selling securities.*

Underwriting syndicate A group of investment bankers that is formed to share the risk of a security offering and also to facilitate the distribution of the securities.*

Unlimited tax bond A bond secured by pledge of taxes that are not limited by rate or amount.**

Unlisted A security not listed on a stock exchange. (See: *Over-the-counter.*)†

Unsecured debt A loan which requires no assets as collateral, but allows the bondholder a general claim against the corporation rather than a lien against specific assets.*

Up tick A term used to designate a transaction made at a price higher than the preceding transaction. Also called a *plus-tick.* A *zero-plus* tick is a term used for a transaction at the same price as the preceding trade but higher than the preceding different price.

Conversely, a *down tick,* or *minus* tick, is a term used to designate a transaction made at a price lower than the preceding trade.

A plus sign, or a minus sign, is displayed throughout the day next to the last price of each company's stock traded at each trading post on the floor of the New York Stock Exchange. (See: *Short sale.*)†

Variable annuity A life insurance policy where the annuity premium (a set amount of dollars) is immediately turned into units of a portfolio of stocks. Upon retirement, the policyholder is paid according to accumulated units, the dollar value of which varies according to the performance of the stock portfolio. Its objective is to preserve, through stock investment, the purchasing value of the annuity which otherwise is subject to erosion through inflation.††

Variable costs Costs that move directly with a change in volume. Examples are raw materials, factory labor, and sales commissions.*

Volume The number of shares traded in a security or an entire market during a given period. Volume is usually considered on a daily basis and a daily average is computed for longer periods.†

Voting right The common stockholder's right to vote their stock in the affairs of a company. Preferred stock usually has the right to vote when preferred dividends are in default for a specified period. The right to vote may be delegated by the stockholder to another person. (See: *Cumulative voting, Proxy.*)††

Warrant A certificate giving the holder the right to purchase securities at a stipulated price within a specified time limit or perpetually. Sometimes a warrant is offered with securities as an inducement to buy. (See: *Rights.*)††

Warrant intrinsic value (See: *Minimum warrant value.*)*

Weighted average cost of capital The computed cost of capital determined by multiplying the cost of each item in the optimal capital structure by its weighted representation in the overall capital structure and summing up the results.*

When issued A short form of "when, as, and if issued." The term indicates a conditional transaction in a security authorized for issuance but not as yet actually issued. All "when issued" transactions are on an "if" basis, to be settled if and when the actual security is issued and the exchange or National Association of Securities Dealers rules the transactions are to be settled.†

Wire house A member firm of an exchange maintaining a communications network linking either its own branch offices, offices of correspondent firms, or a combination of such offices.†

Working capital management The financing and management of the current assets of the firm. The financial manager determines the mix between temporary and permanent "current assets" and the nature of the financing arrangement.*

Working control Theoretically, ownership of 51 percent of a company's voting stock is necessary to exercise control. In practice—and this is particularly true in the case of a large corporation—effective control sometimes can be exerted through ownership, individually or by a group acting in concert, of less than 50 percent.†

Yield Also known as return. The dividends or interest paid by a company expressed as a percentage of the current price. A stock with a current market value of $3.20 is said to return 8 percent ($3.20 ÷ $40.00). The current yield on a bond is figured the same way.††

Yield curve A curve that shows interest rates at a specific point in time for all securities having equal risk but different maturity dates. Usually government securities are used to construct such curves. The yield curve is also referred to as the term structure of interest rates.*

Yield to maturity The yield of a bond to maturity takes into account the price discount from or premium over the face amount. It is greater than the current yield when the bond is selling at a discount and less than the current yield when the bond is selling at a premium.†

Zero coupon bonds Bonds which do not convey a coupon (i.e., do not pay interest) but which are offered at a substantial discount from par value and appreciate to their full value (usually $1,000) at maturity. However, under U.S. tax law, the imputed interest is taxed as it accrues. The appeal of Zero coupon bonds is primarily for IRA and other tax sheltered retirement accounts.

Acquisition Takeover Glossary

Asset Play[1] A firm whose underlying assets are worth substantially more (after paying off the firm's liabilities) than the market value of its stock.

Bear hug An unnegotiated offer, in the form of a letter made directly to the board of directors of the target company. The price and terms are sufficiently detailed so that the directors are obliged to make the offer public. The offer states a time limit for a response and may threaten a tender offer or other action if it is not accepted.

Breakup value[1] The sum of the values of the firm's assets if sold off separately.

Crown jewel option[1] The strategem of selling off or spinning off the asset that makes the firm an attractive takeover candidate.

Four-nine position[1] A holding of approximately 4.9% of the outstanding shares of a company. At 5%, the holder must file a form [13d] with the SEC, revealing his position. Thus, a four-nine position is about the largest position that one can quietly hold.

Black knight[1] A potential acquirer that management opposes and would prefer to find an alternative to (i.e. a *white knight*).

Going private[1] The process of buying back the publicly held stock so that what was heretofore a public firm becomes private.

Golden handcuffs[1] Employment agreement that makes the departure of upper level managers very costly to them. For instance, such managers may lose very attractive stock option rights by leaving prior to their normal retirement age.

Golden handshake[1] A provision in a preliminary agreement to be acquired in which the target firm gives the acquiring firm an option to purchase its shares or assets at attractive prices or to receive a substantial bonus if the proposed takeover does not occur.

Golden parachute[1] Extremely generous separation payments for upper level executives that are required to be fulfilled if the firm's control shifts.

Greenmail[1] Incentive payments to dissuade the interest of outsiders who may otherwise seek control of a firm. The payment frequently takes the form of a premium price for the outsiders' shares, coupled with an agreement from them to avoid buying more stock for a set period of time.

The firm bears the cost of the payment. The stock price generally falls after the payment and the removal of the outside threat.

In play[1] The status of being a recognized takeover candidate.

Junk bonds[1] High-risk, high-yield bonds that are often used to finance takeovers.

LBO[1] A leveraged buyout. A purchase of a company financed largely by debt that is backed by the firm's own assets.

Loaded laggard[1] A stock of a company whose assets, particularly its liquid assets, have high values relative to the stock's price.

Lockup agreement[1] An agreement between an acquirer and target that makes the target very unattractive to any other acquirer; similar to a *golden handshake*.

Mezzanine financing Debt financing subordinate to the claims of the senior debt. This financing often has equity participation in the form of stock options, warrants or conversion to cheap stock.

Nibble strategy A takeover approach involving the purchase in the public market of minority stock position in the target company and a subsequent tender offer for the rest of the target stock.

PacMan defense[1] The tactic of seeking to acquire the firm that has targeted your own firm as a takeover prospect.

Poison pill[1] A provision in the corporate bylaws or other governance documents providing for a very disadvantageous result for a potential acquirer should its ownership position be allowed to exceed some preassigned threshold. For example, if anyone acquires more than 20% of Company A's stock, the

[1]Source: From the *AAII Journal*, American Association of *Individual Investors*, 612 North Michigan Avenue, Chicago, IL 60611. Excerpted from Ben Branch "White Knight Rescues Investors From Terminology."

acquirer might then have to sell $100 worth of its own stock to other shareholders at $50.

Raider A hostile outside party that seeks to take over other companies.

Saturday night special A seven day cash tender offer for all of the target firm's stock. It is usually launched on a Saturday on the assumption that the target company will have difficulty mobilizing its key advisors in reaction to the offer.

Scorched earth defense[1] A tactic in which the defending company's management engages in practices that reduce their company's value to such a degree that it is no longer attractive to the potential acquirer. This approach is more often threatened than actually employed.

Senior debt financing The issuance of debt instruments having first claim on a firm's assets (secured debt) or cash flow (unsecured debt).

Shark repellant[1] Anti-takeover provisions such as the poison pill.

Short swing profit[1] A gain made by an insider (including anyone with more than 10% of the stock) who holds stock for less than six months. Such gains must be paid back to the company whose shares were sold.

Standstill agreement[1] A reciprocal understanding between a company's management and an outside party that usually owns a significant minority position. Each party gives up certain rights in exchange for corresponding concessions by the other party. For example, the outside group may agree to limit its stock purchases to keep its ownership percentage below some level (for instance, 20%). In exchange, management may agree to a minority board representation by the outsider.

Swipe An unnegotiated offer to purchase the shares of a target company's stock made after the target's board has announced its intention to sell the company (usually in a leverage buyout to management). The swipe price is higher than that initially proposed by the board of directors.

Tender offer An offer by a firm to buy the stock of another firm (target) by going directly to the stockholders of the target. The offer is often made over the opposition of the management of the target firm.

13d[1] A form that must be filed with the SEC when a single investor or an associated group owns 5% or more of a company's stock. The form reveals the size of the holding and the investor's intentions.

Two-tier offer[1] A takeover device in which a relatively high per share price is paid for controlling interest in a target and a lesser per share price is paid for the remainder.

White knight defense[1] Finding an alternative and presumably more friendly acquirer than the present takeover threat.

White squire defense[1] Finding an important ally to purchase a strong minority position (for example, 25%) of the potential acquisition's stock. Presumably this ally (the "white squire") will oppose and hopefully block the efforts of any hostile firm seeking to acquire the vulnerable firm.

Stock Exchanges*

Common Stocks (shares of ownership in a corporation) are traded on several exchanges. The best known are the New York Stock Exchange and the American Stock Exchange, both located in Manhattan's financial district. Generally, the stocks of the largest companies are traded on the New York Stock Exchange, while somewhat smaller companies are traded on the American Exchange. There are also a number of regional exchanges such as the Midwest Exchange in Chicago and the Pacific Exchange in San Francisco. These exchanges trade stocks of local corporations as well as stocks listed on the New York and American Exchanges.

In addition, there is the Over-The Counter-Market (OTC) which, unlike the exchanges previously mentioned, does not have a specific location but consists of a network of brokers and dealers linked by telephone and private wires. Smaller or relatively new companies are traded on the OTC. Trading information for many (but far from all) stocks on the OTC market is collected and displayed on a computerized system, the National Association of Security Dealers Automatic Quote System (NASDAQ).

Large institutional traders (mutual and pension funds, insurance companies, etc.) often trade blocks of stocks directly with one another. This information is collected and displayed on the Instinet System.

Major Stock Exchanges

UNITED STATES

AMERICAN STOCK EXCHANGE, INC.
86 Trinity Place
New York, New York 10006

BOSTON STOCK EXCHANGE, INC.
One Boston Place
Boston, Massachusetts 02109

THE CINCINNATI STOCK EXCHANGE, INC.
205 Dixie Terminal Building
Cincinnati, Ohio 45202

MIDWEST STOCK EXCHANGE, INC.
440 South LaSalle Street
Chicago, Illinois 60603

NEW YORK STOCK EXCHANGE, INC.
11 Wall Street
New York, New York 10005

PACIFIC STOCK EXCHANGE, INC.
618 South Spring Street
Los Angeles, California 90014

301 Pine Street
San Francisco, California 94104

PHILADELPHIA STOCK EXCHANGE, INC.
1900 Market Street
Philadelphia, Pennsylvania 19103

SPOKANE STOCK EXCHANGE, INC.
206 Radio Central Building
Spokane, Washington 99201

FOREIGN

AUSTRALIA

SYDNEY STOCK EXCHANGE
Exchange Centre
20 Bond Street
Australia Square
P.O. Box H224
Sydney, 2000

BELGIUM

BRUSSELS STOCK EXCHANGE
Palais de la Bourse
1000 Brussels

CANADA

ALBERTA STOCK EXCHANGE
300–5th Avenue S.W.
Calgary, Alberta T2P 3C4

BOURSE DE MONTRÉAL
The Stock Exchange Tower
800 Victoria Square
Montreal, Quebec H4Z 1A9

TORONTO STOCK EXCHANGE
2 First Canadian Place
Toronto, Ontario M5X 1J2

VANCOUVER STOCK EXCHANGE
Stock Exchange Tower
P.O. Box 10333
609 Granville Street
Vancouver, B.C. V7Y 1H1

* See page 559 for a listing of futures and options exchanges.

WINNIPEG STOCK EXCHANGE
500 Commodity Exchange Tower
360 Main Street
Winnipeg, Manitoba R3C 324

FRANCE

BOURSE DE PARIS—PARIS STOCK EXCHANGE
4, Place de la Bourse
F-75080 Paris Cedex 02

GERMANY

FRANKFURTER WERTPAPIERBORE—FRANKFORT EXCHANGE
Börsenplatz 6, P.O. 100811
D-6000 Frankfurt am Main 1

HONG KONG

STOCK EXCHANGE OF HONG KONG
One and Two Exchange Square
Central Hong Kong

JAPAN

TOKYO STOCK EXCHANGE
2–1 Nihombashi Kayuto-Cho
Cho-Ku, Tokyo 103

THE NETHERLANDS

AMSTERDAMSE EFFECTENBEURS—AMSTERDAM STOCK EXCHANGE
Beursplein 5
1012 JW Amsterdam

SWITZERLAND

GENEVA STOCK EXCHANGE
Rue de la Confédération 8
CH-1204 Geneva

ZÜRICH STOCK EXCHANGE
Bleicherweg 5
P.O. Box CH-8021
Zürich

UNITED KINGDOM

THE INTERNATIONAL STOCK EXCHANGE OF THE UNITED KINGDOM AND THE REPUBLIC OF IRELAND LIMITED
Old Broad Street
London, England EC 2N 1HP

Securities and Exchange Commission

JUDICIARY PLAZA
450 FIFTH STREET, NW
WASHINGTON, DC 20549
PUBLIC AFFAIRS: 202-272-2650
FREEDOM OF INFORMATION ACT:
202-272-7420
FILINGS BY REGISTERED COMPANIES:
202-272-7450

FULL AND FAIR DISCLOSURE

The Securities Act of 1933 requires issuers of securities and their controlling persons making public offerings of securities in interstate commerce or through the mails, directly or by others on their behalf, to file with the Commission registration statements containing financial and other pertinent data about the issuer and the securities being offered. It is unlawful to sell such securities unless a registration statement is in effect. (There are limited exemptions, such as government securities, nonpublic offerings, and intrastate offerings, as well as offerings not exceeding $1,500,000. The effectiveness of a registration statement may be refused or suspended after a public hearing, if the statement contains material misstatements or omissions, thus barring sale of the securities until it is appropriately amended.

Registration of securities does not imply approval of the issue by the Commission or that the Commission has found the registration disclosures to be accurate. It does not insure investors against loss in their purchase but serves rather to provide information upon which investors may make an informed and realistic evaluation of the worth of the securities.

Persons responsible for filing false information with the Commission subject themselves to the risk of fine or imprisonment or both; and persons connected with the public offering may be liable in damages to purchasers of the securities if the disclosures in the registration statement and prospectus are materially defective. Also, the above act contains antifraud provisions which apply generally to the sale of securities, whether or not registered (48 Stat. 74; 15 U.S.C. 77a et seq.).

REGULATION OF SECURITIES MARKETS

The Securities Exchange Act of 1934 assigns to the commission board regulatory re-

Source: This material was abstracted from the United States Government Manual.

sponsibilities over the securities markets, the self-regulatory organizations within the securities industry, and persons conducting a business in securities. Persons who execute transactions in securities generally are required to register with the Commission as broker-dealers. Securities exchanges and certain clearing agencies are required to register with the Commission, and associations of brokers or dealers are permitted to register with the Commission. The Act also provides for the establishment of the Municipal Securities Rulemaking Board to formulate rules for the municipal securities industry.

The Commission oversees the self-regulatory activities of the national securities exchanges and associations, registered clearing agencies, and the Municipal Securities Rulemaking Board. In addition, the Commission regulates industry professionals, such as securities brokers and dealers, certain municipal securities professionals, and transfer agents.

The Securities Exchange Act authorizes national securities exchanges, national securities associations, clearing agencies, and the Municipal Securities Rulemaking Board to adopt rules that are designed, among other things to promote just and equitable principles of trade and to protect investors. The Commission is required to approve or disapprove most proposed rules of these self-regulatory organizations and has the power to abrogate or amend existing rules of the national securities exchanges, national securities associations, and the Municipal Securities Rulemaking Board.

In addition, the Commission has broad rulemaking authority over the activities of brokers, dealers, municipal securities dealers, securities information processors, and transfer agents. The Commission may regulate such securities trading practices as short sales and stabilizing transactions. It may regulate the trading of options on national securities exchanges and the activities of members of exchanges who trade on the trading floors and may adopt rules governing broker-dealer sales practices in dealing with investors. The Commission also is authorized to adopt rules concerning the financial responsibility of brokers and dealers and reports to be made by them.

The Securities Exchange Act also requires the filing of registration statements and annual and other reports with national securities exchanges and the Commission by companies whose securities are listed upon the exchanges, by companies that have assets of $5 million or more and 500 or more shareholders of record. In addition companies that distributed securities pursuant to a registration statement declared effective by the Commission under the Securities Act of 1933, must also file annual and other reports with the Commission. Such applications and reports must contain financial and other data prescribed by the Commission as necessary or appropriate for the protection of investors and to issue fair dealing. In addition, the solicitation of proxies, authorizations, or consents from holders of such registered securities must be made in accordance with rules and regulations prescribed by the commission. These rules provide for disclosures to securities holders of information relevant to the subject matter of the solicitation.

Disclosure of the holdings and transactions by officers, directors, and large (10 percent) holders of equity securities of companies is also required, and any and all persons who acquire more than 5 percent of certain equity securities are required to file detailed information with the Commission and any exchange upon which such securities may be traded. Moreover, any person making a tender offer for certain classes of equity securities is required to file reports with the Commission, if as a result of the tender offer such person would own more than 5 percent of the outstanding shares of the particular class of equity involved. The Commission also is authorized to promulgate rules governing the repurchase by a corporate issuer of its own securities.

REGULATION OF MUTUAL FUNDS AND OTHER INVESTMENT COMPANIES

The Investment Company Act of 1940 (15 U.S.C. 80a–1-80a-64) requires investment companies to register with the Commission and regulates their activities to protect investors. The regulation covers sales and management fees, composition of boards of directors, and capital structure. The act prohibits investment companies from engaging in various transactions, including transactions with affiliated persons unless the Commission first determines that such transactions are fair. In addition, the act provides a somewhat parallel but less stringent regulation of business development companies. Under the act, the Commission may institute court action to enjoin the consummation of mergers and other plans for reorganization of investment companies if such plans are unfair to security holders. It also may impose sanctions by administrative proceedings against investment company managements for violations of the act and other federal securities laws, and file court actions to enjoin acts and practices of management officials involving breaches of fiduciary duty involving personal misconduct and to disqualify such officials from office.

REGULATION OF COMPANIES CONTROLLING UTILITIES

The Public Utility Holding Company Act of 1935 (15 U.S.C. 79–79z-6) provides for regulation by the commission of the purchase and sale of securities and assets by companies in electric and gas utility holding company systems, their intra-system transactions and service and management arrangements. It limits holding companies to a single coordinated utility system and requires simplification of complex corporate and capital structures and elimination of unfair distribution of voting power among holders of system securities.

The issuance and sale of securities by holding companies and their subsidiaries, unless exempt (subject to conditions and terms which the Commission is empowered to impose) as an issue expressly authorized by the state commission in the state in which the issuer is incorporated, must be found by the Commission to meet statutory standards.

The purchase and sale of utility properties and other assets may not be made in contravention of rules, regulations, or orders of the Commission regarding the consideration to be received, maintenance of competitive conditions, fees and commissions, accounts, disclosure of interest, and similar matters. In passing upon proposals for reorganization, merger, or consolidation, the Commission must be satisfied that the objectives of the act generally are complied with and that the terms of the proposal are fair and equitable to all classes of security holders affected.

REGULATION OF INVESTMENT ADVISERS

The Investment Advisers Act of 1940 (15 U.S.C. 80b–1–80b–21) provides that persons who, for compensation, engage in the business of advising others with respect to their security transactions must register with the Commission. The act prohibits certain types of fee arrangements, makes unlawful practices of investment advisers involving fraud or deceit, and requires, among other things, disclosure of any adverse interests the advisers may have in transactions executed for clients. The act authorizes the Commission, by rule, to define fraudulent and deceptive practices and prescribe means to prevent those practices.

REHABILITATION OF FAILING CORPORATIONS

Chapter 11, section 1109(a), of the Bankruptcy Code (11 U.S.C. 1109) provides for Commission participation as a statutory party in corporate reorganization proceedings administered in Federal courts. The principal functions of the Commission are to protect the interests of public investors involved in such cases through efforts to ensure their adequate representation and to participate on legal and policy issues which are of concern to public investors generally.

REPRESENTATION OF DEBT SECURITIES

The interests of purchasers of publicly offered debt securities issued pursuant to trust indentures are safeguarded under the provisions of the Trust Indenture Act of 1939 (15 U.S.C. 77aaa–77bbb). This act, among other things, requires the exclusion from such indentures of certain types of exculpatory clauses and the inclusion of certain protective provisions. The independence of the indenture trustee, who is a representative of the debt holder, is assured by proscribing certain relationships that might conflict with the proper exercise of his duties (15 U.S.C. 77aaa–77bbbb).

ENFORCEMENT ACTIVITIES

The Commission's enforcement activities are designed to secure compliance with the federal securities laws administered by the Commission and the rules and regulations adopted thereunder. These activities include measures to compel obedience to the disclosure requirements of the registration and other provisions of the acts; to prevent fraud and deception in the purchase and sale of securities; to obtain court orders enjoining acts and practices that operate as a fraud upon investors or otherwise violate the laws; to suspend or revoke the registrations of brokers, dealers, investment companies and investment advisers who willfully engage in such acts and practices; to suspend or bar from association persons associated with brokers, dealers, investment companies and investment advisers who have violated any provision of the federal securities laws; and to prosecute persons who have engaged in fraudulent activities, or other willful violations of those laws. In addition, attorneys, accountants, and other professionals who violate the securities laws face possible loss of their privilege to practice before the commission. To this end, private investigations are conducted into complaints or other evidences of securities violations. Evidence thus established of law violations is used in appropriate administrative proceedings to revoke registration or in actions instituted in federal courts to restrain or enjoin such activities. Where the evidence tends to establish fraud or other willful violation of the securities laws, the facts are referred to the Attorney General for criminal prosecution of the offenders. The commission may assist in such prosecutions.

SOURCES OF INFORMATION

Consumer Activities Publications detailing the Commission's activities, which include material of assistance to the potential investor, are available from the Publications Unit. In addition, the Office of Filings, Information and Consumer Services answers questions from investors, assists investors with specific problems regarding their relations with broker-dealers and companies, and advises the Commission and other offices and divisions regarding problems frequently encountered by investors and possible regulatory solutions to such problems. Phone, 202-272-7440.

INVESTOR INFORMATION AND PROTECTION

Complaints and inquiries may be directed to the home office or to any regional office. Registration statements and other public documents filed with the Commission are available for public inspection in the public reference room at the home office. Much of the information also is available in its New York and Chicago regional offices. Copies of the public material may be purchased from the Commission's contract copying service at prescribed rates.

Small Business Activities Information on security laws which pertain to small businesses in relation to securities offerings may be obtained from the Commission. Phone, 202-272-2644.

Reading Rooms The Commission maintains a public reference room (phone, 202-272-7450) and also a library (phone, 202-272-2618) where additional information may be obtained.

REGIONAL OFFICES (Securities and Exchange Commission)

Region	Address
1. New York, New Jersey	75 Park Place, New York, NY 10007 Phone: 212-264-1636
2. Maine, Vermont, New Hampshire, Massachusetts, Connecticut, Rhode Island	90 Devonshire Street, Boston, MA 02109 Phone: 617-223-9900
3. Tennessee, North Carolina, South Carolina, Mississippi, Alabama, Georgia, Florida, Louisiana (southeastern portion only), Virgin Islands	3475 Lenox Road NE, Atlanta, GA 30326 Phone: 404-347-4768
4. Minnesota, Wisconsin, Michigan, Iowa, Missouri, Illinois, Indiana, Ohio, Kentucky	219 S. Dearborn Street, Chicago, IL 60604 Phone: 312-353-7390
5. Kansas, Oklahoma, Texas, Arkansas, Louisiana (except southeastern portion)	411 W. 7th Street, Fort Worth, TX 76102 Phone: 817-334-3821
6. North Dakota, South Dakota, Colorado, Utah, Wyoming, New Mexico	1801 California Street, Denver, CO 80202 Phone: 303-391-6800
7. California, Nevada, Arizona, Hawaii, Guam	5757 Wilshire Boulevard, Los Angeles, CA 90036 Phone: 213-965-3998
8. Washington, Oregon, Alaska, Montana, Idaho	915 Second Avenue, Seattle, WA 98174 Phone: 206-442-7990
9. Pennsylvania, West Virginia, Virginia, Maryland, Delaware, Washington, D.C.	601 Walnut St., Philadelphia, PA 19106 Phone: 215-597-3100

How to Read a Financial Report

If you are a certified public accountant, it is most unlikely that you can learn anything from reading this book. You don't need to be told the basics of understanding what's presented in corporate annual reports. If you aren't a certified public accountant, and you find that annual reports are "over your head," this booklet can help you to grasp the facts contained in such reports and possibly become a better informed investor. That is our principal aim in publishing this booklet, but we also hope that it will be useful to other readers who want to understand how business works and to learn more about the companies that provide them with goods and services or that offer them employment.

Most annual reports can be broken down into three sections: the Executive Letter, the Business Review, and the Financial Review. The Executive Letter gives a broad overview of the company's business and financial performance. The Business Review summarizes recent developments, trends, and objectives of the company. The Financial Review is where business performance is quantified in dollars. This is the section we intend to clarify.

The Financial Review has two major parts: Discussion and Analysis and Audited Financial Statements. A third part might include information supplemental to the Financial Statements.

In the Discussion and Analysis, management explains changes in operating results from year to year. This explanation is presented mainly in a narrative format, with charts and graphs highlighting the comparisons. The operating results are numerically captured and presented in the Financial Statements.

The principal components of the Financial Statements are the balance sheet; income statement; statement of changes in shareholders' equity; statement of cash flows; and footnotes. The balance sheet portrays the financial strength of the company by showing what the company owns and what it owes on a certain date. The balance sheet can be thought of as a snapshot photograph since it reports on financial position as of the end of the year. The income statement, on the other hand, is like a motion picture since it reports on how the company performed during the year and shows whether operations have resulted in a profit or loss. The statement of changes in shareholders' equity reconciles the activity in the equity section of the balance sheet from year to year. Common changes in equity result from company profits or losses, dividends, or stock issuances. The statement of cash flows reports on the movement of cash by the company for the year. The footnotes provide more detailed information on the balance sheet and income statement.

This booklet will focus on illustrating the basic financial statements and footnotes presented in annual reports in accordance with current practice. It will also include examples of financial methods used by investors to better analyze financial statements. In order to provide a framework for illustration, we will invent a company. It will be a public company (one whose shares are freely traded on the open market). The reason for choosing a public company is that it is required to provide the most extensive amount of information in its annual reports in accordance with guidelines issued by the Securities and Exchange Commission (SEC). Our company will represent a typical corporation with the most commonly used accounting and reporting practices. We'll call our company Typical Manufacturing Company, Inc.

A Few Words Before We Begin

The following four pages show a sample Balance Sheet, Income Statement, Statement of Changes in Shareholders' Equity, and a Statement of Cash Flows. These are the statements we will discuss in the first section. To simplify matters, we did not illustrate the Discussion and Analysis nor did we present examples of the Executive Letter or Business Review. In our sample statements, we've presented two years of financial results on the balance sheet and income statement and one year of activity on the statement of changes in shareholders' equity and statement of cash flows. This was also done for ease of illustration. Were we to comply with SEC requirements, we would have had to report the last three years of activity in the Income Statement, Statement of Changes in Shareholders' Equity, and Statement of Cash Flows. Further SEC requirements that we did not illustrate include: presentation of selected quarterly financial data for the past two years, business segment information for the last three years, a listing of company directors and executive officers, and the market price of the company's common stock for each quarterly period within the two most recent fiscal years.

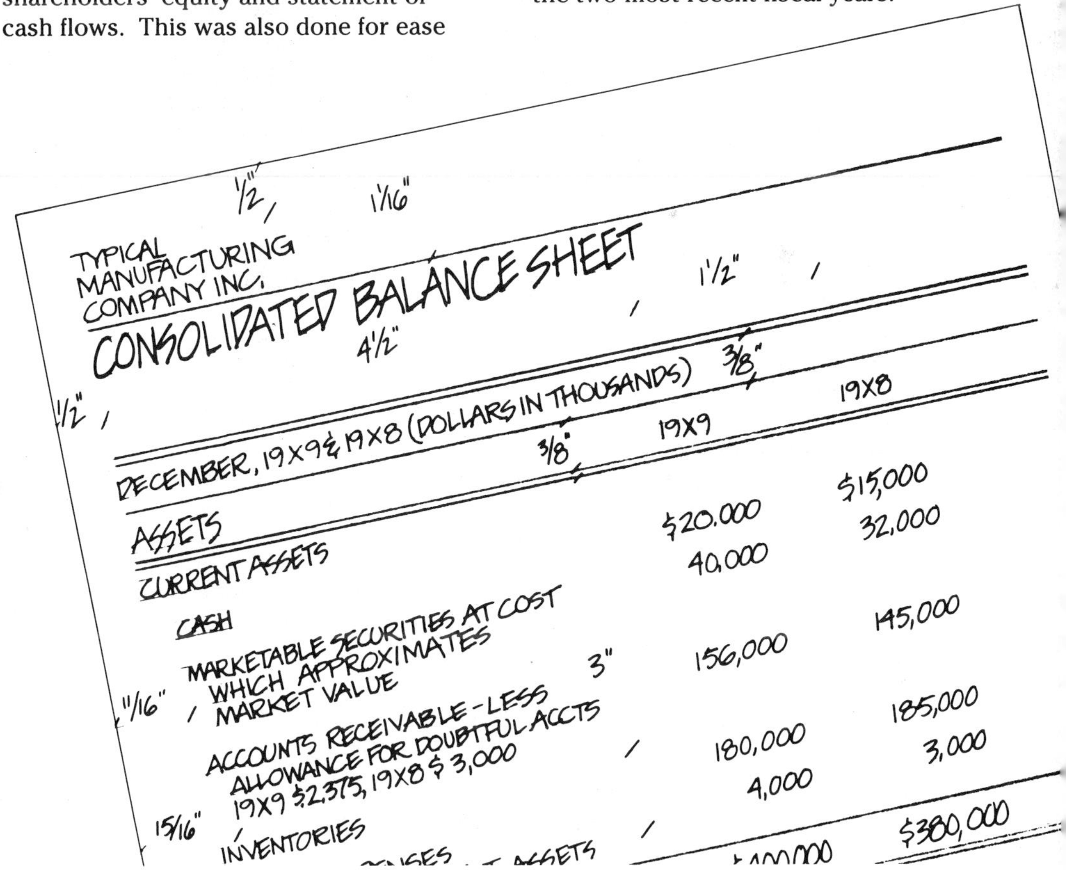

Typical
Manufacturing
Company Inc.

Consolidated Balance Sheet

December 31,19X9 and 19X8 *(dollars in thousands)*

Assets	**19X9**	19X8
Current assets		
Cash	**$ 20,000**	$ 15,000
Marketable securities at cost which approximates market value	**40,000**	32,000
Accounts receivable less allowance for doubtful accounts: 19X9: $2,375, 19X8: $3,000	**156,000**	145,000
Inventories	**180,000**	185,000
Prepaid expenses and other current assets	**4,000**	3,000
Total current assets	**$400,000**	$380,000
Property, plant and equipment		
Land	**$ 30,000**	$ 30,000
Buildings	**125,000**	118,500
Machinery	**200,000**	171,100
Leasehold improvements	**15,000**	15,000
Furniture, fixtures, etc.	**15,000**	12,000
Total property, plant and equipment	**$385,000**	$346,600
Less accumulated depreciation	**$125,000**	$97,000
Net property, plant and equipment	**$260,000**	$249,600
Intangibles (goodwill, patents)—less amortization	**$2,000**	$2,000
Total assets	**$662,000**	$631,600

See accompanying notes to consolidated financial statements.

Typical
Manufacturing
Company Inc.

December 31,19X9 and19X8 *(dollars in thousands)*

Liabilities	**19X9**	19X8
Current liabilities		
Accounts payable	**$ 60,000**	$ 57,000
Notes payable	**51,000**	61,000
Accrued expenses	**30,000**	36,000
Income taxes payable	**17,000**	15,000
Other liabilities	**12,000**	12,000
Total current liabilities	**$170,000**	$181,000
Long-term liabilities		
Deferred income taxes	**$ 16,000**	$ 9,000
12.5% Debentures payable 2010	**130,000**	130,000
Other long-term debt	**0**	6,000
Total liabilities	**$316,000**	$326,000
Shareholders' Equity		
Preferred stock $5.83 cumulative, $100 par value authorized, issued and outstanding 60,000 shares	**$ 6,000**	$ 6,000
Common stock $5.00 par value, authorized 20,000,000 shares, 19X9 issued 15,000,000 shares, 19X8 14,500,000 shares	**75,000**	72,500
Additional paid-in capital	**20,000**	13,500
Retained earnings	**249,000**	219,600
Foreign currency translation adjustments	**1,000**	(1,000)
Less: Treasury stock at cost (19X9–1,000; 19X8–1,000 shares)	**5,000**	5,000
Total shareholders' equity	**$346,000**	$305,600
Total liabilities and shareholders' equity	**$662,000**	$631,600

See accompanying notes to consolidated financial statements.

Typical
Manufacturing
Company Inc.

Consolidated Income Statement

Years ended December 31, 19X9 and 19X8 *(dollars in thousands)*	**19X9**	19X8
Net sales	**$765,000**	$725,000
Cost of sales	**535,000**	517,000
Gross margin	**$230,000**	$208,000
Operating expenses		
Depreciation and amortization	**28,000**	25,000
Selling, general and administrative expenses	**96,804**	109,500
Operating income	**$105,196**	$73,500
Other income (expense)		
Dividends and interest income	**5,250**	9,500
Interest expense	**(16,250)**	(16,250)
Income before income taxes and extraordinary loss	**$94,196**	$66,750
Income taxes	**41,446**	26,250
Income before extraordinary loss	**$52,750**	$40,500
Extraordinary item: Loss on early extinguishment of debt (net of income tax benefit of $750)	**(5,000)**	—
Net income	**$47,750**	$40,500
Common shares outstanding	**$14,999,000**	$14,499,000
Earnings per common share before extraordinary loss	**$3.49**	$2.77
Earnings per share—extraordinary loss	**(.33)**	—
Net income (per common share)	**$3.16**	$2.77

Consolidated Statement Of Changes In Shareholders' Equity

Year ended December 31, 19X9 *(dollars in thousands)*

	Preferred Stock	**Common Stock**	**Additional Paid-in Capital**	**Retained Earnings**	**Foreign Currency Translation Adjustment**	**Treasury Stock**	**Total**
Balance January 1, 19X9	$6,000	$72,500	$13,500	$219,600	($1,000)	($5,000)	$305,600
Net income				47,750			47,750
Dividends paid on:							
preferred stock				(350)			(350)
common stock				(18,000)			(18,000)
Common stock issued		$2,500	$6,500				$9,000
Translation gain					$2,000		2,000
Balance December 31, 19X9	**$6,000**	**$75,000**	**$20,000**	**$249,000**	**$1,000**	**($5,000)**	**$346,000**

See accompanying notes to consolidated financial statements.

Typical
Manufacturing
Company Inc.

Consolidated Statement Of Cash Flows

Year ended December 31, 19X9 *(dollars in thousands)*

Cash flows from operating activities:	
Net income	**$47,750**
Adjustments to reconcile net income to net cash from operating activities:	
Depreciation and amortization	**$28,000**
Increase in marketable securities	**(8,000)**
Increase in accounts receivable	**(11,000)**
Decrease in inventory	**5,000**
Increase in prepaid expenses and other current assets	**(1,000)**
Increase in deferred taxes	**7,000**
Increase in accounts payable	**3,000**
Decrease in accrued expenses	**(6,000)**
Increase in income taxes payable	**2,000**
Total Adjustments	**$19,000**
Net Cash Provided by Operating Activities	**$66,750**
Cash Flows from Investing Activities:	
Purchase of fixed assets	**($38,400)**
Net Cash Used in Investing Activities	**($38,400)**
Cash Flows from Financing Activities:	
Decrease in notes payable	**($10,000)**
Decrease in other long-term debt	**(6,000)**
Proceeds from issuance of common stock	**9,000**
Payment of dividends	**(18,350)**
Net Cash Used in Financing Activities	**($25,350)**
Effect of Exchange Rate Changes on Cash	**$2,000**
Increase in Cash	**$5,000**
Cash at beginning of year	**15,000**
Cash at end of year	**$20,000**

Income tax payments totaled $3,000 in 19X9.
Interest payments totaled $16,250 in 19X9.
See accompanying notes to consolidated financial statements.

The Balance Sheet

(dollars in thousands except per-share amounts)

The balance sheet represents the financial picture as it stood on one particular day, December 31, 19X9, as though the wheels of the company were momentarily at a standstill. Typical Manufacturing's balance sheet not only includes the most recent year, but also the previous year. This lets you compare how the company fared in its most recent years.

The balance sheet is divided into two sides: on the left are shown assets; on the right are shown liabilities and shareholders' equity. Both sides are always in balance. Each asset, liability, and component of shareholders' equity reported in the balance sheet represents an "account" having a dollar amount or "balance." In the assets column, we list all the goods and property owned, as well as claims against others yet to be collected. Under liabilities we list all debts due. Under shareholders' equity we list the amount shareholders would split up if Typical were liquidated at its balance sheet value.

Assume that the corporation goes out of business on the date of the balance sheet. If that occurs, the illustration which follows shows you what Typical Manufacturing's shareholders might expect to receive as their portion of the business.

Total assets (Less: intangibles)	**$660,000**
Amount required to pay liabilities	**316,000**
Amount remaining for the shareholders	**$344,000**

Now, we are going to give you a guided tour of the balance sheet's accounts. We'll define each item, one by one, and explain how they work.

Assets

Current Assets

In general, current assets include cash and those assets which in the normal course of business will be turned into cash in the reasonably near future, i.e., generally within a year from the date of the balance sheet.

Cash

This is just what you would expect—bills and coins in the till (petty cash fund) and money on deposit in the bank.

1 Cash	**$20,000**

Marketable securities

This asset represents investment of excess or idle cash that is not needed immediately. In Typical's case it is invested in preferred stock. Because these funds may be needed on short notice, it is essential that the securities be readily marketable and subject to a minimum of price fluctuation. The general practice is to show marketable securities at cost or market, whichever is lower.

2 Marketable securities at cost which approximates market value	**$40,000**

Accounts receivable

Here we find the amount due from customers but not yet collected. When goods due are shipped prior to collection, a receivable is recorded. Customers are usually given 30, 60, or 90 days in which to pay. The amount due from customers is $158,375. However, experience shows that some customers fail to pay their bills, because of financial difficulties or some catastrophic event (a tornado, a hurricane, or a flood) befalling their business. Therefore, in order to show the accounts receivable item at a figure representing expected receipts, the total is after a provision for doubtful accounts. This year that debt reserve was $2,375.

3 Accounts receivable— less allowance for doubtful accounts of $2,375	**$156,000**

Inventories

The inventory of a manufacturer is composed of three groups: raw materials to be used in the product, partially finished goods in process of manufacture, and finished goods ready for shipment to customers. The generally accepted method of valuation of the inventory is *cost or market, whichever is lower.* This gives a conservative figure. Where this method is used, the value for balance sheet purposes will be cost, or perhaps less than cost if, as a result of deterioration, obsolescence, decline in prices, or other factors, less than cost can be realized on the inventory. Inventory valuation includes an allocation of production and other expenses, as well as the cost of materials.

4	**Inventories**	**$180,000**

Consolidated Balance Sheet

	December 31, 19X9 and 19X8 (dollars in thousands) **Assets**	**19X9**	19X8
	Current Assets		
1	Cash	**$ 20,000**	$ 15,000
2	Marketable securities at cost which approximates market value	**40,000**	32,000
3	Accounts receivable—less allowance for doubtful accounts: 19X9: $2,375, 19X8: $3,000	**156,000**	145,000
4	Inventories	**180,000**	185,000
5	Prepaid expenses and other current assets	**4,000**	3,000
6	**Total current assets**	**$400,000**	$380,000
	Property, plant and equipment		
	Land	**$ 30,000**	$ 30,000
	Building	**125,000**	118,500
	Machinery	**200,000**	171,100
	Leasehold improvements	**15,000**	15,000
	Furniture, fixtures, etc.	**15,000**	12,000
7	**Total property, plant and equipment**	**$385,000**	$346,600
8	Less accumulated depreciation	**$125,000**	$97,000
9	**Net property, plant and equipment**	**$260,000**	$249,600
10	Intangibles (goodwill, patents)—less amortization	**$2,000**	$2,000
11	**Total assets**	**$662,000**	$631,600

Prepaid expenses

Prepaid expenses may arise for a situation such as this: During the year, Typical prepaid fire insurance premiums and advertising charges for the next year. Those insurance premiums and advertising services are as yet unused at the balance sheet date, so there exists an unexpended item, which will be used up over the next 12 months. If the advance payments had not been made, the company would have more cash in the bank. So payments made in advance from which the company has not yet received benefits, but for which it will receive benefits next year, are listed among current assets as prepaid expenses.

5	**Prepaid expenses and other current assets**	**$4,000**

Deferred charges for such items as the introduction of a new product to the market, or for moving a plant to a new location, represent a type of asset similar to prepaid expenses. However, deferred charges are not included in current assets because the benefit from such expenditure will be reaped over several years to come. So the expenditure incurred will be gradually written off over the next several years, rather than fully charged off in the year payment is made. Our balance sheet shows no deferred charges because Typical has none. If it had, they would normally be included just before intangibles on the asset side of the ledger.

To summarize, the *total current assets* item includes primarily: cash, marketable securities, accounts receivable, inventories, and prepaid expenses.

6	**Total current assets**	**$400,000**

You will observe that these assets are mostly *working assets* in the sense that they are in a constant cycle of being converted into cash. Inventories, when sold, become accounts receivable; receivables, upon collection, become cash; cash is used to pay debts and running expenses. We will discover later in the booklet how to make current assets tell a story.

Property, Plant and Equipment

Property, plant and equipment represents those assets not intended for sale that are used over and over again in order to manufacture, display, warehouse, and transport the product. This category includes land, buildings, machinery, equipment, furniture, automobiles, and trucks. The generally accepted and approved method for valuation is *cost minus the depreciation accumulated* by the date of the balance sheet. Depreciation is discussed in the next section.

	Property, plant and equipment	
	Land	**$ 30,000**
	Buildings	**125,000**
	Machinery	**200,000**
	Leasehold Improvements	**15,000**
	Furniture, fixtures, etc.	**15,000**
7	**Total property, plant & equipment**	**$385,000**

The figure displayed is not intended to reflect market value at present or replacement cost in the future. While it is recognized that the cost to replace plant and equipment at some future date might be higher, that possible cost is obviously variable. For this reason, up to now, most companies have followed a general rule: *acquisition cost less accumulated depreciation based on that cost.*

Depreciation

Depreciation is the practice of allocating the cost of a fixed asset over its useful life. This has been defined for accounting purposes as the decline in useful value of a fixed asset due to wear and tear from use and passage of time.

The cost incurred to acquire the property, plant and equipment must be spread over the expected useful life, taking into consideration the factors discussed above. For example: Suppose a delivery truck costs $10,000 and is expected to last five years. Using a "straight-line" method of depreciation, $2,000 of the truck's cost is allocated to each year's income statement. The balance sheet at the end of one year would show:

Truck (cost)	**$10,000**
Less accumulated depreciation	**2,000**
Net depreciated value	**$ 8,000**

At the end of the second year it would show:

Truck (cost)	**$10,000**
Less accumulated depreciation	**4,000**
Net depreciated value	**$ 6,000**

In our sample balance sheet, a figure is shown for accumulated depreciation. This amount is the total of accumulated depreciation for buildings, machinery, leasehold improvements, and furniture and fixtures. Land is not subject to depreciation, and its listed value remains unchanged from year to year.

8 Less accumulated depreciation	**$125,000**

Thus, *net property, plant and equipment* is the valuation for balance sheet purposes of the investment in property, plant and equipment. As explained before, it consists of the cost of the various assets in this classification, less the depreciation accumulated to the date of the financial statement.

9 Net property, plant and equipment	**$260,000**

Depletion is a term used primarily by mining and oil companies or any of the so-called extractive industries. Since Typical Manufacturing is not in the mining business, we do not show depletion on the balance sheet. To deplete means to exhaust or use up. As the oil or other natural resource is used up or sold, a depletion reserve is set up to compensate for the natural wealth the company no longer owns.

Intangibles

These may be defined as assets having no physical existence, yet having substantial value to the company. Examples? A franchise to a cable TV company allowing exclusive service in certain areas, or a patent for exclusive manufacture of a specific article. It should be noted, however, that only intangibles purchased from other companies are shown on the balance sheet.

Another intangible asset sometimes found in corporate balance sheets is *goodwill*, which represents the amount by which the price of acquired companies exceeds the related values of net assets acquired. Company practices vary considerably in assigning value to this asset. Accounting rules now require one firm that buys another to write off the goodwill over a period not exceeding 40 years.

10 Intangibles (goodwill, patents) less amortization	**$2,000**

All of these items added together produce the figure listed on the balance sheet as *total assets.*

11 Total assets	**$662,000**

Liabilities

	Consolidated Balance Sheet		
	December 31, 19X9 and 19X8 **Liabilities**	**19X9**	19X8
	Current Liabilities		
12	Accounts payable	**$ 60,000**	$ 57,000
13	Notes payable	**51,000**	61,000
14	Accrued expenses	**30,000**	36,000
15	Income taxes payable	**17,000**	15,000
16	Other liabilities	**12,000**	12,000
17	**Total current liabilities**	**$170,000**	$181,000
	Long-term liabilities		
18	Deferred income taxes	**$ 16,000**	$ 9,000
19	12.5% Debentures payable 2010	**130,000**	130,000
20	Other long-term debt	**0**	6,000
21	**Total liabilities**	**$316,000**	$326,000
	Shareholders' Equity		
22	Preferred stock $5.83 cumulative, $100 par value, authorized, issued and outstanding 60,000 shares	**$ 6,000**	$ 6,000
23	Common stock $5.00 par value, authorized 20,000,000 shares, issued 19X9 15,000,000 shares, 19X8 14,500,000 shares	**75,000**	72,500
24	Additional paid-in capital	**20,000**	13,500
25	Retained earnings	**249,000**	219,600
26	Foreign currency translation adjustments	**1,000**	(1,000)
27	Less: Treasury stock at cost (19X9–1,000; 19X8–1,000)	**5,000**	5,000
28	**Total shareholders' equity**	**$346,000**	$305,600
29	**Total liabilities and shareholders' equity**	**$662,000**	$631,600

Current Liabilities

This item generally includes all debts that fall due within 12 months. The *current assets* item is a companion to *current liabilities* because current assets are the source from which payments are made on current debts. The relationship between the two is one of the most revealing things to be learned from the balance sheet, and we will go into that later. For now, we need to define the subgroups within current liabilities.

Accounts payable

The *accounts payable* item represents amounts the company owes to its regular business creditors from whom it has bought goods or services on open account.

12 Accounts payable	**$ 60,000**

Notes payable

If money is owed to a bank, individual, corporation, or other lender, it appears on the balance sheet under *notes payable* as evidence that a promissory note has been given by the borrower.

13 Notes payable	**$ 51,000**

Accrued expenses

Now we have defined accounts payable as the amounts owed by the company to its regular business creditors. The company also owes, on any given day, salaries and wages to its employees, interest on funds borrowed from banks and from bondholders, fees to attorneys, insurance premiums, pensions, and similar items. To the extent that the amounts owed and not recorded on the books are unpaid at the date of the balance sheet, these expenses are grouped as a total under *accrued expenses*.

14 Accrued expenses	**$ 30,000**

Income tax payable

The debt due to the various taxing authorities such as the Internal Revenue Service is the same as any other liability under *accrued expenses*. But because of the amount and the importance of the tax factor, it is generally stated separately as *income taxes payable*.

15 Income taxes payable	**$17,000**

Other Liabilities

Simply stated, *other liabilities* includes all liabilities not captured in the specific categories presented.

16 Other liabilities	**$12,000**

Total current liabilities

Finally, the *total current liabilities* item sums up all of the items listed under this classification.

17 Total current liabilities	**$170,000**

Long-term Liabilities

In the matter of current liabilities, you will recall that we included debts due within one year from the balance sheet date. Here, under the heading of *long-term liabilities* are listed debts due after one year from the date of the financial report.

Deferred income taxes

One of the long-term liabilities on our sample balance sheet is *deferred income taxes*. The government provides businesses with tax incentives to make certain kinds of investments that will benefit the economy as a whole. For instance, a company can take accelerated depreciation deductions for investments in plant and equipment. These rapid write-offs in the early years of investment reduce what the company would otherwise owe in current taxes, but at some point in the future the taxes must be paid. Companies include a charge for deferred taxes in their tax calculations on the income statement and show what taxes would be without the accelerated write-offs. That charge then accumulates as a long-term liability on the balance sheet.

18 Deferred income taxes	**$16,000**

Debentures

The other long-term liability on our balance sheet is the *12.5% debentures* due in 2010. The money was received by the company as a loan from the bondholders, who in turn were given a certificate called a bond, as evidence of the loan. The bond is really a formal promissory note issued by the company, which in this case agreed to repay the debt at maturity in 2010 and also agreed to pay interest at the rate of 12.5% per year. Bond interest is usually payable semi-annually. Typical's bond issue is called a debenture because the bonds are backed by the general credit of the corporation rather than by the company's assets. Debentures are the most common type of bond issued by large, well-established corporations today.

Companies can also issue *first mortgage bonds,* which offer bondholders an added safeguard because they are secured by a mortgage on all or some of the company's property. First mortgage bonds are considered one of the highest grade investments because they give investors an undisputed claim on company earnings and the greatest safety. If the company is unable to pay off the bonds in cash when they are due, holders of first mortgage bonds have a claim or lien before other creditors (such as debenture holders) on the mortgaged assets, which may be sold and the proceeds used to satisfy the debt.

19 12.5% Debentures payable 2010	**$130,000**

Other long-term debt

Other *long-term debt* includes all debt other than what is specifically reported on in the balance sheet. In the case of Typical, this debt was extinguished in 1989.

20 Other long-term debt	**0**

Total liabilities

Current and long-term debt are summed together to produce the figure listed on the balance sheet as *total liabilities.*

21 Total liabilities	**$316,000**

Shareholders' Equity

This item is the total equity interest that all shareholders have in this corporation. In other words, it is the corporation's net worth after subtracting all liabilities. This is separated for legal and accounting reasons into the categories discussed below.

Capital Stock

In the broadest sense this represents shares in the proprietary interest in the company. These shares are represented by the stock certificates issued by the corporation to its shareholders. A corporation may issue several different classes of shares, each class having slightly different attributes.

Preferred Stock
These shares have some preference over other shares with respect to dividends and in distribution of assets in case of liquidation. Specific provisions can be obtained from a corporation's charter. In Typical, the preferred stock is a $5.83 *cumulative $100 par value,* which means that each share is entitled to $5.83 in dividends a year, before any dividends are paid to the common shareholders. Cumulative means that if in any year the dividend is not paid, it accumulates in favor of the preferred shareholders and must be paid to them when available and declared before any dividends are distributed on the common stock. Sometimes preferred shareholders have no voice in company affairs unless the company fails to pay them dividends at the promised rate.

22	**Preferred stock $5.83 cumulative, $100 par value, authorized issued and outstanding 60,000 shares**	**$6,000**

Common Stock
Each year before common shareholders receive any dividends, preferred holders are entitled to $5.83 per share, but no more. Common stock has no such limit on dividends payable each year. In good times, when earnings are high, dividends may also be high. And when earnings drop, so may dividends.

23	**Common stock $5.00 par value authorized 20,000,000 shares, issued 15,000,000 shares**	**$75,000**

Additional Paid-In Capital
This is the amount paid in by shareholders over the par or legal value of each share. Typical's common stock has a par value of $5.00 per share. In 1989, Typical sold 500,000 shares of stock for a total of $9,000. The $9,000 was allocated on the balance sheet between capital stock and additional paid-in capital. 500,000 shares at a par value of $5.00 for a total of $2,500 was allocated to common stock. The remaining $6,500 was allocated to additional paid-in capital.

23	**Common stock $5.00 par value authorized 20,000,000 shares issued 15,000,000 shares**	**$75,000**
24	**Additional paid-in capital**	**$20,000**
	Total of capital stock (common) and additional paid-in capital	**$95,000**

Retained Earnings
When a company first starts in business, it has no retained earnings. Retained earnings accumulate as the company earns profits and reinvests or "retains" profits in the company. In other words, retained earnings increase by the amount of profits earned, less dividends declared to shareholders. At the end of its first year, if profits are $80,000 and dividends of $30,000 are paid on the preferred stock but no dividends are declared on the common, the balance sheet will show retained earnings of $50,000. In the second year, if profits are $140,000 and Typical pays $30,000 in dividends on the preferred and $40,000 on the common, the accumulated retained earnings will be $120,000:

Balance at the end of the first year	**$ 50,000**
Net profit for second year	**140,000**
Total	**$190,000**
Less: all dividends	**70,000**
Retained earnings at the end of the second year	**$120,000**

The balance sheet for Typical shows the company has accumulated $249,000 in retained earnings.

25	**Retained earnings**	**$249,000**

Foreign Currency Translation Adjustments

When a company has an ownership interest in a foreign entity and the entity's results are to be captured in the company's consolidated financial statements, the *financial statements* of the foreign entity must be translated to U.S. dollars. Generally, the translation gain or loss should be reflected as a separate component of shareholders' equity called *foreign currency translation adjustment.* This adjustment should be distinguished from adjustments relating to *transactions* which are denominated in foreign currencies. The gain or loss in these cases should be included in a company's net income.

26	**Foreign currency translation adjustments**	**$1,000**

Treasury Stock

When a company reacquires its own stock, it is reported as *treasury stock* and is deducted from shareholders' equity. Of the cost and par methods of accounting, the former method is more commonly applied to treasury stock. Under the cost method, the cost of reacquired stock is deducted from shareholders' equity. Any dividends on shares held in the treasury should never be included as income.

27	**Treasury stock**	**$5,000**

The sum total of stock (net of treasury stock), additional paid-in capital, retained earnings and foreign currency translation adjustments, represents the *total shareholders' equity.*

28	**Total shareholders' equity**	**$346,000**

Just what does the balance sheet show?

In order to analyze balance sheet figures, investors look to certain financial statement ratios for guidance. One of their concerns is whether the business will be able to pay its debts when they come due. They are also interested in the company's inventory turnover and the amount of assets backing corporate securities (bonds, preferred and common stock), along with the relative mix of these securities. In the following section, we will discuss various ratios used for balance sheet analysis.

Net Working Capital

One very important thing to be learned from the balance sheet is *net working capital* or *net current assets,* sometimes called *working capital.* This is the difference between total current assets and total current liabilities. You will recall that current liabilities are debts generally due within one year from the date of the balance sheet. The source from which to pay those debts is current assets. Thus, working capital represents the amount that is left free and clear after all current debts are paid off. For Typical this is:

6	**Current assets**	**$400,000**
17	**Less: current liabilities**	**170,000**
	Working capital	**$230,000**

If you consider yourself a conservative investor, you should invest only in companies that maintain a comfortable amount of working capital. A company's ability to meet obligations, expand volume, and take advantage of opportunities is often determined by its working capital. Moreover, since you want your company to grow, this year's working capital should be larger than last year's.

Current Ratio

What is a comfortable amount of working capital? Analysts use several methods to judge whether a company has a sound working capital position. To help you interpret the current position of a company in which you are considering investing, the *current ratio* is more helpful than the dollar total of working capital. The first rough test for an industrial company is to compare the current assets figure with the total current liabilities. A current ratio of 2 to 1 is generally considered adequate. This means that for each $1 of current liabilities, there should be $2 in current assets.

To find the current ratio, divide current assets by current liabilities. In Typical's balance sheet:

6	**Current assets**	**$400,000**	**2.35**	**or 2.35 to 1**
17	**Current liabilities**	**$170,000**	**1**	

Thus, for each $1 of current liabilities, there is $2.35 in current assets to back it up.

There are so many different kinds of companies, however, that this test requires a great deal of modification if it is to be really helpful in analyzing companies in different industries. Generally, companies that have a small inventory and easily collectible accounts receivable can operate safely with a lower current ratio than those companies having a greater proportion of their current assets in inventory and selling their products on credit.

How Quick is Quick?

In addition to net working capital and current ratio, there are other ways of testing the adequacy of the current position. What are *quick assets*? They're the assets you have to cover a sudden emergency, assets you could take right away to the bank, if you had to. They are those current assets that are quickly convertible into cash. This leaves out merchandise inventories, because such inventories have yet to be sold and are not convertible into cash. Accordingly, quick assets are current assets minus inventories and prepaid expenses.

6	**Current assets**	**$400,000**
4	**Less: inventories**	**180,000**
5	**Less: prepaid expenses**	**4,000**
	Quick assets	**$216,000**

Net quick assets are found by taking the quick assets and subtracting the total current liabilities. A well-fixed industrial company should show a reasonable excess of quick assets over current liabilities. This provides a rigorous and important test of a company's ability to meet its obligations.

	Quick assets	**$216,000**
17	**Less: current liabilities**	**170,000**
	Net quick assets	**$ 46,000**

The *quick assets ratio* is found by dividing quick assets by current liabilities.

	Quick assets	**$216,000**	**1.3**	**or 1.3 to 1**
17	**Current liabilities**	**$170,000**	**1**	

As you see, for each $1 of current liabilities, there is $1.30 in quick assets available.

Debt to Equity

A certain level of debt is acceptable, but too much debt presents a hazardous signal to investors. The *debt-to-equity ratio* is an indicator of whether the company is excessively using debt for financing purposes. For Typical, the debt-to-equity ratio is computed as follows:

21	**Total liabilities**	**$316,000**	= .91
28	**Total shareholders' equity**	**$346,000**	

A debt-to-equity ratio of .91 means the company is using 91 cents of liabilities for every dollar of shareholders' equity in the business. Normally, industrial companies maintain a maximum of a 1 to 1 ratio, to keep debt at a level which is less than the investment level of the owners of the business. Utilities and financial companies can operate safely with much higher ratios.

Inventory Turnover

How big an inventory should a company have? That depends on a combination of many factors. An inventory is large or small depending upon the type of business and the time of the year. An automobile dealer, for example, with a large stock of autos at the height of the season is in a strong inventory position; yet that same inventory at the end of the season is a weakness in the dealer's financial condition.

One way to measure adequacy and balance of inventory is to compare it with sales for the year to get *inventory turnover.* Typical's sales for the year are $765,000, and inventory on the balance sheet date is $180,000. Thus turnover is 4.25 times (765÷180), meaning that goods are bought and sold out more than four times per year on average. (Strict accounting requires computation of inventory turnover by comparing annual *cost of goods sold* with *average inventory.* This information is not readily available in some published statements, so many analysts look instead for *sales* related to *inventory.*)

Inventory as a percentage of current assets is another comparison that may be made. In Typical, the inventory of $180,000 represents 45% of the total current assets, which amount to $400,000. But there is considerable variation between different types of companies, and thus the relationship is significant only when comparisons are made between companies in the same industry.

Book Value of Securities

The balance sheet will reveal *net book value* (the value on the company's books) or *net asset value* of the company's securities. This value represents the amount of corporate assets backing a bond or a common or preferred share. Here's how we calculate values for Typical's securities.

Net Asset Value Per Bond

To state this figure conservatively, intangible assets are subtracted as if they have no value on liquidation. Current liabilities of $170,000 are considered paid. This leaves $490,000 in assets to pay the bondholders. So, $3,769 in net asset value protects each $1,000 bond.

11	Total assets	$662,000
10	Less: intangibles	2,000
	Total tangible assets	$660,000
17	Less: current liabilities	170,000
	Net tangible assets available to meet bondholders' claims	$490,000

$490,000 / 130 (bonds outstanding) = $3,769 net asset value per $1,000 bond

Net Asset Value Per Share of Preferred Stock

To calculate net asset value of a preferred share, we take total assets, conservatively stated at $660,000 (eliminating $2,000 of intangible assets). Current liabilities of $170,000 and long-term liabilities are considered paid. This leaves $344,000 of assets protecting the preferred. So, $5,733 in net asset value backs each share of preferred.

11	Total assets	$662,000
10	Less: intangibles	2,000
	Total tangible assets	$660,000
17	Less: current liabilities	$170,000
18,19, & 20	long-term liabilities	146,000
	Net assets backing the preferred stock	$344,000

$344,000,000 / 60,000 (shares of preferred stock outstanding) = $5,733 net asset value per share of preferred stock

Net Book Value per Share of Common Stock

The net book value per share of common stock can be looked upon as meaning the amount of money each share would receive if the company were liquidated, based on balance-sheet values. Of course, the preferential shareholders would have to be satisfied first. The answer, $22.54 net book value per share of common stock, is arrived at as follows:

11	Total assets		$662,000
10	Less: intangibles		2,000
	Total tangible assets		$660,000
17	Less: current liabilities	$170,000	
18, 19, & 20	long-term liabilities	146,000	
22	preferred stock	6,000	
			$322,000
	Net assets available for the common stock		$338,000

$338,000,000 / 14,999,000 (shares of common stock outstanding) = $22.54 net asset value per share of common stock

An alternative method of arriving at the common shareholders' equity—conservatively stated at $338,000—is:

23	Common stock	$ 75,000
24	Additional paid-in capital	20,000
25	Retained earnings	249,000
26	Foreign currency translation adjustments	1,000
27	Treasury stock	(5,000)
		$340,000
10	Less: intangible assets	(2,000)
	Total common shareholders' equity	$338,000

$338,000,000 / 14,999,000 (shares of preferred stock outstanding) = $22.54 net book value per share of common stock

Do not be misled by book value figures, particularly of common stocks. Profitable companies often show a very low net book value and very substantial earnings. Railroads, on the other hand, may show a high book value for their common stock but have such low or irregular earnings that the stock's market price is much less than its book value. Insurance companies, banks, and investment companies are exceptions. Because their assets are largely liquid (cash, accounts receivable, and marketable securities), the book value of their common stock is sometimes a fair indication of market value.

Capitalization Ratio

The proportion of each kind of security issued by a company is the *capitalization ratio.* A high proportion of bonds sometimes reduces the attractiveness of both the preferred and common stock, and too much preferred can detract from the common's value. That's because bond interest must be paid before preferred dividends, and preferred dividends before common dividends.

To get Typical's *bond ratio* divide the face value of the bonds, $130,000, by the total value of bonds, preferred and common stock, additional paid-in capital, retained earnings, foreign currency translation adjustments and treasury stock, less intangibles, which is $474,000. This shows that bonds amount to about 27% of Typical's total capitalization.

19	**Debentures**	**$130,000**
22	**Preferred stock**	**6,000**
23	**Common stock**	**75,000**
24	**Additional paid-in capital**	**20,000**
25	**Retained earnings**	**249,000**
26	**Foreign currency translation adjustments**	**1,000**
27	**Treasury stock**	**(5,000)**
10	**Less: intangibles**	**(2,000)**
	Total capitalization	**$474,000**

The *preferred stock ratio* is found the same way—divide preferred stock of $6,000 by the entire capitalization of $474,000. The result is about 1%.

The *common stock ratio* will be the difference between 100% and the total of the bond and preferred stock ratio—or about 72%. The same result is reached by combining common stock, additional paid-in capital, retained earnings, foreign currency translation adjustments, and treasury stock.

		Amount	Ratio
19	**Debentures**	**$130,000**	**27%**
22	**Preferred stock**	**6,000**	**1%**
10 & 23 – 27	**Common stock (including additional paid-in capital, related earnings, and foreign currency translation adjustments less: treasury stock and intangibles)**	**338,000**	**72%**
	Total	**$474,000**	**100%**

The Income Statement

(dollars in thousands except per-share amounts)

Now, we come to the payoff for many potential investors: the income statement. It shows how much the corporation earned or lost during the year. It appears on Page 486 of this booklet.

While the balance sheet shows the fundamental soundness of a company by reflecting its financial position at a given date, the income statement may be of greater interest to investors because it shows the record of its operating activities for the whole year. It serves as a valuable guide in anticipating how the company may do in the future. The figure given for a single year is not nearly the whole story. The historical record for a series of years is more important than the figure of any single year. Typical includes two years in its statement and gives a ten-year financial summary as well, which appears on Page 508.

An income statement matches the amounts received from selling goods and services and other items of income against all the costs and outlays incurred in order to operate the company. The result is a *net income* or a *net loss* for the year. The costs incurred usually consist of cost of sales; overhead expenses such as wages and salaries, rent, supplies, depreciation; interest on money borrowed; and taxes.

Consolidated Income Statement

	Years ended December 31, 19X9 and 19X8 (dollars in thousands except per-share amounts)	19X9	19X8
30	Net sales	$765,000	$725,000
31	Cost of sales	535,000	517,000
32	Gross margin	$230,000	$208,000
	Operating Expenses		
33	Depreciation and amortization	28,000	25,000
34	Selling, general and administrative expenses	96,804	109,500
35	Operating income	$105,196	$73,500
	Other income (expense)		
36	Dividends and interest income	5,250	9,500
37	Interest expense	(16,250)	(16,250)
38	Income before income taxes and extraordinary loss	$94,196	$66,750
39	Income taxes	41,446	26,250
40	Income before extraordinary loss	$52,750	$40,500
41	Extraordinary item: Loss on early extinguishment of debt (net of income tax benefit of $750)	(5,000)	—
42	**Net income**	$47,750	$40,500
43	**Common shares outstanding**	$14,990,000	$14,499,000
44	Earnings per share of common stock before extraordinary loss	$3.49	$2.77
45	Earnings per share—extraordinary loss	(.33)	—
46	**Net income (per common share)**	$3.16	$2.77

Net Sales

The most important source of revenue always makes up the first item on the income statement. In Typical Manufacturing, it is *net sales*. It represents the primary source of money received by the company from its customers for goods sold or services rendered. The *net sales* item covers the amount received after taking into consideration returned goods and allowances for reduction of prices. By comparing 19X9 and 19X8, we can see if Typical had a better year in 19X9, or a worse one.

30 Net sales $765,000 $725,000

Cost of Sales

In a manufacturing establishment, this represents all the costs incurred in the factory in order to convert raw materials into finished products. These costs are commonly known as product costs. Product costs are those costs which can be identified with the purchase or manufacture of goods made available for sale. There are three basic components of product cost: direct materials; direct labor; and manufacturing overhead. Direct materials and direct labor costs can be directly traced to the finished product. For example, for a furniture manufacturer, lumber would be a direct material cost and carpenter wages would be a direct labor cost. Manufacturing overhead costs, while associated with the manufacturing process, cannot be traceable to the finished product. Examples of manufacturing overhead costs are costs associated with operating the factory plant (plant depreciation, rent, electricity, supplies, maintenance and repairs, and production foremen salaries).

31 Cost of sales $535,000

Gross Margin

Gross Margin is the excess of sales over cost of sales. It represents the residual profit from sales after considering product costs.

32 Gross margin $230,000

Depreciation and amortization
Each year's decline in value of non-manufacturing facilities would be captured here. Amortization is the decline in useful value of an intangible, such as a 17-year patent.

33 Depreciation and amortization	**$28,000**

Selling, General, and Administrative Expenses
These expenses are generally grouped separately from cost of sales so that the reader of an income statement may see the extent of selling and administrative costs. They include salesmen's salaries and commissions, advertising and promotion, travel and entertainment, executives' salaries, office payroll and office expenses.

34 Selling, general and administrative expenses	**$96,804**

Subtracting all operating expenses from the net sales figure gives us the *operating income.*

35 Operating income	**$105,196**

An additional source of revenue comes from dividends and interest received by the company from its investment in stocks and bonds. This is listed separately under an item called *other income (expense).*

36 Dividends and interest income	**$5,250**

Interest Expense

The interest paid to bondholders for the use of their money is sometimes referred to as a *fixed charge* because the interest must be paid year after year whether the company is making money or losing money. Interest differs from dividends on stocks, which are payable only if the board of directors declares them.

Interest paid is another cost of doing business and is deductible from earnings in order to arrive at a base for the payment of income taxes.

Typical Manufacturing's debentures, carried on the balance sheet as a long-term liability, bear 12.5% interest per year on $130,000. Thus, the interest expense in the income statement is equal to $16,250 per year. It shows up under *other income (expense).*

37 Interest expense	**$16,250**

Income Taxes

Each corporation has a basic tax rate, which depends on the level and nature of its income. Large corporations like Typical Manufacturing are subject to the top corporate income tax rate, but tax credits tend to lower the overall tax rate. Typical's income before taxes is $94,196; the tax comes to $41,446.

38 Income before provision for income taxes	**$94,196**
39 Provision for income taxes	**41,446**

Income Before Extraordinary Loss
After we have taken into consideration all ordinary income (the plus factors) and deducted all ordinary costs (the minus factors), we arrive at *income before extraordinary loss* for the year.

40 Income before extraordinary loss	**$52,750**

Extraordinary Loss

Under ordinary conditions, the above income of $52,750 would be the end of the story. However, there are years in which companies experience unusual and infrequent events called *extraordinary items.* Examples of extraordinary items include debt extinguishments, tax loss carryforwards, pension plan terminations, and litigation settlements. In this case, Typical extinguished a portion of its debt early. This event is isolated on a separate line, net of its tax effect. Its earnings-per-share impact is also segregated from the earnings per share attributable to "normal" operations.

41 Loss on early extinguishment of debt (net of tax benefit of $750)	**($5,000)**

Net Income

Once all income and costs, including extraordinary items, are considered, we arrive at net income.

42	Net income	$47,750

Condensed, the income statement looks like this:

	Plus factors:	
30	Net sales	$765,000
36	Dividends and Interest	5,250
	Total	$770,250
	Minus factors:	
31	Cost of sales	$535,000
33–34	Operating expenses	124,804
37	Interest expense	16,250
39	Provision for income taxes	41,446
	Total	$717,500
40	Net income before extraordinary loss	$ 52,750
41	Extraordinary loss	(5,000)
42	Net income	$ 47,750

Other Items

Two other items that do not apply to Typical could appear on an income statement. First, U.S. companies that do business overseas may have transaction gains or losses related to fluctuations in foreign currency exchange rates.

Second, if a corporation owns more than 20% but less than 51% of the stock of a subsidiary company, the corporation must show its share of the subsidiary's earnings—minus any dividends received from the subsidiary—on its income statement. For example, if the corporation's share of the subsidiary's earnings is $1,200 and the corporation received $700 in dividends from the company, the corporation must include $500 on its income statement under the category *equity in the earnings of unconsolidated subsidiaries.* The corporation must also increase its investment in the company to the extent of the earnings it picks up on its income statement.

Analyzing the income statement

The income statement will tell us a lot more if we make a few detailed comparisons. Before you invest in a company, you want to know its *operating margin of profit* and how it has changed over the years. Typical had sales of $765,000,000 in 19X9 and showed $105,196,000 as the operating income.

35	$105,196 operating income	=	13.8%
30	$765,000 sales		

This means that for each dollar of sales 13.8¢ remained as a gross profit from operations. This figure is interesting but is more significant if we compare it with the profit margin last year.

35	$ 73,500 operating income	=	10.1%
30	$725,000 sales		

Typical's profit margin went from 10.1% to 13.8%, so business didn't just grow, *it became more profitable.* Changes in profit margin can reflect changes in efficiency, product line, or types of customers served.

We can also compare Typical with other companies in its field. If our company's profit margin is very low compared to others, it is an unhealthy sign. If it is high, there are grounds for optimism.

Analysts also frequently use *operating cost ratio* for the same purpose. Operating cost ratio is the complement of the margin of profit. Typical's profit margin is 13.8%. The operating cost ratio is 86.2%.

		Amount	Ratio
30	Net sales	$765,000	100.0%
31, 33, 34	Operating costs	659,804	86.2%
35	Operating income	$105,196	13.8%

Net profit ratio is still another guide to indicate how satisfactory the year's activities have been. In Typical Manufacturing, the year's net income was $47,750. The net sales for the year amounted to $765,000. Therefore, Typical's income was $47,750 on $765,000 of sales or:

42	**$ 47,750 net income**	=	6.2%
30	**$765,000 sales**		

This means that this year for every $1 of goods sold, 6.2¢ in profit ultimately went to the company. By comparing the net profit ratio from year to year for the same company and with other companies, we can best judge profit progress.

Last year, Typical's net income was $40,500 on $725,000 in sales:

42	**$ 40,500 net income**	=	5.6%
30	**$725,000 sales**		

We can compare the U.S. Department of Commerce's latest available average profit margins for all U.S. manufacturers to the profit margins calculated from Typical's 10-year summary on Page 508.

The margin of profit ratio, operating cost ratio, and net profit ratio, like all those we examined in connection with the balance sheet, give us general information about the company and help us judge its prospects for the future. All these comparisons have significance for the long term, because they tell us about the fundamental economic condition of the company. One question remains: are the securities a good investment for you now? For an answer, we must look at some additional factors.

Profit Margins (After Tax)

	19X3	19X4	19X5	19X6	19X7
Average of U.S. Manufacturers	4.1	4.6	3.8	3.8	4.9
Typical	6.1	5.3	5.0	5.1	5.5

Interest Coverage

The bonds of Typical Manufacturing represent a very substantial debt, but they are due many years in the future. The yearly interest, however, is a fixed charge, and we want to know how readily the company can pay the interest. More specifically, we would like to know whether the borrowed funds have been put to good use so that the earnings are ample and thus available to meet interest costs.

The available income representing the source for payment of the bond interest is $110,446 (operating profit plus dividends and interest). The annual bond interest amounts to $16,250. This means the annual interest expense is covered 6.8 times.

37	**$110,446 available income**	=	6.8%
	$ 16,250 interest on bonds		

Before an industrial bond can be considered a safe investment, most analysts say that the company should earn its bond interest requirement three to four times over. By these standards, Typical Manufacturing has a fair margin of safety.

What About Leverage?

A stock is said to have high leverage if the company that issued it has a large proportion of bonds and preferred stock outstanding in relation to the amount of common stock. A simple illustration will show why. Let's take, for example, a company with $10,000,000 of 4% bonds outstanding. If the company is earning $440,000 before bond interest, there will only be $40,000 left for the common stock after payment of $400,000 bond interest ($10,000,000 at 4% equals $400,000). However, an increase of only 10% in earnings (to $484,000) will leave $84,000 for common stock dividends, or an increase of more than 100%. If there is only a small amount of common stock issued, the increase in earnings per share will appear very impressive.

You have probably realized that a decline of 10% in earnings would not only wipe out everything available for the common stock, but also result in the company's being unable to cover its full interest on its bonds without dipping into accumulated earnings. This is the great danger of so-called high-leverage stocks and also illustrates the fundamental weakness of companies that have a disproportionate amount of debt or preferred stock. Conservative investors usually steer clear of them, although these stocks do appeal to people who are willing to assume the risk.

Typical Manufacturing, on the other hand, is not a highly leveraged company. Last year, Typical paid $16,250 in bond interest and its net profit—before this payment—came to $56,750. This left $40,500 for the common stock and retained earnings. Now look what happened this year. Net profit before subtracting bond interest rose by $7,250, or about 13%. Since the bond interest stayed the same, net income after paying this interest also rose $7,250. But that is about 18% of $40,500. While this is certainly not a spectacular example of leverage, 18% is better than 13%.

Preferred Dividend Coverage

To calculate the *preferred dividend coverage* (the number of times preferred dividends were earned), we must use net profit as our base, because federal income taxes and all interest charges must be paid before anything is available for shareholders. Because we have 60,000 shares of $100 par value preferred stock that pays a dividend of $5.83 1/3, the total dividend requirement for the preferred stock is $350,000. Dividing the net income of $47,750,000 by this figure we arrive at approximately 136.4, which means that the dividend requirement of the preferred stock has been earned more than 136 times over. This ratio is so high partly because Typical has only a small amount of preferred stock outstanding.

Earnings Per Common Share

The buyer of common stock is often more concerned with the earnings per share of a stock than with the dividend. This is because earnings per share usually influence stock market prices. Although our income statement separates earnings per share before and after the effect of the extraordinary item, the remainder of our presentation will only consider earnings per share after the extraordinary item. In Typical's case the income statement shows earnings available for common stock.

46	**Earnings per share**	**$3.16**

But if it didn't, we could calculate it ourselves:

42	**Net profit for the year**	**$47,750**
	Less: dividend requirements on preferred stock	**350**
	Earnings available for the common stock	**$47,400**

$$\frac{\text{\$47,400,000 earnings available after preferred dividends}}{\text{14,999,000 number of outstanding common shares}} = \text{\$3.16 earnings per share of common}$$

Typical's capital structure is a very simple one, comprised of common and preferred stock. It's earnings-per-share computation will suffice under this scenario. However, if the capital structure is more complex and contains securities which are convertible into common stock, options, warrants or contingently issuable shares, the calculation requires modification. In fact, two separate calculations must be performed. This is called dual presentation. The calculations are primary and fully diluted earnings per common share.

Primary Earnings Per Common Share

This is determined by dividing the earnings for the year not only by the number of shares of common stock outstanding but by the common stock plus *common stock equivalents if dilutive.*

Common stock equivalents are securities, such as convertible preferred stock, convertible bonds, stock options, warrants and the like, that enable the holder to become a common shareholder by exchanging or converting the security. These are deemed to be only one step short of common stock—their value stems in large part from the value of the common to which they relate.

Convertible preferred stock and convertible bonds offer the holder either a specified dividend rate or interest return, or the option of participating in increased earnings on the common stock, through conversion. They don't have to be actually converted to common stock for these securities to be called a common stock equivalent. This is because they are in substance equivalent to common shares, enabling the holder at his discretion to cause an increase in the number of common shares by exchanging or converting. How do accountants determine a common stock equivalent? A convertible security is considered a common stock equivalent if its effective yield at the date of its issuance is less than two-thirds of the then-current average Aa corporate bond yield.

Now, let's put our new terms to work in an example, remembering that it has nothing to do with our own company, Typical Manufacturing. We start with the facts we have available. We'll say we have 100,000 shares of common stock outstanding plus another 100,000 shares of preferred stock, convertible into common on a share-for-share basis. (Assume they qualify as common stock equivalents.) We add the two and get 200,000 shares altogether. Now let's say our earnings figure is $500,000 for the year. With these facts, our primary computation is easy:

$$\frac{\text{\$500,000 earnings for the year}}{\text{200,000 adjusted shares outstanding}} = \text{\$2.50 primary earnings per share}$$

However, as mentioned earlier, the common stock equivalent shares are only included in the computation if the effect of conversion on earnings per share is dilutive. Dilution occurs when earnings per share decrease or loss per share increases. For example, assume the preferred stock paid $3 a share in dividends. Without conversion, the earnings per share would be $2, as opposed to $2.50 per share, because net income available for common after payment of dividends would be $200,000 ($500,000 less $300,000) divided by the 100,000 common shares outstanding. In this case, the common stock equivalent shares would be excluded from the computation because conversion results in a higher earnings per share (anti-dilutive). Therefore, earnings per share of $2 will be reflected on the income statement.

Fully Diluted Earnings Per Common Share

The primary earnings per share item, as we have just seen in the preceding section, takes into consideration common stock and common stock equivalents. The purpose of *fully diluted earnings per share* is to reflect maximum potential dilution in earnings that would result if all contingent issuances of common stock had taken place at the beginning of the year.

This computation is the result of dividing the earnings for the year by: *common stock* and *common stock equivalents* and *all other securities that are convertible (even though they do not qualify as common stock equivalents).*

How would it work? First, remember that we have 100,000 shares of convertible preferred outstanding, as well as our 100,000 in common. Now, let's say we also have convertible bonds with a par value of $10,000,000 outstanding. These bonds pay 6% interest and have a conversion ratio of 20 shares of common for every $1,000 bond. Assume the current average Aa corporate bond yield is 8%. These bonds are not common stock equivalents, because 6% is not less than two-thirds of 8%. However, for fully diluted earnings per share we have to count them in. If the 10,000 bonds were converted, we'd have another 200,000 shares of stock, so adding everything up gives us 400,000 shares. But by converting the bonds, we could skip the 6% interest payment, which gains us another $600,000 gross earnings. So our calculation looks like this:

Earnings for the year		**$500,000**
Interest on the bonds	**$600,000**	
Less: the income tax applicable to deduction	**300,000**	
		300,000
Adjusted earnings		**$800,000**

$800,000 adjusted earnings / 400,000 adjusted shares outstanding = $2 fully diluted earnings per share

The only remaining step is to test for dilution. Earnings per share without bond conversion would be $2.50 ($500,000 divided by 200,000 shares). Since earnings per share of $2 is less than $2.50 we would assume debt conversion in our calculation of fully diluted earnings per share.

Price-Earnings Ratio

Both the price and the return on common stock vary with a multitude of factors. One such factor is the relationship that exists between the earnings per share and the market price. It is called the *price-earnings ratio*, and this is how it is calculated: If a stock is selling at 25 and earning $2 per share, its price-earnings ratio is 12 1/2 to 1, usually shortened to 12 1/2 and the stock is said to be selling at 12 1/2 times earnings. If the stock should rise to 40, the price-earnings ratio would be 20. Or, if the stock drops to 12, the price-earnings ratio would be 6.

In Typical Manufacturing, which has no convertible common stock equivalents, the earnings per share were calculated at $3.16. If the stock were selling at 33, the price-earnings ratio would be 10.4. This is the basic figure that you should use in viewing the record of this stock over a period of years and in comparing the common stock of this company with other similar stocks.

46 **$ 33 market price / $ 3.16 earnings per share = 10.4 : 1 or 10.4 times**

This means that Typical Manufacturing common stock is selling at approximately 10.4 times earnings.

Last year, Typical earned $2.77 per share. Let's say that its stock sold at the same price-earnings ratio then. This means that a share of Typical was selling for $28.80 or so, and anyone who bought Typical then would be satisfied now. Just remember, in the real world, investors can never be certain that any stock will keep its same price-earnings ratio from year to year. The historical P/E multiple is a guide, not a guarantee.

In general, a high P/E multiple, when compared with other companies in the same industry, means that investors have confidence in the company's ability to produce higher profits in the future.

Statement of Changes in Shareholders' Equity

(dollars in thousands except per-share amounts)

This statement analyzes the changes from year to year in each shareholder's equity account. From this statement, we can see that during the year additional common stock was issued at a price above par. We can also see that Typical experienced a translation gain. The rest of the components of equity, with the exception of retained earnings which we discuss below, remained the same.

Just as the income statement reflects the payoff for shareholders, retained earnings reflects the payoff for the company itself. It shows how much money the company has plowed back into itself for new growth. The Statement of Changes shows that retained earnings increase by net income less dividends on preferred and common stock. Since we have already analyzed net income, we will now analyze dividends.

Dividends

Dividends on common stock vary with the profitability of the company. Common shareholders were paid $18,000 in dividends this year. Since we know from the balance sheet that Typical has 14,999,000 shares outstanding, the first thing we can learn here is what may be the most important point to some potential investors — dividends per share.

$18,000,000 common stock dividends / 14,999,000 shares = $1.20 a share

Once we know the amount of dividends per share, we can easily discover the dividend *payout ratio.* This is simply the percentage of net earnings per share that is paid to shareholders.

46 $1.20 dividend per common share / $3.16 earnings per common share = 38%

Of course, the dividends on the $5.83 preferred stock will not change from year to year. The word *cumulative* in the balance statement description tells us that if Typical's management someday didn't pay a dividend on its preferred stock, then the $5.83 payment for that year would accumulate. It would have to be paid to preferred shareholders before any dividends could ever be declared again on the common stock.

That's why preferred stock is called preferred. It gets at any dividend money first. We've already talked about convertible bonds and convertible preferred stock. Right now, we're not interested in that aspect because Typical Manufacturing doesn't have any convertible securities outstanding. Chances are its 60,000 shares of preferred stock, with a par value of $100 each, were issued to family members of Mr. Isaiah Typical, who founded the company back in 1923. When he took Typical public, he didn't keep any of the common stock. In those days, the guaranteed $5.83 dividend was more important to Isaiah. He was not interested in taking any more chances on Typical.

During the year, Typical has added $29,400 to its retained earnings. Even if Typical has some lean years in the future, it has plenty of retained earnings from which to keep on declaring those $5.83 dividends on the preferred stock and $1.20 dividends on the common stock.

There is one danger in having a lot of retained earnings. It could attract another company—Shark Fast Foods & Electronics, for instance—to buy up Typical's common stock to gain enough control to vote out the current management. Then Shark might merge Typical into itself. Where would Shark get the money to buy Typical stock? By issuing new shares of its own stock, perhaps. And where would Shark get the money to pay the dividends on all that new stock of its own? From Typical's retained earnings. So Typical's management has the obligation to its shareholders to make sure that its retained earnings are put to work to increase the total earnings per share of the shareholders. Or else, the shareholders might cooperate with Shark if and when it makes a raid.

25 Retained earnings $249,000

Return on Equity

Seeing how hard money works, of course, is one of the most popular measures that investors use to come up with individual judgments on how much they think a certain stock ought to be worth. The market itself—the sum of all buyers and sellers—makes the real decision. But the investors often try to make their own, in order to decide whether they want to invest at the market's price or wait. Most investors look for Typical's return on equity, which shows how hard shareholders' equity in Typical is working. In order to find Typical's current return on equity, we look at the balance sheet and take the common shareholders' equity for last year—not the current year—and then we see how much Typical made this year on it. We use only the amount of net profit after the dividends have been paid on the preferred stock. For Typical Manufacturing, that means $47,750 net profit minus $350. Here is what we get:

$47,750 net income — $350 preferred stock dividend
$305,600 last year's stockholders' equity — $6,000 preferred stock value

$ 47,400 / $299,600 = 15.8% return on equity

For every dollar of shareholders' equity, Typical made more than 15¢. Is that good? Well, 15.8¢ on the dollar is better than Typical could have done by going out of business, taking its shareholders' equity and putting that $299,600 in the bank. So Typical obviously is better off in its own line of work. When we consider putting our money to work in Typical's stock, we should compare Typical's 15.8¢ not only to whatever Typical's business competitors make, but to Typical's investment competitors for our money. For instance, the latest available average rate for all U.S. industry, according to the U.S. Federal Trade Commission, was 16¢.

Just remember that 15.8¢ is what Typical itself makes on the dollar. By no means is it what you will make in dividends on Typical's stock. What that return on equity really tells you is whether Typical Manufacturing is relatively attractive as an enterprise. You can only hope that this attractiveness might be translated into demand for Typical stock, and be reflected in its price.

Many analysts also like to see a company's annual return on the total capital available to the company. To get this figure, we use all the equity, plus all available borrowed funds. This becomes the total capital available. And for the total return on this figure we use net income before income taxes and interest charges. This gives us a bigger capital base and a larger income figure. As shareholders, however, what we're most interested in is how hard our own share of the company is working. And that's why we are more interested in return on equity.

Statement of Cash Flows

One more statement needs to be analyzed in order to get the full picture of Typical's financial status. The Statement of Cash Flows examines the changes in cash resulting from business activities. Cash-flow analysis is necessary in order to make proper investing decisions, as well as to maintain operations. Cash flows, although related to net income, are not equivalent. This is because of the accrual concept of accounting. Generally, under accrual accounting, a transaction is recognized on the income statement when the earnings process has been completed or an expense has been incurred. This does not necessarily coincide with the time that cash is exchanged. For example, cash received from merchandise sales often lags behind the time when goods are delivered to customers. However, the sale is recorded on the income statement when the goods are shipped.

Cash flows are separated by business activity. The business activity classifications presented on the statement include investing activities, financing activities, and operating activities. First, we will discuss financing and investing activities. Operating activities basically include all activities not classified as either financing or investing activities.

Financing activities include those activities relating to the generation and repayment of funds provided by creditors and investors. These activities include the issuance of debt or equity securities and the repayment of debt and distribution of dividends. Investing activities include those activities relating to asset acquisition or disposal.

Operating activities involve activities relating to the production and delivery of goods and services. They reflect the cash effects of transactions which are included in the determination of net income. Since many items enter into the determination of net income, the indirect method is used to determine the cash provided by or used for operating activities. This method requires adjusting net income to reconcile it to cash flows from operating activities. Common examples of cash flows from operating activities are interest received and paid, dividends received, salary, insurance, and tax payments.

Qualifying and Certifying

Watch Those Footnotes

The annual reports of many companies contain this statement: "The accompanying footnotes are an integral part of the financial statements." The reason is that the financial reports themselves are kept concise and condensed. Therefore, any explanatory matter that cannot readily be abbreviated is set out in greater detail in footnotes.

Some examples of appropriate footnotes are:

Description of the company's *policy* for depreciation, amortization, consolidation, foreign currency translation, and earnings per share.

Inventory valuation method. This footnote indicates whether inventories shown on the balance sheet or used in determining the cost of goods sold on the income statement are valued on a last in, first out (LIFO) basis or a first in, first out (FIFO) basis. Last in, first out means that the costs on the income statement reflect the actual cost of inventories purchased most recently. First in, first out means the income statement reflects the cost of the oldest inventories. This is an extremely important consideration because a LIFO valuation reflects current costs and does not overstate profits during inflationary times while a FIFO valuation does.

Changes in accounting policy as a result of new accounting rules.

Non-recurring items such as pension-plan terminations or sales of significant business units.

Employment contracts, profit sharing, pension, and retirement plans.

Details of stock options granted to officers and employees.

Long-term leases. Companies which usually lease a considerable amount of selling space must show their lease liabilities on a per-year basis for the next several years and their total lease liabilities over a longer period of time.

Details relating to issuance and maturities of long-term debt.

Contingent liabilities representing claims or lawsuits pending.

Commitments relating to contracts in force that will affect future periods.

Descriptions of the off-balance-sheet credit and market risk associated with certain complex financial instruments include interest rate swaps, forward and futures contracts and options on futures contracts. Off-balance-sheet risk is defined as potential for loss over and above the amount recorded on the balance sheet.

Fair value of financial instruments carried at cost include cash, receivables, investments, liabilities, long-term debt and off-balance-sheet instruments such as swaps and options.

Separate breakdowns of sales and gross profits must be shown for each line of business that accounts for more than 20% of a company's sales. Multinational corporations must also show sales and gross income on a geographic basis by country.

Most people do not like to read footnotes because they may be complicated and are almost always hard to read. This is unfortunate, because footnotes are very informative. Even if they don't reveal that the corporation has been forced into bankruptcy, footnotes can still reveal many fascinating sidelights of the financial story.

Independent Audits

The certificate from the independent auditors, which is printed in the report, says, first, that the auditing steps taken in the process of verification of the account meet the accounting world's approved standards of practice; and second, that the financial statements prepared by management are in conformity with generally accepted accounting principles.

As a result, when the annual report contains financial statements that have a clean opinion from independent auditors, you have added assurance that the figures can be relied upon as having been fairly presented.

However, if the independent accountants' opinion contains words such as "except for," or "subject to," the reader should investigate the reason behind such qualifications. Often the answer can be found by reading the footnotes that pertain to the matter. They are usually referred to in the auditor's opinion.

The Long View

We cannot emphasize too strongly that company records, in order to be very useful, must be compared. We can compare them to other company records, to industry averages or even to broader economic factors, if we want. But most of all, we can compare one company's annual activities to the same firm's results from other years.

This used to be done by keeping a file of old annual reports. Now, many corporations include a ten-year summary in their financial highlights each year. This provides the investing public with information about a decade of performance. That is why Typical Manufacturing included a ten-year summary in its annual report. It's not a part of the statements vouched for by the auditors, but it is there for you to see. A ten-year summary can show you:

- The trend and consistency of sales
- The trend of earnings, particularly in relation to sales and the economy
- The trend of net earnings as a percentage of sales
- The trend of return on equity
- Net earnings per share of common
- Dividends, and dividend policy.

Other companies may include changes in net worth, book value per share, capital expenditures for plant and machinery, long-term debt, capital stock changes by way of stock dividends and splits, number of employees, number of shareholders, number of outlets, and where appropriate, information on foreign subsidiaries and the extent to which foreign operations have been embodied in the financial report.

All of this is really important because of one central point: You are not only trying to find out how Typical is doing *now*. You want to predict how Typical *will* do, and how its stock will perform.

Ten-Year Financial Summary

	19X9	19X8	19X7	19X6	19X5	19X4	19X3	19X2	19X1	19X0
Net Sales	$765,000	$725,000	$690,000	$660,000	$600,000	$520,000	$500,000	$450,000	$350,000	$300,000
Income–before income taxes and extraordinary loss	94,196	66,750	59,750	54,750	50,400	42,000	45,800	40,500	34,350	29,500
Extraordinary loss	(5,000)	–	–	–	–	–	–	–	–	–
Net profit for year	47,750	40,500	37,700	33,650	29,850	27,300	30,360	25,975	21,000	18,100
Earnings per share before extraordinary loss	3.49	2.77	2.57	2.28	2.00	1.83	2.20	1.93	1.69	1.43
Earnings per share after extraordinary loss	3.16	2.77	2.57	2.28	2.00	1.83	2.20	1.93	1.69	1.43
Dividend per share	1.20	1.20	1.20	1.00	1.00	1.00	1.00	.80	.80	.80
Net working capital	230,000	199,000	218,000	223,000	211,000	178,000	136,000	111,000	86,000	96,000
Net plant and equipment	260,000	249,600	205,000	188,000	184,300	187,500	161,600	125,600	92,500	87,600
Long-term debt	130,000	136,000	136,000	–	–	–	–	–	–	–
Preferred stock	6,000	6,000	6,000	6,000	6,000	6,000	6,000	6,000	6,000	6,000
Common stock and surplus	340,000	299,600	275,800	254,700	238,100	220,500	203,250	166,000	133,800	128,000
Book value per share	22.53	20.53	18.39	16.98	15.87	14.70	13.55	11.07	8.92	8.53

Note: All data in thousands except per-share figures.

Selecting Stocks

From the items we've studied in this booklet, Typical Manufacturing appears to be a healthy concern. Which should make Board Chairman Patience Typical, old Isaiah Typical's daughter, and her four nieces, who own most of the shares, happy. But it makes us rather sad, since Typical is fictional, and we can't offer you shares of its stock. When you decide to invest money in real stocks, please remember this:

Selecting common stocks for investment requires careful study of factors other than those we can learn from financial statements. The economics of the country and the particular industry must be considered. The management of the company must be studied and its plans for the future assessed. Information about these other things is rarely in the financial report. These other facts must be gleaned from the press or the financial services or supplied by some research organization. Merrill Lynch's Global Securities Research and Economics Group stands ready to help you get the available facts you need to be an intelligent investor. Ask any Financial Consultant to put Merrill Lynch to work for you.

Tracing Obsolete Securities*

The following is a list of some of the available sources of information on tracing obsolete securities. This list should be useful to those who wonder whether their old securities have any value, to researchers, and to collectors. All of the books listed below should be available in large public libraries or in larger business libraries.

To trace a security, you need to know the name of the company, the date of issue and the state in which the company was incorporated; all three pieces of information should appear on the security. Start with volumes appropriate to the issue date of the security and continue through to the present, if necessary. If the security can not be found, contact the department that registers corporations in the state in which the company was incorporated. In most states this will be the office of the Secretary of State. They maintain records of name changes and bankruptcies and can usually answer your inquiry quickly; some charge a nominal fee for the service. Call the department to see what their procedures and costs are. You may need to send a copy of the certificate. Do not send the original certificate.

For an introduction to searching obsolete securities, the best guide, now out-of-print, is:

Cargiulo, Albert F. and Rocco Carlucci.
The Questioned Stock Manual: A Guide to Determining the True Worth of Old and Collectible Securities. New York: McGraw-Hill, 1979, xiv, 193 p.: ill. tables.
Chapters 3 and 4 deal with locating sources of information on securities. Chapter 6 covers the detection and recognition of fraudulent securities and a description of how securities are printed. The appendix contains a table of the top 100 firms, 1917–1977.

For historical data, beginning with colonial times, the Fisher, Scudder, and Smythe manuals are classics. The manuals are still published and the Smythe firm continues to do research into obsolete securities, charging a fee of $50 for each company. They also serve as dealers and appraisers of obsolete securities for collectors. You can contact them at:

R. M. Smythe & Co.
26 Broadway
New York, NY 10004
(212) 943–1880

* Frederick N. Nesta, formerly Director, Marymount Manhattan College Library.

Robert D. Fisher
Manual of Valuable & Worthless Securities: Showing Companies That Have Been Reorganized, Merged, Liquidated or Dissolved, Little Known Companies and Oil Leases. New York: R. M. Smythe, 1926–. 15 v.
First published in 1926 as the *Marvyn Scudder Manual . . .*, the series was taken over by Robert D. Fisher with vol. 5 in 1937. It has been published by the R. M. Smythe firm since 1971 under the editorship of Robert D. Fisher, Jr. With vol. 6 the series limited itself to securities and the date on which they became worthless. The earlier volumes present brief corporate obituaries. Volume 15, 1984, includes a price guide for collectors of obsolete certificates.

Smythe, Roland M.
Valuable Extinct Securities: the Secret of the Obsolete Security Business. Unclaimed Money and How to Collect It, With a List of . . . Extinct Securities of Good Value From the Records of the Four Principal Dealers. . . . New York: R. M. Smythe, 1929. v, 398 p.
By the author and publisher of *Obsolete American Securities and Corporations*, later the *Robert D. Fisher Manual of Valuable and Worthless Securities.* This list of over 1,500 securities gives due and foreclosure dates and the dates of sale or merger.

Smythe, Roland M.
Obsolete American Securities and Corporations. New York: R. M. Smythe, 1911. liv, 1166 p.: ill.
(*Obsolete American Securities and Corporations:* vol. 2). Pages 1–28 discuss Continental and other early U.S. state and foreign notes and bonds. Twenty plates illustrate some of the bonds discussed. Volume 1 was published in 1904.
Valuable Extinct Securities Guide. 1939 ed. New York: R. M. Smythe, Inc., 1938. 127 p. The first edition was published in 1929 and was the sequel to *Obsolete American Securities and Corporations.*

The books below can be consulted to trace more recent corporate reorganizations:

Capital Changes Reporter for Federal Income Tax Purposes. Clark, NJ: Commerce Clearing House (NJ), 1949–. 6 v., looseleaf.
Securities distributions, taxability of disbursements, splits, offers, rights, etc.

The National Monthly Stock Summary. Jer-

sey City, NJ: National Quotation Bureau, 1926–.
Summary data from the daily service, supplied either from the service or from dealers' lists. Name, par value, exchange, closing price, bids and offerings. May also include shares outstanding, control, reorganization, dividend or other information. Monthly, with bound cumulative volumes issued twice yearly.

Capital Adjustments, Reorganizations and Exchanges, Stock Dividends. Rights and Splits. Englewood Cliffs, NJ: Prentice-Hall, 1980–. 2 v. in 3, looseleaf.
Current changes, disbursements, etc. Includes notes on taxability. Supplements the bound volumes below.

Capital Adjustments: Stock Dividends, Stock Rights, Reorganizations. Englewood Cliffs, NJ: Prentice-Hall, 1962–.
The earlier volumes cover corporate and government securities from early in the century. Updated by looseleaf supplements. Includes name changes, incorporation dates, mergers.

Bank & Quotation Record. Arlington, MA: National News Services, 1928–.
"A publication of the Commercial and Financial Chronicle." Monthly opening and closing prices, highs, lows, etc. Includes equipment trusts, public utility bonds, Chicago Board Options Exchange, foreign exchange rates for the month, CDs, Federal funds, prime banker acceptance rates, commercial paper statistics. Published continuously for over sixty years, it is a fascinating document of American financial history.

FOREIGN CORPORATIONS

Canada

Canadian Mines Register of Dormant and Defunct Companies: Third Supplement. Toronto: Northern Miner Press Limited, 1976. 108 p. Originally published in 1960.

Survey of Predecessor and Defunct Companies. 3rd ed. Toronto: The Financial Post Corporation Service Group, 1985. 208 p.
Covers over 12,000 companies and spans over 50 years. Lists name changes, removals, the exchange basis for new shares, along with the addresses and telephone numbers of Canadian Federal and Provincial corporate registry offices.

United Kingdom

The Stock Exchange Official Year-Book. London: Macmillan, 1934–.
Contains substantial information on the London Stock Exchange, foreign securities, municipal securities, regulations and statistics and a directory of International exchanges. The main body lists each company with parent/subsidiary note, background, financial data, stock history, voting, dividends. Includes the *Register of Defunct and Other Companies Removed from the Stock Exchange Official Year-Book,* a listing of over 23,000 companies removed from the Official Year-Book since 1875, along with a list of Commonwealth Government and Provincial stocks redeemed or converted since 1940. The Register was published separately until 1980.

Australia

Register of Companies Removed from the Stock Exchanges Official Lists. Sydney: Stock Exchange Research Pty., 1984? 104 p.
Lists companies that were traded on one or more Australian exchanges. Historical data, with delistings going back to the early 1930s.

Bonds and Money Market Instruments

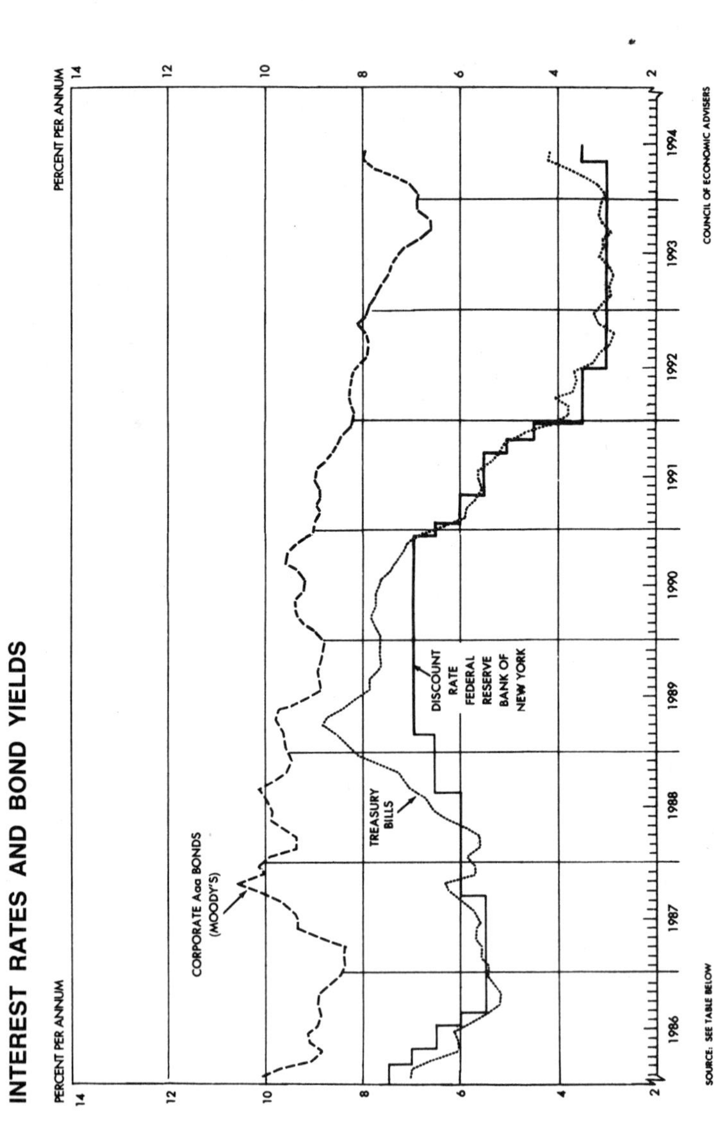

[Percent per annum]

Period	U.S. Treasury security yields			High-grade municipal bonds (Standard & Poor's)[3]	Corporate Aaa bonds (Moody's)	Prime commercial paper, 6 months[1]	Discount rate (N.Y. F.R. Bank)[4]	Prime rate charged by banks[4]	New-home mortgage yields (FHFB)[5]
	3-month bills (new issues)[1]	Constant maturities[2]							
		3-year	10-year						
1984	9.58	11.89	12.44	10.15	12.71	10.16	8.80	12.04	12.38
1985	7.48	9.64	10.62	9.18	11.37	8.01	7.69	9.93	11.55
1986	5.98	7.06	7.68	7.38	9.02	6.39	6.33	8.33	10.17
1987	5.82	7.68	8.39	7.73	9.38	6.85	5.66	8.21	9.31
1988	6.69	8.26	8.85	7.76	9.71	7.68	6.20	9.32	9.19
1989	8.12	8.55	8.49	7.24	9.26	8.80	6.93	10.87	10.13
1990	7.51	8.26	8.55	7.25	9.32	7.95	6.98	10.01	10.05
1991	5.42	6.82	7.86	6.89	8.77	5.85	5.45	8.46	9.32
1992	3.45	5.30	7.01	6.41	8.14	3.80	3.25	6.25	8.24
1993	3.02	4.44	5.87	5.63	7.22	3.30	3.00	6.00	7.20
1993: June	3.10	4.53	5.96	5.73	7.33	3.38	3.00–3.00	6.00–6.00	7.23
July	3.05	4.43	5.81	5.60	7.17	3.35	3.00–3.00	6.00–6.00	7.20
Aug	3.05	4.36	5.68	5.50	6.85	3.33	3.00–3.00	6.00–6.00	7.05
Sept	2.96	4.17	5.36	5.31	6.66	3.25	3.00–3.00	6.00–6.00	6.95
Oct	3.04	4.18	5.33	5.29	6.67	3.27	3.00–3.00	6.00–6.00	6.80
Nov	3.12	4.50	5.72	5.47	6.93	3.43	3.00–3.00	6.00–6.00	6.80
Dec	3.08	4.54	5.77	5.35	6.93	3.40	3.00–3.00	6.00–6.00	6.92
1994: Jan	3.02	4.48	5.75	5.30	6.92	3.30	3.00–3.00	6.00–6.00	6.95
Feb	3.21	4.83	5.97	5.44	7.08	3.62	3.00–3.00	6.00–6.00	6.85
Mar	3.52	5.40	6.48	5.93	7.48	4.08	3.00–3.00	6.00–6.25	6.99
Apr	3.74	5.99	6.97	6.28	7.88	4.40	3.00–3.00	6.25–6.75	7.31
May	4.19	6.34	7.18	6.26	7.99	4.92	3.00–3.50	6.75–7.25	7.43
June	4.18	6.27	7.10	6.14	7.97	4.86	3.50–3.50	7.25–7.25	....
Week ended:									
1994: June 4	4.23	6.29	7.09	6.18	7.96	4.94	3.50–3.50	7.25–7.25	....
11	4.15	6.13	6.97	6.02	7.85	4.82	3.50–3.50	7.25–7.25	....
18	4.16	6.21	7.08	6.12	7.94	4.79	3.50–3.50	7.25–7.25	....
25	4.18	6.32	7.17	6.20	8.02	4.82	3.50–3.50	7.25–7.25	....
July 2 p	4.20	6.45	7.26	6.19	8.10	4.97	3.50–3.50	7.25–7.25	....

[1] Bank-discount basis.
[2] Yields on the more actively traded issues adjusted to constant maturities by the Treasury Department.
[3] Weekly data are Wednesday figures.
[4] Average effective rate for year; opening and closing rate for month and week.
[5] Effective rate (in the primary market) on conventional mortgages, reflecting fees and charges as well as contract rate and assumed, on the average, repayment at end of 10 years.

Sources: Department of the Treasury, Board of Governors of the Federal Reserve System, Federal Housing Finance Board, Moody's Investors Service, and Standard & Poor's Corporation.

Source: *Economic Indicators*, Council of Economic Advisers.

INTEREST RATES Money and Capital Markets

Averages, percent per year; figures are averages of business day data unless otherwise noted

Item	1991	1992	1993	1993	1994			1994, week ending				
				Dec.	Jan.	Feb.	Mar.	Feb. 25	Mar. 4	Mar. 11	Mar. 18	Mar. 25
MONEY MARKET INSTRUMENTS												
1 Federal funds[1,2,3]	5.69	3.52	3.02	2.96	3.05	3.25	3.34	3.25	3.28	3.25	3.19	3.31
2 Discount window borrowing[2,4]	5.45	3.25	3.00	3.00	3.00	3.00	3.00	3.00	3.00	3.00	3.00	3.00
Commercial paper[3,5,6]												
3 1-month	5.89	3.71	3.17	3.35	3.14	3.39	3.63	3.47	3.57	3.61	3.61	3.67
4 3-month	5.87	3.75	3.22	3.36	3.19	3.49	3.85	3.63	3.78	3.84	3.84	3.88
5 6-month	5.85	3.80	3.30	3.40	3.30	3.62	4.08	3.79	3.96	4.06	4.08	4.14
Finance paper, directly placed[3,5,7]												
6 1-month	5.73	3.62	3.12	3.21	3.07	3.30	3.53	3.37	3.45	3.52	3.51	3.59
7 3-month	5.71	3.65	3.16	3.19	3.11	3.40	3.71	3.51	3.62	3.70	3.71	3.75
8 6-month	5.60	3.63	3.15	3.18	3.15	3.39	3.70	3.50	3.62	3.72	3.68	3.73
Bankers acceptances[3,5,8]												
9 3-month	5.70	3.62	3.13	3.23	3.10	3.40	3.73	3.53	3.67	3.75	3.72	3.75
10 6-month	5.67	3.67	3.21	3.30	3.21	3.56	3.96	3.73	3.88	3.95	3.94	4.00
Certificates of deposit, secondary market[3,9]												
11 1-month	5.82	3.64	3.11	3.26	3.08	3.31	3.56	3.41	3.53	3.54	3.52	3.60
12 3-month	5.8[illegible]	3.68	3.17	3.26	3.15	3.43	3.77	3.57	3.71	3.77	3.75	3.81
13 6-month	5.[illegible]1	3.76	3.28	3.35	3.29	3.62	4.03	3.81	3.94	4.01	4.01	4.09
14 Eurodollar deposits, 3-month[3,10]	5.86	3.70	3.18	3.26	3.15	3.43	3.75	3.55	3.68	3.75	3.75	3.79
U.S. Treasury bills												
Secondary market[3,5]												
15 3-month	5.38	3.43	3.00	3.06	2.98	3.25	3.50	3.35	3.47	3.52	3.52	3.49
16 6-month	5.44	3.54	3.12	3.23	3.15	3.43	3.78	3.58	3.68	3.77	3.81	3.81
17 1-year	5.52	3.71	3.29	3.45	3.39	3.69	4.11	3.82	3.95	4.09	4.11	4.15
Auction average[3,5,11]												
18 3-month	5.42	3.45	3.02	3.08	3.02	3.21	3.52	3.33	3.40	3.52	3.57	3.61
19 6-month	5.49	3.57	3.14	3.25	3.19	3.38	3.79	3.53	3.61	3.75	3.85	3.90
20 1-year	5.54	3.75	3.33	3.47	3.52	3.59	4.03	n.a.	n.a.	4.03	n.a.	n.a.
U.S. TREASURY NOTES AND BONDS												
Constant maturities[12]												
21 1-year	5.86	3.89	3.43	3.61	3.54	3.87	4.32	4.01	4.16	4.28	4.31	4.36
22 2-year	6.49	4.77	4.05	4.21	4.14	4.47	5.00	4.67	4.80	4.93	4.98	5.06
23 3-year	6.82	5.30	4.44	4.54	4.48	4.83	5.40	5.03	5.19	5.32	5.37	5.45
24 5-year	7.37	6.19	5.14	5.15	5.09	5.40	5.94	5.60	5.74	5.85	5.91	6.00
25 7-year	7.68	6.63	5.54	5.48	5.43	5.72	6.28	5.94	6.08	6.20	6.24	6.33
26 10-year	7.86	7.01	5.87	5.77	5.75	5.97	6.48	6.15	6.29	6.40	6.45	6.52
27 20-year	n.a.	n.a.	6.29	6.40	6.39	6.57	7.00	6.76	6.86	6.95	6.96	7.02
28 30-year	8.14	7.67	6.59	6.25	6.29	6.49	6.91	6.68	6.79	6.87	6.87	6.92
Composite												
29 More than 10 years (long-term)	8.16	7.52	6.45	6.27	6.24	6.44	6.90	6.63	6.75	6.84	6.86	6.93
STATE AND LOCAL NOTES AND BONDS												
Moody's series[13]												
30 Aaa	6.56	6.09	5.38	5.18	5.14	5.06	5.29	5.12	5.12	5.27	5.32	5.35
31 Baa	6.99	6.48	5.82	5.69	5.60	5.52	5.74	5.58	5.58	5.72	5.78	5.80
32 *Bond Buyer* series[14]	6.92	6.44	5.60	5.35	5.31	5.40	5.91	5.58	5.84	5.88	5.84	5.92
CORPORATE BONDS												
33 Seasoned issues, all industries[15]	9.23	8.55	7.54	7.26	7.25	7.39	7.78	7.54	7.66	7.73	7.75	7.79

Rating group												
34 Aaa	8.77	8.14	7.22	6.93	6.92	7.08	7.48	7.23	7.36	7.44	7.46	7.49
35 Aa	9.05	8.46	7.40	7.12	7.12	7.29	7.69	7.45	7.57	7.65	7.67	7.70
36 A	9.30	8.62	7.58	7.31	7.30	7.44	7.82	7.60	7.70	7.76	7.78	7.82
37 Baa	9.80	8.98	7.93	7.69	7.65	7.76	8.13	7.92	8.01	8.08	8.10	8.15
38 A-rated, recently offered utility bonds[16]	9.32	8.52	7.46	7.28	7.24	7.45	7.82	7.62	7.73	7.80	7.81	7.91
MEMO												
Dividend–price ratio[17]												
39 Preferred stocks	8.17	7.46	6.89	7.01	6.97	7.00	7.07	7.07	7.03	6.86	7.07	7.10
40 Common stocks	3.24	2.99	2.78	2.72	2.69	2.70	2.78	2.72	2.77	2.75	2.74	2.76

1. The daily effective federal funds rate is a weighted average of rates on trades through New York brokers.
2. Weekly figures are averages of seven calendar days ending on Wednesday of the current week; monthly figures include each calendar day in the month.
3. Annualized using a 360-day year or bank interest.
4. Rate for the Federal Reserve Bank of New York.
5. Quoted on a discount basis.
6. An average of offering rates on commercial paper placed by several leading dealers for firms whose bond rating is AA or the equivalent.
7. An average of offering rates on paper directly placed by finance companies.
8. Representative closing yields for acceptances of the highest-rated money center banks.
9. An average of dealer offering rates on nationally traded certificates of deposit.
10. Bid rates for Eurodollar deposits at 11:00 a.m. London time. Data are for indication purposes only.
11. Auction date for daily data; weekly and monthly averages computed on an issue-date basis.
12. Yields on actively traded issues adjusted to constant maturities. Source: U.S. Treasury.
13. General obligations based on Thursday figures; Moody's Investors Service.
14. General obligations only, with twenty years to maturity, issued by twenty state and local governmental units of mixed quality. Based on figures for Thursday.
15. Daily figures from Moody's Investors Service. Based on yields to maturity on selected long-term bonds.
16. Compilation of the Federal Reserve. This series is an estimate of the yield on recently offered, A-rated utility bonds with a thirty-year maturity and five years of call protection. Weekly data are based on Friday quotations.
17. Standard & Poor's corporate series. Preferred stock ratio is based on a sample of ten issues: four public utilities, four industrials, one financial, and one transportation. Common stock ratio is based on the 500 stocks in the price index.

NOTE. Some of the data in this table also appear in the Board's H.15 (519) weekly and G.13 (415) monthly statistical releases. For ordering address, see inside front cover.

Source: *Federal Reserve Bulletin*, Board of Governors of the Federal Reserve System.

PRIME RATE CHARGED BY BANKS on Short-Term Business Loans (percent per year)

Date of change	Rate	Period	Average rate	Period	Average rate	Period	Average rate
1991— Jan. 1	10.00	1991	8.46	1992— Jan.	6.50	1993— Jan.	6.00
2	9.50	1992	6.25	Feb.	6.50	Feb.	6.00
Feb. 4	9.00	1993	6.00	Mar.	6.50	Mar.	6.00
May 1	8.50			Apr.	6.50	Apr.	6.00
Sept. 13	8.00	1991— Jan.	9.52	May	6.50	May	6.00
Nov. 6	7.50	Feb.	9.05	June	6.50	June	6.00
Dec. 23	6.50	Mar.	9.00	July	6.02	July	6.00
		Apr.	9.00	Aug.	6.00	Aug.	6.00
1992— July 2	6.00	May	8.50	Sept.	6.00	Sept.	6.00
		June	8.50	Oct.	6.00	Oct.	6.00
1994— Mar. 24	6.25	July	8.50	Nov.	6.00	Nov.	6.00
Apr. 19	6.75	Aug.	8.50	Dec.	6.00	Dec.	6.00
		Sept.	8.20				
		Oct.	8.00			1994— Jan.	6.00
		Nov.	7.58			Feb.	6.00
		Dec.	7.21			Mar.	6.06
						Apr.	6.45

1. The prime rate is one of several base rates that banks use to price short-term business loans. The table shows the date on which a new rate came to be the predominant one quoted by a majority of the twenty-five largest banks by asset size, based on the most recent Call Report. Data in this table also appear in the Board's H.15 (519) weekly and G.13 (415) monthly statistical releases. For ordering address, see inside front cover.

Source: *Federal Reserve Bulletin*, Board of Governors of the Federal Reserve System.

Reported bond volume and trades on NYSE, 1993 (par value in thousands)

	Par value		No. of	Avg. daily	Avg. trade size
	Total	**Avg. daily**	**trades**	**trades**	**(thousands)**
January	$947,763	$47,388	41,928	2,096	$22.6
February	901,198	47,431	38,239	2,013	23.6
March	1,022,469	44,455	45,032	1,958	22.7
April	1,002,589	47,742	46,737	2,226	21.5
May	827,895	41,395	36,956	1,848	22.4
June	766,782	34,854	35,996	1,636	21.3
July	731,383	34,828	32,935	1,568	22.2
August	706,661	32,121	32,369	1,471	21.8
September	765,001	36,429	33,319	1,587	23.0
October	675,452	32,164	30,620	1,458	22.1
November	706,026	33,620	32,763	1,560	21.5
December	689,755	31,353	32,584	1,481	21.2
Year	**$9,742,974**	**$38,510**	**439,478**	**1,737**	**$22.2** *
		Par value			
High Day		$62,355	February 4		
Low Day		$7,755	November 26		
High Month		$1,022,469	March		
Low Month		$675,452	October		

* New record.

Source: New York Stock Exchange *Fact Book*.

Most active bonds on NYSE, 1993

Issue		Par value of reported volume (thousands)
General Motors Acceptance	zero coupon '15	$285,460
General Motors Acceptance	zero coupon '12	262,210
Stone Container	10¾ s '02	243,056
Stone Container	11½ s '99	220,121
RJR Nabisco Inc.	disc debs due '01	213,766
duPont de Nemours	6 s '01	171,476
RJR Nabisco Inc.	9¼ s '13	168,539
Stone Container	13⅝ s '95	162,549
Stone Container	10¾ s '97	149,564
Stone Container	11⅞ s '98	114,324
MGM/UA Communications	13 s '96	113,912
RJR Nabisco Inc.	7⅝ s '03	111,487
Time Warner	reset notes '02	110,708
McDonnell Douglas	9¼ s '02	105,751
Chrysler Corporation	12 s '15	103,326
RJR Nabisco Inc.	8 s '00	80,390
American Telephone & Telegraph	6 s '00	75,736
Republic Steel	12⅛ s '03	75,349
Chrysler Corporation	10.95 s '17	74,267
USG Corporation	16 s '08	73,286
Time Warner	9⅛ s '13	72,414
Eastman Kodak	LYONS '11	72,232
Stone Container	11 s '99	70,213
Time Warner *	8¾ s '15	69,642
General Motors Acceptance	8¼ s '16	69,003
RJR Nabisco Inc.	10½ s '98	67,715
Time Warner	9.15 s '23	66,560
GPA Delaware	8¾ s '98	64,303
American Telephone & Telegraph	8⅛ s '22	63,634
RJR Nabisco Inc.	8¾ s '04	61,567
Tyco Toys	10⅛ s '02	60,006
RJR Nabisco Inc.	8⅝ s '02	59,362
Sequa Corporation	10½ s '98	57,788
McDonnell Douglas	9¾ s '12	56,842
RJR Nabisco Inc.	8¾ s '05	56,061
RJR Nabisco Inc.	13½ s '01	52,506
General Motors Acceptance	6 s '11	51,192
LTV Corp.	15 s '00	51,161
Revlon Consumers	9½ s '99	48,587
Chiquita Brands	10½ s '04	47,714
Chrysler Corporation	13 s '97	47,670
Marathon Oil	9½ s '94	47,046
Standard Pacific Corp.	10½ s '00	46,759
Storage Technology Corp. *	8 s '15	46,440
Chrysler Corporation	10.4 s '99	46,272
Zenith Electronics *	6¼ s '11	45,640
American Telephone & Telegraph	7⅛ s '02	44,950
Tesoro Petroleum	12¾ s '00	44,532
USAir Inc.	12⅞ s '00	42,196
McDonnell Douglas	8⅝ s '97	40,550

* Convertible

Source: New York Stock Exchange *Fact Book*.

Credit Ratings of Fixed Income and Money Market Securities

KEY TO STANDARD & POOR'S CORPORATE AND MUNICIPAL BOND RATING DEFINITIONS

A Standard & Poor's corporate or municipal debt rating is a current assessment of the creditworthiness of an obligor with respect to a specific debt obligation. This assessment may take into consideration obligors such as guarantors, insurers, or lessees.

The debt rating is not a recommendation to purchase, sell or hold a security, inasmuch as it does not comment as to market price or suitability for a particular investor.

The ratings are based on current information furnished by the issuer or obtained by Standard & Poor's from other sources it considers reliable. Standard & Poor's does not perform an audit in connection with any rating and may, on occasion, rely on unaudited financial information. The ratings may be changed, suspended or withdrawn as a result of changes in, or unavailability of, such information, or for other circumstances.

The ratings are based, in varying degrees, on the following considerations:

I. Likelihood of default—capacity and willingness of the obligor as to the timely payment of interest and repayment of principal in accordance with the terms of the obligation;

II. Nature of and provisions of the obligation;

III. Protection afforded by, and relative position of, the obligation in the event of bankruptcy, reorganization or other arrangement under the laws of bankruptcy and other laws affecting creditor's rights.

AAA

Debt rated **AAA** have the highest rating assigned by Standard & Poor's to a debt obligation. Capacity to pay interest and repay principal is extremely strong.

AA

Debt rated **AA** have a very strong capacity to pay interest and repay principal and differ from the highest rated issues only in a small degree.

A

Debt rated **A** have a strong capacity to pay interest and repay principal although they are somewhat more susceptible to the adverse effects of changes in circumstances and economic conditions than debts in higher rated categories.

BBB

Debt rated **BBB** are regarded as having an adequate capacity to pay interest and repay principal. Whereas they normally exhibit adequate protection parameters, adverse economic conditions or changing circumstances are more likely to lead to a weakened capacity to pay interest and repay principal for debts in this category than for debts in higher rated categories.

BB, B, CCC, CC

Debt rated **BB, B, CCC,** and **CC** are regarded, on balance, as predominantly speculative with respect to capacity to pay interest and repay principal in accordance with the terms of the obligation. **BB** indicates the lowest degree of speculation and **CC** the highest degree of speculation. While such debts will likely have some quality and protective characteristics, these are outweighed by large uncertainties or major risk exposures to adverse conditions.

C

The rating **C** is reserved for income bonds on which no interest is being paid.

D

Debt rated **D** are in default, and payment of interest and/or repayment of principal is in arrears.

Plus (+) or minus (−)

The ratings from **AA** to **B** may be modified by the addition of a plus or minus sign to show relative standing within the major rating categories.

Provisional ratings

The letter *p* indicates that the rating is provisional. A provisional rating assumes the successful completion of the project being financed by the debts being rated and indicates that payment of debt service requirements is largely or entirely dependent upon the successful and timely completion of the project. This rating, however, while addressing credit quality subsequent to completion of the project, makes no comment on the likelihood of, or the risk of default upon failure of, such completion. The investor should exercise his own judgment with respect to such likelihood and risk.

Source: From Standard & Poor's Debt Rating Division.

L*

The letter "L" indicates that the rating pertains to the principal amount of those bonds where the underlying deposit collateral is fully insured by the Federal Savings & Loan Insurance Corp. or the Federal Deposit Insurance Corp.

NR

Indicates that no rating has been requested, that there is insufficient information on which to base a rating or that S&P does not rate a particular type of obligation as a matter of policy.

Debt Obligations

Debt Obligations of issuers outside the United States and its territories are rated on the same basis as domestic corporate and municipal issues. The ratings measure the creditworthiness of the obligor but do not take into account currency exchange and other uncertainties.

Bond Investment Quality Standards

Under present commercial bank regulations issued by the Comptroller of the Currency, bonds rated in the top four categories (**AAA, AA, A, BBB,** commonly known as "Investment Grade" ratings) are generally regarded as eligible for bank investment. In addition, the Legal Investment Laws of various states impose certain rating or other standards for obligations eligible for investment by savings banks, trust companies, insurance companies and fiduciaries generally.

KEY TO STANDARD & POOR'S PREFERRED STOCK RATING DEFINITIONS

A Standard & Poor's preferred stock rating is an assessment of the capacity and willingness of an issuer to pay preferred stock dividends and any applicable sinking fund obligations. A preferred stock rating differs from a bond rating inasmuch as it is assigned to an equity issue, which issue is intrinsically different from, and subordinated to, a debt issue. Therefore, to reflect this difference, the preferred stock rating symbol will normally not be higher than the bond rating symbol assigned to, or that would be assigned to, the senior debt of the same issuer.

The preferred stock ratings are based on the following considerations.

* Continuance of the rating is contingent upon S&P's receipt of an executed copy of the escrow agreement or closing documentation confirming investments and the cash flows.

I. Likelihood of payment—capacity and willingness of the issuer to meet the timely payment of preferred stock dividends and any applicable sinking fund requirements in accordance with the terms of the obligation.
II. Nature of, and provisions of, the issue.
III. Relative position of the issue in the event of bankruptcy, reorganization, or other arrangements affecting creditors' rights.

AAA

This is the highest rating that may be assigned by Standard & Poor's to a preferred stock issue and indicates an extremely strong capacity to pay the preferred stock obligations.

AA

A preferred stock issue rated **AA** also qualifies as a high-quality fixed income security. The capacity to pay preferred stock obligations is very strong, although not as overwhelming as for issues rated **AAA.**

A

An issue rated **A** is backed by a sound capacity to pay the preferred stock obligations, although it is somewhat more susceptible to the adverse effects of changes in circumstances and economic conditions.

BBB

An issue rated **BBB** is regarded as backed by an adequate capacity to pay the preferred stock obligations. Whereas it normally exhibits adequate protection parameters, adverse economic conditions or changing circumstances are more likely to lead to a weakened capacity to make payments for a preferred stock in this category than for issues in the **A** category.

BB, B, CCC

Preferred stock rated **BB, B,** and **CCC** are regarded, on balance, as predominately speculative with respect to the issuer's capacity to pay preferred stock obligations. **BB** indicates the lowest degree of speculation and **CCC** the highest degree of speculation. While such issues will likely have some quality and protective characteristics, these are outweighed by large uncertainties or major risk exposures to adverse conditions.

CC

The rating **CC** is reserved for a preferred stock issue in arrears on dividends or sinking fund payments but that is currently paying.

C

A preferred stock rated **C** is a non-paying issue.

D

A preferred stock rated **D** is a non-paying issue with the issuer in default on debt instruments.

NR

NR indicates that no rating has been requested, that there is insufficient information on which to base a rating, or that S&P does not rate a particular type of obligation as a matter or policy.

Plus (+) **or Minus** (−) To provide more detailed indications of preferred stock quality, the ratings from **AA** to **B** may be modified by the addition of a plus or minus sign to show relative standing within the major rating categories.

The preferred stock rating is not a recommendation to purchase or sell a security, inasmuch as market price is not considered in arriving at the rating. Preferred stock *ratings* are wholly unrelated to Standard & Poor's earnings and dividend *rankings* for common stocks.

MUNICIPAL NOTES

A Standard & Poor's role rating reflects the liquidity concerns and market access risks unique to notes. Notes due in 3 years or less will likely receive a long-term debt rating. The following criteria will be used in making that assessment.

—Amortization schedule (the larger the final maturity relative to other maturities the more likely it will be treated as a note).

—Source of Payment (the more dependent the issue is on the market for its refinancing, the more likely it will be treated as a note).

Note rating symbols are as follows:

SP-1 Very strong or strong capacity to pay principal and interest. Those issues determined to possess overwhelming safety characteristics will be given a plus (+) designation.

SP-2 Satisfactory capacity to pay principal and interest.

SP-3 Speculative capacity to pay principal and interest.

TAX-EXEMPT DEMAND BONDS

Standard & Poor's assigns "dual" ratings to all long-term debt issues that have as part of their provisions a demand or double feature.

The first rating addresses the likelihood of repayment of principal and interest as due, and the second rating addresses only the demand feature. The long-term debt rating symbols are used for bonds to denote the long-term maturity and the commercial paper rating symbols are used to denote the put option (for example, "AAA/A-1+"). For the newer "demand notes," S&P's note rating symbols, combined with the commercial paper symbols, are used (for example, "SP-1+/A-1+").

KEY TO STANDARD & POOR'S COMMERCIAL PAPER RATING DEFINITIONS

A Standard & Poor's Commercial Paper Rating is a current assessment of the likelihood of timely payment of debt having an original maturity of no more than 365 days.

Ratings are graded into four categories, ranging from **A** for the highest quality obligations to **D** for the lowest. The four categories are as follows:

A

Issues assigned this highest rating are regarded as having the greatest capacity for timely payment. Issues in this category are further refined with the designations 1, 2, and 3 to indicate the relative degree of safety.

A-1 This designation indicates that the degree of safety regarding timely payment is very strong.

A-2 Capacity for timely payment on issues with this designation is strong. However, the relative degree of safety is not as overwhelming as for issues designated **A-1.**

A-3 Issues carrying this designation have a satisfactory capacity for timely payment. They are, however, somewhat more vulnerable to the adverse effects of changes in circumstances than obligations carrying the higher designations.

B

Issues rated **B** are regarded as having only an adequate capacity for timely payment. However, such capacity may be damaged by changing conditions for short-term adversities.

C

This rating is assigned to short-term obligations with a doubtful capacity for payment.

D

This rating indicates that the issue is either a default or is expected to be in default upon maturity.

The Commercial Paper Rating is not a recommendation to purchase or sell a security. The ratings are based on current information furnished to Standard & Poor's by the issuer or obtained from other sources it considers reliable. The ratings may be changed, suspended, or withdrawn as a result of changes in, or unavailability of, such information.

KEY TO MOODY'S MUNICIPAL RATINGS*

Aaa

Bonds which are rated **Aaa** are judged to be of the best quality. They carry the smallest degree of investment risk and are generally referred to as "gilt edge." Interest payments are protected by a large or by an exceptionally stable margin and principal is secure. While the various protective elements are likely to change, such changes as can be visualized are most unlikely to impair the fundamentally strong position of such issues.

Aa

Bonds which are rated **Aa** are judged to be of high quality by all standards. Together with the **Aaa** group they comprise what are generally known as high grade bonds. They are rated lower than the best bonds because margins of protection may not be as large as in **Aaa** securities or fluctuation of protective elements may be of greater amplitude or there may be other elements present which make the long term risks appear somewhat larger than in **Aaa** securities.

A

Bonds which are rated **A** possess many favorable instrument attributes and are to be considered as upper medium grade obligations. Factors giving security to principal and interest are considered adequate, but elements may be present which suggest a susceptibility to impairment sometime in the future.

Baa

Bonds which are rated **Baa** are considered as medium grade obligations; i.e., they are neither highly protected nor poorly secured. Interest payments and principal security appear adequate for the present but certain protective elements may be lacking or may be characteristically unreliable over any great length of time. Such bonds lack outstanding investment characteristics and in fact have speculative characteristics as well.

Ba

Bonds which are rated **Ba** are judged to have speculative elements; their future cannot be considered as well assured. Often the protection of interest and principal payments may be very moderate, and thereby not well safeguarded during both good and bad times over the future. Uncertainty of position characterizes bonds in this case.

B

Bonds which are rated **B** generally lack characteristics of the desirable investment. Assurance of interest and principal payments or of maintenance of other terms of the contract over any long period of time may be small.

Caa

Bonds which are rated **Caa** are of poor standing. Such issues may be in default or there may be present elements of danger with respect to principal or interest.

Ca

Bonds which are rated **Ca** represent obligations which are speculative in a high degree. Such issues are often in default or have other marked shortcomings.

C

Bonds which are rated **C** are the lowest rated class of bonds, and issues so rated can be regarded as having extremely poor prospects of ever attaining any real investment standing.

Con.(—)

Bonds for which the security depends upon the completion of some act or the fulfillment of some condition are rated conditionally. These are bonds secured by (a) earnings of projects under construction, (b) earnings of projects unseasoned in operation experience, (c) rentals which begin when facilities are completed, or (d) payments to which some other limiting condition attaches. Parenthetical rating denotes probable credit stature upon completion of construction or elimination of basis of condition.

* **Note:** Those bonds in the **Aa, A, Baa, Ba** and **B** groups which Moody's believes possess the strongest investment attributes are designated by the symbols **Aa 1, A 1, Baa 1, Ba 1** and **B 1.**

Source: Moody's Investors Service, Inc.

KEY TO MOODY'S CORPORATE RATINGS*

Aaa

Bonds which are rated **Aaa** are judged to be of the best quality. They carry the smallest degree of investment risk and are generally referred to as "gilt edge." Interest payments are protected by a large or by an exceptionally

* ***Note:*** Moody's applies numerical modifiers, **1, 2** and **3** in each generic rating classification from **Aa** through **B** in its corporate bond rating system. The modifier **1** indicates that the security ranks in the higher end of its generic rating category; the modifier **2** indicates a mid-range ranking; and the modifier **3** indicates that the issue ranks in the lower end of its generic rating category.

stable margin and principal is secure. While the various protective elements are likely to change, such changes as can be visualized are most unlikely to impair the fundamentally strong position of such issues.

Aa

Bonds which are rated **Aa** are judged to be of high quality by all standards. Together with the **Aaa** group they comprise what are generally known as high grade bonds. They are rated lower than the best bonds because margins of protection may not be as large as in **Aaa** securities or fluctuation of protective elements may be of greater amplitude or there may be other elements present which make the long term risks appear somewhat larger than in **Aaa** securities.

A

Bonds which are rated **A** possess many favorable investment attributes and are to be considered as upper medium grade obligations. Factors giving security to principal and interest are considered adequate but elements may be present which suggest a susceptibility to impairment sometime in the future.

Baa

Bonds which are rated **Baa** are considered as medium grade obligations, i.e., they are neither highly protected nor poorly secured. Interest payments and principal security appear adequate for the present but certain protective elements may be lacking or may be characteristically unreliable over any great length of time. Such bonds lack outstanding investment characteristics and in fact have speculative characteristics as well.

Ba

Bonds which are rated **Ba** are judged to have speculative elements; their future cannot be considered as well assured. Often the protection of interest and principal payments may be very moderate and thereby not well safeguarded during both good and bad times over the future. Uncertainty of position characterizes bonds in this class.

B

Bonds which are rated **B** generally lack characteristics of the desirable investment. Assurance of interest and principal payments or of maintenance of other terms of the contract over any long period of time may be small.

Caa

Bonds which are rated **Caa** are of poor standing. Such issues may be in default or there may be present elements of danger with respect to principal or interest.

Ca

Bonds which are rated **Ca** represent obligations which are speculative in a high degree. Such issues are often in default or have other marked shortcomings.

C

Bonds which are rated **C** are the lowest rated class of bonds and issues so rated can be regarded as having extremely poor prospects of ever attaining any real investment standing.

KEY TO MOODY'S COMMERCIAL PAPER RATINGS

The term "Commercial Paper" as used by Moody's means promissory obligations not having an original maturity in excess of nine months. Moody's makes no representation as to whether such Commercial Paper is by any other definition "Commercial Paper" or is exempt from registration under the Securities Act of 1933, as amended.

Moody's Commercial Paper ratings are opinions of the ability of issuers to repay punctually promissory obligations not having an original maturity in excess of nine months. Moody's makes no representation that such obligations are exempt from registration under the Securities Act of 1933, nor does it represent that any specific note is a valid obligation of a rated issuer or issued in conformity with any applicable law. Moody's employs the following three designations, all judged to be investment grade, to indicate the relative repayment capacity of rated issuers:

Issuers rated **Prime-1** (or related supporting institutions) have a superior capacity for repayment of short-term promissory obligations. Prime-1 repayment capacity will normally be evidenced by the following characteristics:

- -Leading market positions in well established industries.
- -High rates of return on funds employed.
- -Conservative capitalization structures with moderate reliance on debt and ample asset protection.
- -Broad margins in earnings coverage of fixed financial charges and high internal cash generation.
- -Well established access to a range of financial markets and assured sources of alternate liquidity.

Issuers rated **Prime-2** (or related supporting institutions) have a strong capacity for short-term promissory obligations. This will normally be evidenced by many of the characteristics cited above but to a

Source: Moody's Investors Service, Inc.

lesser degree. Earnings trends and coverage ratios, while sound, will be more subject to variation. Capitalization characteristics, while still appropriate, may be more affected by external conditions. Ample alternate liquidity is maintained.

Issuers rated **Prime-3** (or related supporting institutions) have an acceptable capacity for repayment of short-term promissory obligations. The effect of industry characteristics and market composition may be more pronounced. Variability in earnings and profitability may result in changes in the level of debt protection measurements and the requirement for relatively high financial leverage. Adequate liquidity is maintained.

Issuers rated **Not Prime** do not fall within any of the Prime rating categories.

If an issuer represents to Moody's that its Commercial Paper obligations are supported by the credit of another entity or entities, the name or names of such supporting entity or entities are listed within parenthesis beneath the name of the issuer. In assigning ratings to such issuers, Moody's evaluates the financial strength of the indicated affiliated corporations, commercial banks, insurance companies, foreign governments or other entities, but only as one factor in the total rating assessment. Moody's makes no representation and gives no opinion on the legal validity or enforceability of any support arrangement. You are cautioned to review with your counsel any questions regarding particular support arrangements.

KEY TO MOODY'S PREFERRED STOCK RATINGS*

Moody's Rating Policy Review Board Extended its rating services to include quality designations on preferred stocks on October 1, 1973. The decision to rate preferred stocks, which Moody's had done prior to 1935, was prompted by evidence of investor interest. Moody's believes that its rating of preferred stocks is especially appropriate in view of the ever-increasing amount of these securities outstanding, and the fact that continuing inflation and its ramifications have resulted generally in the dilution of some of the protection afforded them as well as other fixed-income securities.

Because of the fundamental differences between preferred stocks and bonds, a variation of our familiar bond rating symbols is being used in the quality ranking of preferred stocks. The symbols, presented below, are designed to avoid comparison with bond quality in absolute terms. It should always be borne in mind that preferred stocks occupy a junior position to bonds within a particular capital structure.

Preferred stock rating symbols and their definitions are as follows:

aaa

An issue which is rated **aaa** is considered to be a top-quality preferred stock. This rating indicates good asset protection and the least risk of dividend impairment within the universe of preferred stocks.

aa

An issue which is rated **aa** is considered a high-grade preferred stock. This rating indicates that there is reasonable assurance that earnings and asset protection will remain relatively well maintained in the foreseeable future.

a

An issue which is rated **a** is considered to be an upper-medium grade preferred stock. While risks are judged to be somewhat greater than in the "**aaa**" and "**aa**" classifications, earnings and asset protection are, nevertheless, expected to be maintained at adequate levels.

baa

An issue which is rated **baa** is considered to be medium grade, neither highly protected nor poorly secured. Earnings and asset protection appear adequate at present but may be questionable over any great length of time.

ba

An issue which is rated **ba** is considered to have speculative elements and its future cannot be considered well assured. Earnings and asset protection may be very moderate and not well safeguarded during adverse periods. Uncertainty of position characterized preferred stocks in this class.

b

An issue which is rated **b** generally lacks the characteristics of a desirable investment. Assurance of dividend payments and maintenance of other terms of the issue over any long period of time may be small.

caa

An issue which is rated **caa** is likely to be in arrears on dividend payments. This rating designation does not purport to indicate the future status of payments.

***Note:** Moody's applies numerical modifiers **1**, **2** and **3** in each rating classification from **1** indicates that the security ranks in the higher end of its generic rating category; the modifier **2** indicates a mid-range ranking; and the modifier **3** indicates that the issue ranks in the lower end of its generic rating category.

Source: Moody's Investors Service, Inc.

"ca"

An issue which is rated "**ca**" is speculative in a high degree and is likely to be in arrears on dividends with little likelihood of eventual payment.

"c"

This is the lowest rated class of preferred or preference stock. Issues so rated can be regarded as having extremely poor prospects of ever attaining any real investment standing.

KEY TO SHORT-TERM LOAN RATINGS

MIG 1/VMIG 1

This designation denotes best quality. There is present strong protection by established cash flows, superior liquidity support or demonstrated broadbased access to the market for refinancing.

MIG 2/VMIG 2

This designation denotes high quality. Margins of protection are ample although not so large as in the preceding group.

MIG 3/VMIG 3

This designation denotes favorable quality. All security elements are accounted for but there is lacking the undeniable strength of the preceding grades. Liquidity and cash flow protection may be narrow and market access for refinancing is likely to be less well established.

MIG 4/VMIG 4

This designation denotes adequate quality. Protection commonly regarded as required of an investment security is present and although not distinctly or predominantly speculative, there is specific risk.

Issues or the features associated with **MIG** or **VMIG** ratings are identified by date of issue, date of maturity or maturities or rating expiration date and description to distinguish each rating from other ratings. Each rating designation is unique with no implication as to any other similar issue of the same obligor. **MIG** ratings terminate at the retirement of the obligation while **VMIG** rating expiration will be a function of each issue's specific structural or credit features.

Collateralized Mortgage Obligation (CMO) Volatility Ratings

Fitch announces ratings of collateralized mortgage obligation (CMO) volatility. V-Ratings offer a balanced view of the relative volatility of total return, price, and maturity for each CMO tranche.

CMOs are fixed income investments supported by U.S. government agency or whole loan collateral and structured into specific classes of securities known as tranches. All CMOs have high credit quality reflecting their support by federal agency certificates of Fannie Mae, Freddie Mac, or Ginnie Mae, or backing from whole loan collateral rated 'AAA.'

Individual tranches, however, have varying degrees of market risk. CMOs differ from pass-through certificates because cash flows from the collateral are structured to prioritize payment among tranches. Pass-through certificates are sold and priced with an expected yield and maturity based on an assumed mortgage prepayment rate. All pass-through certificate holders share symmetrically in this prepayment risk. CMO tranches are individually priced for expected return, maturity, and assumed prepayment rates based on their unique characteristics. Because cash flows are specifically allocated as part of structuring a new issue CMO, there is an asymmetrical distribution of prepayment risk among the tranches.

V-Rating Definitions

Fitch Indicated Volatility: Low to Moderate

Securities rated V1, V2, or V3 perform predictably over a range of various interest rate scenarios. On balance, total return, price, and cash flow indicators are less volatile than current coupon agency certificates.

V1 The security exhibits relatively small changes in total return, price, and cash flow in all modeled interest rate scenarios.

V2 The security exhibits relatively small changes in total return, price, and cash flow in most modeled interest rate scenarios. Under certain adverse interest rate scenarios, one or more of the indicators are more volatile than securities rated V1.

V3 The security exhibits relatively larger changes in total return, price, and cash flow in all modeled interest rate scenarios. However, on balance, total return, price, and cash flow indicators are less volatile than current coupon agency certificates.

Fitch Indicated Volatility: High

Securities rated V4 or V5 perform less predictably over a range of various interest rate scenarios. On balance, total return, price, and cash flow indicators are more volatile than current coupon agency certificates.

V4 The security exhibits greater changes in total return, price, and cash flow than current coupon agency certificates in all modeled interest rate scenarios. However, most indicators show less volatility than securities rated V5.

V5 The security exhibits substantial changes in total return, price, and cash flow in all modeled interest rate scenarios compared to current coupon agency certificates. Under the most stressful interest rate scenario tests, negative total returns may result.

Source: Fitch Investors Service, Inc., One State Street Plaza, New York, NY 10004.

MAJOR MONEY MARKET AND FIXED INCOME SECURITIES

Type	Interest: When Paid	Marketability	Denominations	Maturity
A. Interest Fully Taxable				
Corporate Bonds and Notes	S[1]	Very good to poor depending on quality	$1,000	1 to 50 years
Corporate Preferred Stock (Pays dividends as a fixed percentage of face value. Dividends not obligatory, but if declared must be paid before that of the common stock. Dividends fully taxable for individuals, but 85% exempt from federal tax for corporations)	Generally quarterly	Good to poor depending on quality	$100 or less	No maturity
Federal Home Loan Mortgage Corporate Bonds	S	Fair	$25,000	Up to 25 years
Federal Home Loan Mortgage Certificates	S	Fair	$100,000	Up to 3 years
Farmers' Home Administration Notes and Certificates	Annual	Fair	$25,000	1 to 25 years
Federal Housing Administration Debentures (Guaranteed by the U.S. Government)	S	Very good	$50	1 to 40 years
Federal National Mortgage Association Bonds	S	Fair	$25,000	2 to 25 years
Government National Mortgage Modified Pass through Certificates (interest plus some repayment of principal, guaranteed by U.S. Government)	Monthly	Good	$25,000	30 years; average life 12 years
Federal Home Loan Bank Bonds and Notes	S	Good	$10,000	1 to 20 years
Export-Import Bank Debentures and Certificates	S	Good	$5,000	3 to 7 years
International Bank for Reconstruction Development (World Bank), Inter-American Development Bank, Asia Development Bank	S	Fair to poor	$1,000	3 to 25 years
Foreign and Eurodollar Bonds and Notes	May be Annual or S	Poor	$1,000 (amounts vary in foreign currencies)	1 to 30 years
Bankers Acceptances (short-term debt obligations (resulting from international trade and guaranteed by a major bank)	Discounted[2] on a 360-day year basis	Fair	$5,000	1 to 270 days
Commercial Paper (short-term debt issued by a major corporation)	Discounted on a 360-day year basis	No secondary market	$100,000 (occasionally smaller)	1 to 270 days
Negotiable Certificates of Deposit (short-term debt issued by banks and which can be sold on the open market)	Interest paid on maturity; 360-day year basis	Fair	$100,000 (occasionally smaller)	30 days to 1 year
Non-negotiable Certificate of Deposit (savings certificates)	Interest paid on maturity; 360-day year basis	Non-negotiable	$500 $10,000	30 months 6 months
Collateralized Mortgage Obligations (CMO)	S or monthly	Good	$1,000	typically 2 to 20 years
Repurchase Agreements (generally short term loans by large investors, secured by U.S. Government or other high quality issues)[3]	Interest paid on maturity; 360-day year basis	No secondary market	$100,000	1 to 30 days (sometimes more)

Type	Interest: When Paid	Marketability	Denominations	Maturity
Zero Coupon Bonds (Bonds stripped of coupons)	Bonds issued at deep discount. Full yield realized at maturity	Good	$1,000 on maturity	1 to 30 years
B. Interest Exempt from State and Local Income Taxes				
U.S. Treasury Bonds and Notes	S	Very good	$1,000	1 to 20 years
U.S. Treasury Bills	Discounted on a 360-day basis	Very good	$10,000	90 days to 1 year
U.S. Series EE Savings Bonds[4]	Issued at discount, full interest, paid on maturity	No secondary market: available for resale	$50 minimum $10,000 maximum	10 years (can be redeemed before maturity at reduced yields
U.S. Series HH Savings[5] Bonds	S	No secondary market	$10,000 $15,000 maximum	10 years
Federal Land Bank Bonds	S	Good	$1,000	1 to 10 years
Federal Financing Bank Notes and Bonds	S	Good	$1,000	1 to 20 years
Tennessee Valley Authority Notes and Bonds	S	Fair	$1,000	5 to 25 years
Banks for Cooperatives Bonds	Interest: 360-day year basis	Good	$5,000	180 days
Federal Intermediate Credit Bank Bonds	Interest: 360-day year basis	Good	$5,000	270 days
Federal Home Loan Bank Notes and Bonds	Discounted: 360-day year basis	Good	$10,000	30 to 360-day year basis (some more)
Farm Credit Bank Notes and Bonds	Interest: 360-day year basis	Good	$50,000	270 days (some more)
C. Interest Exempt from Federal Income Tax				
State and Local Notes and Bonds (in-State issues, usually exempt from State and local income taxes)	S	Good to fair depending on rating	$5,000	1 to 50 years
Housing Authority Bonds (in-State issues usually exempt from State and local income taxes)	S	Good to fair	$5,000	1 to 40 years

[1] S means semiannually.

[2] A discount means interest paid in advance, thus a 10% discounted security maturing at $10,000 would cost $9,000 to purchase.

[3] Recently some banks have issued repurchase agreements for smaller amounts of money, i.e., several thousands of dollars.

[4] Since November 1982, U.S. Savings Bonds pay variable interest equal to 85% of the 5 year Treasury securities' rate adjusted semi-annually and have a minimum guaranteed rate which is adjustable. The rate applies to bonds held 5 years or more.

[5] Issued in exchange for EE bonds.

U.S. Treasury Bonds, Notes, and Bills: Terms Defined*

U.S. Treasury bonds, notes and bills are interest paying securities representing a debt on the part of the U.S. Government. Treasury bonds have a maturity of over 5 years, while notes mature within 5 to 7 years. Bills are discussed below. Both Treasury bonds and notes are generally issued in minimum denominations of \$1,000 and pay interest semiannually. The amount of semiannual interest paid is determined by the coupon rate specified on the bond and is calculated on a 365-day year basis. For a \$1,000 face value† bond the interest is given by:

$$\text{semiannual interest} = 1/2\ (\$1{,}000 \times \text{coupon rate})$$

Bonds may be priced higher (at a premium) or lower (at a discount) than the face value (par) depending on current interest rates. The *current yield* is the rate the investor receives based on the prices actually paid for a bond. The price is given by:

$$\text{current yield} = \frac{\$1{,}000 \times \text{coupon rate}}{\text{purchase price}}$$

Thus, a \$1,000 face value bond with an 8% coupon rate purchased at \$850 has a current yield by:

$$\text{current yield} = \frac{\$1{,}000 \times 8\%}{\$850} = 9.41\%$$

The *yield to maturity* (YTM) is the yield obtained on taking into account the years remaining to maturity, annual interest payments, and the capital gain (or loss) realized at maturity. It is obtained from special tables.

However, the yield to maturity (YTM) may be found approximately from the formula

$$\text{YTM} = \frac{\text{I} + \text{A}}{\text{B}}$$

$$\text{I} = \text{annual interest rate}$$

$$\text{A} = \frac{\$1{,}000 - \text{M}}{\text{N}}$$

$$\text{B} = \frac{\$1{,}000 + \text{M}}{2}$$

where M = current market price of the bond

N = years remaining to maturity

As an example, a bond (\$1,000 face value) has a 10% coupon and is currently priced at \$1,100 with 10 years remaining to maturity. What is the approximate YTM?

$$\text{I} = \$1{,}000 \times .1 = \$100 \text{ interest per year}$$

$$\text{A} = \frac{\$1{,}000 - \$1{,}100}{10} = \$-10$$

$$\text{B} = \frac{\$1{,}000 + \$1{,}100}{2} = \$1{,}050$$

$$\text{YTM} = \frac{\$100 - \$10}{\$1{,}050} = .0857 = 8.57\%$$

U.S. Treasury bills (T-bills) are U.S. Government debt obligations which mature within one year. They are offered by the Federal Reserve Bank with maturities of 90 days (3 month bills) and 182 days (six month bills). Nine-month bills and one-year bills are also available. Treasury bills are sold in a minimum denomination of \$10,000. Interest is paid by the discount method based on a 360-day year. With the discount method, interest is, in effect, paid at the time the bill is purchased. Thus a 91-day \$10,000 bill (face value) with an 8% discount interest rate would provide the buyer with \$202.22 (\$10,000 × .08 × 91⁄360) interest at the time of purchase. This amount is deducted from the face value of the bill at the time of purchase so the buyer actually pays a net amount of \$9,797.78 (\$10,000 − \$202.22). When the bill matures, the buyer receives \$10,000 on redemption.

Since T-bills pay interest at the time of purchase (discount basis) on a 360-day year basis, while bonds (and notes) pay interest semiannually on a 365-day year basis, the two rates cannot be compared directly. To compare the two rates, the discount rate must be converted to the so-called *bond equivalent yield*, given by

$$\text{bond equivalent yield} = \frac{365 \times \text{discount rate}}{360 - (\text{discount rate} \times \text{days to maturity})}$$

As an example, a newly issued 91-day note with a discount rate of 12% has a

$$\text{bond equivalent yield} = \frac{365 \times (.12)}{360 - (.12 \times 91)} = 12.55\%$$

Interest from U.S. Treasury bonds, notes, and bills are subject to federal income tax,

* The terms *current yield*, *yield to maturity*, etc. defined in this section are generally applicable to all fixed incomes.

† Face value is the amount of the bond or note payable upon maturity.

but are exempt from state and local income taxes.

How to Read U.S. Government Bond and Note Quotations

TREASURY BONDS AND NOTES

(1) Rate	Maturity (2) Mo/yr	(3) Bid	(4) Asked	(5) Chg	(6) Ask Yld
8½	Feb 92n	100:00	100:02 −	1	0.00
7⅞	Mar 92n	100:11	100:13	. . .	3.25
8½	Mar 92n	100:13	100:15	. . .	3.18
11¾	Apr 92n	101:00	101:02 −	1	3.46
8⅞	Apr 92n	100:27	100:29	. . .	3.51
6⅝	May 92n	100:18	100:20 +	1	3.62

Source: Reprinted by permission of THE WALL STREET JOURNAL,

The above exhibit is an example of U.S. Government bond and note quotations as it appears in *The Wall Street Journal.*

(1) Indicates the coupon rate of interest. Rates are quoted to ⅛ of a percent. Thus 8⅜ means 8.375%. The semiannual interest payments are calculated, as described elsewhere, using this rate.

(2) Indicates the year of maturity and the month in which the bond or note matures. The letter *n* means the security is a note. Otherwise a bond is implied.

(3) The *bid price* per bond or note (the price at which the bond can be sold to the dealer), expressed as a percentage of the face value ($1,000) of the bond. Prices are quoted in terms of 1/32 of a percent. Thus 98.5 means 98 5/32. To find the dollar value of the price, convert 98 5/32 to a decimal (98 5/32 = .98156) and multiply by the face value of the bond to give $981.56 (.98156 × $1,000).

(4) The *ask price* per bond or note (the price at which the dealer will sell the bond). The dollar value is found as indicated above.

(5) The change in the bid price from the closing price of the previous day.

(6) The yield if the bond is held to maturity, based on the ask price.

Some U.S. Treasury bonds can be called back for redemption prior to maturity. These are shown with two dates (under item 2 for example)—*1993–98* indicating that the bonds mature in 1998, but may be called back and redeemed any time after 1993.

Some newspapers (such as *The New York Times*) use a slight modification of the above arrangement, though the various terms have the same meaning as defined above. Thus, a bond maturing in June of 1985 and bearing a 10⅜% coupon is indicated by *May '85 10⅜.*

How to Read U.S. Treasury Bill Quotations

(1) Rate	(2) Days to Mat.	(3) Bid	(4) Asked	(5) Chg	(6) Ask Yld
Feb 27 '92	0	3.59	3.49 +	0.09	0.00
Mar 05 '92	7	3.92	3.82 +	0.09	3.89
Mar 12 '92	14	3.93	3.83 +	0.04	3.90
Mar 19 '92	21	3.93	3.83 +	0.06	3.90
Mar 26 '92	28	3.84	3.80 +	0.04	3.87
Apr 02 '92	35	3.92	3.88 +	0.06	3.96

Source: Reprinted by permission of THE WALL STREET JOURNAL,

The above exhibit is an example of Treasury bill quotations as it appears in *The Wall Street Journal.*

(1) The date of maturity.

(2) Days to maturity.

(3) The bid price at market close quoted as a *discount* rate in percent. This bid price is the price at which the dealer will buy the bill. To convert the discount rate to a dollar price use the formula

$$\text{dollar price} = \$10{,}000 - (\text{discount rate} \times \text{days to maturity} \times .2778)$$

In the above, the discount must be expressed in percent. For example, if the dealer bids 3.82% discount for a bill which matures in 50 days, the dollar price is given by

$$\text{dollar price} = \$10{,}000 - [3.82 \times 50 \times .2778] = \$9{,}946.94$$

(4) The asked price at market close expressed as a discount rate in percent. The asked price is the price at which the dealer will sell a bill to a buyer. To convert to a dollar price use the above formula.

(5) The bond equivalent yield expressed in percent. This is calculated (as explained elsewhere) from the asked price expressed as a discount rate. This rate is used to compare T-bill yields to that of bonds, notes and certificates of deposit.

Some newspapers (e.g., *The New York Times*) use a somewhat different arrangement, though the meaning of the terms is the same as defined above. Thus, a bill maturing on June 4, 1981, is indicated as such. Also included in some newspapers is the change in bid price expressed as a discount rate.

How to Read Corporate Bond Quotations*

Corporate bonds are debt securities issued by private corporations. They generally have a face value (the amount due on maturity) of $1,000 and a specified interest rate (coupon rate) paid semiannually. Many corporate bonds have a *call* provision which permits the company to recall and redeem the bond after a specified date. Call privileges are usually exercised when interest rates fall sufficiently. Investors, therefore, cannot count on *locking in* high interest rates with corporate bonds. Bond quality designations used by Moody's and Standard & Poor's are given elsewhere in the Almanac (pp. 518–524).

The following is an example of price quotations for bonds traded on The New York Stock Exchange as they appear in *The Wall Street Journal.*

CORPORATION BONDS

VOLUME, $18,990,000

(1) Bonds		(2) Cur Yld	(3) Vol	(4) High	(5) Low	(6) Close	(7) Net Chg
AlaP	9s2000	14.	6	63	62	63	2
AlaP	8½s01	15.	10	57½	57½	57¼	. . .
AlaP	8⅞s03	15.	25	60	59½	60	+ ½
AlaP	10⅞05	15.	3	72	72	72	− 2¼
AlaP	10½05	15.	12	70½	70½	70½	− 1
AlaP	12⅝10	16.	7	81¼	81⅛	81⅛	− 1⅝

Source: Reprinted by permission of *The Wall Street Journal,* Dow Jones and Company, Inc. 1981. All rights reserved.

(1) The name of the issue in abbreviated form, followed by the coupon rate of interest in percent (designated by the letter *s*), and the year in which the bond matures. The coupon rate is stated in terms of ⅛ of a percent; 9⅜ means 9.375%.

(2) This is the current yield which is calculated as stated elsewhere. (See U.S. Treasury Bonds, Notes, and Bills, p. 528.)

(3) This item is the number of bonds sold that day.

(4) This is the highest price quoted for the bond sold on that day, expressed as a percentage of face value ($1,000). To convert to dollars, express the price as a decimal and multiply by the face value of the bond. As an example:

$$58\frac{1}{2} = (.5850 \times \$1{,}000.) = \$585$$

(5) This is the lowest price quoted that day. It is converted into dollars as described above.

(6) This is the price at the close of the market that day.

(7) This is the change in the closing price from that of the previous day. To convert to dollars, express as a decimal and multiply by $1,000. Thus, −1⅞ means a decrease per bond of $18.75 (.01875 × $1,000) from that of the previous day.

* Yield terms are the same as those defined in the section on U.S. Treasury Bonds, Notes and Bills, p. 528.

TAX EXEMPT VERSUS TAXABLE YIELDS

tax bracket	To equal a tax-free yield of: 5½%	6%	6½%	7%	7½%	8%	8½%	9%	9½%	10%	10½%	11%
	a taxable investment has to earn:											
28%	7.64%	8.33%	9.03%	9.72%	10.42%	11.11%	11.81%	12.50%	13.19%	13.89%	14.58%	15.28%
30	7.86	8.57	9.29	10.00	10.71	11.43	12.14	12.86	13.57	14.29	15.00	15.71
31	7.97	8.70	9.42	10.14	10.87	11.59	12.32	13.04	13.77	14.49	15.22	15.94
32	8.09	8.82	9.56	10.29	11.03	11.76	12.50	13.24	13.97	14.71	15.44	16.18
34	8.33	9.09	9.85	10.61	11.36	12.12	12.88	13.64	14.39	15.15	15.91	16.67
36	8.59	9.38	10.16	10.94	11.72	12.50	13.28	14.06	14.84	15.63	16.41	17.19
37	8.73	9.52	10.32	11.11	11.90	12.70	13.49	14.29	15.08	15.87	16.67	17.47
39	9.02	9.84	10.66	11.48	12.30	13.11	13.93	14.75	15.57	16.39	17.21	18.03

Tax-Exempt Bonds

Tax exempt (municipal) bonds are issued by state and local governments and are free from federal income tax on interest payments. The bonds are often issued in $5,000 denominations and pay interest semiannually. Capital gains are taxable. In addition, holders of out-of-state bonds may be subject to state and local income taxes of the state in which they reside. For example, a New York City resident holding Los Angeles municipal bonds would be subject to New York State and City income taxes on the interest.

The taxable equivalent yield of a tax exempt bond is obtained by means of the expression

$$\text{taxable equivalent yield} = \frac{\text{tax exempt yield}}{1 - (F + S + L)}$$

where

F is the federal tax bracket of the investor
S is the state tax bracket of the investor
L is the local tax bracket of the investor

Thus, an investor in the 50% federal bracket, 10% state bracket and 3% local bracket who holds a bond with a current yield of 6% which is exempt from all income taxes would enjoy a taxable equivalent yield (TEY) given by

$$\text{TEY} = \frac{6\%}{1 - (.5 + .1 + .03)} = 16.21\%$$

A taxable yield of 16.21% would be necessary to provide the same yield as the 6% current yield on the tax exempt security.

TYPES OF TAX EXEMPT BONDS AND NOTES

General Obligation bonds, also known as GO's, are backed by a pledge of a city's or state's full faith and credit for the prompt repayment of both principal and interest. Most city, county and school district bonds are secured by a pledge of unlimited property taxes. Since general obligation bonds depend on tax resources, they are normally analyzed in terms of the size of the resources being taxed.

Revenue bonds are payable from the earnings of a revenue-producing enterprise such as a sewer, water, gas or electric system, airport, toll bridge, college dormitory, lease payments from property rented to industrial companies, and other income-producing facilities. Revenue bonds are analyzed in terms of their earnings.

Limited and Special Tax bonds are payable from the pledge of the proceeds derived by the issuer from a specific tax such as a property tax levied at a fixed rate, a special assessment, or a tax on gasoline.

Municipal notes are short term obligations maturing from 30 days to a year and are issued in anticipation of revenues coming from the sales of bonds (BANS), taxes (TANS), or other revenues (RANS).

Project notes, issued by local housing and urban renewal agencies, are backed by a U.S. Government guarantee and are also tax exempt.

How to Understand Tax-Exempt Bond Quotations

Generally the prices of municipal bonds are quoted in terms of the yield to maturity (defined elsewhere) rather than in percentage of face value, as with other bonds. The yield to maturity can be converted to a dollar price if the years remaining to maturity and the rate of interest due are known. Certain tables used for this purpose are given in the *Basis Book* (published by the Financial Publishing Company, 82 Brookline Avenue, Boston, Massachusetts). The books list the dollar price (per $1,000 face value of the bond) corresponding to a given coupon rate, yield, and years to maturity.

Some municipal bonds, however, are quoted directly in terms of percentage of face value. Thus, a bid price (the price at which the dealer will buy the bonds from the investor) of 98⅝ for a $5,000 face value bond can be converted to a dollar price by first converting the bid to a decimal expression (.98625) and then multiplying by the face value of the bond. The result in this case is $4,931.25 (.98625 × $5,000). The same calculation applies to the ask price (the price at which the dealer will sell the bond to the investor).

Prices of tax exempt bonds are not quoted in the daily press. They can be obtained by calling municipal bond dealers. Extensive quotations are given in some relatively expensive publications:

The Blue List
Standard & Poor's
25 Broadway
New York, New York 10004
(212) 770-4600

The Daily Bond Buyer
and
The Weekly Bond Buyer
The Bond Buyer
1 State Street Plaza
New York, New York 10004
(212) 943-8200

Bond Week (Formerly Money Manager)
Institutional Investor
488 Madison Avenue
New York, New York 10022
(212) 303-3300

Government National Mortgage Association (GNMA) Modified Pass Through Certificates

A GNMA Mortgage-Backed Security is a government-guaranteed security which is collateralized by a pool of federally-underwritten residential mortgages. The investor receives a monthly check for a proportionate share of the principal and interest on a pool of mortgages whether or not the payments have actually been collected from the borrowers.

The GNMA Mortgage-Backed Security offers the highest yield of any federally-guaranteed security. In addition, the GNMA security offers a very competitive return in comparison to private corporation debt issues. Moreover, the investor receives a monthly return on the GNMA guaranteed investment, rather than semi-annual payments as on most bonds. This monthly payment represents a cash flow available for reinvestment and has the effect of increasing the yield on GNMAs by 10 to 18 basis points (a basis point is 0.1%) when compared to the yield equivalent received on a bond investment with the same "coupon" rate but paying interest semi-annually.

On single-family securities (the most popular form) the maturity is typically 30 years. However, statistical studies have determined that the average life of a single-family security is approximately 12 years, due to prepayments of principal. Nevertheless, some of the mortgages in any pool are likely to remain outstanding for the full 30-year period.

The minimum size of original individual certificates is $25,000 with increments of $5,000 above that amount.

Due to the uncertainties in the maturity of the above mentioned pass-through certificates, collateralized mortgage obligations (CMOs) have been introduced. CMOs are bonds backed by Ginnie Maes, Freddie Macs, and other mortgage instruments providing investors with a wide choice of maturities ranging from 2 to 20 years. Essentially, the monthly payments from the underlying mortgage instruments are initially allocated to the nearest maturity CMO and subsequently to CMO maturities of successively longer duration. CMO interest payments are made semiannually or monthly.

Components—Dow Jones 20 Bond Average

The Dow Jones Bond Averages are a simple arithmetic average compiled daily by using the New York Exchange closing bond prices. A list of the bonds on which these averages are based follows:

10 Public Utilities

Name	Coupon	Maturity
BellSouth Telcm	6⅜%	2004
Comwlth Ed	7⅝%	2003
Consol Nat Gas	7¼%	2015
Michigan Bell	7%	2012
New York Tel	7⅜%	2011
Pacific Bell	7⅛%	2026
Phil Electric	7⅜%	2001
Potmc Elec Pwr	7%	2018
So. Bell Tel	7⅜%	2010
Tucson Elec	7⅝%	2003

10 Industrials

Name	Coupon	Maturity
AT&T	7⅛%	2002
Beth Steel	6⅞%	1999
Champion Intl	6½%	2011
Chrysler Finl	6½%	1998
DuPont	6%	2001
General Signal	5¾%	2002
IBM	6⅜%	2000
Mead Corp.	6¾%	2012
Occid Petrol	10⅛%	2009
Sears Roebuck	9½%	1999

Source: Reprinted by permission of Barron's *Business and Financial Weekly*, © 1994 Dow Jones & Company, Inc. All Rights Reserved Worldwide.

Components—Barron's Confidence Index

Barron's Confidence Index is the ratio of the average yield to maturity on best grade corporate bonds to the intermediate grade corporate bonds average yield to maturity. A list of the bonds on which the confidence index is based follows:

Best Grade Bonds

Name	Coupon	Maturity
AMBAC Inc	9⅜%	2011
Amoco Co	8⅝%	2016
Campbell Soup	8¾%	2021
Ches & Potom T	7⅞%	2022
Genl RE Cp	9%	2009
IBM	8⅜%	2019
McDonalds	8⅞%	2011
Proc & Gamb	8½%	2009
United Parcel	8⅜%	2020
Wisc El Svc	8⅜%	2026

Intermediate Grade Bonds

Name	Coupon	Maturity
Arco Chem	9.80%	2020
Ariz Pub Svc	8¾%	2024
CSX Corp	8⅝%	2022
Dayton Hud	8⅞%	2022
Delta Airl	9¼%	2022
Eastman K	9.20%	2021
GTE Corp	8¾%	2021
NCNB	9⅜%	2009
Philips Pet	9⅜%	2011
Ralston Purina	9¼%	2009

Source: Reprinted by permission of Barron's *Business and Financial Weekly*, © 1994 Dow Jones & Company, Inc. All Rights Reserved Worldwide.

Monetary Aggregates Defined

Money supply data has been revised and expanded to reflect the Federal Reserve's redefinition of the monetary aggregates. The redefinition was prompted by the emergence in recent years of new monetary assets—for example, negotiable order of withdrawal (NOW) accounts and money-market mutual fund shares—and alterations in the basic character of established monetary assets—for example, the growing similarity of and substitution between the deposits of thrift institutions and those of commercial banks.

M1-A has been discontinued with M1-B now designated as "M-1." M-1 is currency in circulation plus all checking accounts including those which pay interest, such as NOW accounts. M-1 excludes deposits due to foreign commercial banks and official institutions.

M-2 as redefined adds to M1-B overnight repurchase agreements (RPs) issued by commercial banks and certain overnight Eurodollars (those issued by Carribbean branches of member banks) held by U.S. nonbank residents, money-market mutual fund shares, and savings and small-denomination time deposits (those issued in denominations of less than $100,000) at all depository institutions. Depository institutions are commercial banks (including U.S. agencies and branches of foreign banks, Edge Act Corporations, and foreign investment companies), mutual savings banks, savings and loan associations, and credit unions.

M-3 as redefined is equal to new M-2 plus large-denomination time deposits (those issued as in denominations of $100,000 or more) at all depository institutions (including negotiable CDs) plus term

RPs issued by commercial banks and savings and loan associations.

L, the very broad measure of liquid assets, equals new M-3 plus other liquid assets consisting of other Eurodollar holdings of U.S. nonbank residents, bankers acceptances, commercial paper, savings bonds, and marketable liquid Treasury obligations.

Federal Reserve Banks

Board of Governors of the Federal Reserve System, Washington, D.C. 20551

Federal Reserve Bank	Telephone Number	District	Address
BOSTON*	617-973-3000	1	600 Atlantic Avenue, Boston, Massachusetts 02106
NEW YORK*	212-720-5000	2	33 Liberty Street (Federal Reserve P.O. Station), New York, New York 10045
Buffalo Branch	716-849-5000		160 Delaware Avenue, Buffalo, New York 14202 (P.O. Box 961, Buffalo, New York 14240-0961)
PHILADELPHIA	215-574-6000	3	Ten Independence Mall, Philadelphia, Pennsylvania 19106 (P.O. Box 66, Philadelphia, Pennsylvania 19105)
CLEVELAND*	216-579-2000	4	1455 East Sixth Street, Cleveland, Ohio 44114 (P.O. Box 6387, Cleveland, Ohio 44101)
Cincinnati Branch	513-721-4787		150 East Fourth Street, Cincinnati, Ohio 45202-0999 (P.O. Box 999, Cincinnati, Ohio 45201-0999)
Pittsburgh Branch	412-261-7800		717 Grant Street, Pittsburgh, Pennsylvania 15219 (P.O. Box 867, Pittsburgh, Pennsylvania 15230)
RICHMOND*	804-697-8000	5	701 East Byrd Street, Richmond, Virginia 23219 (P.O. Box 27622, Richmond, Virginia 23261)
Baltimore Branch	301-576-3300		502 South Sharp Street, Baltimore, Maryland 21201 (P.O. Box 1378), Baltimore, Maryland 21203)
Charlotte Branch	704-358-2100		530 Trade Street, Charlotte, North Carolina 28202 (P.O. Box 30248, Charlotte, North Carolina 28230)
Culpeper Communications and Records Center	703-829-1600		Mount Pony Rd., State Rte. 658 (P.O. Drawer 20, Culpeper, Virginia 22701)
ATLANTA	404-521-8500	6	104 Marietta Street, N.W., Atlanta, Georgia 30303-2713
Birmingham Branch	205-731-8500		1801 Fifth Avenue, North, Birmingham, Alabama 35283 (P.O. Box 830447, Birmingham, Alabama 35283-0447)
Jacksonville Branch	904-632-1000		800 Water Street, Jacksonville, Florida 32204 (P.O. Box 929, Jacksonville, Florida 32231-0044)
Miami Branch	305-591-2065		9100 Northwest 36th Street, Miami, Florida 33178 (P.O. Box 520847, Miami, Florida 33152-0847)
Nashville Branch	615-251-7100		301 Eighth Avenue, North, Nashville, Tennessee 37203 (P.O. Box 4407, Nashville, Tennessee 37203-4407)
New Orleans Branch	504-593-3200		525 St. Charles Avenue, New Orleans, Louisiana 70130 (P.O. Box 61630, New Orleans, Louisiana 70161-1630)
CHICAGO*	312-322-5322	7	230 South LaSalle Street, Chicago, Illinois 60604 (P.O. Box 834, Chicago, Illinois 60690-0834)
Detroit Branch	313-961-6880		160 W. Fort Street, Detroit, Michigan 48226 (P.O. Box 1059, Detroit, Michigan 48231)
ST. LOUIS	314-444-8444	8	411 Locust Street, St. Louis, Missouri 63102 (P.O. Box 442, St. Louis, Missouri 63166)
Little Rock Branch	501-324-8300		325 West Capitol Avenue, Little Rock, Arkansas 72201 (P.O. Box 1261, Little Rock, Arkansas 72203)
Louisville Branch	502-568-9200		410 South Fifth Street, Louisville, Kentucky 40202 (P.O. Box 32710, Louisville, Kentucky 40232)
Memphis Branch	901-523-7171		200 North Main Street, Memphis, Tennessee 38103 (P.O. Box 407, Memphis, Tennessee 38101)
MINNEAPOLIS	612-340-2345	9	250 Marquette Avenue, Minneapolis, Minnesota 55480
Helena Branch	406-447-3800		100 Neill Avenue, Helena, Montana 59601

Federal Reserve Bank	Telephone Number	District	Address
KANSAS CITY	816-881-2000	10	925 Grand Avenue, Kansas City, Missouri 64198
Denver Branch	303-572-2300		1020 16th Street, Denver, Colorado 80202 (Terminal Annex-P.O. Box 5228, Denver, Colorado 80217)
Oklahoma City Branch	405-270-8400		226 Dean A. McGee Avenue (P.O. Box 25129) Oklahoma City, Oklahoma 73125
Omaha Branch	402-221-5500		2201 Farnam Street, Omaha, Nebraska 68102 (P.O. Box 3958 Omaha, Nebraska 68103)
DALLAS	214-651-6111	11	400 South Akard Street (Station K), Dallas, Texas 75222
El Paso Branch	915-544-4730		301 East Main Street, El Paso, Texas 79901 (P.O. Box 100, El Paso, Texas 79999)
Houston Branch	713-659-4433		1701 San Jacinto Street, Houston, Texas 77002 (P.O. Box 2578, Houston, Texas 77252)
San Antonio Branch	512-224-2141		126 East Nueva Street, San Antonio, Texas 78204 (P.O. Box 1471, San Antonio, Texas 78295)
SAN FRANCISCO	415-974-2000	12	101 Market Street, San Francisco, California 94105 (P.O. Box 7702, San Francisco, California 94120)
Los Angeles Branch	213-683-2300		950 South Grand Avenue, Los Angeles, California 90015 (Terminal Annex-P.O. Box 2077, Los Angeles, California 90051)
Portland Branch	503-221-5900		915 S.W. Stark Street, Portland, Oregon 97025 (P.O. Box 3436, Portland, Oregon 97208)
Salt Lake City Branch	801-322-7900		120 South State Street, Salt Lake City, Utah 84111 (P.O. Box 30780, Salt Lake City, Utah 84125)
Seattle Branch	206-343-3600		1015 Second Avenue, Seattle, Washington 98104 (P.O. Box 3567, Seattle, Washington 98124)

*Additional offices of these Banks are located at Lewiston, Maine 04240; Windsor Locks, Connecticut 06096; Cranford, New Jersey 07016; Jericho, New York 11753; Utica Oriskany, New York 13424; Columbus, Ohio 43216; Columbia, South Carolina 29210; Charleston, West Virginia 25328; Des Moines, Iowa 50306; Indianapolis, Indiana 46206; and Milwaukee, Wisconsin 53201.

Source: Board of Governors of the Federal Reserve System, Washington, D.C., 20551.

Options and Futures

What Are Stock Options?

There are two types of stock options—call and put. A call option is the right to buy a specified number of shares of a stock at a given price before a specific date. A put option is the right to sell a specific number of shares of a stock at a given price before a specific date. Options, unlike a futures contract, are a right *not an obligation* to buy or sell stock. The price at which the stock may be bought or sold is referred to as the exercise (or striking) price. The date at which the option expires is the *expiration* date. The term "in-the-money" option refers to either a call option with an exercise price less than that of the market price of the stock, or a put option with an exercise price above the market price of the stock.

Expiration months are set at intervals of three months for the cycles: the January–April–July–October cycle, February–May–August–November cycle, and the March–June–September–December cycle. Options expire at 11:59 P.M. Eastern Standard Time on the Saturday immediately following the third Friday of the expiration month.

The exercise prices are set at 5 point (dollar) intervals for stocks trading below $50, 10 point intervals for stocks trading between $50 to $200, and 20 point intervals for securities trading above $200. Initial exercise prices are set above and below the price of the security. Thus, if a security is priced at 32½ on the New York Stock Exchange at the time new options are opened, the opening exercise prices would be set at 30 and 40. If the price of the security is close to a standard exercise price, three prices are set: at the standard price, as well as above and below the latter.

Standard option contracts are written for 100 shares of stock of the underlying security. The price at which the seller (writer) agrees to sell an option to the buyer is called the *premium.* The premium is quoted *per share* of the underlying stock so that the price per contract is 100 times the quote.

After the option is issued, the premium will fluctuate with the price of the stocks. With call options the premium will increase with an increase in the price of stock. With put options the premium will increase when the stock price declines. The reason should be clear from the following examples. Assume that in January a July call option is written at the exercise price of 50 ($50 per share) on the XYZ Corporation stock. We assume that the stock is selling at $51. The call option writer (seller) asks and receives a premium of $2 ($200 per option contract). After brokerage commission on the sale (say $25 per contract) the option writer nets a profit of $175 per contract. The call option buyer pays $200 for the contract plus the commission or $225. Assume that the stock increases to 60 per share. The option holder (buyer) can, in principle, purchase the stock at 50 (the Exercise price) and sell it at 60 netting a profit on transaction of $10 per share (neglecting commissions). Clearly the call option has acquired increased value which will be reflected in the premium (option price). Let us assume that the premium increases from 2 to 10 ($200 to $1,000 per contract). If the option holder now sells the option, he will make a profit (after commissions) of $750 on a $250 investment ($200 premium and $50 commissions).

Alternatively, the option holder may elect to exercise the option and acquire the shares at 50 (the exercise price). The option writer must then deliver 100 shares of XYZ Corporation at $50 per share.

If the stock price drops below the exercise price and remains so until expiration of the option, the call option buyer can lose his entire investment. Sometimes the loss may be reduced if the option is sold before it matures. The holder then is said to have *closed out* his position.

Similar arguments apply to put options. In this case the option holder benefits if the price of the stock decreases below the exercise price. Assume that the above stock drops to 40. The put holder could, in principle, buy the stock at 40 and sell it at 50 (the exercise price) to the put writer. The put holder would make a profit of $10 per share (neglecting commissions). The put premium would reflect this situation and, as a result, increase.

Instead of selling the option and taking a profit, the put holder may elect to exercise the option and sell 100 shares to the put writer who must purchase these shares at the 50 exercise price.

If the market price of the stock is greater than the exercise price when the put option expires, the holder will lose his investment.

Options are traded on the Chicago Board of Options Exchange, the American Stock Exchange, the Pacific Stock Exchange and the Philadelphia Stock Exchange.

How to Read Option Quotations

The following explains option quotations as they appear in *The Wall Street Journal.*

(1)	(2)	(3)	(4)	(5)	(6)	(7)
			—Call—		—Put—	
Option/Strike		Exp.	Vol.	Last	Vol.	Last
Micron	50	Mar	20	12⅝	106	5/16
62⅝	50	Apr	109	13⅛	110	¾
62⅝	55	Feb	140	7⅞	...	...
62⅝	55	Mar	137	8⅞	37	⅞
62⅝	55	Apr	148	9¾	1001	11/16
62⅝	60	Feb	337	2¾	162	¼

Source: Reprinted by permission of *The Wall Street Journal*

(1) Lists the stock to which the option contract corresponds. The price listed underneath is the closing price of the stock.
(2) Lists the strike price i.e. the price at which the owner of the option can buy or sell the corresponding stock.
(3) Gives the month at which the option expires. All options expire on the third Friday of the expiration month.
(4) Gives the number of option contracts (in this case a call) traded.
(5) Gives the price (premium) per call option at the close of the trading day. Since an option contract is for 100 shares of stock, a contract will trade at 100 times the premium.
(6) Same as 4 above but applies to puts.
(7) Same as 5 above but applies to puts.

Stock Market Futures*

Standard & Poor's 500 Stock Index futures† combine the unique aspects of the futures market with the opportunities of stock ownership and stock options by helping many investors manage their inherent stock market risks, and at the same time allowing others to participate in broad market moves. S&P 500 Index futures can play an important role in an individual's or institution's overall market strategy.

Stock ownership is subject to several risks. Lower earnings reports or changes in industry fundamentals can cause severe declines in individual issues. Or, a promising industry or company might drop because the entire market is heading down. A myriad of decisions go into individual stock selection—but the first question is usually what is the state and direction of the entire market.

The introduction of the Standard & Poor's 500 Stock Index contract allows investors to hedge, and therefore, virtually eliminate their portfolio exposure in a declining market without disturbing their holdings. At the same time, others can purchase or sell the contract according to their expectations of future market activity. This simultaneous ability to hedge the risks of stock ownership and to take advantage of broad market moves creates opportunities for everyone with positions in or opinions about the stock market.

A NEW MARKET FOR TODAY'S INVESTOR

S&P 500 Index futures are traded on the Index and Option Market division of the Chicago Mercantile Exchange. One of the largest commodity exchanges in the world, the CME introduced financial futures trading in 1972 when it formed the International Monetary Market to trade contracts in foreign currencies. Later, the IMM added futures contracts in Gold, 90-Day Treasury Bills, Three-Month Domestic Certificates of Deposit, and Three-Month Eurodollar Time Deposits.

THE S&P 500 INDEX

The Standard & Poor's Stock Price Index has been the standard by which professional portfolio managers and individuals have measured their performance for 65 years. Begun in 1917 as an index based on 200 stocks, the list was expanded to 500 issues in 1957.

Currently, the Index is one of the U.S. Commerce Department's 12 leading economic indicators.

The S&P 500 Index is made up of 400 industrial, 40 public utilities, 20 transportation, and 40 financial companies and represents approximately 80% of the value of all issues traded on the New York Stock Exchange.

The S&P 500 Index is calculated by giving more "weight" to companies with more stock issued and outstanding in the market. Basically, each stock's price is multiplied by its number of shares outstanding. This assures that each stock influences the Index with the same importance that it carries in the actual stock market.

---

* Although every attempt has been made to insure the accuracy of the information in this section, the Chicago Mercantile Exchange assumes no responsibility for any errors or omissions. All matters pertaining to rules and specifications herein are made subject to and are superseded by official Exchange rules.

† Editor's Note: Futures based on the Value Line (Kansas City Exchange) and the New York Stock Exchange (New York Futures Exchange) indices are also traded. The principles are the same as with the S&P 500 futures.

Source: *Opportunities in Stock Futures,* Index and Option Market, Chicago Mercantile Exchange, 444 West Jackson Street, Chicago, IL 60606.

The Index is calculated by multiplying the shares outstanding of each of the 500 stocks by its market price. These amounts are then totaled and compared to a 1941–43 base period.

Calculations are performed continually while the market is open for each of the 500 stocks in the Index. The resulting Index is available minute-by-minute via quote machines throughout the world.

WHAT IS FUTURES TRADING?

The practice of buying or selling goods at prices agreed upon today, but with actual delivery made in the future, dates back to the 12th century. In the United States, organized futures exchanges were active as early as the 1840s. Today, the markets offer futures in grains, meats, lumber, metals, poultry products, currencies and interest-bearing securities.

The ability to contract today at a fixed price for future delivery performs two vital economic functions: risk transfer and price discovery.

For example, suppose a producer of cattle sees that someone is willing to buy his animals for delivery six months hence at a price that insures him an adequate profit. He decides to sell his production, with delivery after the animal matures, at the contracted price. In the process, he has locked in a price that is satisfactory to him and has insulated himself against the risk that the price may fall. In other words, he has transferred the risk of lower prices to someone else. Conversely, the purchaser of his animals has locked in his price and is assured that he will not have to pay a higher price in the future. This transaction could take place directly between the two men, or could be accomplished through futures trading at the CME—without the need for buyer and seller to actually meet. The open public trading system at the CME makes it easy to discover what the market currently considers to be a fair price for future delivery.

If the sale takes place on the Chicago Mercantile Exchange, the Exchange guarantees that both parties adhere to their agreement by placing itself and its resources between them. The Exchange thus becomes the buyer and the seller of the contract. This assures both parties that the contract will be carried out because the Exchange stands behind both parts of the agreement.

When delivery day arrives, the product is delivered to designated delivery points and inspected to make sure it is of the quality stipulated by the contract. The seller receives payment at the agreed price and buyer receives the produce.

Since full payment does not occur until the delivery day, the performance of both parties to the contract requires a good faith deposit or performance bond—known as the margin—when the contract is entered. Margins usually amount to a small percentage of the contract's total face value.

This payment differs from margin for stock purchases in that it is not a partial payment. It serves as a guarantee for both buyer and seller that there are sufficient funds on either side to cover adverse price movements that might otherwise bring the ability to meet contract terms into question.

At the close of business each day, each futures position is revalued at the contract's current closing price. This price is compared to the previous day's close (or if an initial position, the purchase or sale price) and the net gain or loss is calculated. Gains and losses are taken or made from the margin account each day in cash. There are no paper gains or losses in futures trading. If a margin account falls below a specified level, futures traders are required to deposit more money to maintain their positions.

All futures market participants should understand the operation of futures markets and consult with a Registered Commodity Representative before opening a futures trading account.

The S&P 500 Index futures contract is quoted in terms of the actual Index, but carries a face value of 500 times the Index. The contract does not move point-for-point with the actual Index, but it stays close enough to act as an effective proxy for the Index, and by extension, for the stock market as a whole.

If, for example, the futures price is quoted at 108.75, then the face value of the contract would be $54,375 (500 × 108.75). Minimum futures price increments, or movements, are .05 of the Index or $25. So if the futures quote is at 108.75, trades can continue to take place at that level, or move to 108.80 or to 108.70, with each .05 move equal to $25.

Trading opens at 9:00 A.M. and closes at 3:15 P.M. (Chicago time) with contracts trading for settlement in March, June, September and December. The final settlement day is the third Thursday of the contract month. At the close of business on that day all open positions have one final mark-to-market calculation—only on this day the expiration of the contract is marked to the actual closing level of the S&P 500 Index itself. Unlike traditional commodities, there is no physical delivery of the underlying commodity or resulting payment for the commodity in S&P 500 futures.

It is this unique cash settlement feature

of the S&P 500 futures contract that eliminates the prohibitively expensive costs of delivering 500 individual issues in varying amounts. Since there are little or no delivery costs, investors are assured that there will be no institutional factors to influence the futures contract's price. Thus, the price of the futures contract will reflect the current expectations about the direction of future stock prices. The International Monetary Market division of the CME pioneered this innovative concept in 1981, when its Eurodollar Time Deposit contract became the first cash settlement futures contract ever traded.

The S&P 500 futures contract should be viewed as a complement to equity ownership, not a substitute for it. Among the many benefits of S&P futures is the hedging ability that holders of stock can employ to provide an effective, cost efficient means of protecting security holdings against temporary market declines rather than selling and disturbing stock holdings. In addition, investors find the futures market equally as liquid for both buyers and sellers. Unlike the stock exchanges, short sellers do not require an up-tic before a trade can take place and there are no additional margin requirements.

SITUATIONS & STRATEGIES

Outright positions, either long or short, spreading and hedging are all uses for S&P futures. The contract also offers an unusually large number of hedging strategies when combined with equity portfolios and options. The following examples will show some of these uses in more detail.

LONG POSITION

Situation: An individual sees that interest rates are declining, the economy is firming and believes the entire market is undervalued. He notes that the S&P 500 futures contract for September delivery is at 108.85 and the actual S&P 500 Index is at 108.70.

It is apparent that most futures market participants also believe a move up is imminent. As supply and demand factors are bal-

Day	Position	Cost	S&P Future Closing Price	Gain or (Loss) Points × $5 (.01 equals 1 point)		Account Balance	Cumulative Gain or (Loss)
1	Long one contract	108.85	108.90	.05	$ 25	$5,025	$ 25
2	same	108.85	108.60	(.30)	(150)	4,875	(125)
3	same	108.85	108.40	(.20)	(100)	4,775	(225)
4	same	108.85	107.00	(1.40)	(700)	4,075	(925)
5	same	108.85	108.00	1.00	500	4,575	(425)
6	same	108.85	108.70	.70	350	4,925	(75)
7	same	108.85	109.50	.80	400	5,325	325
Sub Total Period one		108.85	109.50	65	$325	$5,325	$325

Period one: Our investor was a little off on his timing and his margin account was debited each day that losses occurred. If his margin balance had fallen to the maintenance minimum ($2,000 per contract) in this example he would have been required to make an additional payment to bring his balance back to the initial margin level ($5.000). As it is, he ended the period with a credit of $325 in cash.

Period two: With minor backing and filling, the trend is up and the S&P futures price closes period two at a level of 115.65.

	Position	Cost	S&P Future Closing Price	Gain or (Loss) Points × $5 (.01 equals 1 point)		Account Balance	Cumulative Gain or (Loss)
Sub Total Period Two	Long one contract	108.85	115.65	6.80	$3,400	$8,400	$3,400

Observations: During the first two weeks our investor's judgment of the market was correct and the S&P futures price advanced 680 index points or 6.25%. This translated into a gain of $3,400 on his initial investment of $5,000 or a gain of 68%.

At this point our investor believes that the market is due for a correction and decides to lock in his profit. He calls his RCR and instructs him to "cover" his September long position. His broker will then enter a sell order. After the close of business, the Exchange Clearing House will match the investor's previous long position and his new short position for a net zero position. All margins will be returned with cash credited to the investor's account with his broker the next day. Brokerage commissions have not been included in this example, but they are usually extremely reasonable and generally are quoted to include *both* the purchase and sale of the contract.

anced in an open marketplace, the intrinsic value of the September contract is established. The market is willing to pay a slight premium (.15) for the futures contract over the actual Index.

He calls his Registered Commodity Representative, enters an order to buy one September S&P 500 futures contract at the market and makes a good faith deposit to his account to guarantee his ability to meet his contractual commitment. For purposes of the following example, a margin account balance of $5,000 will be used. Margin requirements for actual positions vary. Individuals should contact their Registered Commodity Representatives for current information.

SHORT POSITION

If, instead of a rising market our investor believed that tight money would increase interest rates and the economy was weakening, he might have concluded that the S&P 500 Index futures price of 108.85 was an overvaluation and that the price was vulnerable to a decline.

September S&P Index contract to cover his short at the opening.

The opening is down on news that industrial production was weak and his position is covered at 106.55. His gain on his short then amounts to 2.30 at $25 per .05 or $1,150. The money is credited to his account the following day.

REDUCING THE VOLATILITY OF A STOCK PORTFOLIO

One reason for equity ownership is to take advantage of the long-term growth prospects of the company in which stock is purchased. Over time, higher earnings per share might be translated into a higher dividend payout. In the case of a company with a high return on investment and profits that are reinvested in the company's own growth, the expectation is that the growth will be reflected in higher share prices. However carefully constructed and diversified a portfolio may be, it is still subject in varying degrees to the risk that the market will decline. In order to protect principal values in a declining market, investors have traditionally sold stock to raise cash or shifted to more defensive issues with less volatility. These tactics very often are short-run solutions that disturb carefully tailored long-run objectives. S&P 500 Index futures can be used to add protection against a market downturn and allow an investor to maintain his equity holdings based on the prospects of the companies rather than the direction of the market.

Day	Position	Cost	S&P Future Closing Price	Gain or (Loss) Points × $5 (.01 equals 1 point)		Account Balance	Cumulative Gain or (Loss)
1	Short one contract	108.85	110.05	(1.20)	$ 600	$4,400	($ 600)
2	same	108.85	112.50	(2.45)	(1,225)	3,175	(1,825)
3	same	108.85	112.00	(.50)	(250)	3,425	(1,575)
4	same	108.85	109.50	(2.50)	(1,250)	4,675	(325)
5	same	108.85	108.75	.75	375	5,050	50
6	same	108.85	107.40	1.35	675	5,725	725
7	same	108.85	107.05	.35	175	5,900	900
Sub Total		108.85	107.05	1.80	$ 900	$5,900	$ 900

In our hypothetical example, the short position eventually worked. If the price had gone to a closing level of 114.85, the investor's account balance would have dropped to the maintenance margin level of $2,000 and he would have been required to add additional funds to bring his balance back to $5,000.

He decides to call his Registered Commodity Representative and enter a sell order for one September S&P 500 Stock Index future. Selling is just as easy as buying in an open outcry market. All bids to buy and offers to sell must be made publicly in the trading arena and are subject to immediate acceptance by any member. This differs greatly from stock exchanges where specialists or market makers require an up-tic from the previous sale to transact a short sale.

Let's again assume the initial margin required is $5,000. The above table shows the status of the short position over the course of seven trading days.

Our investor decides at this point that he wants to cover his short position and lock in his profit. The next morning before the opening of trading, he enters an order to buy one

SHORT HEDGE AGAINST A DIVERSIFIED PORTFOLIO

Situation: An investor owns a well-diversified portfolio with a current market value of $110,000. The S&P 500 futures contract is at 108.85. The market appears weak and the investor believes that there is substantial downside risk during the next three months. He decides to short S&P 500 futures to protect his portfolio.

Action: The S&P 500 futures contract at 108.85 represents a contract value of $54,425 (500 × 108.85). In order to protect his portfolio, he sells two contracts ($110,000 divided by $54,425 equals 2.02).

This hypothetical example assumed that the volatility of the portfolio very closely matched that of the market as measured by the S&P 500 futures contract prices. In reality, portfolios may be more or less sensitive to market moves. Statistical regression analysis for individual issues and entire portfolios can be calculated to measure past price volatility relative to the market. Expressed as "beta," it is a statistical measure of past movements which may change in the future. However, it is useful when hedging market risk in portfolios that are more volatile than the market.

Day	Position Short 2 Contracts	Closing Price S&P Contract	Gain or (Loss) Contract Points X $5 X 2 Contracts (.01 equals 1 point)		Value of Stock Portfolio	Portfolio Gain or (Loss)
1	108.85	110.05	(1.20)	($1,200)	$111,213	$1,213
18	108.85	109.50	(.65)	(650)	110,657	657
36	108.85	107.40	1.45	1,450	108,535	(1,465)
54	108.85	106.05	2.80	2,800	107,171	(2,829)
72	108.85	103.10	5.75	5,750	104,190	(5,810)
90	108.85	100.65	8.20	8,200	101,714	(8,286)
Position Closed	108.85	100.65	8.20	$8,200	$101.714	($8,286)

Observations: The market dropped and our investor hedged the cash decline in his portfolio with an offsetting gain in his futures position. Of course, if he were wrong about the direction of the market and it went up, he would have had losses in his futures positions but his stocks may have participated in the advance. The investor throughout this period, did not have to disturb his holdings and continued to receive his dividend payments.

Let us assume that the S&P 500 has a beta of 1.00, (that is, a given percentage move in the market gives rise to the same percentage move in the S&P 500) and our hypothetical portfolio has a beta of 1.50. Our portfolio's past market action relative to moves in the market was 50% greater than a given move in the general market. To compensate for this greater volatility, our hedger would require more S&P contracts to offset a greater decline in the value of his portfolio. Known as a hedge ratio, the dollar value of the portfolio is divided by the dollar value of the S&P 500 futures contract, the resulting figure is multiplied by the beta of the portfolio. Using our investor's portfolio and having calculated a beta of 1.5, we arrive at three contracts instead of two when the beta was 1.00:

$$\frac{\$110{,}000}{54{,}425} \times 1.5 = 3.03 \text{ contracts}$$

Thus, our investor would have sold three contracts to offset the portfolio's greater volatility to the market.

The concept of volatility and hedge ratios also may be applied to industry groupings and individual stocks. However, as the number of individual stock holdings that are being hedged decreases, then the greater is the chance that factors affecting that smaller group will make their prices react differently relative to the market than they have in the past.

ADDITIONAL USES OF THE S&P 500 FUTURES CONTRACT

Spreads: The simultaneous purchase and sale of different contract months to take advantage of perceived price discrepancies is called "spreading." The technique is considered by many to be less volatile than an outright long or short position, and as such, spreads generally carry lower margin requirements.

A characteristic of the futures market is that the closest contract date behaves more like the cash market. (In the S&P 500 futures contract, the cash market is the actual S&P 500 Index.) More distant months or back months have a greater component of their price determined by the expectations of what the price will be in the future.

These changing expectations of price levels of the S&P 500 contract into the future creates spreading opportunities. Options strategists will use the S&P 500 futures contract to reduce market risk when writing uncovered puts and calls. Block traders, investment bankers, stock specialists, options principals and anyone with the risk of stock market volatility, now have a vehicle and a well-capitalized liquid market to buy and sell market risk—the Standard & Poor's 500 Stock Index futures contract.

CONTRACT TERMS SUMMARY

Size	500 times the value of the S&P 500 Index
Delivery	Mark-to-market at closing value of the actual S&P 500 Index on Settlement Date
Hours	9:00 am to 3:15 pm Central Time
Months Traded	March, June, September, December
Clearing House Symbol	SP
Ticker Symbol	SP
Prices	Contract quoted in terms of S&P 500 Index
Minimum Fluctuation in Price	05 ($25)
Limit Move	3.00 ($1,500)
Last Day of Trading	3rd Thursday of Contract Month
Settlement Date	Last Day of Trading

Understanding the Commodities Market

COMMODITY EXCHANGES

A Commodity Exchange is an organized market of buyers and sellers of various types of commodities. It is public to the extent that anyone can trade through member firms. It provides a trading place for commodities, regulates the trading practices of the members, gathers and transmits price information, inspects and governs commodities traded on the Exchange, supervises warehouses that store the commodity, and provides means for settling disputes between members. All transactions must be conducted in a pit on the Exchange floor within certain hours.

FUTURES CONTRACT

A futures contract is a contract between two parties where the buyer agrees to accept delivery at a specified price from the seller of a particular commodity, in a designated month in the future, if it is not liquidated before the contract reaches maturity. A futures contract is not an option; nothing in it is conditional. Each contract calls for a specified amount, and grade of product. For example: *A person buying a February Pork Belly contract at 52.40 in effect is making a legal obligation, now, to accept delivery of 38,000 pounds of frozen Pork Bellies, to be delivered during the month of February, for which the buyer will pay 52.40 per pound.*

The average trader does not take delivery of a futures contract, since he normally will close out his position before the futures contract matures. As a matter of fact, a survey conducted by a leading exchange has estimated that less than 3% of the contracts traded are settled by actual delivery.

Editor's Note: The scope of the commodities market has been broadened in recent years to include contracts on financial (debt) instruments (T-bills, bonds, etc.) and composite stock market indices such as Value Line, S&P 500, and the New York Stock Exchange. With the stock market index futures, settlement is made in cash in amount based on the underlying index. Cash, not the securities, is used to offset the long and short positions. The cash value of the contract is defined as the index quotation × 500.

THE HEDGER AND SPECULATOR

A hedger buys or sells a futures contract in order to reduce the risk of loss through price variation. A short hedger sells a futures contract to protect the possible decline in the actual commodity owned by him. A long hedger purchases a futures contract to protect the possible advance in the value of an actual commodity needed to be purchased in the future.

The speculator is an important factor in the volume of future trading today. He, in effect, voluntarily assumes the risk, which the hedger tries to avoid, with the expectations of making a profit. He is somewhat of an insurance underwriter. The largest number of traders on any commodity exchange is the speculator. In order for the hedger to participate, he must have continuous trading interests and activity in the market. This trading activity stems from the role of the speculator, because he involves himself in buying or selling of futures contracts with the idea of making a profit on the advance or decline of prices. The speculator tries to forecast prices in advance of delivery and is willing to buy or sell on this basis. A speculator involves himself in an inescapable risk.

CAN YOU BE A SPECULATOR?

Now, can you be a speculator? Before considering entering into the futures market as a speculator, there are several facts which you should understand about the market and also about yourself. In order to enter into the futures market, you must understand that you are dealing with a margin account. Mar-

Source: Commodity Educational Services, Division of Commodity Cassettes, Inc., 778 Frontage Road, Northfield, IL 60093.

gins are as low as 5 to 10% of the total value of the futures contract, so you are obtaining a greater leverage on your capital.

Fluctuations in price are rapid, volatile, and wide. It is possible to make a very large profit in a short period of time, but also, it is possible to take a substantial loss. In fact, surveys taken by the Agricultural Department have shown that up to 75% of the individuals speculating in commodity markets have lost money. This does not mean that some of their trades were not profitable, but after a period of time with a given sum of money they ended up being a loser.

Now taking you as an individual, let us see whether you have the characteristics to become a commodity trader. Number one and the most important is that you do not take money that you have set aside for your future, or money you need daily to support your family or yourself. Number two, and almost equally important, is that you must be willing to assume losses and be willing to assume these losses with such a temperament that it is not going to affect your everyday life. Money used in the futures market should be money that has been set aside for strictly risk purposes, and if this money is not risk capital, your methods of trading could be seriously affected, because you cannot afford to be a loser.

Another very important factor is that you must not feel that you are going to take a thousand, two thousand, five or ten thousand dollars and place this with a brokerage firm and not follow the daily happenings of the market. Price fluctuations are fast, and as stated before, wide, so you must not only be in contact with your Account Executive daily, but know and study the technical facts that may be affecting the particular market in which you are speculating.

The individual who makes his first trade by buying a contract on Monday and selling this contract on the following Wednesday, making six hundred dollars on a $1,000 investment, in a period of two days, suddenly says to himself, "*Where has this market been all my life? Why am I working? Why not just concentrate on this market, if every two days or so I can make six hundred dollars?*" This is a fallacy, since this is an individual that is going to destroy himself and most likely his family. The next trade he will feel confident that because of his first profitable trade the market will always go his way even though he is now showing a loss in his position. He still feels that the market will turn around in his direction. If you become married to a particular commodity futures contract and constantly feel that the losses you are taking at the present time will reverse into profits, you are really fighting the market and in most cases fighting a losing battle. This could lead to disaster. There is a saying that you let your profits ride, but liquidate your losses fast.

In any way that you are uneasy with a position that you are holding, it is better to liquidate it. If, prior to the time of buying or selling a contract, you are not sure that this is the right step to take, do not take it. To protect yourself against this hazard you should pre-decide on every trade and exactly how much you intend to lose.

Another important point is not to involve yourself in too many markets. It is difficult to know all the technical facts and be able to follow numerous markets. In addition, if you are in a winning position, be conservative as to how you add additional contracts or pyramid your position. Being conservative will sometimes cause you to miss certain moves in certain markets and you may feel this to be wrong, but over a long period of time, this conservatism will be profitable to you.

If at this point you feel that you are ready, both financially and mentally to trade commodities, the next step is to begin the actual mechanics of trading a futures contract.

OPENING AN ACCOUNT

The first important factor is to decide which brokerage firm will afford you the best service. To accomplish this, you should do a little research by checking with the various exchanges about different brokerage firms. You should study their advertising, market letters, and other information. These should all be presented in a business-like manner and have no unwarranted claims, such as a guarantee of profit without indicating the possibility of loss.

The brokerage firm must be able to handle orders on all commodity exchanges. Do not pick just any Account Executive in a firm, but one you feel confident to help you make market decisions. Become acquainted with the Account Executive through phone or personal conversations. His knowledge of the factors entering into the market and the understanding of current market trends are important in your final choice.

After making a decision on the brokerage firm and the Account Executive that would be best for you, contact him and have him send you the literature concerning different contracts, and also, any additional information as to his organization. He will then send you the necessary signature cards required by the firm to open an account, and ask you for a deposit of margin money.

You will be trading in regulated commodities, and margin money will be deposited in a segregated fund at the brokerage firm's bank. A segregated account means that the money will only be used for margin and not for expenses of the brokerage firm.

Now you decide to enter into your first trade. Your Account Executive and you decide to enter into a December Live Cattle contract on the Chicago Mercantile Exchange. Your order will be executed as follows: Your Account Executive will place this order with his order desk who will then transmit the order to the floor of the Chicago Mercantile Exchange. There your order will be executed on the trading floor, in the pit. All technical details connected with the transaction will be handled by the brokerage firm.

Upon filling of your order, the filled order will be transmitted back to your Account Executive, who will then contact you, advising you that you have purchased one December Live Cattle contract at a given price. You will also receive a written confirmation on this transaction. You will now show an open position in December Live Cattle on the books of the brokerage firm.

MECHANICS OF A TRADE

Let us go back one step to explain in detail just how your order to buy one December Cattle was handled on the floor of the exchange. All buying and selling in the pit is done by open out-cry, and every price change is reported on the exchange ticker system. Each firm has brokers in the different pits, a pit meaning a trading area for the purpose of buying and selling contracts.

When your order was received on the exchange floor, it was time stamped and then given to a runner. This is a person who takes the order from the desk on the exchange floor and gives it to one of the brokers in the December Cattle trading pit. He is then responsible to the brokerage firm to fill that order, if possible, at the stated price. After filling the order, he then has the runner return it to the desk where it is time stamped and transmitted back to the order desk at the brokerage house, and the filled order is reported to you.

MARGIN

Futures trading requires the trader to place margin with his brokerage firm. Initial margin is required and this amount varies with each commodity. The minimum margin is established by each commodity exchange. Additional funds are needed when the equity of your account falls below this level. This is known as a maintenance margin call.

All margin calls must be met immediately. Normally you will be given a reasonable amount of time to comply with this request. If you do not comply, the firm has the right to liquidate your trades or a sufficient number of trades to restore your account to margin requirements.

The brokerage firm has the right to raise margin requirements to the customer at any time. This is normally done if the price of the commodity is changing sharply or if it is the brokerage firm's opinion that due to the volatility of the market the margin requirement is not sufficient at that particular time.

Most commodity contracts have a minimum fluctuation and also a maximum fluctuation for any one particular day. For example, if you are trading frozen Pork Bellies on the Chicago Mercantile Exchange the fluctuation is considered in points. A point equals three dollars and eighty cents. this means that if you buy a contract at 52.40 and the next price tick is 52.45, you have made a paper profit of five points or nineteen dollars. The maximum fluctuation on a belly contract is 200 points, so your profit or loss cannot exceed in one day more than 200 points from the previous day's settlement. There are exceptions in some commodity contracts, where the spot month has no limit.

Let us assume that you had originally placed in the hands of your brokerage firm two thousand dollars margin money, and that you and your Account Executive decide to purchase a December Live Cattle contract whose initial margin is $1200 with maintenance of $900.00. After the purchase of the contract your account would show initial margin required $1200 dollars with excess funds of eight hundred dollars. At the end of each day the settlement price of December Cattle would be applied to your purchase price and your account would be adjusted to either an increase due to profit or decrease due to loss in your contract.

Further, assume that in a period of two or three days there is a decline in the price of the December Cattle contract and your account now shows a loss of three hundred dollars. Since maintenance margin is only nine hundred dollars on this contract, you will still show an excess of eight hundred dollars over and above maintenance margin. But, in the next four days suppose there is an additional loss of nine hundred dollars. Your account will now need one hundred dollars to maintain the maintenance margin and four hundred dollars additional in order to bring your account up to initial margin. Your Account Executive, or a man from the margin department of the brokerage firm will then contact you, stating that you must place additional money with the firm in order to maintain the December Cattle contract.

At this point, you must decide whether you should continue with the contract, feeling that it may be profitable in the next few days, and thus sending the brokerage firm the required four hundred dollars to maintain your position, or whether to assume your loss and sell the contract.

Let us assume that you decide to sell your December contract at this point and that the selling price causes a loss of four hundred dollars. Added to this loss would be the commission of forty dollars, so your total loss on the transaction would be four hundred forty dollars. A confirmation and purchase and sales statement will be sent to you, showing the original price paid for the contract, the price for which it was sold, the gross loss of four hundred dollars plus the commission of forty dollars making the total loss four hundred forty dollars, and your new ledger balance on deposit with the firm as fifteen hundred sixty dollars.

As shown in our example, commission was charged only when the contract was closed out. A single commission is charged for each round-turn transaction consisting of the creation and liquidation of a single contract.

CONTROLLED, DISCRETIONARY, AND MANAGED ACCOUNTS

There are two methods of trading your account. The first is the professional approach where you and your Account Executive decide on each trade with no discretion being given directly to your Account Executive. This method was illustrated in the discussion about margins. The second method is called a controlled discretionary or managed account. Under this method, you are giving your Account Executive authorization to trade your account at his discretion at any time and as many times that he considers that a trade should be made. The Chicago Mercantile Exchange, and the Board of Trade have rules governing this type of relationship. The following is an excerpt from the C.M.E. rule regarding controlled, discretionary and managed accounts.

REQUIREMENTS

No clearing member shall accept or carry an account over which any individual or organization, other than the person in whose name the account is carried, exercises trading authority or control, hereinafter referred to as controlled accounts, unless:

> The account is initiated with a minimum of $5000*, and maintained at a minimum equity of $3,750*, regardless of lesser applicable margin requirements. In determining equity the accounts or ledger balances and positions in all commodities traded at the clearing member shall be included. Whenever at the close of any business day the equity, calculated with all open positions figured to the settling price, in any such account is below the required minimum, the clearing member shall immediately notify the customer in person, by telephone or telegraph and by written confirmation of such notice mailed directly to the customer, not later than the close of the following business day. Such notice shall advise the customer that unless additional funds are promptly received to restore the customer's controlled account to no less than $5,000*, the clearing member shall liquidate all of the customer's open futures positions at the Exchange.
>
> In the event the call for additional equity is not met within a reasonable time, the customer's entire open position shall be liquidated. No period of time in excess of five business days shall be considered reasonable unless such longer period is approved in writing by an officer or partner of the clearing member upon good cause shown.

* Minimums can be changed by each exchange, so consult your Account Executive for current regulations.

REVIEWING YOUR CONFIRMATIONS AND STATEMENTS

An important factor in trading is that you must be sure that no errors occur in your account. For every trade made you should receive a confirmation, and for every closeout a profit and loss statement known as a Purchase-and-Sale, showing the financial results of each transaction closed out in your account. In addition, a monthly statement showing your ledger balance, your open position, the net profit or loss in all contracts liquidated since the date of your last previous statement, and the net unrealized profit and loss on all open contracts figured to the market should be sent to you.

You should carefully review these statements. Upon receiving a confirmation of a trade you should immediately check its accuracy as far as type of commodity, month, trading price and quantity of contracts. If this does not agree with your original order, it should be immediately reported to the main office of your brokerage firm, and any differences should be explained and adjustments should be made.

If you do not receive a confirmation on a trade after it was orally reported to you by your Account Executive, be sure to contact him and the main office so that if an error was made it can be corrected immediately.

You should receive written confirmation when you deposit money with your brokerage firm. If within a few days, you have not received this confirmation, report it immediately to the main office of your brokerage firm.

Never assume that an order has been filled until you receive an oral confirmation from your broker. A ticker or a board that you may be observing can be running several minutes behind and is not the determining factor as to whether your trade was executed or not. Until you receive this oral confirmation, never re-enter an order to buy or sell, against that position.

If you receive a confirmation in the mail showing a trade not belonging to you, immediately notify the main office of your brokerage firm and have them explain why this is on a confirmation with your account number. If it is an error, be sure that it is adjusted immediately and a written confirmation sent to you showing the adjustment of the error. If an error is made and it is profitable to you do not consider this any differently than if it was not profitable. Regardless of whether there is a profit or loss, all errors should be immediately reported to the brokerage firm.

Be sure that when you request funds to be mailed from your account that they are received within a few days from the time of your request. If not, contact the accounting department of the brokerage firm to see what is the cause of the delay.

Never make a check out to an individual. Always make your check out to the brokerage firm.

DAY TRADING

Day trading is where there is a buy and sell made during the trading hours on one particular day. Day trading is not considered to be a sound practice for the new speculator and inexperienced trader. Day trading is something that should be executed only by a sophisticated trader who is in frequent communication with the floor, and even then, on a limited basis.

ORDERS

In order to trade effectively in the commodity market there are several basic types of orders. The most common order is a market order. A market order is one which you authorize your Account Executive to buy or sell at the existing price. This is definitely not a predetermined price, but is executed at a bid or offer at that particular moment.

Example: Buy 5 Feb Pork Bellies at the market.

LIMITED OR PRICE ORDERS AND "OB" DESIGNATION

This type of order to buy or sell commodities at a fixed or "limited" price and the ordinary "market" order are the most common types of orders.

Example: Buy Three Jan Silver 463.10. This limit order instructs the floor broker to buy three contracts of January Silver futures at 463.10. Even with this simple order, however, one presumption is necessary—that the market price prevailing when the order enters the pit is 463.10 or higher. If the price is below 463.10, the broker could challenge on the basis that the client may have meant "*Buy Three Jan Silver 463.10 stop.*" Therefore, while it is always assumed that a "limit: order means 'or better,'" if possible, it saves confusion and challenges if the "OB" designation is added to the limit price. This is particularly true on orders near the market, or on pre-opening orders with the limit price based on the previous close, because no one knows whether the opening will be higher or lower than the close, *i.e., Buy Three Jan Silver 463.10 OB.*

STOP ORDERS *(Orders having the effect of market orders)*

Buy Stop Buy stop orders must be written at a price higher than the price prevailing at the time of entry. If the prevailing price for December Wheat is 456 per bushel, a buy stop order must designate a price above 456.

Example: "Buy 20 Dec Wht 456½ Day Stop." The effect of this order is that if December Wheat touches 456½ the order to buy 20 December Wheat becomes a market order. From that point, 456½ on, all the above discussion regarding market orders applies.

Sell Stop Sell stop orders must be written at a price lower than the price prevailing at the time of entry in the trading pit. If the prevailing price of December Wheat is 456 per bushel, a sell stop order must designate a price below 456.

Example: "Sell 20 Dec Wht 455 Day Stop." If this order enters the trading pit with the above price of 456 prevailing, the order to sell 20 December Wheat becomes a market order. From that point 455 on, all the above discussion regarding market orders applies.

Buy stop orders have several specific uses. If you are short a December Wheat at 456, and wish to limit your loss to ½ cent per bushel, the above buy stop order at 456½ would serve this purpose. However, it is important to realize that such *"stop loss"* orders do not actually limit the loss to exactly ½ cent when *"elected"* or *"touched off"* because they become market orders and must be executed at whatever price the market conditions dictate.

Another use is when you are without a position and believe that, because of chart analysis or for other reasons, a buy of December Wheat at 456½ would signal the beginning of an important uptrend in Wheat prices. Thus, the same order to *"Buy 20 Dec Wheat 456½ Day Stop"* would serve this purpose.

Sell stop orders have the same uses in reverse. That is, if you are long 20 December Wheat at 456 and wish to limit this loss to 1 cent per bushel, the above sell stop order at 455 would serve this purpose, within the limitations of the market order possibilities. Similarly, if you are without a position and believe that a sale of December Wheat at 455 would signal a downtrend in wheat prices, and you wish to be short the market, you could use the order to *"Sell 20 December Wheat 455 Day Stop"* for this purpose.

STOP LIMIT ORDERS *(Variations of stop orders)*

Stop limit orders should be used by you when you wish to give the floor broker a limit beyond which he cannot go in executing the order which results when a stop price is *"elected."*

> *Example: "Buy 20 Dec Wheat 456½ Day Stop Limit."* This instructs the broker that when the price of 456½ is reached and *"elects"* this stop order, instead of making it a market order, it becomes a limited order to be executed at 456½ *(or lower)*, but no higher than 456½. Another possibility:

> *Example: "Buy One February Pork Belly 58.10 Day Stop Limit 58.25 (or any other price above 58.10)."* This instructs the broker that when the price of 58.10 *"elects"* the stop order instead of making it a market order, it becomes a limited order to buy at 58.25 *(or lower)*, but no higher as with any limit order.

Stop limit orders are particularly useful to you when you have no position and wish to enter a market via the stop order, but want to put some reasonable limit as to what you will pay. On the other hand, stop limit orders are not useful to you when you have an open position and wish to prevent a loss beyond a certain point. The reason is that by limiting the broker to a certain price after a *"stop loss"* order is elected, **you also run the risk that the market may exceed the limit too fast for the broker to execute.** This would leave you with your original position because the broker would have to wait for the return to the limit before executing. With a straight stop *(no limit)* order, the broker must execute *"at the market."*

> *Example: "Buy One February Pork Belly 58.10 Day Stop Limit 58.25."* Suppose the market moves to 58.10 but then only 20 February Pork Bellies are offered at that price. Your broker bids for one at 58.10 but another broker in the pit catches the seller's eye first and buys 20 and your broker misses the sale. Your broker then bids 58.20 but the best offer is 58.30. He bids 58.25, but the offer at 58.30 remains unchanged. Then another broker bids for and buys February Pork Bellies at 58.30 and the market moves on up. Your broker is left with no execution to your order unless the market later declines to your limit making a fill possible.

If you did not have a position you might be disappointed, but you would be unhurt financially. However, if you had a position and were trying to limit your loss you would have defeated your purpose with the stop limit order, if you truly wanted *"out"* after the stop was elected.

Stop limit orders on the sell side have exactly the same uses, advantages and disadvantages as discussed above, but in reverse:

> *Example: "Sell 20 December Wheat 455 Day Stop Limit."* This means that when the market declines to 455 per bushel, the broker may sell at 455 *(or higher)*, but no lower.

> *Another Example: "Sell One February Pork Belly 58.25 Stop Limit 58.10."* This instructs the broker to sell a belly after the stop price of 58.25 is reached and *"elects"* the stop order, but no lower than 58.10

M.I.T. ORDERS *(Market-if-touched)*

By adding MIT *(Market-If-Touched)* to a limit order, the limit order will have the effect of a market order when the limit price is reached or touched. This type of order is useful to you, when you have an open position and if a certain limit price is reached.

> *Example: "Sell One September Sugar 950 MIT."* The floor broker is told that if and when the price of September Sugar rises to 9½¢ per pound, he is to sell one contract at the market. At this price of 9½¢ all prior discussion on market orders applies.

Under certain market conditions, not

enough contracts are bid at 9½ cents to fill all offers to sell. Thus, you may see your straight limit price appear on the ticker, but your broker fails to make the sale.

But by adding MIT to the limit price, you will receive an execution, because the order becomes a market order, if the price is touched. However, the price will not necessarily be a good one in your eyes, since it became a market order when touched.

The same reasoning is true on the buy side of MIT orders but in reverse. Assume you are short one contract of September Sugar, with the prevailing price at 9½¢ per pound and you want to cover or liquidate your short at 9¢.

Example: "Buy One September Sugar 9¢ MIT." If and when the price of September sugar declines to 9¢ per pound, the floor broker must buy one contract at the market. Aside from the disadvantages of any market order, the MIT designation on the buy order prevents the disappointment which might arise if a straight limit buy at 9¢ were entered without the MIT added.

SPREAD ORDERS

As explained in the Glossary, a spread is a simultaneous long or short position in the same or related commodity. Thus a spread order would be to buy one month of a certain commodity and sell another month of the same commodity, or buy one month of one commodity and sell the same or another month of a related commodity.

Example: "Buy 5 July Beans Market and Sell 5 May Beans Market" or "Buy 10 Kansas City Dec Wheat Market and Sell 10 Chicago May Wheat Market."

Another Example: "Buy 5 May Corn Market and Sell 5 May Wheat Market."

In the example of the related commodity spread, normally the reason you would use such a spread, is that you expect to make a profit out of an expected tightness in the Corn Market, in the hope the corn contract will gain in value faster than wheat.

There may be a situation where you have a position either long or short in a commodity and want to change to a nearer or more distant option of the same commodity. For example you are long 5,000 bushels of May Soybeans on May 20 and want to avoid a delivery notice by moving your position forward into the July option. The basic spread order would be:

"Buy 5 July Beans Market and Sell 5 May Beans Market."

Sometimes you may prefer not to use market orders, in which case you use the difference spread.

Example: "Buy 5 July Beans and Sell 5 May Beans July 2¢ Over." Even though the prices of the two options are not specified, the broker is allowed to execute at any time he can do so with July selling at 2¢ or less above May. Over or under designations are a necessity for clarity to the floor broker. Omitting either is like omitting the price.

All orders, except market orders, can be cancelled, prior to execution. Naturally, a market order is executed immediately upon reaching the pit, so its cancellation is almost impossible.

There are other variations of orders, but for you the new speculator, the types mentioned are sufficient for your trading.

Options on Stock Market Indices, Bond Futures, and Gold Futures

STOCK MARKET INDEX OPTIONS

Stock market index related options are options whose prices are determined by the value of a stock market average such as the Standard and Poor (S&P) 500 Index or the New York Stock Exchange Composite Index, among others. Two types of such options are currently traded; index options and index futures options. The former are settled in cash while the latter are settled by delivery of the appropriate index futures contract.

Both types of options move in the same way in response to the underlying market index, thereby providing investors the opportunity to speculate on the market averages. The buyer of a call index option is betting that the underlying market index value will increase significantly above the strike price (before the option expires) so as to provide a profit when the option is sold. On the other hand, the buyer of a put option is speculating that the market index value will fall sufficiently below the strike price before the option expires so as to provide a profit when the put option is sold. Options writers (sellers), on the other hand, assume an opposite position.

While index futures (page 538) also permit speculation on the market averages, index option tend to be less risky since option *buyers* are not subject to margin calls and losses are limited to the price (premium) paid for the option. However, index option writers (sellers), in return for the premium received, are subject to margin calls and are exposed to losses of indeterminate magnitude. However, writers of call options on index *futures* can protect themselves by holding the underlying futures contract.

Index Options

A number of index options based on the broad market averages are now traded:

- S&P 100 Index [Chicago Board of Options Exchange (CBOE)]
- S&P 500 Index (Chicago Board of Options Exchange)
- Major Market Index [American Exchange (Amex)]
- Institutional Index (American Exchange)
- NYSE Options Index (New York Stock Exchange)
- Value Line Index (Philadelphia Exchange)
- National OTC Index (Philadelphia Exchange)

A brief description of some of the more important indices follows.

The S&P 100 Index is a so-called weighted index obtained by multiplying the current price of each of the 100 stocks by the number of shares outstanding and then adding all of the products to obtain the weighted sum. The weighted sum is then multiplied by a scaling factor to provide an index of a convenient magnitude. The S&P 500 Index is calculated similarly except that all of the S&P 500 stocks are included.

The NYSE Index is based on the weighted sum of all of the stocks traded on the New York Exchange while the AMEX Index is based on the weighted sum of all of the issues traded on the American Exchange. The Institutional Index consists of 75 stocks most widely held by institutional investors.

The Major Market Index differs from the above in that it is just the simple (unweighted) sum of 20 blue chip stocks multiplied by a factor of one tenth. This index behaves very similarly to the Dow Jones Index.

Generally index options expire on the Saturday following the third Friday of the expiration month. Hence the last trading day is on the third Friday of the expiration month. The price of an index option contract is $100 times the premium as quoted in the financial press.

Example: The July 120 (an option with a strike price of 120 expiring in July) Major Market Index call option is quoted (Exhibit 1) at 3.00. The cost of an option contract is $300 ($100 × 3).

Option premiums consist of the sum of two components; the intrinsic value and the time value. The intrinsic value of a *call* option

EXHIBIT 1 INDEX OPTIONS QUOTATIONS

CHICAGO BOARD

CBOE 100 INDEX

Strike Price	Calls—Last June	Calls—Last Sept	Calls—Last Dec	Puts—Last June	Puts—Last Sept	Puts—Last Dec
145	15¼	....	....	1/16	1	....
150	13¾	....	....	⅛	1¾	....
155	9⅛	10	....	7/16	3⅛	....
160	5⅛	9¼	....	17/16	4⅝	8¼
165	2⅛	6½	8⅝	3⅞	7¼	10½
170	11/16	3¾	6	7⅝	12	13½

Total call volume 20846. Total call open int. 62006.
Total put volume 25167. Total put open int. 103733.
The index closed at 163.55, +1.91.

AMERICAN EXCHANGE

MAJOR MARKET INDEX

Strike Price	Calls—Last Jul	Calls—Last Oct	Calls—Last Jan	Puts—Last Jul	Puts—Last Oct	Puts—Last Jan
115	5¾	8⅝	10	1⅞	3¾	5½
120	3	5¾	7	4	5⅞	7½
125	1⅛	3¼	....	7⅜	....	....
130	7/16	2¼	3⅝	....	....	

Total call volume 2351. Total call open int. 14572.
Total put volume 5276. Total put open int. 9593.
The index closed at 118.69, +1.00.

Source: Reprinted by permission of *The Wall Street Journal*, Dow Jones & Co., Inc.

is $100 times the difference obtained by subtracting the strike price from the current value of the index. The instrinsic value of a *put* option is $100 times the difference obtained by subtracting the current value of the index from the strike price. The time value is the money which an option buyer is willing to pay in the expectation that the option will become more valuable (*increase its intrinsic value*) before it expires. Obviously the time value decreases as the time to expiration decreases.

It should be noted that there is a distinction between exercising an index option and selling an index option to close out a position. Exercising an option gives the holder the right to a cash amount equal to the *intrinsic* value of the option. Hence, the time value of the option is lost. When an option is sold to close out a position, the option holder receives a cash amount equal to the *premium* which contains both the intrinsic value and the time value of the option. Thus, in most cases it is more profitable to sell the option. The profit realized (before commissions and taxes) on the *sale* of an option contract is equal to $100 times the difference obtained by subtracting the premium paid when the option was purchased from the premium received when the option was sold.

Example: On May 24 the CBOE 100 Index

was 163.55. In anticipation of a market decline, an investor buys a September 165-put option quoted at 7¼ for a total premium of \$725 (7.25 × 100) per option. Assume that on August 10 the puts were selling at a total premium of \$850 due to a decline in the CBOE 100 Index to 160.10. If the investor sells the put option he will realize a profit, before commissions and taxes, of \$125 (850 − 725). If the market moves in a contrary direction he could lose his entire investment.

Index Futures Options

Index futures options (also called futures options) are the right to buy (call) or sell (put) the underlying index futures contracts (see page 538). Futures options are currently traded on the New York Futures Exchange and the Chicago Mercantile Exchange. The dollar value of the underlying contract for the New York Futures Exchange option is equal to the New York Stock Exchange Composite Index multiplied by 500 while that for the Chicago Mercantile Exchange option is equal to the S&P 500 Index multiplied by 500. Quotations for futures options as they appear in *The Wall Street Journal* are shown in Exhibit 2. The total futures option premium per option is equal to the quoted value multiplied by 500. Gains and losses are calculated in the same way as index options.

The expiration day of the S&P 500 futures option is on the third Thursday of the expiration month while that for the NYSE futures option is the business day prior to the last business day of the expiration month.

Example: On May 24, 1983, the New York Composite Index is 94.39. An investor expects the Index to increase during the next six months and buys a September 96 futures call option at a total premium of \$1750 (3.50 × 500), as indicated in Exhibit 2. Assume that by August 10 the Index is at 100 and that the September call premium is quoted at 8.00 corresponding to a total premium per option of \$4000 (8.00 × 500). By selling the option at the current value the investor can realize a profit of \$2250 (4000 − 1750) before commissions and taxes.

Example: Assume that on May 24, 1983 when the S&P 500 Index is at 163.43, an investor expects a market decline within six months. He purchases a September 155 S&P put option at a total premium per option of \$1150 (2.30 × 500), as indicated in the quotations shown in Exhibit 2. Assume that the Index declines to 150 on August 10 and that the quoted put premium is 6.50 corresponding to a total premium per option of \$3250 (6.50 × 500). By selling the option at the current value the investor can realize a profit of \$2100 (3250 − 1150), before commissions and taxes.

EXHIBIT 2 FUTURES OPTIONS

CHICAGO MERCANTILE EXCHANGE

S&P 500 STOCK INDEX – Price = \$500 times premium.

Strike	Calls—Settle			Puts—Settle		
Price	Jun	Sep	Dec	Jun	Sep	Dec
135	....	....	....	.05	....	....
140	23.90	24.25	....	.05	.45	....
145	18.90	20.20	....	.05	.90	....
150	13.95	15.25	....	.10	1.25	....
155	9.20	11.50	....	.30	2.30	4.50
160	4.95	8.60	....	1.05	3.60	....
165	1.90	5.50	8.75	3.00	5.75	7.80
170	.45	3.50	....	6.50	9.50	....
175	.10	1.80	....	11.15	14.00	....

Estimated total vol. 1,440
Calls: Fri. vol. 766; open int. 6,216
Puts: Fri. vol 532; open int. 6,552

N.Y. FUTURES EXCHANGE

NYSE COMPOSITE INDEX – Price = \$500 times premium.

Strike	Calls—Settle			Puts—Settle		
Price	Jun	Sep	Dec	Jun	Sep	Dec
84	10.90	11.70	....	.05	.40	.75
86	8.90	10.00	11.00	.05	.70	1.50
88	5.95	8.50	9.70	.05	1.00	1.75
90	5.15	7.00	8.30	.25	1.50	2.30
92	3.35	5.50	7.00	.50	2.00	2.95
94	1.95	4.50	6.00	1.15	3.00	3.75
96	.95	3.50	5.00	2.10	3.90	4.95
98	.40	2.75	3.95	3.50	5.25	6.05
100	.15	1.75	3.25	....	6.25	7.00

Estimated total vol. 1,405
Calls: Fri. vol. 844; open int. 4,836
Puts: Fri. vol. 549; open int. 4,801

S&P 500 Index 163.43
New York Composite Index = 94.39

Source: Reprinted by permission of *The Wall Street Journal*, Dow Jones & Co., Inc.

While a number of the same basic concepts apply to both index options and future options, there are differences between the two because the futures options have underlying index futures contracts which are traded on the open market. This makes possible a number of trading strategies with futures options which are not available with index options; for example, simultaneously buying an index futures contract and writing a corresponding call option. Also, for the reason given above, there is a distinction between selling a futures option, the usual procedure, and exercising the option. When a futures option is exercised, the option is exchanged for a position in the index futures market which may result in a loss in the time value of the option.

Investors planning to trade options should read two free booklets available from any of the options exchanges:

Understanding the Risks and Uses of Options

Listed Options On Stock Indices

Subindex Options

Subindex options are based on an index made up of leading publicly traded companies within a specific industry. These options permit speculation on an industry without the necessity of selecting specific stocks within the industry. As with all stock index options they are settled in cash.

U.S. TREASURY BOND FUTURES OPTIONS

Options on U.S. Treasury Bonds (T-Bonds), traded on the Chicago Board of Trade, are the right to buy (call) or sell (put) a T-Bond futures contract. The T-Bond futures contract underlying the option is for $100,000 of Treasury Bonds, bearing an 8% or equivalent coupon, which do not mature (and are non-callable) for at least 15 years. When long term interest rates decline, the value of the futures contract and the call option increases while the value of a put option decreases. The reverse is true when long term rates increase.

Premiums for T-bond futures *options* are quoted in 1⁄64 of 1% (point): Hence each 1⁄64 of a point is equal to $15.63 ($100,000 × .01 × 1⁄64) per option. Thus a premium quote of 2–16 means 2 16⁄64 or (2 × 64 + 16) × $15.63 or $2250.72 per option. It should be noted that prices of T-bond *futures* are quoted in 1⁄32 (of a point) worth $31.25 per futures contract.

As with options trades in general, the profit (before taxes and commissions) is the premium received (per option) when the option is sold minus the premium paid when the option was purchased.

The last trading day for the options is the first Friday, preceded by at least five business days, in the month *prior* to the month in which the underlying futures contract expires. For example, in 1983 a December option stops trading on November 18, 1983.

GOLD FUTURES OPTIONS

The most widely traded gold futures option is on the New York Comex Exchange. The option is the right to buy (call) or sell (put) a gold futures contract for 100 Troy ounces of pure gold. Both the futures contract and the corresponding call option increase or decrease with the price of gold. Put option premiums move in the opposite direction to the price of gold.

Option premiums are in dollars per ounce of gold. Thus a quoted premium of 2.50 corresponds to total premium of $2500 (2.50 × 100) per option.

The profit (before commissions and taxes) to an option buyer is simply the premium received when the option is sold less the premium paid when the option was purchased.

The last trading day for gold futures options is the second Friday in the month *prior* to the expiration date of the underlying gold futures contract. Thus in 1983 a December option expires on Friday November 11, 1983. Example: In August an investor buys a December 400 (an option with a strike price of 400 on a December gold futures contract) Comex call option quoted at 25.00. The total price per option is $2500 (25.00 × 100).

On November 5, the price of gold has increased and the investor sells the option at a quoted premium of 50.00 or $5000.00 (50 × 100) per option. His profit is $2500 (5000 − 2500).

The Commodities Glossary

Acreage allotment The portion of a farmer's total acreage that he can harvest and still qualify for government price supports, low interest crop loans and other programs. It currently applies to specialty crops—tobacco, peanuts and extra long staple cotton—for which complex federal marketing orders have been written to control production closely. Before the 1977 farm bill was passed, the same term also applied more loosely to the portion of a farmer's wheat or feed grain acreage for which government payments would be made. A farmer could harvest 100 acres of wheat, for instance, but he'd receive price support payments only for 70 acres if that was his allotment. The allotment in this sense is called "program acreage" in the new farm bill.

Arbitrage The simultaneous buying and selling of futures contracts to profit from what the trader perceives as a discrepancy in prices. Usually this is done in futures in the same commodity traded on different exchanges, such as cocoa in New York and cocoa in London or silver in New York and silver in Chicago. Some arbitrage occurs between cash markets and futures markets.

Asking price The price offered by one wishing to sell a physical commodity or a futures contract. Sometimes a futures market will close with an asking price when no buyers are around.

Backwardation An expression peculiar to New York markets. It means "nearby" contracts are trading at a higher price, or "premium," to the deferreds. See also *Inverted market*.

Basis A couple of meanings: (1) The difference between the price of the physical commodity (the cash price) and the futures price of that commodity. (2) A geographic reference point for a cash price; for example, the price of a beef carcass is quoted "basic Midwest packing plants."

Bear A trader who thinks prices will decline. "Bearish" is often used to describe news or developments that have, or are expected to have, a downward influence on prices. A bear market is one in which the predominant price trend is down. Some think this term originated with an old axiom about "selling the skin before you've caught the bear."

Bid The price offered by one who wishes to purchase a physical commodity or a futures contract. Sometimes a futures market will close with a bid price when no sellers are around.

Broker An agent who buys and sells futures on behalf of a client for a fee. They work for brokerage firms, some of which have extensive research and analysis departments that occasionally issue trading advice. A few firms have so many customers who follow such advisories that recommendations to buy or sell can influence market prices materially.

Bull A trader who thinks prices will go up. "Bullish" describes developments that have, or are expected to have, an upward influence on prices. A bull market is one in which the predominant price trend is up. Some theorize this term originally related to a bull's habit of tossing its head upward.

Butterfly An unusual sort of spread involving three contract months rather than two. Often used to move profits or losses from one year to the next for tax purposes.

Cash The price at which dealings in the physical commodity take place. Used more sweepingly, it can mean simply the physical commodity itself (as in "cash corn" or "cash lumber"), or refer to a market. For example, the cash hog market is a terminal (or, collectively, all terminals) where live hogs are sold by farmers and bought by meat packers.

Chart A graph of futures prices (and sometimes other statistical trading information) plotted in such a way that the charter believes gives insight into future price movements. Several futures markets regularly are influenced by buying or selling based on traders' price-chart indications.

Clearing house The part of all futures exchanges (usually a separate corporation with its own members, fees, etc.) which clears all trades made on the exchange during the day. It matches the buy transactions with the equal number of sell transactions to provide orderly control over who owns what and who owes what to whom. Although futures traders theoretically trade contracts among themselves, the clearing house technically is in the middle of each transaction—being the buyer to every seller and the seller to every buyer. That's how it keeps track of what is going on.

Close The end of the trading session. On some exchanges, the "close" lasts for several minutes to accommodate customers who have entered buy or sell orders to be consummated "at the close." On those exchanges, the closing price may be a range encompassing the highest and lowest prices of trades consummated at the close. Other exchanges officially use settlement prices as the closing prices.

Source: The *Dow Jones Commodities Handbook*, edited by Dan Ruck, Dow Jones Books, Dow Jones Company, Inc. 1979.

Cold storage Refrigerated warehouses where perishable commodities are stored. In effect, the warehouses are secondary sources of commodities that aren't immediately available from the producers. The Agriculture Department periodically reports the quantities of various commodities stored in warehouses. Futures traders watch these reports to see if the supplies are building or dwindling abnormally fast, which indicates how closely supply and demand are balanced.

Commission The fee charged by a broker for making a trade on behalf of customers.

Contract In the case of futures, an agreement between two parties to make and in turn accept delivery of a specified quantity and quality of a commodity (or whatever is being traded) at a certain place (the delivery point) by a specified time (indicated by the month and year of the contract).

Country Refers to a place relatively close to a farmer where he can sell or deliver his crop or animals. For instance, a country elevator typically is located in a small town and accepts grain from farmers in the immediate vicinity. A country shipping point is a place where farmers in an area combine their marketings for shipment. A country price is the one these elevators, shipping points or whatever pay for the farmers' goods; it's based on the terminal-market prices, less transportation and handling costs.

Covering Buying futures contracts to offset those previously sold. "Short covering" often causes prices to rise even though the overall market trend may be down.

Crop report Estimates issued periodically by the Department of Agriculture on estimated size and condition of major U.S. crops. Similar reports are made on livestock.

Crush The process of reducing the raw, unusable soybean into its two major components, oil and meal. A "crush spread" is a futures spreading position in which a trader attempts to profit from what he believes to be discrepancies in the price relationships between soybeans and the two products. The "crush margin" is the gross profit that a processor makes from selling oil and meal minus the cost of buying the soybeans.

Deferred contracts In futures, those delivery months that are due to expire sometime beyond the next two or three months.

Delivery The tendering of the physical commodity to fulfill a short position in futures. This takes place only during the delivery month and normally takes the form of a warehouse receipt (from an exchange-accredited warehouse, elevator or whatever) that shows where the cash commodity is.

Delivery point The place(s) at which the cash commodity may be delivered to fulfill an expiring futures contract.

Discretionary accounts A futures trading account in which the customer puts up the money but the trading decisions are made at the discretion of the broker or some other person, or maybe a computer. Also known as "managed accounts."

Evening up Liquidating a futures position in advance of a significant crop report or some other scheduled development so as not to be caught on the wrong side of a surprise. In concentrated doses, evening up can cause a bull market to retreat somewhat and a bear market to rebound somewhat.

First notice day The first day of a delivery period when holders of short futures positions can give notice of their intention to deliver the cash commodity to holders of long positions. The number of contracts circulated on first notice day and how they are accepted or not accepted by the longs is often interpreted as an indication of future supply-demand expectations and thus often influence prices of all futures being traded, not just the delivery-month price. This effect also sometimes occurs on subsequent notice days. Rules concerning notices to deliver vary from contract to contract.

F.O.B. Free on Board, meaning that the commodity will be placed aboard the shipping vehicle at no cost to the purchaser, but thereafter the purchaser must bear all shipping costs.

Forward Contract A commercial agreement for the merchandising of commodities in which actual delivery is contemplated but is deferred for purposes of commercial convenience or necessity. Such agreements normally specify the quality and quantity of goods to be delivered at the particular future date. The forward contract may specify the price at which the commodity will be exchanged, or the agreement may stipulate that the price will be determined at some time prior to delivery.

Fundamentalist A trader who bases his buy-sell decisions on supply and demand trends or developments rather than on technical or chart considerations.

Futures Contracts traded on an exchange that call for a cash commodity to be delivered and received at a specified future time, at a specified place and at a specified price. Similar arrangements made directly between buyer and seller are called "forward contracts." They aren't traded on an exchange.

Hedge Using the futures market to reduce the risks of unforeseen price changes that are inherent in buying and selling cash commodities. For example, as an elevator operator buys cash grain from farmer, he can "hedge" his purchases by selling futures contracts; when he sells the cash commodity, he purchases an offsetting number of futures contracts to liquidate his position. If prices rise while he owns the cash grain, he sells the cash grain at a profit and closes out his futures at a loss, which almost always is no greater than his profit in the cash transaction. If prices fall while he owns the cash grain, he sells the cash grain at a loss but recoups all or almost all of the loss by buying back futures contracts at a price correspondingly lower than at which he first sold them. Some users of commodities assure themselves of supplies of their raw materials at a set price by buying futures, which is another form of hedging. When the time comes to acquire inventories, they can either take delivery on their futures contracts or, more likely, simply buy their supplies in the cash market. Futures-contract prices tend to match cash prices at the time the futures expire, so if cash prices have risen the users' higher costs are offset by profits on their futures contracts.

Hedger The Commodity Futures Trading Commission says a hedger in a general sense is someone who uses futures trading as a temporary, risk-reducing substitute for a cash transaction planned later in his main line of business. All other futures traders are classified as speculators. There are more legally specific definitions of hedging and hedgers in such markets as grains, soybeans, potatoes and cotton, where limits are placed on the number of contracts speculators may trade or own. The Commission has broadened these limits to allow hedging in closely related, rather than exactly matching, commodities. A sorghum producer, for instance, can use corn futures as a hedging tool where he couldn't before this rule-broadening. The more general distinction between hedgers and speculators may be important to potential traders. Some may want to use a market like interest rate futures to offset some expected heavy borrowing. The government hasn't set any speculative trading limits in those markets, but lenders or company directors are more apt to back a plan to trade futures for hedging purposes rather than speculation.

Inverted market A futures market where prices for deferred contracts are lower than those for nearby-delivery contracts because of great near-term demand for the cash commodity. Normally, prices of deferred contracts are higher, in part reflecting storage costs.

Last trading day The day when trading in an expiring contract ceases, and traders must either liquidate their positions or prepare to make or accept delivery of the cash commodity. After that, there is no more futures trading for that particular contract month and year.

Life of contract The period of time during which futures trading in a particular contract month and year may take place. This is usually less than a year, but sometimes up to 18 months.

Limit move The maximum that a futures price can rise or fall from the previous session's settlement price. This limit, set by each exchange, varies from commodity to commodity. Some exchanges have variable limits, whereby the limit is expanded automatically if the market moves by the limit for a certain number of consecutive trading sessions. When prices fail to move the expanded limit, or after a specified period of time, the limits revert to normal.

Liquidation Closing out a previous position by taking an opposite position in the same contract. Thus, a previous buyer liquidates by selling, and a previous seller liquidates by buying.

Long A trader who has bought futures, speculating the prices will rise. He is "long" until he liquidates by selling or fulfills his contracts by making delivery.

Margin The amount of "good faith" money that commodity traders must put in order to trade futures. The margins, set by each exchange, usually amount to 5% to 10% of the total value of the commodity contract. The "initial margin" is the amount of money that must be put up to establish a position in a futures market. Exchanges establish this margin, too, but brokerage firms often require even larger amounts to protect their own financial interests. "Maintenance margin" is the money that traders must put up to retain their position in the futures markets.

Margin call A request by a brokerage firm that a customer put up more money. That means the market price has gone against the customer's position and the brokerage firm wants the customer to cover his paper loss, which would become a real loss if the position were liquidated.

Nearby contracts The futures that expire the soonest. Those that expire later are called deferred contracts.

New crop The supply of a commodity that will be available after harvest. The term also is sometimes used in connection with pigs and hogs because the major farrowing periods in the spring and fall are referred to as "crops." There sometimes are substantial price differences between futures contracts related to new-crop supplies and those related to old-crop supplies.

Nominal price An artificial price—usually the midpoint between a bid and an asked price—that gives an indication of the market price level even though no actual transactions may have taken place at that price.

Old crop The supply from previous harvests.

Open The period each session when futures trading commences. Sometimes the open lasts several minutes to accommodate customers who have placed orders to buy or sell contracts "on the open." On these exchanges, opening prices often are reported by the exchange as a range, although these seldom are widely disseminated because of space restrictions in newspapers and periodicals; they are carried on tickers and display panels during that trading day, however.

Open interest Outstanding futures contracts that haven't been liquidated by purchase or sale of offsetting contracts, or by delivery or acceptance of the physical commodity.

Option The right to buy or sell a futures contract over a specified period of time at a set price.

Overbought A term used to express the opinion that prices have risen too high too fast and so will decline as traders liquidate their positions.

Oversold Like "overbought" except the opinion is that prices have fallen too far too fast and so probably will rebound.

Pit The areas on exchange floors where futures trading takes place. Pits usually have three or more levels and can accommodate a large number of traders. On several New York exchanges the trading areas are called rings and consist of open-center, circular tables around which traders sit or stand.

Position A trader's holdings, either long or short. A position limit is the maximum number of contracts a speculator can hold under law; it doesn't apply to bona-fide hedgers, although there really isn't any objective way of telling whether a person in position to hedge actually is hedging or is speculating instead.

Profit taking A trader holding a long position turns paper profits into real ones by selling his contracts. A trader holding a short position takes profits by buying back contracts.

Reaction A decline in prices following a substantial advance.

Recovery An increase in prices following a substantial decline.

Settlement price The single closing price, determined by each exchange's price committee of directors. It is used primarily by the exchange clearing house to determine the need for margin capital to be put up by brokerage-firm members to protect the net position of that firm's total accounts. It's also issued by some exchanges as the official closing price, and it is used to determine the price limits and net price changes on the following trading day. (See also: *Close*.)

Set-aside Acreage withdrawn from crop production for a season and used for soil conservation under a production-control program. Wheat farmers this year must set aside two acreas of land for each 10 acres they plant to wheat in order to get any federal price support or disaster aid. The Agriculture Department has also said corn, sorghum and barley producers similarly may be required to set aside some of their acreage if it appears that surpluses will grow too much otherwise.

Short A trader who has sold futures, speculating that prices will decline. He is "short" until he liquidates by buying back contracts or fulfills his contracts by taking delivery.

Short squeeze A situation in which "short" futures traders are unable to buy the cash commodity to deliver against their positions and so are forced to buy offsetting futures at prices much higher than they'd ordinarily be willing to pay.

Speculation Buying or selling in hopes of making a profit. The word connotes a high degree of risk.

Spot The same as cash commodities. Literally, delivery "on the spot" rather than in the future.

Spreads and straddles Terms for the simultaneous buying of futures in one delivery month and selling of futures in another delivery month (or even the simultaneous buying of futures in one commodity and selling of futures in a different but related commodity). One purpose is to profit from perceived discrepancies in price relationships. Another purpose is to transfer current trading profits to some future time to avoid immediate tax liability.

Stop-loss order An open order given to a brokerage firm to liquidate a position when the market reaches a certain price so as to prevent losses from mounting or profits from eroding. Sometimes market price trends are accelerated when concentrations of stop-loss orders are touched off.

Support price A level below which the government tries to keep the agricultural-commodity prices that farmers receive from falling. They're set basically by Congress when farm legislation is passed and adjusted from time to time by the President or Agriculture Secretary. Subsidy payments, commodity purchases, production controls or commodity-secured loans are among the devices used to make up the difference when market prices dip below the support level. Futures and cash prices often tend to remain near the support level when there are large crop surpluses because lower prices keep commodities off the market and higher ones quickly draw willing sellers.

Switch A trading maneuver in which a trader liquidates his position in one futures delivery and takes the position in another delivery month in expectation that prices will change more rapidly in the second contract than in the first. Thus, a trader might switch out of a position in an October silver futures contract into a position in a December silver futures contract. Warning: Some people use the word "switch" when they mean "spread" or "straddle." Feel free to correct them.

Technical factors Futures prices often are affected by influences related to the market itself, rather than to supply-demand fundamentals of the commodity with which the market is concerned. For example, if a market moves up or down the limit several days in succession there frequently is a subsequent "technical reaction" caused in part by the liquidation of contracts held by traders on the wrong side of the price move.

Terminal Refers to an elevator or livestock market at key distribution points to which commodities are sent from a wide area.

Trading range The amount that futures prices can fluctuate during one trading session—essentially, the price "distance" between limit up and limit down. If, for instance, the soybean futures price can advance or fall by a maximum of 20 cents per bushel in one day, the trading range is double that, or 40 cents per bushel. In one market, cocoa, price movements are restricted to a daily range of six cents a pound.

Visible supply The amount of a commodity that can be accounted for and computed accurately, usually because it is being kept in major known storage places.

Warehouse or elevator receipt The negotiable slip of paper that a short can hand over to fulfill an expiring futures contract's delivery requirement. The receipt shows how much of the commodity is in storage.

Dow Jones Futures and Spot Commodity Indexes

The method for arriving at the Dow Jones Futures and Spot Commodity Indexes differs from some others in the order in which the computations are made. Instead of first weighting each price, then adding them up and finally calculating the percentage or index, this method first turns each price into an index or percentage of its base-year price, then weights each individual index, and finally adds them up. Stated mathematically, the more usual method calculates the percentage relation of one average to another, while the Dow Jones Commodity Index method calculates the average of a set of percentage changes. These two methods do not result in exactly the same figures. However, they are equally valid when used consistently, and the indexes they produce are of the same general magnitude.

The Dow Jones Commodity Index method has two advantages. One is that it saves computation, because the factors or multipliers perform two computations at once. They calculate the individual percentages and weight them at one stroke. The other advantage is that if you have yesterday's index, you can apply the multipliers to today's individual price changes. Then all you do is add the resulting figures to yesterday's index, or subtract them from it, depending on whether they're up or down. That gives today's index. No need to recalculate the whole thing each day.

As for the weights, they were obtained by the usual mathematical methods. Basically, the weight of each commodity is the percentage of its commercial production value to the total commercial production value of all commodities in the index, in this case for the years 1927–31. In calculating the weights, consideration also was given to the relation between volume of trading in each commodity and its commercial production.

A further refinement was necessary because price changes of the various commodities are quoted in different units. Grain prices change in eighths of a cent, wool prices change in tenths of a cent, and all the other staples in the Dow Jones index move in hundredths of a cent. This adjustment merely required appropriate treatment in each case of the multiplier, so that it would give the

Source: The *Dow Jones Commodities Handbook*, edited by Dan Ruck, Dow Jones Books, Dow Jones & Company, Inc.

right figure for any price change. In the case of grains it meant an adjustment of 20%, since one-tenth is that much smaller than one-eighth. In other cases a mere adjustment of decimal points was sufficient.

The twelve commodities, with the weight of each and the multiplier applied to the price changes of each, are:

	Weight	**Multiplier**
Wheat	19.5	16
Corn	8	11
Oats	5	13
Rye	4	5
Wool Tops	5.5	4
Cotton	23	10
Cottonseed Oil	4.5	4
Coffee	7	3
Sugar	8.5	27
Cocoa	5	5
Rubber	6	3
Hides	4	3

These are the essentials for calculating the spot index. However, the futures index requires one more set of unusual steps. That's because several times a year an actual quoted "future" disappears. For instance, while early in the year it is possible to buy wheat to be delivered in December, when the month of December actually arrives that "delivery" expires and is no longer quoted.

The result is that futures prices are affected not only by market conditions but also by how close the delivery date looms. Interest charges and other such factors influence them. On July 1, the December delivery is just five months off, but a month later it is only four months away, and a five-month delivery should not, in a precise index, be compared with a four-month delivery.

This problem is overcome by the use of two futures quotations for each commodity. They are combined to produce on each market day the calculated price that would apply to a delivery exactly five months off.

On the first day of July, only the December delivery is used, since it is just five months away and thus no adjustment need be made. On the second day, the two quotations used are those for the same December delivery and the one for May of the following year. The quoted price for December is adjusted by one day's proportion of the difference between it and May's quoted price. Since there are 151 days between December and May (except in leap years) the figure for one day's proportion is 1/151 of the price difference between the two. The resulting fraction is added to December's price, or subtracted from it, depending on whether May is quoted above or below December.

The following day 2/151 of the difference are added or subtracted, the third day 3/151 and so on until December 1, on which day only the May contract's price is used. On December 2, the combination used is May and July, and so on around the year.

To facilitate the work of calculating the futures index every hour of each business day and the spot index once a day, tables have been prepared—resembling somewhat tables of logarithms or bond yields—which give the figures arrived at by multiplying the various quotational units of each commodity by its factor or multiplier. For instance, the tables show the proper multiples for one-eighth, one-quarter, three-eighths, etc., when each is multiplied by each grain's factor or multiplier.

The commodity futures index is published once an hour and as of the close of commodity markets each day on the Dow Jones News Service, where also the spot index is published once daily. Both are published likewise in *The Wall Street Journal*.

Commodity Futures Trading Commission (CFTC)

Federal laws regulating commodity futures trading are enforced by the Commodity Futures Trading Commission. For information on commodity brokers call (202) 254-8630.

National Office

Commodity Futures Trading Commission
2033 K Street, NW
Washington, DC 20581
Telephone: (202) 254-6387
Public Information: 202-254-8630

Regional Offices

Eastern Region
1 World Trade Center
New York, NY 10048
Telephone: (212) 466-2061

Central Region
233 S. Wacker Drive
Chicago, IL 60606
Telephone: (312) 353-5991

Southwestern Region
4900 Main Street
Kansas City, MO 64112
Telephone: (816) 374-6602

Minneapolis Office
510 Grain Exchange Building
Minneapolis, MN 55415
Telephone: (612) 370-2025

Western Region
10880 Wilshire Boulevard
Los Angeles, CA 90024
Telephone: (213) 209-6783

The Commodity Futures Trading Commission (CFTC), the Federal regulatory agency for futures trading, was established by the Commodity Futures Trading Commission Act of 1974 (88 Stat. 1389; 7 U.S.C. 4a), approved October 23, 1974. The Commission began operation in April 1975, and its authority to regulate futures trading was renewed by Congress in 1978, 1982, and 1986.

The CFTC consists of five Commissioners who are appointed by the President with the advice and consent of the Senate. One Commissioner is designated by the President to serve as Chairman. The Commissioners serve staggered 5-year terms, and by law no more than three Commissioners can belong to the same political party.

ACTIVITIES

The Commission regulates trading on the 13 U.S. futures exchanges, which offer active futures and options contracts. It also regulates the activities of numerous commodity exchange members, public brokerage houses (futures Commission merchants), Commission-registered futures industry salespeople and associated persons, trading advisers, and commodity pool operators. Some off-exchange transactions involving instruments similar in nature to futures contracts also fall under CFTC jurisdiction.

The Commission's regulatory and enforcement efforts are designed to ensure that the futures trading process is fair and that it protects both the rights of customers and the financial integrity of the marketplace. The CFTC approves the rules under which an exchange proposes to operate and monitors exchange enforcement of those rules. It reviews the terms of proposed futures contracts, and registers companies and individuals who handle customer funds or give trading advice. The Commission also protects the public by enforcing rules that require that customer funds be kept in bank accounts separate from accounts maintained by firms for their own use, and that such customer accounts be marked to present market value at the close of trading each day.

Futures contracts for agricultural commodities were traded in the United States for more than 100 years before futures trading was diversified to include trading in contracts for precious metals, raw materials, foreign currencies, financial instruments, commercial interest rates, and U.S. Government and mortgage securities. Contract diversification has grown in exchange trading in both traditional and newer commodities.

Source: U.S. Government Manual and the Commodity Futures Trading Commission.

Futures and Options Exchanges: Addresses

UNITED STATES

American Stock Exchange (AMEX)
86 Trinity Place
New York, NY 10006
(212) 306-1000

Chicago Board of Trade (CBOT)
141 West Jackson Boulevard
Chicago, IL 60604
(312) 435-3620

Chicago Board Options Exchange (CBOE)
400 South LaSalle
Chicago, IL 60605
(312) 786-5600

Chicago Mercantile Exchange (CME) and International Monetary Market Division of the CME (IMM) and Index and Option Market Division (IOM) of the CME
30 South Wacker Drive
Chicago, IL 60606
(312) 930-1000

Citrus Associates of the New York Cotton Exchange
4 World Trade Center
New York, NY 10048
(212) 938-2702

Coffee, Sugar & Cocoa Exchange (CSCE)
4 World Trade Center
New York, NY 10048
(212) 938-9863

Commodity Exchange, Inc. (COMEX)
4 World Trade Center
New York, NY 10048
(212) 938-2900

Financial Instrument Exchange (FINEX)
4 World Trade Center
New York, NY 10048
(212) 938-2634

GLOBEX
30 S. Wacker Drive
Chicago, IL 60606
(312) 456-6700

International Monetary Market (see Chicago Mercantile Exchange)

Index and Option Market (see Chicago Mercantile Exchange)

Kansas City Board of Trade (KCBT)
4800 Main Street
Kansas City, MO 64112
(816) 753-7500
(816) 821-4444 (hotline)

Midamerica Commodity Exchange (MidAm)
141 West Jackson Boulevard
Chicago, IL 60604
(312) 341-3000

Minneapolis Grain Exchange (MGE)
400 S. Fourth Street
Minneapolis, MN 55415
(612) 338-6212

New York Cotton Exchange (NYCE)
4 World Trade Center
New York, NY 10048
(212) 938-2702

New York Futures Exchange (NYFE)
20 Broad Street
New York, NY 10005
(212) 656-4949

New York Mercantile Exchange (NYMEX)
4 World Trade Center
New York, NY 10048
(212) 938-2222

New York Stock Exchange Options (NYSE)
11 Wall Street
New York, NY 10005
(212) 656-8533
(800) 692-6973 (Out-of-State)

Pacific Stock Exchange (PSE)
301 Pine Street
San Francisco, CA 94104
(415) 393-4000

Philadelphia Board of Trade (PHLX)
1900 Market Street
Philadelphia, PA 19103
(215) 496-5000

Philadelphia Stock Exchange (PBOT)
1900 Market Street
Philadelphia, PA 19103
(215) 496-5000

Selected Foreign Exchanges

AUSTRALIA

Australian Options Market
Australian Stock Exchange Derivatives Market
20 Bond Street
Sydney, NSW 2000, Australia
Phone: 61-2-227-0000

Sydney Futures Exchange (SFE)
30-32 Grosvenor St.
Sydney, NSW 2000, Australia
Phone: 61-2-256-0555

CANADA

Montreal Exchange (ME)
800 Victoria Square
Montreal, Quebec, Canada H4Z 1A9
Phone: (514) 871-2424

Toronto Futures Exchange (TFE)
2 First Canadian Place
Exchange Tower
Toronto, Ontario, Canada M5X 1J2
Phone: (416) 947-4487

Toronto Stock Exchange (TSE)
2 First Canadian Place
Exchange Tower
Toronto, Ontario, Canada M5X 1J2
Phone: (416) 947-4700

Vancouver Stock Exchange (VSE)
609 Granville Street
Vancouver, British Columbia
Canada V7Y 1H1
Phone: (604) 689-3334

The Winnipeg Commodity Exchange (WCE)
500 Commodity Exchange Tower
360 Main Street
Winnipeg, Manitoba
Canada R3C 3Z4
Phone: (204) 949-0495

FRANCE

Marche á Terme International de France (MATIF)
176 Rue Montmartre
75002 Paris, France
Fax: 33-1-40-28-80-01

Marche des Options Negociables de Paris (MONEP)
39 Rue Cambon
75001 Paris, France
Fax: 33-1-49-27-18-23

GERMANY

Deutsche Terminböerse (DTB)
Grueneburgweg 102
Postfach 17 02 03
6000 Frankfurt 1, Germany
Fax: 49-69-15-303-310

HONG KONG

Hong Kong Futures Exchange (HKFE)
Asia Pacific Finance Tower
3 Garden Road
Hong Kong
Fax: 852-810-5089

JAPAN

Osaka Securities Exchange
8-16 Kitahama, 1-chome, Chuo-ku
Osaka 541, Japan
Fax: 81-6-231-2639

Tokyo Commodity Exchange (TOCOM)
10-8 Nihonbashi Horidomecho
1-chome, Chuo-ku
Tokyo 103, Japan
Fax: 81-3-3661-7568

Tokyo International Financial Futures Exchange (TIFFE)
NTT Data Otemachi Bldg.
2-2-2 Otemachi, Chiyoda-ku
Tokyo 100, Japan
Fax: 81-3-3275-2862

Tokyo Stock Exchange (TSE)
2-1 Nihombashi-Kabuto-Cho
Chuo-ku, Tokyo 103, Japan
Fax: 81-3-3663-0625

NETHERLANDS

European Options Exchange (EOE)
Rokin 65, Amsterdam
1012 KK, The Netherlands
Fax: 31-20-6230-0012

Financiële Termijnmarkt Amsterdam N.V. (FTA)
Nes 49, Amsterdam
1012 KD, The Netherlands
Fax: 31-20-6245416

SINGAPORE

Singapore International Monetary Exchange Ltd. (SIMEX)
1 Raffles Place, #07-00
OUB Centre, Singapore 0104
Fax: 65-535-7282

SWITZERLAND

Swiss Options and Financial Futures Exchange AG (SOFFEX)
Neumattstrasse 7
8953 Dietikon, Switzerland
Fax: 41-1-740-1776

UNITED KINGDOM

International Petroleum Exchange of London Ltd. (IPE)
International House
1 St. Katharine's Way
London, England E1 9UN
Phone: 44-71-481-0643

London International Financial Futures and Options Exchange (LIFFE)
Cannon Bridge
London, England EC4R 3XX
Phone: 44-71-623-0444

London Fox Futures and Options Exchange
1 Commodity Quay
St. Katharine Docks
London, England E1 9AX
Phone: 44-71-481-2080

London Metal Exchange
Plantation House, Fenchurch Street
London, England EC3M 3AP
Phone: 44-71-626-3311

OM London Ltd. (OML)
107 Cannon Street
London EC4N 5AD
Phone: 44-71-283-0678

Futures and Securities Organizations

UNITED STATES

Chicago Futures/Options Society
50 S. LaSalle Street
Chicago, IL 60675
(312) 444-7810

Futures Industry Association, Inc.
2001 Pennsylvania Avenue, NW
Washington, DC 20006
(202) 466-5460

Futures Industry Institute
2001 Pennsylvania Avenue
Washington, D.C. 20006
(202) 223-1528

Managed Futures Association
182 University Avenue, P.O. Box 287
Palo Alto, CA 94302
(415) 325-4533

1919 Pennsylvania Avenue
Washington, DC 20006
(202) 872-9186

Market Technicians Association Inc.
71 Broadway
New York, NY 10006
(212) 344-1266

National Association of Securities Dealers (NASD)
1735 K Street, NW
Washington, DC 20006
(202) 728-8300

National Futures Association (NFA)
200 West Madison Street
Chicago, IL 60606
(312) 781-1300
(800) 621-3570

National Option & Futures Society Inc.
170 Old Country Road
Mineola, NY 11501
(212) 213-0241

North American Securities Administrators Association, Inc. (NASAA)
1 Massachusetts Avenue, NW
Washington, DC 20004
(202) 737-0900

FOREIGN

Canada

International Organization of Securities Commissions
800 Square Victoria, P.O. Box 4510
Montreal, Quebec, H4Z 1C8 Canada
(514) 875-8278

Investment Dealers Association of Canada
121 King Street West
Toronto, Ontario M5H 3T8
(416) 364-6133

Japan

Federation of Bankers Associations of Japan
3-1 Marunouchi, 1-chome
Chiyoda-ku, Tokyo 100, Japan

Japan Securities Dealers Association
5-8 Kayabacho, 1-chome
Nihonbashi, Chuo-ku
Tokyo 103, Japan

Switzerland

Swiss Commodities, Futures and Options Association
11 Route de Drize
P.O. Box 1181
CH-1227 Carouge/Geneva, Switzerland

United Kingdom

Association for Futures Investment
1 New Inn Square
Bateman's Row
London EC2A 3PY, UK

European Managed Futures Association
St. Katharine's Way
London E1 9, UK

COMMODITY PRICE CHARTS[1]

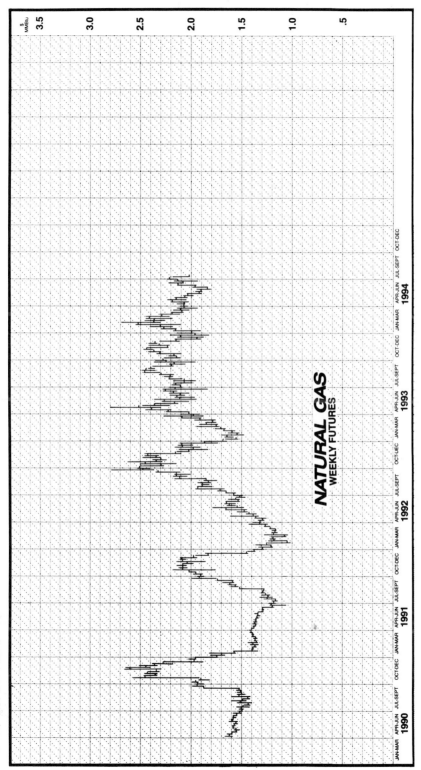

[1] See page 590.

Source: Courtesy of Commodity Price Charts, 219 Parkade, Cedar Falls, Iowa 50613.

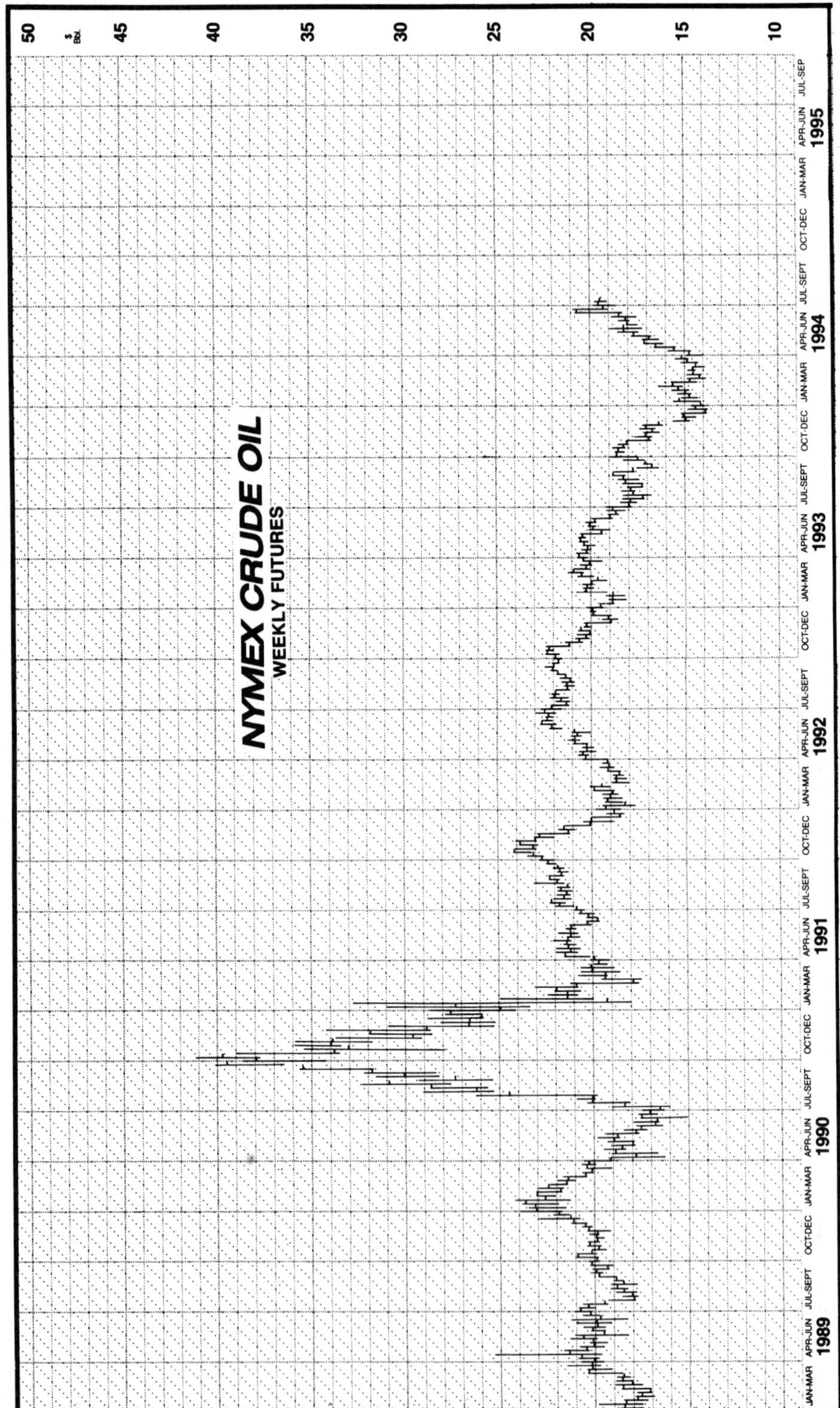
NYMEX CRUDE OIL
WEEKLY FUTURES
50
$ Bbl.
45
40
35
30
25
20
15
10
JAN-MAR APR-JUN JUL-SEPT OCT-DEC
1989
1990
1991
1992
1993
1994
1995
JUL-SEP

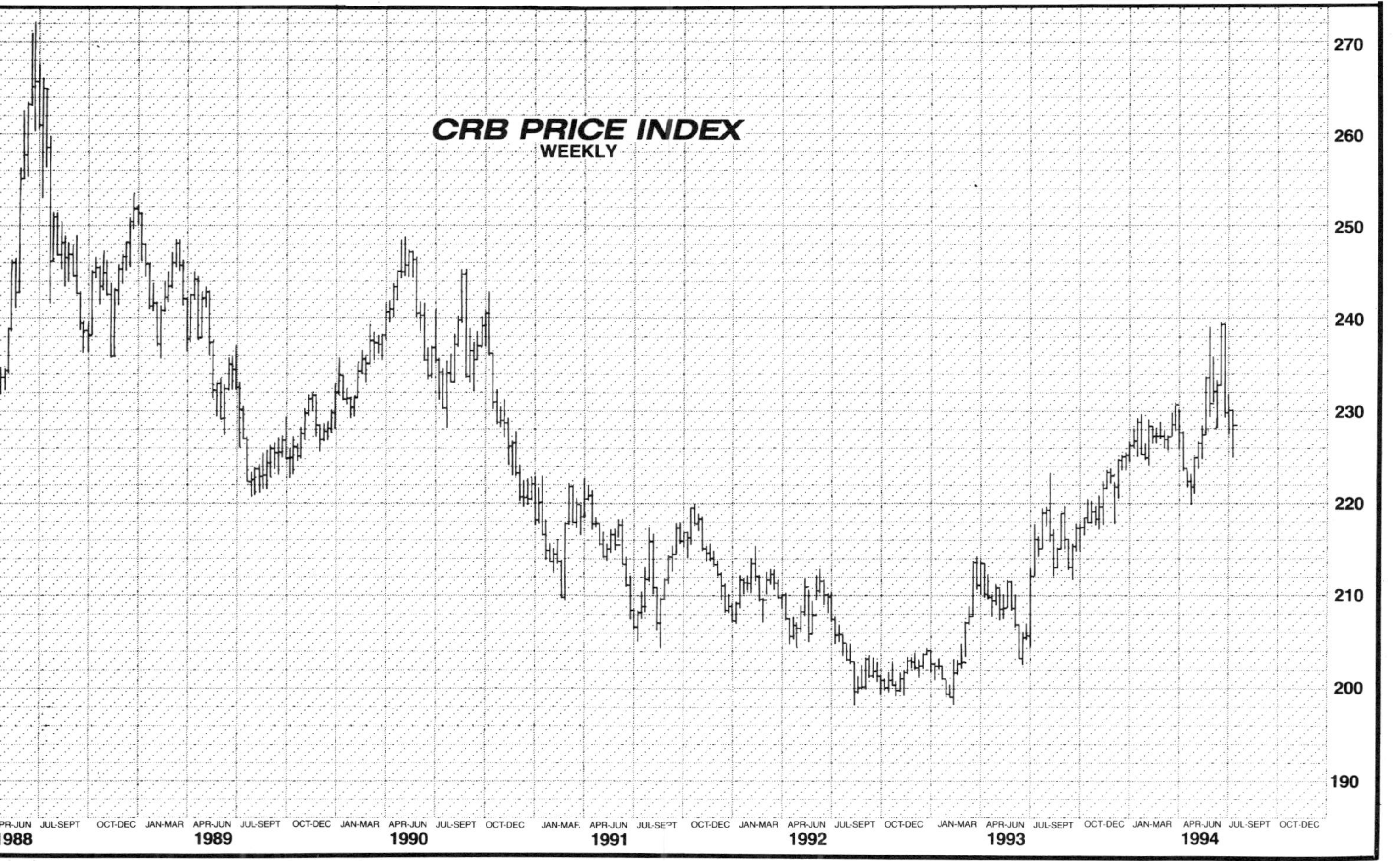

Source: Courtesy of Commodity Price Charts, 219 Parkade, Cedar Falls, Iowa 50613.

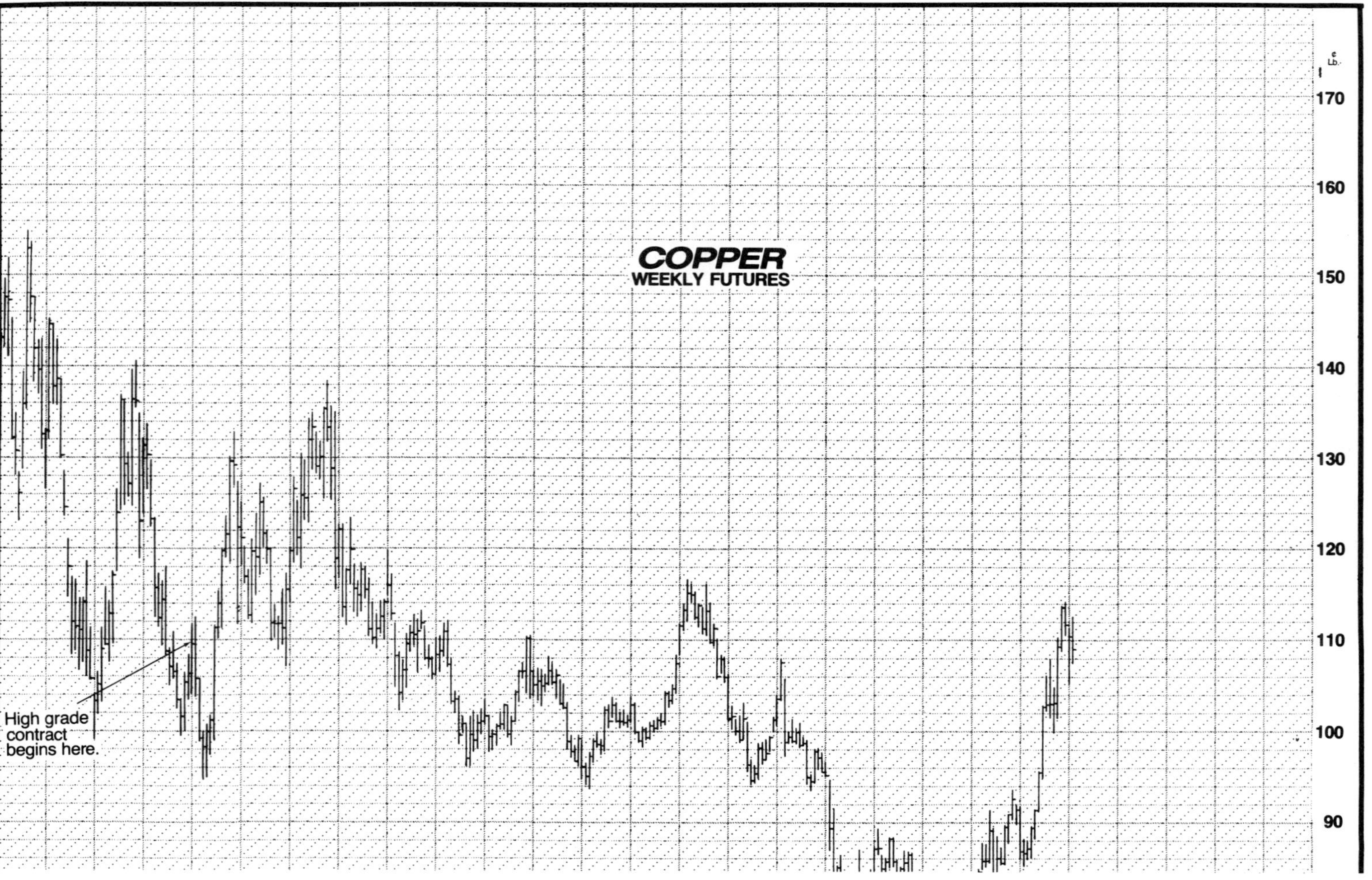
COPPER
WEEKLY FUTURES
170
160
150
140
130
120
110
100
90
High grade
contract
begins here.

Source: Courtesy of Commodity Price Charts, 219 Parkade, Cedar Falls, Iowa 50613.

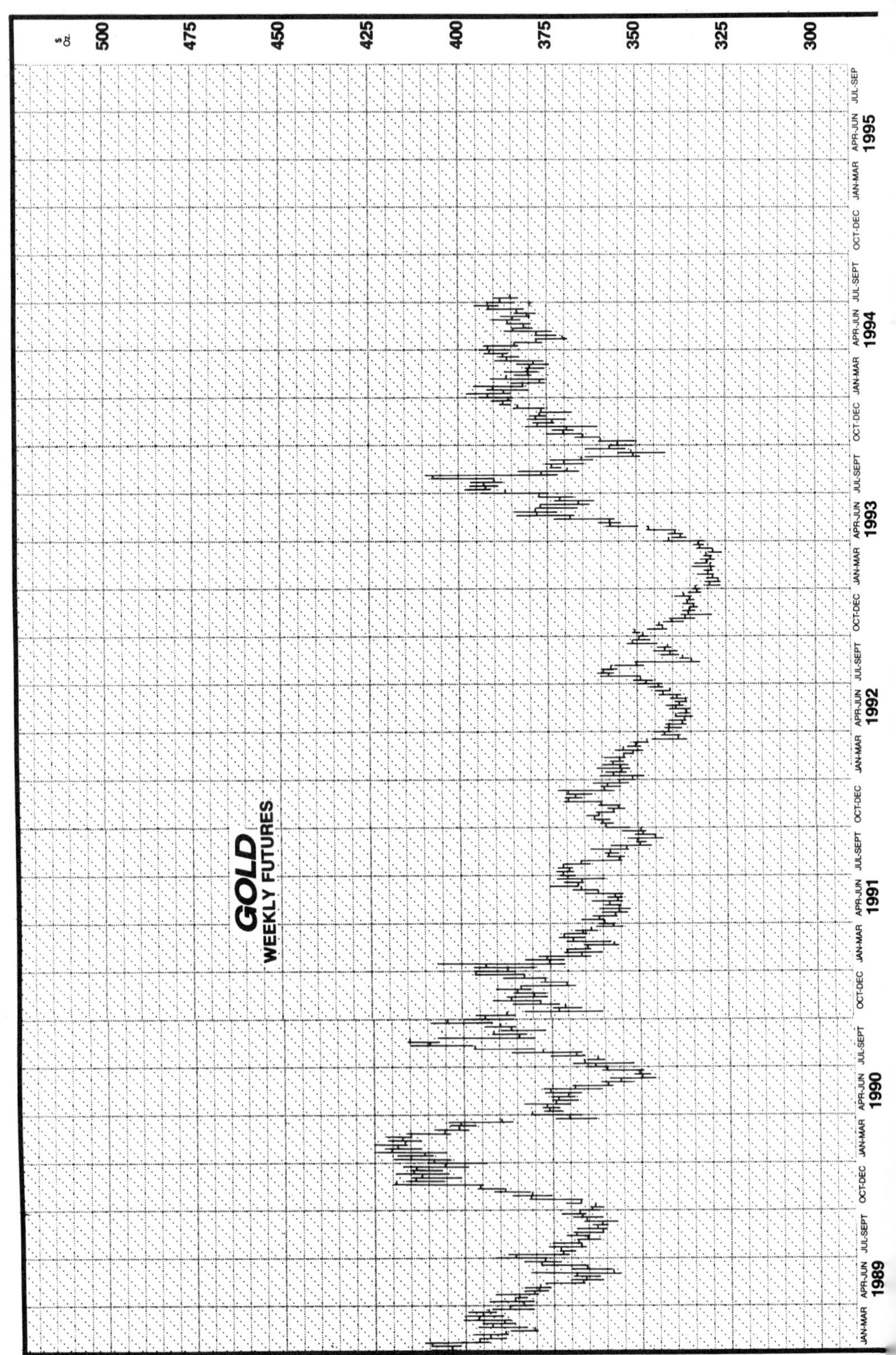
GOLD
WEEKLY FUTURES
$ Oz.
500
475
450
425
400
375
350
325
300
JAN-MAR APR-JUN JUL-SEPT OCT-DEC
1989
1990
1991
1992
1993
1994
1995
JUL-SEP

Source: Courtesy of Commodity Price Charts, 219 Parkade, Cedar Falls, Iowa 50613.

COMEX SILVER
WEEKLY FUTURES

$/Oz

11.0
10.5
10.0
9.5
9.0
8.5
8.0
7.5
7.0
6.5

Source: Courtesy of Commodity Price Charts, 219 Parkade, Cedar Falls, Iowa 50613.

T-BILLS
WEEKLY FUTURES
2
3
4
5
6
7
8
9
98
97
96
95
94
93
92
91
98
JUL-SEPT OCT-DEC JAN-MAR APR-JUN JUL-SEPT OCT-DEC JAN-MAR APR-JUN JUL-SEPT OCT-DEC JAN-MAR APR-JUN JUL-SEPT OCT-DEC JAN-MAR APR-JUN JUL-SEPT OCT-DEC JAN-MAR APR-JUN JUL-SEPT OCT-DEC JAN-MAR APR-JUN JUL-SEPT OCT-DEC
1989
1990
1991
1992
1993
1994

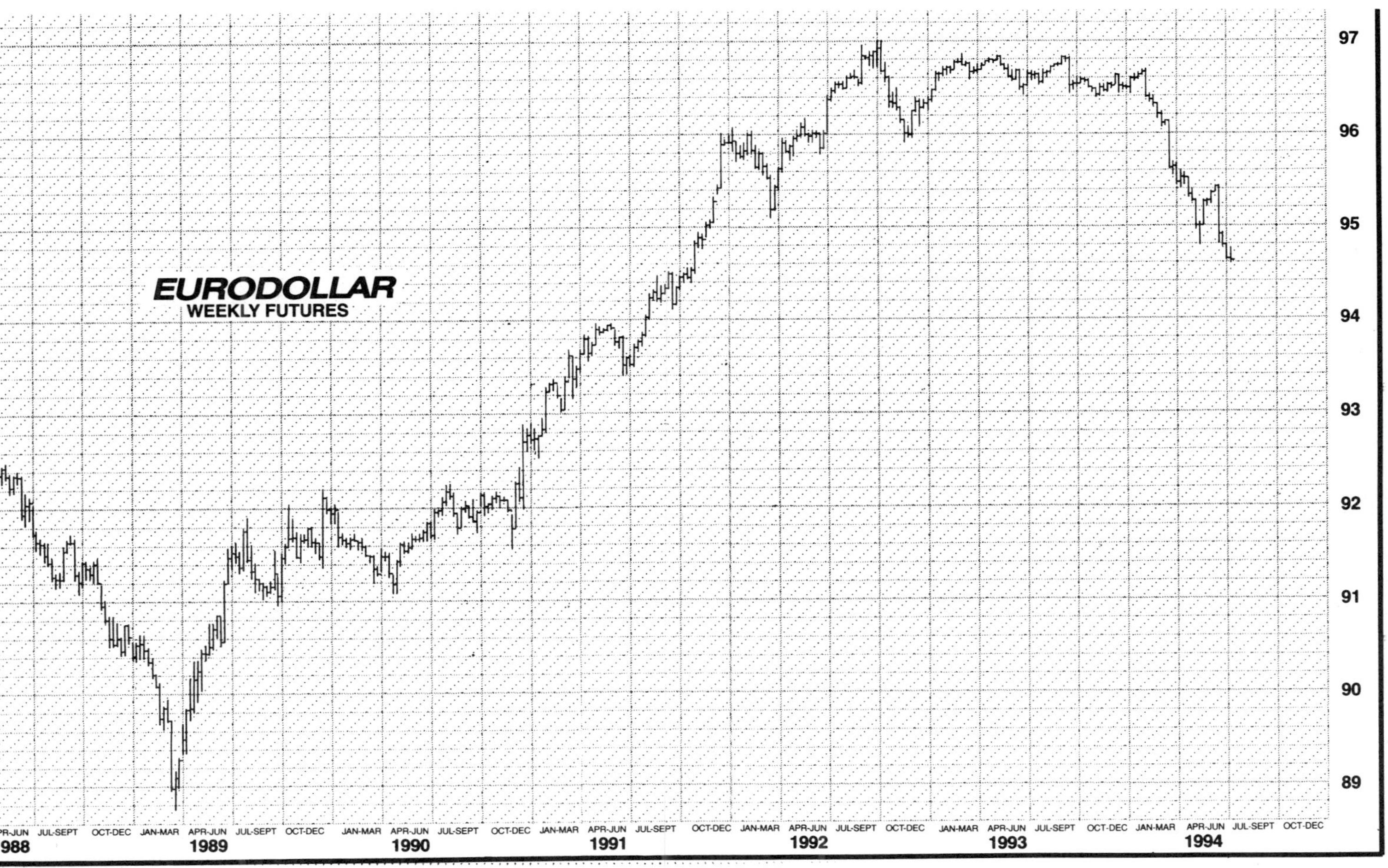

Source: Courtesy of Commodity Price Charts, 219 Parkade, Cedar Falls, Iowa 50613.

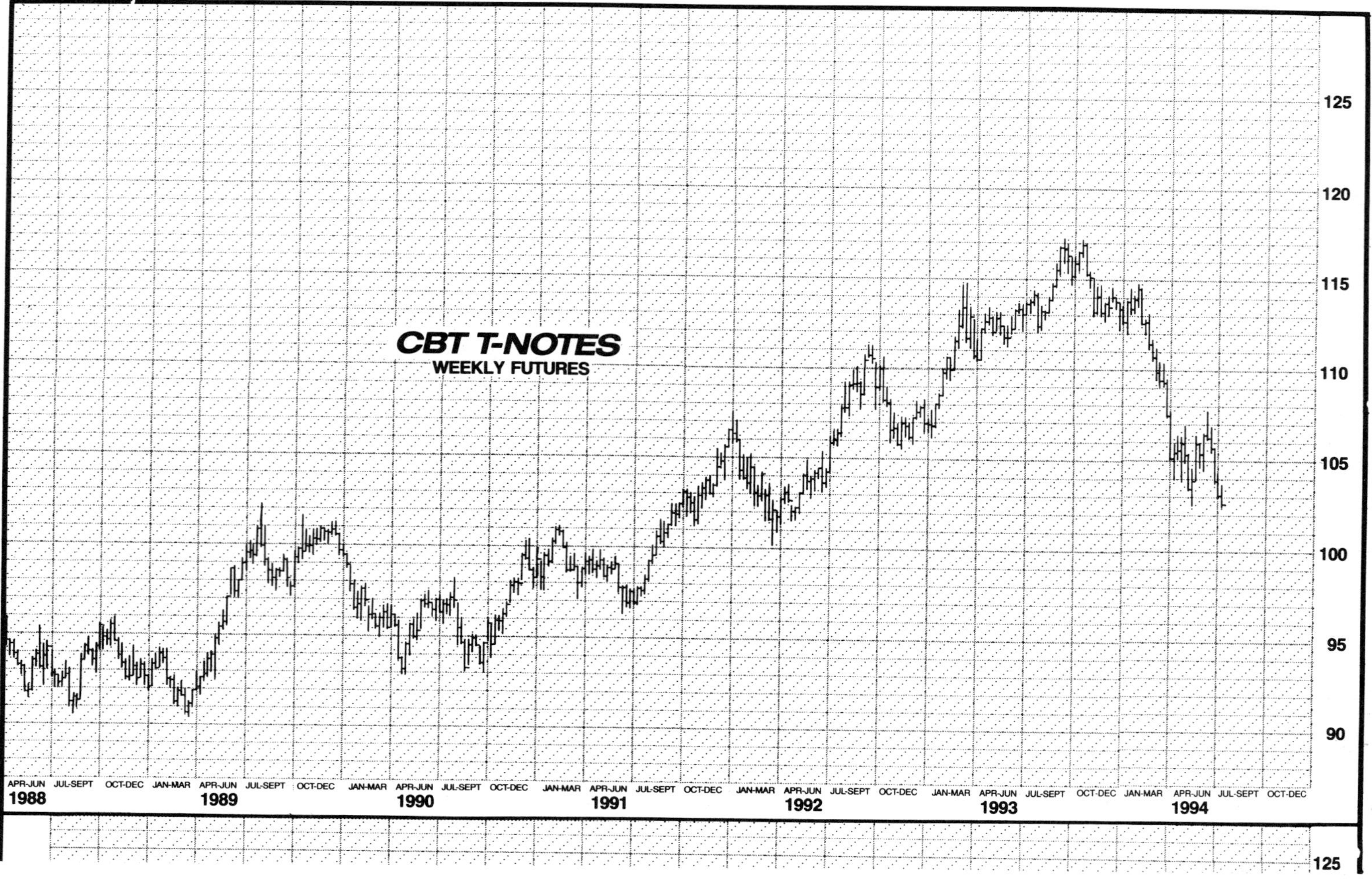
CBT T-NOTES
WEEKLY FUTURES
125
120
115
110
105
100
95
90
APR-JUN JUL-SEPT OCT-DEC
1988
JAN-MAR APR-JUN JUL-SEPT OCT-DEC
1989
JAN-MAR APR-JUN JUL-SEPT OCT-DEC
1990
JAN-MAR APR-JUN JUL-SEPT OCT-DEC
1991
JAN-MAR APR-JUN JUL-SEPT OCT-DEC
1992
JAN-MAR APR-JUN JUL-SEPT OCT-DEC
1993
JAN-MAR APR-JUN JUL-SEPT OCT-DEC
1994
125

Source: Courtesy of Commodity Price Charts, 219 Parkade, Cedar Falls, Iowa 50613.

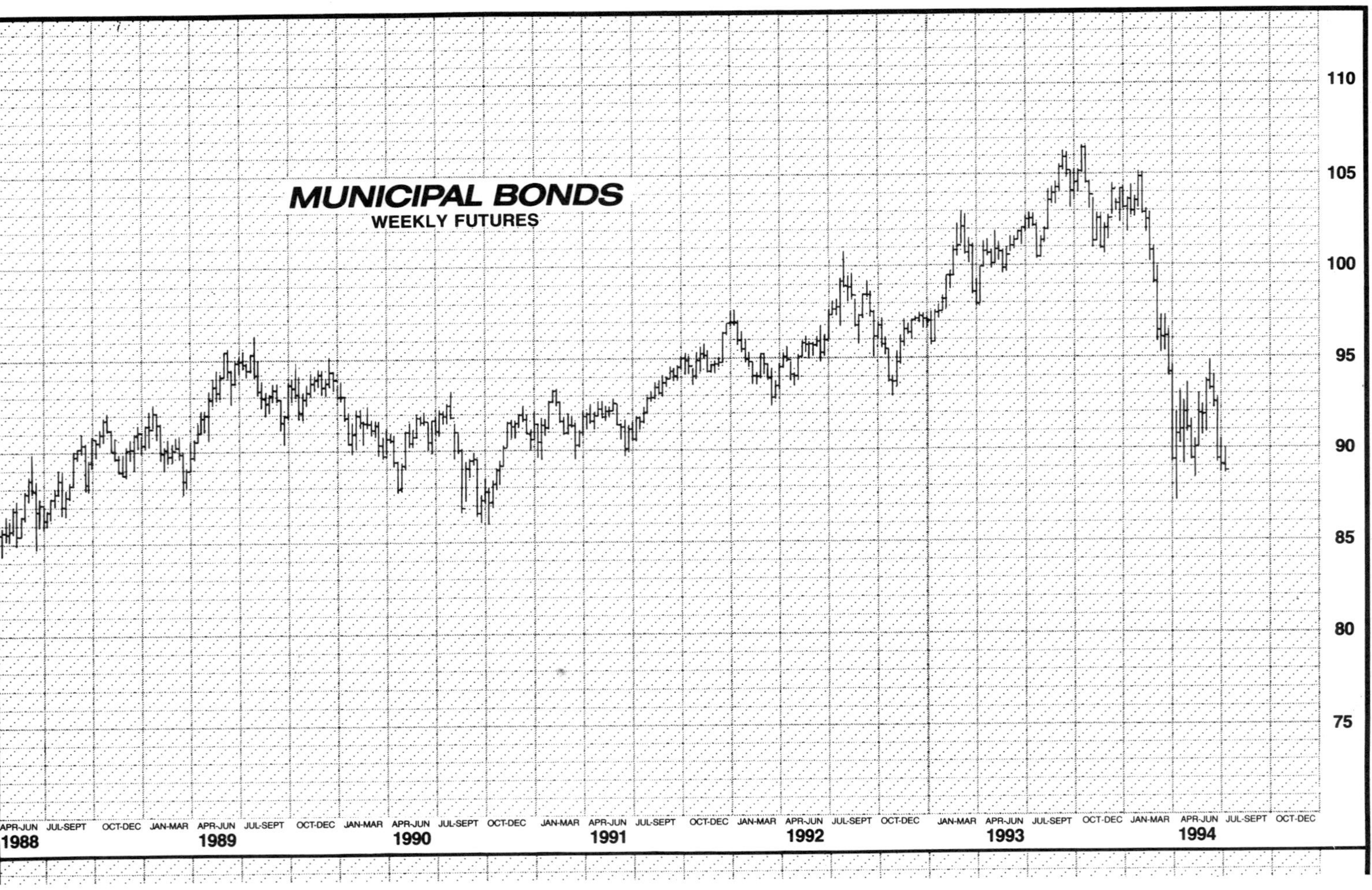
MUNICIPAL BONDS
WEEKLY FUTURES
110
105
100
95
90
85
80
75
APR-JUN JUL-SEPT OCT-DEC
1988
JAN-MAR APR-JUN JUL-SEPT OCT-DEC
1989
JAN-MAR APR-JUN JUL-SEPT OCT-DEC
1990
JAN-MAR APR-JUN JUL-SEPT OCT-DEC
1991
JAN-MAR APR-JUN JUL-SEPT OCT-DEC
1992
JAN-MAR APR-JUN JUL-SEPT OCT-DEC
1993
JAN-MAR APR-JUN JUL-SEPT OCT-DEC
1994

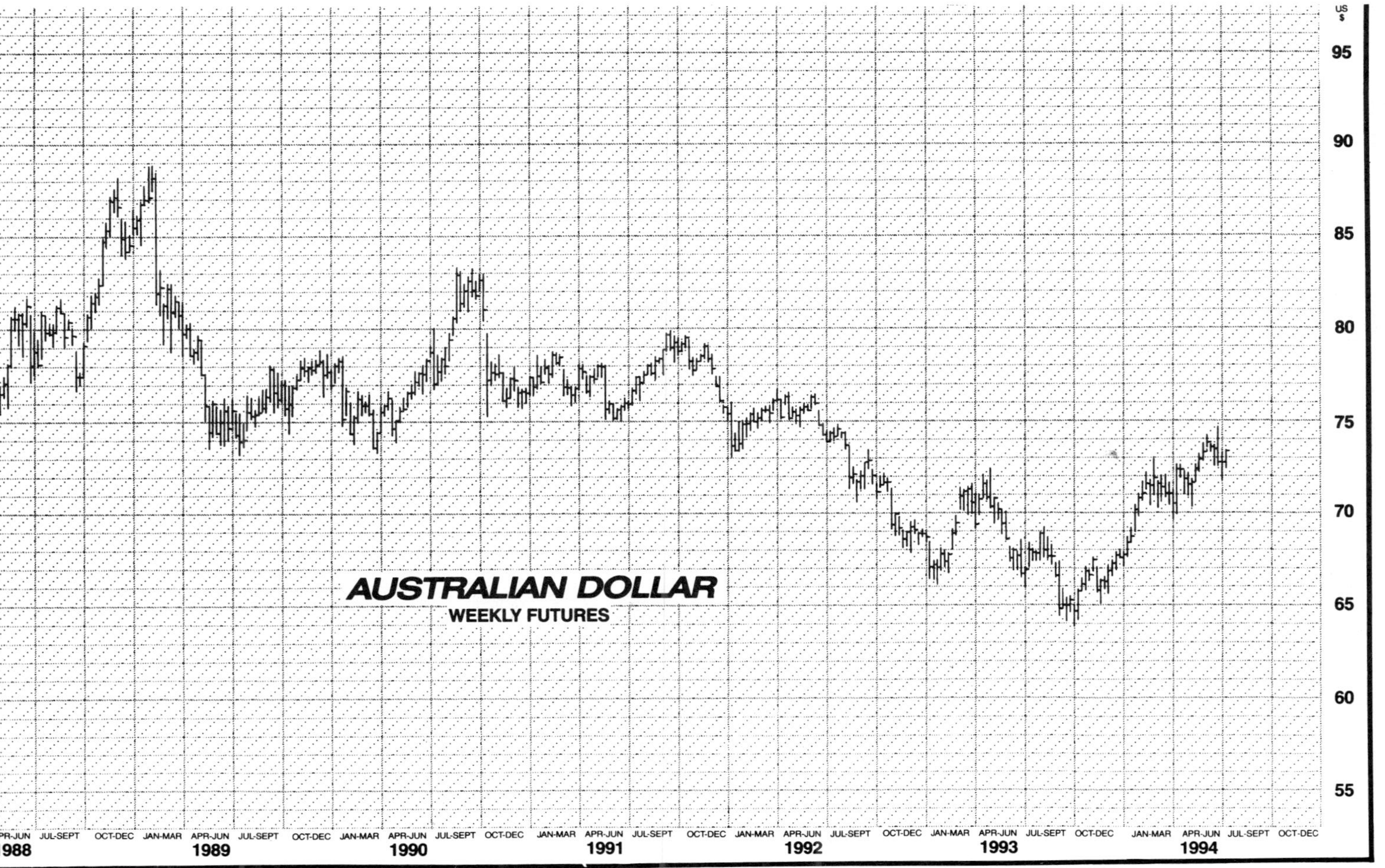

Source: Courtesy of Commodity Price Charts, 219 Parkade, Cedar Falls, Iowa 50613.

BRITISH POUND
WEEKLY FUTURES
U.S. $
2.100
2.000
1.900
1.800
1.700
1.600
1.500
1.400
1.300
JUL-SEPT OCT-DEC
JAN-MAR APR-JUN JUL-SEPT OCT-DEC
1989
JAN-MAR APR-JUN JUL-SEPT OCT-DEC
1990
JAN-MAR APR-JUN JUL-SEPT OCT-DEC
1991
JAN-MAR APR-JUN JUL-SEPT OCT-DEC
1992
JAN-MAR APR-JUN JUL-SEPT OCT-DEC
1993
JAN-MAR APR-JUN JUL-SEPT OCT-DEC JAN-MAR
1994

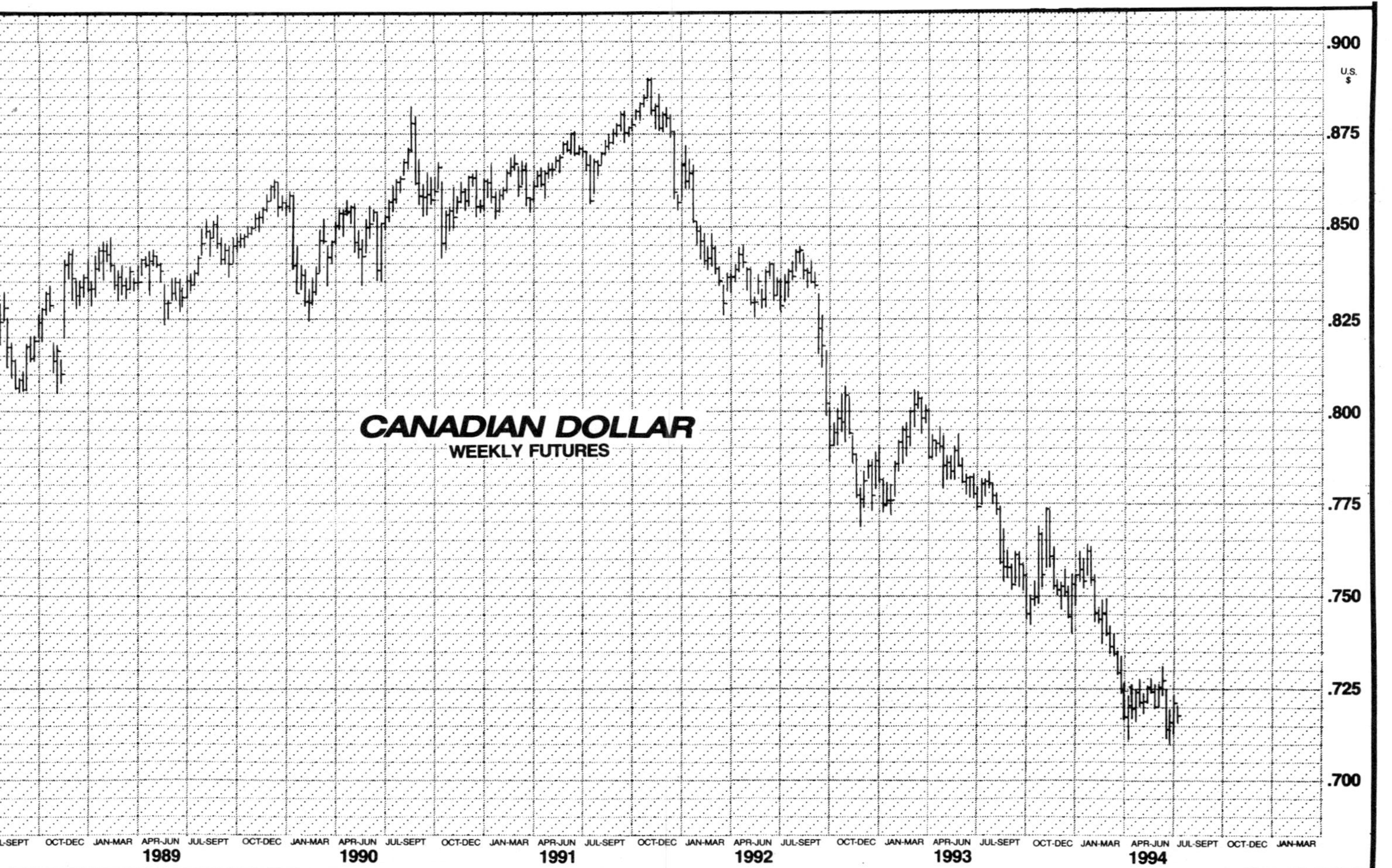

Source: Courtesy of Commodity Price Charts, 219 Parkade, Cedar Falls, Iowa 50613.

DEUTSCHE MARK
WEEKLY FUTURES
U.S. $
.750
.700
.650
.600
.550
.500
.450
.400
U.S. ¢
JUL-SEPT OCT-DEC JAN-MAR APR-JUN JUL-SEPT OCT-DEC JAN-MAR APR-JUN JUL-SEPT OCT-DEC JAN-MAR APR-JUN JUL-SEPT OCT-DEC JAN-MAR APR-JUN JUL-SEPT OCT-DEC JAN-MAR APR-JUN JUL-SEPT OCT-DEC JAN-MAR APR-JUN JUL-SEPT OCT-DEC JAN-MAR
1989
1990
1991
1992
1993
1994

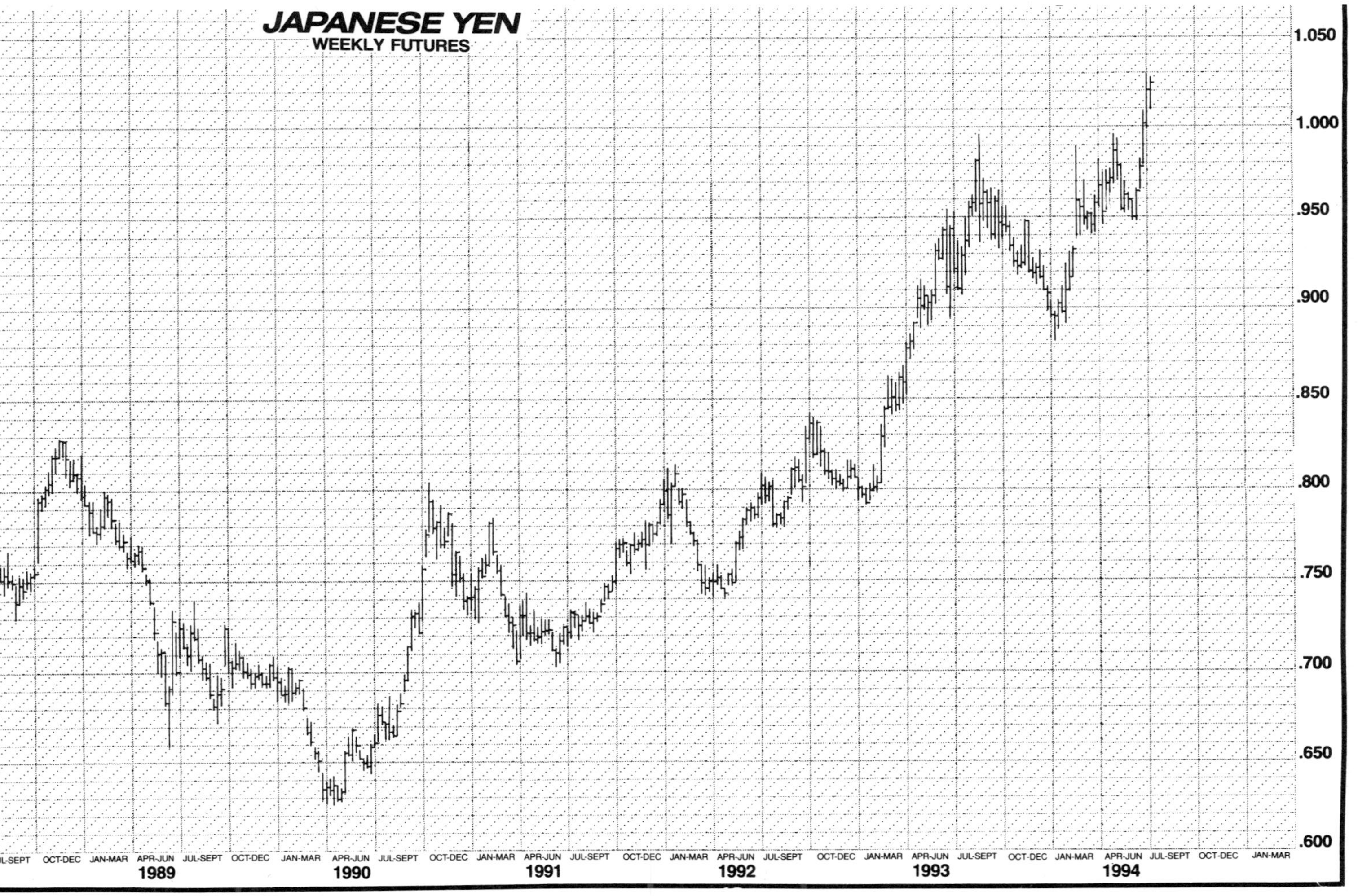

Source: Courtesy of Commodity Price Charts, 219 Parkade, Cedar Falls, Iowa 50613.

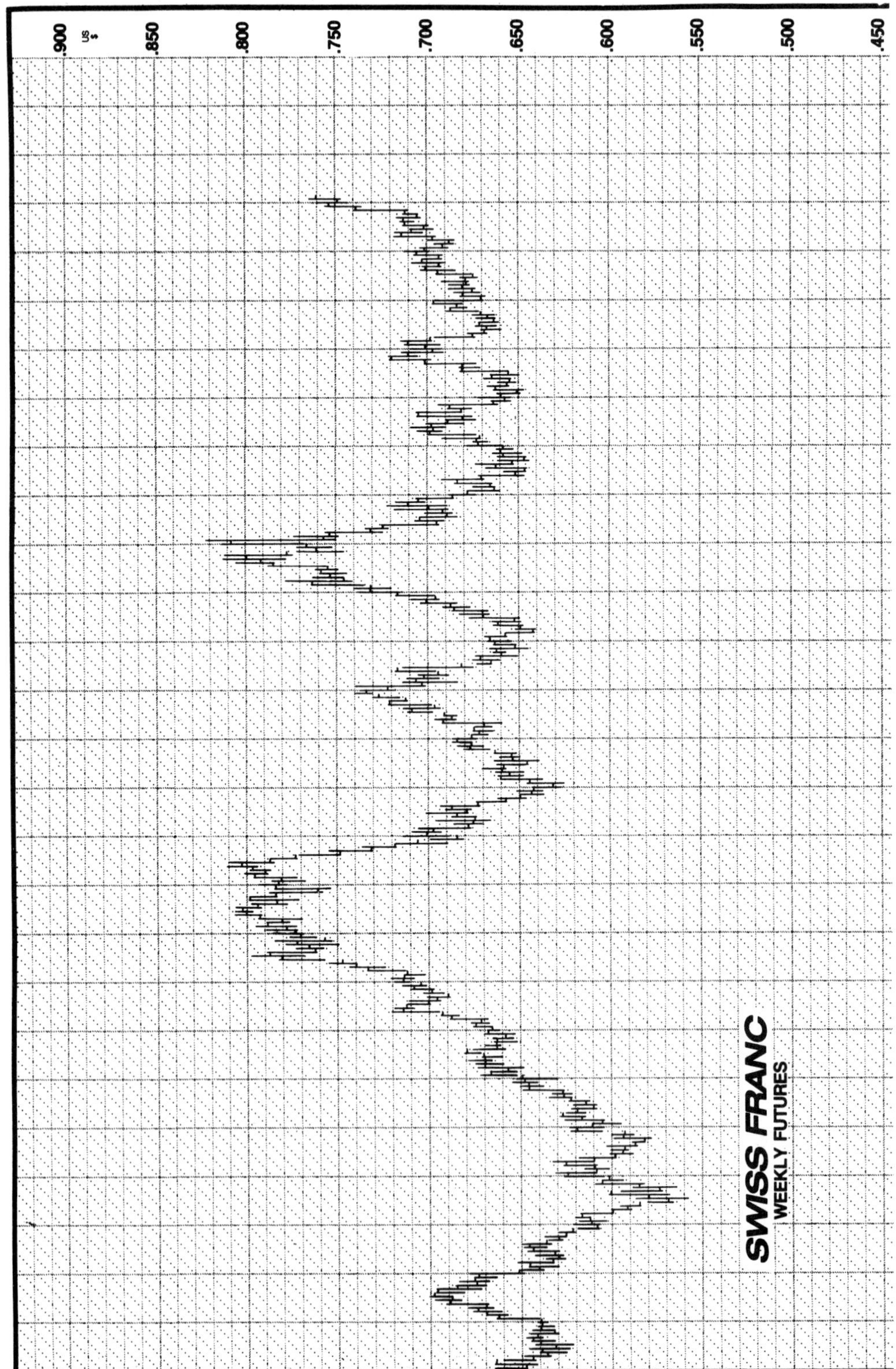
SWISS FRANC
WEEKLY FUTURES
US $
.900
.850
.800
.750
.700
.650
.600
.550
.500
.450

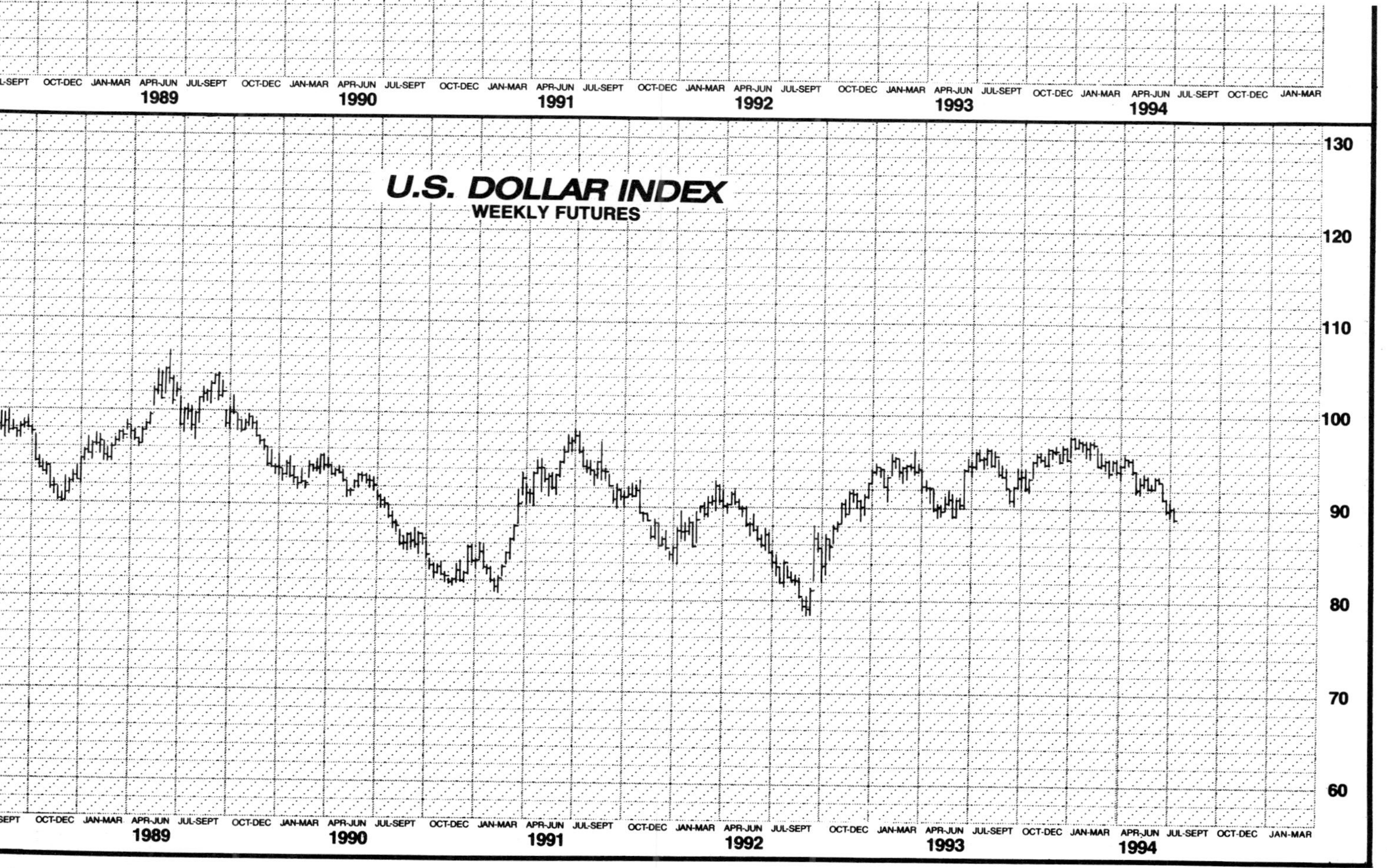

Source: Courtesy of Commodity Price Charts, 219 Parkade, Cedar Falls, Iowa 50613.

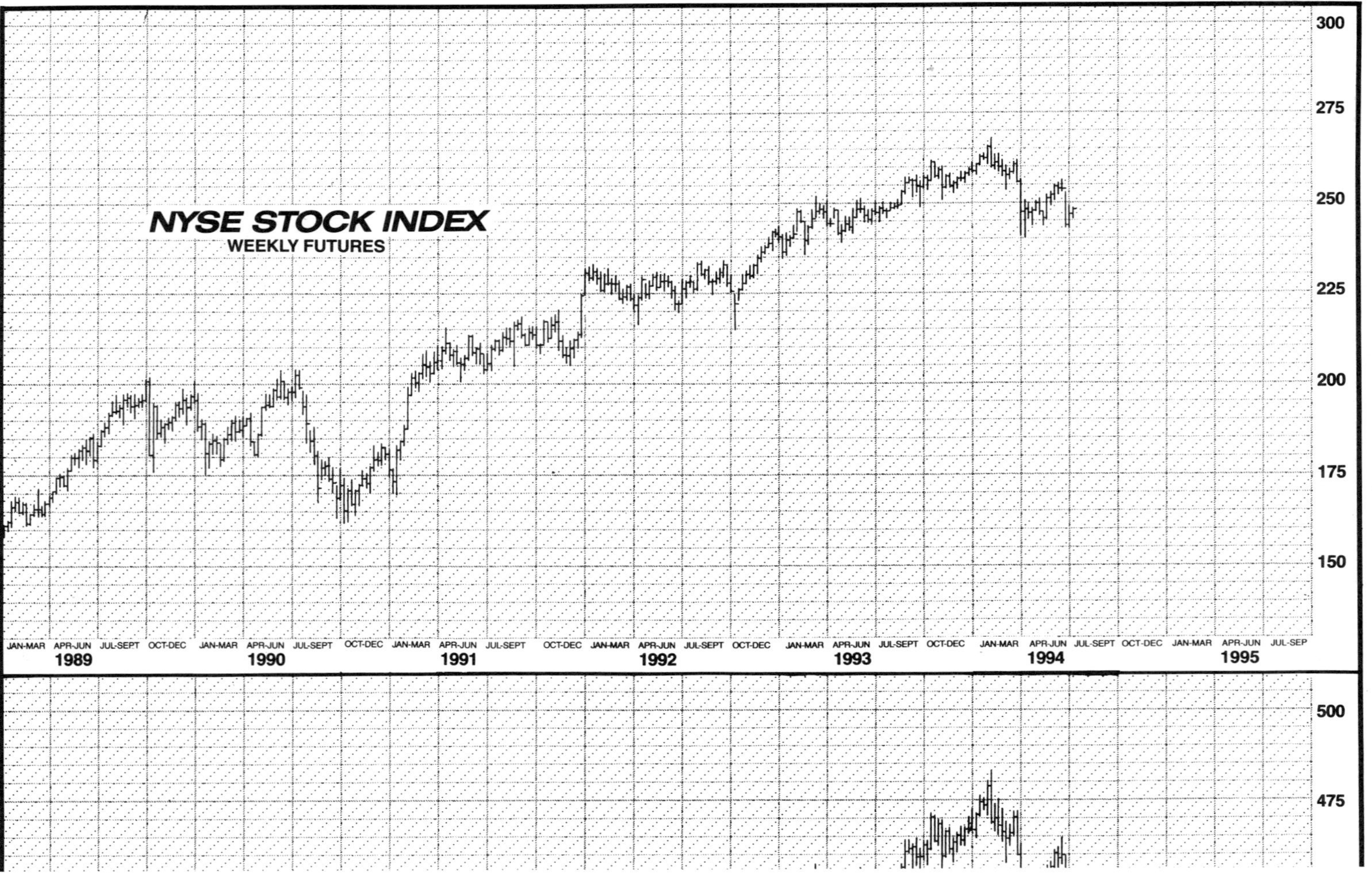
NYSE STOCK INDEX
WEEKLY FUTURES
300
275
250
225
200
175
150
500
475
JAN-MAR APR-JUN JUL-SEPT OCT-DEC
1989
JAN-MAR APR-JUN JUL-SEPT OCT-DEC
1990
JAN-MAR APR-JUN JUL-SEPT OCT-DEC
1991
JAN-MAR APR-JUN JUL-SEPT OCT-DEC
1992
JAN-MAR APR-JUN JUL-SEPT OCT-DEC
1993
JAN-MAR APR-JUN JUL-SEPT OCT-DEC
1994
JAN-MAR APR-JUN JUL-SEP
1995

Source: Courtesy of Commodity Price Charts, 219 Parkade, Cedar Falls, Iowa 50613.

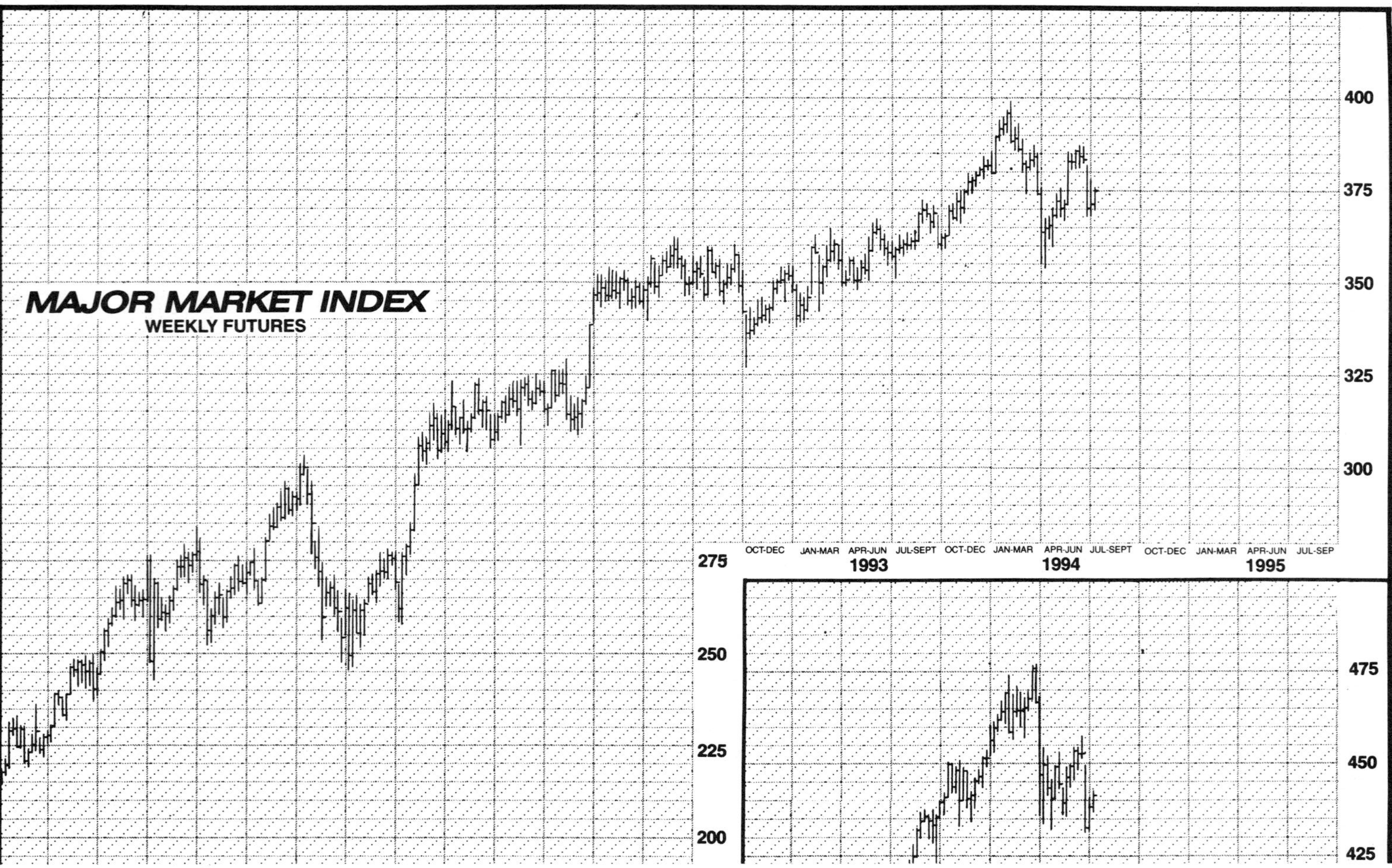
MAJOR MARKET INDEX
WEEKLY FUTURES
400
375
350
325
300
275
250
225
200
475
450
425
OCT-DEC
JAN-MAR
APR-JUN
1993
JUL-SEPT
OCT-DEC
JAN-MAR
APR-JUN
1994
JUL-SEPT
OCT-DEC
JAN-MAR
APR-JUN
1995
JUL-SEP

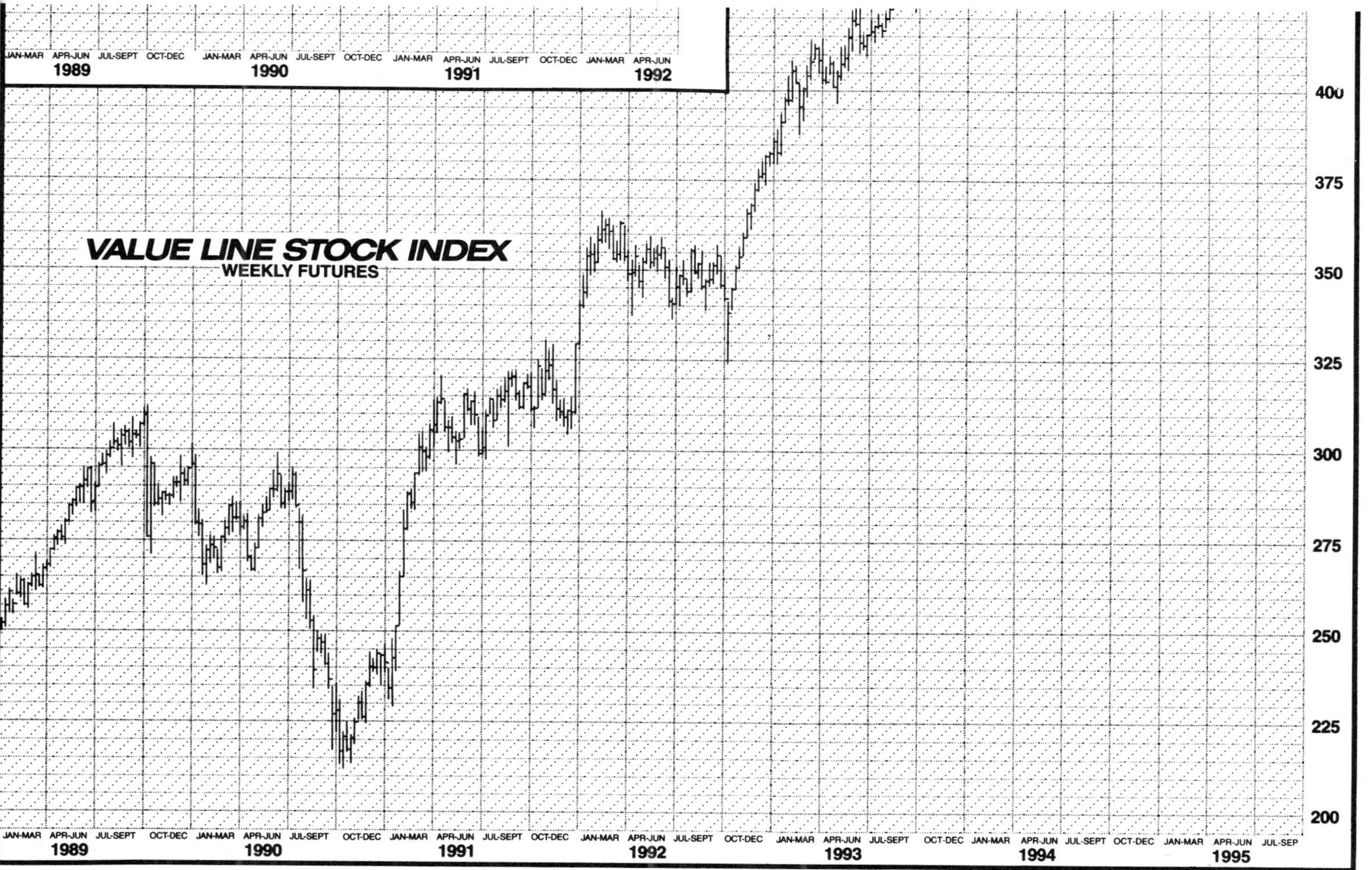

Source: Courtesy of Commodity Price Charts, 219 Parkade, Cedar Falls, Iowa 50613.

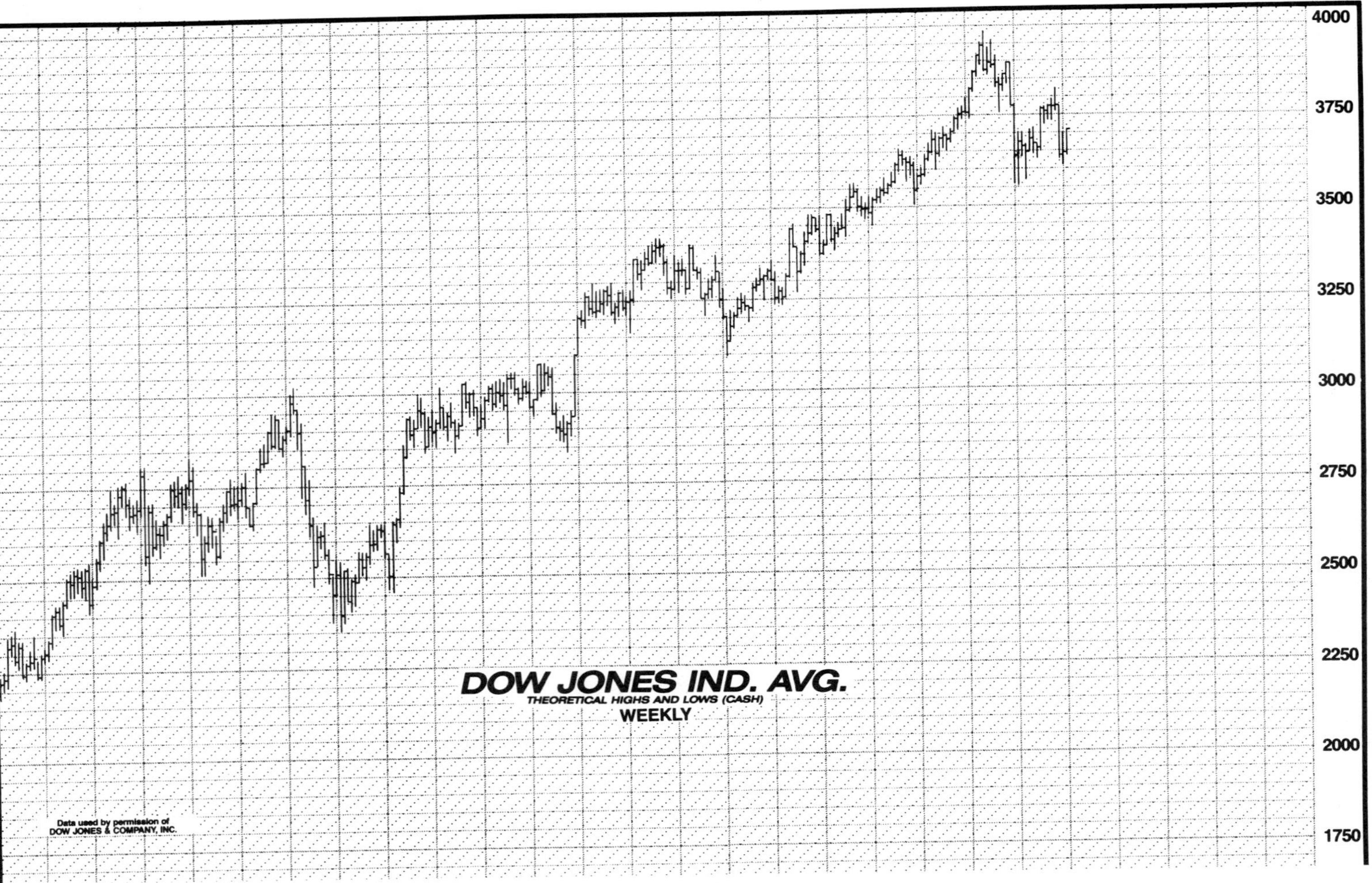
4000
3750
3500
3250
3000
2750
2500
2250
2000
1750
DOW JONES IND. AVG.
THEORETICAL HIGHS AND LOWS (CASH)
WEEKLY
Data used by permission of
DOW JONES & COMPANY, INC.

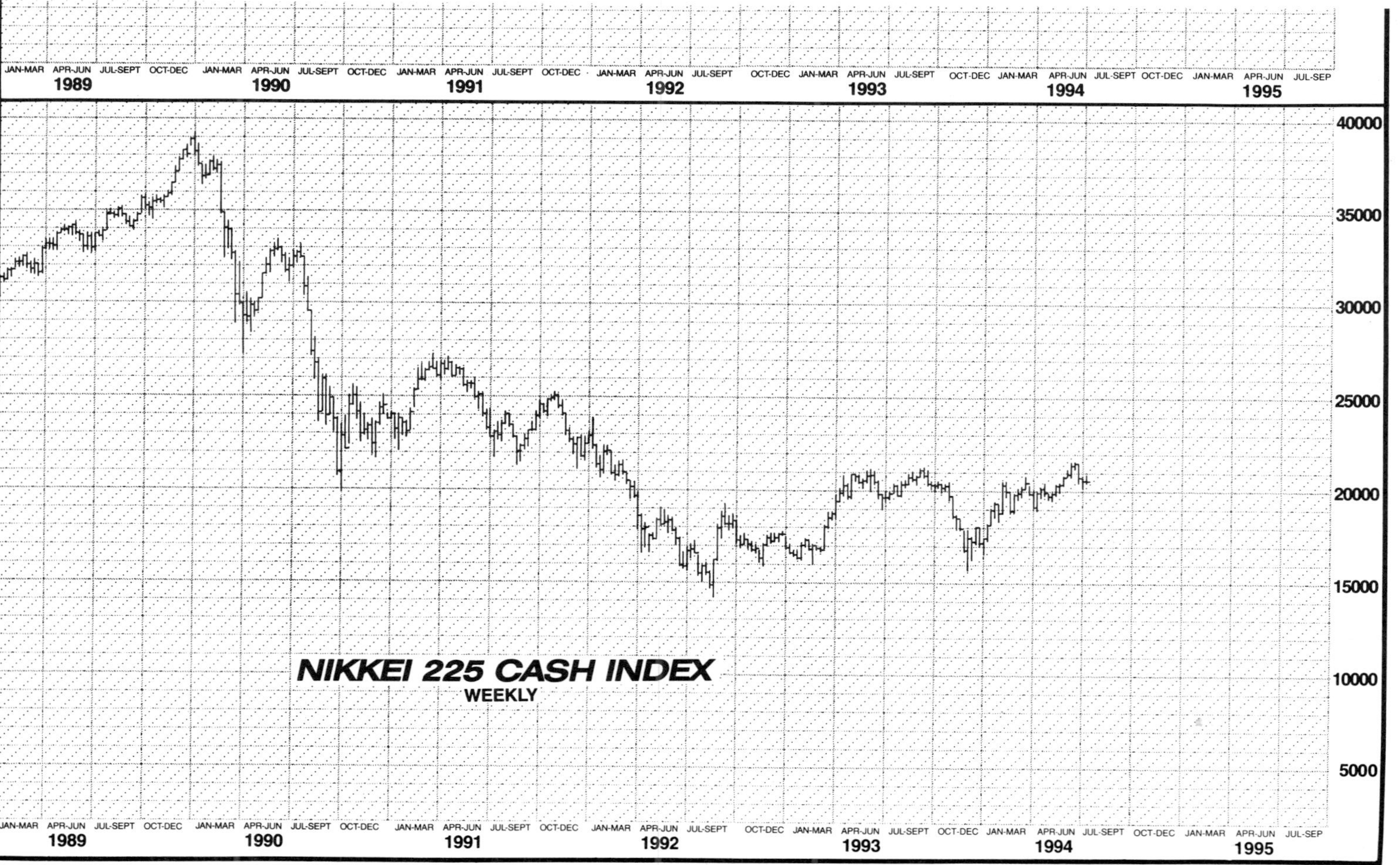

Source: Courtesy of Commodity Price Charts, 219 Parkade, Cedar Falls, Iowa 50613.

These weekly Charts are plotted through July 8, 1994. Weekly charts are published on a quarterly schedule, and the next mailing is on Oct. 7, 1994. Monthly charts are published semi-annually. The next mailing will be August 12, 1994.

Weekly High, Low & Close Charts of the Nearest Futures Contract: Long-term charts are plotted for the nearest futures contract on a weekly basis. During the week of change-over, the price action of both the expiring contract and the next one are included in the week's range.

Contract months used for plotting CPC weekly and monthly supplements.

Cattle	Feb., Apr., June, Aug., Oct., Dec.,
Hogs	Feb., Apr., June, July, Aug., Oct., Dec.,
Feeder Cattle	Jan., March, Apr., May, Aug., Sept., Oct., Nov.
Pork Bellies	Feb., March, May, July, Aug.
Corn	March, May, July, Sept., Dec.
Oats	March, May, July, Sept., Dec.
Soybeans	Jan., March, May, July, Aug., Sept., Nov.,
Soybean Meal	Jan., March, May, July, Aug., Sept., Oct., Dec.
Soybean Oil	Jan., March, May, July, Aug., Sept., Oct., Dec.
Chicago Wheat	March, May, July, Sept., Dec.
K.C. Wheat	March, May, July, Sept., Dec.
Mpls. Wheat	March, May, July, Sept., Dec.
Cotton	March, May, July, Oct., Dec.
Lumber	Jan., March, May, July, Sept., Nov.
Crude Oil	All contracts
Reg. Gas	All contracts
Heating Oil	All contracts
Currencies	March, June, Sept., Dec.
Int. Rates	March, June, Sept., Dec.
Stock Indices	March, June, Sept., Dec. (except MMI)
Major Market Index	All contracts
Cocoa	March, May, July, Sept., Dec.
Coffee	March, May, July, Sept., Dec.
Orange Juice	Jan., March, May, July, Sept., Nov.
Sugar	March, May, July, Oct.
Copper	March, May, July, Sept., Dec.
Silver	March, May, July, Sept., Dec.
Gold	Feb., June, Aug., Oct., Dec.
Palladium	March, June, Sept., Dec.
Platinum	Jan., Apr., July, Oct.

Source: Courtesy of Commodity Price Charts, 219 Parkade, Cedar Falls, Iowa 50613.

Computer Services and Educational Material for Business and Finance

Selected On-Line Business/ Financial Data Bases

On-line data bases are collections of computer stored data which are retrievable by remote terminals. The data bases are collected and organized by a so-called *producer*. The latter provides the data base to a *vendor* who distributes the data by means of a telecommunication network to the user. Often a vendor will offer a large number of different data bases. In some instances the producer and vendor are the same.

Using an on-line data base requires: (1) a *terminal* (a typewriter-like device usually equipped with a video display) to receive data and send commands to the vendor's computers, and (2) a *modem* for coupling the terminal to a telephone line. Printouts (hard copy) of the desired information can be obtained with the aid of electronic printers located at the user's terminal or, alternatively, ordered from the vendor.

The user accesses the data base by dialing a telephone number and then typing (on the terminal keyboard) a password provided by the vendor. Searching the data base is done with special commands and procedures peculiar to each base.

The contents of data bases vary. Some provide statistical data only—usually in the form of time series. Other bases provide bibliographic references and, in some instances, abstracts or the full text of articles.

Specifics concerning data base contents, instructions, and prices are available from vendors. Listed below are some major business data bases and vendors. More complete information concerning data bases is available from the sources given below.

ABI Inform

Provides references on all areas of business management with emphasis on "how-to" information.

Producer: Data Courier Inc. (Louisville, KY)

Vendors: BRS, DIALOG, SDC

Accountants Index

Contains reference information on accounting, auditing taxation, management and securities.

Producer: American Institute of Certified Public Accountants (New York, NY)

Vendors: SDC

American Profile

Provides statistical information on U.S. households including population, income, dependents, and also data on types of businesses in an area.

Producer: Donnelley Marketing (Stamford, CT)

Vendors: Business Information Service

Business Credit Service

Provides business credit and financial information.

Producer: TRW, Inc. (Orange, CA)

Vendors: TRW

Canadian Business and Current Affairs

English language business and popular periodicals

Producer: Micromedia Limited (Toronto, Ontario)

Vendor: DIALOG, CISTI

CIS Index

Contains references and abstracts from nearly every publication resulting from Senate and House Committee meetings since 1970.

Producer: Congressional Information Services, Inc. (Washington, DC)

Vendors: Dialog, SDC

Commodities

Contains over 41,000 times series of current commodity prices for the U.S., Canada, U.K., and France.

Producer: Wolff Research (London, U.K.)

Vendor: I. P. Sharp

Compendex (Computerized Engineering Index)

Contains over 1 million citations and abstracts to the world wide engineering literature.

Producer: Engineering Information Inc. (New York)

Vendor: BRS, D-STAR, DIALOG.

CompuServe, Inc.

Provides reference, statistical and full text retrieval of information of personal interest including health, recipes, gardening, financial and investment data including the Compustat and Value Line data bases.

Producer: CompuServe, Inc. (Columbus, OH)

Vendor: CompuServe

Compustat

Provides very extensive financial data on companies.

Producer: Standard And Poor's Compustat Service, Inc. (Englewood, CO)

Vendors: ADP, Business Information Services, CompuServe, Data Resources, Chase Econometrics/Interactive Data Corp.

Disclosure II

Provides extracts of 10K and other reports filed with the Securities and Exchange Commission.

Producer: Disclosure Inc. (Bethesda, Maryland)

Vendors: Business Information Services (Control Data). Dialog, Dow Jones, New York Times Information Services, Mead Data Central.

Dow Jones News/Retrieval Service and Stock Quote Reporters

Contains text of articles appearing in major financial publications including the *Wall Street Journal* and *Barrons*. Quote Service provides quotes on stocks, bonds, mutual funds.

Producer: Dow Jones & Company (New York, NY)

Vendors: BRS, Dow Jones & Company

DRI Capsule/EEI Capsule

Provides over 3700 U.S. social and economic statistical time series such as population, income, money supply data, etc.

Producers: Data Resources, Inc. (Lexington, MA) and Evans Economics Inc. (Washington, DC)

Vendors: Business Information Services, United Telecom Group, I. P. Sharp

Federal Register Abstracts

Provides coverage of federal regulatory agencies as published in the Federal Register.

Producer: Capitol Services (Washington, DC)

Vendors: DIALOG, SDC

GTE Financial System One Quotation Service

Provides current U.S. and Canadian quotations and statistical data on stocks, bonds, options, commodities and other market data.

Producer: GTE Information Systems (Reston, VA)

Vendor: GTE Information Systems, Inc.

The Information Bank

Provides an extensive current affairs data source consisting of abstracts from numerous English language publications.

Producer: The New York Times Information Service

Vendor: The New York Times Information Service

LEXIS

Contains full text references to a wide range of legal information including court decisions, regulations, government statutes.

Producer: Mead Data Central (New York, NY)

Vendor: Mead Data Central

Media General Financial Services

Provides extensive historical fundamental and technical data and calculations on U.S. publicly owned companies. Also provides data on industries, the financial markets, mutual funds and corporate bonds.

Producer: Media General Financial Services (Richmond, VA)

Vendors: Dow Jones News Retrieval, Dialog, Thomson Financial Networks, Randall—Helms Fiduciary Consultants, Telescan, Lotus One Source (CDROM)

NEXIS

Provides full text business and general news including management, technology, finance, science, politics, religion.

Producer: Mead Data Central (New York, NY)

Vendor: Mead Data Central

PTS Marketing and Advertising Reference Service

Provides citations with abstracts & articles on the marketing and advertising of consumer goods and services.

Producer: Predicast, Inc. (Cleveland, OH)

Vendors: DIALOG, BRS, DATA-STAR

PTS Prompt

Covers world wide business news on new products, market data, etc.

Producer: Predicast, Inc. (Cleveland, OH)

Vendors: ADP, BRS, DIALOG

Quick Quote
Provides current quotations, volume, high-low data for securities of U.S. public corporations.
Producer: CompuServe Inc.
Vendor: CompuServe

Quotron 800
Provides up to the minute quotation and statistics on a broad range of securities such as stocks, bonds, options, commodities.
Producer: Quotron Systems Inc. (Los Angeles, CA)
Vendor: Quotron Systems Inc.

The Source (has been acquired by CompuServe)
Producer: Source Telecomputing (McLean, VA)
Vendor: Source Telecomputing Corp.

Trinet Company Data Base
Provides data on about 250,000 companies in the U.S.
Producer: Trinet, Inc. (Parsippany, NJ)
Vendors: DRI, DIALOG, Mead Data Central

For further information on data bases:

Computer Readable Data Bases, Gale Research (835 Penobscot Building, Detroit, MI 48226) A comprehensive data base and CD-ROM directory, revised annually.

Data Base Vendors

ADP Data Services, Inc.
175 Jackson Plaza
Ann Arbor, MI 48106
313-769-6800

BRS, Inc.
1200 Route 7
Latham, NY 12110
518-783-1161
800-235-1209

Chase Econometrics/Interactive Data Corporation
95 Hayden Avenue
Lexington, MA 02173
617-890-8100

CompuServe, Inc.
5000 Arlington Centre Boulevard
Columbus, OH 43220
614-457-8600
800-848-8990

Data Resources, Inc. (DRI)
1750 K Street NW
Washington, DC 20006
202-663-7720

DIALOG Information Services, Inc.
3460 Hillview Avenue
Palo Alto, CA 94304
415-858-3810
800-334-2564

Dow Jones & Company, Inc.
P.O. Box 300
Princeton, NJ 08540
609-452-2000
800-257-5114

General Electric Information Services Company
401 North Washington Street
Rockville, MD 20850
301-294-5405

GTE Education Services
8505 Freeport Parking
Irving, TX 75063
214-929-3000

Mead Data Central
P.O. Box 933
Dayton, OH 45401
800-227-4908

The New York Times Information Services, Inc.
229 West 43 Street
New York, NY 10036
800-543-6862

Quotron Systems, Inc.
12731 West Jefferson Boulevard
P.O. Box 66914
Los Angeles, CA 90066
213-827-4600

SDC Search Service/Orbit
8000 Westpark Drive
McLean, VA 22102
703-442-0900
800-456-7248

I. P. Sharp Associates
Exchange Tower
Toronto, Ontario, Canada M5X IE3
416-364-5361
800-387-1588

TRW Information Services Division
505 City Parkway West
Orange, CA 92668
714-385-7000

Noteworthy Software of Interest to Investors

The following provides a brief description of moderately priced software products of special interest to investors.

The EQUALIZER (Charles Schwab & Co., 101 Montgomery Street, San Francisco, CA 94104)

To use this software it is necessary to open an account with the discount brokerage firm of Charles Schwab & Co. The EQUALIZER includes the following features:

- access to financial information and data via Dow Jones News Retrieval and Standard and Poor's Marketscope
- price quotes on securities and mutual funds provided by Schwab, Dow Jones, or Warner Communications
- portfolio maintenance and record keeping
- trading capabilities (via Charles Schwab, of course)

This is excellent software for the active investor. The instruction manual which accompanies the software is first class.

QUICKEN (Intuit, 66 Willow Place, Menlo Park, CA 04025)

This is a leading program for maintaining records and managing personal finances. QUICKEN permits users to record deposits, monitor investments, keep track of saving, and print out checks as they become due. The software can also be used for small business and bookkeeping.

A 'help' program is provided which facilitates start up. The instruction manual accompanying QUICKEN is excellent. Also available at bookstores are other manuals.

WEALTHBUILDER (developed for *Money Magazine* by Reality Technologies, Inc., 3624 Market Street, Philadelphia, PA 19104) is a program intended to guide users on the development of investment strategies to meet their goals (home purchase, college education, retirement, etc.). Given the investor's financial goals, risk tolerance, net worth, and the like, the program provides an allocation of investments among equities, mutual funds, bonds, precious metals, and money market funds.

Information for allocating funds among each type of investment is available (for a price) on quarterly updated disks which contain data provided by Standard & Poor. CompuServe, the online data base, now provides a service for users of WEALTHBUILDERS.

The program is recommended for serious financial planning.

MANAGING YOUR MONEY (MECA Ventures, Inc., 355 Riverside Avenue, Westport, CT 06801) is a popular personal financial program providing the following features:

- budget and checkbook program
- a tax estimator
- an estate and insurance planner
- a financial calculator
- a portfolio manager

In addition to the above the program has a built in name filing capability and a word processor.

QUANT IX (Quant Software, 5900 North Port Washington Road, Milwaukee, WI 53217) is an excellent and relatively inexpensive portfolio managtock analyzer with record keeping capability. The software also provides for downloading data from CompuServe and Warner Communications. A unique feature is the availability of six different methods for evaluating stocks.

OPTIONS TOOLS DELUX (Richard Kedrow, 25 Illinois Avenue, Schaumburg, IL 60913). This helpful software provides option investors with the capability of calculating theoretical option values using the Black-Scholes and binomial models, hedge ratios, volatility, breakeven values, and covered call analysis.

BUSINESS PLAN GENERATOR (Essex Financial Group, 714 Market Street, Philadelphia, PA 19106) is a very useful computer program intended to help in the development of business plans. The underlying philosophy is that of Dynamic Planning which views planning as an ongoing procedure responding to changes in the business environment, and provides for feedback into the planning process. The program generates all of the expected planning projections; profit and loss statements, balance sheets, cash flows, and numerous financial ratios. The program also permits taking into account the effects of acquisitions. The *Business Plan Generator* requires the use of lotus 1-2-3 since it functions as an overlay of the latter.

DEALMAKER II (ValueSource, 1939 Grand Avenue, San Diego, CA 92109) is a sophisticated business evaluation program intended for buyers, sellers, and brokers. Other applications include evaluations of businesses for such purposes as marital dissolution, estate and gift taxes, employee stock options, and going public.

Twelve evaluation methods are provided, including book value, liquidation value, discounted earnings, the use of industry P/E ratios, and others.

The program also allows for consideration of projected post acquisition financial statements and for the effects on buyer and seller of different ways of financing the acquisition.

Screening Software

With thousands of companies listed on the exchanges, identifying promising investment opportunities is a daunting task. Fortunately this arduous chore can be greatly facilitated with the screening programs described below.

Investor's Alliance

Investor's Alliance provides a data base service to members comprising nearly 5000 companies traded over the counter and on the exchanges. The data are provided on diskettes which are updated quarterly. However, users can also update more frequently by going online. A screening capability is also included. Though the cost of this service is very modest the available data are surprisingly extensive.

Investor's Alliance, Inc.
219 Commercial Boulevard
Fort Lauderdale, FL 33308-4440
Telephone: 305-491-5100

MarketBase

MarketBase is an impressive software package providing key financial and market data on *all* companies traded in the NYSE, AMEX, and NASDAQ exchanges—over 5200 companies in all. The data spans a five year period. Updates are provided (depending on the subscription terms) on a weekly, monthly, or quarterly basis. Bi-Monthly and bi-Weekly updates are also available.

Over fifty financial and market criteria are included for screening. Companies may be screened by selecting a combination of criteria; for example, the PE ratio, revenues, earnings growth, market capitalization, SIC Code, and others. *MarketBase* also permits users to define their own selection criteria. Once screened, companies may be further explored by obtaining annual reports, 10-Q, press releases, and other materials by phoning the company. Although *MarketBase* software does not provide phone numbers, these may be obtained by calling the vendor. The software also lacks online communication capability.

MarketBase is an important resource for the serious investor. For further information contact:

MarketBase, Inc.
368 Hillside Avenue
P.O. Box 37
Needham Heights, MA 02194
Telephone: 800-735-0700

Value/Screen

Value/Screen provides access to about 1600 stocks composing the Value Line data base. Reportedly, these account for 90% of all trading on U.S. exchanges. Screening is carried out utilizing a wide variety of financial, market, and rating variables. Provisions are also available for user defined screening criteria. A rather elegant screening option displays particular screening criteria by means of a histogram.

Value/Screen is equipped with an online communications capability providing access to the Dow Jones News Retrieval Services.

Updates are available weekly, monthly, or quarterly. Data can also be down loaded online.

For complete details, contact:

Value Line Publishing, Inc.
711 Third Avenue
New York, NY 10017
Telephone: 800-654-0508

Home Study Course for Investors

Several very good self study courses of interest to investors are worthy of mention here.

CEI FUTURES AND OPTIONS HOME STUDY COURSE (Commodities Educational Institute, 219 Parkade, Cedar Falls, IA 50613) is intended to train professionals and consists of some 21 audio tapes and two binders of notes and supplemental materials. The emphasis of this course is on commodity futures though some attention is given to financial futures and options on futures. Topics covered include the economic function of the futures market, how the futures market works, technical analysis, hedging, rules and regulations, financial futures, stock indexes, options on futures.

Purchasers of this course can attend 5 day work shops held in various cities at reduced rates.

FUTURES TRADING COURSE (Futures Industry Association, 2001 Pennsylvania Avenue, N.W., Washington, D.C. 20006) is comprised of three volumes which cover much of the same ground as the CEI course described above. The Institute also runs seminars and workshops for those wishing to acquire professional qualifications.

HOME STUDY COURSE OF THE AMERICAN ASSOCIATION OF INDIVIDUAL INVESTORS (AAII), (AAII, 625 North Michigan Avenue, Chicago, IL 60611) is an excellent course which provides coverage of the entire field of investments; stocks, bonds, mutual funds, futures, options, real estate, and more. Purchasers of this course receive updated material from time to time. The association also holds comprehensive national investment seminars on topics of current interest which are also available on audio tape. A recent seminar occupied some 25 tapes and is accompanied by a substantial set of notes.

FORBES STOCK MARKET COURSE (Forbes, Inc., 60 Fifth Avenue, New York, NY 10011) is somewhat more elementary than the AAII described above and focuses almost exclusively on the stock market. A small section of the course is devoted to options and warrants. The course should appeal to investors who want a readable basic survey of the equities market.

Employment

Future Employment Opportunities

Every 2 years, the Bureau of Labor Statistics develops projections of the labor force, economic growth, industry output and employment, and occupational employment under three sets of alternative assumptions—low, moderate, and high. These projections cover a 10- to 15-year period and provide a framework for the discussion of job outlook in each occupational statement in the *Handbook*. All of the approximately 250 statements in this edition of the *Handbook* identify the principal factors affecting job prospects, then discuss how these factors are expected to affect the occupation. This chapter uses the moderate alternative of each projection to provide a framework for the individual job outlook discussions.

Population Trends

Employment opportunities are affected by population trends in several ways. Changes in the size and composition of the population between 1992 and 2005 will influence the demand for goods and services. For example, the population aged 85 and over will grow about four times as fast as the total population, increasing the demand for health services. Population changes also produce corresponding changes in the size and characteristics of the labor force.

The U.S. civilian noninstitutional population, aged 16 and over, is expected to increase from about 192 to 219 million over the 1992–2005 period—growing more slowly than it did during the previous 13-year period, 1979–92. However, even slower population growth will increase the demand for goods and services, as well as the demand for workers in many occupations and industries.

The age distribution will shift toward relatively fewer children and teenagers and a growing proportion of middle-aged and older people into the 21st century. The decline in the proportion of teenagers reflects the lower birth rates that prevailed during the 1980's; the impending large increase in the middle-aged population reflects the aging of the "baby boom" generation born between 1946 and 1964; and the very rapid growth in the number of old people is attributable to high birth rates prior to the 1930's, together with improvements in medical technology that have allowed most Americans to live longer.

Minorities and immigrants will constitute a larger share of the U.S. population in 2005 than they do today. Substantial increases in the number of Hispanics, Asians, and Blacks are anticipated, reflecting immigration, and higher birth rates among Blacks and Hispanics. Substantial inflows of immigrants will continue to have significant implications for the labor force. Immigrants tend to be of working age but of different educational and occupational backgrounds than the U.S. population as a whole.

Population growth varies greatly among geographic regions, affecting the demand for goods and services and, in turn, workers in various occupations and industries. Between 1979 and 1992, the population of the Midwest and the Northeast grew by only 3 percent and 4 percent, respectively, compared with 19 percent in the South and 30 percent in the West. These differences reflect the movement of people seeking new jobs or retiring, as well as higher birth rates in some areas than in others.

Projections by the Bureau of the Census indicate that the West and South will continue to be the fastest growing regions, increasing 24 percent and 16 percent, respectively, between 1992 and 2005. The Midwest population is expected to grow by 7 percent, while the number of people in the Northeast is projected to increase by only 3 percent.

Geographic shifts in the population alter the demand for and the supply of workers in local job markets. Moreover, in areas dominated by one or two industries, local job markets may be extremely sensitive to the economic conditions of those industries. For these and other reasons, local employment opportunities may differ substantially from the projections for the Nation as a whole presented in the *Handbook*. Sources of information on State and local employment prospects are identified on page 606.

Labor Force Trends

Population is the single most important factor governing the size and composition of

Source: *Occupational Outlook Handbook* 1994–1995, U.S. Department of Labor, Bureau of Labor Statistics.

Chart 1

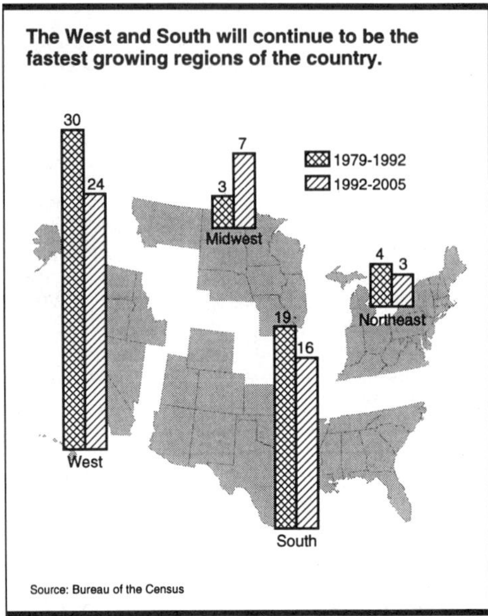

the labor force, which includes people who are working, or looking for work. The civilian labor force, 127 million in 1992, is expected to reach 151 million by 2005. This projected 19-percent increase represents a slight slowdown in the rate of labor force growth, largely due to slower population growth (chart 2).

America's workers will be an increasingly diverse group as we move toward 2005. White non-Hispanic men will make up a slightly smaller proportion of the labor force, and women and minority group members will comprise a larger share than in 1992. White non-Hispanics have historically been the largest component of the labor force, but their share has been dropping, and is expected to fall from 78 percent in 1992 to 73 percent by 2005. Whites are projected to grow more slowly than Blacks, Asians, and others, but because of their size, whites will experience the largest numerical increase. Hispanics will add about 6.5 million workers to the labor force from 1992 to 2005, increasing by 64 percent. Despite this dramatic growth, Hispanics' share of the labor force will only increase from 8 percent to 11 percent, as shown in chart 3. Blacks, Hispanics, and Asians and other racial groups will account for roughly 35 percent of all labor force entrants between 1992 and 2005.

Women will continue to join the labor force in growing numbers. The percentage increase of women in the labor force between 1992 and 2005 will be larger than the percentage increase in the total labor force, but smaller than the percentage increase for women in the previous 13-year period. In the late 1980's, the labor force participation of women under age 40 began to increase more slowly than in the past. Women were only 42 percent of the labor force in 1979;

Chart 2

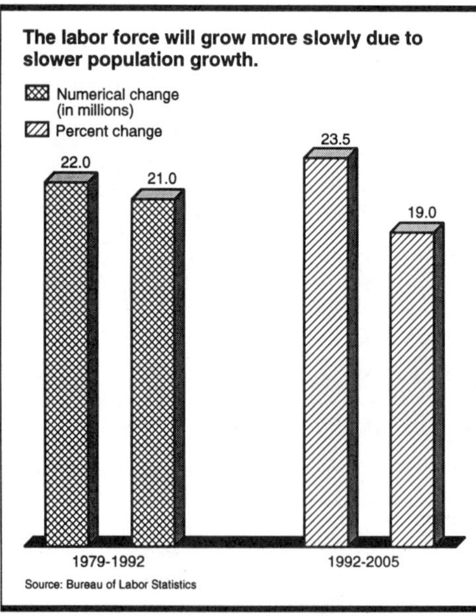

Chart 3

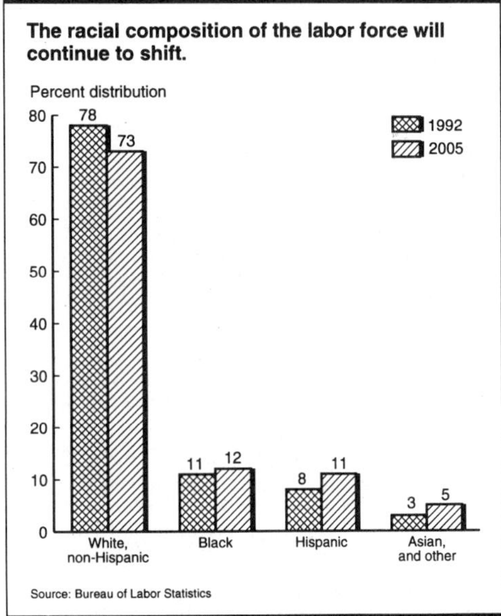

by 2005, they are expected to constitute 48 percent.

The changing age structure of the population will directly affect tomorrow's labor force. Compared to young workers, the pool of experienced workers will increase. In 1992, the median age of the labor force was 37.2 years; by 2005, it will be 40.5 years.

Between 1979 and 1992, the youth labor force (16 to 24 years of age) dropped by 5 million, a 20-percent decline. In contrast, the number of youths in the labor force will increase by 3.7 million over the 1992–2005 period, reflecting an increase of 18 percent, compared to 19 percent growth for the total labor force. As a result, young people are expected to comprise roughly the same percentage of the labor force in 2005 as in 1992. Among youths, the teenage labor force (16 to 19 years of age) will increase by 31 percent over the 1992–2005 period, a numerical increase of 2.1 million. The labor force 20 to 24 years of age is projected to increase by 12 percent, a numerical increase of 1.6 million. The total youth labor force accounted for 24 percent of the entire labor force in 1979, fell to 16 percent in 1992, and should stay about the same through 2005.

The scenario should be somewhat different for prime-age workers (25 to 54 years of age). The baby boom generation will continue to add members to the labor force, but their share of the labor force peaked in 1985. These workers accounted for 62 percent of the labor force in 1979, and rose significantly to 72 percent in 1992, but should decline slightly to 70 percent by 2005. The proportion of workers in the 25–34 age range will decline dramatically, from 28 percent to 21 percent in 2005. On the other hand, the growing proportion of workers between the ages of 45 and 54 is equally striking. These workers should account for 24 percent of the labor force by the year 2005, up from 18 percent in 1992. Because workers in their mid-forties to mid-fifties usually have substantial work experience and tend to be more stable than younger workers, this could result in improved productivity and a larger pool of experienced applicants from which employers may choose.

The number of older workers, aged 55 and above, is projected to grow about twice as fast as the total labor force between 1992 and 2005, and about 15 times as fast as the number of workers aged 55 and above grew between 1979 and 1992. As the baby boomers grow older, the number of workers aged 55 to 64 will increase; they exhibit higher labor force participation than their older counterparts. By 2005, workers aged 55 and over will comprise 14 percent of the labor force, up from 12 percent in 1992.

In recent years, the level of educational attainment of the labor force has risen dramatically. In 1992, 27 percent of all workers aged 25 and over had a bachelor's degree or higher, while only 12 percent did not possess a high school diploma. The trend toward higher educational attainment is expected to continue. Projected rates of employment growth are faster for occupations requiring higher levels of education or training than for those requiring less.

Three out of the 4 fastest growing occupational groups will be executive, administrative, and managerial; professional specialty; and technicians and related support occupations. These occupations generally require the highest levels of education and skill, and will make up an increasing proportion of new jobs. Office and factory automation, changes in consumer demand, and movement of production facilities to offshore locations are expected to cause employment to stagnate or decline in many occupations that require little formal education—apparel workers and textile machinery operators, for example. Opportunities for those who do not finish high school will be increasingly limited, and workers who are not literate may not even be considered for most jobs.

Those who do not complete high school and are employed are more likely to have low paying jobs with little advancement potential, while workers in occupations requiring higher levels of education have higher incomes. In addition, many of the occupations projected to grow most rapidly between 1992

Chart 4

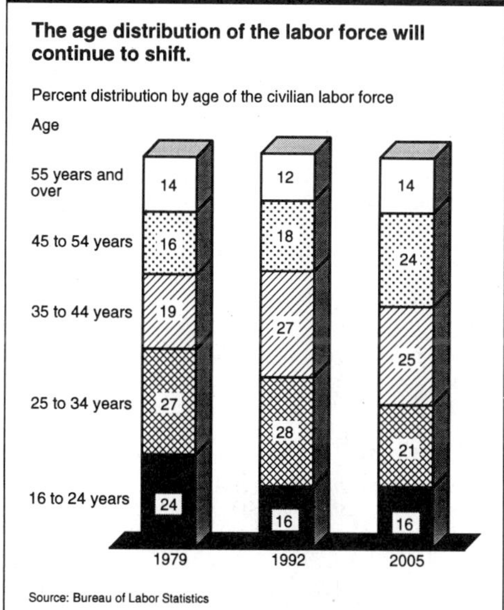

and 2005 are among those with higher earnings.

Nevertheless, even slower growing occupations that have a large number of workers will provide many job openings, because the need to replace workers who leave the labor force or transfer to other occupations account for most job openings. Consequently, workers with all levels of education and training will continue to be in demand, although advancement opportunities generally will be best for those with the most education and training.

Employment Change

Total employment is expected to increase from 121.1 million in 1992 to 147.5 million in 2005, or by 22 percent. The 26.4 million jobs that will be added to the U.S. economy by 2005 will not be evenly distributed across major industrial and occupational groups, causing some restructuring of employment. Continued faster than average employment growth among occupations that require relatively high levels of education or training is expected. The following two sections examine projected employment change from both industrial and occupational perspectives. The industrial profile is discussed in terms of wage and salary employment, except for agriculture, forestry, and fishing, which includes self-employed and unpaid family workers. The occupational profile is viewed in terms of total employment (wage and salary, self-employed, and unpaid family workers).

Industrial Profile

The long-term shift from goods-producing to service-producing employment is expected to continue (chart 5). For example, service-producing industries, including transportation, communications, and utilities; retail and wholesale trade; services; government; and finance, insurance, and real estate are expected to account for approximately 24.5 million of the 26.4 million job growth over the 1992–2005 period. In addition, the services division within this sector—which includes health, business, and educational services—contains 15 of the 20 fastest growing industries. Expansion of service sector employment is linked to a number of factors, including changes in consumer tastes and preferences, legal and regulatory changes, advances in science and technology, and changes in the way businesses are organized and managed. Specific factors responsible for

Chart 5

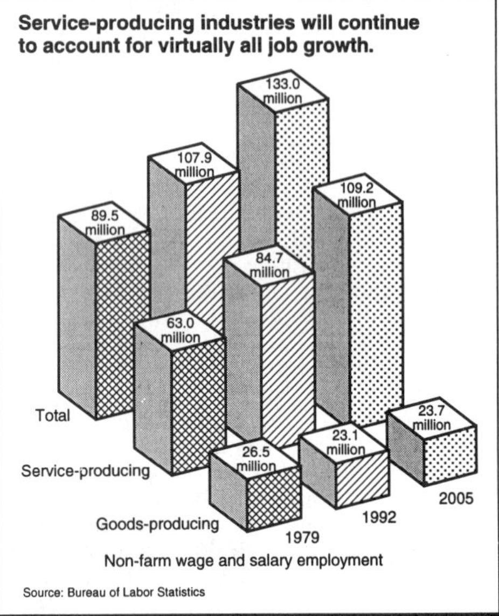

varying growth prospects in major industry divisions are discussed below.

Service-Producing Industries

Services. Services is both the largest and the fastest growing division within the service-producing sector (chart 6). This division provided 38.6 million jobs in 1992; employment is expected to rise 40 percent to 54.2 million by 2005, accounting for almost two-thirds of all new jobs. Jobs will be found in small firms and in large corporations, and in industries as diverse as hospitals, data processing, and management consulting. Health services and business services are projected to continue to grow very fast. In addition, social, legal, and engineering and management services industries further illustrate this division's strong growth.

Health services will continue to be one of the fastest growing industries in the economy with employment increasing from 9.6 to 13.8 million. Improvements in medical technology, and a growing and aging population will increase the demand for health services. Employment in home health care services—the second fastest growing industry in the economy—nursing homes, and offices and clinics of physicians and other health practitioners is projected to increase rapidly. However, not all health industries will grow at

Chart 6

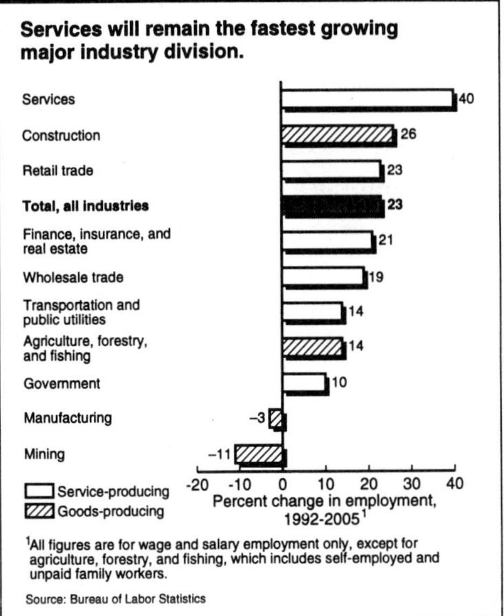

the same rate. Despite being the largest health care industry, hospitals will grow more slowly than most other health services industries.

Business services industries also will generate many jobs. Employment is expected to grow from 5.3 million in 1992 to 8.3 million in 2005. Personnel supply services, made up primarily of temporary help agencies, is the largest sector in this group and will increase by 57 percent, from 1.6 to 2.6 million jobs. However, due to the slow-down in labor force participation by young women, and the proliferation of personnel supply firms in recent years, this industry will grow more slowly than during the 1979–92 period. Business services also includes one of the fastest growing industries in the economy, computer and data processing services. This industry's rapid growth stems from advances in technology, world wide trends toward office and factory automation, and increases in demand from business firms, government agencies, and individuals.

Education is expected to add 2.8 million jobs to the 9.7 million in 1992. This increase reflects population growth and, in turn, rising enrollments projected for elementary, secondary, and postsecondary schools. The elementary school age population (ages 5–13) will rise by 2.8 million between 1992 and 2005, the secondary school age (14–17) by 3.4 million, and the traditional postsecondary school age (18–24) by 2.2 million. In addition, continued rising enrollments of older, foreign, and part-time students are expected to enhance employment in postsecondary education. Not all of the increase in employment in education, however, will be for teachers; teacher aides, counselors, and administrative staff also are projected to increase.

Employment in social services is expected to increase by 1.7 million, bringing the total to 3.7 million by 2005, reflecting the growing elderly population. For example, residential care institutions, which provide around-the-clock assistance to older persons and others who have limited ability for self-care, is projected to be the fastest growing industry in the U.S. economy. Other social services industries that are projected to grow rapidly include child daycare services and individual and miscellaneous social services, which includes elderly daycare and family social services.

Wholesale and retail trade. Employment in wholesale and retail trade is expected to rise by 19 and 23 percent, respectively; from 6 to 7.2 million in wholesale trade and from 19.3 to 23.8 million in retail trade. Spurred by higher levels of personal income, the fastest projected job growth in retail trade is in apparel and accessory stores, and appliance, radio, television, and music stores. Substantial numerical increases in retail employment are anticipated in large industries, including eating and drinking places, food stores, automotive dealers and service stations, and general merchandise stores.

Finance, insurance, and real estate. Employment is expected to increase by 21 percent—adding 1.4 million jobs to the 1992 level of 6.6 million. The strong demand for financial services is expected to continue. Bank mergers, consolidations, and closings—resulting from overexpansion and competition from nonbank corporations that offer bank-like services—are expected to limit job growth among commercial banks and savings and loan associations. The fastest growing industries within this sector are expected to be holding and investment offices and mortgage bankers and brokers. Insurance agents, brokers, and services is expected to register the largest numerical increase in jobs.

Transportation, communications, and public utilities. Overall employment will increase by 14 percent. Employment in the transportation sector is expected to increase by 24 percent, from 3.5 to 4.3 million jobs. Truck transportation will account for 50 percent of all new jobs; air transportation will account for 29 percent. The projected gains in transportation jobs reflect the continued shift from rail to road freight transportation, rising personal incomes, and growth in foreign trade. In addition, deregulation in the transportation industry has increased personal and business travel options, spurring strong job growth in the passenger transportation arrangement industry, which includes travel agencies. Reflecting laborsaving technology and industry competition, employment in communications is projected to decline by 12 percent. Employment in utilities, however, is expected to grow, adding 117,000 new jobs, highlighted by strong growth in water supply and sanitary services.

Government. Between 1992 and 2005, government employment, excluding public education and public hospitals, is expected to increase 10 percent, from 9.5 million to 10.5 million jobs. Growth will be driven by State and local government. Employment in the Federal Government and U.S. Postal Service is expected to decline by 113,000 and 41,000 jobs, respectively.

Goods-Producing Industries

Employment in this sector has not recovered from the recessionary period of the early 1980's and the trade imbalances that began in the mid-1980's. Although overall employment in goods-producing industries is expected to show little change, growth prospects within the sector vary considerably.

Construction. Construction is expected to increase by 26 percent from 4.5 to 5.6 million. The need to improve the Nation's infrastructure, resulting in increases in road, bridge, and tunnel construction, will offset the slowdown in demand for new housing, reflecting the slowdown in population growth and the overexpansion of office building construction in recent years.

Agriculture, forestry, and fishing. After declining for many decades, overall employment in agriculture, forestry, and fishing is projected to grow by 14 percent, from 1.7 million to 2 million jobs. Strong growth in agricultural services will more than offset an expected continued decline in crops, livestock and livestock products.

Manufacturing. Manufacturing employment is expected to decline by 3 percent from the 1992 level of 18 million. The projected loss of manufacturing jobs reflects productivity gains achieved from increased investment in manufacturing technologies.

The composition of manufacturing employment is expected to shift since most of the jobs that will disappear are production jobs. On the other hand, the number of professional positions in manufacturing firms will increase.

Mining. Mining employment is expected to decline 11 percent from 631,000 to 562,000. Underlying this projection is the assumption that domestic oil production will drop and oil imports will rise, reducing employment in the crude petroleum industry. In addition, employment in coal mining should continue to decline sharply due to the expanded use of laborsaving machinery.

Occupational Profile

Continued expansion of the service-producing sector conjures up an image of a work force dominated by cashiers, retail sales workers, and waiters. Although service sector growth will generate millions of these jobs, it also will create jobs for financial managers, engineers, nurses, electrical and electronics technicians, and many other managerial, professional, and technical workers. As indicated earlier, the fastest growing occupations will be those that require the most formal education and training.

This section furnishes an overview of projected employment in 12 categories or "clusters" of occupations based on the Standard Occupational Classification (SOC). The SOC is used by all Federal agencies that collect occupational employment data, and is the organizational framework for grouping statements in the *Handbook.*

In the discussion that follows, projected employment change is described as growing faster, slower, or the same as the average

Chart 7

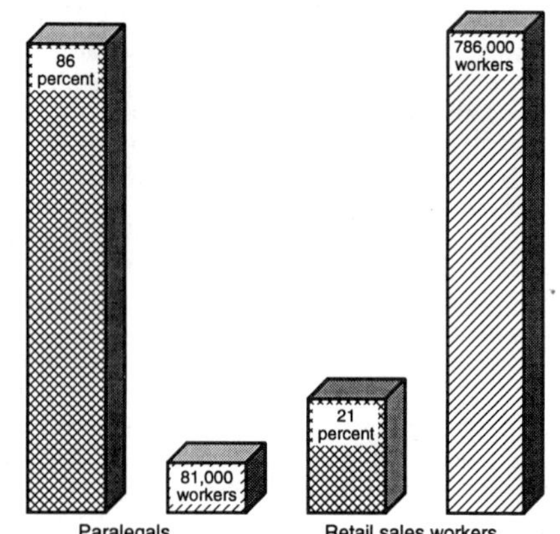

for all occupations. (These phrases are explained on page 605.) While occupations that are growing fast generally offer good opportunities, the numerical change in employment also is important because large occupations, such as retail sales workers, may offer many more new jobs than a small, fast-growing occupation, such as paralegals (chart 7). For a more detailed discussion of occupational growth, see the discussion of job outlook in the chapter, Keys to Understanding What's in the *Handbook*.

Professional specialty occupations. Workers in these occupations perform a wide variety of duties, and are employed in almost every industry. Employment in this cluster is expected to grow by 37 percent, from 16.6 to 22.8 million jobs, making it the fastest growing occupational cluster in the economy (chart 8). Human services workers, computer scientists and systems analysts, physical therapists, special education teachers, and operations research analysts are among the fastest growing professional specialty occupations.

Service occupations. This group includes a wide range of workers in protective services, food and beverage preparation, health services, and cleaning and personal services. Employment in these occupations is expected to grow by 33 percent, faster than average, from 19.4 to 25.8 million. Service occupations that are expected to experience both fast growth and large job growth include homemaker-home health aides, nursing aides, child care workers, guards, and correction officers.

Chart 8

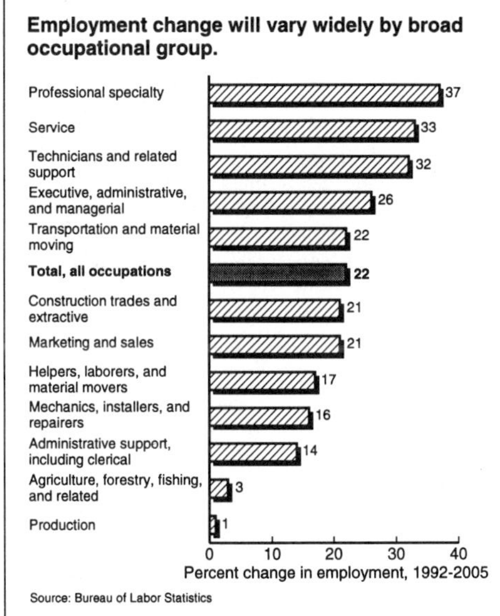

Technicians and related support occupations. Workers in this group provide technical assistance to engineers, scientists, physicians, and other professional workers, as well as operate and program technical equipment. Employment in this cluster is expected to increase 32 percent, faster than average, from 4.3 to 5.7 million. Employment of paralegals is expected to increase much faster than average as use of these workers in the rapidly expanding legal services industry increases. Health technicians and technologists, such as licensed practical nurses and radiological technologists, will add large numbers of jobs. Growth in other occupations, such as broadcast technicians, will be limited by laborsaving technological advances.

Executive, administrative, and managerial occupations. Workers in this cluster establish policies, make plans, determine staffing requirements, and direct the activities of businesses, government agencies, and other organizations. Employment in this cluster is expected to increase by 26 percent, from 12.1 to 15.2 million, reflecting average growth. Growth will be spurred by the increasing number and complexity of business operations and result in large employment gains, especially in the services industry division. However, many businesses will streamline operations by employing fewer managers, thus offsetting increases in employment.

Like other occupations, changes in managerial and administrative employment reflect industry growth, and utilization of managers and administrators. For example, employment of health services managers will grow much faster than average, while wholesale and retail buyers are expected to grow more slowly than average.

Hiring requirements in many managerial and administrative jobs are becoming more stringent. Work experience, specialized training, or graduate study will be increasingly necessary. Familiarity with computers will continue to be important as a growing number of firms rely on computerized management information systems.

Transportation and material moving occupations. Workers in this cluster operate the equipment used to move people and equipment. Employment in this group is expected to increase by 22 percent, from 4.7 to 5.7 million jobs. Average growth is expected for bus drivers, reflecting rising school enrollments. Similar growth is expected for truck drivers and railroad transportation workers due to growing demand for transportation services. Technological improvements and automation should result in material moving equipment operators increasing more slowly than the average. Water transportation workers are projected to show little change in employment as technological advances increase productivity.

Construction trades and extractive occupations. Workers in this group construct, alter, and maintain buildings and other structures, and operate drilling and mining equipment. Overall employment in this group is expected to increase 21 percent, about as fast as average, from 3.7 to 4.5 million. Virtually all of the new jobs will be in construction. Spurred by new projects and alterations to existing structures, average employment growth is expected in construction. On the other hand, increased automation, continued stagnation in the oil and gas industries, and slow growth in demand for coal, metal, and other materials will result in a decline in employment of extractive workers.

Marketing and sales occupations. Workers in this cluster sell goods and services, purchase commodities and property for resale, and stimulate consumer interest. Employment in this cluster is projected to increase by 21 percent, from 13 to 15.7 million jobs, about as fast as average. Demand for travel agents is expected to grow much faster than average. Due to strong growth in the industries that employ them, services sales representatives, securities and financial services sales workers, and real estate appraisers will experience faster than average growth. Many part- and full-time job openings are expected for retail sales workers and cashiers due to the large size and high turnover associated with these occupations. Opportunities for higher paying sales jobs, however, will tend to be more competitive.

Helpers, laborers, and material movers. Workers in this group assist skilled workers and perform routine, unskilled tasks. Overall employment is expected to increase by 17 percent, about as fast as average, from 4.5 to 5.2 million jobs. Some routine tasks will become increasingly automated, limiting employment growth among machine feeders and offbearers. Employment of service station attendants will decline, reflecting the trend toward self-service gas stations. Employment of construction laborers, however, is expected to increase about as fast as average, reflecting growth in the construction industry.

Mechanics, installers, and repairers. These workers adjust, maintain, and repair automobiles, industrial equipment, computers, and many other types of equipment. Overall employment in these occupations is expected to grow by 16 percent, from 4.8 to 5.6 million, due to increased use of mechanical and electronic equipment. The fastest growing occupation in this group is expected to be data processing equipment repairers, reflecting the increased use of these types of machines. Communications equipment mechanics, installers, and repairers, and telephone and cable television line installers and repairers, in sharp contrast, are expected to record a decline in employment due to labor-saving advances.

Administrative support occupations, including clerical. Workers in this largest major occupational group perform a wide variety of administrative tasks necessary to keep organizations functioning smoothly. The group as a whole is expected to grow by 14 percent, from 22.3 to 25.4 million jobs, about as fast as the average. Technological advances are projected to slow employment growth for stenographers and typists and word processors. Receptionists and information clerks will grow faster than average, spurred by rapidly expanding industries such as business services. Because of their large size and substantial turnover, clerical occupations will offer abundant opportunities for qualified jobseekers in the years ahead.

Agriculture, forestry, fishing, and related occupations. Workers in these occupations cultivate plants, breed and raise livestock, and catch animals. Although demand for food, fiber, and wood is expected to increase as the world's population grows, the use of more productive farming and forestry methods and the consolidation of smaller farms are expected to result in only a 3-percent increase in employment, from 3.5 to 3.6 million jobs. Employment of farm operators and farm workers is expected to rapidly decline, reflecting greater productivity; the need for skilled farm managers, on the other hand, should result in average employment growth in that occupation.

Production occupations. Workers in these occupations set up, install, adjust, operate, and tend machinery and equipment and use hand tools to fabricate and assemble products. Little change in the 1992 employment level of 12.2 million is expected due to increases in imports, overseas production, and automation. Relative to other occupations, employment in many production occupations is more sensitive to the business cycle and competition from imports.

Replacement Needs

Most jobs through the year 2005 will become available as a result of replacement needs. Thus, even occupations with little or no employment growth or slower than average employment growth still may offer many job openings.

Replacement openings occur as people leave occupations. Some transfer to other occupations as a step up the career ladder or change careers. Others stop working in order to return to school, assume household responsibilities, or retire.

The number of replacement openings and the proportion of job openings made up by replacement needs varies by occupation. Occupations with the most replacement openings generally are large, with low pay and status, low training requirements, and a high proportion of young and part-time workers. Occupations with relatively few replacement openings tend to be associated with high pay and status, lengthy training requirements, and a high proportion of prime working age, full-time workers. Workers in these occupations generally acquire education or training that often is not applicable to other occupations. For example, among professional specialty occupations, only 38 percent of total job opportunities result from replacement needs, as opposed to 78 percent among production occupations (chart 9).

Chart 9

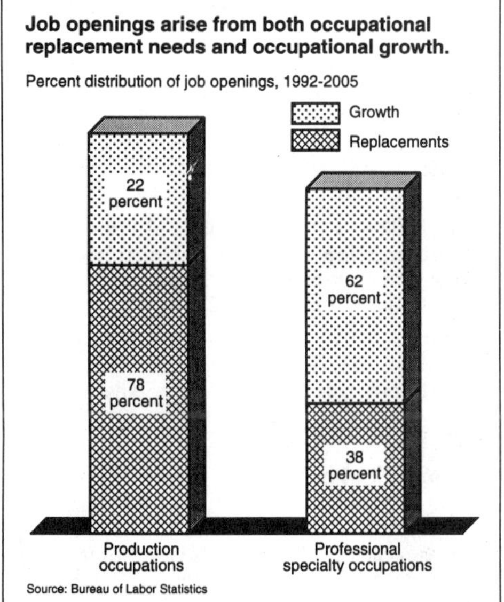

Interested in More Detail?

Readers interested in more information about projections and detail on the labor force, economic growth, industry and occupational employment, or methods and assumptions should consult the November 1993 *Monthly Labor Review* or *The American Work Force: 1992–2005*, BLS Bulletin 2452. Information on the limitations inherent in economic projections also can be found in either of these two publications. For additional occupational data, as well as statistics on educational and training completions, see the 1994 edition of *Occupational Projections and Training Data*, BLS Bulletin 2451.

Key Phrases in the *Handbook*

Changing employment between 1992 and 2005

If the statement reads . . .	Employment is projected to . . .
Grow much faster than the average	Increase 41 percent or more
Grow faster than the average	Increase 27 to 40 percent
Grow about as fast as the average	Increase 14 to 26 percent
Little change or grow more slowly than the average	Increase 0 to 13 percent
Decline	Decrease 1 percent or more

Opportunities and competition for jobs

If the statement reads . . .	Job openings compared to jobseekers may be . . .
Excellent opportunities	Much more numerous
Very good opportunities	More numerous
Good or favorable opportunities	About the same
May face competition	Fewer
May face keen competition	Much fewer

Where to Find State and Local Job Information

State and local job market and career information is available from State employment security agencies and State Occupational Information Coordinating Committees (SOICC's). State employment security agencies develop occupational employment projections and other job market information. SOICC's provide or help locate labor market and career information. The following list provides the title, address, and telephone number of State employment security agency directors of research and SOICC directors.

Alabama
Chief, Labor Market Information, Alabama Department of Industrial Relations, 649 Monroe St., Room 422, Montgomery, AL 36131. Phone: 205-242-8855.

Director, Alabama Occupational Information Coordinating Committee, Alabama Center for Commerce, Room 364, 401 Adams Ave., P.O. Box 5690, Montgomery, AL 36103-5690. Phone: 205-242-2990.

Alaska
Chief, Research and Analysis Section, Alaska Department of Labor, P.O. Box 25501, Juneau, AK 99802-5501. Phone: 907-465-4500.

Executive Director, Alaska Department of Labor, Research and Analysis Section, P.O. Box 25501, Juneau, AK 99802-5501. Phone: 907-465-4518.

American Samoa
Statistical Analyst, Research and Statistics, Office of Manpower Resources, American Samoa Government, Pago Pago, AS 96799. Phone: 684-633-5172.

Director, American Samoa State Occupational Information Coordinating Committee, Office of Manpower Resources, American Samoa Government, Pago Pago, AS 96799. Phone: 684-633-4485.

Arizona
Research Administrator, Arizona Department of Economic Security, P.O. Box 6123, Site Code 733A, Phoenix, AZ 85005-6123. Phone: 602-542-3871.

Executive Director, Arizona State Occupational Information Coordinating Committee, P.O. Box 6123, Site Code 897J, 1789 West Jefferson St., First Floor North, Phoenix, AZ 85005-6123. Phone: 602-542-6466.

Arkansas
Manager, Labor Market Information, Arkansas Employment Security Division, P.O. Box 2981, Little Rock, AR 72203-2981. Phone: 501-682-3198.

Executive Director, Arkansas Occupational Information Coordinating Committee, Arkansas Employment Security Division, Employment and Training Services, P.O. Box 2981, Little Rock, AR 72203. Phone: 501-682-3159.

California
Chief, Labor Market Information Division, Employment Development Department, P.O. Box 942880, MIC 57, Sacramento, CA 94280-0001. Phone: 916-427-4675.

Executive Director, California Occupational Information Coordinating Committee, 1116 9th St., Lower Level, P.O. Box 94244-2220, Sacramento, CA 95814. Phone: 916-323-6544.

Colorado
Director, Labor Market Information, Colorado Department of Labor and Employment, 393 S. Harlan St., 2nd Floor, Lakewood, CO 80226-3509. Phone: 303-937-4947.

Director, Colorado Occupational Information Coordinating Committee, State Board Community College, 1391 Speer Blvd., Suite 600, Denver, CO 80204-2554. Phone: 303-866-4488.

Connecticut
Director, Research and Information, Employment Security Division, 200 Folly Brook Blvd., Wethersfield, CT 06109. Phone: 203-566-2120.

Executive Director, Connecticut Occupational Information Coordinating Committee, Connecticut Department of Education, 25 Industrial Park Rd., Middletown, CT 06457. Phone: 203-638-4042.

Delaware
Chief, Office of Occupational and Labor Market Information, Delaware Department of Labor, P.O. Box 9029, Newark, DE 19702-9029. Phone: 302-368-6962.

Executive Director, Office of Occupational and Labor Market Information, Delaware Department of Labor, University Office Plaza, P.O. Box 9029, Newark, DE 19714-9029. Phone: 302-368-6963.

District of Columbia
Chief, Division of Labor Market Information, District of Columbia Department of Employment Services, 500 C St. NW., Room 201, Washington, DC 20001. Phone: 202-724-7213.

Executive Director, District of Columbia Occupational Information Coordinating Committee, Department of Employment Security

Services, 500 C St. NW., Room 215, Washington, DC 20001. Phone: 202-639-1090.

Florida

Chief, Bureau of Labor Market Information, Florida Department of Labor and Employment Security, 2012 Capitol Circle SE., Room 200, Tallahassee, FL 32399-2151. Phone: 904-488-1048.

Manager, Florida Department of Labor and Employment Security, Bureau of Labor Market Information, 2012 Capitol Circle SE., Hartman Bldg., Suite 200, Tallahassee, FL 32399-0673. Phone: 904-488-1048.

Georgia

Director, Labor Information Systems, Georgia Department of Labor, 148 International Blvd. NE., Atlanta, GA 30303. Phone: 404-656-3177.

Executive Director, Georgia Occupational Information Coordinating Committee, Department of Labor, 148 International Blvd., Sussex Place, Atlanta, GA 30303. Phone: 404-656-9639.

Guam

Administrator, Department of Labor, Bureau of Labor Statistics, Government of Guam, P.O. Box 9970, Tamuning, GU 96911-9970.

Executive Director, Guam State Occupational Information Coordinating Committee, Human Resource Development Agency, Jay Ease Bldg., Third Floor, P.O. Box 2817, Agana, GU 96910. Phone: 671-646-9341.

Hawaii

Chief, Research and Statistics Office, Department of Labor and Industrial Relations, P.O. Box 3680, Honolulu, HI 96813. Phone: 808-548-7639.

Executive Director, Hawaii State Occupational Information Coordinating Committee, 830 Punchbowl St., Room 315, Honolulu, HI 96813. Phone: 808-586-8750.

Idaho

Chief, Research and Analysis, Idaho Department of Employment, 317 Main St., Boise, ID 83735-0670. Phone: 208-334-6169.

Director, Idaho Occupational Information Coordinating Committee, Len B. Jordan Bldg., Room 301, 650 West State St., Boise, ID 83720. Phone: 208-334-3705.

Illinois

Director, Economic Information and Analysis, Illinois Department of Employment Security, 401 South State St., Room 215, Chicago, IL 60605. Phone: 312-793-2316.

Executive Director, Illinois Occupational Information Coordinating Committee, 217 East Monroe, Suite 203, Springfield, IL 62706. Phone: 217-785-0789.

Indiana

Program Manager, Labor Market Information, Indiana Workforce Development, 10 North Senate Ave., Indianapolis, IN 46204. Phone: 317-232-7460.

Executive Director, Indiana Occupational Information Coordinating Committee, 309 West Washington St., Room 309, Indianapolis, IN 46204. Phone: 317-232-8528.

Iowa

Supervisor, Audit and Analysis Department, Iowa Department of Employment Services, 1000 East Grand Ave., Des Moines, IA 50319-0209. Phone: 515-281-8181.

Acting Executive Director, Iowa Occupational Information Coordinating Committee, Iowa Department of Economic Development, 200 East Grand Ave., Des Moines, IA 50309. Phone: 515-242-4890.

Kansas

Chief, Labor Market Information Services, Kansas Department of Human Resources, 401 SW. Topeka Blvd., Topeka, KS 66603-3182. Phone: 913-296-5058.

Director, Kansas Occupational Information Coordinating Committee, 401 Topeka Ave., Topeka, KS 66603. Phone: 913-296-2387.

Kentucky

Branch Manager, Research and Statistics, Department for Employment Services, 275 East Main St., Frankfort, KY 40621. Phone: 502-564-7976.

Information Liaison/Manager, Kentucky Occupational Information Coordinating Committee, Workforce Development Cabinet, 500 Mero St., Capital Plaza Tower, Room 305, Frankfort, KY 40601. Phone: 502-564-4258.

Louisiana

Director, Research and Statistics Section, Louisiana State Department of Labor, P.O. Box 94094, Baton Rouge, LA 70804-4094. Phone: 504-342-3141.

Acting Director, Louisiana Occupational Information Coordinating Committee, P.O. Box 94094, Baton Rouge, LA 70804-9094. Phone: 504-342-5149.

Maine

Director, Division of Economic Analysis and Research, Maine Department of Labor, Bureau of Employment Security, 20 Union St., Augusta, ME 04330. Phone: 207-289-2271.

Acting Executive Director, Maine Occupational Information Coordinating Committee, State House Station 71, Augusta, ME 04333. Phone: 207-624-6200.

Maryland

Director, Office of Labor Market Analysis and Information, Economic and Employment Development, 1100 North Eutaw St., Room 601, Baltimore, MD 21201. Phone: 410-333-5000.

Director, Maryland State Occupational Information Coordinating Committee, State Department of Employment and Training, 1100 North Eutaw St., Room 205, Baltimore, MD 21201. Phone: 410-333-5478.

Massachusetts

Director of Research, Massachusetts Department of Employment and Training, 19 Staniford St., 2nd Floor, Boston, MA 02114. Phone: 617-727-6868.

Director, Massachusetts Occupational Information Coordinating Committee, Massachusetts Division of Employment Security, Charles F. Hurley Bldg., 2nd Floor, Government Center, Boston, MA 02114. Phone: 617-727-6718.

Michigan

Deputy Director, Financial and Management Services, Michigan Employment Security Commission, 7310 Woodward Ave., Detroit, MI 48202. Phone: 313-876-5904.

Executive Coordinator, Michigan Occupational Information Coordinating Committee, Victor Office Center, Third Floor, 201 North Washington Square, Box 30015, Lansing, MI 48909. Phone: 517-373-0363.

Minnesota

Director, Research and Statistics Office, Minnesota Department of Jobs and Training, 390 North Robert St., St. Paul, MN 55101. Phone: 612-296-6546.

Director, Minnesota Occupational Information Coordinating Committee, Department of Jobs and Training, 390 North Robert Street, St. Paul, MN 55101. Phone: 612-296-2072.

Mississippi

Chief, Labor Market Information Division, Mississippi Employment Security Commission, P.O. Box 1699, Jackson, MS 39215-1699. Phone: 601-961-7424.

Director, Mississippi Occupational Information Coordinating Committee Office, 301 West Pearl St., Jackson, MS 39203-3089. Phone: 601-949-2240.

Missouri

Chief, Research and Analysis, Missouri Division of Employment Security, P.O. Box 59, Jefferson City, MO 65104-0059. Phone: 314-751-3591.

Director, Missouri Occupational Information Coordinating Committee, 400 Dix Rd., Jefferson City, MO 65109. Phone: 314-751-3800.

Montana

Chief, Research and Analysis, Department of Labor and Industry, P.O. Box 1728, Helena, MT 59624-1728. Phone: 406-444-2430.

Program Manager, Montana Occupational Information Coordinating Committee, P.O. Box 1728, 1327 Lockey St., Second Floor, Helena, MT 59624. Phone: 406-444-2741.

Nebraska

Director, Labor Market Information, Nebraska Department of Labor, P.O. Box 94600, Lincoln, NE 68509-4600. Phone: 402-471-9964.

Administrator, Nebraska Occupational Information Coordinating Committee, P.O. Box 94600, State House Station, Lincoln, NE 68509-4600. Phone: 402-471-4845.

Nevada

Chief, Employment Security Research, Nevada Employment Security Department, 500 East Third St., Carson City, NV 89713. Phone: 702-687-4550.

Director, Nevada Occupational Information Coordinating Committee, 1923 North Carson St., Suite 211, Carson City, NV 89710. Phone: 702-687-4577.

New Hampshire

Director, Economic Analysis and Reports, New Hampshire Department of Employment Security, 32 South Main St., Concord, NH 03301-4587. Phone: 603-228-4123.

Director, New Hampshire State Occupational Information Coordinating Committee, 64B Old Suncook Rd., Concord, NH 03301. Phone: 603-228-3349.

New Jersey

Assistant Commissioner, Policy and Planning, New Jersey Department of Labor, Labor and Industry Bldg., P.O. Box CN056, Trenton, NJ 08625-0056. Phone: 609-292-2643.

Staff Director, New Jersey Occupational Information Coordinating Committee, 609 Labor and Industry Bldg., CN056, Trenton, NJ 08625-0056. Phone: 609-292-2682.

New Mexico

Chief, Economic Research and Analysis Bureau, Employment Security Department, P.O. Box 1928, Albuquerque, NM 87103. Phone: 505-841-8645.

Director, New Mexico Occupational Information Coordinating Committee, 401 Broadway NE., Tiwa Bldg., P.O. Box 1928, Albuquerque, NM 87103. Phone: 505-841-8455.

New York

Director, Division of Research and Statistics, New York State Department of Labor, State

Campus, Bldg. 12, Room 400, Albany, NY 12240-0020. Phone: 518-457-6181.

Executive Director, New York Occupational Information Coordinating Committee, Department of Labor, Research and Statistics Division, State Campus, Bldg. 12, Room 400, Albany, NY 12240. Phone: 518-457-6182.

North Carolina
Director, Labor Market Information Division, Employment Security Commission of North Carolina, P.O. Box 25903, Raleigh, NC 27611-5903. Phone: 919-733-2936.

Executive Director, North Carolina Occupational Information Coordinating Committee, 1311 Saint Mary's St., Suite 250, P.O. Box 27625, Raleigh, NC 27611. Phone: 919-733-6700.

North Dakota
Director, Research and Statistics, Job Service of North Dakota, P.O. Box 1537, Bismarck, ND 58502-1537. Phone: 701-224-2868.

Coordinator, North Dakota State Occupational Information Coordinating Committee, 1720 Burnt Boat Dr., P.O. Box 1537, Bismarck, ND 58502-1537. Phone: 701-224-2733.

Northern Mariana Islands
Executive Director, Northern Mariana Islands Occupational Information Coordinating Committee, P.O. Box 149, Room N-1, Building N, Northern Mariana College, Saipan, CM 96950. Phone: 670-234-1457.

Ohio
Director, Labor Market Information Division, Ohio Bureau of Employment Services, P.O. Box 1618, Columbus, OH 43215. Phone: 614-752-9494.

Director, Ohio Occupational Information Coordinating Committee, Division of Labor Market Information, Ohio Bureau of Employment Services, 1160 Dublin Rd., Bldg. A, Columbus, OH 43215. Phone: 614-752-6863.

Oklahoma
Director, Research and Planning Division, Oklahoma Employment Security Commission, 2401 North Lincoln, Room 310, Oklahoma City, OK 73105. Phone: 405-557-7116.

Executive Director, Oklahoma Occupational Information Coordinating Committee, Department of Voc/Tech Education, 1500 W. 7th Ave., Stillwater, OK 74074. Phone: 405-743-5198.

Oregon
Assistant Administrator, Research and Statistics, Employment Division, Oregon Department of Human Resources, 875 Union St. NE., Room 207, Salem, OR 97311-9986. Phone: 503-378-3220.

Acting Director, Oregon Occupational Information Coordinating Committee, 875 Union St. NE., Salem, OR 97311. Phone: 503-378-5490.

Pennsylvania
Director, Research and Statistics Division, Department of Labor and Industry, 1213 Labor and Industry Building, Harrisburg, PA 17121. Phone: 717-787-6466.

Director, Pennsylvania Occupational Information Coordinating Committee, Pennsylvania Department of Labor and Industry, 1224 Labor and Industry Bldg., Harrisburg, PA 17120. Phone: 717-787-8646.

Puerto Rico
Director of Bureau of Labor Statistics, Department of Labor and Human Resources, Research and Analysis Division, 505 Munoz Rivera Ave., 17th Floor, Hato Rey, PR 00918. Phone: 809-754-5332.

Director, Puerto Rico Occupational Information Coordinating Committee, 202 Del Cristo St., P.O. Box 366212, San Juan, PR 00936-6212. Phone: 809-723-7110.

Rhode Island
Supervisor, Labor Market Information and Management Services, Rhode Island Department of Employment, 107 Friendship St., Providence, RI 02903. Phone: 401-277-3704.

Director, Rhode Island Occupational Information Coordinating Committee, 22 Hayes St., Room 133, Providence, RI 02908. Phone: 401-272-0830.

South Carolina
Director, Labor Market Information Division, South Carolina Employment Security Commission, P.O. Box 995, Columbia, SC 29202-0995. Phone: 803-737-2660.

Director, South Carolina Occupational Information Coordinating Committee, 1550 Gadsden St., P.O. Box 995, Columbia, SC 29202. Phone: 803-737-2733.

South Dakota
Director, Labor Market Information Division, South Dakota Department of Labor, P.O. Box 4730, Aberdeen, SD 57402-4730. Phone: 605-622-2314.

Director, South Dakota Occupational Information Coordinating Committee, South Dakota Department of Labor, 420 South Roosevelt St., P.O. Box 4730, Aberdeen, SD 57402-4730. Phone: 605-622-2314.

Tennessee
Director, Research and Statistics Division, Tennessee Department of Employment Security, 500 James Robertson Pkwy., 11th Floor, Nashville, TN 37245-1000. Phone: 615-741-2284.

Executive Director, Tennessee Occupational Information Coordinating Committee, 500 James Robertson Pkwy., 11th Floor Volunteer Plaza, Nashville, TN 37219. Phone: 615-741-6451.

Texas
Chief, Economic Research and Analysis, Texas Employment Commission, 1117 Trinity St., Room 208-T, Austin, TX 78778. Phone: 512-463-2616.

Director, Texas Occupational Information Coordinating Committee, Texas Employment Commission Building, 3520 Executive Center Dr., Suite 205, Austin, TX 78731. Phone: 512-502-3750.

Utah
Director, Labor Market Information, Utah Department of Employment Security, P.O. Box 11249, Salt Lake City, UT 84147-1249. Phone: 801-536-7425.

Executive Director, Utah Occupational Information Coordinating Committee-c/o Utah Department of Employment Security, P.O. Box 11249, 140 East 300 South, Salt Lake City, UT 84147. Phone: 801-536-7806.

Vermont
Chief, Policy and Public Information, Vermont Department of Employment and Training, P.O. Box 488, Montpelier, VT 05602. Phone: 802-229-0311.

Director, Vermont Occupational Information Coordinating Committee, 5 Green Mountain Dr., P.O. Box 488, Montpelier, VT 05601-0488. Phone: 802-229-0311.

Virginia
Director, Economic Information Service, Virginia Employment Commission, P.O. Box 1358, Richmond, VA 23211. Phone: 804-786-7496.

Executive Director, Virginia Occupational Information Coordinating Committee, Virginia Employment Commission, 703 East Main St., P.O. Box 1358, Richmond, VA 23211. Phone: 804-786-7496.

Virgin Islands
Director, Virgin Islands Department of Labor, Bureau of Labor Statistics, Labor/Research and Analysis Division, P.O. Box 3359, St. Thomas, U.S. Virgin Islands 00801-3359. Phone: 809-776-3700.

Coordinator, Virgin Islands Occupational Information Coordinating Committee, P.O. Box 3359, St. Thomas, U.S. Virgin Islands 00801. Phone: 809-776-3700.

Washington
Director, Labor Market and Economic Analysis, Washington Employment Security Department, 605 Woodview Dr., SE, Lacey, WA 98503. Phone: 206-438-4800.

Acting Executive Director, Washington Occupational Information Coordinating Committee, c/o Employment Security Department, P.O. Box 9046, Olympia, WA 98507-9046. Phone: 206-438-4803.

West Virginia
Director, Labor and Economic Research Section, West Virginia Bureau of Employment Security, 112 California Ave., Charleston, WV 25305-0112. Phone: 304-348-2660.

Executive Director, West Virginia Occupational Information Coordinating Committee, One Dunbar Plaza, Suite E, Dunbar, WV 25064. Phone: 304-293-5314.

Wisconsin
Director, Bureau of Workforce Policy and Information, Department of Industry, Labor, and Human Relations, P.O. Box 7944, Madison, WI 53707-7944. Phone: 608-266-5843.

Administrative Director, Wisconsin Occupational Information Coordinating Council, Division of Employment and Training Policy, 201 East Washington Ave., P.O. Box 7972, Madison, WI 53707. Phone: 608-266-8012.

Wyoming
Manager, Research and Planning, Employment Security Commission, P.O. Box 2760, Casper, WY 82602-2760. Phone: 307-265-6715.

Executive Director, Wyoming Occupational Information Coordinating Council, Post Office Box 2760, 100 West Midwest, Casper, WY 82602. Phone: 307-265-7017.

U.S. Demographics

Highlights from the Bureau of the Census Middle Series

Population Size and Growth

- In the middle series, the population is projected to reach 276 million by 2000—a growth of 26.9 million or 10.8 percent since 1990. Only during the 1950's were more people added to the Nation's population than are projected to be added during the 1990's.
- The population may top 300 million by 2010. By the middle of the next century, the population may increase to 392 million—more than a 50 percent increase from the 1990 population.
- Despite these large increases in the number of persons in the population, the rate of population growth is projected to decrease during the next six decades by about 50 percent. From 2030 to 2050, the U.S. would grow more slowly than ever before in its history.

Age Distribution

- The age group under 18 may increase about 6 million by the turn of the century, then grow another 20 million by 2050. Even so, this age group's proportion of the total population may never again be as large as it is today.
- During the next decade, the largest growing age group is the 45 to 54 year olds, increasing 44 percent from 1990 to 2000.
- During the next two decades, the rate of population growth of the elderly population (aged 65 and over) is projected to be slower than at any time during this century.
- The most rapidly growing age group would be the 85 and over age group, doubling in size from 1990 to the year 2020, and increasing sixfold by the year 2050.

Source: Excerpted from *Population Projections of the United States, by Age, Sex, and Race, and Hispanic Origin, 1993 to 2050* by Jennifer Cheeseman Day, U.S. Bureau of the Census, Current Population Reports, Series P25–1104. The tables in this section are from the same source.

Race and Hispanic-Origin Distribution

- The race and Hispanic-origin distribution of the U.S. population is projected to change. A combination of three factors contributes to this shift: differential fertility, net immigration, and age distribution among the race and Hispanic-origin groups.
- Although three-quarters of the population was non-Hispanic White in 1990, this group would contribute only 35 percent of the total population growth during this decade. After 2030, the non-Hispanic White population would contribute nothing to the nation's population growth because it would be declining in size.
- The non-Hispanic White share of the U.S. population would steadily fall from 76 percent in 1990 to 72 percent in 2000, 60 percent in 2030, and 53 percent in 2050.
- By the middle of the next century, the Black population would double its 1990 size to 62 million. After 2012, more Blacks than non-Hispanic Whites would be added to the population each year.
- The fastest-growing race/ethnic group (with the highest rate of increase) would be the Asian and Pacific Islander population with annual growth rates that may exceed 4 percent during the 1990's.
- The race/ethnic group adding the largest number of people to the population would be the Hispanic-origin population. In fact, after 1996 the Hispanic population is projected to add more people to the United States every year than would any other race or origin group. By 2010, the Hispanic-origin population may become the second-largest race/ethnic group.
- By the year 2030, the non-Hispanic White population would be less than half of the U.S. population under age 18. In that year, this group would still comprise three-quarters of the 65 and over population.

Components of Change

- Between 1993 and 2050, the aging of the population would cause the annual total number of deaths to increase by about 85 percent, from 2.2 million in 1993 to 4.1

million in 2050. Most of the deaths would occur to the non-Hispanic White population.

- The number of births in the United States is projected to decrease slightly as the century ends, and then increase progressively throughout the projection period. After 2011 the number of births each year would exceed the highest annual number of births ever achieved in the United States during the 20th century.
- In 1995, about 63 percent of all births would be non-Hispanic White, about 1 in 6 would be Black, and 1 in 6 would be of Hispanic origin. By the middle of the 21st century, less than one-half of all births would be non-Hispanic White, 1 in 3 would be Hispanic, 1 in 5 would be Black, and 1 in 10 would be Asian and Pacific Islander.
- The middle series assumes that every year 2 of every 3 people added to the population through net immigration would be Hispanic or Asian, 1 in 5 would be non-Hispanic White, and 1 in 10 would be Black.
- In 1993, almost one-third of the population growth would be caused by net immigration. By 2000, the nation's population is projected to be 7.8 million (2.9 percent) larger than it would have been if there had been no net immigration after July 1, 1992.

Population, by Race and Hispanic Origin: 1990 to 2050

(As of July 1. Resident population)

Year	Total	Race				Hispanic Origin[3]	Not of Hispanic origin, by race			
		White	Black	American Indian[1]	Asian[2]		White	Black	American Indian[1]	Asian[2]
ESTIMATE										
1990	249,415	209,150	30,620	2,075	7,570	22,554	188,559	29,400	1,806	7,096
PROJECTIONS										
Lowest Series										
2050	285,502	214,054	42,026	3,323	26,099	57,643	161,382	38,933	2,807	24,738
Middle Series										
1995	263,434	218,334	33,117	2,226	9,756	26,798	193,900	31,648	1,927	9,161
2000	276,241	226,267	35,469	2,380	12,125	31,166	197,872	33,741	2,055	11,407
2005	288,286	233,343	37,793	2,543	14,608	35,702	200,842	35,793	2,190	13,759
2010	300,431	240,297	40,224	2,719	17,191	40,525	203,441	37,930	2,336	16,199
2020	325,942	254,791	45,409	3,090	22,653	51,217	208,280	42,459	2,641	21,345
2030	349,993	267,457	50,596	3,473	28,467	62,810	210,480	46,934	2,960	26,810
2040	371,505	277,232	55,917	3,894	34,461	75,130	209,148	51,489	3,314	32,424
2050	392,031	285,591	61,586	4,346	40,508	88,071	205,849	56,346	3,701	38,064
Highest Series										
2050	522,098	378,408	79,722	5,039	58,930	128,255	262,855	71,675	4,221	55,093

[1]American Indian represents American Indian, Eskimo, and Aleut.
[2]Asian represents Asian and Pacific Islander.
[3]Persons of Hispanic origin may be of any race.

Percent Distribution of the Population, by Race and Hispanic Origin

(As of July 1. Resident population)

Series and year	Race					Hispanic origin[3]	Not of Hispanic origin, by race			
	Total	White	Black	American Indian[1]	Asian[2]		White	Black	American Indian	Asian
ESTIMATE										
1990	100.0	83.9	12.3	0.8	3.0	9.0	75.7	11.8	0.7	2.8
PROJECTIONS										
Lowest Series										
2050	100.0	75.0	14.7	1.2	9.1	20.2	56.5	13.6	1.0	8.7
Middle Series										
1995	100.0	82.9	12.6	0.8	3.7	10.2	73.6	12.0	0.7	3.5
2000	100.0	81.9	12.8	0.9	4.4	11.3	71.6	12.2	0.7	4.1
2005	100.0	80.9	13.1	0.9	5.1	12.4	69.7	12.4	0.8	4.8
2010	100.0	80.0	13.4	0.9	5.7	13.5	67.7	12.6	0.8	5.4
2020	100.0	78.2	13.9	0.9	7.0	15.7	63.9	13.0	0.8	6.5
2030	100.0	76.4	14.5	1.0	8.1	17.9	60.1	13.4	0.8	7.7
2040	100.0	74.6	15.1	1.0	9.3	20.2	56.3	13.9	0.9	8.7
2050	100.0	72.8	15.7	1.1	10.3	22.5	52.5	14.4	0.9	9.7
Highest Series										
2050	100.0	72.4	15.3	1.0	11.3	24.6	50.3	13.7	0.8	10.6

[1]American Indian represents American Indian, Eskimo, and Aleut.
[2]Asian represents Asian and Pacific Islander.
[3]Persons of Hispanic origin may be of any race.

Women in Business: Information Sources

Not only are women starting businesses at twice the rate of men but women owned businesses are also growing in diversity. If the present trend continues, almost 40% of small businesses will be owned by women by the year 2000. As the number of women entrepreneurs continues to increase so does the amount of business related information targeted to them. The following is a selected list of information sources that should prove helpful.

OFFICE OF WOMEN'S BUSINESS OWNERSHIP (OWBO)
SMALL BUSINESS ADMINISTRATION (SBA)
409 Third Street SE
Washington, DC 20416
OWBO Tel: 202-205-6673
TDD: 202-205-7333
Fax: 202-205-7064

The Office of Women's Business Ownership (OWBO) offers both current and potential women business owners access to a variety of services and resources. These include prebusiness workshops, technical, financial and management information and training conferences on exporting, access to capital, and selling to the Federal Government (see below).

Each SBA office has a women's representative who can explain the resources that are available and provide guidance on how to access them. The regional coordinator for your area will direct you to your local representative. The coordinator's telephone numbers are given below:

ME, VT, MA, NH, CT, RI	617-565-8695
NY, NJ, PR, VI	716-263-6700
PA, DE, MD, VA, DC, WV	215-897-5406
NC, SC, KY, TN, GA, AL, MS, FL	404-347-2386
MN, WI, MI, OH, IN, IL	312-353-5000 Ext. 764
NM, TX, OK, AR, LA	214-767-7858
KS, MO, IA, NE	816-426-5311
MT, ND, SD, WY, UT, CO	303-294-7067
CA, NV, AZ, HI	415-744-8491
WA, OR, ID, AK	206-553-8547

The following are a number of OWBO sponsored programs.

Access to Capital

OWBO sponsors "Access to Capital" conferences throughout the country and markets the SBA guaranteed loan programs including the Small Loan Incentive, which targets small businesses searching for $50,000 or less; and has developed a directory.

Alternative Financing Sources is available to women business owners seeking new sources of capital. To obtain a copy call 202-205-6673.

For businesses needing smaller amounts of capital, the SBA has the Microloan Program that emphasizes small loans up to a maximum of $25,000. This program is not yet available in every state.

Women's Network for Entrepreneurial Training

A national mentoring program, the Women's Network for Entrepreneurial Training (WNET), is available in all 50 states. This program links established women business owners with entrepreneurs whose businesses are ready to grow. Through the year-long, one-on-one mentor relationship, successful women entrepreneurs pass on knowledge, skills, information, inspiration and support.

Demonstration Project Program for Women Business Owners

Currently there are 20 Demonstration Centers established by the SBA and private companies to provide long-term training and counseling for women interested in either starting or expanding a small business. These Centers provide one to one, woman-to-woman counseling on all aspects of business and include for example, legal, marketing, accounting, and budgeting information. These non-profit Centers charge only a nominal charge for their services.

To locate the Demonstration Center nearest your area call 202-205-6673.

Selling to the Federal Government

OWBO sponsors conferences to train women on how to do business with the federal government and encourages women business owners to register on the Procurement Automated Source System (PASS), Telephone: 202-205-6469, which lists potential small business suppliers for federal agencies and prime contractors. OWBO also refers women business owners to SBA procurement personnel who can assist them in the procedures of selling to the federal government.

OWBO negotiates women-owned procurement goals with each federal department and agency, encouraging procurement officials to seek out women-owned firms to provide the goods and services they need.

Opportunities in the Global Marketplace

Together with SBA's Office of International Trade, OWBO offers training and resources for women entrepreneurs considering expanding their businesses beyond domestic borders.

To prepare women entrepreneurs for the global marketplace, OWBO hosts training conferences, "Women Going International," around the country. Topics include export financing, legal considerations, strategic marketing and a focus on service related businesses.

Small Business Development Centers (SBDCs)

SBDCs are sponsored by SBA in partnership with state and local governments, the educational community and the private sector. They provide high-quality, low-cost assistance, counseling and training to prospective and existing small business owners. To locate the lead SBDC nearest you see page 243.

SERVICE CORPS OF RETIRED EXECUTIVES (SCORE)
409 Third Street SW
Washington, DC 20024

This organization of volunteers provides counseling to small business people. Volunteers include former or active accountants, business owners, corporation executives and lawyers. To obtain the name of the National SCORE Women's Business Ownership Coordinators nearest you call the National Volunteer Director at 410-266-8746.

STATE SPONSORED WOMEN ASSISTANCE PROGRAMS

Many states have specific programs geared for women-owned businesses. To locate the nearest office call your state's Department of Economic Development, listed in the State Information Guide on page 682.

SELECTED ASSOCIATIONS FOR BUSINESS WOMEN

NATIONAL ASSOCIATION FOR FEMALE EXECUTIVES, INC. (NAFE)
30 Irving Place
New York, NY 10003
Telephone: 212-477-2200

The National Association for Female Executives, Inc. (NAFE) is the largest businesswomen's organization in the United States. It is a professional association dedicated to the advancement of women in the workplace through education, networking and public advocacy. NAFE functions to support women in business and to help them succeed in achieving their career goals and financial independence.

Among the benefits of membership are a venture capital fund to assist entrepreneurial members; satellite conferences, seminar programs and special events to encourage education and networking; *Executive Female* magazine; low-interest unsecured loan programs, credit card, group health and auto insurance, resume service and "How-To" career guides; flat-fee debt collection service; restaurant discounts plus many other discount services for your business. Membership is $29 per year.

AMERICAN WOMEN'S ECONOMIC DEVELOPMENT CORPORATION (AWED)
71 Vanderbilt Avenue
New York, NY 10169
Telephone: 212-688-1900
Fax: 212-692-9296

The American Women's Economic Development Corporation (AWED) is a non-profit organization providing entrepreneurial women with management training and business counseling. Some of the courses offered by AWED are: Starting Your Own Business, Managing Your Own Business, Finance, as well as Chief Executive Roundtables and a Business Development Roundtable. Admission to AWED training programs is based on an application and a personal interview. Modest fees are charged for the above.

ADDITIONAL ASSOCIATIONS

AMERICAN ASSOCIATION OF UNIVERSITY WOMEN
1111 16th Street, NW
Washington, DC 20036
Telephone: 202-785-7700

AMERICAN BUSINESS WOMEN'S ASSOCIATION
9100 Ward Parkway
P.O. Box 8728
Kansas City, MO 64114
Telephone: 816-361-6621

AMERICAN WOMEN'S SOCIETY OF CERTIFIED PUBLIC ACCOUNTANTS
401 N. Michigan Avenue
Chicago, IL 60611
Telephone: 312-644-6610

BUSINESS AND PROFESSIONAL WOMEN/USA
2012 Massachusetts Avenue, NW
Washington, DC 20036
Telephone: 202-293-1100

ASSOCIATION OF BLACK WOMEN ENTREPRENEURS, INC.
1301 N. Kenter Avenue
Los Angeles, CA 90049
Telephone: 310-472-4927

FEDERALLY EMPLOYED WOMEN
1400 Eye Street, NW
Washington, DC 20005
Telephone: 202-898-0994

FEDERATION OF ORGANIZATIONS FOR PROFESSIONAL WOMEN
2001 S Street, NW
Washington, DC 20009
Telephone: 202-328-1415

FINANCIAL WOMEN INTERNATIONAL
Bethesda, MD 20814-3015
Telephone: 301-657-8288
Fax: 301-913-0001

HISPANIC WOMEN'S COUNCIL
5803 East Beverly Boulevard
Los Angeles, CA 90022
Telephone: 213-725-1657

LATIN BUSINESS & PROFESSIONAL WOMEN
P.O. Box 45-0913
Miami, FL 33245-0913
Telephone: 305-446-9222

NATIONAL ASSOCIATION FOR THE COTTAGE INDUSTRY
P.O. Box 14850
Chicago, IL 60616
Telephone: 312-871-4900

NATIONAL ASSOCIATION OF DEMONSTRATING COMPANIES
P.O. Box 1476
Buzzards Bay, MA 02532
Telephone: 508-564-5918

NATIONAL ASSOCIATION OF INVESTMENT COMPANIES
1111 14th Street, NW
Washington, DC 20005
Telephone: 202-289-4336

NATIONAL ASSOCIATION OF MINORITY WOMEN IN BUSINESS
906 Grand Avenue
Kansas City, MO 64106
Telephone: 816-421-3335
Fax: 816-421-3336

NATIONAL ASSOCIATION OF SMALL BUSINESS INVESTMENT COMPANIES
1199 N. Fairfax Street
Washington, DC 20005
Telephone: 703-683-1601

NATIONAL ASSOCIATION OF WOMEN BUSINESS ADVOCATES
Women's Business Resource Program
Ohio Department of Development
77 South High Street
Columbus, OH 43215
Telephone: 614-466-4945

NATIONAL ASSOCIATION OF WOMEN BUSINESS OWNERS
710 44th Street
Chevy Chase, MD 20815
Telephone: 301-951-9411

NATIONAL FEDERATION OF BUSINESS & PROFESSIONAL WOMEN CLUBS
2012 Massachusetts Avenue, NW
Washington, DC 20036
Telephone: 202-293-1100

NATIONAL FOUNDATION FOR WOMEN BUSINESS OWNERS
1377 K Street, NW
Washington, DC 20005
Telephone: 301-495-4975

NATIONAL WOMEN'S ECONOMIC ALLIANCE FOUNDATION
1440 New York Avenue
Washington, DC 20005
Telephone: 202-393-5257

NATIONAL WOMEN'S POLITICAL CAUCUS
1275 K Street, NW
Washington, DC 20005
Telephone: 202-898-1100

9 TO 5: NATIONAL ASSOCIATION OF WORKING WOMEN
614 Superior, NW
Cleveland, OH 44113
Telephone: 216-566-9308

ORGANIZATION OF CHINESE AMERICAN WOMEN
1439 Rhode Island Avenue
Washington, DC 20005
Telephone: 202-638-0330

WOMEN'S BUSINESS DEVELOPMENT CORPORATION
P.O. Box 658
Bangor, ME 04402-0658
Telephone: 207-623-0065

WOMEN'S WORLD BANKING
8 West 40th Street
New York, NY 10018
Telephone: 212-768-8513

WOMEN EXECUTIVES IN STATE GOVERNMENT
122 C Street, NW
Washington, DC 20001
Telephone: 202-628-9374

WOMEN IN FRANCHISING
53 West Jackson Boulevard
Chicago, IL 60604
Telephone: 312-431-1467

SOCIETY OF WOMEN ENGINEERS
345 East 47th Street
New York, NY 10017
Telephone: 212-705-7855

PUBLICATIONS:

A list of SBA publications and video tapes for starting and managing a small business is available from your local SBA office or by writing: Small Business Directory, P.O. Box 1000, Ft. Worth, TX 76119.

An SBA publication *Women Business Owners: Selling to the Federal Government* is designed to help women business owners by providing them with information about marketing their goods and services to the federal government. Available from your local U.S. Government Bookstore or by mail or telephone from the Superintendent of Documents in Washington, D.C. Telephone: 202-783-3238.

For Women: Managing Your Own Business includes material on business planning, marketing, personnel management, insurance and much more. Available from the Office of Women's Business Ownership by calling 202-205-6673 or the Superintendent of Documents at 202-783-3238.

The Women's Bureau of the U.S. Department of Labor publishes a variety of material for women business owners, including:

A Working Woman's Guide To Her Job Rights
Directory of Non Traditional Training and Employment Programs Serving Women
Alternative Work Patterns
State Maternity/Parental Leave Laws
Women Business Owners
Women in Labor Unions

Single copies of publications are available free of charge from the Department of Labor, 200 Constitution Avenue, NW Washington, DC 20210, Telephone: 202-219-6611.

The *Encyclopedia of Women's Associations Worldwide*, edited by L. R. Greenfield, contains thousands of organizations throughout the world concerning women and women's issues. Among the information included are the purpose of the organization, languages of correspondence, publications, conventions, and meetings. Entries are arranged by subject and organized alphabetically. Published by Gale Research Co., 835 Penobscot Building, Detroit, MI 48226.

Women and Credit Histories is available from the Federal Trade Commission (FTC). Telephone: 202-326-2222. This free pamphlet tells you how to establish credit and what to do if you feel you have been unfairly denied credit. Also includes an explanation of your legal credit rights as well as information on how to establish credit.

Entrepreneurial Woman, published by *Entrepreneur Magazine*, contains information appropriate to its title. Address: 2392 Morse Avenue, Irvine, CA 92714-6234. Telephone: 714-261-2325.

Executive Female is the official bimonthly publication of the National Association for Female Executives (NAFE). Issues contain articles on a variety of subjects such as career strategies, the best solutions to management problems, tips from successful entrepreneurs on starting and growing a business, better ways to manage money, your staff, and your company. Membership in NAFE includes a subscription to *Executive Female*. Contact NAFE at 212-477-2200.

50/50 By 2000: *The Woman's Guide to Political Power* is available from NAFE. Covers such topics as women in politics, and women's issues. Contact NAFE at 212-477-2200.

SELECTED PUBLICATIONS ON FINANCING

In addition to the generally known publications, the following are some lesser known publications which should be of interest to the business woman.

Alternative Financing, prepared by the Office of Women's Business Ownership, contains a listing and description of Federal small business funding sources, organizations active in development finance, as well as a list of loans that are only available in specific states. To obtain a free copy call 202-205-6673.

The State and Small Business, produced by the Office of Advocacy of the Small Business Administration, includes information on sources of financing, state legislation that affects business, and much more. Available through the Superintendent of Documents at 202-783-3238.

Steps to Small Business Financing is an informative booklet developed through a joint project with the American Banker's Association and the National Federation of Independent Business. Available from the American Banker's Association at 202-663-5456.

Investing in Gold and Diamonds

Investing in Gold

Gold has been one of the more widely promoted investment vehicles over the last several years. Prices moved from about $140 per ounce in early 1977 to over $800 in early 1980. However, by August 1985 prices declined to $291 an ounce but climbed to over $380.00 by May 1993. Because of such large fluctuations, the metal has stimulated a great deal of speculative interest among many investors.

Investment in gold can be made in a variety of ways:

Gold bullion (bars and wafers) This can be purchased through many stock brokers, bullion currency dealers, and some investment (mutual fund) companies. The purity of gold is indicated by the fineness. Pure gold has a fineness of 1.000 and corresponds to 24 karats.* Each bar is stamped with the fineness as determined by an assay, the refiner's number, a bar identification number and the weight. A bar fineness of .995 or better is acceptable.

Individuals who accept delivery of gold bars and who subsequently wish to resell must have the bar reassayed prior to sale because of the possibility of adulteration with cheaper metals. Because of the latter possibility, individuals should always buy from reputable dealers, and the bar should bear the stamp of well recognized refiners or assayers. Individuals taking physical possession of the metal also have sales taxes, storage, and insurance costs.

The purchaser may arrange to have the dealer (or agent) retain physical possession of the bullion. In this case, evidence of ownership is provided by a *gold deposit certificate* (receipt) issued by the dealer. Since gold certificates are generally non-negotiable or assignable, there is no loss if it is stolen. The gold deposit certificate method of buying bullion eliminates sales taxes, storage risks (though the dealer will charge a modest storage fee) and the need for assay on resale. It is probably the most convenient way of purchasing gold.

Gold bullion coins Bullion coins are issued in large number by several governments which guarantee their gold content. They have no numismatic value. The best known gold bullion coins are the U.S. Gold One Ounce, South African Krugerrand, Canadian Maple Leaf, Austrian 100 Corona and the Gold Mexican 50 peso. The first three coins have a pure gold content of one ounce. The Austrian Corona has a gold content of .9802 ounce and the Mexican peso 1.2057 ounces. The premium (cost above the gold value) varies from dealer to dealer. For those who do not want to take physical possession, deposit certificates are available for the coins.

One of the largest bullion dealers is Gold Line International (800-289-3325) headquartered in Santa Monica, California. Gold coins can also be purchased at banks where there is generally a very low premium over the gold content value.

Gold stocks The stocks of a number of Canadian and U.S. gold mining companies are traded on the New York (N), American (A) and Over-The-Counter (O) exchanges. Of course, with stocks, the investor is not just buying into gold, but also into the many special problems associated with running a company—production costs, quality of the ore, lifetime of the deposit, etc. However, many gold stocks pay dividends, whereas other gold investments do not pay any return during the holding period.

South African gold mines are traded on the Over-The-Counter Market by means of ADR (American Depository Receipt). ADR is a claim on foreign stocks (South African gold shares, in this case) held by the foreign branches of large U.S. banks. Holders of ADRs are entitled to dividends which, in the case of South African gold shares, may be substantial. The ADRs of these companies are listed in *The Wall Street Journal.*

Mutual funds specializing in gold and precious metals A number of mutual funds specializing in gold and precious metals stocks provide diversification among a number of issues thereby reducing risk associated with any particular stock.

Options on gold stocks Put and call options are available on Homestake Mining (Chicago Options Exchange) and on ASA Limited (American Options Exchange). These options may be used for leveraged speculation or for hedging existing gold

* This "karats" is not to be confused with the "carats" that apply to diamonds.

holdings. Holders of call options gain if the gold shares increase, while holders of put options benefit if prices decline.

The Philadelphia Stock Exchange trades a gold/silver option based on an index of seven different stocks in the industry.

Options on gold bullion Put and call options on gold bullion are traded on the International Options Market (IOM) of the Montreal Stock Exchange. IOM options are on 10 ounces of gold. Contract months are Feb/May/Aug/Nov.

Monex (Newport Beach, CA) provides put and call options on 32.15 ounces of gold. The Monex options are not tradeable but can be exercized during the option period. Expiration periods are 30, 60, 90, and 185 days.

Since options are paid in full, they are not subject to margin calls or forced liquidation as is the case with futures contracts. At this time, quotations on bullion options are not available in the daily press.

Gold futures contract Gold futures contracts are obligations to buy or sell 100 ounces of gold on or before a specified date at a specified price. Futures contracts must be exercised if held to maturity, while options contracts need not be exercised if held to maturity. Futures contracts are purchased on margin, and hence, are subject to margin call and possible forced liquidation. They are widely quoted in the financial press, and the market is highly organized.

As with options, futures contracts may be used for leveraged speculation or for hedging. Speculators will buy contracts if they anticipate a price increase or sell contracts in anticipation of a price decrease.

Gold futures are traded on the N.Y. Commodity Exchange, the International Monetary Market of the Chicago Mercantile Exchange, and other markets.

Options on Gold Futures Contracts Options on Gold Futures contracts (the right to buy and sell a gold futures contract rather than the metal) are actively traded on the New York Comex. The futures contract underlying the options is for 100 ounces of gold. Contract months are April/Aug./Dec. Gold futures options premiums are reported daily in the *Wall Street Journal*.

Investing in Diamonds

Diamond prices are very volatile. For example, they have appreciated on the average of about 12.6% over the ten-year period 1969–1979 (compared to a consumer price index of 6.1% during the same period of time). There have been periods (the recession of 1973—1974 and in 1981) when the price of investment quality diamonds slipped as much as 40%. A major factor stabilizing the market is DeBeers, a South African diamond company which handles as much as 80% of the world's diamonds. While the appreciation of diamonds has been impressive, potential buyers should be aware that prices are not quoted in the daily newspapers; therefore, selling the stones at a profit may be difficult. Quotes are available in the *Rappaport Diamond Report*, 15 West 47 Street, New York, NY 10036, (212) 354-0575. Another good source of information on the diamond industry is the Diamond Registry, 580 Fifth Avenue, New York, NY 10036, (212) 575-0444. The registry publishes a monthly newsletter which includes price ranges, trends, and forecasts as well as other pertinent material.

To locate reputable gem dealers check with the Diamond Registry (address above) or the

American Gem Society
1050 East Flamingo Road
Las Vegas, NV 89109
(702) 255-6500

American Diamond Industry Association

71 West 47 Street
New York, NY 10036
(212) 575-0525

Buyers should only deal with reputable firms, and the stones should be certified by an independent laboratory such as the Gemological Institute of America, tel: (212) 221-5858 and International Gemological Institute, tel: (212) 398-1700.

Diamonds are ranked in terms of the 4 C's—carat (one carat equals 1/142 ounces weight), color, clarity, and cut.

Carat For investment purposes the diamond should be more than .5 carat. However, diamonds of more than 2 carats may be difficult to sell.

Color There are six main categories, each with subdivisions:

D,E,F—Colorless
G,H,I,J—Near colorless
K,L,M—Faint yellow
N,O,P,Q,R—Very light yellow
S,T,U,V,W,X,Y,Z—Light yellow
Fancy yellow stone

Color should be in the range from D to H. However, Fancy Yellow Stones often command very high prices because of their scarcity.

Clarity Although bubbles, lines, and specks (inclusions) are natural to diamonds, they may interfere with the passage of light through the diamond. With a 10X magnification, a professional appraiser can grade the diamond according to the ten clarity grades:

- **FL**—Flawless
- **IF**—Internally flawless
- **VVS-1, VVS-2**—Very, very slight inclusions
- **VS-1, VS-2**—Very slight inclusions
- **SI-1, SI-2**—Slight inclusions
- **I-1, I-2, I-3**—Imperfect

Investment grade stones should be in the range FL to VS-2.

Cut There are several types of cuts—oval, marquise, pear shaped, round brilliant and emerald. Round brilliant stones are preferred for investment purposes. Proportions are important, and the preferred values are:

- Depth % (total depth divided by girdle diameter): 57% to 63%.
- Table (table diameter divided by girdle diameter): 57% to 66%.
- Girdle thickness should be neither very thick nor very thin.

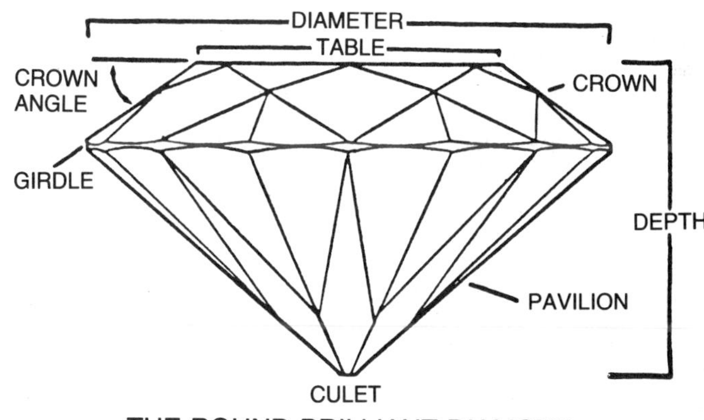

THE ROUND BRILLIANT DIAMOND

MEDIAN SALES PRICE OF EXISTING SINGLE-FAMILY HOMES (in thousands of dollars)

Metropolitan Area*	1991	1992	1993	1993 I	1993 II	1993 III	1993 IV	1994 Ir
				(Not Seasonally Adjusted)				
Akron, OH	$71.8	$79.3	$83.2	$77.4	$85.4	$84.0	$84.2	$81.6
Albany/Schenectady/Troy, NY	110.3	111.4	112.3	109.9	110.6	111.9	115.4	112.5
Albuquerque, NM	86.8	92.0	100.4	94.4	100.8	102.6	102.9	103.1
Amarillo, TX	57.5	58.1	63.2	59.7	63.5	63.5	65.3	63.6
Orange Cnty. (Anaheim/Santa Ana MSA), CA**	239.7	234.8	220.7	219.4	219.9	221.3	214.7	209.5
Appleton/Oshkosh/Neenah, WI	66.4	71.0	75.4	74.6	75.7	73.6	77.9	78.6
Atlanta, GA	87.6	89.5	91.8	88.3	92.4	93.2	92.4	93.2
Atlantic City, NJ	110.6	109.1	106.7	101.4	110.2	102.8	109.7	104.9
Aurora/Elgin, IL	114.4	118.8	121.7	116.7	123.2	124.8	119.1	124.2
Austin/San Marcos, TX	N/A	83.8	91.3	86.6	92.3	92.1	93.2	95.5
Baltimore, MD	110.1	113.4	115.7	113.7	113.3	118.9	115.9	115.7
Baton Rouge, LA	69.4	73.6	75.9	72.8	74.8	77.8	77.5	78.4
Beaumont/Port Arthur, TX	57.5	61.5	63.2	60.3	65.0	62.4	64.9	65.6
Biloxi/Gulfport, MS	58.2	62.4	67.2	60.8	65.4	70.6	71.3	72.4
Birmingham, AL	86.0	90.9	96.5	89.0	95.9	99.1	100.2	99.5
Boise City, ID	76.8	83.1	91.4	86.4	87.8	94.8	95.3	97.3
Boston, MA	170.1	171.1	173.2	160.5	175.6	176.9	172.7	170.6
Bradenton, FL	N/A	82.1	86.5	84.3	87.6	86.9	87.4	86.4
Buffalo/Niagara Falls, NY	79.7	81.7	83.5	84.2	85.0	80.9	83.6	82.4
Canton, OH	67.3	71.1	75.4	67.1	76.4	76.0	78.2	76.3
Cedar Rapids, IA	62.9	71.9	78.0	73.4	76.4	80.6	80.3	80.6
Champaign/Urbana/Rantoul, IL	65.9	66.6	69.7	68.7	67.9	70.8	71.3	68.2
Charleston, SC	79.4	82.3	89.9	86.2	95.5	91.6	87.2	91.3
Charleston, WV	65.7	70.3	74.8	75.4	73.6	77.0	73.5	72.4
Charlotte/Gastonia/Rock Hill, NC/SC	101.4	102.2	106.1	102.8	105.6	108.8	106.0	104.0
Chattanooga, TN/GA	70.8	73.0	73.6	69.8	74.6	75.1	73.9	76.1
Chicago, IL	131.1	136.8	142.0	135.3	143.9	145.9	140.9	135.5
Cincinnati, OH/KY/IN	84.9	88.6	91.4	85.6	91.7	95.1	92.3	93.6
Cleveland, OH	86.2	90.7	95.0	89.2	95.8	96.6	95.8	94.2
Colorado Springs, CO	N/A	86.9	93.7	88.5	94.6	95.0	95.2	97.9
Columbia, SC	80.5	84.7	85.1	82.3	85.3	84.5	87.5	82.9
Columbus, OH	85.2	91.0	91.8	88.0	92.7	92.9	92.0	92.8
Corpus Christi, TX	64.3	67.5	70.5	66.6	69.6	71.6	73.5	71.7
Dallas, TX	88.3	91.3	94.5	89.5	95.9	95.7	95.5	95.1

Davenport/Moline/Rock Island, IA/IL	N/A	54.8	58.3	54.5	58.3	59.6	59.1	60.8
Dayton/Springfield, OH	76.3	81.2	82.1	78.4	82.1	86.1	80.5	82.5
Daytona Beach, FL	66.3	66.2	67.8	67.6	65.7	68.4	69.6	66.2
Denver, CO	89.1	96.2	104.7	96.9	104.7	105.0	109.0	111.2
Des Moines, IA	68.2	73.0	78.8	71.6	78.7	80.2	82.3	77.4
Detroit, MI	80.6	81.3	86.0	92.2	83.6	87.4	83.9	84.5
El Paso, TX	66.0	67.5	71.8	67.9	72.1	72.6	74.1	73.6
Eugene/Springfield, OR	73.7	79.7	84.4	80.4	83.5	83.9	88.7	90.1
Fargo/Moorhead, ND/MN	67.2	70.7	75.5	67.3	74.9	76.4	79.3	78.2
Ft. Lauderdale/Hollywood/Pompano Beach, FL	96.2	99.1	103.1	99.5	103.5	105.1	103.5	100.1
Ft. Myers/Cape Coral, FL	71.3	71.1	77.1	74.3	79.0	78.2	76.3	78.9
Ft. Worth/Arlington, TX	77.6	80.2	82.9	79.7	82.5	84.2	84.4	83.5
Gainesville, FL	74.9	79.1	82.9	80.4	82.0	83.7	85.8	82.1
Gary/Hammond, IN	70.3	76.1	82.8	79.4	82.0	84.3	84.2	84.1
Grand Rapids, MI	70.7	73.1	76.5	73.9	76.5	77.3	78.0	76.6
Green Bay, WI	66.1	72.9	81.5	76.9	83.4	80.0	83.1	84.4
Greensboro/Winston-Salem/High Point, NC	86.1	88.4	94.7	89.3	93.1	96.6	98.1	96.2
Greenville/Spartanburg, SC	77.5	82.9	84.9	82.8	84.0	86.1	86.1	83.0
Hartford, CT	148.2	141.1	135.3	135.5	137.0	134.8	134.2	132.9
Honolulu, HI	340.0	349.0	358.5	347.0	358.5	365.0	360.0	355.0
Houston, TX	74.0	80.3	80.9	78.0	81.8	81.8	81.0	84.8
Indianapolis, IN	79.1	83.7	86.6	83.8	86.4	87.6	87.4	90.5
Jacksonville, FL	73.7	76.8	77.1	74.1	75.2	77.7	79.9	79.7
Kalamazoo, MI	64.9	69.6	71.1	66.0	71.6	73.1	72.8	74.7
Kansas City, MO/KS	76.6	79.5	83.6	79.1	84.5	84.9	83.6	84.9
Knoxville, TN	78.8	80.1	85.3	82.4	85.1	85.8	86.9	88.6
Lake County, IL	113.9	119.6	130.1	121.4	128.0	133.5	131.3	N/A
Lansing/East Lansing, MI	66.7	69.9	73.2	69.8	74.1	72.7	74.9	73.0
Las Vegas, NV	101.4	104.3	108.2	105.2	107.8	109.0	109.9	110.4
Lexington/Fayette, KY	75.6	78.7	82.5	76.9	81.3	85.1	84.2	83.0
Lincoln, NE	62.7	67.7	72.5	69.0	70.2	74.5	74.3	74.1
Little Rock-N. Little Rock, AR	67.5	N/A	N/A	N/A	79.0	80.6	79.5	74.5
Los Angeles Area, CA**	218.9	213.1	197.9	197.8	200.6	194.6	193.0	188.5
Louisville, KY/IN	65.4	69.5	74.5	69.9	74.6	77.5	74.6	77.4
Madison, WI	87.7	94.9	104.6	97.7	100.0	107.6	111.0	111.5

(continued)

MEDIAN SALES PRICE OF EXISTING SINGLE-FAMILY HOMES (in thousands of dollars) *(concluded)*

Metropolitan Area*	1991	1992	1993	1993 I	1993 II	1993 III	1993 IV	1994 Ir
				(Not Seasonally Adjusted)				
Melbourne/Titusville/Palm Bay, FL	$72.0	$74.8	$75.3	$72.7	$74.7	$77.7	$75.9	$74.9
Memphis, TN/AR/MS	82.5	85.3	87.0	84.2	85.5	90.6	86.7	85.6
Miami/Hialeah, FL	93.7	97.1	98.8	96.8	99.8	99.1	99.2	105.0
Milwaukee, WI	90.0	97.0	104.1	98.4	103.7	104.1	107.9	106.5
Minneapolis/St. Paul, MN/WI	91.1	94.2	98.2	96.4	99.6	96.2	99.4	100.0
Mobile, AL	60.8	64.8	68.2	66.2	69.3	70.5	66.7	69.5
Montgomery, AL	76.2	79.7	83.2	79.1	81.9	85.0	85.2	81.7
Nashville, TN	86.9	88.8	90.4	87.0	89.9	91.3	92.9	95.2
New Haven/Meriden, CT	153.2	145.8	142.5	142.6	144.5	145.8	137.9	137.6
New Orleans, LA	71.8	73.6	76.8	73.0	79.6	77.0	76.7	75.4
New York/N. New Jersey/Long Island, NY/NJ/CT	173.5	172.7	173.2	168.0	173.5	176.9	173.0	170.3
Bergen/Passaic, NJ	187.1	187.6	188.4	182.8	193.0	193.2	181.4	188.3
Middlesex/Somerset/Hunterdon, NJ	158.4	168.9	168.8	158.5	170.1	173.3	168.8	161.1
Monmouth/Ocean, NJ	134.4	139.2	137.1	135.3	139.7	136.1	137.7	135.2
Nassau/Suffolk, NY	159.2	158.6	159.2	158.0	159.0	158.7	161.1	158.8
Newark, NJ	178.8	184.4	185.1	174.6	185.8	191.9	184.9	181.4
Norfolk/Virginia Bch/Newport News, VA	91.7	94.8	98.2	94.0	95.7	101.5	103.4	104.7
Ocala, FL	56.1	56.2	57.8	55.2	56.7	56.1	62.4	58.1
Oklahoma City, OK	57.0	61.6	64.9	60.6	65.5	65.7	66.1	67.6
Omaha, NE/IA	66.5	69.4	72.7	64.3	75.3	74.1	73.2	72.8
Orlando, FL	86.3	87.6	90.1	86.9	89.8	92.1	91.5	89.9
Pensacola, FL	64.9	67.2	71.9	67.2	72.6	72.0	74.8	74.8
Peoria, IL	55.8	59.1	63.2	57.5	65.0	65.8	63.1	65.9
Philadelphia, PA/NJ	118.4	117.0	118.0	108.9	118.6	123.3	117.9	116.8
Phoenix, AZ	85.5	86.8	89.1	86.3	88.2	90.2	91.0	89.2
Pittsburgh, PA	74.2	78.6	82.2	75.9	82.7	85.2	82.4	80.0
Portland, OR	88.5	97.7	106.0	99.6	104.8	107.7	109.6	111.2
Providence, RI	124.3	118.5	116.3	112.5	119.0	116.8	116.5	115.6
Raleigh/Durham, NC	100.8	105.9	109.2	101.3	109.7	112.5	108.5	110.1
Reno, NV	115.1	117.9	126.3	119.2	124.4	128.1	131.3	130.7
Richland/Kennewick/Pasco, WA	70.3	84.2	101.9	96.4	99.1	102.9	108.8	105.3
Richmond/Petersburg, VA	92.5	93.9	94.1	89.4	95.0	97.9	92.4	94.0
Riverside/San Bernardino, CA**	137.6	136.2	134.5	135.3	135.0	135.5	131.9	131.0

Rochester, NY	81.5	84.7	84.8	83.3	83.8	86.5	84.5	85.3
Rockford, IL	71.2	75.7	81.3	77.6	78.8	83.3	83.7	82.5
Sacramento, CA**	137.7	134.0	129.4	130.4	129.7	129.8	127.7	127.3
Saginaw/Bay City/Midland, MI	51.5	N/A	58.3	56.4	61.1	58.9	56.8	59.2
Saint Louis, MO/IL	79.4	83.2	84.8	82.1	85.5	86.8	83.5	83.1
Salt Lake City/Ogden, UT	72.8	76.5	84.9	78.0	81.9	88.4	89.2	92.8
San Antonio, TX	64.9	70.4	77.0	72.6	78.6	79.4	75.8	76.8
San Diego, CA**	187.5	183.1	177.4	175.1	178.9	177.2	177.5	177.8
San Francisco Bay Area, CA**	258.5	254.7	250.2	246.6	252.7	254.1	248.2	246.9
Sarasota, FL	89.0	93.2	94.1	88.9	94.6	93.8	96.8	97.1
Seattle, WA	143.1	145.7	150.2	145.0	150.5	151.3	152.1	152.9
Shreveport, LA	64.0	66.3	69.0	66.1	71.0	71.6	66.3	68.8
Sioux Falls, SD	63.6	69.0	74.8	70.7	75.1	76.4	75.8	77.8
South Bend/Mishawaka, IN	59.1	62.9	63.6	63.0	65.4	62.0	63.5	N/A
Spokane, WA	64.5	76.3	85.5	79.1	84.3	86.8	88.6	90.7
Springfield, IL	66.6	67.7	72.6	67.6	75.3	72.2	73.0	70.9
Springfield, MA	117.1	115.1	112.4	106.3	113.8	115.6	110.9	108.4
Springfield, MO	N/A	62.8	68.1	64.3	66.9	69.4	70.0	69.3
Syracuse, NY	77.7	80.4	84.7	85.6	84.0	85.3	83.7	82.1
Tacoma, WA	98.2	107.8	113.5	109.1	113.3	116.7	114.1	115.0
Tallahassee, FL	84.3	87.3	92.5	86.5	93.0	92.6	96.8	95.7
Tampa/St. Petersburg/Clearwater, FL	71.3	72.6	75.0	69.9	75.1	76.9	76.7	74.3
Toledo, OH	68.8	71.5	72.3	65.8	72.7	73.9	74.6	72.8
Topeka, KS	58.2	64.7	67.5	62.9	69.1	69.7	66.8	66.4
Trenton, NJ	147.5	138.1	133.4	132.9	140.7	137.3	124.5	128.9
Tucson, AZ	N/A	N/A	88.2	80.3	87.5	93.4	91.2	88.5
Tulsa, OK	65.4	68.3	71.3	68.2	70.9	73.5	72.0	73.5
Washington, DC/MD/VA	156.7	157.8	158.3	153.5	159.1	161.2	157.5	154.9
Waterloo/Cedar Falls, IA	45.4	47.2	50.5	44.3	50.1	52.9	52.5	48.1
W. Palm Beach/Boca Raton/Delray Beach, FL	116.3	114.1	114.6	108.8	109.6	118.1	119.1	114.0
Wichita, KS	65.9	68.6	71.4	69.3	71.1	71.8	72.6	73.4
Wilmington, DE/NJ/MD	116.5	117.2	N/A	115.7	117.8	N/A	N/A	N/A
Worcester, MA	N/A	128	129	122.4	126.3	134.5	129.9	129.2
Youngstown/Warren, OH	54.5	57.6	61.2	58.6	62.4	60.6	62.2	66.3

* *All areas are metropolitan statistical areas (MSA) as defined by the U.S. Office of Managment and Budget as of 1992. They include the named central city and surrounding areas.*
** *Provided by the California Association of REALTORS®. N/A Not Available r Revised p Preliminary*

Source: Reprinted with permission from the ***REAL ESTATE OUTLOOK: Market Trends and Insights,*** NATIONAL ASSOCIATION OF REALTORS®, Washington, DC.

SALES AND MEDIAN SALES PRICE OF APARTMENT CONDOS AND CO-OPS

Year		United States	Northeast	Midwest	South	West	United States	Northeast	Midwest	South	West
		Unit Volume Seasonally Adjusted Annual Rate					Median Sales Price Not Seasonally Adjusted				
1991		339,000	66,000	61,000	109,000	103,000	$85,700	$106,800	$73,700	$68,200	$106,100
1992		366,000	78,000	67,000	115,000	106,000	84,900	103,200	75,800	69,600	107,100
1993		401,000	86,000	73,000	131,000	111,000	83,500	99,200	76,400	69,000	103,500
1993	I	384,000	81,000	72,000	125,000	105,000	$82,400	$98,500	$74,100	$67,900	$105,900
	II	369,000	74,000	68,000	124,000	103,000	83,400	98,800	76,100	69,500	104,100
	III	405,000	92,000	71,000	132,000	110,000	83,500	100,900	76,500	69,200	98,700
	IV	445,000	96,000	79,000	143,000	127,000	84,400	98,500	78,400	69,300	106,500
1994	I r	439,000	95,000	77,000	144,000	124,000	85,100	100,800	80,700	68,900	106,600

r Revised p Preliminary

Source: Reprinted with permission from the ***REAL ESTATE OUTLOOK: Market Trends and Insights,*** NATIONAL ASSOCIATION OF REALTORS®, Washington, DC.

HOUSING AFFORDABILITY

Year		Median Priced Existing Single-Family Home	Mortgage Rate*	Monthly P & I Payment	Payment as % Income	Median Family Income	Qualifying Income**	Affordability Indices Composite	Fixed	ARM
1991		$100,300	9.30%	$663	22.1%	$35,939	$31,825	112.9	109.9	124.2
1992		103,700	8.11	615	20.1	36,812	29,523	124.7	120.1	145.0
1993		106,800	7.16	578	18.3	37,970	27,727	136.9	131.9	159.1
1993	Apr	$105,500	7.26%	$576	18.6%	$37,198	$27,664	134.5	129.0	158.0
	May	106,500	7.30	584	18.8	37,294	28,037	133.0	128.4	153.1
	Jun	109,200	7.23	595	19.1	37,391	28,549	131.0	125.6	151.8
	Jul	108,400	7.14	585	18.7	37,487	28,086	133.5	129.4	153.5
	Aug	108,800	7.05	582	18.6	37,584	27,936	134.5	131.2	154.8
	Sep	107,200	6.93	567	18.0	37,680	27,194	138.6	134.8	158.9
	Oct	106,600	6.75	553	17.6	37,777	26,550	142.3	138.4	162.4
	Nov	107,100	6.77	557	17.6	37,873	26,729	141.7	137.0	164.2
	Dec	107,400	6.84	562	17.8	37,970	26,996	140.6	133.9	165.1
1994	Jan	107,900	6.89	568	17.9	38,083	27,260	139.7	133.8	162.1
	Feb r	107,200	6.83	561	17.6	38,197	26,919	141.9	136.4	165.6
	Mar r	107,600	7.01	573	18.0	38,310	27,517	139.2	133.5	161.7
	Apr p	108,900	7.21	592	18.5	38,424	28,414	135.2	127.6	154.9
								This Month	Month Ago	Year Ago
Apr p	Northeast	$139,200	7.52%	$780	22.0%	$42,626	$37,443	113.8	115.5	112.4
	Midwest	87,500	7.64	496	15.3	38,812	23,818	163.0	171.9	171.1
	South	96,000	7.57	541	18.8	34,481	25,951	132.9	139.7	141.8
	West	145,600	7.59	822	24.4	40,337	39,437	102.3	105.7	106.3

* *Effective rate on loans closed on existing homes – Federal Housing Finance Board. Regional interest rate from HSH Associates, Butler, NJ*

** *Based on current lending requirements of the Federal National Mortgage Association using a 20% down payment.*

r Revised p Preliminary

Source: Reprinted with permission from the ***REAL ESTATE OUTLOOK: Market Trends and Insights,*** NATIONAL ASSOCIATION OF REALTORS®, Washington, DC.

FIRST-TIME HOMEBUYER AFFORDABILITY

Year		Starter Home Price	10% Down Payment	Loan Amount	Effective Interest Rate*	Effective I Rate Plus PMI	Monthly Payment	Prime First-Time Median Income	Qualifying Income	Affordability Indices: First-Time Buyer	Affordability Indices: Composite
1991		$85,300	$8,530	$76,770	9.30%	9.55%	$648	$23,345	$31,120	75.0	112.9
1992		88,100	8,810	79,290	8.11	8.36	602	23,625	28,887	81.8	124.7
1993		90,800	9,080	81,720	7.16	7.41	566	24,249	27,186	89.2	136.9
1993	I	$88,200	$8,820	$79,380	7.55%	7.80%	$571	$23,781	$27,429	86.7	132.5
	II	91,000	9,100	81,900	7.26	7.51	573	23,937	27,514	87.0	133.1
	III	91,900	9,190	82,710	7.04	7.29	566	24,093	27,191	88.6	135.9
	IV	91,000	9,100	81,900	6.79	7.04	547	24,249	26,260	92.3	141.9
1994	I r	91,500	9,150	82,350	6.91	7.16	557	24,436	26,724	91.4	140.6

* *Effective rate on loans closed on existing homes – Federal Housing Finance Board*

r Revised p Preliminary

Source: Reprinted with permission from the ***REAL ESTATE OUTLOOK: Market Trends and Insights,*** NATIONAL ASSOCIATION OF REALTORS®, Washington, DC.

AVERAGE PER ACRE VALUE OF FARM REAL ESTATE, BY STATE, 1977–94

State	1977	1982	1987	1990	1991	1992	1993	1994	Percent change 1993-94
	Dollars								Percent
Northeast:	887	1,364	1,491	1,722	1,703	1,711	1,749	1,927	10.2
Maine	414	680	885	1,019	978	931	992	1,081	9.0
New Hampshire	696	1,136	1,847	2,237	2,148	2,045	2,178	2,374	9.0
Vermont	533	815	1,114	1,190	1,142	1,087	1,158	1,262	9.0
Massachusetts	1,138	1,874	3,012	3,763	3,612	3,439	3,662	3,992	9.0
Rhode Island	1,821	2,729	3,389	5,028	4,827	4,595	4,894	5,334	9.0
Connecticut	1,780	2,610	3,557	4,417	4,240	4,036	4,299	4,686	9.0
New York	587	821	960	974	1,031	1,051	1,119	1,251	11.8
New Jersey	2,211	3,181	3,729	4,634	4,912	4,774	4,536	4,840	6.7
Pennsylvania	994	1,513	1,540	1,807	1,757	1,820	1,747	1,910	9.3
Delaware	1,250	1,787	1,677	2,259	2,248	2,126	2,362	2,641	11.8
Maryland	1,353	2,376	2,009	2,420	2,196	2,255	2,521	2,866	13.7
Lake States:	669	1,234	707	841	906	916	950	980	3.2
Michigan	778	1,278	924	1,005	1,085	1,105	1,130	1,212	7.3
Wisconsin	598	1,144	777	803	853	870	932	975	4.6
Minnesota	672	1,272	587	805	873	873	896	900	0.4
Corn Belt:	1,098	1,642	900	1,096	1,129	1,158	1,193	1,285	7.7
Ohio	1,099	1,629	1,097	1,204	1,217	1,249	1,267	1,386	9.4
Indiana	1,188	1,804	1,061	1,244	1,275	1,303	1,366	1,473	7.8
Illinois	1,458	2,023	1,149	1,389	1,433	1,500	1,503	1,645	9.4
Iowa	1,259	1,889	786	1,102	1,157	1,178	1,245	1,316	5.7
Missouri	548	945	604	679	689	689	715	762	6.6
Northern Plains:	325	547	331	425	440	449	462	497	7.6
North Dakota	274	455	303	340	368	358	388	409	5.4
South Dakota	194	349	238	328	351	365	370	388	4.9
Nebraska	420	730	400	550	556	569	580	635	9.5
Kansas	398	628	373	462	467	484	494	537	8.7
Appalachia:	650	1,083	1,004	1,111	1,059	1,089	1,129	1,162	2.9
Virginia	701	1,096	1,154	1,516	1,295	1,363	1,295	1,338	3.3
West Virginia	430	723	633	613	625	719	696	713	2.4
North Carolina	759	1,297	1,259	1,263	1,243	1,264	1,319	1,349	2.3
Kentucky	619	1,058	878	981	962	993	1,084	1,144	5.5
Tennessee	618	1,040	936	996	988	985	1,049	1,054	0.5
Southeast:	636	1,095	1,055	1,253	1,254	1,212	1,229	1,305	6.2
South Carolina	600	980	792	909	948	931	871	923	6.0
Georgia	581	926	889	1,012	995	902	964	983	2.0
Florida	861	1,518	1,605	2,085	2,133	2,062	2,074	2,205	6.3
Alabama	477	885	786	839	791	832	863	964	11.7
Delta States:	543	1,135	757	782	797	771	802	845	5.4
Mississippi	461	981	685	728	754	738	757	814	7.5
Arkansas	542	1,096	724	750	770	724	759	800	5.4
Louisiana	665	1,414	921	915	905	905	945	973	3.0
Southern Plains:	318	576	532	495	482	472	480	502	4.6
Oklahoma	394	725	475	497	486	494	512	534	4.3
Texas	299	539	546	495	481	466	471	493	4.7
Mountain:	174	325	257	267	286	288	295	325	10.2
Montana	157	271	200	238	243	252	270	302	11.9
Idaho	454	839	552	661	659	687	691	784	13.5
Wyoming	110	193	157	149	153	138	149	169	13.4
Colorado	256	451	368	358	410	367	383	430	12.3
New Mexico	101	195	156	196	230	239	225	240	6.7
Arizona	138	302	299	263	285	302	305	314	3.0
Utah	271	589	451	389	403	425	464	508	9.5
Nevada	112	268	240	194	219	231	215	229	6.5
Pacific:	595	1,346	1,084	1,163	1,206	1,198	1,189	1,242	4.5
Washington	535	922	756	779	798	792	782	898	14.8
Oregon	342	705	541	571	583	603	657	740	12.6
California	759	1,900	1,554	1,704	1,787	1,765	1,722	1,722	0.0
48 States	474	823	599	668	681	684	699	744	6.4

Value of farmland and buildings in nominal dollars. Value data as of Feb. 1 for 1977 and 1987, April 1 for 1982, and Jan. 1 for 1990-94.

Source: *Agricultural Land Values,* Economics Research Service, U.S. Department of Agriculture.

Industrial Real Estate Market: Selected Cities*

Atlanta, Georgia: Industrial

Atlanta, Georgia

Market Data

Inventory (sf)	Central City	Suburban
Total	43,200,000	219,500,000
Vacant	8,800,000	30,100,000
Vacancy Rates	20.4%	13.7%
Under Construction	0	3,200,000
Net Absorption	50,000	10,950,000

Site Prices ($/sf)	Central City	Suburban
Improved Sites		
Less than 2 acres	-	2.00-3.00
2 to 5 acres	1.50-2.00	1.75-3.00
5 to 10 acres	-	1.50-2.75
Over 10 acres	-	1.50-2.50
Unimproved Sites		
Less than 10 acres	-	1.00-2.00
10 to 100 acres	.50-1.00	.75-1.75
Over 100 acres	-	.50-1.25

Prime Source of Financing: Commercial Banks, Pension Funds, Owner Financing

Mortgage Money Supply: Tight

Current Trends

Composition of Absorption	
Warehouse/Distr.	90.0%
Manufacturing	0.0%
High Tech/R&D	10.0%
Composition of Inventory	
Warehouse/Distr.	90.0%
Manufacturing	0.0%
High Tech/R&D	10.0%
Rate of Construction	
Warehouse/Distr.	Up 1-5%
Manufacturing	Same
High Tech/R&D	Same
Dollar Volume - Sales	
Warehouse/Distr.	Up 6-10%
Manufacturing	Up 1-5%
High Tech/R&D	Same
Dollar Volume - Leases	
Warehouse/Distr.	Up 6-10%
Manufacturing	Same
High Tech/R&D	Same

Outlook

Sales Prices	
Warehouse/Distr.	Up 6-10%
Manufacturing	Up 1-5%
High Tech/R&D	Same
Lease Prices	
Warehouse/Distr.	Up 6-10%
Manufacturing	Up 1-5%
High Tech/R&D	Same
Site Prices	Up 1-5%
Absorption	
Warehouse/Distr.	Up 11-15%
Manufacturing	Same
High Tech/R&D	Up 1-5%
Construction	
Warehouse/Distr.	Up 6-10%
Manufacturing	Up 1-5%
High Tech/R&D	Same
Dollar Volume - Sales	Up 6-10%
Dollar Volume - Leases	Up 1-5%

	Sales Prices ($/sf)		Gross Lease Prices ($/sf)		Construction	Vacancy
	Central City	Suburban	Central City	Suburban	($/sf)	Indicators
Less than 5,000 sf	25.00-30.00	35.00-45.00	3.00-4.00	3.50-5.00	40.00-50.00	Balanced Market
5,000 to 19,999 sf	20.00-25.00	30.00-35.00	2.50-3.50	3.00-4.50	25.00-35.00	Balanced Market
20,000 to 39,999 sf	16.00-20.00	18.00-25.00	2.25-3.00	2.75-3.75	20.00-25.00	Moderate Oversupply
40,000 to 59,999 sf	15.00-18.00	16.00-18.00	2.00-2.50	2.50-3.25	16.00-20.00	Moderate Oversupply
60,000 to 99,999 sf	12.00-15.00	14.00-16.00	1.50-2.00	2.00-3.00	15.00-16.00	Moderate Shortage
More than 99,999 sf	10.00-14.00	12.00-15.00	1.50-1.75	1.75-2.75	14.00-15.00	Substantial Shortage
High Tech/R&D	40.00-60.00	45.00-70.00	6.00-7.00	5.00-8.00	30.00-50.00	Moderate Oversupply

	Operating Expenses				Tax Expenses			
	Warehouse		Factories		Warehouse		Factories	
	Central City	Suburban	Central City	Suburban	Central City	Suburban	Central City	Suburban
Less than 5,000 sf	n/a	n/a	n/a	n/a	n/a	n/a	n/a	n/a
5,000 to 19,999 sf	n/a	n/a	n/a	n/a	n/a	.40	n/a	n/a
20,000 to 39,999 sf	n/a	n/a	n/a	n/a	n/a	n/a	n/a	n/a
40,000 to 59,999 sf	n/a	1.00	n/a	n/a	n/a	n/a	n/a	n/a
60,000 to 99,999 sf	n/a	n/a	n/a	n/a	n/a	.30	n/a	n/a
More than 99,999 sf	n/a	n/a	n/a	n/a	n/a	n/a	n/a	n/a
High Tech/R&D	n/a	1.50*	n/a	n/a	n/a	.70	n/a	n/a

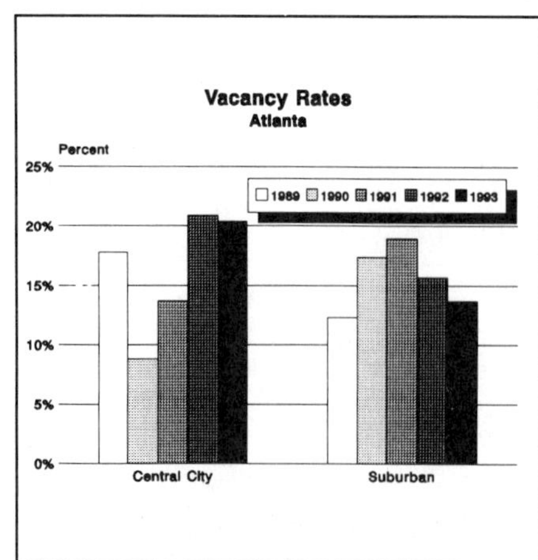

1993 Review

Suburban Atlanta saw active development of build-to-suits: 20 new buildings came on-line in 1993 or are currently under-construction. By contrast, the city's inventory fell by 200,000 sq. ft. As the southeast's primary distribution center, demand for warehouse/distribution space pushed the suburban vacancy rate down to 13.7 percent and held the city's rate steady at about 20 percent. Sales and lease prices for warehouse/distribution space rose six to 10 percent in 1993. Atlanta's economy is experiencing a temporary boost induced by the 1996 Olympic Games. However, some businesses have downsized and/or consolidated operations to combat recessionary pressures.

1994 Forecast

Higher site acquisition and construction costs will limit new construction in 1994. A shortage of larger spaces, greater than 60,000 sq. ft., however will prompt build-to-suit development. Absorption of warehouse/distribution space is projected to increase 11 to 15 percent in 1994 despite increase in sales and lease prices. Growth will likely slow after 1996.

* includes cleaning

Source: Reprinted from the 1994 edition of *Comparative Statistics of Industrial and Office Real Estate Markets* with permission of the Society of Industrial and Office REALTORS®.

* See Glossary of Terms on page 652.

Chicago, Illinois: Industrial

Central City and Suburban-Chicago, Illinois

Market Data

Inventory (sf)	Central City	Suburban
Total	184,315,000	548,685,000
Vacant	20,000,000	52,100,000
Vacancy Rates	10.9%	9.5%
Under Construction	0	1,065,000
Net Absorption	315,000	3,685,000

Site Prices ($/sf)	Central City	Suburban
Improved Sites		
Less than 2 acres	1.50-6.00	4.00-4.50
2 to 5 acres	2.00-6.00	2.50-3.50
5 to 10 acres	2.00-4.00	2.25-3.00
Over 10 acres	1.50-4.00	1.75-3.50
Unimproved Sites		
Less than 10 acres	n/a	n/a
10 to 100 acres	n/a	1.00-1.50
Over 100 acres	n/a	.50-1.00

Prime Source of Financing: Commercial Banks, Owner Financing, REITS

Mortgage Money Supply: Tight

Current Trends

Composition of Absorption	
Warehouse/Distr.	70.0%
Manufacturing	25.0%
High Tech/R&D	5.0%
Composition of Inventory	
Warehouse/Distr.	35.0%
Manufacturing	62.5%
High Tech/R&D	2.5%
Rate of Construction	
Warehouse/Distr.	Up 6-10%
Manufacturing	Same
High Tech/R&D	Same
Dollar Volume - Sales	
Warehouse/Distr.	Up 6-10%
Manufacturing	Same
High Tech/R&D	Same
Dollar Volume - Leases	
Warehouse/Distr.	Up 6-10%
Manufacturing	Same
High Tech/R&D	Same

Outlook

Sales Prices	
Warehouse/Distr.	Down 1-5%
Manufacturing	Down 6-10%
High Tech/R&D	Same
Lease Prices	
Warehouse/Distr.	Down 6-10%
Manufacturing	Down 6-10%
High Tech/R&D	Same
Site Prices	Down 6-10%
Absorption	
Warehouse/Distr.	Up 6-10%
Manufacturing	Up 6-10%
High Tech/R&D	Up 1-5%
Construction	
Warehouse/Distr.	Same
Manufacturing	Up 1-5%
High Tech/R&D	Up 1-5%
Dollar Volume - Sales	Up 6-10%
Dollar Volume - Leases	Up 6-10%

	Sales Prices ($/sf)		**Net Lease Prices** ($/sf)		**Construction**	**Vacancy**
	Central City	Suburban	Central City	Suburban	($/sf)	**Indicators**
Less than 5,000 sf	35.00	45.00	4.00	5.50	40.00	Moderate Shortage
5,000 to 19,999 sf	25.00	40.00	2.75	4.25	35.00	Balanced Market
20,000 to 39,999 sf	18.00	35.00	2.50	3.80	28.00	Moderate Oversupply
40,000 to 59,999 sf	16.50	32.50	2.50	3.35	23.00	Substantial Oversupply
60,000 to 99,999 sf	14.00	25.00	2.50	3.25	20.00-22.00	Substantial Oversupply
More than 99,999 sf	12.50	22.00	2.25	3.30	20.00	Balanced Market
High Tech/R&D	n/a	n/a	n/a	8.00	40.00-70.00	Substantial Oversupply

	Operating Expenses				**Tax Expenses**			
	Warehouse		**Factories**		**Warehouse**		**Factories**	
	Central City	Suburban	Central City	Suburban	Central City	Suburban	Central City	Suburban
Less than 5,000 sf	n/a	n/a	n/a	n/a	1.75	1.50	1.75	1.50
5,000 to 19,999 sf	n/a	n/a	n/a	n/a	1.75	1.50	1.75	1.50
20,000 to 39,999 sf	n/a	n/a	n/a	n/a	1.50	1.30	1.50	1.30
40,000 to 59,999 sf	n/a	n/a	n/a	n/a	1.25	1.00	1.25	1.25
60,000 to 99,999 sf	n/a	n/a	n/a	n/a	1.15	1.00	1.15	1.20
More than 99,999 sf	n/a	n/a	n/a	n/a	1.00	1.00	1.00	1.00
High Tech/R&D	n/a	n/a	n/a	n/a	n/a	3.00	3.00	3.00

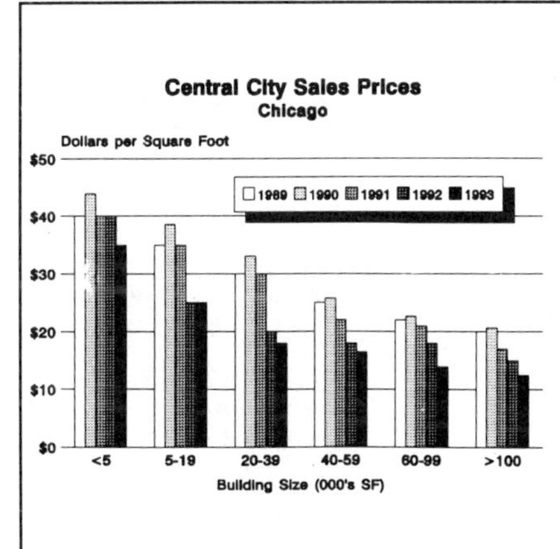

1993 Review

Net absorption hit 4 million sq. ft. in 1993 as demand for large spaces, 150,000 to 450,000 sq. ft., soared. The "Big Box" build-to-suit phenomenon, which began in late 1992, has not yet let up. SIOR's correspondents report that 3.5 million sq. ft. of build-to-suit deals and 1.0 million sq. ft. of speculative space was completed in 1993. Rising rents propelled development. Corporate consolidations and restructurings placed some bigger blocks of space into the market. Conversions to other uses, such as retail, are reducing the industrial inventory.

1994 Forecast

Total vacancy in Chicago stands at 72,100,000 sq. ft. Few cities in the U.S. contain industrial markets of this size. The sheer volume of available space will depress market conditions. Market rents will depreciate by six to 10 percent in 1994. Demand for specialized-use facilities will result in another round of build-to-suit developments. Investors will find bargains, as sales prices continue to fall in 1994.

HOUSTON, TEXAS: INDUSTRIAL

Houston, Texas

MARKET DATA

Inventory (sf)	Central City	Suburban
Total	70,000,000	200,000,000
Vacant	16,000,000	18,000,000
Vacancy Rates	22.9%	9.0%
Under Construction	0	1,000,000
Net Absorption	0	0

Site Prices ($/sf)	Central City	Suburban
Improved Sites		
Less than 2 acres	1.50-6.00	.70-5.00
2 to 5 acres	1.50-6.00	.70-5.00
5 to 10 acres	1.50-5.00	.70-4.00
Over 10 acres	1.00-5.00	.50-4.00
Unimproved Sites		
Less than 10 acres	1.50-5.00	.25-2.50
10 to 100 acres	1.00-3.00	.20-2.00
Over 100 acres	n/a	.10-1.00

Prime Source of Financing: Insurance Companies, Commercial Banks, Owner Financing

Mortgage Money Supply: Tight

CURRENT TRENDS

Composition of Absorption	
Warehouse/Distr.	50.0%
Manufacturing	20.0%
High Tech/R&D	30.0%
Composition of Inventory	
Warehouse/Distr.	40.0%
Manufacturing	40.0%
High Tech/R&D	20.0%
Rate of Construction	
Warehouse/Distr.	Up 1-5%
Manufacturing	Same
High Tech/R&D	Same
Dollar Volume - Sales	
Warehouse/Distr.	Down 1-5%
Manufacturing	Down 1-5%
High Tech/R&D	Down 1-5%
Dollar Volume - Leases	
Warehouse/Distr.	Down 1-5%
Manufacturing	Down 1-5%
High Tech/R&D	Down 1-5%

OUTLOOK

Sales Prices	
Warehouse/Distr.	Up 1-5%
Manufacturing	Same
High Tech/R&D	Up 6-10%
Lease Prices	
Warehouse/Distr.	Up 6-10%
Manufacturing	Same
High Tech/R&D	Up 6-10%
Site Prices	Same
Absorption	
Warehouse/Distr.	Up 1-5%
Manufacturing	Same
High Tech/R&D	Up 1-5%
Construction	
Warehouse/Distr.	Up 1-5%
Manufacturing	Down 1-5%
High Tech/R&D	Same
Dollar Volume - Sales	Same
Dollar Volume - Leases	Same

	Sales Prices ($/sf)		**Gross Lease Prices** ($/sf)		**Construction**	**Vacancy**
	Central City	Suburban	Central City	Suburban	($/sf)	**Indicators**
Less than 5,000 sf	20.00-40.00	15.00-45.00	2.50-4.00	2.50-4.00	25.00-40.00	Balanced Market
5,000 to 19,999 sf	20.00-35.00	15.00-35.00	2.20-4.00	2.20-4.00	20.00-35.00	Balanced Market
20,000 to 39,999 sf	18.00-30.00	15.00-35.00	2.00-3.55	2.00-3.50	20.00-35.00	Moderate Shortage
40,000 to 59,999 sf	15.00-30.00	15.00-30.00	2.00-3.25	2.00-3.25	18.00-30.00	Substantial Shortage
60,000 to 99,999 sf	12.00-25.00	12.00-25.00	1.80-3.00	1.80-3.00	15.00-28.00	Substantial Shortage
More than 99,999 sf	12.00-20.00	12.00-25.00	1.80-2.80	1.80-2.80	14.00-25.00	n/a
High Tech/R&D	15.00-50.00	15.00-50.00	3.50-8.00	3.50-8.00	25.00-50.00	Balanced Market

	Operating Expenses				**Tax Expenses**			
	Warehouse		**Factories**		**Warehouse**		**Factories**	
	Central City	Suburban	Central City	Suburban	Central City	Suburban	Central City	Suburban
Less than 5,000 sf	.95-1.20	.95-1.20	1.00-1.40	1.10-1.50	.45-.60	.40-.60	.45-.60	.40-.60
5,000 to 19,999 sf	.95-1.15	.95-1.15	1.00-1.35	1.10-1.40	.45-.55	.40-.60	.45-.60	.40-.60
20,000 to 39,999 sf	.80-.92	.80-.92	.90-1.00	.95-1.10	.45-.55	.40-.50	.45-.60	.40-.60
40,000 to 59,999 sf	.80-.92	.80-.92	.90-1.00	.95-1.10	.45-.55	.40-.50	.45-.55	.40-.50
60,000 to 99,999 sf	.70-.80	.70-.80	.80-.90	.90-1.00	.40-.50	.35-.45	.40-.50	.35-.45
More than 99,999 sf	.70-.80	.70-.80	.80-.90	.90-1.00	.40-.50	.35-.45	.40-.50	.35-.45
High Tech/R&D	1.40-1.80	1.40-1.80			.45-.60	.40-.60	.40-.60	.40-.60

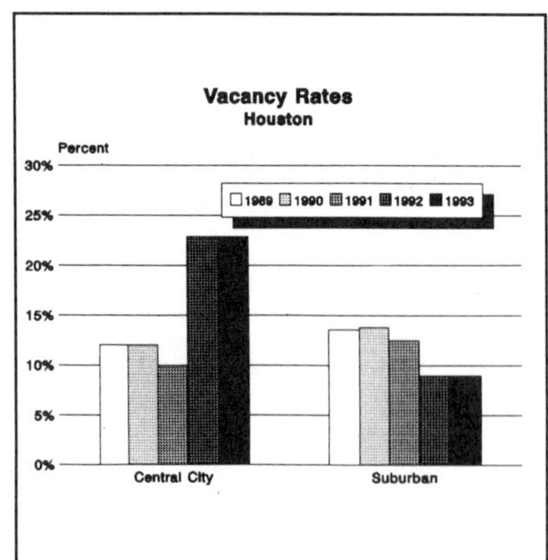

1993 REVIEW

SIOR's Houston correspondent reports no change in market conditions for industrial properties from 1992 to 1993. This is not good news for a market with 24 million sq. ft. of vacant space. Although Houston experienced moderate employment growth, most of the new jobs created have been in the services sector and have not translated into industrial demand. Sales and leasing activity was down slightly for the year but prices have remained firm.

1994 FORECAST

With over 260 academic and government research centers, Houston is poised to be one of the country's high-tech manufacturing leaders. Although the energy industry is still vital to the Houston economy, an increasing number of new manufacturing jobs are expected in such fields as biotechnology, computers, and engineering. About 30 percent of Houston's inventory is used for high-tech/R&D functions and more will be needed once job growth picks up steam. Both lease and sales rates are projected to increase during 1994.

Los Angeles-Central, California: Industrial

Los Angeles-Central, California

Market Data

Inventory (sf)	Central City	Suburban
Total	322,000,000	-
Vacant	32,000,000	-
Vacancy Rates	9.9%	-
Under Construction	100,000	-
Net Absorption	n/a	-

Site Prices ($/sf)	Central City	Suburban
Improved Sites		
Less than 2 acres	9.00-30.00	-
2 to 5 acres	9.00-20.00	-
5 to 10 acres	8.00-15.00	-
Over 10 acres	9.00	-
Unimproved Sites		
Less than 10 acres	9.00	-
10 to 100 acres	9.00	-
Over 100 acres	n/a	-

Prime Source of Financing: Commercial Banks, SBA thru Comm. Bank

Mortgage Money Supply: Tight

Current Trends

Composition of Absorption	
Warehouse/Distr.	75.0%
Manufacturing	20.0%
High Tech/R&D	5.0%
Composition of Inventory	
Warehouse/Distr.	75.0%
Manufacturing	20.0%
High Tech/R&D	5.0%
Rate of Construction	
Warehouse/Distr.	Down 6-10%
Manufacturing	Down 6-10%
High Tech/R&D	Down 6-10%
Dollar Volume - Sales	
Warehouse/Distr.	Down 6-10%
Manufacturing	Down 6-10%
High Tech/R&D	Down 6-10%
Dollar Volume - Leases	
Warehouse/Distr.	Up 1-5%
Manufacturing	Down 6-10%
High Tech/R&D	Down 6-10%

Outlook

Sales Prices	
Warehouse/Distr.	Down 1-5%
Manufacturing	Down 1-5%
High Tech/R&D	Down 1-5%
Lease Prices	
Warehouse/Distr.	Down 1-5%
Manufacturing	Down 1-5%
High Tech/R&D	Down 1-5%
Site Prices	Down 1-5%
Absorption	
Warehouse/Distr.	Up 1-5%
Manufacturing	Up 1-5%
High Tech/R&D	Down 6-10%
Construction	
Warehouse/Distr.	Down 1-5%
Manufacturing	Down 1-5%
High Tech/R&D	Down 1-5%
Dollar Volume - Sales	Up 1-5%
Dollar Volume - Leases	Up 1-5%

	Sales Prices ($/sf)		Net Lease Prices ($/sf)		Construction	Vacancy
	Central City	Suburban	Central City	Suburban	($/sf)	Indicators
Less than 5,000 sf	60.00-100.00	-	5.50-7.00	-	30.00	Moderate Oversupply
5,000 to 19,999 sf	50.00-80.00	-	4.00-6.00	-	27.00	Moderate Oversupply
20,000 to 39,999 sf	40.00-60.00	-	4.00-5.00	-	25.00	Balanced Market
40,000 to 59,999 sf	35.00-50.00	-	2.50-4.00	-	19.00	Balanced Market
60,000 to 99,999 sf	30.00-45.00	-	2.50-4.00	-	18.00	Moderate Oversupply
More than 99,999 sf	30.00-40.00	-	2.50-3.50	-	15.00	Substantial Oversupply
High Tech/R&D	60.00-100.00	-	6.00-10.00	-	45.00	Moderate Oversupply

	Operating Expenses				Tax Expenses			
	Warehouse		Factories		Warehouse		Factories	
	Central City	Suburban	Central City	Suburban	Central City	Suburban	Central City	Suburban
Less than 5,000 sf	n/a	n/a	n/a	n/a	n/a	n/a	n/a	n/a
5,000 to 19,999 sf	n/a	n/a	n/a	n/a	n/a	n/a	n/a	n/a
20,000 to 39,999 sf	n/a	n/a	n/a	n/a	n/a	n/a	n/a	n/a
40,000 to 59,999 sf	n/a	n/a	n/a	n/a	n/a	n/a	n/a	n/a
60,000 to 99,999 sf	n/a	n/a	n/a	n/a	n/a	n/a	n/a	n/a
More than 99,999 sf	n/a	n/a	n/a	n/a	n/a	n/a	n/a	n/a
High Tech/R&D	n/a	n/a	n/a	n/a	n/a	n/a	n/a	n/a

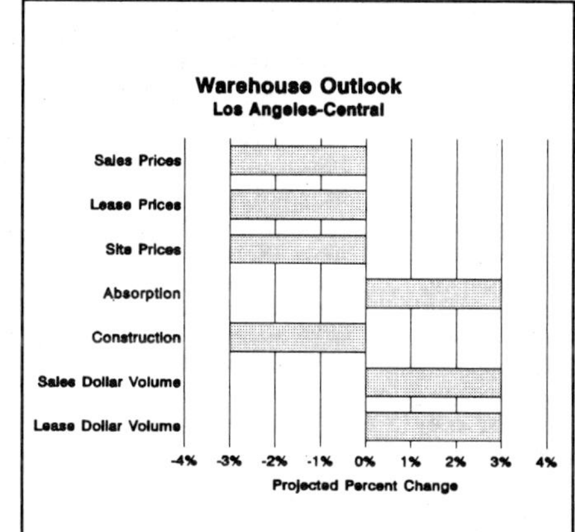

1993 Review

Central Los Angeles' massive industrial market is dominated by warehouse space. About 75 percent of the market's 322 million sq. ft. inventory is used for warehouse/distribution, underscoring not only Los Angeles' role as the center of commerce for Southern California, but the increased importance of U.S. trade with the Pacific Rim. Space available increased again in 1993, rising to 32 million sq. ft. (up from 31.7 million in 1992) representing a vacancy rate of 9.9 percent. Not surprisingly, the added vacancy depressed sales and lease prices.

1994 Forecast

Southern California's weakened economy will provide little support for the Los Angeles-Central industrial market in 1994. Speculative construction will come to a virtual halt, allowing from some positive net absorption, but not enough to stabilize sales and lease prices. After falling by as much as 10 percent in 1993, the dollar volume of sales and leases is expected to decline by as much five percent in 1994 for all industrial property types.

New Jersey-Central: Industrial

Central New Jersey

Market Data

Inventory (sf)	Central City	Suburban
Total	n/a	n/a
Vacant	n/a	26,800,000
Vacancy Rates	n/a	n/a
Under Construction	n/a	0
Net Absorption	n/a	7,200,000

Site Prices ($/sf)	Central City	Suburban
Improved Sites		
Less than 2 acres	n/a	n/a
2 to 5 acres	n/a	n/a
5 to 10 acres	n/a	n/a
Over 10 acres	-	n/a
Unimproved Sites		
Less than 10 acres	n/a	n/a
10 to 100 acres	n/a	n/a
Over 100 acres	n/a	n/a

Prime Source of Financing: Insurance Companies

Mortgage Money Supply: Tight

Current Trends

Composition of Absorption	
Warehouse/Distr.	80.0%
Manufacturing	5.0%
High Tech/R&D	15.0%
Composition of Inventory	
Warehouse/Distr.	n/a
Manufacturing	n/a
High Tech/R&D	n/a
Rate of Construction	
Warehouse/Distr.	Up 6-10%
Manufacturing	Same
High Tech/R&D	Same
Dollar Volume - Sales	
Warehouse/Distr.	Up 6-10%
Manufacturing	Same
High Tech/R&D	Same
Dollar Volume - Leases	
Warehouse/Distr.	Up 6-10%
Manufacturing	Same
High Tech/R&D	Same

Outlook

Sales Prices	
Warehouse/Distr.	Up 6-10%
Manufacturing	Same
High Tech/R&D	Same
Lease Prices	
Warehouse/Distr.	Up 6-10%
Manufacturing	Same
High Tech/R&D	Same
Site Prices	Same
Absorption	
Warehouse/Distr.	Up 6-10%
Manufacturing	Same
High Tech/R&D	Same
Construction	
Warehouse/Distr.	Up 6-10%
Manufacturing	Down 11-15%
High Tech/R&D	Same
Dollar Volume - Sales	Up 6-10%
Dollar Volume - Leases	Up 6-10%

	Sales Prices ($/sf)		Net Lease Prices ($/sf)		Construction	Vacancy
	Central City	Suburban	Central City	Suburban	($/sf)	Indicators
Less than 5,000 sf	25.00	45.00	3.50	6.00	50.00	Balanced Market
5,000 to 19,999 sf	22.00	39.00	3.00	5.25	40.00-45.00	Balanced Market
20,000 to 39,999 sf	15.00	38.00	3.00	5.00	35.00	Balanced Market
40,000 to 59,999 sf	12.00	38.00	2.50	4.00	33.00	Substantial Oversupply
60,000 to 99,999 sf	12.00	30.00	2.50	4.00	30.00	Moderate Oversupply
More than 99,999 sf	10.00	33.00	2.50	3.50	30.00	Balanced Market
High Tech/R&D	n/a	60.00	7.50	7.00	70.00	Moderate Oversupply

	Operating Expenses				Tax Expenses			
	Warehouse		Factories		Warehouse		Factories	
	Central City	Suburban	Central City	Suburban	Central City	Suburban	Central City	Suburban
Less than 5,000 sf	n/a	n/a	n/a	n/a	n/a	n/a	n/a	n/a
5,000 to 19,999 sf	n/a	n/a	n/a	n/a	n/a	n/a	n/a	n/a
20,000 to 39,999 sf	n/a	n/a	n/a	n/a	n/a	n/a	n/a	n/a
40,000 to 59,999 sf	n/a	n/a	n/a	n/a	n/a	n/a	n/a	n/a
60,000 to 99,999 sf	n/a	n/a	n/a	n/a	n/a	n/a	n/a	n/a
More than 99,999 sf	n/a	n/a	n/a	n/a	n/a	n/a	n/a	n/a
High Tech/R&D	n/a	n/a	n/a	n/a	n/a	n/a	n/a	n/a

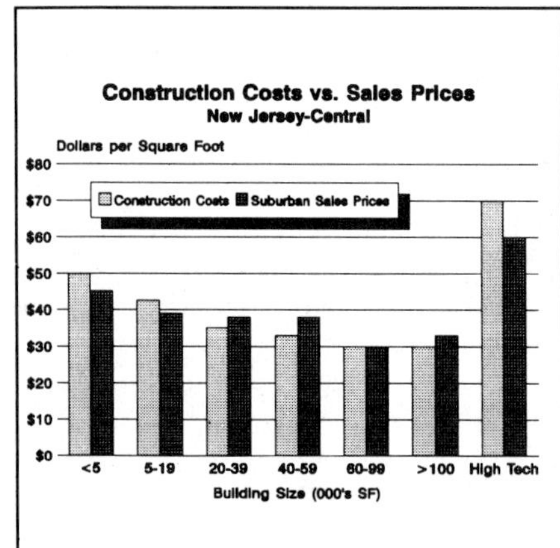

1993 Review

Since central New Jersey serves as a major distribution point for New York City and other East Coast markets, much of its industrial market is comprised of warehouse/distribution space. Slowly recovering national and regional economies have boosted trade and transportation activity in the market, pushing demand for industrial space up significantly in 1993. The dollar volume of sales and leasing in warehouse properties increased by a range of six to 10 percent for the year while activity among other property types remained stagnant.

1994 Forecast

Steady job growth over the next two years forecasted by Data Resources Inc. for the counties that comprise New Jersey — Central bodes well for the industrial market. Although manufacturing and high-tech space will record another year of lackluster activity in 1994, demand for warehouse space is expected to rise again, supporting healthy gains in both sales and lease rates.

New Jersey-Northern: Industrial

New Jersey-Northern

Market Data

Inventory (sf)	Central City	Suburban
Total	n/a	n/a
Vacant	n/a	57,900,000
Vacancy Rates	n/a	n/a
Under Construction	n/a	0
Net Absorption	n/a	6,300,000

Site Prices ($/sf)	Central City	Suburban
Improved Sites		
Less than 2 acres	7.00	7.00
2 to 5 acres	6.00	6.50
5 to 10 acres	5.00	6.50
Over 10 acres	n/a	6.00
Unimproved Sites		
Less than 10 acres	n/a	4.00
10 to 100 acres	n/a	3.50
Over 100 acres	n/a	n/a

Prime Source of Financing: Insurance Companies

Mortgage Money Supply: Tight

Current Trends

Composition of Absorption	
Warehouse/Distr.	75.0%
Manufacturing	5.0%
High Tech/R&D	20.0%
Composition of Inventory	
Warehouse/Distr.	n/a
Manufacturing	n/a
High Tech/R&D	n/a
Rate of Construction	
Warehouse/Distr.	Same
Manufacturing	Same
High Tech/R&D	Same
Dollar Volume - Sales	
Warehouse/Distr.	Up 6-10%
Manufacturing	Same
High Tech/R&D	Same
Dollar Volume - Leases	
Warehouse/Distr.	Up 6-10%
Manufacturing	Same
High Tech/R&D	Same

Outlook

Sales Prices	
Warehouse/Distr.	Up 6-10%
Manufacturing	Same
High Tech/R&D	Same
Lease Prices	
Warehouse/Distr.	Up 6-10%
Manufacturing	Same
High Tech/R&D	Same
Site Prices	Same
Absorption	
Warehouse/Distr.	Up 6-10%
Manufacturing	Down 6-10%
High Tech/R&D	Same
Construction	
Warehouse/Distr.	Up 6-10%
Manufacturing	Same
High Tech/R&D	Same
Dollar Volume - Sales	Up 1-5%
Dollar Volume - Leases	Up 1-5%

	Sales Prices ($/sf)		Net Lease Prices ($/sf)		Construction	Vacancy
	Central City	Suburban	Central City	Suburban	($/sf)	Indicators
Less than 5,000 sf	45.00	63.00	5.00	6.50	50.00	Balanced Market
5,000 to 19,999 sf	35.00	54.00	4.50	5.75	40.00-45.00	Balanced Market
20,000 to 39,999 sf	35.00	50.00	4.00	5.25	35.00	Moderate Oversupply
40,000 to 59,999 sf	30.00	40.00	3.75	4.75	33.00	Moderate Oversupply
60,000 to 99,999 sf	25.00	40.00	3.50	4.50	30.00	Moderate Oversupply
More than 99,999 sf	25.00	35.00	3.50	4.50	30.00	Moderate Shortage
High Tech/R&D	n/a	65.00	n/a	7.00	70.00	n/a

	Operating Expenses				Tax Expenses			
	Warehouse		Factories		Warehouse		Factories	
	Central City	Suburban	Central City	Suburban	Central City	Suburban	Central City	Suburban
Less than 5,000 sf	n/a	n/a	n/a	n/a	n/a	n/a	n/a	n/a
5,000 to 19,999 sf	n/a	n/a	n/a	n/a	n/a	n/a	n/a	n/a
20,000 to 39,999 sf	n/a	n/a	n/a	n/a	n/a	n/a	n/a	n/a
40,000 to 59,999 sf	n/a	n/a	n/a	n/a	n/a	n/a	n/a	n/a
60,000 to 99,999 sf	n/a	n/a	n/a	n/a	n/a	n/a	n/a	n/a
More than 99,999 sf	n/a	n/a	n/a	n/a	n/a	n/a	n/a	n/a
High Tech/R&D	n/a	n/a	n/a	n/a	n/a	n/a	n/a	n/a

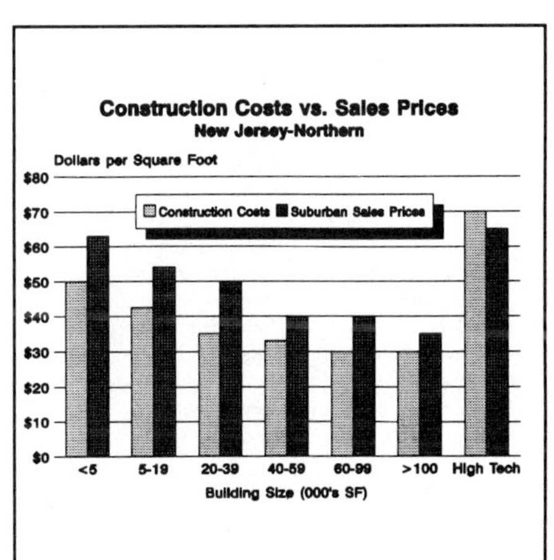

1993 Review

Northern New Jersey's supply of vacant industrial space dropped to 57.9 million sq. ft. in 1993, down from 64.3 million sq. ft. in 1992. Driven primarily by job growth in the trade and transportation sectors, demand for industrial properties gained momentum during the second half of the year. Still, most market segments are oversupplied. Warehouse/distribution space continues to be the strongest performer among industrial property types. The dollar volume of warehouse sales and leasing transaction increased by a range of six to 10 percent during 1993.

1994 Forecast

Northern New Jersey's continued investment in infrastructure, including the extension of I-287, the Route 24 link between I-287 and I-78, and the rail system connecting downtown Newark, Elizabeth, and Newark International Airport are expected to facilitate future job growth. These transportation improvements will be especially beneficial to the region's distributors and should serve to boost demand for industrial property. Speculative construction in 1994 will, for the most part, be dormant, although SIOR's correspondent projects a slight increase in warehouse development.

New Jersey-Southern: Industrial

Camden, Gloucester, and Burlington Counties, New Jersey

Market Data

Inventory (sf)	Central City	Suburban
Total	-	27,590,190
Vacant	-	3,586,725
Vacancy Rates	-	13.0%
Under Construction	-	n/a
Net Absorption	-	n/a

Site Prices ($/sf)	Central City	Suburban
Improved Sites		
Less than 2 acres	-	1.70
2 to 5 acres	-	1.70
5 to 10 acres	-	1.40
Over 10 acres	-	1.38
Unimproved Sites		
Less than 10 acres	-	1.00
10 to 100 acres	-	.90
Over 100 acres	-	.85

Prime Source of Financing: Insurance Companies, Commercial Banks, Owner Financing

Mortgage Money Supply: Tight

Current Trends

Composition of Absorption	
Warehouse/Distr.	85.0%
Manufacturing	5.0%
High Tech/R&D	10.0%
Composition of Inventory	
Warehouse/Distr.	80.0%
Manufacturing	15.0%
High Tech/R&D	5.0%
Rate of Construction	
Warehouse/Distr.	Same
Manufacturing	Same
High Tech/R&D	Same
Dollar Volume - Sales	
Warehouse/Distr.	Down 6-10%
Manufacturing	Down 6-10%
High Tech/R&D	Same
Dollar Volume - Leases	
Warehouse/Distr.	Up 1-5%
Manufacturing	Up 1-5%
High Tech/R&D	Up 1-5%

Outlook

Sales Prices	
Warehouse/Distr.	Same
Manufacturing	Same
High Tech/R&D	Same
Lease Prices	
Warehouse/Distr.	Up 6-10%
Manufacturing	Up 1-5%
High Tech/R&D	Up 1-5%
Site Prices	Same
Absorption	
Warehouse/Distr.	Same
Manufacturing	Same
High Tech/R&D	Same
Construction	
Warehouse/Distr.	Same
Manufacturing	Same
High Tech/R&D	Same
Dollar Volume - Sales	Same
Dollar Volume - Leases	Same

	Sales Prices ($/sf)		**Net Lease Prices** ($/sf)		**Construction**	**Vacancy**
	Central City	Suburban	Central City	Suburban	($/sf)	**Indicators**
Less than 5,000 sf	-	n/a	-	3.50-4.00	40.00-60.00	Balanced Market
5,000 to 19,999 sf	-	n/a	-	3.50-4.00	40.00-45.00	Moderate Oversupply
20,000 to 39,999 sf	-	n/a	-	3.25-3.50	35.00-40.00	Moderate Oversupply
40,000 to 59,999 sf	-	n/a	-	3.25-3.50	30.00-34.00	Moderate Oversupply
60,000 to 99,999 sf	-	35.00	-	3.25-3.50	26.00-32.00	Balanced Market
More than 99,999 sf	-	19.00-23.00	-	3.25-3.50	24.00-27.00	Balanced Market
High Tech/R&D	-	n/a	-	5.00	24.00-27.00	Moderate Oversupply

	Operating Expenses				**Tax Expenses**			
	Warehouse		**Factories**		**Warehouse**		**Factories**	
	Central City	Suburban	Central City	Suburban	Central City	Suburban	Central City	Suburban
Less than 5,000 sf	-	.90-1.60	-	.90-1.60	-	.65-1.00	-	.65-1.00
5,000 to 19,999 sf	-	.90-1.60	-	.90-1.60	-	.55-.90	-	.55-.90
20,000 to 39,999 sf	-	.90-1.60	-	.90-1.60	-	.55-.90	-	.55-.90
40,000 to 59,999 sf	-	.90-1.60	-	.90-1.60	-	.55-.85	-	.55-.90
60,000 to 99,999 sf	-	.90-1.60	-	.90-1.60	-	.55-.85	-	.55-.85
More than 99,999 sf	-	.90-1.60	-	.90-1.60	-	.55-.85	-	.55-.85
High Tech/R&D	-	.90-1.60	-	-	-	.85-1.10	-	.85-1.10

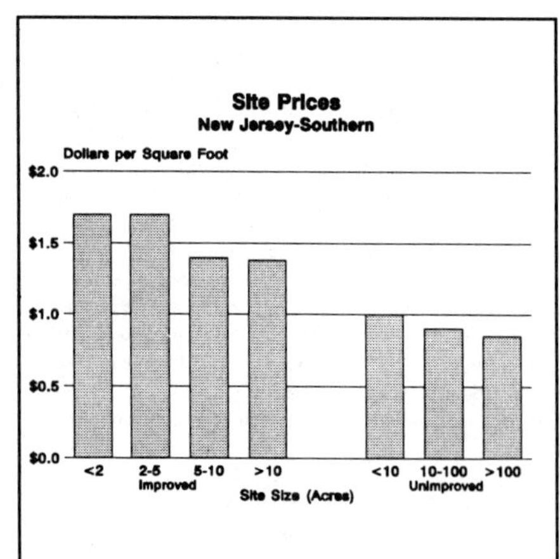

1993 Review

Cutbacks in defense spending have had a negative effect on employment levels in the southern New Jersey region and have served to limit demand for area industrial space. During 1993, space in the 10,000 to 20,000 sq. ft. range and for properties over 90,000 sq. ft. experienced a moderate increase in demand. Most of the leasing involved firms already present in the southern New Jersey market. Little improvement in sales activity occurred and most transactions remain extremely price sensitive.

1994 Forecast

A 195,000 sq. ft. building in the Commodore I-295 Business Park in Gloucester County represents the only significant speculative construction currently planned for 1994. With downsizing still likely to occur among some of the region's major employers, this low level of new development is welcome news. As of third quarter 1993, the average vacancy rate in southern New Jersey industrial properties was a comparatively high 13 percent.

New York City, New York: Industrial

Manhattan, New York, New York (Generally represents loft buildings)

Market Data

Inventory (sf)	Central City	Suburban
Total	n/a	-
Vacant	n/a	-
Vacancy Rates	n/a	-
Under Construction	n/a	-
Net Absorption	n/a	-

Site Prices ($/sf)	Central City	Suburban
Improved Sites		
Less than 2 acres	n/a	n/a
2 to 5 acres	n/a	n/a
5 to 10 acres	n/a	n/a
Over 10 acres	n/a	n/a
Unimproved Sites		
Less than 10 acres	n/a	n/a
10 to 100 acres	n/a	n/a
Over 100 acres	n/a	n/a

Prime Source of Financing: Insurance Companies, Commercial Banks, Owner Financing

Mortgage Money Supply: Tight

Current Trends

Composition of Absorption	
Warehouse/Distr.	n/a
Manufacturing	n/a
High Tech/R&D	0.0%
Composition of Inventory	
Warehouse/Distr.	40.0%
Manufacturing	60.0%
High Tech/R&D	0.0%
Rate of Construction	
Warehouse/Distr.	Same
Manufacturing	Same
High Tech/R&D	Same
Dollar Volume - Sales	
Warehouse/Distr.	Same
Manufacturing	Same
High Tech/R&D	Same
Dollar Volume - Leases	
Warehouse/Distr.	Down Moderately%
Manufacturing	Down Moderately%
High Tech/R&D	Down

Outlook

Sales Prices	
Warehouse/Distr.	Same
Manufacturing	Same
High Tech/R&D	Same
Lease Prices	
Warehouse/Distr.	Down 1-5%
Manufacturing	Down 1-5%
High Tech/R&D	Same
Site Prices	Same
Absorption	
Warehouse/Distr.	Up 1-5%
Manufacturing	Up 1-5%
High Tech/R&D	Same
Construction	
Warehouse/Distr.	Same
Manufacturing	Same
High Tech/R&D	Same
Dollar Volume - Sales	Up 1-5%
Dollar Volume - Leases	Up 1-5%

	Sales Prices ($/sf)		**Net Lease Prices** ($/sf)		**Construction**	**Vacancy**
	Central City	Suburban	Central City	Suburban	($/sf)	**Indicators**
Less than 5,000 sf	30.00-120.00	-	5.00-20.00	-	n/a	Moderate Oversupply
5,000 to 19,999 sf	30.00-120.00	-	5.00-20.00	-	n/a	Moderate Oversupply
20,000 to 39,999 sf	25.00-110.00	-	4.50-15.00	-	n/a	Balanced Market
40,000 to 59,999 sf	25.00-110.00	-	4.50-15.00	-	n/a	Balanced Market
60,000 to 99,999 sf	25.00-110.00	-	4.00-15.00	-	n/a	Balanced Market
More than 99,999 sf	25.00-110.00	-	4.00-15.00	-	n/a	Moderate Shortage
High Tech/R&D	n/a	-	n/a	-	n/a	Substantial Shortage

	Operating Expenses				**Tax Expenses**			
	Warehouse		**Factories**		**Warehouse**		**Factories**	
	Central City	Suburban	Central City	Suburban	Central City	Suburban	Central City	Suburban
Less than 5,000 sf	n/a	n/a	n/a	n/a	n/a	n/a	n/a	n/a
5,000 to 19,999 sf	n/a	n/a	n/a	n/a	n/a	n/a	n/a	n/a
20,000 to 39,999 sf	n/a	n/a	n/a	n/a	n/a	n/a	n/a	n/a
40,000 to 59,999 sf	n/a	n/a	n/a	n/a	n/a	n/a	n/a	n/a
60,000 to 99,999 sf	n/a	n/a	n/a	n/a	n/a	n/a	n/a	n/a
More than 99,999 sf	n/a	n/a	n/a	n/a	n/a	n/a	n/a	n/a
High Tech/R&D	n/a	n/a	n/a	n/a	n/a	n/a	n/a	n/a

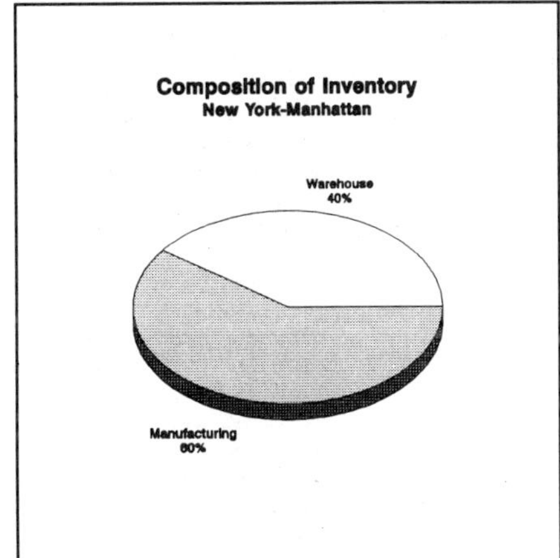

1993 Review

Housing a variety of functions, ranging from garage and auto service stations to light-assembly plants, print shops, and apparel industry facilities, Manhattan's industrial market has been shrinking for decades. High costs hasten the conversion of industrial space into higher uses. Softness in the office market has slowed this process, and new zoning regulations promoting Manhattan's manufacturing businesses could reverse the trend. Compared to national standards, lease rates are extremely high.

1994 Forecast

Another stagnant year is projected for the industrial market. No improvement is expected in sales prices, and lease rates, which have fallen over the last three years, and are likely to drop again. The rate of attrition of industrial properties may be stanched if zoning regulations designed to make it easier for Manhattan businesses to expand are adopted.

New York City-Bronx, New York: Industrial

New York City-Bronx, New York

Market Data

Inventory (sf)	Central City	Suburban
Total	30,000,000	-
Vacant	4,500,000	-
Vacancy Rates	15.0%	-
Under Construction	0	-
Net Absorption	-200,000	-

Site Prices ($/sf)	Central City	Suburban
Improved Sites		
Less than 2 acres	-	-
2 to 5 acres	-	-
5 to 10 acres	-	-
Over 10 acres	-	-
Unimproved Sites		
Less than 10 acres	-	-
10 to 100 acres	-	-
Over 100 acres	-	-

Prime Source of Financing: -

Mortgage Money Supply: Tight

Current Trends

Composition of Absorption	
Warehouse/Distr.	75.0%
Manufacturing	25.0%
High Tech/R&D	-
Composition of Inventory	
Warehouse/Distr.	75.0%
Manufacturing	25.0%
High Tech/R&D	-
Rate of Construction	
Warehouse/Distr.	n/a
Manufacturing	n/a
High Tech/R&D	n/a
Dollar Volume - Sales	
Warehouse/Distr.	n/a
Manufacturing	n/a
High Tech/R&D	n/a
Dollar Volume - Leases	
Warehouse/Distr.	n/a
Manufacturing	n/a
High Tech/R&D	n/a

Outlook

Sales Prices	
Warehouse/Distr.	Down 11-15%
Manufacturing	Down 11-15%
High Tech/R&D	Down 11-15%
Lease Prices	
Warehouse/Distr.	Down 11-15%
Manufacturing	Down 11-15%
High Tech/R&D	Down 11-15%
Site Prices	n/a
Absorption	
Warehouse/Distr.	n/a
Manufacturing	n/a
High Tech/R&D	n/a
Construction	
Warehouse/Distr.	n/a
Manufacturing	n/a
High Tech/R&D	n/a
Dollar Volume - Sales	n/a
Dollar Volume - Leases	n/a

	Sales Prices ($/sf)		Gross Lease Prices ($/sf)		Construction	Vacancy
	Central City	Suburban	Central City	Suburban	($/sf)	Indicators
Less than 5,000 sf	6.00	-	-	-	-	Moderate Oversupply
5,000 to 19,999 sf	4.50	-	-	-	-	Moderate Oversupply
20,000 to 39,999 sf	4.50	-	-	-	-	Moderate Oversupply
40,000 to 59,999 sf	4.50	-	-	-	-	Moderate Oversupply
60,000 to 99,999 sf	4.00	-	-	-	-	Moderate Oversupply
More than 99,999 sf	4.00	-	-	-	-	Moderate Oversupply
High Tech/R&D	-	-	-	-	-	Moderate Oversupply

	Operating Expenses				Tax Expenses			
	Warehouse		Factories		Warehouse		Factories	
	Central City	Suburban	Central City	Suburban	Central City	Suburban	Central City	Suburban
Less than 5,000 sf	0.00	-	0.00	-	1.25	-	1.25	-
5,000 to 19,999 sf	0.00	-	0.00	-	1.25	-	1.25	-
20,000 to 39,999 sf	0.00	-	0.00	-	1.25	-	1.25	-
40,000 to 59,999 sf	0.00	-	0.00	-	1.25	-	1.25	-
60,000 to 99,999 sf	0.00	-	0.00	-	1.25	-	1.25	-
More than 99,999 sf	0.00	-	0.00	-	1.25	-	1.25	-
High Tech/R&D	0.00	-	-	-	1.25	-	1.25	-

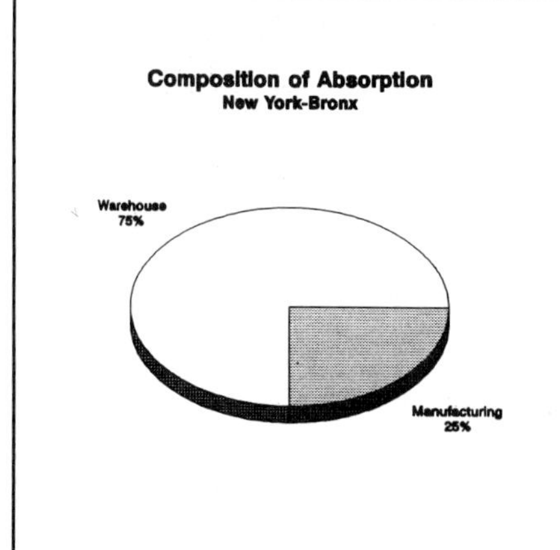

1993 Review

Located north of Manhattan, the Bronx industrial market totals approximately 30 million sq. ft. and is still evolving from manufacturing uses to warehouse/distribution functions. Like much industrial property in the five boroughs, the Bronx market is in decline due to decreasing manufacturing employment and pressure to convert available space into higher uses. With the recession, however, gentrification has stalled, which in effect causes vacancy to rise. Negative net absorption of two million sq. ft. was reported for 1993 as the vacancy rate rose to an average of 15 percent.

1994 Forecast

Sales and lease prices have dropped on average by 30 percent in the Bronx industrial market and are expected to fall further in 1994. A soft Manhattan market has sapped demand since a number of tenants who traditionally sought cheaper space in the Bronx are finding good deals in Manhattan. Prices are expected to drop another 11 to 15 percent in 1994 which may, in the long run, be beneficial. The Bronx, along with most of the city, has suffered a tremendous out-migration of production jobs due to high costs. Lower rents may induce some businesses to forego relocation plans.

New York City-Brooklyn/Queens, New York: Industrial

New York City-Brooklyn/Queens, New York

Market Data

Inventory (sf)	Central City	Suburban
Total	330,000,000	-
Vacant	56,000,000	-
Vacancy Rates	17.0%	-
Under Construction	0	-
Net Absorption	15,000,000	-

Site Prices ($/sf)	Central City	Suburban
Improved Sites		
Less than 2 acres	10.00-20.00	-
2 to 5 acres	8.00-15.00	-
5 to 10 acres	7.00-15.00	-
Over 10 acres	6.00-15.00	-
Unimproved Sites		
Less than 10 acres	n/a	-
10 to 100 acres	n/a	-
Over 100 acres	n/a	-

Prime Source of Financing: Owner Financing

Mortgage Money Supply: Tight

Current Trends

Composition of Absorption	
Warehouse/Distr.	78.0%
Manufacturing	21.0%
High Tech/R&D	1.0%
Composition of Inventory	
Warehouse/Distr.	60.0%
Manufacturing	30.0%
High Tech/R&D	10.0%
Rate of Construction	
Warehouse/Distr.	n/a
Manufacturing	n/a
High Tech/R&D	n/a
Dollar Volume - Sales	
Warehouse/Distr.	Down 11-15%
Manufacturing	Down 40%
High Tech/R&D	Down 90%
Dollar Volume - Leases	
Warehouse/Distr.	Down 11-15%
Manufacturing	Down 11-15%
High Tech/R&D	Down 35%

Outlook

Sales Prices	
Warehouse/Distr.	Down 6-10%
Manufacturing	Down 6-10%
High Tech/R&D	Down 11-15%
Lease Prices	
Warehouse/Distr.	Down 11-15%
Manufacturing	Down 11-15%
High Tech/R&D	Down 20%
Site Prices	Same
Absorption	
Warehouse/Distr.	Same
Manufacturing	Same
High Tech/R&D	Same
Construction	
Warehouse/Distr.	n/a
Manufacturing	n/a
High Tech/R&D	n/a
Dollar Volume - Sales	Down 11-15%
Dollar Volume - Leases	Down 11-15%

	Sales Prices ($/sf)		**Gross Lease Prices** ($/sf)		**Construction**	**Vacancy**
	Central City	Suburban	Central City	Suburban	($/sf)	**Indicators**
Less than 5,000 sf	20.00-35.00	-	3.75-5.75	-	45.00	Moderate Oversupply
5,000 to 19,999 sf	15.00-30.00	-	3.35-4.50	-	40.00	Moderate Oversupply
20,000 to 39,999 sf	17.00-30.00	-	2.75-4.25	-	40.00	Balanced Market
40,000 to 59,999 sf	12.00-30.00	-	2.50-4.25	-	35.00	Substantial Oversupply
60,000 to 99,999 sf	10.00-30.00	-	2.25-3.75	-	32.00	Substantial Oversupply
More than 99,999 sf	10.00-25.00	-	2.25-3.75	-	30.00	Substantial Oversupply
High Tech/R&D	30.00-40.00	-	4.00-5.00	-	110.00	Moderate Oversupply

	Operating Expenses				**Tax Expenses**			
	Warehouse		**Factories**		**Warehouse**		**Factories**	
	Central City	Suburban	Central City	Suburban	Central City	Suburban	Central City	Suburban
Less than 5,000 sf	n/a	-	n/a	-	1.25	-	1.25	-
5,000 to 19,999 sf	n/a	-	n/a	-	1.25	-	1.25	-
20,000 to 39,999 sf	n/a	-	n/a	-	1.35	-	1.35	-
40,000 to 59,999 sf	n/a	-	n/a	-	1.35	-	1.35	-
60,000 to 99,999 sf	n/a	-	n/a	-	1.35	-	1.35	-
More than 99,999 sf	n/a	-	n/a	-	1.35	-	1.35	-
High Tech/R&D	n/a	-	-	-	2.50	-	2.50	-

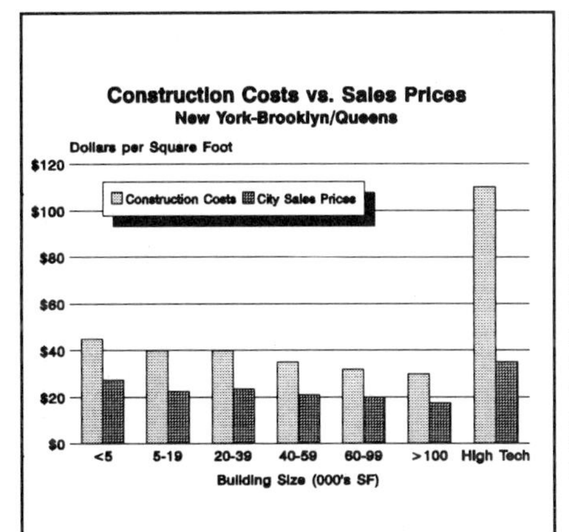

1993 Review

Given the sluggish pace of the New York City economy, demand for industrial property in the Brooklyn and Queens market was surprisingly strong in 1993. The supply of vacant space dropped by an estimated 15 million sq. ft. over the year and as of third quarter, the vacancy rate averaged 17 percent, down from 18.5 percent in 1992. Demand was especially strong for small buildings totalling 50,000 sq. ft. or less. Sales volumes continued to fall, dropping for manufacturing space and in the comparatively small high tech/R&D market.

1994 Forecast

SIOR's reporter expects some market indicators to further deteriorate in 1994. Sales and lease prices are projected to drop again, falling from six to 20 percent depending upon the property type and size. New construction will be negligible and the only development activity is likely to be the sale and conversion of industrial buildings or sites into "big box" retail discount operations. But net absorption should match 1993's performance, further reducing the market's overhang of unoccupied space.

San Francisco, California: Industrial

San Francisco, California

Market Data

Inventory (sf)	Central City	Suburban
Total	28,000,000	-
Vacant	2,440,000	-
Vacancy Rates	8.7%	-
Under Construction	0	-
Net Absorption	-60,000	-

Site Prices ($/sf)	Central City	Suburban
Improved Sites		
Less than 2 acres	45.00	-
2 to 5 acres	35.00	-
5 to 10 acres	25.00	-
Over 10 acres	22.00	-
Unimproved Sites		
Less than 10 acres	n/a	-
10 to 100 acres	n/a	-
Over 100 acres	n/a	-

Prime Source of Financing: Pension Funds

Mortgage Money Supply: Tight

Current Trends

Composition of Absorption	
Warehouse/Distr.	60.0%
Manufacturing	30.0%
High Tech/R&D	10.0%
Composition of Inventory	
Warehouse/Distr.	60.0%
Manufacturing	30.0%
High Tech/R&D	10.0%
Rate of Construction	
Warehouse/Distr.	Same
Manufacturing	Same
High Tech/R&D	Same
Dollar Volume - Sales	
Warehouse/Distr.	Down 6-10%
Manufacturing	Down 6-10%
High Tech/R&D	Down 6-10%
Dollar Volume - Leases	
Warehouse/Distr.	Down 11-15%
Manufacturing	Down 11-15%
High Tech/R&D	Down 11-15%

Outlook

Sales Prices	
Warehouse/Distr.	Up 6-10%
Manufacturing	Up 1-5%
High Tech/R&D	Up 1-5%
Lease Prices	
Warehouse/Distr.	Up 1-5%
Manufacturing	Same
High Tech/R&D	Same
Site Prices	Same
Absorption	
Warehouse/Distr.	Down 6-10%
Manufacturing	Down 6-10%
High Tech/R&D	Down 11-15%
Construction	
Warehouse/Distr.	Same
Manufacturing	Same
High Tech/R&D	Same
Dollar Volume - Sales	Down 6-10%
Dollar Volume - Leases	Down 6-10%

	Sales Prices ($/sf)		Net Lease Prices ($/sf)		Construction	Vacancy
	Central City	Suburban	Central City	Suburban	($/sf)	Indicators
Less than 5,000 sf	64.00-68.00	-	7.80	-	40.00	Balanced Market
5,000 to 19,999 sf	52.00-62.00	-	6.00	-	35.00	Balanced Market
20,000 to 39,999 sf	42.00-53.00	-	4.25	-	35.00	Balanced Market
40,000 to 59,999 sf	40.00-51.00	-	4.25	-	35.00	Moderate Oversupply
60,000 to 99,999 sf	40.00-50.00	-	4.25	-	35.00	Moderate Oversupply
More than 99,999 sf	38.00-40.00	-	4.20	-	25.00	Moderate Oversupply
High Tech/R&D	70.00-95.00	-	9.00	-	55.00	Moderate Oversupply

	Operating Expenses				Tax Expenses			
	Warehouse		Factories		Warehouse		Factories	
	Central City	Suburban	Central City	Suburban	Central City	Suburban	Central City	Suburban
Less than 5,000 sf	n/a	n/a	n/a	n/a	n/a	n/a	n/a	n/a
5,000 to 19,999 sf	n/a	n/a	n/a	n/a	n/a	n/a	n/a	n/a
20,000 to 39,999 sf	n/a	n/a	n/a	n/a	n/a	n/a	n/a	n/a
40,000 to 59,999 sf	n/a	n/a	n/a	n/a	n/a	n/a	n/a	n/a
60,000 to 99,999 sf	n/a	n/a	n/a	n/a	n/a	n/a	n/a	n/a
More than 99,999 sf	n/a	n/a	n/a	n/a	n/a	n/a	n/a	n/a
High Tech/R&D	n/a	n/a	n/a	n/a	n/a	n/a	n/a	n/a

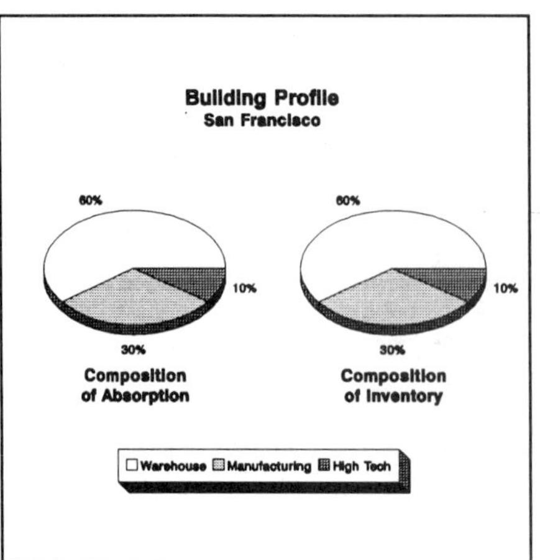

1993 Review

SIOR's correspondent reports no change in market conditions in San Francisco during 1993. Vacancy is stuck at 8.7 percent, representing 2.4 million sq. ft. of unoccupied space. Another 60,000 sq. ft. of negative net absorption was recorded in the market over the last year, reflecting the ongoing weakness of the California economy and the exodus of industrial users to locations outside the MSA.

1994 Forecast

The San Francisco industrial market will continue to soften in 1994. As consolidations and cutbacks among Bay area firms enter into another year, demand for industrial property types is projected to decline. As a result, landlords will be forced to lower sales and lease rates yet again in an effort to compete for the shrinking pool of potential tenants.

TUCSON, ARIZONA: INDUSTRIAL

Tucson, Arizona

MARKET DATA

Inventory (sf)	Central City	Suburban
Total	7,363,456	-
Vacant	986,608	-
Vacancy Rates	13.4%	-
Under Construction	253,000	-
Net Absorption	487,551	-

Site Prices ($/sf)	Central City	Suburban
Improved Sites		
Less than 2 acres	1.75	-
2 to 5 acres	1.60	-
5 to 10 acres	1.50	-
Over 10 acres	1.40	-
Unimproved Sites		
Less than 10 acres	.50	-
10 to 100 acres	.20	-
Over 100 acres	.10	-

Prime Source of Financing: Commercial Banks, SBA

Mortgage Money Supply: Tight

CURRENT TRENDS

Composition of Absorption	
Warehouse/Distr.	35.0%
Manufacturing	30.0%
High Tech/R&D	35.0%
Composition of Inventory	
Warehouse/Distr.	35.0%
Manufacturing	50.0%
High Tech/R&D	15.0%
Rate of Construction	
Warehouse/Distr.	Up 70%
Manufacturing	Up 40%
High Tech/R&D	Same
Dollar Volume - Sales	
Warehouse/Distr.	Same
Manufacturing	Up 11-15%
High Tech/R&D	Up 25%
Dollar Volume - Leases	
Warehouse/Distr.	Up 6-10%
Manufacturing	Up 6-10%
High Tech/R&D	Up 11-15%

OUTLOOK

Sales Prices	
Warehouse/Distr.	Up 6-10%
Manufacturing	Up 6-10%
High Tech/R&D	Up 11-15%
Lease Prices	
Warehouse/Distr.	Up 11-15%
Manufacturing	Up 11-15%
High Tech/R&D	Up 11-15%
Site Prices	Up 6-10%
Absorption	
Warehouse/Distr.	Up 1-5%
Manufacturing	Up 6-10%
High Tech/R&D	Up 11-15%
Construction	
Warehouse/Distr.	Up 30%
Manufacturing	Up 11-15%
High Tech/R&D	Up 11-15%
Dollar Volume - Sales	Down 6-10%
Dollar Volume - Leases	Down 1-5%

	Sales Prices ($/sf)		**Net Lease Prices** ($/sf)		**Construction**	**Vacancy**
	Central City	Suburban	Central City	Suburban	($/sf)	**Indicators**
Less than 5,000 sf	30.00	-	3.60	-	35.00	Balanced Market
5,000 to 19,999 sf	25.00	-	3.36	-	30.00	Balanced Market
20,000 to 39,999 sf	25.00	-	3.00	-	30.00	Balanced Market
40,000 to 59,999 sf	25.00	-	3.00	-	28.00	Moderate Shortage
60,000 to 99,999 sf	23.00	-	3.00	-	26.00	Moderate Shortage
More than 99,999 sf	23.00	-	3.00	-	20.00	Moderate Shortage
High Tech/R&D	32.00	-	4.80	-	45.00	Moderate Shortage

	Operating Expenses				**Tax Expenses**			
	Warehouse		**Factories**		**Warehouse**		**Factories**	
	Central City	Suburban	Central City	Suburban	Central City	Suburban	Central City	Suburban
Less than 5,000 sf	.48	-	.48	-	1.20	-	1.30	-
5,000 to 19,999 sf	.60	-	.60	-	1.20	-	1.40	-
20,000 to 39,999 sf	.60	-	.60	-	1.20	-	1.40	-
40,000 to 59,999 sf	.60	-	.60	-	1.20	-	1.40	-
60,000 to 99,999 sf	.48	-	.48	-	1.20	-	1.40	-
More than 99,999 sf	.48	-	.48	-	1.00	-	1.20	-
High Tech/R&D	.72	-	-	-	1.40	-	1.80	-

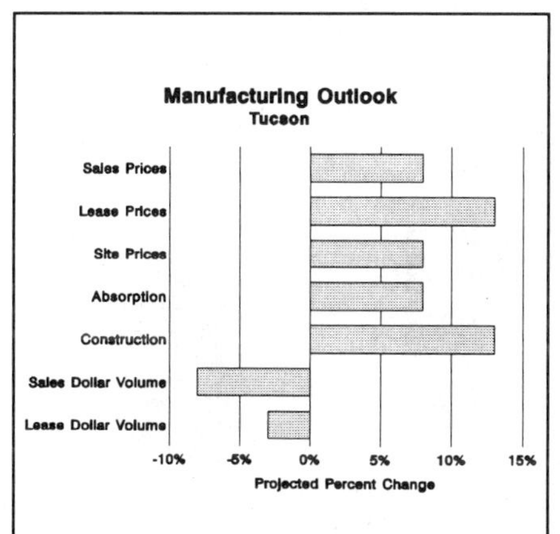

1993 REVIEW

Benefiting from relocations from California, most notably Hughes' decision to consolidate its missile systems operations in Tucson, industrial indicators improved again in 1993. Limited new construction over the past several years combined with strong net absorption has lowered Tucson's vacancy rate to 13.4 percent, down from 12.7 percent in 1991. Land sales have increased and while no speculative projects are currently on the drawing table, a few well-capitalized groups are reportedly discussing industrial development opportunities.

1994 FORECAST

With a much improved balance between supply and demand and sales of the most distressed properties complete, Tucson's industrial market is poised for a promising year in 1994. Lease prices are projected to rise by as much as 15 percent, accompanied by a slightly less robust increase in sales prices. The biggest increase in demand is expected to be for high-tech/R&D space, driven by expanding software development companies, biomedical firms, and the optic technology industry.

Office Real Estate Market: Selected Cities*

ATLANTA, GEORGIA: Office

Atlanta, Georgia

MARKET DATA

	Class A		Class B	
Inventory (sf)	**CBD**	**Outside CBD**	**CBD**	**Outside CBD**
Total	32,411,196	64,972,839	-	-
Vacant	5,047,149	8,303,088	-	-
Vacancy Rate	15.6%	12.8%	-	-
Vacant Sublease	n/a	n/a	-	-
Under Construction	0	850,000	-	-
Substantial Rehab	620,000	112,000	-	-
Net Absorption	357,742	1,011,925	-	-
Rental Rates ($/sf)				
Lowest	19.71	18.05	11.57	11.56
Highest	21.19	18.46	12.83	12.21
Weighted Average	22.83	19.57	13.20	11.83
Sales Prices ($/sf)				
Lowest	n/a	n/a	n/a	n/a
Highest	n/a	n/a	n/a	n/a
Weighted Average	n/a	n/a	n/a	n/a
Operating Expenses ($/sf)				
Lowest	6.50	6.00	5.00	4.50
Highest	9.50	8.95	8.00	7.00
Weighted Average	n/a	n/a	n/a	n/a
Tax Expenses ($/sf)				
Lowest	n/a	n/a	n/a	n/a
Highest	n/a	n/a	n/a	n/a
Weighted Average	n/a	n/a	n/a	n/a

Utility Rates: CBD $1.75 per sf; Outside CBD $1.75 per sf; Not Separately Metered

Parking Ratio: CBD - 1 per 500 sf; Outside CBD - 1 per 250 sf

Standard Work Letter: n/a, typically based on dollars per square foot

Operating Cost Escalation: Base Year

Rate of Return: Cap Rate: n/a; IRR: 9.0%

Mortgage Money Supply: Tight
Prime Source of Financing: Insurance Companies

Cumulative Discount Rate: 20%
Landlord Concessions
Parking, Rental Abatement, Moving Allowance, Interior Improvements

Leasing Activity Profile
Major Activity - Fortune 500 Firms, Legal/Accounting, Business Services, Finance/Banking
Minor Activity - Sales, Engineering/Architecture, Government, Energy

Outlook

Absorption			Up 1-5%
Construction			Up 1-5%
Vacancies			Down 1-5%
Rental Rates			Up 1-5%
Landlord Concessions			Same
Sales	Class A	CBD	n/a
Prices		Outside CBD	n/a
	Class B	CBD	n/a
		Outside CBD	n/a

1993 REVIEW

While Atlanta's overall vacancy is down again this year and leasing activity is reported to be strong, net absorption dropped 52.3 percent from a year ago. A large sublease market appears to be the culprit, with large users such as IBM putting up 500,000 sq. ft. for sublease and HBO trying to sublease 350,000 sq. ft. In spite of stronger suburban absorption, rental rates in the outlying areas have continued to erode while rental rates in the CBD have edged upward. The completion of Georgia 400 to Buckhead is sparking new and revised development plans, but there is still strong pressure for substantial preleasing.

1994 FORECAST

Atlanta's current rate of "Olympics-driven" economic growth is not expected to be sustainable over the next several years. However, led by the trade and service sectors, the present economic recovery is expected to continue. While the current lack of construction has caused a tightening in the market, the completion of a new UPS headquarters and Hewlett-Packard facility should free up more space by 1995. Reportedly, a number of previously planned office sites are now being developed as retail centers.

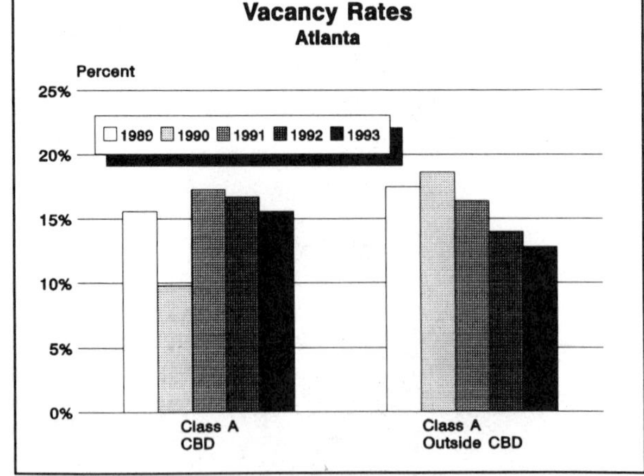

Source: Reprinted from the 1994 edition of *Comparative Statistics of Industrial and Office Real Estate Markets* with permission of the Society of Industrial and Office REALTORS®.

* See Glossary of Terms on page 652.

Chicago, Illinois: Office

Chicago, Illinois

Market Data

Inventory (sf)	Class A CBD	Class A Outside CBD	Class B CBD	Class B Outside CBD
Total	43,750,978	24,631,879	47,258,914	32,899,406
Vacant	9,481,767	3,813,207	10,305,015	6,175,867
Vacancy Rate	21.7%	15.5%	21.8%	18.8%
Vacant Sublease	624,555	534,044	1,401,112	424,311
Under Construction	0	150,000	0	50,590
Substantial Rehab	0	0	0	0
Net Absorption	1,627,085	678,214	29,083	1,799,277
Rental Rates ($/sf)				
Lowest	20.00	16.00	12.00	14.00
Highest	47.00	33.25	30.00	27.75
Weighted Average	29.74	25.30	21.30	17.80
Sales Prices ($/sf)				
Lowest	50.00	40.00	30.00	30.00
Highest	120.00	100.00	60.00	70.00
Weighted Average	n/a	n/a	n/a	n/a
Operating Expenses ($/sf)				
Lowest	4.39	3.50	3.80	2.50
Highest	8.00	7.92	10.00	6.15
Weighted Average	n/a	n/a	n/a	n/a
Tax Expenses ($/sf)				
Lowest	4.43	1.10	2.58	1.00
Highest	10.00	7.25	7.90	6.44
Weighted Average	n/a	n/a	n/a	n/a

Utility Rates: CBD $1.40 per sf; Outside CBD $1.00 per sf; Separately Metered

Parking Ratio: CBD - n/a; Outside CBD - 1 per 250 sf

Standard Work Letter: $20.00 per sf, typically based on dollars per square foot

Operating Cost Escalation: Base Year and Stop

Rate of Return: Cap Rate: 10.0%-40.0%; IRR: n/a

Mortgage Money Supply: Moderate
Prime Source of Financing: Insurance Companies, Commercial Banks, Owner Financing

Cumulative Discount Rate: 10%
Landlord Concessions
Parking, Rental Abatement, Lease Assumptions, Moving Allowance, Interior Improvements, Architectural Fees

Leasing Activity Profile
Major Activity - Legal/Accounting, Insurance, Business Services, Finance/Banking, Engineering/Architecture, Government, Software
Minor Activity - Fortune 500 Firms, Sales

Outlook

Absorption		Same
Construction		Same
Vacancies		Down 6-10%
Rental Rates		Same
Landlord Concessions		Same
Sales Prices	Class A CBD	Same
	Class A Outside CBD	Up 1-5%
	Class B CBD	Down 1-5%
	Class B Outside CBD	Down 1-5%

1993 Review

After one of the most severe recessions in the Midwest, Chicago turned the corner, with 1992's employment loss followed by a 1.3 percent gain in jobs in 1993. Demand seems to be improving, with absorption in the downtown market turning positive for the first time in two years. Suburban absorption has been steady and spot shortages of space are being experienced in several submarkets. With most of the large corporate downsizings complete, much of the bad news facing the office market has been seen.

1994 Forecast

Early renegotiations of leases, especially in the downtown market, are becoming a trend. A historically high vacancy rate burdened downtown in the past year, but positive absorption and a construction hiatus will move this indicator off its peak. Class "A" vacancy rates in the north and west suburbs are at a 10-year low. Rental rates should start to respond. Only small amounts of speculative construction are expected in 1994. Construction should be concentrated in the western and northern suburbs where large tenants have difficulty finding suitable space.

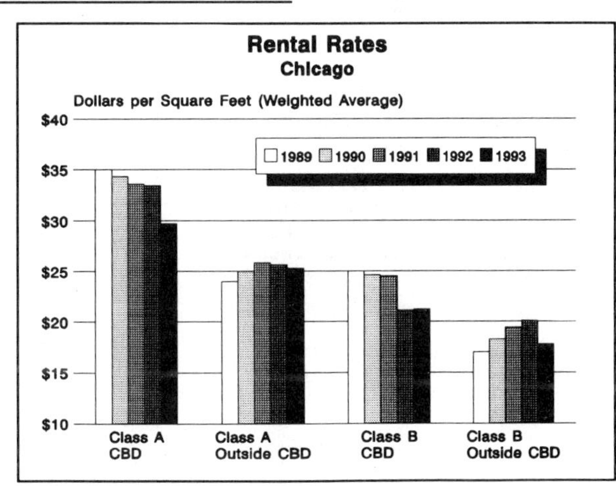

Houston, Texas: Office

Houston, Texas

Market Data

Inventory (sf)	Class A CBD	Class A Outside CBD	Class B CBD	Class B Outside CBD
Total	25,155,656	35,191,773	11,021,508	64,880,326
Vacant	4,203,144	3,344,759	2,883,817	12,391,925
Vacancy Rate	16.7%	9.5%	26.2%	19.1%
Vacant Sublease	n/a	n/a	n/a	n/a
Under Construction	0	637,000	0	0
Substantial Rehab	0	0	0	0
Net Absorption	-301,536	-30,870	-498,273	499,235
Rental Rates ($/sf)				
Lowest	13.00	13.00	9.00	9.00
Highest	18.00	21.00	15.00	14.00
Weighted Average	14.82	14.29	12.24	11.05
Sales Prices ($/sf)				
Lowest	50.00	50.00	25.00	20.00
Highest	90.00	75.00	50.00	40.00
Weighted Average	80.00	55.00	30.00	30.00
Operating Expenses ($/sf)				
Lowest	6.13	4.50	4.50	3.50
Highest	8.68	9.25	7.50	10.00
Weighted Average	6.92	6.38	5.81	5.35
Tax Expenses ($/sf)				
Lowest	n/a	n/a	n/a	n/a
Highest	n/a	n/a	n/a	n/a
Weighted Average	n/a	n/a	n/a	n/a

Utility Rates: CBD n/a, Outside CBD n/a

Parking Ratio: CBD - 11 per 2,500 sf, Outside CBD - 1 per 300 sf

Standard Work Letter: $11.00 per sf, typically based on dollars per square foot

Operating Cost Escalation: Base Year

Rate of Return: Cap Rate: 10.0%-12.0%, IRR: 8.0%-8.5%

Mortgage Money Supply: Tight
Prime Source of Financing: Owner Financing

Cumulative Discount Rate: 15-20%
Landlord Concessions
Parking, Rental Abatement, Lease Assumptions, Moving Allowance, Interior Improvements

Leasing Activity Profile
Major Activity - Fortune 500 Firms, Legal/Accounting, Insurance, Engineering/Architecture
Minor Activity - Business Services, Sales, Finance/Banking, Government, Energy

Outlook

Absorption		Up 1-5%
Construction		Same
Vacancies		Down 1-5%
Rental Rates		Same
Landlord Concessions		Same
Sales Prices	Class A CBD	Same
	Outside CBD	Same
	Class B CBD	Same
	Outside CBD	Same

1993 Review

Decline in Houston's oil and gas industry has had a highly negative impact on the local economy, affecting everything from mining and manufacturing employment to finance, insurance, and real estate. Countering gains in the services sector and at NASA have not been enough to offset energy-related losses. Demand for office space continues to languish. Sublease inventories are growing as area banks, accounting, and law firms continue to break up, go out of business, or downsize.

1994 Forecast

Although the service and trade sectors are expected to jump-start the Houston economy over the next year, massive amounts of office employment will have to be generated to consume existing vacancies. Several build-to-suits are occurring for larger tenants who have been unable to secure contiguous space in a specific location. This will compound the oversupply problem as these large tenants move out of older space. There is currently no speculative development in Houston and none is expected in the near term.

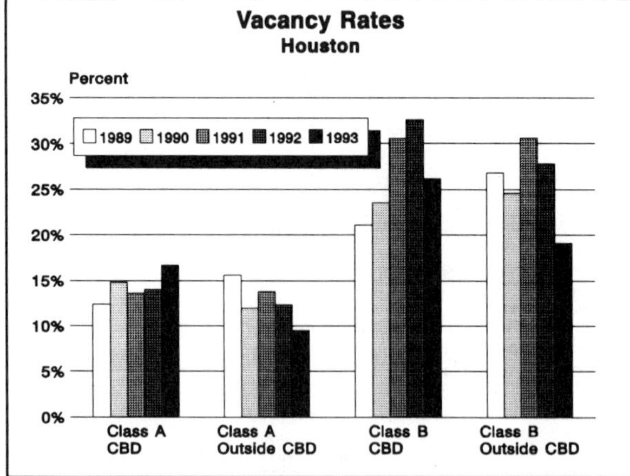

Los Angeles-Central, California: Office

Downtown Los Angeles, California

Market Data

	Class A		Class B	
Inventory (sf)	**CBD**	**Outside CBD**	**CBD**	**Outside CBD**
Total	25,243,000	-	5,957,000	-
Vacant	4,457,000	-	904,200	-
Vacancy Rate	17.7%	-	15.2%	-
Vacant Sublease	1,495,000	-	76,000	-
Under Construction	0	-	0	-
Substantial Rehab	0	-	0	-
Net Absorption	2,681,666	-	284,310	-
Rental Rates ($/sf)				
Lowest	15.00	-	10.00	-
Highest	24.00	-	18.00	-
Weighted Average	18.00	-	13.00	-
Sales Prices ($/sf)				
Lowest	70.00	-	30.00	-
Highest	150.00	-	90.00	-
Weighted Average	110.00	-	50.00	-
Operating Expenses ($/sf)				
Lowest	7.90	-	7.50	-
Highest	12.00	-	10.00	-
Weighted Average	10.50	-	9.00	-
Tax Expenses ($/sf)				
Lowest	n/a	-	n/a	-
Highest	n/a	-	n/a	-
Weighted Average	n/a	-	n/a	-

Utility Rates: CBD $1.80 per sf
Outside CBD - Not Separately Metered

Parking Ratio: CBD - 1 per 1,000 sf
Outside CBD - -

Standard Work Letter: $40.00 per sf, typically based on dollars per square foot

Operating Cost Escalation: Stop - $10.00

Rate of Return: Cap Rate: 12.0%
IRR: 20.0%

Mortgage Money Supply: Tight
Prime Source of Financing: Commercial Banks

Cumulative Discount Rate: 25%
Landlord Concessions
Rental Abatement, Lease Assumptions, Moving Allowance, Interior Improvements

Leasing Activity Profile
Major Activity - Legal/Accounting, Insurance, Government, Energy
Minor Activity - Fortune 500 Firms, Business Services, Sales, Finance/Banking

Outlook

Absorption		Up 11-15%
Construction		Up 1-5%
Vacancies		Down 6-10%
Rental Rates		Same
Landlord Concessions		Down 1-5%
Sales Prices	Class A CBD	Up 1-5%
	Outside CBD	n/a
	Class B CBD	Down 6-10%
	Outside CBD	n/a

1993 Review

With almost no new office space being added to the central Los Angeles market in 1993, supply of space was steady. But, demand was not. Layoffs, decentralization, and corporate downsizing continued to cause instability within the market place. Primary absorption in the central Los Angeles market was up strongly and vacancies dipped from 27.5 percent to 17.7 percent among Class "A" buildings in 1993. But add another six percent to the total to account for sublease space. There is reported to be increasing activity among users moving up to Class "A" as well as purchasing space.

1994 Forecast

With no real recovery in Los Angeles' near future, its office market performance looks to be weak in 1994. Absorption of Class "A" space in central Los Angeles will likely come at the expense of other markets within the MSA. There is presently no new speculative development planned for the market and build-to-suit construction is limited to a handful of projects preleased to government agencies.

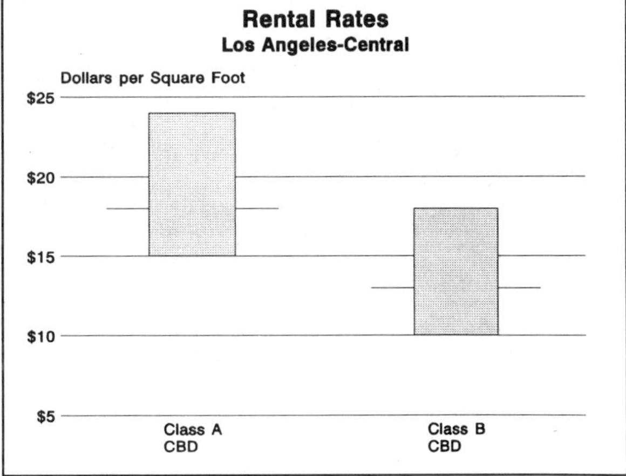

New Jersey-Central, New Jersey: Office

Hunterdon, Mercer, Middlesex, Monmouth, Somerset, and Union Counties, New Jersey

Market Data

	Class A		Class B	
Inventory (sf)	**CBD**	**Outside CBD**	**CBD**	**Outside CBD**
Total	-	38,047,000	-	30,915,000
Vacant	-	3,487,000	-	5,976,000
Vacancy Rate	-	9.2%	-	19.3%
Vacant Sublease	-	461,000	-	375,000
Under Construction	-	0	-	0
Substantial Rehab	-	0	-	0
Net Absorption	-	105,000	-	-86,000
Rental Rates ($/sf)				
Lowest	-	17.50	-	9.00
Highest	-	28.00	-	22.00
Weighted Average	-	21.50	-	16.15
Sales Prices ($/sf)				
Lowest	-	n/a	-	33.00
Highest	-	n/a	-	75.00
Weighted Average	-	n/a	-	50.00
Operating Expenses ($/sf)				
Lowest	-	3.50	-	3.50
Highest	-	5.50	-	5.00
Weighted Average	-	5.00	-	4.50
Tax Expenses ($/sf)				
Lowest	-	1.75	-	1.50
Highest	-	2.50	-	2.50
Weighted Average	-	2.25	-	2.00

Utility Rates: CBD n/a
Outside CBD $2.75 per sf
Not Separately Metered

Parking Ratio: CBD - n/a
Outside CBD - 1 per 400 sf

Standard Work Letter: $20.00 per sf, typically based on dollars per square foot

Operating Cost Escalation: Base Year

Rate of Return: Cap Rate: 10.0%
IRR: 10.0%

Mortgage Money Supply: Tight
Prime Source of Financing: Owner Financing

Cumulative Discount Rate: 20%
Landlord Concessions
Parking, Rental Abatement, Lease Assumptions, Moving Allowance, Interior Improvements

Leasing Activity Profile
Major Activity - Legal/Accounting, Insurance, Business Services
Minor Activity - Fortune 500 Firms, Sales, Finance/Banking, Energy, Media/Advertising

Outlook

Absorption		Up 6-10%
Construction		Up 1-5%
Vacancies		Down 1-5%
Rental Rates		Same
Landlord Concessions		Same
Sales Prices	Class A CBD	n/a
	Outside CBD	Same
	Class B CBD	n/a
	Outside CBD	Same

1993 Review

Central New Jersey unemployment has decreased from a year ago to roughly the national average, however, the industries that are typically large office users have not reached their former levels of employment. Demand for office space was disappointing in 1993. What progress was made in the Class "A" sector was nullified by losses in the Class "B" sector as users moved up to better space in this weak market. Sales have consisted exclusively of Class "B" buildings with buyers being mostly users taking advantage of the opportunity to purchase an office building at nearly half its replacement cost.

1994 Forecast

For the short term, New Jersey's growth outlook is tied to the national recovery. However, long-term prospects appear promising, with a high concentration of R&D firms that will hopefully be in the forefront of creating new industries in the future. Possible constraints to growth in the market could come from state government regulation and requirements in the Clean Air Act that will affect companies that employ a large number of people.

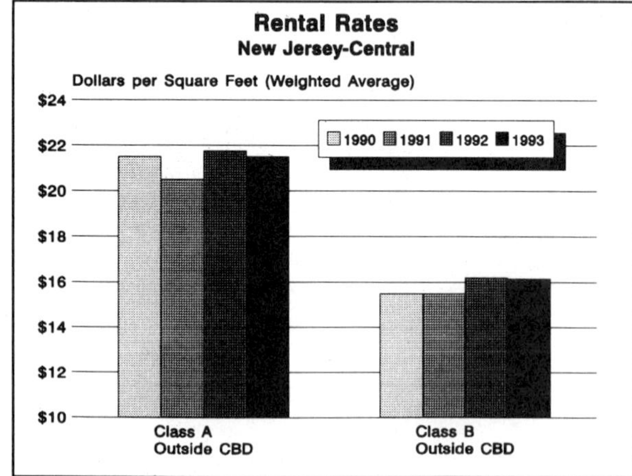

New Jersey-Northern, New Jersey: Office

Bergen, Essex, Hudson, Morris, and Passaic Counties, New Jersey

Market Data

	Class A		Class B	
Inventory (sf)	**CBD**	**Outside CBD**	**CBD**	**Outside CBD**
Total	-	52,348,000	-	45,409,000
Vacant	-	8,882,000	-	11,784,000
Vacancy Rate	-	17.0%	-	26.0%
Vacant Sublease	-	733,000	-	354,000
Under Construction	-	0	-	0
Substantial Rehab	-	0	-	0
Net Absorption	-	1,171,000	-	-560,000
Rental Rates ($/sf)				
Lowest	-	17.50	-	10.00
Highest	-	30.00	-	24.00
Weighted Average	-	21.50	-	16.50
Sales Prices ($/sf)				
Lowest	-	65.00	-	40.00
Highest	-	80.00	-	55.00
Weighted Average	-	75.00	-	50.00
Operating Expenses ($/sf)				
Lowest	-	4.60	-	3.25
Highest	-	5.50	-	4.50
Weighted Average	-	5.00	-	4.00
Tax Expenses ($/sf)				
Lowest	-	2.00	-	1.50
Highest	-	2.50	-	2.00
Weighted Average	-	2.25	-	1.75

Utility Rates: CBD n/a; Outside CBD $2.75 per sf; Not Separately Metered

Parking Ratio: CBD - n/a; Outside CBD - 1 per 400 sf

Standard Work Letter: n/a, typically based on dollars per square foot

Operating Cost Escalation: Base Year

Rate of Return: Cap Rate: 10.0%; IRR: 10.0%

Mortgage Money Supply: Tight
Prime Source of Financing: Owner Financing

Cumulative Discount Rate: 15%
Landlord Concessions
Parking, Rental Abatement, Lease Assumptions, Moving Allowance, Interior Improvements

Leasing Activity Profile
Major Activity - Fortune 500 Firms, Business Services, Finance/Banking, Engineering/Architecture
Minor Activity - Legal/Accounting, Insurance, Sales, Government, Energy

Outlook

Absorption		Up 6-10%
Construction		Same
Vacancies		Down 1-5%
Rental Rates		Same
Landlord Concessions		Same
Sales Prices	Class A CBD	n/a
	Outside CBD	Same
	Class B CBD	n/a
	Outside CBD	Same

1993 Review

Unemployment has decreased, however office demand has not increased. Market activity in 1993 was dominated by companies moving from Manhattan to the Hudson County Waterfront market. The 1.2 million sq. ft. 101 Hudson Street office building in Jersey City came on line this year, adding more than 600,000 sq. ft. of occupied space. Also, major leases were signed at the Harbor Side office complex. Demand for space in the remaining Northern New Jersey office market was weak. Encouragingly, negative absorption came to a halt in Morris County.

1994 Forecast

Infrastructure investment will aid growth; the northern extension of I-287 will be completed next year, Route 24 now links I-287 to I-78 making North-Central New Jersey more accessible from the east. A rail system that will link downtown Newark, Elizabeth, and Newark International Airport is under construction. State regulations and taxes could restrict growth. No speculative or build-to-suit construction is planned for 1994. However, BASF is finishing its corporate facility in Mt. Olive and American Home Products will soon build a facility in Giralda Farms, both in Morris County.

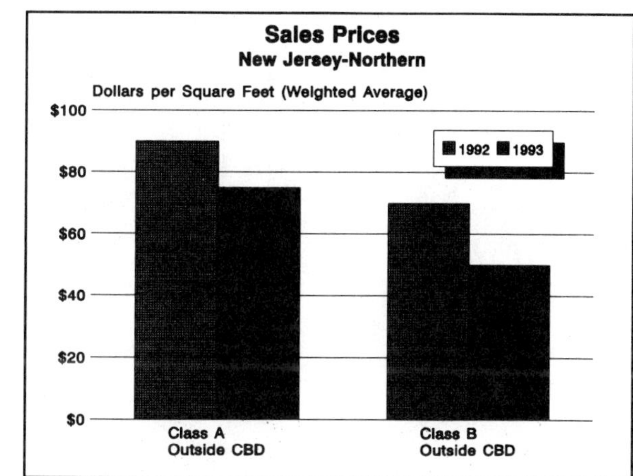

New Jersey-Southern, New Jersey: Office

Burlington, Camden, and Gloucester Counties, New Jersey

Market Data

	Class A		Class B	
Inventory (sf)	**CBD**	**Outside CBD**	**CBD**	**Outside CBD**
Total	-	14,062,904	-	-
Vacant	-	375,097	-	-
Vacancy Rate	-	2.7%	-	-
Vacant Sublease	-	157,275	-	-
Under Construction	-	677,000	-	-
Substantial Rehab	-	n/a	-	-
Net Absorption	-	n/a	-	-
Rental Rates ($/sf)				
Lowest	-	13.00	-	8.50
Highest	-	21.50	-	17.75
Weighted Average	-	17.00	-	15.00
Sales Prices ($/sf)				
Lowest	-	50.00	-	40.00
Highest	-	80.00	-	60.00
Weighted Average	-	65.00	-	55.00
Operating Expenses ($/sf)				
Lowest	-	7.00	-	5.00
Highest	-	n/a	-	n/a
Weighted Average	-	n/a	-	n/a
Tax Expenses ($/sf)				
Lowest	-	1.50	-	1.25
Highest	-	2.00	-	1.50
Weighted Average	-	1.75	-	1.38

Utility Rates: CBD n/a
Outside CBD $1.75-2.25 per sf
Not Separately Metered

Parking Ratio: CBD - n/a
Outside CBD - 1 per 222 sf

Standard Work Letter: $19.00 per sf, typically based on dollars per square foot

Operating Cost Escalation: Base Year

Rate of Return: Cap Rate: 10.0%-12.0%
IRR: 10.0%

Mortgage Money Supply: Tight
Prime Source of Financing: Commercial Banks, Pension Funds

Cumulative Discount Rate: n/a%
Landlord Concessions
Moving Allowance, Interior Improvements

Leasing Activity Profile
Major Activity - None
Minor Activity - Insurance, Sales, Finance/Banking

Outlook

Absorption	Up 1-5%
Construction	Up 1-5%
Vacancies	Down 1-5%
Rental Rates	Same
Landlord Concessions	Same
Sales Prices Class A CBD	n/a
Outside CBD	n/a
Class B CBD	n/a
Outside CBD	n/a

1993 Review

With the erosion of jobs in Burlington and Gloucester Counties, the availability of white collar employment was significantly reduced. however, SIOR's local correspondent reports a gradual increase in activity from companies expanding within the market, although there is still evidence of downsizing due to layoffs. Demand for office space (specifically Class "A" midrise and Class "B" space) has not shown significant improvement and the vacancy rate is still above 20 percent. The sale of commercial properties continues to be difficult. It is estimated that 10 percent of the office buildings in the area have been foreclosed on by their lending institutions.

1994 Forecast

Absorption is expected to pick up slightly in 1994, however, prices will not be affected due to the lack of supply-side pressure. With respect to construction in the tri-county market, there will be almost no new speculative development. A scant amount of construction for physician/medical use is possible, but the developer must have a viable tenant in place before securing financing. As was the case in 1993, build-to-suit construction will dominate development activity in 1994.

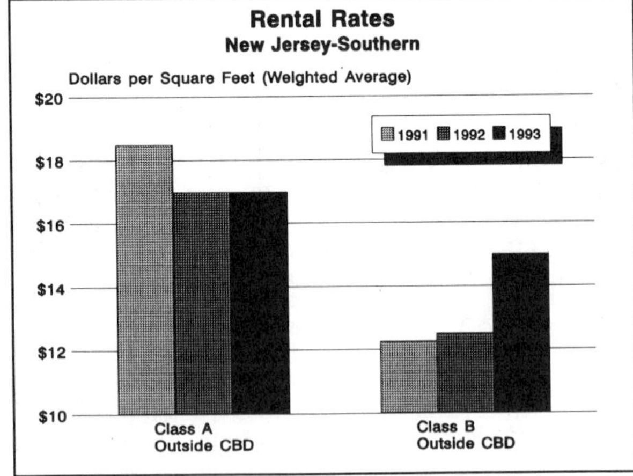

New York City, New York: Office

Manhattan, New York

Market Data

	Class A		Class B	
Inventory (sf)	**Midtown**	**Downtown**	**Midtown**	Downtown
Total	180,400,000	88,500,000	80,700,000	32,000,000
Vacant	29,900,000	16,400,000	16,700,000	8,800,000
Vacancy Rate	16.6%	18.5%	20.7%	27.5%
Vacant Sublease	n/a	n/a	n/a	n/a
Under Construction	0	0	0	0
Substantial Rehab	n/a	n/a	n/a	n/a
Net Absorption	-300,000	-300,000	-500,000	-300,000
Rental Rates ($/sf)				
Lowest	28.00	23.00	18.00	14.00
Highest	50.00	38.00	29.00	25.00
Weighted Average	32.00	29.00	25.00	22.00
Sales Prices ($/sf)				
Lowest	130.00	n/a	40.00	13.00
Highest	345.00	n/a	200.00	71.00
Weighted Average	200.00	n/a	125.00	40.00
Operating Expenses ($/sf)				
Lowest	7.00	7.00	5.00	5.00
Highest	12.00	12.00	10.00	10.00
Weighted Average	8.50	8.50	8.50	8.50
Tax Expenses ($/sf)				
Lowest	8.50	7.00	6.00	3.50
Highest	12.00	10.00	9.00	5.00
Weighted Average	9.00	8.50	8.00	4.50

Utility Rates: CBD $2.50 per sf; Outside CBD $2.50 per sf; Not Separately Metered

Parking Ratio: CBD - n/a; Outside CBD - n/a

Standard Work Letter: n/a, typically based on dollars per square foot

Operating Cost Escalation: Base Year

Rate of Return: Cap Rate: 7.0-9.0%; IRR: 12.0%

Mortgage Money Supply: Tight
Prime Source of Financing: Commercial Banks, Pension Funds

Cumulative Discount Rate: 20-25%
Landlord Concessions
Rental Abatement, Moving Allowance, Interior Improvements, Signing Bonuses

Leasing Activity Profile
Major Activity - Fortune 500 Firms, Legal/Accounting, Finance/Banking, Government
Minor Activity - Insurance, Business Services, Sales

Outlook

Absorption		Up 1-5%
Construction		Same
Vacancies		Same
Rental Rates		Same
Landlord Concessions		Same
Sales Prices	Class A CBD	Down 6-10%
	Outside CBD	Down 1-5%
	Class B CBD	Down 1-5%
	Outside CBD	Down 1-5%

1993 Review

Although services turned the corner toward recovery, New York City employment continues to contract. While Connecticut and New Jersey have drawn NYC relocations with incentives, this trend has slowed due to falling rents in the city. Marked by Berttlesman and Morgan Stanley transactions, the West Side Midtown market is heating up. The result has been an equalization of vacancy rates among Midtown districts. Large users are among the most active, but the availability of large blocks of space (larger than 500,000 sq. ft.) are becoming scarce.

1994 Forecast

Employment gains in services, FIRE, and trade will fuel the New York City office market in 1994. Although the market will not see significant improvement, gradual increases in absorption and a realization that the bottom has been reached will begin to spark the interest of investors. Foreign investors are already looking actively as evidenced by the recent sale of 150 E. 58th Street. Financing is made only when conservative requirements are met, but the pace should pick up in 1994. However, the market will not justify new construction for several years.

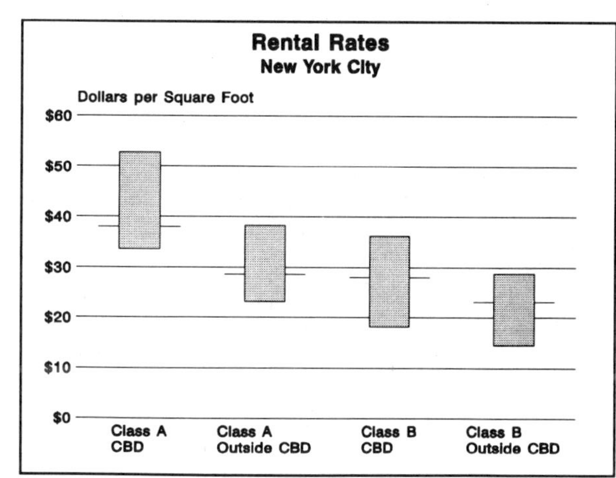

San Francisco, California: Office

San Francisco, California

Market Data

Inventory (sf)	Class A CBD	Class A Outside CBD	Class B CBD	Class B Outside CBD
Total	32,283,000	5,588,000	15,813,000	12,757,000
Vacant	3,058,000	565,000	2,280,000	979,000
Vacancy Rate	9.5%	10.1%	14.4%	7.7%
Vacant Sublease	725,000	37,000	151,000	55,000
Under Construction	0	0	0	0
Substantial Rehab	0	0	0	0
Net Absorption	-81,000	22,000	-236,000	-181,000
Rental Rates ($/sf)				
Lowest	15.00	14.00	9.00	9.00
Highest	40.00	24.00	22.00	34.00
Weighted Average	21.83	19.16	15.38	14.14
Sales Prices ($/sf)				
Lowest	91.00	83.00	19.00	23.00
Highest	117.00	223.00	164.00	110.00
Weighted Average	103.00	111.00	75.00	37.00
Operating Expenses ($/sf)				
Lowest	9.00	8.00	8.00	7.00
Highest	12.10	11.00	10.00	9.00
Weighted Average	10.50	9.50	9.25	8.50
Tax Expenses ($/sf)				
Lowest	1.00	1.00	.75	.50
Highest	2.00	2.00	2.00	1.50
Weighted Average	1.50	1.50	1.25	1.00

Utility Rates: CBD $1.60 per sf; Outside CBD $1.60 per sf; Not Separately Metered

Parking Ratio: CBD - 1 per 3,500 sf; Outside CBD - 1 per 1,000 sf

Standard Work Letter: $30.00 per sf, typically based on dollars per square foot

Operating Cost Escalation: Base Year

Rate of Return: Cap Rate: 9.0%; IRR: n/a

Mortgage Money Supply: Tight
Prime Source of Financing: Owner Financing

Cumulative Discount Rate: 10-15%
Landlord Concessions
Rental Abatement, Moving Allowance, Interior Improvements

Leasing Activity Profile
Major Activity - Business Services, Health & Software
Minor Activity - Legal/Accounting, Insurance, Sales, Finance/Banking, Government

Outlook

Absorption		Same
Construction		Same
Vacancies		Down 1-5%
Rental Rates		Same
Landlord Concessions		Same
Sales Prices	Class A CBD	Down 6-10%
	Outside CBD	Down 11-15%
	Class B CBD	Down 6-10%
	Outside CBD	Down 6-10%

1993 Review

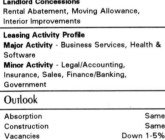

Weakness in local financial and business services have contributed to San Francisco's lingering recession. The availability of space in the CBD continues to rise as local firms reduce overhead by moving to suburban markets or to neighboring states. Landlords continued to reduce CBD rental rates in an effort to entice potential tenants as well as to retain their existing buildings occupants. Although the CBD market experienced more than 300,000 sq. ft. of negative absorption, this was offset by a decrease in available sublease space from more than 1.5 million sq. ft. in 1992 to 876,000 sq. ft. this year.

1994 Forecast

Led by tourism and the convention industry, San Francisco's service sector will provide one of the few stimuli to growth over the next two years. Consolidation and shrinkage of space requirements will prevail, but the quantity of available sublease space should start to dry up by the end of next year. Sales prices are expected to be down sharply in 1994 as reduced rents take their toll on values. Tight financing and a weak rental market will shut down speculative development in the foreseeable future.

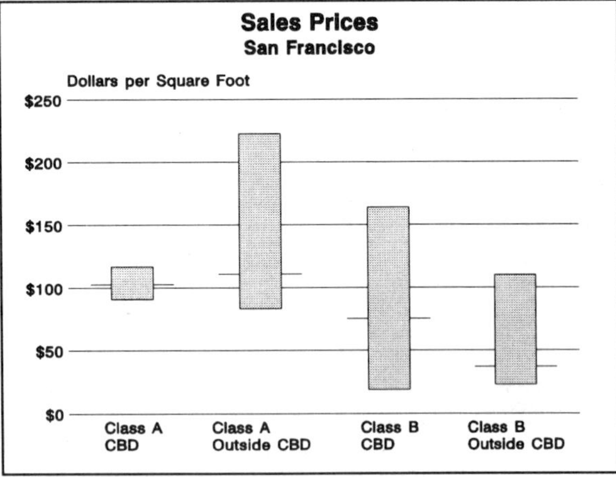

Tucson, Arizona: Office

Tucson, Arizona

Market Data

	Class A		Class B	
Inventory (sf)	**CBD**	**Outside CBD**	**CBD**	**Outside CBD**
Total	490,423	2,278,389	925,820	2,538,058
Vacant	105,113	254,224	199,208	501,927
Vacancy Rate	21.4%	11.2%	21.5%	19.8%
Vacant Sublease	15,000	32,000	12,000	29,000
Under Construction	0	0	0	10,000
Substantial Rehab	0	0	15,000	0
Net Absorption	2,500	52,600	13,500	51,200
Rental Rates ($/sf)				
Lowest	17.85	14.00	12.50	11.50
Highest	20.50	18.50	14.50	14.00
Weighted Average	18.10	16.05	13.20	13.25
Sales Prices ($/sf)				
Lowest	n/a	44.00	19.00	27.00
Highest	n/a	66.00	52.00	44.00
Weighted Average	n/a	58.00	37.00	41.00
Operating Expenses ($/sf)				
Lowest	6.85	6.25	5.70	5.50
Highest	7.25	6.75	6.10	6.25
Weighted Average	7.00	6.50	5.95	5.75
Tax Expenses ($/sf)				
Lowest	2.05	1.05	1.15	.81
Highest	2.85	2.25	1.68	1.72
Weighted Average	2.10	1.65	1.52	1.45

Utility Rates: CBD $1.50-1.75 per sf
Outside CBD $1.50-1.75 per sf
Not Separately Metered

Parking Ratio: CBD - 1 per 200 sf
Outside CBD - 1 per 250 sf

Standard Work Letter: $15.00 per sf, typically based on dollars per square foot

Operating Cost Escalation: Base Year

Rate of Return: Cap Rate: 10.5%-11.0%
IRR: 12.0%-15.0%

Mortgage Money Supply: Moderate
Prime Source of Financing: Owner Financing

Cumulative Discount Rate: 5-10%
Landlord Concessions
Parking, Interior Improvements, Cash Flow Lease Structures

Leasing Activity Profile
Major Activity - Legal/Accounting, Insurance, Business Services, Sales
Minor Activity - Fortune 500 Firms, Finance/Banking, Engineering/Architecture, Government

Outlook

Absorption		Up 6-10%
Construction		Up 1-5%
Vacancies		Down 1-5%
Rental Rates		Up 1-5%
Landlord Concessions		Same
Sales Prices	Class A CBD	Same
	Outside CBD	Up 6-10%
	Class B CBD	Same
	Outside CBD	Up 1-5%

1993 Review

The Tucson market posted positive absorption in all submarkets, and overall vacancy dropped to 17.0 percent in 1993. The last time the market reported such uniform improvement was almost 10 years ago. Moves to Tucson by telemarketing, catalog ordering, and reservation centers have absorbed most large contiguous spaces. No speculative construction has occurred since 1986. Additionally, many "user" purchases have reduced overall square footage of multi-tenant space. Continued absorption and a shrinking inventory base are forcing vacancy rates down and lease rates up.

1994 Forecast

Expansions and/or relocations by Artisoft, Hughes, Sunquest, Chipsoft, Breault Research, Northwestern National Life and others (including many HMOs) will continue to fuel employment growth and office absorption in 1994. The lack of suitable space will force many firms to consider build-to-suit opportunities, as land is still relatively inexpensive and abundant. No new speculative development is anticipated until 1996 since lease rates need to increase an average of $6.00 per sq. ft. to justify new development.

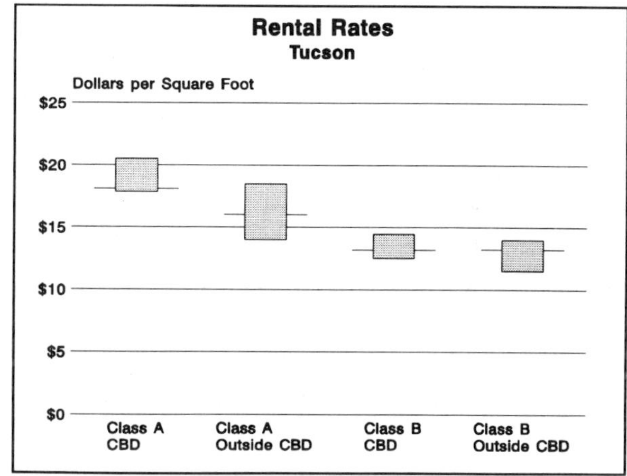

Glossary of Terms

DEMOGRAPHICS

Population. The 1993 population projection for the MSA. Figures are based on data from National Planning Data Corporation.

Population Growth Rate. The annual percentage change in populations between 1983 and 1993 for the MSA. Figures are based on data from National Planning Data Corporation.

Unemployment Rate. The percent of labor force unemployed in September 1993 as published by the Bureau of Labor Statistics in Employment and Earnings.

Median Household Income. The estimated median household income for 1993 as published by National Planning Data Corporation.

Cost of Living Index. Measures relative price levels for consumer goods and services in participating areas, as published by American Chamber of Commerce Researchers Association (ACCRA).

Demographic Rankings. This ranks local statistics against other U.S. Metropolitan markets.

INDUSTRIAL MARKETS

Prime Industrial Building. A prime industrial building is in the top 25 percent of the most desired industrial properties in a given market area. Such buildings are considered to be for general purpose uses such as industrial, research, warehouse and/or manufacturing.

Central City/Suburban. Since the definition of urban and suburban varies widely, it is the responsibility of the individual survey respondent to reflect his or her area's particular characteristics.

Total Inventory. Total square footage (sq. ft.) of rentable industrial space, vacant and occupied, ready for tenant finish. Includes owner occupied space.

Vacant Inventory. Total square footage of vacant rentable industrial space, including sublease.

Net Absorption. Net change in occupied space.

Under Construction. Industrial space in construction stages; ground has been broken. Does not include planned projects.

Construction Costs. Construction costs reflect only hard construction costs such as general contractor, overhead, and profit, but exclude architectural and engineering fees, financing fees, and mortgage/brokerage fees for both construction and permanent financing.

Lease Prices. A gross lease is one in which the tenant's rent includes real estate taxes, fire and extended coverage insurance, as well as maintenance of the roof structure and outside walls. A net lease is one in which the tenant assumes the operating expenses of the leased premises.

Improved Sites. Improved sites are in the top 25 percent of overall desirability of the existing inventory. Such sites are in a "ready-to-build" condition and are essentially level and graded and serviced with all necessary utilities. Rail service may or may not be available.

Unimproved Sites. These sites are also in the top 25 percent of overall desirability of the existing inventory and zoned for industrial use. Streets and utilities may not yet be installed, but are reasonably close and available. Rail service may or may not be available.

Prime High-Technology Building. Generally, high-technology (high-tech) buildings are 50 percent or more office, fully air-conditioned, 12-18′ clear height, have extensive landscaping and parking, and are architecturally impressive. In some areas of the country where high-tech industries are not prevalent, this building could be used as a showroom or as pure office. These properties are sometimes called "flex buildings."

Operating Expenses. Outlays pertaining to real estate operations, exclusive of tenant's on-going businesses costs. Includes building payroll, maintenance, utilities, insurance, general and administrative costs, etc. Expessed in dollars per sq. ft., annually. [Note: survey questionaire did not define this item for reporters, and local practices vary. Please refer inquiries about specifics to local reporters.]

Real Estate Taxes. Local property taxes on land and building, expressed in dollars per sq. ft., annually.

OFFICE MARKETS

CBD. Central Business District space located near the historical urban core, commonly associated with traditional government and financial districts in most cities.

Outside CBD. Outside the CBD includes both suburban area and "urban clusters" with areas of high office space concentrations that often rival nearby CBDs.

Class "A." Excellent locations, high-quality tenants, high-quality finish, well-maintained, professionally managed, and usually new, or old buildings that are competitive with new buildings.

Class "B." Good location, professionally managed, fairly high-quality construction and tenancy. Class "B" buildings generally show very little functional obsolescence and deterioration.

Total Inventory. Total square footage (sq. ft.) of rentable space, vacant and occupied, ready for tenant finish. Includes owner occupied space.

Vacant Inventory. Total square footage of vacant rentable space, including sublease.

Current Construction. Total square footage presently under construction includes any space that will be available for occupancy before the end of 1993.

Substantial Rehabilitation. Repair/replacement of building interior finish and/or systems requiring temporary displacement of tenants.

Net Absorption. Net change in occupied stock.

Rental Rate. Minimum, maximum, and weighted average quoted gross rental rate for competitive office space in each class, in U.S. dollars per square foot ($/sq. ft.).

Gross Rental. Services included in the rental rate vary from market to market.

Sales Prices. Minimum, maximum, and weighted average sales prices for competitive office space in each class, in U.S. dollars per square foot ($/sq. ft.).

Weighted Average Rental Rate. Average quoted rental rate weighted by the vacant space available at the rental rate, in each class.

Average Utility Rates. Figures presented are dollars per square foot per year.

Standard Work Letter. Sometimes called a construction rider, this refers to the work that the landlord will do for the tenant, typically to finish out the interior of the space.

Typical Parking Ratio. The ratio refers to the availability of parking spaces per number of square feet leased by a tenant.

Operating Cost Escalation. Operating cost escalation refers to the procedure used to adjust rents over the term of a lease.

Cumulative Discount Rate. The rental rate discount factor is the cumulative effect of landlord lease concessions on gross rental rates. It is expressed as a percentage of base rent.

Operating Expenses. Outlays pertaining to real estate operations, exclusive of tenant's on-going businesses costs. Includes building payroll, maintenance, utilities, insurance, general and administrative costs, etc. Expessed in dollars per sq. ft., annually. [Note: survey questionaire did not define this item for reporters, and local practices vary. Please refer inquiries about specifics to local reporters.]

Real Estate Taxes. Local property taxes on land and building, expressed in dollars per sq. ft., annually.

Cap Rate. Rate of return to real estate investment, expressed as a ratio of net operating income to sales price. Excludes the impact of mortgage.

Internal Rate of Return. The annualized rate of return on investment capable of being generated over a period of ownership, including the periodic cash flows and the ultimate termination of the investment. Discounts all returns to equal the original investment. In practice, often used synonymously with **discount rate** to indicate the return on capital used to convert all future receipts into net present value. [Note: this term was introduced into the SIOR questionaire for the first time this year, but a definition was omitted. Inconsistencies may therefore appear in its usage. Please refer inquiries about specifics to local reporters.]

MISCELLANEOUS TERMS

Maquiladora. The twin plant operation that has grown up along the U.S./Mexico border, in which goods are shipped into Mexico for assembly and finishing work using lower cost labor, and then are distributed through the U.S. market. Import duties are payable only on the imputed value added in the assembly process. The Maquiladora program served as a spring board for U.S./Mexico trade cooperation, which has culminated in the North American Free Trade Agreement. The treaty agreements under NAFTA will eventually supercede the Maquiladora arrangements.

FIRE Sector. An acronym standing for Finance, Insurance and Real Estate, one of the major industry groupings in the Standard Industrial Classification system established by the U.S. Department of Commerce.

Backfilling. A colloquialism referring to the re-leasing of space once occupied by a tenant that has relocated elsewhere.

Source: Reprinted from the 1994 *Comparative Statistics of Industrial and Office Real Estate Markets* with permission of the Society of Industrial and Office REALTORS®.

Real Estate Investment Trusts (REITs)

WHAT IS A REIT?

A REIT is essentially a corporation or trust that combines the capital of many investors to acquire or provide financing for all forms of real estate. A REIT serves much like a mutual fund for real estate. Its shares are freely traded, often on a major stock exchange.

A corporation or trust that qualifies as a REIT generally does not pay corporate income tax to the Internal Revenue Service (IRS). This is a unique feature and one of the most attractive aspects of a REIT. Most states honor this federal exemption and do not require REITs to pay state income tax. This means that nearly all of a REITs income can be distributed to shareholders, and there is no double taxation of the income to the shareholder.

WHAT QUALIFIES A REIT?

In order for a corpotation or trust to qualify as a REIT it must comply with certain provisions within the Internal Revenue Code. As required by the Tax Code, a REIT must:

- be a corporation, business trust or similar association;
- be managed by a board of directors or trustees;
- have shares that are fully transferable;
- have a minimum of 100 shareholders;
- have no more than 50 percent of the shares held by five or fewer individuals during the last half of each taxable year;
- invest at least 75 percent of total assets in real estate assets;
- derive at least 75 percent of gross income from rents from real property, or interest on mortgages on real property;
- derive no more than 30 percent of gross income from the sale of real property held for less than four years, securities held for less than six months or certain prohibited transactions;
- pay dividends of at least 95 percent of REIT taxable income.

Source: *Real Estate Investment Trusts: Frequently Asked Questions About REITS*, National Association of Real Estate Investment Trusts, Inc., 1129 Twentieth Street, N.W., Washington, D.C. 20036.

WHY WERE REITS CREATED?

REITs were created to provide investors with the opportunity to participate in the benefits of ownership of larger-scale commercial real estate or mortgage lending, and receive an enhanced return, because the income is not taxed at the REIT entity level. This means that a diverse range of investors can realize investment opportunities otherwise available only to those with larger resources. This opportunity first became available when President Eisenhower signed the real estate investment trust tax provisions into law in 1960. The basic provisions of this law remain unchanged, although there have been a number of improvements to the law over the past 30 years.

The REIT industry has benefitted from tax reform initiatives enacted in the 1980s. These initiatives were meant to eliminate the incentive of tax-sheltered real estate vehicles and promote a return to the fundamentals of capital formation and investment in real estate for income and appreciation.

WHO INVESTS IN REITS?

Thousands of investors, both American and foreign, own shares of REITs. So do pension funds, endowment funds, bank trust departments and mutual funds.

An individual who chooses to invest in a REIT seeks to achieve current income distributions and long-term stock appreciation potential. An investor also has the benefit of liquidity, if needed.

REIT shares typically may be purchased from $2 to $40 each, with no minimum purchase required.

ARE REITS LIMITED PARTNERSHIPS?

No. REITs are not partnerships. There are important organizational and operational differences between REITs and limited partnerships.

One of the major differences between REITs and limited partnerships is how annual tax information is reported to investors. An investor in a REIT receives IRS Form 1099 from the REIT, indicating the amount and type of income received during the year. An investor in a partnership receives a very complicated Internal Revenue Service Schedule K-1.

The oversight/corporate governance features of a REIT are believed to be far superior to the partnership.

Other important differences between REITs and limited partnerships are shown in the accompanying chart.

IMPORTANT DIFFERENCES: REITS VS. PARTNERSHIPS

	REITs	Partnerships
Liquidity	*Yes, most REITs are listed on stock exchanges*	*No, when liquidity exists, generally much less than REITs*
Minimum Investment Amount	*None*	*Typically $2,000-$5,000*
Reinvestment Plans	*Yes, including some at discounts*	*No*
Ability to Leverage Investments without Incurring UBIT for Tax-Exempt Accounts	*Yes, this makes REITs suitable for individual IRAs, KEOGH and other pension plans*	*No*
Investor Control	*Yes, investors re-elect directors and, in some cases, approve advisors annually*	*No, controlled by general partner who cannot be easily removed by limited partners*
Independent Directors	*Yes, state law typically requires majority to be independent of management*	*No*
Beneficial Ownership	*At least 100 shareholders required -- most REITs have thousands*	*Shared between any number of limited and general partners*
Ability to Grow by Additional Public Offerings of Stock	*Yes*	*No*

HOW MANY REITS ARE THERE?

There are over 230 REITs operating in the United States today. Their assets total $53 billion. About two-thirds of these trade on the national stock exchanges:

- New York Stock Exchange—93 REITs
- American Stock Exchange—60 REITs
- NASDAQ National Market System—19 REITs

HOW ARE REIT STOCKS VALUED?

Like all companies whose stocks are publicly traded, REIT share prices are quoted daily. To determine a value for these shares, typical analysis involves one or more of the following criteria:

- Underlying asset value of the real estate and/or mortgages, and other assets;
- Anticipated total return from the stock, calculated from the anticipated price change and the prevailing yield;
- Current prevailing dividend yield relative to other yield-oriented investments (e.g., bonds, utility stocks);
- Dividend coverage from funds from operations;
- Management quality structure; and
- Anticipated growth (or lack thereof) in funds from operations per share.

WHAT TYPES OF REITS ARE THERE?

The REIT industry has a diverse profile, which offers many attractive opportunities to

INDUSTRY PROFILE

by Asset Profile Mix

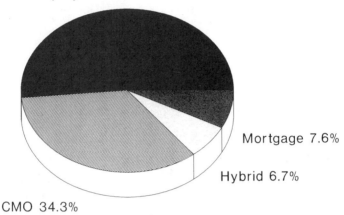

June 30, 1993

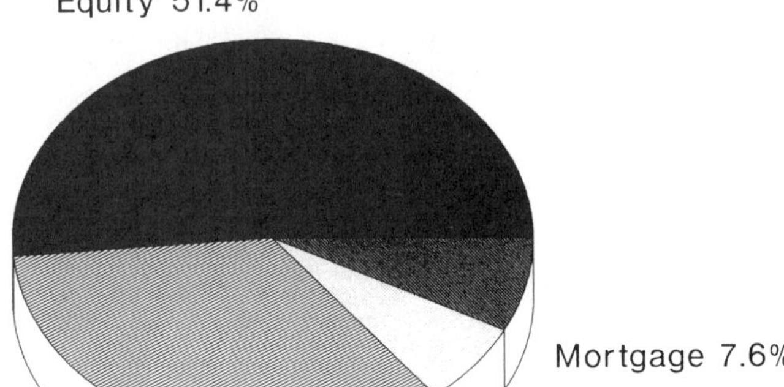

TOTAL REAL ESTATE INVESTMENT

Publicly Traded REITs

September, 1992

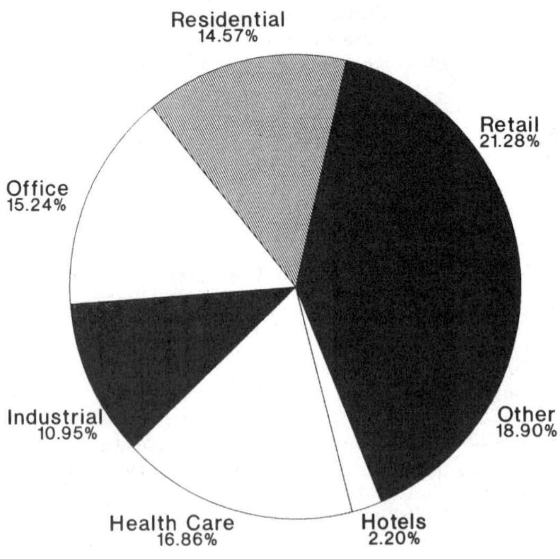

Note: Net of Residential Mortgage Backed Security Investments

Source: *Real Estate Investment Trusts: Frequently Asked Questions About REITS*, National Association of Real Estate Investment Trusts, Inc., 1129 Twentieth Street, N.W., Washington, D.C. 20036.

investors. REIT industry analysts often classify REITs in one of three investment approaches:

Equity REITs own real estate. Their revenue comes principally from rent. REIT industry investments in property ownership have increased steadily for 30 years.

Mortgage REITs loan money to real estate owners. Their revenue comes principally from interest earned on their mortgage loans.

Hybrid REITs combine the investment strategies of both equity REITs and mortgage REITs.

REITs can also be distinguished by . . .

Type of Property . . .

Some REITs invest in a variety of property types—office buildings, shopping centers, apartments, warehouses, etc. Other REITs specialize in one property type only, such as shopping centers. Health care REITs specialize in health care facilities: hospitals, including acute care, rehabilitation and psychiatric, medical office buildings, nursing homes, and congregate and assisted living centers.

Geographic Focus . . .

Some REITs invest throughout the country. Others specialize in one region only or even a single metropolitan area.

WHO DETERMINES A REIT'S INVESTMENTS?

A REIT's investments are determined by its board of directors or trustees. Directors are elected by, and responsible to, the shareholders. In turn, the directors appoint the management personnel. REIT directors are typically well-known and respected members of the real estate, business and professional communities.

HOW ARE REITS MANAGED?

REITs employ professional management, individuals who are hired and periodically reviewed by the REIT's board of directors. REIT managers are selected based upon their extensive real estate background and expertise. REITs can be either internally managed or externally advised.

WHAT MAKES A REIT ATTRACTIVE TO INVESTORS?

In addition to avoiding double taxation and requiring no minimum investment, REITs also offer investors:

- Current income: usually stable and often provides an attractive return;
- Liquidity: shares of publicly traded REITs are readily converted into cash because they are traded on the major stock exchanges;
- Professional management: REIT managers are skilled, experienced real estate professionals;
- Portfolio diversification: minimizes risk;
- Performance Monitoring: A REIT's performance is monitored on a regular basis by independent directors of the REIT, independent analysts, independent auditors, and the business and financial media. This scrutiny provides the investor a measure of protection and more than one barometer of the REIT's financial condition.

HOW DO I INVEST IN A REIT?

An individual may invest in a publicly traded REIT, which in most cases is listed on a major stock exchange, by purchasing shares through a stock broker. An investor can enlist the services of a broker, investment advisor or financial planner to help analyze his or her financial objectives. These individuals also may be able to recommend an appropriate REIT for the investor.

An investor can also contact a REIT directly for a copy of the company's annual report, prospectus and other financial information.

Potential investors can also contact the National Association of Real Estate Investment Trusts (NAREIT) for a free listing of all publicly traded REITs, with exchange symbols, and a list of educational publications available.

For more information, contact NAREIT, 1129 Twentieth Street, N.W., Suite 705, Washington, D.C., 20036 (202) 785-8717.

PUBLICLY TRADED REITS

AMERICAN STOCK EXCHANGE

ASR Investments Corporation	ASR
Angeles Mortgage Investment Trust	ANM
Angeles Participating Mortgage Trust	APT
Arizona Land Income Corporation	AZL
Banyan Hotel Investors Trust	VHT
Banyan Short Term Income Trust	VST
Boddie-Noell Restaurant Properties, Inc.	BNP
Bradley Real Estate Trust	BTR
CNL Realty Investors, Inc.	NNN
California Jockey Club	CJ
Capital Housing and Mortgage Partners	CAP
Columbia Real Estate Investments, Inc.	CIV
Copley Properties, Inc.	COP
EastGroup Properties	EGP
EquiVest, Inc.	EVI
HMG/Courtland Properties, Inc.	HMG
HealthVest	HVT
Income Opportunity Realty Trust	IOT
Koger Equities, Inc.	KE
Landsing Pacific Fund	LPF
Lincoln N.C. Realty Fund Incorporated	LRF
Linpro Specified Properties Trust	LPO
MIP Properties	MIP
MSA Realty Trust	SSS
Medical Properties, Inc.	MPP
Meridian Point Realty Trust IV	MPD
Meridian Point Realty Trust VI	MPF
Meridian Point Realty Trust VII	MPG
Meridian Point Realty Trust VIII	MPH
Metropolitan Realty Corporation	MET
One Liberty Properties, Inc.	OLP
PS Business Parks, Inc.	PSB
Partners Preferred Yield, Inc.	PYA
Partners Preferred Yield II, Inc.	PYB
Partners Preferred Yield III, Inc.	PYC
Pennsylvania Real Estate Investment Trust	PEI
Pittsburgh West Virginia Railroad	PW
Presidential Realty Corporation	PDL.A
Property Capital Trust	PCT
Public Storage Properties VI, Inc.	PSF
Public Storage Properties VII, Inc.	PSH
Public Storage Properties VIII,Inc.	PSJ
Public Storage Properties IX, Inc.	PSK
Public Storage Properties X, Inc.	PSL
Public Storage Properties XI, Inc.	PSM
Public Storage Properties XII, Inc	PSN
Public Storage Properties XIV, Inc	PSP
Public Storage Properties XV, Inc.	PSQ
Public Storage Properties XVI, Inc	PSU
Public Storage Properties XVII, Inc	PSV
Public Storage Properties XVIII, Inc	PSW
Public Storage Properties XIX, Inc .	PSY
Public Storage Properties XX, Inc.	PSZ
RYMAC Mortgage Investment Corporation	RMI
Resort Income Investors, Inc.	RII
Storage Properties, Inc.	PSA
Southwestern Property Trust, Inc.	SWP
Vanguard Real Estate Fund I	VRO
Vanguard Real Estate Fund II	VRT
Washington Real Estate Investment Trust	WRE
Western Investment Real Estate Trust	WIR

NEW YORK STOCK EXCHANGE

Americana Hotels and Realty Corporation	AHR
American Health Properties, Inc.	AHE
Asset Investors Corporation	AIC
BRE Properties, Inc.	BRE
BRT Realty Trust	BRT
Banyan Mortgage Investment Fund	VMG
Berkshire Realty Company	BRI
Burnham Pacific Properties, Inc.	BPP
CRI Insured Mortgage Investments II, Inc.	CMM
CRI Liquidating REIT, Inc	CFR
CV REIT	CVI
California Real Estate Investment Trust	CT
Capstead Mortgage Corporation	CMO
Carr Realty Corporation	CRE
Countrywide Mortgage Investments, Inc.	CWM
Cousins Properties Incorporated	CUZ
Del-Val Financial Corporation	DVL
Developers Diversified Realty Corporation	DDR
Dial REIT, Inc.	DR
Duke Realty Investments. Inc.	DRE
EQK Realty Investors I	EKR
Federal Realty Investment Trust	FRT
First Union Real Estate Investments	FUR
HRE Properties	HRE
Health & Rehabilitation Properties Trust	HRP
Health Care Property Investors, Inc.	HCP
Health Care REIT, Inc.	HCN
Health Equity Properties, Inc.	EQP
Homeplex Mortgage Corporation	HPX
Hotel Investors Trust	HOT
ICM Property Investors Incorporated	ICM
IRT Property Company	IRT
Kimco Realty Corporation	KIM
Kranzco Realty Trust	KRT
LNH REIT, Inc.	LHC
LTC Properties, Inc.	LTC
Liberte Investors	LBI
MGI Properties	MGI
Manufactured Home Communities, Inc.	MHC
Meditrust	MT
Merry Land & Investment Company	MRY
Mortgage and Realty Trust	MRT
National Health Investors	NHI
Nationwide Health Properties, Inc.	NHP
New Plan Realty Trust	NPR
Omega Healthcare Investors, Inc.	OHI
Property Trust of America	PTR
Prudential Realty Corporation	PRT
RPS Realty Trust	RPS
Real Estate Investment Trust of California	RCT
Realty Refund Trust	RRF
Resource Mortgage Capital, Inc.	MR
Rockefeller Center Properties, Inc.	RCP
Santa Anita Realty Enterprises, Inc.	SAR
Sizeler Property Investors, Inc.	SIZ
Storage Equities, Inc.	SEQ
TIS Mortgage Investment Company	TIS
Taubman Centers, Inc.	TCO
Trammell Crow Real Estate Investors	TCR
Transcontinental Realty Investors	TCI
United Dominion Realty Trust	UDR
Universal Health Realty Income Trust	UHT
Weingarten Realty Investors	WRI
Wellsford Residential Property Trust	WRP

NASDAQ NATIONAL MARKET SYSTEM

Allied Capital Commercial Corp.	ALCC
Banyan Strategic Land Fund II	VSLF

Banyan Strategic Land Trust	VLANS
Chicago Dock and Canal Trust, The	DOCKS
CleveTrust Realty Investors	CTRIS
Continental Mortgage and Equity Trust	CMETS
Crocker Realty Investors	CRKR
Eastover Corporation	EASTS
INVG Mortgage Securities Corporation	INVG
Mellon Participating Mortgage Trust	MPMTS
Meridian Point Realty Trust '83	MPTBS
Monmouth Real Estate Investment Corp.	MNRTA
National Income Realty Trust	NIRTS
Nooney Realty Trust, Inc.	NRTI
Price REIT	PRET
Sierra Real Estate Equity Trust '84	SETC
Vinland Properties, Inc.	VIPTS
Wetterau Properties, Inc.	WTPR
Royale Investments, Inc.	RLIN
USP Real Estate Investment Trust	USPTS

OTHER OVER-THE-COUNTER

Arlington Realty Investors	RYNMS
Central Realty Investors	CMRT
Century Realty Trust	CRLTS
Commonwealth Equity Trust	CWLES
Fifty Associates	FFTY
First Real Estate Investment Trust of New Jersey	FRET
Harbor American Health Care Trust, Inc.	HAHC
The Mortgage Trust Corporation	RRR
Pacific Real Estate Investment Trust	PCIFS
Real Estate Fund Investment Trust	REFI

NASDAQ SUPPLEMENTAL LIST

Cedar Income Fund 1, Ltd.	CEDR
First Continental REIT	FCRES

Source: National Association of Real Estate Investment Trusts, Inc., 1129 20th Street, N.W., Washington, D.C. 20036.

Glossary of Real Estate and REIT Terms

This glossary of terminology used in conjunction with discussions of real estate investment trusts has been prepared by the Research Department of the National Association of Real Estate Investment Trusts. Credit should be given to Realty Income Trust, a NAREIT member, which produced a glossary of terms upon which NAREIT drew heavily.

Acceleration clause A condition in a loan contract or mortgage note which permits the lender to demand immediate repayment of the entire balance if the contract is breached or conditions for repayment occur, such as sale or demolition.

Accrued interest or rent An amount of interest or rent which has been earned but which may not have been received in the same period as earned. On many short-term first mortgages, accrued interest is not received in cash until permanent financing is obtained.

Acquisition loan See C&D loan.

Advisor A REIT's investment advisor (usually pursuant to a renewable one-year contract) provides analysis of proposed investments, servicing of the portfolio, and other advisory services. Fee limits for advisory services are prescribed by many state securities regulators. Also spelled "adviser."

Amortization The process of retiring debt or recovering a capital investment through scheduled, systematic repayments of principal; that portion of fixed mortgage payment applied to reduction of the principal amount owed.

Anchor tenant An important tenant, usually with an excellent credit rating (also known as a triple-A tenant), which takes a large amount of space in a shopping center or office building and is usually one of the first tenants to commit to lease. The anchor tenant usually is given lower rent because of the desirability of having that tenant at the property, both because of its credit rating and its ability to generate traffic.

Appraisal An opinion by an expert of the value of a property as of a specified date, supported by the presentation and analysis of relevant data. The appraisal may be arrived at by any or all of three methods: the cost approach (cost to reproduce), the market approach (comparison with other similar properties), or the income approach (capitalization of actual or projected income figures).

Assessed value The value of a property which is assigned to it by a taxing authority for purposes of assessing property taxes; often assessed value bears a fixed relationship by local statute to market value.

Asset swaps See swap program.

Assets Anything of value owned by the company. Assets are either financial, as cash or bonds; or physical, as real or personal property. For REIT tax purposes, more than 75% of the trust's assets must be property owned or securities backed by real estate.

Assumption of mortgage When the responsibility for repaying existing indebtedness secured by property is "assumed" by the second purchaser. In most jurisdictions, this relieves the first owner of the original obligations, at least to the extent that can be satisfied by sale of this asset after foreclosure.

Attribution More than 50% of a REIT's shares cannot be held by fewer than six people (otherwise it becomes a personal holding company for tax purposes). When someone has indirect control over someone else's shares (such as a trustee over shares held for the benefit of another) then "control" for personal holding company purposes may be "attributed." This complicated legal topic of "attribution" arises, however, only when the REIT's shares are held by a few.

Audit An examination of the financial status and operations of an enterprise, based mostly on the books of account, and undertaken to assure conformity to generally accepted accounting principles and to secure information for, or to check the accuracy of, the enterprise's balance sheet, income statement, and/or cash flow statement.

Balloon mortgage A mortgage loan which provides for periodic payments, which may include both interest and principal, but which leaves the loan less than fully amortized at maturity, requiring a final large payment which is the "balloon." Usually the term does not apply to an "interest only" loan whose full principal is due upon maturity or upon call during its life.

Bankrupt When liabilities exceed assets, Federal laws enable the entity to dissolve in an orderly fashion (Chapter VII), or permit a court officer to restructure the company into a survivor "going business" (Chapter X), or permit existing management to do the same under court supervision (Chapter XI), or to do so despite the preferred position of secured creditors if real property is the only asset of the business (Chapter XII).

Source: National Association of Real Estate Trusts, 1101 Seventeenth Street, N.W., Washington, D.C. 20036.

Beneficial owner The person who ultimately benefits from ownership of shares or other securities—in contrast to "nominees" (often pseudonyms for control of investment professionals so as to facilitate security transactions without having to track down beneficial owners to participate in each step of the procedures).

Blue sky laws State laws regulating conditions of sale of securities of companies (particularly those just starting out of the "clear blue sky") for the protection of the investing public. National stock exchange rules usually supercede state laws pursuant to a "blue chip" exemption contained in such state laws. The federal securities laws dovetail with state laws and pertain to publicly held companies, primarily as to accounting and disclosure practices.

Bond A debt certificate which (a) represents a loan to a trust, (b) bears interest, and (c) matures on a stated future date. Short term bonds (generally with a maturity of five years or less from the date of issuance) are often called notes. See debentures.

Book value per share Shareholder equity as adjusted to tangible net worth (assets minus liabilities plus paid-in capital) per share outstanding.

Borrower A person or entity who received something of value, ordinarily money, and is obligated to pay it back, as the debtor to the creditor, usually pursuant to a note or "IOU" containing terms and conditions.

Broker A person who is paid to act as an intermediary in connection with a transaction, in contrast to a dealer or principal who buys or sells for his own account. In the REIT world, the term "broker" usually refers to a real estate salesman, although the term is also used for "stockbrokers" too.

Building lien An encumbrance upon the property by the contractor or subcontractors. Also known as a "mechanic's" or "materialman's" lien.

Building permit Written permission by the local municipality (usually through the building inspector or other agent) allowing construction work on a piece of property in accordance with plans which were submitted and conforming to local building codes and regulations.

Business trust An unincorporated business in which assets are given to trustees for management to hold or to sell, as investments. The business trust form was first fully developed in Massachusetts, under common law, and the term "Massachusetts business trust" is sometimes used to describe entities formed in other states. It is a form of business through a trustee or trustees who hold legal title to the property of the business. Capital contributions are made to the trustees by the beneficiaries whose equitable title and interest in the property of the trust are evidenced by trust certificates, usually called shares of beneficial interest. The earnings of the trust are paid to them, as dividends are paid to stockholders. The beneficiaries generally enjoy limited liability, as the control and management of the trust rests solely with the trustees, but the trust form or organization can be distinguished from a corporation. Early REIT tax laws relied on this distinction to define eligible real estate operations.

Capital gain The amount by which the net proceeds from resale of a capital item exceed the adjusted cost (or "book value") of the asset. If a capital asset is held for more than twelve months before disposition it is taxed on a more favorable basis than a gain after a shorter period of time.

Capitalization rate The rate of return utilized to value a given cash flow, the sum of a Discount Rate and a Capital Recapture Rate. It is applied to any income stream with a finite term over which the invested principal is to be returned to the investor or lender.

Cash flow The revenue remaining after all cash expenses are paid, i.e., non-cash charges such as depreciation are not included in the calculation.

Cash flow per share. Cash flow divided by the common shares outstanding. Shareholders must make this computation themselves since the SEC has prohibited companies from stating this calculation.

Net cash flow. Generally determined by net income plus depreciation less principal payments on long-term mortgages.

Cash on cash return The "cash flow" from a property expressed as a percentage of the cash "equity" invested in a property.

Chapter X See bankrupt.

Collateral An item of value, such as real estate or securities, which a borrower pledges as security. A mortgage gives the creditor the right to seize the real estate collateral after non-performance of the debtor.

Commitment A promise to make an investment at some time in the future if certain specified conditions are met. A REIT may charge a fee to the borrower at the time of making the commitment. A REIT's level of commitments minus expected repayments can be regarded as an indication of future funding requirements.

"Take-out" commitment is one provided by the anticipated long-term lender, usually with complicated terms and conditions that must be met before the "take-out" becomes effective.

"Gap" commitment is an anticipated short-term loan to cover part of the final "take-out" that the long-term lender refuses to advance until certain conditions are met (like 90% rent-up of an apartment after construction is completed). The amount above the "floor" or basic part of the loan is the "gap," and the gap commitment is issued to enable the construction lender to make a construction loan commitment for the full amount of the take-out loan instead of only for the "floor" amount.

"Standby" commitment is one that the lender and borrower doubt will be used. It exists as reassurance to a short-term construction lender that if, after completion of a building, the borrower cannot find adequate long-term "take-out" financing, the construction lender will be repaid.

Compensating balances Money which is sometimes required by banks to be held in checking accounts by borrowers, as part of their loan agreement.

Condominium A form of fee ownership of whole units or separate portions of multi-unit buildings which facilitates the formal filing, recording and financing of a divided interest in real property. The condominium concept may be used for apartments, offices and other professional uses. See cooperatives.

Conduit tax treatment So long as most (if not all) earnings are passed along by an entity, then federal taxation is avoided at the entity's level. REITs, mutual funds, and certain kinds of holding companies are eligible for "conduit tax treatment" under certain conditions.

Constant The agreed-upon periodic (usually monthly) payment to pay the face interest rate, with any residual amount going to amortize the loan.

Construction and development loan (C&D) A short-term loan for the purpose of constructing a building, shopping center, or other improvement upon real estate, or developing a site in preparation for construction. A C&D loan is normally disbursed in increments (called *draws* or *draw-downs*) as building proceeds, rather than in a single disbursement, and is conditioned upon compliance with a variety of factors. It is usually repaid with the proceeds of the permanent loan. A land loan or purchase and development loan is sometimes made for the purpose of acquiring unimproved vacant land, usually as a future building site and for financing improvements to such land (street, sewers, etc.) as a prerequisite to construction of a building upon the site.

Contingent interest Interest on a loan that is payable only if certain conditions occur, in contrast to interest that becomes an accrued liability (whether or not paid) at a specific time.

Cooperative A form of ownership whereby a structure is owned by a corporation or trust with each individual owner holding stock in the corporation representative of the value of his apartment. Title to the apartment is evidenced by a proprietary lease which often does not qualify as adequate collateral for some lenders.

Cost-to-carry The concept specified by the accounting profession to be used by REITs in computing anticipated interest cost on debt needed to "carry" non-earning or partially-earning assets until they're restored to earning status or sold.

Current liabilities Money owed and due to be paid within one year.

Dealer Someone who buys property with the purpose of selling it at a profit rather than holding it as an investment. A dealer's profits are taxed at the ordinary income rate rather than the capital gains rate regardless of how long the property is held for resale (in contrast to the investor who sells a property after a year and pays at the capital gains rate). A REIT is not permitted to be a dealer unless it is willing to pay a 100% tax on gains from such sales in the year in which it is deemed to be a dealer; sales of foreclosed property do not fall within this definition. See principal.

Debenture An obligation which is secured only by the general credit of the issuing trust, as opposed to being secured by a direct lien on its assets, real estate or otherwise. A debenture is a form of a bond.

Declaration of trust Similar to articles of incorporation for a corporation, this document contains rules for operation of the trust, selection of its governing trustees, etc., and is the keystone of a REIT.

Deed A legal instrument which conveys title from one to another. It must be (a) made between competent parties (b) have legally sound subject matter (c) correctly state what is being conveyed (d) contain good and valuable consideration (e) be properly executed by the parties involved and (f) be delivered to be valid.

Deed in lieu of foreclosure The device by which title to property is conveyed from the mortgagor (borrower) to the mortgagee (lender) as an alternative to foreclosure. While this procedure can transfer effective control more quickly, many lenders eschew it because undiscovered prior liens (from a workman who was never paid but hadn't gotten around to filing his valid, but late, claim for example) remain enforceable in contrast to the more formal foreclosure procedures which wipe out prior claims after due notice.

Deferred maintenance The amount of repairs that should have been made to keep a property in good running condition, but which have been put off. The term contemplates the desirability of immediate expenditures, although it does not necessarily denote inadequate maintenance in the past.

Deficiency dividend The process of paying an "extra" dividend after the close of the fiscal year so as to comply with REIT tax requirements to pay out more than 90% of income. See dividend.

Depreciation The loss in value of a capital asset, due to wear and tear which cannot be compensated for by ordinary repairs, or an allowance made to allow for the fact that the asset may become obsolete before it wears out. The purpose of a depreciation charge is to write off the original cost of an asset by equitably distributing charges against its operation over its useful life, matching "cost" to the period in which it was used to generate earnings. Depreciation is an optional noncash expense recognizable for tax purposes. If the REIT pays out more than its taxable earnings, then it is distributing a "return of capital" or—as is commonly stated in the industry—"paying out depreciation."

Development loans See Construction and development loan.

Dilution The situation which results when an increase occurs in a company's outstanding securities without a corresponding increase in the company's assets and/or income.

Discount rate An interest rate used to convert a future system of payments into a single present value. See capitalization rate.

Dividend or distribution The distribution of cash or stock to shareholders of a company which is made periodically as a means of distributing all or a portion of net income or cash flow. Technically, a dividend can be paid only from net taxable income, so many REITs distribute cash and later characterize their distributions as capital gains or a tax-free return of capital if net taxable income is less than the cash paid out.

Dividend or distribution yield The annual dividend or distribution rate for a security expressed as a percent of its market price. For most REITs, the "annualized" rate is the previous quarter's distribution times four, regardless of how the distribution is characterized.

Draw A request from a borrower to obtain partial payment from the lender pursuant to a loan commitment. The lender reassures himself that the borrower has completed the required steps (such as putting in the concrete properly) before advancing money. Often, the borrower submits bills from subcontractors, which are then "paid" by the lender after inspecting the subcontractor's work. In such cases, the check is usually made out to the subcontractor but must be signed by the borrower, too, so that the lender ends up only with one borrower. See construction and development loan.

Effective borrowing costs The cost of borrowing after adjustment for compensating balances or fees in lieu of compensating balances, and selling expenses in the case of publicly sold debt.

Encumbrance A legal right or interest in real estate which diminishes its value. Encumbrances can take a number of forms, such as easements, zoning restrictions, mortgages, etc.

Entrepreneur An individual who is responsible for a commercial or real estate activity who takes a certain risk of loss in a transaction for the right to enjoy any profit which may result.

Equity The interest of the shareholders in a company as measured by their paid-in capital and undistributed income. The term is also used to describe (i) the difference between the current market value of a property and the liens or mortgages which encumber it or (ii) the cash which makes up the difference between the mortgage(s) and the construction or sale price.

Equity leveraging The process by which shares are sold at a premium above book value (in anticipation of greater earnings).

Equity participation Usually, the right of an investor to participate to some extent in the increased value of a project by receiving a percentage of the increased income from the project. If a REIT were to participate in a percentage of the net income of a venture (such as the shopping center's owner/lessor), then it could be deemed to be a partner in an active business. Thus, most REIT leases spell out the "equity participation" as a percentage of gross receipts or sales (which is a more stable measure of sales activity, anyway, and one readily identifiable from the lessor's federal income tax statement).

Escrow A deposit of "good faith" money which is entrusted to a third party (often a bank) until fulfillment of certain conditions and agreements, when the escrow may be released or applied as payment for the purchase of property or for services rendered.

Estoppel certificate An instrument used

when a mortgage or lease is assigned to another. The certificate sets forth the exact remaining balance of the lease or mortgage as of a certain date and verifies any promises to tenants that may have been made by the first owner for which the second owner may be held accountable.

Exculpatory clause A clause which relieves one of liability for injuries or damages to another. Exculpatory clauses are placed in REIT documents with the intention of eliminating personal liability of its trustees, shareholders and officers.

Expenses The costs which are charges against current operations or earnings of a building, company or other reporting entity. They may have been "paid out" in cash, or accrued to be paid later, or charged as a bookkeeping procedure to reflect the "using up" of assets (as in depreciation) utilized in the production of income during the period of current operations.

Face value The value which is shown on the face of an instrument such as a bond, debenture or stock certificate. The "face rate" of a debt instrument is often known as its "coupon rate."

Fair market value See Market value.

Fee or fee simple Title to a property which is absolute, good and marketable; ownership without condition.

Fiduciary A relationship of trust and confidence between a person charged with the duty of acting for the benefit of another and the person to whom such duty is owed, as in the case of guardian and ward, trustee and beneficiary, executor and heir.

First mortgage That mortgage which has a prior claim over all other liens against real estate. In some jurisdictions, real estate taxes, mechanics liens, court costs, and other involuntary liens may take priority over such a contractual lien: title companies "clear" properties so as to reassure first mortgage lenders (and owners) of their uncontested position and to guarantee them of that position under certain conditions.

Fiscal year The 12-month period selected as a basis for computing and accounting for a business. A fiscal year need not coincide with the calendar year, except for all REITs initially qualifying for special tax treatment after 1976.

Fixed assets Assets, such as land, buildings and machinery, which cannot be quickly converted into cash. For REITs, most "fixed assets" are real property although some (like furniture in an apartment lobby) may be personal property.

Fixed charges Those interest charges, insurance costs, taxes and other expenses which remain relatively constant regardless of revenue. See net lease.

Floating rate A variable interest rate charged for the use of borrowed money. It is determined by charging a specific percentage above a fluctuating base rate, usually the prime rate as announced by a major commercial bank.

Floor loan A portion or portions of a mortgage loan commitment which is less than the full amount of the commitment and which may be funded upon conditions less stringent than those required for funding the full amount, or the "ceiling" of the loan. For example, the floor loan, equal to perhaps 80% of the full amount of the loan, may be funded upon completion of construction without any occupancy requirements, but substantial occupancy of the building may be required for funding the full amount of the loan, which is referred to as the "ceiling." See commitment, gap.

Foreclosure The legal process of enforcing payment of a debt by taking the properties which secure the debt, once the terms of the obligation are not followed. Upon foreclosure, the entire debt might not be fully discharged by transfer and disposition of the property (as determined by the courts). If so, a "deficiency judgment" may be obtained, at which point the lender is like any other creditor in attempting to get the debtor to pay the deficiency. Collection of the deficiency judgment in major real estate transactions is rare, but it becomes a major factor in negotiations if the borrower decides to return to the real estate business in the future.

Fully diluted earnings The hypothetical earnings per share of a company, computed after giving effect to the number of shares which would be outstanding if all convertible debt and warrants were exercised, and also to any reduction in interest payments resulting from such exercise.

Gap commitment See commitment, gap. Also see floor loan.

General lien A lien against the property of an individual or other entity generally, rather than against specific items of realty or personal property.

Ground lease See sale-leaseback.

Holding company A corporation that owns or controls the operations of various other companies. Many REITs were sponsored by bank or insurance holding companies whose subsidiary companies advise and manage REITs, pursuant to contracts with the REIT's trustees.

Independent contractor A firm hired to actively manage property investments. A tax-qualified REIT must hire an independent contractor to manage and operate its property, so as to distinguish itself as an investor rather than an active manager.

Income property Developed real estate, such as office buildings, shopping centers, apartments, hotels and motels, warehouses and some kinds of agricultural or industrial property, which produce a flow of income—in contrast to non-income generating real estate like raw land which would be bought and held for a speculative profit upon resale or development.

Indenture The legal document prepared in connection with, for example, a bond issue, setting forth the terms of the issue, its specific security, remedies in case of default, etc. It may also be called the "deed of trust."

Indentured trustee A trustee, generally the trust department of a major bank, which represents the interest of bondholders under a publicly offered issue.

Insider A person close to a trust who has intimate knowledge of financial developments before they become public knowledge.

Interest rate The percentage rate which an individual pays for the use of borrowed money for a given period of time.

Intermediate-term loan A loan for a term of three to ten years which is usually not fully amortized at maturity. Often, developers will seek interim loans by which to pay off construction financing, in anticipation of obtaining long-term financing at a later date on more favorable terms, either because long-term rates decline generally or because the project can show an established, stable earnings history.

Interim loan A type of loan which is to be repaid out of the proceeds of another loan. Ordinarily, not self-liquidating (amortized), the lender evaluates the risk of obtaining refinancing as much as the period risk. See C&D loans.

Investment advisor See advisor.

Joint venture The entity which is created when two or more persons or corporate entities join together to carry out a specific business transaction of real estate development. A joint venture is usually of limited duration and usually for a specific property; it can be treated as a partnership for tax purposes. The parties have reciprocal and paralleling rights and obligations.

Junior mortgage loan Any mortgage loan in which the lien and the right of repayment is subordinate to that of another mortgage loan or loans. A "second mortgage" is a junior mortgage. "Third, fourth," etc. mortgages are always deemed to be secondary.

Land loan See Construction and development loan.

Land-purchase leaseback See sale-leaseback.

Late charge The charge which is levied against a borrower for a payment which was not made in a timely manner.

Lease A contract between the owner of property (lessor) and a tenant (lessee) setting forth the terms, conditions and consideration for the use of the property for a specified period of time at a specified rental. See sale-leaseback and net lease.

Leasehold improvements The cost of improvements or betterments to property leased for a period of years, often paid for by the tenant. Such improvements ordinarily become the property of the lessor (owner) on expiration of the lease; consequently their cost is normally amortized over the life of the lease if the lessor pays for them.

Leverage The process of borrowing upon one's capital base with the expectation of generating a profit above the cost of borrowing.

Liability management The aspect of the management of a company concerned with the planning and procurement of funds for investment through the sale of equity, public debt and bank borrowings. In the REIT industry, the phrase contrasts to "asset management" or the real estate side of the business.

Line of credit Usually, an agreement between a commercial bank and a borrower under which the bank agrees to provide unsecured credit to the borrower upon certain terms and conditions. Normally, the borrower may draw on all or any part of the credit from time to time.

Limited partnership A partnership which limits certain of the partners' (the limited partners) liability to the amount of their investment. At least one partner (the "general partner") is fully liable for the obligations of the partnership and its operations, usually with the limited partners participating as investors only.

Loan loss reserve A reserve set up to offset asset values in anticipation of losses that are reasonably expected. Initially, REITs had insufficient operating experience to anticipate losses in any one class of investments or for a portfolio as a whole, so tax authorities would not permit substantial contributions toward a reserve as an allowable period expense. When difficulties arose, the conversion of short-term loans to longer-term property holdings required some form of recognition of likely losses in the financial statements. A novel procedure for REITs was devised by requiring, for book purposes, computation of additions to the reserve based in part on the probable cost of sustaining the troubled assets over the longer period of time necessary to "cure" the problem. Also known as "allowance for losses."

Loan run-off The rate at which an existing mortgage portfolio will reduce (or "run-off") to zero if no new loans are added to the portfolio.

Loan swaps See asset swaps.

Long-term mortgage Any financing, whether in the form of a first or junior mortgage, the term of which is ten years or more. It is generally fully amortized.

Loss carry forwards The net operating loss (NOL) incurred in prior years, which may be applied for tax purposes against future earnings, thereby reducing taxable income. For REITs (which must pay out most of their taxable income), NOLs can be carried forward eight years; for non-REIT-taxed companies, NOL can be carried forward for only seven years.

Market value The highest price in terms of money which a property will bring in a competitive and open market under all conditions requisite to a fair sale—the buyer and the seller each acting prudently, knowledgeably, and at arm's length. See appraisal.

Moratorium A period in which payments of debts or other performance of a legal obligation is suspended temporarily, usually because of unforeseen circumstances which make timely payment or performance difficult or impossible. This forebearance can be whole or partial.

Mortgage A publicly recorded lien by which the property is pledged as security for the payment of a debt valid even beyond death ("mort" is death in French). In some states a mortgage is an actual conveyance of the property to the creditor until the terms of the mortgage are satisfied. While there is always a "note" secured by a mortgage document, both the note and mortgage instrument are commonly called "the mortgage." For types, see: first, junior, short-term, long-term, wrap-around and construction and development mortgage definitions.

Mortgage banker A non-depository lender who makes loans secured by real estate and then usually packages and sells those loans in large groups to institutional investors, pursuant to a "long-term commitment" he has negotiated with the life insurance company or other institutional investor. Mortgage bankers frequently arrange to service these mortgages for the out-of-town institutions, collecting regular payments, keeping the lender up to date on the progress of the loan, escrowing payments for taxes and insurance premiums, and, if necessary, administering foreclosure proceedings. Many REITs were sponsored by mortgage bankers.

Mortgage constant The total annual payments of principal and interest (annual debt service) on a mortgage with level-payment amortization schedule, expressed as a percentage of the initial principal amount of the loan.

Mortgagee in possession A lender or one who holds a mortgage who has taken possession of a property in order to protect an interest in the property. Usually, this is done with commercial properties as to which rents, management fees and other disbursements continue even if the mortgage is in default. The possession must be taken with the consent of the mortgagor (or a court, in cases of foreclosure) and the mortgagee must be careful to do only those things to the property that the mortgagor (or court) will agree to accept, should it resume its role as a credit-worthy owner.

Net Income The dollar amount that remains after all expenses, including taxes, are deducted from gross income. For regular companies, it is also called after-tax profit, the "bottom line" figure of how a company has performed with its investors' money. For REITs, it is net taxable income which, if fully distributed, is not taxed.

Net lease A lease, sometimes called a net-net (insurance and taxes) or even a net-net-net lease (insurance, taxes, and maintenance) in which the tenant pays all costs, including insurance, taxes, repairs, upkeep and other expenses, and the rental payments are "net" of all these expenses. See lease and fixed charges.

Net worth The remaining asset value of a property company or other entity after deduction of all liabilities against it.

Non-accrual loans See non-earning investments.

Non-earning investments The category of loans or investments which are not earning the originally anticipated rate of return. Some may be characterized as "partially earning." When interest is recorded as earned rather than as received (accrued interest), "non-accrual investments" are those which management expects not to receive interest as originally contemplated. In the vernacular, nonearning investments are "problem loans" or "troubled properties."

Non-qualified REIT A REIT that was formerly qualified, or conducts its affairs as if it is qualified, but that has elected for the tax year in question to be treated like a normal business corporation for tax purposes. Thus, some restraints (primarily against active management and holding property for sale) are lifted, while REIT conduit tax treatment is lost.

Occupancy rate The amount of space or number of apartments or offices or hotel rooms which are rented as compared with the total amount or number available. The rate is usually expressed as a percentage.

Operating expenses Expenses arising out of or relating to business activity such as interest expense, professional fees, salaries, etc.

Operating income Income received directly from business activity in the normal course, as contrasted with capital gains income, or other extraordinary income.

Option A right to buy or lease property at a certain specified price for specified terms. Consideration is typically given for the option, which is exercisable over a limited time span. If the option is not exercised, the consideration is forfeited. A loan to a developer secured by his option to obtain real estate is considered a "qualified" REIT asset.

Origination The process by which a loan is created, including the search for (or receipt of) the initial plans, the analysis and structuring of the proposed financing, and the review and acceptance procedures by which the commitment to make the investment is finally issued.

Overage income Rental income above a guaranteed minimum depending on a particular level of profit or retail sales volume by the tenant, payable under the terms of a lease.

Participations A lender often "participates out" or sells a portion of his loan to another lender while retaining a portion and managing the investment. REITs buy real estate secured participations as well as originating them.

Par value The face value assigned to a security when it is issued. The stated par value of a security generally has nothing to do with its market or book value.

Passivity The state of owning investments but not actively managing them (as a property management firm does for the investor) or engaging in trading the securities (like a broker or dealer). This "passivity" test is implicit behind several of the REIT tax requirements.

Pension funds Money which is accumulated in trust to fund pensions for companies or unions and which is frequently invested in part in real estate. A co-mingled real estate pension fund account is managed, usually under contract to a financial institution, much like a REIT except that its shares are not publicly traded but instead sold to other pension funds.

Permanent financing See long-term loan.

Point An amount which represents 1% of the maximum principal amount of an investment. Used in connection with a discount from, or a share of, a principal amount deducted at the time funds are advanced, it represents additional compensation to the lender.

Portfolio The investments of a company, including investments in mortgages and/or ownership of real property. REIT portfolios usually consist of equity in property, short-term mortgages, long-term mortgages and/or subordinated land sale-lease-backs.

Portfolio turnover The average length of time from the funding of investments until they are paid off or sold.

Preferred shares Stocks which have prior claim on distributions (and/or assets in the event of dissolution) up to a certain definite amount before the shares of beneficial interest are entitled to anything. As a form of ownership, preferred shares stand behind senior subordinated and secured debtholders in dissolution, as well as other creditors.

Prepayment penalty The penalty which is imposed on the borrower for payment of the mortgage before it is due. Often a mortgage contains a clause specifying that there is to be no prepayment penalty, or limits the prepayment penalty to only the first few years of the mortgage term.

Price earning ratio A ratio which consists of the market price divided by current annualized earnings per share. Such a computation is now found in most daily stock listings. For REITs, annualization of quarterly earnings is computed by multiplying the most recent distribution by four, regardless of the distribution's later characterization as a dividend, return-of-capital, or capital gains.

Prime lending rate The rate at which commercial banks will lend money from time to time to their most credit-worthy customers, used as a base for most loans to financial intermediaries such as REITs.

Principal The buyer or seller in a real estate transaction as distinguished from an agent.

Principal The sum of money loaned. The amount of money to be repaid on a loan excluding interest charges.

Prior lien A lien or mortgage ranking ahead of some other lien. A prior lien need not itself be a first mortgage.

Pro forma Projected or hypothetical as opposed to actual as related, for example, to a balance sheet or income statement.

Problem investments See nonearning investments.

Prospectus A document describing an investment opportunity; the detailed description of new securities which must be supplied to prospective interstate purchasers under the Securities Act of 1933.

Provision for loan losses Periodic allocation of funds to loan loss reserves in recognition of a decline in the value of a loan or loans in a trust's portfolio due to a default on the part of the borrowers.

Proxy An authorization given by a registered security holder to vote stock at the annual meeting or at a special meeting of security holders.

Purchase and leaseback See sale-leaseback.

Pyramiding In stock market transactions, this term refers to the practice of borrowing against unrealized "paper" profits in securities to make additional purchases. In corporate finance, it refers to the practice of creating a speculative capital structure by a series of holding companies, whereby a relatively small amount of voting stock in the parent company controls a large corporate system. In real estate, it refers to the practice of financing 100% or more of the value of the property.

Qualified assets Assets which meet tax requirements for special REIT tax treatment, i.e. real property. In any tax year, 75% of a REIT's assets must be invested in real property, either through ownership or by securities secured by real estate. A "partially qualified" asset is one that qualifies under the 90% test of being a passive investment in a security, but not under the 75% real estate test.

Qualified income That portion of income which is classified as interest, rents, or other gain from real property, as spelled out in the REIT tax laws.

Raw land Land which has not been developed or improved.

RCA See revolving credit agreement.

Real estate investment trust (REIT, pronounced "reet") A trust established for the benefit of a group of investors which is managed by one or more trustees who hold title to the assets for the trust and control its acquisitions and investments, at least 75% of which are real estate related. A major advantage of a REIT is that no federal income tax need be paid by the trust if certain qualifications are met. Congress enacted these special tax provisions to encourage an assembly method, which is essentially designed to provide for investment in real estate what the mutual provided for investment in securities. The REIT provides the small investor with a means of combining his funds with those of others, and protects him from the double taxation that would be levied against an ordinary corporation or trust.

Revolving credit agreement (or "revolver") A formal credit agreement between a group of banks and a REIT, the terms of which are reviewed periodically when it is "rolled over" or "revolved" or refinanced by a similar agreement. For many trusts, "revolvers" have replaced informal lines of credit extended by individual banks to REITs, thereby providing a uniform (and usually restrictive) approach by all creditors, reassuring each bank that others in the RCA would not be paid off preferentially.

Registration statement The forms filed by a company with the Securities and Exchange Commission in connection with an offering of new securities or the listing of outstanding securities on a national exchange.

Reserves for loss See loan loss reserve.

Return of capital A distribution to shareholders in excess of the trust's earnings and profits, usually consisting of either depreciation or repayment of principal from properties or mortgages held by the trust. Each shareholder receiving such a distribution is required to reduce the tax basis of his shares by the amount of such distribution. For financial accounting purposes, what constitutes a return of capital may differ from that determined under Federal income tax requirements.

Return on equity A figure which consists of net income for the period divided by equity and which is normally expressed as a percentage.

Right of first refusal The right or option granted by a seller to a buyer, to have the first opportunity of acquiring a property.

Rights offering The privilege extended to a shareholder of subscribing to additional stock of the same or another class or to bonds, usually at a price below the market and in an amount proportional to the number of shares already held. Rights must be exercised within a time limit and often may be sold if the holder does not wish to purchase additional shares.

Sale-leaseback A common real estate transaction whereby the investor buys property from and simultaneously leases it back to, the seller. This enables the previous owner (often a developer) to "cash out" on an older property while retaining control.

Land sale-leaseback—this procedure,

made common by several REITs that specialize in the transaction, affects only the land under income—producing improvements (such as shopping centers, etc.)—leaving the depreciable improvements in the hands of those who might benefit from the tax consequences. Since the improvements were probably financed with the proceeds of a first mortgage which remains in effect, the rights of the new investor are made second, or junior, to those of the first mortgage holder. Hence the common phrase "subordinated land sale-leaseback." In return for accepting a less secure position, the new investor usually obtains an "overage" clause whereby additional rent is paid anytime gross income of the shopping center (or whatever) exceeds a pre-determined floor.

Seasoned issues Securities of large, established companies which have been known to the investment public for a period of years, covering good times and bad.

Second mortgages See junior mortage loan.

Secured mortgages See junior mortgage loan.

Secured debt For REITs, senior mortgage debt secured by specific properties. In case of default on "nonrecourse" debt, the lender may assume property ownership but may not pursue other assets of the lender.

Senior mortgage A mortgage which has first priority.

Senior unsecured debt Funds borrowed under open lines without security. Most bank lines to REITs were unsecured.

Shares of beneficial interest Tradable shares in a REIT. Analogous to common stock in a corporation.

Shareholders' equity Primarily money invested by shareholders through purchase of shares, plus the accumulation of that portion of net income that has been reinvested in the business since the commencement of operations.

Short-term mortgage A loan upon real estate for a term of three years or less, bearing interest payable periodically, with principal usually payable in full at maturity.

Sinking fund An arrangement under which a portion of a bond or preferred stock issue is retired periodically, in advance of its fixed maturity. The company may either purchase a stipulated quantity of the issue itself, or supply funds to a trustee or agent for that purpose. Retirement may be made by call at a fixed price, or by inviting tenders, or by purchase in the open market.

Sponsor The entity which initiated the formation of a REIT and usually acts (often via a subsidiary) as investment advisor to the trust thereafter. The sponsor puts the reputation of its institution on the line for the REIT and usually arranges lines of credit, provides support services and, occasionally, compensating balances.

Spread Difference between percentage return on an investment and cost of funds to support the investment.

Standby commitment See commitment, standby.

Standing loan Usually not amortized, the loan is secured by completed property that has not yet been refinanced with a "permanent" long-term mortgage.

Subordinated debt Debt which is junior to secured and unsecured senior debt, it may be convertible into shares of beneficial interest for REITs. Senior subordinated debt is senior to other subordinated debt.

Subordinated ground lease See sale-leaseback.

Swap program A procedure for reducing debt (by a troubled REIT) by trading an asset to the creditor in return for cancellation of part of a loan to the REIT. Often a cash premium payment is made in addition to reduction of the debt. The premium may then be distributed to the other creditors pro rata. The amount of the cash premium, or the ratio of cash-to-debt reduction to be applied against the value of the asset, is sometimes determined by a sealed-bid "auction" process as set forth in the "revolving credit agreement" between the creditors and the REIT. See RCA.

Syndicate A group of investors who transact business for a limited period of time and sometimes with a single purpose. It is a short-term partnership.

Take-out commitment See commitment.

Tax shelter The various aspects of an investment which offer relief from income taxes or opportunities to claim deductions from taxable income. Although tax shelters are an important facet of real estate investment, they do not have a direct influence on REIT investment choices because qualified trusts are exempt from income taxes.

Usury The charging of interest rates for the use of money higher than what's allowed by local law.

Warrants Stock purchase warrants or options give the holder rights to purchase shares of stock, generally running for a longer period of time than ordinary subscription rights given shareholders. Warrants are often attached to other securities, but they may be issued separately or detached after issuance.

Working capital Determined by subtracting current liabilities from current assets. It represents the amount available to carry on the day-to-day operation of the business.

Work-out When a borrower has problems, the process undertaken by the lender to help the borrower "work out" of the problems becomes known itself as a "work out." The presumption during a "work out" is that the borrower will eventually resume a more normal debtor's position once problems are solved within (presumably) a reasonably short time.

Wrap-around mortgage A type of junior mortgage used to refinance properties on which there is an existing first mortgage loan. The face amount of the wrap-around loan is equivalent to the unpaid balance on the existing mortgage plus cash advanced to the property owner upon funding. Such loans carry a higher interest rate than the existing mortgage. The wrap-around lender assumes the obligation to maintain payments of principal and interest on the existing mortgage so as to enhance his right to make claim from his secondary position.

Yield In the stock market, the rate of annual distribution or dividend expressed as a percentage of price. Current yield is found by dividing the market price into the distribution rate in dollars. In real estate, the term refers to the effective annual amount of income which is being accrued on an investment expressed as a percentage of its value.

Business Information Directory

General Reference Sources

Business Information Sources by Lorna M. Daniells. A classic source of information covering such topics as finance, industry, statistics, management, marketing and much more. Published by the University of California Press, Berkeley and Los Angeles, California.

Business Organizations, Agencies and Publications Directory, lists organizations, agencies and information services that promote, coordinate, and regulate commercial activity in the U.S. Gale Research Co., 835 Penobscot Building, Detroit, MI 48226.

Directory of Marketing Research Houses and Services is an annual available from the American Marketing Association, 250 South Wacker Drive, Chicago, IL 60606.

Encyclopedia of Banking and Finance, is a comprehensive source on subjects indicated in the title. Bankers Publishing Co., 210 South Street, Boston, MA.

Encyclopedia of Business Information Sources edited by James Woy. A wide range of information sources are listed under 1,100 alphabetically arranged business subjects. Easy identification of key live, print, and electronic sources of information. Also covers subjects of current interest, new technologies, and new industries in addition to basic business subjects. Available from Gale Research Co., 835 Penobscot Building, Detroit, MI 48226.

Encyclopedia of Business Information Sources: Europe, edited by M. Balachandran covers business information sources from more than 50 Eastern and Western European countries. Sources are listed under alphabetically arranged business subjects and then by type of resources. There is also a section in which these entries are arranged by title or organization name. Available from Gale Research Co., 835 Penobscot Building, Detroit, MI 48226.

Encyclopedia of Information Systems and Services. Provides comprehensive international coverage of computer-based information systems and services. Includes details on information providers, access services, sources of information, and support services. Listings are arranged in a single volume covering about 5,000 information organizations, systems, and services located in the United States and some 70 other countries. More than 30,000 organizations, services and products are identified. Published by Gale Research Co., 835 Penobscot Building, Detroit, MI 48226.

Guide to American Directories, published by B. Klein Publications, Inc., P.O. Box 8503, Coral Springs, FL 33065.

Lesko's Info Power contains thousands of sources of free and low cost information covering a wide variety of subjects such as investments, businesses, job opportunities and much more. Published by Information USA, P.O. Box E, Kingston, MD 20895.

National Directory of Addresses and Telephone Numbers. A national business directory that lists all SEC registered companies, major accounting and law firms, banks, and financial institutions, associations, unions, etc. Included are 50,000 fax numbers. Published by Omnigraphics, Penobscot Building, Detroit, MI 48226.

Standard Rate and Data Service provides information on periodical circulation and advertising rates. Published by Standard Rates and Data Service, Inc., 5201 Old Orchard Road, Skokie, IL 60077–1021.

Statistical Abstract of the United States, published annually by the Bureau of the Census, is the standard summary on the social, political, and economic statistics of the United States. It includes data from both government and private sources. Appendix I gives a comprehensive list of sources. Available from the Superintendent of Documents, Government Printing Office, Washington, DC 20402.

The *United States Government Manual* is an annual publication. It describes the organization, purposes, and programs of most government agencies and lists top personnel. Available from the Superintendent of Documents, Government Printing Office, Washington, DC 20402.

Washington Information Directory is an annual publication listing, by topic, organizations and publications which provide information on a wide range of subjects. It also lists congressional committee assignments, regional federal offices, embassies, and state and local officials. Published by the Congressional Quarterly, Inc., 1414 22nd Street NW, Washington, DC 20037.

Who Knows: A Guide to Washington Experts, Washington Researchers, 2612 P Street NW, Washington, DC 20007.

Professional and trade organizations and

publications are a major source of contacts and information. Key directories to these sources are listed below.

Directories in Print, contains more than 16,000 detailed entries on directories published in the United States and Canada. Directories outside the U.S. and Canada are listed in *International Directories in Print* and city and state directories are listed in *City and State Directories in Print.* Available from Gale Research Co., 835 Penobscot Building, Detroit, MI 48226.

Encyclopedia of Associations contains detailed entries on over 22,000 active organizations, clubs, and other non-profit organizations. Available from Gale Research Co., 835 Penobscot Building, Detroit, MI 48226.

The Gale Directory of Publications and Broadcast Media, a guide to newspapers, magazines and other periodicals, as well as radio, television and cable companies. Available from Gale Research Co., 835 Penobscot Building, Detroit, MI 48226.

National Trade and Professional Associations of the United States. A comprehensive listing of professional trade and labor associations, including addresses, membership size, publications by the associations, and convention schedules. An annual published by Columbia Books, 1212 New York Avenue NW, Washington, DC.

Standard Periodical Directory covers U.S. and Canadian periodicals. Published by Oxbridge Communications, Inc., 150 Fifth Avenue, New York, NY 10011.

The World Guide to Trade Associations gives a comprehensive national and international listing of associations. Published by R. R. Bowker Co., 245 West 17th Street, New York, NY 10011.

Ulrich's International Periodical Directory covers both domestic and foreign periodicals. Published by R. R. Bowker Co., 245 West 17th Street, New York, NY 10011.

World Business Directory edited by Linda Irvin contains information on more than 130,000 companies interested in international trade opportunities. Lists contact, financial, and business information and includes an Alphabetic Index, SIC Index and Product Index. Available from Gale Research Co., 835 Penobscot Building, Detroit, MI 48226.

Population information on all aspects of national and world population is provided by the Population Reference Bureau, Inc., 1875 Connecticut Avenue NW, Washington, DC 20009.

BUSINESS AND ECONOMICS INFORMATION

Government publications referred to below may be obtained from the Government Printing Office (GPO), Washington, DC, 20402, unless otherwise indicated.

Census Catalog and Guide is an annual one-step guide to Census Bureau resources. Includes explanations of the censuses and surveys of business, manufacturing, and population, names and phone numbers of over 1,600 sources of assistance—Census Bureau specialists, State and local agencies, and private companies.

Business and economic information is provided by the following key references.

Annual Survey of Manufacturers. General statistics of manufacturing activity for industry groups, individual industries, states, and geographical regions are provided. (GPO)

County Business Patterns is an annual publication on employment and payrolls, which includes a separate paperbound report for each state. (GPO)

Current Industrial Reports are a series of over 100 monthly, quarterly, semiannual, and annual reports on major products manufactured in the United States. For subscription, contact the Bureau of the Census, U.S. Department of Commerce, Washington, DC 20233. (GPO)

The Economic Bulletin Board of the Department of Commerce includes same day postings of data provided by both the Bureau of Labor Statistics and the Bureau of Economic Analysis. There are updates from the Bureau of the Census on the principal indicators, monetary statistics and foreign trade. For information call (202) 482-1986.

Economic Indicators is a monthly summary-type publication prepared by the Council of Economic Advisers. It contains charts and tables on natural output, income, spending, employment, unemployment, wages, industrial production, construction, prices, money, credit, federal finance, and international statistics. (GPO)

Federal Reserve Bulletin is a monthly issued by the Federal Reserve System, containing articles and very extensive tabulated data on all aspects of the monetary situation, credit, mortgage markets, interest rates, and stock and bond yields. Available from the Board of Governors, Federal Reserve System, Washington, DC 20551.

Foreign Trade is a Bureau of the Census publication giving monthly reports on U.S. foreign trade. (GPO)

Monthly Labor Review. This monthly publication provides articles and statistics on employment, productivity, wages, earnings, prices, wage settlements, and work stoppages. (GPO)

Population: Current Report is a series of monthly and annual reports covering population changes and socioeconomic characteristics of the population. (GPO)

Quarterly Financial Report for Manufacturing, Mining, and Trade Corporations is issued by the Bureau of the Census of the U.S. Department of Commerce. It covers corporate financial statistics including sales, profits, assets, and financial ratios, classified by industry group and size. (GPO)

Retail Sales: Current Business Report is a weekly report which provides retail statistics. (GPO)

State and Metropolitan Area Data Book contains information on personal income, population characteristics, business, health, and crime among other topics. Prepared by the Bureau of the Census. (GPO)

Survey of Current Business is a major publication which is supplemented on a weekly basis with *Current Statistics*. The publication contains articles as well as comprehensive statistics on all aspects of the economy, including data on the GNP, employment, wages, prices, finance, foreign trade, and production by industrial sector. (GPO)

Wholesale Trade, Sales and Inventories: Current Business Report provides a monthly report on wholesale trade. (GPO)

U.S. Industrial Outlook is an annual providing evaluations and projections of all major industrial and commercial segments of the domestic economy. (GPO)

U.S. Occupational Outlook is an annual providing information on employment opportunities, and projections. (GPO)

U.S. CORPORATE INFORMATION

The major sources of information on publicly held corporations (as well as government and municipal issues) are:

Moody's Investor Services, Inc., owned by Dun & Bradstreet, 99 Church Street, New York, NY 10007, and

Standard & Poor's Corp., owned by McGraw-Hill, 25 Broadway, New York, NY 10004.

Standard & Poor's *Corporate Records* and Moody's *Manuals* are large multivolume works published annually and kept up to date with daily (for Standard & Poor's) or semiweekly (for Moody's) reports. The services provide extensive coverage of industrials, public utilities, transportation, banks, and financial companies. Also included are municipal and government issues.

In addition, the above corporations provide computerized data services and magnetic tapes. Compustat tapes, containing major corporate financial data, are available from Investor's Management Services, Inc., Denver, CO, a subsidiary of Standard & Poor's. Time-sharing access to Compustat and other financial data bases is available through Interactive Data Corporation, Waltham, MA.

Media General Financial Services, 301 East Grace Street, Richmond, VA, 23219, maintains a database of corporate and industry information on 5500 companies. It can be accessed via Dow Jones News Retrieval, Dialog, Thomson Financial Networks, Randall-Helms Fiduciary Consultants, Lotus One Source (CD-ROM). Media General Financial Services also provides data on the financial markets, mutual funds and corporate bonds.

The Media General Financial Services proprietary product line also includes direct sales of its data through magnetic tapes, diskettes, custom research applications, specialized screening and report services.

DISCLOSURE II, available from Disclosure, Inc., (5161 River Road, Bethesda, MD 20816) provides an on line data base of corporate information for some 10,000 companies. Disclosure II can be used via the Dow Jones Retrieval Service, New York Times Information Service, Lockheed's DIALOG Information Services, Inc., ADP, CompuServe, among others.

Also available from Disclosure is MICRO/SCAN: Disclosure II, a monthly diskette service which provides information on dividends per share, 4-year growth rate in earnings per share, price/book value, etc. For information call 800–638–8076.

The 10-K and other corporate reports are filed with the Securities and Exchange Commission and are available at local SEC offices, investor relations departments of publicly traded companies, as well as various private services, such as Disclosure Inc. which provides a complete microfiche service. *The SEC News Digest*, formerly published by the government, is now available from Disclosure, Inc. (address above). Included in the *Digest* is a daily listing of 8K reports, a daily Acquisitions of Securities Report, as well as information about what's happening inside the SEC.

Disclosure Inc. has two additional services helpful for researching a corporation. Through the *SEC Watch Service* any report filed by a company with the SEC can be retrieved while corporate information such as prospective supplements and tender offers can be retrieved through the *SEC Research Service*.

Betchel Information Service located at 1801 Research Boulevard, Rockville, MD 20850 is another SEC document retrieval service. The Index of financial documents is updated several times a day.

Major trade directories include the annual *Thomas Register of American Manufacturers* (published by Thomas Publishing Company, 1 Pennsylvania Plaza, New York, NY 10005) and Dun & Bradstreet's *Reference Book of Manufacturers*.

Thomas Register includes in two volumes

an alphabetical listing of manufacturers, giving address, phone number, product, subsidiaries, plant location, and an indication of assets. Dun & Bradstreet's *Reference Book* covers similar information, including sales and credit. Dun & Bradstreet's *Million Dollar Directory* series provides data on U.S. companies whose net worth is $1,000,000 and up, including information on privately held corporations; also published is a companion volume the *Billion Dollar Directory* which tracks America's corporate families.

How to Find Information About Private Companies includes strategies for private company investigation, sources for private company intelligence, and how to find information about private companies. Published by Washington Researchers, 2612 P Street NW, Washington, DC 20007.

The *Corporate Directory*, published by Cambridge Information Group, 7200 Wisconsin Avenue, Bethesda MD 20814 is a two volume compendium of over 9500 public companies. Included is such information as corporate officers, majority stockholders, SIC members, major subsidiaries, P/E ratio, etc.

Monitor Publishing, 104 Fifth Avenue, New York, NY 10011 publishes four directories that list, among other items, names, titles, and addresses of the managers of the listed companies in the U.S. and abroad. The volumes are: *The Corporate 1000* (a quarterly), *The Financial 1000, The Over-the-Counter 1000*, and *The International 1000.* Monitor also publishes the *Blue Book of Canadian Business.*

Directory of Investment Research, an annual published by Nelson Publishing, 1 Gateway Plaza, Port Chester, NY lists security analysts with a subject specialty, top corporate officers, and brokerage firms researching a given company.

Register of Corporations is published by Standard and Poor's Corp., 345 Hudson Street, New York, NY 10014.

Directory of Corporate Affiliations and International Directory of Corporate Affiliations are references to the structure of major domestic and international corporations. Published by National Register Publishing Company, 3004 Glen View Road, Wilmette, IL 60091.

How to Find Company Intelligence in State Documents provides information filed by companies with the state governments and also business related data collected by the states. Washington Researchers Publishing, 2612 P Street NW, Washington, DC 20007.

How to Find Information About Companies: The Corporate Intelligence Source Book provides information on sources helpful in researching either private or public companies. Available from Washington Researchers Publishing. (See above for the address.)

Ward's Business Directory of U.S. Private and Public Companies. Company profiles on over 142,000 private and public U.S. businesses—over 90% of which are privately held. Available from Gale Research, Inc., 835 Penobscot Building, Detroit, MI 48226.

Future earnings projections of listed companies based on surveys by securities analysts are provided by Lynch, Jones, and Ryan, 345 Hudson Street, New York, NY 10013.

Zacks Investment Research, Inc., 155 North Wacker Drive, Chicago, IL 60606 also provides future earnings projections.

The Corporate Finance Sourcebook, published by the National Register Publishing Company, Macmillan Directory Division, P.O. Box 609, Wilmette, IL 60091, provides information on sources of capital, financial intermediaries and specialized financial sources.

Information on foreign corporations is provided in *World Trade Data Reports,* distributed by the District Offices of the U.S. Department of Commerce.

TRACKING FEDERAL GOVERNMENT DEVELOPMENTS

Commerce Business Daily (*CB*). This daily provides information on contract awards and subcontract opportunities, Defense Department awards, and surplus sales. *CB* is available on-line from: United Communications Group, 8701 Georgia Avenue, Silver Springs, MD 20910; DIALOG Information Services, 3460 Hillview Avenue, Palo Alto, CA 94304; or Data Resources, Inc., 2400 Hartwell Avenue, Lexington, ME 02173. Available from the Superintendent of Documents, Government Printing Office, Washington, DC 20402.

Federal Register. This daily provides information on federal agency regulations and other legal documents. Available from the Superintendent of Documents, Government Printing Office, Washington, DC 20402.

CQ Weekly Report. This major service follows every important piece of legislation through both houses of Congress and reports on the political and lobbying pressures being applied. Available from the Congressional Quarterly Service, 1414 22nd Street, Washington, DC 20037.

Daily Report for Executives. A daily series of reports giving Washington developments that affect all aspects of business operations. Available from the Bureau of National Affairs, Inc., 1231 25th Street NW, Washington, DC 20037.

The Bureau of National Affairs, Inc. (address above) and the *Commerce Clearing House, Inc.* (4025 West Peterson Avenue, Chicago, IL 60646), publish a large number of valuable weekly loose-leaf reports covering developments in all aspects of law, government regulations, and taxation.

INDEX PUBLICATIONS

Indexes of a wide variety of articles appearing in periodicals, trade presses, and financial services dealing with corporations, industry, and finance are given in the following:

Business Periodicals Index published by H. W. Wilson Co., 950 University Avenue, Bronx, NY.

Funk and Scott Index of Corporations and Industries, published by Predicast, Inc., 11001 Cedar Street, Cleveland, OH 44141.

Major newspaper indexes are:

Wall Street Journal Index published by Dow Jones & Co. Inc., 22 Cortlandt Street, New York, NY 10007 (monthly).

New York Times Index published by the New York Times Company, 229 W. 43rd Street, New York, NY 10036 (semimonthly, cumulates annually).

TRACKING ECONOMIC INDICATORS

Composite Index of Leading Economic Indicators: Each month the Bureau of Economic Analysis compiles this data from the 12 leading economic indicators. This material appears each month in the *Bureau's Survey of Current Business* available by subscription from:

Superintendent of Documents
Government Printing Office
Washington, DC 20402

Consumer Price Index (*CPI*) (changes in cost of goods to customers): For these monthly reports prepared by the Bureau of Labor Statistics write:

Bureau of Labor Statistics
Department of Labor
Postal Square Building
2 Massachusetts Avenue NE
Washington, DC 20212

CPI 24 hour hotline: 202-606-7828.

Producer Price Index (*PPI*) (measures changes in prices received in primary markets by producers). For monthly reports write:

Bureau of Labor Statistics
Department of Labor
Postal Square Building
2 Massachusetts Avenue NE
Washington, DC 20212

PPI 24 hour hotline: 202-606-7828.

Available from the Bureau of Labor Statistics (BLS) are press releases on *State and Metropolitan Area Unemployment* (issued monthly), the *Employment Cost Index* (issued quarterly, and the *Employment Situation Study* (released monthly). To subscribe write:

Bureau of Labor Statistics
Department of Labor
Postal Square Building
2 Massachusetts Avenue NE
Washington, DC 20212

Unemployment Insurance Claims Weekly may be obtained by calling or by writing:

Employment and Training Administration
Department of Labor
Postal Square Building
2 Massachusetts Avenue NE
Washington, DC 20212

Releases on the *Money Supply* (Report H-6, issued weekly) and on *Consumer Credit* (Report G-19, issued monthly) may be obtained from the

Publications Services
Federal Reserve Board
Washington, DC 20551
202-452-3244

Personal Consumption Expenditure Deflator is prepared monthly by the Bureau of Economic Analysis of the Department of Commerce. This information appears in a press release *Personal Income and Outlays* and can be obtained in writing from the

Public Information Office Order Desk
Bureau of Economic Analysis
Department of Commerce
Washington, DC 20230

For information call 202-523-0777.

Monthly Trade Report (index of retail sales and accounts receivable) is compiled by the Bureau of the Census and published in *Current Business Reports* as part of what is known as the BR series. Also available are *Current Business Reports Wholesale Trade* and *Current Business Reports Selected Services.* To subscribe contact the Superintendent of Documents (Address given below). For a sample copy call: 301-763-4100.

Value of New Construction Put in Place is a Census Bureau monthly report (part of the C-30 Series) which charts the dollar amount of new construction. It is available on an annual subscription basis from the Superintendent of Documents, Government Printing Office, Washington, DC 20402. For a sample copy call: 301-763-5717.

Joint Economic Committee of Congress Reports

Reports on the economic issues studied by the Joint Economic Committee are available free of charge from:

Joint Economic Committee of Congress
Dirksen Senate Office Building
Washington, DC 20510
202–224–5321

TRACKING CONGRESSIONAL ACTION

Congressional action information can be obtained from several sources. The Legis Office will provide information on whether legislation has been introduced, who sponsored it, and its current status. For House or Senate action, call 202–225–1772.

Cloakrooms of both houses will provide details on what is happening on the floor of the chamber.

House cloakrooms:
Democrat 202–225–7330
Republican 202–225–7350

Senate cloakrooms:
Democrat 202–224–4691
Republican 202–224–6391

ASSISTANCE FROM U.S. GOVERNMENT AGENCIES

The **Office of Business Liaison (OBL)** serves as the focal point for contact between the Department of Commerce and the business community. Through the *Business Assistance Program* individuals and firms are guided through the entire government complex. Other services include dissemination of information and reports such as *Outlook*.

Write Office of Business Liaison, U.S. Department of Commerce, Washington, DC 20230. This office is also a focal point for handling inquiries for domestic business information.

OBL telephone numbers:

Office of the Director . . (202) 482-3942
Office of Private Sector Initiatives 3717
Business Assistance Program 3176
TDD 5691

Industry experts in the International Trade Administration can provide specifics about an industry.

Country experts in the Department of State provide up to date economic and political information on countries throughout the world, as well as background reports on specific countries. For information contact:

Country Desk Officers
U.S. Department of State
2201 C Street NW
Washington, DC 20520
Telephone: 202–647–4000

Major Bureau of Labor Statistics Indicators are available daily from a recorded message at 202–606-7828.

Economic news and highlights of the day are provided by phone from the Department of Commerce. For economic news call 202–393–4100. For news highlights call 202–393–1847.

The Energy Information Center will provide free information on energy and related matters. Write National Energy Information Center, Forrestal Building, 1000 Independence Avenue SW, Washington, DC 20585. Call 202–586–8800.

Technical and scientific information are provided by the **National Technical Information Service** of the Department of Commerce, 5285 Port Royal, Springfield, VA 22161, which handles requests about government-sponsored research of all kinds. There is a basic charge to research a subject. For information call 703–487–4600.

The **Census Bureau** produces detailed statistical information for the U.S. Information is available on population, housing, agriculture, manufacturing, retail trade, service industries, wholesale trade, foreign trade, mining, transportation, construction, and the revenues and expenditures of state and local governments. The Bureau also produces statistical studies of many foreign countries.

Information Sources in the Bureau of the Census

As the Federal Government's principal fact-finding agency, the Census Bureau collects, processes, analyzes, and disseminates statistics on important aspects of the Nation's social and economic life.

User Services

Product Information .... (301) 763-4100
Guides: Catalogs and
Directories .... (301) 763-1584
Data User Training .... (301) 763-1510

Government, Commerce and Industry Subjects

Agriculture Data .... (301) 763-1113
Business Data (Retail,
Wholesale, Services) .... (301) 763-7564
Construction Statistics .... (301) 763-7163
Foreign Trade Data .... (301) 763-5140
State Exports .... (301) 763-2725
Government Data .... (301) 763-7366
Industry Data .... (301) 763-5850
Manufacturers Data .... (301) 763-7666

Population, Housing and Income Subjects

Housing Data .... (301) 763-8553
International Statistics .... (301) 763-4221
Neighborhood Statistics .... (301) 763-4282
Population Data .... (301) 763-5020
Special Surveys .... (301) 763-2767

Regional Assistance

Atlanta, Georgia .... (404) 730-3832
Boston, Massachusetts .... (617) 565-7100
Charlotte, North Carolina .... (704) 344-6142
Chicago, Illinois .... (312) 353-6251
Dallas, Texas .... (214) 767-7500
Denver, Colorado .... (303) 969-6750
Detroit, Michigan .... (313) 259-0056
Kansas City, Kansas .... (913) 236-3728
Los Angeles, California .... (818) 904-6393
New York, New York .... (212) 264-3860
Philadelphia, Pennsylvania ...... (215) 597-4920
Seattle, Washington .... (206) 728-5300

For a detailed telephone
contact list .... (301) 763-4100

Information Sources in the U.S. Department of Commerce: Quick Reference List

Procurement Forecast	(202) 482-1472
Sea Grant Research	(301) 713-2438
Small Business Administration Answer Desk	(800) 827-5722
Small Business Innovation Research (SBIR)	(301) 763-4240
Small Business Set Asides	(202) 482-3387
Small Business Technology Assistance	(301) 975-6343
Standards Code and Information Program	(301) 975-4029
Technology Administration	(202) 482-1397
U.S. Travel and Tourism Administration	(202) 482-0137
Women-Owned Business	(202) 482-5614
PUBLICATIONS	
"Business America" Magazine	(202) 482-3251
"Commerce Business Daily"	(202) 482-0632
"Survey of Current Business"	(202) 606-9900
STATISTICS	
Business Cycles	(202) 606-5365
Capital Investment	(202) 606-5308
Export Statistics	(202) 482-2185
Foreign Travelers to U.S.	(202) 482-4028
Gross Domestic Product	(202) 606-9700
Housing Starts	(301) 763-5731
Income Data	(301) 763-8579
International Investment	(202) 606-9800
International Trade Balance	(202) 606-9545
Leading Economic Indicators	(202) 606-5366
National Economic, Social & Environmental Data Bank (Domestic)	(202) 482-1986
Personal Income, Outlays and Savings	(202) 606-5301
Personal Income by County	(202) 606-5360
Population	(301) 763-5002
Price Indexes	(202) 606-9700
Regional Projections	(202) 606-5344
Retail Trade Data	(301) 763-5294
Export Statistics	(202) 482-2185
TRADE AND EXPORTS	
Advocacy Center	(202) 482-3896
Business Information Service for the Newly Independent States	(202) 482-4655
District Export Councils	(202) 482-2976
Eastern Europe Business Information Center	(202) 482-2645
Export Contact List Service	(202) 482-2505
Export Licensing Voice Information System (ELVIS)	(202) 482-4811
Export License Application and Information Network (ELAIN)	(202) 482-4811
Export Promotion Coordination	(202) 482-4501
Export Trading Companies	(202) 482-5131
Fish Exports	(301) 713-2328
Foreign Availability	(202) 482-0074
Foreign Trade Zones	(202) 482-2862
Industry/Products Information	(202) 482-1461
International Trade Administration	(202) 482-3808
Latin America/Caribbean Business Development Center	(202) 482-0841
National Trade Data Bank	(202) 482-1986
System for Tracking Export License Application (STELA)	(202) 482-2752
Trade Information Center, for any information on Federal programs and activities that support U.S. exports	(202) 482-0543 or (800) USA-TRADE (800) 482-8723
WEATHER	
Climate for Farming	(301) 713-1677
Historic Weather Conditions w/certified copies	(704) 271-4800
Selected Cities Forecast	(703) 260-0806
Tide Predictions	(301) 713-2815

COMMODITIES: SOURCES OF GOVERNMENT INFORMATION

Information on various commodities may be obtained by calling the following:

Office of Industries
International Trade Commission
Telephone: 202-205-3296

Bureau of Mines
Ferrous and Nonferrous Metals
Telephone: 202-501-9465
Industrial Minerals
Telephone: 202-501-9401

Crops Bulletin Board
Department of Agriculture
Telephone: 202-720-4020

Crops Statistics
Bureau of the Census
Telephone: 301-763-8567

Metals and Minerals
Trade Development
Telephone: 202-482-5157

Minerals Industries
Bureau of the Census
Telephone: 301-763-5938

Industry and Commodity Classification
Bureau of the Census
Telephone: 202-763-1935

Federal Agricultural Service: Commodity and Marketing Divisions

Dairy, Livestock and Poultry	800-523-3215
Grain and Feed Division	800-523-3215
Horticulture and Tropical Products	800-523-3215
Oilseed and Oilseed Products	301-763-4476
Tobacco, Cotton and Seeds	800-523-3215
Forest Products	202-205-0957

Available through the Government Printing Office (202–783–3238) are the Bureau of the Census Publications, *U.S. Imports, U.S.A. Commodities by Country* and *U.S. Exports Schedule 13, Commodities by Country*.

DOING BUSINESS WITH THE FEDERAL GOVERNMENT

Publications

Doing Business with the Federal Government contains helpful material for marketing products or services to the Government, i.e., how to make products known, how and where to obtain the necessary forms and papers to get started, and how to bid on Government contracts. It also provides a geographical listing of Business Service Centers that have information about contract opportunities, as well as whom to contact and where to go for the information needed to sell to individual Government agencies. A list of Business Service Centers is given below.

The *Commerce Business Daily* tells, for example, what products and services the Government is buying, which agencies are buying, due dates for bids, how to get complete specifications. Each weekday, the *Commerce Business Daily* gives a complete listing of products and services wanted by the U.S. Government. Each listing includes product or service, along with a short description, name and address of agency, deadline for proposals or bids, phone number to request specifications, and solicitation numbers of product or service needed. Issued Monday through Friday.

The *Federal Acquisition Regulation* (FAR) is the primary source of procurement regulations used by all Federal agencies in their acquisition of supplies and services. It sets forth all the provisions and clauses that are used in Government contracting. Because the clauses in a specific solicitation for bids refer to a numbered provision of FAR rather than providing the full text, the FAR is necessary to understand the solicitation. Subscription service consists of a basic manual and supplementary material for an indeterminate period.

The *United States Government Purchasing and Sales Directory* contains an alphabetical listing of the products and services bought by all military departments and a separate listing for civilian agencies. It also includes an explanation of the ways in which the Small Business Administration can help a business obtain Government prime contracts and subcontracts, data on Government sales of surplus property, and comprehensive descriptions of the scope of the Government market for research and development.

The *Small Business Subcontracting Directory* is designed to aid small business professionals interested in subcontracting opportunities within the Department of Defense (DOD). The guide is arranged alphabetically by state and includes the name and address of each current DOD prime contractor as well as the product or service being provided to DOD. It also includes the name and telephone number for each DOD Small Business Liaison Officer who knows what the subcontracted products and services are, what the prime contracting firm has purchased in the past, what it is presently purchasing, and what it may be planning to purchase in the future.

The *Federal Register* provides the official version of public regulations issued by the Federal agencies. It also includes announcements of grants and other funding information, as well as data on the availability of Government contracts.

U.S. GENERAL SERVICES ADMINISTRATION (GSA): BUSINESS SERVICE CENTERS

The Business Service Centers are a one stop, one point of contact for information on General Services Administration and other Government contract programs. The primary function is to provide advice on doing business with the Federal Government. The Centers provide information, assistance, and counseling and sponsor business clinics, procurement conferences, and business opportunity meetings.

Many Government purchases must be made from a GSA "Federal Supply Schedule"—a list of vendors from which agencies can place their orders directly with contractors at pre-established prices. Business representatives interested in selling products and services to the Government should contact the nearest Business Service Center given below.

Region	Area of Service	Telephone
National Capitol	District of Columbia, nearby Maryland, Virginia	202-708-5804
1	Connecticut, Maine, Massachusetts, New Hampshire, Rhode Island, and Vermont	617-565-8100
2	New Jersey, New York, Puerto Rico, and Virgin Islands	212-264-1234
3	Delaware, Pennsylvania, West Virginia, Virginia, Maryland (except for D.C. metropolitan area)	215-597-9613
4	Alabama, Florida, Georgia, Kentucky, Mississippi, North Carolina, South Carolina, and Tennessee	404-331-5103
5	Illinois, Indiana, Ohio, Michigan, Minnesota, and Wisconsin	312-353-5383
6	Iowa, Kansas, Missouri, and Nebraska	816-926-7203
7	Arkansas, Louisiana, New Mexico, Oklahoma, and Texas	817-334-3284
8	Colorado, Montana, North Dakota, South Dakota, Utah, and Wyoming	303-236-7408
9	California (northern), Hawaii, and Nevada (except Clark County)	415-744-5050
	Arizona, Los Angeles, California (southern), and Nevada (Clark County only)	213-894-3210
10	Alaska, Idaho, Oregon, and Washington	206-931-7956

BUSINESS ASSISTANCE PROGRAM: COMMERCE DEPARTMENT

The Business Assistance program is designed to shorten the time it takes a businessperson to track down information within the labyrinth of government bureaus and agencies. Business Assistance Program staffers can provide information or direct inquiries to the proper authority on such subjects as regulatory changes, government programs, services, policies, and even relevant government publications for the business community. For information call 202–482–3176 or write: Business Assistance Program Business Liason Office, Department of Commerce, Washington, DC 20230.

FEDERAL INFORMATION CENTER (FIC)

The FIC is a focal point for obtaining information about the federal government and often about state and local governments. A member of the center's staff can either provide information or direct inquiries to an expert who can.

To call the Center, dial the telephone number given below for your metropolitan area. The Center is open from 9 A.M. to 5 P.M., local time, unless otherwise noted. If you are not in one of the areas listed, call (301) 722-9000.

Alabama
Birmingham, Mobile .... (800) 366-2998

Alaska (8 A.M.–4 P.M.)
Anchorage .... (800) 729-8003

Arizona
Phoenix........................... (800) 359-3997

Arkansas
Little Rock .... (800) 366-2998

California
Los Angeles, San Diego,
San Francisco,
Santa Ana .... (800) 726-4995
Sacramento .... (800) 726-4995

Colorado
Colorado Springs,
Denver, Pueblo .... (800) 359-3997

Connecticut
Hartford, New Haven .... (800) 347-1997

Florida
Fort Lauderdale, Jacksonville, Miami, Orlando, St. Petersburg, Tampa, West Palm Beach . . . . (800) 347-1997

Georgia
Atlanta . . . . (800) 347-1997

Hawaii (7 A.M.–3 P.M.)
Honolulu . . . . (800) 733-5996

Illinois
Chicago . . . . (800) 366-2998

Indiana
Gary . . . . (800) 366-2998
Indianapolis . . . . (800) 347-1997

Iowa
All locations . . . . (800) 735-8004

Kansas
All locations . . . . (800) 735-8004

Kentucky
Louisville . . . . (800) 347-1997

Louisiana
New Orleans . . . . (800) 366-2998

Maryland
Baltimore . . . . (800) 347-1997

Massachusetts
Boston . . . . (800) 347-1997

Michigan
Detroit, Grand Rapids . . . . (800) 347-1997

Minnesota
Minneapolis . . . . (800) 366-2998

Missouri
St. Louis . . . . (800) 366-2998
All other locations . . . . (800) 735-8004

Nebraska
Omaha . . . . (800) 366-2998
All other locations . . . . (800) 735-8004

New Jersey
Newark, Trenton . . . . (800) 347-1997

New Mexico
Albuquerque . . . . (800) 359-3997

New York
Albany, Buffalo, New York, Rochester, Syracuse . . . . (800) 347-1997

North Carolina
Charlotte . . . . (800) 347-1997

Ohio
Akron, Cincinnati, Cleveland, Columbus, Dayton, Toledo . . . . (800) 347-1997

Oklahoma
Oklahoma City, Tulsa . . . . (800) 366-2998

Oregon
Portland . . . . (800) 726-4995

Pennsylvania
Philadelphia, Pittsburgh . . . . (800) 347-1997

Rhode Island
Providence . . . . (800) 347-1997

Tennessee
Chattanooga . . . . (800) 347-1997
Memphis, Nashville . . . . (800) 366-2998

Texas
Austin, Dallas, Fort Worth, Houston, San Antonio . . . . (800) 366-2998

Utah
Salt Lake City . . . . (800) 359-3997

Virginia
Norfolk, Richmond, Roanoke . . . . (800) 347-1997

Washington
Seattle, Tacoma . . . . (800) 726-4995

Wisconsin
Milwaukee . . . . (800) 366-2998

Users of Telecommunications Devices for the Deaf (TDD/TTY) may call toll-free from any point in the United States by dialing (800) 326-2996.

State Information Guide

Regional Manufacturers Directories

Connecticut/Rhode Island Manufacturers Directory, Commerce Register®, 190 Godwin Avenue, Midland Park, NJ 07432

Directory of Central Atlantic States Manufacturers, George D. Hall Company, 50 Congress Street, Boston, MA 02109

Directory of New England Manufacturers, The, George D. Hall Company, 50 Congress Street, Boston, MA 02109

Maine/New Hampshire/Vermont Directory of Manufacturers, MacRAE's, 817 Broadway, New York, NY 10003

Maryland/DC/Delaware Manufacturers Directory, MacRAE's, 817 Broadway, New York, NY 10003

Massachusetts/Rhode Island Manufacturers Directory, MacRAE's, 817 Broadway, New York, NY 10003

New York Metro Directory of Manufacturers, Commerce Register®, 190 Godwin Avenue, Midland Park, NJ 07432

New England Manufacturers Directory, George D. Hall Company, 50 Congress Street, Boston, MA 02109

New York Upstate Directory of Manufacturers, Commerce Register®, 190 Godwin Avenue, Midland Park, NJ 07432

North/South Carolina/Virginia, MacRAE's, 817 Broadway, New York, NY 10003

State Sales Guides, Dun & Bradstreet, Inc., 299 Park Avenue, New York, NY 10171

Upstate New York Directory of Manufacturers, Commerce Register®, 190 Godwin Avenue, Midland Park, NJ 07432

State Business Assistance Publications

Directory of Federal and State Business Assistance—A Guide for New and Growing Companies, presents full descriptions to financial, management, innovation, and information programs and services established to help both large and small firms in their day-to-day operations. To order write the National Technical Information Service, 5285 Port Royal Road, Springfield, VA 22161 or call 703-487-4650.

Directory of Incentives for Business Investment and Development in the U.S., The Urban Institute Press, available from United Press of America, 4720 Boston Way, Lanham, MD 20706. State by state guide to economic business incentives. Included are descriptions of state assistance and financial assistance programs.

How to Do Business with the States: A Guide for Vendors. A list of primary state entities with independent purchasing authority and information. Includes a listing of states that publish vendor guides and vendor commodity definition guidelines. Available from the Council of State Governments. Call: 800-800-1910.

Monthly Checklist of State Publications, Superintendent of Documents. Washington, DC 20402. A monthly list of documents and publications received from the States.

State Administrative Officials Classified by Function, Council of State Governments, Iron Works Pike, P.O. Box 1190, Lexington, KY 40578. Names, titles, telephone numbers and addresses of state officials and administrators.

State and Local Government Purchasing is available from the Council of State Governments. A resource to a better understanding of laws, regulations and procedures associated with the acquisition of goods and services. Call: 800-800-1910.

State and Metropolitan Area Data Book is prepared by the Bureau of the Census of the U.S. Department of Commerce. Presents a wide variety of information on States and metropolitan areas in the United States. Available from the Government Printing Office by calling 202-783-3238.

State Executive Directory is available from Carroll Publishing at 1058 Thomas Jefferson Street, NW., Washington, D.C. 20007. Telephone: 202-333-8620. Contains names, titles, addresses and phone numbers.

The States and Small Business: A Directory of Programs and Activities. A guide to state programs designed to assist small business. Includes sources of financing, new state legislation affecting business and more. Prepared by the Office of Advocacy, U.S. Small Business Administration and available from the Superintendent of Documents at 202-783-7954.

Business/Industry Data Centers and State Data Centers

Business/Industry Data Centers (BIDC's) offer assistance in business related matters. Such assistance includes information gathering, location of expert help, and guidance on new technologies. Most of these centers also are able to offer other types of assistance, such as market feasibility, or at least link businesses with appropriate contacts.

Access to the many statistical products available from the Bureau of the Census is provided through the services of the joint federal-state cooperative State Data Center Program. Through the Program, the Bureau furnishes statistical products, training in the data access and use, technical assistance, and consultation to states which, in turn, disseminate the products and provide assistance in their use.

Additional information on the State Data Program and a list of the State Data Centers can be obtained by contacting the User Services staff in any of the Bureau's regional offices or by calling the Data User Services Division of the Bureau of the Census at 301-763-1580.

State Information Offices*

Alabama

State Capitol, Montgomery, AL 36130
(205) 242-8000

INFORMATION OFFICES

Commerce/Economic Development
Alabama Development Office
401 Adams Avenue
Montgomery, AL 36130

Department of Economic & Community Affairs
401 Adams Avenue
Montgomery, AL 36130

Corporate
Secretary of State
P.O. Box 5616
Montgomery, AL 36103

Taxation
Department of Revenue
Gordon Persons Building
50 Ripley Street
Montgomery, AL 36132

State Chamber of Commerce
Business Council of Alabama
2 N. Jackson Street
P.O. Box 76
Montgomery, AL 36101

International Commerce
Department of International Trade
Alabama Development Office
401 Adams Avenue
Montgomery, AL 36130

Banking
State Banking Department
101 S. Union Street
Montgomery, AL 36130

Securities
Alabama Securities Exchange Commission
770 Washington Street
Montgomery, AL 36130

Labor and Industrial Relations
Department of Industrial Relations
649 Monroe Street
Montgomery, AL 36130

Alabama Department of Labor
Administrative Building
1789 Congressman W. L. Dickinson Drive
National Guard Credit Union
Montgomery, AL 36130

Insurance
Department of Insurance
135 S. Union Street
Montgomery, AL 36130

Uniform Industrial Code
Alabama Development Office
401 Adams Street
Montgomery, AL 36130

INDUSTRIAL AND BUSINESS DIRECTORIES

Alabama Directory of Mining and Manufacturing, Alabama Development Office, State Capitol, Montgomery, AL 36130

Alabama Manufacturers Register, Manufacturers' News, Inc., 1633 Central Street, Evanston, IL 60201

Alabama International Trade Directory, Alabama Development Office, State Capitol, Montgomery, AL 36130

Top Businesses in Alabama, State Capitol, Montgomery, AL 36130

Birmingham Industrial Directory, Birmingham Chamber of Commerce, 1914 6th Avenue, Birmingham, AL 35203

Alaska

State Capitol, Juneau, AK 99811
(907) 465-2111

INFORMATION OFFICES

Commerce/Economic Development
Department of Commerce & Economic Development
P.O. Box 110800
Juneau, AK 99811-0800

Corporate
Department of Commerce & Economic Development
Corporation Section
P.O. Box 110808
Juneau, AK 99811-0808

* See page 236 for Small Business Administration Regional Office telephone numbers.

Taxation
Department of Revenue
P.O. Box 110420
Juneau, AK 99811-0420

State Chamber of Commerce
Alaska State Chamber of Commerce
310 2nd Street
Juneau, AK 99801

International Commerce
Office of International Trade
3601 C Street
Anchorage, AK 99503-5934

Banking
Division of Banking, Securities and Corporations
Department of Commerce & Economic Development
P.O. Box 110808
Juneau, AK 99811-0808

Securities
Division of Banking, Securities and Corporations
Department of Commerce and Economic Development
P.O. Box 11808
Juneau, AK 99811-0808

Labor and Industrial Relations
Department of Labor
P.O. Box 21149
Juneau, AK 99802-1149

Insurance
Division of Insurance
Department of Commerce and Economic Development
P.O. Box 110805
Juneau, AK 99811-0805

Uniform Industrial Code
Uniform Commercial Code Office
Division of Management
Department of Natural Resources
P.O. Box 107005
Anchorage, AK 99510-7005

INDUSTRIAL AND BUSINESS DIRECTORIES

Alaska Petroleum and Industrial Directory, 409 W. Northern Lights Boulevard, Anchorage, AK 99603

Arizona

State Capitol, Phoenix, AZ 85007
(602) 542-4331

INFORMATION OFFICES

Commerce/Economic Development
Department of Commerce
3800 N. Central Avenue
Phoenix, AZ 85012

Corporate
Arizona Corporation Commission
1200 W. Washington Avenue
Phoenix, AZ 85007

Taxation
Department of Revenue
1600 W. Monroe
Phoenix, AZ 85007

State Chamber of Commerce
Arizona State Chamber of Commerce
1221 E. Osborn Road
Phoenix, AZ 85014

Banking
Banking Department
2910 N. 44th Street
Phoenix, AZ 85018

Insurance
Insurance Department
2910 N. 44th Street
Phoenix, AZ 85018

Securities
Arizona Corporation Commission
1200 W. Washington Avenue
Phoenix, AZ 85007

International Commerce
International Trade
Department of Commerce
3800 N. Central Avenue
Phoenix, AZ 85012

Labor and Industrial Relations
Industrial Commission
800 W. Washington Street
Phoenix, AZ 85007

INDUSTRIAL AND BUSINESS DIRECTORIES

Arizona Industrial Directory, Phoenix Chamber of Commerce, 201 N. Central Avenue, Phoenix, AZ 85004; Manufacturers' News, 1633 Central Street, Evanston, IL 60201

Arizona USA International Trade Directory, Arizona State Department of Commerce, 3800 N. Central Avenue, Phoenix, AZ 85012

Directory of Arizona Manufacturers, Phoenix Chamber of Commerce, 201 N. Central Avenue, Phoenix, AZ 85004

Arkansas

State Capitol, Little Rock, AR 72201
(501) 682-3000

INFORMATION OFFICES

Commerce/Economic Development
Arkansas Industrial Development Commission
Big Mac Building
One State Capitol Mall
Little Rock, AR 72201

Corporate
Secretary of State
Corporations Department
State Capitol
Little Rock, AR 72201

Taxation
State Revenue Office
Department of Finance and Administration
Joel Y. Ledbetter Building
7th and Wolfe Streets
Little Rock, AR 72201

State Chamber of Commerce
Arkansas State Chamber of Commerce
410 South Cross
Little Rock, AR 72201

International Commerce
Arkansas Industrial Development Commission
Big Mac Building
One State Capitol Mall
Little Rock, AR 72201

Banking
State Bank Department
323 Center Street
Tower Building
Little Rock, AR 72201

Securities
Arkansas Securities Department
Heritage West Building
201 East Markham
Little Rock, AR 72201

Labor and Industrial Relations
Arkansas Department of Labor
10421 West Markham
Little Rock, AR 72205

Insurance
Arkansas Insurance Department
400 University Tower Building
Little Rock, AR 72204

Ombudsman
State Claims Commission
State Capitol
Little Rock, AR 72201

INDUSTRIAL AND BUSINESS DIRECTORIES

Arkansas Directory of Manufacturers, Arkansas Industrial Development Commission, One State Capitol Mall, Little Rock, AR 72201; Manufacturers' News, 1633 Central Street, Evanston, IL 60201

Arkansas State and County Economic Data (annual), Research and Public Service, Division of Regional Economic Analysis, 2801 South University, Little Rock, AR 72204

California

State Capitol, Sacramento, CA 95814
(916) 332-9900

INFORMATION OFFICES

Commerce/Economic Development
Trade and Commerce Agency
801 K Street
Sacramento, CA 95814

Corporate
Secretary of State
1230 "J" Street
Sacramento, CA 95814

Taxation
Board of Equalization
450 N Street
Sacramento, CA 95814

State Chamber of Commerce
California Chamber of Commerce
1027 10th Street
P.O. Box 1736
Sacramento, CA 95814

International Commerce
California State World Trade Commission
801 K Street
Sacramento, CA 95814

Banking
State Banking Department
11 Pine Street
San Francisco, CA 94111-5613

Securities
Department of Corporations
1107 9th Street
Sacramento, CA 95814

Labor and Industrial Relations
Department of Industrial Relations
455 Golden Gate Avenue
P.O. Box 420603
San Francisco, CA 94842
or
2422 Arden Way
Sacramento, CA 95825

Insurance
Department of Insurance
600 S. Commonwealth Avenue
Los Angeles, CA 90005
or
770 "L" Street
Sacramento, CA 93814

INDUSTRIAL AND BUSINESS DIRECTORIES

California Handbook, California Institute of Public Affairs, P.O. Box 49040, Sacramento, CA 95818

California International Trade Register, Database Publishing Company, P.O. Box 7440, Newport Beach, CA 92658; Manufacturers' News, Inc., 1633 Central Street, Evanston, IL 60201

California Manufacturers Register, Database Publishing Company, P.O. Box 7440, Newport Beach, CA 92658; Manufacturers' News, Inc., 1633 Central Street, Evanston, IL 60201

California Manufacturers Register, Database Publishing Company, P.O. Box 7440, Newport Beach, CA 92658; Manufacturers' News, Inc., 1633 Central Street, Evanston, IL 60201

California Services Register, Database Publishing Company, P.O. Box 7440, Newport Beach, CA 92658; Manufacturers' News, Inc., 1633 Central Street, Evanston, IL 60201

San Francisco County Commerce and Industry Directory, Database Publishing Company, P.O. Box 7440, Newport Beach, CA 92658; Manufacturers' News, Inc., 1633 Central Street, Evanston, IL 60201

Southern California Business Directory and Buyers Guide, Database Publishing Company, P.O. Box 7440, Newport Beach, CA 92658; Manufacturers' News, Inc., 1633 Central Street, Evanston, IL 60201

Colorado

State Capitol, Denver, CO 80203
(303) 866-5000

INFORMATION OFFICES

Commerce/Economic Development
Office of Business Development
World Trade Center
1625 Broadway
Denver, CO 80202

Corporate
Secretary of State
Civic Center Plaza
1560 Broadway
Denver, CO 80202

Taxation
Colorado Department of Revenue
Department of Revenue
1375 Sherman Street
Denver, CO 80203

State Chamber of Commerce
Colorado Association of Commerce and Industry
1776 Lincoln Street
Denver, CO 80203

International Commerce
Office of Business Development
International Trade Office
1625 Broadway
Denver, CO 80202

Banking
Division of Banking
1560 Broadway
Denver, CO 80202

Securities
Division of Securities
Department of Regulatory Agencies
1580 Lincoln Street
Denver, CO 80203

Labor and Industrial Relations
Division of Labor
1120 Lincoln Street
Denver, CO 80203-2140

Insurance
Division of Insurance
1560 Broadway
Denver, CO 80202

Uniform Commercial Code
Commercial Recordings Division
1560 Broadway
Denver, CO 80202

INDUSTRIAL AND BUSINESS DIRECTORIES

Directory of Colorado Manufacturers, Business Research Division, Graduate School of Business Administration, Campus Box 420, University of Colorado, Boulder, CO 80309; Manufacturers' News, Inc., 1633 Central Street, Evanston, IL 60201

Connecticut

State Capitol, Hartford, CT 06106
(203) 566-4200

INFORMATION OFFICES

Commerce/Economic Development
Department of Economic Development
865 Brook Street
Rocky Hill, CT 06067

Corporate
Secretary of State
Corporations Division
30 Trinity Street
Hartford, CT 06106

Taxation
Department of Revenue Services
92 Farmington Avenue
Hartford, CT 06105

State Chamber of Commerce
Connecticut Business and Industry Association
370 Asylum Street
Hartford, CT 06103

International Commerce
Department of Economic Development
865 Brook Street
Rocky Hill, CT 06067

Banking
Department of Banking
44 Capitol Avenue
Hartford, CT 06106

Securities
Divisions of Securities & Business Investments
Department of Banking
44 Capitol Avenue
Hartford, CT 06106

Labor and Industrial Relations
Department of Labor
200 Folly Brook Boulevard
Wethersfield, CT 06109
Insurance
Department of Insurance
165 Capitol Avenue
Hartford, CT 06106
Uniform Industrial Code
Department of Economic Development
865 Brook Street
Rocky Hill, CT 06107
Business Ombudsman
Department of Economic Development
865 Brook Street
Rocky Hill, CT 06067

INDUSTRIAL AND BUSINESS DIRECTORIES

Classified Business Directory—State of Connecticut, Connecticut Directory Co., Inc., 322 Main Street, Stamford, CT 06901
Connecticut Classified Business Directory, Connecticut Directory Co., Inc., 322 Main Street, Stamford, CT 06901
Connecticut Service Directory, George D. Hall Co., 50 Congress Street, Boston, MA 02109
Directory of Connecticut Manufacturers, George D. Hall Co., 50 Congress Street, Boston, MA 02109
Directory of Connecticut Manufacturing Establishments, Connecticut Department of Labor, 200 Folly Brook Boulevard, Wethersfield, CT 06109
MacRAE's State Industrial Directory Connecticut/Rhode Island, MacRAE's Industrial Directories, 817 Broadway, New York, NY 10003

Delaware

LEGISLATIVE HALL, DOVER, DE 19901
(302) 739-4101

INFORMATION OFFICES

Commerce/Economic Development
Delaware Development Office
99 Kings Highway
P.O. Box 1401
Dover, DE 19903
Corporate
Secretary of State
Corporations Department
Townsend Building
P.O. Box 898
Dover, DE 19903
Taxation
Department of Finance
Division of Revenue
Carvel State Office Building
820 N. French Street
Wilmington, DE 19801
International Commerce
Delaware Development Office
99 Kings Highway
P.O. Box 1401
Dover, DE 19903
State Chamber of Commerce
Delaware State Chamber of Commerce, Inc.
One Commerce Center
Wilmington, DE 19801
Banking
State Bank Commission
Department of State
Thomas Collins Building
P.O. Box 1401
Dover, DE 19903
Labor and Industrial Relations
Division of Industrial Affairs
Department of Labor
Carvel State Office Building
820 N. French Street
Wilmington, DE 19801
Insurance
State Insurance Commission
841 Silver Lake Boulevard
Rodney Building
Dover, DE 19901

INDUSTRIAL AND BUSINESS DIRECTORIES

Delaware Directory of Commerce and Industry, Delaware State Chamber of Commerce, One Commerce Center, Wilmington, DE 19801; Manufacturers' News, Inc., 1633 Central Street, Evanston, IL 60201
MacRAE's State Industrial Directory Maryland/DC/Delaware, MacRAE's Industrial Directories, 817 Broadway, New York, NY 10003

Florida

STATE CAPITOL, TALLAHASSEE, FL 32399
(904) 488-1234

INFORMATION OFFICES

Commerce/Economic Development
Department of Commerce
Collins Building
107 W. Gaines Street
Tallahassee, FL 32399-2000

Division of Economic Development
Department of Commerce
Collins Building
Tallahassee, FL 32399-2000

Corporate
Secretary of State
Division of Corporations
409 E. Gaines Street
Tallahassee, FL 32301

Taxation
Department of Revenue
Carlton Building
Tallahassee, FL 32399-0100

State Chamber of Commerce
Florida Chamber of Commerce
P.O. Box 11309
Tallahassee, FL 32302-3309

International Commerce
Florida Department of Commerce
Division of International Trade and Development
Collins Building
107 W. Gaines Street
Tallahassee, FL 32399-2000

Banking
Florida Department of Banking & Finance
The Capitol
Tallahassee, FL 32399-0350

Securities
Florida Department of Banking & Finance
Division of Securities
The Capitol
Tallahassee, FL 32399-0350

Labor and Industrial Relations
Florida Department of Labor and Employment Security
303 Hartman Building
2012 Capital Circle, SE
Tallahassee, FL 32399-2152

Insurance
Florida Department of Insurance
The Capitol
Tallahassee, FL 32399-0300

Commercial Information Services
Florida Department of State
Bureau of Information Services
409 E. Gaines Street
Tallahassee, FL 32301

Business Ombudsman
Florida Department of Commerce
Bureau of Business Assistance
Collins Building
107 W. Gaines Street
Tallahassee, FL 32399

INDUSTRIAL AND BUSINESS DIRECTORIES

Florida Manufacturers Register, Manufacturers' News, Inc., 1633 Central Street, Evanston, IL 60201

South Florida International Trade and Services Directory 1990, World Trade Center Miami, One World Trade Plaza, 80 SW 8th St., Suite 1800, Miami, FL 33130

Directory of International Manufacturing and Commercial Operations In Florida, Florida Department of Commerce, Division of International Trade and Development, Collins Building, Tallahassee, FL 32399-2000

Directory of Florida Industries, Florida Chamber of Commerce, Trend Book Division, P.O. Box 611, St Petersburg, FL 33731

Georgia

State Capitol, Atlanta, GA 30334
(404) 656-2000

INFORMATION OFFICES

Commerce/Economic Development
Department of Industry, Trade, and Tourism
P.O. Box 1776
285 Peachtree Center Avenue, N.E.
Atlanta, GA 30301-1776

Corporate
Business Services and Regulations Division
Secretary of State
2 Martin Luther King Jr. Drive, S.E.
Atlanta, GA 30334

Taxation
Department of Revenue
270 Washington Street, S.W.
Atlanta, GA 30334

State Chamber of Commerce
Business Council of Georgia
233 Peachtree Street
Atlanta, GA 30303-2705

International Commerce
Department of Industry and Trade
P.O. Box 1776
285 Peachtree Center Avenue
Atlanta, GA 30303-1776

Banking
Department of Banking and Finance
2990 Brandywine Road
Atlanta, GA 30341

Securities
Business Services and Regulations Division
Secretary of State
2 Martin Luther King Jr. Drive, S.E.
Atlanta, GA 30334

Labor and Industrial Relations
Department of Labor
148 International Boulevard
Atlanta, GA 30303

Insurance
Office of Commissioner of Insurance
2 Martin Luther King Jr. Drive, S.E.
Atlanta, GA 30334

INDUSTRIAL AND BUSINESS DIRECTORIES

Georgia Manufacturers Register, Manufacturers' News, Inc., 1633 Central Street, Evanston, IL 60201

Georgia Manufacturing Directory, Department of Industry, Trade, and Tourism, P.O. Box 1776, 285 Peachtree Center Avenue, Atlanta, GA 30301-1776

Georgia World Trade Directory, Business Council of Georgia, 233 Peachtree Street, Atlanta, GA 30303

Industrial Sites in Georgia, Georgia Power Company, Box 4545, Atlanta, GA 30303

Georgia International Trade Directory, Department of Industry, Trade, and Tourism, P.O. Box 1776, 285 Peachtree Center Avenue, Atlanta, GA 30301-1776

Georgia Directory of International Services, World Congress Institute, 1 Park Place S, Fulton Federal Building, Atlanta, GA 30303

International Companies with Facilities in Georgia. Department of Industry, Trade, and Tourism, P.O. Box 1776, 285 Peachtree Center Avenue, Atlanta, GA 30301-1776

Hawaii

STATE CAPITOL, HONOLULU, HI 96813
(808) 548-6222

INFORMATION OFFICES

Commerce/Economic Development
Department of Business, Economic Development & Tourism
737 Bishop Street
Honolulu, HI 96813

Department of Commerce and Consumer Affairs
1010 Richards Street
Honolulu, HI 96813

Corporate
Department of Commerce and Consumer Affairs
Business Registration Division
P.O. Box 40
Honolulu, HI 96810

Taxation
Department of Taxation
830 Punchbowl Street
Honolulu, HI 96813

State Chamber of Commerce
Chamber of Commerce of Hawaii
735 Bishop Street
Honolulu, HI 96813

International Commerce
International Business Center of Hawaii
201 Merchant Street
Honolulu, HI 96813

Hawaii Foreign-Trade Zone No. 9
Pier 2
Honolulu, HI 96813

Banking
Financial Institutions Division
Department of Commerce and Consumer Affairs
1010 Richards Street
Honolulu, HI 96813

Securities
Financial Institutions Division
Department of Commerce and Consumer Affairs
1010 Richards Street
Honolulu, HI 96813

Labor and Industrial Relations
Department of Labor and Industrial Relations
830 Punchbowl Street
Honolulu, HI 96813

Insurance
Insurance Division
Department of Commerce and Consumer Affairs
1010 Richards Street
Honolulu, HI 96813

Business Ombudsman
Office of the Ombudsman
465 S. King Street
Honolulu, HI 96813

INDUSTRIAL AND BUSINESS DIRECTORIES

Directory of Manufacturers, State of Hawaii, Chamber of Commerce of Hawaii, Dillingham Building, 735 Bishop Street, Honolulu, HI 96813

Hawaii Business Directory, Hawaii Business Directory, Inc., 1164 Bishop Street, Honolulu, HI 96813

Idaho

STATE CAPITOL, BOISE, ID 83720
(208) 334-2411

INFORMATION OFFICES

Mailing address for all state offices is:
Statehouse
Boise, ID 83720

Commerce/Economic Development
Department of Commerce
700 W. State Street
Boise, ID 83720

Corporate
Secretary of State
State Capitol
Boise, ID 83720

Taxation
Department of Revenue and Taxation
80 Park Boulevard
Boise, ID 83722

State Chamber of Commerce
Idaho Association of Commerce and Industry
805 West Idaho
Boise, ID 83702

International Commerce
Department of Commerce
700 W. State Street
Boise, ID 83720

Banking
Department of Finance
700 W. State Street
Boise, ID 83720

Securities
Department of Finance
700 W. State Street
Boise, ID 83720

Labor and Industrial Relations
Department of Labor and Industrial Services
277 N. 6th Street
Boise, ID 83720

Insurance
Department of Insurance
700 W. State Street
Boise, ID 83720

Uniform Industrial Code
Department of Labor and Industrial Services
277 N. 6th Street
Boise, ID 83720

Business Ombudsman
Department of Commerce
700 W. State Street
Boise, ID 83720

INDUSTRIAL AND BUSINESS DIRECTORIES

Idaho Manufacturing Directory, Center for Business and Research, University of Idaho, Moscow, ID 83843; Manufacturers' News, Inc., 1633 Central Street, Evanston, IL 60201

Idaho Opportunities, Department of Commerce, 700 W. State Street, Boise, ID 83720

Illinois

State House, Springfield, IL 62706
(217) 782-2000

INFORMATION OFFICES

Commerce/Economic Development
Department of Commerce and Community Affairs
620 E. Adams Street
Springfield, IL 62701

Corporate
Secretary of State
Business Services
Michael Howlett Building
Springfield, IL 62756

Taxation
Department of Revenue
101 W. Jefferson Street
Springfield, IL 62794

State Chamber of Commerce
Illinois State Chamber of Commerce
311 S. Wacker Drive
Chicago, IL 60606

International Commerce
Department of Commerce and Community Affairs
100 W. Randolph Street
Chicago, IL 60601

Banking
Department of Financial Institutions
100 W. Randolph Street
Chicago, IL 60601

Securities
Secretary of State
900 S. Spring Street
Springfield, IL 62704

Labor and Industrial Relations
Department of Labor
One W. Old State Capitol Plaza
Springfield, IL 62701

Department of Commerce & Community Affairs
620 E. Adams Street
Springfield, IL 62701

Insurance
Department of Insurance
320 W. Washington Street
Springfield, IL 62767

Uniform Industrial Code
Secretary of State
Uniform Commercial Code
Michael Howlett Building
Springfield, IL 62756

Business Ombudsman
Attorney General
500 South Second Street
Springfield, IL 62706

INDUSTRIAL AND BUSINESS DIRECTORIES

Chicago Cook County and Illinois Industrial Directory, Manufacturers' News, Inc., 1633 Central Street, Evanston, IL 60201

Illinois Manufacturers Directory, Manufacturers' News, Inc., 1633 Central Street, Evanston, IL 60201

Illinois Services Directory, Manufacturers' News, Inc., 1633 Central Street, Evanston, IL 60201

Development Finance Programs, Department of Commerce and Community Affairs, 620 E. Adams, Springfield, IL 62701

Indiana

State House, Indianapolis, IN 46204
(317) 232-3140

INFORMATION OFFICES

Commerce/Economic Development
Department of Commerce
1 N. Capitol Avenue
Indianapolis, IN 46204
Corporate
Secretary of State
Corporation Section
Indiana Government Center South
Indianapolis, IN 46204
Taxation
Department of Revenue
100 N. Senate Avenue
Indianapolis, IN 46204
State Board of Tax Commissioners
150 W. Market Street
Indianapolis, IN 46204
State Chamber of Commerce
Indiana Chamber of Commerce
1 N. Capitol Avenue
Indianapolis, IN 46204
International Commerce
International Trade Division
Indiana Department of Commerce
1 N. Capitol Avenue
Indianapolis, IN 46204
Banking
Department of Financial Institutions
Indiana Government Center South
Indianapolis, IN 46204
Securities
Secretary of State
Securities Commission
1 N. Capitol Avenue
Indianapolis, IN 46204
Labor and Industrial Relations
Indiana Department of Labor
Indiana Government Center South
Indianapolis, IN 46204
Insurance
Indiana Department of Insurance
311 W. Washington Street
Indianapolis, IN 46204
Uniform Industrial Code
Secretary of State
Uniform Commercial Code Division
Indiana Government Center South
Indianapolis, IN 46204
Business Ombudsman
Business Ombudsman Office
Department of Commerce
1 N. Capitol Avenue
Indianapolis, IN 46204

INDUSTRIAL AND BUSINESS DIRECTORIES

Indiana Manufacturers Directory, Manufacturers' News, Inc., 1633 Central Street, Evanston, IL 60201

Iowa

State Capitol, Des Moines, IA 50319
(515) 281-5011

INFORMATION OFFICES

Commerce/Economic Development
Department of Economic Development
200 E. Grand Avenue
Des Moines, IA 50309
Corporate
Secretary of State
Corporation Division
Hoover Building
Des Moines, IA 50319
Taxation
Department of Revenue and Finance
Hoover Building
Des Moines, IA 50319
International Commerce
Department of Economic Development
200 E. Grand Avenue
Des Moines, IA 50309
Banking
Department of Commerce
Banking Division
200 E. Grand Avenue
Des Moines, IA 50309
Iowa Housing Finance Authority
200 E. Grand Avenue
Des Moines, IA 50309
Securities
Department of Commerce
Insurance Division
Securities Bureau
Lucas Building
Des Moines, IA 50319
Labor
Department of Employment Service
Division of Industrial Services
1000 E. Grand Avenue
Des Moines, IA 50319
Bureau of Labor
1000 E. Grand Avenue
Des Moines, IA 50319
Insurance
Department of Commerce
Insurance Division
Lucas Building
Des Moines, IA 50319

INDUSTRIAL AND BUSINESS DIRECTORIES

Iowa Manufacturers Register, Iowa Department of Economic Development, 200 E. Grand Avenue, Des Moines, IA 50309; Manufacturers' News, Inc., 1633 Central Street, Evanston, IL 60201

Doing Business in Iowa, Iowa Department of Economic Development, 200 E. Grand Avenue, Des Moines, IA 50309

Kansas

STATE HOUSE, TOPEKA, KS 66612
(913) 296-0111

INFORMATION OFFICES

Commerce/Economic Development
Department of Commerce
400 S.W. 8th Street
Topeka, KS 66603-3957

Corporate
Secretary of State
State House
Corporation Department
Topeka, KS 66612

Taxation
Department of Revenue
Docking State Office Building
915 Harrison Street
Topeka, KS 66612-1588

State Chamber of Commerce
Kansas Chamber of Commerce and Industry
500 Bank IV Tower
One Townsite Plaza
Topeka, KS 66603-3460

International Commerce
Department of Commerce
400 S.W. 8th Street
Topeka, KS 66603-3959

Banking
Banking Department
700 Jackson Street
Topeka, KS 66603-3714

Securities
Securities Commissioner of Kansas
618 S. Kansas
Topeka, KS 66603-3804

Labor and Industrial Relations
Department of Human Resources
401 Topeka
Topeka, KS 66603-3182

Insurance
Insurance Department
420 S.W. 9th Street
Topeka, KS 66612-1678

Business Ombudsman
Department of Commerce
400 S.W. 8th Street
Topeka, KS 66603-3957

INDUSTRIAL AND BUSINESS DIRECTORIES

Directory of Kansas Manufacturers and Products, Kansas Department of Commerce, 400 W. 8th Street, Topeka, KS 66603-3957; Manufacturers' News, Inc., 1633 Central Street, Evanston, IL 60201

Kansas Association Directory, Kansas Department of Commerce, 400 S.W. 8th Street, Topeka, KS 66603-3957

Kansas Aerospace Directory, Kansas Department of Commerce, 400 S.W. 8th Street, Topeka, KS 66603-3957

Kansas Agribusiness Directory, Kansas Department of Commerce, 400 S.W. 8th Street, Topeka, KS 66603-3957

Kansas International Trade Resource Directory, Kansas Department of Commerce, 400 S.W. 8th Street, Topeka, KS 66603-3957

Kansas Job Shop Directory, Kansas Department of Commerce, 400 S.W. 8th Street, Topeka, KS 66603-3957

Kentucky

STATE CAPITOL, FRANKFORT, KY 40601
(502) 564-3130

INFORMATION OFFICES

Commerce/Economic Development
Kentucky Economic Development Cabinet
Capital Plaza Office Tower
Frankfort, KY 40601

Corporate
Office of Secretary of State
Corporation Division
Capitol Building
Frankfort, KY 40601

Taxation
Kentucky Revenue Cabinet
Fair Oaks Lane
Frankfort, KY 40601

State Chamber of Commerce
Kentucky Chamber of Commerce
Versailles Road
P.O. Box 817
Frankfort, KY 40602

International Commerce
Kentucky Economic Development Cabinet
Office of International Marketing
Capitol Plaza Tower
Frankfort, KY 40601

Banking
Kentucky Department of Financial Institutions
Division of Banking and Thrift Institutions
477 Versailles Road
Frankfort, KY 40601

Securities
Kentucky Department of Financial Institutions
Division of Securities
477 Versailles Road
Frankfort, KY 40601

Labor Industrial Relations
Kentucky Labor Cabinet
The 127 Building
Frankfort, KY 40601

Insurance
Kentucky Department of Insurance
229 West Main Street
P.O. Box 517
Frankfort, KY 40602

Uniform Industrial Code
Kentucky Department of Housing, Buildings, and Construction
The 127 Building
Frankfort, KY 40601

Business Ombudsman
Kentucky Department of Existing Business and Industry
Capitol Plaza Tower
Frankfort, KY 40601

INDUSTRIAL AND BUSINESS DIRECTORIES

Kentucky International Trade Directory, Kentucky Economic Development Cabinet, Capitol Plaza Tower, Frankfort, KY 40601

Kentucky Directory of Manufacturers, Kentucky Economic Development Cabinet, Capitol Plaza Tower, Frankfort, KY 40601

Kentucky Manufacturers Register, Manufacturers' News, Inc., 1633 Central Street, Evanston, IL 60201; Harris Publishing Co., 2057 Aurora Road, Twinsburg, OH 44087-1999

Louisiana

STATE CAPITOL, BATON ROUGE, LA 70804
(504) 342-7015

INFORMATION OFFICES

Commerce/Economic Development
Department of Economic Development
P.O. Box 94185
Baton Rouge, LA 70804-9185

Corporate
Secretary of State
Division of Corporation
P.O. Box 94125
Baton Rouge, LA 70804-9125

Taxation
Department of Revenue and Taxation
P.O. Box 3440
Baton Rouge, LA 70823

State Chamber of Commerce
Louisiana Association of Business and Industry
P.O. Box 80258
Baton Rouge, LA 70898

International Commerce
Department of Economic Development
Office of International Trade, Finance and Development
P.O. Box 94185
Baton Rouge, LA 70804-9185

Banking
Department of Economic Development
Office of Financial Institutions
P.O. Box 94095
Baton Rouge, LA 70804

Securities
Louisiana Securities Commission
1100 Poydras Street
325 Loyola Avenue
New Orleans, LA 70163

Labor and Industrial Relations
Department of Labor
P.O. Box 94094
Baton Rouge, LA 70804-9094

Insurance
Office of Insurance Rating Commission
P.O. Box 94157
Baton Rouge, LA 70804

Uniform Industrial Code
Department of Economic Development
P.O. Box 94185
Baton Rouge, LA 70804-9185

Department of Labor
Department of Labor
P.O. Box 94094
Baton Rouge, LA 70804-9094

Business Ombudsman
Department of Economic Development
P.O. Box 94185
Baton Rouge, LA 70804-9185

INDUSTRIAL AND BUSINESS DIRECTORIES

Louisiana Manufacturers Register, Manufacturers' News, Inc., 1633 Central Street, Evanston, IL 60201

Louisiana Directory of Manufacturers, Department of Economic Development, 101 France Street, Baton Rouge, LA 70802; Harris Publishing Co., 2057 Aurora Rd, Twinsburg, OH 44087

Louisiana International Trade Directory, World Trade Center, 2 Canal Street, New Orleans, LA 70130

Maine

STATE HOUSE, AUGUSTA, ME 04333
(207) 289-1110

INFORMATION OFFICES

Commerce/Economic Development
Department of Economic and Community Development
193 State Street
State House Station #59
Augusta, ME 04333

Corporate
Department of State
Division of Corporations
State House Station #101
Augusta, ME 04333

Private Development Associations
Maine Development Foundation
45 Memorial Circle
Augusta, ME 04330

Taxation
Bureau of Taxation
Department of Administrative & Financial Services
State House Station #24
Augusta, ME 04333

State Chamber of Commerce
Maine State Chamber of Commerce and Industry
126 Sewall Street
Augusta, ME 04330

International Commerce
Department of Economic and Community Development
193 State Street
State House Station #59
Augusta, ME 04333

Banking
Bureau of Banking
Hallowell Annex
Correspondence to:
State House Station #36
Augusta, ME 04333-0036

Securities
Bureau of Banking
Securities Division
State House Station #121
Augusta, ME 04333

Labor and Industrial Relations
Department of Labor
Bureau of Labor Standards
State House Station #45
Augusta, ME 04333

Insurance
Bureau of Insurance
Hallowell Annex
Hallowell, ME 04347
Correspondence to:
State House #34
Augusta, ME 04333

INDUSTRIAL AND BUSINESS DIRECTORIES

Maine Marketing Directory, Department of Economic and Community Development, State House Station #59, Augusta, ME 04333

MacRAE's State Industrial Directory Maine/New Hampshire/Vermont, MacRAE's Industrial Directories, 817 Broadway, New York, NY 10003

Maine Manufacturing Directory, Tower Publishing Company, 34 Diamond Street, Portland, ME 04101; Manufacturers' News, Inc., 1633 Central Street, Evanston, IL 60201

Maryland

State House, Annapolis, MD 21401
(410) 974-3901

INFORMATION OFFICES

Commerce/Economic Development
Department of Economic and Employment Development
217 E. Redwood Street
Baltimore, MD 21202

Corporate
State Department of Assessments and Taxation
301 W. Preston Street
Baltimore, MD 21201

Taxation
Comptroller of the Treasury
Louis L. Goldstein Treasury Building
P.O. Box 466
Annapolis, MD 21404-0466

State Chamber of Commerce
Maryland Chamber of Commerce
60 West Street
Annapolis, MD 21401

International Commerce
Department of Economic and Employment Development
Maryland International Division
World Trade Center
401 East Pratt Street
Baltimore, MD 21202

Maryland Port Administration
World Trade Center
401 E. Pratt Street
Baltimore, MD 21202

Banking
State Banking Commissioner
Department of Licensing and Regulation
501 St. Paul Place
Baltimore, MD 21202

Securities
Division of Securities
Office of the Attorney General
200 St. Paul Place
Baltimore, MD 21202

Labor and Industrial Relations
Division of Labor and Industry
Department of Licensing and Regulation

501 St. Paul Place
Baltimore, MD 21202

Insurance
Maryland Insurance Administration
Department of Licensing and Regulation
501 St. Paul Place
Baltimore, MD 21202

Business Ombudsman
Department of Economic and Employment Development
Office of Business Assistance
217 East Redwood Street
Baltimore, MD 21202

INDUSTRIAL AND BUSINESS DIRECTORIES

Maryland Manufacturers Directory, Harris Publishing Company, 2057 Aurora Road, Twinsburg, OH 44087

Maryland/D.C. Manufacturers Directory, Manufacturers' News, Inc., 1633 Central Street, Evanston, IL 60201

Maryland High-Tech Directory, Corporate Technology Information Services, Inc., Suite 200, 12 Alfred Street, Woburn, MA 01801

Massachusetts

State House, Boston, MA 02133
General Information: (617) 727-2121

INFORMATION OFFICES

Commerce/Economic Development
Executive Office of Economic Affairs
2101 McCormack Building
1 Ashburton Place
Boston, MA 02108

Massachusetts Department of Commerce and Development
Division of Economic Development
100 Cambridge Street
Boston, MA 02202

Department of Commerce and Development
Leverett Saltonstall Building
100 Cambridge Street
Boston, MA 02202

Corporate
Secretary of State
1 Ashburton Place
Boston, MA 02108

Taxation
Accounting Bureau/Department of Revenue
Leverett Saltonstall Building
100 Cambridge Street
Boston, MA 02202

International Commerce
Office of International Trade and Investment
100 Cambridge Street
Boston, MA 02202

Banking
Division of Banks and Loan Agencies
100 Cambridge Street
Boston, MA 02202

Securities
Secretary of State
Securities Division
1 Ashburton Place
Boston, MA 02108

Labor and Indusrial Relations
Executive Office of Labor
1 Ashburton Place
Boston, MA 02108

Department of Labor and Industries
Executive Office of Economic Affairs
100 Cambridge Street
Boston, MA 02202

Insurance
Division of Insurance
100 Cambridge Street
Boston, MA 02202

INDUSTRIAL AND BUSINESS DIRECTORIES

Directory of Directors in the City of Boston and Vicinity, Bankers Service Co., 14 Beacon Street, Boston, MA 02108

Directory of Massachusetts Manufacturers, George D. Hall Co., 50 Congress Street, Boston, MA 02109

MacRAE's State Industrial Directory Massachusetts/Rhode Island, MacRAE's Industrial Directories, 817 Broadway, New York, NY 10003

Massachusetts Service Directory, George D. Hall Co., 50 Congress Street, Boston, MA 02109

Massachusetts State Industrial Directory, State Industrial Directories Corp., 2 Penn Plaza, New York, NY 10001

Michigan

State Capitol, Lansing, MI 48913
(517) 373-1837

INFORMATION OFFICES

Commerce/Economic Development
Michigan Jobs Commission
Customer Assistance and Research
201 N. Washington Square
Victor Office Center
Lansing, MI 48913

Corporate
Corporation and Securities Bureau
6546 Mercantile Way
Lansing, MI 48909
Taxation
Bureau of Collection
Department of Treasury
Treasury Building
P.O. Box 30199
Lansing, MI 48909
State Chamber of Commerce
Michigan State Chamber of Commerce
600 S. Walnut
Lansing, MI 48933
International Commerce
Michigan International Office
Department of Commerce
525 W. Ottawa Street
P.O. Box 30225
Lansing, MI 48909
Banking
Financial Institutions Bureau
Department of Commerce
Grand Plaza
206 E. Michigan
P.O. Box 30224
Lansing, MI 48909
Securities
Corporation and Securities Bureau
Department of Commerce
6546 Mercantile Way
P.O. Box 30199
Lansing, MI 48909
Labor and Industrial Relations
Bureau of Employment Relations
Department of Labor
State of Michigan Plaza Building
1200 Sixth Street
Detroit, MI 48226

Department of Labor
Victor Office Center
201 North Washington
P.O. Box 30015
Lansing, MI 48909
Insurance
Ottawa Building
P.O. Box 30220
Lansing, MI 48913
Business Ombudsman
Michigan Jobs Commission
Customer Assistance and Research
Victor Office Center
Lansing, MI 48913

INDUSTRIAL AND BUSINESS DIRECTORIES

Harris Michigan Marketers Industrial Directory, Harris Publishing Company, 2057 Aurora Road, Twinsburg, OH 44087

Michigan Manufacturers Directory, Manufacturers' News, Inc., 1633 Central Street, Evanston, IL 60201

Minnesota

State Capitol, St. Paul, MN 55155
(612) 296-6013

INFORMATION OFFICES

Commerce/Economic Development
Department of Trade and Economic Development
500 Metro Square
121-7th Place East
St. Paul, MN 55101-2146

Minnesota Department of Commerce
Commerce Building
133 E. 7th Street
St. Paul, MN 55101
Corporate
Secretary of State
Domestic or Foreign Corporations
180 State Office Building
St. Paul, MN 55155
Taxation
Department of Revenue
10 River Park Plaza
St. Paul, MN 55146
State Chamber of Commerce
Minnesota Chamber of Commerce
480 Cedar Street
St. Paul, MN 55101
International Commerce
Minnesota Trade Office
1000 World Trade Center
St. Paul, MN 55101
Banking
Minnesota Department of Commerce
Banking Division
Commerce Building
133 E. 7th Street
St. Paul, MN 55101
Securities
Minnesota Department of Commerce
Registration Unit
Commerce Building
133 E. 7th Street
St. Paul, MN 55101
Labor and Industrial Relations
Minnesota Department of Labor and Industry
443 Lafayette Road
St. Paul, MN 55155
Insurance
Minnesota Department of Commerce
Policy Analysis Division
Commerce Building
133 E. 7th Street
St. Paul, MN 55101
Business Ombudsman
Department of Trade and Economic Development
Small Business Assistance Office
500 Metro Square
121-7th Place East
St. Paul, MN 55101-2146

INDUSTRIAL AND BUSINESS DIRECTORIES

Minnesota Directory of Manufacturers, Manufacturers' News, Inc., 1633 Central Street, Evanston, IL 60201; State Industrial Directories Corp., 2 Penn Plaza, New York, NY 10001

Minnesota Manufacturer's Register, Manufacturers' News, Inc., 1633 Central Street, Evanston, IL 60201

Mississippi

OFFICE OF THE GOVERNOR, JACKSON, MS 39205
(601) 359-3150

INFORMATION OFFICES

Commerce/Economic Development
Mississippi Department of Economic and Community Development
P.O. Box 849
Jackson, MS 39205

Division of International Development
P.O. Box 849
Jackson, MS 39205

Corporate
Secretary of State
P.O. Box 136
Jackson, MS 39205

Taxation
Tax Commission
102 Woolfolk Building
P.O. Box 22828
Jackson, MS 39225

State Chamber of Commerce
P.O. Box 1849
Jackson, MS 39205-1849

Banking
Department of Banking and Consumer Finance
1206 Woolfolk State Office Building
P.O. Drawer 23729
Jackson, MS 39225-3729

International Commerce
Department of Economic and Community Development
P.O. Box 849
Jackson, MS 39205

Securities
Secretary of State's Office
Securities Division
P.O. Box 136
Jackson, MS 39205

Labor and Industrial Relations
Employment Security Commission
1520 W. Capitol Street
P.O. Box 1699
Jackson, MS 39215-8711

Insurance
Department of Insurance
1804 Sillers Building
P.O. Box 79
Jackson, MS 39205

INDUSTRIAL AND BUSINESS DIRECTORIES

Mississippi Manufacturers' Directory, Research Division, Department of Economic and Community Development, P.O. Box 849, Jackson, MS 39205; Manufacturers' News, Inc., 1633 Central Street, Evanston, IL 60201

Missouri

STATE INFORMATION, JEFFERSON CITY, MO 65101
(314) 751-2000

INFORMATION OFFICES

Commerce/Economic Development
Department of Economic Development
Economic Development Programs
P.O. Box 118
Jefferson City, MO 65102

Corporate
Secretary of State
Corporations Division
600 West Main Street
P.O. Box 778
Jefferson City, MO 65102

Taxation
Department of Revenue
Division of Taxation and Collections
Truman State Office Building
P.O. Box 629
Jefferson City, MO 65105

State Chamber of Commerce
Missouri Chamber of Commerce
428 East Capitol Avenue
P.O. Box 149
Jefferson City, MO 65102

International Commerce
International Business Development
Economic Development Program
Truman State Office Building
P.O. Box 118
Jefferson City, MO 65102

Banking
Missouri Division of Finance
Truman State Office Building
P.O. Box 716
Jefferson City, MO 65102

Securities
Office of the Secretary of State
Securities Division
600 West Main Street
P.O. Box 778
Jefferson City, MO 65102

Labor and Industrial Relations
Missouri Dept. of Labor & Industrial Relations
3315 West Truman Boulevard
Jefferson City, MO 65109
Insurance
Missouri Division of Insurance
Truman State Office Building
P.O. Box 690
Jefferson City, MO 65102
Uniform Industrial Code
Missouri Division of Labor Standards
P.O. Box 449
Jefferson City, MO 65102

INDUSTRIAL AND BUSINESS DIRECTORY

Contacts Influential: Commerce and Industrial Directory (for Kansas City Area), Contacts Influential, Inc., 2405 Grand Avenue, Kansas City, MO 64108
Missouri Manufacturers' Register, Manufacturers' News, Inc., 1633 Central Street, Evanston, IL 60201

Montana

STATE CAPITOL, HELENA, MT 59620
(406) 444-3111

INFORMATION OFFICES

Commerce/Economic Development
Department of Commerce
1424 9th Avenue
Helena, MT 59620-0501

Census and Economic Information Center
Department of Commerce
1429 9th Avenue
Helena, MT 59620-0501
Corporate
Secretary of State
Business Services Bureau
State Capitol Building
Helena, MT 59620-2801
State Chamber of Commerce
Montana Chamber of Commerce
P.O. Box 1730
Helena, MT 59624
International Commerce
International Trade Office
Montana Department of Commerce
1424 9th Avenue
Helena, MT 59620-0501
Banking
Commissioner of Financial Institutions
Montana Department of Commerce
1520 East 6th Avenue
Helena, MT 59620-0543
Securities
Securities Division
State Auditor's Office
Sam Mitchell Building
Helena, MT 59620-0301
Labor & Industrial Relations
Commissioner's Office
Montana Department of Labor & Industry
Lockey and Roberts
Helena, MT 59620-1501
Insurance
Insurance Department
State Auditor's Office
Sam Mitchell Building
Helena, MT 59620-0301
Uniform Commercial Code
Secretary of State
Uniform Commercial Code Bureau
State Capitol Building
Helena, MT 59620-2801
Business Ombudsman
Small Business Advocate
Montana Department of Commerce
1424 9th Avenue
Helena, MT 59620-0501

INDUSTRIAL AND BUSINESS DIRECTORIES

Montana Manufacturers Directory, Department of Commerce, 1424 9th Avenue, Helena, MT 59620; Manufacturers' News, Inc., 1633 Central Street, Evanston, IL 60201
Montana Business & Industrial Location Guide, Department of Commerce, 1424 9th Avenue, Helena, MT 59620

Nebraska

STATE CAPITOL, LINCOLN, NE 68509
(402) 471-2311

INFORMATION OFFICES

Commerce/Economic Development
Department of Economic Development
301 Centennial Mall South
P.O. Box 94666
Lincoln, NE 68509-4666
Corporate
Secretary of State
Corporation Division
P.O. Box 94608
Lincoln, NE 68509-4608
Taxation
Department of Revenue
301 Centennial Mall South
P.O. Box 94818
Lincoln, NE 68509-4818
State Chamber of Commerce
Nebraska Chamber of Commerce and Industry
1320 Lincoln Mall
P.O. Box 95128
Lincoln, NE 68509

International Commerce
Nebraska Department of Economic Development
Business Recruitment Division
P.O. Box 94666
Lincoln, NE 68509-4666

Banking
Department of Banking and Finance
301 Centennial Mall South
P.O. Box 95006
Lincoln, NE 68509-5006

Securities
Department of Banking and Finance
The Atrium
1200 N Street
P.O. Box 95006
Lincoln, NE 68509-5006

Labor and Industrial Relations
Nebraska Department of Labor
550 South 16th Street
P.O. Box 94600
Lincoln, NE 68509-4600

Insurance
Department of Insurance
The Terminal Building
941 O Street
Lincoln, NE 68508

Uniform Industrial Code
Uniform Commercial Code Division
301 Centennial Mall South
P.O. Box 95104
Lincoln, NE 68509-5104

Business Ombudsman
One-Stop Center
Department of Economic Development
P.O. Box 94666
Lincoln, NE 68509-4666

INDUSTRIAL AND BUSINESS DIRECTORIES

A Directory of Lincoln, Nebraska Manufacturers, Lincoln Chamber of Commerce, 1221 N. Street, Lincoln, NE 68508

Nebraska Manufacturers Register, Manufacturers' News, Inc., 1633 Central Street, Evanston, IL 60201

Directory of Nebraska Manufacturers and Their Products, Nebraska State Department of Economic Development, P.O. Box 94666, Lincoln, NE 68509-4666

Directory of Manufacturers for the Omaha Metropolitan Area, Omaha Economic Development Council, 1301 Harney, Omaha, NE 68102.

Directory of Major Employers for the Omaha Area, Omaha Economic Development Council, 1301 Harney, Omaha, NE 68102

Nevada

State Capitol, Carson City, NV 89710
(702) 687-5670

INFORMATION OFFICES

Commerce/Economic Development
Department of Commerce
1665 Hot Springs Road
Carson City, NV 89710

Commission on Economic Development
5151 S. Carson Street
Carson City, NV 89710

Corporate
Secretary of State
Capitol Complex
Carson City, NV 89710

Taxation
Department of Taxation
1340 S. Curry Street
Carson City, NV 89710

State Chamber of Commerce
Nevada Chamber of Commerce Association
P.O. Box 3499
Reno, NV 89505

International Commerce
Commission on Economic Development
International Office
3770 Howard Hughes Parkway #295
Las Vegas, NV 89158

Banking
Financial Institutions Division
406 E. Second Street
Carson City, NV 89710

Securities
Secretary of State
Capitol Complex
Carson City, NV 89710

Labor and Industrial Relations
Labor Commission
1445 Hot Springs Road
Carson City, NV 89710

Department of Industrial Relations
1390 S. Curry Street
Carson City, NV 89710

Insurance
Insurance Department
1665 Hot Springs Road
Carson City, NV 89710

INDUSTRIAL AND BUSINESS DIRECTORIES

Directory of Nevada Mine Operations, Division of Mine Inspection Department of Industrial Relations, 1380 S. Curry Street, Carson City, NV 89710

Nevada Industrial Directory, Gold Hill Publishings Co., Inc., P.O. Drawer F, Virginia City, NV 89440; Manufacturers' News, Inc., 1633 Central Street, Evanston, IL 60201

New Hampshire

State House, Concord, NH 03301
(603) 271-1110

INFORMATION OFFICES

Commerce/Economic Development
Department of Resources and Economic Development
Division of Economic Development
172 Pembroke Road
Concord, NH 03302

Corporate
Secretary of State
Corporations Division
State House Annex
Concord, NH 03301

Taxation
Board of Taxation
61 S. Spring Street
Concord, NH 03301

Department of Revenue Administration
61 S. Spring Street
Concord, NH 03301

State Chamber of Commerce
Business and Industry Association of New Hampshire
122 N. Main Street
Concord, NH 03301

International Commerce
Department of Resources & Economic Development
Division of Economic Development
172 Pembroke Road
Prescott Park—Concord, NH 03302

Banking
Banking Department
State of New Hampshire
169 Manchester Street
Concord, NH 03301

New Hampshire Banking Association
125 N. Main Street
Concord, NH 03301

Securities
Insurance Department, Securities Division
State of New Hampshire
State House
Concord, NH 03301

Labor and Industrial Relations
Department of Employment Security
State of New Hampshire
32 S. Main Street
Concord, NH 03301

Department of Labor
95 Pleasant Street
Concord, NH 03301

Insurance
Insurance Department
State of New Hampshire
169 Manchester Street
Concord, NH 03301

Standard Industrial Code
Department of Employment Security
State of New Hampshire
32 S. Main Street
Concord, NH 03301

INDUSTRIAL AND BUSINESS DIRECTORIES

Made in New Hampshire, New Hampshire Office of Industrial Development, Department of Resources, Concord, NH 03301

MacRAE's State Industrial Directory Maine/New Hampshire/Vermont, MacRAE's Industrial Directories, 817 Broadway, New York, NY 10003

New Hampshire Manufacturing Directory, Tower Publishing Company, 34 Diamond Street, Portland, ME 04111

New Jersey

State House, Trenton, NJ 08625
(609) 777-2500

INFORMATION OFFICES

Commerce/Economic Development
Department of Commerce and Economic Development
20 W. State Street, CN 820
Trenton, NJ 08625

Division of Travel and Tourism
20 W. State Street, CN 826
Trenton, NJ 08625

Economic Development Authority
Capitol Place One, CN 990
200 S. Warren Street
Trenton, NJ 08625

Corporate
Secretary of State
Division of Commercial Recording
820 Bear Tavern Road, CN 308
W. Trenton, NJ 08625

Taxation
Department of Treasury
Division of Taxation
50 Barrack Street, CN 240
Trenton, NJ 08625

State Chamber of Commerce
New Jersey State Chamber of Commerce
1 State Street Square
50 W. State Street
Trenton, NJ 08608

International Commerce
Division of International Trade
28 W. State Street, CN 836
Trenton, NJ 08625-0836

Banking
Department of Banking
20 W. State Street, CN 040
Trenton, NJ 08625

Securities
Bureau of Securities
2 Gateway Center
Newark, NJ 07102

Labor and Labor Relations
Department of Labor and Industry
John Fitch Plaza, CN 110
Trenton, NJ 08625

Insurance
Department of Insurance
20 W. State Street, CN 325
Trenton, NJ 08625

Business Ombudsman
Department of State
State House CN 300
Trenton, NJ 08625

INDUSTRIAL AND BUSINESS DIRECTORIES

New Jersey Manufacturers Directory, George D. Hall Co., 50 Congress Street, Boston, MA 02109; Manufacturers' News, Inc., 1633 Central Street, Evanston, IL 60201

MacRAE's New Jersey State Industrial Directory, MacRAE's Industrial Directories, 817 Broadway, New York, NY 10003

The New Jersey Directory of Manufacturers, Commerce Register®, Inc., 190 Godwin Avenue, Midland Park, NJ 07432

New Mexico

State Capitol, Santa Fe, NM 87503
(505) 827-3000

INFORMATION OFFICES

Commerce/Economic Development
Economic Development Department
Joseph M. Montoya Building
1100 St. Francis Drive
Santa Fe, NM 87503

Corporate
State Corporation Commission
P.E.R.A. Building
P.O. Drawer 1269
Santa Fe, NM 87504

Taxation
Taxation and Revenue Department
P.O. Box 630
Manuel Lujan Sr. Building
Santa Fe, NM 87504-0630

State Chamber of Commerce
Association of Commerce and Industry of New Mexico
4001 Indian School NE
Albuquerque, NM 87110

International Commerce
Trade Division
Economic Development Department
Joseph M. Montoya Building
1100 St. Francis Drive
Santa Fe, NM 87503

Banking
Financial Institutions Division
Regulation and Licensing Department
725 St. Michael's Drive
Santa Fe, NM 87503

Securities
Securities Division
Financial Institutions Division
Regulation and Licensing Department
725 St. Michael's Drive
Santa Fe, NM 87503

Labor and Industrial
Labor and Industrial Division
1596 Pacheso Street
Aspen Plaza Building
Santa Fe, NM 87504

Insurance
State Corporation Commission
P.E.R.A. Building
P.O. Drawer 1269
Santa Fe, NM 87501

INDUSTRIAL AND BUSINESS DIRECTORIES

New Mexico Manufacturing Directory, Manufacturers' News, Inc., 1633 Central Street, Evanston, IL 60201

New Mexico Directory of Manufacturers, Economic Development Division, New Mexico Economic Development, Joseph M. Montoya Building, 1100 St. Francis Drive, Santa Fe, NM 87503

New York

State Capitol, Albany, NY 12224
(518) 474-2121

INFORMATION OFFICES

Commerce/Economic Development
Department of Economic Development
One Commerce Plaza
Albany, NY 12245

Division of Regional Economic Development
One Commerce Plaza
Albany, NY 12245

Corporate
Secretary of State
162 Washington Avenue
Albany, NY 12231

Taxation
Department of Taxation and Finance
State Campus Building #9
Albany, NY 12227

State Chamber of Commerce
Business Council of New York State
152 Washington Avenue
Albany, NY 12210

Small Business Advisory Board
Division for Small Business
1515 Broadway
New York, NY 10036
International Commerce
Department of Economic Development
1515 Broadway
New York, NY 10036
Banking
Department of Banking
194 Washington Avenue
New York, NY 12210
Labor and Industrial Relations
Department of Labor
State Campus
Albany, NY 12240
Insurance
Department of Insurance
Empire State Plaza
Agency Building #1
Albany, NY 12257
Business Ombudsman
Department of Economic Development
Division for Small Business
1515 Broadway
New York, NY 10036
Uniform Commercial Code
Department of State
107 Washington Avenue
Albany, NY 12231

INDUSTRIAL AND BUSINESS DIRECTORIES

New York Manufacturers' Directory, George D. Hall Co., 50 Congress Street, Boston, MA 02109; Manufacturers' News, 1633 Central Street, Evanston, IL 60201
MacRAE's New York State Industrial Directory, MacRAE's Industrial Directories, 817 Broadway, New York, NY 10003
The New York State Directory, Cambridge Information Group, 7200 Wisconsin Avenue, Bethesda, MD 20814–9777

North Carolina

General Assembly
State Legislative Building,
Raleigh, NC 27601-1096
(919) 733-1110 (government information)
733-7928 (legislators)

INFORMATION OFFICES

Commerce/Economic Development
Department of Commerce
430 N. Salisbury Street
Raleigh, NC 27603-5900
Corporate
Secretary of State
Corporation Division
300 N. Salisbury Street
Raleigh, NC 27603-5909
Taxation
Department of Revenue
501 N. Wilmington Street
Raleigh, NC 27604-8001
State Chamber of Commerce
North Carolina Citizens for Business and Industry
P.O. Box 2508
Raleigh, NC 27602
International Commerce
International Development
Department of Commerce
430 N. Salisbury Street
Raleigh, NC 27603
Banking
Banking Commission
Department of Commerce
430 N. Salisbury Street
Raleigh, NC 27603
Securities
Secretary of State
Securities Division
300 N. Salisbury Street
Raleigh, NC 27603-5909
Labor and Industrial Relations
Department of Labor
4 W. Edenton Street
Raleigh, NC 27601-1092
Insurance
Department of Insurance
430 N. Salisbury Street
Raleigh, NC 27603-5908

INDUSTRIAL AND BUSINESS DIRECTORIES

North Carolina Manufacturers Register, Manufacturers' News, Inc., 1633 Central Street, Evanston, IL 60201
MacRAE's State Industrial Directory North/South Carolina/Virginia, MacRAE's Industrial Directories, 817 Broadway, New York, NY 10003
North Carolina Manufacturers Directory, George D. Hall Co., 50 Congress Street, Boston, MA 02109

North Dakota

State Capitol, Bismarck, ND 58505
(701) 224-2000

INFORMATION OFFICES

Commerce/Economic Development
Economic Development & Finance
1833 East Bismarck Expressway
Bismarck, ND 58504
Corporate
Office of the Secretary of State
Corporation Department
600 East Boulevard Avenue
Bismarck, ND 58505-0500

Taxation
Tax Department
600 East Boulevard Avenue
Bismarck, ND 58505-0599

State Chamber of Commerce
Greater North Dakota Association
State Chamber of Commerce
Box 2639
2000 Shafer Street
Bismarck, ND 58502

International Commerce
International Trade
Economic Development & Finance
1833 East Bismarck Expressway
Bismarck, ND 58504

Banking
State Banking Commission
600 East Boulevard Avenue
Bismarck, ND 58505-0510

Securities
Securities Commissioner
600 East Boulevard Avenue
Bismarck, ND 58505

Labor and Industrial Relations
State Commissioner of Labor
600 East Boulevard Avenue
Bismarck, ND 58505

Insurance
Insurance Commissioner
600 East Boulevard Avenue
Bismarck, ND 58505-0320

Uniform Industrial Code
Secretary of State
600 East Boulevard Avenue
Bismarck, ND 58505-0500

INDUSTRIAL AND BUSINESS DIRECTORIES

North Dakota Directory of Manufacturers, Economic Development & Finance, 1833 East Bismarck Expressway, Bismarck, ND 58504; Manufacturers' News, Inc., 1633 Central Street, Evanston, IL 60201

Strictly Business, Frontier Directory Co., Inc., 515 E. Main Street, Bismarck, ND 58501

Ohio

State House, Columbus, OH 43215
(614) 466-3455
State Operator: (614) 466-2000

INFORMATION OFFICES

Commerce/Economic Development
Ohio Department of Development
77 S. High Street
P.O. Box 1001
Columbus, OH 43266-0101

Corporate
Secretary of State
Corporation Section
30 E. Broad Street
Columbus, OH 43266-0418

Taxation
Department of Taxation
30 E. Broad Street
Columbus, OH 43266-0420

State Chamber of Commerce
Ohio Chamber of Commerce
35 E. Gay Street
Columbus, OH 43215-1192

International Commerce
Ohio Department of Development
International Trade Division
77 S. High Street
P.O. Box 1001
Columbus, OH 43266-0101

Banking
Ohio Department of Commerce
Division of Banks
77 S. High Street
Columbus, OH 43266-0544

Securities
Ohio Department of Commerce
Division of Securities
77 S. High Street
Columbus, OH 43266-0544

Labor and Industrial Relations
Ohio Department of Industrial Relations
2323 W. Fifth Avenue
P.O. Box 825
Columbus, OH 43266-0567

Insurance
Ohio Department of Insurance
2100 Stella Court
Columbus, OH 43266-0566

Uniform Industrial Code
Industrial Commission of Ohio
Division of Safety and Hygiene
246 N. High Street
Columbus, OH 43266-0589

Business Ombudsman
Ohio Department of Development
Small and Developing Business Division
Minority Business Development Division
77 S. High Street
P.O. Box 1001
Columbus, OH 43266-0101

INDUSTRIAL AND BUSINESS DIRECTORIES

Akron, Ohio Membership Directory and Buyers Guide, Akron Regional Development Board, 1 Cascade Plaza, Akron, OH 44308-1192

The Chamber Directory, Toledo Area Chamber of Commerce, 218 Huron Street, Toledo, OH 43604

Manufacturers Directory, Columbus Regional Information Service, 37 North High Street, Columbus, OH 43215-3181

Harris Ohio Industrial Directory, Harris Publishing Company, 2057 Aurora Road, Twinsburg, OH 44087

Ohio Manufacturers Directory, Manufacturers' News, Inc., 1633 Central Street, Evanston, IL 60201

Oklahoma

State Capitol, Oklahoma City, OK 73105
(405) 521-2011

INFORMATION OFFICES

Commerce/Economic Development
Department of Commerce
P.O. Box 26980
Oklahoma City, OK 73126

Corporate
Secretary of State
State Capitol
Oklahoma City, OK 73105

Taxation
Tax Commission
M. C. Connors Building
2501 N. Lincoln Boulevard
Oklahoma City, OK 73105

State Chamber of Commerce
Oklahoma State Chamber of Commerce & Industry
4020 N. Lincoln Boulevard
Oklahoma City, OK 73105

International Commerce
International Trade Division
Department of Commerce
6601 Broadway Extension
P.O. Box 26980
Oklahoma City, OK 73126

Banking
Oklahoma Banking Department
4100 N. Lincoln Boulevard
Oklahoma City, OK 73105

Securities
Oklahoma Securities Commission
Will Rogers Building
2401 N. Lincoln Boulevard
Oklahoma City, OK 73105

Labor and Industrial Relations
Oklahoma Labor Department
4001 N. Lincoln Boulevard
Oklahoma City, OK 73105

Insurance
Insurance Commission
1901 N. Walnut Street
P.O. Box 53408
Oklahoma City, OK 73152-3408

Uniform Industrial Code
Universal Commercial Code Division
County Clerk's Office
County Court House
Oklahoma City, OK 73102

INDUSTRIAL AND BUSINESS DIRECTORIES

Oklahoma Directory of Manufacturers and Processors, Department of Commerce, P.O. Box 26980, Oklahoma City, OK 73126

Oklahoma Manufacturers Register, Manufacturers' News, Inc., 1633 Central Street, Evanston, IL 60201

Oregon

State Capitol, Salem, OR 97310
(503) 986-1388

INFORMATION OFFICES

Commerce/Economic Development
Economic Development Department
775 Summer Street N.E.
Salem, OR 97310

Corporate
Corporation Division
Office of Secretary of State
Commerce Building
158 12th Street N.E.
Salem, OR 97310

Taxation
Department of Revenue
Revenue Building
955 Center Street
Salem, OR 97310-0210

International Commerce
International Trade Division
Economic Development Department
One World Trade Center
121 S.W. Salmon
Portland, OR 97204

Banking
Division of Finance and Corporate Securities
Department of Consumer and Business Services
21 Labor and Industries Building
Salem, OR 97310

Securities
Division of Finance and Corporate Securities
Department of Consumer and Business Services
21 Labor and Industries Building
Salem, OR 97310

Labor and Industry
Bureau of Labor and Industries
800 N.E. Oregon Street
Portland, OR 97232

Insurance
Insurance Division
Department of Consumer and Business Services
Labor and Industries Building
Salem, OR 97310

Uniform Industrial Code
Building Codes Division
Department of Consumer and Business Services
1535 Edgewater N.W.
Salem, OR 97310

INDUSTRIAL AND BUSINESS DIRECTORIES

Directory of Oregon Manufacturers, International Trade Directory, and *Directory of Oregon Wood Products Manufacturers,* Economic Development Department, 775 Summer Street N.E., Salem, OR 97310; Manufacturers' News, Inc., 1633 Central Street, Evanston, IL 60201

Oregon Business Directory, American Directory Publishing Co., Inc., 5711 S. 86th Circle, P.O. Box 27347, Omaha, NE 68127

Pennsylvania

Main Capitol Building, Harrisburg, PA 17120
(717) 787-2121

INFORMATION OFFICES

Department of Commerce
Department of Commerce
Office of the Secretary
Forum Building
Harrisburg, PA 17120

Office of International Development
Department of Commerce
Forum Building
Harrisburg, PA 17120

Office of Program Management
Department of Commerce
Forum Building
Harrisburg, PA 17120

Business Resource Network
Department of Commerce
Forum Building
Harrisburg, PA 17120

Office of Technology Development
Department of Commerce
Forum Building
Harrisburg, PA 17120

International Commerce
Department of Commerce
Office of International Development
Forum Building
Harrisburg, PA 17120

Corporate
Department of State
Bureau of Corporations
308 North Office Building
Harrisburg, PA 17120

Taxation
Department of Revenue
P.O. Box 8903
Harrisburg, PA 17105

State Chamber of Commerce
Pennsylvania Chamber of Business and Industry
417 Walnut Street
Harrisburg, PA 17101-1596

Banking
Department of Banking
333 Market Street
Harristown II
Harrisburg, PA 17101-2290

Securities
Securities Commission
East Gate Office Building
1010 N. 7th Street
Harrisburg, PA 17102

Labor and Industrial Relations
Department of Labor & Industry
Labor & Industry Building
7th & Forester Streets
Harrisburg, PA 17120

Insurance
Department of Insurance
1321 Strawberry Square
Harrisburg, PA 17120

INDUSTRIAL AND BUSINESS DIRECTORIES

Harris Pennsylvania Industrial Directory of Pennsylvania, Harris Publishing Company, 2057 Aurora Road, Twinsburg, OH 44087

MacRAE's State Industrial Directory Pennsylvania, MacRAE's Industrial Directories, 817 Broadway, New York, NY 10003

Pennsylvania Manufacturers Register, Manufacturers' News, Inc., 1633 Central Street, Evanston, IL 60201

Rhode Island

State House, Providence, RI 02903
(401) 277-2000

INFORMATION OFFICES

Commerce/Economic Development
Department of Economic Development
7 Jackson Walkway
Providence, RI 02903

Taxation
Division of Taxation
Department of Administration
One Capitol Hill
Providence, RI 02908

Corporate
Secretary of State
Corporation Department
100 N. Main Street
Providence, RI 02903

State Chamber of Commerce
Rhode Island Chamber of Commerce
30 Exchange Terrace
Providence, RI 02903
International Commerce
Rhode Island Department of Economic Development
7 Jackson Walkway
Providence, RI 02903
Banking
Department of Business Regulation
Banking Division
233 Richmond Street
Providence, RI 02903
Securities
Department of Business Regulation
Banking Division
233 Richmond Street
Providence, RI 02903
Labor and Industrial Relations
Department of Labor
220 Elmwood Avenue
Providence, RI 02907
Insurance
Department of Business Regulation
Insurance Division
233 Richmond Street
Providence, RI 02903
Business Ombudsman
Business Development Division
Department of Economic Development
7 Jackson Walkway
Providence, RI 02903

INDUSTRIAL AND BUSINESS DIRECTORIES

MacRAE's State Industrial Directory Massachusetts/Rhode Island, MacRAE's Industrial Directories, 817 Broadway, New York, NY 10003

Rhode Island Directory of Manufacturers, Department of Economic Development, 7 Jackson Walkway, Providence, RI 02903; Manufacturers' News, Inc., 1633 Central Street, Evanston, IL 60201

South Carolina

Governors Office
State House, Columbia, SC 29211
(803) 734-9818
State Operator (803) 734-1000

INFORMATION OFFICES

Commerce/Economic Development
South Carolina State Department of Commerce
P.O. Box 927
1201 Main Street
Columbia, SC 29202
Taxation
Department of Revenue
P.O. Box 125
Columbia Mill Building
Columbia, SC 29214
Corporate
Secretary of State
P.O. Box 11350
Columbia, SC 29211
State Chamber of Commerce
South Carolina Chamber of Commerce
1201 Main Street
Columbia, SC 29202
International Commerce
South Carolina Department of Commerce
1201 Main Street
P.O. Box 927
Columbia, SC 29202
Labor and Industrial Relations
South Carolina Department of Labor, Licensing, and Regulation
Landmark Center, 3600 Forest Drive
P.O. Box 11329
Columbia, SC 29211-1329
Insurance
South Carolina Department of Insurance
1612 Marion Street
P.O. Box 100105
Columbia, SC 29202-3105
Banking
State Treasurer's Office
Wade Hampton Building
Banking Operations
P.O. Drawer 11778
Columbia, SC 29211
Securities
Secretary of State
Securities Division
P.O. Box 11350
1205 Pendleton Street
Columbia, SC 29201
Business Ombudsman
SC Department of Consumer Affairs
P.O. Box 5757
2801 Devine Street
Columbia, SC 29250-5757

INDUSTRIAL AND BUSINESS DIRECTORIES

Industrial Directory of South Carolina, South Carolina Department of Commerce, P.O. Box 927, 1201 Main Street, Columbia, SC 29202; Manufacturers' News, Inc., 1633 Central Street, Evanston, IL 60201

MacRAE's State Industrial Directory North Carolina/South Carolina/Virginia, MacRAE's Industrial Directories, 817 Broadway, New York, NY 10003

South Dakota

State Capitol, Pierre, SD 57501-5070
(605) 773-3011

INFORMATION OFFICES

Commerce/Economic Development
Governor's Office of Economic Development
711 Wells Avenue
Pierre, SD 57501

Department of Commerce and Regulation
910 E. Sioux
Pierre, SD 57501

Corporate
Secretary of State
Corporation Division
Capitol Building
Pierre, SD 57501

Taxation
Department of Revenue
Kneip Building
Pierre, SD 57501

State Chamber of Commerce
Industry & Commerce Association of South Dakota
P.O. Box 190
Pierre, SD 57501

International Commerce
Governor's Office of Economic Development
711 Wells Avenue
Pierre, SD 57501

Banking
Department of Commerce and Regulation
Division of Banking
105 S. Euclid
Pierre, SD 57501

Securities
Department of Commerce and Regulation
Division of Securities
910 E. Sioux
Pierre, SD 57501

Labor and Industrial Relations
Department of Labor
Division of Labor and Management
Kneip Building
Pierre, SD 57501

Insurance
Department of Commerce and Regulation
Division of Insurance
910 E. Sioux
Pierre, SD 57501

INDUSTRIAL AND BUSINESS DIRECTORIES

South Dakota Manufacturers and Processors Directory, Governor's Office of Economic Development, 711 Wells Avenue, Pierre, SD 57501; Manufacturers' News, Inc., 1633 Central Street, Evanston, IL 60201

South Dakota Export Directory, Governor's Office of Economic Development, 711 Wells Avenue, Pierre, SD 57501

Tennessee

State Capitol, Nashville, TN 37243-0001 (615) 741-2001

INFORMATION OFFICES

Commerce/Economic Development
Department of Economic and Community Development
Rachel Jackson Building
320 6th Avenue North
Nashville, TN 37243-0405

Corporate
Secretary of State
Records Division
James K. Polk Building
Nashville, TN 37243-0306

Taxation
Department of Revenue
1200 Andrew Jackson Building
500 Deaderick Street
Nashville, TN 37242-1099

International Commerce
Department of Economic & Community Development
International Sales & Marketing
Rachel Jackson Building
320 6th Avenue North
Nashville, TN 37243-0405

Banking
Department of Financial Institutions
John Sevier Building
500 Charlotte Avenue
Nashville, TN 37243-0705

Securities
Department of Commerce & Insurance
Securities Division
500 James Robertson Parkway
Nashville, TN 37243

Labor and Industrial Relations
Department of Labor
710 James Robertson Parkway
Nashville, TN 37243-0661

Insurance
Department of Commerce & Insurance
Insurance Division
500 James Robertson Parkway
Nashville, TN 37243

Business Ombudsman
Department of Economic & Community Development
Business & Industry Services Division
Rachel Jackson Building
320 6th Avenue North
Nashville, TN 37243-0405

INDUSTRIAL AND BUSINESS DIRECTORIES

Directory of Tennessee Manufacturers, M. Lee Smith Publishers, 162 Fourth Avenue, P.O. Box 198867, Nashville, TN 37219; Manufacturers' News, Inc., 1633 Central Street, Evanston, IL 60201

Texas

STATE CAPITOL, AUSTIN, TX 78701
State Information: (512) 463-4630

INFORMATION OFFICES

Commerce/Economic Development
Texas Department of Commerce
P.O. Box 12728, Capitol Station
Austin, TX 78711
Corporate
Secretary of State
P.O. Box 12697
Austin, TX 78711
Taxation
Comptroller of Public Accounts
P.O. Box 13528
Austin, TX 78711-3528
State Chamber of Commerce
Texas State Chamber of Commerce
900 Congress Avenue
Austin, TX 78711-3528
Rio Grande Chamber of Commerce
P.O. Box 1499
Weslaco, TX 78599-1499
International Commerce
Texas Department of Commerce
P.O. Box 12728, Capitol Station
Austin, TX 78711
Banking
Texas Department of Banking
2601 N. Lamar
Austin, TX 78705-4294
Securities
State Securities Board
P.O. Box 13167
Austin, TX 78711-3167
Licensing and Regulation
P.O. Box 12157
Austin, TX 78711
Insurance
Texas Department of Insurance
P.O. Box 149104
Austin, TX 78711-9104
Uniform Industrial Code
Secretary of State
Uniform Commercial Code Section
P.O. Box 12697
Austin, TX 78711

INDUSTRIAL AND BUSINESS DIRECTORIES

Dallas Business Guide, Greater Dallas Chamber of Commerce, 1201 Elm Street, Dallas, TX 75270-2014

Directory of Texas Manufacturers, Bureau of Business Research, University of Texas at Austin, TX 78712

Fort Worth Directory of Manufacturers, Fort Worth Area Chamber of Commerce, 777 Taylor Street, Fort Worth, TX 76102-4997

Texas Manufacturers Register, Manufacturers' News, Inc., 1633 Central Street, Evanston, IL 60201

Utah

STATE CAPITOL, SALT LAKE CITY, UT 84114
(801) 538-3000

INFORMATION OFFICES

Commerce/Economic Development
Department of Commerce
160 East 300 South
Salt Lake City, UT 84111

Division of Business and Economic Development
160 East 300 South
Salt Lake City, UT 84111

Office of Planning & Budget
Data Resources Section
116 Capitol Building
Salt Lake City, UT 84114
Corporate
Division of Corporations
Heber M. Wells Building
160 E. 300 South
Salt Lake City, UT 84111
Taxation
Utah State Tax Commission
Heber M. Wells Building
160 E. 300 South
Salt Lake City, UT 84134
International Commerce
International Business Development
Division of Business & Economic Development
160 East 300 South
Salt Lake City, UT 84111
Banking
Financial Institutions
324 S. State
P.O. Box 89
Salt Lake City, UT 84110-0089
Securities
Division of Securities
Heber M. Wells Building
P.O. Box 45811
Salt Lake City, UT 84111
Labor and Industrial Relations
Industrial Commission of Utah
Heber M. Wells Building
160 E. 300 South
Salt Lake City, UT 84111
Insurance
Department of Insurance
3110 State Office Building
Salt Lake City, UT 84114

Licensing
Division of Occupational and Professional Licensing
160 East 300 South
P.O. Box 45802
Salt Lake City, UT 84145-0802

Uniform Industrial Code
Employment Security/Job Service
140 East 300 South
Salt Lake City, UT 84111

INDUSTRIAL AND BUSINESS DIRECTORIES

Utah Directory of Business and Industry, Utah Division of Business and Economic Development, 140 East 300 South, Salt Lake City, UT 84111; Manufacturers' News, Inc., 1633 Central Street, Evanston, IL 60201

Vermont

STATE HOUSE, MONTPELIER, VT 05602
(802) 828-3333

INFORMATION OFFICES

Commerce/Economic Development
Agency of Development and Community Affairs
Department of Economic Development
109 State Street
Montpelier, VT 05602

Corporate
Secretary of State
Corporation Department
26 Terrace Street
Montpelier, VT 05602

Taxation
Department of Taxes
Agency of Administration
109 State Street
Montpelier, VT 05602

International Commerce
Agency of Development and Community Affairs
Pavillion Office Bldg
109 State Street
Montpelier, VT 05609

State Chamber of Commerce
Vermont State Chamber of Commerce
P.O. Box 37
Montpelier, VT 05602

Insurance
Department of Banking and Insurance
89 Main Street
Montpelier, VT 05602

Banking
Department of Banking and Insurance
89 Main Street
Montpelier, VT 05602

Securities
Department of Banking and Insurance
89 Main Street
Montpelier, VT 05602

Labor and Industrial Relations
Department of Labor and Industry
National Life Building
Montpelier, VT 05602

Uniform Commercial Code
Department of Banking and Insurance
89 Main Street
Montpelier, VT 05602

Business Ombudsman
Agency Development and Community Affair
Department of Economic Development
109 State Street
Montpelier, VT 05602

INDUSTRIAL AND BUSINESS DIRECTORIES

MacRAE's State Industrial Directory Maine/New Hampshire/Vermont, MacRAE's Industrial Directories, 817 Broadway, New York, NY 10003

Vermont Manufacturing Directory, Tower Publishing, 34 Diamond Street, Portland, ME 04112; Manufacturers' News, Inc., 1633 Central Street, Evanston, IL 60201

Vermont Directory of Manufacturers, Vermont Agency of Development and Community Affairs, Montpelier, VT 05602

Vermont Yearbook, The National Survey, Chester, VT 05143

Virginia

STATE CAPITOL, RICHMOND, VA 23219
(800) 422-2319

INFORMATION OFFICES

Commerce/Economic Development
Department of Economic Development
P.O. Box 798
1021 East Cary Street
Richmond, VA 23206-0798

Corporate
State Corporation Commission
Tyler Building
1300 East Main Street
Richmond, VA 23219

Taxation
Department of Taxation
2200 W. Broad Street
P.O. Box 1880
Richmond, VA 23282-1880

State Chamber of Commerce
Virginia Chamber of Commerce
9 South Fifth Street
Richmond, VA 23219

International Commerce
Department of Economic Development
P.O. Box 798
1021 East Cary Street
Richmond, VA 23206-0798

Banking
State Corporation Commission
Bureau of Financial Institutions
Tyler Building
1300 East Main Street
Richmond, VA 23219

Securities
State Corporation Commission
Division of Securities and Retail Franchising
Tyler Building
1300 East Main Street
Richmond, VA 23219

Labor and Industrial Relations
Department of Labor and Industry
Powers-Taylor Building
13 S. 13th Street
Richmond, VA 23219

Insurance
State Corporation Commission
Bureau of Insurance
Tyler Building
1300 East Main Street
Richmond, VA 23219

Employment and Unemployment Information
Virginia Employment Commission
Economic Information Services Division
703 E. Main Street
Richmond, VA 23219

Consumer Ombudsman
Department of Agriculture and Consumer Services
Division of Consumer Affairs
P.O. Box 1163
Richmond, VA 23209

INDUSTRIAL AND BUSINESS DIRECTORIES

Virginia Industrial Directory, Chamber of Commerce, 9 South Fifth Street, Richmond, VA 23219

Virginia Manufacturers Directory, Manufacturers' News, Inc., 1633 Central Street, Evanston, IL 60201

MacRAE's State Industrial Directory North Carolina/South Carolina/Virginia, MacRAE's Industrial Directories, 817 Broadway, New York, NY 10003

Washington

101 General Administration Building,
Olympia, WA 98504
(206) 753-5630

INFORMATION OFFICES

Commerce/Economic Development
Department of Trade and Economic Development
101 General Administration Building
Olympia, WA 98504

Corporate
Secretary of State
Corporate Division
505 E. Union
Olympia, WA 98504

Taxation
Department of Revenue
412 General Administration Building
Olympia, WA 98504

State Chamber of Commerce
Association of Washington Business
1414 S. Cherry Street
Olympia, WA 98501

International Commerce
Department of Trade & Economic Development
Domestic & International Trade Division
2600 Westin Building
2001 Sixth Avenue
Seattle, WA 98121

Banking
General Administration Building
Banking & Consumer Finance
219 General Administration Building
Olympia, WA 98504

Securities
Department of Licensing Building
Att: Securities Division
7240 Martin Way
Olympia, WA 98506

Labor and Industrial Relations
Department of Labor & Industries
Employment Standards—Apprenticeship
Crime Victims Division
406 Legion Way SE
Olympia, WA 98504

Insurance
Insurance Commissioner's Office
Insurance Building
Olympia, WA 98504

Uniform Commercial Code
Department of Licensing
Business License Services
405 Black Lake Boulevard
Olympia, WA 98504

Business Ombudsman
Department of Trade & Economic Development

Business Assistance Center
919 Lakeridge Way, S.W.
Olympia, WA 98504

INDUSTRIAL AND BUSINESS DIRECTORIES

Directory of Advanced Technology Industries in Washington State, Economic Development Partnership for Washington State, 18000 Pacific Highway South, Seattle, WA 98188

Business Assistance in Washington State, Washington State International Trade Directory, Department of Trade and Economic Development, 101 General Administration Building, Olympia, WA 98504

Minority Women Business Enterprises, Office of Minority Women Business Enterprises, 406 S. Water Street, Olympia, WA 98504

Washington Manufacturers Register, Times Mirror Press, P.O. Box 7440, Newport Beach, CA 92658

Washington Forest Industry Mill Directory (1984), Department of Natural Resources, 1065 S. Capitol Way, Olympia, WA 98504

Directory of Washington Mining Operations, Department of Natural Resources, Division of Geology, Olympia, WA 98504

Washington Manufacturers Register, Database Publishing, 523 Superior Avenue, Newport Beach, CA 92663; Manufacturers' News, Inc., 1633 Central Street, Evanston, IL 60201

West Virginia

State Capitol, Charleston, WV 25305
(304) 558-3456

INFORMATION OFFICES

Commerce/Economic Development
West Virginia Development Office
State Capitol
Charleston, WV 25305

Corporate
Secretary of State
Corporate Division
Building 1
1900 Washington Street East
Charleston, WV 25305

Taxation
Department of Tax and Revenue
Building 1
1900 Washington Street East
Charleston, WV 25305

State Chamber of Commerce
P.O. Box 2789
1101 Kanawha Valley Building
Charleston, WV 25330-2789

International Commerce
West Virginia Development Office
1900 Washington Street East
Building 6
Charleston, WV 25305

Banking
Division of Banking
1900 Washington Street East
Charleston, WV 25305

Securities
Auditor's Office
Building 1
Charleston, WV 25305

Labor & Industrial Relations
Division of Labor
1900 Washington Street East
Building 1
Charleston, WV 25305

Insurance
Insurance Commission
2019 Washington Street East
Charleston, WV 25305

Uniform Industrial Code
Secretary of State
1900 Washington Street East
Building 1
Charleston, WV 25305

Business Ombudsman
West Virginia Development Office
Building 6
Charleston, WV 25305

INDUSTRIAL AND BUSINESS DIRECTORIES

West Virginia Manufacturers Register, Manufacturers' News, Inc., 1633 Central Street, Evanston, IL 60201, Harris Publishing, 2057 Aurora Road, Twinsburg, OH 44087

Wisconsin

State Capitol, Madison, WI 53702
(608) 266-2211

INFORMATION OFFICES

Commerce/Economic Development
Department of Development
123 W. Washington Avenue
Box 7970
Madison, WI 53707-7970

Corporate
Secretary of State
Corporate Division
30 W. Miffin Street
Box 7848
Madison, WI 53707-7848

Taxation
Department of Revenue
125 S. Webster Avenue
P.O. Box 8933
Madison, WI 53708-8933

State Chamber of Commerce
Wisconsin Association of Manufacturers and Commerce
501 E. Washington Avenue
Box 352
Madison, WI 53701

International Commerce
International Business Services
Department of Development
Box 7970
123 W. Washington Avenue
Madison, WI 53707-7970

Banking
Banking, Office of the Commissioner
131 W. Wilson Avenue
P.O. Box 7876
Madison, WI 53707-7876

Securities
Securities—Office of the Commissioner
111 W. Wilson Avenue
Box 1768
Madison, WI 53701-1768

Labor and Industrial Relations
Department of Industry, Labor, and Human Relations
201 E. Washington Avenue
P.O. Box 7946
Madison, WI 53707-7946

Insurance
Office of the Commissioner of Insurance
121 E. Wilson Street
Box 7873
Madison, WI 53707-7873

Uniform Industrial Code
Department of Industry, Labor and Human Relations
201 E. Washington Avenue
Box 7969
Madison, WI 53707

Business Ombudsman
Small Business Ombudsman
Department of Development
123 W. Washington Avenue
Box 7970
Madison, WI 53707

INDUSTRIAL AND BUSINESS DIRECTORIES

Classified Directory of Wisconsin Manufacturers, Wisconsin Association of Manufacturers and Commerce, 501 E. Washington Avenue, Box 352, Madison, WI 53701; State Industrial Directories Corp., 2 Penn Plaza, New York, NY 10001

Wisconsin Exporters Directory, Wisconsin Department of Development, 123 W. Washington Avenue, Box 7920, Madison, WI 53707

Wisconsin Manufacturers Register, Manufacturers' News, Inc., 1633 Central Street, Evanston, IL 60201

Wisconsin Local Development Organizations (annual), Wisconsin Department of Development, 123 W. Washington Avenue, Box 7970, Madison, WI 53707

Wisconsin Services Directory, Wisconsin Association of Manufacturers and Commerce, 501 E. Washington Avenue, Box 352, Madison, WI 53701

Wyoming

State Capitol, Cheyenne, WY 82002
(307) 777-7220

INFORMATION OFFICES

Commerce/Economic Development
Department of Commerce
Division of Economic and Community Development
Barrett Building
Cheyenne, WY 82002

Corporate
Secretary of State
Corporate Division
State Capitol
Cheyenne, WY 82002

Taxation
Department of Revenue and Taxation
Herschler Building
Cheyenne, WY 82002

International Commerce
International Trade Office
Herschler Building
Cheyenne, WY 82002

Banking
State Examiner
Herschler Building
Cheyenne, WY 82002

Securities
Secretary of State
Securities Division
State Capitol
Cheyenne, WY 82002

Labor and Industrial Relations
Department of Employment
Herschler Building
Cheyenne, WY 82002

Insurance
Insurance Commission
Herschler Building
Cheyenne, WY 82002

Business Ombudsman
Division of Economic and Community Development
Barrett Building
Cheyenne, WY 82002

INDUSTRIAL AND BUSINESS DIRECTORIES

Wyoming Directory of Manufacturing and Mining, Manufacturers' News, Inc., 1633 Central Street, Evanston, IL 60201

Puerto Rico

Capitol, San Juan, PR 00901
(809) 724-6040 (House of Representatives)
(809) 724-2030 (Senate)

INFORMATION OFFICES

Commerce/Economic Development
Puerto Rico Department of Commerce
P.O. Box S 4275
San Juan, PR 00902

Puerto Rico Economic Development Administration
P.O. Box 362350
San Juan, PR 00936

Puerto Rico Planning Board
P.O. Box 41119
San Juan, PR 00940

Government Development Bank
P.O. Box 42001
Minillas Station
San Juan, PR 00940

Economic Development Bank
P.O. Box 5009
San Juan, PR 00919-5009

Taxation
Puerto Rico Department of Treasury
P.O. Box S-4515
San Juan, PR 00902

Office of Industrial Tax Exemption
P.O. Box 2519
San Juan, PR 00919

International Commerce
Foreign Export
P.O. Box 362350
San Juan, PR 00936

Chamber of Commerce
Chamber of Commerce of Puerto Rico
P.O. Box 3789
San Juan, PR 00902

Puerto Rico Manufacturers Association
P.O. Box 192410
San Juan, PR 00919

Securities
Office of the Commissioner of Financial Institutions
Centre Europa Building
1492 Ponce de León Building
San Juan, PR 00907

Labor and Industrial Relations
Puerto Rico Labor Relations Board
P.O. Box 4048
San Juan, PR 00905

National Labor Relations Board
Federal Building
Charlos E. Chardon Street
San Juan, PR 00918

Insurance
Office of the Insurance Commissioner
P.O. Box 8330
San Juan, PR 00910

Puerto Rico Insurance Companies Association, Inc.
P.O. Box 3395
San Juan, PR 00936

Uniform Industrial Code
Department of Labor and Human Resources
505 Muñoz Rivera Avenue
Prudencio Rivera Martínez Building
San Juan, PR 00918

Business Ombudsman
Ombudsman Office
1205 Ponce de León Avenue
Banco de San Juan
San Juan, PR 00907-3995

International Commerce
Puerto Rico Department of Commerce
External Trade Promotion Program
P.O. Box S 4275
San Juan, PR 00902

US Department of Commerce
International Trade Administration
Charlos E. Chardon Street
Federal Building
San Juan, PR 00918

Puerto Rico Chamber of Commerce
International Trade Division
P.O. Box 3789
San Juan, PR 00902

Banking
Puerto Rico Bankers Association
820 Banco Popular Center
San Juan, PR 00918

INDUSTRIAL AND BUSINESS DIRECTORIES

Puerto Rico Official Industrial and Trade Directory, Witcom Group, Inc., P.O. Box 2310, San Juan, PR 00902

The Businessman's Guide to Puerto Rico, Puerto Rico Almanacs, Inc., P.O. Box 9582, Santurce, Puerto Rico 00908

International Trade

EC MEMBER COUNTRIES

Population & Gross Domestic Product

1991	Population millions	GDP current - $bn	Per Capita dollars	Exports as % of GDP	Imports as % of GDP
United States	252.7	5,677.5	22,467	7.5	8.8
EC-12	346.3	6,251.7	18,053	21.9	23.4

Source: OECD, Main Economic Indicators, November 1992

EC INFORMATION SOURCES AND CONTACTS

EC Washington Office

The EC delegation in Washington can provide a wide variety of information about Community institutions and policies, including a number of useful publications. Some of the publications are free. They can be obtained from the Delegation of the European Communities, 2100 M Street, NW., 7th Floor, Washington, D.C. 20037; Tel: 202-862-9500.

Unipub

Publications can be purchased from the European Communities' sales agent, UNIPUB, 4611F Assembly Drive, Lanham, MD. 20706–4391; Tel: 800-274-4888 or 301-459-7666:

European Trade Development Offices[1]

These offices provide commercial information resources developed by the European governments themselves.

Embassy of Belgium
Economic Section
Belgian Foreign Trade Office Representative
3330 Garfield Street, NW
Washington, D.C. 20008
Tel: (202) 333-6900 Fax: (202) 333-3079

Royal Danish Embassy
Economic Section
3200 Whitehaven Street, NW
Washington, D.C. 20008
Tel: (202) 234-4000 Fax: (202) 378-1470

German-American Chamber of Commerce
New York Head Office
40 West 57th Avenue
New York, N.Y. 10103
Tel: (212) 974-8830 Fax: (212) 974-8867

[1] The U.S. Government relays these addresses for the benefit of the reader but cannot vouch for the information provided by each addressee.

French Industrial Development Agency
610 Fifth Avenue
New York, N.Y. 10020
Tel: (212) 757-9340 Fax: (212) 245-1568

Embassy of Greece
Economic Office
1636 Connecticut Avenue, NW
Washington, D.C. 20009
Tel: (202) 745-7100 Fax: (202) 265-4291

Industrial Development Authority of Ireland
Two Grand Central Towers
140 East 45th Street
New York, N.Y. 10017
Tel: (212) 972-1000 Fax: (212) 687-8739

Italian Trade Commission
499 Park Avenue
New York, N.Y. 10022
Tel: (212) 980-1500 Fax: (212) 758-1050

Board of Economic Development (Luxembourg)
801 Second Avenue
New York, N.Y. 10017
Tel: (212) 370-9870 Fax: (212) 697-5529

Netherlands Foreign Investment Agency
One Rockefeller Plaza
New York, N.Y. 10020
Tel: (212) 246-1434 Fax: (212) 246-9769

Portuguese Trade Commission
1900 L Street, NW
Washington, D.C. 20036
Tel: (202) 331-8222 Fax: (202) 331-8236

Embassy of Spain
Minister for Economic and Commercial Affairs
2558 Massachusetts Avenue, NW
Washington, D.C. 20008
Tel: (202) 265-8600 Fax: (202) 265-9478

British Trade Development Office
Inward Investment Bureau
845 Third Avenue
New York, N.Y. 10020
Tel: (212) 593-2258 Fax: (212) 326-0456

Single Internal Market: 1992 Information Service (SIMIS)

For information on the 1992 Single Internal Market Program, copies of the Single Internal Market regulations, background information on the European Community, or assistance regarding specific opportunities or potential problems, contact:

Office of European Community Affairs
U.S. Department of Commerce
14th and Constitution Ave., NW.
Washington, D.C. 20230
Tel: 202-482-5276
Fax: 202-482-2155

The Single Internal Market Information Service (SIMIS) in the Office of European Community (EC) Affairs is a primary contact point within the U.S. government for U.S. business questions on the commercial and trade implications of the EC 1992 program. SIMIS staff maintain a comprehensive data-base of EC directives and regulations, as well as copies of specialized documentation published by the EC Commission, the U.S. government and the private sector. SIMIS offers U.S. exporters a variety of services, including a basic information packet on EC 1992; a quarterly newsletter, *Europe Now;* specialized guides to EC legislation; information on EC duties, taxes, and customs requirements; informational seminars; and individual business counseling. SIMIS staff field business inquiries on EC 1992 issues and refer inquiries to various Commerce specialists for counseling and assistance.

Internal Trade Administration (ITA)

If you want advice or information about any aspect of exporting to the EC, contact your ITA District Office or an ITA European country desk officer:

Belgium, Luxembourg	202-482-5401
Denmark	3254
France	6008
Germany	2434
Greece	3945
Ireland	2177
Italy	2177
Netherlands	5401
Portugal	3945
Spain	4508
United Kingdom	3748

Commerce Department industry specialists can answer questions about the marketability of specific products in Europe, as well as in other overseas markets.

Free brochures can be obtained by writing the Delegation of the Commission of the European Communities (DEC), 2100 M St. NW., Washington, D.C. 20037. DEC official publications and studies on the EC 1992 program can be obtained by contacting UNIPUB, 3611-F Assembly Drive, Lanham, MD. 20706–4391, or Tel: 301-459-7666, or 800-274-4888.

National Institute of Standards and Technology

For information on European Standards the National Institute of Standards and Technology has prepared an extensive summary of the EC initiatives on standards and other related materials. These can be obtained by contacting the National Center for Standards and Certification Information (NCSCI), National Institute of Standards and Technology, Administration Building, Room A629, Gaithersburg, MD. 20899, Tel: 301-975-4040 (GATT Hotline: 301-975-4041), or GATT Inquiry Point/Technical Office, Office of Standards Code and Information, National Institute of Standards and Technology, Administration Building, Room A629, Gaithersburg, MD. 20899, Tel: 301-975-4040.

U.S. Department of State

U.S. Department of State, Europe/Regional, Political and Economic Affairs, Room 6519, Washington, D.C. 20520, Tel: 202-647-1708.

U.S. Mission to the EC

The primary objective of the U.S. and Foreign Commercial Service at U.S. embassies around the world is to promote the sale of U.S. products, technology, and services. The same could be said of the Foreign Commercial Service at the U.S. Mission to the European Communities (USEC) in Brussels, Belgium.

While it is not a marketing organization, the primary objective of the Commercial Section at USEC is to help U.S. industry, especially small- and medium-sized companies, participate in the growing EC marketplace. Trade between the United States and European Community totals nearly $200 billion annually. It is a large market and one that U.S. companies cannot afford to neglect or to take for granted.

To contact the Mission from the United States, write: U.S. and Foreign Commercial Service, U.S. Mission to the EC, PSC 82, Box 002, APO AE 09724.

The location in Brussels is: Blvd. du Regent 40, B-1000 Brussels; tel: 011-32-2-513-4450, fax: 011-32-2-513-1228.

Additional Information Services on EC 1992[1]

A number of additional information services on EC 1992 are now available. Several services are listed below.

- *Conformity for Export (COMFEX), Detroit Testing Laboratory, Inc., P.O. Box 869, Warren, Mich. 48090–0869.* COMFEX's testing and certification services facilitate acceptance of a company's products in Europe. COMFEX will assess a firm's quality assurance system and assist in gaining European certification, approvals, and marks. Call Lynne Neumann or Silviu Vals at (313) 754-9000, ext. 1300, or fax them at (313) 754-9045.
- *Key to Europe, Waitsfield, VT. 05673.* Key to Europe is an international non-profit association for education, training, and research on the European Community. It organizes educational and training programs on the EC for U.S. companies to give them a better understanding about doing business in the changing European market. For more information, tel: (802) 496-2428; fax: (802) 496-4548.
- *Prentice Hall Legal and Financial Services, 15 Columbus Circle, New York, N.Y. 10023–7773.* Prentice Hall Legal and Financial Services has published guides detailing basic requirements for incorporating in each European Community country. Guides are also available explaining partnerships, sole proprietorships, and joint ventures in the EC. For information, call 1-800-221-0770; fax: (212) 373-7679.
- *Single Market Ventures, 87 Rue Faider, B-1050, Brussels, Belgium.* Single Market Ventures supplies information services covering the rules exporters must meet to gain EC-wide acceptance for their products. Services include: an introduction to EC product approval rules, EC product approval briefings, and the *Europe Link* newsletter. For information, call (011) 322-537-2603; fax: (011) 322-537-1078.
- *USAssist, 3400 International Drive, NW., Washington, D.C. 20008.* USAssist provides for emergency medical, legal, security, and financial help for U.S. overseas travelers or for U.S. workers in foreign countries. USAssist has representatives in almost every country to handle problems. For information, call 1-800-765-5900 or (202) 686-8492; fax: (202) 537-0000.

[1] Citation of these titles and firms is done as a public service and does not constitute an endorsement by the U.S. Department of Commerce or the *International Almanac*.

U.S. Government Publications

Department of State, Bureau of European and Canadian Affairs

The European Community's Program to Complete a Single Market by 1992 (July 1988)

Financial Services and the European Community's Single Market Program (January 1989)

Copies are available from the U.S. Department of State, EUR/RPE, 2201 C St., NW., Washington, D.C. 20520; Tel: 202-647-2395.

Department of State, Bureau of Public Affairs

The European Community's Program for a Single Market in 1992 (November 1988)

Copies are available from the Department of State, Bureau of Public Affairs, 2201 C St., NW., Washington, D.C. 20520; Tel: 202-647-6575.

Office of the U.S. Trade Representative

Completion of the European Community Internal Market: An Initial Assessment of Certain

Economic Policy Issues Raised by Aspects of the EC's Program (December 1988)

Available from USTR, 600 17th St., NW., Washington, D.C. 20506; Tel: 202-395-3230.

Europe Now/A Report (Quarterly): Newsletter providing summaries of the latest developments of the EC's 1992 Program.

Available from Office of European Community Affairs, Room H3036, International Trade Administration, U.S. Department of Commerce, Washington, D.C. 20230

EC 1992: Growth Markets: Provides information for U.S. firms interested in taking advantage of the expanding opportunities created by the EC's 1992 Internal Market Program. This is available from the Superintendent of Documents, U.S. Government Printing Office, Washington, D.C. 20402; Tel: 202-783-3238.

Congressional Research Service

The European Communities' 1992 Plan: An Overview of the Proposed Single Market (September 1988). Copies can be obtained by contacting your congressional representative.

Small Business Administration

Exporter's Guide to Federal Resources for Small Business. A specially designed guide for smaller firms interested in exporting, prepared by the Small Business Administration and AT&T. Available from the U.S. Government Printing Office, Washington, D.C. 20402.

National Institute of Standards and Technology

A Summary of the New European Community Approach to Standards Development, NSBIR 88–3793. An extensive summary of the EC initiatives on standards. Obtain this review and other related materials through the Office of Standards Code and Information, National Institute of Standards and Technology, Administration Building, Gaithersburg, MD. 20899; Tel: 301-975-4040.

U.S. International Trade Commission

The Effects of Greater Economic Integration within the European Community on the United States (April 1993). The ITC has prepared a major analytical report on EC 1992 for Congress. Copies of this publication are available from the U.S. International Trade Commission, 500 E St., SW., Washington, D.C. 20436; Tel: 202-205-2000.

Non-U.S. Government Publications

Europe 1992: A Practical Guide for American Business, U.S. Chamber of Commerce, Washington, D.C., November 1993

This publication analyzes the effects of the EC 1992 program in its developmental stage on U.S. business. Covers major trade issues. Tel: 202-463-5469.

Europe 1992: A Practical Guide for American Business, Action Bulletin Update 4, U.S. Chamber of Commerce, Washington, D.C., 1993

These updates provide analysis of ongoing EC 1992 issues affecting U.S. business and trade. Tel: 202-463-5469.

EC Information Handbook 1992, American Chamber of Commerce, Brussels, Belgium, 1991

Where to Find Export/Import Sources, Market Information, Trade Leads, and Services

U.S. GOVERNMENT SOURCES

Department of Commerce

The Commerce Department's Trade Information Center provides a full range of information on federal export assistance programs and activities, overseas markets, and industry trends to U.S. companies. It features a nationwide 800-number-based system—1-800-USA-TRADE (872-8723)—making access to the center available at no cost.

The central export information source within the Department of Commerce is the International Trade Administration (ITA), which promotes the growth of U.S. industry and commerce, both foreign and domestic.

Public Affairs: 202-482-3808

Helpful services of the ITA are listed below:

Business Services for the newly Independent States (former Soviet Union) .... (BISNIS, see below) (202) 482-4655
Consortia of American Business in Eastern Europe (CABEE)............... 482-5131
Eastern Europe Business Information Center (EEBIC)............. 482-2645
Japan Export Information Center (JEIC)..... 482-2425
Latin American/Caribbean Business Development Center (LA/CBD).......... 482-0841

U.S. Department of Commerce/Trade Opportunities Program—TOP provides companies with current sales leads from international firms seeking to buy or represent their products or services. TOP leads are printed daily in leading commercial newspapers and are also distributed electronically via the Economic Bulletin Board. The fee varies.

Contact: For your nearest Department of Commerce District Office call 202-482-2000. For the Department of Commerce Economic Bulletin Board, call 202-482-1986.

International Economic Policy (IEP)—the office organized on a country and regional basis which develops and implements policy concerning U.S. international trade, investment, and commercial relations with foreign businesses and governments, and which gives market-specific counsel to American business

Useful IEP Telephone Numbers

Headquarters..................... (202) 482-3022
GATT Division........................ 482-3681
International Organizations............... 482-3227
U.S. Trade by Region
Africa.............................. 482-2175
Canada............................. 482-3101
Caribbean Basin........................ 482-2527
Eastern Europe........................ 482-2645
Europe............................. 482-5638
European Community.................. 482-5276
Israel Information Center................ 482-4652
Japan.............................. 482-4527
Mexico............................. 482-5327
Near East........................... 482-4441
Newly Independent States (former U.S.S.R.)..................... 482-4655
Pacific Basin.......................... 482-4008
People's Republic of China............... 482-3583
Hong Kong........................... 482-2462
South America........................ 482-2436
South Asia........................... 482-2954
Western Europe....................... 482-5324

IEP Flash Facts is a resource for obtaining information quickly. Simply dial number from your desk touch-tone phone, follow instructions and information will be automatically faxed to you!

Business Information Services for the newly Independent States (Central Asia/Russia/Ukraine)............. (202) 482-3145
Eastern Europe Business Information Center (Albania/Balkan States/Bulgaria/Czech/Poland/Hungary/Slovak Republic/Romania).......................... 482-5745
Africa, Near East, and South Asia (Afghanistan/Algeria/Bahrain/Bangladesh/Bhutan/Egypt/India/Iran/Iraq/Israel/Jordan/Kuwait/Lebanon/Maldives/Morocco/Namibia/Nepal/Nigeria/Oman/Pakistan/Qatar/Saudi Arabia/South Africa/Sri Lanka/Syria/Tunisia/UAE/Yemen).................. 482-1064
Office of Mexico........................ 482-4464
Office of the Pacific Basin (ASEAN/Australia/Cambodia/Indonesia/Korea/Malaysia/New Zealand/Philippines/Singapore/Taiwan/Thailand/Vietnam).......................... 482-3875
482-3646

U.S. and Foreign Commercial Service (US&FCS)—the framework within which ITA gathers accurate and timely commercial information, distributes it through a world-wide network of trade specialists, and provides in-depth counseling, assistance, and support to the business community both in the U.S. and abroad.

Useful US&FCS Telephone Numbers:

Headquarters..................... (202) 482-5777
Domestic Operations.................... 482-4767
Export Promotion Services............... 482-8220
Office of Information Systems............. 482-4641
Foreign Operations:
Western Hemisphere.................. 482-2736
Europe............................ 482-1599
East Asia/Pacific..................... 482-2422
Africa/Near East..................... 482-4836

U.S. Department of Commerce/ITA/Agent/Distributor Service—A customized search helps identify agents, distributors, and foreign representatives for U.S. firms based on the foreign companies' examination of U.S. product literature. A fee per country is charged.

Contact: Your nearest Department of Commerce District Office.

U.S. Department of Commerce/Bureau

of the Census/Center for International Research—CIR compiles and maintains up-to-date global demographic and social information for all countries in its International Data Base (IDB), which is accessible to U.S. companies seeking to identify potential markets overseas. The information in the IDB can be purchased.

Contact: Systems Analysis and Programming Staff, 301-763-4811, Fax: 301-763-7610.

U.S. Department of Commerce/ITA/ *Business America*—The principle Commerce Department publication for presenting domestic and international business news. Each biweekly issue includes a "how to" article for new exporters, a discussion of U.S. trade policy, news of government actions that may affect trade, and a calendar of upcoming trade shows, exhibitions, fairs, and seminars. An annual subscription fee is charged.

Contact: ITA Office of Public Affairs, 202-482-3801, Fax: 202-482-5819. Subscriptions: U.S. Government Printing Office, 202-783-3238.

U.S. Department of Commerce/ US&FCS Commercial Information Management System/National Trade Data Bank—Local Commerce District Office specialists can tailor information packages drawing from statistical trade and economic data, market research reports, and foreign traders indices. CIMS/NTDB house all relevant international trade publications published by ITA, including Foreign Economic Trends reports, Overseas Business Reports, and Industry Sector Analyses.

Contact: Your nearest Department of Commerce District Office.

U.S. Department of Commerce/ITA/ *Commercial News USA*—A monthly magazine published by the US&FCS to promote U.S. products and services to overseas markets, which is disseminated through 240 U.S. embassies and consular posts around the world. Selected portions are reprinted in newsletters that are tailored in content and language to the individual country and distributed to potential buyers, agents, American Chambers of Commerce abroad, and other multipliers. U.S. firms can have their products or services highlighted for a small fee.

Contact: For the address and phone number of your nearest Department of Commerce District Office, call *Commercial News USA* at 202-482-4918, Fax: 202-482-0115.

U.S. Department of Commerce/ITA/ Comparison Shopping Service—A custom-tailored service provides firms with targeted information on marketing and foreign representation for specific products in specific countries. Fee varies.

Contact: Your nearest Department of Commerce District Office.

The U.S. Department of Commerce/The Economic Bulletin Board—The EBB, a personal computer-based electronic bulletin board, is your online source for trade leads as well as for the latest statistical releases from the Bureau of the Census, the Bureau of Economic Analysis, the Bureau of Labor Statistics, the Federal Reserve Board, and other federal agencies.

Subscribers to the EBB pay an annual registration fee which allows two hours of free access to the system. Continued access is billed quarterly per minute between 8 A.M. and 12 noon EST. There are other per minute charges between noon and 6 P.M. EST, as well as other charges per minute at all other times and on weekends and holidays.

Contact: EBB, 202-482-1986, Fax: 202-482-2164; or try the EBB as a guest user by dialing 202-482-3870 with your personal computer and modem (8 bit words, no parity, 1 stop bit).

U.S. Department of Commerce/ITA/Export Counseling—Trade specialists are available at ITA district and branch offices for individualized export counseling. Call 202-482-4811.

U.S. Department of Commerce/ITA/ Gold Key Service—Offered by many Foreign Commercial Service units at overseas posts, this is a custom-tailored service for U.S. firms planning to visit a country. It combines orientation briefings, market research, introductions to potential partners, an interpreter for meetings, and assistance in developing a sound market strategy and an effective follow-up plan. The fee varies.

Contact: Your nearest Department of Commerce District Office.

U.S. Department of Commerce/Minority Business Development Agency/Minority Export Development Consultants Program—This program helps develop marketing plans, identify potential overseas markets, and trade leads for minority business. It also provides assistance in documentation, short-term financing and shipping.

Contact: Business Development Specialist, 202-482-2414.

U.S. Department of Commerce/National Trade Data Bank (NTDB)—The NTDB is a "one-stop" source for export promotion and international trade data collected by 15 U.S. Government agencies. Updated each month and released on one CD-ROM, the NTDB enables a user with an IBM-compatible personal computer equipped with a CD-ROM reader to access over 100,000 trade-related documents. The NTDB contains the latest Census data on U.S. imports and exports by commodity and country; the complete CIA *World Factbook;* current market research reports compiled by the U.S. and Foreign and Commercial Service; the complete Foreign Traders Index, which contains over 45,000 names and addresses of individuals and firms abroad interested in importing U.S. products; and many other data series.

The NTDB is available at over 600 federal depository libraries nationwide, and can be purchased per single disc or as a 12-month subscription.

Contact: For the address and phone number of your nearest Department of Commerce District Office, call 202-482-1986; for ordering and other information, Fax: 202-482-2164.

U.S. Department of Commerce/ITA/Overseas Catalog and Video-Catalog Shows—Companies can gain market exposure for their product or service without the cost of traveling overseas by participating in a catalog or video-catalog show sponsored by the Commerce Department. Provided with the firm's product literature or promotional video, an industry will display the material to select foreign audiences in several countries. Call 202-482-3808 or your local ITA District Office.

U.S. Department of Commerce/ITA/Overseas Trade Missions—Officials of U.S. firms can participate in a trade mission which will give them an opportunity to confer with influential foreign business and government representatives. Commerce Department staff will identify and arrange a full schedule of appointments in each country. Call 202-482-3808 or for your local ITA District Office.

U.S. Department of Commerce/ITA/Overseas Trade Fairs—U.S. exporters may participate in overseas trade fairs which will enable them to meet customers face-to-face and also to assess the competition. The Commerce Department creates a U.S. presence at international trade fairs, making it easier for U.S. firms to exhibit and gain international recognition. The Department selects international trade fairs for special endorsement, called certification. This cooperation with the private show organizers enables U.S. exhibitors to receive special services designed to enhance their market promotion efforts. There is a service charge. Call 202-482-3808 or your local ITA District Office.

U.S. Department of Commerce/ITA/Matchmaker Events—Matchmaker Trade Delegations offer introductions to new markets through short, inexpensive overseas visits with a limited objective: to match the U.S. firm with a representative or prospective joint-venture/licensee partner who shares a common product or service interest. Firms learn key aspects of doing business in the new country and meet in one-on-one interviews the people who can help them be successful there. Call 202-482-3808 or your local ITA District Office.

U.S. Department of Commerce/U.S. Travel and Tourism Administration—USTTA promotes export earnings through trade in tourism. USTTA stimulates demand for travel to the United States; encourages and facilitates promotion in international travel markets by U.S. travel industry concerns; works to increase the number of new-to-market travel businesses participating in the export market; forms cooperative marketing opportunities for private industry and regional, state, and local governments; provides timely data; and helps to remove government-imposed travel barriers.

Contacts: Private Sector Marketing, 202-482-4003, and Public Sector Marketing, Fax: 202-482-8887.

U.S. Department of Commerce/ITA/World Traders Data Report—A method for checking the reputation, reliability, and financial status of a prospective trading partner. For a fee, an exporter can obtain this information, along with a recommendation from commercial officers at the U.S. Embassy as to the suitability of the company as a trading partner. Call 800-USA-Trade.

Business Information Service for the Newly Independent States (BISNIS)— BISNIS is the new information service at the U.S. Department of Commerce providing "one-stop shopping" for U.S. firms interested in doing business in the Newly Independent States (NIS) of the former Soviet Union. BISNIS provides information on commercial opportunities in the NIS, sources of financing, up-to-date lists of trade officials and enterprise contacts, as well as information on all U.S. Government programs supporting trade and investment in the region. The office is staffed with trade specialists who may be contacted by phone or through scheduled appointments. The countries covered are:

Russia, Ukraine, Belarus, Moldova, Georgia, Armenia, Azerbaijan, Uzbekistan, Turkmenistan, Tajikistan, Kazakhstan, Kyrgyzstan.
For information call 202-482-4655.

Trade Development (TD)—the industry unit responsible for formulating trade policy and promotion activities.

Useful TD Telephone Numbers

Headquarters	(202) 482-1461
Foreign Trade Reference Room	482-2185
Major Projects Reference Room	482-4876
Aerospace	482-1872
Automotive	482-0554
Chemicals and Allied Products	482-0128
Consumer Goods	482-0337
Computer and Business Equipment	482-0572
Energy	482-1466
Export Trading Companies	482-5131
Forest Products and Domestic Construction	482-0384
Instrumentation	482-5466
Medical Services	482-2796
Major Projects and International Construction	482-5225
Metals, Minerals and Commodities	482-0575
Micro Electronics & Instrumentation	482-2587
Service Industries	482-3575
Special Industrial Machinery	482-0302
Telecommunications	482-4466
Textiles	482-5078
Trade Information Analysis	482-1316
Export Statistics and Trade Data (Foreign)	482-4211
Export Statistics and Trade Data (Domestic)	482-4356

This is a partial listing of industry sectors; for others not listed, call 202-482-1461.

Import Administration (IA)—the office responsible for safeguarding the national interest through effective administration of U.S. trade laws.

Useful IA Telephone Numbers

Office of Assistant Secretary	(202) 482-1780
Deputy Assistant Secretary for Investigations	482-5497
Investigations	
Office of Antidumping Investigations	482-1779
Office of Countervailing Investigations	482-2438
Compliance	482-2104
Office of Antidumping Compliance	482-2104
Office of Countervailing Compliance	482-2786
Office of Agreements Compliance	482-3793
Foreign Trade Zones Staff	482-2862
Statutory Import Programs Staff	482-1600

Bureau of Export Administration (BXA)—responsible for export licensing, technology and policy analysis, and foreign availability determinations. Public Affairs: 202-482-2721.

Useful BXA Telephone Numbers:

Press and Public Information	(202) 482-2721
Headquarters	482-5491
Exporter Assistance Staff	482-4811

STELA (System for Tracking Export License Applications) answers the question most frequently asked by business: What is the status of my license application?

Information about STELA ..... (202) 482-2752

ELAIN (Export License Application and Information Network) .... (202) 482-4811
Accepts export license applications electronically for all freeworld destinations.

ELVIS (Export Licensing Voice Information System)...................... (202) 482-4811
An automated attendant that offers a range of licensing information and emergency handling procedures.

Emergency Licensing Requests	(202) 482-4811
Trade Fair Licenses	482-4811
General Regulations Information	482-4811
Export Seminar Program	482-8731

Major Offices Administering Export Controls:

Office of Export Licensing	(202) 482-4811
Special Licensing Division	482-3287
Office of Technology and Policy Analysis	482-4188
Capital Goods Technical Center	482-5695
Computer Systems Technical Center	482-2279
Telecommunications Technical Center	482-0730
Electronic Components and Instrumentation	482-1641
Foreign Availability	482-8074
Assessments	482-5953
Export Enforcement	482-1561

Major Offices Administering Export Enforcement:

Washington, D.C.	(202) 482-5282
	(202) 482-8208

BXA Enforcement Field Offices:

California—Los Angeles	(818) 904-6019
California—San Jose	(408) 291-4204
Florida—Miami	(305) 523-1401
Illinois—Chicago	(312) 353-6640
Massachusetts—Boston	(617) 565-6030
New York—New York	(212) 264-1365
Texas—Dallas	(214) 767-9294
Virginia—Springfield	(703) 487-4950
Office of Antiboycott Compliance	(202) 482-5914
Office of Export Intelligence	(202) 482-4255

Department of Agriculture

U.S. Department of Agriculture/Economic Research Service—The ERS staff provides economic data, models and research information about agricultural economies and policies of foreign countries and bilateral agricultural trade and development relationships. The ERS maintains files on the production and marketing of major commodities; pricing data; use, development, and conservation of natural resources; and overseas performance of the U.S. agricultural industry. It also publishes regional agriculture and trade reports, commodity outlook circulars, and a variety of research publications on country-specific issues.

Contact: Agriculture and Trade Analysis Division, 202-219-0700, Fax: 202-219-0759.

U.S. Department of Agriculture/AgExport Connections—The AgExport Action Kit provides information which can help put U.S. exporters in touch quickly and directly with foreign importers of food and agricultural products. To receive a free copy of the Action Kit, Fax your request to the number listed below.

There are four specific services of AgExport Connections:

- Trade Leads are inquiries from foreign buyers sent daily to USDA by the Foreign Agricultural Service's 80 overseas offices. They are made available daily on electronic bulletin boards, several times a week in the *Journal of Commerce*, weekly on the AgExport Fax polling system, and weekly in the *AgExport Trade Leads* bulletin. Fees vary.
- *Buyer Alert* is a weekly overseas newsletter which can introduce your food and agricultural products to foreign buyers at no charge. *Buyer Alert* is electronically transmitted from Washington to FAS attaches and trade officers, who distribute it within their countries of responsibility.
- Foreign Buyer Lists may be used to match products to prospective buyers worldwide. The data base contains over 18,000 foreign firms covering 70 countries and over 235 food and agricultural commodities. Lists are processed by either specific commodity or specific country and are available for a fee.
- U.S. Supplier Lists may be used to source food and agricultural products for export. Over 6,500 names comprise this data base, which is also distributed worldwide to FAS overseas offices. Listings by commodity are available for a fee.

Contact: AgExport Connections Staff, 202-447-7103, Fax: 202-472-4374.

U.S. Department of Agriculture/Computerized Information Delivery Service (CIDS)—CIDS provides instant access to USDA reports and news releases, making time-sensitive agricultural information available to any location within seconds of release. Among the information available, for a fee, through CIDS are trade leads, market reports, economic outlooks, and certain statistics.

Contact: 202-447-5505, Fax: 202-447-8098.

U.S. Department of Agriculture/Country Market Profiles—Country-specific 2–4 page descriptions of 40 overseas markets for high value agricultural products. They provide a market overview, market trends, and information on the U.S. market position, the competition, and general labeling and licensing requirements.

Contact: FAS Information Division, 202-447-7937, Fax: 202-382-1727.

U.S. Department of Agriculture/Trade and Marketing Information Centers— These centers, part of the National Agricultural Library, help locate relevant material from their large collection of trade and marketing information and provide copies of research and data from their AGRICOLA data base.

Contact: Information Center Branch, 301-344-3704, Fax: 301-344-5472.

Department of Energy

U.S. Department of Energy/Coal and Technology Export Program—This program promotes the export of U.S. clean coal products and services by acting as an information source on coal and coal technologies.

Contact: Office of Fossil Energy, 202-586-7297, Fax: 202-586-1188.

U.S. Department of Energy/Fossil Energy-AID Database—The Office of Fossil Energy forwards prospective energy-related leads to AID for inclusion in its growing trade opportunities data base in an effort to reach an extended audience seeking energy-related trade opportunities.

Contact: Office of Fossil Energy, 202-586-9680, Fax: 202-586-1188.

Department of Labor

U.S. Department of Labor/Foreign Labor Trends—A series of reports, issued annually, that describe and analyze labor trends in more than 70 foreign countries. The reports, which are prepared by the American Embassy in each country, cover labor-management relations, trade unions, employment and unemployment, wages and working conditions, labor and government, international labor activities, and other significant developments. A list of key labor indicators is also included.

Contact: Office of Foreign Relations, 202-523-6257, Fax: 202-523-9613.

Small Business Administration

Office of International Trade—OIT works in cooperation with other federal agencies and public and private sector groups to encourage small business exports and to assist small businesses seeking to export. The office's outreach efforts include sponsoring and developing "how to" and market-specific publications for exporters. OIT directs and coordinates SBA's export initiatives, including the Export Legal Assistance Network (ELAN) and Export Information System (XIS), and promotes SBA's two loan guaranty programs designed specifically for international trade.

Contact: Office of International Trade, 202-205-6720, Fax: 202-205-7272.

Agency for International Development (AID)

Trade and Investment Monitoring System—TIMS, a user-friendly computer-based system, provides a broad array of trade and investment information to potential U.S. investors and exporters on 42 developing countries, e.g., general economic and business data; trade and investment policies and prospects; government regulation and incentives; sources of funding and corporate tax structures; production and labor forces; and business facilities and infrastructure.

Contact: 202-647-3805.

Overseas Private Investment Corporation (OPIC)

1100 New York Avenue, NW., Washington, D.C. 20527. Phone: 202-336-8400.

Investor Information Service—This information clearinghouse provides "one-stop-shopping" for basic economic, business, and political information and data from a variety of sources on 118 developing countries and 16 geographic regions. This service is available for purchase in country- and region-specific kits.

Contact: 202-336-8662.

Overseas Private Investment Corporation/Investor Services—A new OPIC initiative designed to assist smaller U.S. firms with their overseas investment planning and implementation needs. Fee-based services provide counseling to American firms on business plan development, project structuring, joint-venture partner identification, and location of project financing services.

Contact: Investor Services, 202-336-8620.

Overseas Private Investment Corporation/Opportunity Bank—This computer data system matches a U.S. investor's interest with specific overseas opportunities. A modest fee is charged.

Contact: 202-336-8662.

Private Export Funding Corporation (PEFCO)

Address: 280 Park Avenue, New York, NY 10017. Telephone: 212-557-3100.

PEFCO, owned mostly by commercial banks, lends only to finance export of goods and services of U.S. manufacture and origin. PEFCO's loans generally have maturities in the medium-term area and all are unconditionally guaranteed by Eximbank as to payment of interest and repayment of principal. PEFCO's funds supplement the financing of U.S. exports available through commercial banks and Eximbank.

Before contacting PEFCO, the potential borrower (a foreign buyer) or the U.S. exporter should obtain an indication from Eximbank that its board will issue a Financial Guarantee for part of the required financing. Exporters or foreign buyers with no experience in using Eximbank or PEFCO funding should first approach an experienced commercial bank; the bank will then determine whether a PEFCO loan would be a reasonable supplement to the funds provided by other sources.

U.S. Export-Import Bank

811 Vermont Avenue, NW., Washington, D.C. 20571. Public Affairs: 202-566-8990.

The Export-Import Bank of the United States (Eximbank) is the principal government agency responsible for aiding the export of U.S. goods and services through a variety of loan, guarantee, and insurance programs.

Eximbank's financial programs generally are available to any U.S. export firm, regardless of size. A list of Eximbank loan officers and country specialists can be obtained by calling the public affairs office at 202-566-8990.

The following programs, however, are particularly helpful to small business exporters.

Export Credit Insurance—An exporter may reduce its financing risks by purchasing export credit insurance from Eximbank's agent, the Foreign Credit Insurance Association (FCIA). Policies available include insurance for financing or operating leases, medium-term insurance, the new-to-export policy, insurance for the service industry, the umbrella policy, and multibuyer and singlebuyer policies.

Working Capital Guarantee—The Working Capital Loan Guarantee Program assists small businesses in obtaining crucial working capital to fund their export sales. The program guarantees working capital loans extended by banks to eligible U.S. exporters with exportable inventory or export receivables as collateral.

Direct and Intermediary Loans—Eximbank provides two types of loans: direct loans to foreign buyers of U.S. exports and intermediary loans to fund responsible parties that extend loans to foreign buyers of U.S. capital and quasi-capital goods and related services. Both the local and guarantee programs cover up to 85 percent of the U.S. export value, with repayment terms of one year or more.

Guarantees—Eximbank's guarantee provides repayment protection for private sector loans to creditworthy buyers of U.S. capital equipment and related services. The guarantee is available alone or with an intermediary loan.

Most guarantees provide comprehensive coverage of both political and commercial risks, but political-risks-only coverage is also available.

Small Business Advisory Service—To encourage small business to sell overseas, Eximbank maintains a special office to provide information on the availability and use of export credit insurance, guarantees, and direct and intermediary loans to finance the sale of U.S. goods and services abroad. Its toll-free number, open all the time, is 1-800-424-5201; or within the Washington, D.C., area or from Alaska and Hawaii, the number is 202-566-4423.

Briefing Programs—Eximbank offers briefing programs available to small business. For scheduling information, call 202-566-4490.

Electronic Bulletin Board for Eximbank information—In operation all the time, telephone 202-566-4699.

PRIVATE EXPORT/IMPORT SOURCES AND CONTACTS

American Association of Exporters and Importers provides a number of useful sources including *The Weekly International Trade Alert* and *The Daily Alertfax,* a daily one page summary of events affecting trade. Contact the American Association of Exporters and Importers, 11 West 42nd Street, New York, N.Y. 10036; Tel: 212-944-2230.

AT&T and several multinational corporations operate "The Export Hotline," a fax information retrieval system designed to help U.S. companies learn about worldwide markets. The database contains up-to-date information on 50 key industries of all major trading partners of the United States; it can be accessed from anywhere in the United States 24 hours a day. Companies can find out how to use the service by calling 1-800-USA-XPORT, toll-free. The only expense for users is the cost of the fax calls. The AT&T hotline complements the Trade Information Center (Tel: 1-800-USA-TRADE), which offers one-on-one attention.

The Bureau of National Affairs publishes the *Export Shipping Manual,* updated weekly and the weekly, *International Trade Reporter.* Available from the Bureau of National Affairs, Inc., Distribution Center, Key West Avenue, Rockville, MD. 20850; Tel: 800-372-1033.

Dun and Bradstreet publishes an annual *Exporters Encyclopedia* which covers over 220 countries. Available from Dun's Marketing Services, 3 Sylvan Way, Parsippany, N.J. 07054; Tel: 800-526-0651.

The **International Trade Institute** publishes a number of manuals including a *Guide to Export Documentation* and a *Guide to International Shipping.* Contact: International Trade Institute, 5055 North Main Street, Dayton, OH. 45415; Tel: 800-543-2455.

Journal of Commerce is a daily newspaper covering all aspects of Commerce. Address: 110 Wall Street, New York, N.Y. 10005; Tel: 212-425-1616.

Predicasts makes available a large number of sources including the *F & S Index International, F & S Index Europe,* and the multivolume *Worldcasts* containing abstracts of forecasts and markets outside the United States. Contact: Predicasts, 1101 Cedar Avenue, Cleveland, OH. 44106; Tel: 800-321-6388.

The above information is also available on **Dialog.**

TRADE ORGANIZATIONS

Several additional private sector organizations that focus on export and trade issues are listed below:

Academy of International Business
Tulane University
New Orleans, LA. 70118
Tel: 504-865-5563

Affiliated Advertising Agencies International
World Headquarters
2280 South Xanadu Way
Aurora, CO. 80014
Tel: 303-671-8551

American Arbitration Association
140 West 51st Street
New York, N.Y. 10020
Tel: 212-484-4000

American Association of Exporters and Importers
11 West 42nd Street
New York, N.Y. 10036
Tel: 212-944-2230

American Enterprise Institute for Public Policy Research
1150 17th Street, NW.
Washington, D.C. 20036
Tel: 202-862-5800

American Importers Association
11 West 42nd Street
New York, N.Y. 10036
Tel: 212-944-2230

American Institute of Marine Underwriters
14 Wall Street
New York, N.Y. 10005
Tel: 212-233-0550

American Management Association
135 West 50th Street
New York, N.Y. 10020
Tel: 212-586-8100

American National Metric Council
1735 N. Lynn Street
Arlington, VA. 22209
Tel: 703-857-0474

American Society of International Law
2223 Massachusetts Avenue, NW.
Washington, D.C. 20008
Tel: 202-265-4313

Bankers Association for Foreign Trade
1600 M Street, NW.
Washington, D.C. 20036
Tel: 202-452-0952

Brazil-U.S. Business Council (U.S. Section)[1]
Tel: 202-463-5485

Brookings Institution (The)
1775 Massachusetts Avenue, NW.
Washington, D.C. 20036
Tel: 202-797-6000

Carribbean Central American Action
1211 Connecticut Avenue, NW.
Washington, D.C. 20036
Tel: 202-466-7464

Chamber of Commerce of the United States
1615 H Street, NW.
Washington, D.C. 20062
Tel: 202-659-6000
Tel: 202-463-5460 (International)

Coalition for Employment Through Exports, Inc.
1801 K Street, NW.
Washington, D.C. 20006
Tel: 202-296-6107

Committee for Economic Development
1700 K Street, NW.
Washington, D.C. 20006
Tel: 202-296-5860

Committee on Canada-United States Relations (U.S. Section)[1]
Tel: 202-463-5478

Conference Board (The)
845 Third Avenue
New York, N.Y. 10022
Tel: 212-759-0900

[1] Address: Chamber of Commerce of the United States, International Division, 1615 H Street NW., Washington, D.C. 20062.

Council of the Americas
680 Park Avenue
New York, N.Y. 10021
Tel: 212-628-3200

Council on Foreign Relations, Inc.
56 East 68th Street
New York, N.Y. 10021
Tel: 212-734-0400

Customs and International Trade Bar Association
℅ Ross & Hardies
65 East 55th Street
New York, N.Y. 10002
Tel: 212-421-5555

Czech and Slovak U.S. Economic Council (U.S. Section)[1]
Tel: 202-463-5482

E.C.-U.S. Conference on Agriculture
Tel: 202-463-5533

Export Managers Association of California
14549 Victory Boulevard
Van Nuys, CA. 91411
Tel: 213-749-8698

Foreign Policy Association
729 7th Avenue
New York, N.Y. 10019
Tel: 212-764-4050

Federation of International Trade Associations
1851 Alexander Bell Drive
Reston, VA. 22091
Tel: 703-391-6108

Foreign Credit Interchange Bureau/National Association of Credit Managers
520 Eighth Ave.
New York, N.Y. 10018
Tel: 212-947-5368

Fund for Multi-National Management Education (FMME)
40 East 49 Street
New York, N.Y. 10017
Tel: 212-758-3007

Hungarian-U.S. Economic Council (U.S. Section)[1]
Tel: 202-463-5482

Ibero American Chamber of Commerce
1316 Pennsylvania Avenue, SE.
Washington, D.C. 20005
Tel: 202-990-1255

India-U.S. Business Council (U.S. Section)[1]
Tel: 202-463-5477

International Advertising Association
342 Madison Avenue
New York, N.Y. 10017
Tel: 212-557-1133

International Bank for Reconstruction and Development
1818 H Street, NW.
Washington, D.C. 20006
Tel: 202-477-1234

International Cargo Gear Bureau
17 Battery Place
New York, N.Y. 10004
Tel: 212-425-2750

International Economic Policy Association
12605 Native Dancer Place
Darnestown, MD.
Tel: 301-990-1255

International Finance Corporation
1818 H Street, NW.
Washington, D.C. 20433
Tel: 202-477-1234

National Association of Export Companies (NEXCO)
Murray Hill Station
P.O. Box 1330
New York, N.Y. 10156
Tel: 212-725-3311

National Association of Manufacturers
1331 Pennsylvania Avenue, NW.
Washington, D.C. 20006
Tel: 202-626-3000

National Association of State Development Agencies
444 North Capitol, NW.
Washington, D.C. 20001
Tel: 202-624-5411

National Committee on International Trade Documentation (The)
350 Broadway
New York, N.Y. 10013
Tel: 212-925-1400

National Council on International Trade and Documentation
350 Broadway
New York, N.Y. 10013
Tel: 212-925-1400

National Customs Brokers and Forwarders Association of America
Five World Trade Center
New York, N.Y. 10048
Tel: 212-432-0050

National Export Traffic League
234 Fifth Avenue
New York, N.Y. 10001
Tel: 212-697-5895

National Foreign Trade Council
100 East 42nd Street
New York, N.Y. 10017
Tel: 212-399-7128

National Industrial Council
1331 Pennsylvania Avenue, NW.
Washington, D.C. 20006
Tel: 202-637-3000

Organization of American States
19th & Constitution Avenue, NW.
Washington, D.C. 20006
Tel: 202-458-3000

Overseas Development Council
1717 Massachusetts Avenue, NW.
Washington, D.C. 20036
Tel: 202-234-8701

Pan American Development Foundation
1889 F Street, NW.
Washington, D.C. 20006
Tel: 202-458-3969

Partners of the Americas
1424 K Street, NW.
Washington, D.C. 20005
Tel: 202-628-3300

Philippine-U.S. Economic Council (U.S. Section)[1]
Tel: 202-463-5668

Polish-U.S. Economic Council (U.S. Section)[1]
Tel: 202-463-5482

Private Export Funding Corporation
280 Park Avenue
New York, N.Y. 10017
Tel: 202-557-3100

Romanian-U.S. Economic Council (U.S. Section)[1]
Tel: 202-463-5482

Turkish-U.S. Economic Council (U.S. Section)[1]
Tel: 202-463-5489

U.S. ASEAN Council for Business and Technology
1400 L Street, NW.
Washington, D.C. 20005
Tel: 202-289-1911

U.S. China Business Council
1818 N Street, NW.
Washington, D.C. 20036
Tel: 202-429-0340

U.S.-Japan Business Council
1020 19th Street NW.
Washington, D.C. 20036
Tel: 202-728-0068

The Trade and Economic Council (previously the U.S.-U.S.S.R. Trade and Economic Council)
805 Third Avenue
New York, N.Y. 10022
Tel: 212-644-4550

The U.S.A.-Republic of China Economic Council
200 Main Street
Crystal Lake, IL. 60014
Tel: 815-459-5875

United States Council for International Business
1212 Avenue of the Americas
New York, N.Y. 10036
Tel: 212-354-4480

United States Trade Relations Council
1 Church Street
Rockville, MD. 20850
Tel: 202-309-8660

World Trade Centers Association
One World Trade Center
New York, N.Y. 10048
Tel: 212-313-4600

Contact for other World Trade Centers

World Trade Institute
1 World Trade Center
New York, N.Y. 10048
Tel: 212-466-4044

PUBLICATIONS

American Export Register. A two volume annual that contains among other information, product listings in more than 4000 categories, product listings in 10 languages, an alphabetical list of almost 43000 companies as well as a directory of import/export services. Available from Thomas Publishing Co., 5 Penn Plaza, New York, N.Y. 10001.

Bergano's Register of International Importers. Includes a list of some 2000 agents, dealers, distributors, and representatives for more than 75 international markets. Available from Bergano's. P.O. Box 190, Fairfield, CT. 06430.

Building An Import/Export Business, edited by Kenneth D. Weiss. Provides practical advice needed to start up and operate import and export businesses. Includes marketing information, shipping practices, regulations, importing procedures, and much more. Published by John Wiley & Sons, 605 Third Avenue, N.Y. 10158.

Directory of United States Exporters and *Directory of United States Importers.* These world trade directories feature numerical product listings and company profiles. Published by the Journal of Commerce Business Directories, 445 Marshall Street, Phillipsburg, N.J. 08965.

Exporters' Enclyclopedia. An annual that covers country by country information for more than 200 markets. Included are such topics as business travel, communication, country profiles, documentation, marketing, trade regulations, and transportation. Published by Duns Marketing Services, 3 Sylvan Way, Parsippany, N.J. 07054.

Export Reference Manual. A three-volume

looseleaf service with weekly updates covering U.S. export controls on a country-to-country basis, foreign import regulations and coverage on each country. Information is also included on a wide range of topics, including advertising, banking, currency, marketing weights and measures, and shipments. Published by the Bureau of National Affairs, Inc., 1231 25th Street, NW., Washington, D.C. 20037.

Export Sales and Marketing Manual by John R. Jagoe. This is a practical step-by-step looseleaf service with quarterly updates. Among the many subjects included are: Agents, Distributors, and EMCs, Budgeting for Export, Identifying Foreign Markets, Pricing Products for Exports, and Selecting a Foreign Freight Forwarder. Published by Export USA Publications, 4141 Parklawn Avenue South, Minneapolis, MN. 55435.

The Export Yellow Pages. This Directory covers a broad range of resources available to companies seeking to begin or expand their export operations. Includes a listing of export services, trading companies, technical support services, and a listing of export producers. Sponsored by U.S. West in cooperation with the U.S. Department of Commerce. To obtain a copy free of charge contact the U.S. Department of Commerce District Office nearest you. Outside the U.S. contact the U.S. Embassy or Consulate.

Guide to Incoterms. Contains explanations of international commercial trade terms most widely used in international commerce. Published by ICC Publishing Corporation, 156 Fifth Avenue, New York, N.Y. 10010.

Importing Into The United States. This publication outlines essential import requirements and regulations. Prepared by the Department of the Treasury, U.S. Customs Service. Available from the Superintendent of Documents, U.S. Government Printing Office, Washington, D.C. 20402–9328.

"International Business" is a monthly devoted to all aspects of international business. Available from International Business, 500 Mamaroneck Avenue, Harrison, N.Y. 10528.

International Direct Marketing Guides: Regional Markets and Selected Countries, edited by William A. Delphos. Contains useful information for marketing products internationally. Includes brief overviews of the regions of the world, detailed information on selected countries and examples of their potential markets. Also included are several case studies of companies that are marketing globally. In cooperation with the U.S. Postal Service, this Guide is published by Braddock Communications, Inc., Alexandria, VA. 221314–1555.

The McGraw-Hill Handbook of Global Trade and Investment Financing by Lawrence W. Tuller. Includes information and sources of financing throughout the world, specific contacts for starting the financing process, and more. Published by McGraw-Hill, Inc., 1221 Avenue of the Americas, New York, N.Y. 10020.

Trade Shows Worldwide. Annual publication that includes more than 5000 scheduled trade shows, exhibits, and association conventions. Gale Research, Inc. 835 Penobscot Building, Detroit, MI. 48226.

Practical country business guides are available from the following major accounting firms:

Price Waterhouse
153 East 53rd Street
New York, N.Y. 10022

Ernst & Young
787 Seventh Avenue
New York, N.Y. 10019

KPMG (Peat Marwick)
Publications Distribution
3 Chestnut Ridge Road
Montvale, N.J. 07645

Foreign Trade Zones

Foreign or "free" trade zones are secured areas legally outside a nation's customs territory. Their purpose is to attract and promote international trade and commerce. The Foreign-Trade Zones Board authorizes operations based upon showing that the intended operations are not

Source: Excerpted from *Importing into the United States*, Department of the Treasury, United States Customs Service.

detrimental to the public interest. Subzones are special-purpose facilities for companies unable to operate effectively at public zone sites. Foreign-trade zones are usually located in or near Customs ports of entry, at industrial parks, or terminal warehouse facilities. Foreign-trade zones must be within 60 miles or 90 minutes' driving time from the Customs supervising office, while subzones have no limit and are located in the zone user's private facility. A Foreign-Trade Zones Board, created by the Foreign-Trade Zones Act of 1934, reviews and approves applications to establish, operate, and maintain foreign-trade zones. It is important to note that although foreign-trade zones are legally outside the Customs territory of the United States, other federal laws, such as the Federal Food, Drug, and Cosmetic Act, are applicable to products and establishments with such zones.

Foreign exporters planning to expand or open up new American outlets may forward their goods to a foreign-trade zone in the United States to be held for an unlimited period while awaiting a favorable market in the United States or nearby countries without being subject to customs entry, payment of duty or tax, or bond.

Merchandise lawfully brought into these zones may be stored, sold, exhibited, broken up, repacked, assembled, distributed, sorted, graded, cleaned, mixed with foreign or domestic merchandise, or otherwise manipulated or manufactured. However, imported merchandise for use in the zone, such as construction material and production equipment, must be entered for consumption before it is taken into a zone. . . .

An important feature of foreign-trade zones for foreign merchants entering the American market is that the goods may be brought to the threshold of the market, making immediate delivery certain and avoiding possible cancellation of orders due to shipping delays after a favorable market has closed. . . .

Production of articles in zones by the combined use of domestic and foreign materials makes unnecessary either the sending of the domestic materials abroad for manufacture or the duty-paid or bonded importation of the foreign materials. . . .

Another feature under the zone act is the authority to exhibit merchandise within a zone. Zone facilities may be utilized for the full exhibition of foreign merchandise without bond, for an unlimited length of time, and with no requirement of exportation or duty payment. . . .

Savings may result from manipulations and manufacture in a zone. For example, many products, shipped to the zone in bulk, can be dried, sorted, graded, or cleaned and bagged or packed, permitting savings of duties and taxes on moisture taken from content or on dirt removed and culls thrown out. From incoming shipments of packaged or bottled goods, damaged packages or broken bottles can be removed. Where evaporation results during shipment or while goods are stored in the zone, contents of barrels or other containers can be regauged and savings obtained, as no duties are payable on the portions lost or removed. In other words, barrels or other containers can be gauged at the time of transfer to customs territory to insure that duties will not be charged on any portion of their contents which has been lost due to evaporation, leakage, breakage, or otherwise. These operations may also be conducted in bonded warehouses.

Savings in shipping charges, duties, and taxes may result from such operations as shipping unassembled or disassembled furniture, machinery, etc., to the zone and assembling or reassembling it there.

Merchandise may be remarked or relabeled in the zone (or in a bonded warehouse) to conform to requirements for entry into the commerce of the United States if otherwise up to standard. Remarking or relabeling that would be misleading is not permitted in the zone. Substandard foods and drugs may, in certain cases, be reconditioned to meet the requirements of the Food, Drug, and Cosmetics Act.

There is no time limit as to how long foreign merchandise may be stored in a zone, or when it must be entered into customs territory, reexported, or destroyed.

Location of, and general information on United States Foreign-Trade Zones may be obtained from the Foreign-Trade Zones Board, Department of Commerce, Washington, D.C. 20230.

Questions relating to legal aspects of Customs Service responsibilities in regard to foreign trade zones should be addressed to: Chief, Entry Rulings Branch, U.S. Customs Service, 1301 Constitution Avenue, NW., Washington, D.C. 20229.

Questions relating to operational aspects of such responsibilities should be addressed to the appropriate district/area director of Customs.

The *Foreign-Trade Zones Manual* for grantees, operators, users, Customshouse brokers, may be purchased from the Superintendent of Documents, U.S. Government Printing Office, Washington, D.C. 20402. When ordering refer to GPO Stock No. 048-002-00111-7 and Customs Publication No. 559.

U.S. Customs

Customs Regions and Districts

Headquarters
U.S. Customs Service
1301 Constitution Ave., NW
Washington, D.C. 20229
Tel: 202-927-2095

Northeast Region—
Boston, MA. 02222–1056
Districts:
Portland, Maine 04112
St. Albans, VT. 05478
Boston, MA. 02222–1056
Providence, R.I. 02905
Buffalo, N.Y. 14202
Ogdensburg, N.Y. 13669
Philadelphia, PA. 19106
Baltimore, MD. 21202
Norfolk, VA. 23510
Washington, D.C. 20041

New York Region—
New York, N.Y. 10048
New York Seaport Area
New York, N.Y. 10048

Kennedy Airport Area
Jamaica, N.Y. 11430

Newark Area
Newark, N.J. 07102

Southeast Region—
Miami, FL. 33131
Districts:
Wilmington, N.C. 28401
San Juan, P.R. 00901
Charleston, S.C. 29402
Savannah, GA. 31401
Tampa, FL. 33605
Miami, FL. 33131
St. Thomas, V.I. 00801

South Central Region—
New Orleans, LA. 70130
Districts:
Mobile, AL. 36602
New Orleans, LA. 70130

Southwest Region—
Houston, TX. 77057
Districts:
Port Arthur, TX. 77642
Houston/Galveston, TX. 77029
Laredo, TX. 78041–3130
El Paso, TX. 79985
Dallas/Fort Worth, TX. 75261

Pacific Region—
Los Angeles, CA. 90831–0700
Districts:
Nogales, AZ. 85621
San Diego, CA. 92188
Los Angeles/Long Beach, CA. 90731
San Francisco, CA. 94126
Honolulu, HI. 96806
Portland, OR. 97209
Seattle, WA. 98104
Anchorage, AK. 99501
Great Falls, MT. 59405

North Central Region—
Chicago, IL. 60603–5790
Districts:
Chicago, IL. 60607
Pembina, N.D. 58271
Minneapolis-St. Paul, MN. 55401
Duluth, MN. 55802–1390
Milwaukee, WI. 53237–0260
Cleveland, OH. 44114
St. Louis, MO. 63105
Detroit, MI. 48226–2568

U.S. Customs Officers in Foreign Countries

Austria
Customs Attaché
American Embassy
Boltzmanngasse 16, A-1091
Vienna

Belgium
Customs Attaché
U.S. Mission to the European Communities
PSC 82 Box 002
APO AE 09724

Canada
Customs Attaché
American Embassy
100 Wellington St.
Ottawa, Ontario
Canada, KIP 5TI

France
Customs Attaché
American Embassy
58 bis Rue la Boetie
76008 Paris

Hong Kong, B.C.C.
Senior Customs Representative
American Consulate General
St. John's Building
33 Garden Road

Italy
Customs Attaché
American Embassy
Via Veneto 119
Rome, Italy

Senior Customs Representative
American Consulate General
Via Principe Amedeo
2/10–20121 Milano

Japan
Customs Attaché
American Embassy
10–5 Akasaka 1-Chome
Minato-ku, Tokyo 107
Japan

Korea
Customs Attaché
82 SeJong Ro
Chongro-Ku
Seoul 110–050

Mexico
Customs Attaché
American Embassy
Paseo De La Reforma 305
Colonia Cuahtemoc
Mexico City, Mexico

Sr. Customs Representative
American Consulate General
No. 139 Morelia
Hermosillo Son., Mexico

Sr. Customs Representative
American Consulate
Paseo Montejo 453
Merida, Yucatan
Mexico 97000

Sr. Customs Representative
American Consulate General
Avenida Constitucion
411 Poniente
Monterrey N.L., Mexico

The Netherlands
Customs Attaché
American Embassy
Lange Voorhout 102
2514EJ The Hague, Netherlands

Panama
Customs Attaché
Calle 38 & Avenida Balboa
Panama, R.P.

Singapore
Customs Attaché
American Embassy
30 Hill Road
Singapore 0617

Thailand
Customs Attaché
American Embassy
95 Wireless Road
Bangkok

United Kingdom
Customs Attaché
American Embassy
24/31 Grosvenor Square
London, W. 1A 1AE

Uruguay
Customs Attaché
American Embassy
APO Miami, FL. 34035

West Germany
Customs Attaché
American Embassy
Deichmanns Aue. 29
5300 Bonn 2

Index

A

B

C

J

K

L